Keys to BUSINESS COMMUNICATION

Keys to BUSINESS COMMUNICATION

SUCCESS IN COLLEGE, CAREER, & LIFE

Carol Carter

Prentice Hall
Boston Columbus Indianapolis New York San Francisco Upper Saddle River
Amsterdam Cape Town Dubai London Madrid Milan Munich Paris Montreal Toronto
Delhi Mexico City São Paulo Sydney Hong Kong Seoul Singapore Taipei Tokyo

Editorial Director: Sally Yagan
Editor in Chief: Eric Svendsen
Acquisitions Editor: James Heine
Director of Development: Steve Deitmer
Development Editor: Amy Ray
Senior Editorial Development Manager: Kate Allyn Moore
Director of Editorial Services: Ashley Santora
Assistant Editor: Karin Williams
Editorial Assistant: Jason Calcano
Director of Marketing: Patrice Lumumba Jones
Senior Marketing Manager: Nikki Ayana Jones
Marketing Assistant: Ian Gold
Senior Managing Editor: Judy Leale
Production Project Manager: Jacqueline A. Martin
Senior Operations Supervisor: Arnold Vila
Manager of Design Development: John Christiana
Text and Cover Designer: John Christiana
Cover Images: Yuri Arcurs/Shutterstock; Tammy Hanratty/Corbis RF; Yuri Arcurs/Shutterstock; Jupiter Images/Thinkstock/Comstock/Getty Images; David Mager/Pearson Learning Photo Studio
Lead Media Project Manager: Lisa Rinaldi
Media Editor: Joan Waxman
Full-Service Project Management: S4Carlisle Publishing Services
Composition: S4Carlisle Publishing Services
Printer/Binder: R.R. Donnelley/Willard
Cover Printer: Phoenix Color Corp., Hagerstown
Text Font: 10/12 Minion

Credits and acknowledgments borrowed from other sources and reproduced, with permission, in this textbook appear on appropriate page within text (photos credits appear on page PC-1).

Library of Congress Cataloging-in-Publication Data

Carter, Carol.
Keys to business communication : success in college, career, & life / Carol Carter.
p. cm.
Includes index.
ISBN-13: 978-0-13-610333-2
ISBN-10: 0-13-610333-2
1. Business communication. I. Title.
HF5718.C27 2011
650.101′4—dc22 2010045886

Prentice Hall
is an imprint of

www.pearsonhighered.com

10 9 8 7 6 5 4 3 2 1
ISBN 10: 0-13-610333-2
ISBN 13: 978-0-13-610333-2

Dedication

For my husband, Norton. Thank you for being my inspiration.

—Carol

Brief Contents

About the Author xiii
Preface xv

Chapter 1 Strategic Thinking for Smart Business Communication 3
Chapter 2 Teamwork, Leadership, and Business Communication 29
Chapter 3 Communicating Across Cultures and Generations 59
Chapter 4 Preparing Business Messages 79
Chapter 5 Writing, Revising, and Editing Messages 111
Chapter 6 Designing, Proofreading, and Distributing Messages 143
Chapter 7 Positive, Everyday Messages 171
Chapter 8 Negative Messages 203
Chapter 9 Strategies for Persuasive Messages 235
Chapter 10 Writing Reports and Proposals 265
Appendix 10A Example Reports 294
Chapter 11 Business Presentations 315
Chapter 12 Effective Visual Aids in Presentations 339
Chapter 13 Career Exploration and the Job Search 367
Chapter 14 The Tools for Finding a Job 399
Chapter 15 Job Interviewing 433
Chapter 16 Becoming a World-Class Employee and Leader 465

Appendix A Social Networking and Media A-1
Appendix B Formats for Business Documents B-1
Appendix C A Basic Guide to Documenting Sources C-1
Appendix D Brief Handbook of Grammar, Punctuation, Mechanics, and Conventions D-1
Appendix E Commonly Used Revision and Proofreading Symbols E-1

Glossary G-1
References R-1
Photo Credits PC-1
Index I-1

Contents

About the Author xiii
Preface xv

CHAPTER 1 **Strategic Thinking for Smart Business Communication: Preparing to Succeed in the 21st Century 3**

How Can You Prepare Yourself for Today's Business World? 4
How Does Communication Affect Business Successes and Failures? 7
What Are the Four Elements of Any Communication Exchange? 10
What Are the Three Levels of Listening, and How Do They Relate to Communication? 13
- ***REAL INSIGHTS*** *from a New Professional* 13

What Three Questions Will Help You Think Strategically about Any Communication Exchange? 16
How Can the Skills You Learn in This Course Help You in College, Your Career, and Life? 19
- ***REAL INSIGHTS*** *from a Seasoned Professional* 20

Summary Synthesize What You Have Learned 21
Know It Reflect, Respond, and Express 23
Write It Draft, Revise, and Finalize 23
Speak It Discuss, Listen, and Understand 24
Do It Document Your Success Track Record 24
Business in Action Skype's Influence on Business Communication 25
Key Terms 25
Review Questions Test Yourself 26
Grammar Review Mastering Accuracy: Nouns 26
Extra Resources Tools You Can Use 27

CHAPTER 2 **Teamwork, Leadership, and Business Communication: Motivating and Inspiring Others 29**

What Are Business Teams Like Today? 30
What Do You Have to Offer a Team? 31
What Makes a Team Work Together Effectively? 36
- ***REAL INSIGHTS*** *from a New Professional* 41

What Causes Teams to Break Down? 46
How Can You Become an Effective Team Leader? 49
- ***REAL INSIGHTS*** *from a Seasoned Professional* 50

Summary Synthesize What You Have Learned 52
Know It Reflect, Respond, and Express 53
Write It Draft, Revise, and Finalize 53
Speak It Discuss, Listen, and Understand 54
Do It Document Your Success Track Record 54
Business in Action Kraft-ing a Leadership Plan for Long-term Success 55
Key Terms 55
Review Questions Test Yourself 56
Grammar Review Mastering Accuracy: Pronouns 56
Extra Resources Tools You Can Use 57

CHAPTER 3 **Communicating across Cultures and Generations 59**

Why Is It Important to Know Your Audience? 60
What Are 10 Cultural Components of Communication? 62
What Are Six Major Barriers to Effective Intercultural Communication? 64
- ***REAL INSIGHTS*** *from a Seasoned Professional* 64
- ***REAL INSIGHTS*** *from a New Professional* 67

How Can You Learn to Become a Good Intercultural Communicator? 68
How Can You Effectively Communicate with the Four Generations That Now Share the Workplace? 70
Summary Synthesize What You Have Learned 72
Know It Reflect, Respond, and Express 73
Write It Draft, Revise, and Finalize 74
Speak It Discuss, Listen, and Understand 75
Do It Document Your Success Track Record 75
Business in Action How Envirofit Tailors Its Messages to People of Other Cultures 76
Key Terms 76
Review Questions Test Yourself 76
Grammar Review Mastering Accuracy: Verbs 77
Extra Resources Tools You Can Use 77

CHAPTER 4 **Preparing Business Messages 79**

Why Is Planning Important for Communicating Business Messages? 80
What Are the Six Questions You Should Ask as You Prepare Business Messages? 82
- ***REAL INSIGHTS*** *from a New Professional* 89

When Should You Use Oral versus Written Communication for Business Messages? 92
How Do You Gather Information and Organize a Written Business Message? 94

How Can You Set Yourself Up to Be a Successful Writer? 101
■ **REAL INSIGHTS** *from a Seasoned Professional* 103
Summary Synthesize What You Have Learned 103
Know It Reflect, Respond, and Express 105
Write It Draft, Revise, and Finalize 106
Speak It Discuss, Listen, and Understand 106
Do It Document Your Success Track Record 107
Business in Action Turning Blogging into a Business 107
Key Terms 108
Review Questions Test Yourself 109
Grammar Review Mastering Accuracy: Adjectives 109
Extra Resources Tools You Can Use 109

CHAPTER 5 Writing, Revising, and Editing Messages 111
What Preparations Will Make Your Writing Powerful? 112
How Can Words, Sentences, Paragraphs, and Tone Be Combined to Create a Compelling Message? 115
■ **REAL INSIGHTS** *from a New Professional* 120
How Can Reviewing and Revising Your Draft Affect the Impact of Your Message? 126
■ **REAL INSIGHTS** *from a Seasoned Professional* 134
How Can Getting Feedback Result in a Positive Response to Your Message? 135
Summary Synthesize What You Have Learned 136
Know It Reflect, Respond, and Express 137
Write It Draft, Revise, and Finalize 138
Speak It Discuss, Listen, and Understand 138
Do It Document Your Success Track Record 139
Business in Action Writing Plays a Critical Role at Hanley Wood 139
Key Terms 139
Review Questions Test Yourself 140
Grammar Review Mastering Accuracy: Adverbs 141
Extra Resources Tools You Can Use 141

CHAPTER 6 Designing, Proofreading, and Distributing Messages 143
What Design Choices Will Make Your Message Stand Out? 145
■ **REAL INSIGHTS** *from a Seasoned Professional* 147
How Do Headings and White Space Affect a Message's Readability? 150
What Makes a Message Visually Interesting? 154
Why Is It Important to Proofread Your Message? 159
What Is the Best Way to Distribute Your Message? 160
■ **REAL INSIGHTS** *from a New Professional* 163
Summary Synthesize What You Have Learned 164
Know It Reflect, Respond, and Express 165
Write It Draft, Revise, and Finalize 165
Do It Document Your Success Track Record 166
Speak It Discuss, Listen, and Understand 166
Business in Action Getting the Word Out on the Brunetti Language School 167
Key Terms 168
Review Questions Test Yourself 168
Grammar Review Mastering Accuracy: Prepositions and Conjunctions 169
Extra Resources Tools You Can Use 169

CHAPTER 7 Positive, Everyday Messages: Letters, Memos, and Electronic Communications 171
What Are Positive, Everyday Messages? 172
Why Is Effective Writing Critical for Communicating Positive, Everyday Messages? 175
■ **REAL INSIGHTS** *from a Seasoned Professional* 178
What Channels Are Used to Deliver Positive, Everyday Messages? 178
Why Should You Separate Your Professional Communications from Your Personal Communications? 195
■ **REAL INSIGHTS** *from a New Professional* 196
Summary Synthesize What You Have Learned 196
Know It Reflect, Respond, and Express 197
Write It Draft, Revise, and Finalize 198
Speak It Discuss, Listen, and Understand 199
Do It Document Your Success Track Record 199
Business in Action How Phreesia's Communication Technology Helps Doctors Deliver Health-Related Messages to Patients 200
Key Terms 200
Review Questions Test Yourself 201
Grammar Review Mastering Accuracy: Capitalization 201
Extra Resources Tools You Can Use 201

CHAPTER 8 Negative Messages: Fostering Goodwill during Difficult Communication Exchanges 203
What Is a Negative Message, and Why Is It Important to Plan One? 204
How Do You Organize Negative Messages? 208
What Are the Different Types of Negative Messages? 210
What Is the Best Way to Respond to Negative Messages? 222

■ *REAL INSIGHTS from a Seasoned Professional* 223
■ *REAL INSIGHTS from a New Professional* 226
Summary Synthesize What You Have Learned 227
Know It Reflect, Respond, and Express 228
Write It Draft, Revise, and Finalize 228
Speak It Discuss, Listen, and Understand 229
Do It Document Your Success Track Record 230
Business in Action Toyota Delay Tactics Lead to Deaths, Lawsuits, and Investigation 230
Key Terms 231
Review Questions Test Yourself 232
Grammar Review Mastering Accuracy: Commas 232
Extra Resources Tools You Can Use 233

CHAPTER 9 **Strategies for Persuasive Messages: Using the Right Words at the Right Time 235**
What Are Persuasive Messages? 236
What Makes a Message Persuasive? 237
What Types of Messages Use Persuasion? 241
■ *REAL INSIGHTS from a Seasoned Professional* 242
How Do You Persuade Ethically? 250
■ *REAL INSIGHTS from a New Professional* 255
Summary Synthesize What You Have Learned 257
Know It Reflect, Respond, and Express 258
Write It Draft, Revise, and Finalize 259
Speak It Discuss, Listen, and Understand 259
Do It Document Your Success Track Record 260
Business in Action Tom Cruise Fails to Persuade Brooke Shields . . . and a Lot of Other People 260
Key Terms 261
Review Questions Test Yourself 261
Grammar Review Mastering Accuracy: Colons and Semicolons 262
Extra Resources Tools You Can Use 263

CHAPTER 10 **Writing Reports and Proposals: Compiling and Interpreting Business Information 265**
When Do Reports and Proposals Need to Be Written in the Workplace and for Whom? 266
What Types of Personal Reports and Logs Do Employees Typically Keep? 268
What Types of Informal Progress Reports Do Employees Write? 269
■ *REAL INSIGHTS from a New Professional* 271
What Types of Formal Reports and Proposals Do Employees Write? 273
How Are Research Reports Written and Organized? 279
What Are Feasibility Reports and What Do They Consist Of? 285
■ *REAL INSIGHTS from a Seasoned Professional* 287
Summary Synthesize What You Have Learned 288
Know It Reflect, Respond, and Express 289
Write It Draft, Revise, and Finalize 290
Speak It Discuss, Listen, and Understand 290
Do It Document Your Success Track Record 291
Business in Action AIG's Reporting Practices Underscore the Importance of Ethical Communication 291
Key Terms 292
Review Questions Test Yourself 292
Grammar Review Mastering Accuracy: Exclamation Points, Periods, and Questions Marks 293
Extra Resources Tools You Can Use 293

APPENDIX 10A Example Reports 294

CHAPTER 11 **Business Presentations: Making an Impact 315**
What Are the Three Basic Types of Presentations? 316
How Do You Plan a Presentation? 317
■ *REAL INSIGHTS from a Seasoned Professional* 324
How Can You Be a Better Presenter? 325
■ *REAL INSIGHTS from a New Professional* 328
How Should Different Types of Audiences Be Handled? 329
What Is the Key to Making a Successful Team Presentation? 331
Summary Synthesize What You Have Learned 332
Know It Reflect, Respond, and Express 332
Write It Draft, Revise, and Finalize 333
Speak It Discuss, Listen, and Understand 334
Do It Document Your Success Track Record 334
Business in Action IDEO—Making Business Presentations the Unconventional Way 335
Key Terms 335
Review Questions Test Yourself 336
Grammar Review Mastering Accuracy: Dashes and Hyphens 336
Extra Resources Tools You Can Use 337

CHAPTER 12 **Effective Visual Aids in Presentations: Engaging the Audience and Commanding Attention 339**
What Types of Visual Aids Are Used in Presentations? 340
What Makes a Slideshow Effective? 343
■ *REAL INSIGHTS from a Seasoned Professional* 346

How Can You Make Your Slides Look Professional? 351
■ *REAL INSIGHTS from a New Professional* 351
How Can You Deliver Your Slideshow Effectively? 354
How Can the Web Be Used to Make Presentations? 356
Summary Synthesize What You Have Learned 359
Know It Reflect, Respond, and Express 360
Write It Draft, Revise, and Finalize 360
Speak It Discuss, Listen, and Understand 361
Do It Document Your Success Track Record 362
Business in Action Engaging Audiences with iClickers 363
Key Terms 363
Review Questions Test Yourself 364
Grammar Review Mastering Accuracy: Quotation Marks, Parentheses, Apostrophes, and Italics 364
Extra Resources Tools You Can Use 365

CHAPTER 13 **Career Exploration and the Job Search: Starting Out on the Path to Future Success 367**
How Can You Pinpoint Your Best Skills to Use Professionally? 368
How Can Networking and Research Help You Target a Career and a Company? 371
■ *REAL INSIGHTS from a New Professional* 379
What Can Make You a Desirable Employee? 380
How Do You Effectively Search for a Job? 381
■ *REAL INSIGHTS from a Seasoned Professional* 387
What Steps Can You Take in a Difficult Job Market? 388
Summary Synthesize What You Have Learned 391
Know It Reflect, Respond, and Express 392
Write It Draft, Revise, and Finalize 392
Speak It Discuss, Listen, and Understand 393
Do It Document Your Success Track Record 394
Business in Action Bonobos Founders Created Their Own Opportunities—and Some for Others 395
Key Terms 395
Review Questions Test Yourself 396
Grammar Review Mastering Accuracy: Numbers 396
Extra Resources Tools You Can Use 397

CHAPTER 14 **The Tools for Finding a Job: Cover Letters, Résumés, and Portfolios 399**
What Makes Up a Winning Application Packet? 400
What Are the Different Types of Cover Letters? 401
How Can You Make Your Cover Letter Stand Out? 403
Which Résumé Formats Are Most Common? 407
■ *REAL INSIGHTS from a New Professional* 409
How Do You Write a Winning Résumé? 413
■ *REAL INSIGHTS from a Seasoned Professional* 419
How Does Technology Affect Résumé Writing? 420
How Can You Create an Impressive Portfolio? 423
Summary Synthesize What You Have Learned 425
Know It Reflect, Respond, and Express 427
Write It Draft, Revise, and Finalize 427
Speak It Discuss, Listen, and Understand 428
Do It Document Your Success Track Record 429
Business in Action How Does Google Attract and Retain the Best? 429
Key Terms 430
Review Questions Test Yourself 430
Grammar Review Mastering Accuracy: Common Preposition and Pronoun Errors 431
Extra Resources Tools You Can Use 431

CHAPTER 15 **Job Interviewing: Securing a Position and Negotiating Your Salary 433**
How Do You Respond to or Set Up an Interview? 434
What Types of Interviews Do Employers Utilize? 435
How Do You Prepare for an Interview? 438
■ *REAL INSIGHTS from a New Professional* 439
What Should You Do on the Day of the Interview? 443
How Do You Close the Interview? 448
How Should Job Offers, Job Rejections, and Resignations Be Handled? 451
■ *REAL INSIGHTS from a Seasoned Professional* 452
Summary Synthesize What You Have Learned 456
Know It Reflect, Respond, and Express 458
Write It Draft, Revise, and Finalize 458
Speak It Discuss, Listen, and Understand 459
Do It Document Your Success Track Record 460
Business in Action Interview Tips from Zest Recruitment 460
Key Terms 461
Review Questions Test Yourself 461
Grammar Review Mastering Accuracy: Accurate Word Choices 462
Extra Resources Tools You Can Use 463

CHAPTER 16 **Becoming a World-Class Employee and Leader: Communicate Your Own Success Story 465**
How Do Good Business Communication Skills Help Organizations Succeed? 466

How Do You Find and Keep Your Passion for Your Work? 466

Why Is It Important to Establish Healthy Boundaries at Work? 467

How Do You Exceed Expectations on the Job? 469

How Can You Advance Your Career with Communication? 471

■ ***REAL INSIGHTS** from a New Professional* 477

How Can Feedback Improve Your Professionalism? 478

What Is the Key to Ethical Communication in the Business World? 479

How Do You Know When Your Job Is No Longer a Good Fit? 482

■ ***REAL INSIGHTS** from a Seasoned Professional* 483

Summary Synthesize What You Have Learned 485

Know It Reflect, Respond, Express 486

Write It Draft, Revise, and Finalize 486

Speak It Discuss, Listen, and Understand 487

Do It Document Your Success Track Record 487

Business in Action Goals Lead a Former Cattle Herder to Achieve Her Dreams 488

Key Terms 489

Review Questions Test Yourself 489

Grammar Review Mastering Accuracy: Wordiness 489

Extra Resources Tools You Can Use 490

APPENDIX A Social Networking and Media: Getting the Word Out in the 21st Century A-1

APPENDIX B Formats for Business Documents B-1

APPENDIX C A Basic Guide to Documenting Sources C-1

APPENDIX D Brief Handbook of Grammar, Punctuation, Mechanics, and Conventions D-1

APPENDIX E Commonly Used Revision and Proofreading Symbols E-1

Glossary G-1

References R-1

Photo Credits PC-1

Index I-1

About the Author

Carol Carter

Carol Carter is a different kind of teacher to students. She and her staff teach students in her company, LifeBound, who are for-credit interns. Instead of facilitating in front of the class, Carol works with students firsthand on everything from research to marketing to developing training programs for students. For the last 10 years, Carol has been the president and founder of LifeBound, a student success company that publishes books, conducts training in academic coaching skills, and provides teacher training in the K–12 and college areas. LifeBound's goal is to eradicate developmental education at the college level in the next decade by better preparing incoming freshmen with college-level skills. Carol's passion is solving tough problems in practical ways. Like most students, she thrives when she is challenged.

Carol began her career in the business world of publishing in 1984. In 1987, at age 26, she was promoted and became the first female assistant vice president at Prentice Hall. That same year, she published her first book, *Majoring in the Rest of Your Life: Career Secrets for College Students*, now in a fifth edition. Two years later, Carol co-authored a book for college freshmen entitled *The Keys to Success*, which is used throughout the United States, Latin America, and Canada to help freshmen succeed. Fifteen years after publication, the series has helped over a million students do well in college and in their careers. Finally at Pearson, she became the vice president and director of student programs for the company's education group, a position she held until 1998, when she left to join the Learning Network.

In addition to writing books and operating LifeBound, Carol is a national and international keynote speaker. She has spoken at the East Asian Regional Council of Schools in Bangkok, the Tri-Association Educator's Conference in the Dominican Republic, and the Teachers Matter Conference in Australia and New Zealand. She is the proud stepmother of Chris and Michelle, who are both college students, and the aunt to one niece and three nephews in college. She and her husband, Norton, enjoy bike riding, skiing, hiking, yoga and, most of all, spending time with family.

Preface

One of the comments most frequently made by reviewers about *Keys to Business Communication* is that it is a truly refreshing, more practical, new kind of business communication textbook. This book connects business communication skills with a person's college, career, and life aspirations. Helping students make this connection is not only the goal of this book but the goal of author Carol Carter's company, LifeBound. LifeBound is dedicated to fostering success in students at all education levels.

Book Features

To help you learn the business communications skills you need to enhance your college experience, career, and life, *Keys to Business Communication* offers the following features:

Professional and Personal Business Communication Examples

There is a saying that all politics is local. Similarly, all business communication is ultimately personal. We become what we communicate to other people in all realms of our lives. For this reason *Keys to Business Communication* includes examples of both professional business communication and personal business communication. The examples range from delivering messages not only to a company's customers and stakeholders, but also messages asking instructors for letters of recommendation, messages to one's employer seeking a promotion, and messages about how to communicate with firms when making a claim. This book encourages you to apply real-world communication techniques to your daily lives and in your business transactions as you attend college. In other words, the book encourages you to practice the skills you learn in the book now and over the course of your careers and your lives. You do not have to wait until you graduate.

An Action Framework for Practicing Business Communication Skills

To help you apply the business communication concepts covered in the text, the book provides a framework of actions to master the skills you need. The exercises in the following innovative end-of-chapter sections reinforce this framework by providing you with practical, everyday exercises you can use to begin honing your business communication and strategic thinking skills.

- ***Know It:*** Critical thinking questions and scenarios
- ***Write It:*** Exercises to strengthen your writing skills
- ***Speak It:*** Group discussion topics and activities
- ***Do It:*** Self-directed activities that build experience

Industry Themes Illustrating Communication in Context

Industry themes that permeate the chapters expose you to 15 possible career paths and provide you with a way to look at business messages in context. For example, Chapter 5 focuses on the industry of real estate while discussing the concept of writing, editing, and revising material. As you learn the content of the chapters, you are also exposed to real-world situations in which you will inevitably find yourself—everything from being in the position of negotiating the sale of a home to writing a persuasive proposal for a business.

Professional Profiles of Successful Business Communicators

New and seasoned professionals from the industries profiled in each chapter share their views on business communication success. New professionals have been out of college for only a few years and are discovering firsthand how to communicate in a variety of business situations. In contrast, seasoned professionals, or professionals with a number of years of experience on the job, share how their communication skills have contributed to their career achievements. You will see how real people use the very skills you are reading about to succeed in their lives and make a difference in their companies and the world.

Resources for Students

mybcommlab.com, which is located online, offers you multiple ways of reviewing each chapter, including a customizable "Study Plan," "Self-Tests," "PowerPoints," "FlashCards," and "Interactive Lectures." Multiple activities are also provided to get you interacting with the material: "Video Exercises" show you how textbook concepts are put into practice every day; "Document Makeovers" provide hands-on, scored practice of document writing; and "Mini-simulations" help you think critically and prepare to make choices in the business world. "Mini-simulations" are real-world scenarios that invite you to assume the role of a decision maker at a company and apply the concepts you have just learned. You are scored on the five-minute simulation and then directed to the eText, quizzes, and other learning aids to help reinforce the concepts.

mybcommlab.com also features pretest questions that generate a personalized "Study Plan" for you based on your incorrect answers. The "Study Plan" links to multiple learning aids, such as videos, and the flashcards, for additional help. After you work through the learning aids, you can take a posttest to check your improvement. The "Video Library" features a variety of topical business videos that correspond to each chapter topic. "Document Makeovers" ask you to analyze and correct business documents such as e-mail messages, letters, memos, outlines, blogs, and résumés. Immediate feedback is provided.

Each element of **mybcommlab.com**, including the chapter specific content and learning objective-based student activities described above, is created to help you master the textbook concepts and focus strategically on those areas where you may need extra work.

Acknowledgments

Many, many people, including teachers, industry professionals, students, the staff at Pearson, and others made *Keys to Business Communication* what it is today. I am deeply indebted to all of them.

Academic Reviewers

Literally scores of professors contributed their ideas to the book. The following professors provided me with invaluable insight, comments, and examples. I am deeply grateful to all of these people for their input.

Barbara Alpern, Siena Heights University
Janine Diane Anderson, Brown Mackie College–Tucson
Sherry Baker, Rich Mountain Community College
Cynthia Barnes, Lamar University
Lise-Pauline Barnett, Harrisburg Area Community College
Julie Basler, Platt College
Eric Bauer, Brown Mackie College–Akron
Rhonda Baughman, Brown Mackie College–North Canton
Cheryl Beese, Vatterott College
Shasta Bennett, Olney Central College
Ashley Bennington, Texas A&M University–Kingsville
Jill Bernaciak, John Carroll University
Janel Bloch, Northern Kentucky University
Mary Bowers, Northern Arizona University
Lori Braunstein, Central Washington University
Steve Bryant, Antonelli College
Terry Buchanan, Metropolitan State College of Denver
Randy Bullis, Career Point College
Phyllis Bunn, Delta State University Division of Managment, Marketing, and Business Administration
Brennan Carr, Long Beach City College
Rod Carveth, Fitchburg State University
Jennifer Chunn, Harrisburg Area Community College
Ned Cummings, Bryant and Stratton College
Cathy Dees, DeVry University
Sandee Dillon, College of the Siskiyous
Terry Don, Keiser University and University of South Florida
Veronica Dufresne, Finger Lakes Community College
Deb Dusek, North Dakota State College of Science & Technology
Daniel Filipek, Oakland Community College
Melissa Fish, American River College
Catherine Flynn, Kaplan University
Edwin Fowler, El Paso Community College
Gail Garton, Ozarks Technical Community College
Darin Gerdes, Liberty University
Robert Goldberg, Prince George's Community College
Laura Goodman, Pima Medical Institute
Georgia Hale, University of Arkansas
Susan Hall, University of West Georgia
Victoria Hess, Central Wyoming College–Jackson Campus
Sheila Hostetler, Orange Coast College
Michael Hricik, Westmoreland County Community College
Rebecca Hubbard, Horry-Georgetown Tech College
Pat Hurley, University of Hawai'i–Leeward Community College
Rae Ann Ianniello, Chabot College
Rusty Juban, Southeastern Louisiana University
Patrick Knisley, Fashion Institute of Technology
Melinda Kramer, Prince George's Community College
Sarah Kravits, co-author, *Keys to Success*
Karna Kurtz, Anoka Ramsey Community College
Ruth Levy, Westchester Community College
Brent Madalinski, Bay de Noc Community College
Lisa Martin, Piedmont Technical College
Joseph Martinez, El Paso Community College
Lisa McCormick, Community College of Allegheny County
Annie Laurie I. Meyers, Northampton Community College
Alexa North, University of West Georgia
Claudia Orr, Northern Michigan University
Mary Padula, Borough of Manhattan Community College
Marvin Parker, Fort Valley State University
Jessica Ponto, Miami University of Ohio
Carole Quine, Baltimore City Community College
Richard David Ramsey, Southeastern Louisiana University
Monica Rausch, Armstrong Atlantic State University
Ann Marie Rigdon, Trinidad State Junior College
Loreen Ritter, Salter College
Raymond Rodgers, Harcum College
Melinda Rose, Lee College
Mary Rowe, Miami Dade College–North
Kevin Sager, State University of New York
Danielle Scane, Orange Coast College
Peggy J. Scott, Tidewater Community College
Liz Simmons, Lamar University
Brenda Siragusa, Corinthian Colleges
Jason Snyder, Central Connecticut State University

Steve Soucy, Santa Monica College
Debra Thomas, Harrisburg Area Community College
Cindy Thompson, University of Arkansas Community College at Morrilton
John Turner, Lone Star College–Kingwood
Pam Uhlenkamp, Iowa Central Community College
Nathan Ullger, Catawba Valley Community College
Betty Wanielista, Valencia Community College, East Campus
Kelli Wilkes, Wiregrass Technical College
Beth Williams, Stark State College of Technology
Diane Williams, Colby Community College
Donna K. Young, Ivy Tech Community College of Indiana
Diane Youngblood, Greenville Technical College
Alex Yousefi, ECPI College of Technology
Lale Yurtseven, Mission College

In addition to reviewers of the main text, the following professors contributed outstanding work toward this project's supplemental materials. Their contributions will enhance the book's success tremendously. Special thanks go to Rhonda Baughman, Brown Mackie College; Christine Laursen, Red Rock Community College; Beth Williams, Stark State College; Cheryl Beese, Vatterott College; Randy Gerber; Macomb Community College; Jay Stubblefield, North Carolina Wesleyan College; Jean Fennema, Pima Medical Institute; Catherine Flynn, Kaplan University; Melinda Kramer, Prince George's Community College; John Waltman, Eastern Michigan University; and the team at ANSRSource Group for all of their efforts.

Professional Profiles

My sincerest thanks go to the following many professionals who contributed their wisdom and workplace experience to the "Real Insights from a New Professional / Seasoned Professional" feature:

Michelle Aleti, Procter & Gamble
Jessica Bennett, Organic People, Inc.
Lauren Berger, Superior Lexus North
Dave Bouwman, DTS Agile
Scott Carter, HBO
Sacha Chua, IBM
Rebecca Cummings, Aloha Guide
Amy Dohr, Renaissance Care for Internal and Preventative Medicine
Jenna Drobnick, Freelancer
Vanessa Evans, Ron Brown Scholar Program
Cliff Ho, Sandia National Laboratories
Frank Jedlicka, Adtran, Inc.
Susan Katz, HarperCollins Children's Books
Lynette Luis, Major computer makers
Diandra Macias, Duarte Inc.
Joe Martin, New Teacher University, Real World University, and the Academic Coaching Company
Brooke Meacham, Omation Animation Studios
Cole Mehlman, Odyssey International
David Packer, Rich Products
Ritika Puri, Claremont McKenna College
Alexa Robinson, Pizza Hut, Inc.
Paul Rosengard, Li & Fung USA
Aron Rosenthal, Orbis Institute
Brianne Schmidt, BMO Capital Markets
David Secunda, Avid4 Adventure
Gary Siedenburg, Farmer's Insurance
Jordan Simon, Venture West
Laurie Guevara-Stone, Solar Energy International (SEI)
Tim Thwaites, Coda Coffee Company
Karen Travis, Sigma Performance Solutions, Inc.
Ana Valdez, Teach for America and Weill Cornell Medical College
Nicole Yoder-Barnhart, Real Living, Inc.

Nonacademic (Industry) Reviewers

Many nonacademic business professionals, including some who also agreed to be profiled in the chapters, contributed their thoughts and expertise to the book as well. They include Tiffany Yore, Martha Roden, Maureen Breeze, Diane Fromme, Suzanne Stromberg, Don Cameron, Gary Izumo, Dan Oltersdorf, Norton Ewart, Rich Matteson, Maya Gumennik, Darrin Duber-Smith, Rama Moorthy, David Koutsoukis, Rebecca Wardlow, Jim Goddard, Sebastian Waszak, Jessica Lavery, Keith Hanenberg, Michael Portee, Ben Beierwaltes, David Katz, Alana Zdinak, Douglas Rath, and Sandy Steiner. These people took a great deal of time out of their busy schedules to help make the book the best it can be, and I thank them.

Student Reviewers

Keys to Business Communication was not reviewed only by professors and business professionals but by an army of student reviewers who combed over the material, helped catch typos, and offered suggestions about what confused them and what could be improved. They include Natalie Vielkind, Elizabeth Fritzler, Miriam Evangelista, Austin Correll, Angelica Jestrovich, Drew Rudebusch, Allyn Delozier, Roger Emmelheinz, Amy Piazza, Kristen Fenwick, and Bennett Delozier. Thanks also to Jeremy Pape, who served as our Internet expert and digital guru.

The Pearson Dream Team

I was very blessed to have the contributions of one of the most talented teams at Pearson. Sally Yagan, Pearson Business Publishing's vice president and editorial director, first came to me to ask if I would consider writing this book. She saw potential synergies between my business experience and my work in the area of student success. After six months of thinking about it, I became excited to help students understand how to communicate effectively in school, their careers, and their personal lives. I thank Sally for her faith in me. James Heine, my acquisitions editor, has been an absolute pleasure even during times of disagreements and misunderstandings. His wit, good nature, and even temper always inspired me to do a better job. I also admire his teamwork skills; he knew how to motivate our entire group to get the best from each and every person.

Steve Deitmer, director of development, has been a friend of mine for 20 years. Steve has the most gentle and reassuring way of asking really tough questions and giving difficult feedback. His sense of humor had me laughing in e-mails and smiling through conference calls. Kate Moore, senior editorial development manager, has been a friend even longer than Steve has. If I had to think of an accurate title for Kate relative to this book, it would be "relationship manager." She knows how to connect with each and every person on the planet, and she never forgets people's birthdays or their children's names. Her passion for her kids, her work, and her life in general is something I want to emulate. Her heart is huge, and she is a tremendous asset and a dear friend.

Amy Ray, my developmental editor, helped me make sense of my rough ideas and smooth them into something sharp and sensible. We shared many stories as we discussed the particulars of chapters, features, supplements, and household pets. She is first-rate. Karin Williams, my project manager, kept me on a schedule in the most diplomatic and encouraging way. Like her team members, Karin has a great sense of humor, which would always hook me into moving her requests up my priority list.

Nikki Jones, my marketing manager, has been involved with this project since its inception. Her enthusiasm for the approach of the book and her ebullient personality allow her to be a high-impact rainmaker. She knows how to make things happen, and her follow-through is impeccable. Judy Leale, Jackie Martin, and Lori Bradshaw did a fabulous job producing this book. John Christiana, the director of design, was the mastermind behind the look and the feel of the interior and the cover. He nailed our sample chapter the first time out and listened with a true understanding of how to make the first pass on the cover a little bit better than his already strong design.

Patrice Jones was the force behind our strategic company-wide marketing initiatives, especially with the career sales team. Jerome Grant, in his role as president, set the stage for all of these talented people to do their best work. I would also like to thank Brian Kibby, senior vice president, Sales, Marketing, and Business Development; Walt Kirby, vice president, Career College Sales; and Tim Bozik, CEO, Pearson Professional & Career.

Special Thanks

I also must express my special thanks to the following people, whose friendship and guidance have helped me so much through this project and throughout my journey as an author:

Melinda Kramer and I met 25 years ago when we were both working in the area of freshman composition. About five years ago, we met again, this time in the area of student success. Melinda is a professor of business communication at Prince George's Community College, teaches student success, and is the chair of the college's English department.

I knew that Melinda would give me honest and sometimes scathing feedback on the chapters in the book. I have always valued and admired Melinda's candor, and in writing this book found her to be as harsh and helpful as my most challenging English professor in college. Without Melinda's input, this book would be far less developed and certainly less accurate. I know my weaknesses. I was thrilled to have Melinda's red marks on my drafts. The best students aren't without mistakes, but they do know their weaknesses and take action to get help when they need it.

Personally, what I love about Melinda is her relationship with her husband, her foreign travels, and her ski vacations. She has a zest for life and she is not a sidelines sitter. I am grateful to her for being an outstanding professor, colleague, and friend.

Dan Oltersdorf is a vice president for the firm Student Advantage. He and I work in the same office, and I have marveled at how someone just over 30 years old can be as successful as Dan. In college, Dan started a Web site for all of the resident advisors around the country. Once he graduated, the company he works for now bought the firm. How many undergrads know that they can start their own businesses in college or right out of college? As a first-generation college student, Dan looked at how he could become involved in college as a leader and gain experiences beyond the scope of his family, neighborhood, and town. He is a role model for today's students, and his instincts have shaped the direction of this book. His leadership provides a model for all young people who start from scratch to create their own advantages.

While Dan has a wonderful career, his greatest achievement is his marriage to Erin and his beautiful daughters, Grace and Lydia. He is a model of life/work balance and he is a manager who promotes this throughout his company. He knows it is not about working long hours. It is about working smart so that you can have time with the people you love. I appreciate Dan's savvy instincts on what today's students need to be strong business communicators and strong people overall. I expect to be seeing him and Campus Advantage on the cover of *Inc.* magazine. Mark my words!

Gary Izumo and I have worked together for the past 15 years writing books and conducting training linking student success to career success. Along with Joe Martin, the founder of New Teacher University, Real World University, and the Academic Coaching Company, we co-authored the *Career Tool Kit, Keys to Career Success,* and *Stop Parenting and Start Coaching.* Gary is a national leadership expert and conducts trainings on how institutions and companies—from school districts to Fortune 500 companies—can be more effective with an inspired, mission-driven, and focused charge. He knows firsthand what makes businesspeople successful and what can cost them their jobs. He is direct, honest, and practical.

What I love about Gary is that he is a wonderful human being. He is a business colleague who starts every conversation by asking how I am personally and how things are in my life and family. I'm a firm believer that good business comes from strong relationships. Without the underpinning of respect, personal connection, and concern, we aren't capable of our best business outcomes. Strong business deliverables come from people who enjoy, help, and understand each other on a human level first. My hope is that today's undergraduates will understand that basic life truth from the people they meet in this book. I thank Gary for his insight, his courage in facing life, his compassion, and for his ability to be fully human.

Chelsey Emmelheinz began as an intern with my company. After six months, her for-credit internship was over, and I hired her as an editorial assistant for her remaining year-and-a-half of college. Chelsey's skills were far beyond her age. That, combined with her insights as a student, provided the best guidance I could have asked for when my ideas were not entirely relevant to students. I don't think exactly like today's undergrads, but Chelsey helped me better understand her and all of the other students she managed in the student-reviewing process. She also made it clear to me that today's students are visual learners and contributed to the visual design of this book.

Over the course of two years, I saw Chelsey grow and mature not just as an editor, but as a person who learned how to truly create a positive and sustainable environment that could continue after she began her career in children's publishing. She learned how to ask the most important questions while "holding all the possible answers." She learned how to challenge herself, how to contribute to a process and how to sit squarely in the middle of chaos without losing her cool for herself or her team. Chelsey gives me hope for young people in our country, and I hope that students who read this book will be emboldened by her contributions as they read each chapter.

It was so great to work with Chelsey on this and all the other projects she ran. I am sure that I will see her someday as the president of a children's publishing company or her own firm. On that day, I will look back and say I knew her when!

Angelica Jestrovich is a recent graduate—a very talented one—who took over for Chelsey. She worked on all of the final edits of the book, helped me with photo research, and reviewed the supplements from a student and now a graduate perspective. Angelica has excellent instincts, a great sense of humor, and is extremely versatile. It was great to run the last part of this marathon with her.

For all of my incredible staff members at LifeBound who were willing to help with this book—Maureen Breeze, Tiffany Yore, Heather Brown, Diane Fromme, Renee Brown, Don Cameron, and most of all, Martha Roden—I thank them profusely for their many hours of contribution, insight, and feedback. They are the most committed and consummate professionals and I am very honored to work with them on this project and the other important work we undertake.

I would also like to thank Sandra Steiner, one of my longtime friends whom I met 20 years ago this year. I appreciate her faith, instincts, and encouragement. Finally, I would like to thank my husband, Norton, who read many chapters but especially pored over the chapter on presentations while offering his perspective as a former executive with Hewlett-Packard. Norton keeps my life fun and silly, and I love him!

Carol J. Carter
Author and President of Lifebound, LLC.
January 2011

Lifebound
1530 High Street
Denver, CO 80218
Toll-Free Office: 877-737-8510
Office: 303-327-5688
Fax: 303-327-5684

www.caroljcarter.com
www.lifebound.com
www.keystobuscom.com

Keys to BUSINESS COMMUNICATION

"Communication—the human connection—is key to personal and career success."

—**Paul J. Meyer,** author and global business executive

CHAPTER 1

Strategic Thinking for Smart Business Communication

Preparing to Succeed in the 21st Century

>>> **Right** out of college, Stephen took a job with a small public relations firm. During his first performance review, his manager praised his work ethic and his willingness to learn all facets of the business. The manager also applauded Stephen's teamwork and ability to prioritize various tasks while maintaining focus in the midst of chaos. However, she recommended Stephen work on his communication skills. "Although your interpersonal communication skills are top rate, there is room for improvement in your writing and oral presentation skills," she wrote in the review. Specifically, she commented that his contributions to proposals and client presentations often required extensive editing. In particular, he tended to take a long time to get to the point and used vocabulary unfamiliar to clients. She also said his writing needed some work because it was too academic and did not seem direct or friendly enough.

In spite of receiving a pay raise and an above-average performance review, Stephen was devastated. He had always received top marks on his college papers, so he figured his writing skills were adequate. Although he had never participated on his high school or college's speech and debate teams, he felt his public speaking skills were better than average. Business communication was more complex than he thought.

LEARNING OBJECTIVE QUESTIONS

1. How can you prepare yourself for today's business world?
2. How does communication affect business successes and failures?
3. What are the four elements of any communication exchange?
4. What are the three levels of listening, and how do they relate to communication?
5. What three questions will help you think strategically about any communication exchange?
6. How can the skills you learn in this course help you in college, your career, and life?

PEARSON **mybcommlab** Access interactive videos, simulations, sample documents, document makeovers, and assessment quizzes in Chapter 1 of **mybcommlab.com** for mastery of this chapter's objectives.

Stephen >>>

DID YOU KNOW?

A survey of recruiters from major companies by the University of Pittsburgh's Katz Business School found that the major factors they look for in candidates are good communication skills, including a person's ability to make written and oral presentations and work well with other people. The survey also found that good communication skills are the single most important criterion firms look at when hiring managers.[1]

Stephen's story is common. After students graduate and enter the workforce, they often realize the business world demands different communication abilities than the classroom did. Writing for work is very different than writing for school, where the objective is usually to express what is known about a subject. In business, there are three basic overarching goals for communicating: to inform others, to elicit a response, and/or to incite an action. Time is usually of the essence. As a result, business communication needs to be direct, concise, and to the point.

Stephen's story demonstrates that in the business world you will be judged by the way you think, write, and speak before you start your first professional job. You can't get an interview without a high-impact, well-written résumé showcasing your experiences. You can't get a second interview or a job offer without being able to orally communicate what you have to offer a prospective employer. You can't get promoted from an entry-level job to one with more responsibility without strong thinking, writing, and speaking skills. Even seasoned managers need to constantly improve their own communication skills. These skills and more are required and rewarded in the world of work. They are not "nice to have." They are "must haves."

1 How Can You Prepare Yourself for Today's Business World?

Many professionals agree that the world of business is dynamically changing. Evolving technologies are rapidly affecting the way we work and communicate. The globalization of many industries is shifting who we work for and how we conduct business. The increasing diversity of the workforce demands that we know more about different cultures, attitudes, and beliefs so that we can work together in productive ways. Emerging laws and regulatory policies require employees to be well-versed in business ethics and best legal practices. A survey of Fortune 500 executives concluded that effective communication skills are more important than ever before and will continue to be a critical component of the information society.[2]

■ For an interactive, real-world example of this topic, access this chapter's bcomm mini sim entitled Learning to Listen at Second City Communications, located at **mybcommlab.com**

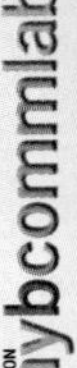

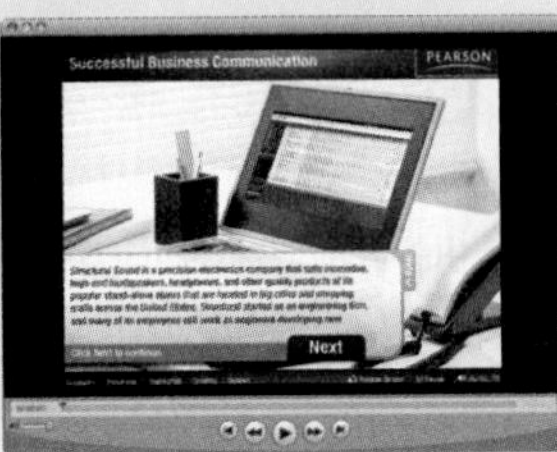

Consider the typical day in the lives of the following four professionals in today's workforce:

Chad

Chad works for an information technology firm in Los Angeles, California. His coworker Naileesh lives in Delhi, India. Chad and Naileesh sometimes communicate via computer using voice over Internet protocol (VoIP) and instant messaging. However, because of the time difference between Los Angeles and Delhi, the two workers must coordinate when they can directly communicate with one another in real time. Otherwise, they have to rely on e-mails for correspondence.

Maria

Maria works as a customer service representative from 6 P.M. to 2 A.M. from her home office in New Jersey. Her company, which produces medical equipment, is headquartered in Calgary, Canada. Maria has never met her direct supervisor face to face. She uses her Spanish-speaking skills to communicate with clients all over the world in Spanish-speaking countries.

Jeff

Jeff is a sales representative with a furniture manufacturing company. He spends 20 percent of his time traveling throughout the United States, meeting with retailers in the industry. He spends another 60 percent of his time maintaining these relationships around the country via e-mail, thank-you notes, and phone calls. The remaining 20 percent of his time is spent communicating with the factories in Asia, where his company's furniture is manufactured, and the freight companies that ship the products to the United States.

Sasha

Sasha works on Wall Street for an investment bank. Her team analyzes home-mortgage portfolios to be purchased, bundled, and then traded on the secondary market. Because of the changing real estate and investment climate, Sasha and her team must comply with stringent new regulatory policies.

Clearly, the way people work today is very different than the way they worked 20 years ago. The types of jobs available to business graduates are continually evolving, too. In fact, according to the forecasts of several business schools, the top 10 jobs of 2015 most likely don't even exist today.[3] So how do you prepare yourself for jobs that don't yet exist? You do so by knowing how to operate in a diverse workforce, compete in the global market, and remain flexible and employable despite uncertain economic times—all of which will require you to hone the communication skills this book will teach you.

Diversity in the Workforce

Chapter 3 discusses diversity in the workforce in greater detail. But for now, let's briefly consider what diversity means in the professional world. Some people think of diversity in terms of race and gender, but **diversity** in the workforce can show up in many ways, from varying skill levels and professional backgrounds, to differing work habits, age levels, cultural values, and so forth. Diversity can affect how people work together.

Exhibit 1-1 uses an iceberg to illustrate both the highly visible and less visible ways in which people differ from one another on the job. The cap of an iceberg can be seen above the surface of water. Similarly, some of the differences between people are readily visible. The cap represents "above the waterline" characteristics you can see. The bulk of the iceberg remains below the surface, though. "Below the waterline" characteristics are not as easy to identify. However, even visible differences are not always as clear as you think they might be. Consider gender. Have you ever found it hard to tell which gender someone was?

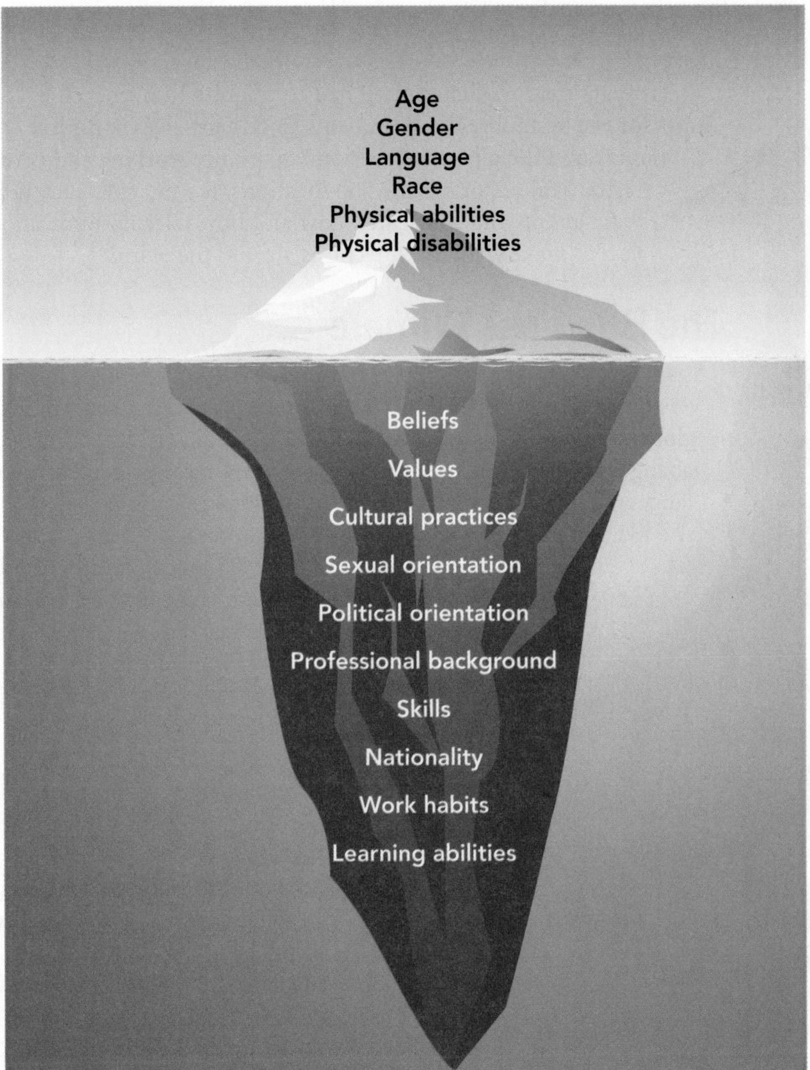

Exhibit 1-1
Examples of Diversity in the Workforce

It is almost certain that at some point in your career you will work with a group of people whose diverse skill sets will challenge you and your fellow team members. Developing the ability to collaborate with people of diverse backgrounds is more important than ever because businesses today rely heavily on teamwork. Chapter 2 discusses how to be a strong team member and leader.

Global Competition

You will not only be working with people from diverse backgrounds. You will be competing with them for the best jobs in the market. Becoming gainfully employed today is different from 20 years ago. During 2000 to 2003, somewhere between one-quarter to a half-million U.S. service jobs moved to low-wage countries.[4] This trend continues today. Alan S. Blinder, a Princeton University economist, lists the following 10 most vulnerable occupations that face competition from overseas workers:[5]

- Computer programmers
- Data entry workers
- Electrical and electronic drafters
- Mechanical drafters
- Computer and information specialists
- Actuaries
- Mathematicians
- Statisticians
- Math science occupations
- Film and video editors

Fifteen years ago, graduates often had to migrate to bigger cities in the United States for the best jobs. Today, students find themselves considering opportunities around the globe, some of which require working and communicating from remote, or off-site, job locations. It's smart to start thinking globally about your job search now and how telecommunications can help you to make virtual connections around the world.

The Business Climate

As already noted, the makeup of the workforce you are preparing to enter is diversifying. The competition you will be up against is expanding across the globe, and the types of jobs that will be available to you are dramatically changing. On top of this, the last few years have presented economic challenges that have affected all areas of business. Beginning in 2008, industries shrank, and unemployment rates rose around the world.

You can't do much about the state of the economy. However, you can be smart about your education to position yourself to take advantage of the best career opportunities in the marketplace. For example, did you know that the number of jobs for producing and marketing goods in the United States has been stagnant since the 1980s and is expected to decline by 3.3 percent from 2006 to 2016? By contrast, the service-oriented sector, especially in the healthcare, social assistance, and education industries are expected to produce 15.7 million new jobs from 2006 to 2016. Three of 10 new jobs will be in these fields.[6]

You might think, "I'm a business major, not in medical school," or "What does the education service sector have to do with my business degree?" A lot. The service sector needs business-minded individuals. It will be up to you to position yourself to capture these opportunities. You can do so by developing superb communication skills.

Communication in the 21st Century

How can you best prepare yourself for the 21st century job market, where globalization and the digital revolution are redefining business priorities? The Partnership for 21st Century Skills, an organization made up of education and business professionals across the country, addresses this question. The leaders of the organization have taken a careful look at what the 21st century workplace demands of employees and what it rewards. In response, they have developed a "Framework for 21st Century Learning" identifying the knowledge and the skills employees need to be successful. **Exhibit 1-2** outlines them.

Keys to Business Communication is designed to help you develop media literacy. If you have these skills, you have the chance to close the gap between what the world needs workers to do and what you as a graduating college student can offer the working world. This course is your ticket to being a ready-for-hire applicant when you graduate.

Exhibit 1-2
The Framework for 21st Century Learning

Core Subjects & 21st Century Themes

- Global awareness
- Financial, economic, business, and entrepreneurial literacy
- Civic literacy—community service
- Health literacy

Information, Media, & Technology Skills

- Information literacy
- Media literacy
- ICT (Information, communications, and technology)

Life & Career Skills

- Flexibility and adaptability
- Initiative and self-direction
- Social and cross-cultural skills
- Productivity and accountability
- Leadership and responsibility

Learning & Innovation Skills

- Creativity and innovation
- Critical thinking and problem solving
- Communication and collaboration

Source: Reprinted with permission from Partnership for 21st Century Skills; 177 N. Church Avenue, Ste 305, Tucson, AZ 85701. PH: 520-623-2466.

2 How Does Communication Affect Business Successes and Failures?

In any business, people produce goods or services in exchange for some form of trade or payment. Business does not occur if the products or services do not transfer from the producer to the consumer. The means for this transfer is communication. It lies at the heart of business.

There will be no business if the greatest tennis shoes ever made are never purchased and worn. Similarly, the most innovative financial model for investment will never generate revenue if its developers cannot communicate its value to potential investors. Communication, which is the lifeblood of any successful business enterprise, takes many forms: internal and external communication; and communication in writing, on the phone, and in person.[7]

Exhibit 1-3 When Communication Fails

What Suffers When Communication Fails...			
Time	**Opportunity**	**Talent**	**Reputation**
A memo went out to 100 employees detailing changes to their health-care and benefits structure. However, because the manager did not want to upset the staff, she embedded several important points in long paragraphs. The result was a confusing, long-winded memo that caused many employees to call Human Resources and complain. After hours of calming distraught employees, another memo was sent to clarify the message.	A sales representative for a lumber company called on the largest home builder in his territory. Due to his poor sales presentation and lack of follow-up skills, the unimpressed customer went elsewhere for his lumber purchases. The sales representative's lack of training cost the lumber company the account—and millions of dollars in business.	A senior manager failed to listen, clarify goals and procedures, and support her staff through effective communication. This caused her talented employees to look elsewhere for work. The costs of recruiting and training talent, and then losing employees because of failed communication, can add up quickly and cause troubling morale problems. Communicating effectively to retain the best and brightest workers must be a priority for any company.	Merck, the pharmaceutical company, went to trial to defend its drug Vioxx. The company was unable to effectively communicate scientific explanations about the drug to the jury, which ultimately cost Merck the verdict. Losing a highly visible trial not only hurt the company's bottom line, but its reputation as well.

PEARSON mybcommlab

Apply Exhibit 1-3's key concepts by revising a new document. Go to Chapter 1 in mybcommlab.com and select Document Makeovers.

When businesses communication failures occur, not only do exchanges not occur, but time, opportunities, and revenues are lost. The firm's reputation can suffer, which can cause talented employees to leave the organization. **Exhibit 1-3** outlines some of the scenarios that can occur within businesses when this happens.

Poor communication costs businesses billions. According to a study conducted by the consulting company Accenture, consumers returned $13.8 billion worth of electronics in America in 2007. Surprisingly, the majority of these returns were not due to faulty equipment but due to problems with customer communication, confusing interfaces, and weak product documentation.[8]

Without communication, products and services will never be known to their potential customers.

Because poor communication can produce crippling results, companies assess their applicants' communication skills. **Exhibit 1-4** illustrates how employers rate the qualities they look for when interviewing candidates for employment. As you can see, good written and verbal communication skills top the list.

Firms and their employees must also be able to communicate well on an intrapersonal and interpersonal level. **Intrapersonal communication** means how you talk to yourself; **interpersonal communication** means how you talk with others. It is the process of sending and receiving messages between people in one-on-one settings, in small groups, or public speaking situations. It includes both verbal and written communication, and encompasses how people relate to one another in the communication process.

Exhibit 1-5 describes the differences between intrapersonal and interpersonal communication.

An impressive résumé and a high GPA might land you an interview, but you'll need an arsenal of tangible and intangible skills to make a grade-A impression. These are some of the skills and qualities employers value the most:

- Critical-thinking skills
- Written communication skills
- Verbal communication skills
- Listening skills
- Conflict-resolution skills
- Problem-solving skills
- Computer/technical skills
- Arithmetic/math skills
- Ability to be organized
- Ability to work well with others/teamwork
- Energy/passion/positive attitude
- Dedication/loyalty/reliability
- Flexibility
- Self-confidence
- Self-motivation
- Ability to multitask
- Ability to meet deadlines
- Honesty/integrity/morality
- Creativity/innovation
- Sense of humor

Others

- Proofreading/attention to detail
- Money management/budget skills
- Willingness to learn
- Leadership abilities
- Long-term potential
- Analytical skills
- Interpersonal abilities
- Professional attitude
- Enthusiasm/initiative
- Intelligence
- Social skills

Exhibit 1-4
Skills and Qualities Employers Value the Most

Because building relationships is the key to conducting business, employers say interpersonal skills are critical for success and essential for effective leadership. Begin practicing your interpersonal skills every time you interact with people by considering the following tips:

- If the communication is face to face, maintain eye contact.
- Don't multitask during conversations.
- Try to express your points clearly and concisely while providing the background information listeners need.
- Concentrate on hearing others, even if you don't agree with what they are saying.

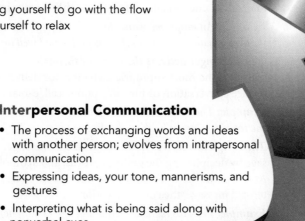

Intrapersonal Communication
• The communication you have with yourself that then informs how you communicate with others
• Having internal thoughts and conversations
• Listening to your "inner voice"
• Reminding yourself to go with the flow
• Telling yourself to relax
Interpersonal Communication
• The process of exchanging words and ideas with another person; evolves from intrapersonal communication
• Expressing ideas, your tone, mannerisms, and gestures
• Interpreting what is being said along with nonverbal cues

Exhibit 1-5
Intrapersonal Communication and Interpersonal Communication

- Don't let your mind race ahead to what you want to say next. Instead stay in the moment and listen to what others are saying.
- Ask questions if you don't understand, and use questions to draw others into the conversation if necessary.
- If the conversation is emotionally charged, take a breath before you respond. Don't raise your voice.
- Try to avoid making assumptions about the person with whom you are speaking. Instead, concentrate on the information being conveyed.

Well-honed communication skills are not necessary only during exchanges with one's customers. These skills are also critical during the production process and after the sale of products and services, especially when there is a crisis. Consider, Johnson & Johnson, the healthcare products and pharmaceutical maker. In 1982, Johnson & Johnson faced a crisis when several deaths were linked to its Extra-Strength Tylenol capsules. Someone had taken bottles of Tylenol from stores, laced the capsules with deadly cyanide, and returned them to the shelves.

However, even before the discovery, Johnson & Johnson's effective communication and swift action spared the firm its reputation. Executives recalled 31 million bottles and immediately advised consumers not to take the capsules and throw away any bottles they had at home. The company also suspended all regular product advertising, and replaced it with messages explaining how they would exchange consumers' capsules for tablets not vulnerable to tampering. The firm also sent direct messages to doctors, hospitals, pharmacies, and distributors, to clarify the situation and outline the company's actions. It then designed tamper-proof packaging.[9] Communication is the major tool in crisis management.

3 What Are the Four Elements of Any Communication Exchange?

Whether you are writing a letter, composing an e-mail, reciting a speech, or presenting an idea to a teammate, the keys to communication are the same. As the famous journalist Edward R. Murrow once said: "The newest computer can merely compound, at speed, the oldest problem in the relations between human beings, and in the end the communicator will be confronted with the old problem of what to say and how to say it."[10]

As you reflect on what to say and how to say it, look at the **four-step communication model** shown in **Exhibit 1-6.**

1. ***The messenger formulates the idea to be communicated.*** The communication process begins when a messenger identifies an idea to be communicated. At this stage, the messenger considers the purpose of the message, assumptions regarding both the situation surrounding the message and the recipient's knowledge about the subject, along with expectations of how the message will be received. The messenger then tries to mentally encapsulate, or formulate, the message in a way the receiver will understand.

   Example: *An employee wants to ask her boss for a raise. She has been with the company for over a year and believes she has performed well on the job.*
2. ***The messenger delivers the message through a channel.*** At this stage, the messenger considers the most appropriate channel for delivering the message, such as via a face-to-face conversation or meeting, phone call, e-mail, letter, or formal presentation.

   Example: *The employee sends a formal letter to her boss requesting a raise and detailing the reasons why she believes she deserves it.*
3. ***The recipient receives and interprets the message.*** The receiver interprets the message by deciphering the gestures, words, and symbols, and attaching meaning to them. At this point the communication flow is complete. If the recipient understands the intended message, the communication is successful.

   Example: *The boss reads the letter and agrees with her employee's justifications for a raise. She decides to increase her salary at the start of the next month.*
4. ***The recipient provides the sender with feedback.*** The feedback helps the messenger determine if the communication was actually a success or not. Many obstacles

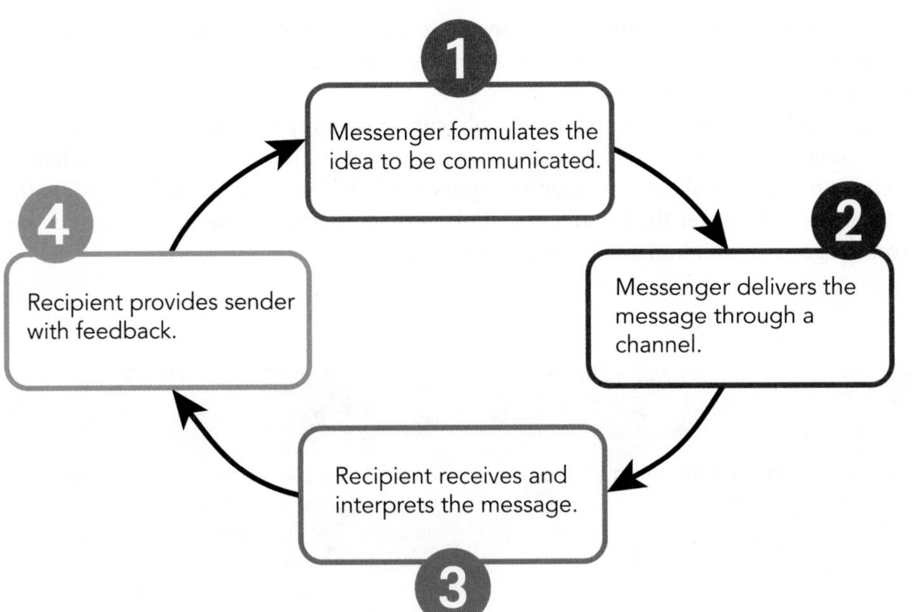
1
Messenger formulates the idea to be communicated.
2
Messenger delivers the message through a channel.
3
Recipient receives and interprets the message.
4
Recipient provides sender with feedback.

Exhibit 1-6
A Four-Step Communication Model

can prevent the recipient from completely understanding the message. They include the following:

- Incorrect assumptions made on the messenger's part
- Poorly chosen words or visuals to express an idea
- Problems with the delivery channel, incompatible communication technology, and so on
- A different perspective of the situation by the recipient

Example: *An employee fails to submit his justification for a raise in a well-documented and well-written e-mail format. His poor business communication, in his manager's view, matches his average job performance. He doesn't get a raise.*

Communication Breakdowns

Consider the following example in which interference breaks down the communication flow. A sales representative for a publishing company meets with a group of school superintendents in Virginia with the hopes of selling her company's math curriculum to the state's district high schools. She develops her message in the form of a speech and multimedia presentation and delivers it to the superintendents. These recipients sit in a dark conference room as they listen to and decode her message. Even though this communication is face to face, let's consider the communication gaps that could interfere with her message:

Level of Formality	Poor Lighting	Audience Receptivity	No Diversity in Visual Aids
The presentation is in the form of a speech, which is less conducive to the audience asking immediate questions to clarify information.	The members of the audience have had a long day and several of them are tired. Sitting in a dark room can reduce their attention spans.	New math textbooks are not a priority for some of the superintendents in the audience who deal with large budget cuts. This fact clouds their receptivity to the speaker's message.	The slides contain images of Caucasian males only. However the student population is more diverse. On a subliminal level, many members of the audience do not directly connect their students with the product being pitched.

The breakdowns in this example show how a significant amount of interference can take place even when messages are delivered face to face. Let's look at another example with even greater potential for interference.

Jim, a college senior, aims to secure a job with a company that manufactures and distributes a new line of ski wear. Because he has a personal connection with the president of the company, he formulates a message asking about the job and delivers it via e-mail to the president. Let's consider the interference Jim's message might receive as it makes its way across the gap between him and the president:

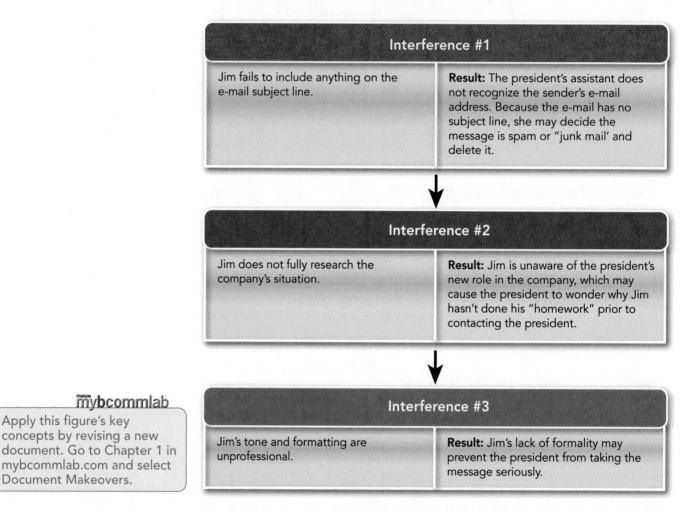

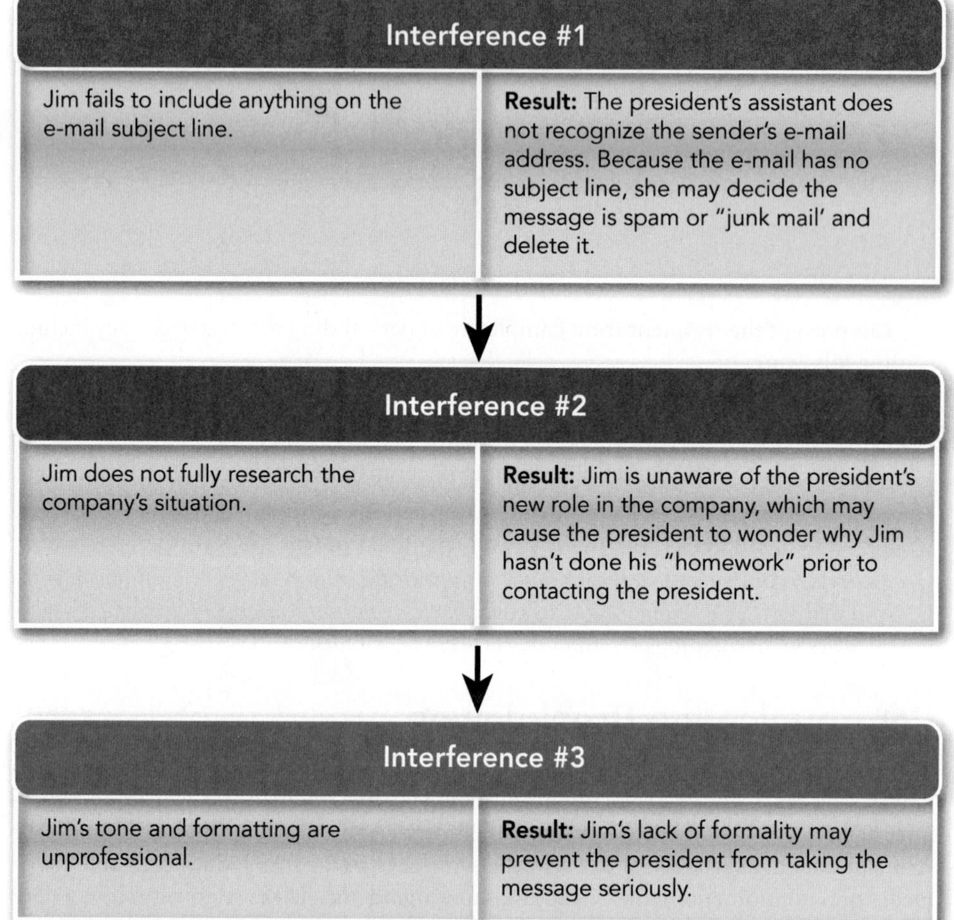

Interference #1
Jim fails to include anything on the e-mail subject line.
Result: The president's assistant does not recognize the sender's e-mail address. Because the e-mail has no subject line, she may decide the message is spam or "junk mail' and delete it.
Interference #2
Jim does not fully research the company's situation.
Result: Jim is unaware of the president's new role in the company, which may cause the president to wonder why Jim hasn't done his "homework" prior to contacting the president.
Interference #3
Jim's tone and formatting are unprofessional.
Result: Jim's lack of formality may prevent the president from taking the message seriously.

PEARSON mybcommlab

Apply this figure's key concepts by revising a new document. Go to Chapter 1 in mybcommlab.com and select Document Makeovers.

As you can see, communication breakdowns can occur in many different ways. Whenever possible, the sender should look for feedback to ensure the receivers understood the message. The feedback can come in the form of nods, smiles, verbal, and written responses. The actions taken by the recipients of the message are also a form of feedback. Companies rely on surveys, customer complaint records, and other evaluation tools to garner critical feedback so that they can evaluate the quality of their communication efforts. It will be your job as an employee to consider each stage of the communication process and gather the feedback necessary to ensure your messages are effective.

REAL INSIGHTS from a New Professional

Name: *Sacha Chua*
Title: *Enterprise 2.0 Evangelist/IT Specialist*
Organization: *IBM*
Location: *Toronto, Canada*

FIFTEEN SECONDS INTO A PHONE CONVERSATION with IBM consultant Sacha Chua, it's apparent that "Living an Awesome Life" is the perfect title for her popular blog. Chua is enthusiastic, forward-thinking, intelligent, and creative.

"I really am living an awesome life," Chua says. "There are a lot of people who find a large organization like IBM to be intimidating. They feel like they're lost or not appreciated or they don't know how to fit in, but because I'm working in a role that really takes advantage of my strengths and interests, I can't imagine a better place to be."

A 26-year-old from Makati, Philippines, Chua now calls Toronto, Canada, her home. But she seldom spends a day in a Toronto frame of mind, because Internet technology lets her spread IBM's "smarter planet" gospel. "The fact is, IBM spans the entire world, and that I can reach out and talk to people around the world easily is such an amazing thing."

Chua has technical skills, honed from computer science studies at Ateneo de Manila University and a graduate program in mechanical and industrial engineering at the University of Toronto. She also has a grade-A work ethic and passion for social networking. As a consultant at IBM, she develops Web applications, presents executive-level workshops, facilitates virtual brainstorming discussions, and helps people use Web 2.0 tools such as blogs, wikis, and social bookmarking to maximize collaboration.

"I gain so much more by sharing things," Chua says. "If I keep things to myself, not only do I have to figure out things on my own, but I wouldn't be able to help others. . . . The main challenge is making sense of all the information, all the possibilities, all the potential connections. Who do you talk to about what? What's going on where? Working with my social network means I don't need to know everything or everyone, as long as I know connectors and mavens who can point me in the right direction."

In addition to fostering a can-do attitude and generating smiles, Chua's blog offers unique insight on how to improve your business presentation skills. "When you're giving a presentation, don't force yourself to stick to the script," she says. "Give yourself permission to ad-lib and adapt. When I give a presentation online, I almost always have a chat channel where people can ask questions and share their thoughts throughout the presentation. I love it! It's a great way to learn from people. They're not 'your audience,' they're individuals with their own perspectives and insights."

Chua urges people to communicate with energy and passion. Be active, not passive. "It's not just the content but also the emotional labor that you put into this," she says. "I like using passion and enthusiasm and happiness because it's fun for me and people really appreciate that. . . . Your emotional investment in something, that happiness gets communicated as well, and people like that. . . . Especially in distance communication, there's a feeling inside you that makes people hide behind passive sentences. You have to remember that a real person is going to be reading what you're writing. You have a choice between communicating one way or another, so you might as well pick the one that works."

Questions

1. Why does Chua believe it's important to communicate with energy and passion?
2. What are some pointers Chua offers for improving presentations?

Source: Sacha Chua in discussion with the author, June 2010.

4 What Are the Three Levels of Listening, and How Do They Relate to Communication?

Listening is not simply the act of hearing. It is a process of actively gathering information through hearing and the ability to read nonverbal cues, such as a person's hand gestures, facial features, and body language. More than 35 business studies indicate that listening is a top skill needed for success in business.[11] It is one of the very first communication skills we develop as humans. As infants and toddlers, most of us learned to react, respond, and ultimately talk, by listening. Yet failing to listen is a major cause of communication interference.

How do you know if you are listening effectively? Take a look at the following three levels of listening and see where you find yourself most often.

Level 1: Surface Listening

Surface listening is when you listen but are not fully engaged. You might be thinking about something else or planning your response to what is being said. Even though you may be making eye contact with the speaker and nodding your head in response to her words, you aren't completely processing the content of the message or absorbing the subtleties of the speaker's nonverbal communication.

Skimming the text of written material is the equivalent of surface listening. You might capture the highlights of what you're skimming and take note of the section heads, but you miss the details of the content.

Level 2: Listening for Meaning

Listening for meaning is listening on a deeper level. You process the words being said and extract meaning from the message. You might ask yourself or the sender questions to confirm that you correctly interpreted the message. Listening at this level takes more effort on your part, particularly if you aren't especially interested in the message being delivered.

It is similar with reading. You read and process the word and assign meaning to the content. You are able to report back what you read.

Level 3: Perceptive Listening

Perceptive listening takes Level 2 a step further. You are not only actively listening for meaning, but you look for nonverbal cues, interpret body language, and consider the timing, tone, and context of the message. You carefully listen to what is being said, and supplement the message with your perceptions of the messenger and the surrounding situation. You formulate questions.

When reading, you again assign meaning to the content; you also "read between the lines," by considering both what has been written and what has not been written. You connect what you read with other knowledge you have, relate it to outside experiences, and ask questions. Level 3 reading serves as a jumping-off point for deeper thinking about the subject.

Consider this example:

Andrea is a senior in college and hopes to find a job in the finance industry when she graduates. One day she unexpectedly finds herself in the office of a woman who manages a division at an investment bank. Andrea acts on the opportunity and asks the woman if there are any openings in her division. The manager tells her "No. I have nothing here in my department. We're overstaffed right now, and I can hardly find enough projects for the employees I oversee. There are other departments scrambling to make deadlines and are short on help, but I've got more people here than I know what to do with." The manager then stopped what she was doing and walked around from behind her desk.

- If Andrea is listening at the Level 1 stage, she might only hear "no." Her mind might wander as she tries to come up with a way to politely excuse herself from the situation. Or, she might find herself thinking, "I shouldn't have tried this. I could have just sent a letter."

Exhibit 1-7
Barriers to Effective Listening

Source: Based on Webb, Michael, "Eliminate Barriers to Effective Listening," March 2006.

Barriers to Effective Listening	Strategies for Dealing with Listening Barriers
Assuming you know the answer or what is going to be said. Making assumptions limits your ability to fully listen. They can lead you to interrupt the speaker, prejudge the message, or formulate a hasty response.	Don't comment until the speaker is completely finished. Remind yourself to keep an open mind.
Trying to be helpful and offer solutions. Although your intention might be to help the speaker, your efforts to offer solutions can short circuit your hearing the complete message. You can get caught up in delivering the best advice at the expense of hearing the whole problem.	Listen to the speaker as if you are a detective gathering information. Later, if appropriate, offer any advice you might have.
Aiming to impress or influence. Trying to come up with great comebacks, interesting questions, and so forth, can distract you from fully hearing the message.	People enjoy being heard. The fact that you are a capable and conscientious listener will impress people and make them want to communicate with you.
Reacting to strong words or red flags. Certain phrases, words, or examples can cause an emotional reaction that is unintended. This, in turn, can color your listening and become a barrier to your understanding the true meaning of the message.	Ask the speaker for clarification, if possible. Generally, your desire to clearly understand the message will be appreciated. If the situation doesn't allow you to ask for clarification, keep an open mind. Know that people interpret different phrases, words, and examples differently.

- Now imagine Andrea is listening at the Level 2 stage. She would hear the same, "no," but would also hear the manager talk about the other departments within the investment bank. She could take the opportunity to ask the manager about these other departments or other possibilities within the finance industry.
- If Andrea listens at the Level 3 stage, she would notice the manager had stopped what she was working on, stood up, and walked around from behind her desk. Andrea could interpret she was making herself comfortable—a subtle sign that she was willing to take a moment to engage in a longer conversation.

By listening at Level 3, Andrea could turn the communication exchange into a golden opportunity—one that she would have missed if she had remained listening at Level 1. Sophisticated listeners are able to use these listening skills to extract valuable information in business. **Exhibit 1-7** includes common barriers to effective listening and strategies for overcoming these barriers.[12]

Listening is a skill you can practice, just like a musical instrument or a sport. You can see the results quickly, and it can make a tremendous difference in your ability to lead others and work in teams. In fact, good listeners are generally well liked by others, and many effective leaders demonstrate a keen ability to listen.

DID YOU KNOW?

Approximately 45 percent of communication time is spent listening, 30 percent talking, 16 percent reading, and 9 percent writing. However, studies show most people listen well only 25 percent of the time.[13]

5 What Three Questions Will Help You Think Strategically about Any Communication Exchange?

One of the keys to business success is to think strategically about the message by asking yourself the following three questions:

- What is the purpose of my communication?
- How can I adapt the message for the intended recipient or audience?
- How can I create goodwill and make a positive impact?

Thinking about these questions can save you time and headaches in the long run. Next, we'll consider each of them in more depth.

What Is the Purpose of My Communication?

What do you want to accomplish? For example, if your purpose is to inform others of a changing policy, you must first understand the policy, consider the consequences changing it will create, and the questions the new policy might generate. The bottom line: Do your homework. Know all that you can about what you are trying to communicate. Purpose is different from context. Purpose is why you communicate.

If you are simply asking a question, think about why it is relevant. Consider secondary questions you might need to ask as a follow-up to your primary question. Imagine that you call your boss to ask when the deadline is for an upcoming proposal your team is submitting to your company's board of directors. Your boss gives you the date, you thank her, and then hang up the phone. Seconds later, you wonder if she wants to see a draft of the proposal before it goes to the board. Now you have to call her a second time. Had you thought through your question and its consequences before the initial call, you could have saved both you and your boss time. Your boss would also be more likely to view you as someone who is organized and efficient.

How Should the Message Be Adapted for the Recipient or Audience?

You will see this important point repeated several times throughout this textbook because it is crucial for effective communication. Not considering the audience is perhaps the number-one cause for failed communication. The following are obvious blunders people make when they don't know their audiences:

An executive delivers a speech that includes terms that are unfamiliar to the audience.
An employee sends an e-mail with an attached file in .docx format, but the recipient can open only files that are in a .doc format.
A salesperson for a tent manufacturing company makes a sales call to a retailer that has shifted the focus of his business and no longer sells camping goods.
A company spends hundreds of dollars mailing a brochure to thousands of households that are ineligible for the services it sells.

Mistakes such as these can be avoided if you take the time to think about the audience you are targeting with your communication.

Consider the following more subtle situations:

You ask for time off from work when your boss is scrambling to make a deadline.
While having a face-to-face conversation, you are standing too close to someone who happens to be from a culture in which greater personal-space distances are preferred.
You send a contract for immediate review to your company's in-house lawyer, who has posted notification to the effect that he's out on vacation for two weeks.

Knowing your audience can make or break your communication efforts, which is why you need to think about the following additional communication aspects.

The audience's communication medium preferences: Do the recipients prefer e-mails or hard copy memos? Do they like to talk on the phone or send text messages? Is receiving a message in real-time important to them? If the message needs to be sent as a letter and delivered by the post office, are they comfortable with a lapse of time?

The audience's abilities and limitations: Knowing the technological capability of the recipients of your message is important in this era of ever-changing technology. Other considerations include knowing whether your audience has enough background information to make sense of your message. What if your audience lacks the ability to understand your point of view on an issue? What if they have had experiences in the past that limit their level of enthusiasm for the project you are pitching? What if English isn't their native language? Knowing these types of details about your audience will help you understand how much supporting and persuasive information you need to include in your communication.

Timing of the message: Often the success of communication depends on how its timing will affect your audience. Are they facing a deadline? Is there anything else happening at the same time that might affect how they will receive your message? What other timing factors are relevant to them?

How Can Goodwill Be Created and a Positive Impact Be Made?

Business relationships are built as a result of goodwill. **Goodwill** is the value a company creates for itself by developing positive business relationships, demonstrating loyalty to its customers, employees, and community, and committing to conscientious and ethical business practices. Although it can be hard to put a dollar value to goodwill, many professionals know it improves a company's bottom line over and above its immediate profits. Customers are more likely to do business with the company in the future, and the value of the overall business increases.

Many employees miss the opportunity to create goodwill for their companies because they don't see it as being immediately relevant to their business communications. Suppose a sporting-goods store manager must e-mail a supplier to see why the inventory he ordered hasn't been shipped on time. Even with messages as simple as this, goodwill can be created. Perhaps the manager can include a comment on how he appreciates the supplier's usual quick response to his questions, adding that it is a pleasure doing business with the company.

People like to feel appreciated. A quick thank you in the form of a phone call or written card also creates goodwill. Acknowledging the efforts of other people creates goodwill as well. When you are working with a team, point out the efforts of your teammates. When you are resolving conflicts, quickly acknowledging that together you have moved past other challenging issues can pave the way for future success. As you can probably guess, goodwill gestures can not only benefit your company but help you personally in your career.

The late Indira Gandhi, who was India's prime minister before her assassination in 1984, is famous for having said, "You cannot shake hands with a clenched fist." Gandhi's quote is a good way to discuss the next aspect of creating goodwill: with your tone. The **tone** of a message refers to the attitude conveyed by a speaker or writer, either consciously or unconsciously. Using the right tone in a message will help you create goodwill. The best messages are both businesslike *and* friendly. They should never be angry sounding. You don't want them to be too formal and stilted. Nor do you want them to be too informal and unprofessional.

Exhibit 1-8
Conversational, Informal, and Formal Tones: An Example

Conversational	Informal	Formal
Ari, Here is the signed commitment letter with both of our signatures. I hope it meets your approval. David	Ari, Here's the letter you asked for. It has both of our signatures. Hope everything's OK. David	Ari, In reponse to your request, I have attached the signed commitment letter with both of our signatures. I hope it meets your company's needs. David

A *conversational tone* is clear and straightforward, yet professional. It is the tone you should strive for most of the time. An *informal tone* should be used only when you are communicating with friends. Use a *formal tone* for formal occasions such as conferences, business meetings, charity functions, award ceremonies, and so forth. The following table illustrates the three types of tones. **Exhibit 1-8** shows an example for each type of tone.

Even if you use the right tone, you still might not come across as sensitive to your audience's needs and create the goodwill you hope to unless you adopt the "you" attitude in your communication. A **"you" attitude** emphasizes your readers' interests and concerns rather than yours. It makes them feel important and treats them the way they like to be treated. To convey a "you" attitude, replace terms that refer to you and your company with terms that refer to your audience. For example, try to use words like *you* and *your* more than *I, me, mine, we, us,* and *ours*.

"I" Attitude	"You" Attitude
I received the application and am currently reviewing it.	The application you sent is under review.
Our human resources department needs to schedule an interview with you.	Please schedule an interview with our human resources department.
We just sent you a new employee packet. We are available to answer any questions you might have.	Your new employee packet should reach you any day. Please call us if you have any questions.

Remember that every time you communicate you are given the opportunity to make a positive impact. Your communication often becomes your "face" in the business world. **Exhibit 1-9** lists questions you can ask to ensure you are making a positive impact.

Finally, not only should your messages create goodwill and be delivered with the right tone, they must also comply with the law. When you communicate on behalf of a company, you are liable for accurate and truthful disclosure, especially in the areas of financial reporting and product labeling. Copyright infringement—reproducing someone's written work or visual images without their permission—is a federal offense. Making false claims or statements that adversely affect a person's or organization's reputation can also result in legal repercussions. A detailed discussion of business communication ethics appears in the final chapter of this textbook. For now, know that communicating honestly and with integrity is a direct reflection of you as a person, you as an employee, and you as a representative of your company. Looking like a professional is important for landing a job. Communicating like one is critical to keeping it.

CHECKLIST

Think strategically about your communication:

- ☑ What is the purpose of my communication?
- ☑ How should the message be adapted for the recipient or audience?
- ☑ How can goodwill be created and a positive impact made?

Exhibit 1-9
Making a Positive Impact

- How does it appear?
- Is it neat and well organized?
- Is it free of mechanical errors?
- Are your word choices clear and understandable?
- Are your words upbeat even when delivering difficult news?
- Do your words come across as genuine?
- Are you writing with a "you" attitude?

- Is your tone positive and upbeat?
- Do you sound focused or distracted?
- Do your gestures and body language convey the same message?
- Do you exude confidence?
- Do you convey genuine enthusiasm?
- Are you speaking with a "you" attitude?

6 How Can the Skills You Learn in This Course Help You in College, Your Career, and Life?

You have probably already experienced the need for business communication firsthand. Did you have to write an essay to get into college? Perhaps you wrote to someone requesting a letter of recommendation. Perhaps you petitioned your department in an effort to craft a unique major. You may have worked on group projects that required team communication skills. This book will help you develop these skills and use them now as well as in the future. Why wait to put them into action?

Today: College

This textbook reflects the content you will be studying in your other business courses. If you are a business major, you will most likely be required to study finance, sales, marketing, accounting, human resources, and other business-related functions. Each chapter of this book features examples related to different industries and functions within these industries. For example, while you are learning about marketing theory in another class, your business communication class allows you to study real-world communication dealing with marketing issues.

You will also complete exercises and compile pieces for an e-portfolio that addresses a pressing business need you have now: preparing yourself to find a job after you graduate. Part of this process will include composing a personal mission statement, prospecting for

REAL INSIGHTS from a Seasoned Professional

Name: *Cole Mehlman*
Title: *President and Owner*
Organization: *Odyssey International*
Location: *Phoenix, Arizona, and Shanghai, China*

AS A PARTNER IN TWO NATIONAL FURNITURE VENTURES, Cole Mehlman's livelihood depends on the efficient interaction with his factories in China. Mehlman has learned to expect the unexpected, such as a middle-of-the-night exodus by a dependable factory owner. "This factory was about 80 percent of our production. Overnight, we had a new owner who doesn't speak a word of English," Mehlman says.

A managing partner and owner of Flexx Market Umbrellas and Odyssey International, Mehlman and his business partner, his brother Andrew, acted swiftly and strategically to forge a bond with the new owner. In need of an interpreter, the brothers hired a bilingual lawyer—at $600 an hour—who had strong business communication skills. "It was very important for us to have it be a native Chinese person so they could better understand body language and emotions and things like that to give us some direction," Mehlman says.

While modern technology allows for videoconferencing and other instant collaboration, Mehlman stresses the need to be in China frequently to supervise operations. "We've found that to be successful, and to keep our factory partners in tune and in line with what we need them to do, we need to be in front of them. We need to be at the factories constantly," Mehlman says.

A 1985 graduate of Claremont McKenna College, Mehlman worked as a marketing analyst for Honeywell just after college, and then served as assistant vice president at Fremont Capital Resources. In 1991, he began a 15-year career at Kincaid Furniture, rising from district sales manager to the award-winning vice president of sales. "I thought I would retire there," he says.

A proposition by a Chinese-American who wanted to expand capacity and output for his Shanghai-based factory led Mehlman to resign from Kincaid and take the plunge into business ownership. Odyssey International, with offices in Arizona and Colorado, sells products to four of the top 10 U.S. furniture retailers. "That's a huge accomplishment," Mehlman says. "The majority of furniture manufacturers never get into any of the top 10. . . . We're the envy of a lot of people in the industry."

Flexx is a niche company, offering a patented patio umbrella designed to withstand high winds.

Mehlman has some specific advice for business professionals: Use e-mail with caution, and listen. "E-mail can be a very dangerous tool if not used professionally or in a well-thought-out manner," Mehlman says. "I've established a new rule for myself: Never send an e-mail when I'm emotional. I can write it, but I can't send it until I've calmed down or reread it, or had others read it. You can't take it back. It's worse than a conversation, because the receiver can keep going back to it daily and reread it. It can be damaging."

Being a good listener has helped Mehlman fine-tune presentations to address hot-button concerns and lock down lucrative contracts. "Typically when I go into a meeting with a buyer, I try to get them talking a bit before I go into my presentation," Mehlman says. "Usually they will be forthcoming about the state of their business and often about the competition, who's performing, who's doing well and not. You can really tailor your presentation to find things they are looking for. The problem with a lot of salespeople is they don't listen enough, and spend too much time talking."

Questions

1. Why do you think Mehlman finds it necessary to communicate face to face to accomplish goals with his business contacts in China?
2. What specific rule has Mehlman established for his business communications?

Source: Cole Mehlman in discussion with the author, August 2010.

internship opportunities, and writing sample résumés. The key to success will be to practice and apply the material you read in this textbook today and throughout your career, regardless of where your talents take you.

Tomorrow: Your Career

Exploring the business opportunities in a variety of industries will open your mind and help you become a more diverse, flexible, and versatile businessperson. The beginning of each chapter introduces the industry being featured and its employment opportunities. Each chapter also features interviews with new and seasoned professionals in the industry. Real-world business scenarios from the industry are illustrated. You will get a closer look at the possibilities that await you in the field and how professionals in the industry conduct their business communication.

This approach will make you more aware of different fields in case you ever want to change careers. It will also make you a more well-rounded business person who understands people from many backgrounds. Whether you are a dental technician or a financial advisor, you will be able to better understand your patients or your clients and their lines of work. As a result, you will be able to build more solid interpersonal relationships with them.

Finally, you will draw on these industries in your personal and academic life. For instance, in the future, you might want to buy a home or invest your money more wisely. Reading about the real estate and finance industries might prove useful for your future endeavors. If you haven't selected a career or major yet, each chapter will give you more information about fields that may interest you.

Each chapter also contains a case study that relates the content you have read to a real company. The case studies offer insight as to how organizations handle various communication issues. Our goal is to provide you an opportunity to see diverse communication practices in a variety of business and industry settings.

Future: Your Life

Business communication skills are life skills. How you position and promote yourself ultimately depends on how well you communicate. To show how real people successfully communicate, we have profiled a young graduate as well as a seasoned manager in each chapter. Both share their personal advice.

Their stories are designed to inspire you to practice your communication skills so you are prepared for the business opportunities that await you. Says Jim Rohn, author and business philosopher: "Take advantage of every opportunity to practice your communication skills so that when important occasions arise, you will have the gift, the style, the sharpness, the clarity and emotions to affect other people." In Chapter 2, you will see how these skills will help you become a valuable team player and leader in the field you decide to pursue.

Summary *Synthesize What You Have Learned*

1. How can you prepare yourself for today's business world?

The business world of today is very different than it was 20 years ago. Evolving technologies, increased globalization, a diverse workforce, and the fluctuating economy demand that you be as prepared as possible to maximize your career opportunities. As you begin your job search, think globally. You will be competing for many of the top-notch jobs with candidates from around the world. Developing the best business communication skills possible will help you to work well with others from diverse backgrounds in this rapidly changing business climate.

2. How does communication affect business successes and failures?

Communication lies at the heart of business. It is critical in all its forms: internal, external, on the phone, in writing, and in person. When communication fails it can cost companies time, opportunities, talent, and reputation. Well-developed communication skills are one of the most important factors managers consider when interviewing candidates for a job. The most valuable employees possess well-developed intrapersonal and interpersonal skills, and are able to communicate effectively in small teams and large groups both within and outside of their organizations.

3. What are the four elements of any communication exchange?

The four elements of communication are:

1. The messenger formulates the idea to be communicated.
2. The messenger delivers the message through a chosen channel.
3. The recipient receives and interprets the message.
4. The recipient provides the messenger with feedback.

These elements apply to both written and spoken communication. Interference causes communication to break down and can happen anywhere in the process. This communication gap, caused by interference, can come in many forms: from the obvious, such as the message being delivered in a language that is foreign to the recipient, to the subtle, such as the tone of an e-mail clouding how the recipient perceives the message.

4. What are the three levels of listening, and how do they relate to communication?

Listening is a critical element of communication. For any successful communication exchange to take place, active listening must occur. In this chapter, we discussed three levels of listening, along with its counterpart, reading, which applies to written communication.

- Level 1 is surface listening, where a person's mind is not fully engaged in the exchange.
- Level 2 is listening for meaning. At this level, the listener understands and extracts meaning from the message.
- Level 3 is perceptive listening, where the listener gathers clues from both what is said, as well as from what is observed: the messenger's tone, body language, and other nonverbal cues. Successful business people know how to actively listen at this deeper level and capitalize upon what they both hear and see.

5. What three questions will help you think strategically about any communication exchange?

When you are preparing to speak or write, ask yourself these questions so you communicate in an effective manner:

- ***What is the purpose of my communication?*** Reflecting on your purpose will help you organize your thoughts so that you include all the essential elements in your message. This step aligns your message with the expected outcomes you hope to achieve.
- ***Who is my audience?*** Considering your audience will help ensure you have crafted your message so that it will be well received by your recipients. This step will help you to eliminate many of the interference factors that can derail your communication.
- ***How can I create goodwill?*** Creating goodwill should always be a goal in your business communication, especially when you are dealing with conflict or delivering bad news. Taking the extra time to connect with your recipient in a positive way can build and sustain business relationships, and adds value to the company.

6. How can the skills you learn in this course help you in college, your career, and life?

Many business students don't aspire to be brilliant writers or polished speakers. But to be successful in the world of work, you must be able to write and speak professionally. Even if your specialty is numbers, you will probably need to make presentations and write reports. By developing your writing and speaking abilities, you will be prepared to express yourself more capably at work, perform effectively on teams, and one day emerge as a leader in your chosen industry.

PEARSON
mybcommlab

Are you an active learner? Go to **mybcommlab.com** to master Chapter 1's content. Chapter 1's interactive activities include:

- Customizable Study Plan and Chapter 1 practice quizzes
- Chapter 1 Simulation, Successful Business Communication, that helps you think critically and prepare to make choices in the business world
- Chapter 1 Video Exercise, Learning to Listen at Second City Communications, which shows you how textbook concepts are put into practice every day
- Flash cards for mastering the definition of chapter terms
- Interactive Lessons that visually review key chapter concepts
- Document Makeovers for hands-on, scored practice in revising documents

Know It *Reflect, Respond, and Express*

Build Your Critical Thinking Skills

Critical Thinking Questions

1. List the college courses in your degree curriculum and determine how communication skills apply to each course.
2. Create a two-column list putting your communication strengths in one column and your weaknesses in the other column. As you work your way through the course, refine your strengths and address and remedy your weaknesses, keeping the original column as a point of reference.
3. Research the academic honesty policy for your institution. What is the tone of the policy? Who is the intended audience? How does the policy protect both the institution (business) and the intended audience (students)? Write a brief explanation of your findings to present to the class.
4. What industry are you preparing to enter after you graduate? What has attracted you to that industry?

Critical Thinking Scenario

Rakash was thrilled when she was hired at a small business in her hometown after graduating from college. Her pay was decent, her benefits were awesome, and her coworkers seemed genuinely pleasant. Shortly after starting work with the company, Rakash noticed that things seemed to get "lost in translation." Orders got misplaced and instructions were misinterpreted. Rakash sometimes felt like her questions remained unanswered because the recipients responded to unimportant details rather than the thrust of her messages. For the first time in her career, Rakash is feeling overwhelmed.

Questions

1. What might be causing the misplaced orders and misinterpretations? What could Rakash and her coworkers do to improve the situation?
2. What might be causing the lack of appropriate response to Rakash's questions? What could Rakash and her coworkers do to improve the situation?

Write It *Draft, Revise, and Finalize*

Create Your Own Success Story

1. Think of a situation you faced in which your communication with someone broke down. Were you babysitting and expected the children's parents to return at a certain time, only to have them show up several hours late? Have you dealt with a customer who became angry about a miscommunication? Perhaps the person expected a product to be a certain price but became frustrated after discovering it was not.
   a. Briefly summarize the situation and how you handled it. Were you guilty of surface listening? Did you consider the audience with which you were interacting? Did you attempt to create goodwill?
   b. Script out how you could have handled the situation better using tactics like perceptive listening and making a positive impact. How might the situation have turned out? How can arming yourself with these skills make you better prepared for these types of situations in the future?
   c. Share your ideas with a partner. Does your partner believe the tactics you suggested would be effective? Why or why not?

2. Revise the following short memo to make it more direct, concise, and to the point:

   TO: Supervisor Jon Miller

   FROM: Kate Smith

   DATE: December 23, 2013

   RE: Holiday Vacation

   Since the next couple of days are holidays and most people will be on vacation and we'll be closed for part of it, jeans and sweaters sound so much more comfortable than the stuffy clothes we wear all the time. Most people would appreciate such a wonderful gesture and enjoy the comfort of working in comfortable clothes. I'd be happy to send notification to everyone to let all the employees know we will be wearing casual clothes to work for a couple days—how many days would you think is feasible for us to have casual dress codes?

3. Revise the following e-mail for a formal audience. Analyze both the original and revised versions for the intended audiences. What are the differences in interpretation between formal and informal writing?

   Dude!

   I am sooo sorry I was late today by like, only 20 minutes. You would not believe the traffic! *especially since I got up late—must be a lot of late people today. Haha. Won't happen again, trust me.

Speak It *Discuss, Listen, and Understand*

Build Your Leadership and Teamwork Skills

How do you communicate in a team? What agreements are important for teams to follow to ensure their communication is effective and productive? To start with, get into groups. Next, as a team, answer the following questions. Have one person serve as the facilitator and one as the note taker.

1. Will the team members be held accountable for their actions and contributions? How?
2. What will the consequences be for not participating and contributing fairly to the team?
3. What role will each person play (the facilitator, note taker, and so forth)? Will the roles switch? If so, how often?
4. What behavioral expectations does the team have? How will teammates treat one another when the group is coming up with ideas and presenting them?

Next, have each member list one thing they believe makes a successful team. Write each person's response on a separate sheet of paper. Then, discuss how the team can work together to achieve each person's suggestion. Lastly, present your ideas to the class. Compile the responses into a class list and edit it as needed. If competing beliefs exist, discuss them openly with the class and decide together on the best course of action. When the class has created an agreed-upon set of rules for working in teams, ask students to commit to signing off on them to make the most of their group work in this class.

Do It *Document Your Success Track Record*

Build Your e-Portfolio

A personal portfolio is a collection of the best examples of your work, which you can use to showcase your talents and accomplishments during interviews. Every chapter in this book will give you an opportunity to add something to your personal portfolio. You might be asked to create a letter to inquire about a potential internship, to write a blog, or to create a personal mission statement. Think of your portfolio as a place to begin your professional career: What you contribute to your portfolio today could help you land your dream job in the future.

Your first portfolio assignment is to write a description of your dream job, its responsibilities, location, and salary. What type of company would you like to work for? Would you be running the company? Consider all possibilities. Remember, this is your *dream* job.

When you're finished, save a copy of the job description to a folder on your hard drive and label it "My Portfolio." Then print the job description and tape it to the front of a regular folder you will use to store printed samples from your portfolio. When you look at the job description, it should serve as a reminder of the direction you want your career to take. Remember: Seeing is believing.

Business in Action
Skype's Influence on Business Communication

Many companies operating in the global market face challenges of communicating with employees and customers on the other side of the world. Fortunately, advances in technology are helping reduce the interferences and gaps caused by geographical barriers.

Skype has helped to reduce such communication gaps. Skype Inc. was founded by Niklas Zennstrom and Janus Friis in 2003. The company's Skype software allows people to share files, send instant messages, and engage in voice or video chat at the click of a button. In most cases, using Skype is free.

Since its launch, Skype has grown immensely and become a marvel of communication in itself. According to writer James Gaskin, Skype's total bill for the marketing and advertising of its service came to an astonishing zero dollars. That is, Skype's 25 million registered users became customers of their own will—by word of mouth alone.

Skype quickly gained credibility among businesses. In fact, it is believed to have increased global business communication by about 35 percent. According to Skype, businesses that use the service have experienced the following results:

- 95 percent indicated they are able to save money because they can use their own computers and telephones—eliminating the need to buy new equipment.
- 62 percent say they communicate better with customers using Skype.
- 80 percent say they are seeing increased productivity within their companies.

Questions

1. What communication gaps or interferences do you believe technology such as Skype can best eliminate? What gaps or interferences might still be present even with such innovative technology?
2. What other technology exists to help reduce communication gaps and interferences in the global business world?
3. Can you imagine other innovations that might one day further reduce communication gaps and interferences?

Sources: Stefan Oberg, "The Future of Business Communications," *Skype.com*, May 20, 2009, accessed at http://share.skype.com/sites/business/2009/05/the_future_of_business_communi.html; James E. Gaskin, "What Is Skype?" *O'Reilly Media*, August 4, 2005, accessed at http://www.oreillynet.com/pub/a/network/2005/08/04/whatisSkype.html.

Key Terms

Diversity (both visible differences and nonvisible). Things about people that differ, such as their races, genders, skill levels, professional backgrounds, differing work habits, and cultural values. *(p. 5)*

Four-step communication model. Four steps involved in communicating with others: (1) the messenger formulates the idea to be communicated; (2) the messenger delivers the message through a channel; (3) the recipient receives and interprets the message; (4) the recipient provides the sender with feedback. *(p. 10)*

Goodwill. The value a company creates for itself by developing positive business relationships, demonstrating loyalty to its customers, employees, and community, and committing to conscientious business practices. *(p. 17)*

Interpersonal communication. Communication you have with others to exchange ideas. This communication includes words, gestures, and tone. *(p. 8)*

Intrapersonal communication. Communication you have with yourself, such as internal thoughts and conversations. The way you think about and talk to yourself affects how you think about and talk to others. *(p. 8)*

Listening. A process of actively gathering information through hearing and reading nonverbal cues. *(p. 13)*

Listening for meaning. You listen on a deeper level to process words and extract meaning from the message. This involves asking questions to confirm that you are correctly interpreting the message. This is mid-level listening, requiring more effort on your part. *(p. 14)*

Perceptive listening. You are fully present and actively listening for meaning by looking for nonverbal cues, interpreting body language, and considering the timing, tone, and context of the message. This is the deepest level of listening, requiring the most effort on your part. *(p. 14)*

Surface listening. You appear to be listening, but are probably thinking about other things or planning your response. This is superficial listening, requiring very little effort on your part. *(p. 14)*

Tone. The attitude conveyed by the writer, either consciously or unconsciously. The best messages are both businesslike *and* friendly. Typical tones include conversational, informal, and formal. *(p. 17)*

"You" attitude. A way of writing that makes the reader feel as if you are speaking directly to him or her, in terms that are meaningful to the reader. Your attitude shows that you have taken into account the reader's point of view. This typically involves using words like *you* and *your* more than *I, me, mine, we, us,* and *ours.* *(p. 18)*

Review Questions *Test Yourself*

1. Why is communication a critical component of business?
2. How do you prepare yourself for jobs that do not yet exist?
3. Define diversity in the workforce and explain how it relates to business communication.
4. What possible fallouts can occur if communication fails?
5. What methods create effective communication during a crisis?
6. How do intrapersonal communication skills affect interpersonal communication skills?
7. What obstacles could prevent complete understanding of a message?
8. What tools do companies rely on for feedback? How effective are those tools? How are they used?
9. Define surface listening and give an example of a time you have experienced it.
10. Describe examples of when you have experienced listening for meaning and perceptive listening. How well did you retain and/or interpret the information you received? What are the differences between the two types of listening?
11. What strategies for dealing with listening barriers have you used and why?
12. Why is purpose the first consideration to analyze when communicating?
13. How do medium preferences, abilities and limitations, and timing affect your intended audience? Why are they important considerations to have when developing your message's delivery?
14. Define goodwill and describe why it is important to business communication.
15. What is the importance of analyzing different industries before you enter the workforce?
16. Why is successful communication important in life in general?

Grammar Review *Mastering Accuracy*

Nouns

Section I

Each of the following sentences contains one or more common errors in word usage, grammar, or style. Identify the errors. If you have trouble finding the errors, review Sections 1.1.1. and 3.1.2. in the handbook (Appendix D) at the back of this textbook.

1. Janice's Dog, Bucky, a stubborn, short-tempered Dachshund, does not understand the complexities of Business; yet, neither does janice.
2. "Holiday shopping is like running a Business! It requires planning and patience if you wish to purchase all of the gifts for the Loved one's on your list," susie's Mother shouted.
3. At a recent company-sponsored regatta: the Departmental's leader failed to notice a school of fishes alongside his craft; however, luckily for his Team, he did notice the iceberg.
4. When asked a question about Holiday protocol, Stephen's Boss replied, "we will not close our offices on halloween or arbor day."
5. Our Professor, a graduate of Yale university, indicated he enjoyed studying Math and Science in school, but found japanese to be his most difficult course.
6. In my second proposal i wrote that i conducted outside meetings during all Seasons, but my third proposal's was more detailed: I stated during the Winter, all Employees could choose to attend an indoor meeting instead.
7. The committee appreciate three week's notice before an employee steps down from a position.
8. A Students' intelligence is often reflected by His/Her ability to communicate in a clear, concise, and confident manner.
9. A successful Global economy demand a diverse Workforce.
10. Students should ask themselfs how they can prepare for jobs that might not yet exist: this type of critical analysis are actually one skills employers highly values.

Section II

On a separate sheet of paper, rewrite the following sentences so they are clearer, more professional sounding, grammatically correct, and goodwill oriented.

1. I really liked your first idea about the mission statement; however, I think your second idea was rather silly.
2. The right to vote was not just given all of a sudden without lots of hardship: moreover: many folks worked tirelessly to see this effort come to a realization.
3. On his résumé, John states that he believes he has a diligent nature, and he thinks hiring managers are looking for this personality trait.
4. Our place of business thinks that all managers need to be super sharp, very intelligent, and know how to think quickly.
5. It's a dumb idea to text your pals during a company meeting.
6. Wheelchair ramps for the physically afflicted were added to all the stairs and guard rails were also put up for safety reasons.
7. Parking is free and the parking lot is really close to the building you need to go to for the meeting tomorrow.

8. The employee lounge begins breakfast at 9am in the morning with a buffet every day offering gourmet food.
9. Actually, I just wanted to let you know that I really care very much about you.
10. Students might wanna prep for an awful economy by maintaining a good outlook and looking for good opportunities.

Extra Resources *Tools You Can Use*

Books

- Canfield, Jack, Leslie Hewitt, and Mark Victor Hansen. *The Power of Focus: How to Hit Your Business, Personal and Financial Targets with Absolute Certainty.* Deerfield Beach, FL: Health Communications, Inc., 2000.
- Misner, Ivan R., and Don Morgan. *Masters of Success: Proven Techniques for Achieving Success in Business and Life.* Irvine, CA: Entrepreneur Press, 2004.
- Pincott, Jena. *Success: Advice for Achieving Your Goals from Remarkably Accomplished People.* New York: Random House, 2005.

Web Sites

- *Global Business Success Foundation*
- *International Business Center*
- *Business Know-How*

"If your actions inspire others to dream more, learn more, do more and become more, you are a leader." —**John Quincy Adams,** sixth president of the United States

CHAPTER 2

Teamwork, Leadership, and Business Communication

Motivating and Inspiring Others

LEARNING OBJECTIVE QUESTIONS

1. What are business teams like today?
2. What do you have to offer a team?
3. What makes a team work together effectively?
4. What causes teams to break down?
5. How can you become an effective team leader?

PEARSON **mybcommlab** Access interactive videos, simulations, sample documents, document makeovers, and assessment quizzes in Chapter 2 of **mybcommlab.com** for mastery of this chapter's objectives.

>>> **Maria** is a sophomore majoring in business at the University of Vermont. She is currently an intern for a company that makes high-protein snack bars for athletes on the go. Maria is one of three interns working for the company. One intern is studying finance, one is studying market research, and Maria is studying marketing. Because the company is small and only five years old, Maria is doing many types of business tasks with the firm, tasks ranging from accounting and finance, to sales and market development, to answering the phones and filling orders. The interns do their tasks on a rotating basis, so they have to be able to communicate well with one another.

The CEO of the company wants to target a new market for one of its bars: working women and moms who exercise at their local gyms and have very tight schedules. She has asked Maria to work with the other interns to set up five focus, or research, groups with consumers around the country to gather feedback about the bar's taste, what to name it, and how to market it.

Maria uses her writing skills to notify the team about the project and explain its goals and objectives. She also communicates how the results will be interpreted and by whom. Finally, she clearly identifies what the group is expected to deliver to the CEO and the time frame for doing so. As the project progresses, she runs effective meetings. One of her team members takes notes, summarizes the information, and gives it back to Maria. Maria then reviews the summary, and after making a few grammar and spelling changes, distributes it to the entire team.

During the course of the project, each intern is required to summarize in writing the results of the focus groups he or she oversees. The summary includes feedback about the taste of the product, recommendations for its improvement, and any other pertinent information. At the end of the summer, Maria must create an executive summary of all of the findings, and the team must deliver them to the CEO.

Maria >>>

Perhaps you were working on a class project and there was a power struggle between teammates. Perhaps you were on a team in which several members failed to fully participate. Although teamwork can be difficult, teams are an integral part of business. The following are some of the advantages and disadvantages of working on teams:

Advantages	Disadvantages
Multiple ideas can be generated for solving problems.	Although teams can at times speed up the problem-solving process, they can also slow it down as their size grows larger.
Various talents of team players are brought to the table.	Employees who prefer working alone can become frustrated.
Employees can energize one another.	Meeting tight deadlines can be more difficult.
Teamwork can add a social element to jobs, strengthening the bonds between employees and improving their job satisfaction.	Frequently, team members don't all participate equally on the team.
Large tasks can be more easily tackled.	If not effectively managed, teams can damage the morale of a company.

Most of the disadvantages of teams can be overcome if team members know how to communicate with one another. How you communicate with and function on a team can, in fact, make or break your career.[1] As Lee Iacocca, the businessman credited with reviving the Chrysler Corporation in the 1980s, once said, "A major reason capable people fail to advance is that they don't work well with colleagues."[2] The best employees know that being a good team player is one of the key competencies managers look at when assessing leadership potential.[3]

The goal of this chapter is to help you develop communication skills that will make you an effective team player and a good leader. This chapter's examples relate to the food and beverage industry. It is one of the largest industries in our economy, generating $54.7 billion a year. The industry includes companies that process, package, and distribute goods meant for human consumption. An estimated 258,000 positions will be available for graduates between now and the year 2016 in just the franchise and restaurant ownership portion of the industry alone.[4]

Opportunities for business graduates in the food and beverage industry cover a wide spectrum. They range from restaurant management, to product development, packaging design, supply chain management, and organic farming. Jobs exist throughout the country (and the world), and are not concentrated in only one region.

Rich Matteson, the director of national marketing for Pizza Hut, says, "One area I have seen change significantly in the food and beverage industry over the past 5 years is go-to market development time lines for products. What used to have an 18-month time line may now have a 6-month time line. Business is moving faster than ever, thus the importance of teamwork across functions is critical."

1 What Are Business Teams Like Today?

Work teams today look very different than they did 20 years ago. Before the 1970s, companies were generally organized into divisions representing their different operations. However, this structure led to many managerial levels. It also led to duplicated roles, with each division relying on its own accountants, engineers, and so forth, and limited the ways teams across different divisions worked together.

Organizations are much flatter today. In other words, there are few layers of managers, and teams are the norm. (We will look more at organizational structures in Chapter 4.) "Employees are consistently asked to take on new and different tasks as part of teams," says

Matteson. "Working in teams helps them build a stronger skill set and enables them to become as flexible as possible."

Many firms utilize geographically dispersed teams. Geographically dispersed teams consist of members who work in different locations both inside and outside of an organization. Consider a donut and coffee company based in Philadelphia. The board of directors had decided to expand operations and open 400 new sites in the next two years. The company then assembled the following team to lead the initiative:

- The senior vice president of finance to manage the financial operations for the expansion
- A marketing associate from an independent marketing firm to oversee market analyses for each potential site
- The head of franchise development to review and select franchise owners
- A third-party real estate broker and professional to manage the real estate selection, leases, and purchases on behalf of the company
- An in-house lawyer to regulate all negotiations and transactions

The senior vice president of finance works from the parent company's headquarters in San Francisco, while the marketing associate works from her firm's offices in Maryland. The head of franchise development travels extensively, meeting with potential franchise owners, while the real estate professional scouts sites around the country for future development. Not only is this team geographically dispersed, but its members are not all employed by the same company. As a result, it is a **virtual team**, and members must rely on technology to work together.

The team begins each week with a Monday-morning **conference call**, during which time members give a brief status report on the work they are doing. **Videoconferencing** allows them to interface with the board of directors. To prepare written documents, the team members collaborate on the writing using software such as Google Docs. **Web conferencing** allows them to work together on different phases of the process without having to all travel to one location.

Later in this text, we will discuss the many ways teams use these forms of technology. It is not only advancements in technology that help teams operate successfully. Much of their success depends on the leader and team members knowing the strengths and weaknesses they bring to the group. Ideally the members learn to make the most of one another's strengths and minimize each of their weaknesses.

2 What Do You Have to Offer a Team?

Self-awareness is critical for functioning well in any group. From chief executive officers to entry-level associates, successful businesspeople share a common ability to maximize their strengths and compensate for their weaknesses. Understanding how you process information, read the signals other people are sending, and express yourself will help you succeed in teams and emerge as a leader. **Emotional intelligence** is the ability to monitor and control your emotions, thoughts, and feelings, while remaining sensitive to and aware of others' feelings. Your **emotional quotient (EQ)** is said to measure your emotional intelligence, much like your intelligence quotient (IQ) measures your intellectual intelligence.

Author Daniel Goleman claims that in business, your EQ is arguably more important than your IQ. What you know is not necessarily a measure of what you can do. Moreover, your ability to communicate effectively is correlated with your emotional intelligence.[5] You might have the greatest ideas in the world, but if you don't listen to others, if you become hostile when someone questions you, or fail to acknowledge other people's efforts, you won't get far in the world of business.

Assessing Your Personality Strengths and Weaknesses

How can you learn about yourself and develop your emotional intelligence? There are many self-assessments available, including the Keirsey Sorter and Myers/Briggs personality tests and the VARK questionnaire. A number of versions of them can be found on the Web and taken for free. The assessments are like maps. People refer to hundreds of types of maps—

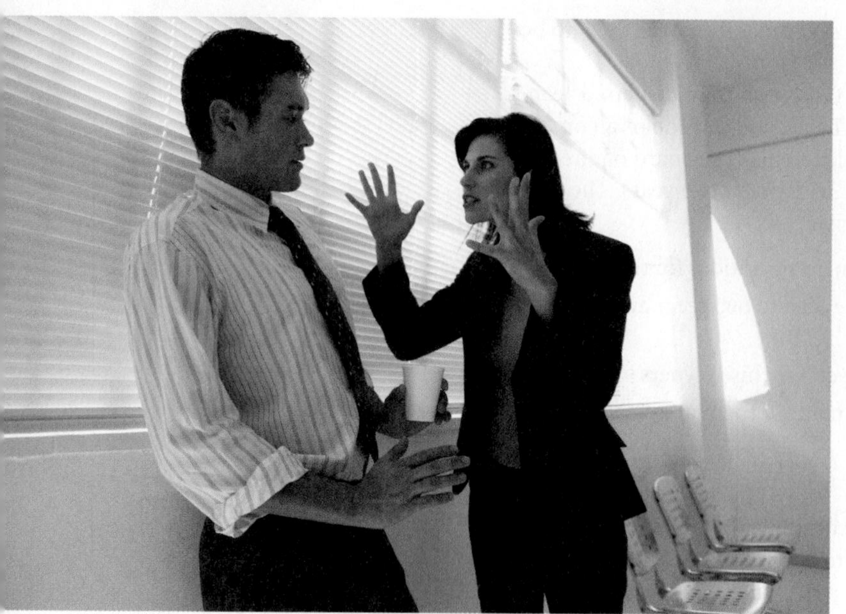

A low EQ can hamper your ability to effectively communicate with others and succeed in business.

highway maps, topographical maps, atmospheric maps, and so forth. They all show a different view of the landscape. Self-assessments work in the same way. They show different aspects about who you are.

Are self-assessments absolute and unchanging? No. They simply provide you with information that will enable you to communicate and operate more effectively in the world. Nor are they infallible or always accurate. Nonetheless, many companies now use assessment tools to identify the individual traits and tendencies of their employees and prospective employees. The assessment in this chapter is based on the **Keirsey Sorter personality types** test. It will allow you to see your dominant strengths and your lower-scoring areas, which we call "growth areas."

1. Take a few minutes to complete the assessment in **Exhibit 2-1a** by answering the questions quickly and honestly.
2. Next, chart your responses in **Exhibit 2-1b** by plotting your total score for each of the following quadrants: *giver, thinker, adventurer,* and *organizer.* Now connect the points from thinker to giver, from giver to adventurer, from adventurer to organizer, and finally from organizer back to thinker. If you are evenly balanced, your figure will look like a square. If you are predominately a thinker and organizer, your shape could look more like a trapezoid.

Exhibit 2-1a Personality Spectrum

Rank order the 4 responses to each question by placing a 1, 2, 3, or 4 in each box.

4 = MOST LIKE YOU, 1 = LEAST LIKE YOU

1. I like instructors who
   - A. tell me exactly what is expected of me.
   - B. make learning active and exciting.
   - C. maintain a safe and supportive classroom.
   - D. challenge me to think at higher levels.
2. I learn best when the material is
   - A. well organized.
   - B. something I can do hands-on.
   - C. about understanding and improving the human condition.
   - D. intellectually challenging.
3. A high priority in my life is to
   - A. keep my commitments.
   - B. experience as much of life as possible.
   - C. make a difference in the lives of others.
   - D. understand how things work.
4. Other people think of me as
   - A. dependable and loyal.
   - B. dynamic and creative.
   - C. caring and honest.
   - D. intelligent and inventive.
5. When I experience stress, I would most likely
   - A. do something to help me feel more in control of my life.
   - B. do something physical and daring.
   - C. talk with a friend.
   - D. want to be alone and think about it.
6. I would probably not choose someone as a best friend who was
   - A. irresponsible.
   - B. unwilling to try new things.
   - C. selfish and unkind to others.
   - D. an illogical thinker.
7. My vacations could be best described as
   - A. traditional.
   - B. adventuresome.
   - C. pleasing to others.
   - D. a new learning experience.
8. One word that best describes me is
   - A. sensible.
   - B. spontaneous.
   - C. giving.
   - D. analytical.

Total Columns

A B C D

Plot these totals on the brain diagram below.

Exhibit 2-1b Personality Spectrum—Thinking Preferences

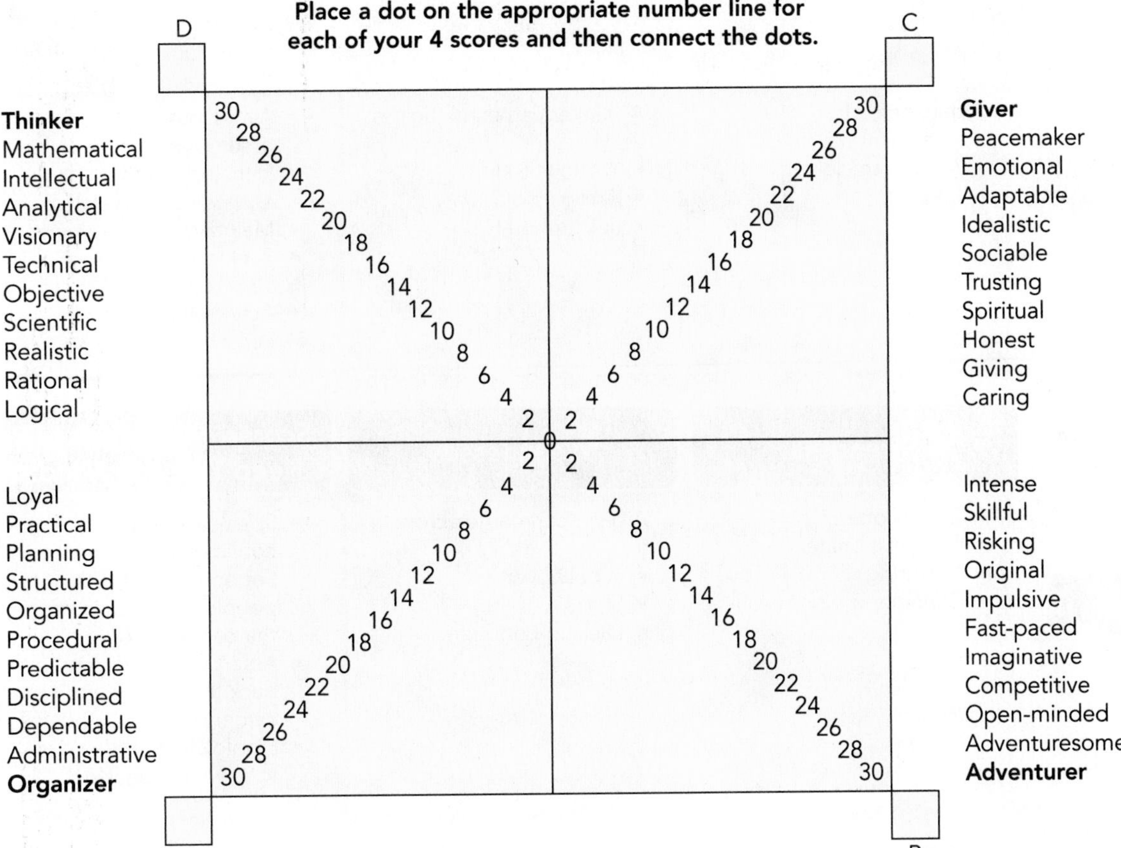

Now that you have assessed yourself and learned about the four personality types, examine **Exhibit 2-2**. It illustrates potential strengths and weakness for each of the four personality types, along with communication tips for you to consider.

Keirsey Sorter Personality Types in the Workplace

When you enter the workforce, you will see Keirsey Sorter personality types reflected in your coworkers. You may also see some of them in yourself. In this section, we will look at the types. The personality types are a tool you can use to better understand yourself and others, especially when it comes to working together in a team. However, people are not objects that can be easily categorized and put into boxes like nuts and bolts, sorted by size. Never assume you know everything about a person just because you think you have figured out his or her personality type.

The Thinker

Marcus works for a national chain, Just Juice, and is part of an upper-level management team responsible for reducing overhead and cutting operation costs. The company CEO has demanded quick action. After thoroughly analyzing all operating costs and revenues, Marcus believes 300 of the 900 stores across the country need to be closed within three months. Others on the team don't feel that such drastic measures are needed.

Although Marcus is extremely confident that his solution is the best for the company, he understands that consensus for this management team is important. As a result, he takes time to meet with other team members to ask them for their suggestions, and give them an opportunity to voice their concerns regarding his proposal.

In addition, he makes sure that all team members then have a copy of his written proposal, which includes numbers, figures, and explanations that take into account their concerns.

Exhibit 2-2 The Strengths and Weaknesses of Thinkers, Givers, Organizers, and Adventurers

	Strengths	Weaknesses	Scored Highest Here? Keep These in Mind:
Thinker	A thinker is often: • Analytical • A problem solver • Logical	A thinker can come across as: • A know-it-all • Arrogant • Judgmental	• Avoid making assumptions. • Develop patience for slower learning styles. • Maintain an open mind. • Seek opposing viewpoints. • Acknowledge others' contributions.
 Giver	A giver is often: • Compassionate • Nurturing • Connected emotionally	A giver can come across as: • A pushover • Shy • Lacking confidence	• Speak up with confidence. • Set boundaries with people who dominate the conversation. • Assert your ideas and back them up with evidence. • Employ a confident tone when speaking.
 Organizer	An organizer is often: • Responsible • Orderly • Efficient	An organizer can come across as: • Rigid • Inflexible • Close-minded	• Embrace change; work on being flexible. • See alternate solutions and points of view. • Avoid being locked down into your own way of doing things. • Try to think outside the box.
 Adventurer	An adventurer is often: • Playful • Spontaneous • Creative	An adventurer can come across as: • Unfocused • Domineering • Over excited	• Organize your thoughts. • Be prepared. • Enlist others and be open to the ideas of teammates. • Keep passion level efficient. • Communicate slowly and deliberately.

Marcus has thought about this situation in more depth than several of his teammates. However, he realizes that he must be patient and will benefit if he can help others see the problem and potential solution from his perspective.

The Giver

Marissa is a sales associate for Emerald Food Distribution in Miami, Florida, where she sells food and kitchen equipment to restaurants throughout the city. She attends monthly meetings with her manager and fellow associates, in which they review the sales figures for all of the company's accounts and develop promotional marketing plans to sell overstocked inventory and seasonal items.

Although Marissa comes to meetings with well-thought-out suggestions, she has a hard time asserting herself and getting others to listen to her ideas. She feels more comfortable being the champion for others, but knows that it is important for her career to be able to speak up and contribute ideas to the team.

For the next month's meeting, she approaches her manager and asks to be put on the agenda, guaranteeing her an opportunity to present her ideas to the team. In the meantime she's practicing her delivery and has prepared a graph and spreadsheet illustrating the benefits her associates and the company will receive by adopting her suggestions.

The Organizer

Janice is the vice president of human resources for The American Grill, a national restaurant chain. For the last 10 years she organized the company's annual weekend planning retreat for the firm's top executives. At a recent meeting, several executives suggested they change the location of the retreat and restructure the events for the weekend. Janice panicked. She had developed a system for producing the event that worked well—a system that she took great pride in. "Why change something that works?" she thought. However, her teammates felt the event needed something new and invigorating. Janice realized that although she had effectively organized a great event for 10 years, she needed to "let go" and be flexible. After listening to everyone's suggestions, she resolved to let her teammates help her explore new possibilities for the weekend, knowing that the changes would be good for the event and her as well.

The Adventurer

Alberto and his three brothers formed a company with several private investors in Los Angeles, with a mission to sell frozen meals featuring his great aunt's recipes from San Felipe, Mexico. As Alberto prepared for an upcoming meeting to finalize the company's product line, his creative juices started flowing. He envisioned a partnership with a tortilla chip company headquartered in Massachusetts that could help foster his firm's East Coast expansion. An idea for a logo design using his great aunt's picture came to him in the middle of the night. A cookbook featuring the company's best-selling recipes, each accompanied by traditional folklore, could be a hit.

However, Alberto knew that several of the private investors would be at the meeting, and that his adventurous spirit might create the perception that he lacked focus and commitment to the meeting's agenda. So, Alberto decided to wait to bring up his new ideas until after the meeting's objectives were met and the product line was finalized.

When the time was right, Alberto presented his two best ideas, remembering to talk slowly and invite others to comment and offer feedback. At the end of the meeting he followed up by distributing a written memo detailing the ideas he had brainstormed, with space included for his teammates to comment and add suggestions for each.

Communicating with Managers Who Have Different Personality Types

Knowing about the Keirsey Sorter personality types will not only help you communicate better with your team members, but also enable you to understand and work more efficiently with people to whom you report. Think about each personality profile mentioned earlier and identify which profiles fit your managers, college professors, or teachers. Then, incorporate some of the suggestions from **Exhibit 2-3** in your communication.

Exhibit 2-3 Tips for Communicating with Managers Who Have Different Personality Types

Manager's Personality	Communication Tips
Thinker	Give a thinker well-analyzed memos and oral summaries. Have your data and your facts handy and double check their accuracy. Do your homework, in other words.
Giver	Provide communication that is genuine and interesting. Use stories to illustrate an accomplishment or a job well done. Be willing to give feedback and acknowledgement for work being done.
Organizer	Provide solid information presented in an organized way. Proofread, prepare, rehearse, and re-rehearse your delivery. Find the most attractive and effective way to package information.
Adventurer	Be interesting, challenging, or entertaining. Use stories and humor to illustrate your message with visuals, music, and an element of surprise. Be creative and convey passion.

❸ What Makes a Team Work Together Effectively?

You have seen how important it is to understand what you have to contribute to a team, and how to communicate effectively. However, what happens when you simply do not like a team member? The fact is you are not going to like everyone with whom you work. However, liking or disliking someone is very different than working well with him or her. Regardless of your feelings, behave professionally and communicate respectfully with the person. One way to do this is to remain focused on the team's desired outcomes.

Understanding Group Dynamics: Going from Forming to Performing

In 1965, Bruce Tuckman, a psychologist and education specialist, attempted to explain the dynamics of groups by describing their stages of development. Tuckman maintained that the stages are necessary and inevitable for teams to go through in order to plan, strategize,

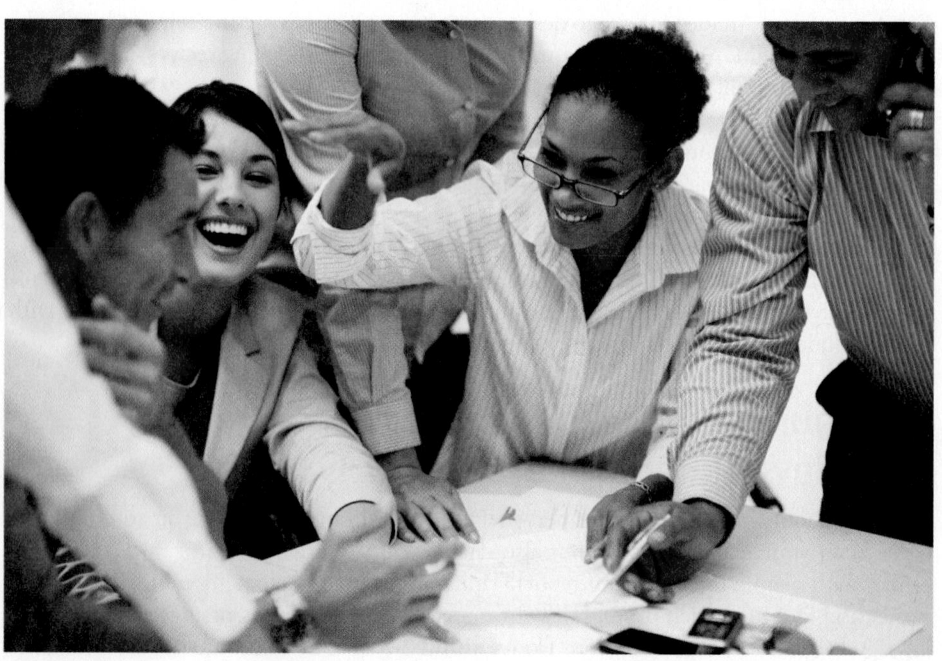

address problems, and deliver results. The easy-to-remember stages are forming, storming, norming, performing, and adjourning.[6] Consider the following scenario.

Jennifer is a 24-year-old sales manager for Northside Beverages. Her supervisor, Rosanne, has asked her to join a group of employees to develop a strategy for expanding the presence of Northside's products in large grocery store chains. Jennifer has teamed up with John from the company's product development group, Amy from the firm's marketing department, and Benny, a regional sales representative for Northside.

Forming: Because the members of the group have never worked together, they engage in a series of initial meetings to get the project started. This is the group's "forming" stage. They explore different approaches to product research and development, vendor outreach, and customer assessment. The members observe and assess one another and gauge their chances of pursuing mutually beneficial goals.

Storming: Three weeks after the initial meeting, a number of conflicts surface. The team is now in the "storming" stage. Benny is traveling a lot and has attended only one meeting, leaving most of the sales strategy planning to Jennifer. John seems disconnected because he feels his product-development skills are not needed until the other team members figure out which new products the group is actually going to develop. Jennifer and Amy have begun to meet alone, and communication among all four team members has nearly stopped.

Norming: After Rosanne gets a status update, she pulls the group together for a meeting to discuss all of the issues and concerns. The team members revisit their goals and discuss the importance of each member's role. Finally, they make a plan for what they will do if communication breaks down or conflict occurs as the process moves forward. This is the "norming" stage, or the stage in which the group recommits, accepts roles and responsibilities, and begins to build consensus.

Performing: Eight weeks after the initial meeting, the team has been conducting tactical meetings once a week and communicating regularly. The members have a good understanding of one another's strengths and have come together and developed a formal proposal for Northside's board of directors. The proposal includes a marketing strategy, industry research, and an action plan for expansion. The stage at which the group delivers what it has set out to accomplish is the "performing" stage.

Adjourning: After the team has completed its task, Rosanne brings the team members together to congratulate them on their success. This is the "adjourning stage." Based on the effectiveness they showed, she informs them that she will bring them together again for future projects.

Team Sizes

A team's size affects its ability to communicate effectively. If a team is too large, it becomes difficult for everyone to voice their opinions, and consensus can be difficult to build. If a team is too small, it often lacks the multiple perspectives that are advantageous in teamwork. According to Edward Hall, a noted anthropologist and psychoanalyst, the ideal business team has between 8 and 12 members. This size allows members to know one another well enough to utilize their talents while accomplishing tasks. In groups larger than 12, Hall warns that leadership doesn't develop naturally and instead can become political. Also, in larger groups, the team members' participation and commitment can suffer.

How Teams Make Decisions

Imagine you are on a different team at Northside Beverages. Your group's responsibility is to design packaging for your product and determine where the packaging will be manufactured. After months of meetings, the team has finally agreed on the packaging it believes will attract the most attention from customers and increase sales.

The problem is you cannot agree on where the packaging should be manufactured. One-third of your team believes the packaging should be made in the same factory where the juice is produced, even though the cost of production is significantly higher. Other team

Exhibit 2-4 Decision-Making Models Used by Teams

members believe the packaging should be manufactured at different factories, but they are divided as to which factory is best. How do you come to a decision?

Authoritarian
One person, often the team leader, makes a decision that is adopted and followed without question by the group. This decision-making process is quick, and perhaps best used in emergency situations. However, it fails to give the members of the team any say in the decision-making process.
Group Deciders
A subgroup with authority makes the decision on behalf of the team. You might see this process in action when a team designates a committee to research and decide upon a solution for the group. This process is more representative of the entire team, but it still fails to give the members of the team much of a role in the decision-making process.
Majority Rules
Team members vote on an issue and the position with the majority of votes wins. The group determines what constitutes a majority. A simple majority means whichever side has the most number of votes wins. A two-thirds majority means that one side must have two-thirds of all votes to claim victory. This strategy is perceived as being fair, but may still leave team members feeling as if their viewpoints have not been heard.
Consensus
Most effective model for building team morale and communication. It allows all team members to express their stance on an issue. After lengthy debate, team members come to a unanimous decision. All members might not agree with each and every provision of the chosen solution, but they can live with resulting decision. This strategy requires the greatest communication skills because everyone must be heard and differing viewpoints must be considered to reach an ultimate consensus. This strategy can take a long time and may not be best in an emergency situation.

One of the biggest challenges teams face is making decisions that reflect the thinking of the entire group. **Exhibit 2-4** shows four common decision-making models teams use. Regardless of the model a team chooses for its decision-making process, the best communication occurs when:

- The team has a clearly defined goal.
- The need for making the decision is understood by all members.
- Supporting information has been gathered to aid in the decision-making process.
- Some time is dedicated to coming up with alternate solutions.

Establishing Ground Rules for Teams

Many teams find it beneficial to share a common set of "ground rules," or agreed-upon standards, for the group. **Exhibit 2-5** provides some suggestions for you to consider. In addition, during this phase, the roles of the participants are decided, including who becomes the time keeper, recorder, facilitator, and so on. Meetings can become time wasters if they aren't organized well. Make every effort to use the time in meetings wisely by preparing for them. Having a well-thought-out agenda is an important part of this preparation. **Exhibit 2-6** is an example of a meeting agenda.

Etiquette in Teams

Working on a team can be a slow process, but proper team etiquette can help teams avoid the frustrations described in the following scenario: Imagine a team of business associates from Wok Fast, a Chinese fast food chain, meeting to explore ways for man-

Exhibit 2-5 Making Teams Work: Setting Ground Rules for Teams

Identify Desired Outcomes	Begin with the End in Mind	Define Expectations	Use Diversity	Plan Ahead in Detail
Outline the team's goals and how you will know when those goals have been met. This will help each member be accountable to the overall objectives.	Identify the end result. This will prevent members from falling off course and becoming distracted by other issues.	Name attainable goals to increase motivation: • Use an agenda every time • Agree to work through conflict • Start and end meetings on time	Solicit different points of view and examine the pros and cons. This allows you to see the big picture when solving problems. Starting with a diverse team can make this easier.	Create well-defined action steps and time frames for completion. This is a good way to summarize a meeting and have all members on the same page.

mybcommlab

Apply Exhibit 2-5's key concepts by revising a new document. Go to Chapter 2 in mybcommlab.com and select Document Makeovers.

aging the inventory and shipment of food supplies to their 120 franchises across the country. The session begins at 4:00 P.M. but two members walk in at 4:15 so the top items on the agenda have to be repeated. One member fails to adequately prepare for the meeting, and is therefore unable to report on the two software options being considered for the project. The company controller, who's involved in several concurrent projects, sends text messages from his Blackberry under the table while others are speaking. At 4:45, the vice president of Wok Fast gets up and walks out, frustrated that the team is behind schedule.

mybcommlab

Apply Exhibit 2-6's key concepts by revising a new document. Go to Chapter 2 in mybcommlab.com and select Document Makeovers.

Exhibit 2-6 A Meeting Agenda

Training Team Meeting Agenda

December 2, 2011, 9:00 A.M.–10:30 A.M.

Location: 2nd floor conference room

Remote members: Dial 1-800-672-2345, PIN: 2534.
Access screen-sharing at: gotomeeting.com, PIN: 2534.

Attendees: Jose Oliff, Jeff Tartun, Aaron Kneel, Amy Lassiter, Maria Dennen
Absent: Leo Kahn (Amy will send notes to Leo)
Agenda:

1. Check-in: 5 minutes
2. Review of action items from Nov. 1 meeting: 30 minutes
   - Jeff: Status on training module template
   - Amy: Update on new training software
   - Maria: Reporting system progress
3. Module rollout discussion: 10 minutes
4. Identify next training topics: 10 minutes
5. Timing of launch: 10 minutes
6. Other: 5 minutes
7. Action items for next meeting: 10 minutes
8. Open-discussion period: 10 minutes

Note the items in the agenda: (start and end time, date, location, and attendees).

Review: summarizes the last meeting and previous action plans.

Agenda items: provides structure for the meeting and assignments for the next meeting.

Open discussion: allows members to bring up other relevant information.

To avoid situations like the one described, consider these tips:

- Show up on time.
- Be prepared. If you miss a meeting, find out what occurred during your absence so that you are prepared when the team gathers for its next session.
- Try to sit where you can see all of the other team members. Sitting in a circle-type configuration usually works best with smaller teams.
- Be courteous. Don't interrupt someone who's speaking, and raise your hand if you want to speak or ask a question.
- Use polite language. Remember to say please and thank you. Don't use inappropriate language.
- Respect the team's confidentiality. Be discerning about the information you share from the meetings with others outside of the team.
- If you have an issue with a teammate, talk to the person directly. Avoid talking to others about the problem unless the issue specifically involves them.
- Make a point to acknowledge team members when appropriate. Giving credit to others when good work has been done is a great way to build allies on the team.
- Keep your personal business outside of the meeting. Although sharing what you did over the weekend might be a good icebreaker to start a meeting, discussing a recent break-up with your partner is inappropriate.
- Avoid sending text messages, e-mails, and instant messages during meetings.
- Clean up after yourself. Don't leave papers, coffee cups, and other items for other people to dispose of. Don't eat at a meeting unless everyone is being served food.

Student teams can experience the same dynamics as work teams. Participating in student teams is an excellent way to learn more about how they develop and to practice tips to help make them work better. Whether you are on your college's debate team, a sports team, or working on a group project for class, take charge by incorporating the following ideas at each stage of team development:

1. Know what you have to offer.
2. Help the team clarify its objectives.
3. Deliver more than is expected.
4. Document your success.
5. Use your diplomacy skills to keep your team on track, focused, and motivated.

Let's look at how Jonathan managed to incorporate these ideas to help a student team work on a project for entrepreneurship class. Jonathan and four of his teammates had to come up with an idea for a business and then develop a business plan. The team chose to explore launching a unique lunch service program on campus where fresh, wholesome sandwiches and soups would be made in an onsite campus kitchen, and sold from kiosks at various sites on campus. Students would manage and operate the lunch service program as part of a work-study program. They would be paid hourly wages, and all profits from the operation would go toward an international scholarship fund for students in war-torn countries.

- ***Know what you have to offer.*** Jonathan knew he was a thinker-organizer with strong interpersonal skills. Once the team settled on a business idea, he came to the next meeting prepared with spreadsheets and graphs to help communicate some of his ideas on how the lunch service could operate successfully on the campus.
- ***Help the team clarify its objectives.*** Jonathan took notes at meetings and kept a running list of things that needed to be done. At the end of each meeting, he wrote the list on a large sheet of butcher paper so that the team members could review as a group their overall objectives and each teammate could then choose what he or she would be responsible for delivering at the next meeting.
- ***Deliver more than what is expected, and document your success.*** Whatever Jonathan signed up to do, he tried to do really well. For example, when he committed to exploring

CHECKLIST

Etiquette in team meetings:

- ☑ Show up on time.
- ☑ Be prepared.
- ☑ Be courteous and use polite language.
- ☑ Respect the team's confidentiality.
- ☑ If you have an issue with a teammate, talk to the person directly and not to other people about it.
- ☑ Acknowledge your team members' contributions.
- ☑ Don't share too many personal details.
- ☑ Don't send text messages, e-mails, and instant messages while participating in a meeting.
- ☑ Clean up after yourself.

REAL INSIGHTS from a New Professional

Name: Alexa Robinson
Title: Coordinator, PR & Emerging Media
Organization: Pizza Hut, Inc.
Location: Dallas, Texas

THINGS HAPPEN FAST IN THE PIZZA WORLD. And it's not just pies that are speeding out to customers. In Alexa Robinson's role as Coordinator, PR & Emerging Media for Pizza Hut, Inc., the flow of information is turbocharged. "An immediate response isn't fast enough for them," Robinson said of Pizza Hut's 30,000 followers on Twitter.

A 2009 University of North Carolina journalism grad and the daughter of a newspaper editor and a journalist, Robinson, 23, sends Tweets for a living. She's a public relations staffer for Yum! Brands' Pizza Hut, with the mission of enhancing the brand through social networking, mobile marketing, and technologies that are evolving daily. "We are always looking for the next big thing," Robinson said. "Just because something is new and the hot thing, if it's not the right fit for your brand, it's not going to be successful for you. We are always looking at where Pizza Hut can fit in with the new technology and the newest social networking tools."

Robinson had visions of a career in advertising, not the food and beverage marketing realm. But that changed when she landed a gig as a "Twintern," an intern dedicated to managing Pizza Hut's Twitter presence. Sending text messages of 140 characters or less offers its own communication challenges, but Robinson's ability to connect with customers using everyday language helped the company's Twitter numbers rise from 3,000 to now more than 30,000. After her three-month internship ended, Pizza Hut offered her a full-time position at its Dallas headquarters. "I had the drive and ambition to find my place in the company. People recognized that social media was important and I was the right person to bring that to the company," she said.

In addition to her Twitter duties, Robinson energizes Pizza Hut's Facebook presence, shares photos supporting the company brand on Flickr, posts travel updates to Foursquare, a mobile phone application people use to explore areas, and spearheads mobile ventures such as the Pizza Hut iPhone application. As the company's social media guru, she tutors staffers on social media technology and supports other marketing and communication efforts, such as press release writing.

"If we are launching a new product and one of our brand managers wants to do some product support online, social media is an inexpensive way to get the word out about the new product," Robinson said. "There are different brand managers and advertising team members, so social media has a lot to do with teamwork. We want everything to look fluid, from our print advertising to TV advertising, social media and anything else we do in print or digitally. It requires a lot of teamwork to make sure that everyone understands how the different parts work."

On Twitter, she's developed her own personality, and speaks to customers and followers using her own voice. On Facebook, she speaks in a slightly more formal tone, using the third-person Pizza Hut brand. In press release tasks, she is adept at ramping up her grammar and style and presenting information in a more traditional manner. "It's great to build those lasting relationships with our customers on Twitter and Facebook," she said. "They become your brand advocates for you, often through word of mouth to their friends."

Questions

1. According to Robinson, is every new social networking technology right for every brand?
2. Why is teamwork important to Pizza Hut's social media initiatives?

Source: Alexa Robinson in discussion with the author, June 2010.

the competition for selling lunches on campus, he analyzed four different campuses that already had services similar to the one his team was proposing, and created a report on their sales, pricing, marketing, and operations for his teammates. He also kept a large binder with all of the agendas, notes, and reports generated by the team that it used to create a final business plan and report for the class's instructor.

- ***Use your diplomacy skills to keep your team on track, focused, and motivated.*** Jonathan tried to motivate his teammates to work together, even though he was never officially assigned to be the leader of the group. He knew that a semester-long project could be challenging because students get busy and distracted by other demands on their time. To combat the problem, he spearheaded a unique plan: at each meeting, someone would bring an item of food from the proposed menu and conduct a taste test. He knew that food would be an effective motivator for getting the group together. It was.

The experience taught Jonathan that although getting people to work together is worthwhile, it's very hard. Rosalynn Carter, the former first lady of the United States once said, "A leader takes people where they want to go. A great leader takes people where they don't necessarily want to go, but ought to be."

Using Technology to Facilitate Communication in Teams

As we explained at the beginning of the chapter, a virtual team is any team whose members are rarely, if ever, in the same physical location. Virtual teams are becoming increasingly common because companies recognize that the best people for projects are often in different locations. Working across geographical distances, time zones, and cultures can be challenging, but the core principles of team dynamics remain the same.

Technology can assist in bridging the physical gaps virtual teams experience. For example, **Exhibit 2-7** illustrates how Google Docs software allows team members to coordinate their efforts to launch a new product using a joint calendar.

Communication technology can also help companies save time and money because they don't have to spend thousands of dollars on airfare and other travel costs for employees to meet in person. Employees benefit, too, because they spend less time traveling and away from home and work.

Consider this 21st-century business team. A small coffee roasting company is introducing a new line of coffee to be distributed across the country, and expanding its coffee shops into new markets. As part of this effort, the company is creating a marketing campaign around social responsibility, highlighting its relationships with coffee bean growers in Costa Rica. The business team consists of two company executives, one who works in New York City, and another who works in Seattle. A marketing specialist from an independent public relations firm is also on the team, and she works in Chicago. The company's product specialist is based in Costa Rica for the next three months.

In the beginning, this virtual team brainstorms and develops ideas for the campaign. These initial meetings are conducted by conference calls that allow simultaneous conversation between all team members. As ideas develop, the team begins to identify potential partners for the campaign. When meeting with potential partners, the team relies on

Exhibit 2-7
Sharing and Publishing Documents with Google Docs

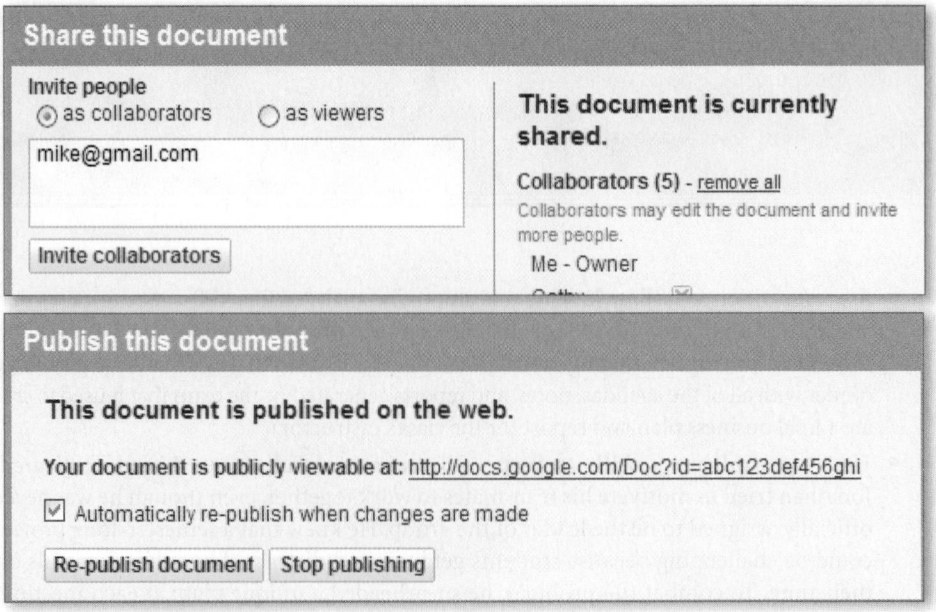

Share this document
Invite people
as collaborators as viewers
mike@gmail.com
Invite collaborators
This document is currently shared.
Collaborators (5) - remove all
Collaborators may edit the document and invite more people.
Me - Owner

Publish this document
This document is published on the web.
Your document is publicly viewable at: http://docs.google.com/Doc?id=abc123def456ghi
Automatically re-publish when changes are made
Re-publish document Stop publishing

Videoconferencing can help make geographically dispersed teams more cohesive.

videoconferencing, technology that streams audio and video communications in real time in multiple places. Videoconferencing lets the team members see and hear one another while they hold a conference call.

For everyday telephone communication between team members, the group uses **voice over Internet protocol (VoIP)**, technology that transfers analog audio signals to digital data and transmits the data over the Internet. VoIP allows team members to talk to one another across long distances via their computers without paying long-distance telephone charges.

The team also relies on **online chat**, a form of instant messaging and e-mails for quick, everyday written correspondence. Online-chat technology allows team members to stay connected in the same way that members who work on site together casually stop by one another's offices for brief exchanges. In addition, some companies and teams are now using **social networking** types of Web sites similar to Facebook to facilitate their communication. For example, the yogurt maker Danone, based in France, has an internal social network which its employees in 100 countries use to communicate with one another about products, customers, and market opportunities.

Instant messaging makes it possible for team members to communicate with one another in real time.

As the team begins the planning and writing process for their campaign, they turn to groupware to facilitate these hands on-meetings. **Groupware** is any type of collaborative software that allows teams to work cooperatively with their computers. The members are able to view the same computer screen at the same time and work with the application on that screen. The control of the screen shifts back and forth between the members of the meeting.

The team uses Web conferences to conduct live, real-time meetings at which members connect via the Internet on their computers. Each meeting attendee has a Webcam that captures and streams video to the other members' screens so everyone can see and hear one another. Instant messaging built into the software allows people to ask questions of specific team members without interrupting the meeting. The entire meeting can be recorded for later reference.

When the team puts things in writing, the members use **collaborative writing software** to read, edit, and create documents. Programs such as Google

Exhibit 2-8
A Collaborative Press Release Created Using Wiki Technology

Organic Chips Launches New Chipotle Line

San Antonio, TX -- December 02, 2010 -- (PR.com) – Organic Chips, known for its all-natural snack foods, has announced a new line of Chipotle flavored chips, called "Chipotle Smoke." The new line will debut January 15, 2011, in markets in San Antonio, Houston, and Chicago. According to Steve Coppell, Organic Chips' vice president of marketing, the line sold exceptionally in test markets in all three cities.

Organic Chips, which opened in San Antonio in 2003, made a name for itself by creating unique chips with organically grown potatoes and other natural ingredients while promoting social responsibility. Organic Chips' business model ensures that above-market prices are paid to farmers for their organically grown, pesticide-free crops.

(ASchmidt SAN ANTONIO-12/1/10-8:03am) We need to add some information in about our social responsibility initiatives. Maria - can you add some information?

In the past five years, the company has awarded over $250,000 in grants to projects in North, South, and Central America that promote earth-friendly agricultural practices and help with global hunger relief. Following this year's exceptionally dry summer, the company donated $100,000 to Global Hunger Relief, Inc., a nonprofit organization that delivers food aid to hundreds of nations around the world.

(MValez CHICAGO -12/1/10-9:10am) - Here is that information. Rochelle, we will also need some specifics on our partnership with Students for Sustainability.

In addition, Organic Chips supports Students for Sustainability, a nationwide effort to use research and education to create a healthier, sustainable environment for today and tomorrow's generations.

(RKruse HOUSTON-12/1/10-2:41pm) Hello, Andy and Maria. Let's add the following to our press release; to foreshadow our release of the salted version. Rochelle

According to Coppell, a sea-salted version of Chipotle Smoke chips is currently being test marketed by Organic Chips, and is expected to be released within 6–8 months.

DMarcus-SAN ANTONIO-12/1/10-3:56pm) This looks great. Nice job on the collaboration!

Docs, Writeboards, and Wikis allow this coordinated writing effort. **Exhibit 2-8** illustrates the team using a form of Wiki technology that supports online collaboration. The comments that appear in color are the notes the team members have created for one another.

When the team makes a formal presentation to a larger audience, they turn to Webcasts. **Webcasts** have a higher production value, requiring special cameras to capture video footage, and are often created with formal lighting and professional filming crews. Webcasts are often used for formal presentations to large, dispersed audiences, not for hands-on, highly interactive meetings. These on-demand or live presentations are then streamed over the Internet. In a nutshell, this is broadcasting over the Internet. **Exhibit 2-9** outlines the communication tools virtual teams are using today.

Tips for Working in Virtual Teams

Working in virtual teams requires extra attention to the communication process to combat the obstacles that could result from not having regular face-to-face interaction.

Make a Personal Connection

In a face-to-face meeting, the interpersonal connections between individuals are much easier to make than through collaborative meeting software. Jokes, friendly discussions, and informal chatter can enhance the working relationships among team members in a face-to-face meeting.

Exhibit 2-9 Electronic Communication Tools Used by Teams

Telephone Conferences

Three or more team members converse simultaneously. Participants dial one number and then punch in a code to connect to the call.—*OR*—A moderator calls all the participants and connects them to the call.

Videoconferences

Two or more sites interact by two-way video and audio transmissions through interactive telecommunications technology. Video images are projected onto large screens for viewing.

VoIP (voice over Internet protocol)

This technology transfers audio signals to digital data, which is transmitted through the Internet. This allows team members to speak directly with one another and avoid long-distance telephone charges.

Online Chat and Social Networking

Internet-based communication tools that let team members send messages and share ideas using e-mails, instant messaging software such as Instant Messenger, Google, or Tok Box, and social-networking Web sites similar to Facebook.

Web Conferences

Team members conduct meetings through the Internet, using a Web-based application, where each member uses a separate computer with attached Web cam. The technology is ideal for small, interactive sessions. Examples include: Web Train, Microsoft Office Live Meeting, Acrobat Connect, and WebEx.

Collaborative Writing Software

Teams use software such as Google Docs, White-board, and Wikis to collaboratively create, edit, and revise written reports and documents.

Webcasts

Teams use Webcasts for formal presentations to large and dispersed audiences. They can broadcast their presentations over the Internet.

Making a personal connection tends to be more difficult in virtual teams. Videoconferencing helps because it allows team members to see one another's facial expressions during meetings. The management consulting firm Accenture has developed an internal form of Facebook. The social networking site helps employees get to know one another and understand what one another's strengths are. Other helpful tactics include introducing team members before meetings and incorporating "icebreaker" activities. An icebreaker activity can be as simple as having team members introduce themselves by saying a few things about their role in the company or what they like to do in their free time.

Choose the Right Communication Tools

Many different tools are available to aid virtual teams. When selecting among them, consider the following: the technical proficiency of the team's members, the technology available to each member, and the goals of the team. The most advanced collaboration software is useless if the members of the team don't have the proper equipment or technological savvy to use it.

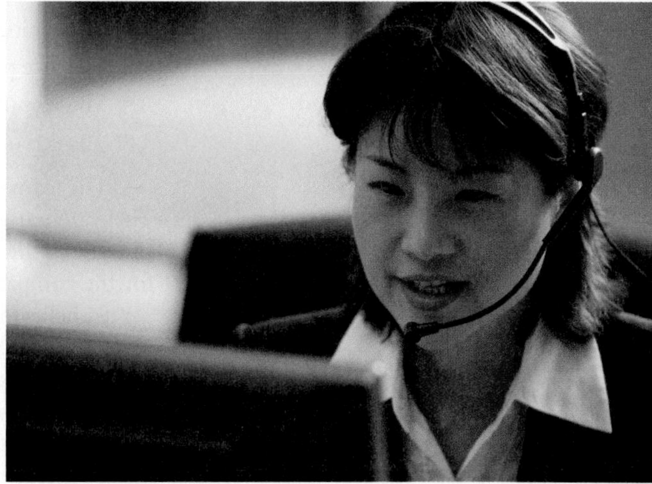

Speak Clearly

Working in a virtual team often means working with people who live in different parts of the country or world. People's accents can sometimes be difficult to understand. Speak clearly, not too fast, and loudly enough for everyone to hear. It doesn't hurt to ask, "Can you hear me?" Lastly, try to eliminate any background noise.

Pick Up the Phone

E-mail, instant messaging, and other electronic communication allow for easy communication. However, the personal touch can get lost in the mix. Taking the time to have a phone conversation can help bridge the gap that can result from electronic communication. Picking up the phone can also help when several e-mail messages have not produced the results you want.

4 What Causes Teams to Break Down?

Even the best-managed teams have problems. In this section we will discuss problems teams can experience, and how to use your communication skills to work through these problems.

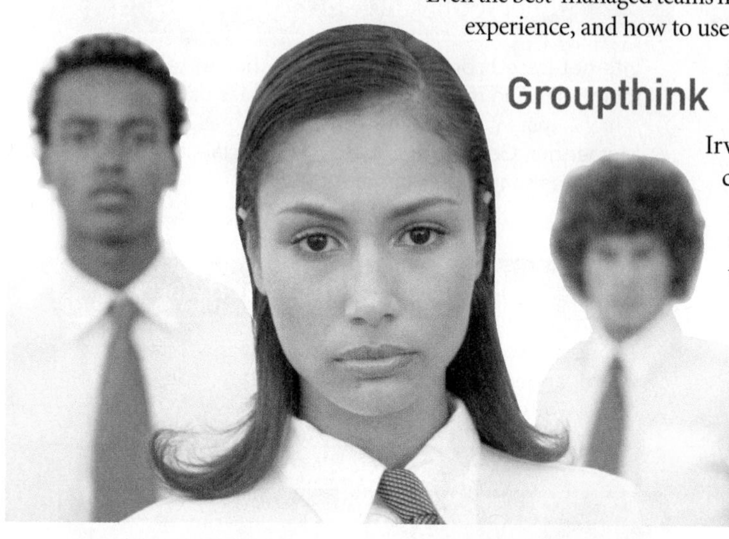

Groupthink is a negative consequence of teams.

Groupthink

Irving Janis, a research psychologist from Yale University, coined the term **groupthink** to describe the phenomenon that occurs when the members of a group "go with the flow," or tacitly agree with one another's ideas to avoid conflict—even when they might silently object to those ideas. Groupthink creates a false consensus. Janis cites incidents such the Bay of Pigs Invasion and the Vietnam War, as political examples of failed policy where some leaders in the decision-making process went along with the flow, despite personal objections to the decisions being made.[7]

Decisions made under the pressures of groupthink are often worse than the decisions people make alone. When the desire for a consensus overrides the ability of a team's members to think thoroughly and critically about a situation, the advantages of working as a team are lost. Dissension during the group decision-making process is critical. If there is no dissension, the group will not achieve the best outcome. To prevent groupthink, teams need to agree to listen to dissenting ideas and explore them.

Team Conflicts

Team conflicts can result from power struggles, personality differences, limited resources, opposing interests, and a lack of clarity regarding the roles each member plays in the group. **Exhibit 2-10** illustrates some of the common sources of conflict in the workplace and ways to address each.

Consider the following example. Green Line Food Distributors sells and delivers food and kitchen supplies to over 200 restaurants in a large metropolitan city. The firm's upper-management team consists of the following five executives:

- The senior vice president of sales
- The senior manager of operations
- The vice president of human resources
- The vice president of finance
- The senior manager of service

The team is in conflict. Two record-breaking snowstorms have limited their resources. The warehouses are low and they do not have enough fresh produce to fill their orders on time. The senior vice president of sales insists that the five new accounts she recently opened for the company should have their orders filled first. The senior manager of service disagrees, believing that the longest-standing customers should have priority. The senior vice president of sales is allied with new customers, whereas the senior manager of service is allied with the existing customers.

The team members are hoping to consider other options for getting the produce they need to stock their warehouses, including flying in extra shipments from South America. However, no one knows who was supposed to research the options and bring the informa-

Exhibit 2-10 Sources of Workplace Conflicts and Strategies for Solving Them

Conflict	Conflicts of Interest	Lack of Clarity about Roles	Limited Resources	Power Struggles	Personality Differences
Source	Individuals can get caught up in their own agendas and lose site of organizational goals.	Team members can experience conflict when their roles and boundaries are not clearly defined.	Lack of time, money, resources, supplies, and space can cause conflict.	The need to control a project or outcome often causes conflict.	Differences in personalities can result in conflict due to differing approaches and work styles.
Strategy for Resolution	Consistently remind team members how the roles they play fit into the broader mission of the organization.	Clarify what each member is expected to deliver to the team. Make sure a time frame is agreed upon and that everyone has the necessary, up-to-date information.	Include teams in resource allocation discussions so they understand why resources are distributed the way they are.	Promote an environment that fosters positive relationships. Teach team members how to effectively navigate political "minefields" or situations where conflicts are likely to occur.	Work toward understanding your own personality. Share what you know about yourself and discuss with the team how to work with people with various personalities.

tion to the meeting for review. As a result, team members begin pointing fingers and blaming one another for the lack of viable solutions.

The vice president of human resources is also concerned because many of the company's truck drivers have been unable to report to work due to closed roads and stranded vehicles. The company must pay overtime wages to the few workers who are able to make it to work. She wants to reduce the number of trucks going out on delivery so that payroll remains in check. However, the senior manager of operations, vying for a promotion, demands that all trucks are on the road, despite the costs for paying drivers overtime. He wants his division to look productive.

To make matters worse, the vice president of human resources, a "giver" who resists conflict, is up against the senior manager of operations, an "adventurer" who will do whatever it takes to get his agenda accomplished. Tensions are running high and these two team members storm out of the meeting.

Conflicts can also arise because of the behaviors of the team members. Think back to a time when you were on a dysfunctional team. Were there one or two people who made the team miserable? Can you remember the behaviors these people exhibited? **Toxic team members** prevent a team from reaching its potential. Toxic members become the interference in the communication model mentioned in Chapter 1.

If we are honest with ourselves, we have probably all been a toxic team member at one time or another. The following is a list of team member stereotypes demonstrating "toxic" behaviors, and what you can do to prevent yourself from falling into these traps.

- ***The Lone Ranger.*** The lone ranger tends to have an introverted, highly competitive personality. Lone rangers prefer to work alone, without others slowing them down. They often become entrepreneurs who work for themselves. A lone ranger's team members can feel overwhelmed by his or her intelligence and fast pace. If you have lone-ranger tendencies, be patient when working with other people and work on building consensus so the group can reach a common goal.

- ***The Know-It-All.*** The know-it-all often believes she knows everything. Some teammates avoid voicing their ideas rather than continue not to be heard by the know-it-all. If you have know-it-all tendencies, listen to others without judging them and before you focus on your own ideas exclusively.
- ***The Passive Aggressive.*** The passive aggressive desperately wants to make his ideas heard but blames others for not giving him a voice. Rather than disagree with others, he will wait until the moment of opportunity has passed and then fail to turn in an assignment, withhold information, or in some other way "hurt" the person on his team with whom he has an issue. If you have these tendencies, work on being direct in your communication. People can't solve a problem they don't know about. Muster up the courage to plainly and simply state your point of view.
- ***The Intimidated.*** If you think others on your team are smarter or more talented than you, you may become easily intimidated. Remind yourself of your strengths and pledge to dismiss any inferiority thoughts. You will be most effective if you can be strong and humble at the same time.
- ***The Gossip.*** The gossip has developed a pattern of gossiping about others to feel better, stronger, or more powerful about himself. If you are not willing to say something to someone directly, don't say it to someone else. Let go of the tendency to criticize others. As you do, you will begin to breed goodwill and positive results.
- ***The Taker.*** The taker often takes credit for the work of others. If you notice this pattern in yourself, acknowledge the contributions of other people on a daily basis. The next time an opportunity comes up to "steal" the credit, remain silent and realize that you are on your way toward developing a more mature, professional communication style.
- ***The Slacker.*** The slacker avoids volunteering for assignments because she may not believe in herself. If you have these tendencies, make a pact with yourself to start taking more responsibility so you become a finisher. Employers do not retain employees who are not strong finishers.
- ***The Seat Filler.*** The seat filler resembles the slacker. The slacker does the minimum required, while the seat filler does nothing. If you are a seat filler, you may have to do some soul searching and start taking responsibility in your life. Ask yourself what it will cost you if you don't.

The Conflict-Resolution Process

As we have mentioned, conflicts within teams are inevitable and can even be positive. The following tips can help you resolve conflict, regardless of its source:

- What are you trying to accomplish? Keep the outcome in mind.
- Avoid personality disputes. Focus on the problem, not the person.
- Maintain a positive outlook and attitude toward other members of the group.
- Have confidence that you will get to a win-win outcome.

Let's look again at Green Line Food Distributors. The team needs to focus on its immediate goal: to meet its customers' needs and deliver their food and supplies on schedule as promised. By maintaining a solutions-driven outlook, they can generate ideas that go beyond flying supplies in from South America. Perhaps they can network with competing suppliers, or work with customers to restructure their orders.

Staying focused on the problem and not the personalities of team members keeps the team from getting stuck. The vice president of human resources can avoid shutting down in response to the senior manager of operations' adventurer tendencies. Instead, she can remain focused on the problem and how she might approach it with an adventuresome attitude to discover new solutions. The bottom line is this: the crisis will pass, but the team members will still need to work together and manage the conflicts that arise in such situations. By addressing the problem from a "we" perspective, these team players can navigate through the trying week, orchestrate solutions that serve the entire company, and move forward together once the snowstorms pass. **Exhibit 2-11** offers a step-by-step approach you can use to work through team conflicts and impasses.

Exhibit 2-11 Steps to Working through Team Conflicts and Impasses

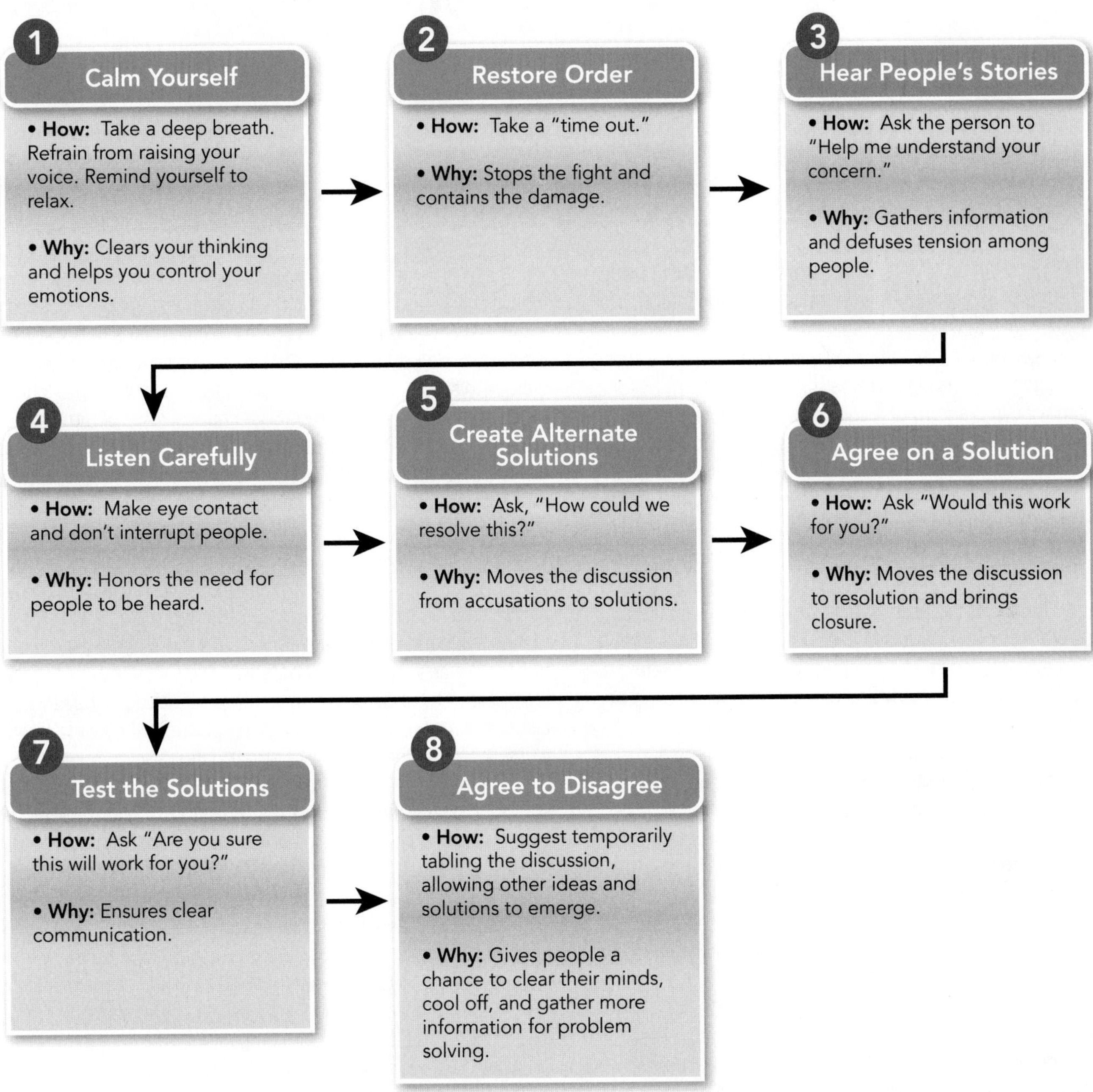

1
Calm Yourself
• How: Take a deep breath. Refrain from raising your voice. Remind yourself to relax.
• Why: Clears your thinking and helps you control your emotions.
2
Restore Order
• How: Take a "time out."
• Why: Stops the fight and contains the damage.
3
Hear People's Stories
• How: Ask the person to "Help me understand your concern."
• Why: Gathers information and defuses tension among people.
4
Listen Carefully
• How: Make eye contact and don't interrupt people.
• Why: Honors the need for people to be heard.
5
Create Alternate Solutions
• How: Ask, "How could we resolve this?"
• Why: Moves the discussion from accusations to solutions.
6
Agree on a Solution
• How: Ask "Would this work for you?"
• Why: Moves the discussion to resolution and brings closure.
7
Test the Solutions
• How: Ask "Are you sure this will work for you?"
• Why: Ensures clear communication.
8
Agree to Disagree
• How: Suggest temporarily tabling the discussion, allowing other ideas and solutions to emerge.
• Why: Gives people a chance to clear their minds, cool off, and gather more information for problem solving.

When conflict abounds and tensions run high, bringing in an outside mediator, such as someone from Human Resources, can be helpful. Although working in teams can be difficult, its rewards are many. As Henry Ford once said:

"Coming together is the beginning.
Keeping together is progress.
Working together is success."[8]

❺ How Can You Become an Effective Team Leader?

Maybe you think a leader is someone famous with a formal title or position, a big salary, and lots of power. However, according to Dr. Howard Gardner, a professor at Harvard Graduate School of Education, "A **leader** is an individual (or, rarely, a set of individuals) who significantly affects the thoughts, feelings, and/or behaviors of a significant number of individuals."[9] More formally,

REAL INSIGHTS from a Seasoned Professional

Name: *David Packer*
Title: *Distribution Manager, Western Zone*
Organization: *Rich Products*
Location: *Buffalo, New York*

DAVID PACKER HAS THREE ENERGETIC BOYS. So it's a given that there's teamwork involved to get through a week filled with work, school, sports, and other agenda items big and small.

Teamwork, in the form of a collaborative spirit, is one key to Packer's success on the job too. "For an organization to be healthy and grow and promote their people and retain their people, you need to have collaboration and communication. Without collaboration, you're not going to have strong communication," said Packer, the Western Zone distribution manager for Rich Products, a foodservice giant specializing in baked goods, desserts, barbecued meats, and Italian cuisine. Packer manages the Rich Products' partnerships with large national foodservice distributors such as Sysco Foodservice, U.S. Foodservice, Shamrock Foods, and Food Services America. He spearheads marketing programs for Rich and is responsible for growing the company's sales.

Packer, 44, who holds a degree in hotel and restaurant management from the University of Nevada–Las Vegas, has an all-star résumé in terms of foodservice sales. He didn't start small. Right out of college, he landed a job as distributor sales representative for Kraft Foodservice in Chicago. "I was the youngest person they had ever hired for a distributor sales rep position," Packer noted. "The people that hired me could sense my passion for sales and for wanting to help people. I had good communication skills and a strong desire to succeed and make a difference."

Packer grew his territory sales from $250,000 to almost $2 million and earned Kraft's Circle of Excellence Award for sales and gross profit in 1991 and 1992. He enjoyed similar success at Land O'Lakes, Specialty Brands, and Windsor Foods before joining Otis Spunkmeyer as the director of sales foodservice distribution in 2007. There, he increased Sysco-branded cookie dough sales by $4.7 million, among other achievements.

"The salespeople that do well are the ones who can separate themselves from being just a salesperson to being more of a consultant, as if you're a partner in their business," Packer said. "You want them to come to you for solutions to issues they are having, not to your competitor. Going along with communication is being a good listener. Your customer will tell you what they're looking for. It's about putting yourself on their agenda and seeing what their needs are, and not necessarily what your needs are."

Creativity also helps. To generate excitement and boost the product launch of "Cowboy Cookie" at Spunkmeyer, Packer rewarded distributors who exceeded sales targets with a dude ranch getaway in the Colorado high country. Most of the 'ranchers' were East Coasters who had never been on a horse. "It was like a scene out of 'City Slickers,'" Packer said. "The first half of the first day, they were real tentative. By the end of the last day, they were all saying it was the best trip they'd ever been on."

Packer earned supplier achievement awards and exceeded sales targets at Spunkmeyer, but ultimately, he felt stagnated by an upper-level executive who stifled the team spirit. "He didn't want his subordinates to appear to have more knowledge than him, so it was very non-collaborative," Packer said. "Their opinions weren't even asked for. They weren't involved in the key decision making with the aspects of the business they were hired to manage. You need to have strong internal communication, which leads to collaboration, and you have to be able to express your idea. You need a culture that promotes that, so there's a comfort level in being able to express what needs to be done to move the company forward."

Packer said the forecast for careers in the food and beverage sector is strong. "People have to eat, so as far as being recession-proof, our business has been affected by the downturn of the economy but not nearly to the extent of other industries. It's very stable, with a lot of different avenues as far as career directions go. . . . To differentiate yourself from your competitors, you want to present yourself as someone who is excited about the industry, wants to learn and put in long hours, and has a clear direction of where you want your career to go."

Questions

1. What traits and skills allowed Packer to land a key role with Kraft right out of college?
2. Why does Packer believe good communication and teamwork are vital to firms?

Source: David Packer in discussion with the author, June 2010.

leadership can be defined as the ability and process of motivating people to move toward a common goal.[10] As Microsoft founder Bill Gates puts it, "As we look ahead into the next century, leaders will be those who empower others."

Every team has a leader, and that leader could be you. Think of the leaders who have inspired you. Are they business leaders such as Henry Ford or Bill Gates? Perhaps you immediately think of humanitarian heroes such as Mother Teresa or Nelson Mandela. Or do you look up to social change–agents like Martin Luther King, Jr.? Maybe your leadership inspiration falls closer to home. Perhaps your family members, teachers, coaches, or local athletes demonstrate good leadership abilities you would like to acquire.

All leaders have detractors and supporters. **Detractors** are the people who do not support the leader and can be derisive or coercive. If the leader is a new manager and determines there is a detractor on the team, he or she will usually first give the person a chance to accept the new philosophy and goals. If the person continues to be a detractor, the manager might try to find him or her a different job within the company or let the person go.

Supporters are the people who support the leader and show their commitment by meeting deadlines, coming up with new and original ideas, and creating a culture and an environment that is positive and affirms the leader's goals and vision. Although not everyone needs to agree with the leader, the leader needs the support of the members of the team or it will not succeed.

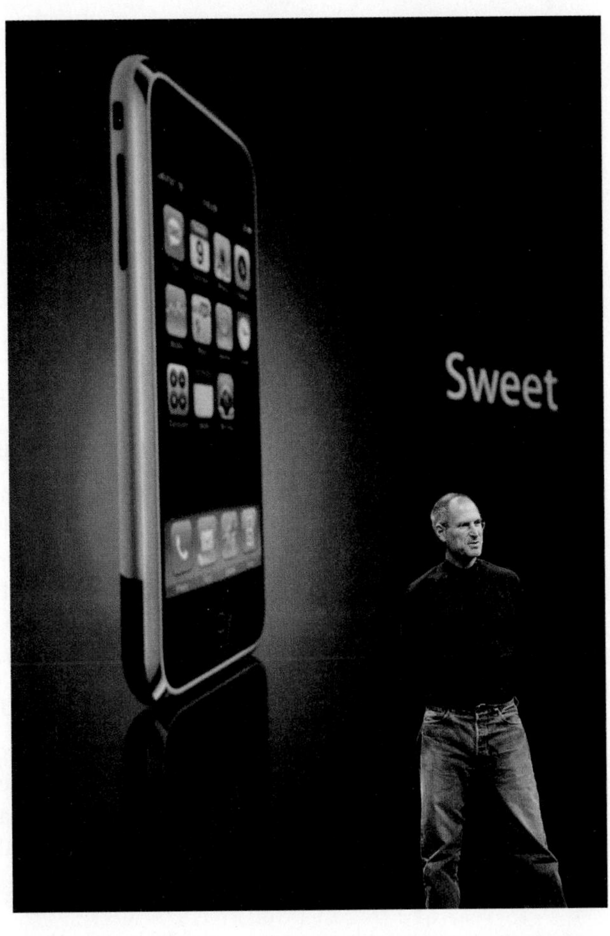

Great leaders like Steve Jobs, the CEO of Apple, have qualities that inspire and motivate others.

Consider people who are in leadership positions in your life: your manager in your part-time job, your academic advisor, and your professors. What role do you play in these relationships? Are you a supporter or are you a detractor? How would these people describe you to your future manager? If you observe your behavior and find you are a detractor, what can you do to turn that around, and how would that help you become the successful professional you want to be?

What do leaders have in common? What characteristics do they possess that you can apply to your own life? The most effective leaders demonstrate some, or all, of the attributes shown in **Exhibit 2-12**. You can develop these attributes by studying good leaders around

Exhibit 2-12 Elements of Effective Leadership

Ability to Influence	Exemplary Behavior	Follow-Through Skills	Positive Self-Identity	Values	Vision
Leaders garner support for causes by influencing others. They motivate others to embrace a vision, do their best work, and become part of a solution.	Leaders model best behaviors and take responsibility for their actions. They "walk their talk" and demonstrate how to do things, rather than simply telling others what to do.	Effective leaders consistently deliver on their promises. They meet deadlines and follow through with their commitments.	The best leaders are self-aware. They understand their strengths AND weaknesses. They believe in themselves and what they can contribute to a cause.	Leaders possess values that reflect the team's best interests. They look to these values to inform and guide their actions.	The best leaders hold fast to a vision of what is possible. They inspire others through this vision to work toward a common goal, despite obstacles met along the way.

you and joining teams with effective leaders. Once you see these leadership skills in action, try them out by assuming greater responsibility in your work and academic settings. Is there an organization on campus that interests you? Join the organization and take an active role. Do you have a part-time job? Think about how to improve a product or procedure and discuss it with your manager. These types of experiences will help you develop effective leadership skills for the business world. If you are faced with a tricky communication situation, think about how the leader you most admire would handle it and act how he or she would. Leaders are not born. They are made.

Summary *Synthesize What You Have Learned*

1. What are business teams like today?

Business teams today look very different than they did 20 years ago. With advances in technology and increased globalization you might find yourself on a team with members from around the world, communicating through interactive software, and rarely meeting face to face. Having a clear understanding of how teams are organized, how they operate, the role communication plays, and what you bring to the table will make you stand out as an employee and business leader.

2. What do you have to offer a team?

Being aware of your strengths and weaknesses helps you determine what you bring to a team. This type of self-awareness will also help you communicate with team members, managers, and employees who report to you. A team is more effective when its members know their strengths and weaknesses and what they have to offer the group.

3. What makes a team work together effectively?

To be effective in business communication, you must have a clear understanding of how teams operate. By applying your understanding of the stages of team development, the ground rules for teamwork, and how to resolve team conflict, you will ensure peak team performance.

4. What causes teams to break down?

Common barriers to team effectiveness include: groupthink, conflict in the workplace, and toxic team members. Combat groupthink by freely allowing dissent and encouraging questions. Deal with conflicts by focusing on team outcomes, not personal goals. Deal with toxic team members by understanding why they behave the way they do and addressing the underlying causes.

5. How can you become an effective team leader?

Look for opportunities in both school and work to develop the following leadership attributes: ability to influence, exemplary behavior, follow-through skills, positive self-identity, values, and vision. By seeing yourself as a leader and practicing these skills with every opportunity, you will learn to share your vision and influence those around you.

PEARSON **mybcommlab**™ Are you an active learner? Go to **mybcommlab.com** to master Chapter 2's content. Chapter 2's interactive activities include:

- Customizable Study Plan and Chapter 2 practice quizzes
- Chapter 2 Video Exercise, Creativity at Second City, which shows you how textbook concepts are put into practice every day
- Flash cards for mastering the definition of chapter terms
- Interactive Lessons that visually review key chapter concepts
- Document Makeovers for hands-on, scored practice in revising documents

Know It *Reflect, Respond, and Express*

Build Your Critical Thinking Skills

Critical Thinking Questions

1. How can Web conferencing help a business team that is not virtual?
2. Complete an Internet search for the Myers-Briggs Personality Test. Complete a free test online and bring the results to class. How do the results compare to the outcome of the Keirsey Sorter test?
3. List the five areas for student team development and discuss their relevance to business communication. In which areas have you had the best and worst experiences?
4. What "icebreaker" exercises have you experienced in a class or workplace setting? What information is the most effective when trying to get to know team members?
5. In groups, discuss the definition of leadership and what makes someone an effective leader.

Critical Thinking Scenario

While visiting the student union between classes, Juan, a college junior, noticed how few healthy options were available to students. Juan spoke with some of his friends and other people around the campus and realized that many students felt the same way. Armed with his nutrition professor's support, Juan and several friends founded the SHO (Students for Healthy Options) club with the goal of working with the student government and the campus food buyers to make sure a healthy diet was represented on campus.

During one of SHO's first meetings, Juan noticed that there were some conflicting personalities in the group. Lee, the SHO's treasurer, refused to consider others' points of view and Matt, the vice president, wasn't willing to back Juan's leadership role as president. Juan is beginning to feel that the effectiveness of the group will be compromised if its members don't find a way to work together. He believes it might be beneficial to create some ground rules for the team.

Questions

1. What are four rules that he might consider? How would each of these benefit the group and contribute to its success?
2. What about you? Have you have had an instance when similar rules have helped a group you have been involved in? What was the result? Looking back, would different rules have yielded a better result?
3. After implementing Juan's new ground rules, things begin to run a little more smoothly for the club. As the group gets ready to meet with the student government and food suppliers on campus, Juan realizes that he needs to outline how he will go about conveying SHO's ideas both orally and on paper. He must decide what communication strategies to use. Will Juan write the student government discussing specific reasons why healthy options should be available? Will he deliver an oral speech to the suppliers about how healthier options will reduce food costs for the school? What would you do in Juan's place? Write out your strategy for conveying Juan's ideas effectively to these audiences.

Write It *Draft, Revise, and Finalize*

Create Your Own Success Story

1. If you could build a strong business team and direct it toward any goal you can think of, what would you do? Who would you want on your team?
   a. Describe your own strengths as a team member and as a leader.
   b. Describe the specific qualities of the people you would recruit to your team based on balancing your own strengths and weaknesses.
   c. Finally, write a letter to an investor describing the strengths of your team, your leadership abilities, and your potential contribution that would warrant the investment.
2. With a partner, use Google Docs to create a memo to your instructor explaining the importance of using technology in business communication. E-mail the completed document to your instructor.
3. Take the tour on Wikispaces.com and explore the possibilities of the Web site. Analyze the site's usability and write a memo to your classmates describing its features and hindrances.
4. Visit Skype.com and explore the possibilities available using the service. Write a memo to the class explaining the top features the Web site offers and how to best utilize those features in business communication.

Speak It *Discuss, Listen, and Understand*

Build Your Leadership and Teamwork Skills

1. Get into groups of four. Ask the groups to imagine they work for competing paper-cup companies. Summer is just around the corner and the companies are gearing up for increased sales due to barbecue season. Have each group think of all of the things it would need to do to launch a successful new paper-cup design. Consider areas like marketing, finance, and distribution. Allow 15 minutes for the discussion.
   a. After 15 minutes, go through the stages of group dynamics discussed on page 37. Ask each team to try and pinpoint when each of the initial stages occurred and what the outcome of each was.
      - Forming:
      - Storming:
      - Norming:

   b. For the fourth stage (performing) have each group synthesize its paper-cup concept and present it as a group to the class. After all the groups have presented their ideas, the class will vote on which one they as consumers would be most likely to buy. After the paper-cup design is chosen, resume groups and discuss the last step. What was the result of your presentation? Looking back, was there something your group could have done to make the performing step more successful?
   c. Now personally consider how you worked within your group. What did you notice about yourself and how you related to others? How hard was it to come up with an innovative concept with someone else?
2. In groups or as a class, discuss the benefits of having a project manager oversee a team project.
3. In groups, review your results for the Keirsey Sorter test. Next, how does what you learned about emotional quotient (EQ) help you understand your classmates and future colleagues? What are the limitations to such tests?
4. In groups, discuss the definition of leadership and what makes someone an effective leader.
5. In groups, practice using the tips for effective interpersonal communication. Look each group member in the eye and focus on listening to one another. Take turns explaining a specialized aspect of your major and ensure everyone understands your message through their reactions and questions.

Do It *Document Your Success Track Record*

Build Your e-Portfolio

Many future employers will be interested in the leadership and teamwork skills you develop during your college years. This exercise is an opportunity for you to review and document various roles you have played on teams, and the leadership and teamwork skills you developed as a result.

Think back to times when you participated in a group, inside or outside of school, where the group was responsible for accomplishing a particular goal. Then answer the following questions and save your "Leadership and Teamwork" document for your e-portfolio.

1. Identify a group where you played a leadership role:
   - What was the group and what was its goal?
   - How did you become the leader and what did you do in that role?
   - Were there any toxic members on your team? How did you deal with them?
   - Discuss your leadership style: what worked well and what would you do differently in the future?
   - What skills did you develop as a result of your experience?
2. Now identify a group where you played a team worker role:
   - What was the group and what was its goal?
   - What did you do in the group?
   - What is your personality style? What different personality styles did you have in the group and how did you learn to work with them?
   - Discuss your team's working style: what worked well and what you would do differently in the future?
   - What skills did you develop as a result of your experience?
3. Based on your own experience:
   - What qualities do you think make a good leader? A good team worker?
   - Are they similar or different qualities?

Business in Action
Kraft-ing a Leadership Plan for Long-Term Success

From Cadbury confections to Maxwell House coffee, Oscar Mayer cold cuts and Nabisco snacks, Kraft Foods brands encompass the culinary spectrum. The world's second-largest food company with annual revenues of $48 billion, Kraft counts on leaders with the ability to inspire and motivate its staff.

"Providing a workplace that is safe, inclusive, and rewarding is a proven strategy for keeping good people and inspiring them to do great things," the Kraft Foods Responsibility Report states. "And that's the best way we know to grow a great company."

A variety of strategies and employee development tools keep Kraft thriving:

- The company identifies skills gaps and manages the development of its employees' capabilities through a special managing-and-appraising-performance program. Kraft also encourages people at all levels to communicate upwards and generate ideas. For example, a junior manager is welcome to approach the company's CEO with a critical problem, bypassing her boss so to collaborate directly with the CEO. This breeds communication between all levels of the business. The company's motto—"company before individuals"—encourages a sense of community versus self-promotion. The firm also stresses that success is a team effort that is only possible through constant communication.
- Kraft's "Leadership Competency Model" provides the organization with a common language that outlines its expectations of all employees regardless of their levels in the organization, locations, functions, or business-product line. The company also provides employees with a Web-based toolkit—translated into 28 languages—that helps them develop each competency.
- Kraft fosters an "open and inclusive" workplace, with diversity and inclusion training, diversity-focused employee councils, and diversity goals that are factored into its executive compensation.
- In 2007 Kraft decentralized its organizational structure and gave more responsibility to smaller local business units. This gave employees more power to make decisions and instilling pride. "We had let the pendulum swing much too far toward centralization," Kraft Foods CEO Irene Rosenfeld said in a 2009 *strategy + business magazine* report. "We had a structure that was 80/20 global versus local. We needed to move that pendulum back."

Questions

1. What are the advantages of the "communicating upwards" philosophy that Kraft practices? What are some potential disadvantages of this business communication philosophy?
2. What effect does decentralizing a company's decision making have on communication? Is the effect good or bad?

Key Terms

Collaborative writing software. Software that allows multiple people to work on the same document together. *(p. 43)*

Conference call. Simultaneous phone conversation between all team members. *(p. 31)*

Detractors. Team members who do not support a group's leader and can be derisive or coercive. *(p. 51)*

Emotional intelligence. The ability to monitor and control your emotions, thoughts, and feelings, while remaining sensitive to and aware of others' feelings. *(p. 31)*

Emotional quotient (EQ). The measurement of one's emotional intelligence; much like the intelligence quotient (IQ) is a measurement of one's intellectual intelligence. *(p. 31)*

Groupthink. The phenomenon where members of a group begin to tacitly agree with one another's ideas to avoid conflict—even when they might silently object to those ideas. Everyone appears to think alike. *(p. 46)*

Groupware. Software that allows users to hold meetings and collaborate over the Web. As they work, they can see one another's screens and collaboratively use their software applications. *(p. 43)*

Keirsey Sorter personality types. Four common types of personalities that exhibit certain strengths and weaknesses. The types are giver, thinker, adventurer, and organizer. *(p. 32)*

Leader. An individual (or, rarely, a set of individuals) who significantly affects the thoughts, feelings, and/or behaviors of a significant number of individuals. *(p. 49)*

Online chat. A form of instant messaging and e-mails for quick, everyday written correspondence. *(p. 43)*

Self-awareness. The ability to understand how you process information, read the signals other people are sending, and express yourself as perceived by others. *(p. 31)*

Social networking. A Web site or a network of Web sites that allows people with common interests to communicate with one another. *(p. 43)*

Supporters. Team members who support the leader and show their commitment by meeting deadlines, coming up with new and original ideas, and creating a culture and an environment that is positive and affirms the leader's goals and vision. *(p. 51)*

Toxic team members. Team members that behave poorly and negatively impact the performance of the team. Toxic members include Lone Ranger, Know-it-All, Passive Aggressive, Intimidated, Gossip, Taker, Slacker, Seat Filler. *(p. 47)*

Videoconferencing. Technology that allows team members to see and hear one another, such as when they hold a conference call. *(p. 31)*

Virtual team. A team that is not physically in the same location and relies on technology to communicate. *(p. 31)*

Voice over Internet protocol (VoIP). Technology that transfers audio signals to digital data and transmits the data over the Internet. *(p. 43)*

Webcasts. On-demand or live presentations streamed over the Internet. Webcasts are typically formal presentations made to large, dispersed audiences. *(p. 44)*

Web conferencing. The process of conducting live, real-time meetings where each member uses his or her computer to connect through the Internet. Attendees see and hear one another with Webcams, and typically use groupware to collaborate. *(p. 31)*

Review Questions *Test Yourself*

1. Define a virtual team and describe the different components that enable it to work.
2. Why is self-awareness important to business communication?
3. Define emotional intelligence and describe its importance to business communication.
4. Describe Tuckman's five stages of group dynamics and explain the importance of each to a cohesive team project.
5. What circumstances create the best communication within a group?
6. Define interpersonal communication and explain its importance to business communication.
7. What benefits do you obtain from receiving feedback?
8. What key elements should you keep in mind when giving feedback?
9. What personality traits do you need to be a good leader?
10. How can personality tests help you in the workplace?
11. In what ways can you become an effective leader?
12. In what ways can you utilize your college experience to develop your leadership skills?
13. What strategies can you utilize if you do not like a team member?

Grammar Review *Mastering Accuracy*

Pronouns

Section I

Each of the following sentences contains one or more common errors in word usage, grammar, or style. Identify the errors. If you have trouble finding the errors, review Sections 1.1.1. and 3.1.2. in the handbook (Appendix D) at the back of this textbook.

1. David and her were in several classes together.
2. Who are you calling?
3. Our instructor taught David and I many chemistry lessons.
4. The boss is her.
5. This is the professor which taught me English.
6. If I were her, I would start running for office.
7. Proceed with caution as this issues are extremely difficult.
8. Our current salary is extremely low: us worker need raises.
9. Those lengthy reports needs to be submitted on time for final evaluation.
10. I delivered a copy of *The new England Tribune* to my Supervisor, and then walked to the deli to purchase Breakfast for my Team: Spanish Rice and eggs.

Section II

On a separate sheet of paper, rewrite the following sentences so they are clearer, more professional sounding, grammatically correct, and goodwill oriented.

1. This is the guy that taught me how to write.
2. That is the proposal that that gangly chick wrote.
3. Any drunk employees at the company party need to pipe down.
4. Why can't Steven learn to keep it real and ask for help?

5. Do you ever know what you're talking about?
6. Your taste in film is awful: why would you even watch that?
7. It has the best management of any company in town.
8. You're in big trouble; do you know to whom you'll have to answer?
9. Each desk comes equipped with one accessible wall-mounted electrical outlet; moreover, don't bogart someone's outlet.
10. They will always ask questions after the meeting.

Extra Resources *Tools You Can Use*

Books

- Schein, Edward H. *Organizational Culture and Leadership* (San Francisco, CA: Jossey-Bass, 2004).
- Goleman, Daniel. *Emotional Intelligence: Why It Can Matter More Than IQ* (New York: Bantam Dell, 2006).

Web Sites

- *Keirsey Temperament Sorter (KTS-II)*
- "Before You Search: Self-Assessment Tools," *The Riley Guide.*

"Know thy audience . . . for it is not you." —**Dr. Eric Shaffer,** CEO of Human Factors International

CHAPTER 3

Communicating across Cultures and Generations

>>> **We** have all experienced being misunderstood by someone—a member of our family, a friend, or a coworker. Now imagine how easy it is for a misunderstanding to occur when you communicate with someone from another culture who doesn't speak the same language or have the same background or experiences as you. Just think about the communication problems that Robert, Shawna, and Jodi might encounter in their lines of work as they interact with people around the world.

Robert, Shawna, and Jodi all work for "green" companies. Although green companies may seem like a relatively new phenomenon, the green industry grew out of the environmental movement that started in 1970 with the first Earth Day. Green companies typically provide goods and services that seek to improve the quality of the environment or reduce the negative impact of production upon the environment. Many green companies also take into consideration various aspects of social responsibility, such as human rights, animal protection, community involvement, and social justice.

Robert is a mechanical engineering student in Northern Illinois in his junior year of college. He's an intern with a small company developing nonpolluting cook stoves for use in rural India. Several times a year Robert travels to India with his boss and a small team of engineers to demonstrate the stoves to families who live in small villages.

Shawna is a software developer in California, working remotely via e-mail, phone, and Web conferences with programmers in Michigan, Germany, and Japan. She and her coworkers are currently developing software that controls the pollution systems in cars. Shawna has noticed that the young programmers in Japan seem to favor Web conferences, whereas a senior programmer in Michigan prefers to talk on the phone.

Jodi is director of the English Language Studies (ELS) program on an Oregon university campus. This program provides intensive English language training for international students. Every day Jodi meets students from around the world who want to improve their English skills and knowledge of American culture so they are prepared to study at universities in the United States.

LEARNING OBJECTIVE QUESTIONS

1. Why is it important to know your audience?
2. What are 10 cultural components of communication?
3. What are six major barriers to effective intercultural communication?
4. How can you learn to be a good intercultural communicator?
5. How can you effectively communicate with the four generations that now share the workplace?

PEARSON **mybcommlab** Access interactive videos, simulations, sample documents, document makeovers, and assessment quizzes in Chapter 3 of **mybcommlab.com** for mastery of this chapter's objectives.

Companies within the green industry make everything from solar panels, wind turbines, and bio-fuel to cleaning, body care, and pet care products. These companies also provide services, such as environmental consulting, education, and urban planning. One such company is the social networking site Care2. The site educates people about sustainability, allows people to sign up for petitions, and informs them about green events. With a great diversity in products and services, the green industry generates revenues of roughly $3.7 billion a year. Experts are optimistic about the future, projecting that the industry will grow 25 percent by 2016. Employment opportunities in this industry include environmental and conservation science, program management, forestry, government policy-making, rural development, and urban planning. By 2016, experts project that there will be upward of 125,000 job openings for graduates.[1]

■ For an interactive, real-world example of this topic, access this chapter's bcomm mini sim entitled Communicating Effectively in the Global Workplace, located at **mybcommlab.com**

PEARSON mybcommlab

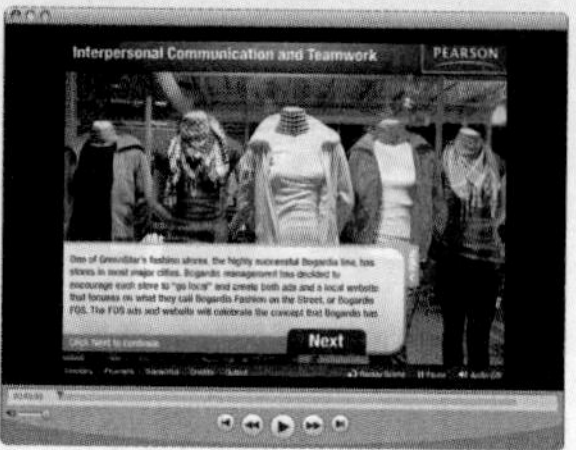

Companies in the green industry must communicate with people of all ages, from all over the planet, many of whom have never considered the environmental or social impact of the products they buy. These companies must also recruit employees from around the world. As a result, many companies provide online courses, workshops, and other forms of education to better adapt their message to their audience and effectively communicate across borders and generation gaps. Regardless of the type of industry you end up working in, sooner or later you will be working with someone from another culture or generation. Today's global workplace consists of communicating with people of all ages, from all over the world by phone, by e-mail, or in person. The workplace also challenges us to figure out the best ways to ask questions, answer questions, and connect without offending anyone.

1 Why Is It Important to Know Your Audience?

As you learned in Chapter 1, good communication starts with understanding your audience. Understanding your audience makes it easier to customize your message for your listener. You also learned in Chapter 1 that communication involves both a messenger (you) and a receiver (your audience). We have all been in situations where we said something and thought we were understood, but it turned out we weren't. Somehow, the words we used just didn't make sense to our listeners, or worse, offended them.

Audience Characteristics Affect Interpretation

People interpret what you say differently. The differences among people lie above and below the surface of the communication iceberg. Those differences that lie above the surface of the iceberg are those you can easily observe and adjust your message accordingly. They are as follows:

1. ***Age.*** How old is your audience? Working with people of different ages is often a challenge. A **generation** is a particular age group, usually consisting of people born within the same 25-year time period. People in one generation have different shared experiences than people in another. They use different words. They wear different clothes. They behave differently and have different comfort levels with technology.

   Points to keep in mind: Use age-neutral words that do not involve generation-specific slang. That way, everyone will know what you are talking about. Don't fall prey to stereotypes when you are talking to people of another generation. For example, don't assume that everyone knows what an "emoticon" is or uses the terms "LOL," "BFF," or "OMG."

   Most younger students are comfortable multitasking with different devices and switching their attention back and forth between equipment and people. For example, you might text while talking to a friend and possibly surf the Internet at the same time. However, if you were talking to an older person, he or she might consider this behavior rude. Remember, every person has a unique perspective to offer, regardless of his or her age. These different perspectives actually help people and businesses solve problems.

DID YOU KNOW?

Car companies have created "aging suits" for young designers to wear when they design vehicles. The aging suits simulate the restricted mobility and vision that many older drivers experience. As a result, designers know, for example, how large to make the buttons on the car, dashboard symbols, and so forth.

2. ***Gender.*** Is your audience male or female? The brains of men and women process information differently, resulting in different communication styles. The more you understand how men and women use language, the better you can communicate your ideas to both genders.
   - Women tend to use language to develop connections, whereas men tend to use language to convey information and status.[2]
   - Women tend to ask more questions when they don't understand or are interested in learning more. Men are less likely to ask questions because they don't want to appear unknowledgeable.[3]

   Points to keep in mind: If your audience consists primarily of women, take time to share stories to connect and ask questions. If your audience consists primarily of men, stay on topic, use fewer words, and get to the point quickly. If your audience consists of both genders, it will require all your talents to get to the point without too many detours for the men but still ask questions and build rapport with the women.

The members of each generation should be treated with respect when you communicate with them.

3. ***Physical abilities and disabilities.*** Do your audience members have any physical disabilities that might prevent them from easily understanding you? Are you making assumptions about them based on those disabilities? It is easy to make assumptions based on how people look—and physical disabilities are often the most visible aspect of a person's appearance.

   Points to keep in mind: Don't refer to people as handicapped or disabled either in speaking or writing. In fact, don't refer to their disabilities at all, unless doing so is absolutely essential to your message. If you must do so, always put the person first and the disability second. For example, say "employees with physical disabilities" rather than "handicapped employees." That way, your focus is on the whole person, not the disability. Finally never use outdated terminology that stigmatizes individuals, such as the words crippled, retarded, afflicted, or diseased. When talking to someone with a physical disability, you may need to alter your verbal or nonverbal methods to accommodate the person. For example, you might need to make an extra effort to enunciate your words and face the person you are talking to when that person cannot hear well.

4. ***Education.*** How educated is your audience? This affects the words you use and the examples you present.

   Points to keep in mind: Not everyone graduates from high school or goes to college, but that doesn't mean they are unintelligent. It simply means they haven't had a college experience. However, they have probably had plenty of other experiences, many of which you haven't had. Make sure the vocabulary you use and the examples you choose match your audience's experiences, and never talk down to them.

5. ***Technological background.*** What knowledge of technology does your audience have? This will affect the words and acronyms you should use as well as the level of technological detail you go into. For example, technologically-savvy people often use terms in their communication other people don't understand. Examples include GUI (graphical user interface), VoIP (voice over Internet protocol), and WYSIWYG ("what you see is what you get"). If terms such as these leave you clueless, you're not alone.

   Points to keep in mind: Don't assume that everyone uses the same equipment or the same vocabulary you do. Not everyone has a Blackberry, an iPhone, and broadband Internet. Not everyone works in the same industry with the same vocabulary. Use plain English and explain acronyms and abbreviations the first time you use them.

CHECKLIST

Note the characteristics of your audience:

- ☑ What are their ages?
- ☑ What gender are they?
- ☑ What are their physical abilities and disabilities?
- ☑ What are their education levels?
- ☑ What are their technological backgrounds?
- ☑ What race/ethnicity are they?

6. ***Race and ethnicity:*** What race or ethnic background does your audience consist of? How diverse is your audience? What cultural aspects of race are specific to that audience? For example, if you are addressing people at a synagogue, what subtleties will you need to learn about in advance to communicate successfully? What might your sources of information be?

   Points to keep in mind: If your audience is racially or ethnically diverse, be sure to provide various examples to connect with their differing experiences. Try to avoid stereotypes, and if you need to check your examples, consult a trusted source who has insight about the audience to tell you if your message is or is not on target.

Communication Is about Collaboration

Conversation is not a competition. It is a collaborative effort between people. The purpose of communication is not to force another person to agree with you or to prove you know more than he or she does. It is to connect and learn, to find out what you have in common with someone else, and exploit your similarities and differences so you can accomplish a goal together.

You can't demand that everyone adjust to your communication style. If you make no attempt to learn about your audience or relate to them, you will fail. Failure can mean a lost friend, a lost sale, or a lost business deal. At the extreme, it might even mean a serious conflict, or at an international level, a war. Adjusting your message to your audience takes a little more time and thought, but it is part of being a good communicator.

2 What Are 10 Cultural Components of Communication?

Culture includes all of the socially transmitted behavior patterns of a particular society. Next, we explain the cultural components of communication.

Language Fluency. Does your audience consist of native-English speakers? If not, how much English does your audience know? Did your audience members learn it in school or on the job? Are they fluent?

Nonnative English speakers might not understand you if you talk too fast or use slang or idioms. Carefully consider your words to make sure they will not confuse or offend your listeners. For example, "off-the-wall," "hanging out," or "chill out" might have very different meanings to non-English speakers who take the words literally.

Age. How does your audience view younger or older people? Are you older or younger than your audience? How does this impact their perception of you?

People in some cultures show more respect for older people than Americans typically do. In many of these cultures, you are to address older people by their titles (Mr., Ms., Mrs., Dr., and so forth).

Gender. Are gender roles strongly defined in the culture? This goes beyond the male and female communication styles you learned about earlier.

In many regions of the world, gender roles are very strongly defined, affecting how people dress and how they are supposed to interact publicly with the opposite sex. For example, in some cultures in the Middle East, men and women are forbidden from interacting in many public and social situations without an intermediary.

Family. How important is family to your audience? How does this impact their lives? In many cultures, including India, Mexico, and Saudi Arabia, a person's family is the most important aspect of his or her life.

In cultures such as these, asking personal questions about family is considered normal and vital when you first meet someone.

Religion. How important is religion to members of the culture, and how does it affect people's lives? This will affect how you should interact with them. In many cultures, religion permeates all aspects of life, both at home and at work.

For example, it affects when you can do business (holidays), how you must dress, and what you should eat. Some foods are forbidden in certain cultures. For example, devout Hindus would never eat beef and might be offended if you did so in their presence.

Eating Behavior. How do people in the culture eat? With their hands? A particular hand? Utensils? What type? What do people eat or, more importantly, not eat? This will affect what you eat when visiting others and how you eat without embarrassing yourself or offending others.

Holiday office parties can be a big issue in any business. If you are involved in holiday planning at work, avoid offending coworkers by taking into account differences in people's tastes in foods, as well as religious practices. This may mean eliminating gift exchanges with Jehovah's Witnesses, providing Kosher food for Jews, serving nonalcoholic beverages for Muslims, or providing nonmeat alternatives for vegetarians. It is worth the time to accommodate others because it shows you are considering their needs, which builds a more supportive, cohesive work team.

Greeting Behavior. Do people in the culture shake hands? Hug? Bow? Air kiss? Should you take off your shoes when entering their homes? Bring a gift?

Good greeting behavior creates a good first impression. Regardless of the culture, people often make up their minds about you in less than 30 seconds, just about the time that's required to greet one another.

Business and Public Behavior. How do you address someone when you first meet at work? By first name or last name? Should you make small talk before discussing business? Can you ask personal questions? Is bribery an accepted business practice? (In some countries it is, but U.S. law forbids U.S. companies from offering or accepting bribes.) Should you always negotiate?

Some business cultures, such as the Japanese business culture, are more formal than others and adhere to a strict hierarchy; other business cultures, such as the American business culture, are informal and collaborative. Some cultures view the negotiating process as an enjoyable part of business and therefore take their time. In other cultures, people just want to make a decision as quickly as possible.

Personal Space. **Personal space** refers to how close you can stand next to someone without invading his or her comfort. Can you make direct eye contact without offending people?

In some cultures, such as Indian and Southeast Asian, people are comfortable standing closely together. In other cultures this is taboo. In some cultures, people expect you to look at them when you talk to them. In others, people do not.

Perception of Time. How important is punctuality?

Some cultures are more rigid about time, whereas others are more fluid. People in the United States adhere pretty rigidly to deadlines and times—give or take 10 minutes. However, in some countries, such as Mexico, it is common for people to show up an hour late and no offense is taken. In other countries, being five minutes late for an appointment is considered very rude.

Are you curious to learn more about how people communicate in different countries? Visit mybcommlab.com for a closer look at the cultural components of six major countries.

DID YOU KNOW?

The Web site of Executive Planet serves as on online reference source for people searching for information about the cultural practices of different countries. If you have a chance, visit the site. You will be surprised at what you learn.

PEARSON mybcommlab

For a closer look at the cultural components of six major countries visit Chapter 3 in mybcommlab.com.

REAL INSIGHTS from a Seasoned Professional

Name: *Laurie Guevara-Stone*
Title: *International Program Manager*
Organization: *Solar Energy International (SEI)*
Location: *The United States, Nicaragua, and Ecuador*

LAURIE GUEVARA-STONE IS A 43-YEAR-OLD international program manager at Solar Energy International (SEI). SEI teaches people how to use renewable energy and sustainable building technologies to improve their lives.

When Stone graduated from high school, she had no idea what she wanted to do. Since math always came easily to her, she decided to major in math at Colorado College in Colorado Springs, Colorado. During her studies, she got involved with a college group focused on Central American issues. After graduation, she traveled to Nicaragua to see the country firsthand.

During her two-month stay there, Stone picked coffee, lived with a local family, and immersed herself in the Spanish language. She fell in love with the laid-back, family-oriented culture of Nicaragua, and the political atmosphere in the nation at the time. She then returned to the United States, saved her money, and later went back to Nicaragua.

Her second time in Nicaragua, Stone joined a construction brigade to build warehouses. Then she and a friend went off to work on other construction projects in hurricane-damaged areas. She also traveled to Guatemala and Mexico.

Stone soon learned that the American concept of time—with milestones, deadlines, appointments, and punctuality—had absolutely no meaning in Central America. She learned to have patience and to not get frustrated. Things moved at a slower pace. There were two-hour breaks in the middle of days, lots of time for conversation, and plenty of time for family.

While traveling, Stone became aware of the huge, unmet need Central Americans have for electricity. She decided to return to the United States and do graduate work at the University of Colorado, Boulder. Her graduate work was in energy engineering, with a focus on solar energy. During graduate school, she returned again to Central America and developed solar water distillation units for rural communities in need of clean water.

In terms of intercultural communication, Stone learned that Americans must avoid the superiority trap. "Just because you're from the United States, don't think you have all the answers. You have as much to learn as you have to teach. Go with an open mind."

Stone experienced firsthand the importance of speaking a second language. Although she had studied Spanish in high school, she still struggled to speak it during her first couple of trips to Central America. "Even if all you can say is 'please' or 'thank you,' it shows you're making an effort and people appreciate it." Of course, her immersion in the language while living with local families boosted her Spanish fluency considerably.

In Nicaragua, Stone met many people who wanted to learn more about solar cooking and solar lighting. She decided to finish graduate school and get more solar experience. She discovered SEI, signed up for every solar energy class offered, and became an SEI intern. Then it was back to El Salvador to bring solar cooking and lighting to rural communities. One year later, she became an SEI employee. She says, "I was in the right place at the right time." She now coordinates and teaches international trainings on solar energy in Latin America. She also does a lot of writing—articles, newsletters, publications, and proposals. The skills most critical to her job have become writing, organizing, and speaking—not math or engineering.

Stone says she has learned a lot through her Latin American travels and work with SEI. She sums it up with this statement: "The three most important things you need are patience, open-mindedness, and a sense of humor."

Questions

1. According to Stone, what is the biggest difference between how Nicaraguans and Americans perceive time?
2. What did Stone find vital for good intercultural communication during her time in Nicaragua?

Source: Laurie Guevara-Stone in discussion with the author, March 2009.

3 What Are Six Major Barriers to Effective Intercultural Communication?

The components discussed in the previous section should give you an idea of what to expect when communicating with someone from another culture. Armed with this knowledge, you are ready to confront the barriers that many people face when they try to communicate cross-culturally.

Ethnocentrism—"It's My Way or the Highway"

Ethnocentrism is the belief that your own culture is superior and the standard by which all other cultures should be measured.[4] Basically, ethnocentrism means, "We are right. Everyone else is wrong. We are better than everyone else, too."

Ethnocentrism not only makes communication difficult, it almost guarantees misunderstanding and anger at an individual level, and potential conflict at a national level. As you have learned, different countries, including the United States, have certain ways of viewing the world and certain ways of doing things. Some are probably more ethnocentric than others. However, every culture has something to offer, so why not learn as much as we can about people, cultures, and their views?

DID YOU KNOW?

Only 3 percent of American undergraduates ever study abroad.[5] However, there are many ways to explore the world without ever leaving home. Films, books, music, and the Internet are great ways to get to know another culture. For example, at Live-Radio.net, you can listen to thousands of radio stations around the world.

Assumptions

Assumptions are beliefs, not objective truths. They are typically based on stereotypes, and they negatively impact our perception of people from other cultures. Unfortunately, we all make assumptions from time to time.

Why do we make assumptions based on stereotypes? Probably because it is so hard to mentally process all of the complicated information about other people in the world and spend time understanding the different ways people behave. Instead, we find it easier to put people into categories and to accept cultural stereotypes, especially those promoted by the media. After all, if we don't have the time or money to travel to other countries, the only ideas we have about the people who live there are based on what other people tell us or on popular opinion.

Sadly, stereotypes narrow our perspective, limit our ideas, and have little to do with reality. In fact, a widespread study by the National Institute of Health found there was no correlation between perceived cultural characteristics and the actual traits rated for real people.[6]

Think about the following stereotypes:

- Americans are obsessed with money, fanatical about their appearance, and rude and pushy.
- Arabs are religious fanatics, terrorists, and evil oil sheiks.
- Jewish people are cheap, shrewd in business, and typically doctors or lawyers.
- Asians are great students, martial artists, gangsters, or laundry owners.

Now, think about actual individuals you know from each of these cultures. Do they resemble these stereotypes? Probably not.

The next time you meet someone from another culture, observe your own reactions. Do you find yourself thinking any of these thoughts? "Oh, she's from [country name]. I know what she is like." Or, "That's weird. Why does she do that? That's stupid." Or, "I can't understand him at all."

If thoughts such as these cross your mind, you are probably thinking in terms of stereotypes. Say "no" to those thoughts. Instead, ask questions and get to know the person. Once you begin to examine your assumptions, you are on your way to overcoming a significant barrier to good intercultural communication.

Language Differences

We said it once, but it is worth saying again: Language differences are a huge barrier when it comes to intercultural communication. Most Americans do not speak a second language, but they often expect people from other cultures to know English. Nonnative English speakers might know English, but they may not be fluent and understand all local dialects.

Slang causes serious intercultural communication problems, as you can see by the cartoon on the next page. For those of you who are unfamiliar with British rhyming slang, the cartoon character on the left is saying, "Please buddy. Give me some money for the phone." Speaking louder won't help make a nonnative speaker better understand what you are saying. Instead, it is best to speak clearly, repeat things, and use examples. The same is true when you find someone else's accent difficult to understand. Listen carefully. As you do so, you will become more familiar with the accent. Don't hesitate to ask people to repeat themselves as many times as necessary.[7]

PEARSON mybcommlab

Apply these key concepts by revising a new document. Go to Chapter 3 in mybcommlab.com and select Document Makeovers.

Source: Reprinted with permission from CartoonStock. www.cartoonstock.com

Lastly, don't talk down to nonnative speakers. Just because someone has an accent or doesn't speak English fluently, doesn't mean the person is unintelligent or lazy. Anyone who has attempted to learn a second language should be respected. In fact, one of the best things an American can do is learn another language, or at least learn some basic words to use in conversation. Your attempt to speak another language opens cultural doors that might otherwise remain closed.

Close-mindedness

Close-mindedness is closely related to ethnocentrism. If you are close-minded, you might not think your culture is the greatest on earth, but you have absolutely no interest in learning about any other cultures. What's the problem with this attitude? By keeping a closed mind, you miss out on interesting conversations, beneficial ideas, and novel solutions to problems you might be trying to solve. You are also less likely to do things like make new friends and eat new foods. In short, you will confine yourself to a world with very rigid boundaries and limited potential.

For example, suppose a friend from your band suggests going to an Ethiopian restaurant for dinner and musical entertainment. You have never heard of that kind of a restaurant and immediately turn down the invitation. Not only do you miss out on a great meal, you also miss out on meeting a group of interesting musicians from Africa.

Or, maybe a mechanical engineering classmate from India wants to talk about what it was like living in Mumbai and driving a scooter to and from school every day. However, you are not interested. Little do you know that the classmate retrofitted the scooter with a special carburetor to reduce pollution. By closing your mind to new people and new ideas, you miss out. Remember, minds are like parachutes. They only function when open.[8]

Ignorance—It's Different Than Stupidity

Being ignorant about a culture is different than being stupid. **Ignorance** simply means you are uninformed or lack personal experience with the culture. Stupidity means you have no interest in learning, period. Ignorance can be cured with education. Stupidity can't.

Ignorance can be a serious impediment when it comes to communicating with people from other cultures. What if you had no idea that it was against the law to kiss in public in Dubai

REAL INSIGHTS from a New Professional

Name: *Cliff Ho*
Title: *Researcher*
Organization: *Sandia National Laboratories*
Location: *Albuquerque, New Mexico*

CLIFF HO IS A LEAD RESEARCHER and engineer at Sandia National Laboratories, a research and engineering facility that develops energy and other sustainable solutions designed to protect the security of the United States. The son of Chinese immigrants, Ho grew up in Wisconsin. He was the lone minority student in his school and was often bullied by other students. "I look back at that, and it has shaped me. I'm very sensitive to when people are disrespectful," he says.

Ho earned an undergraduate degree in mechanical engineering from the University of Wisconsin–Madison, and then headed to the University of California at Berkeley for his master's and doctorate studies. He began his career at Sandia by developing thermal-hydrologic transport models. Since then he has conducted water-treatment and solar power research, among other things.

Ho's presentations at industry conferences have impressed his peers. He has won numerous awards, including the 2010 Asian American Engineer of the Year Award presented by the Chinese Institute of Engineers, USA.

"I think one thing engineers and scientists can be better at is to make our message a little more concise and clear, hit on just two or three main points in an easy-to-follow manner," he says. You must also respect your audience. "If you can effectively convey the information without saying things that are disrespectful or demeaning, you'll be doing well regardless of their culture."

Both on the job and off, Ho tries to create consensus among people. "One thing I'm always working on is communicating in what are called 'crucial conversations'—times when the stakes are high and there are differing opinions or strong emotions. The key is to develop mutual understanding, mutual respect, and a safe environment in which people can communicate and collaborate with one another," he says.

Questions

1. What kind of intercultural communication barriers has Ho experienced in his lifetime? What do you think led to them?
2. How does Ho personally try to break down intercultural-communication barriers with his audience? How has he managed to successfully do so?

Source: Cliff Ho in discussion with the author, June 2010.

or taboo to shake a woman's hand in Iran? What if you didn't realize that pointing at a Japanese gentleman was an obscene gesture? What if you didn't know to initially ask about an Indian businessman's family before jumping right into business talk? Or what if you were unaware that arriving 10 minutes late to a business appointment in Germany is extremely rude?

What is the worst-case scenario for the situations we just described? That would be kissing in public in Dubai. Doing so could land you in jail. Two English tourists were jailed for three months in Dubai because they kissed each other in public. Additionally, they had to pay 1,000 Dirham ($280).[9]

What is the best-case scenario of the situations we described? It is a toss-up among the other three cultural gaffes. Any one of them could cause you to lose potential friends and business partners.

Fear

A huge impediment to intercultural communication is fear. When you are afraid of people from another culture, you feel uncomfortable around them, and it is very difficult to spend time with them, listen to them, or understand them. What's worse is that fear is an emotion that can develop into hatred.

Emotions like fear and hatred interfere with communication. Instead of hearing what someone is truly saying, we misinterpret what's said. We may start imagining we have heard all sorts of hidden, negative nuances. We may become irrational and reactive.

Think of it this way: it is difficult to have a meaningful conversation with loud music blaring in the background. Likewise, it is difficult to have a conversation when strong emotions are blaring in our bodies and minds.

❹ How Can You Learn to Become a Good Intercultural Communicator?

Good communication helps cultures connect.

At this point you might be wondering, "How am I ever going to talk to someone from another country without offending him or her? There are so many things I could say and do wrong." You may even be asking yourself, "When am I going to have a chance to even meet someone from another country?"

Have no fear. You can start slowly by getting out and seeing more of your own town or city or by visiting nearby cities or states. You never know who you might meet and what interesting conversations you might have. Your goal should be to reach a point where you want to communicate and are willing to do what it takes to do so, even if that means altering your natural style of communication.

Ten Tips for Facilitating Global Communication

The following 10 guidelines will help you become a good global communicator.

1. ***Take into account all components of the regional culture.*** Make sure you know what is similar and different about your own culture and the culture of the individual you are talking to. Revisit the 10 cultural components presented earlier in this chapter.
2. ***Become familiar with the language and speak clearly.*** Learn a few phrases of another language and use them. People will be grateful because it shows you are interested in their culture and willing to meet them halfway. Use simple, accurate words and avoid contractions or slang. Otherwise, you may be misunderstood.
3. ***Understand body language and its nuances.*** As you become familiar with the behaviors of the culture you are addressing, you will discover that gestures have different meanings. Observe others and their body language. For example, when you attend a meeting, pay attention to the way people from other cultures sit. Asians, for example, feel it is rude for people to cross their legs when they don't know you. Hand signals are particularly problematic. Pointing with your index finger is an obscene gesture in many cultures.
4. ***Be an active listener.*** When you talk to someone from another culture, you are probably talking to a nonnative English speaker or someone who speaks with an accent. The person is likely to use different words or put words together in a different order to communicate a message. Listen carefully. Let the person finish the entire message and don't interrupt. You should be able to figure out what the speaker means, even if he or she doesn't say things the way you would.

   For example, a German speaker just learning English might say, "Can I with you speak?" Or a French speaker might say, "The weather makes cold today." You should be able to figure out what he or she means by the context of the conversation. As Jodi Weber, the director for the English Language School (ELS) Center of Southern Oregon University, reminds her students: "The speaker may only have the English skills of a 5-year-old, but they have the intellect of an adult. Think how frustrating it is for them."[10]
5. ***Be curious.*** We live in a big, diverse world, full of extraordinary people and places. Take the time to learn about some of them by reading books or watching movies. For example, Rick Steves is a well-known guidebook author and tour guide. His guidebook, *Europe Through the Back Door,* and his travel show on PBS focus on interacting with the locals in European countries he visits. *Globetrekker* (also known as Lonely Planet), another PBS travel show, similarly focuses on getting to know the culture of out-of-the-way locations. Both shows are also available on video and DVD.

   If you prefer movies or television to books, *Outsourced* is a wonderful movie (and now a television show) that tells the tale of a Seattle call center manager whose entire call center is outsourced to India. He must travel to India to train the replacement team.

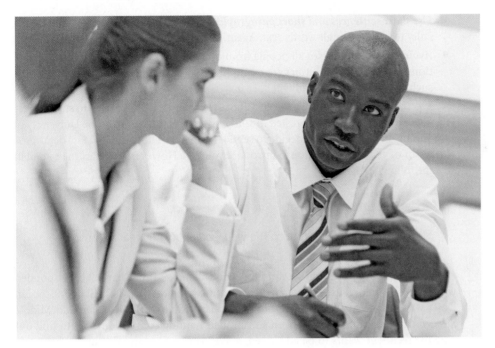

Listen intently, and you will learn more during intercultural conversations.

A series of realistic culture clashes ensues that challenge the stereotypes the manager holds, resulting in a tremendous learning experience for him. The movie is now used in high school and college curriculums and can be found on the Web. The books and Web sites listed at the end of this chapter will provide you with a good start as well.

6. ***Be globally oriented.*** Remember, the United States is not the center of the universe, nor are its attitudes and behaviors the only acceptable ones in the world. Be humble and respect the cultures of others.
7. ***Keep your message simple.*** Keep your writing clear and to the point to avoid confusing nonnative English speakers, by doing the following:
   - ***Use correct capitalization and punctuation.*** Don't use texting language to write. Without capital letters and periods to guide them, nonnative English speakers may have difficulty reading your message. Capital letters tell readers where new sentences begin, and periods tell them where sentences end.

Correct Capitalization and Punctuation	Texting (Hard to Read)
Are you going to the solar hot water workshop? I might go, but I am not sure. How much does it cost?	r u going to solar hot water workshop i might go but not sure how much $?
I am buying an electric bike to help me ride up hills on the way to school. What do you think?	buying e-bike 2 get up hills on the way 2 school what do u think?

   - ***Avoid "filler" words.*** Every culture has **filler words**, or words that fill in gaps in conversations but mean little or nothing. "Like" and "all" are often used as filler words by Americans. Filler words can confuse people who don't speak English or who are from other cultures.

Filler-Free Communication	Filler-Full Communication
He wanted to try a new restaurant, but I said "No."	He wanted to try like a new restaurant, but, um, I said "No."

PEARSON mybcommlab

Apply these key concepts by revising a new document. Go to Chapter 3 in mybcommlab.com and select Document Makeovers.

- ***Use short sentences and short paragraphs.*** Nonnative English speakers have difficulty reading through wordy text. Again, keep your message short and simple.
- ***Avoid contractions.*** Not all people from other cultures are familiar with contractions. *Can't, don't,* and *won't* are examples of contractions. Instead, use full words such as *cannot, do not,* and *will not.*
- ***Use the correct salutation.*** A **salutation** is the proper greeting used to start a message. Imagine you are interested in studying general linguistics at the University of Tubingen, Germany. You decide to send an e-mail to Dr. Erhard W. Hinrichs, professor of general linguistics, to introduce yourself. However, you start the e-mail in the following way.

> Dear Doc Erhard,
>
> I read about your program on the web, and it looked great to me! 

What kind of impression do you think you will make? If you haven't corresponded with someone before, use the person's correct title, such as Mr., Ms., Miss, Mrs., or Dr. Don't write too casually. Also, keep in mind that people's titles in Asian and Middle Eastern cultures can be complicated, as can their naming conventions. Try to find out how the recipient wants to be addressed. A Web site such as the Executive Planet can also help you determine how to address your recipient.

8. ***Use correctly formatted dates and numbers.*** Not all cultures write dates and numbers the same way. Imagine you are sending an e-mail to a German coworker to tell her when you will arrive in Stuttgart, Germany. You will be there on the 8th of July, so you write 7-8-2011. Unfortunately, you should have written 8.7.2011. Instead of thinking you will arrive on the 8th day of July, your German coworker thinks you are arriving on the 7th day of August. She probably won't be waiting for you at the airport.

   Suppose you send an e-mail to your European coworker telling her you sold 1,500 units of a product. You later find out your coworker is very disappointed with your sales level. You should have written 1.500. Instead, your coworker thinks you sold 1 and 500/1000 units, or one-and-a-half units. The following are examples of date and number differences.

American	European
1,500	1.500
December 10, 2009 12-10-09	10 December 2009 10.12.2009

5 How Can You Effectively Communicate with the Four Generations That Now Share the Workplace?

We have talked about different cultures, but what about different generations? Did you know that this is the first time in American history that we have had four different generations employed side by side in the workplace? **Exhibit 3-1** identifies the various names and years associated with each generation.

Exhibit 3-2 shows their personal and lifestyle characteristics. Remember, though, that people are individuals. Just because they were born in a particular year doesn't mean they have all the characteristics of their generation or even identify with it. The differences in personal and lifestyle characteristics shown in Exhibit 3-2 lead to differences in workplace behaviors as well. **Exhibit 3-3** summarizes some key behavioral characteristics of each generation in the workplace.

1922–1945	1946–1964	1965–1980	1981–2000
Veterans Traditionalists Silent Generation	Baby Boomers	Gen X Generation X Xers	Gen Y Generation Y Millennials Echo Boomers

Exhibit 3-1
Generation Timeline[11]

Source: Courtesy of Fairleigh Dickinson University.

When we study the communication and interaction styles of the generations as well as what motivates them, we can see some differences and similarities:

- *GenY'ers* make up the most tech-savvy generation, communicating much more online than face to face. They are very comfortable collaborating via online chats and Wikis. They generally prefer text messages to e-mails. GenY'ers are motivated to cooperate with other people and do meaningful work.
- *GenXers* are fairly tech-savvy. They like quick responses and prefer e-mail and voice mail over in-person meetings. Because they are more independent than the other generations, they typically are not as comfortable working in groups or having face-to-face meetings. They are motivated by the opportunity to do things their own way without a lot of structure.
- *Baby Boomers* like to talk in person, so meetings are no problem for them. They are somewhat tech-literate and typically don't have problems with e-mail or voice mail. However, texting and social media are not generally something they use as often. They are motivated by knowing that their teams value and need them.
- *Veterans* are the least tech-literate of the group and often need some technological support. They prefer formal memos and written communications or phone calls for important matters. They are also more accustomed to work situations that rely on the chain of command than collaboration. Knowing that other people respect their experience often motivates them.

Exhibit 3-2 Personal and Lifestyle Characteristics by Generation[12]

Characteristics	Veterans (1922–1945)	Baby Boomers (1946–1964)	Gen X (1965–1980)	Gen Y (1981–2000)
Core Values	Respect for authority Conformity Discipline	Optimism Involvement	Skepticism Fun Informality	Realism Confidence Extreme fun Socially inclined
Family	Traditional	Disintegrating	Latchkey kids	Merged families
Education	A dream	A birthright	A way to get there	An incredible expense
Communication Tool	Rotary phone One-on-one Memo	Touch-tone phone Call anytime	Cell phone Call me at work E-mail	Internet Smartphone E-mail Text message
Money Approach	Save Pay cash	Buy now, pay later	Conservative Save, save, save	Earn to spend

Source: Courtesy of Farleigh Dickinson University.

Exhibit 3-3 Workplace Characteristics by Generation[13]

Characteristics	Veterans (1922–1945)	Baby Boomers (1946–1964)	Gen X (1965–1980)	Gen Y (1981–2000)
Communication Style	Formal Memos	Informal Meetings	Immediate E-mail Voice mail	Immediate Text messages Social media
Interaction Style	Individual	Team player	Entrepreneur	Participative
Leadership Style	Directive Command-and-control Hierarchical	Consensual Collaborative	Everyone is the same Challenge others Ask why	To be determined*
Messages That Motivate	Your experience is respected	You are valued and needed	Do it your own way Forget the rules	You will work with other creative people
Preferred Reward	Satisfaction in a job well done	Title Recognition Money	Freedom	Meaningful work
Work Ethic	Hard work Respect authority Duty before fun Adhere to rules	Workaholic Desire quality Crusade causes Question authority	Eliminate the task Need structure and direction Skeptical	Goal oriented Multitasking Entrepreneurial Tolerant
Work Is ...	An obligation	An exciting adventure	A difficult challenge	A means to an end

*The members of Generation Y have not spent much time in the workforce, so their characteristics have yet to be determined.
Source: Courtesy of Farleight Dickinson University.

Good business communication is based on understanding others, including people from other generations. Find out how the people around you prefer to communicate and let them know your preferences as well.[14] As Heather Neely, author of the book *The Next Wave of Young Workers* puts it, "Each generation is an expression of the social, political, and economic world in which they were raised. Our task is to learn what makes them tick so we can maximize the talents they possess."

Summary *Synthesize What You Have Learned*

1. Why is it important to know your audience?

Knowing your audience will help adjust your message to reach them. This means being sensitive to five visible differences: people's ages, genders, physical disabilities, educational levels, and technical background. Use age-neutral words and age-related stereotypes and assumptions. Understand that male and female brains process information differently, which makes their communication styles different. Be aware of people's disabilities and alter your communication style to accommodate them. For example, enunciate your words and face the person who is hearing impaired, avoid gestures when speaking to a person who is blind, and slow down and listen when speaking to someone with a speech impediment. Because people's education levels vary, make sure your vocabulary is appropriate. Similarly, not all audiences are tech-savvy. Keep this in mind when you use technical words or acronyms.

2. What are 10 cultural components of communication?

It is easy to see someone's age or gender and adjust your message accordingly. It is harder to "see" culture, which affects people's behavior, beliefs, and attitudes. The

10 cultural components to be aware of as you communicate with someone from another culture: The language, the roles age, gender, family, and religion play; eating, greeting, and business behaviors, personal-space constraints, and the culture's perception of time.

3. **What are six major barriers to effective intercultural communication?**

The six barriers to communication you might encounter: (1) ethnocentrism; (2) the assumptions people make based on stereotypes; (3) language differences, including a person's speech speed, accent, and slang; (4) close-mindedness, or the unwillingness to learn about other cultures; (5) ignorance about other cultures; and (6) the fear of people in other cultures.

4. **How can you learn to be a good intercultural communicator?**

Take into account all cultural components of a particular region and be curious about it. Get familiar with the language and speak clearly. Understand the culture's body language and its nuances, and be an active listener. Write clearly and simply. Keep your sentences and paragraphs short and pay attention to salutations, contractions, and dates and numbers.

5. **How do you effectively communicate with the four generations that now share the workplace?**

Treat people as individuals and do not assume that just because they are members of a particular generation, they share all that generation's traits. Get to know their interaction styles, communication styles, and motivations. Then, communicate with them in ways that make them feel comfortable.

PEARSON **mybcommlab**™ Are you an active learner? Go to **mybcommlab.com** to master Chapter 3's content. Chapter 3's interactive activities include:

- Customizable Study Plan and Chapter 3 practice quizzes
- Chapter 3 Simulation, Interpersonal Communication and Teamwork, that helps you think critically and prepare to make choices in the business world
- Chapter 3 Video Exercise, Communicating Effectively in the Global Workplace, which shows you how textbook concepts are put into practice every day
- Flash cards for mastering the definition of chapter terms
- Interactive Lessons that visually review key chapter concepts
- Document Makeovers for hands-on, scored practice in revising documents

Know It *Reflect, Respond, and Express*

Build Your Critical Thinking Skills

Critical Thinking Questions

1. List the 10 cultural components of communication and describe one or two you had not considered before when analyzing your audience.
2. What is the importance of reviewing cultural components of your native country?
3. What is the connection between communication and collaboration?
4. How do the personal and lifestyle characteristics differ across the generations? For example, how is the Generation X core value of fun different from the Generation Y core value of extreme fun?
5. What assumptions do you commonly make based on someone's educational and degree level? How do those assumptions affect a message's delivery and interpretation?
6. List the ways work ethics vary across the generations. How do these work ethics relate to and affect the preferred communication styles of generations?
7. Imagine your company has a new policy regarding cell phone use in the office that permits cell phones to be used only during breaks. Would you create an e-mail or letter or make a phone call to communicate the new policy to the employees? Which generation would prefer which type of delivery? How can you reach all generations?

Critical Thinking Scenario

Shawna works as a trainer for Solar Energy International (SEI), the U.S.-based, nonprofit organization that you learned about earlier in Laurie Guevara-Stone's profile. SEI provides education and training to decision makers, technicians, and users of renewable energy sources (solar, wind, and water).

SEI holds workshops in the Americas, Africa, Micronesia, and the Caribbean. Shawna has always been involved in the U.S. workshops, teaching many photovoltaic design and installation workshops in Arizona, Texas, and Colorado. However, last year, for the first time, Shawna had the opportunity to teach her workshops in Costa Rica. Her focus was installing and upgrading systems with current renewable energy equipment in developing nations. She couldn't wait to go.

She arrived at Rancho Mastatal, a sustainable living center in the last virgin rainforest in Costa Rica, and was amazed at the incredible habitat, full of endangered plants and animals. However, she didn't give herself much time to enjoy the beautiful environment because she was worried about getting ready for her workshop—she had to set up a lot of equipment. She felt somewhat nervous and arrived early on the first day of her class to wait for her students . . . and waited . . . and waited.

Finally, 30 to 45 minutes later, students started straggling in. They sat down, chatting to one another. One hour after the class was supposed to start, all the students had arrived. Shawna introduced herself and started to go over the agenda. However, the students had other ideas and started asking all sorts of questions about Shawna's home and her family. By the time she got on track again, another hour had passed. At noon, the students crowded around her and wanted to join her for lunch. The food was delicious and the conversation was good, but no one made a move to return to class at 1:00. Everyone wanted to go for a swim. Two hours later, her wet but happy students were back in class, ready to learn more about solar photovoltaics . . . and more about Shawna and the United States.

This went on every day—people arriving late for class and taking two-hour lunch breaks to swim, hike, or visit cultural locations. In class, no matter how hard Shawna tried to stay on topic, her students always wanted to talk about their lives and ask Shawna questions about hers. Shawna wondered how she was ever going to finish teaching the class. She felt stressed and resentful that no one cared about her schedule. She hoped she never had to come back and teach another class.

Questions

1. What cultural differences contributed to Shawna's distress?
2. What could Shawna have done to improve the situation?
3. If you were Shawna, what would you have done differently?
4. What did Shawna miss out on by being so focused on a schedule?

Write It *Draft, Revise, and Finalize*

Create Your Own Success Story

1. Look at the following types of people and write down your first thoughts about the characteristics of each in terms of their social behaviors.

   - Mexican
   - Arab
   - Man
   - Woman
   - Teenager
   - Senior citizen
   - Chinese
   - Indian

   a. Examine what you have written. Which characteristics are negative? Which are based on movies or television? Which are based on what other people have told you? Did you write down anything based on real people you actually know?

   b. Ask another student about his or her culture. Use the following "10 cultural components" as your guideline to help you formulate your questions.

   - Language fluency
   - Age
   - Gender
   - Family
   - Religion
   - Eating behavior
   - Greeting behavior
   - Business and public behavior
   - Personal space
   - Perception of time

   c. Does the student break with his or her culture on any of the answers?

   d. Do the answers you get support or challenge the stereotypes you may hold?

   e. Based on your conversation with your classmate, revise your original descriptions of the people in step a. Once both of you have revised your descriptions, compare each list of characteristics and write a final description.

2. Create a short list of slang words specific to your generation. Choose one word and explain how the meaning of a message could be misinterpreted because of the use of the slang word.
3. Research different idioms that could affect a message's meaning for non-English speakers. Prepare a summary of your findings for the class.
4. Visit the Traveler's Notebook Web site and search for the article "12 Things You Don't Want to Be Caught Doing in Foreign Lands." Analyze what the different laws tell you about different cultures. Write a short summary explaining your reaction to what you discovered in the article and your analysis of the different cultures.
5. Visit ExecutivePlanet.com and look up one specific country not discussed in the exhibits in Chapter 3. Explore a few of the links provided for etiquette, and prepare a short memo addressed to your classmates explaining what you have learned.

6. Write down one stereotype about your own culture and analyze why people may believe it. Discuss the stereotypes with the full class and analyze their validity.
7. Revise the following paragraph to omit helping verbs and clarify the message.
The meeting is being held in the main conference hall. The content of the meeting is intended to focus on cutting costs in the production department. Production is in need of an overhaul—we should be streamlining the process.
8. Revise the following paragraph written in texting language by properly capitalizing, punctuating, and spelling out the content.
i got ur message. Idk when i can b their. r u alrdy there? c u soon!
9. Write the following dates and numbers in both U.S. and European formats.
    a. Seven thousand eight hundred
    b. 17th day of June, 1987
    c. Six thousand seventy-nine and eighteen one hundredths
10. Look up the four generations' names online using a basic search engine and find the origins of the titles. Write a short explanation of the labels.

Speak It *Discuss, Listen, and Understand*

Build Your Leadership and Teamwork Skills

Imagine that you work for Vestas, an international company that develops wind turbines and equipment. The company headquarters are in Denmark, but there are facilities all over the world. You work in Windsor, Colorado, in blade production. A business associate from a Vestas facility in India is coming to visit you.

Your Indian associate has never visited the United States and is unfamiliar with American culture. You want to make your associate feel as comfortable as possible, then discuss some business concerns. You also plan to take the person to dinner that evening.

Pair up with another person and pretend he or she is your Indian associate. Then talk through the following scenarios.

1. You meet your associate for the first time in your office. Greet and seat your associate and then have a short conversation.
    a. How should you greet your associate?
    b. How would you start up a conversation?
    c. How should you approach business topics?
2. Your facility is having problems with quality assurance and you hope your associate can come up with solutions. You share the problems with your associate and throw out some ideas.
    a. Your associate agrees with every idea. How can you find out what your associate really thinks?
    b. Your associate then shares some ideas, which seem very strange to you. How can you voice your concerns without offending your associate?
3. You want to make reservations for 7 P.M. and take your associate to dinner.
    a. What kind of restaurant might you suggest?
    b. What can you do to make sure your associate is ready for dinner at 7 P.M.?
4. Repeat these scenarios, but this time, pretend the other person is a business associate from Germany.
5. Discuss the biggest differences between the Indian and German scenarios with your role-play partner.
6. In groups or as a class, discuss how each generation views work. How do their perspectives differ? How are they similar? How can all four generations effectively work together?
7. In small groups, discuss technological acronyms such as GUI, URL, and WYSIWYG. How would using such terms alienate different generations of audience members? What other technological terms need to be defined for all generations? Give a few examples.
8. In groups or class discussion, analyze the importance of learning another language, even if it's just a few expressions. Why do people have a tendency to speak loudly or "down" to foreign speakers? How are the preceding questions related to ethnocentrism and close-mindedness?

Do It *Document Your Success Track Record*

Build Your e-Portfolio

Think about a country you would like to visit or work in. Based on what you learned in this chapter and any independent research you may have done, create a "cheat sheet" you could use during your travels. Focus on greetings, appointments, and conversation behavior in the country you selected.

- Greetings
- Appointments and punctuality
- Conversation and public behavior

Business in Action

How Envirofit Tailors Its Messages to People of Other Cultures

Roberta is an intern at Envirofit, a U.S. company that develops and distributes products that address major environmental problems in the developing world. In India, many people still burn wood, dung, and other organic matter to cook and heat their homes. Their existing stoves produce smoke that causes an alarming number of deaths each year. Envirofit has developed a nonpolluting cook stove to prevent such deaths.

Envirofit's primary customers will be poor women in rural Indian villages because they do almost all the cooking for their families.

The team members' study of Indian culture has revealed that wives and mothers spend most of their days taking care of children and have no time or means to travel. Also, in India, everything revolves around one's family. The greatest success for parents is to see their children happily married.

Based on this cultural knowledge, Roberta's team came up with a unique plan. To address the fact that the women for whom the stoves are designed cannot travel, they take the tiny stoves from village to village during the day. They introduce the women to the stove and let them handle it. The team then shows them a special short video. It tells the story of a family with a daughter about to get married. However, the daughter is becoming ill from the smoke of the dung-burning fire. A neighbor gives the daughter a new Envirofit stove as a wedding gift, and in no time at all, the home is smoke free, the daughter is well, and the wedding is a success.

The women who see the stove and watch the video want to buy it. One woman even mentions that because the little stove looks like a rice cooker, her neighbors will think she has electricity. She is so proud.

Questions

1. What would have happened if Roberta's team had used a traditional U.S. marketing campaign with television ads and brochures?
2. What would have happened if Roberta's team had aimed their marketing campaign at Indian men, who typically control the money in the households?
3. Why did the wedding video work so well?
4. How does the appearance similar to a rice cooker affect its potential customers?

Key Terms

Assumptions. Beliefs that are typically based on stereotypes and negatively impact our perceptions of other people. *(p. 65)*

Close-mindedness. The characteristic of having absolutely no interest in learning. *(p. 66)*

Culture. Includes all the socially transmitted behavior patterns of a particular society, such as language, religion, eating, greeting, business, and public behavior, treatment of people based on age and gender, perception of time, and acknowledgement of personal space. *(p. 62)*

Ethnocentrism. The belief that your own culture is superior to all others and is the standard by which all other cultures should be measured. *(p. 65)*

Filler words. Words that have little or no meaning but merely fill gaps in conversation. *(p. 69)*

Generation. A particular age group, usually consisting of people born within the same 25-year time period. *(p. 60)*

Ignorance. The failure to understand a culture due to lack of experience with the culture or lack of education about it. *(p. 66)*

Nonnative English speaker. A person in or from another country learning English as a second language. *(p. 62)*

Personal space. The space immediately surrounding a person's body; the size of someone's personal space influences how they interact with others. *(p. 63)*

Religion. A specific, fundamental set of beliefs and practices generally agreed upon by a number of persons or sects. *(p. 63)*

Salutation. The greeting with which to start a letter. *(p. 70)*

Review Questions *Test Yourself*

1. What characteristics affect your audience's interpretation of your message?
2. What is a "generational gap" and how would such a gap affect a person's interpretation of messages?
3. How do men and women communicate differently? How do the different styles affect interpretation of a message?
4. Define *ethnocentrism* and explain how it can create problems with communication.

5. How are ethnocentrism and close-mindedness related? How can they affect clear communication?
6. In what ways can the emotion of fear affect communication?
7. How can body language affect your abilities as a global communicator?
8. How does active listening impact your abilities as a good intercultural communicator?
9. List a few techniques for keeping written communication simple.
10. What motivational tactics can be used to appeal to all generations?

Grammar Review *Mastering Accuracy*

Verbs

Section I

Each of the following sentences contains one or more common errors in word usage, grammar, or style. Identify the errors. If you have trouble finding the errors, review Section 1.1.2. in the handbook (Appendix D) at the back of this textbook.

1. Sasha has declined to have run for public office.
2. Each public official run for the office of the president.
3. Perishable items should not be left for more than 24 hours.
4. Margaret believes she be a victim of discrimination, as she were passed over for the promotion.
5. Tucker decided sleep during the meeting; however, his colleagues was shocked at his callous disregard for his managerial position.
6. At the end of each business day, please proceed to emptying the shavings from your pencil sharpener into the receptacle provided.
7. The face of the employee should be smiling, as it is a face that be pleasing and representative of the company; therefore, a slovenly appearance will not be tolerated.
8. Mr. Polcek thought he was scary as creeped up the back stairs and hided behind the curtains.
9. He says that everyone be seated in rows according to rank.
10. The company must strive to remain and be in compliance with all regulations and policies.

Section II

On a separate sheet of paper, rewrite the following sentences so they are clearer, more professional sounding, grammatically correct, and goodwill oriented.

1. Where might one intend or think I should go to get this so-called training?
2. Nancy will do a spreadsheet to ensure we got all the data necessary for tomorrow's retention meeting.
3. You got to review our affirmative action policies before you make any new hiring decisions.
4. The computer lab was left unlocked and turned into a complete pig sty!
5. Our conference room comfortably seats 20 individuals of average to bigger size.
6. A good-looking and well-formatted portfolio is one way to grab a potential employer's attention.
7. Even though the economy sucks, I'm still thinking I might find a good job.
8. People are often hired when employers know that they have not just the know-how, but the can-do.
9. I think maybe Gayle should cool down before she says something stupid and then we all have to go to conflict management training.
10. Technology stuff changes so fast that all people who want a job need to be on top of changes and things.

Extra Resources *Tools You Can Use*

Books

- Baron-Cohen, Simon. *The Essential Difference: The Truth About the Male and Female Brain.* New York: Basic Books, 2003.
- Elmer, Duane. *Cross-Cultural Connections: Stepping Out and Fitting in Around the World.* Downers Grove, IL: InterVarsity Press, 2002.
- Glaser, Connie. *Gender Talk Works: Seven Steps for Cracking the Gender Code.* New York: Windsor Hall Press, 2007.
- Peterson, Brooks. *Cultural Intelligence: A Guide to Working with People from Other Cultures.* Boston: Intercultural Press, 2004.
- Tannen, Deborah. *You Just Don't Understand: Women and Men in Conversation.* New York: Harper Paperbacks, 2001.

Web Sites

- *Brave New Traveler*
- *Executive Planet*
- *Kwintessential Cross Cultural Solutions*
- *Traveler's Notebook*

Online Videos

- *International Communication,* Village Videos.
- *International Written Communication,* eHow.com.

"Before everything else, getting ready is the secret to success." — Henry Ford, inventor and entrepreneur

Preparing Business Messages

Making Yourself Clear

CHAPTER

4

LEARNING OBJECTIVE QUESTIONS

1. Why is planning important for communicating business messages?
2. What are the six questions you should ask as you prepare business messages?
3. When should you use oral versus written communication for business messages?
4. How do you gather information and organize a written business message?
5. How can you set yourself up to be a successful writer?

PEARSON **mybcommlab** Access interactive videos, simulations, sample documents, document makeovers, and assessment quizzes in Chapter 4 of **mybcommlab.com** for mastery of this chapter's objectives.

>>> **During** Catherine's senior year of college she submitted a business plan for her Young Entrepreneur's course. The plan described an e-zine (Internet magazine) designed for the young, international traveler. Although she had been mulling over her idea for years, Catherine spent two months preparing the business plan, one month writing it, and one month revising and editing it. As she wrote it, Catherine considered not only her professor but other people who should see the plan: private investors, venture capitalists, and loan officers. Her plan included an analysis of her target markets, a strategy for attracting advertisers for income, and detailed graphs projecting the company's appreciated value in five years.

With a formal, no-nonsense writing style, Catherine described the feasibility of her concept and its attractiveness to investors. She offered a simple exit strategy, showing she had thoroughly considered the challenging conditions she might face when she launches the e-zine.

After submitting her business plan to her professor, Catherine received more than just an "A" for the project. Her professor was so inspired by her preparation and clear writing that he encouraged her to submit the plan to a young entrepreneur's business plan contest. Catherine entered the contest, won first place, and is now presenting her plan to several venture capital companies. When asked about the success of her writing, she said, "It was all in the preparation."

Catherine >>>

The ability to communicate well in writing cleared Catherine's path to success, and it can do the same for you. This chapter focuses on how to prepare business messages for all types of audiences, whether the messages are to be delivered by telephone, e-mails, letters, or formal reports.

Preparing to communicate is important for all business professionals, perhaps even more so for entrepreneurs. Entrepreneurs launching new businesses face the daunting task of making their ideas a reality. They must be able to communicate their ideas to others. Whether they are explaining a newly patented technology to potential investors, creating a marketing brochure for a tradeshow, or writing a business plan to be submitted with a loan application, their chances of success will improve if they carefully prepare their messages.

This chapter's examples focus on messages entrepreneurs create. Consider Nick Kellet, the inventor of the board game GiftTRAP. Kellet prepared to pitch his product through various social networking sites. He first connected with a former coworker through LinkedIn who had connections to a Chinese company that manufactured board games and arranged an introduction to the factory owners. Kellet then turned to the photo-sharing site Flickr for photographs to legally use for his game. Lastly, via the Web, Kellet connected with influential players in tabletop gaming to find people reviewers. Kellet's planning and hard work paid off: *Games Magazine* declared GiftTRAP the best party game of 2008 and it has since been translated into eight languages.[1]

The Kauffman Index of Entrepreneurial Activity indicates that in 2008, 530,000 new businesses were started in the United States each month. "The entrepreneurial sector is a critical factor in our nation's economic growth. Even during times of recession, new firms have been responsible for the bulk of new jobs and innovations in America," said Robert W. Fairlie, professor of economics at the University of California, Santa Cruz, who developed the Kauffman Index.[2]

One reason so many new businesses are started is that people like to work for themselves. According to the Gallup-Healthways Well-Being Index, business owners claim to enjoy the greatest job satisfaction when compared to workers in all other occupations.[3] However, entrepreneurs face a stark reality: seven out of 10 new businesses last at least two years, but 50 percent of all new businesses fail within the first five years of opening.[4] Whether you choose to work alone as an entrepreneur or become an employee of a start-up company, your communication skills will be essential to your success. If you are wondering what types of work you can do as a business graduate involved in a start-up company, look at **Exhibit 4-1** for a few ideas.

As an entrepreneur, you typically have the freedom to set your own hours and create your own work environment. However, you also are typically responsible for doing your own marketing and finding your own clients. Your writing is often the first thing potential clients see, so it becomes a reflection of you and your company. Professional versus unprofessional copy can mean the difference between winning or losing a client, so take pride in writing well. Your ability to write clearly, using correct grammar, punctuation, and spelling, will make you stand out from your competition.

DID YOU KNOW?

- Roughly 51 percent of entrepreneurs were the first of their family to launch a business.
- Almost half of all businesses in the United States are owned by women.
- Women business owners contribute to the overall employment of 18 million workers and generate anywhere from \$2 to \$3 trillion in revenue to the U.S. economy.[5]

1 Why Is Planning Important for Communicating Business Messages?

You probably understand why it's important to plan your message if it's a report or presentation. However, what if it is a simple message delivered by voice mail or e-mail? Suppose you have to make a call about an erroneous charge on your cell phone bill. The customer service representative who takes your call asks you for the amount of the charge and the day it appeared on your bill. She also asks about the terms of your contract. If you have to get back to her with the answers because you don't have the information in front of you, you have wasted valuable time along with the opportunity to fix the situation. However, if you plan ahead by anticipating the representative's questions, and have the bill and contract in front of you, you will be able to resolve the situation more easily.

It doesn't matter whether you are a newly hired assistant or a chief executive officer, you can increase your chances of being successful by planning how to best communicate your messages. Rarely do you climb into your car without having a route in mind. Nor do you at-

Exhibit 4-1
Sample Departments and Job Duties with Start-up Businesses

Operations
- Develop business plans
- Pursue patents, copyrights, and legal protection
- Establish manufacturing and warehouse procedures

Finance
- Secure loans and financing
- Track project revenues and expenses
- Ensure financial compliance

Human Resources
- Recruit and hire employees
- Determine employee procedures
- Establish benefits packages

Accounting
- Manage bookkeeping
- Create budgets and forecasts
- Prepare financial statements

Sales & Marketing
- Develop sales and marketing tools
- Create public relations campaigns and media strategies
- Secure markets for goods and services

tempt to cook a meal for others without considering the ingredients you have on hand, the time to prepare the meal, and the tastes and appetites of those you're cooking for. It's the same for preparing business messages. Communicating without a plan can lead you down the wrong path.

But how do you "plan to communicate"? It's similar to young students who are told to study. "Just study and you will do well," teachers claim. But until a student learns how to study—to memorize, to comprehend, to review and recite, and to compare and connect ideas—simply being told to study doesn't help. It is the same with planning business messages. That is why this chapter focuses on the specific tactical steps you need to take to plan messages. Whether you are calling a colleague, meeting with your boss, composing a blog post, or writing a proposal, you need a communication strategy.

As you learned in Chapter 1, effective business messages have a defined purpose, are adapted for the audience, and create goodwill.

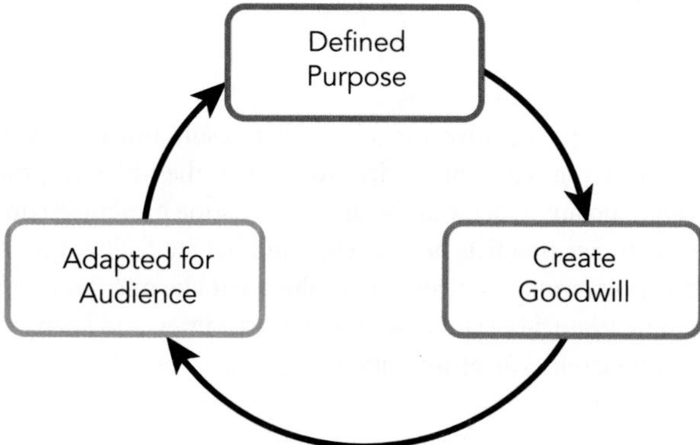

- A defined **purpose** includes knowing why you are communicating and what you want the communication to achieve. In other words, what action do you want the receivers of the message to take? Or, what emotion do you want them to feel?
- **Adapted for the audience** means you know your audience and have adjusted your message accordingly. Are you communicating with your boss or a high-level decision maker, a colleague, an employee who reports to you, a customer, or the general public? Your answers

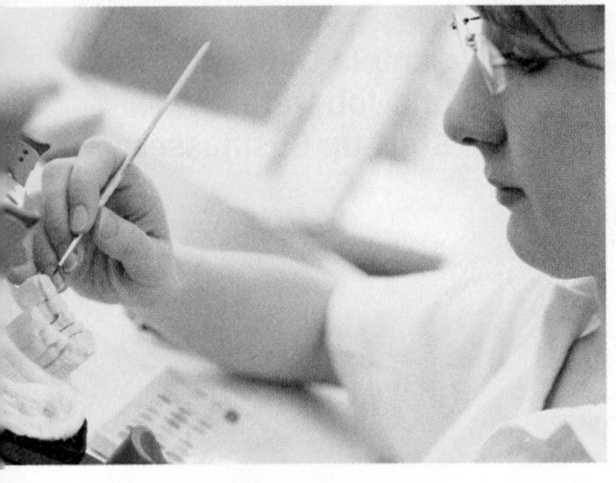

will affect the tone you use, the amount of background information you provide, and the way in which you choose to deliver your message. Adapting a message also includes using the "you attitude" you learned about in Chapter 1. In a nutshell, your messages should have more "you" words and fewer "I" and "we" words. For example, *instead of saying:*

"I am sending you the proposal today,"

you could say:

"You will receive the proposal today" to emphasize the reader's point of view.

- Whenever you communicate, you have an opportunity to create goodwill. It can be expressed in many ways, from a smile, to an understanding nod, to a written sentence acknowledging you value the party with whom you are communicating. Even when you deliver bad-news messages, you must strive to create goodwill. (We will talk more about bad-news messages in Chapter 8.)

Taking time to plan will help you create messages that achieve these three objectives. Of course, time is a factor. Every day you will need to think quickly and communicate on the spot. However, by developing the habit of thinking about messages in these three terms—purpose, audience, and goodwill—you will be better able to communicate both quickly and successfully. The following story about Christina illustrates how she made a great impression on her boss by effectively preparing her message.

Christina works as a dental technician at a busy clinic in San Diego. The clinic serves thousands of patients and operates at maximum capacity. As a result, the staff is extremely busy. Christina had an idea to purchase a medical-records scanning device that would streamline the process for maintaining patient records while relieving the clerical staff's workload.

Her message has a clear purpose.

Before Christina approached her boss with her idea, she prepared for the conversation by:

- Determining the price of the equipment.
- Analyzing how long it would take for the machine to pay for itself in terms of hours spent by the staff.
- Researching several manufacturers of similar technology to determine the machine of greatest value.
- Outlining the benefits the technology would provide to patients and staff.

Research helps Christina express the benefits of the technology from her boss's point of view.

When the right opportunity presented itself, Christina shared her idea with her boss, explaining how it could contribute to the practice's success. She was able to support her ideas as a result of the preparation she had done before their conversation. Not only did her boss like the idea and commit to adopting it, but she commended Christina for being proactive.

Christina's concern for the practice's success helps create goodwill.

This example shows the positive outcomes that result from preparing a message. If Christina simply stated that a scanning device would help the office run more smoothly, her boss might have been reluctant to act. But the details Christina presented convinced the boss of the technology's value to her practice, her patients, and her staff. The story also demonstrates that although Christina was not an entrepreneur, she acted like one. Managers seek employees who can formulate new strategies, create unusual opportunities, and keep a company competitive. Whether you see yourself as an entrepreneur or not, it helps to know how to think like one.

2 What Are the Six Questions You Should Ask as You Prepare Business Messages?

Ask yourself the following questions to ensure your communication has a clearly defined purpose, speaks to your intended audience, and generates a positive impression for both you and your organization.

- Who are you in the organization?
- What is the purpose of your message?
- Where do you want your message to land?
- When does your message need to be received?
- Why might objections be raised to your message?
- How should your message be received?

Who Are You in the Organization?

Who are you are as the sender of the message? Although knowing your audience is essential, knowing who you are as the sender must come first.

Knowing Your Role in a Company

The messages you send in business depend on your role in the company. Are you the president creating a mission statement for a start-up company manufacturing electric scooters? Or are you the marketing assistant for a clothing company in charge of writing copy for a trade magazine? Having a clear understanding of your position in the company will help you communicate effectively with people inside and outside of the organization.

The communication channels for sending and receiving messages from supervisors and those reporting to you are determined by your company's **chain of command.** **Exhibit 4-2** demonstrates a flat chain of command, while **Exhibit 4-3** illustrates a more vertical chain of command. A **flat chain of command** gives staff members easier access to superiors because there are fewer levels of management above them. A **vertical chain of command** has more levels of hierarchy, which can make it harder for staff members, managers, and executives to access and communicate with one another.

As you study Exhibits 4-2 and 4-3, imagine you are a staff member in the finance department (highlighted in yellow). Notice that you could face a greater challenge getting a message to the president in a company with a vertical command chain than in a company with a flat command chain. You would have to go through four levels of hierarchy rather than two. Generally speaking, a flatter communication chain allows for faster communication within the ranks, whereas a vertical chain creates a more complex communication flow. Understanding where you are within the structure will help clarify your communication responsibilities.

Also, know that messages you send *up* the chain of command will be more formal, professional, and serious in tone. Messages sent *across* the chain of command to colleagues or *down* the chain to those who report to you can be slightly less formal. However, they must remain professional.

Exhibit 4-2 **Flat Chain of Command**

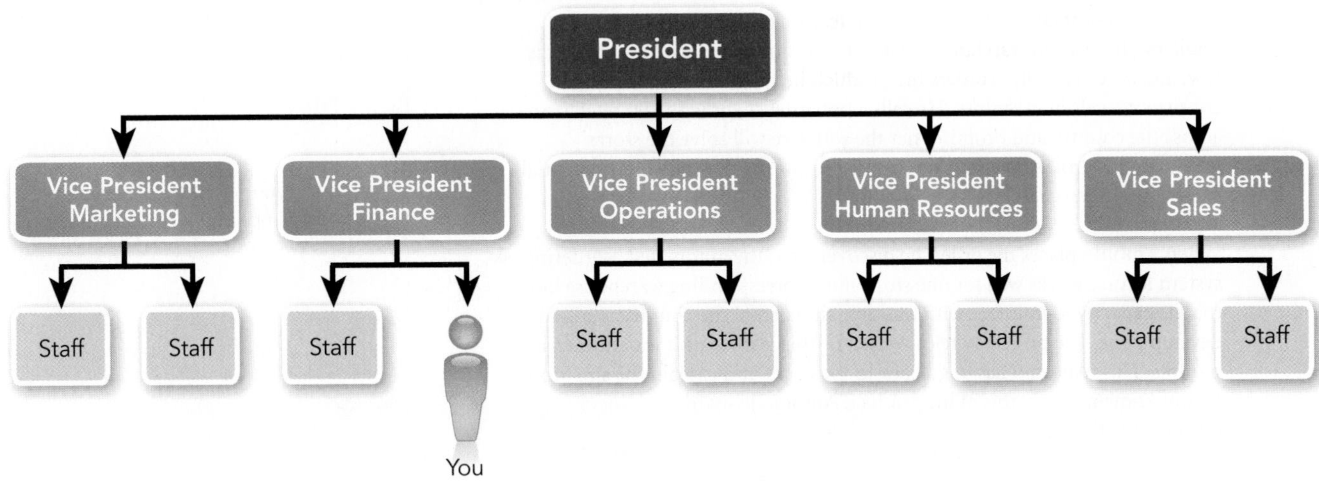

Exhibit 4-3
Vertical Chain of Command

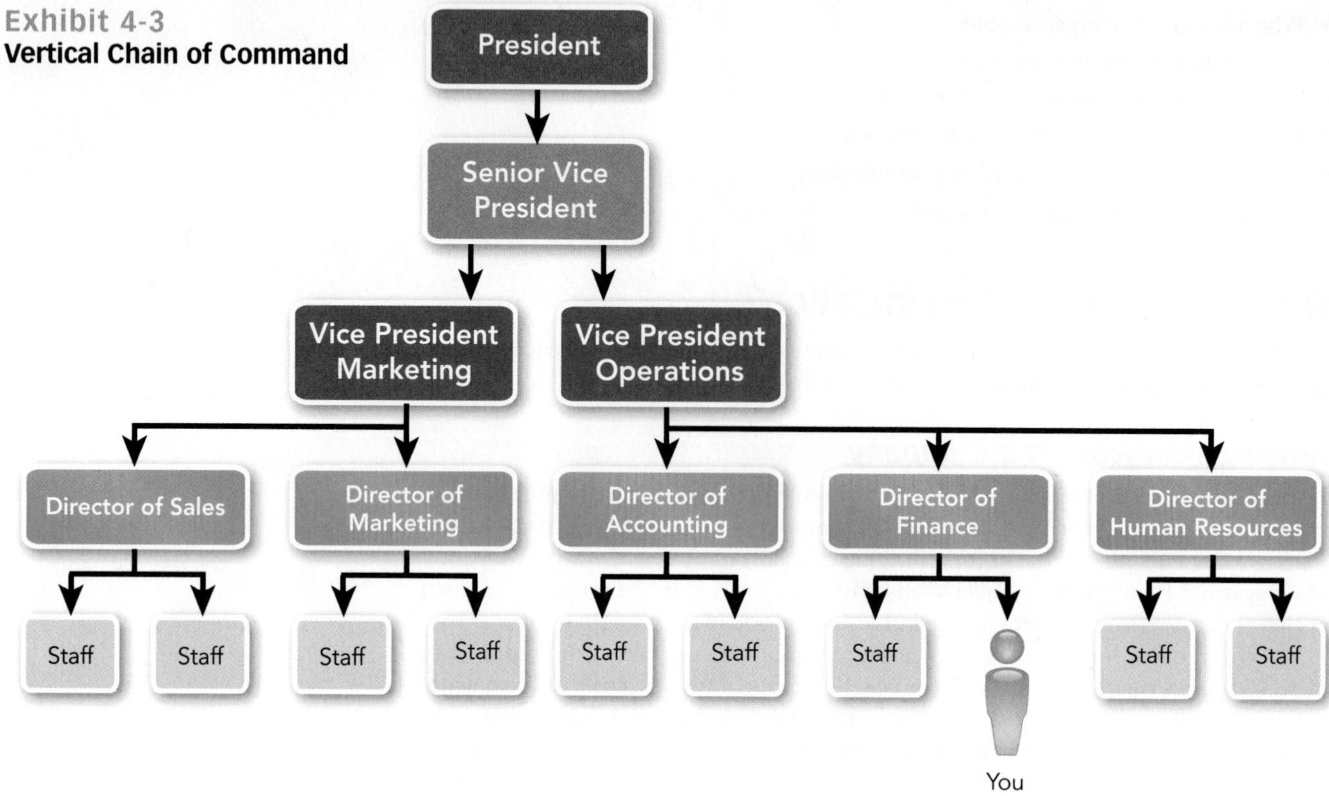

Understanding your role in a company as you prepare messages to customers or people outside of the organization is equally important. Know that promises you make on behalf of the organization are, in most instances, legally binding. For example, if you write a letter agreeing to reverse charges on a customer's account and later find out that you lack the authority to make such a decision, you could end up costing your company money. Your goal is to communicate effectively yet not overstep your bounds.

Knowing Your Company

Believe it or not, understanding how your company operates can be challenging, especially in organizations with many locations and divisions. Knowing what your company is doing, how it functions, and when and why things are happening will affect your ability to successfully communicate.

Antonio is a sales associate for a software company. One of the products he sells has an automatic reordering system feature that tracks inventory on retailers' shelves and warehouses. The system is triggered when inventory is low, and automatically reorders the product, helping retailers maintain consistent levels of inventory. He calls a potential client with 100 retail stores across the country and promises her the software will solve the stores' inventory-control problems. The client is thrilled by the software's potential and agrees to purchase it.

When Antonio places the order, he discovers that the automated reordering system feature works well for one store and a corresponding warehouse but that its capacity to interface with multiple sites across the country is still in development. The projected release date for this feature isn't for another six months. Now Antonio has to go back to the client and explain the situation. By not knowing the status of his product, Antonio jeopardized a lucrative business relationship.
Antonio fails to know important details about his company's products.

In an effort to jump right into business, people in start-up organizations sometimes overlook defining who they are, what they do, and why they do it. One of the first planning exer-

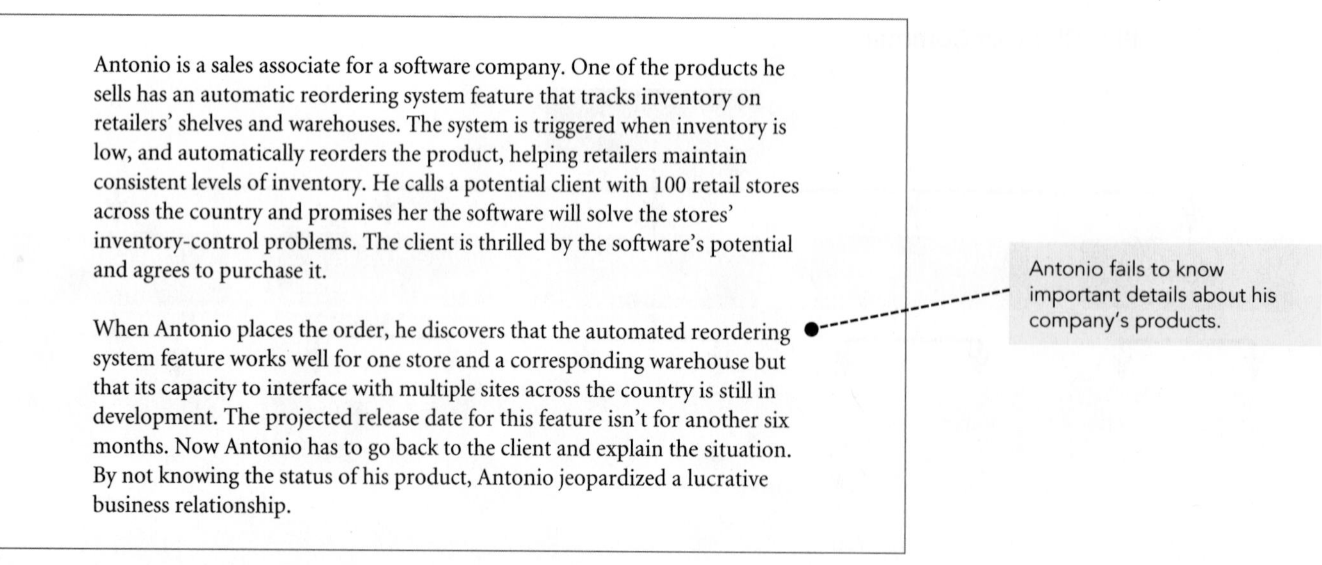

cises a start-up company should do is write a mission statement. A company's **mission statement** usually consists of several sentences summarizing its purpose, goals, overarching philosophy, and values. The mission statement serves as a compass for the organization and helps employees chart a proper course for organization. In addition, crafting the mission statement gives businesspeople a way to explore who they are before they face the challenge of communicating this information to people outside of the organization. Communicating on behalf of a company that lacks a clear mission is like batting from a home plate that keeps drifting. It's hard to know where the strike zone is. By contrast, standing with a bat in hand over a solid home plate increases your chances of hitting a grand slam.

Consider the following mission statement:

> The mission of Angelica's Organic Coffee is to provide the highest quality coffee products to consumers worldwide.
> In doing so, we will:
>
> - Buy coffee beans grown without the use of pesticides and chemicals.
> - Provide products that are healthier for consumers.
> - Pay growers ethical prices so as to improve their lives and those of their families. Operate in an environmentally sustainable way and continue to search for ways to reduce our carbon footprint on the planet.

The writers of the mission statement for Angelica's Organic Coffee clearly address who they are and what they do; they are the producers of organic coffee products. The mission statement also explains whom they target—as many consumers worldwide as possible. The writers then go on to state how the company will achieve its mission—by utilizing coffee beans free of pesticides and chemicals. Finally, the mission statement reflects the company's core values—providing healthier products to consumers, sustaining the livelihoods of growers and their families, and reducing the firm's carbon footprint on the environment. A mission statement such as this one also gives employees a clear idea of who they are as they communicate on the company's behalf.

Now read International Furniture Express, Inc.'s mission statement:

> Our mission at International Furniture Express is to continue to strengthen the "partnership" aspect of Techlink, and offer both unique designs, as well as custom projects, to our customer base with a focus on product that is saleable in broad markets, value and uniqueness being paramount to the end result.

This statement fails to clarify exactly who International Furniture Express is and what it does. We can assume it is a furniture business, but does it manufacture or simply import? Who is Techlink? Who is the company's customer base? What differentiates International Furniture Express from its competitors, and how does this affect the business? The writers of this mission statement seem to have collected ideas that describe aspects of the company without strategically planning to make the statement direct, powerful, and clear.

Now read the revised mission statement for International Furniture Express:

> The mission of International Furniture Express is to maximize our unique partnership with China's Techlink factory to manufacture original, value-oriented furniture for the largest furniture retailers in North America. We stand apart from our competitors by offering retailers a diverse product line manufactured in one factory. This simplifies their buying process while allowing us to keep our prices competitive and shipping times to a minimum.

The revised mission statement tells us who International Furniture Express is—a manufacturing company that partners with a Chinese factory. We know who the furniture company's customer base is: large North American furniture retailers. Finally, we learn what

DID YOU KNOW?

Mission statements help a company:

- Meet its objectives by clearly stating goals and standards that serve as benchmarks for the firm's performance.
- Stay on track by establishing what the business is designed to do and what it is not designed to do.
- Succinctly describe its unique story and reason for existing.
- Save time by keeping employees and key decision makers focused on the intent and objectives of the business.
- Bolster its reputation by highlighting the core values and essence of the firm.

the company's competitive edge is: being able to produce multiple products in one factory, which streamlines the buying process for retailers as well as International Furniture Express' shipping process. A potential investor in the company might be enticed to further explore the firm because its mission statement makes it clear it's doing something different than traditional furniture manufacturers and importers.

What Is the Purpose of Your Communication?

As you prepare a message, ask yourself whether the purpose is to inform, ask a question, respond to an inquiry, or request an action. Then, ask what you want the outcome of the communication to be. Consider the following example: Dianne's company is preparing a marketing plan to launch a new sports drink. She needs sales figures from other sports drinks companies in order to analyze her organization's competition. Roshanda writes her assistant the message illustrated in **Exhibit 4-4**.

Roshanda's purpose for communicating is clear. But her request is too general. It fails to request specific information that could benefit her marketing plan. If she has a savvy assistant, she might be in luck. Roshanda could improve her request if she considered the specific outcomes she needs from the e-mail: information about the company's biggest competitors, including their market shares and how they have changed over the last five years; and comparison statistics for sports drinks, soda pop, and juice. Roshanda can create a more effective message if she knows exactly what she wants and is able to articulate it. **Exhibit 4-5** shows a revised e-mail that will produce a more desirable outcome.

Suppose an executive needs to inform his staff that his company did not receive an important business loan it was expecting. On the one hand, he can simply write an interoffice memo relaying this information. On the other hand, he can also think specifically about the outcome he wants to achieve—keeping the firm's staff informed and yet upbeat. If he does this, he will craft a better message—one that delivers the bad news but also includes positive information about the firm's future funding possibilities.

Where Do You Want Your Message to Land?

Chapter 3 discussed evaluating your audience, including their ages, genders, educational levels, technical backgrounds, and so forth. Asking yourself the following additional questions will also help you prepare a better message.

- Who is your primary audience and who is your secondary audience?
- Will your message be received by people within the organization, outside of it, or both?

Exhibit 4-4 A Message Requesting Information

To: stevesmith@oxygenwater.com
From: roshandakent@oxygenwater.com
Subject: Sales Statistics for Marketing Plan

Hi Steve,

Can you please research the sales figures for sports drinks across the country?

These numbers will be used for the marketing plan, which will be presented to the board of directors in two weeks. If you can get this information to me by Friday before noon, I would appreciate it.

Best regards,

Roshanda

The purpose is clear, but the message fails to specifically request the numbers needed.

Exhibit 4-5 A More Effective Message Requesting Information

To: stevesmith@oxygenwater.com
From: roshandakent@oxygenwater.com
Subject: Sales Statistics for Marketing Plan

Hi Steve,

Please research the following statistics for sports drinks so we can prepare our marketing plan:

- The gross sales for all sports drinks both across the country and by regions.
- The names of the three biggest competitors in each region, and their market shares.
- Each competitor's percentage of increased or decreased market share over the past five years.
- Sales figures for sports drinks versus soda pop and juice drinks across the country and by region.

I will need the information by Friday noon so I can get the marketing plan ready for the board of directors' meeting on Monday afternoon.

Thank you for your help,

Roshanda

The detailed request clarifies the message's purpose and specific information requested.

Sentence explains when the information is needed and why.

PEARSON mybcommlab

Apply Exhibit 4-5's key concepts by revising a new document. Go to Chapter 4 in mybcommlab.com and select Document Makeovers.

- What assumptions can you make or not make about your audience?
- What details should be included in the message?

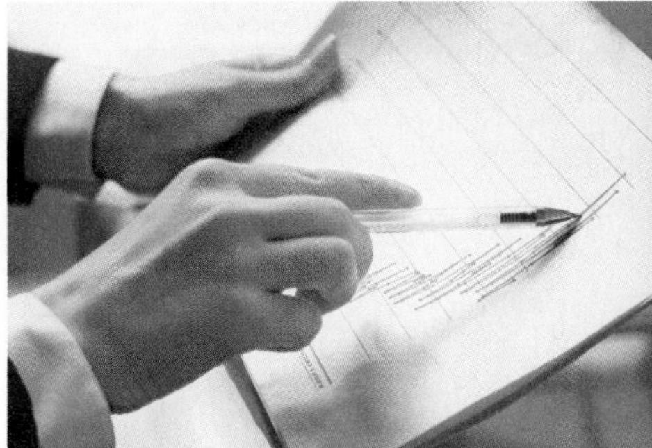

Exhibit 4-6 explains why these questions are important.

Next, ask yourself where you want your message to land or end up. If you are applying for a business loan from a local bank, your written application needs to reach the loan officer. However, where you really want your message to end up is in the bank's boardroom, where the trustees sign off on approved loans. How do you plan for your message to reach its optimal destination and not just its first stop? By researching, asking questions, and positioning your message to land in the right hands.

Imagine you work for a start-up solar energy company and are submitting a response to an RFP (request for proposal) from your city's government. Your firm wants the job of installing solar panels in the city's new convention center. Your research might include:

- Investigating who sits on the city's review committee.
- Reading other RFPs submitted for similar projects.
- Reviewing criteria set out by the city to ensure you are in compliance with the technical standards for installation.
- Attending any informational meetings open to the public.
- Asking questions of the city's staff and review committee.

Legwork such as this can make the difference between your proposal being rejected by a gatekeeper in the first round versus in front of the final review committee. A **gatekeeper** is someone who controls or monitors access to decision makers. Usually a gatekeeper is an administrative staff member who screens their phone calls and e-mails.

When Does Your Message Need to Be Received?

What is the timeframe for your communication? The motto for selling real estate is "location, location, location." The motto for selling your communication could easily be "timing, timing,

Exhibit 4-6 Additional Questions to Consider When Preparing a Message

Who Is Your Primary Audience? Who Is Your Secondary Audience?	Will Your Message Be Received by People Within the Organization, Outside of It, or Both?
Consider your main target but also think about others who might receive your message. For example, if you send a message to a potential investor about your new company, consider whether he or she might share your message with other investors or professionals. This concept is especially important when you are using electronic communication where messages can easily be forwarded to others beyond your primary target.	Consider how much the recipient knows about the issue. When you communicate with a colleague you have been working with, your message might be brief. However, when conveying the same information to someone up the command chain, you might have to provide more background information to familiarize your reader with information being discussed.
What Assumptions Can You Make or Not Make about Your Audience?	**What Details Should Be Included In the Message?**
Challenge assumptions by asking questions: What background does the audience already understand? What background information needs to be included? What experience does the reader have that might affect how the message is understood? What questions will the reader have? What perspectives will influence the reader's point of view?	Understanding the complexities of your message and the special needs of your audience will influence how you shape your content. This also helps you determine what should accompany your message (graphs, explanations, testimonials, etc.).

timing." Consider the solar energy example we discussed. Imagine the company secured the financing it needed to install solar panels in the convention center and just completed the installation. The convention center is now about to be unveiled. You are responsible for sending a press release to announce the grand opening. Do you send it to the media a month in advance, two weeks in advance, the week of the opening, or all of the above? To answer this question, you will need to know what else is happening in your city. What other events might hamper or enhance your efforts? When should your story be released?

Think, too, about how the timing affects the person receiving the message. Imagine you're the office manager for a landscape company. It's October. The owner of the company hates to lay off valuable seasonal employees. However, as the business slows down in the winter, he must reduce his labor costs. You have an idea to expand the company's operations to include hanging holiday lights for both businesses and residents. Proposing your idea to the owner at a time when he wants to keep valuable employees on staff and still has time to advertise a new service will help the chances of your idea being adopted.

Why Might Objections to Your Message Be Raised?

Anticipating **objections**, or negative reactions to messages, and ways to address them, pays off for communicators. What objections might there be to your message? Are any parts of it confusing? Are there ideas or claims that need additional explanation or justification? What might raise a red flag in the recipient's mind? Put yourself in the recipient's shoes and play the devil's advocate. Look for any issues that might interfere with your message producing your desired outcome and address them.

Suppose you are a private investor reviewing a request for capital from a start-up company, Sound Helmets. Sound Helmets manufactures snowboarding helmets. The innovative helmets have speakers built into the back of them that can be connected to MP3 players. The following are two different approaches to describing the product in a proposal.

REAL INSIGHTS from a New Professional

Name: ***Tim Thwaites***
Title: ***Co-President***
Organizations: ***Coda Coffee Company***
Locations: ***Phoenix, Arizona, and Denver, Colorado***

EVEN THOUGH HE GREW UP IN SEATTLE, "the coffee mecca of the world," Tim Thwaites didn't see the coffee business as his end goal. Even though as a teenager he worked with his brother Tommy for a coffee roaster in Seattle, he chose to pursue his college degree in aviation management in 2001 from Central Washington University.

However, one path led to another and a few years later Tommy invited him to work together again for a coffee roaster in Denver. This round, Tim Thwaites realized his passion for doing the coffee industry right. In July 2005, Thwaites decided to co-found Coda Coffee Company with his brother and now business associate. Coda is a wholesale roaster with residual customers they must communicate with regularly.

"I am the classic example of thinking I could not be an entrepreneur," Thwaites says. But having put time into working in the roasting business already, he comments, "This move made so much sense." Of course, start-up wasn't easy. Thwaites' financial advice when starting a business is "to always plan to go over budget . . . it always costs more than what you see on the surface." Loans of approximately $300,000 from relatives gave him a good base start-up with some cash to stay afloat for a year.

During this start-up period, Thwaites realized how closely clear communication is tied to acquiring finances. "When you begin to gather resources for a business, you must know your audience," says Thwaites. "Who is reading your letter asking for money? Is it your uncle, someone who would be an equal business partner, or a bank?" He points out that messages must be tailored to each audience—a letter to a bank would likely be more formal than a letter to your uncle.

He also encourages young professionals to scour the communication to make sure the message is clear. "Treat this type of business communication like a résumé," Thwaites says. "Every word counts and the first lines have to be eye-grabbing."

Thwaites advocates for honesty in business communication. "Let people see who you are through your messages. Don't act like you have everything all figured out because that will raise more questions than if you are honest."

When dealing with prospective coffee customers, Thwaites employs a two- or three-pronged communication approach. "I always start with an e-mail introducing our company, but in my business an e-mail is never enough," he says. "I have to follow up with verbal communication over the phone or ultimately face to face. This way I can appeal to their personal circumstances and personal style."

Thwaites says his e-mails have a clear, concise message about the value of Coda Coffee that includes how Coda differentiates itself from its competitors. "We are high quality and socially responsible," says Thwaites. The two go hand-in-hand: Coda works directly at the farm level to ensure sustainability through directly sourced coffees. Thwaites explains, "We help farmers make a better living and we get better quality coffee." Coda also helps some of its farmers improve the quality of their coffee beans with upgraded equipment or educational opportunities.

The biggest communication struggle Thwaites faces with regular clients is putting his emotions aside and realizing the value of any one customer. "I have learned to bite my tongue when a situation out of my control occurs and the customer is not happy," he says. "For example, if a customer doesn't receive his Tanzanian Peaberry coffee on time, I have to recognize that he doesn't understand it was held up in customs because there was a snail on the bag. The customer doesn't care about that—he just wants me to make it right."

Thwaites sums up his most valuable lessons learned about business communication. "First, start with an extremely clear message. Second, follow up—it's your fault if you don't. Third, put your emotions aside, and last, know your audience."

Questions

1. Give two specific examples of how Coda Coffee Company capitalizes on the value of clear messages?
2. What business communication lesson lies in Thwaites' comment: "Follow up—it's your fault if you don't"? How is following up part of delivering clear messages?

Source: Tim Thwaites in discussion with the author, June 2010.

Poor Approach: Doesn't Anticipate Possible Objections

> Sound Helmets will provide snowboarders with the latest technology so they can enjoy their music while riding on the mountain. Consumers will no longer have to worry about irritating ear phones. This product is certain to become the rage at every winter resort.

Successful Approach: Anticipates Possible Objections by Addressing Safety Concerns

> The hip design and X Games' endorsement of Sound Helmets guarantee they will be a hit with style-conscious snowboarders. Moreover, unlike earphones, which can cause irreparable hearing damage, Sound Helmets provide snowboarders with a safe, surround-sound listening experience. The National Ski Patrol has endorsed Sound Helmets. The helmets are cut above the ear so snowboarders can hear other sounds in addition to the music from their MP3 players, reducing the risks of accidents.

An investor reading the first proposal might not understand the advantages of the product or question its safety. By contrast, the second proposal calls attention to the potential safety objection up front. It addresses the concerns the investor might have and entices him or her with the product's marketability and the ski patrol's safety endorsement.

How Should Your Message Be Received?

What's the best medium for your message? Is it urgent? Is it formal or informal? Will it have greater impact if the recipient can linger over a letter, make notes on the paper, and underline key concepts? Or, will it be better received in person with a smile and a handshake?

Consider Amy, a young woman who hoped to receive a job at an advertising firm with which she had interviewed. After a month of waiting to hear back from the company, she decided to write the interviewing manager a card with a cat and a garden scene on its cover. Inside the card she wrote that she was looking forward to hearing from the manager. Unfortunately, when she finally did hear from the manager, no job was offered. Whether the cutesy card kept her from getting the position or not, she didn't know. However, it's likely that her message would have been better received if she had written a brief e-mail or made a polite phone call within two weeks of her interview. Her choice of timing and the medium did not work for her. Later in the chapter you will learn when to send messages through oral communication channels and when to send them through written channels.

Exhibit 4-7
Planning Template for Business Messages

Who Are You?
• Your Role • Your Company
What Is Your Purpose for Communicating?
• Primary Purpose • Desired Outcomes
Where Do You Want Your Message to Land?
• Primary versus Secondary Targets • External and/or Internal Audiences • Assumptions to Clarify • Accompanying Details • Other Influencing Factors
When Does Your Message Need to Be Received?
• Sense of Immediacy • Timing Considerations for Sender • Timing Considerations for Receiver
Why Might Objections Be Raised?
• Potential Red Flags • Proactive Steps to Be Taken
How Should Your Message Be Received?
• Best Medium for Delivery

Exhibit 4-7 is a quick checklist, or template, you can use to organize your thoughts prior to sending a message. Eventually the process of planning messages will become second nature to you. Until then, the template will help you become a better communicator. **Exhibit 4-8** shows how the owners of Clean Green Grow, a manufacturer of environmentally friendly cleaning products, used the template to plan for their writing a small business loan application.

Exhibit 4-8 Filled-In Template for Completing a Loan Application

Who Are You?	
• Your Role	Founder and chief executive officer; secure financial resources and generate community support for Green Clean Glow.
• Your Company	Green Clean Glow, a producer of nontoxic, environmentally friendly cleaning products for industrial use.
What Is Your Purpose for Communicating?	
• Primary Purpose	To receive a Small Business Association loan for $25,000.
• Desired Outcomes	Secure a start-up loan—$25,000. Secure a revolving line of credit—$15,000. Build community support and a potential product sponsorship.
Where Do You Want Your Message to Land?	
• Primary versus Secondary Targets • Gatekeeper(s)	Loan officer at South Dakota Community Bank, Rapid City, South Dakota; loan committee and bank trustees.
• External and/or Internal Audiences	External audience.
• Assumptions to Clarify	Explanation of start-up costs, manufacturing issues, and costs of green requirements for products.
• Accompanying Details	Graphs showing market distribution of competition; testimonials from product trials.
• Other Influencing Factors	Tie application into city's green initiatives; demonstrate job creation and tax revenue to be generated by company's presence within city limits.
When Does Your Message Need to Be Received?	
• Sense of Immediacy	Proposal should be completed by December 1, 2011.
• Timing Considerations for Sender	Submit the application before end of fiscal year 2011.
• Timing Considerations for Receiver	To be received before end-of-year funding cycle and just after mayor's announcement of new "green" initiative.
Why Might Objections Be Raised?	
• Potential Red Flags	Costs for manufacturing set up; competition in current market; perceptions of higher product costs.
• Proactive Steps to Be Taken	Complete and submit reports from test markets showing cost effectiveness, product effectiveness, and environmental impact study.
How Should Your Message Be Received?	
• Best Medium for Delivery	A formal report with visual aids illustrating the competition, their market shares, and a cost analysis.

Exhibit 4-9 Oral Communication Methods

Methods for Oral Communication	Situation
Face-to-Face Meetings	Appropriate for interactive discussions, building consensus, or developing interpersonal relationships; offer opportunities to capture nonverbal feedback and provide immediate responses.
Phone Calls	Useful for obtaining quick answers and delivering basic information; allow for addressing nonverbal feedback in terms of tone and pauses, and for answering questions; highly accessible method of communication.
Voice Mails	Effective for delivering short informative messages or asking simple questions; allow receivers to respond at their convenience.
Teleconferences	Appropriate when one or more of the communicators are in different locations.
Skype	Provides an inexpensive way for people who are separated geographically to communicate using voice over Internet protocol (VoIP) technology.

3 When Should You Use Oral versus Written Communication for Business Messages?

Continually changing communication technology has made choosing the best channels for sending business messages today challenging. Remember Amy, the young woman who followed up on her interview too late and did so with a card instead of a phone call? You don't want to be like her. This section will help you determine whether your message is best suited for verbal or written delivery.

Oral Communication for Business Messages

Exhibit 4-9 lists the methods available for oral communication and the situations in which it is most appropriate. In general, oral communication is best when interaction with the receiver is needed for a rapid response. **Exhibit 4-10** lists the advantages and disadvantages of oral communication.

Exhibit 4-10
The Advantages and Disadvantages of Oral Communication

Advantages of Oral Communication	Disadvantages of Oral Communication
When face to face or during video conferences, provides the opportunity to respond to nonverbal cues	Participants must be in same location or have same time availability
Allows for immediate feedback	Doesn't provide a permanent record unless conversations are recorded
Provides opportunity to answer questions and address misunderstandings	Senders are unable to revise or refine message
Allows for spontaneous discussion and interaction	Details can be lost or more easily misconstrued
Helps develop consensus, team building, and rapport	Messages are more susceptible to lose focus

One of the pitfalls of oral communication is that people often fail to plan in the same way they do for written communication. When conducting face-to-face meetings, teleconferences, and phone calls, you need to be able to speak spontaneously and planning ahead of time will help you do so.

Before you pick up the phone or walk into a meeting, think about the upcoming exchange. Write down the main points you want to cover. Then, list any concerns or potential objections you might face and how you might respond in these instances. Once you enter the meeting or begin the phone conversation, take notes. Keep track of the main points discussed and the actions that need to be taken once the conversation is finished. With more formal meetings and conversations, a follow-up e-mail outlining the highlights discussed and actions to be taken is a great way to demonstrate professional communication habits.

One final point: When leaving voice mail messages, organize your thoughts beforehand to keep from rambling and sounding disorganized. Clearly state your purpose and the action you will be taking or the action you need the receiver to take. Keep your message short and simple. Like all messages, define the purpose of the communication, adapt the message for your receiver, and deliver it in a positive and professional manner.

CHECKLIST

When making phone calls:

- ☑ Have a notepad in front of you.
- ☑ Before dialing, list the important points that need to be covered.
- ☑ Take notes during the call.
- ☑ Record follow-up actions that need to be taken.

When Writing Is Your Best Option

Writing is the best choice for communicating when:

- You need a legal record of the communication.
- The message contains complicated details or numbers.
- The sender needs time to compose and organize the message.
- The receiver needs the freedom to take in the information at his or her own pace.
- The message is formal.

Exhibit 4-11 lists the pros and cons of written communication. After looking these over, we will explore how effective planning helps you maximize the advantages that writing offers and minimize its disadvantages.

In general, written communication offers the sender control, whereas spoken communication provides the sender flexibility. So, when drafting a written message, how do you maximize the control writing offers, yet minimize the need for flexibility? By careful planning. Two of the most widely cited researchers studying the writing process claim that planning is the

DID YOU KNOW?

Two-thirds of salaried employees in large American companies are expected to write messages and other documents. Says one human resources director: "All employees must have writing ability. . . . Manufacturing documents, operating procedures, reporting problems, lab safety, waste disposal operations—all have to be crystal clear."[6]

Exhibit 4-11
The Advantages and Disadvantages of Sending a Written Message

Advantages of a Written Message	Disadvantages of a Written Message
Gives the sender time to design the message	Time lapse between sending and receiving the message
Offers the sender control over how the reader receives the message, such as the order of information and its format	Does not allow the sender to interpret the receiver's immediate reaction by his or her voice or body language
Provides control over word choice and rhythm of the message to create the greatest impact	Does not allow the sender to immediately address the receiver's concerns
Gives the sender an opportunity to communicate from a distance when dealing with an emotionally charged situation	Keeps the sender from knowing when and where communication is breaking down
Creates documentation for later reference	Does not allow the sender to suddenly inject the emotion necessary to inspire and persuade the receiver
Provides legal documentation, ensures accountability, prevents misunderstandings	Is not always easy to confirm the message was received

hallmark of the expert writer and that expert writers differ from novice writers in both the amount and type of planning they do before writing.[7]

A general rule of thumb for writing for business is to spend one-half of your time planning, one-quarter of your time putting your ideas into words, and the final quarter revising and editing. For a busy employee, spending so much time planning might seem daunting. But for longer, more formal communications, planning will save you time.

Keep in mind that many business managers must answer hundreds of e-mails a day, making in-depth planning impossible. When fast communication is required, pause for a brief moment to define your purpose and consider your recipient's point of view. Even a few seconds of planning can make your message more effective and leave a good impression.

For formal reports or other types of in-depth messages, you will probably need to do more than address the questions in the template we discussed. You might also need to generate ideas and gather information and data. If you are writing to create a legal record of the message, you will need to plan for a more formal tone and style. If your message must convey a logical progression of ideas, you must organize your thoughts in a way that can be easily followed by your audience. If you need to emphasize supporting details, you might plan for accompanying visuals such as graphs and tables. Finally, if you need to persuade a reader, you will probably want to build your case up front. Chapter 9 will help you become a good persuasive writer.

4 How Do You Gather Information and Organize a Written Business Message?

When faced with a writing task for business, assess its formality and complexity to determine the type of planning and research needed. On the one hand, you might need to draft a simple e-mail with little or no additional research. On the other hand, writing a lengthy proposal might require supporting evidence from outside sources, interviews with primary sources, or statistics from experimental research. The remainder of this section will discuss how to generate ideas, gather pertinent information, and organize the material.

Generating Ideas

As we have explained, you can prepare for any writing task by using the planning template in Exhibit 4-7. However, you might need to generate other ideas to bring your message to life. Perhaps historical examples or testimonials can enhance your message and give it credibility. The following are several ways you can generate ideas.

Here are a few that you might try.

- **Brainstorm.** Brainstorming is the process of capturing as many individual ideas as possible about a given topic without censoring them. Specify a certain amount of time for the activity and capture any and all items on paper or a computer as they come to mind. Once the time is up, go back and analyze each idea to see if it can truly enhance your message. The following is an example of ideas generated for a newsletter promoting an animal daycare business.

Ideas for Newsletter	
Quotes from customers	Fees
Pictures of the facility	Vet endorsements
Mission statement	Article: exercise tips
Training services	Advertisements
Article: new dog park	Article: animal vitamins
Pricing	Recall notices on leashes and collars
Staff biographies	Pets and infants
Article: pet vaccinations	Training methods
Pet vitamins	Grooming tips

- ***Make lists.*** Making lists with categories can help you generate ideas. Lists can help you focus on one category at a time instead of having to generate ideas that cover the entire gamut of your task. The following example shows how lists can be used to generate ideas for the same newsletter.

Topics	Fees/Charges	Pictures
Pet vitamins	Hour	Kennels
Grooming tips	Half day	Dog park
Pets and infants	Full day	Grooming
Training methods	Package rates	Staff

Free-writing can help you come up with ideas you might otherwise not have thought of.

- ***Free-write***. To free-write, put your pen to paper and let your ideas flow freely, narrative style, without censoring them. Free-writing can help you not only generate ideas but make connections between them you might not otherwise see. Once you have your thoughts down, you can then evaluate them to see how well they serve your purpose.
- ***Use a mind map***. Mind maps, which are especially valuable for visual thinkers, can help you generate secondary ideas from main ideas. To create a mind map like the one below, begin by writing a main idea in a circle. As new ideas are triggered from the idea, draw offshoots to record them. In addition to doing a mind map on paper, you can download free mind-mapping software from the Internet to help you with the process. Cmap is such a tool.

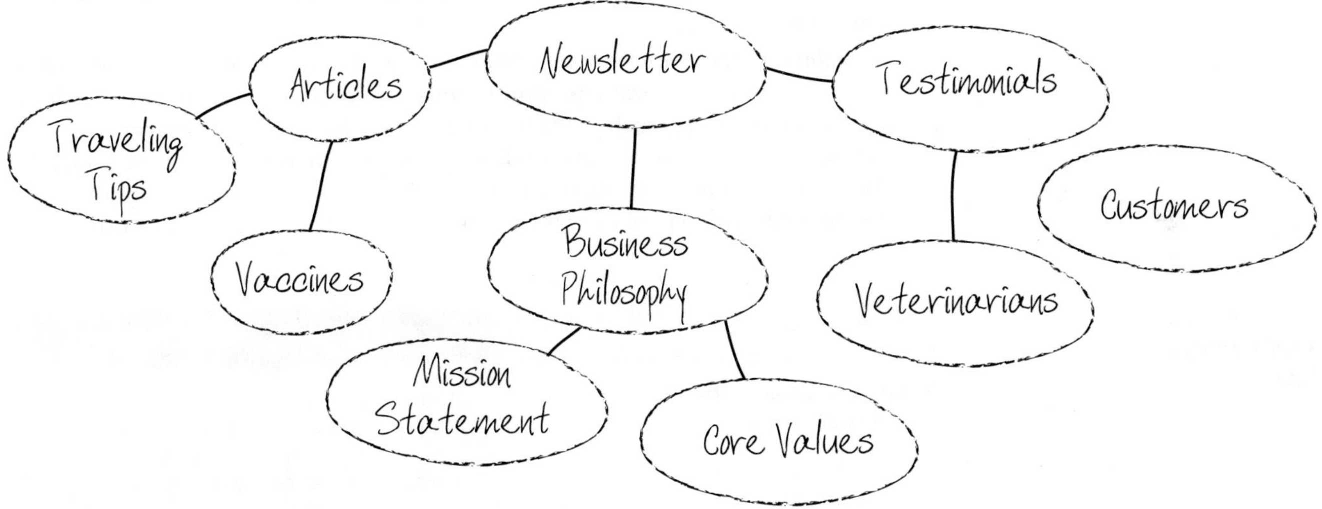

- ***Consider other viewpoints.*** Look at your message from different angles and multiple perspectives. How would you write it if you were the CEO of your firm? How would you write it if you had been employed by your company for 10 years rather than two months? How might being a consultant to the company instead of an employee shape your writing? Considering other viewpoints can help you generate ideas, make connections, and more deeply analyze the issue you're trying to write about.

Gathering Additional Information

Sometimes your message will need to be more complex. Your ideas alone won't be enough to get your point across, so you will need to gather additional information. For example, you might need to obtain numbers from your accountant, quote consumer-spending reports, or cite a marketing research blog. Two types of information gathering are informal research and formal research.

Informal Research

Informal research refers to using methods such as the following, which can be used to gather informal information that can be used to explore a problem for a writing task.

- ***Refer to company files and documents for needed information.*** The information you need might already exist in your company's databases but in a department other than your own.
- ***Talk with your supervisor, colleagues, department heads, and customers.*** Doing so will give you insights that will help you with your writing task.
- ***Talk to your audience.*** Find out what they expect to hear. Whenever possible, craft your message to meet their needs. This step is especially important if the message you need to deliver differs from what they expect to hear.

Formal Research

Longer, complex writing projects often demand that you expand your research to include references and supporting data from surveys and experiments, often called **formal research**. The information can come from either primary or secondary sources.

- ***Primary sources.*** **Primary sources** are sources of information you gather firsthand. The information can be obtained by interviewing and surveying customers, gathering your firm's sales data, and conducting studies or experiments that provide empirical data. The research you do using primary sources can be further broken down into two categories: qualitative research and quantitative research. **Qualitative research** involves systematically talking to individuals or small groups of people and summarizing the general information they give you. By contrast, **quantitative research** gathers data that is then statistically calculated. A formal survey of a large group of people, the gathering of special sales data, lab data, manufacturing data, and so forth, are examples of quantitative research.
- ***Secondary sources.*** **Secondary sources** are sources of information already gathered by other people and organizations. Most business professionals begin their research using secondary sources such as the Internet because it's faster and cheaper than conducting experiments or surveys. Online databases such as Business Source Premier offer writers easy access to published articles and data. Secondary source research can also be conducted in public libraries or at colleges and universities, or by using trade

Exhibit 4-12
Tips for Evaluating the Validity of Resources[8]

Questions to Ask	Things to Look For
Is the material supported by references?	The material is backed up by the thought, research, and statistics of other professionals. The arguments may demonstrate effective reasoning.
Do the experiments generate sound data?	The experiments are conducted with reasonable sample sizes and parameters, the details of which are readily available for review.
Is the material written well?	The material is written and published in a professional manner.
Does the material align with other sources?	The material presents factual information that is in agreement with other reputable sources.
Who publishes the material and for what purpose? What is the URL?	The domain name suffix lends support to the source's credibility. See Exhibit 4-13 for more information.

books, encyclopedias, and other reference material. Firms can also purchase data from companies that specialize in gathering primary research. The Nielsen Company gathers information like the number of viewers watching television programs or scanner information from checkout stands in stores.

The Credibility of Sources

Not all sources, including Internet sources, are equally credible. **Exhibit 4-12** lists questions you can ask to evaluate the reliability of the sources you're consulting. **Exhibit 4-13** shows you how to determine level of credibility based on the domain extension. As you can see, .gov Web sites are more credible than .com Web sites.

Copyright Infringement

Did you know that any and all original copy you write is protected by copyright laws? So are the pictures, cartoons, and graphics you create. No one else can publish them without your permission. Material does not necessarily have to show a copyright notice or be registered to be protected under U.S. copyright laws.

Cutting and pasting information from the Web is easy, but it's not legal. Plagiarism and proper citation are discussed in detail in Chapter 16. For now, keep the following tips in mind: Contact the writer or creator of the material and ask for permission to use it. Even if permission is granted, you may have to pay a fee. Search for comparable sources that are in the public domain. The public domain includes material with expired copyrights and material that will never be copyrighted, such as government documents.[9] If

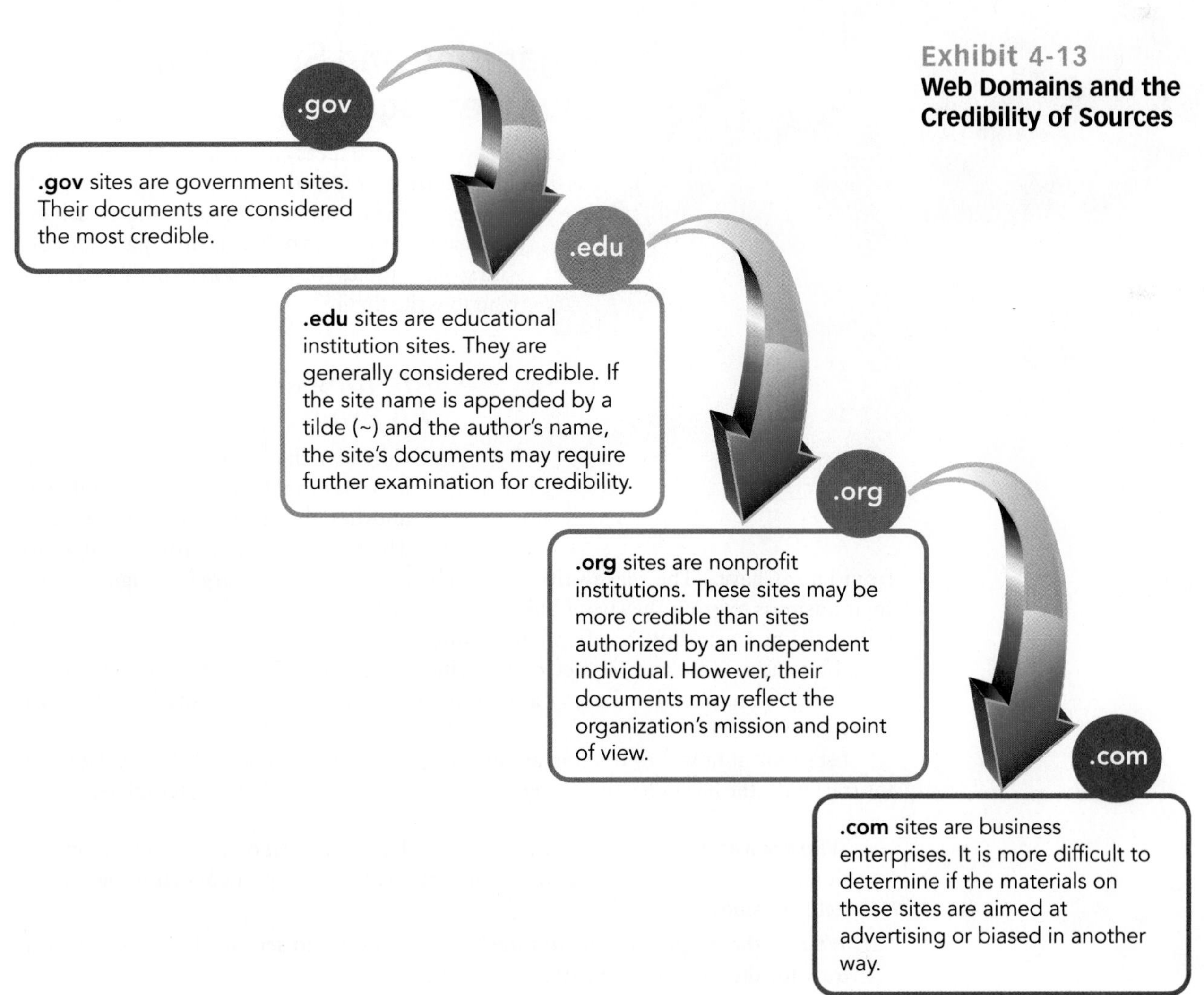

.gov
.gov sites are government sites. Their documents are considered the most credible.
.edu
.edu sites are educational institution sites. They are generally considered credible. If the site name is appended by a tilde (~) and the author's name, the site's documents may require further examination for credibility.
.org
.org sites are nonprofit institutions. These sites may be more credible than sites authorized by an independent individual. However, their documents may reflect the organization's mission and point of view.
.com
.com sites are business enterprises. It is more difficult to determine if the materials on these sites are aimed at advertising or biased in another way.

Exhibit 4-13
Web Domains and the Credibility of Sources

you are still in doubt, consult the U.S. Copyright Office's *Fair Use Provisions for Copyrighted Material.* You can find it online.

Accurate and Ethical Messages

One final note about preparing and researching business messages—they need to be accurate and ethical. What you write about your product can be legally binding. It is also critical that you disclose, in simple, everyday language, warnings about your product that can adversely affect consumers.

Companies that don't hold themselves to the highest legal and ethical standards can find themselves beleaguered with problems. Consider McNeil Nutritionals, the manufacturer of artificial sweetener Splenda. McNeil Nutritionals was sued because its advertising claimed Splenda was "made from sugar, so it tastes like sugar." (Splenda does start out as pure cane sugar. However, the final product contains no sugar. The active ingredient is a chemical that does not occur in nature.) McNeil settled the suit and changed its slogan but not before incurring a significant amount of legal fines and fees, not to mention a loss of credibility among consumers.[10]

Organizing and Structuring Your Message

Once you have generated ideas and gathered information, it is time to organize your material. Using an outline can help you structure your message logically and to achieve the greatest impact. An **outline** is simply a guide consisting of the topics you plan to write in the order you plan to write them.

Creating an Outline: An Example

Consider the following scenario: Gina and Joe Donatello started a floral shop and design business several years ago. They rented a storefront retail space from Lucy Chavez. The space suits them well, and because it is large enough to allow their business to grow, they would like to purchase it. Mrs. Chavez has never mentioned selling the property, but she often talks about retiring to Florida and getting out of the rental business. Gina and Joe decide to write to her about buying her property when she's ready to retire. They believe a lease-to-own option would be the best thing for everyone involved.

Let's look at how they develop an outline to write their message. First, the Donatellos start with the basics by answering the questions from the planning template.

1. ***Who are we?*** We are three-year tenants who have paid rent on time, and take exceptional care of the property. We are also successful entrepreneurs running a profitable business.
2. ***What is the purpose of the message?*** The purpose is to set up a lease-to-own contract for the space we are currently renting.

3. ***Where does the message need to land?*** The primary person is Lucy Chavez. A secondary audience might include her grown children and her attorney.
4. ***When does the message need to be sent?*** The message needs to be sent before the current lease is up for renewal.
5. ***What objections might be raised?*** Mrs. Chavez might not be ready to sell the property because of sentimental ties to it or financial concerns.
6. ***How should the message be delivered?*** A letter is optimal. She can share it with her children and attorney for advice. The letter will also give her time to process the idea.

Using the ideas from the template they filled in, as **Exhibit 4-14** shows, Gina and Joe created an outline that consists of three parts: an introduction, body, and closing. The **introduction** of a message typically informs the readers about the purpose of the document or attracts the interest of the reader. The **body** supports the message's purpose with details and explanations. The **closing** highlights the main ideas and presents any conclusions. It should contain the information you want the reader to remember. In some cases, the closing tells the reader what you will do, or it contains a "call to action," which is what the reader should do. The closing should also create goodwill.

The Direct Approach versus the Indirect Approach

The most common method for structuring business messages is the direct approach. The **direct approach** presents the main point of the message in the introduction so the reader quickly understands its purpose. Use the direct approach when the reader is interested in or excited about the main point you are making or is at least neutral about it.

Sometimes you will want to organize your information using the indirect approach. When you use an **indirect approach**, you wait to mention your main purpose

Exhibit 4-14
An Example of an Outline

Introduction
1. Thank Mrs. Chavez for being an honorable landlord. Remind her that she has mentioned she wants to move to be near her children and grandchildren.

Body
1. Explain the lease-to-own idea, which works as follows:
   - Gina and Joe pay an upfront fee of several thousand dollars, which gives them the opportunity to buy the property at specified price at a future date. A portion of their rent is applied to the property's down payment.
   - Mrs. Chavez is guaranteed Gina and Joe will pay their rent on time until she sells her property. She also won't have to market the property or pay a realtor's commission.
2. Tell Mrs. Chavez why they would be candidates to purchase the property:
   - They love the space and have always taken care of it, both inside and out.
   - They have money for a down payment and have been prequalified by a mortgage lender.
   - They have a successful record as business owners.
   - As young entrepreneurs, it is their dream to be owners, not renters.

Closing
1. Invite Mrs. Chavez to meet and discuss the idea by asking for a convenient date and time.
2. End with a positive note such as thanking Mrs. Chavez for being a good landlord.

in the body of the message and use your introduction to build up to the main point. The indirect approach is often used when bad or sensitive news must be delivered or when the reader might have a negative reaction to your main point, or be uninterested in it.

Notice in Exhibit 4-14 that the Donatellos took the indirect approach: They used the introduction to build up to their main idea and then placed their purpose for writing in the body of the message. They used the indirect approach because they did not know if Mrs. Chavez would respond negatively. However, they trusted that she would continue reading beyond the introduction because of their good relationship with her. **Exhibit 4-15** and **Exhibit 4-16** illustrate the direct approach and indirect approach, respectively.

Suppose the writer had opened the letter shown in Exhibit 4-16 by saying, "The Sunfarer model will be discontinued as of October 1," which is the direct approach. An opening such as this would likely elicit a negative reaction from the reader. Instead, the indirect approach gave the sender an opportunity to express Garden Umbrellas' appreciation for the customer and build up to the bad news being delivered.

Exhibit 4-15 The Direct Approach

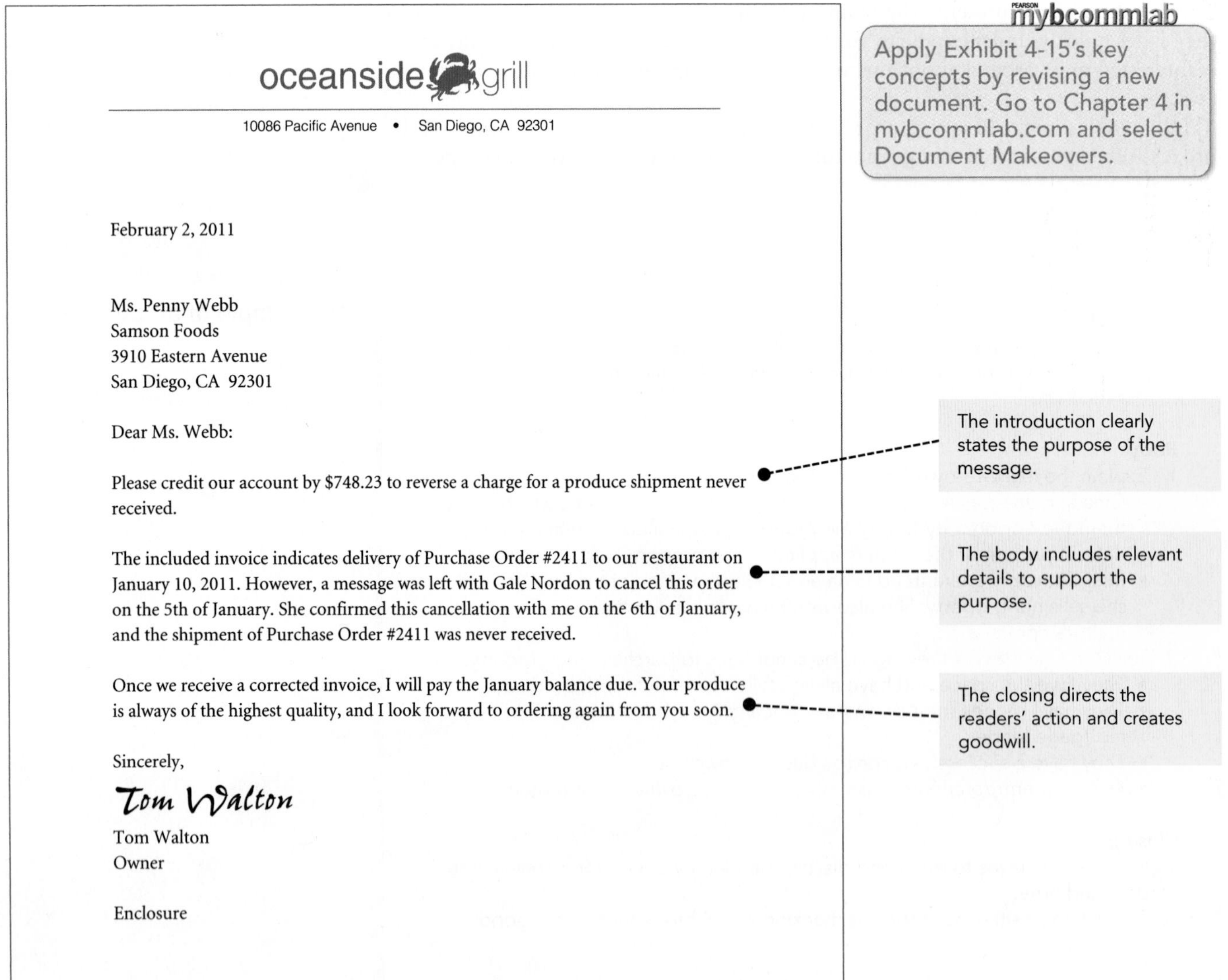

oceanside grill

10086 Pacific Avenue • San Diego, CA 92301

February 2, 2011

Ms. Penny Webb
Samson Foods
3910 Eastern Avenue
San Diego, CA 92301

Dear Ms. Webb:

Please credit our account by $748.23 to reverse a charge for a produce shipment never received.

The included invoice indicates delivery of Purchase Order #2411 to our restaurant on January 10, 2011. However, a message was left with Gale Nordon to cancel this order on the 5th of January. She confirmed this cancellation with me on the 6th of January, and the shipment of Purchase Order #2411 was never received.

Once we receive a corrected invoice, I will pay the January balance due. Your produce is always of the highest quality, and I look forward to ordering again from you soon.

Sincerely,

Tom Walton

Tom Walton
Owner

Enclosure

PEARSON mybcommlab
Apply Exhibit 4-15's key concepts by revising a new document. Go to Chapter 4 in mybcommlab.com and select Document Makeovers.

Exhibit 4-16 The Indirect Approach

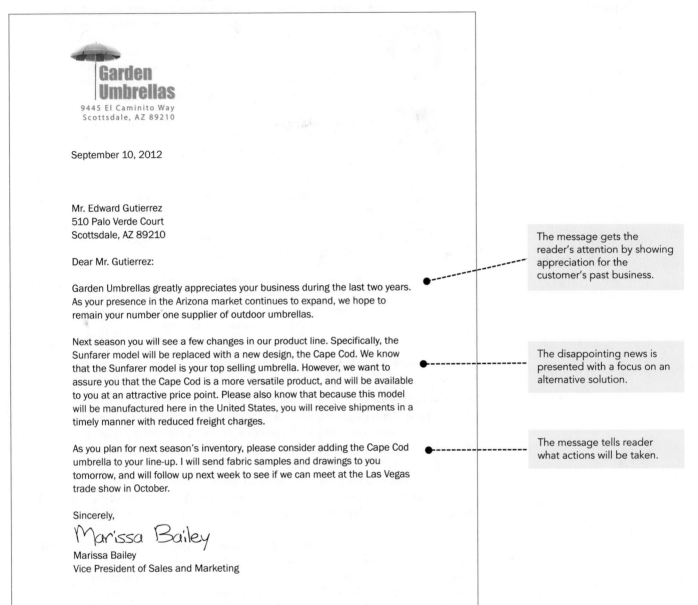

Garden Umbrellas
9445 El Caminito Way
Scottsdale, AZ 89210

September 10, 2012

Mr. Edward Gutierrez
510 Palo Verde Court
Scottsdale, AZ 89210

Dear Mr. Gutierrez:

Garden Umbrellas greatly appreciates your business during the last two years. As your presence in the Arizona market continues to expand, we hope to remain your number one supplier of outdoor umbrellas.

The message gets the reader's attention by showing appreciation for the customer's past business.

Next season you will see a few changes in our product line. Specifically, the Sunfarer model will be replaced with a new design, the Cape Cod. We know that the Sunfarer model is your top selling umbrella. However, we want to assure you that the Cape Cod is a more versatile product, and will be available to you at an attractive price point. Please also know that because this model will be manufactured here in the United States, you will receive shipments in a timely manner with reduced freight charges.

The disappointing news is presented with a focus on an alternative solution.

As you plan for next season's inventory, please consider adding the Cape Cod umbrella to your line-up. I will send fabric samples and drawings to you tomorrow, and will follow up next week to see if we can meet at the Las Vegas trade show in October.

The message tells reader what actions will be taken.

Sincerely,

Marissa Bailey

Marissa Bailey
Vice President of Sales and Marketing

5 How Can You Set Yourself Up to Be a Successful Writer?

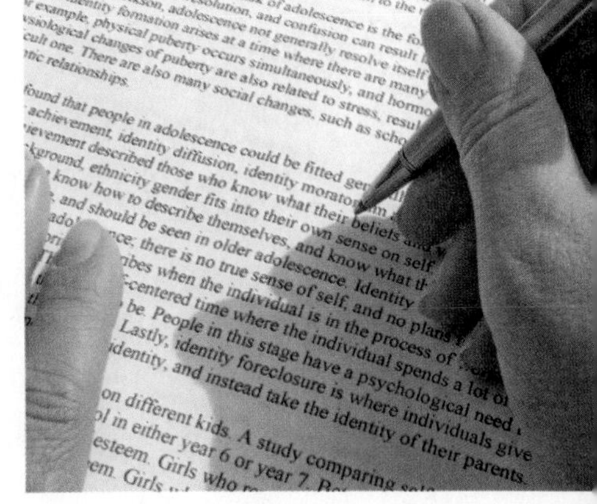

Once you have completed your research, organized your material, and decided upon the best structure for your message, it is time to start writing. Although some people jump into the process with no forethought or planning, other people procrastinate and linger in the planning stage for too long. If you procrastinate before writing, read through **Exhibit 4-17**, which contains some tips to help you get started.

Positioning yourself to be the best writer possible will help propel you forward in the business world. If you need to improve your basic writing skills, find a mentor. Consider visiting your college's writing center or asking a professor, an upperclassman, a family member, or counselor from your career center to read and critique your work on a regular basis. You will be amazed at the progress you can make with one-on-one support. If you can't find a mentor, sign up for additional writing classes. Even creative writing groups will help you develop skills you can transfer to the business arena.

Exhibit 4-17
Tips for Writing

- **Identify your best time of day for planning and writing**. Find the time of day when you write with the greatest ease. Many people claim that early in the morning when their minds aren't cluttered with the day's details is best. Others prefer late in the afternoon, after the barrage of phone calls and e-mails have subsided. Experiment to see when you're most productive and then schedule your writing projects accordingly.

- **Limit distractions**. Writing is more difficult when you're distracted. Find a quiet space. Shut your door. Turn off your cell phone and focus on your topic.

- **Break down your task**. Divide your work into smaller chunks—the opening, body, and closing we discussed—or sections, headings, paragraphs. Then tackle the task in increments. It is much easier to commit to completing a section of a proposal than to sit down with the intention of writing an entire proposal from start to finish.

- **End your day in the middle of an idea**. Some writers quit each session's writing in the middle of an idea. Knowing the direction in which your message is headed can make it easier to get started during the next writing session.

Another tip for improving your skills is to practice editing other people's writing. Get in the habit of asking yourself, "How could I rewrite this material to make it better?" Make it a game. Text messages, e-mails, and postings on social networking sites can give you ample opportunities to rewrite others' messages.

Try reading a business letter, putting it away, and then recreating it in your own words. Or consider writing a blog entry and then rewrite it from a different point of view. Experiment by composing an e-mail as if you were an intern, a mid-level manager, and a CEO, delivering the same message in all three instances. How does your writing change with each role you play?

Outside of practicing, nothing can help your writing more than reading. Study how the experts write by reading business magazines, trade magazines, newspapers, and company blog sites. Time invested in improving your abilities will never be wasted. According to a report released by the National Commission on Writing, "Writing appears to be a 'marker' attribute of high skill, high wage professional work."[11] Remember that writing well will open doors for you. It is one skill you can develop that will set you apart in the business world.

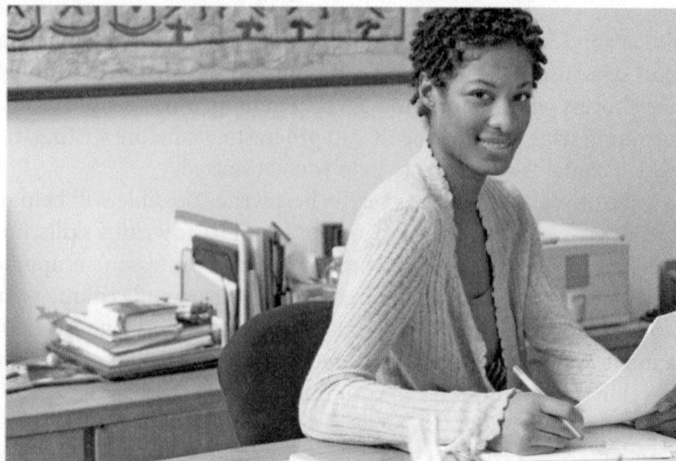

One way to become a better writer is by reading and editing other people's writing.

REAL INSIGHTS from a Seasoned Professional

Name: Joe Martin
Title: Co-Founder, Owner
Organizations: New Teacher University, Real World University, and the Academic Coaching Company
Location: Tallahassee, Florida

Dr. Joe Martin was raised in the projects of Miami (Liberty City), the son of a single parent who happened to be a teenaged, alcoholic mother. In high school, Martin was told he wasn't "college material" by educators and a local U.S. Navy recruiter. Undaunted, he decided that he didn't want to live in the projects the rest of his life. After watching several of his high-school friends die as a result of gang violence, Martin set his sights on college, which he knew would be his ticket out of a life of squalor. He enrolled at Okaloosa-Walton Jr. College and later transferred to the University of West Florida, where he earned his EdD in Curriculum Development. He has made it his life's work to help others realize their full potential. Moreover, he always envisioned his own success, which along with a lot of hard work, has allowed him to make his dreams happen.

Martin's entrepreneurial instincts began early. He owned a clothing store when he was 22, which he managed with his wife. He also ran a special events agency as well as worked for the both the federal and state government, including a stint with the Florida Governor's Office as the communications director for community service.

However, Martin knew, he would someday start a business teaching others about his own life lessons and success strategies. Today, he owns three such companies: New Teacher University, which is a teacher training company for K–12 teachers; Real World University, which helps students get the insights they need to succeed both in and out of the workplace; and the Academic Coaching Company, operated in conjunction with the author of this textbook, Carol Carter. The Academic Coaching Company teaches professors, teachers, principals, and school executives question-asking skills.

Martin is also one of the highest-paid speakers on the college and K–12 speech circuits. Annually, he addresses thousands of teachers, students, and undergraduates. In addition, he has authored or co-authored nine books, which he publishes and distributes himself. At 5'5" tall, he often jokes, "I'm a little guy with a big mouth." The truth is that his communication skills have been central to his success as an entrepreneur. He says he enjoys working for himself and would have it no other way.

When he prepares to write, Martin says he first considers his ultimate goal, and then asks himself what "power questions" will result in answers that lead his readers and audiences toward that goal. He then researches those answers to see if they are in line with what other successful people have used to achieve similar outcomes. "When you really think about it, success is never achieved in a vacuum or in isolation; it leaves clues," he says. "We just have to ask the right questions that will help us uncover those clues and then chart our own course."

Martin believes his job as a communicator and educator is to challenge his audiences to do one thing: "Think." He describes himself more as an "irritational speaker" rather than a "motivational" one. "If my words, whether on paper or in person don't make you a little uncomfortable, then I haven't done my job," says Martin. He continues, "No one will ever move out of their self-manufactured comfort zone until they become uncomfortable with the status quo, and that's my job: to irritate, educate, and then motivate people to take action."

Questions

1. To what does Martin attribute his success?
2. What entrepreneurial tasks required him to use his communication skills?
3. How does Martin prepare to write?

Source: Joe Martin in discussion with the author, June 2010.

Summary *Synthesize What You Have Learned*

1. Why is planning important for communicating business messages?

Planning your messages helps maximize the advantages of both written and oral communication while minimizing their limitations. Effective messages have a clearly defined purpose, are adapted for their audiences, and create goodwill. By taking the time to plan, you will be able to prepare messages that produce desired outcomes and pave the way for positive business relationships.

2. What are the six questions you should ask as you prepare business messages?

A well-prepared communicator considers the following who, what, where, when, why, and how questions before composing messages ranging from voice mails to detailed annual reports.

1. ***Who are you in the organization?*** Consider both your role in your job as well as your role as a representative of your company.
2. ***What is the desired outcome of your communication?*** Look beyond your basic purpose for communicating and ask yourself what the best possible reaction and outcome to your message could be; in other words, what do you need the receiver to do? Then prepare your message accordingly.
3. ***Where do you want your message to land?*** Separate this question into two parts. Where do you *need* it to land and where do you *want* it to land? Prepare for both purposes so your message goes the distance.
4. ***When is the best time for your message to be sent and to be received?*** Consider this aspect from both the sender and the reader's point of view. Strategically planning the timing of your message can affect the outcome you desire.
5. ***Why might objections be raised?*** If you can anticipate your readers' reactions and address them up front, your communication will appear well-thought-out and prepared.
6. ***How will you distribute your message?*** Careful consideration of the best medium for delivering your message will ensure that it has the greatest impact.

3. When should you use oral versus written communication for business messages?

Use oral communication when you need quick answers to a question or need to respond immediately to any concerns, objections, or questions that stem from the message. Oral communication provides an opportunity for interaction and immediate feedback from both verbal and nonverbal cues.

Use written communication when you need legal documentation of your exchange, are trying to relate complex information with fact and figures, or need time to plan how best to deliver your message. Writing things also helps clarify who is responsible for what, documents working relationships and understandings, and prevents misunderstandings. Finally, written communication also allows you to emotionally distance yourself from a situation when you need to communicate objectively. In general, writing offers more control, whereas oral communication provides more flexibility.

4. How do you gather information and organize a written business message?

Methods such as brainstorming, making lists, and mind mapping help generate ideas for any given writing task. When additional information is necessary, perform informal research by talking with your supervisor or colleagues, questioning your audience, or reviewing company documents and files. Conduct more formal research by looking into both primary and secondary sources, as well as conducting and analyzing surveys and experiments.

Once you collect all the information you need for your writing task, use an outline to organize the material. At this point, determine whether your message should be structured in a direct or indirect manner, depending on the receptivity of your audience.

5. How can you set yourself up to be a successful writer?

Although planning is critical for effective writing, you eventually have to put your pen to the paper or your fingers to the keyboard. Getting started can be a struggle, even for the most accomplished writers. Tips for jumpstarting your writing include finding the time of day when you write the best and setting this time aside for your writing projects; limiting distractions; breaking down longer writing projects into smaller sections; ending your day's writing knowing exactly where you will begin the next day.

Writing is a skill that can be developed. Rewriting your own work, as well as other messages you encounter, will help you hone your skills. Finally, read. Seek out good writing in books, professional blogs, and magazines in order to study how the experts write.

Know It *Reflect, Respond, and Express*

Build Your Critical Thinking Skills

Critical Thinking Questions

1. How do you define a purpose, create goodwill, and adapt your message for an audience during an everyday business transaction, such as making a deposit at the bank or checking out groceries? Do you invest the time to truly interact with the people with whom you come in contact? How do the people with whom you interact respond to you? What impression does it leave you?
2. To analyze the role of record keeping and its importance in business processes, compile a list of all the items you need to file your income taxes every spring. How many documents do you need to best prepare your taxes? What are the penalties for not filing by April 15? How does planning affect the process of filing your taxes?
3. Imagine you are a store manager who needs to communicate the store's new holiday hours to your employees. The hours will change from 10 A.M.–9 P.M. to 9 A.M.–10 P.M. in a week, so you need to quickly convey the information. What method of communication do you use? For what objections should you prepare? Write a brief explanation of how you would convey your message clearly.
4. How does time of day affect your focus on writing? What time of day works best for you?
5. Describe ways you organize your writing tasks. Do you break them up into smaller chunks? Do you write in a straightforward or linear fashion, or do you approach different aspects of the task at different times?
6. What are a few ways you limit distractions when you write? What is your environment like when you write?

Critical Thinking Scenario

Remember Catherine from the earlier chapter? She won the Young Entrepreneur's Business Plan contest. Imagine she successfully secured a round of venture capital funding, convinced five private investors to put up capital funds, and hired a team of technology experts to launch her e-zine, *Youth Travel International.*

Two weeks before her e-zine is ready to go live, she receives a letter from someone claiming that he had the idea for an Internet-based magazine featuring teen travelers. Although he has not yet launched his site, he charges Catherine with stealing his concept. Catherine contacts her attorney, who suggests she write him a letter before pursuing legal action. He tells her to explain that her idea came out of a college writing project from several years ago and inform him of the proper legal steps she's taken to start her company.

Questions

1. Take a moment to reflect:
    - How should Catherine prepare to write this letter?
    - What information should she gather before writing?
    - Who should be copied on her correspondence?
2. Your job is to help Catherine prepare for this written communication by considering these questions and using the planning grid on page 90. You don't need to write the letter, only identify the information she needs to gather, and answer the questions she needs to consider to write the most effective letter possible for this situation.

Write It *Draft, Revise, and Finalize*

Create Your Own Success Story

1. The following scenarios each require written communication. Your job is to prepare to write for each scenario. Use the planning grid on page 90 to make an action plan for writing as you consider all the elements for crafting the best correspondence possible. List your responses to the questions as you plan to write a letter for each scenario. The purpose of this exercise is to *prepare* for the writing, *not* to actually write the letters.

Scenario 1: You have learned that a new company has formed in your city that operates an online cycling equipment store. As a cycling enthusiast, you would love to be an intern for this company and gain valuable business experience. You decide to write the president a letter asking for an internship.

Scenario 2: You're employed as assistant to the director of an organization that has just been nominated for the "Best of the City: Innovation Award." Your boss asks you to draft a letter to the board of directors announcing this prestigious recognition.

Scenario 3: You just secured your patent for a one-of-a-kind squirt gun. You hope to enlist the support of a successful financer and entrepreneur in your community to mentor you as you set up your company. You decide to send him a letter introducing yourself and asking for a meeting.

2. Select a word or phrase related to your major or future profession. Perform a key word or subject search on the Internet using a search engine or your library's Web site and choose one Web site or article that sparks your interest. Analyze the source's credibility using the following questions: Is the material supported by references? Is the material well written and authoritative? Who is the author? When was the source written or last updated? Write a short memo to your class with the source information and your analysis of its credibility.
3. As the landlord of an apartment complex, you must write a letter to your 25 tenants explaining a raise in rent due to an increase in the complex's property taxes. Write two versions of a letter, one with the direct approach and one with the indirect approach. Analyze the differences between the two versions and choose which one would be best in this situation. Write a short summary at the end to explain your choice.
4. Write a short explanation for your daily activities over the time period of a week but change the times you write it every day. After you write at various times for a week, what time do you find works best for you?
5. Find a mentor to help read your writing on a regular basis. What communication method did you use to request the help of your chosen mentor? Prepare a short description of the person and explain the method you used to request his or her help.
6. Rewrite one of the e-mails you received in your school e-mail account during the last several weeks, either using a direct approach or indirect approach depending upon the approach used by the original e-mail. Bring both the original e-mail and the revised copy to class to discuss the similarities and differences.
7. What information should be included in a voice mail or answering machine greeting? Write a brief script of what you would say, listing the information that would help you to leave an effective voice-mail message.
8. Explain why all employees must have strong writing abilities. List the types of documents you will have to compose in your future careers.

Speak It *Discuss, Listen, and Understand*

Build Your Leadership and Teamwork Skills

1. Divide into teams of four. Your team will act as a start-up company preparing to launch a new product or service into the marketplace.
   a. First, come up with your team's imaginary product or service.
   b. Once you have identified your company's purpose, write a mission statement for your organization and present it to your class.
   c. Then poll the members of your class by asking the following questions:
      - Is the mission statement clear?
      - Has any important information about what the company is or what it does been left out?
      - Based on the information in the mission statement, would the people in your class want to do business with the company? Why or why not?
2. Find your college's mission statement, which is commonly posted on its Web site. Analyze how it serves as a compass for your institution. How does it summarize the college's pur-

pose and goals? In groups or as a class, discuss how the mission statement demonstrates a clear understanding of the purpose of the institution.

3. In groups or as a class, imagine you are proposing a new parking deck for your institution's campus. What research would you conduct to gather enough evidence for the need and cost of a new deck? What audiences would read your proposal? Who would be your primary audience? Secondary audience? Who would make the ultimate decision to accept the proposal or not?

4. Prepare a short oral explanation of your major and the reasons you chose it. Communicate the information in an impromptu speech to your classmates. What assumptions do you make or not make about your audience as you prepare? Do you share the same or similar majors as your classmates? How much background information does your audience need? What questions do you anticipate them to have? Consider your audience and anticipate their reactions as you prepare your explanation.

Do It *Document Your Success Track Record*

Build Your e-Portfolio

Setting professional goals and identifying core values will help shape your job search. Writing a personal mission statement is a concrete way to express these goals and core values. This statement can help you chart a successful course for your career, just as mission statements help start-up companies evolve into highly functioning businesses.

1. As you prepare to write your personal mission statement, reflect on the following questions:
   - What brings you joy and satisfaction?
   - What skills do you hope to acquire?
   - What qualities do you wish to embrace?
   - What goals do you plan to strive for?
   - What accomplishments do you wish to attain?
   - What values do you wish to live by?
2. Now write a three-to-five-sentence personal mission statement. Keep it simple, clear, and direct. Know that personal mission statements may change down the road. But having this statement in your e-portfolio now will serve as a rudder when you consider different career options. In the years to come it will offer you a snapshot of where you were at this moment in time.

Business in Action

Turning Blogging into a Business

When you meet Gia Lipa you realize one thing very quickly—she is not a stereotypical engineer. Lipa is creative, outgoing, and enthusiastic. She is the very definition of an entrepreneur.

At 43, she is two years into her successful new career as author of two personal finance blogs, "The Digerati Life," and "The Smarter Wallet." So, how did a former database guru and Java developer become a successful blogger?

In the mid-1980s, Lipa came to the United States from the Philippines to study computer science at the University of California, Berkeley. After graduation, she worked as a database expert and Java developer for a number of Silicon Valley giants and small dot-com start-ups. Working for start-ups fostered her entrepreneurial spirit and ignited a personal interest in financial management.

Then Lipa discovered blogging. Many of her friends were doing it and she was curious. She decided to write a blog for fun. And what did she write about? Finances. Blogging for fun turned into a full-fledged obsession. She was hooked. "It was like a compulsion. I had to say something every day," she says.

Initially, Lipa didn't know who her audience was or what they cared about, so she wrote for her own personal fulfillment. But as her audience grew and responded to her posts, she learned more about them and the topics they liked. She began thinking about the impact her words had on readers and developed a friendly, conversational writing style.

Lipa has developed a successful routine that allows her to write every day: She jots down ideas, free-writes, and then organizes and edits her work. In the morning, her creative "right brain" is in charge. She lets her mind wander as she does chores and runs errands, considering possible blog topics for the week. In the afternoon she writes down the topics, prioritizes them, and decides which one will be the day's post.

Thereafter, Lipa's analytical "left brain" kicks in. She begins researching her topic. Once she has her research in place, she writes quickly, trying to get everything down. She then organizes the information and does light editing. In the evening, she does her heavy editing and publishes her post.

Does she ever suffer from writer's block? Not often. But when she does, she's prepared. Lipa writes ideas in a journal, day and night. When a day arrives that she can't think of a thing to write, she has her journal to fall back on. And if that fails her, she can find inspiration in magazines, newspapers, articles on the Internet, or other people's blogs. Taking walks, breathing deeply, and doing yoga also helps.

Lipa believes the following skills and talents are essential in her line of work: an innate love of writing and strong language skills—so you connect with people through your writing; the ability to research—because you don't always know all the facts; marketing skills—so you can persuade people; the ability to multitask—because you're often working on more than one topic; and lastly, an entrepreneurial spirit—so you can take risks.

What's Lipa's advice for someone who's considering blogging for a living?

1. Write about something you enjoy, something you're passionate about. And think about your audience and the impact your words will have on them.
2. Be realistic. Do not expect to make a lot of money at first. Instead, expect to learn about your audience, your subject, and yourself. Adopt the attitude that "I'm going to have fun and see what happens."
3. Treat your blog as a hobby, not a job. Make daily posts for three months and then assess whether you still enjoy what you're doing. Writing a blog is a big commitment, and some people find that after a trial period, it's really not for them.

Lipa's journey from software developer to professional blogger has been a journey of self-discovery. She has learned that she is not just an analytical, problem-solving engineer—she is a very creative writer. She believes that "You can do anything with determination, drive, and interest." Indeed, she is a real-life example of the saying "Do what you love and the money will follow."

Questions

1. As a blogger, what does Lipa ask and expect of her audience?
2. Lipa follows a routine: mornings she looks for ideas, afternoons she researches and writes, and evenings she revises and edits. What routines help you write?
3. If you were to write a daily blog, what would be your topic of interest?

Source: Gia Lipa in discussion with the author, June 2010.

Key Terms

Adapted for the audience. Involves knowing your audience and adjusting your message accordingly. *(p. 81)*

Body. The largest section of the message. Here you identify and discuss points you must make to achieve your purpose. *(p. 99)*

Brainstorm. The process of capturing as many ideas about a given topic without censoring your ideas. *(p. 94)*

Chain of command. An organization structure that determines the communication channels for sending and receiving messages from supervisors and those reporting to you. *(p. 83)*

Closing. An element at the end of a message that tells your reader what you will do or what the reader should do. *(p. 99)*

Direct approach. An approach that presents the main point of the message at the beginning so readers understand its purpose as quickly as possible. *(p. 99)*

Flat chain of command. An organization structure that gives staff members easier access to their superiors because there are fewer levels of hierarchy above them. *(p. 83)*

Formal research. Defined ways to gather information for longer, more complex writing projects. See *qualitative* and *quantitative research.* *(p. 96)*

Free-write. A method of writing whereby you write whatever comes to your mind without mentally censoring your ideas *(p. 95)*

Gatekeeper. Someone who controls or monitors access to someone else—usually an administrative staff member who screens phone calls and e-mails. *(p. 87)*

Indirect approach. An approach that waits to mention the main purpose until the body of the message, and uses the introduction to "build up" to the main point. *(p. 99)*

Informal research. Informal ways to gather information, such as asking questions, referring to company files, and talking with colleagues, for smaller or daily writing tasks. *(p. 96)*

Introduction. Information at the beginning of a message that informs readers about the purpose of the document. *(p. 99)*

Mind map. An idea-generating device whereby you write a main idea in a circle. As new ideas are triggered from this idea, you draw offshoots to record them. *(p. 95)*

Mission statement. A statement that usually consists of several sentences summarizing the purpose and goals of a company, while highlighting its overarching philosophies and values. *(p. 85)*

Objections. Negative reactions to a message. *(p. 88)*

Outline. A guide that lists the topics you plan to write in the order you plan to write them. *(p. 98)*

Primary sources. Information you gather firsthand. *(p. 96)*

Purpose. Involves knowing why you are communicating and what you want the communication to achieve. *(p. 81)*

Qualitative research. Informal, firsthand surveys of small groups of people. *(p. 96)*

Quantitative research. Formal surveys of large groups of individuals, the results of which are statistically calculated. *(p. 96)*

Secondary sources. Information that was already gathered by others and is already published or accessible. It might include information in databases, libraries, trade books, or other reference material. *(p. 96)*

Vertical chain of command. An organization structure with numerous levels of hierarchy, which can make it harder for staff members, managers, and executives to access and communicate with one another. *(p. 83)*

Review Questions *Test Yourself*

1. What three aspects create an effective business message?
2. What tools can you use to define the purpose of an effective message?
3. In what ways can you adapt your message to your audience?
4. Why is it important to know your role and company when you communicate?
5. What is the difference between a primary audience and a secondary audience?
6. How can preparing for objections help your message achieve its goals?
7. What are the different methods of oral communication? When is which type the most appropriate?
8. What are some disadvantages to oral communication? What methods of written communication can eliminate the disadvantages?
9. When is writing your best option for sending your messages?
10. What are some examples of methods for generating ideas? Which one have you had the most experience with?
11. What is the difference between primary and secondary sources?
12. List the differences between using the direct approach and the indirect approach for messages.
13. What techniques can be used to create goodwill in written communication? How can they solidify business relationships?

Grammar Review *Mastering Accuracy*

Adjectives

Section I

Each of the following sentences contains one or more common errors in word usage, grammar, or style. Identify the errors. If you have trouble finding the errors, review Section 1.1.3. in the handbook (Appendix D) at the back of this textbook.

1. There are at least 36 rules to remember for our next meeting in Austin-Texas.
2. You will not get lost if you continue North-West on Decatur Rd.
3. I sometimes miss my ex supervisor's freespirited-like demeanor.
4. Between Dennis and Steven, Dennis is the richest of the two.
5. Stacey has two beautiful apartments in Cleveland and Chicago, respectively, but I think her condo in Malibu is the nicer building.
6. Jason is the more stronger of the two managers.
7. Our company resort in the Bahamas was all inclusive and included my favorite dessert every night for dinner: chocolate covered cashew-sundaes.
8. We interviewed a flaky candidate today and I doubt we will give her a chance for the job.

Section II

On a separate sheet of paper, rewrite the following sentences so they are clearer, more professional sounding, grammatically correct, and goodwill oriented.

1. I know Melissa would not take your stupid and foolish advice.
2. You're delusional if you think this is going to work.
3. Your suggestion is worthless.
4. I can't believe you were so faint-hearted at the autopsy!
5. Carol's insipid contractual rhetoric needs to be fixed.
6. It is my request that you please leave me alone.
7. The attitudes of the employees really suck.
8. Hurry up and e-mail that janitor who fixes our stuff.
9. Jeffrey's cubicle is a mess! I just can't see how he gets anything done with that junk in there.
10. No one except the folks up top ever reads these boring, wordy memos.

Extra Resources *Tools You Can Use*

Books

- Cleland, Jane. *Business Writing for Results: How to Create a Sense of Urgency and Increase Response to All of Your Business Communications.* New York: McGraw-Hill, 2003.
- Lindsell-Roberts, Sheryl. *Writing Successful Business Documents: Write It So They'll Read It.* Boston: Houghton Mifflin Company, 2003.

Web Sites

- *Bacal and Associates Strategic Planning Methods Models and Planning Skills*
- *The Business Writing Center*

Video

- "The Writing Workshop Video Clips," *The Writing Workshop (online).*

"The difference between the right word and almost the right word is the difference between lightning and the lightning bug." —**Mark Twain,** American author and humorist

CHAPTER

5

Writing, Revising, and Editing Messages

>>> **Carmen and Arturo Aquino** lived in a small apartment until their baby, Corazon, came along. The next thing the couple knew, they were in the market for a home. They bought a small house in a not-so-great part of town but felt proud of their purchase. They put a lot of time and energy into fixing up the house, and then the bottom dropped out of their world. Arturo lost his job. Unfortunately for them, they had been talked into a sub-prime loan when they bought the house, and the interest rate was skyrocketing. It became more and more difficult to make their mortgage payments, and it looked like they would lose their home to foreclosure.

Carmen and Arturo decided to write a hardship letter to their lender, explaining their circumstances and asking if their payments could be reduced or delayed to prevent foreclosure. They did their research on the Internet and visited a local Home Buyers Assistance (HBA) representative in their city. Then they drafted their letter, reviewed, and revised it. Next they asked their HBA representative to review it because she better understood what mortgage companies needed. Finally, they put in the representative's comments and submitted the letter. Ultimately, the mortgage lender revised their mortgage payment and schedule. This gave Carmen and Arturo the breathing room they needed while Arturo searched for a new job.

LEARNING OBJECTIVE QUESTIONS

1. What preparations will make your writing powerful?
2. How can words, sentences, paragraphs, and tone be combined to create a compelling message?
3. How can reviewing and revising your draft affect the impact of your message?
4. How can getting feedback result in a positive response to your message?

PEARSON mybcommlab Access interactive videos, simulations, sample documents, document makeovers, and assessment quizzes in Chapter 5 of **mybcommlab.com** for mastery of this chapter's objectives.

Carmen and Arturo >>>

Have you ever faced a writing assignment and said, "I have a lot of good ideas, but I don't know where to start?" Or, perhaps thought, "I know what I want to say, but something goes wrong when I try to write it down"?

You might think that good writing is a mysterious talent that only a few people have. Not so. Good writing is more about practice than it is about innate talent. Yes, some people find it easier than others to express themselves with words. But in the end, to be a good writer, you have to write and rewrite. The more you write, the better you'll become. After reading this chapter, you will be able to write effective e-mails, memos, notes, and other documents.

This chapter features examples from the real estate industry, which is expected to grow 11 percent between now and 2016.[1] Writing and revising messages are an everyday part of working in the real estate business. The industry requires you to constantly think of better ways to communicate in order to sell or lease properties and deal effectively with buyers, sellers, renters, suppliers, vendors, banks, and investors.

An area of real estate you might be interested in now and in the future is the student-housing market. "Many students and recent college graduates are employed in our field," says Dan Oltersdorf, the president of Campus Advantage, Inc., a student-housing management firm with operations throughout the United States. "Of my 900 employees, I have over 300 student staff members who are getting tremendous professional experience while in college. We work to groom these individuals to move up in the company and stay in the industry." The student-housing market is also a somewhat recession-resistant area of the economy, he notes, because during recessions, more people tend to enroll in colleges and need a place to live.

Campus Advantage's leasing agents constantly engage in written communication: They follow up on Internet leads from property owners and prospective renters by e-mail, post Facebook and Twitter messages, and write notifications to current residents and their parents. The agents also write ad copy for Web sites and often publish resident newsletters. "Writing skills are obviously critical to their success on the job and to upward mobility," explains Oltersdorf, noting that communicating via social media has become a driving force in his business. For example, sites such as MindMeister are teaching real estate professionals and investors how to communicate via social networks to close more real estate deals.

❶ What Preparations Will Make Your Writing Powerful?

Good basic writing skills are the foundation upon which you can build any successful written message. Without this firm foundation, it won't matter how educated or clever you are—people won't understand your messages. In fact, poor writing skills are likely to cause your readers to draw the wrong conclusions about you. If your writing is awkward and clumsy, readers might think you are disorganized and don't know your topic very well. Poor grammar and spelling may make people think you're uneducated or careless. Worse yet, readers might think you don't care about what you're writing, so why should they? Good writing is powerful. The better you are at it, the better you will be at your job, and the more respect you will get from your colleagues and managers.

In this chapter, we will cover the first three steps in the writing process: writing, reviewing and revising, and getting feedback to edit the message. In Chapter 6, we will discuss the remaining steps: designing and formatting the message, proofreading, and distributing it. **Exhibit 5-1** shows all the steps in the process.

You might not go through all of these steps with every document you write. A short e-mail to a coworker, for example, is only likely to involve writing the message, editing it, and sending it.

From the Outline to the Draft

Perhaps you have heard people say that they hate to write. But have you ever heard people say they hate to think? Probably not. Writing is really just an extension of thinking. It is the

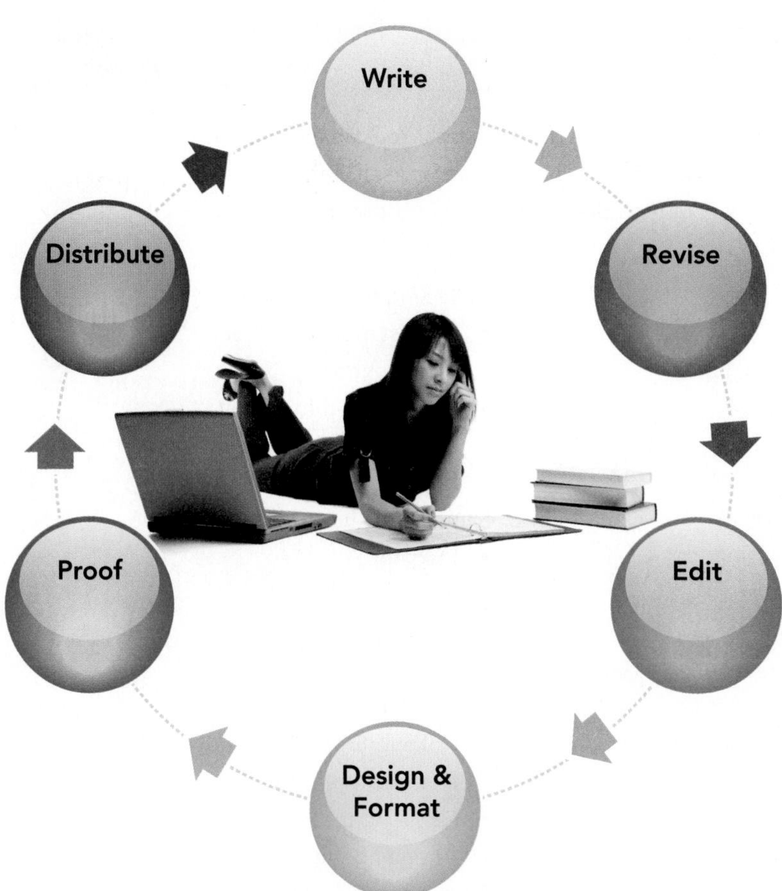

Exhibit 5-1
The Writing Process

process of capturing your thoughts, organizing them, and putting them on paper. As you learned in Chapter 4, good writing starts with a good blueprint or an outline. An architect would never build a house without a plan, and you shouldn't write anything without some kind of an outline.

Use your outline as a starting point for whatever you plan to write. Consider developing it further into an **annotated outline**. An annotated outline is more than just a bare-bones outline. It's an outline with additional notes, quotes, and reference information that help you "fill in the blanks." Sometimes it contains the actual introduction and closing because those sections help define the contents. An annotated outline is not written to be read by your audience; it's written for you, so all the information you need is in one place.

Regardless of whether you are a fast writer or a slow writer, give yourself permission to write a less-than-perfect first draft.

Exhibit 5-2 shows an annotated outline for a book titled *How to Sell Your Own Home . . . And Live to Tell about It,* which is designed for first-time home sellers. The original outline contained only the words "Introduction," "Body," and "Closing," and then was fleshed out from there.

Some writers prefer using index cards to create their annotated outlines. If they want to change the order of their outlines, they do so by simply changing the order of their cards.

Writing your first draft becomes a lot easier once you have created an annotated outline. Your first draft will generally be roughly written, meaning it may have spelling or grammar mistakes, and it may even be missing information. However, it should flow logically from topic to topic, and address most of the information in your annotated outline.

If your annotated outline is extremely detailed, you may only have to connect its points to make the information flow so it becomes a first draft. If your annotated outline is more sparse, you will need to

Exhibit 5-2
An Annotated Outline

How to Sell Your Own Home ... *And Live to Tell about It!*

You might think that selling a house is a daunting task. You can either work with a reat estate agent or decide to sell your home yourself. There are pros and cons to both options, but regardless of what you choose, the steps below will help you get ready. *Introduction*

1. Preparing the inside
   - Structural repairs
   - Paint and furnishings
2. Preparing the outside
   - Structural repairs
   - Paint
3. Preparing the yard
   - Curb appeal
   - Garden and lawn
4. Studying the market
   - Assessing current home prices
   - Assessing your home's value
5. Creating a flyer
   - Photos
   - Specifications
   - Layout and text
6. Networking
   - Mortgage companies and brokers
   - First-time home buyer classes
   - Friends, family, and associates
7. Collecting the paperwork
   - Earnest money contract
   - Sales contract
   - Home walk-through list
   - List of helpful tips for buyers
8. Showing the house
   - Staging
   - Advertising
   - Holding the open house
   - Following-up
9. Making the sale
   - Holding the walk-through and identifying fixes
   - Finalizing the contract
   - Attending the closing
10. Ending the journey
    - Getting ready
    - Moving out
    - Handing over the keys

Body

After you complete all of these exercises, you should be ready to sell your home. *Closing*

fill in the blanks between outline topics, jot down additional ideas for each point, and put in placeholders like "???" or "XXX" for items you can't think of at the moment.

Different people have different writing processes. You might prefer to write your first draft as quickly as possible to keep up with your thoughts. This is called free-writing. Or, you might prefer to write more slowly and deliberately, thinking through each sentence before you write it. Whatever your method, remember that it is your first draft. It does not have to be perfect. It just needs to be done.

Writer's block refers to a state of mind in which you believe you cannot think of anything to write. The truth is, you can always think of something to write. The actual block is caused by the anxiety that what you write won't be good enough. Eliminate the worry by giving yourself permission to write a not-so-great first draft knowing that you will rewrite the copy several times until it's good. Writing anything, although it might not immediately turn out the way you want it to, is better than writing nothing at all.

❷ How Can Words, Sentences, Paragraphs, and Tone Be Combined to Create a Compelling Message?

If an outline is the blueprint for writing, then words, sentences, paragraphs, and tone are the bricks and mortar. They help you build your message. The material to come contains a number of guidelines to keep in mind as you work with your "bricks and mortar" to build your first draft.

Choose Your Words Wisely

Use Positive Words

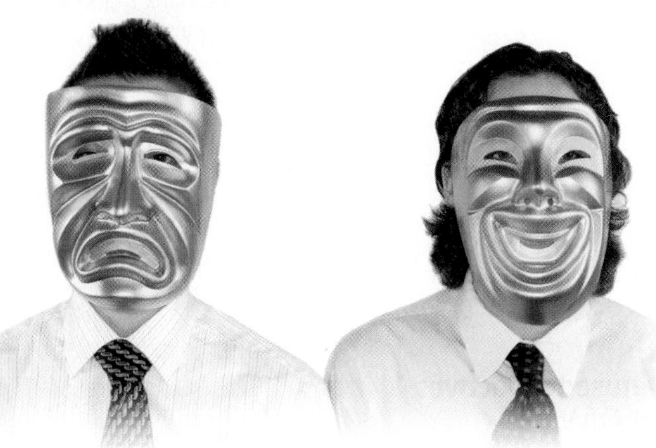

Positive words help put the reader in the right frame of mind to accept your message and act on it. Positive words also build goodwill. Negative words have the opposite effect. They increase the reader's resistance to your message and goals and erode goodwill. For example, imagine you were in the process of purchasing your first home and made an offer on a small townhouse. The real estate agent sent you a note letting you know that the owner rejected your offer. Which of the following messages would you rather receive from the real estate agent?

Negatively Worded Message	Positively Worded Message
I am sorry to tell you that the seller rejected your offer. She felt it was far below market price. I can show you another townhouse, but it has only 1-1/2 bathrooms instead of 2.	The seller seriously considered your offer but decided to accept a higher offer. I have another motivated seller with a townhouse in your price range and your preferred location. It has 2 bedrooms and 1-1/2 bathrooms, and I can show it to you anytime this week.

Both messages tell the potential buyer that the offer was rejected. However, you will be more motivated to call the real estate agent and set up an appointment to see the other townhouse after reading the positively worded message.

Use Powerful Words

Avoid using weak terms. Use nouns and verbs that convey real power. **Exhibit 5-3** illustrates the difference between weak phrases and powerful words. In addition, people often use nouns when they should use verbs. Nouns that end in "–ment," "-ion," and "–al" are more powerful rewritten as verbs. See **Exhibit 5-4** for some examples.

Exhibit 5-3
Weak versus Powerful Words

Weak Phrase	Powerful Word
provide assistance	assist
take into consideration	consider
brilliant scientist	genius
huge house	mansion

Exhibit 5-4
Weak Nouns versus Strong Verbs

Weak Word	Strong Verb
The loan officer provided **assistance**.	The loan officer assisted us. –OR- The loan officer **helped** us.
We made the **decision** to buy the house.	We **decided** to buy the house.
The bank made a **referral** to an excellent appraiser.	The bank **referred** us to an excellent appraiser.

Avoid Overusing Adverbs and Adjectives

Avoid overusing adjectives and adverbs like the ones in **Exhibit 5-5,** which can result in cluttered writing. ("Very" is one of the commonly overused modifiers.) Use exactly the right word instead of the wrong word with too many modifiers.

Exhibit 5-5
Overused Adjectives and Adverbs

Too Many Adverbs or Adjectives	Improved Copy
ran really fast	raced
walked slowly	lumbered
very, very angry	enraged
really terrible	horrific

Use Bias-Free Language

Avoid words and phrases that needlessly or unfairly categorize people in ways related to their genders, races, ethnicities, ages, or disabilities.

- ***Gender bias:*** Avoid sexist language by using the same terms for both men and women. For example, don't refer to a woman as a congresswoman and a man as a congressman. Instead refer to both of them as representatives or members of Congress. Also, avoid using only male pronouns, such as "he," "him," or "his." An easy way to do this is to make your subjects plural. For example, use "they," "them," or "theirs." You can also alternate "he" with "she," using both throughout your document. Or, you can use "he or she" if it doesn't sound too awkward. Some writers prefer using the word "you" to avoid the entire problem.

  If you don't know the gender of the person you are writing about, don't refer to him or her as they or them. For example, suppose you do not know whether the real estate agent you are meeting is a man or a woman, so you erroneously write:

  The real estate agent is supposed to arrive at 3:00 P.M. I will talk to them *at that time.*

  This sentence is incorrect. *Real estate agent* is singular; *them* is plural. Instead, you should write:

  The real estate agent is supposed to arrive at 3:00 P.M. I will talk to him or her *at that time.* See **Exhibit 5-6** for more examples of how gender-bias can be corrected.

- ***Racial and ethnic bias:*** Avoid identifying people by race or ethnic origin unless that information is relevant to your message.
- ***Age bias:*** Avoid mentioning the age of a person unless it is relevant to your message.
- ***Disability bias:*** Avoid using terms that label a person's disabilities unless they are relevant to your message. As you learned in Chapter 3, "put the person first and the disabil-

Gender-Biased Language	Improved Copy
A first-time **homebuyer** is often so proud to own a home that **he** feels like **his** home is the best on the block.	First-time **homebuyers** are often so proud to own homes that **they** feel like **their** homes are the best on the block. -or- A first-time **homebuyer** is often so proud to own a home that **he or she** feels like it is the best on the block. -or- As a first-time **homebuyer**, **you will** be so proud to own your home, **you will** feel like **it** is the best on the block.
The model home has an oversized bathtub constructed of **man-made** marble.	The model home contains a bathtub made of **faux** marble.
When you talk to the manager at the title company, make sure **he** understands your concerns. If the manager isn't there, ask the **receptionist** if **she** knows when the manager will return.	When you talk to the manager at the title company, make sure **he or she** understands your concerns. If the manager is not there, ask the **person at the front desk** when the manager will return.

Exhibit 5-6
Correcting Gender-Biased Language

ity second" and avoid derogatory terms such as crippled and handicapped. Avoid calling attention to someone's physical appearance (either attractive or unattractive) in any business message you write.

Avoid Slang Words, Unknown Acronyms, Jargon, and Idioms

Acronyms are abbreviations that contain the first letters of the words involved and are pronounced as a word. **Exhibit 5-7a** contains some examples of acronyms used in the real estate market and how they can be eliminated.

If you must use an acronym, spell it out the first time you use it. The following is an example:

> If you are a real estate agent with a frequently accessed Web site, make sure to use an ISP (Internet service provider) that provides broadband Internet and has friendly technical-support people.

Jargon is language that's particular to a culture, profession, or group. For example, a lawyer might tell his assistant, "I've got *depo* in a few minutes," which means, "I have a deposition in a few minutes." Jargon often consists of acronyms. Using jargon is hard to avoid in many industries. If you know your audience members well enough, you might decide they will understand your jargon. Otherwise, ordinary words and simple explanations are best. Likewise, avoid idioms. **Idioms** are expressions that mean something other

Abbreviation	Improved Copy
ARM	adjustable-rate mortgage
FDR	formal dining room
MLS	multiple listing service
HVAC	heating, ventilation, and air conditioning

Exhibit 5-7a
Examples of Acronyms

Exhibit 5-7b
Examples of Idioms

Idiom	Improved Copy
boot camp	basic course, class, seminar, session
cutting edge, bleeding edge	innovative, new
keep an eye out	watch
left in the dust	outpaced
lion's share	majority

Exhibit 5-7c
Examples of "Text-lish"

Text-Message Term	
BTW	by the way
LOL	laughing out loud
OMG	oh my gosh
TTYL	talk to you later

than the actual words being used. They are usually specific to a certain language or culture. **Exhibit 5-7b** contains some examples of idioms and how they can be eliminated. Nonnative English speakers are often confused by the jargon of other languages.

In business messages, do not use text-message-like terms, which is sometimes referred to as "text-lish." (See **Exhibit 5-7c** for some examples.) It can be difficult to understand and undermine your professionalism.

Eliminate Trite Phrases

Trite phrases are the jargon of the business world. They mean nothing and take up space. Worse, they become dated over time. **Exhibit 5-8** shows how trite phrases can be improved.

Exhibit 5-8
Correcting Trite Phrases

Trite Phrases	Improved Copy
as per your question regarding	regarding
as per your request	as you requested
at this point in time	now
due to the fact	because
enclosed please find	enclosed is/are
feel free to	please
please do not hesitate to	please
thank you in advance	thank you

Use Fewer Words for Greater Impact

Readers do not like to wade through lengthy sentences and then re-read them to get the point. Shorter sentences are generally less confusing and convey messages better. **Exhibit 5-9** shows how wordy sentences can be rewritten to be more effective.

Wordy	Concise
Real estate agents facilitate the process of selling a home.	Real estate agents sell homes.
Complicated, verbose sentences tend to discourage full comprehension in readers.	Wordy sentences are difficult for readers to understand.
This application is designed to be completed by the applicant with the lender's assistance.	Please fill out this application with your lender's assistance.

Exhibit 5-9
Making Sentences More Concise

Use Simple Words

Some people believe that longer words make them look smarter and more sophisticated. The truth is, long words can interfere with understanding. Short words are easier to read. For example, a two-syllable word will be easier to read than a three-syllable word. A larger vocabulary is a sign of a person's knowledge, but be sure your vocabulary matches your audience. When in doubt, use shorter, simpler words. **Exhibit 5-10** illustrates how long words can be replaced with short words that are easier for readers to understand.

PEARSON mybcommlab

Apply these key concepts by revising a new document. Go to Chapter 5 in mybcommlab.com and select Document Makeovers.

Harder to Understand	Easier to Understand
enumerate	count
originated	started
utilize	use

Exhibit 5-10
Simplifying Words

CHECKLIST

To make writing as effective as possible:

- ☑ Use positive words.
- ☑ Choose powerful verbs.
- ☑ Avoid overusing adverbs and adjectives.
- ☑ Use bias-free language.
- ☑ Avoid slang words, unknown acronyms, and jargon.
- ☑ Eliminate trite phrases.
- ☑ Use fewer words for greater impact.
- ☑ Use simple words.

Write Effective Sentences

Next, let's consider the framework of writing—using words to build sentences, and sentences to build paragraphs. Well-written sentences ensure readers grasp the meaning of a message quickly and accurately. Keep the following ideas in mind to compose well-written sentences.

Use Active Voice

Do you want your readers to stay awake when they read your writing? Do you want them to understand what you're saying? Then use active voice whenever possible. **Active voice** means the subject of your sentence is performing the action. **Passive voice** means the subject is not doing the acting. **Exhibit 5-11** shows examples of each type of voice. Instead, it's receiving the action. You will notice that passive voice sentences typically use helping verbs like *be, is, are, was, were,* or *have.*

Passive Voice	Active Voice
Receiver ← Action The noteholder must be notified by the bank.	Actor → Action The bank must notify the note holder.
Receiver ← Action The following items are being returned.	Actor → Action We are returning the following items.
Receiver ← Action The open house was hosted by the real estate agent.	Actor → Action The real estate agent hosted the open house.

Exhibit 5-11
Passive versus Active Voice

REAL INSIGHTS from a New Professional

Name: *Nicole Yoder-Barnhart*
Title: *Real Estate Agent*
Organization: *Real Living, Inc.*
Location: *Columbus, Ohio*

"ONCE I STARTED WORKING [IN REAL ESTATE], I developed a passion for it," says Nicole Yoder-Barnhart, a top-selling real estate agent. Based in Columbus, Ohio, Yoder has been working in the real estate industry since she was 16. She obtained her real estate license when she was 18. Her story, though unusual for someone so young, is inspirational for real estate agents of any age.

Yoder's verbal and written communication skills, as well as her attention to detail, have helped her succeed. She quickly climbed to the top of her field. By age 20, she was inducted into the Columbus Board of Realtor's One Million Dollar Club. By 27, she was a member of the Twenty-Five Million Dollar Club. She is currently a part of the Real Living Network's "Winners Circle Elite," putting her in the network's top 1 percent of its agents; the honor is a significant accomplishment because Real Living is the fifth-largest real estate network in the country.

Yoder's writing skills are essential to her work. "We don't use the phone," she explains, "so e-mail is a big part of being a real estate agent." She and other Real Living agents write e-card notifications and e-mails to clients as well as develop and customize online newsletters. Because she must keep her communications brief in newsletters and paid advertisements, she arranges her thoughts carefully to "get the most out of those fifty characters to best describe the home."

When sending a message, she usually asks someone else to proofread her writing and offer feedback. "I want to make sure the e-mail is received as what I perceive it to be," she says. Although she admits that she and other agents sometimes make typos and editing mistakes, proofreading is a definite priority to minimize the number of errors.

Yoder's team also helps edit Real Living's online newsletter. This includes shaping the information into intriguing key points and making sure the tone correctly reflects the subject matter and audience, something crucial to communicating effectively with readers.

In her 10 years in real estate, Yoder's dedication to the details of her writing has resulted in the continued recognition of her many accomplishments.

Questions

1. What types of written communications does Yoder work on?
2. Why do you think it takes more planning to write very brief communications?
3. Why does Yoder use someone else to proofread her work?

Source: Tara Rogers, "Real Living Agent Named Realtor Magazine's Thirty Under 30,"*Real Living/HER,* June 16, 2003, accessed at www.realliving.com/data%5C0%5Cextra%5Cnews%5CNPR_061603.pdf.

DID YOU KNOW?

Eighty percent or more of the companies in the service, finance, insurance, and real estate (FIRE) sectors assess candidates' writing during the hiring process. "Applicants who provide poorly written letters wouldn't likely get an interview," commented one insurance executive.[2]

Sentences written in passive voice are often longer, more difficult to understand, and less personal than those written in active voice.

Write in Second Person When Appropriate

Writing in second person is often better than writing in third person. When you write in second person, you refer directly to your reader with the word "you." When you do so, people who read your writing will feel like you are speaking directly to them—which you are. Second person is direct and takes up less room. **Exhibit 5-12** shows the difference between second and third person. Notice how second person is more personal so it commands the reader's attention.

Structure Sentences Effectively

Whenever possible, put the important idea or action at the beginning of a sentence (preferably within the first seven words), as the column on the right in **Exhibit 5-13** illustrates. That way, the reader does not have to wait until the end of the sentence to understand the point.

Exhibit 5-12
Using Second Person

Third Person	Second Person
This form helps **the buyer** document the purchase price, accurately record terms, and professionally submit her offer to purchase a home.	This form helps **you** document your purchase price, accurately record terms, and professionally submit your offer to purchase a home.
The buyer might consider hiring a real estate attorney to attend the closing. The attorney will advise **the buyer** during contract signing and generally represent his interests at the closing	Consider hiring a real estate attorney to attend **your** closing. The attorney can advise **you** during contract signing and generally represent **your** interests at the closing meeting.

Exhibit 5-13
Effectively Structuring Sentences

Important Idea at the End of the Sentence	Important Idea at the Beginning of the Sentence
If you have not received a copy of your credit report, **please resend your request**.	**Please resend your request** if you have not received a copy of your credit report.
To determine the amount due, **we personally contacted the credit card company.**	**We personally contacted the credit card company** to determine the amount due.
To eliminate fees and pass on savings to the homebuyer, **we want to sell our home without a real estate agent.**	**We want to sell our home without a real estate agent** to eliminate fees and pass on savings to the homebuyer.

Choose the Right Type of Sentence

Every sentence must have a noun and a verb, but the structure of sentences can differ.

- **Simple sentence.** A simple sentence consists of a **subject** (person, place, or thing) and a **verb** (action). **Clauses** consist of related groups of words. As **Exhibit 5-14a** illustrates, in a simple sentence, there is only one main clause. Use simple sentences as often as possible because they are the easiest to write and read.
- **Compound sentence.** A compound sentence consists of two main clauses connected by a **conjunction** such as *or, and,* or *but.* In other words, each clause can stand on its own as a complete sentence if ended with a period. **Exhibit 5-14b** shows how a compound sentence is constructed. Use compound sentences to combine ideas that are of equal importance.

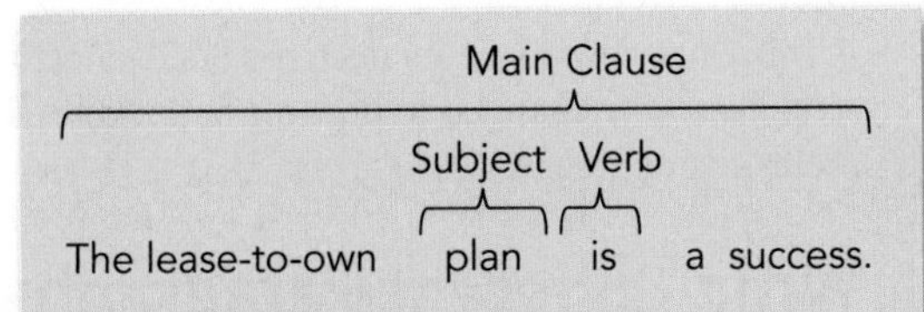

Exhibit 5-14a
Simple Single-Clause Sentence

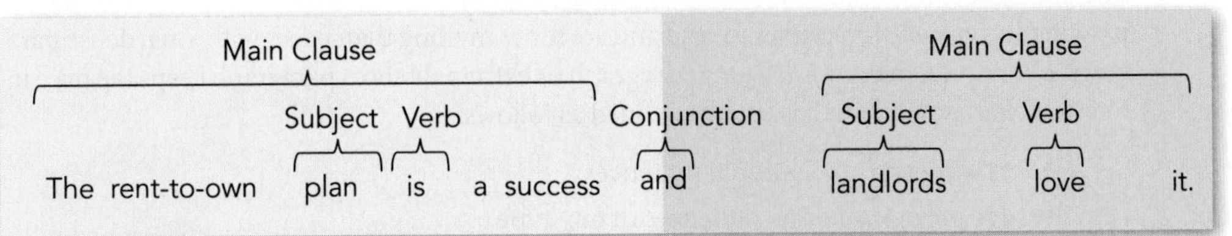

Exhibit 5-14b
Compound Sentence

DID YOU KNOW?

Most word-processing programs have a function that displays the readability of a document. The readability score generally comes up as part of the spell-checking function. Readability is generally measured by grade level. If you want everyone to read your document easily, aim for a readability level of the seventh-to-ninth grade. Above all, match the readability to your intended audience.

You might also consider breaking a compound sentence into two shorter sentences. For example:

The rent-to-own plan is a success. Landlords love it.

- **Complex sentence.** A complex sentence consists of one major idea (the most important idea) and one or more minor ideas (less important ideas). The major idea is called the **independent clause** because it can stand on its own as a complete sentence. The minor idea is called the **dependent clause** because it cannot stand on its own as a sentence and depends on the independent clause for meaning. **Exhibit 5-14c** shows how a complex sentence is constructed. It's a good idea to mix simple sentences with compound sentences so that your message doesn't sound choppy.

Exhibit 5-14c Complex Multi-Clause Sentence

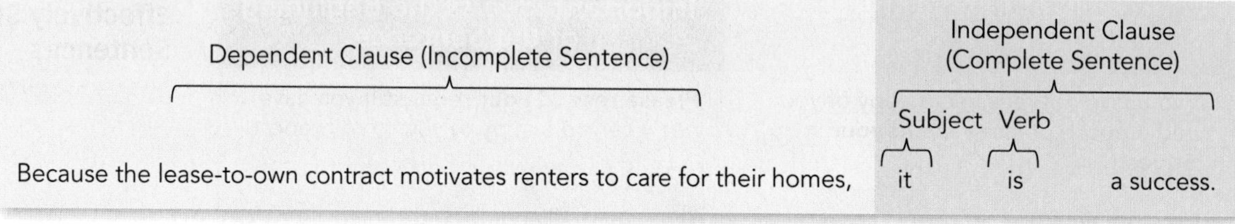

Watch the Length of Sentences

Just as short words are easier to read than long words, short sentences are easier to read than long sentences. This is especially true when a person is reading online. In fact, online readers tend to scan text rather than read it word for word, so the shorter the sentence, the better. **Exhibit 5-15,** shows how easy or hard a sentence is to read depending on its length.

Exhibit 5-15
Readability and the Number of Words in a Sentence

Number of Words	Readability
8 words or less	very easy to read
11 words	easy
14 words	fairly easy
17 words	standard
21 words	fairly difficult
25 words	difficult
29 words or more	very difficult

Let's review some ineffective versus effective sentences. Pay attention to how the bad sentences were changed to become better ones. **Exhibit 5-16** shows you how to improve an ineffective sentence.

CHECKLIST

To write effective sentences:

- ☑ Use active voice.
- ☑ Write in second person.
- ☑ Structure the sentence correctly.
- ☑ Use the right type of sentence.
- ☑ Watch the sentence length.

Write Coherent Paragraphs

Effective sentences are a good start. However, they aren't enough. You still must organize them into coherent paragraphs. The length of a paragraph has an effect on readers. Pages with shorter paragraphs typically look easier to read and are more inviting than pages with long, dense paragraphs. However, an occasional long paragraph or extremely short paragraph keeps the pace interesting. Paragraph length is usually defined as follows:

- ***Short paragraph:*** 1–2 simple sentences
- ***Average paragraph:*** 3–5 sentences of any type
- ***Long paragraph:*** 6 or more sentences of any type

Exhibit 5-16
Ineffective versus Effective Sentences

Ineffective Sentence	It is required by law that the estimated closing costs must be provided to you by the lender.
Good Sentence	According to the law, your lender must provide you with an estimate of your closing costs.
Better Sentence	The law requires your lender to provide you with an estimate of your closing costs.
Best Sentence	The law requires your lender to give you an estimate of your closing costs.

Develop a Main Sentence

Every paragraph, regardless of its size, has a main sentence. The main sentence introduces the topic or conveys the main idea of the paragraph. Keep the sentence as concise as possible. Doing so lets your reader know what you're going to address. Alternately, you can make the main sentence a **hook**—something that grabs the attention of readers and encourages them to read on.

After you write the main sentence, it's time to add supporting details. Each supporting sentence should relate in some way to the main sentence. Otherwise, it belongs in another paragraph. **Exhibit 5-17a** shows a paragraph from a book on home ownership. We have added a hook sentence to the beginning of the paragraph. Notice how it gets your attention and then the other sentences explain or support it.

Exhibit 5-17a
A Paragraph with a Hook

How much can you afford to spend on a home? An often-quoted guideline is that you can afford a house that costs up to two-and-one-half times your annual gross income. Your gross income is the amount you make before taxes are deducted from your income. If you are buying a house with someone else, such as a spouse, parent, or companion, you can also consider your co-purchaser's annual gross income when determining how expensive a home you can buy. Remember, however, your co-purchaser's debts and credit history will also be considered in determining how much you can borrow.[3]

Arrange the Paragraph

Some paragraph arrangements work well for informing or educating, whereas others work better for persuading. The typical arrangements include the following:

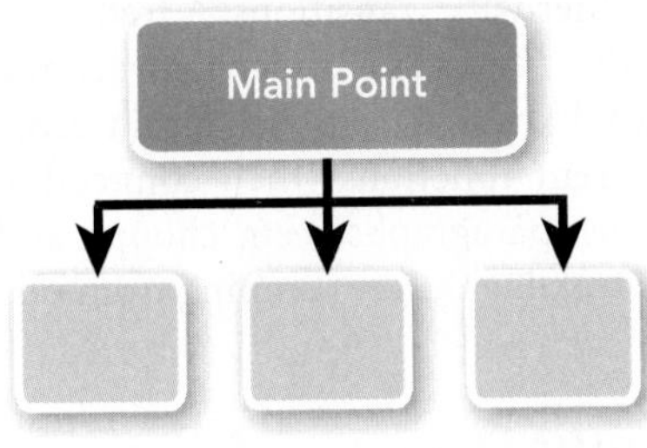

A **direct paragraph** like the one shown in **Exhibit 5-17b** begins with the main sentence, followed by supporting sentences. This arrangement is best when you want to define, explain, or describe something. It's probably the most common way to arrange a paragraph, and the easiest. The following is an example of a direct paragraph.

Exhibit 5-17b A Direct Paragraph

A lease-to-own contract is a win-win situation for landlords and renters alike. The contract helps a renter who is desperate to buy a home but lacks the down payment to do so. The renter gets time to improve her credit score and find a mortgage lender. The renter also gets a chance to apply a percentage of the rent toward the purchase of the home. Lease-to-own contracts give landlords peace of mind because they know the renters will care for the house; after all, they're going to buy it. Better yet, lease to-own contracts provide landlords with upfront money and regular rent payments until the house is sold.

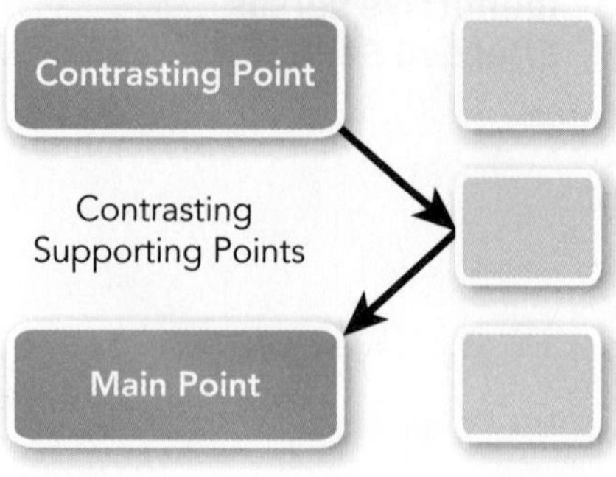

A **pivoting paragraph** starts with a sentence that offers a contrasting or negative idea before delivering the main idea. This arrangement is useful when you are comparing and contrasting ideas within a single paragraph. **Exhibit 5-17c** shows an example of a pivoting paragraph. The main idea in the paragraph is the last one. It pivots away, or contrasts, with the previous sentence.

Exhibit 5-17c A Pivoting Paragraph

> Lease-to-own contracts aren't for everyone. Landlords don't always like locking in the price of a home, not knowing whether real estate prices will go up or down in the future. Renters might not appreciate having to come up with a couple of thousand dollars for the option fee. However, for the most part, lease-to-own options work very well for both landlords and renters.

However, if you place too many negative ideas before the main point, readers might not understand that you are actually making a positive point.

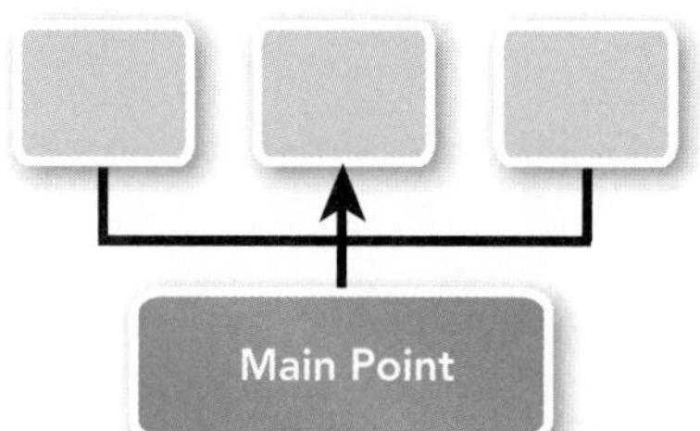

An **indirect paragraph** begins with supporting sentences and ends with the main sentence. This arrangement is useful for persuading people. It lets you make all of your points before you present your conclusion. **Exhibit 5-17d** shows an example of an indirect paragraph.

Exhibit 5-17d An Indirect Paragraph

> A lease-to-own contract helps a renter who is desperate to buy a home but lacks the down payment to do so. The renter is given time to improve her credit score and find a mortgage lender. The renter also gets a chance to apply a percentage of the rent toward the purchase of the home. Lease-to-own contracts give landlords peace of mind because they know the renters will care for the house—after all, they're going to buy it. Better yet, lease-to-own contracts provide landlords with upfront money and regular rent payments until the house is sold. Lease options are a win-win situation for landlords and renters alike.

Transitions tie paragraphs together, forming the fabric of a well-written message.

Use Transitions between Paragraphs

Paragraphs must be tied to one another to create a coherent message. Think of the paragraphs as squares of a quilt. They must be sewn together to create a coherent pattern in the quilt. Otherwise, they're nothing more than a pile of fabric squares.

Of course, you don't sew paragraphs together with needle and thread—you tie them together with transitions. A **transition** is a word, phrase, or sentence that serves as a bridge between the previous idea and the next idea. **Exhibit 5-18** lists typical transition words that perform different functions when connecting paragraphs. Without transitions, paragraphs seem choppy and unconnected, and readers can feel like they're jumping from one paragraph to the next.

Dovetail Your Paragraphs

Another way to achieve transition between paragraphs is called dovetailing. **Dovetailing** is accomplished by fitting one paragraph into the next by repeating words at the end of the first paragraph and the beginning of the second. The words boldfaced in the paragraphs in **Exhibit 5-19** show how they link together.

Exhibit 5-18 Transition Words That Connect Paragraphs

Strengthen	Continue	Contradict	Contrast	Emphasize	Conclude
accordingly	again	although	as opposed to	above all	as a result
also	also	actually	at the same time	in other words	in closing
in addition	additionally	but	however	most importantly	therefore
in other words	again	despite	on the other hand	without a doubt	
similarly	because	even so			
specifically	furthermore	however			
what's more	generally	in fact			
		instead			
		otherwise			
		still			

Exhibit 5-19 Examples of Dovetailing Ideas

> The exterior is what people see first. The homebuyer's first impression is based on how a house looks from the outside. Remember, outside appearances include both your house and your **yard**.
>
> Is your **yard** at least average for your neighborhood? If not, buy a few bushes and plant them. Fill in your flowerbed with annuals for color and some perennials for later bloom. Cover your bare earth with mulch. Mow your lawn. Add some potted plants. It's amazing what some hands-on time outdoors can do to improve your yard's appearance.

CHECKLIST

To write coherent paragraphs:

- ☑ Develop a main sentence.
- ☑ Write supporting sentences.
- ☑ Arrange the paragraph (direct, pivoting, indirect approaches).
- ☑ Use transitions.
- ☑ Dovetail your paragraphs.

Properly arranging paragraphs, using transitions, and dovetailing will all help your message read smoothly so your reader has an easy time grasping your meaning. The readability statistics available in Microsoft Word's spell-checker can help you determine if your message is easy to read.

Use the Appropriate Tone

As you have learned, the tone of a message refers to the attitude conveyed by the writer, either consciously or unconsciously. Sometimes the tone is formal and sometimes it's informal. However, in general, the best writing is conversational—both businesslike and friendly—and always courteous. Never write anything you're ashamed of or wouldn't want the general public to read. Also, remember to adopt the "you" attitude.

If you followed the steps in this chapter, you should have a decent first draft. However, a first draft is by no means perfect. It probably has some long sentences, grammar and punctuation mistakes, and perhaps a few spelling errors. Because it's only the first draft, there is plenty of room for improvement.

Does the tone of your message convey a friendly attitude? If it doesn't, the receiver might reject it.

3 How Can Reviewing and Revising Your Draft Affect the Impact of Your Message?

As the suspense novelist Ken Follett points out, "The first draft is the hardest because every word of the outline has to be fleshed out. . . . The rewrite is very satisfying."[4] Think of your first draft as a raw gemstone that's been roughly cut. Now you have to polish it.

If you can, it is best to wait a day or at least a few hours after finishing your draft before reviewing it. Doing so will gives you a certain distance from the material and makes you more objective when you revise it later. The idea is to get away from the draft long enough to view it like another reader.

Measure the Message against Its Goals

The first step in the review process is to determine whether your document conveys the ideas you intended. Don't worry about sentence and paragraph construction at this point. Instead, look over the document and ask yourself these questions:

1. Do I clearly state the purpose of the document?
2. Do I cover the main points identified in my outline?
3. Do the points appear in a logical order that my reader can follow? Are they clear?
4. Have I provided enough evidence to back up my points? Is there any evidence missing?
5. Is the information I provided true?
6. Is the information presented clearly?
7. Do I use both logic and emotion?
8. Do I need to provide a call to action at the end?

If you answer "no" to any of these questions, mark the sections of the document that need work. You might have to move sections around. Or, you might have to add more facts or check your facts. You might also need to strengthen your hook or clearly state your call to action. The ending of any communication should make clear what happens next.

Keep Your Message Concise

Once you complete any reorganization of your message, get rid of any extra words that add bulk but no meaning to your draft. Your reader's time is limited, so get to the point. The following are some things you can do to tighten up your writing.

Shorten Clauses to Phrases

- ***Wordy:*** The home, **which is very spacious,** will go on the market next month.
- ***Tight:*** **The spacious home** goes on the market next month.

Shorten Phrases to Words

- ***Wordy:*** I hired a real estate agent **for the purpose of selling** my home as quickly as possible.
- ***Tight:*** I hired a real estate agent **to sell** my home quickly.

Eliminate Repetitive Ideas

- ***Wordy:*** **Prior to the closing on Tuesday,** please collect all the necessary documents before we close.
- ***Tight:*** Please gather the necessary **documents before the closing on Tuesday.**

Eliminate Trite Phrases

- ***Wordy:*** **As per our agreement,** the buyers will pay all closing costs.
- ***Tight:*** **As we agreed,** the buyers will pay all closing costs.

CHECKLIST

To keep your message concise:

- ☑ Shorten clauses to phrases.
- ☑ Shorten phrases to words.
- ☑ Eliminate repetitive ideas.
- ☑ Eliminate filler words.

Eliminate Irrelevant Words (Filler Words) and Ideas

- *Wordy:* My new real estate agent is **originally from Michigan** and very experienced.
- *Tight:* My new real estate agent is **very experienced.**

Keep Your Message Easy to Read

What stops readers from understanding a message? How can you make your message easier to read? The following are some things you can to do to improve the readability of your message.

Break Up Overly Long Sentences

Readers don't like re-reading long sentences to figure out what they mean. Break them up into several short sentences instead. See **Exhibit 5-20** for some examples of how sentences can be effectively broken up.

Exhibit 5-20
Breaking a Long Sentence into Two Smaller Ones

One Long Sentence	Two Short Sentences
We process thousands of requests for information each month, estimating that it takes approximately one hour to respond to each request.	We process thousands of requests for information each month. We estimate it takes approximately one hour for each response.

Rewrite Vague Sentences

A vague sentence is one where you don't come right out and say what you mean. Readers can detect when you're hedging. It's better to state clearly what you mean. Readers will respect you for it. Keep in mind that "clearly" does not mean "rudely." **Exhibit 5-21** shows some examples of vague sentences that have been rewriten so that the messages are clearer.

Exhibit 5-21
Vague and Clear Sentences

Vague Sentence	Clear Sentence
I believe that you agreed to send me the rent by the first of the month. However, it's the tenth and I still haven't received it.	We agreed that the rent was due the first of the month. However, it's the tenth and I still haven't received it.
I would really like it if you could call me tomorrow to tell me what's going on.	I realize you have had some financial problems, so please call me tomorrow to discuss the situation.

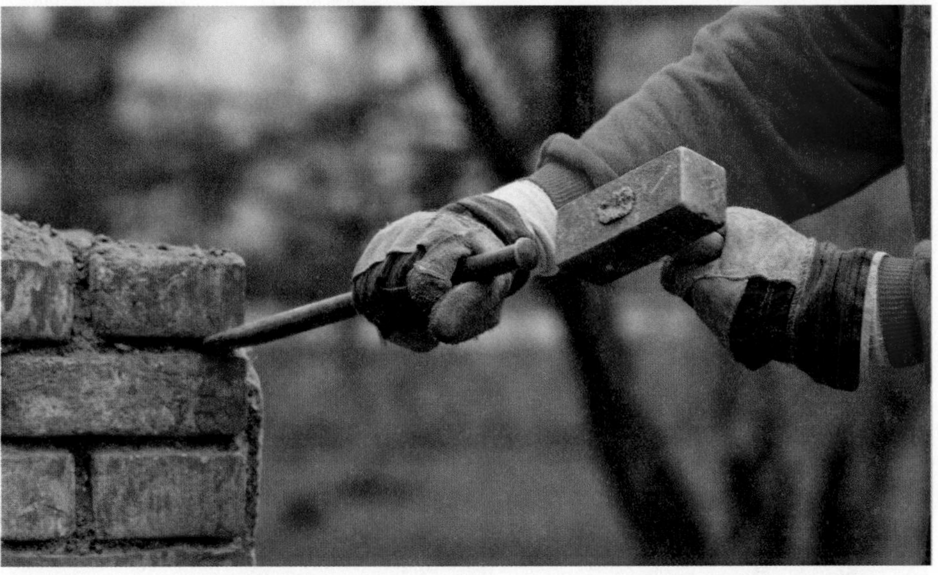

Readers don't like wading through long paragraphs. As with sentences, it's better to break up one long paragraph into several shorter ones. Divide paragraphs where you move from one subtopic, or aspect of the topic, to another.

Keep Your Paragraphs Short

Readers don't like wading through long paragraphs. As with sentences, it's better to break up one long paragraph into several shorter ones, as **Exhibit 5-22** shows. Divide paragraphs when you move from one subtopic, or aspect of the topic, to another.

Exhibit 5-22
Breaking Up Large Paragraphs

One Long Paragraph	Three Shorter Paragraphs
Condominiums are the starter home of choice for many homebuyers because they are usually smaller and less expensive than conventional, single-family homes. The term "condominium" does not describe a type of architectural style, but rather a type of joint ownership. Each condo unit is individually owned, even though walls may be shared with another owner's unit. The common areas (land, hallways, elevators, recreational facilities) are jointly owned by all owners. Owners pay a monthly condo fee to cover the maintenance of the common areas.	Condominiums are the starter home of choice for many homebuyers because they are usually smaller and less expensive than conventional, single-family homes. The term "condominium" does not describe a type of architectural style, but rather a type of joint ownership. Each condo unit is individually owned, even though walls are often shared with another owner's unit. The common areas (land, hallways, elevators, recreational facilities) are jointly owned by all owners. Owners pay a monthly condo fee to cover the maintenance of the common areas.

Use Lists to Call Out Important Information

Large, dense blocks of text easily hide important ideas until those ideas become almost invisible. The fastest way to make them visible again is to put them in a list, as **Exhibit 5-23** illustrates.

Exhibit 5-23
Using Bullet Points within a List

Ideas Hidden in a Paragraph	Ideas Visible in a List
The printout provided by the real estate agent includes the asking price, mortgage balance, seller's monthly payments, and information indicating whether the mortgage is assumable.	The printout provided by the real estate agent includes the following: • asking price • mortgage balance • seller's monthly payments • information indicating whether the mortgage is assumable

There are two types of lists: numbered and bulleted.

- ***Numbered lists.*** Use numbers when the order of your points matters. Numbered lists are used to describe step-by-step instructions.
- ***Bulleted lists.*** Use bullets when the order of your points is not important. Bulleted lists are often used to group points that are related.

CHECKLIST

To break up dense blocks of text:

- ☑ Use numbered lists when order matters.
- ☑ Use bulleted lists when order is unimportant.
- ☑ Use parallel construction for all lists.

When you start a list, always introduce it with an introductory sentence, as **Exhibit 5-24** shows. Notice in the exhibit that when a list is numbered (see the left-hand side of the exhibit), the steps within it must be completed in the prescribed order. By contrast, when a list is bulleted (as the right-hand side of the exhibit shows), the steps can be performed in any order. Writers often omit the period at the end of item in a bulleted list when the item is short and is not a complete sentence. Whatever you decide to do, be consistent.

Regardless of whether you use numbered or bulleted lists, make sure to use **parallel construction**. Parallel construction means that each item on the list should be constructed similarly. For example, if the first item begins with a verb, the rest of the items should as well. If the first item begins with a noun, the rest of the items should also begin with a noun. Par-

Numbered List	Bulleted List
Steps for buying a house: 1. Decide what you want in a house. 2. Shop around and find the house you want. 3. Negotiate the purchase. 4. Inspect the house. 5. Shop for a loan. 6. Apply for a loan. 7. Prepare for closing. 8. Attend closing.	Remove clutter to make your kitchen more appealing to buyers: • Get everything off the counters. • Clear out your junk drawer. • Get rid of old canned and dry goods. • Clean out the area beneath the sink. • Remove pots, pans, and dishes you rarely use.

Exhibit 5-24
Numbered versus Bulleted Lists

allel construction keeps readers from mentally stumbling as they read. Readers might not be aware that a list uses parallel construction, but they certainly know when the list sounds odd or is difficult to read.

Exhibit 5-25 shows two lists from a home-for-sale advertisement. Can you tell which one uses parallel construction? You should have picked List A. All its items are phrases, not complete sentences, and every item starts with an adjective that modifies a noun. List B is a mix of styles. Some of the items are phrases, while others are complete sentences. Some items start with a verb, whereas others start with noun or an adjective. List B does not use parallel construction and does not read as smoothly.

List A	List B
• Expansive greenbelt in back. • Mature, perennial, low-water landscaping and shade trees. • Cathedral ceiling in living room with skylight. • New office cabinetry in third bedroom. • Updated master bath with skylight, new tile, shower, floor, and vanity. • New paint in master bedroom, master bath, and third bathroom. • Dry-walled, insulated, and wired garage.	• Backs to expansive greenbelt. • Comes with mature, perennial, low-water landscaping and shade trees. • Cathedral ceiling in living room with skylight. • New office cabinetry in third bedroom. • See updated master bath with skylight, new tile, shower, floor, and vanity. • We painted the master bedroom, master bath, and third bedroom. • Garage has been dry-walled, insulated, and wired.

Exhibit 5-25
Parallel Construction: A Comparison

The next step in the review process is checking for accuracy in your grammar, spelling, and punctuation. Though these steps may seem tedious, they're essential to ensuring that your message is received in the best light.

Edit for Grammar

No matter what types of documents you write, even text messages and e-mails, you will need to edit them. Your goal is for the reader to understand what you have written and get a good impression of you. Good grammar helps you achieve that goal. At the end of this book, there is a very useful grammar handbook for your reference.

Grammar checkers merely suggest words that might be incorrect. Consequently, you need to look at the flagged words to decide whether or not they are incorrect. The following grammar rules will help you do this.

Subject and Verb Agreement

Nothing can make your writing look more amateurish than when the subject and verb in a sentence do not agree. This means, if the subject is singular, the verb must be as well. If the subject is plural, so is the verb. **Exhibit 5-26** illustrates proper subject-verb agreement.

CHECKLIST

To make your message more readable:

- ☑ Break up overly long sentences.
- ☑ Rewrite vague sentences.
- ☑ Keep your paragraphs short.
- ☑ Use bullets or numbers to clarify.

Exhibit 5-26
Subject-Verb Agreement

Incorrect	Each program has **their** own guidelines.
Correct	Each program has **its** own guidelines.
Why	Program = singular; its = singular
Incorrect	Your real estate agent and lender **ensures** that you meet program guidelines.
Correct	Your real estate agent and lender **ensure** that you meet program guidelines.
Why	Real estate agent and lender (they) = plural; ensure = plural

Case

This has to do with using the correct pronoun (for example, "I" versus "me") in a sentence. An easy way to figure out what pronoun to use is to break up the sentence and use the pronoun by itself to see if it sounds right. **Exhibit 5-27** shows incorrect and correct examples of case agreement.

Exhibit 5-27
Case Agreement

Incorrect	The title company and **me** have an appointment next Wednesday.
Correct	The title company and **I** have an appointment next Wednesday.
Why	You would say, "**I** have an appointment," not "**me** have an appointment."
Incorrect	The mortgage specialist and **myself** will follow up on the status of the loan application
Correct	The mortgage specialist and **I** will follow up on the status of the loan application.
Why	You would say, "**I** will follow up," not "**myself** will follow up."

Dangling Participle

Participles are action words that provide more information about the subject of a sentence. A **dangling participle** is an action that appears to be performed by the subject but actually has nothing to do with the subject.

In **Exhibit 5-28**, the boldfaced text indicates the participle (action); the italicized text indicates a subject. The participle is considered dangling when it is not associated with the subject because the subject is not performing the action. In the correct examples, the subject is performing the action, so the participle is no longer dangling.

Misplaced Modifier

A misplaced modifier is a modifier that's in the wrong place in a sentence. In its incorrect location it appears to modify the wrong item. **In Exhibit 5-29**, the misplaced modifiers are boldfaced.

That versus Which

People commonly misuse "that" and "which." You will stand out as an excellent writer if you keep these rules in mind. Use *that* for **restrictive clauses** that deliberately limit the scope of the noun and are essential for understanding. Use *which* for **nonrestrictive clauses** that are considered nonessential. Always put a comma (,) before and after a nonrestrictive clause beginning with which. The commas are not necessary for the restrictive clause beginning with *that.* If the definition sounds complicated, consider the following two sentences:

> The **real estate agent** said the home **that had solar panels** sold almost immediately.
> The **real estate agent** said the home, **which had solar panels,** sold almost immediately.

Incorrect	**Trying to find the right lender,** *the real estate agent's suggestions* were bypassed.
Correct	**Trying to find the right lender,** *the homeowner* bypassed the real estate agent's suggestions.
Why lender;	"The real estate agent's suggestions" did not try to find the right the homeowner did. You have to indicate "who" bypassed the real estate agent's suggestions.
Incorrect	**Sitting through the long closing,** *the chairs* were very uncomfortable.
Correct	**Sitting through the long closing,** *the couple* found the chairs very uncomfortable.
Why	The chairs did not sit through the long closing; the couple did. You have to indicate "who" found the chairs uncomfortable.
Incorrect	**Studying the home loan application,** *the signature* was missing.
Correct	**Studying the home loan application,** *the loan officer* noticed the signature was missing.
Why	The signature did not study the loan application; the loan officer did. You have to indicate "who" noticed the missing signature.

Exhibit 5-28
Dangling Participles

Incorrect	The couple looked for homes that had old-fashioned porches **in the morning.**
Correct	**In the morning**, the couple looked at homes that had old-fashioned porches.
Why	"In the morning" refers to when the homebuyer looked for homes; it has nothing to do with the porches.
Incorrect	**Overflowing with wildflowers**, the couple stared at their beautiful garden.
Correct	The couple stared at their beautiful garden **overflowing with wildflowers.**
Why	"The couple" was not covered with the wildflowers; the garden was.

Exhibit 5-29
Misplaced Modifiers

In the first sentence, "that had solar panels" is a restrictive clause. It limits the scope of the word "home," indicating the writer doesn't mean just any home, but only the one with solar panels. If you remove that clause, the reader doesn't know which house sold and the sentence loses crucial information.

In the second sentence, the clause "which has solar panels," is nonrestrictive. The writer is merely giving additional information about a house she's describing or pointing out. It is additional information that is not essential to the meaning and could be taken out. **Exhibit 5-30** contains more examples about how to correctly use *that* and *which.*

Who versus Whom

Many people have a hard time figuring out when to use *who* and when to use *whom.* Both words are pronouns, so what is the difference between using one or the other? The answer

DID YOU KNOW?

More than 40 percent of the firms that responded to a survey by the National Commission on Writing offer or require training for salaried employees with writing deficiencies. "We're likely to send out 200–300 people annually for skills-upgrade courses like business writing or technical writing," said a representative for one of the firms that responded. By some estimates, American firms spend as much as $3.1 billion annually remedying their employees' writing deficiencies.[5]

Exhibit 5-30
That versus Which

Incorrect	Please call the department, **which** administers the Home Buyer Assistance Program.
Correct	Please call the department **that** administers the Home Buyer Assistance Program.
Why	The phrase after *that* is essential to understand the sentence. Without it, the reader would not know which department to call.
Incorrect	Let's buy the three-bedroom house, **which** has radiant heating.
Correct	Let's buy the three-bedroom house **that** has radiant heating.
Why	The phrase after *that* is essential to understand the sentence. Without it, the reader would have no idea which three-bedroom house you're talking about.

is simple: Use *who* when you are talking about the subject of a sentence, and *whom* when you are talking about the object of a sentence. "Subject" and "object" might sound abstract, but their definitions are straightforward. The subject of the sentence is the person or thing doing something, and the **object** is the person or thing having something done to it. Consider the following sentence:

The homebuyer called the real estate agent.

The homebuyer is the subject of the sentence, and the real estate agent is the object of the sentence. Now, look at **Exhibit 5-31** to find out when to use *who* and when to use *whom* when you have questions about the sentence.

Exhibit 5-31
Whom versus Who

Whom	*Whom* did the homebuyer call? Use *whom* because it refers to the real estate agent, and the real estate agent is the object of the sentence.
Who	*Who* called the real estate agent? Use who because it refers to the homebuyer, and the home buyer is the subject of the sentence.

Sentence Fragment

A **sentence fragment** is an incomplete sentence, which means it does not have a subject and a verb. **Exhibit 5-32** shows some examples of sentence fragments and how to correct them.

Exhibit 5-32
Correcting Sentence Fragments

Incorrect	The mortgage company declined our loan application. **Because our credit rating is poor.**
Correct	The mortgage company declined our loan application because our credit rating is poor.
Why	"Because or credit rating is poor" is not a complete sentence.
Incorrect	We decided to sell our home without a real estate agent for a good reason. **To save money.**
Correct	We decided to sell our home without a real estate agent to save money.
Why	"To save money" is not a complete sentence.

Exhibit 5-33
Run-On Sentences

Incorrect	We identified what we were looking for in a home **then we started searching the for-sale-by-owner ads.**
Correct	We identified what we were looking for in a home. **Then we started searching the for-sale-by-owner ads.** *(Made run-on sentence two separate sentences.)* We identified what we were looking for in a home, **and then we started searching the for-sale-by-owner ads.** *(Added the conjunction, "and.")* We identified what we were looking for in a home; **then we started searching the for-sale-by-owner ads.** *(Added a semicolon.)*

Run-On (Fused) Sentence

A **run-on sentence,** or fused sentence, results when two independent clauses are fused together without punctuation or a conjunction. Consequently, one clause runs into the other. You can fix a run-on sentence in a number of ways, including making it into two separate sentences, adding a conjunction (such as *or, and, but, yet,* or, *so*) or adding a semicolon (;). **Exhibit 5-33** shows an example of a run-on sentence and the various ways in which it can be fixed.

Comma Splice

A **comma splice** is very similar to a run-on sentence. It occurs when a comma joins, or splices, two independent clauses in a sentence without any conjunction. You can fix the situation by replacing the comma with a period (.) or a conjunction. **Exhibit 5-34** shows you how.

Exhibit 5-34
Comma Splice

Incorrect	It's nearly noon, we can't get to the title company before the loan officer leaves for lunch.
Correct	It's nearly noon, **and** we can't get to the title company before the loan officer leaves for lunch. It's nearly noon. We can't get to the title company before the loan officer leaves for lunch. It's nearly noon; we can't get to the title company before the loan officer leaves for lunch.

Pay Attention to Punctuation, Numbers, and Dates

Now that your message appears to be grammatically correct, it's time to check your punctuation. You are probably familiar with basic punctuation as well as the rules for writing numbers and dates. However, if you need a quick review, see the grammar handbook at the end of this textbook and check your message for any punctuation errors.

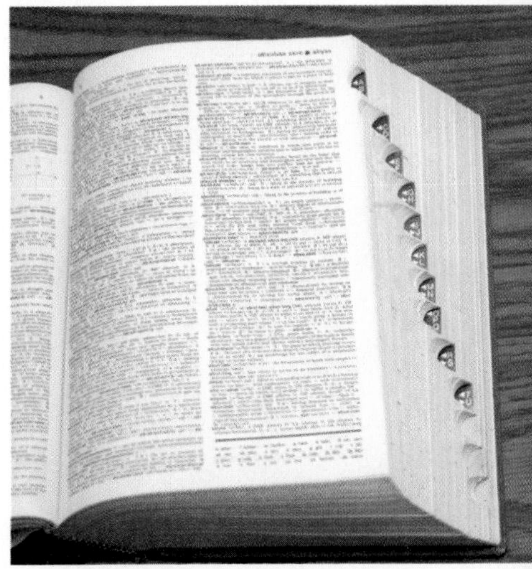

Online or offline, dictionaries are a writer's best friend.

Check Your Spelling

Don't forget to run your spell-checker. Each time it finds a mistake, look at the word it suggests as a replacement before you accept the change; sometimes the spell-checker makes incorrect suggestions. You may have to add words to your spell-checker if you're using technical terms that the spell-checker doesn't recognize.

The spell-checker will not find all mistakes. It is particularly bad at finding instances in which you use the wrong word, but the word is nonetheless spelled correctly. "I through the contract in the trash" is an example. Although "through" is spelled correctly, it's the wrong word. "Threw" is the right word. "Threw" and "through" are **homonyms.**

REAL INSIGHTS from a Seasoned Professional

Name: Jordan Simon
Title: Vice President
Organization: Venture West
Location: Tucson, Arizona

WHEN IT COMES TO REAL ESTATE, Jordan Simon insists "good writing skills are the essential component for success." Simon, who is the vice president of Venture West, an Arizona-based commercial real estate development, construction, and management company, says it is essential to pay attention to every detail.

After 25 years in the industry, Simon takes those details very seriously. In a typical day at the office, Simon's writing tasks include everything from casual e-mails to formal legal documents.

Being detail-oriented is essential when it can result in legal action: "Every 'i' must be dotted and 't' must be crossed," says Simon. "The difference in one word, such as 'and' versus 'or' can completely change the meaning of the document." The ramifications of these mistakes can also be costly. In one lawsuit Simon cited, the missing two-letter word "or" led to a judgment in favor of a plaintiff, a mistake that cost a landlord over $150,000 in lost rent, or as Simon puts it, "$75,000 per letter."

To protect against such catastrophes, Simon notes the importance of hiring people who write well, know how to edit, and how to proofread carefully for mistakes. He believes that "professional communication is part of your calling card to your clients." That's why it's vital he has trustworthy staff members with good writing skills. This ensures that his firm receives the positive attention it deserves and that his customers end up viewing the company in the best light possible.

"If you are looking for an adventure where multiple skill sets are used on a daily basis, commercial real estate could be looking for you," says Simon. Just make sure you have dotted your "i"s and crossed your "t"s.

Questions

1. Why is attention to detail and proofreading so important to Simon?
2. What kind of skills does Simon suggest looking for in new hires?

Source: Jordan Simon in discussion with the author, June 2010.

Both words sound alike, but they have completely different meanings. A spell-checker won't flag errors such as these. The following is a humorous poem that illustrates the limits of a spell-checker when it comes to homonyms. At best, the spell-checker is a rough spelling check. You still need to proofread to find other mistakes.

I have a spell checker,
It came with my PC;
It marks **four** my **revue,**
Mistakes I cannot **sea.**
I've run this poem **threw** it,
And I'm sure you're pleased to **no,**
It is letter perfect in **it's weigh,**
My checker **tolled** me **sew.**

Source: Reprinted with permission from Cartoon Stock. www.CartoonStock.com.

4 How Can Getting Feedback Result in a Positive Response to Your Message?

The last step in the review and revision process is getting and incorporating feedback to make your writing stronger and more effective. Depending upon the type of document you're writing, you may or may not want to ask another person to read it and give you feedback. If you are sending a routine e-mail to someone, you can probably skip this step.

It's best if the people who review your document know your actual audience or are similar to your audience. That way, you get feedback from a realistic virtual audience before you distribute the document to your real audience.

Take the following steps when soliciting and incorporating feedback.

1. ***Send a cover letter.*** When you send out your final draft for review outside the organization, provide a **cover letter,** which can consist of either a letter or an e-mail message. If you send an e-mail message, attach your document to it. Feedback from within your organization is most common and usually solicited with either a memo or e-mail. Either way, the letter should include the following information:
   - The purpose of the document and its intended audience.
   - The type of feedback you want. This might include asking your reviewers to look for any, but not necessarily all, of the following items: missing information, incorrect information, extraneous information, inappropriate tone, typos, and grammar mistakes.
   - The date that feedback is due. Ask the reviewer to contact you if he or she cannot review the document in the time allotted.
   - A heartfelt thank-you. People are busy and need to know you appreciate them taking the time to review your document. They also need to know that their feedback is important to the success of the document.

   Figure 5-35 shows the cover letter (e-mail) a young couple sent a friend who is a real estate agent, Sharon, regarding a letter they planned to send to their landlady.

To: showell@comcast.net

From: jolopez@frii.com

Subject: Can you review our letter?

```
Dear Sharon,

We attached the one-page letter we plan to send our
landlady. The letter presents the idea of a lease-to-own
option, which we would like her to consider. Our goal is
to set an appointment with her to discuss the idea, and,
ultimately, to draw up a lease-to-own contract.

We value your opinion and would like you to review our
letter to make sure it:
* Is logically organized and makes sense.
* Correctly explains a lease-to-own option and its
  benefits.
* Contains no typos or grammar mistakes.

If possible, please send us your comments by the end of
the week.

Thank you for your help,

Angela and Joseph Lopez
```

Figure 5-35
A Cover Letter to a Reviewer

PEARSON mybcommlab

Apply Exhibit 5-35's key concepts by revising a new document. Go to Chapter 5 in mybcommlab.com and select Document Makeovers.

CHECKLIST

The 10-steps to successful writing are:

- ☑ **1.** Know the *who, what,* and *why.*
- ☑ **2.** Develop an outline.
- ☑ **3.** Choose the appropriate words.
- ☑ **4.** Write effective sentences.
- ☑ **5.** Develop coherent paragraphs with good transitions.
- ☑ **6.** Use lists for clarity.
- ☑ **7.** Use the appropriate tone.
- ☑ **8.** Check grammar, punctuation, numbers, and dates.
- ☑ **9.** Check the spelling.
- ☑ **10.** Solicit and incorporate feedback.

2. ***Consolidate the feedback.*** When you receive your feedback from multiple people, consolidate the feedback into one document to make it easier to read. This may mean printing out a clean copy of the document and transferring everyone's corrections and suggestions onto it. Or it may mean taking the most marked-up copy from one reviewer and adding the other reviewers' comments to it.
3. ***Resolve any conflicting feedback.*** Sometimes one reviewer says one thing and another says the opposite. If you believe that one set of feedback is obviously right and one is obviously wrong, use the right feedback. If you're not sure, do some research. This could involve talking to the people who gave you the conflicting feedback to figure out what to do. You might also need to do some research on the Internet or talk to another professional.
4. ***Incorporate the feedback.*** Once the feedback is consolidated, start making changes.

When all the feedback is in, your draft is finished and you can move on to formatting, proofreading, and distributing it, which you will learn about in the next chapter.

Summary *Synthesize What You Have Learned*

1. What preparations will make your writing powerful?

You must be clear about who your audience is, what the purpose of the document is, and why a reader would be interested in reading the document before you begin writing any message. Next, create an annotated outline with additional notes, quotes, and reference information to help you "fill in the blanks" as you write your first draft.

2. How can words, sentences, paragraphs, and tone be combined to create a compelling message?

Words: Consider whether your message needs to be conversational, formal, or informal. Then write with a "you" attitude. Use positive words, and powerful verbs. Avoid overusing adverbs and adjectives. Use bias-free language. Avoid slang words, unknown acronyms, and jargon. Use fewer words and simple words for greater impact.
Sentences: Use active voice and write in second person when appropriate. Put important information at the beginning of the message. Keep your sentences short, but vary their lengths for interest.
Paragraphs: Develop a main sentence that introduces the paragraph, conveys the main idea of the paragraph, or also provides a hook to get readers interested. Then write supporting sentences that relate to the main sentence or idea you are trying to convey. Use the direct approach in paragraphs to explain or define. The pivoting approach should be used to compare or contrast. Use the indirect approach to persuade and provide reasons. Use transition words, phrases, and sentences to create connections between your paragraphs.

3. How can reviewing and revising your draft affect the impact of your message?

Keep your messages concise by shortening clauses to phrases and phrases to words, and eliminating repetitive ideas, filler words, and irrelevant words or ideas. Make your messages more readable by breaking up overly long sentences, rewriting vague sentences, keeping paragraphs short, and using bullets or numbers to clarify. Ensure messages are grammatically correct by editing for grammar, using proper punctuation, and formatting numbers and dates correctly.

4. How can getting feedback result in a positive response to your message?

To obtain feedback, send the document to your reviewer(s), along with a cover letter containing this information: the purpose of the document, the type of feedback you're looking for, the date the feedback is due, and a heartfelt thank-you. Then consolidate the feedback, resolve any conflicting feedback, and incorporate it.

PEARSON **mybcommlab**™ Are you an active learner? Go to **mybcommlab.com** to master Chapter 5's content. Chapter 5's interactive activities include:

- Customizable Study Plan and Chapter 5 practice quizzes
- Flash cards for mastering the definition of chapter terms
- Interactive Lessons that visually review key chapter concepts
- Document Makeovers for hands-on, socred practice in revising documents

Know It *Reflect, Respond, and Express*

Build Your Critical Thinking Skills

Critical Thinking Questions

1. Review your curriculum guide or brochure for your major. Who is the intended audience for the guide? What is the purpose of the communication? How does it hold your interest and advertise the major?
2. Find an article from a newspaper or magazine (online or print). Who is the intended audience for the article? What is the purpose of the article? Why are readers interested in the article? How does it hold the audience's interest?
3. Explore the review section of your word processing program. What tools do you have available to use electronically when you review documents?
4. What methods of communication could you use to resolve conflicting feedback? Would you contact both reviewers? Would you send an e-mail, make a phone call, send a letter, or use multiple methods of communication?

Critical Thinking Scenario

Michael Vodzner is a young real estate agent who has been in business for two years. He just composed the first draft of a letter he plans to mail to prospective clients to drum up business. Most of his clients have been young couples purchasing their first home. However, he now wants to market his services to retired couples who are downsizing and need to purchase smaller homes, townhouses, or condominiums.

The body of Michael's first draft reads as follows:

> To Whom It May Concern:
>
> Hi, my name is Michael Vodzner, and I am the "new guy" in town when it comes to real estate agents. I recently graduated with a bachelor's degree in business and a minor in marketing.
>
> I've been working with At Home Real Estate for two years and am considered its "star pupil." I've been serving clients aged 18–30, but want to gain experience with older clients.
>
> I'm cool with whatever kind of home you're looking for. I'm a great networker and know how to research the market to find the perfect home for you. I'm a hard worker and a friendly kind of guy.
>
> Please consider me when you think about looking for a new home.

Review Michael's draft and consider the following aspects of the message:

- The goal of the message
- Michael's knowledge of the audience
- The tone
- Use of the "you" attitude
- Jargon
- Any other aspects you can think of

Based on your evaluation of these aspects, how would you revise the message to improve it?

Write It *Draft, Revise, and Finalize*

1. On a separate sheet of paper, revise the following sentences and paragraph to make them more effective. Your revisions could involve correcting spelling or grammar, changing passive to active voice, eliminating words, or taking any of the steps suggested in the checklists throughout this chapter.
   a. The appraisal report is provided to the lender which contains an accurate and adequately supported opinion of the market value of the property.
   b. You are hereby notified that as of December 3, 2011, morgage payments will begin to be collected from you by the Five Star Bank.
   c. If you have any questions about the transfer of your morgage loan, the Customer Service Department should be notified.
   d. Your mortgage loan, which was owned by Fannie Mae, has been transferred to Five Star Bank. However, Five Star Bank does not service your loan. It is important that your monthly payments be sent directly to Five Star Bank and not to Fannie Mae. All correspondence and inquiries concerning your mortgage loan should be addressed to the bank. The bank has authority to respond to any questions about your mortgage loan.
2. Compose a rough draft of a message to your classmates explaining your view of collaborative work. Analyze your audience to best convey your purpose. Revise the rough draft at least once and bring at least two copies to class. Exchange messages with one other classmate and revise for clarity of purpose and the overall structure of the message.
3. Create an annotated outline for how you approach the writing process. Use your text for quotes and reference information. Be thorough about the steps you take while working through the process of writing.
4. Edit the following sentences to make them bias-free:
   a. The student left his books in class.
   b. The elderly couple enjoyed a stroll.
   c. I met the Venezuelan flight attendant in the terminal.
   d. The blind woman is next in line.
   e. I sat next to the pretty blonde in the waiting room.
5. Give an example of a trite phrase and revise it for clarity.
6. Revise the following run-on sentences:
   a. Barack Obama is the President of the United States he is the first African-American to serve in that position.
   b. Business Communication enables various majors to prepare for the workplace, more employers seek good communication skills in their employees.
   c. Fused sentences and comma splices cause run-on sentences, most writers fix run-ons by reading them out loud.
7. Compose a cover letter requesting feedback on a business proposal you have due in four weeks. What deadline would you give a reviewer? What type of feedback would you look for?

Speak It *Discuss, Listen, and Understand*

Build Your Leadership and Teamwork Skills

1. Get together in small groups. Then make a list of the jargon, popular sayings, and trite expressions or filler words you use: (a) in conversation or online, (b) hear on TV or radio, or (c) read in magazines or on the Internet.
   a. Write the words down in a column.
   b. For each word, write a more widely understood word in a second column next to the first column.
   c. In a third column, indicate how frequently you personally use the ineffective words: **R** = rarely, **S** = sometimes, **O** = often, **A** = always. Armed with information, work toward using the ineffective words as little as possible.
   d. Discuss with your group when and with what audience(s) jargon and popular sayings might be appropriate and when and with what audience(s) they wouldn't be.
2. In small groups, create an annotated outline for a new product proposal. What is the product? Who is your consumer or audience? How would you discuss the costs? What market research needs to be completed? Organize your information in an outline format with additional information added where it is needed. Be as thorough as possible.
3. In small groups, come up with some ideas for writing effective introductions that hook the reader. Organize the ideas into an annotated outline of how you might present the material to the class.
4. In groups, discuss the difference between the restrictive clause *that* and the nonrestrictive clause *which*. How can you determine if the clause is essential to the sentence's meaning?
5. In groups or as a class, discuss why second person (you) is often used in business communication.

Do It *Document Your Success Track Record*

Build Your e-Portfolio

1. Imagine that you have been working at the job of your dreams for the last two years. You ask your manager to write a letter of recommendation for your file in case someday you decide to leave your job and move on. Your manager has agreed to do it.

   Now imagine you are the manager. Write the letter following these steps:

   a. Determine the purpose of the letter.
   b. Understand the audience for the letter.
   c. Develop a mind map, list of important points, or outline to help you organize your thoughts.
   d. Create the first draft following the checklists in this chapter.
   e. Review and edit the draft following the checklists in this chapter.
   f. Ask a teacher, parent, or friend to review the first draft. Compose a covering e-mail, and refer to the attached letter, explaining what you want the reviewer to look for.
   g. Incorporate any feedback and finalize your letter of recommendation. Keep the letter on hand to read whenever you feel discouraged so that you have the motivation to persist.

Business in Action
Writing Plays a Critical Role at Hanley Wood

Producing the best possible product is a common goal for most businesses, but remaining committed to that goal for more than 30 years and succeeding is another story—especially when the product is a written one. Hanley Wood, based in Washington, DC, connects real estate and construction buyers with manufacturers. How do they do this? With over 30 publications, online media, annual conferences and events, and house plans.

Hanley Wood's success depends on the accuracy of its publications. Mistakes in the building industry are costly. That's why Hanley Wood is meticulous about writing, revising, and editing its publications. All content must be thoroughly reviewed and error-free. For example, incorrectly written figures about the cost of roofing materials or insulation could be devastating if a large number of construction companies used those figures in their bids for construction projects.

Such a mistake could result in lost contracts and revenue for the construction firms, which could result in layoffs for their employees. This, in turn, would result in lost clients for Hanley Wood because its publications would appear unreliable. The quality of editing and revising actually means the difference between gaining and losing customers, money, and jobs.

Hanley Wood, however, is known for its staff of all-star editors and writers, as well as the wealth of accurate knowledge the company passes on to its clients. In fact, the company's Business Media division has been the recipient of multiple awards for its writing in the field of real estate.

What's the result of such dedication? Perhaps it is Hanley Wood's legacy: the company has spent more than 25 years in the research and publication market and it's still growing. One of Hanley Wood's editorial directors, Boyce Thompson, sums up this attitude of success and growth through dedication: "I believe that the media has the power to transform and lead an industry. When your medium is the written word, its power cannot be understated."

Questions

1. Given the type of media Hanley Wood produces, why do you think editing and proofreading are so important to the company?
2. Who is the audience for Hanley Wood publications? How do you imagine Hanley Wood ensures that the information in its publications is appropriate and accurate for that audience?

Key Terms

Acronyms. Acronyms are formed from the first letters of the words for which they stand. An acronym is usually pronounced as a word rather than as individual letters: POTUS (President of the United States). *(p. 117)*

Active voice. A sentence in which the subject performs the action of the verb. *(p. 119)*

Annotated outline. An outline with additional notes, quotes, and reference information that can aid a writer in creating a first draft. *(p. 113)*

Clause. A related group of words containing a subject and a verb. *(p. 121)*

Comma splice. When a comma joins, or splices, two independent clauses in a sentence without a conjunction. *(p. 133)*

Complex sentence. A sentence consisting of a major idea in the independent main clause and one or more minor ideas in one or more dependent clauses. *(p. 122)*

Compound sentence. A sentence consisting of two main clauses connected by a conjunction such as *or, and,* or *but. (p. 121)*

Conjunction. A word such as *or, and, but, because, although,* or *whereas* that connects one clause to another clause. *(p. 121)*

Cover letter: A letter or message that accompanies other material to explain what it consists of and who sent it. *(p. 135)*

Dangling participle. An action word or phrase that appears to be performed by the subject but actually has nothing to do with the subject. *(p. 130)*

Dependent clause. The minor idea of a complex sentence. It cannot stand on its own and is not a complete sentence. *(p. 122)*

Direct paragraph. A paragraph that begins with the main sentence, followed by supporting sentences. *(p. 123)*

Dovetailing. A sentence that serves as a bridge between one paragraph and the next by repeating words. *(p. 124)*

Homonyms. Two words that sound alike but have completely different meanings and spellings. *(p. 133)*

Hook. An interesting phrase or sentence that begins a paragraph and gets the reader "hooked" into reading the rest. *(p. 123)*

Idiom. Expressions that mean something other than the actual words being used. *(p. 117)*

Independent clause. The major idea of a simple or complex sentence; it can stand on its own as a complete sentence. Compound sentences have two or more independent clauses. *(p. 122)*

Indirect paragraph. A paragraph that begins with supporting sentences and ends with the main sentence. *(p. 124)*

Jargon. Language that is particular to a culture, profession, or group. Jargon often consists of acronyms. *(p. 117)*

Nonrestrictive clauses. A clause that adds information, but is not essential to meaning. *(p. 130)*

Object. A person, place, or thing that receives the action of the verb. *(p. 132)*

Parallel construction. Words or phrases using the same grammatical form to establish coherence, particularly in lists. *(p. 128)*

Passive voice. A sentence in which the subject receives the action of the verb. *(p. 119)*

Pivoting paragraph. A paragraph that starts with a sentence that offers a contrasting or negative idea before delivering the main idea. *(p. 124)*

Restrictive clauses. A clause that deliberately limits the scope of the noun and is essential to meaning. *(p. 130)*

Run-on sentence. A fused sentence that results when two independent clauses are fused together without punctuation or a conjunction. *(p. 133)*

Sentence fragment. A grammatically incomplete sentence lacking either a subject, a verb, or both. *(p. 132)*

Simple sentence. A sentence consisting of a subject (person, place, thing, or idea) and a verb (action). *(p. 121)*

Subject. A person, place, or thing that performs the action of a sentence. *(p. 121)*

Transition. A word, phrase, or sentence that serves as a bridge between the previous idea and the next idea. *(p. 124)*

Verb. The action of a sentence. *(p. 121)*

Writer's block. A state of mind in which you believe you cannot think of anything to write. *(p. 114)*

Review Questions *Test Yourself*

1. Why should you know who is in your audience before you begin to write?
2. How does purpose add power and clarity to your message?
3. What are the advantages of knowing your audience's reasons for reading your message?
4. How can an outline help you create your message?
5. What features can be added to an annotated outline to help you expand and organize your ideas?
6. Define free writing and explain how it may be able to help you with the writing process.
7. How do powerful verbs affect your message?
8. In what situations are acronyms or jargon acceptable to use?
9. What is the difference between active and passive voice? Why is active voice preferred in business communication? When is passive voice used?
10. In what ways does organization help make the document readable?
11. What are a few suggestions for keeping your message concise?
12. List a few ideas for making your message easy to read.
13. What qualities should you look for in a reviewer?
14. List the information you should include in a cover letter to a reviewer.
15. How can you effectively consolidate the feedback you receive?

Grammar Review *Mastering Accuracy*

Adverbs

Section I

Each of the following sentences contains one or more common errors in word usage, grammar, or style. Identify the errors. If you have trouble finding the errors, review Section 1.1.3. in the handbook (Appendix D) at the back of this textbook.

1. David seldomly arrives to class on time.
2. I have quite of recent wrecked my car.
3. Paula has not got no information regarding her promotion.
4. She has rarely makes a mistake on tests.
5. In high school, I very well learned how to play chess.
6. The professor began to carefully regard Shane's exam.
7. John decided on the more better and expensive tuxedo for his company mixer.
8. Amy don't like no extra attention during her speech.
9. James became angry when another student would not try nothing to help him cheat.
10. Quite often and occasionally I place adverbs correctly within sentences.

Section II

On a separate sheet of paper, rewrite the following sentences so they are clearer, more professional sounding, grammatically correct, and goodwill oriented.

1. I barely have any time to get my work done when my coworkers chatter and hover next to me.
2. Nobody in the cop car hardly noticed when I turned the corner too fast.
3. David acted very lazy during our early morning meeting.
4. Megan acted spacey and out of it during rehearsal.
5. Sarah has little time for questions in the middle of her speech.
6. The team leader doesn't care about our questions.
7. I really hate the traffic around our parking lot!
8. Well, what do you need me to do today?
9. Maybe I think I will go to the conference.
10. Keep your trap shut when the head honcho gets here.
11. You're in denial if you ever think you're going to get the perks our bosses receive.

Extra Resources *Tools You Can Use*

Books

- Conn, Earl L., and R. Carl Largent. *Effective Business Writing: Write Tight and Right.* Davenport, IA: Robin Vincent Publishing LLC, 2000.
- Magnan, Robert. *1001 Commonly Misspelled Words: What Your Spell Checker Won't Tell You,* 1st ed. Columbus, OH: McGraw-Hill, 2000.
- O'Conner, Patricia T. *Woe Is I: The Grammarphobe's Guide to Better English in Plain English,* 2nd ed. New York: Riverhead Trade, June 2004.
- Pelligrino, Victor C. *A Writer's Guide to Powerful Paragraphs.* Wailuku, HI: Maui Thoughts Company, 2002.
- *Practical Spelling: The Basics Made Easy,* 2nd ed., ed. LearningExpress. New York: LearningExpress, LLC, 2006.
- Strunk, William, and E. B. White. *Elements of Style,* 4th ed. Needham Heights, MA: Allyn & Bacon, 2000.
- Truss, Lynn. *Eats, Shoots & Leaves: The Zero Tolerance Approach to Punctuation.* New York: Gotham Books, 2004.

Web Sites

- "Just Say No to These Three Enemies of Clear and Direct Writing," *Copyblogger.*
- "Drafting Legal Documents: Principles of Clear Writing," *Archives.gov.*
- "Grammar Girl: Quick and Dirty Tips for Better Writing," *Quick and Dirty Tips.*
- "Improving Communication from the Federal Government to the Public," *Plain Language.gov.*

"Appearance is everything." —**Steve Jeffes,** American author

Designing, Proofreading, and Distributing Messages

LEARNING OBJECTIVE QUESTIONS

1. What design choices will make your message stand out?
2. How do headings and white space affect a message's readability?
3. What makes a message visually interesting?
4. Why is it important to proofread your message?
5. What is the best way to distribute your message?

PEARSON **mybcommlab** Access interactive videos, simulations, sample documents, document makeovers, and assessment quizzes in Chapter 6 of **mybcommlab.com** for mastery of this chapter's objectives.

>>> **Kobe** was a senior manager in the European Division for Sylvan Learning Systems, a company providing educational support for K–12 education. After working in both the United States and overseas in Spain and France, Kobe decided he wanted to make a difference in the public education system in his hometown of San Antonio, Texas. He applied to be the superintendent of the largest school district in San Antonio. The application was a long shot because Kobe did not have a teaching degree. However, he did have a degree in political science from the University of Texas at Austin, and an MBA from Princeton. Most importantly, he had a very impressive track record with his jobs up to and including his tenure with Sylvan. At 40 years of age, Kobe had a lot to offer, including his fluency in Spanish.

Kobe decided to take a unique approach and write letters to both the school board and the citizens and parents in San Antonio. In his letter to the community and parents, he realized he needed to be clear about his vision and outline the specific changes he thought were necessary for the district: 1) create higher expectations for teachers by inspiring them to teach in an interactive and participatory way, 2) measure the performance of schools by more than just test scores, and 3) urge parents to turn off their televisions and set higher expectations for their children.

After getting feedback on the message from his colleagues, Kobe then formatted the letters to make sure they were as readable and attractive as possible. He proofread them and asked a number of other people to proofread them as well. He then corrected the letters and mailed a copy to each member of the board. To reach the citizens and parents in the community, he paid to have the letter printed in a local community newspaper. Both letters contained links to a Web site where visitors could get more information about Kobe as well as view his résumé and personal information.

The school board and community found Kobe's ideas—informed in large part by Kobe's strong business instincts and communication skills—to be just what the district needed. His efforts paid off. He was hired.

TIPS FOR THE WEB

Throughout this chapter you will interject special tips for formatting and delivering your message on the Web, rather than in print.

Kobe >>>

By now, you already have a good idea of how to organize and write documents so people can easily read and understand them. However, Kobe's story should illustrate the importance of a document's accuracy and appearance. Typos, strange fonts, and crowded text can easily cause people to conclude before they even read your document that you are unprofessional or don't know what you are talking about. That's why you need to pay attention to the layout and format of a document as well as proofread it. Attractive, engaging documents without errors are particularly important in the field of education.

If you are interested in written communication, enjoy interacting with others, and love to explain things, the field of education might be a good fit for you.

Besides traditional teaching jobs in primary and secondary schools or colleges, other jobs in the field of education you might be interested in are included in the following chart. All of these jobs require their holders to have the ability to communicate clearly and produce and distribute well-written, professional-looking materials.

Technical Writer

Technical writers write materials that will be printed in textbooks or workbooks for traditional and correspondence schools, or that will appear on Web pages for online schools. These writers are also employed in high-tech industries such as software, electronics, and scientific instruments industries to write user manuals and product specifications.

Copyeditor

A copyeditor reads and revises material, making sure its organization makes sense to readers, and its spelling, grammar, and punctuation are correct.

Adult-Education Instructor

Adult-education instructors are often teachers with life or work experience in certain subjects. They often work for technical schools.

Tutor

Tutors can be freelancers who work one-on-one with children or adults, at schools or at home. They can also be employees of colleges and organizations such as Sylvan Learning.

Instructional Designer

Instructional designers are in charge of creating courses or textbooks. They work with subject matter experts to develop course outlines and identify activities, tests, and supplemental materials that enhance learning. However, they do not write the actual course material.

Instructional Coordinator

Instructional coordinators play a large role in improving the quality of education in the classroom by developing curricula, selecting textbooks, and other materials, training teachers, assessing educational programs, and implementing new technology in the classroom.

Communications Officer

Communications officers are responsible for all external communication for large school districts or county offices of education. Their duties include acting as spokespeople, drafting reports, writing pages, etc.

Health Educator

Health educators promote, maintain, and improve the health of individuals and communities by helping them to adopt healthy behaviors. Health educators collect and analyze data to identify a community's health needs and evaluate programs designed to encourage healthy lifestyles, policies, and environments.

Educational Administrator

Educational administrators manage the day-to-day activities in schools, preschools, day care centers, and colleges and universities. They also direct the educational programs of businesses, correctional institutions, museums, and job training and community service organizations.

Corporate Trainer

Corporate trainers develop training materials and teach employees and customers. They typically work for large companies.

❶ What Design Choices Will Make Your Message Stand Out?

In this chapter, you will follow the journey of the document shown in **Exhibit 6-1** on p. 146. The exhibit shows a flyer advertising an internship with an educational publisher. Throughout the chapter, you will discover how the flyer undergoes a "makeover" and is improved.

■ For an interactive, real-world example of this topic, access this chapter's bcomm mini sim entitled The Communication Process, located at **mybcommlab.com**

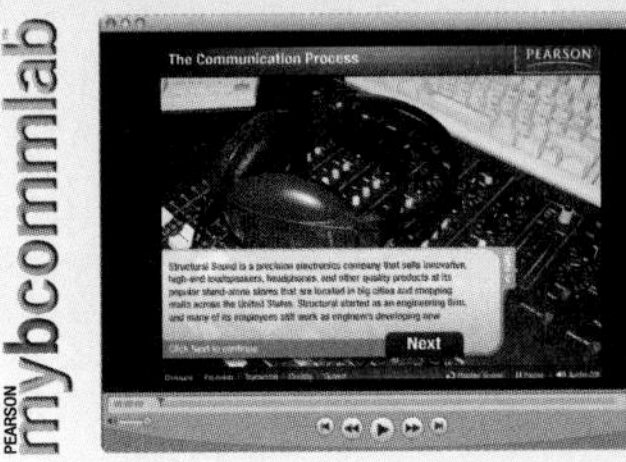

Designing the Message

Making a document look good is actually easier than making sure it has good content. Following the guidelines in this section will help you create a document that's visually appealing. Your words might be terrific, but if the message is poorly designed, readers might see you and the organization you represent as unprofessional. As a result, your message could be ignored or rejected. Just as people judge others by their appearance and form quick opinions, so do they judge documents by their appearance. Make sure your document makes a great first impression.

Not all documents require extensive formatting. For example, a text message will require very little, perhaps just some spacing and punctuation to make the information clear. However, a multipage report with charts and graphs or a section of a textbook will require a great deal of formatting.

Choosing Fonts

A **font** is the technical name for a typeface. There are two major categories of fonts: sans-serif fonts and serif fonts. A **serif** font contains small vertical or horizontal marks called "serifs" at the end of strokes. A **sans-serif** font does not have serifs at the end of strokes. The term comes from the French word sans, which means "without."[1]

Exhibit 6-2 illustrates the difference between sans-serif and serif fonts. The serifs appear as extra vertical and horizontal lines attached to the ends of each letter. **Exhibit 6-3** shows some of the most commonly used fonts. Once you choose a font, use it throughout the body of your document. Mixing different fonts and sizes of fonts in the body of your text will make your document look amateurish. However, you can use different fonts for headings or tables. Just do not mix and match too many types of fonts.

Just because there are a seemingly endless number of fonts available to you, doesn't mean you should use all of them.

Exhibit 6-1
Original Flyer

Seeking Interns

Are you someone who loves to write?
Enjoys learning?
Can't get enough of talking to people?

Consider Becoming a Developmental Editor Intern

Success Unlimited is offering a summer internship to sophomores, juniors, or seniors who would like to work remotely from home or work in a small-office environment. An internship is a great opportunity to learn and earn money and credits.

Success Unlimited is a small educational publishing house, dedicated to providing academic success skills to students of all backgrounds, ages, and learning styles.

Job Description
Revise copy for educational workbooks
Check grammar and punctuation
Research projects and gather information
Gather permissions and references for bibliography
Help manage projects

Necessary Skills
Able to write clearly
Good at explaining things
Comfortable talking to others to gather information
Able to make short presentations
Well-organized and a self-starter

"Nice-to-Have" Skills
Working knowledge of MS Word and PowerPoint (optional)
Prior writing experience (articles, instructions, proposals, blogs, web content)

Requirements
Working toward degree in English, Business, Communication, Education, Journalism
GPA of 3.0 or higher

Compensation
6 units of work study credit toward your degree

Apply Today
We are accepting applications through the end of June. If you are interested in an internship, please email your cover letter to Cherie White at: jobs@successunlimited.com

Attach the following:
Resume (include any honors, writing classes, teaching experience, or publications)
Two letters of reference
Two short writing examples that show your writing style

Exhibit 6-2
Sans-Serif and Serif Fonts

EeFfGg	Sans-serif font (Verdana)
EeFfGg	Serif font (Georgia)

Exhibit 6-3
Commonly Used Fonts

Serif Fonts	Sans-Serif Fonts
Bookman Antiqua	Arial
Century Schoolbook	Tahoma
Georgia	Trebuchet
Times New Roman	Verdana

REAL INSIGHTS from a Seasoned Professional

Name: *Susan Katz*
Title: *President and Publisher*
Organization: *HarperCollins Children's Books*
Location: *New York City, New York*

SUSAN KATZ BEGAN HER CAREER in publishing after graduate school in 1972. At the time, there were few teaching jobs in New York City, which is what Katz had originally planned to do. After a friend encouraged her to consider a career in educational publishing instead, Katz, who loves the English language, jumped at the opportunity to become an editorial assistant for Random House. Her passion was well placed.

It wasn't long before Katz advanced through the ranks, breaking barriers in what was, at the time, a male-dominated field. She worked on books for seventh to twelfth graders and was quickly promoted to an associate editor's position. She later accepted a job with Holt, Rinehart, and Winston, a publisher of college textbooks, before going on to become its editor in chief. Later she was recruited by HarperCollins' college publishing division before being promoted to her current position.

Katz has seen dramatic changes in her 38 years in the publishing industry, especially with regard to the technology used. One of her goals for HarperCollins is to continue harnessing new technologies to help readers learn in all kinds of ways. "We don't want to be left behind," Katz says about her company. "We want to lead the way."

Part of leading the way includes finding better ways to communicate with HarperCollins' employees, customers, and shareholders. HarperCollins is part of the global media company News Corporation, which owns a host of movie, television, newspaper, magazine, and book-publishing companies. On the 9th floor of HarperCollins is an entire communication center. Katz uses the center to create internal videos to get her message across and conduct Web and video conferences with live question-and-answer sessions. However, the richest method of communicating is still face to face, she says.

Katz's advice to students seeking careers in publishing is to research areas about which they are passionate. If you are interested in children's publishing, go to bookstores, talk to parents about the best books they have read and why they like them, watch children reading books, and so on. The same is true if you are looking for a job in college or high school publishing. "Put yourself squarely in the center of what interests you and learn as much as you can about that area," Katz suggests.

Having passion for your job isn't enough, though. You also have to be able to communicate your ideas and motivate people to act on them. Many new graduates need to work on their communication skills, Katz says. Sloppy speech, writing, dress, and interpersonal communications styles can take a toll on a graduate's career advancement. "We have communication breakdowns daily when people are too casual, when they don't do their homework, or when they don't speak up in meetings," she says.

Some new grads under-communicate. They have information, but they don't come forth to share it in useful ways. Others make assumptions without getting the facts or talking to people who know the answers. She says the most successful new hires take the initiative in meetings, see problems and solve them, do their homework, and are prepared to contribute in ways beyond the standard "job" mentality.

Questions

1. In what ways does Katz distribute messages to HarperCollins' employees?
2. Think of a situation where you had to communicate something important to a particular audience in writing. What was the message, and who was the audience? How did you make sure that the message was formatted professionally and distributed appropriately?

Source: Susan Katz in discussion with the author, July 2010.

TIPS FOR THE WEB: FONTS

Not everyone has the same fonts installed on their computers. Unusual fonts might not show up right on people's computers, even though they look fine on yours. To avoid the problem use common fonts such as Times New Roman, Georgia, Arial, or Verdana, which are typically available on all computers. Also, for online reading, research has shown people find sans-serif fonts easier to discern.

Sizes

Fonts in larger point sizes are easier to read than smaller fonts. A **point** is a unit of measure for fonts (about 1/72 of an inch). The body of your text should be 10 to 12 points in size so that your readers can see the text easily. For most online documents, 12 point is best.

You might be wondering about the range of point sizes. Why shouldn't one point size be used in all messages? The reason it shouldn't is because not all fonts are created equal. For example, 10-point Times New Roman looks smaller than 10-point Verdana. Look at the point sizes of the fonts in **Exhibit 6-4** to see the differences.

Exhibit 6-4
Different Fonts and Sizes

9 Point	10 Point	11 Point	12 Point
Georgia	Georgia	Georgia	Georgia
Times New Roman	Times New Roman	Times New Roman	Times New Roman
Arial	Arial	Arial	Arial
Verdana	Verdana	Verdana	Verdana

TIPS FOR THE WEB: FONT SIZES

People of all ages surf the Web, which means your font needs to be visible to people with less-than-perfect eyesight. To ensure Web visitors can read what you write, use a font size that is at least 10 points or larger.

Styles

You can vary a font's style for different purposes. The following are common font styles.

- ***Boldface.*** **Boldface** type is generally used for the beginning of items in bulleted lists as well as for headings. The key terms in textbooks, such as this one, are often set in boldface. Boldfaced words get attention. However, too much boldfacing is overwhelming. Use it sparingly.
- ***Italics.*** **Italics** are characters set in rightward-leaning typeface. They are generally used for emphasis, as the following sentence shows:

  When negotiating a selling price, do not *automatically suggest you are willing to pay more.*

  Do not overuse italics because they are more difficult to read than standard text.
- ***Underlining.*** Online, **underlines** are generally used to indicate "hot links" you click to go to another Web page or part of a Web page.

  In printed documents, the rules are a little different. No underlines are necessary because readers cannot click the link on a printed page and actually go to the Web. Also, do not use underlines for headings. Underlines can make your document look old-fashioned. They were commonly used with manual typewriters to distinguish headings.

  Avoid using boldface, italics, and underlines in e-mails. Many people receive their e-mails in a plain-text format, which means the styles don't show up in their messages. However, you can still make your e-mails look nice with good spacing, asterisks (*) and dashes (—), as **Exhibit 6-5** shows.

Colors

When it comes to text color, less is more. Most professional documents use only one color for text. However, some use a different color for headings, and others use an accent color as well. For example, in some chapters of this book, different colors are used to highlight certain text and make it stand out.

Too many text colors make your document look like "fruit punch" and give it an unprofessional appearance. Additionally, a sizable proportion of the populace is color-blind and find it particularly difficult to distinguish between green and red text.

Subject: Internship opportunities

```
Attached is a flyer I received about an internship with a
company called Success Unlimited. You might be interested
in it if you are looking for a summer job in an area
associated with your major.  Please read the attached
flyer for specific details. Below are some of the flyer's
main points:

* Compensation *
--------------------
You can earn six units of college credits.

* Type of Work*
--------------------
You will be doing a lot of writing and editing (which I
know is your strength), and you will get to talk to many
different people and do research.

* Requirements *
---------------------
Study the requirements in the flyer. Many of you meet all
of them.

Dr. Margaret Ashfield
```

Exhibit 6-5
E-mail Formatting

Regardless of the colors you use, make sure the **color contrast** is strong. In other words, the color of the text should contrast strongly with the background color. Dark text on a light background is best. **Exhibit 6-6** shows some examples of good versus poor color contrasts.

Finally, be consistent with the colors you use. For example, perhaps all your headings are dark gray, and the body of your text is always black. Readers will see the pattern and begin to scan for dark gray text as they look for the headings. Most readers will assume blue, underlined text is a link to a Web page, so keep this in mind when you are choosing font colors and styles.

TIPS FOR THE WEB: COLORS

Every monitor and every browser show colors a little differently. Consequently, the color you see in your browser when viewing a Web page might not be exactly the same color someone else sees on his or her monitor when viewing the page. If you want the colors on your Web page or document to look the same in all browsers, use Web-safe colors. There are 216 colors that look the same on all Web browsers. To see a palette of these colors, do an online search for *Web-safe colors*.

Exhibit 6-6
Color Contrast

Poor Contrast	Good Contrast
Blue text on dark gray	Black text on a white background
Red text on black background (Difficult to see)	Black text on a light gray background
Red text on blue background (Difficult to see)	Dark blue text on pale blue background
White text on a black background (Use only for headings because the color combination tends to fatigue the eyes)	Dark brown text on light yellow

2 How Do Headings and White Space Affect a Message's Readability?

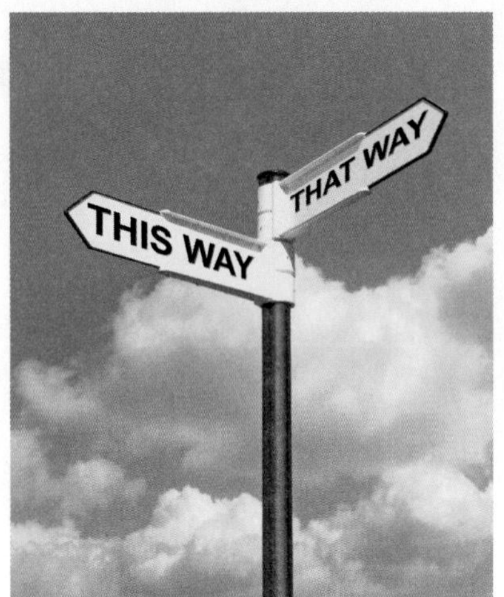

Headings act as signposts, guiding the reader through a document.

A document's headings, subheadings, and white space can make a difference in terms of the message's readability. Specifically, they can make it easier or harder for your reader to scan the message for important information.

Creating Headings and Subheadings

Headings typically identify major sections in a document. **Subheadings** indicate subsections. Both headings and subheadings should be clear, compelling, and concise. Use them to grab the attention of readers and encourage them to keep reading. Headings and subheadings also serve as guideposts for readers by helping them scan quickly through a document to find what they need. Consequently, when you write a heading, focus on what your readers really need to know as they scan the text. In general, headings should be no more than eight words long.[2]

Major headings are generally much larger than **body text**. Often the headings are 16 to 20 points. We mentioned earlier that they can also be a different font or color. Subheadings are usually four points smaller than headings, but should still be at least two points larger than body text size. **Exhibit 6-7** illustrates the difference between those types of headings.

Exhibit 6-7
Major Headings and Subheadings

> **This Is a Major Heading**
> The major heading is 16 points in size.
>
> **This Is a Minor Heading**
> The minor heading is 12 points in size.

The size of the heading is not the only aspect you need to think about. You need to consider the wording as well. Headings are like newspaper headlines—critical attention-getters that allow your readers to determine in just a few seconds if the information is relevant to them. Readers use headings to grasp the content on a page and decide if they want to read more of it.

Make sure you capitalize your headings in a consistent way. Some people prefer newspaper-style capitalization, where you capitalize the first letter of each major word in the heading. Others prefer sentence-style capitalization, where you capitalize only the first letter of the first word of the heading. Whichever form of capitalization you choose, use it throughout your document.

Newspaper Capitalization: Great News for Educational Publishing Interns
Sentence Capitalization: Great news for educational publishing interns

TIPS FOR THE WEB: HEADINGS

Headings make Web pages easier for people to read because they "chunk," or categorize, information so people can quickly skim the pages and find what they are looking for. Use headings with words that mean something important to the reader, either consciously or unconsciously.

CHECKLIST

Use headings to:

- Break up long blocks of text.
- Get the reader's attention and guide the reader.

Let's revisit the internship flyer (see **Exhibit 6-8**) to see how the font style, color, and heading principles you learned about have been applied to the first part of the flyer. We will continue to follow this part of the flyer throughout the rest of the chapter.

Exhibit 6-8 Top Section of Flyer: Changing Fonts, Styles, and Colors

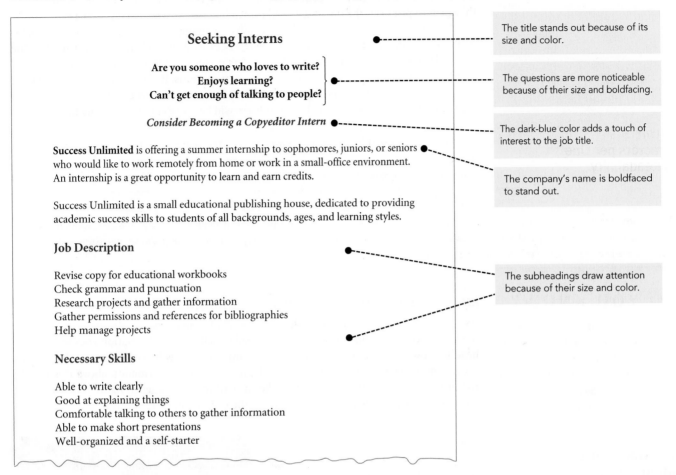

Seeking Interns

Are you someone who loves to write?
Enjoys learning?
Can't get enough of talking to people?

Consider Becoming a Copyeditor Intern

Success Unlimited is offering a summer internship to sophomores, juniors, or seniors who would like to work remotely from home or work in a small-office environment. An internship is a great opportunity to learn and earn credits.

Success Unlimited is a small educational publishing house, dedicated to providing academic success skills to students of all backgrounds, ages, and learning styles.

Job Description

Revise copy for educational workbooks
Check grammar and punctuation
Research projects and gather information
Gather permissions and references for bibliographies
Help manage projects

Necessary Skills

Able to write clearly
Good at explaining things
Comfortable talking to others to gather information
Able to make short presentations
Well-organized and a self-starter

The title stands out because of its size and color.

The questions are more noticeable because of their size and boldfacing.

The dark-blue color adds a touch of interest to the job title.

The company's name is boldfaced to stand out.

The subheadings draw attention because of their size and color.

Using White Space

What you don't put on the page is almost as important as what you do. **White space** is the part of the document that does not contain any text. White space enhances your document by separating ideas into manageable segments readers can easily digest, defining sections, and giving the reader's eyes a rest. A document without enough white space looks cluttered and complicated. A document with too much white space looks empty and simplistic. Try to achieve a good balance between the two. Catherine S. Hibbard, a business writing expert with the Cypress Media Group, puts it this way: "Think of white space as you would a five-course meal served in a nice restaurant. Served in distinct courses, the food's visual impact is much greater than that of a crowded buffet table, which is laden with as much food as possible in as little space as possible."[3]

White space typically appears:

- At the top, bottom, and side margins
- Before and after headings
- Between paragraphs
- Between bulleted items in a list
- Between columns of words or numbers
- Before indented sentences

Let's look at the first four items in the list. These are the most effective ways to provide white space.

Margins act as a frame around your page.

Margins

Margins are the blank areas at the top, bottom, and sides of the document. If the margins are too small, the text can appear dense and hard to read. If possible, use at least 1″ margins for the top, bottom, and sides of your document. Some people use 1.25″ for the left margin if they plan to print out the document and punch holes in it so it can be put in a binder.

If you need to adjust the margins, consider changing the top or bottom ones in 0.25″ increments rather than the side margins. Why? Because as the side margins get smaller, the line width gets longer. Studies show that readers prefer shorter lines because they can read them faster. That's why newspapers are laid out in columns. It's best to use 50 to 60 characters per line.[4] Notice how much easier **Exhibit 6-9a** is to read than **Exhibit 6-9b** because of the width. If you are using a smaller font, there will be more characters in the line.

Exhibit 6-9
Characters per Line and Readability

A

These lines of text are easy to read because they are not so long. The sentences are fine, and the text width of the line is not too great. The narrower width takes less time to scan. The reader's eyes do not become fatigued, and the reader perceives the text as uncluttered.

B

These lines of text are difficult to read because they are so long. The sentences are fine, but the text width is too great. The extra width takes longer to scan. The reader's speed may slow down, but more importantly, the reader's eyes may become fatigued. Worse, the reader will perceive the text as too dense and complicated and stop reading.

DID YOU KNOW?

To specify spacing between list items in Microsoft Word, use the **Format** > **Paragraph** command. You can then set the number of points you want before (above) and after (below) paragraphs. Whatever spacing you use, be consistent.

Line Spaces before and after Headings

As you learned earlier, headings indicate the start of a new type of information. However, the line space above and below them helps readers tell which information goes with which heading. Always use more space above a heading than below it. This indicates that the information below the heading is associated with it and the information above it is not. In **Exhibit 6-10**, the spacing on the left makes it hard for the reader to figure out which text goes with which heading, but the spacing on the right makes it quite clear.

Exhibit 6-10
Using Line Spaces with Headings

Incorrect Spacing for Headers	Correct Spacing for Headers
Heading 1 This text belongs with Heading 1. This text belongs with Heading 1. This text belongs with Heading 1. **Heading 2** This text belongs with Heading 2. This text belongs to Heading 2. This text belongs to Heading 2.	**Heading 1** This text belongs with Heading 1. This text belongs with Heading 1. This text belongs with Heading 1. **Heading 2** This text belongs with Heading 2. This text belongs to Heading 2. This text belongs to Heading 2.

Line Spaces between Paragraphs

Readers need white space between paragraphs to tell them where one paragraph begins and one ends. A single line space is common in business documents.

Line Spaces between List Items

Readers also need some white space between items in a list to make the items more readable. A single line space may be too little, but a few points more might be just right.

Exhibit 6-11 shows two lists created by an instructional designer who develops workbooks for a correspondence school. Notice how the numbered list on the right, which uses 3 points of space between each item in the list, is less dense and easier to read.

TIPS FOR THE WEB: SPACING

Use ample white space on Web pages. Great information in dense blocks of text on Web pages often doesn't get read. Break up long paragraphs (more than five lines is too long) and maintain adequate margins and line spacing.

Exhibit 6-11
Using Spacing between List Items

Too Little Space between Items	Right Amount of Space between Items
Things to Think About 1. Know your learner. 2. Identify measurable learning objectives. 3. Develop activities to demonstrate objectives. 4. Write instructions for activities. 5. Present concepts that must be in place before students try the activities. 6. Present real-life stories and examples to engage students.	**Things to Think About** 1. Know your learner. 2. Identify measurable learning objectives. 3. Develop activities to demonstrate objectives. 4. Write instructions for activities. 5. Present concepts that must be in place before students try the activities. 6. Present real-life stories and examples to engage students.

Spaces between Columns

Presenting information in multiple columns saves space when you are trying to use as little vertical area as possible. Word processing tools allow you to specify the number of columns, as well as their width and the amount of space between them. Do not use too many columns or make them too narrow because the text will become very difficult to read. **Exhibits 6-12a** and **6-12b** show good and bad examples of column spacing.

Exhibit 6-12
Using Multiple Columns

Two columns is usually the maximum number you need for your document to use up less space but still remain professional looking and easy to read. The two columns are sufficiently wide to contain enough words to make reading easy.	Also, the amount of space between columns is adequate to clearly separate them. The result is easy to read and professional in appearance.

A

Using multiple columns to save space won't necessarily make your document	attractive or easy to read. You can see from this example that the columns	are too narrow, resulting in too few words on each line. This makes reading	difficult. Also, the amount of space between columns is too narrow, making them appear to run together.

B

How could white space help our example flyer? **Exhibit 6-13** shows the difference with added spacing.

Helping the Reader Skim and Scan

Most people tend to scan before they read anything in depth. You have already learned that boldface, white space, and headings all draw the reader's eye and improve his or her scanning. Bullets are another way to help people's eyes quickly slide down the page.

Listing items with bullets makes it much easier for the reader to get useful information. Readers can quickly scan all the information to find out if it satisfies their needs. Compare the text in **Exhibit 6-14.** It is easy to see that the text in the right column is easier to scan because it has bullets, more white space, and boldfaced words.

Exhibit 6-13 **Top Section of Flyer: Better Spacing**

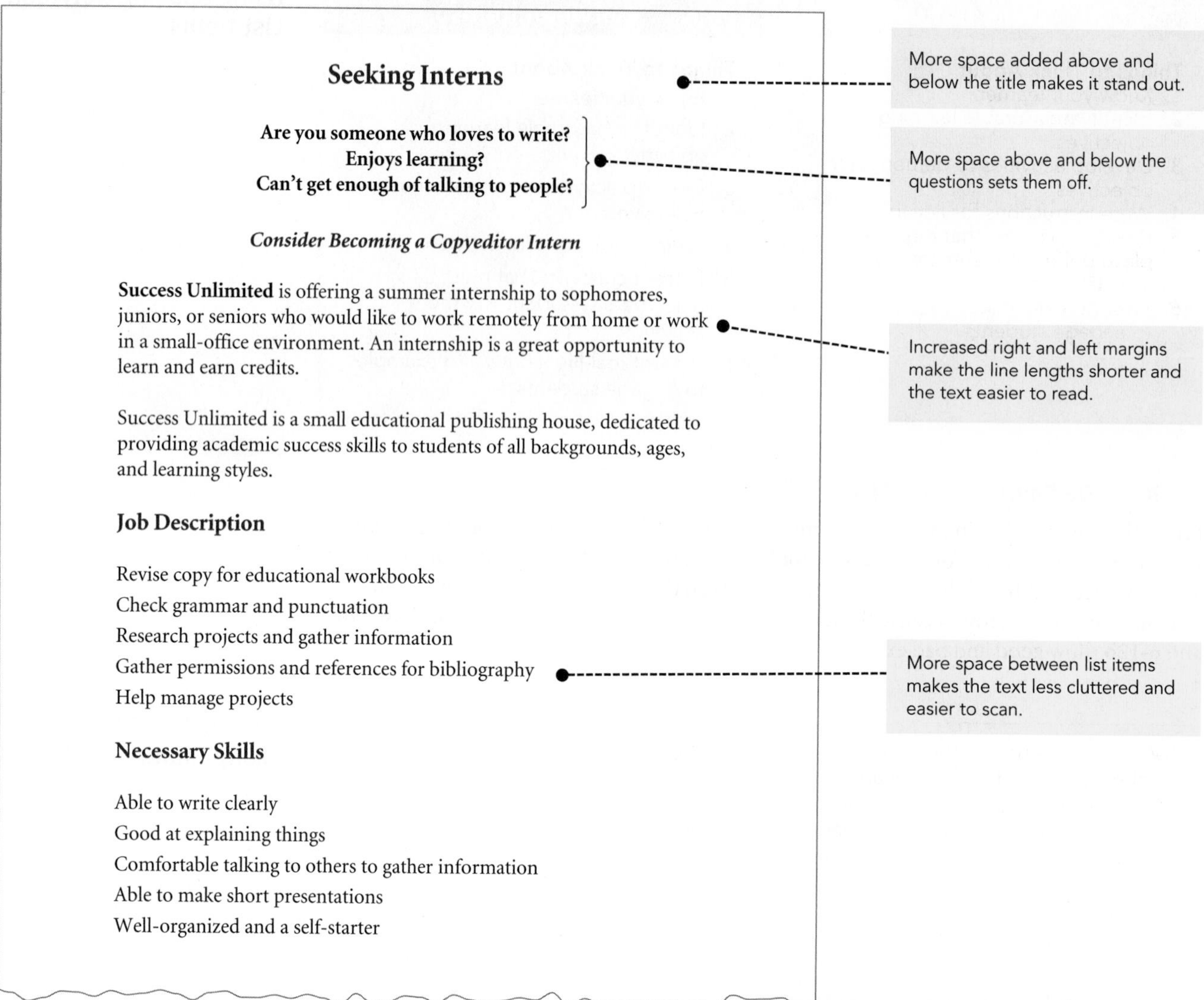

Seeking Interns

Are you someone who loves to write?
Enjoys learning?
Can't get enough of talking to people?

Consider Becoming a Copyeditor Intern

Success Unlimited is offering a summer internship to sophomores, juniors, or seniors who would like to work remotely from home or work in a small-office environment. An internship is a great opportunity to learn and earn credits.

Success Unlimited is a small educational publishing house, dedicated to providing academic success skills to students of all backgrounds, ages, and learning styles.

Job Description

Revise copy for educational workbooks
Check grammar and punctuation
Research projects and gather information
Gather permissions and references for bibliography
Help manage projects

Necessary Skills

Able to write clearly
Good at explaining things
Comfortable talking to others to gather information
Able to make short presentations
Well-organized and a self-starter

More space added above and below the title makes it stand out.
More space above and below the questions sets them off.
Increased right and left margins make the line lengths shorter and the text easier to read.
More space between list items makes the text less cluttered and easier to scan.

Exhibit 6-14
Using Bullets to Make Scanning Easier

Copy without Bullets	Copy with Bullets
Internships are a great way to learn more about the subject you are studying in college. They provide real experience in your chosen profession. They give you the opportunity to interact with people who studied what you studied. They help you find out if you really want to go into the field you are studying. Better yet, they let you earn money and college credits while you learn.	Internships are a great way to learn more about the subject you are studying in college. They do the following: • Provide experience in your chosen profession. • Give you a chance to interact with people who studied what you studied. • Help you find out if you really want to go into the field you are studying. • Let you earn money and college credits while you learn.

3 What Makes a Message Visually Interesting?

No one wants to read a document that puts him or her to sleep. You need to keep your readers interested in what you have to say and wanting to read more. The right graphic elements and layout can add to the visual appeal of your message, which will help keep the reader's attention.

Using Graphic Elements

Graphic elements such as tables, charts, and illustrations can add interest to your document and help you convey information more effectively than words alone can.

Tables

Tables are useful for displaying and comparing information in an easy-to-read format. Readers more easily scan data in a table than data in a paragraph. When you create a table, keep these guidelines in mind.

- ***Use a sans-serif font.*** Sans-serif font is easier to read not only on the Web but in tables, especially when you are displaying a lot of information. You can also use a smaller-sized font than serif font, and the table will still be readable. For example, if the text in your document is 12-point Times New Roman, use 9-point Verdana for the table.
- ***Left-align words.*** People typically read text from left to right. Consequently, names, addresses, and other textual information should be left-aligned. Studies indicate that right-aligned text is more difficult to read.[5]
- ***Right-align numbers.*** Numbers are typically right-aligned so the ones, tens, and hundreds places line up for ease of reading and math operations. **Exhibit 6-15** shows how words should be aligned left in a table and numbers should be aligned right.

CHECKLIST

To properly format a table:

- ☑ Use a sans-serif font.
- ☑ Left-justify text.
- ☑ Right-justify numbers.

Exhibit 6-15
Table with the Correct Alignment of Words and Numbers[6]

Job	Gross Annual Income
Chief executive officer	$160,720
Corporate trainer	$51,450
Instructional designer (also called instructional coordinator)	$56,880
Technical writer	$61,620
Tutor (or teaching assistant)	$25,000
Vocational education instructor	$47,330

Visuals

A document's visuals usually consist of charts, photos, or illustrations.

- ***Insert visuals where applicable.*** Sometimes you need a picture to explain a concept, get the reader's attention, or break up text. You can allow text to wrap around the picture or place the picture in line with the text. It depends on the page layout. Make sure the visual is large enough for the reader to see. (You will learn more about the use of visuals in Chapter 12.)

TIPS FOR THE WEB: VISUALS

Visuals are just as important on the Web as on the printed page. However, an image's file size has to be considered before you post it to a Web page. Large files take longer to download, so visitors with slower Internet connections will have to wait longer for the image to appear on their screens.

An image's format also needs to be considered. For most Web images, use a *JPEG (Joint Photographic Experts Group)* file. JPEGs result in smaller-sized files. If your image contains a large variety of colors or needs to appear with sharper resolution, use a *PNG (Portable Network Graphics)* file. Finally, if your image is an animation, use a *GIF (Graphics Interchange Format)* file.

Layout and Alignment

The last thing to look at when formatting a message is its overall layout. This means evaluating where the text, graphics, headings, and white space appear on the page. You are looking for simplicity, balance, and professionalism.

- ***Avoid centered text.*** Centered text is fine for headings and subheadings but not standard text. Readers prefer left margins that are set consistently straight (left-justified) so they can easily scan down the page.

> Notice how difficult it is to read a large block of text that is centered. A straight (justified) left margin makes it easier to scan the page. When the text is centered, it results in a ragged left margin that hinders scanning down the page.

- ***Avoid full-justification.*** **Justification** refers to the vertical alignment of the text. If you left-justify (align the left side) of the body of your text, don't right-justify (align the right side). If you do, the result will be **full justification,** or a straight left margin and a straight right margin. The spacing varies between words in lines that are fully justified, which can distract the reader. This is especially true when the column of text is not very wide, as the following example shows.

> Do not make the mistake of using full justification to form a straight left margin and a straight right margin. When you do, the spacing changes between words and disrupts the reader's attention.

- ***Avoid right-justification.*** If you think centered or full-justified text is difficult to read, try reading right-justified text. **Right-justified** text is text with a **ragged,** or uneven, left margin and a straight right margin. People read from top to bottom and left to right. A ragged left margin prevents them from moving down the left margin and easily reading and scanning.

> Notice how difficult it is to read the right-justified text shown in this paragraph. The text is crammed against the right margin, making it hard for readers to scan down the left margin.

- ***Use left justification.*** Use left justification for your text. Text that is **left-justified** has a straight left margin and a ragged right margin.

> Notice how much easier it is to read text that is left-justified, with a straight left margin and a ragged right margin. Now you can easily scan down the left margin and read the text quickly. Also, spacing is much more natural between the words

- ***Use a grid.*** Using a **grid,** a temporary table with horizontal and vertical lines called *gridlines,* can help you line up text and images for a clean look. When your space is limited, double columns can help. You can later remove the grid's lines once all of your

Exhibit 6-16
Using Grid Lines

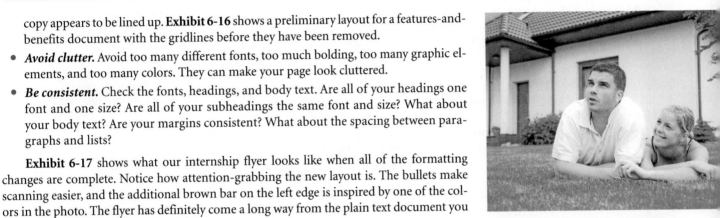

<table>
<tr><td colspan="2">Title</td></tr>
<tr><td>Photo can be placed here.</td><td>Attention-getting questions and introductory text goes here.</td></tr>
<tr><td>Features
Text text text text text Text text text text text Text text text text text Text text text text text</td><td>Benefits
Text text text text text Text text text text text Text text text text text Text text text text text Text text text text text Text text text text text Text text text text text</td></tr>
</table>

copy appears to be lined up. **Exhibit 6-16** shows a preliminary layout for a features-and-benefits document with the gridlines before they have been removed.

- ***Avoid clutter.*** Avoid too many different fonts, too much bolding, too many graphic elements, and too many colors. They can make your page look cluttered.
- ***Be consistent.*** Check the fonts, headings, and body text. Are all of your headings one font and one size? Are all of your subheadings the same font and size? What about your body text? Are your margins consistent? What about the spacing between paragraphs and lists?

Exhibit 6-17 shows what our internship flyer looks like when all of the formatting changes are complete. Notice how attention-grabbing the new layout is. The bullets make scanning easier, and the additional brown bar on the left edge is inspired by one of the colors in the photo. The flyer has definitely come a long way from the plain text document you saw at the beginning of the chapter.

A document that is laid out well is like a well-designed home: easy on the eyes and easy to navigate.

Technology Shortcuts

You don't have to be a formatting guru to produce a professional-looking document. Microsoft Word and other word processing programs have a number of technology shortcuts or tools that can give your documents a polished, professional appearance.

The following are a few technology shortcuts:

- **Default settings**: When you open an empty document, it will already have specific settings in place for the orientation of the document (horizontal or vertical), its margins, its headers and footers, which consist of repeated information at the top and bottom of each page, and spacing between lines. You can either use the settings as they are or change them if they don't meet your needs.
- **Styles**: If fonts and formatting confuse you, styles can help. Styles are predefined formats you can use repeatedly throughout a document to format heads, lists, texts, and other elements. When you open an empty document, certain default styles are automatically available to you. For example, suppose the "Heading1" style is defined as centered, bold, 14 point, Verdana font. All you have to do is highlight your text and select the "Heading1" style from your toolbar, and your text will be automatically transformed to match the Heading 1 style, as shown below:

  Formatted text for Heading1

  Using the style menu this way will save you many mouse clicks and ensure that all of your headings are consistently formatted. You can use the predefined styles as is, edit them, or create your own.
- ***Table of Contents:*** Most word processing programs let you automatically generate a table of contents from your document, complete with your headings and page numbers. This will save you time and mistakes when you create a table of contents for your document. All you have to do is tag your headings with the appropriate styles and specify

CHECKLIST

To improve a document's layout:

- ☑ Avoid centering blocks of text.
- ☑ Use a ragged-right margin.
- ☑ Balance text with visuals and white space.
- ☑ Use a grid or table to line up items.
- ☑ Get rid of clutter.
- ☑ Be consistent.

Exhibit 6-17 Finished Flyer: Improved Layout, Color, and an Image

Seeking Interns

Are you someone who loves to write?
Enjoys learning?
Can't get enough of talking to people?

Consider Becoming a Copyeditor Intern

Success Unlimited is offering a summer internship to sophomores, juniors, or seniors who would like to work remotely from home or work in a small-office environment. An internship is a great opportunity to learn and earn credits.

Success Unlimited is a small educational publishing house, dedicated to providing academic success skills to students of all backgrounds, stages, and learning styles.

Job Description

- Revise copy for educational workbooks
- Check grammar and punctuation
- Research projects and gather information
- Gather permissions and references for bibliography
- Help manage projects

Necessary Skills

- Able to write clearly
- Good at explaining things
- Comfortable talking to others to gather information
- Able to make short presentations
- Well-organized and a self-starter

"Nice-to-Have" Skills

- Working knowledge of MS Word and PowerPoint (optional)
- Prior writing experience (articles, instructions, proposals, blogs, Web content)

Academic Requirements

- Working toward degree in English, Business, Communication, Education, Journalism
- GPA of 3.0 or higher

Compensation

- 6 units of work study credit toward your degree

Apply Today

We are accepting applications through the end of June. If you are interested in an internship, please e-mail your cover letter to Cherie White at: jobs@successunlimited.com

Attach the following:

- Résumé (include any honors, writing classes, teaching experience, or publications)
- Two letters of reference
- Two short writing examples that show your writing style

The image grabs attention.

The left-justified copy is easy to read.

The vertical, colored bar adds attention.

The double columns take up less space and are easy to read.

The colored bullets make the list easier to scan.

The boldfaced white type on the dark background stands out.

The boldfaced text calls out information students need for the application process.

PEARSON mybcommlab

Apply Exhibit 6-17's key concepts by revising a new document. Go to Chapter 6 in mybcommlab.com and select Document Makeovers.

which styles should appear as part of the table of contents. The word processing program does the rest.

- **Templates:** Templates are the ultimate formatting shortcut. A template is a document with a predefined layout, sample text (which you can edit), and built-in styles. You simply choose a template with the look and layout you like and then substitute your own content. Templates come with most word processing programs, and many are available online. **Exhibit 6-18** shows a sample template for a memo.

Exhibit 6-18
Template for a Memo

Company Name Here

Memo

To: [type name]
From: [type name]
CC: [type name]
Date: 2/23/2011
Re: [type subject]

How to Use This Memo Template

Select text you would like to replace, and type your memo. Use styles such as *Heading* and *Body Text* in the *Style* control on the *Formatting* toolbar. To save changes to this template for future use, Choose *Save As* from the *File* menu. In the *Save As Type* box, choose *Document Template.* Next time you want to use it, choose *New* from the *File* menu, and then double-click your template.

Technology shortcuts may make your document more attractive, but only your writing skills can make your document readable. Good content and good layout are signs of a professional document that gets the reader's attention, keeps it, and produces results. Spend some time looking at other well-designed documents to get ideas for the layout and format of your documents. The more documents you read and write, the better writer and formatter you will become.

4 Why Is It Important to Proofread Your Message?

At this point, you will have looked for errors in organization, flow, and content. You have chosen fonts and determined the best layout for the message. Now, it's time to **proofread** it, or inspect for problems your readers might spot: typos, formatting, grammar, spelling, and punctuation errors missed during any of the previous stages. Typos cause real problems in business documents. In the case of the internship flyer, what if you mistakenly typed "16 units of credit hours" instead of "6"? Those mistakes could cause serious problems for both Success Unlimited and for the students who respond to the flyer. As with revising, if you have the time, wait at least a few hours after finishing your draft before proofreading it. This will help give you a certain amount of distance from the draft so that you can see it as another reader would.

Before you start proofreading, print the document. People read documents more easily in print than on computers. They also pay more attention to detail in print than online.

The following are different ways to proofread:

1. Read the document out loud.
2. Read the document from top to bottom in one sitting.
3. Read in chunks in several sittings (for very large documents).
4. Read from the bottom of the document, sentence by sentence, to the top in one sitting.

Try the various methods and then choose the one that enables you to proofread the most accurately. Whichever method you choose, take your time. If you rush the process, you will make mistakes. It is also a good idea to proofread your work in several passes:

- ***One pass to check for typos, spelling, and grammar.*** Pay particular attention to high-priority items, such as names, numbers, and addresses. These items are important because (a) they lend credibility to your document and (b) if they are wrong, they can

Exhibit 6-19
Proofreading Symbols

Symbol	Meaning
(delete mark)	Delete copy
^	Insert copy
¶	Start a new paragraph
(transpose mark)	Transpose (reverse)
/	Lowercase (do not capitalize)
≡	Capitalize
⊙	Add a period
[	Move left
]	Move right
#	Insert a space
(close-up mark)	Close up
‖	Align vertically
stet	Let it stand (don't make marked change after all)

cause serious problems both for you and the reader. For example, what if the internship flyer accidentally called the company "Success Limited" instead of "Success Unlimited?" What if there was a typo in the company's e-mail address?

- ***One pass to check the document's formatting and layout.*** Consider this the final polishing pass as you ask yourself: Is the spacing above and below headings consistent? Are the fonts the correct size and type? Are the bullets all the same shape? Are the margins consistent? If you try to do both checks at once, you will probably miss something.

As you proofread, mark errors when you find them. **Exhibit 6-19** contains a list of commonly used proofreading symbols. Take a look at **Exhibit 6-20,** which shows the body of a letter a student created to apply for the Success Unlimited internship. Notice how he marked it up with proofreading symbols. **Exhibit 6-21** on page 162 shows the corrected copy.

Very few people can proofread their own work without making some mistakes. Depending upon how critical your message is, it is a good idea to ask another person to proofread your message after you. Of course, you won't always be able to do this with all of your e-mails and text messages, but at least read through them several times before sending them.

5 What Is the Best Way to Distribute Your Message?

Once your message is written, formatted, and proofread, you must choose the appropriate channel for distributing it. You can do so either as hard copy, via e-mail, or on the Web. Chapter 7 explains these mediums in more detail.

Print Distribution

Send a printed version of the document in the following situations:

- ***Your distribution list is small.*** If all of the recipients are in your company, you can hand-deliver your document or use interoffice mail. If the recipients are outside of your company, you can mail it without incurring a large mailing cost.

Exhibit 6-20
Proofread Copy

Dear Cherie,

My Technical Journalism Instructor, Dr. Ashfield, told everyone in class about you internship.

I am currently a Junior in the Technical Journalism program at Wesley College. During hte summer of my freshman year, I had the opportunity to proofread sections of text books for two professors at Wesley—one in the biology department and one in the archeology department. Not only did I gain valuable experience identifying spelling, grammar, and punctuation errors, I also learned a lot about Biology and Archeology.

During the summer of my sophomore year, i worked with the same Professors, this time helping them put together lecture materials and presentations. I found that I really enjoyed learning about new subjects and figuring out how to present them to students in exciting ways. Both Professors said my assistance was invaluable in getting their text books finished on time and making sure their lecture materials were top quality. I visited your Web site and was very impressed by the books you've published and the coaching you provide to students and teachers. You are definitely making a difference in education, on book at a time and I want to be a part of that difference.

With my writing, editing, proofreading, love of learning, i think I'm an excellent candidate for your internship. I've attached my résumé, writing samples, and letters of recommendations from the 2 professors I worked with. Feel free to contact them with any questions. Their contact information is in the letters

I hope to hear from you soon.

- ***Your document is large.*** Large documents attached to e-mails can be a nightmare for recipients. People with modems or slow Internet connections will have to wait a long time to download the attachments. Some Internet providers have rules about the size of attachments. If the attachments are too large, they are rejected as undeliverable. It's better to send a large document by mail.
- ***Your document contains many colors.*** If your document has a lot of colored visuals, only people with color printers will be able to print them. If the colors are important, you might choose to print the document in color and mail it to recipients.

E-mail Distribution

E-mailing your document makes sense in the following situations:

- ***Your distribution list is large.*** If you are sending the document to a large number of people inside or outside your company, hand delivery is out of the question. Physically mailing the document might be costly, so e-mail could be your best way to send the document.
- ***Your document is small.*** Small documents are usually acceptable as e-mail attachments. People with modems or slow Internet connections can easily download them. Internet providers generally have no problems transmitting small documents to recipients.
- ***Your document contains little color.*** If your document has a minimum of colored visuals, or the colors are not that important, e-mailing them is fine. The people who receive the document can print it in black and white without it losing meaning.

Whenever you distribute a document by e-mail, consider using a **PDF** (which stands for Portable Document Format). PDF files can be viewed by anyone with any operating system,

Exhibit 6-21
Corrected Copy

Dear Ms. White:

My Technical Journalism instructor, Dr. Ashfield, told everyone in class about your internship.

I'm currently a junior in the Technical Journalism program at Wesley College. During the summer of my freshman year, I had the opportunity to proofread sections of textbooks for two professors at Wesley—one in the Biology Department and one in the Archeology Department. Not only did I gain valuable experience identifying spelling, grammar, and punctuation errors, I also learned a lot about biology and archeology.

During the summer of my sophomore year, I worked with the same professors again; this time helping them put together lecture materials and presentations. I found that I really enjoyed learning about new subjects and figuring out how to present them to students in exciting ways. Both professors said my assistance was invaluable in getting their textbooks finished on time and making sure their lecture materials were top quality.

I visited your Web site and was very impressed by the books you've published and the coaching you provide to students and teachers. You are definitely making a difference in education, one book at a time. I want to be part of the difference you are making.

My writing, editing, and proofreading experience as well as my love of learning make me a good fit for the internship. I've attached my résumé, writing samples, and letters of recommendation from the two professors I worked with. Feel free to contact them if you have any questions. Their contact information is in the letters.

I hope to hear from you soon.

PEARSON mybcommlab

Apply Exhibit 6-21's key concepts by revising a new document. Go to Chapter 6 in mybcommlab.com and select document makeovers.

as long as Adobe Reader is installed on the computer. Adobe Reader is free and downloadable from the Web.

When you convert your message to a PDF, an electronic image, or picture, of it is created in the process. All margins, footers, headers, and unusual fonts or formatting are preserved in the document. If the recipients have the software application Adobe Reader, they can open the file, and it will look exactly like it did on your system. A PDF format ensures that no one can edit your document, which is important when you send a résumé, a contract, or a proposal that you want no one to change. You should create a PDF file if it is important for the electronic version the recipient receives to look exactly like the document you sent.

Web Distribution

Sometimes it is easier to publish a document on the Web and let people download it than send it out as an e-mail attachment. This is particularly true when the document is very large or has the potential to be viewed by hundreds or thousands of people. Common company documents posted to the Web include the following:

- Résumés
- News articles
- Press releases

REAL INSIGHTS from a New Professional

Name: *Ana Valdez*
Title: *Medical student and former teacher*
Organizations: *Teach for America and Weill Cornell Medical College*
Locations: *New York City, New York*

ANA VALDEZ IS 24 YEARS OLD and as ambitious as they come. After graduating from Columbia University in 2008 and getting a premedical degree in the area of neuroscience and behavior, Valdez joined forces with Teach for America. Teach for America is an organization dedicated to ending educational inequality. It hires outstanding recent college graduates from all backgrounds and career interests to teach for two years in urban and rural public schools.

Valdez signed up to teach high school chemistry and physics at the same Texas high school she attended as an adolescent. Teach for America intrigued Valdez in part because of where she grew up: the Rio Grande Valley. "The Valley," as it is called, lies on the southernmost border of Texas. The region is infamous for teenage pregnancies and high schools that are referred to as "drop-out factories." As a Valley native, the statistics worked against her as she pursued her educational and career ambitions.

While teaching for Teach for America, Valdez's professional responsibilities included prioritizing learning objectives for students, developing lesson plans, and coordinating laboratory experiments. She also helped students master basic, functional science skills and developed and implemented intervention strategies for low-performing students.

Valdez, who is now enrolled as a student at Cornell University's medical school, found that teaching required her to concisely organize and disseminate her knowledge in a way that was both logical and that engaged students. This has altered her own processing and acquisition of knowledge in a way that she believes might be beneficial for many areas of study or work. When communicating with fellow teachers and administrative professionals, she learned that it's important to communicate simply, concisely, and accurately.

You also have to understand the needs and backgrounds of a diverse group of people, Valdez says, be it people in the classroom or in the workforce, and to approach situations in terms of challenges and solutions. Because she was a product of the high school at which she taught, she understands what it's like for students to venture into the educational and professional world outside of the Valley. As a teacher, she tried to tailor her communication to the diverse needs of not only her students, but also the teachers and administrators.

Valdez says she was impressed by Teach for America, and as a corps member felt she received a great deal of support. Corps members gain invaluable skills that are transferable to almost any field. They are sought after, and succeed, in many different careers. Once she graduates from medical school Valdez hopes to use her career and communication skills to achieve positive changes within the healthcare industry, much as she did in the field of education.

Questions

1. According to Valdez, what key aspects should you remember when disseminating your communication in the world of work?
2. Why is it important to understand the needs of the people with whom you are communicating?

Source: Ana Valdez in discussion with the author, July 2010.

- Job descriptions
- Product datasheets
- White papers
- Instruction manuals
- Product or course catalogs
- Case studies and success stories

The PDF format is also a good choice when you want people to download a document from the Web. They will be able to easily view it but not edit it. In the case of our internship flyer, if the publishing company had a "Jobs" or "Careers" link on its Web page, the firm might have opted to post the flyer there. Often companies combine e-mail and Web distributions: They send out an e-mail or e-newsletter with a link to the location on the Web where they have posted their latest documents.

CHECKLIST

When distributing a message:

- ☑ Consider the number of recipients.
- ☑ Consider the size of the document.
- ☑ Consider the amount of color.

After your message goes out and recipients respond to it, you will be able to measure the results it gets against your original goals. Consider the Success Unlimited internship flyer. If the publisher's goal is to reach the widest number of students possible, the firm might measure the flyer's success by the number of times it had been downloaded from the company's Web site or number of résumés, calls, or e-mails it produced. Good documents are read and acted upon. You will learn more about how to create messages that persuade people to take action in Chapter 9.

Summary *Synthesize What You Have Learned*

1. What design choices will make your message stand out?

Use a good layout and professional formatting. A major formatting focus should be the fonts. Choose one font family, if possible—either sans-serif or serif. Avoid too many instances of italics or boldface. Use a font size that's easy to read, at least 10 to 12 point. Remember, certain fonts look smaller than others and may require a larger font size to be readable.

2. How do headings and white space affect a message's readability?

Headings break up blocks of text, grab the reader's attention, and guide scanning. Margins, paragraph spacing, and list spacing keep documents from looking too cluttered and dense.

3. What makes a message visually interesting?

Tables, charts, and images help add interest to documents. Layout also has an impact on the appearance of a document. Balance text with visuals and white space. Using technology shortcuts such as styles and templates can make formatting documents easier.

4. Why is proofreading your message important?

Proofreading your document is critical. It can be done in a variety of ways (top to bottom, bottom to top, in chunks, and in several passes).

5. What is the best way to distribute your message?

Identify the right distribution method (hardcopy, e-mail, or on the Web) based on the number of recipients, size of the document, and amount of color in it.

PEARSON mybcommlab™ Are you an active learner? Go to **mybcommlab.com** to master Chapter 6's content. Chapter 6's interactive activities include:

- Customizable Study Plan and Chapter 6 practice quizzes
- Chapter 6 Simulation, The Communication Process, that helps you think critically and prepare to make choices in the business world
- Flash cards for mastering the definition of chapter terms
- Interactive Lessons that visually review key chapter concepts
- Document Makeovers for hands-on, scored practice in revising documents

Know It *Reflect, Respond, and Express*

Build Your Critical Thinking Skills

Critical Thinking Questions

1. Explore the templates available in your word processing program. Print out a template for a business letter. What elements of the template create a simple, balanced, professional document? Make notes on the printed template indicating what aspects create a successful document design. Would you change anything?
2. Research a prominent company within your field of study by visiting the firm's Web site. What documents do they have available to view? The policy and procedures manual? Job descriptions? What is the purpose of placing the documents online?

Critical Thinking Scenario

Daiva Chezny recently accepted a nine-month paid internship with a distance-learning school. She is now working in the school's marketing communications department. The department is responsible for developing all print and online communications that promote the school to potential students and their parents.

The department currently focuses the majority of its efforts on printed marketing materials, such as letters, brochures, and catalogues. However, the department wants to devote more attention to online materials such as e-mails, Web articles, and blog postings.

Daiva's task is to review the school's current online materials, and offer suggestions for improving them. As she reviews the materials, she notices that the e-mails are written like printed letters; the online articles are written like long magazine articles; and the blog posts are written like short magazine articles. Everything is too long, too hard to scan, and not very attractive.

The current writers have worked in the department for more than 10 years, and Daiva is concerned about criticizing their work. Luckily for Daiva, they are very open to new ideas and welcome her suggestions.

Question

1. If you were Daiva, what are some of the ideas you would share about formatting materials for the Web?

Write It *Draft, Revise, and Finalize*

Create Your Own Success Story

1. On a separate piece of paper, rewrite the e-mail on the following page to make it as readable as possible. Your revision could include correcting typos, breaking up paragraphs, and changing some wording.
2. In your word processing program, write the same sentence using four different types of font. Analyze how the fonts appear on the computer versus on the printed page. List any differences and similarities you find. What are the different aspects of readability for the different font types? To what different types of audiences would each one appeal?
3. Visit the Web site Vischeck.com and explore the different ways people who are color-blind see colors on Web pages. Write a memo to your instructor explaining your findings.
4. Open a blank word-processing document and experiment with heading and subheading design using different fonts, font sizes, and font styles. Bring the examples you create to class and compare your designs with those of your classmates. How do the different design choices affect the presentation of the documents?
5. Look at a Web site you frequent and answer the following questions about it: How is the information chunked on the page? How are headings and subheadings used and organized? Does the structure of the information aid in usability? Prepare an analysis of your findings in a brief paragraph or two.
6. Create a numbered or bulleted list describing the process you use to proofread a document. Use the design tips in the chapter when formatting the list.
7. Practice using the proofreading symbols discussed in the chapter. Proofread the following paragraph twice: once for typos, spelling, and grammar, and once for formatting and layout.

   > Business communication enables you to be prepared for the workplace. Learning to write memos, e-mails, and letters will enable you market yourself as a adaptable writer. Purpose and audience considerations guide your content to best reach the audience.

   Using your revised paragraph, create three different documents with three different alignments (left-justification, full-justification, and right-justification) and three different types of fonts (of your choice). Choose the one that is the easiest to read and explain why.
8. Visit a bank's Web site and find contact information for customer service. Compose a brief message (often through a supplied template) inquiring about current interest rates for savings accounts or IRA accounts. Send the e-mail inquiry and keep track of any responses you receive. Did you receive an auto-reply indicating the bank received your e-mail? What response, if any, did you receive from a customer service agent? Print a copy of your inquiry and record any responses you received and bring them to class to compare with your classmates. Were some of you more successful than others in terms of getting a good response?

To: UpperDivMathList@turnercollege.edu

Cc: Barti.Sunjanil@turnercollege.edu

Subject: We Need Math Tutors!

Dear Upper Division Math Students,

It has come to my atention that many first year students are struggle with college Algebra. Some recieve failing grades on tests and others drop their Math classes entirely. For many student, this is their first experience with college level Mathematics. A bad expereince can leave a lasting impression, including a life long distaste for math. It can can also handicap students in future classes and possibly in life.

I believe we can improve the situation by providing non threatening, informal, one on one tutoring for any student who needs help. I call you to recall in the past when you were struggling with math concepts and then consider helping those who are struggling now. The Math department will offer two units of credit for tutoring two nights a week during the semester, which includes tutoring training sessions, as well as support during preexam study sessions.

We will hold the "Introduction to Math Tutoring" kick-off session on Tuesday, April 8, from 5:00 – 6:30 pm in 154 Clark Building. For more information, contact me: barti.sunjanil@turnercollege.edu

Please considering attending the kick-off session and join our tutoring team.

Barti Sunjanil
Tutoring Team Leader

Do It *Document Your Success Track Record*

Build Your e-Portfolio

Format the e-mail document you rewrote in "Write It" Exercise 1 and make it an interoffice memo. Pay attention to:

- Fonts
- Color
- White space
- Illustrations
- Layout

1. Proofread the document and make any corrections.
2. Check the document for:
   - Layout
   - Balance
   - Consistency
3. Revise the document accordingly.
4. Think through how this document is an example of your ability to proof and ensure accuracy in communicating. You may need to use this as an example in a future job interview.

Speak It *Discuss, Listen, and Understand*

Build Your Leadership and Teamwork Skills

1. Suppose the flyer on the following page appeared on a bulletin board in your university library. Next, form groups of three. Make sure at least one person in each group has good word processing skills. As a group, review the flyer for layout, formatting, spacing, font, and color issues. Then circle the problem areas. Based on the circled areas, list the specific problems you found and offer suggestions for improvement.

NaNoWriMo
National Novel Writing Month
November 1–30
30 days and nights of literary abandon

What Is It?

National Novel Writing Month is a fun, seat-of-your-pants approach to novel writing. Participants begin writing November 1. The goal is to write a 175-page (50,000-word) novel by midnight, November 30.

Why Do It?

New writers are notorious for giving up on their first novels because they can't make progress and they can't write perfectly. With its 30-day writing limit, the *only* thing that matters in NaNoWriMo is output. It's all about quantity, not quality. The kamikaze approach forces you to lower your expectations, take risks, and write on the fly.

Make no mistake: You will be writing a lot of junk. That's a good thing. By forcing yourself to write so intensely, you are giving yourself permission to make mistakes. Those mistakes can easily be taken care of ... *after* your first draft is written.

How Do You Participate?

Come to McAllister Library, on November 1 for the university's NaNoWriMo kick-off meeting, from 1:00 P.M. to 5:00 P.M. Bring a laptop, pencil, paper, and whatever else you need to write. We will walk you through the process and then set you free. We will meet once a week at the library, through November 30, to keep you on track.

Need Help?

Our official "NaNoWriMo Mentors" will be available at the weekly meetings and via e-mail. We also highly recommend the hilarious and official handbook for NaNoWriMo—*Plot? No Problem!* Pick up a signed copy today at the University Bookstore!

Questions?

Contact the University Writing Center at: uniwritingcenter@caltech.edu

2. In groups or as a class, discuss the different ways to proofread a document. What methods have you used before? Which ones would you try? How can they be used together?
3. In groups, discuss the most effective way you receive information from your instructor or institution. Most schools are moving toward electronic communication as the primary means of communication, for everything from catalogs to applications for federal student aid. Outline the advantages and disadvantages of the different methods of distribution.

Business in Action

Getting the Word Out on the Brunetti Language School

For global companies, distributing a message often means more than deciding whether to deliver it by e-mail, print, or in person. It means deciding what language to use. Whether it is French, German, or Spanish, the Brunetti Language School in St. Louis, Missouri, provides businesspeople with the language tools they need to successfully communicate in a global climate. By helping businesspeople learn to better communicate and disseminate their messages, Brunetti has, unwittingly, distributed its own message of growth as well.

The influx of for-profit education companies, such as Brunetti, could not come at a better time in the field of education. American public and private schools are being forced to slash their foreign language programs, which will definitely affect the ability of U.S. students to compete on a global level. The loss of foreign language programs has increased Brunetti's business, though. Brunetti has even begun sending its own instructors to schools that can no longer afford to keep language teachers on the payroll.

According to Laura Morsch of CareerBuilder, being fluent in more than one language can increase a worker's salary substantially—usually between 5 to 20 percent more than the position's base pay. This fact makes the loss of language programs at colleges all the more alarming—and businesses like Brunetti all the more appealing. Determining the language that will give the message its greatest impact and how to best get it to people gives the writer a leg-up on the competition. Now that's job security.

Questions

1. What is driving individuals and businesses to learn other languages?
2. How might delivering a message in a different language affect its audience?
3. What changes in the educational world are leading students to Brunetti? Does your college provide language courses? Are you attending any?

Source: Based on Laura Morsch, "Why It Pays to Be Bilingual," *CareerBuilder.com*, January 26, 2009, accessed at http://jobs.aol.com/articles/2009/01/26/why-it-pays-to-be-bilingual/.

Key Terms

Body text. Text that makes up the majority of a document. *(p. 150)*

Boldface. A typeface that appears thicker than regular text. *(p. 148)*

Color contrast. The contrast between the background color and the foreground text. *(p. 149)*

Default settings. The settings that are automatically in place when you open a new document on your computer. *(p. 157)*

Font. A typeface. *(p. 145)*

Full-justified. Text that is flush against both the right and left margins. *(p. 156)*

Grid. A temporary table with vertical and horizontal lines that help a person line up text and illustrations on a page. *(p. 156)*

Headings. Phrases that identify major sections in a document and act like newspaper headlines. *(p. 150)*

Italics. Characters set in rightward-leaning type. *(p. 148)*

Justification. The vertical alignment of the text. *(p. 156)*

Left-aligned (left-justified). Text that is flush against the left margin. *(p. 156)*

Margins. The white space at the top, bottom, and sides of a page. *(p. 151)*

PDF. An acronym for Portable Document Format. A PDF is essentially a photo of the original document that retains all special fonts and formatting. *(p. 161)*

Point. A unit of measure for font sizes. A point is about 1/72 of an inch. *(p. 148)*

Proofreading. A detailed read-through of a document for the purpose of finding typos, formatting, grammar, punctuation, and spelling errors. *(p. 159)*

Ragged. Text that is not vertically aligned and has an uneven edge. *(p. 156)*

Right-aligned (right-justified). Text that is flush against the right margin. *(p. 156)*

Sans-serif. A typeface style that does not have a serif (a vertical or horizontal mark, sometimes called a "tail") at the end of the stroke. *(p. 145)*

Serif. A typeface style that has a small feature called a serif (a vertical or horizontal mark, sometimes called a "tail") at the end of the stroke. *(p. 145)*

Styles. Formatting applications in word processing applications that specify fonts, sizes, justification, and boldface. *(p. 157)*

Subheadings. Phrases that indicate subsections in a document. *(p. 150)*

Templates. Special documents with a predefined layout, sample text, and built-in styles. *(p. 158)*

Underlining. A typeface often used to highlight Internet links in electronic documents. It is rarely used in print documents. *(p. 148)*

White space. The part of the document that is blank and does not contain text, images, or graphics. *(p. 151)*

Review Questions *Test Yourself*

1. Why is it important that your document make a good first impression? What tools can help you?
2. What are the different aspects to consider when choosing a font?
3. What issues can arise when you are using boldface, italics, or underlines in e-mails? What tools can you use instead, to help information stand out?
4. How does white space enhance your document, and where do you typically provide it?
5. What are the two major categories of fonts and what is the difference between them?
6. What text design elements should you avoid to create a simple and balanced document?
7. What are a few technology shortcuts available in word processing programs?

8. What is the goal of proofreading?
9. How can typos cause problems in business documents?
10. What are the two different forms of proofreading you should perform when reviewing a document?
11. What proofreading symbols have you seen in your previous papers from instructors? Which ones have you not seen before?
12. List the situations that call for the printed distribution of a document.
13. What situations call for e-mail distribution of a document?
14. What is a PDF file and how can it be utilized to distribute a document?

Grammar Review *Mastering Accuracy*

Prepositions and Conjunctions

Section I

Each of the following sentences contains one or more common errors in word usage, grammar, or style. Identify the errors. If you have trouble finding the errors, review Section 1.1.4. in the handbook (Appendix D) at the back of this textbook.

1. Both Janice an Theodore are able to attend the policy meeting next month.
2. Part of the hiring process includes not only a demonstration but only a panel discussion.
3. It's is up to the current supervisor, but I don't believe neither icy rain or frigid winds will cancel tomorrow's policy meeting.
4. It certainly may appear so, but when we move closer to the date we will have more information.
5. The meeting will begin shortly, yet it is only a matter of whether John takes minutes or Jeremy does.
6. The petty cash drawer is not really a drawer, but rather it's is just a small metal box.
7. All paperwork must be completed in blue ink, but neither red or black ink is acceptable.
8. Since once communication has been established, please remember to follow additional protocol so as you can continue to maintain contact.
9. It has been established thru out history: mankind is neither just man or always kind.
10. John will not address the court and in fact, he will only speak of the record.

Section II

On a separate sheet of paper, rewrite the following sentences so they are clearer, more professional sounding, grammatically correct, and goodwill oriented.

1. It's bad business, so please don't leave people hanging by the telephone for a long time.
2. Writing and talking skills should be practiced by people who want to be professional in order to keep your skills up-to-date.
3. The President of SoarTech is going vacationing for five days, so all employees need to behave and act as if he is still here til he gets back.
4. Employees should get into the habit of being on time.
5. We will be working off of the hard copies located in the second file drawers.
6. Managers of the department managers should work closely with employees to ensure communication between departments occurs.
7. Fire marshals will demonstrate the best ways for exiting around the doors and up the stairs.
8. The law says we must not discriminate about our hiring practices.
9. Two things that are necessary to the successful business of any organization are diversity and collaboration.
10. Don't just whine and moan, you should give the boss a real solution to a difficult issue, instead of just complaints.

Extra Resources *Tools You Can Use*

Books

Printed Layout

- Cullen, Kristen. *Layout Workbook: A Real World Guide to Building Pages in Graphic Design.* Beverley, MA: Rockport Publishers, 2007.
- Graham, Lisa. *Basics of Design: Layout and Typography for Beginners,* 1st ed. Florence, KY: Delmar Cengage Learning, 2001.
- Salz, Ina. *Typography Essentials: 100 Design Principles for Working with Type.* Beverley, MA: Rockport Publishers, 2009.
- Tondreau, Beth. *Layout Essentials: 100 Design Principles for Using Grids.* Beverley, MA: Rockport Publishers, 2009.

Web Layout

- Beaird, Jason. *The Principles of Beautiful Web Design,* 1st ed. Collingwood, Victoria, Australia: SitePoint, January 2007.
- Krug, Steve. *Don't Make Me Think—A Common Sense Approach to Web Usability,* 2nd ed. Berkeley, CA: New Riders Press, 2005.
- Wroblewski, Luke. *Site Seeing—Communicating Successfully with Visual Design,* 1st ed. Hoboken, NJ: Wiley, 2002.

"If you just communicate, you can get by. But if you skillfully communicate, you can work miracles." —**Jim Rohn,** business philosopher

Positive, Everyday Messages

Letters, Memos, and Electronic Communications

LEARNING OBJECTIVE QUESTIONS

1. What are positive, everyday messages?
2. Why is effective writing critical for communicating positive, everyday messages?
3. What channels are used to deliver positive, everyday messages?
4. Why should you separate your professional communications from your personal communications?

PEARSON **mybcommlab** Access interactive videos, simulations, sample documents, document makeovers, and assessment quizzes in Chapter 7 of **mybcommlab.com** for mastery of this chapter's objectives.

>>> **When Roxanna** started school at her local community college, she knew the college required students to have health insurance. If a student lacks health insurance, a mandatory $600 is applied to his or her yearly tuition to cover the cost of him or her being insured through the school. Although the school's health insurance plan was comprehensive, Roxanna couldn't believe its price. She was sure she could find something more reasonable. After all, she rarely got sick, didn't engage in dangerous behavior, and could really use any extra money she could get.

Roxanna began her quest with a politely worded letter to the college's student services department inquiring about the policy. In her letter, she asked what the protocol was for a student wishing to purchase outside health insurance coverage. If she could get it, would the school reimburse her the $600 she had already paid? Within a few days, she received an e-mail back with more information on the policy and, to her delight, information on being reimbursed.

Roxanna's next contact was her employer. Although she was only a part-time cashier, she knew the grocery store she worked at offered health benefits to many of its employees. Because her boss was in and out of his office often, Roxanna created a memo detailing her problem and requesting health insurance through the grocery store. Unfortunately, when her boss returned, he informed her that the store couldn't insure part-time employees. He suggested she find a low-premium personal plan from a major health insurance provider.

Taking her boss's advice, Roxanna compared prices on the Internet and finally located a reasonable insurance plan. She was thrilled and signed up for coverage immediately. In her final e-mail to the student services department, Roxanna outlined her new coverage and attached several documents to prove she was insured. She was ready to be reimbursed and sure enough, a month later, she opened her mailbox to find a check for $600 inside.

Roxanna >>>

Roxanna's story, and this chapter, show how people communicate in writing on a daily basis. From composing letters and e-mails to sending Twitter messages, you will discover the best practices for formatting messages and determining the appropriate channels for sending them.

The examples in this chapter illustrate scenarios you would find in the healthcare industry, a promising sector of the economy that generates approximately $265 billion in revenues annually. As the Baby Boomer generation retires over the next decade, for the first time in history there will be more people over 65 than under 65, creating an even greater demand for healthcare. "The healthcare industry is becoming broader and bigger every day," says Eve Tahmincioglu, a contributor to the cable network MSNBC. "So think outside the box, especially if you have a business background. Opportunities abound for those with higher degrees, even if their area of education is not healthcare-related."[1]

The healthcare industry hires graduates for jobs in accounting, finance, marketing, sales, manufacturing, and human resources, among others. You may already be familiar with some healthcare companies, such as UnitedHealthCare, CIGNA, and Pfizer. Other healthcare–related organizations that employ business students include those listed below.

Healthcare-Related Organizations						
Hospitals	Long-term care facilities and the companies that own and operate them	Private physician practices and healthcare clinics	Pharmaceutical companies	Medical technology companies	Health insurance companies	Government agencies that determine healthcare policies and oversee their administration

As you learn to write positive, everyday messages in this chapter, consider the opportunities the healthcare industry might offer you.

1 What Are Positive, Everyday Messages?

■ For an interactive, real-world example of this topic, access this chapter's bcomm mini sim entitled Routine Messages, located at **mybcommlab.com**

Positive, everyday messages are routine messages that deliver good news or neutral news. In this chapter, we will look at positive, everyday messages written in a direct, rather than indirect, structure. Negative messages that use an indirect writing organization will be covered in Chapter 8. Persuasive messages will be covered in Chapter 9.

Most business communication is sent via everyday messages. These are the "glue" that holds organizations together. Changes in the workplace such as remote office sites, telecommuting, and globalization have reduced the amount of time employees spend together. Instead of being able to walk into a coworker's office to ask a question, you may need to e-mail a colleague on the other side of the world. As a result, writing effective, everyday messages is a necessary skill for succeeding in business.

Everyday messages fall into one of the following five categories. They are messages that:

- Inform
- Ask questions
- Respond to questions
- Request action
- Express appreciation

Messages That Inform

A message that informs simply updates the reader. Imagine you are preparing a budget for a low-income health clinic. Your boss is anxious for the numbers, so you send her a message about your progress and your expected completion date. Or perhaps you are a program director for a hospital foundation, and you send letters to agencies that have applied for grants, informing them that their requests are currently being processed.

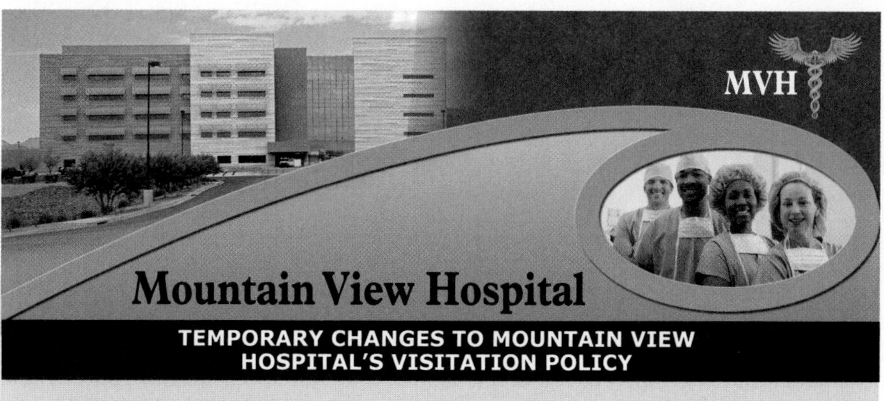

MVH
Mountain View Hospital
TEMPORARY CHANGES TO MOUNTAIN VIEW HOSPITAL'S VISITATION POLICY

FOR IMMEDIATE RELEASE

Flu Concerns Lead to New Visitation Policies
Mountain View, CA, Sept. 20, 2011—Because of the growing number of flu cases reported daily, Mountain View Hospital is changing its visitation policies to protect the patients, staff, and other visitors. Effective today, visiting children under the age of 12 will not be allowed in any unit in the hospital. Visitors older than 12 years of age must not be sick or have fevers, coughs, sore throats, or any other flu-like symptoms.

"The change in policy reflects the national trend hospitals across the country are adopting to minimize the spread of the flu virus," reported Dr. Lucinda Benito, Chief of Staff for Mountain View Hospital. *"We recognize this new policy is inconvenient for families and visitors. However, our patients' health is our primary concern during this flu season."*

Notices have been placed throughout the hospital explaining the temporary change in the visitation policy. In addition, brochures are available for all patients and visitors providing information regarding precautions, symptoms, and treatment for the flu virus.

# # #

For media inquiries only, contact Mountain View Hospital's Media Relations at 319-602-8764.

Exhibit 7-1
A Message That Informs

Exhibit 7-1 shows an example of a message that informs: a notification of a change in a hospital visitation policy. The message appears as a press release on the hospital's Web site.

Messages That Ask Questions

Messages that ask direct questions and require a response fall into this category. **Exhibit 7-2** is an example of such a message. They might be as simple as clarifying the time for the ribbon-cutting ceremony for a hospital's new wing or as complex as asking a sales team for a detailed explanation of why the company's market share has dropped 10 percent in California, Oregon, and Washington.

Aidan,

Do you have the start date for the new marketing associate hired to work with the hospital's foundation staff?

Jan

Exhibit 7-2
A Message That Asks a Question (sent via instant messaging)

Messages That Respond to Questions

Messages that respond to questions can include simple one-line answers, such as a date, a time, a name, or a resource. **Exhibit 7-3** is an example of this type of message. They can also include longer responses, such as detailed explanations, action plans, and recommendations. During a typical hour, a sales manager for a pharmaceutical company might respond to questions from his boss regarding quarterly sales projections, questions from a sales representative regarding the release date of a new drug, and questions from an assistant regarding a vacation request.

Exhibit 7-3
A Message That Responds to a Question (sent via instant messaging)

Jan,

The new marketing associate is starting on September 16. I have set up her orientation for the following day.

Aidan

Messages That Request Action

Examples of messages that request action include a request to a hospital supplier to delete an incorrect item from an invoice, a request to a government agency to send information outlining a Medicaid policy, or a request to a construction company to bid on architectural plans for a new medical building. The requests can range from simple to complex. **Exhibit 7-4** shows a request that may require a more involved response.

Exhibit 7-4
A Message That Requests Action

From: dean.provo@StJosephsHospital.org

To: Staff Doctors—St. Joseph's Hospital

Subject: Survey for St. Joseph's Maternity Wing Expansion Plans
1 Attachment

Staff Doctors:

Please complete the attached questionnaire to help the Planning and Development Committee explore possibilities for expanding St. Joseph's maternity wing. Any additional comments you have can be added at the bottom of the survey and submitted online.

Your participation in this process is greatly appreciated during this exciting time at St. Joseph's Hospital. The ideas you offer will be invaluable and benefit the hospital, the staff, and the community.

Please return your responses by December 9, 2010, so we can include your ideas in our planning process.

Regards,

Dean Provo
Director of Facility Development
St. Joseph's Hospital
dean.provo@StJosephsHospital.org

Messages That Express Appreciation

People frequently fail to express their appreciation in business messages. This is a mistake. Writing a thank-you note to acknowledge a job well done, a favor granted, or a gift received goes a long way toward showing your appreciation. Although sending an e-mail is acceptable, a letter or handwritten note on an appropriate card or stationery makes a longer-lasting impression and will set you apart in the minds of both your managers and colleagues. **Exhibit 7-5** is a good example of a thank-you letter.

Exhibit 7-5
A Message That Expresses Appreciation

38 Cook Street
Canton, OH 44708

December 7, 2009

Mr. Raymond Atelier
Director of Finance
St. Joseph's Hospital
2380 West 34th Avenue
Canton, OH 44708

Dear Mr. Atelier:

Thank you for the letter of recommendation you submitted for my graduate school applications. Your willingness to discuss the work I did at St. Joseph's and your letter's detailed description of my final performance review are greatly appreciated.

Your commitment as my mentor helped me learn a great deal during my two years of employment at St. Joseph's. Thank you again for your support. I will let you know my admission status as soon as I hear from the schools.

Sincerely,

Tom Esquibol

Tom Esquibol

2 Why Is Effective Writing Critical for Communicating Positive, Everyday Messages?

The ability to write effective messages affects both how business is conducted and how your managers and fellow workers perceive you. The following story illustrates how a new graduate's inability to write positive, everyday messages adversely affected his career.

Fresh out of college with a business degree in hand, Robert accepted a marketing position with a medical technology company. Robert looked like an aspiring business professional. He dressed in nice suits, arrived at work promptly every morning, and demonstrated top-notch office etiquette. However, when promotions were later being awarded, Robert was overlooked. Why?

Although Robert looked and acted the part of a business professional, he did not write like one. He sent lengthy memos that were difficult for his team members to follow. He buried important points in paragraphs of text, and failed to offer action plans and timeframes for taking necessary steps. He typed his instant messages in all capital letters, which made many of his coworkers feel as if he were shouting at them. Worse, he always "replied to all" when responding to e-mails, cluttering people's inboxes with irrelevant correspondence. In a nutshell, Robert's writing got in the way of his message. In a company where your written word becomes your professional face, poor writing skills can be your downfall. For Robert, they became the reason his boss overlooked him when deciding whom to groom for the management track.

In business, the ability to write well is also important for conveying essential details. Imagine a hospital administrator sending a poorly written e-mail informing nurses' aides that their benefits were being reduced. If the wording was confusing and the message did little to build confidence and goodwill, the e-mail would create havoc for the hospital's human resources department. The nurses' aides could become disgruntled, the human resources manager might receive formal complaints, and employees could quit. Similarly, consider a manager sending an instant message to advise all accounting personnel at a health clinic of a mandatory meeting. What if the manager accidentally typed 11:00 and not 1:00? The accounting staff would show up for the meeting, but the manager wouldn't be there. Time would be wasted, employees would be irritated, and the manager would lose credibility.

Strategies for Writing Effective Positive, Everyday Messages

Today's fast-paced communications can make it challenging for a person to take the time needed to write well-conceived messages. However, your communication can still be effective if you keep in mind the following writing practices covered in the previous two chapters:

- Plan your message before you write, even if you must do so quickly.
- Strive for simplicity in terms of the message's language and formatting.
- Review and revise your message before distributing it.

Avoid multitasking and other distractions when you write messages. A poorly conceived letter, a rambling e-mail, or misspelled words distract from the intent of the message and negatively affect how people view your work. Many successful business communicators set aside specific times each day to send and respond to messages. By giving this part of your job your undivided attention, you will communicate more effectively.

It takes skill and practice to write quickly and efficiently. The best way to develop this skill is to learn to distill a message, thought, or idea down to its essence. How do you learn to do this? Throughout your day, ask yourself, "What is the main idea of the conversation I'm having?" Or, if you are watching television, ask yourself, "What is the purpose of this scene?" Reread the messages you write and find a way to eliminate words, phrases, and sentences that aren't necessary. Over time, you will become good at stating things as simply as possible. Knowing how to zero in on a situation and put the most important idea into one sentence will help you learn to communicate directly.

Keep your message positive by paying attention to the words you use.

Open with the Message's Main Objective

Whether you are sending an everyday, positive letter, memo, or e-mail, being clear about your main idea will help you write a direct opening to your message. Are you responding to a request or complaint, asking a question, or informing the reader about a policy? The first one or two sentences of a positive or neutral, everyday message should be straightforward and designed to let the reader know why you are writing.

Exhibits 7-6a and **7-6b** illustrate two openings to a letter sent to the patients of a public health clinic. Three sentences into the letter in Exhibit 7-6a, you will notice that the writer's intent is still unclear. By contrast, the message in Exhibit 7-6b gets to the point much more quickly.

Explain the Message's Information in a Logical and Positive Way

The opening of your message should be followed with further details organized in a clear and logical way. Using lists, bullet points, italics, and other graphical devices can help you structure your content in a way that is easy to understand. In addition, the tone of your message should be positive. Avoid negative words such as *unfortunately, error, mistake, regret, fault,* and so forth. Words such as these immediately get a reader's guard up. Instead, focus on the solutions being pursued or changes being made that will benefit the reader. For ex-

Exhibit 7-6a A Message with an Unclear Opening

October 15, 2012

Ms. Gina Valez
888 Princeton Way
Canton, OH 44704

Dear Ms. Valez:

Flu season is on its way. The number of whooping cough cases reported has spiked for two consecutive years. Hepatitis B can cause serious liver damage. When did you last update your child's vaccines?

Exhibit 7-6b A Message with a Clear Opening

October 15, 2012

Ms. Gina Valez
888 Princeton Way
Canton, OH 44704

Dear Ms. Valez:

Updating your child's vaccines will safeguard his or her health. Our clinic is ready to help you with all of your children's vaccine needs.

ample, instead of saying "We regret we won't have flu shots available until November 15," say, "Flu shots will be available for you and your family on November 15."

End the Message with a Goodwill Closing and Any Directions for Action

Don't miss the opportunity to create goodwill in your closing. **Exhibit 7-7** illustrates a goodwill closing. If the reader of the message needs to take action, outline what needs to be done, by what date, and why. If you are taking action to benefit the reader, explain what you will do and when the reader can expect the action to be completed.

Exhibit 7-7 A Closing That Exhibits Goodwill

Your child's health is important to us at the Cleveland Public Health Clinic. To receive free vaccinations in November, please call today for your appointment.

Sincerely,

Edward Dwight
Chief Administrator
Cleveland Public Health Clinic

REAL INSIGHTS from a Seasoned Professional

Name: *Amy Dohr*
Title: *Director of Practice Management*
Organization: *Renaissance Care for Internal and Preventative Medicine*
Location: *Denver, Colorado*

AMY DOHR EARNED HER BA IN ART HISTORY from the University of Notre Dame in 1991. After graduating, she pursued a career in the field of continuing medical education. She developed ongoing education opportunities for practicing physicians to keep up to date on advancements in medicine and the delivery of care.

In 2006, Dohr became the director of practice management for Renaissance Care for Internal and Preventative Medicine. As the director of practice management, she helped pioneer an innovative, new type of business model known as "concierge practices," or "boutique practices." Concierge, or boutique, practices allow physicians to deliver more rapid, personalized care to patients who pay an additional annual out-of-pocket fee.

Patients who pay the extra fee demand great service. Effectively communicating with them is part of the service, and it is a key part of Dohr's job. So is communicating how the service works to the general public. "One of our greatest challenges is communicating who we are to the general public so that they understand how our practice operates and what we have to offer," Dohr says. In addition to communicating with the public, she writes messages every day to physicians, staff members, patients, insurance carriers, and the employees of other private companies.

The advice Dohr offers today's business students is as follows: "Make your messages brief, clear, and to the point. And always consider who you are serving."

Questions

1. What are Dohr's on-the-job communication challenges?
2. Why do you think Dohr advises business communicators to consider who they are serving?

Source: Amy Dohr in discussion with the author, March 2009.

③ What Channels Are Used to Deliver Positive, Everyday Messages?

One of the greatest challenges a communicator faces is choosing the most effective communication medium for a given situation. The following discussion explains the advantages and disadvantages of using different channels for written communication.

Letters

A letter is the most formal way to communicate an everyday message. Letters are often used to correspond with people outside of an organization to communicate information about a company's products, services, policies, promotions, and so forth. Letters are also sent to people both outside of the organization and within it when the communication needs to be legally documented or confidentiality is important. Finally, letters can also be sent to make messages stand out from the large number of e-mails received daily by businesspeople.

There are two types of standard designs for business letters. They can be written in block style or modified block style. In **block style** letters, almost all of the components begin at the left-hand margin. In **modified block style** letters, some of the elements, including the date of the letter and the sender's signature, begin at the center of the page. **Exhibits 7-8** and **7-9** show examples of the two styles. Although both formats are acceptable, the block style is more common and easier to create.

Set the margins for business letters at 1.0 to 1.5 inches on all sides. As Chapter 6 explained, don't justify the right-hand margin of a letter. A ragged-right margin is easier to read. Now let's look at each of the written components that make up a business letter.

Exhibit 7-8
A Block Style Letter

American Alliance of Actuaries

3090 Connecticut Street, NW, Suite 500
Washington, D.C. 20049
Phone: 202-596-8357 • Fax: 202-596-8399 • www.amalac.com

February 3, 2010

Mr. Raymond Jordan
Colorado State Representative, District 82
315 East River Avenue
Denver, CO 80203

Dear Representative Jordan:

You and your fellow members of the Medicaid Steering Committee are invited to attend the keynote address at our upcoming conference.

Sarah Knight, Senior Health Fellow at the Brighton Center for Health Policy, will be speaking about the fundamentals of risk classification to help policymakers and the public better understand its role in the health insurance market. With health insurance being one of the top concerns expressed by your constituents this year, you will find Ms. Knight's presentation informative and timely.

My assistant, Deborah Jones, will be following up with you in a week to see if we can reserve a special table for you and your committee members. We hope to see you at this informative presentation.

Sincerely,

Lena Atwater

Lena Atwater
Chief Advisor

Letterhead

The **letterhead** appears at the top of the page and includes the company's logo (if there is one), name and address, and sometimes the firm's phone, fax number, e-mail, and Web address.

Example:

American Alliance of Actuaries

3090 Connecticut Street, NW, Suite 500
Washington, D.C. 20049
Phone: 202-596-8357 • Fax: 202-596-8399 • www.amalac.com

Always use your organization's letterhead for business correspondence. Conversely, if you are writing a personal message, *don't* put it on your company's letterhead. Doing so could confuse the reader and get you in trouble with your company. If you are sending a personal business letter, and you lack stationery with a letterhead, you can create one by typing your name and contact information at the top of the page. Or, you can simply type your address at the top left margin of the page above the date.

Exhibit 7-9
A Modified Block Style Letter

American Alliance of Actuaries

3090 Connecticut Street, NW, Suite 500
Washington, D.C. 20049
Phone: 202-596-8357 • Fax: 202-596-8399 • www.amalac.com

February 3, 2010

Mr. Raymond Jordan
Colorado State Representative, District 82
315 East River Avenue
Denver, CO 80203

Dear Representative Jordan:

You and your fellow members of the Medicaid Steering Committee are invited to attend the keynote address at our upcoming conference.

Sarah Knight, Senior Health Fellow at the Brighton Center for Health Policy, will be speaking about the fundamentals of risk classification to help policymakers and the public better understand its role in the health insurance market. With health insurance being one of the top concerns expressed by your constituents this year, you will find Ms. Knight's presentation informative and timely.

My assistant, Deborah Jones, will be following up with you in a week to see if we can reserve a special table for you and your committee members. We hope to see you at this informative presentation.

Sincerely,

Lena Atwater

Lena Atwater
Chief Advisor

Return Address

The **return address** is your address if you don't use letterhead Type the return address roughly four-to-six lines down from the top of the page. Be prepared to increase or decrease the space as necessary to center the letter vertically on the page. Use the two-letter state abbreviation and include the zip code in the return address.

Example:

407 Shaw Street
Richland, WA 99354

Date

Position the date at least one blank line below the letterhead or return address. If you need to vary the space for better vertical alignment of the letter on the page, you can do so. In a block letter, the date should be left-justified. In a modified-block letter, it should begin in the center of the page. Type out the full month, followed by the day and a comma, followed by the year. If you are sending a letter to another country, use the appropriate date format. (See Chapter 3.)

Example (block style):

February 3, 2010

Example (modified block style, European date format):

3 February 2010

Inside Address

A letter's **inside address** consists of the recipient's name, title, and address. Leave at least one blank line between the date and the inside address. If letterhead is being used, type the inside address two to seven blank lines down from the date. Adjust the space as necessary to center the letter vertically on the page. Always use the two-letter state abbreviation and include the zip code.

Example:

Mr. Aaron Kessler
Practice Administrator
Union Valley Health Clinic
4290 Valley Road
Englewood, NJ 06418

Salutation

The **salutation** is the greeting that begins the letter. Type the salutation one blank line down from the inside address and insert a colon after it. Always try to identify the right person to receive the letter and the spelling of his or her name. In addition, find out the way in which the person prefers to be addressed, such as *Dr., Mr., Ms., Mrs.,* or *Miss.* If the recipient is a woman, and you don't know her, it is best to use *Ms.* as the salutation.

Example:

Dear Mr. Kessler:

Body

Begin the body of the message one blank line down from the salutation. Start the body by telling the reader why you are writing, and then explain the details of the message. Single space the paragraphs and insert a double space between them.

End the letter with a positive statement that creates goodwill and outlines any specific actions that need to be taken. Keep the letter to one page, if possible. If you must use additional pages, use plain paper of the same color and quality as the first page and include the following heading at the left margin, one inch from the top of the paper. The continued text then follows two blank lines down after the second page heading.

Example:

Mr. Aaron Kessler
Page 2
March 8, 2010

Closing and Signature Block

Use a standard closing such as *Sincerely, Sincerely yours,* or *Cordially* followed by a comma. The **signature block** consists of the writer's name, title, and signature at the end of the letter. Align and type your name and title three blank lines down from the closing. Both your name and title can appear on the same line. Or, if your title is long, you can put your name on the first line and your title on the second. The positioning depends on the length of the letter and how it best looks from top to bottom on the page. Some writers include their phone numbers one line below their titles, and their e-mail addresses one below that. If you have used letterhead or an inside address, there is no need for you to type in your company's name in the signature block because it already appears at the top of the page. Sign your name in blue or black ink in the space between the closing and your typed name and title.

Example:

Sincerely,

Marilyn Franklin

Marilyn Franklin
Account Executive

Reference Initials

If you compose a letter, but someone else types it, include reference initials. **Reference initials** indicate both the writer and typist who prepared the message and should appear one blank line down from the writer's printed name and title. The writer's initials should be capitalized and followed by a colon and the typist's initials in lowercase.

Example:

Marilyn Franklin
Account Executive

MEF: lhv

Enclosures

If you include other materials with your letter, type "Enclosure" or "Enclosures" one blank line below your name and title or reference initials, if you have enough space vertically on the page to do so. If you are including multiple enclosures, you have the option of adding the number of enclosures in parentheses.

Example:

Marilyn Franklin
Account Executive

MEF: lhv
Enclosures (2)

Exhibit 7-10a An Ineffective Letter

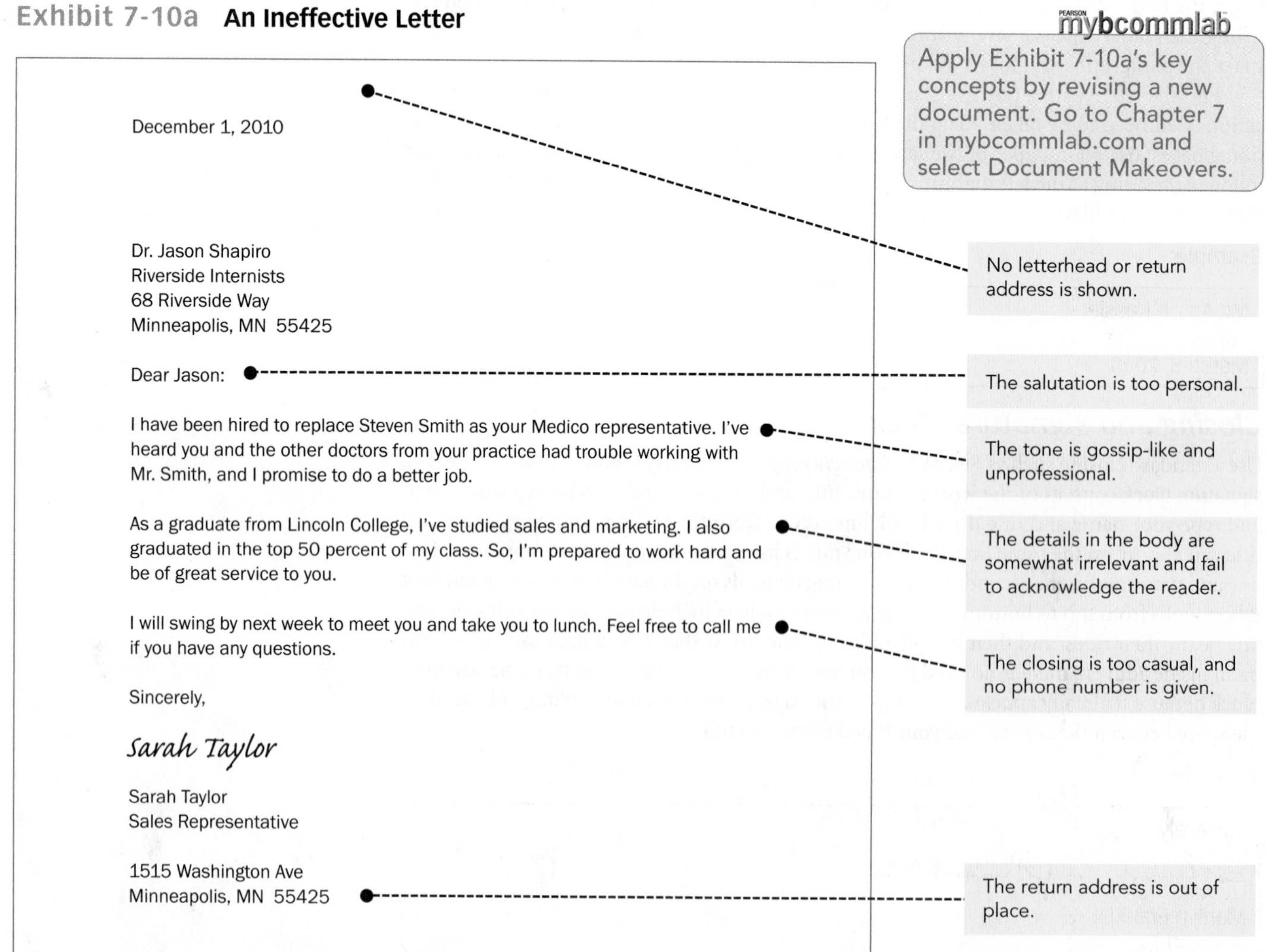

December 1, 2010

Dr. Jason Shapiro
Riverside Internists
68 Riverside Way
Minneapolis, MN 55425

Dear Jason:

I have been hired to replace Steven Smith as your Medico representative. I've heard you and the other doctors from your practice had trouble working with Mr. Smith, and I promise to do a better job.

As a graduate from Lincoln College, I've studied sales and marketing. I also graduated in the top 50 percent of my class. So, I'm prepared to work hard and be of great service to you.

I will swing by next week to meet you and take you to lunch. Feel free to call me if you have any questions.

Sincerely,

Sarah Taylor

Sarah Taylor
Sales Representative

1515 Washington Ave
Minneapolis, MN 55425

No letterhead or return address is shown.
The salutation is too personal.
The tone is gossip-like and unprofessional.
The details in the body are somewhat irrelevant and fail to acknowledge the reader.
The closing is too casual, and no phone number is given.
The return address is out of place.

Copies

If you are sending copies of the letter to other readers, type *cc* followed by the person or people to which you are also sending the letter. (The abbreviation *cc* stands for "carbon copy." It is a term that was used before photocopiers were invented and people used carbon paper to make duplicates of letters and memos. People still use the abbreviation.) Or, you can simply type *c*, which stands for "copy," followed by a colon and the names of the people being copied.

Example:

cc: Ross Turnbow

Example:

c: Ross Turnbow

Fold the letter horizontally into thirds before placing it in its envelope. Position the letter in the envelope so that the bottom fold of the letter sits at the bottom of the envelope. (See Exhibit B-4 in Appendix B at the back of this textbook for an illustration.)

Exhibit 7-10a demonstrates the elements of an ineffective letter and **Exhibit 7-10b** demonstrates the elements of an effective letter. Can you see the difference between the two? The second letter is direct and concise, yet maintains a positive and upbeat tone. The letter stays on topic and introduces the writer to the reader in a professional manner. It states what the writer is prepared to do for the reader and demonstrates the "you" attitude.

Exhibit 7-10b An Effective Letter

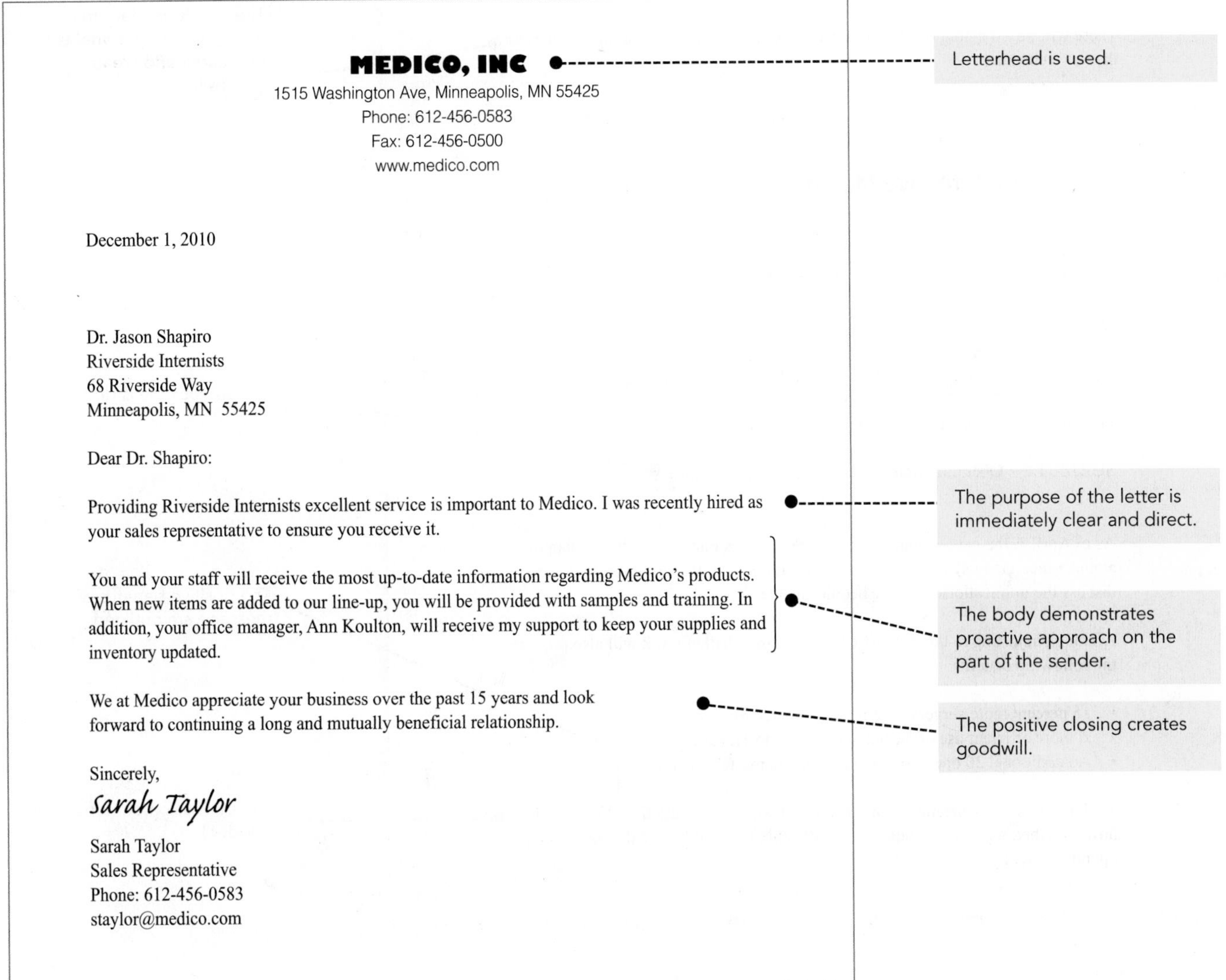

MEDICO, INC
1515 Washington Ave, Minneapolis, MN 55425
Phone: 612-456-0583
Fax: 612-456-0500
www.medico.com

December 1, 2010

Dr. Jason Shapiro
Riverside Internists
68 Riverside Way
Minneapolis, MN 55425

Dear Dr. Shapiro:

Providing Riverside Internists excellent service is important to Medico. I was recently hired as your sales representative to ensure you receive it.

You and your staff will receive the most up-to-date information regarding Medico's products. When new items are added to our line-up, you will be provided with samples and training. In addition, your office manager, Ann Koulton, will receive my support to keep your supplies and inventory updated.

We at Medico appreciate your business over the past 15 years and look forward to continuing a long and mutually beneficial relationship.

Sincerely,

Sarah Taylor

Sarah Taylor
Sales Representative
Phone: 612-456-0583
staylor@medico.com

Memos

Memos are usually reserved for messages sent within an organization. Managers use memos when they must present important messages in a formal manner, when they need to convey confidential details such as legal or salary information, or have to send longer messages. Memos can also serve as official records when they are used for employee performance appraisals, changes in policy, or other documentation.

Exhibit 7-11a An Ineffective Memo

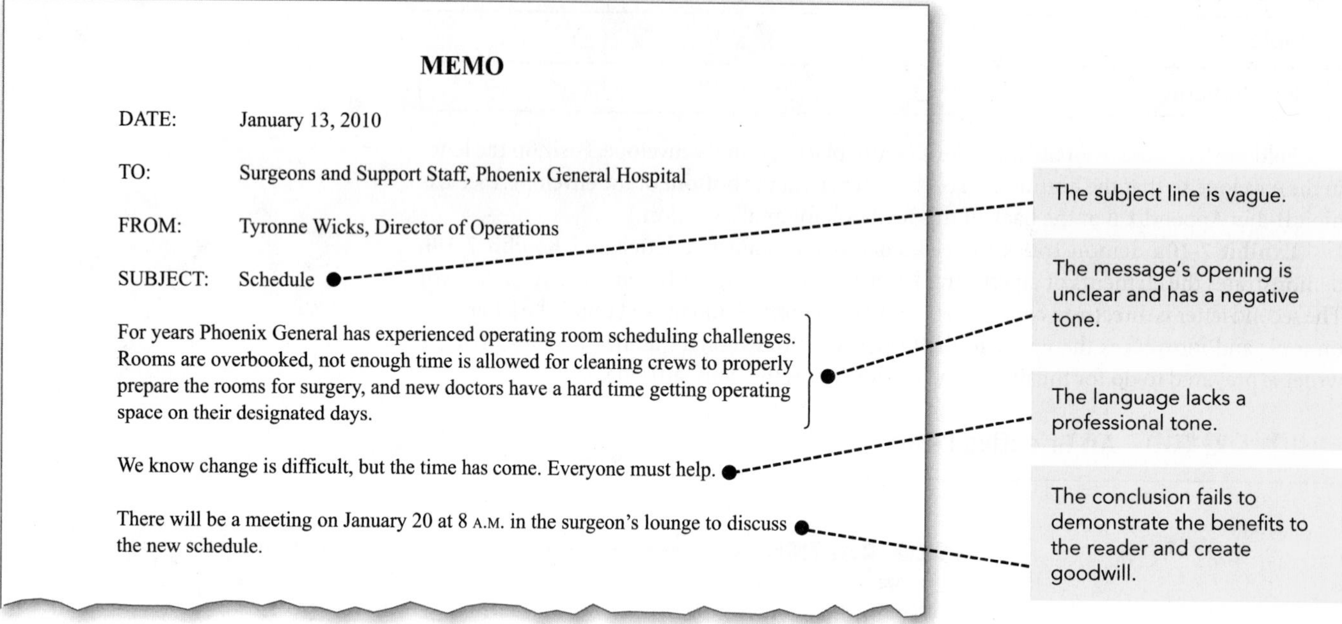

MEMO

DATE: January 13, 2010

TO: Surgeons and Support Staff, Phoenix General Hospital

FROM: Tyronne Wicks, Director of Operations

SUBJECT: Schedule

For years Phoenix General has experienced operating room scheduling challenges. Rooms are overbooked, not enough time is allowed for cleaning crews to properly prepare the rooms for surgery, and new doctors have a hard time getting operating space on their designated days.

We know change is difficult, but the time has come. Everyone must help.

There will be a meeting on January 20 at 8 A.M. in the surgeon's lounge to discuss the new schedule.

Exhibit 7-11b An Effective Memo

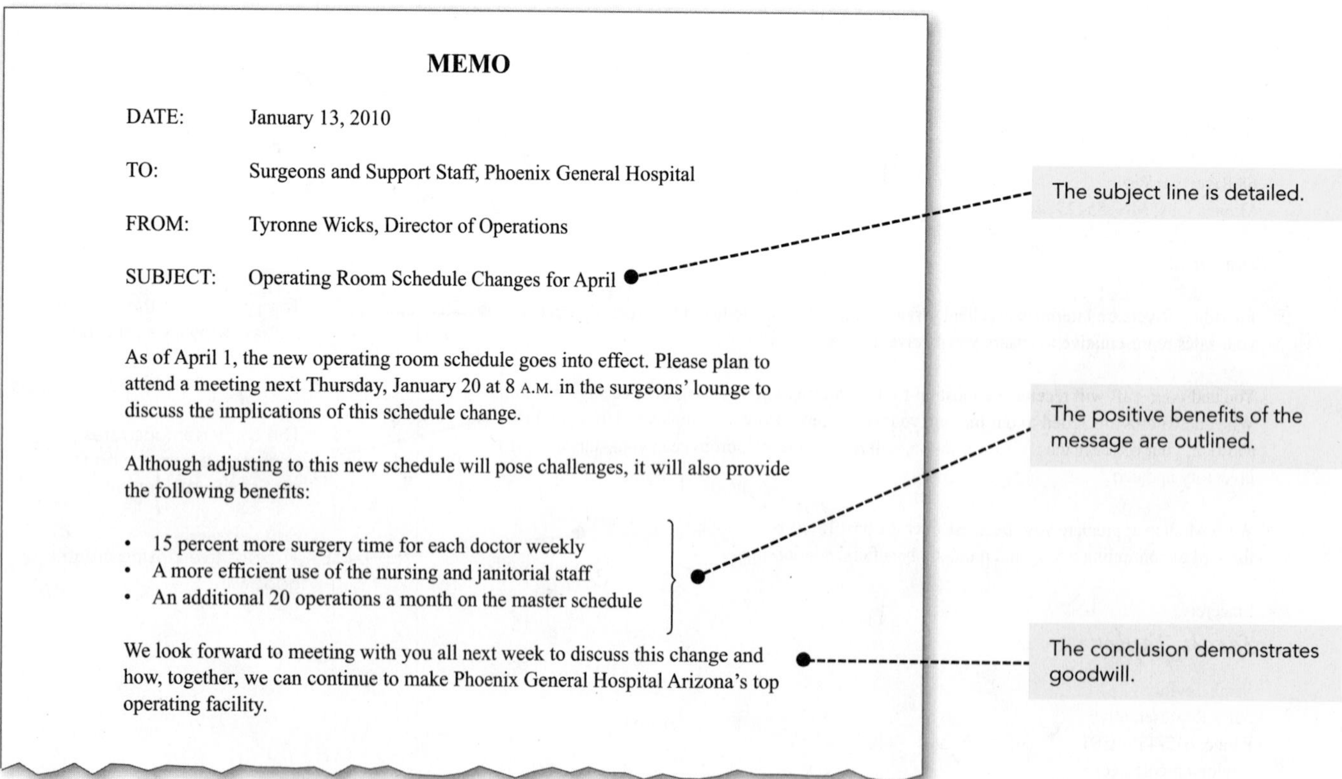

MEMO

DATE: January 13, 2010

TO: Surgeons and Support Staff, Phoenix General Hospital

FROM: Tyronne Wicks, Director of Operations

SUBJECT: Operating Room Schedule Changes for April

As of April 1, the new operating room schedule goes into effect. Please plan to attend a meeting next Thursday, January 20 at 8 A.M. in the surgeons' lounge to discuss the implications of this schedule change.

Although adjusting to this new schedule will pose challenges, it will also provide the following benefits:

- 15 percent more surgery time for each doctor weekly
- A more efficient use of the nursing and janitorial staff
- An additional 20 operations a month on the master schedule

We look forward to meeting with you all next week to discuss this change and how, together, we can continue to make Phoenix General Hospital Arizona's top operating facility.

A standard memo includes:

- Routing instructions, including "To," "From," and "Date" lines.
- A clear and concise "Subject" line that accurately and quickly informs the reader about the message's content.
- A short opening paragraph explaining the purpose of the memo.
- Follow-up information explaining or justifying the main idea presented in the opening.
- A conclusion summarizing the message and stating any actions to be taken and timetables to be considered.

Exhibit 7-11a demonstrates an ineffective memo. **Exhibit 7-11b** demonstrates an effective memo. The second memo states the message's purpose right away. Its opening relates to the subject line, and the benefits for the change are clearly outlined for the reader. Finally, the conclusion creates goodwill and is upbeat.

E-mails

For many organizations, e-mails have replaced memos as the primary form of internal written communication. E-mails are similar to memos but less formal. They are quick to send, inexpensive, and easy to distribute around the globe, and they don't create a lot of paper waste. As a result, they have become the predominant channel for delivering everyday, positive messages.

You are probably accustomed to sending personal e-mails. **Exhibit 7-12** offers some general guidelines for sending e-mails in the workplace. Let's now look at the elements of business e-mails and some tips for composing them.

To: Enter the recipient's e-mail address. To avoid sending e-mails to the wrong people, consider completing this line after you finish writing your message. You can't accidentally send an e-mail without the "To" line completed.

From: Unless you have permission from your manager, be sure to use your work e-mail address rather than your personal e-mail address for all business.

Subject: Busy employees often have to read through hundreds of e-mails a day, so, include a clear and specific subject line.

Cc: Copy others who need to be informed about the discussion.

Bcc: *Bcc* stands for "blind carbon copy." Complete the "Bcc" line when you want to send a third party the e-mail but you do not want your reader to know the third party has been copied on it.

DID YOU KNOW?

- A single U.S. office worker uses 10,000 sheets of paper each year.
- Americans threw away over 4.5 million tons of office paper between 2000 and 2010.
- It takes one 15-year-old tree to produce half a box of paper.
- One tree can filter up to 60 pounds of pollutants from the air each year.

Source: Reprinted with permission from "Shocking Statistics," CompuMentor, 2008. TechSoup Global.

Exhibit 7-12
General Guidelines for Sending E-mails in the Workplace

Remember	Respond
Business e-mails are more formal than personal e-mails.	Consider your audience and adjust your level of formality.
It is your responsibility to know your company's e-mail policies and adhere to the guidelines for using the company's e-mail for personal use.	Activate a separate e-mail account for your personal communication needs.
E-mails can be easily forwarded. Don't write anything you wouldn't want other people to read.	Practice asking yourself, "Would I say this to someone's face?" or "Would I show this to my boss?" before sending e-mails.
Your e-mails represent you and your company, as a professional in the workplace.	Revise, edit, and proofread, and format your messages for clarity, grammar, punctuation, and spelling.

Salutation: Greet your reader with a simple salutation. The following examples are all acceptable.

- Dear Ms. Rivers:
- Hello, John:
- David:
- Greetings:

If you are sending an e-mail to a close colleague, you can be less formal and use greetings such as:

- Hi, Jasmine.
- Good morning, Michael.

Body: Organize your ideas so that your main point is stated in the first paragraph. Keep e-mails brief. Longer messages are best reserved for paper memos. Summarize your message at the end and clarify any actions that need to be taken. Add a statement of goodwill, reminding the reader how he or she will benefit from the actions.

Closing: Close your message with a simple expression such as one of the following:

- Regards,
- Sincerely,
- Thanks,

Signature Block: Follow the closing information with your name, title, company's name, and your contact information, including your e-mail address. Some people also like to include their companies' Web site addresses. Most e-mail applications allow you to create a personalized signature block that will automatically appear at the bottom of every e-mail message you send.

Attachments: Send attachments with your e-mail message when your information:

- Is longer than a page or two.
- Has complicated formatting such as detailed outlines, multiple subheadings, or varied margins.
- Consists of a non-text file such as an "html" file or PowerPoint file.

Some Internet providers have spam and virus detectors that reject e-mails with large files attached or files with certain extensions, such as .zip files. You may need to follow up with your recipients to make sure they received your attachments.

Exhibit 7-13a demonstrates an ineffective e-mail requesting action. **Exhibit 7-13b** demonstrates an effective e-mail requesting action. Compare the two e-mails for their effectiveness and clarity.

The first e-mail fails to clarify its objective up front. Although it discusses the goals for improving customer satisfaction, it fails to direct the reader's actions. The second e-mail clearly asks the reader to review the attachment. It then provides supporting details explaining why the proposals have been collected and the procedure being followed. Finally, it explains what the reader must do and by when.

E-mail allows for quick and efficient communication, but beware of its pitfalls. It is very easy to make mistakes when sending e-mails. Take a little time to plan, organize, and review them before they are sent. Once you hit the send button, you usually cannot retrieve a message. Ask any business employee about a time he or she hit "send" too soon. He or she will probably have an embarrassing story to tell you. Some programs, such as Microsoft Exchange Server and Microsoft Outlook, do allow a sender to retrieve a sent e-mail if it hasn't been opened by the recipient, but both the sender and receiver must have the software on their computers.

In addition, don't overwhelm your coworkers by overusing the "Reply to All" button. Many employees receive huge numbers of e-mails on a daily basis. Consider who does and does not need to receive your messages and keep them short to save your readers time. Don't forward a string of e-mails and expect the receiver to read through them all to find the information you want the person to have. Instead, cut and paste or summarize the pertinent information from the previously sent e-mails. To save yourself

Exhibit 7-13a An Ineffective E-mail

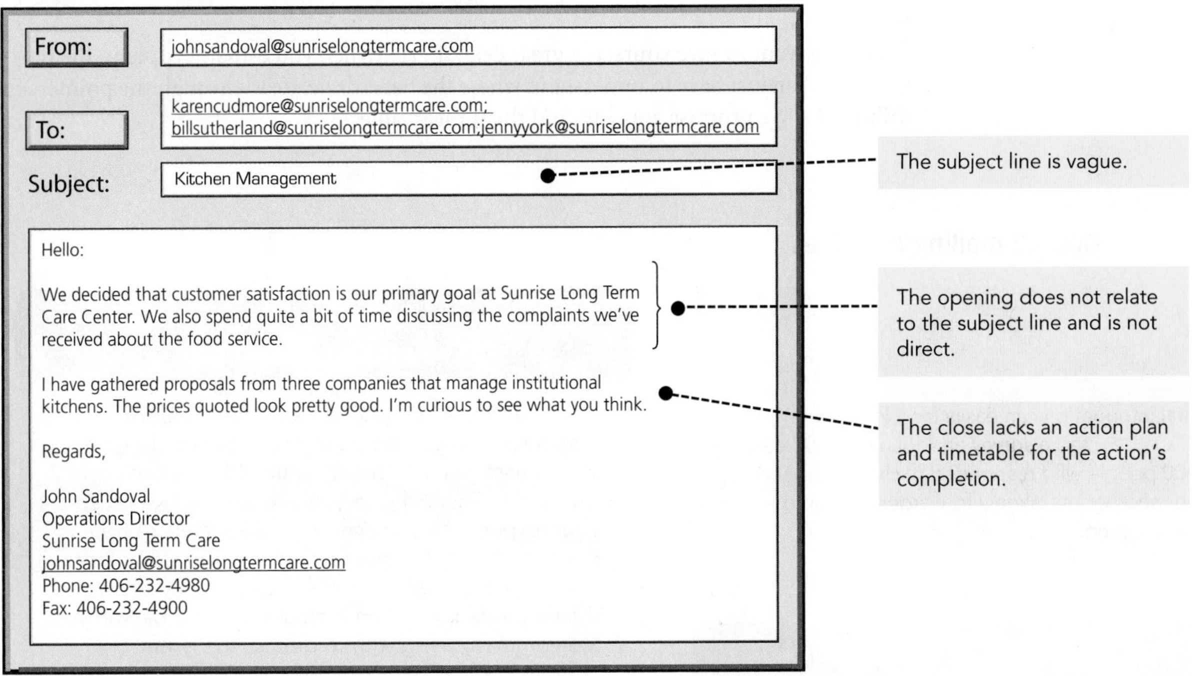

From: johnsandoval@sunriselongtermcare.com

To: karencudmore@sunriselongtermcare.com; billsutherland@sunriselongtermcare.com;jennyyork@sunriselongtermcare.com

Subject: Kitchen Management

Hello:

We decided that customer satisfaction is our primary goal at Sunrise Long Term Care Center. We also spend quite a bit of time discussing the complaints we've received about the food service.

I have gathered proposals from three companies that manage institutional kitchens. The prices quoted look pretty good. I'm curious to see what you think.

Regards,

John Sandoval
Operations Director
Sunrise Long Term Care
johnsandoval@sunriselongtermcare.com
Phone: 406-232-4980
Fax: 406-232-4900

The subject line is vague.
The opening does not relate to the subject line and is not direct.
The close lacks an action plan and timetable for the action's completion.

Exhibit 7-13b An Effective E-mail

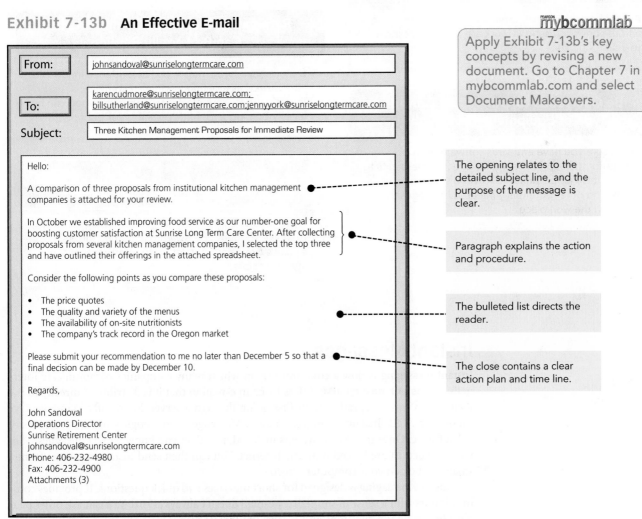

From: johnsandoval@sunriselongtermcare.com

To: karencudmore@sunriselongtermcare.com; billsutherland@sunriselongtermcare.com;jennyyork@sunriselongtermcare.com

Subject: Three Kitchen Management Proposals for Immediate Review

Hello:

A comparison of three proposals from institutional kitchen management companies is attached for your review.

In October we established improving food service as our number-one goal for boosting customer satisfaction at Sunrise Long Term Care Center. After collecting proposals from several kitchen management companies, I selected the top three and have outlined their offerings in the attached spreadsheet.

Consider the following points as you compare these proposals:

- The price quotes
- The quality and variety of the menus
- The availability of on-site nutritionists
- The company's track record in the Oregon market

Please submit your recommendation to me no later than December 5 so that a final decision can be made by December 10.

Regards,

John Sandoval
Operations Director
Sunrise Retirement Center
johnsandoval@sunriselongtermcare.com
Phone: 406-232-4980
Fax: 406-232-4900
Attachments (3)

The opening relates to the detailed subject line, and the purpose of the message is clear.

Paragraph explains the action and procedure.

The bulleted list directs the reader.

The close contains a clear action plan and time line.

PEARSON mybcommlab

Apply Exhibit 7-13b's key concepts by revising a new document. Go to Chapter 7 in mybcommlab.com and select Document Makeovers.

time, create folders to organize your e-mails after you have read them. Employees lose a significant amount of time each year trying to retrieve e-mails they thought they kept but can't find.

Do you want to save yourself a great deal of grief when you e-mail people in the business world? You just have to understand where the hazards lie. Read through the pointers in **Exhibit 7-14.** We promise you will find them invaluable.

Exhibit 7-14 Good E-mailing Practices

Be Cautious about Forwarding E-mails.

Confidential information can easily land in the wrong hands. AOL conducted a survey and found that 32 percent of the 4,000 people who responded to the survey had at one time or another mistakenly forwarded e-mail to an unintended recipient.

Consider Every E-mail You Send to Be Available to the Public.

Always be professional. E-mails are easily distributed, and the ones you send at work are legally accessible to your employer.

Be Courteous to Others and Consider the Type of Equipment They Might Have.

Make sure you have anti-virus software on your computer to keep from sending infected messages to others. It is inappropriate to forward spam, hoaxes, jokes, and other potentially infected messages to others in the workplace.

Avoid Replying to an E-mail when You Are Angry.

If you receive an upsetting e-mail, wait before responding so you are calm. If you decide to type your message immediately, wait 24 hours before sending it. This will give you time to review and edit your response. If you cannot give yourself 24 hours, have another colleague read your response before you send it. E-mail messages often sound harsher than intended, so when in doubt, call the person you are communicating with to discuss the issue.

Remember, Electronic Communication Can Be Legally Binding.

E-mails have been introduced as evidence in lawsuits and viewed as legal documents in criminal investigations. Your electronic communication can be legally binding and made available for public scrutiny.

Be Aware of Font Styles and Sizes.

Never use all capital letters in your messages. They read like shouting. Be aware that some readers' e-mail systems are not set up to interpret font types, styles, or sizes.

Instant Messages

Instant messaging is now a common way in which many companies communicate internally. An **instant message (IM)** differs from an e-mail in that it is distributed directly to the recipient in real time, rather than first going through a server. Microsoft's Windows Live Messenger, AOL's Instant Messenger, Yahoo! Messenger, and Google Chat are examples of IM software. Once the IM software is installed, it will let you know when colleagues from your contact list are logged onto the Internet. You can then send instant messages from a small text box on your computer screen.

Instant messaging is designed for short messages and quick questions. It provides communicators with a sense of immediacy e-mail doesn't always afford. You can ask other people who are online questions and receive immediate responses from them without having to check your e-mail. Virtual team members often use instant messaging software so they can determine which of their coworkers are in their offices and available for phone calls or longer e-mail conversations.

There are a number of drawbacks to using instant messages. Unlike e-mails, they can't be widely disseminated. They occur between a sender and a receiver only. Security and archiving issues have also been a problem with instant messaging. Instant messages generally disappear once a communication exchange has occurred. This is problematic because if companies do not properly archive instant messages, their communication records will not comply with various regulatory agencies, including the SEC (Securities Exchange Commission), the FERC (Federal Energy Regulation Commission), and the Sarbanes Oxley Act. Some companies have invested in software to manage and archive in-house instant messages as well as download and review them. You can also print or cut and paste instant messages into other documents.

Another downside is that instant messages popping up on your computer screen can be distracting. As a result, some companies ban instant messaging at work. Before you send instant messages on the job, check your company's policies. If instant messaging is part of your company's communication culture, know when to make yourself unavailable if you need to focus on a task. This is similar to knowing when to shut your office door to think, finish a project, or meet a deadline.

Instant messaging is also a fast-paced communication medium that lets you carry on multiple electronic conversations at once. This makes it easy to accidentally send a message to the wrong recipient or forget about a colleague who is waiting for a response while you respond to another instant message. Be professional, discreet, and pay close attention to the instant messages you are sending.

Text Messages

Text messaging is showing up in the workplace as well. Some retail companies use **text messages**, or short messaging service, to alert consumers of sales. Travel companies use it to notify customers if their flight times or hotel accommodations change. Doctors are now sending automated text messages to remind patients of their appointments. Text messages even notify people of dangerous weather conditions.

Proper spelling and punctuation apply to business-related text messages, just as they do to formal letters. Sending the following text message would be inappropriate in a business setting:

Gratz R U here

You should send this message instead:

Congratulations on your promotion. Are you in the office?

Messages written without punctuation or in lowercase letters are very difficult to read because readers cannot tell where one thought ends and another begins. The messages also look unprofessional.

Blogs

A **blog** is a shortened expression for the two words *Web log*. Blogs are similar to the articles newspaper columnists write, except that they appear on the Web. A writer posts his or her message on the blog (a Web site), and readers can then post follow-up comments about the message.

Blogs are typically used to deliver good or neutral news. The following are some of the purposes for which companies use blogs:

- ***Public or Media Relations.*** To inform the general public about events involving the company or new products, services, or company policies.
- ***Customer Support.*** Tips for customers regarding company products and services.
- ***Discussion Forums.*** Entries that stimulate discussion on pertinent policies and issues relevant to the company and consumers.
- ***Crisis Management.*** Postings conveying time sensitive information in response to a pending crisis.
- ***Recruiting.*** Listings to inform potential employees about job offerings and opportunities within the organization.

CHECKLIST

Before sending an instant message or a text message:

- ☑ Stop and think before you send a message or respond to one.
- ☑ Keep your messages short and concise.
- ☑ Maintain a professional tone.
- ☑ Use proper punctuation and capitalization.
- ☑ Avoid acronyms and common text abbreviations.
- ☑ Reread your message before sending it.
- ☑ Edit and proofread it as necessary.

Consider a cancer center using a blog to post articles about experimental treatments and links to scientific journals detailing advancements in chemotherapy or make announcements about the facility's expansion. A national health organization might use a blog during a crisis, posting commentary about a pandemic sweeping across the country. A medical-products manufacturing company might post blog entries to answer consumers' questions and keep them informed about new drugs. **Exhibit 7-15** shows how a vaccine manufacturing company hosts a pediatric expert on its blog to market the benefits of flu vaccines.

A blog can be a great business tool. However, it is only as good as the material on it and the audience it attracts. Simply creating a blog does not ensure that anyone will know it exists or will read it once they know it does. A frequently visited blog is one that is advertised, has well-written content, and is updated regularly.

How do you advertise a blog? Companies often advertise blogs on their Web sites, through e-mail, or direct marketing campaigns. What about content? Once readers become aware of the blog, they will continue visiting it only if the content is relevant and interesting. Keep the following tips in mind when you create and maintain a blog:

- The blog is *not* a personal diary—its contents must be meaningful to your readers. Choose innovative topics that resonate with your audience and are aligned with your company's goals.
- Make sure your posts are short, clear, and to the point. Revisit Chapter 5 for tips on clear writing.
- Encourage audience members to post comments to your entries and make an effort to read and respond to their comments. You can also embed online surveys and polls in your blog to get an idea about what the readers of it are thinking and to engage them.

Exhibit 7-15 An Example of a Blog Posting

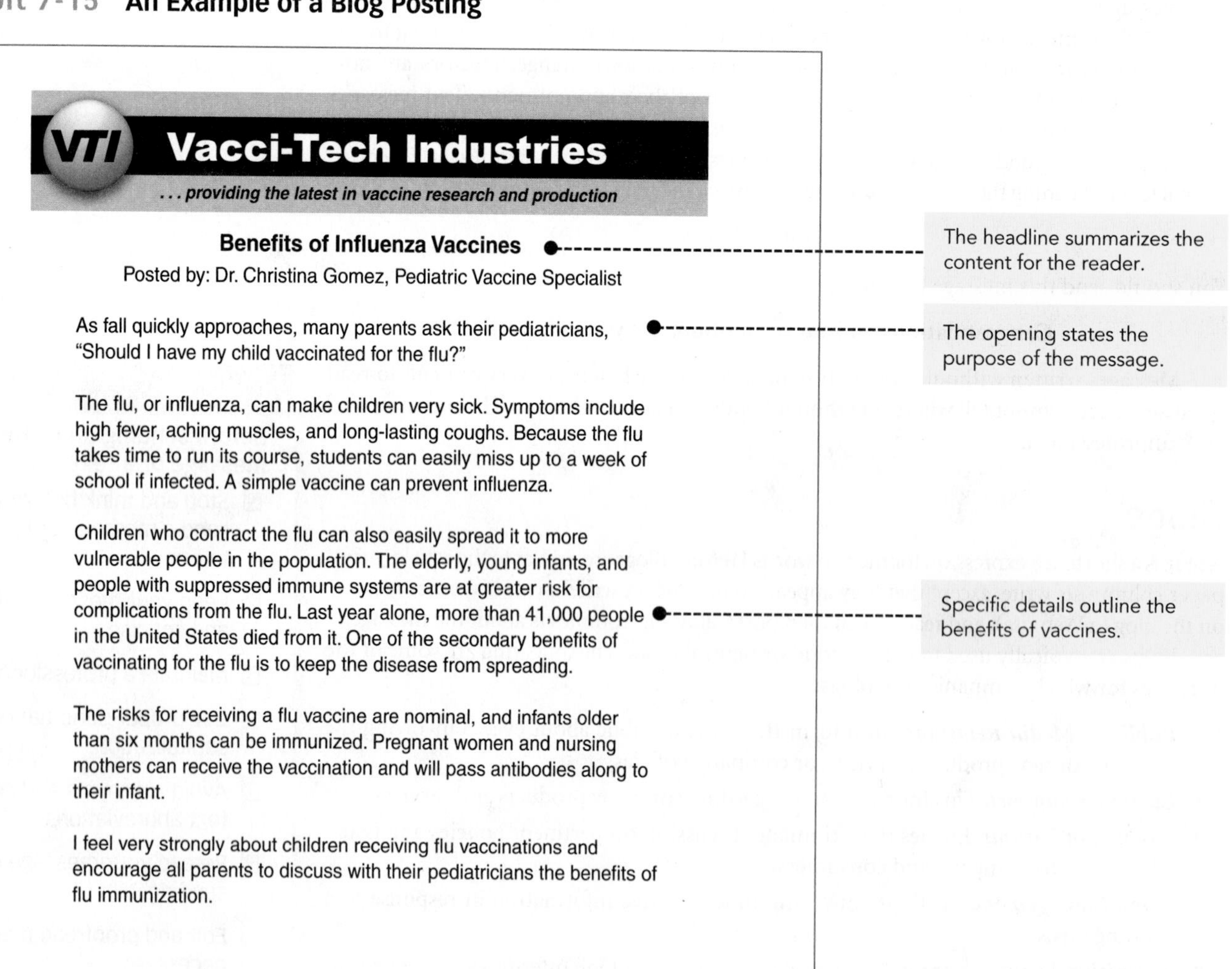

Remember, once you post a blog entry, it's on the Internet for everyone to see. People can also copy the information and store it on their computers, even if you eventually remove the material. At a small company, your manager might approve your blog posts.

If you write a blog for a large company, you might need to have your material reviewed by your public relations department or even your legal team before you post it. Whatever you write and post on the Web will obviously be subject to scrutiny.

Consider the problems Think Secret ran into. Think Secret, a once-popular rumor Web site that revealed details about Apple's soon-to-be released products, was sued by Apple for allegedly revealing its trade secrets. The creators of the small Web site tried to have the lawsuit dismissed, claiming the First Amendment gave the site the right to report such information. However, Apple has a strong copyright claim on its images and products. It also has a lot of money it can spend to pursue lawsuits. Eventually Think Secret was forced to shut down its site as part of a legal settlement with Apple.[2]

Social Networking Communications

We first discussed social networking in Chapter 2. **Social networking sites** are Web sites that allow people to connect with one another online for personal or professional reasons. Many people and businesses use social networking sites on a daily basis to deliver positive, everyday messages. The idea behind social networking is that as your social network grows, so does your influence.

Two of the most popular U.S.-based social networking sites are LinkedIn and Facebook. Each site has a different purpose and target audience.

LinkedIn

People use LinkedIn to connect with their coworkers, people who could become their coworkers and share their interests, and potential employers. LinkedIn gives you a way to present your "professional face" to the online world. Users of the site generally post information about their current and past employment history, business interests, and résumés, join online groups in their fields of expertise, and ask or answer job-related questions. The site allows companies to post job listings and people to search for them. According to a survey by Laura Aronsson and Bianca Male of *Business Insider*, there were 24 million unique LinkedIn visitors in the United States in December 2009. The visitors had the following characteristics:[3]

- There were slightly more male visitors than female.
- Most visitors have at least a college education, with 33 percent having a graduate degree.
- They are generally older, educated, and more affluent.

Facebook

Both professionals and individuals use Facebook. However, more people use Facebook to connect with their friends and acquaintances, play games, and present their "public face" to the online world. According to the same survey by Aronsson and Male, there were 116 million unique Facebook visitors in the United States in December 2009. The visitors had the following characteristics:[4]

- There were slightly more female visitors than male visitors.
- The visitors follow the Internet average pretty closely in terms of their affluence, education, and household sizes.
- They are mostly younger, aged 13–34.

Companies use social networking sites to promote their brands and listen to what their customers are saying. Recently Ford Motor Company announced it would begin unveiling its newest car models not at Detroit auto shows or to reports but on Facebook. Companies also hire employees who specialize in media to search sites, like LinkedIn, Facebook, and the Web in general, for negative messages people are posting about their firms. Then the employees post messages countering the negative comments. If a customer is unhappy with a firm's service, the firm's social media professional can sometimes offer to make the situation right.

Human resource recruiters also troll sites like LinkedIn using key words in profiles to find top-notch employees who might not be looking for jobs but could be persuaded to change companies given the right offer. LinkedIn and Facebook aren't the only two social networks on the Web, though. Many social networks are also being used for collaborative business communications. For example, Within3.com is a social network for doctors to discuss medical journal articles.

There are a number of pitfalls related to social networking sites, so consider the following information and pointers:

- Recruiters, bosses, coworkers, friends, and family can search social networking sites for information about you—and they do. Is there any content in your profile that you would not want other people reading or seeing?
- Make sure what you write is grammatically correct, spelled correctly, and looks professional. Why? Because employers routinely use LinkedIn to look for people to fill job openings.
- Your online profile is the property of the social networking site upon which you created it. Even if you choose to delete your account, everything you have posted is archived and belongs to the site.
- Spending all your time surfing and posting to a social networking site won't make you successful. You have to actually do your work and not just tell others about what you are doing or read about what they are doing.

Businesses have to consider the downsides of social networking sites as well. They can facilitate communication, but they can also be huge time wasters if employees are spending too much time on them. According to the Information Overload Research Group (IORG), the United States alone loses $650 billion per year in lowered productivity and hampered innovation because of employees surfing social networking sites. To help control the problem, some firms block, or make it impossible, for employees to access sites like Facebook and LinkedIn on their work computers.

Emerging Business Communications

Other emerging technologies are finding their way into mainstream business communications. Some examples follow:

Microblogs: A **microblog** is a short message sent to specific networks of people. The messages are generally no more than 140 characters and are designed to accomplish the following:

- Make company announcements.
- Report on relevant news or events.
- Ask or answer questions.
- Build a community of supporters and/or followers.
- Offer customers limited-time-only goods and services.

With instant messages, you send messages to individuals or groups that you specify by name. However, with microblogs, you send messages to a network of people who have "subscribed" to follow your posts—you do not have to specify their names. For example, a manager overseeing a large sales force can rely on microblogging to keep employees updated on pricing changes, inventory reductions, and shipment dates. Other managers may use it to notify their employees about impromptu meetings and other information demanding immediate attention.

Some of the more popular microblogging sites include:

- Twitter
- Tumblr
- Yammer
- Jaiku

Some people erroneously use microblogs to tell others everything they are doing throughout the day, or to inflate their own egos. This is both unprofessional and useless to subscribers. Instead, use your microblog posts to inform subscribers of events and information that are important to them, especially if the information is time-sensitive. Because you

HealthNorth

HealthNorth has expanded its services by partnering with First Medical: http://tinyurl.com/xl23

6:14 AM Nov 18th from web

Exhibit 7-16
A Microblog Post

must limit your word count, consider providing a link to a Web site where readers can get more details. For example, the link in the microblog post in **Exhibit 7-16** lets readers get more information about a new service.

Wikis: **Wikis** are Web sites that allow workers to collaborate on documents and projects by directly editing them on the Internet. Originally developed for software teams to share information during product development, Wikis are becoming a highly valued project management tool. Using the Web, multiple users can edit documents, calendars, organization notes, and other information from remote locations. *Wikipedia,* the popular online encyclopedia, is a popular example of this technology.

Other popular collaborative writing Web-based applications include:

- Google Docs
- Zoho Writer
- Socialtext
- Near-Time
- Writeboard

Fluwikie.com, a flu-pandemic planning site, is an example of a Wiki designed to help communities plan for public-health emergencies.

E-Zines: Electronic magazines, commonly referred to as **E-zines,** communicate information much like printed magazines. E-zine articles and newsletters generally focus on specific topics and are delivered by e-mail to subscribers. Some companies rely on e-zines as a marketing tool, using them to drive traffic to their Web sites. *Elderly Care Industry Ezine,* for healthcare professionals and elder care business owners, and *Health Care Recruitment E-zine,* for job seekers exploring the medical field are two examples of healthcare industry related e-zines.

RSS: **RSS** stands for *really simple syndication.* An RSS "feed" lets you receive news from your favorite Web sites, blogs, and Internet magazines on your computer or mobile device without actually having to visit the sites. RSS feeds also don't get screened by spam filters like e-mails do. Businesses use RSS feeds to communicate information about new products, services, and promotions to customers as well as send updates to their employees and suppliers.

To use RSS technology, click the RSS logo on the Web site you're interested in following. Updates from the site will then be delivered to you via text, video, audio, or images. You will need an RSS reader application to read the feeds. Common RSS readers include Feed Demon, Net News Wire, and Tristana.

Choosing the Best Channel for Sending Positive, Everyday Messages

Imagine you are a sales representative for a medical technology company, and you have just landed a new account that will increase your sales by 115 percent. Or, perhaps you are the finance manager at a long-term healthcare facility and have secured some additional financing for the facility. How should you communicate? Do you send an e-mail, write a formal letter, or tweet your team?

Ask yourself the following questions to determine which channels of communication best suit your needs:

- ***Is a phone call or face-to-face communication more effective than a letter or e-mail?*** At times, it may seem easier to write a letter or send an e-mail than to talk directly to a person. However, business is about people working together and making things happen. Resist hiding behind technology, since face-to-face communication can help

Exhibit 7-17 **The Advantages and Disadvantages of Today's Written Communication Channels**

Communication Channel	Advantages	Disadvantages
Paper		
Letters	Make a formal first impression Are confidential and private Are conducive to planning during the writing process Are a strong marketing tool Can be retained for future reference Can be certified and the receipt verified through the post office	Are more expensive to produce and distribute than electronic communication Take longer to distribute Make it challenging to reach wide audiences
Memos	Provide a written record Are confidential and private Are good for longer messages Conducive for planning during the writing process	Are less immediate than e-mail Are more expensive to generate than electronic communication
Electronic		
E-mails	Are quick and easy to send Are cost effective Make it easy to reach wide audiences Are environmentally friendly	Can be overused Make it difficult to ensure privacy and confidentiality Make it easy for senders to ramble and neglect good writing practices
Instant Messages	Communicate in real time Facilitate quick communication Are good for questions and informal messages Are environmentally friendly	Work for short messages only Are more susceptible to mistakes Make it difficult to ensure privacy Can be disruptive Can be challenging for companies to monitor for compliance
Web-Based		
Blogs	Are effective marketing and promotional tools Give companies an online presence Are effective for sharing information with wide audiences Are environmentally friendly	Can't target specific audiences Are not as effective with direct inquiries and responses for one-on-one communication
Social Networking Sites	Give you access to a large number of people whom you may not know personally, but are known by members of your network Let you find contacts within companies for job research Make you visible to recruiters	Provide limited privacy Can be time-consuming to maintain and use on a regular basis Own all content you have posted
Emerging Communication Technologies (Wikis, Twitter, E-zines, etc.)	Are cutting edge Are quick Are adaptive Are environmentally friendly Appeal to younger, technologically savvy audiences	Are problematic when companies and workers are not up to speed on the latest technologies Can become a distraction when technologies change rapidly

foster important connections inside and outside of your organization. Phone calls can be particularly helpful when you are a member of a remote team and are having a difficult time getting answers by electronic means.

- ***What is the communication culture in your industry?*** Hospitals, insurance companies, and banks tend to use more formal methods of communication than small, start-up technology companies, film production companies, or sporting goods companies. Know the culture and standards expected in your industry.
- ***How can you best communicate to preserve the important details of a message?*** If you have procedures to document and numbers to relay, formal written messages will clarify your communication and document the facts.
- ***How urgent is your message?*** Electronic media helps you reach your audience almost immediately. Consider the cost to your organization if your message is received in several days as opposed to several hours.
- ***How private is your message?*** As we explained earlier, confidentiality cannot be guaranteed when you are using e-mail and other electronic media. If privacy is a concern, consider writing a letter or confidential paper memo.
- ***Is cost an issue?*** If you are trying to reach 500 people across the globe, sending an e-mail versus letters will save you a considerable amount of money. You might also want to consider your company's attitude on sustainability and the environment. For example, does your company recycle and actively try to reduce waste? If so, you probably don't want to blanket your office with paper copies of documents.
- ***Is your message complicated?*** Longer, complicated messages are often better received in writing so readers can slowly process the information at their convenience. Incorporating headings and bullet points in the message (much like we have done with this list of suggestions) also makes a message easier to understand.
- ***Does your message need to be archived for future reference?*** If your message contains information that needs to be retrieved or kept for permanent record, formal written communication in the form of a memo or letter is appropriate.
- ***How does your audience typically receive messages?*** When possible, communicate with your audience using the methods most familiar and comfortable to them. Tweeting a message to an audience that does not regularly follow microblogs will be ineffective.

Exhibit 7-17 outlines the additional "pros" and "cons" related to various business communication media.

4 Why Should You Separate Your Professional Communications from Your Personal Communications?

It is easy to feel anonymous behind your computer, and just as easy to loosen the boundaries between your personal and professional life when using technology. To be as productive as possible on the job, separate the two. People who do not draw such boundaries run into trouble.

Consider the employee who writes a response on a blog that relates to his profession but injects personal commentary that is not representative of his company. Or the sales representative who tracks down a potential client on Facebook, realizes he knows the client from the past, and carries on a lengthy electronic conversation during business hours. Or the employee who receives "feeds" from her favorite Web sites and takes time to read the regular updates when she should be writing a proposal. Sitting at your desk reading a magazine that you brought in from home is not appropriate; neither is perusing the Internet for your own purposes on company time.

Although you might think checking your Facebook page only takes a minute, it shifts your attention. You are then likely to need several more minutes to refocus on your work and finish your projects. Also, consider when you need to distance yourself from the information that flows to you every day via technology. Information overload is a common reason why people cease to be productive. The computer chipmaker Intel, for example, learned that each of its employees was losing about eight hours of productivity per week due to electronic interruptions.[5]

REAL INSIGHTS from a New Professional

Name: Ritika Puri, College Senior
Title: Student Manager
Organization: Claremont McKenna College
Location: Claremont, California

RITIKA PURI IS A SENIOR AT Claremont McKenna College in Claremont, California. Puri already has an impressive résumé and is earning a reputation as someone who knows what she wants to do and how to do it. Puri recently completed her tenure as the student manager of the Rose Institute where she conducted and published research on California government policy. Last year, she traveled to New Delhi, India, to intern with Adharshila, an organization that provides legal services to residents in a local slum.

The *Wall Street Journal* featured Puri for designing an internship that allowed her to explore the relationship between people's socioeconomic status and their access to education and healthcare facilities. By interviewing families and talking with the residents in the slums of New Delhi, she documented the urgent need for basic healthcare there. Although services existed to treat AIDS and cancer in New Delhi, there was nowhere for residents to go who had a common cold. As a result of her research, Puri helped launch a clinic in the slums that provides services to approximately 20 patients a day.

Toward the end of her internship, Puri also raised money for the students she tutored through a quick e-mail campaign. She used the donations to purchase English textbooks and school supplies for 100 children. "Because time was of the essence," she explained, "I chose to solicit support by writing e-mails instead of writing grant proposals that require greater turnaround time."

Her work at both the Rose Institute and Adharshila demanded that Puri break down complex ideas, organize technical data from surveys, and communicate the ideas and data in writing for the general public. She claims that her ability to write creatively and effectively, a benefit of her literature major, helped her achieve business success so early in her career.

Her writing advice to business students? Take time to plan. "Step back and reflect on the comprehensive view of what you want to communicate. Between work, school, and friends, it's difficult to carve out the time for planning," she says. She recently pulled an "all-nighter," writing well into the morning to submit a paper on time. She admits receiving her worst grade ever as a result. Given the opportunity to rewrite the paper, she took three days to think about the assignment and plan. When it came time to write, she finished it in less than two hours, and received a better grade.

Questions

1. What communication methods did Puri use to raise money for a clinic and for school textbooks and supplies?
2. How did Puri's literature major help her communicate?
3. What does Puri think is most important to produce a well-written message?

Source: Ritika Puri in discussion with the author, March 2009.

When you have a report to complete, close your e-mail application and silence your phone, if possible. Let technology serve you rather than becoming a slave to it. Your success in business will depend upon your ability to manage your time effectively while still using electronic resources.

Finally, assume that your employer monitors all company electronic communication. Avoid forwarding inappropriate jokes, messages, blog postings, and so forth. Messages sent by electronic media can be used against you in court, just as official letters and memos can. Always communicate at work in a way that you would feel comfortable revealing to the whole world.

Summary *Synthesize What You Have Learned*

1. What are positive, everyday messages?

Positive, everyday messages are typical messages sent on a daily basis that deliver good or neutral news. They include messages that relay information, ask or answer questions, request action, or express appreciation.

2. **Why is effective writing critical for communicating positive, everyday messages?**

You must be able to compose messages that are accurate and concise. The many communication technologies available today will do nothing for you if your messages lack focus or fail to build goodwill with your reader. Well-developed writing and critical thinking skills will always be necessary to ensure that you convey the right information, communicate with the appropriate style and tone, and choose the most effective channel for distribution. Develop the best writing skills possible and then master specific technologies for sending messages. Your time will be well spent learning how to distill messages to their essence so you become a confident and successful business communicator.

3. **What channels are used to deliver positive, everyday messages?**

The various communication channels include letters, memos, e-mails, instant messages, blogs, social networking sites, and other emerging business communication technologies. As technology changes and business cultures shift, the channels for sending these messages continue to evolve. Yet the need for effective writing skills remains the same. You, the sender, must be able to express your ideas clearly no matter what communication channel you choose.

4. **Why should you separate your professional communications from your personal communications?**

Because technology lends itself to both personal and professional communication, it is easy to blur the lines between the two. Drawing boundaries between your personal and professional life while on the job is imperative for effective business communication, productivity, and career success.

PEARSON **mybcommlab**™ Are you an active learner? Go to **mybcommlab.com** to master Chapter 7's content. Chapter 7's interactive activities include:

- Customizable Study Plan and Chapter 7 practice quizzes
- Chapter 7 Simulation, Routine Messages, that helps you think critically and prepare to make choices in the business world
- Chapter 7 Video Exercise, Technology and the Tools of Commuication, which shows you how textbook concepts are put into practice every day
- Flash Cards for mastering the definition of chapter terms
- Interactive Lessons that visually review key chapter concepts
- Document Makeovers for hands-on, scored practice in revising documents

Know It *Reflect, Respond, and Express*

Build Your Critical Thinking Skills

Critical Thinking Questions

1. List the guidelines for writing an e-mail message. How are they similar to the guidelines for writing a memo? How are they different?
2. As a student, outline strategies you can use to accomplish your tasks without being interrupted by technology. Do you think the strategies would differ in the workplace? If so, how?
3. How does the idea of representing your company while you are at work relate to the Web sites you visit during office hours?
4. Review the chapter's tips for using e-mail wisely. Then, locate your institution's policy on e-mail and computer usage, which may be available on your institution's Web site. How does the policy compare to the chapter's tips? Are the legal issues of e-mail addressed in your institution's policy?
5. Review popular blogs on the Internet, such as the blogs available on ESPN.com or CNN.com. How are blogs changing how the media delivers news stories? How does the interactive aspect of blogging affect the reader? What are the business communication implications?

Critical Thinking Scenario

Amanda, a former marketing assistant at a pharmaceutical company, was laid off when her company downsized. Before Amanda left, the human resources manager told her about the Consolidated Omnibus Budget Reconciliation Act of 1985, commonly referred to as COBRA. COBRA requires most employers with group health insurance plans to offer temporary coverage to employees leaving the company if those employees would otherwise lose coverage. Amanda was eligible for COBRA insurance and her company agreed to pay for this expense for six months after her termination.

A month after she left the company, Amanda fell and broke her arm, landing her in the emergency room. Within two weeks, bills and letters started arriving, claiming that her insurance had lapsed and she had no coverage. Shocked and frustrated, Amanda tried to call the hospital and the insurance company, but kept getting caught in the telephone menu system and was unable to reach anyone to help her. Now, unless Amanda is able to remedy this mistake, she will be stuck paying the medical bills out of her own pocket.

- Because direct communication over the telephone failed, perhaps a written message would be more effective. Considering the avenues already tried, to whom should Amanda direct her written message? Name at least three possibilities.
- What type of written communication would be most beneficial to reach each of the three possible people you listed?
- Compose three messages, one for each person you indicated. Write as if you were Amanda in this situation.

Write It *Draft, Revise, and Finalize*

Create Your Own Success Story

1. Read through the four following scenarios and determine which channels of communication would be best suited for each one. Because there are multiple ways to handle these situations, consider each communication channel's advantages and disadvantages before making your decision. Then draft a message for each scenario using your chosen channel for communicating.
   - **a.** You want to be considered by your boss for an upcoming project that could open many professional doors for you. The project involves coordinating programs to help young children develop healthy eating habits. Your findings will be presented to state authorities on nutrition.
   - **b.** You are employed by a medical research facility and your boss asks you to get the following information from the city's largest hospital:
     - i. The average length of a patient's stay
     - ii. The average cost of a patient's stay
     - iii. The percentage of patients utilizing Medicaid
     - iv. The average number of deaths each month
     - v. The nurse-to-patient ratio
   - **c.** You work for a small healthcare clinic and need to inform the patients that the clinic now accepts three new insurance carriers, along with Medicare and Medicaid.
   - **d.** You work for a health insurance provider and have tried contacting a customer about lapsed insurance several times over the phone. You care about your job and the health of the customer, but each call has gone unreturned.
2. Distill the meaning of this chapter into a one-paragraph summary. Break down the idea even more by distilling the meaning of the entire chapter into one sentence.
3. Compose a short e-mail message that informs your classmates what your schedule looks like for the current term or semester. Would you list your classes? Write a short paragraph? Use a bulleted or numbered list? Consider the design of the message as you compose the content.
4. Compose a short message to your instructor asking for clarification on a homework assignment for the course. On the same page, create a short response to your inquiry.
5. Write a thank-you note showing appreciation to someone who has recently helped you. Handwrite the note since handwriting is considered more personable than an e-mail.
6. Write a paragraph summary of the day's class, putting the essence of the lecture and/or discussion into a short statement.
7. Compose a letter to a credit card company requesting they close your credit card account. Include all the format protocols used for business letters, such as a date at the top and salutation before the content begins. Choose either block or modified block format for the text design. Carefully consider what to include in the introduction, body, and conclusion of the content.
8. Read a couple of pages in your textbook and then write down the time you stop. Log into your personal e-mail or a social network like Facebook and browse the Web site for a couple of minutes. Shut the Web site down and resume focus on the textbook. How did the Web site distraction affect your concentration? Write a brief description of your findings.

Speak It *Discuss, Listen, and Understand*

Build Your Teamwork and Leadership Skills

1. Find three other classmates to form a team. Within your group, each person chooses one of the following departments to represent:
   - Accounting
   - Manufacturing
   - Marketing
   - Sales

   Imagine you work at a medical technology company and your boss has placed you on a team that is preparing to launch a new product.

   a. First, as a team, decide what healthcare–related product your company has developed. Is it a new breathing apparatus? Pacemaker? Or perhaps a new, compact set of surgical tools?

   b. Next, determine what characteristics set your product apart from others. The following list offers a few ideas to consider but feel free to come up with more.

      i. Do you offer a longer warranty?

      ii. How has the product tested in clinical trials?

      iii. Is the price point lower than that of your competitors?

      iv. Is the product manufactured in the United States? Does that affect the price positively?

      v. Is the product eco-friendly?

      vi. Do you offer free training seminars for staff members with the purchase of your product?

   c. Once you decide on a product, determine the best way to introduce your new product to the various independent practices and hospitals in your company's area. Remember the departments you are representing. Consider the different perspectives you might have. Someone from accounting might be more concerned with the costs, whereas a representative from sales might aim for the widest distribution of your message. Decide on the channels of communication you will use. Based on the examples throughout this chapter and the following brief list, pick at least three channels for sending your message.

      i. Letters accompanying samples

      ii. Memos to the gatekeepers of the organizations

      iii. E-mail notices

      iv. Blog postings

   d. Collaborating as a team, draft a message for each of your three channels for communication. Concentrate on the benefits your product provides to your recipients. Feel free to look back through the chapter for formatting suggestions and answers to other questions you might have.

   e. Now partner with another team from your class. Allow the other team to read your messages. The other team will then give you feedback on both the choices you made for distributing your messages and the content of each message. Switch roles so you read the other team's messages and then provide feedback on their work.

2. In groups or as a class, discuss your primary and secondary audiences of the e-mails you send. Who is your primary audience? Who makes up your secondary audiences? What are the legal implications of each type of audience?

3. In groups or as a class, take 5 minutes to jot down a description of your ideal profession and why you are interested in it. How do you best describe the profession and why it interests you? Keep the message simple. After the initial 5 minutes, take 5 minutes to review and revise your message. Pass the description to a neighbor. Once you receive someone else's description, distill the essence of what the writer is trying to express down to one sentence. After you have completed the sentence, review the information. Have you conveyed the basic meaning of the writer's description?

Do It *Document Your Success Track Record*

Build Your e-Portfolio

Imagine that your college has an electronic newsletter on health and wellness it sends to new freshman throughout the year. The e-newsletter includes tips on adjusting to college life, discovering student life on campus, and additional information helpful for a first-time college student.

You have been asked to write a brief article for the e-newsletter because, as a current student, you have experiences and knowledge that freshmen coming into school do not have. The e-newsletter publisher asks that you keep the article to fewer than 500 words, since it may eventually become a blog post.

As you compose your short article, keep in mind these tips for effective writing:

- Be clear with the intent of the message.
- Keep your audience in mind.
- Focus on relevant information.
- Keep the article brief.

Business in Action

How Phreesia's Communication Technology Helps Doctors Deliver Health-Related Messages to Patients

What do you get when you combine emerging technology, healthcare, and the need for accurate information? Chaim Indig, CEO of Phreesia, based in New York City, answers this question with his invention of Phreesia Tablets. Phreesia Tablets are wireless electronic devices that replace the forms, pens, and clipboards used in most physicians' offices and emergency rooms to capture patients' medical histories and insurance information.

When mistakes occur in the patient information intake process, problems can range from simple billing errors, to prescription mix-ups, to operations performed on the wrong patients. It is critical to communicate accurate patient information to all attending physicians and nurses.

Indig created Phreesia Tablets to solve this communication problem. The tablets use touch-screen and swipe-card technology to link patient information captured in the waiting room with the doctor's software. Once data is in the system, it is saved and securely stored. Doctors can then access patient files from their offices, hospitals, and homes.

A secondary benefit to this technology allows doctors to relay everyday messages to their patients. After a patient completes the intake process using the Phreesia Tablet, a message on the screen appears asking the patient if he or she would like to see some health-related information. If the patient agrees, the individual receives messages from the doctor including practical pointers for healthy living, information concerning the hospital or practice, pharmaceutical-sponsored messages, and relevant information concerning specific diseases or illnesses. This ingenious technology gives healthcare providers the opportunity to deliver empowering information to patients who might not otherwise have access to it.

Indig states, "Given the push by the new administration towards advanced healthcare IT adoption, this is an exciting time to be at the forefront of technology for patient-centered care." His product has been supported by several venture capital funding sources and might someday become a mainstay for delivering health-related messages throughout doctors' offices and hospitals across the nation.

Questions

1. Based on this story, how can everyday messages improve patient care?
2. What other types of everyday messages could Indig's technology send?

Source: Brian Dolan, "Patient Check-in Tablet Company Gets $16 Million," MobiHealthNews, June 2, 2010, accessed at http://mobihealthnews.com/775/patient-check-in-tablet-company-gets-16-million/.

Key Terms

Block style. A letter style in which the basic elements (the date, signature, and so forth) begin at the left-hand margin. *(p. 178)*

Blog. A shortened expression for the two words *Web log.* A blog is a Web site upon which a writer posts informative messages on a daily or frequent basis. People who read the blog can then post their follow-up comments on the site. *(p. 189)*

E-zines. Electronic magazines delivered by e-mail to subscribers. *(p. 193)*

Inside address. Consists of the recipient's name, title, and address. *(p. 181)*

Instant messages (IM). Messages that are electronically distributed directly to a recipient computer in real time. *(p. 188)*

Letterhead. The heading at the top of a piece of stationery that contains the sender's name and contact information. *(p. 179)*

Microblog. A short blog posting of small amounts of text, images, and videos sent to people in a restricted group. *(p. 192)*

Modified block style. A letter style in which date and signature are aligned to begin at the center of the page. *(p. 178)*

Positive, everyday messages. Messages sent on a daily basis. They deliver either good news or neutral news. *(p. 172)*

Reference initials. Initials that indicate both the writer and typist who prepared the message. They should appear one blank line down from the writer's printed name and title. *(p. 182)*

Return address. The sender's typed address on a letter. It appears below the letter's date and above the recipient's address. *(p. 180)*

RSS. An acronym that stands for *really simple syndication.* An RSS feed allows subscribers to electronically receive updated information from specific Web sites without having to check their e-mail inboxes. *(p. 193)*

Salutation. The greeting that begins a letter. *(p. 181)*

Signature block. A set of information containing the name, title, and contact information of a message's sender. *(p. 181)*

Social networking site. A Web site that allows people to connect with one another online for personal or professional reasons. *(p. 191)*

Text messages. Short text messages that are sent by phone to a recipient in real time. *(p. 189)*

Wikis. Web sites that allow workers to collaborate on documents and projects by directly editing them online. *(p. 193)*

Review Questions *Test Yourself*

1. Define everyday messages and why they are used more now than ever before.
2. List the five categories of everyday messages.
3. What are the characteristics of each of the five different categories of everyday messages?
4. List the best writing practices from the first two chapters of the book you should focus on when composing a message.
5. What factors should you consider when replying to messages?
6. How are letters used in business communication?
7. What are the elements of a standard memo? When are memos used in business communication?
8. Why is it important to separate your personal communications from your professional communications?

Grammar Review *Mastering Accuracy*

Capitalization

Section I

Each of the following sentences contains one or more common errors in word usage, grammar, or style. Identify the errors. If you have trouble finding the errors, review Sections 3.1.1. and 3.1.2. in the handbook (Appendix D) at the back of this textbook.

1. Tim said, i do not know how to fix this sentence.
2. "Please return the oreo cookies to the break room," nancy said, as she walked away.
3. Mario's most difficult class, principles of Physics, was facilitated by professor James Newstend.
4. Tim once said "we should learn to take notes at meetings", and he was right.
5. "Should we attend the first conference," asked James, our new supervisor.
6. While i enjoyed our Company trip to the local River, it was really the Great Mississippi River i wanted to visit.
7. Does this document contain obvious errors; if so, what are they?
8. Our first term paper will address our hopes, dream, and goals for the future—However, our second term paper will address how we will reach those hopes, dreams, and goals?
9. When visiting the Museum (Our instructor says we should visit museums several times a year), we took the longest and most expensive tour.
10. We can assert our positive position on the following items:
    a. To protect all Confidentiality agreements
    b. to annually review all claims of discrimination under the eeoc policy

Section II

On a separate sheet of paper, rewrite the following sentences so they are clearer, more professional sounding, grammatically correct, and goodwill oriented.

1. We should help find some jobs for all students within the criminal justice department.
2. The ancient time clock is on its last legs and will be replaced with the latest electronic model in two weeks.
3. The art piece in the lobby is by the World Famous artist Damien Hirst.
4. The artificial orange tree in the First Floor lobby is for decorative purposes only; therefore, people should be more aware and not try to eat the fake fruit.
5. Please make sure that you take the time to familiarize yourself with the locations of all the obviously marked Fire Exits.
6. Employees have been very sloppy lately, moreover, employees should clean their shoes before trampling through the building.
7. "A clean workspace is a duty, not an option. We need to increase efficiency and also inspire a feeling of confidence in our clients" said Mario at our last Manager's meeting.
8. The scary freight elevator near the ramp will be out of service for two weeks while modifications are made to get the mechanism up to snuff.
9. Hector will be informed of his rights and options under AdA, section 504 of the RA. and the IDEA.
10. Keeping tally of industry changes and trends will set students apart from the mindless herd who doesn't know how to do it.

Extra Resources *Tools You Can Use*

Books

- Forsyth, Patrick. *Effective Business Writing.* Philadelphia, PA: Kogan Page, 2009.
- Smith, Lisa. *Business E-mail: How to Make It Look Professional and Effective.* San Anselmo, CA: Writing & Editing at Work, 2002.

Web Sites

- *Business Netiquette International*
- "Letter Writing Useful Phrases," *AskOxford.com.*

"One of the toughest challenges for a communicator is to deliver bad news."

—**Curtis Sittenfeld,** American novelist

CHAPTER

8

Negative Messages

Fostering Goodwill during Difficult Communication Exchanges

LEARNING OBJECTIVE QUESTIONS

1. What is a negative message, and why is it important to plan one?
2. How do you organize negative messages?
3. What are the different types of negative messages?
4. What is the best way to respond to negative messages?

PEARSON mybcommlab Access interactive videos, simulations, sample documents, document makeovers, and assessment quizzes in Chapter 8 of **mybcommlab.com** for mastery of this chapter's objectives.

>>> **Irena** is the leasing manager for Execu-Fleet, an auto-leasing firm specializing in providing and maintaining fleets of automobiles to large corporations and government agencies. These cars are typically used by executives, traveling sales reps, and visiting dignitaries. Irena's team handles the initial contracts, and then subcontracts all maintenance and cleaning work out to a local garage and car wash.

At the moment, Irena is not very excited about the phone call she must make. She dreads telling Marc, the nice guy from Clean Cars car wash, about his apparent lack of attention to detail. Three cars just came back without any interior work—the floors and seats unvacuumed, the dashboards dusty, and the inside of the windows dirty. All three cars were to be used by visiting dignitaries from Europe. Irena knew from experience that the European visitors would take a dim view of Execu-Fleet once they stepped foot into those cars. So instead, Irena had to scramble to find three other cars that would fit the bill.

Unfortunately, this wasn't the first of Marc's slip-ups. An unvacuumed interior here, a neglected wax job there, and shoddy detail work overall. And now, Irena finally has to let Marc know that his actions have cost him the account with Execu-Fleet. Of course, it isn't Irena's choice. Her boss just let her know that he's had enough of Marc's carelessness, and feels it is Irene's job, as leasing manager, to let Marc know that Execu-Fleet will be switching to another company. But how can she break the bad news to someone who has been nice enough to offer ongoing discounts and always sends holiday cards with cookie tins?

Irena knows the conversation will be a delicate balance of building goodwill and delivering the bottom line. Before ever picking up the phone, she decides to plan her message. Thinking critically, Irena thinks about what it means to write a negative message. She identifies her audience, her purpose, and what she wants to accomplish. She even practices the conversation with her boss, who gives her pointers on tone and inflection. A few hours later, Irena feels confident that the conversation will be a success. Taking a deep breath, Irena picks up the phone and dials Marc's number.

Irena >>>

So far, the chapters in this book have dealt with communicating primarily positive messages. However, what about negative ones? Not everything goes according to plan. During your career, you will have to deliver or receive negative news. No one is immune, not even CEOs. Consider the CEOs in the automotive industry. U.S. automakers have had to ask for government bailouts and adjust their sales messages to attract customers worried they would go out of business. No matter what type of work you end up doing, no matter what industry, this chapter will help you better understand the fine art of effectively composing and delivering negative messages.

1 What Is a Negative Message, and Why Is It Important to Plan One?

■ For an interactive, real-world example of this topic, access this chapter's bcomm mini sim entitled Negative Messages, located at **mybcommlab.com**

A **negative message** is any type of information construed as bad news because it's not what your audience expected or wanted to hear. A negative message needs to be presented in a way that does the following:

- Helps the audience or receiver accept it
- Promotes goodwill
- Resolves the situation
- Maintains your reputation and that of your business
- Avoids legal liability

That's a lot for a message to convey, but it's not impossible to do. Disappointing someone is never a pleasant task. However, with some preparation, you will be able to deliver a negative message without coming across as a negative person. Like other types of business communication, when you're developing a negative message, you need to ask yourself these questions:

1. Who is my audience?
2. Why am I sending this message?
3. What outcome do I want from this message?

To get an idea of how to think about these questions, consider the following scenario. You are responsible for purchasing cars for your company's sales team. You buy a new car off the lot one Sunday afternoon. You drive the car around town, take it home, and park it in your garage. On Monday morning the car won't start, so you're going to be late to an important meeting. You're angry and want to tell the car dealer how upset you are.

- ***Who needs to receive this message?*** If you contact the salesperson who sold you the car, you are probably talking to the wrong person. He or she is probably not in a position to do much about your problem. It might be better to talk to the sales manager.
- ***Why am I sending this message?*** You need your car to run so you can go to work. It is also brand new, so it should work. You need to deal with the problem and get it resolved.
- ***What outcome do I want from this message?*** Chances are you haven't even thought of the outcome you want because you're mad and all you want to do is vent your anger. However, if you do this, you will probably end up making your listener mad, getting into a yelling match, or slamming down the phone. Instead, think about what you really want to happen, such as getting a loaned car so you can drive to work and getting your car repaired for free.

If you ask yourself these questions and answer them, you will probably make a different, much more productive phone call to the dealership.

Once you know who is supposed to get the message, why you're sending it, and the outcome you want, answer these content-specific questions:

1. ***What information must your message include?*** Jot down the points you want to cover.
2. ***What evidence supports your position?*** Make sure you have done your research and have all the facts.

3. ***What objections can you expect your receiver to have?*** Think about how the receiver may react. What negative reactions will your message have to overcome?
4. ***How will the situation affect the receiver's response?*** Consider the factors leading up to the message. Be sensitive to how they could affect the receiver's reaction to your message.

Setting the Tone

Delivering bad news is no fun. However, the right tone can make the difference between a message that's ignored and a message that's read; a message that breeds contempt and one that cultivates goodwill; and a message that creates disappointment and one that offers hope. The following sections contain suggestions for setting the right tone.

Explain Yourself Clearly

Minimize the space and time devoted to the bad news, but do not trivialize it. Present the information the way you would like to receive it, with the seriousness and care it deserves.

Avoid Negative Language

Unless you are taking responsibility for an action or inaction, avoid **negative language,** or words that convey unhappy and unpleasant thoughts. Words such as these predispose the receiver of the message to react negatively to your message. Examples of words such as these include:

- unfortunate
- regret
- mistake
- problem
- refuse
- stop

In other words, do not give your receiver of the message a reason to fear or avoid reading or hearing what you have to say. **Exhibit 8-1** shows a few examples of negative versus positive wording. Which message would you rather receive?

Exhibit 8-1
Negative versus Positive Wording

Negative Wording	Positive Wording
We regret to inform you that the seat cover you ordered is out of stock and will not be available for another week.	Thank you for your recent order. Due to increased demand, the seat cover you ordered is out of stock. We anticipate it will be available in two weeks.
You do the worst job of installing batteries. I bought one from you last month, and the top is already all corroded and disgusting looking. I'm bringing it in to get my money back!	I purchased one of your top-of-the-line batteries last month and had it installed by your expert crew. Last week I noticed some corrosion on the top and would like to bring it in for inspection.

Use Consequence-Oriented Language

Be clear about the consequences of your news. If you deliver a layoff notice, make sure the receiver understands what is going to happen and when. If you deliver a reprimand, make sure the receiver understands what you expect of him or her. If you deliver a delayed-order notice, explain when the customer will get her order.

Avoid Careless Language

Do not say anything that is untrue just to protect the receiver's feelings. For example, if you must terminate staff members because your company is going out of business, do not give an employee false hope by saying "We will be sure to rehire you when the company reopens." You can't make this promise because you have no way of knowing if or when the company will reopen. Legally, such a statement could imperil you and your company.

Never Use Angry or Abusive Language

The worst thing you can do when delivering bad news is to use angry or abusive language.

Take Responsibility

If the bad news is due to a mistake you made, acknowledge your error. Acknowledging your mistake and taking measures to correct it can earn you and your company respect, resulting in loyal customers. Dodging responsibility will have the opposite effect and could create legal problems for your company.

Apologize Sincerely

Let people know that you understand the news you're delivering is inconveniencing them, hurting them financially, or causing them distress. There is nothing wrong with saying you feel bad about delivering bad news; people appreciate heartfelt apologies. **Exhibit 8-2** illustrates an example of an ineffective apology versus an effective apology.

Exhibit 8-2a
An Ineffective Apology

> The ENKEI EKM3 rims you ordered are out of stock. We will let you know when they are back in stock.

Exhibit 8-2b
An Effective Apology

> Thank you for your order. The ENKEI EKM3 rims you ordered are so popular they are currently out of stock. We anticipate they will be back in stock within two weeks. We are sorry for the delay and are happy to offer you similar ENKEI LF-10 rims, which are currently in stock, for the same price. Please let us know which rims you would like to purchase.

Accentuate the Positive

No matter how bad the news is, try to say something positive, which will go a long way with your receiver. Don't, however, make promises your firm can't keep. Because you are a representative of your company, your promises are legally binding.

Use Passive Voice Sparingly

As you learned in Chapter 5, sentences written in active voice are easier to read than those written in passive voice. Passive voice sentences are typically longer and do not specify who or what is doing the acting. The reason people use passive voice is because they either don't know who or what was doing the acting, or the actor wants to remain anonymous.

Why would the "actor" want to remain anonymous? Generally because the message contains negative news. **Exhibit 8-3** shows the difference between messages delivered in the active voice versus the passive voice.

As the examples in Exhibit 8-3 show, using the passive voice seems to soften the blow of bad news. However, it also conveys a lack of accountability on the part of the writer as well as a certain distance or lack of caring. Readers generally resent this tone. If you must use it, try to make it more personal, as the following example shows:

The passive voice can be overused when conveying bad news. Receivers of messages written in passive voice can get the idea that you are trying to avoid accountability.

We're sorry your request for financing has been denied.

The sentence still does not indicate who's doing the denying, but at least it says, "We're sorry," which indicates some accountability. Consider how the receiver is likely to feel about your message. If you write a message that you would feel comfortable receiving, the message will likely be more acceptable to your audience.

Passive Voice	Active Voice
Your **car will be repossessed.** *The writer does not want to come out and say who's doing the repossessing, which leaves the reader wondering.*	Our bank **will be repossessing your car.**
Your request for financing **has been denied.** *The writer does not want to say who's denying the request, which leaves the reader wondering.*	First Lending, LLC has **denied** your request for financing.

Exhibit 8-3
Negative Messages Delivered Using Passive Voice versus Active Voice

Delivery Methods

Is it better to deliver bad news in print or in person? It depends on the situation, the people, and the timing of a message's delivery. The following are some guidelines to help you choose the best delivery method.

In Person

The worse the news is, the more important in-person delivery becomes.

- ***Personal contact.*** For difficult messages, personal contact is always best. Seeing a person's face helps you gauge his or her reaction to your news so you can adjust your message. Unfortunately, people often do everything possible to avoid personal contact because they do not want to deal with the receiver's reaction.
- ***Phone.*** If you cannot physically be in the same room with the person due to distance or timing, delivering the message via phone is the next best alternative. Be polite and give listeners your full attention. (They can tell when you are working on the computer, texting, or doing something else.) A person receiving bad news prefers to hear it from someone who sounds caring. Above all, give people time to respond to the news and listen to what they say. It is also generally a wise idea to send a written follow-up message to make sure the listener accurately perceived what you intended to say.

Consider how you would like to get the news if you were the receiver. Then write a script of the message and read it aloud for practice. Anticipate the receiver's reaction and be prepared to respond to it.

Dr. Robert Buckman is a cancer specialist who teaches doctors and high-level executives how to break bad news. Buckman has had plenty of personal experience delivering it to patients. He was also on the receiving end of it when he was diagnosed with an autoimmune disease. The following is advice a manager might give an employee based on Buckman's advice when it comes to actually delivering bad news:[2]

- ***Start by listening, not talking.*** Don't begin by immediately delivering the bad news. Instead, ask the person some open-ended ended questions such as "How have things been going for you?" Then sit back and listen so that you truly understand the person's point of view.
- ***Explore the receiver's perceptions.*** Find out what your receiver thinks is going on. For example, if you have to give a bad performance review, you might start by asking the employee, "How do you think you have done this year? Is there anything you're really proud of? Is there anything you want to work on?"
- ***Acknowledge people's emotions.*** Accept that people will be upset by the news, and let them be upset. Acknowledging their emotions shows them you understand. There's nothing more powerful than saying to someone, "This must be awful for you." It gives the person permission to feel what he or she is feeling without embarrassment or guilt.
- ***Don't get emotional yourself.*** Even though the other person is upset, stay calm. Listen to the other person's feedback without reacting to his or her emotion.

When you're done with the difficult conversation, review the ground you have covered, identify a plan of action, and agree on a time and date for the next contact—if there is going to be one.

DID YOU KNOW?

The electronics retailer RadioShack discovered that e-mail is not a good way to deliver extremely bad news, such as news about a layoff. In 2006, RadioShack decided to lay off 400 employees by e-mail, a bad move, according to management specialists.

The e-mail read:

The work force reduction notification is currently in progress. Unfortunately your position is one that has been eliminated.

Derrick D'Souza, a management professor at the University of North Texas, was surprised that RadioShack did not use face-to-face meetings with supervisors to implement the layoff. A massive e-mail layoff could be seen as dehumanizing, says D'Souza. "If I put myself in their [the employees'] shoes, "I'd say, 'Didn't they have a few minutes to tell me?' "[1]

In Print

Printed messages—e-mails, memos, and letters—are useful in terms of conveying news that is not too painful but must be documented. Delivering a printed message is also a good way to document negative news that was already delivered in person.

- ***E-mails.*** E-mails are good for sending routine negative messages that must be received immediately. E-mails are more common for companies that do business online, such as Amazon or eBay. When you send an e-mail, be prepared to follow up by phone to make sure the recipient understood the message. If you don't follow up, be prepared to answer questions by phone, memo, or e-mail.
- ***Letter or memo.*** Letters and memos are good for delivering formal messages or for situations in which you need a paper trail. After you meet with someone in person or via phone to deliver bad news, you can later send a letter or memo as a record of the conversation. Sometimes letters and memos are sent first and then followed up by phone or in person. When sending an important letter or memo as an e-mail attachment consider providing it in PDF format so the content cannot be changed by the receiver.

Other Electronic Delivery Methods

People often take extremely bad news personally. Certain online media are inappropriate for delivering it. Using text messages and instant messages to deliver extremely bad news is a poor choice. The abbreviated nature of them can make you come across as unfeeling. In the case of an instant message, if the recipient's computer is unattended, people dropping by his or her desk might see the message in a popup window on the person's computer. Using Twitter is an equally poor choice to deliver bad news to an individual because anyone following your tweets can read the message. Posting the news on a blog is poor practice, unless you want to broadcast the news to a very large audience. Again, when choosing the delivery method for the message, consider how you would like to receive it.

Timing the Delivery

No news is good news, right? Well, not exactly. Some people dread being the bearer of bad news so much that they put off delivering it. Refusing to talk about problems won't make them go away. In many cases, the longer you put off delivering negative news, the more serious the consequences become. "No news" then becomes "extremely bad news."

Timing is more important with negative messages than with positive ones. For example, you wouldn't deliver a negative performance evaluation at the end of a day to an employee who spent most of the afternoon in the emergency room with an injured child. Nor would you tell a team of software developers that a project was canceled after the developers pulled an all-nighter to finish the project. In both cases, you might want to wait until the people got some rest.

In general, people tend to have more energy in the morning and during the beginning of the week. If you have to deliver bad news in person, consider doing it then. If you are delivering bad news by mail and the news is time sensitive, consider the time it will take for the message to arrive so the recipient gets it in time.

2 How Do You Organize Negative Messages?

When planning to write a negative message, keep these goals in mind:

1. Make sure the reader understands the news.
2. Get the receiver to accept the bad news.
3. Maintain a positive image of you and your organization.

Let's start with the subject line of your bad news message, which is discussed next.

The Subject Line

Writing the subject line of a negative memo or e-mail can be tricky. Because you want your news to be read, you need to word your subject line so you don't scare off readers or anger them. However, you also need to avoid being so casual that those who receive the e-mail discard it without reading the message. **Exhibit 8-4** shows some examples of good and bad subject lines for negative messages.

Exhibit 8-4
Good and Bad Subject Lines

Topic	Bad Subject Line	Good Subject Line
A meeting to discuss a disciplinary action needs to be set up.	Upcoming disciplinary meeting	Discussion regarding your performance
Your claim has been denied.	Claim denied	The results of your auto claim
The company was bought out, and 50 percent of the employees will be laid off.	Bad news about company	News about the company's purchase

The Body

As you learned in Chapter 4, there are two ways to approach the body of a message: direct or indirect. With negative messages, the indirect approach is always best and that is the approach we demonstrate in this chapter.

When you use the **indirect approach,** you avoid stating the bad news at the beginning of your message. The indirect approach reduces the impact of the negative news by providing explanations first. This helps prepare the reader, softens the blow, and shows some sensitivity on your part. The approach is useful when you believe the bad news may come as a shock, the audience may be upset with the news.

The basic structure of a negative message using the indirect approach is as follows:

1. ***Present a buffer.*** A **buffer** is a neutral message that engages the reader without stating the reason for the message. A buffer is not a lie, nor is it an unrealistic promise. It is simply a noncontroversial statement related to the point of the message. Never use negative language in the buffer. The following sentences are an example of a good buffer:

   As a long-time writer of car reviews, I appreciate the continued opportunity to test drive and comment on your company's vehicles. To date, Kacey Motors has been a driving force in automotive excellence.

2. ***Outline the reason for the bad news.*** Outline the facts and the reason for the bad news, but don't initially discuss the news itself. Use positive language and demonstrate to the reader that the matter was treated seriously and fairly.

   Test driving Kacey automobiles has certainly resulted in a positive relationship with your company. However, time constraints and external demands have recently taken a toll on the quality of my reviews.

3. ***Position the bad news.*** Position the bad news strategically. Unlike the lead in a news story, position the negative news near the middle of the message. When you present it, apologize if necessary. Finally, offer an alternative, if possible. In the case of customers, suggest other products that might meet their needs or suggest a compromise to lessen the impact of the bad news.

   Therefore, I must withdraw my services from the Drive-and-Write program, effective today. I would be glad to provide Kacey with the names of several other writers with whom I work. All are competent, knowledgeable auto reviewers, and I would proudly stand by their reviews.

Exhibit 8-5 A Negative-News Message Using the Indirect Approach

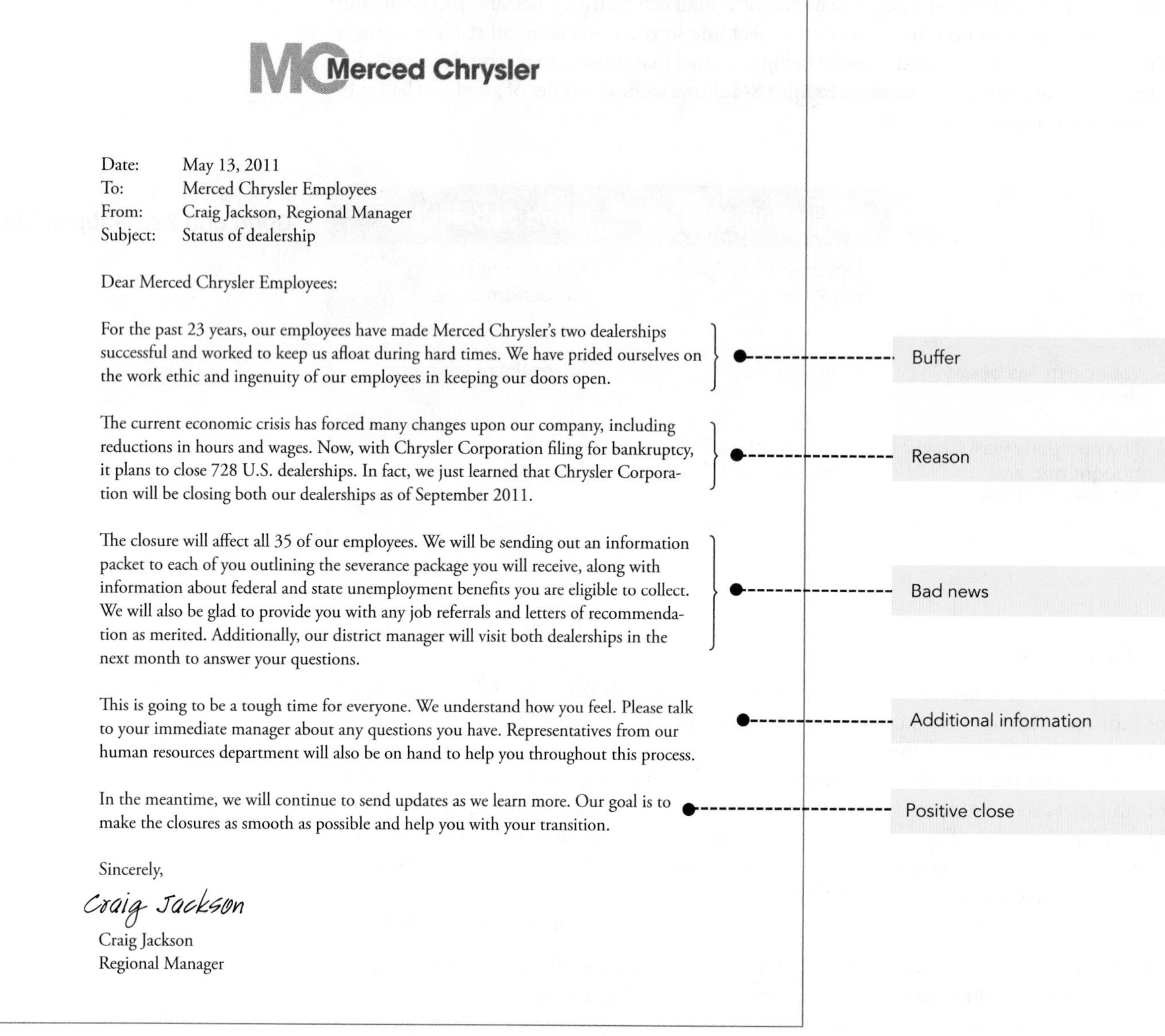

Merced Chrysler

Date: May 13, 2011
To: Merced Chrysler Employees
From: Craig Jackson, Regional Manager
Subject: Status of dealership

Dear Merced Chrysler Employees:

For the past 23 years, our employees have made Merced Chrysler's two dealerships successful and worked to keep us afloat during hard times. We have prided ourselves on the work ethic and ingenuity of our employees in keeping our doors open.

The current economic crisis has forced many changes upon our company, including reductions in hours and wages. Now, with Chrysler Corporation filing for bankruptcy, it plans to close 728 U.S. dealerships. In fact, we just learned that Chrysler Corporation will be closing both our dealerships as of September 2011.

The closure will affect all 35 of our employees. We will be sending out an information packet to each of you outlining the severance package you will receive, along with information about federal and state unemployment benefits you are eligible to collect. We will also be glad to provide you with any job referrals and letters of recommendation as merited. Additionally, our district manager will visit both dealerships in the next month to answer your questions.

This is going to be a tough time for everyone. We understand how you feel. Please talk to your immediate manager about any questions you have. Representatives from our human resources department will also be on hand to help you throughout this process.

In the meantime, we will continue to send updates as we learn more. Our goal is to make the closures as smooth as possible and help you with your transition.

Sincerely,

Craig Jackson

Craig Jackson
Regional Manager

4. ***Close positively.*** The close is your chance to emphasize your respect for your audience, even though you delivered some bad news. Avoid insincere clichés and references to possible problems. The close is also a good place to indicate that you would like to continue the business relationship, if that is your intention.

   Thank you again for the rare opportunity to participate in this program with your company. I regret my departure, but I do hope to continue our business relationship again sometime in the future.

   Exhibit 8-5 shows a letter that delivers news about a layoff using the indirect approach.

3 What Are the Different Types of Negative Messages?

Think about the negative messages you might be asked to deliver in the workplace. Some might be delivered to your manager, your employees, or your coworkers. Others might be delivered to a customer or client.

This section contains a variety of examples for you to review. The messages are written using the indirect method. The salutations of many of the examples include the recipients' titles and last names. However, if you know recipients well, it might be appropriate to use their first names, depending on the formality and content of the communication.

Negative Messages to Clients and Customers

When working with clients and customers, there will be times when you need to say "no" to a request or convey disappointing news. Because words in print can seem cold and unfeeling, it's often best to speak with clients or customers in person. If that's not possible, call them first and then send a letter or e-mail.

Claude Breton fell in love with the faux tie-dyed look of a Smart Car he saw on the streets of Ottawa, Canada—but only after he had already purchased his own Smart Car through a local dealer. Claude then contacted the dealer to see if he could purchase the tie-dyed panels and switch out his original panels. Unfortunately, the dealer was forced to refuse Claude's request. **Exhibit 8-6** is an example of the dealer's response.

Sometimes customers or would-be customers request something that a business cannot supply. When this happens, respond to the request honestly, tell them the bad news, and then offer an alternative, if possible.

Not all customers' requests can be met. Learning to deliver bad news to customers while building goodwill with them is part of doing business.

Exhibit 8-6 A Negative-News Letter to a Customer

OTTAWA PREMIER MOTORS

1414 3rd Ave, Seattle, WA 98101-2105
Phone: (206) 623-4392
Fax: (206) 623-4393
www.ottawamotors.com

March 5, 2011

Dear Mr. Breton:

We are pleased to learn that you are happy with your new Smart for two. We are sure it will get you around Ottawa quickly and easily, especially when you are trying to fit into those hard-to-find parking spaces. — Buffer

The popular color panel you requested, Numeric Blue, is no longer manufactured by Smart, so we cannot sell it to you. However, we are aware of a number of online Smart enthusiast groups that can help you locate existing panels so you can swap yours out. We recommend www.clubsmartcar.com and www.smartmania.co.uk to get you started. — Reason for bad news

Please contact me if you have any questions after you visit the websites I mentioned. In the meantime, I wish you the best of luck with your Numeric Blue panel hunt. — Positive close

Sincerely,

Charles McLauren

Charles McLauren
Manager

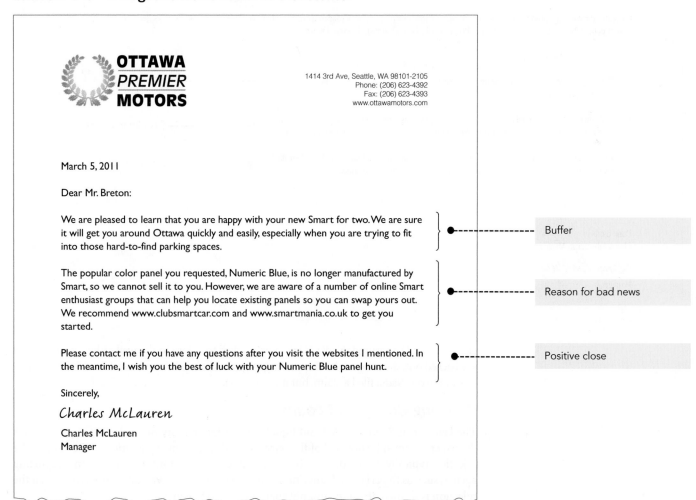

Denying Claims

Claims are demands for something customers feel are due them. When a customer makes a claim, he or she is emotionally involved. It is not always possible to grant the customer's request. It is, however, important to acknowledge the problem without accepting responsibility for it. When dealing with angry clients, avoid blaming them, or getting defensive or upset.

When you break the bad news, it's helpful to use the indirect approach. Doing so helps the customer understand first why you're refusing the request. Begin by restating the customer's claim to show you understand the issue, explain why the claim cannot be accepted, and then clearly state the refusal. If possible, suggest an alternative. End on a positive note to indicate the desire for a continued relationship with the customer. **Exhibit 8-7** is an example of an insurance

Exhibit 8-7 A Denial of a Customer's Claim

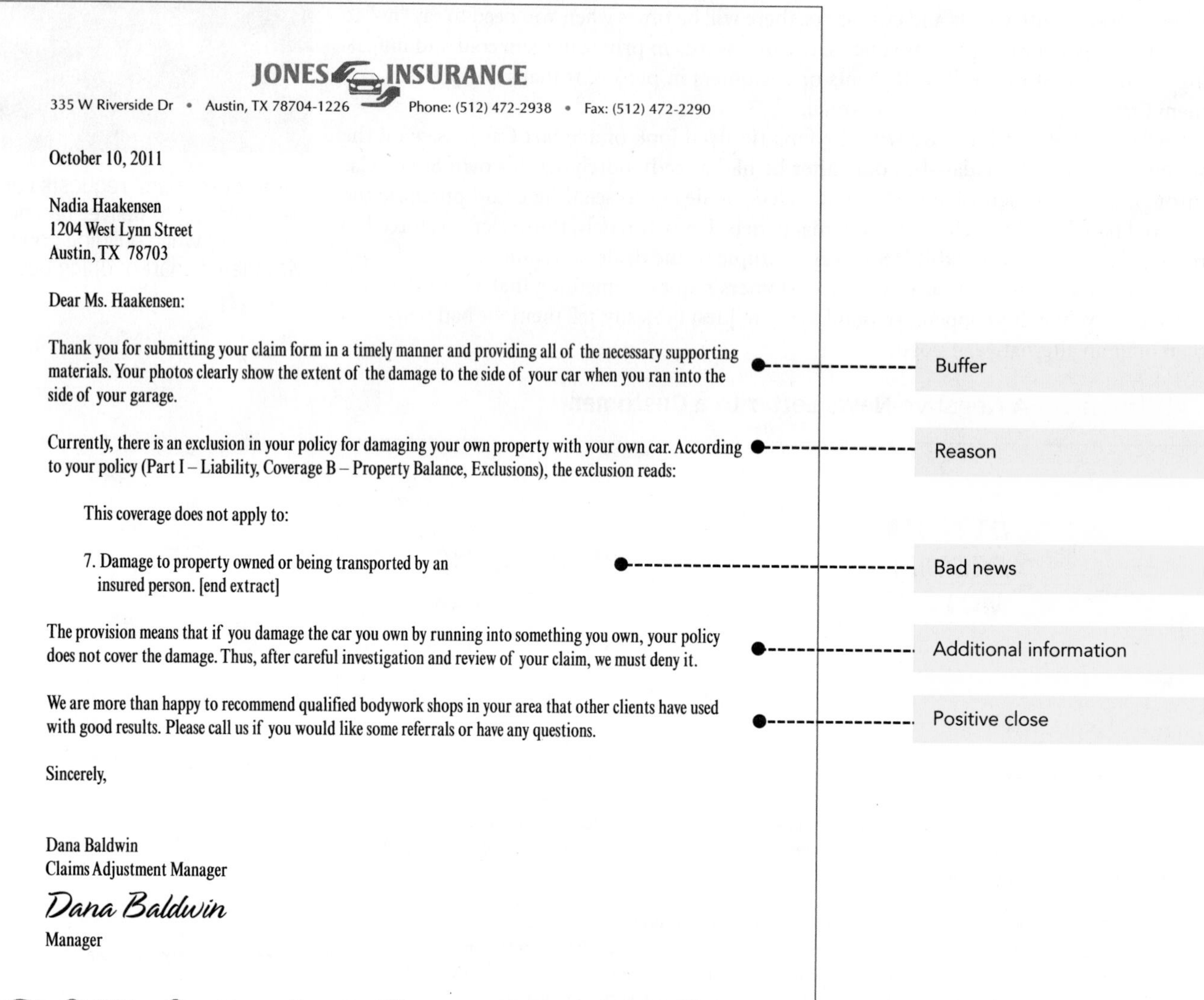

JONES INSURANCE
335 W Riverside Dr • Austin, TX 78704-1226 Phone: (512) 472-2938 • Fax: (512) 472-2290

October 10, 2011

Nadia Haakensen
1204 West Lynn Street
Austin, TX 78703

Dear Ms. Haakensen:

Thank you for submitting your claim form in a timely manner and providing all of the necessary supporting materials. Your photos clearly show the extent of the damage to the side of your car when you ran into the side of your garage.

Currently, there is an exclusion in your policy for damaging your own property with your own car. According to your policy (Part I – Liability, Coverage B – Property Balance, Exclusions), the exclusion reads:

> This coverage does not apply to:
>
> 7. Damage to property owned or being transported by an insured person. [end extract]

The provision means that if you damage the car you own by running into something you own, your policy does not cover the damage. Thus, after careful investigation and review of your claim, we must deny it.

We are more than happy to recommend qualified bodywork shops in your area that other clients have used with good results. Please call us if you would like some referrals or have any questions.

Sincerely,

Dana Baldwin
Claims Adjustment Manager
Dana Baldwin
Manager

claim denial. The insured, Nadia Haakensen, parked too close to the wall of her garage. When she backed out, she scraped the side of the garage, damaging the door panels and fender on one side of the car. Nadia filed a claim, but it was denied.

Refusing Credit and Loans

The Fair Credit Reporting Act and Equal Credit Opportunity Act state that anyone who is denied credit must be notified of the rejection and receive an explanation of the denial. The rejection typically comes directly from the lender, based on information from a reporting agency, such as Experian or TransUnion. However, the lender typically must explain that the rejection is its own decision, and not that of the credit agency.

As with other forms of negative messages, try to suggest a helpful, positive alternative. In the case of denying credit and loan applications, recommend that the customer contact the credit-reporting bureau. Sometimes the credit-reporting bureau has outdated information. To get it corrected, the applicant needs to contact the bureau. **Exhibit 8-8** is an example of a loan rejection letter. The applicant, Mark Hoffner, applied for a loan to buy a new hybrid Insight from a local Honda dealership. The dealer denied the request based on Mark's credit record, which was provided by Experian.

Dealing with an Upset Customer

Frustrated customers are an occasional reality in any line of work. Deal with the problem immediately, personally and politely by contacting the customer, apologizing, and explain-

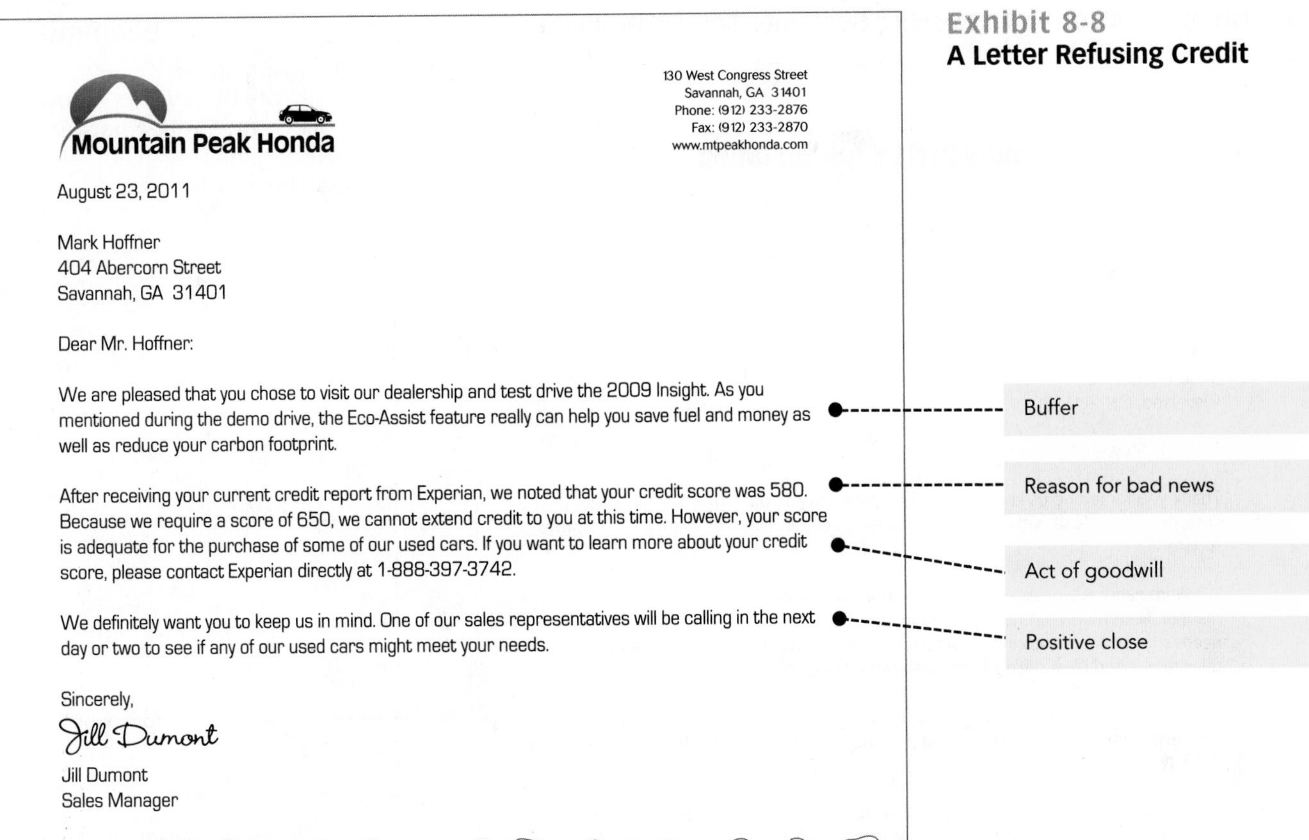

Mountain Peak Honda

130 West Congress Street
Savannah, GA 31401
Phone: (912) 233-2876
Fax: (912) 233-2870
www.mtpeakhonda.com

August 23, 2011

Mark Hoffner
404 Abercorn Street
Savannah, GA 31401

Dear Mr. Hoffner:

We are pleased that you chose to visit our dealership and test drive the 2009 Insight. As you mentioned during the demo drive, the Eco-Assist feature really can help you save fuel and money as well as reduce your carbon footprint.

After receiving your current credit report from Experian, we noted that your credit score was 580. Because we require a score of 650, we cannot extend credit to you at this time. However, your score is adequate for the purchase of some of our used cars. If you want to learn more about your credit score, please contact Experian directly at 1-888-397-3742.

We definitely want you to keep us in mind. One of our sales representatives will be calling in the next day or two to see if any of our used cars might meet your needs.

Sincerely,

Jill Dumont

Jill Dumont
Sales Manager

Exhibit 8-8
A Letter Refusing Credit

ing how the problem will be dealt with or prevented in the future. Offering something in the way of a discount or a gift certificate can also help the situation. If you choose to call the customer, make sure to follow up with a written letter to confirm the phone conversation took place and show that you take the matter seriously.

When Jack Stewart visited an Auto Parts Plus store to buy seat covers, he had difficulty with an over-aggressive salesperson. The salesperson kept following Jack around, pestering him to buy more products. He felt so intimidated that he left the store. He later wrote the store manager and told her what had happened. **Exhibit 8-9** shows the letter the manager immediately wrote back to Mr. Stewart.

Dealing with Problematic Orders

In business, not everything goes exactly as planned. The unexpected happens and delays occur. Sometimes products are no longer available because companies run out of them due to increased demand or difficulties with production equipment or vendors.

Although you might have little control over situations such as these, you nonetheless must deal effectively with your customer's disappointment. When you write a letter to a customer about a problem with an order, acknowledge the problem, apologize to the customer, and provide a solution. Again, it can be beneficial to offer a discount or a temporary solution until the order can be fulfilled.

Exhibit 8-10 is an example of a response to Iman Kasar, a customer who ordered a Mini convertible with all the accessories—sport suspension, traction control, challenge wheel spokes, leather interior, hood stripes, high-definition radio, and an onboard computer. Unfortunately, all the extras caused a delay in shipping.

Negative Messages to Superiors

Superiors, or bosses, are anyone who works at a level in the corporate hierarchy above you. No one likes disappointing the boss, but it happens. Usually, the disappointment revolves around making a mistake, not meeting a deadline, or running over budget. However, most

Exhibit 8-9 A Letter Addressing Customer Service Problems

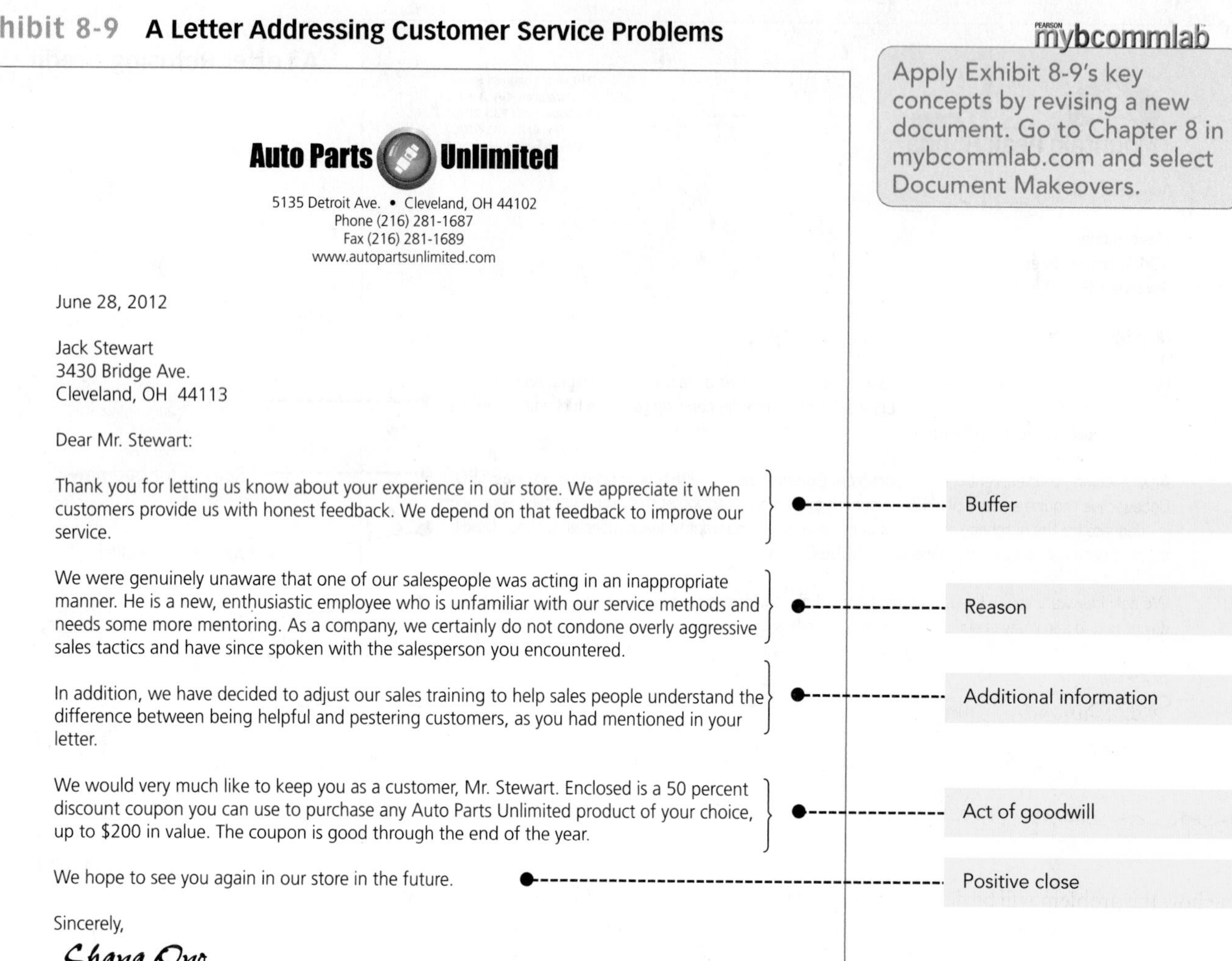
Auto Parts Unlimited
5135 Detroit Ave. • Cleveland, OH 44102
Phone (216) 281-1687
Fax (216) 281-1689
www.autopartsunlimited.com

June 28, 2012

Jack Stewart
3430 Bridge Ave.
Cleveland, OH 44113

Dear Mr. Stewart:

Thank you for letting us know about your experience in our store. We appreciate it when customers provide us with honest feedback. We depend on that feedback to improve our service.

We were genuinely unaware that one of our salespeople was acting in an inappropriate manner. He is a new, enthusiastic employee who is unfamiliar with our service methods and needs some more mentoring. As a company, we certainly do not condone overly aggressive sales tactics and have since spoken with the salesperson you encountered.

In addition, we have decided to adjust our sales training to help sales people understand the difference between being helpful and pestering customers, as you had mentioned in your letter.

We would very much like to keep you as a customer, Mr. Stewart. Enclosed is a 50 percent discount coupon you can use to purchase any Auto Parts Unlimited product of your choice, up to $200 in value. The coupon is good through the end of the year.

We hope to see you again in our store in the future.

Sincerely,

Shana Ono

Shana Ono
Director of Sales and Service

mybcommlab

Apply Exhibit 8-9's key concepts by revising a new document. Go to Chapter 8 in mybcommlab.com and select Document Makeovers.

managers would rather be made aware of an impending problem than be told about it after it's too late to intervene. Regardless of the situation, don't just tell your manager there's a problem: offer a potential solution. It demonstrates that you are solution oriented, which employers like.

When delivering a negative message to a superior, organize it as follows:

Describe the Problem
Describe what is wrong as clearly and unemotionally as possible. Avoid placing blame, which won't solve the problem, and will usually reflect badly on you.

Provide the Details
Briefly provide some background information and then explain how the problem occurred.

Offer Alternatives
Provide one or more suggestions for fixing the problem.

Ask for Action
If you provided multiple suggestions, ask your manager for feedback regarding which suggestion to pursue. If you provided only one suggestion, ask for your manager's approval so you can make the necessary changes and fix the problem.

Exhibit 8-10 A Letter Explaining a Delivery Delay

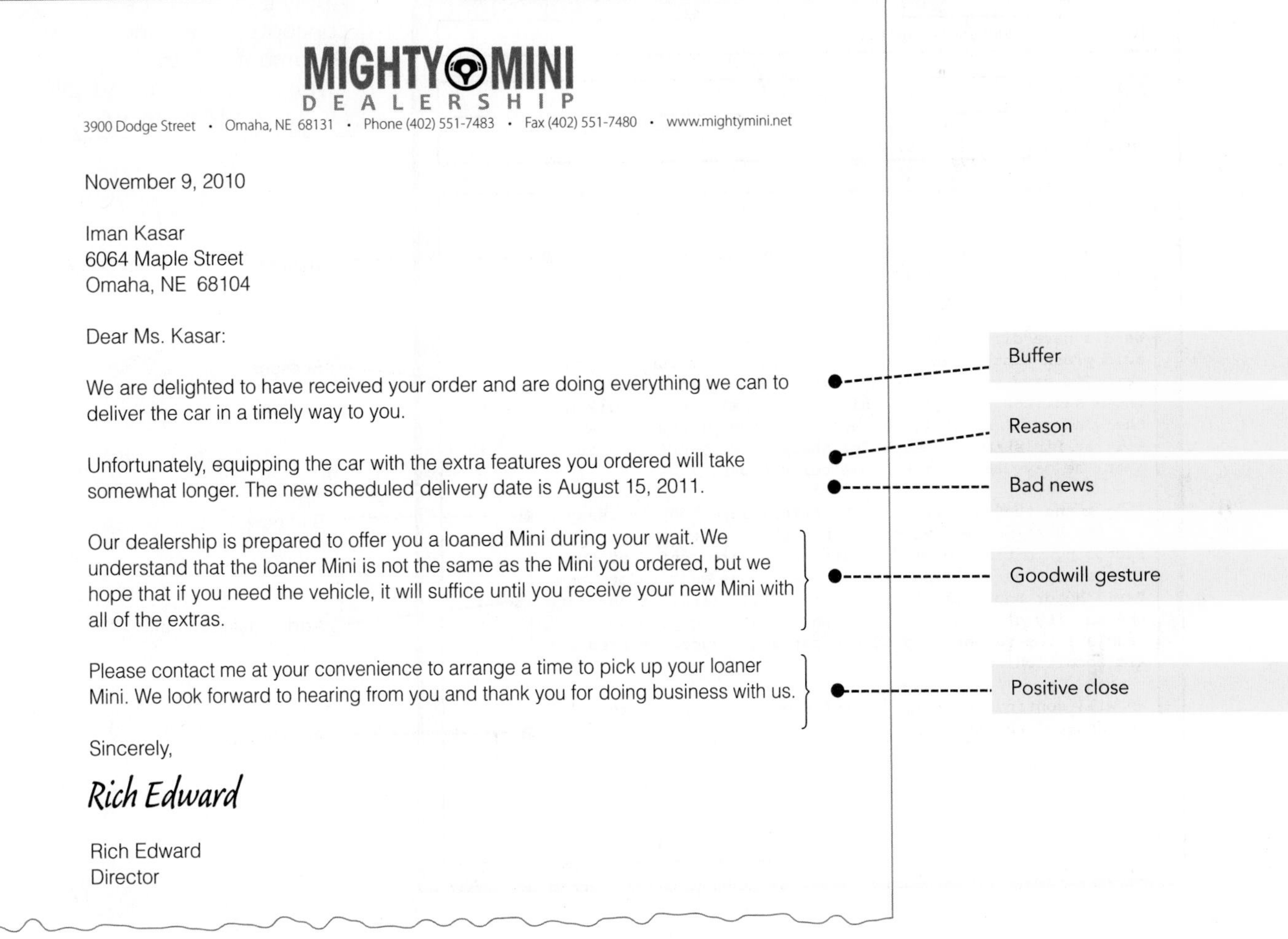
MIGHTY MINI
DEALERSHIP
3900 Dodge Street • Omaha, NE 68131 • Phone (402) 551-7483 • Fax (402) 551-7480 • www.mightymini.net

November 9, 2010

Iman Kasar
6064 Maple Street
Omaha, NE 68104

Dear Ms. Kasar:

We are delighted to have received your order and are doing everything we can to deliver the car in a timely way to you.

Unfortunately, equipping the car with the extra features you ordered will take somewhat longer. The new scheduled delivery date is August 15, 2011.

Our dealership is prepared to offer you a loaned Mini during your wait. We understand that the loaner Mini is not the same as the Mini you ordered, but we hope that if you need the vehicle, it will suffice until you receive your new Mini with all of the extras.

Please contact me at your convenience to arrange a time to pick up your loaner Mini. We look forward to hearing from you and thank you for doing business with us.

Sincerely,

Rich Edward

Rich Edward
Director

The following section looks at some real examples of messages you might send to your superiors.

Delivering Bad News about Project Budgets

Budgets are based on forecasts; and like the weather, forecasts can change. For example, the cost of a project can go up due to the need for additional people, or expensive custom parts, or other assistance.

As an employee, it's your responsibility to keep your manager informed of your progress and let him or her know when a project is running over budget. If possible, outline the potential benefits of any cost overruns as you present them. If you're responsible for a budget overrun, own up to it. Your boss will respect you more than if you try to dodge blame.

Delivering Bad News about Project Timelines

It is not uncommon in the business world for projects to take longer than planned. No one can accurately predict exactly how long a project will take, unless the project is exactly like another that has already been completed. Often, there are new factors that enter the picture that could delay a project. Regardless, managers still want to know when the project will be done, despite the obstacles encountered.

At some point in your career, you're probably going to have to tell your manager that a project is late. If you have neglected to keep your manager informed about how the project has been going, this type of news will be difficult for your manager to accept. After all, your manager has been operating under the misconception that everything is fine because you

Exhibit 8-11 An E-mail Informing a Manager of a Project Delay

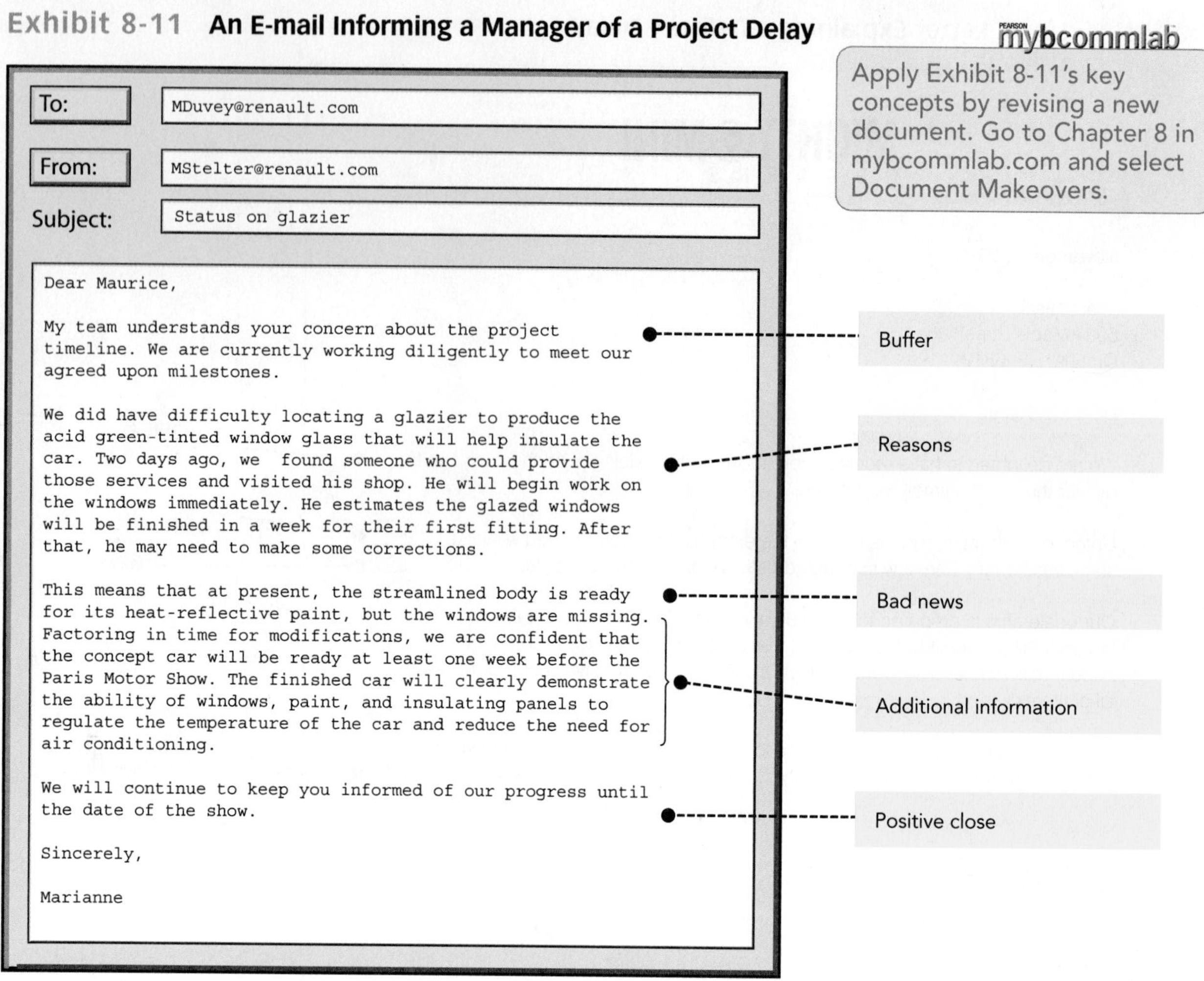
To: MDuvey@renault.com

From: MStelter@renault.com

Subject: Status on glazier

Dear Maurice,

My team understands your concern about the project timeline. We are currently working diligently to meet our agreed upon milestones.

We did have difficulty locating a glazier to produce the acid green-tinted window glass that will help insulate the car. Two days ago, we found someone who could provide those services and visited his shop. He will begin work on the windows immediately. He estimates the glazed windows will be finished in a week for their first fitting. After that, he may need to make some corrections.

This means that at present, the streamlined body is ready for its heat-reflective paint, but the windows are missing. Factoring in time for modifications, we are confident that the concept car will be ready at least one week before the Paris Motor Show. The finished car will clearly demonstrate the ability of windows, paint, and insulating panels to regulate the temperature of the car and reduce the need for air conditioning.

We will continue to keep you informed of our progress until the date of the show.

Sincerely,

Marianne

mybcommlab

Apply Exhibit 8-11's key concepts by revising a new document. Go to Chapter 8 in mybcommlab.com and select Document Makeovers.

have never said anything to the contrary. Don't make the mistake of thinking, "I don't want to let anyone know that I'm having problems." Instead, let your manager know when you encounter serious difficulties so there is time to get assistance. Better yet, offer a potential solution if you can. **Exhibit 8-11** is an example of an e-mail a lead car designer sent her manager regarding a delay in the development of a new zero-emissions concept car. The developer had to explain the reason for the delay, as well as reassure her manager that the car would be ready for the Paris Motor Show.

Negative Messages to Subordinates and Peers

If you become a manager, there will be times when you need to deliver a negative message to a **subordinate,** who is anyone who works a level below you, or to a **peer,** who is anyone who works at the same level as you do. Negative messages to subordinates and peers are a way to warn people and hold them accountable for their actions. The message should be organized in the same way as when you deliver negative news to a superior: describe what's wrong, as clearly and unemotionally as possible, and provide some details.

For review, the organization should look similar to the following. Note that a buffer is included to retain and build goodwill:

Open with a Buffer	Describe the Problem	Provide Details	Offer Solutions	Ask for Action
Start by reaffirming the value and importance of the recipient. Often a negative message is directed at a behavior or event, not the person.	Describe the issue.	Explain what is expected of the recipient.	Provide one or more suggestions for fixing the problem.	End on a positive note by performing a call to action. Clearly state what is expected to come of the message.

Delivering Negative Performance Appraisals

Generally, a manager is required to give performance appraisals to employees at least once a year. Appraisals help employees identify their strengths and weaknesses, perform better, and put themselves in a position for advancement. As a manager, you must accurately assess your employees, tactfully point out what they don't do so well, and offer suggestions for their improvement.

When employees have more weaknesses than strengths, appraising them can be difficult. Make sure to acknowledge their strengths, but be honest about their weaknesses. Provide them with actual examples they can understand and offer guidance. It is possible that with your guidance, employees can make dramatic improvements.

Even if an appraisal is negative, it should be realistic. Don't distort the reality of the situation by using absolutes. The following are examples of absolutes:

- You're never on time.
- You're always defensive.
- You will never get your ideas accepted.

Exhibit 8-12 contains a section of a performance evaluation that addresses an employee's interpersonal skills. The evaluation is very specific, uses examples to describe the employee's behavior, and offers suggestions for the employee's improvement.

Exhibit 8-12
An Excerpt from a Negative Performance Appraisal

Interpersonal Skills
Chris is an excellent problem solver and often comes up with very innovative solutions. However, he needs to improve his method of communicating. Specifically, he needs to learn to be less defensive when his ideas are questioned. Based on my observations, the questions are typically asked for clarification purposes only.

By asking for his team members' feedback and improving his communication skills, Chris will get his ideas accepted more readily and could eventually end up in a position as a team leader. It should be noted that Chris does not mean to intimidate his teammates, as he is very personable in all other situations.

I recommend that Chris attend a series of communication workshops provided by Career Tracks. I will monitor his behavior in meetings and assess his progress in three months. That should give him a chance to begin exercising his new communication skills so as to improve them. Then we will check in again after six months.

Delivering Disciplinary Notices

As a manager, you might be forced to deal with an employee who is particularly disruptive or problematic. It is generally best to deal with the issue immediately and in person. Be explicit about where and when the problem occurred, explain the consequences of the action, and specify how the employee needs to change his or her behavior. When an employee's behavior is particularly harmful, an in-person meeting should be followed up with a written reprimand (memo or letter) for both employee and company records (or files).

Delivering Messages Related to Layoffs and Firings

Messages about layoffs and firings are normally delivered in person. However, they are also often accompanied by written statements, usually letters.

If you must write a termination letter, you will typically have three goals:

1. Explain the reasons for the termination.
2. Avoid statements that expose the company to wrongful termination lawsuits. These are statements that do any of the following:[3]
   - Violate oral and written employment agreements
   - Violate federal and state anti-discrimination laws
   - Constitute a form of sexual harassment
   - Violate labor laws
   - Act as retaliation against an employee for having filed a complaint or claim against the employer
3. Leave the relationship between the terminated employee and firm as favorable as possible.

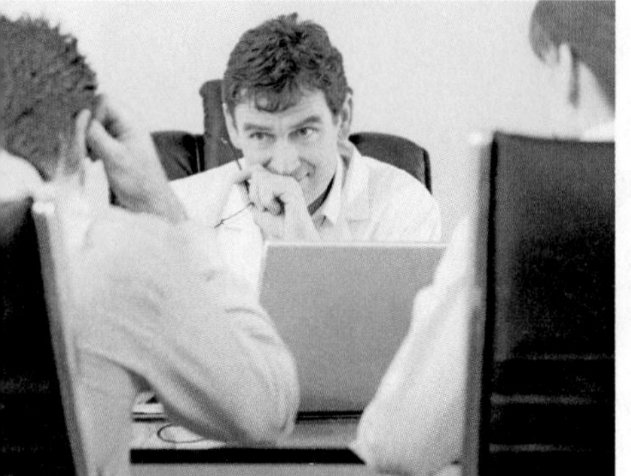

Messages about layoffs are generally delivered in person and then followed up with messages in writing.

Most companies have specific guidelines for handling terminations. However, if you find yourself in a situation in which you need to perform the action without having any written guidelines, keep the following information in mind:

1. ***Check the facts.*** Before you start writing, make sure your reasons are accurate and verifiable. Make sure the employee was told about the problem and knew he or she would be terminated if it were not corrected.
2. ***Avoid vague statements.*** Be specific. Avoid statements that are open to interpretation by the employee.
3. ***Be honest.*** Tell the truth about the termination and help as much as you can to make the employee's transition as smooth as possible.

Exhibit 8-13 is an example of a letter written to the employee Daniel Mercer after he attended a meeting during which he and the rest of the workers at a small auto parts factory were laid off. Notice that Daniel is addressed by name, rather than "Dear Employee," even though the entire workforce is being terminated. This makes the letter more personal.

Saying "No" to Job Applicants

The indirect approach works best for these types of letters. Letters that reject job applicants should be polite but not go into much detail about why the candidate was not the best person for the job. Not only can such information be disheartening to an already disappointed recipient, it can also result in legal problems, such as discrimination lawsuits.

To avoid complications such as these, many companies develop standard rejection letters that meet the criteria we have discussed. The letters thank candidates for applying and inform them that their résumés will remain on file and under consideration should future positions open up. This creates a positive view of the company in the minds of applicants.

If you believe an applicant is well qualified but not a fit for the advertised position, consider suggesting the person apply for other openings within your company or others. Doing so will take the sting out of the rejection and leave the applicant feeling good about your company.

Negative Messages to Peers

When delivering bad news to peers, use the same method you would with superiors and subordinates: share the problem, provide the details, discuss alternatives, and ask for a specific action.

DID YOU KNOW?

Experts still don't agree on the best way to let job candidates know you're rejecting them.

Elaine Dobra, the president of Temporary Associates in Roselle, Ill., sees value in the human aspect of the telephone. "A letter is so cold," she says. On the other hand, Bob Adams, president of Career City, recommends writing a letter. "On the phone, you're more likely to get an argumentative situation," Adams says. "Also, it's embarrassing for the candidate."

Some companies address the issue by using a letter or e-mail for candidates who sent résumés and a phone call for those who were interviewed.

Exhibit 8-13 A Letter of Termination

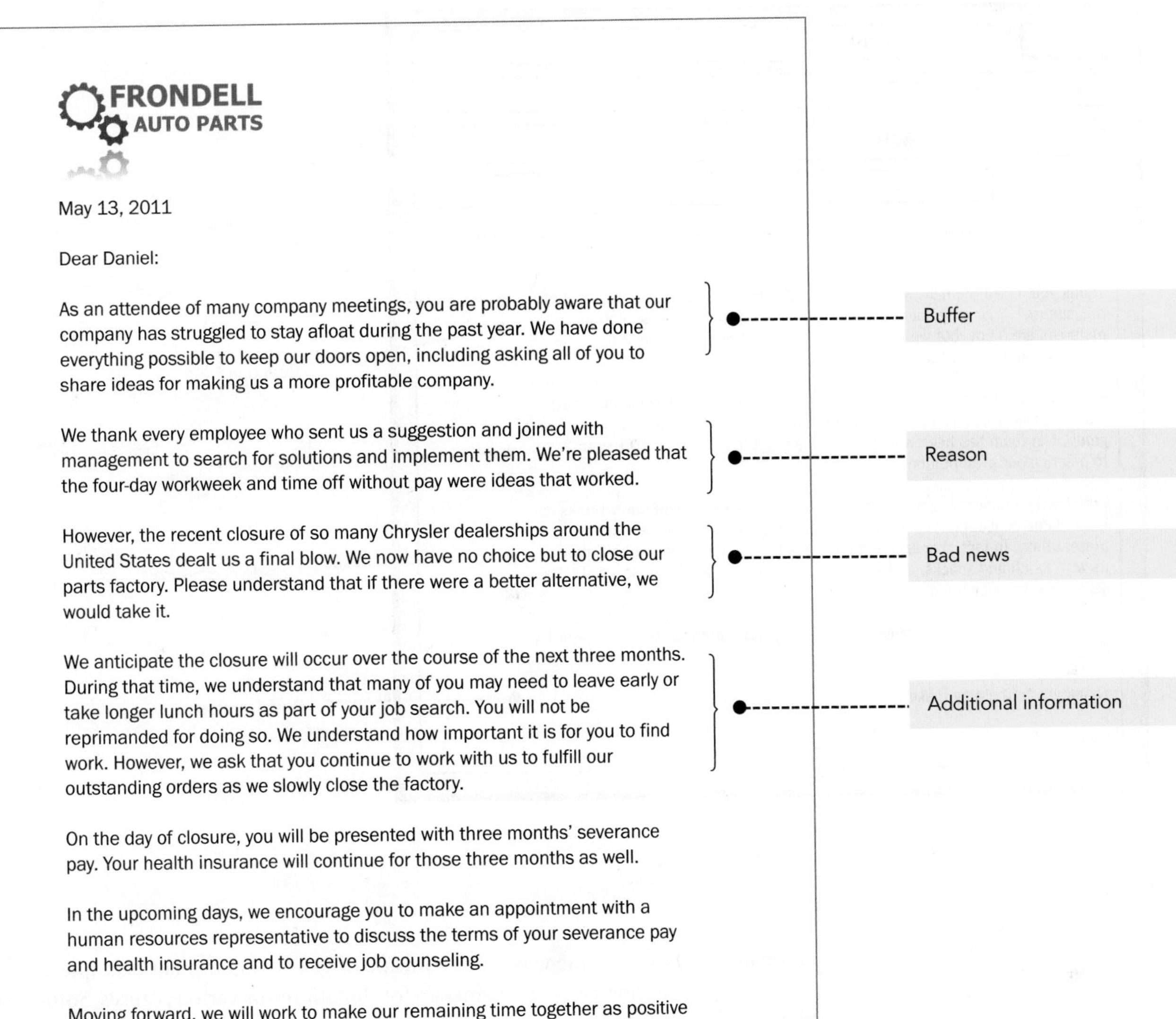

FRONDELL AUTO PARTS

May 13, 2011

Dear Daniel:

As an attendee of many company meetings, you are probably aware that our company has struggled to stay afloat during the past year. We have done everything possible to keep our doors open, including asking all of you to share ideas for making us a more profitable company.

We thank every employee who sent us a suggestion and joined with management to search for solutions and implement them. We're pleased that the four-day workweek and time off without pay were ideas that worked.

However, the recent closure of so many Chrysler dealerships around the United States dealt us a final blow. We now have no choice but to close our parts factory. Please understand that if there were a better alternative, we would take it.

We anticipate the closure will occur over the course of the next three months. During that time, we understand that many of you may need to leave early or take longer lunch hours as part of your job search. You will not be reprimanded for doing so. We understand how important it is for you to find work. However, we ask that you continue to work with us to fulfill our outstanding orders as we slowly close the factory.

On the day of closure, you will be presented with three months' severance pay. Your health insurance will continue for those three months as well.

In the upcoming days, we encourage you to make an appointment with a human resources representative to discuss the terms of your severance pay and health insurance and to receive job counseling.

Moving forward, we will work to make our remaining time together as positive and effective as possible.

Sincerely,

Charles Frondell

Charles Frondell
CEO

Make every effort not to alienate your peers when you write to them. A good way to avoid alienating them is to think about what you would say if you were talking to them in person, and then write it down. Be friendly, get to the point, and ask for what you need. If you are on good terms with your coworkers, you might even try a bit of humor. Most importantly, deliver the news in a way you would like to receive it. If you follow this advice, your message will be better received. **Exhibit 8-14** is an example of an e-mail written by an employee, informing his teammates they will have to come into work on Saturday.

Turning Down External Parties and Internal Employees

When you work for a company, you will be surprised at the number of favor-types of requests that routinely come across your desk or your e-mail inbox including those from

Exhibit 8-14 A Negative Message to Peers

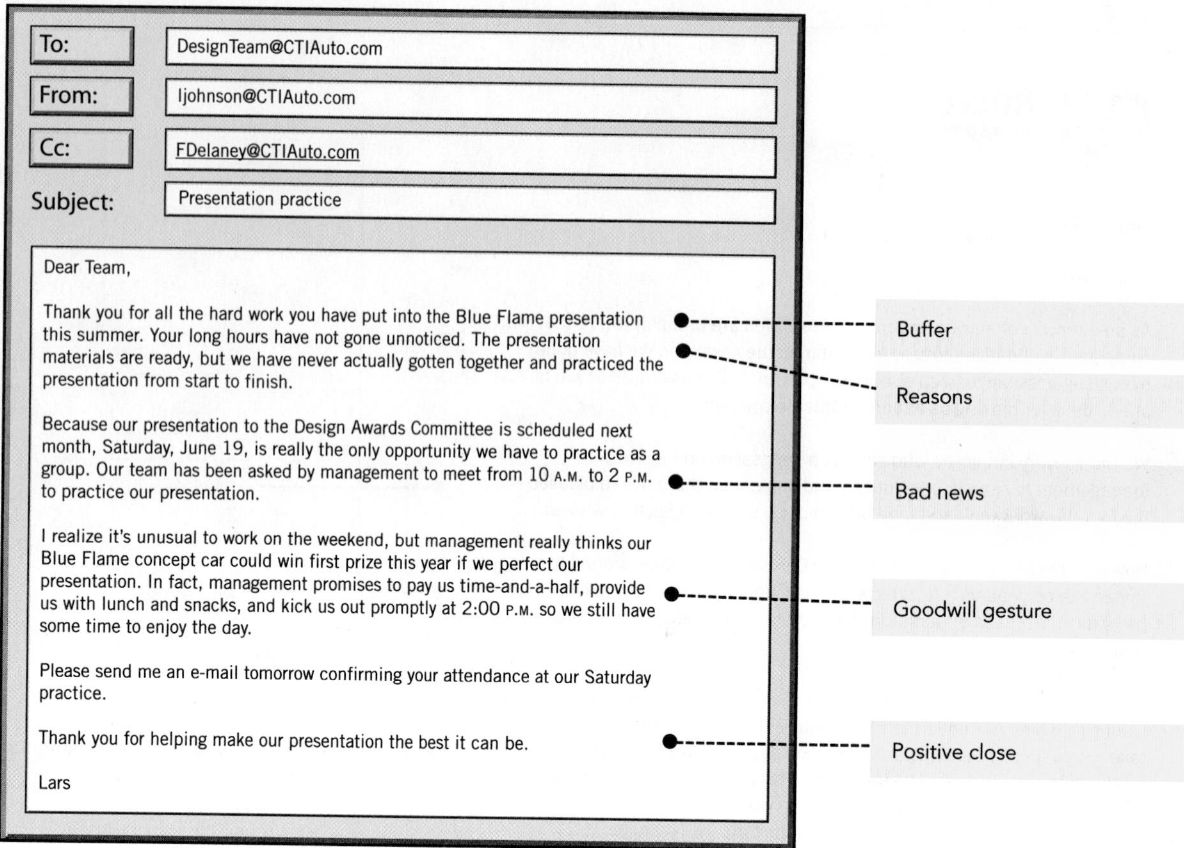

To: DesignTeam@CTIAuto.com

From: ljohnson@CTIAuto.com

Cc: FDelaney@CTIAuto.com

Subject: Presentation practice

Dear Team,

Thank you for all the hard work you have put into the Blue Flame presentation this summer. Your long hours have not gone unnoticed. The presentation materials are ready, but we have never actually gotten together and practiced the presentation from start to finish.

Because our presentation to the Design Awards Committee is scheduled next month, Saturday, June 19, is really the only opportunity we have to practice as a group. Our team has been asked by management to meet from 10 A.M. to 2 P.M. to practice our presentation.

I realize it's unusual to work on the weekend, but management really thinks our Blue Flame concept car could win first prize this year if we perfect our presentation. In fact, management promises to pay us time-and-a-half, provide us with lunch and snacks, and kick us out promptly at 2:00 P.M. so we still have some time to enjoy the day.

Please send me an e-mail tomorrow confirming your attendance at our Saturday practice.

Thank you for helping make our presentation the best it can be.

Lars

external parties, or anyone who works outside of your company. For example, many community organizations ask local businesses for donations for various causes. Sometimes employees ask their firms to support the causes they are involved with. Not all of these requests can be granted.

It's vital that you learn to process the requests quickly, deciding which requests you can accommodate and which you can't. You can't say yes to everything. There isn't enough time and money in the world to do so. Know your company's policies, learn to set limits, and get comfortable saying no. Your biggest challenge will be to give a clear negative response to requests without generating negative feelings.

When you deliver a negative response to a routine request, organize it like this:

Say Something Positive

Always thank individuals for asking and acknowledging their reasons for doing so.

Answer Clearly but Gently

Don't make requesters guess whether you are saying "yes" or "no." Do supplement any refusal with phrasing that builds goodwill.

Explain Why You Said "No"

Different situations determine whether you should be specific about why you declined the request and when you should be more vague. For examples and reasons to use each, read "Declining Invitations" later in the chapter.

Close

If you want to leave a matter open for future consideration, you can do so in the close. If the matter is closed, do not imply that it's open for negotiation.

Rejecting Requests for Favors, Money, or Information

People have a right to ask you for something; it's part of the relationship-building process firms and individuals engage in when they do business with one another. However, you also have the right to say "no." When verbally declining a request, do so in a confident and friendly tone. Compliment the person for asking, even though you cannot grant the request. Remember, your goal is to maintain a positive relationship with the requester.

Exhibit 8-15 is a manager's response to a heartfelt request for financial assistance from Jared Spencer, a car designer in Indiana. Jared would like his manager to pay for his airfare and lodging so he can attend this year's Detroit Autorama and meet the winner of the prestigious Ridler Award. Each year, the Ridler Award is given to "the most creatively designed vehicle" at the Detroit Autorama, sponsored by the Michigan Hot Rod Association. Jared wants to check out the cars, get some new ideas, and shake hands with the Ridler Award winner. Although Jared's manager refuses his request, his refusal e-mail shows empathy for Jared's situation and offers a possible alternative.

Declining Invitations

Businesspeople often receive invitations to professional and civic events, not all of which they can or want to attend. When you are personally invited to an event and choose to decline, always start by thanking the person who invited you. If you have no interest in attending the event, it is best to simply apologize for not being able to attend without offering specific reasons why. If you genuinely want to go but cannot because of current obligations, let the requester know you are interested in similar events in the future. Then close your communication on a positive note.

Exhibit 8-16 shows two messages written in response to an invitation to attend an annual charitable event. The example on the left politely indicates that the receiver of the invitation has no interest in attending the function but is willing to donate money. The example on the right leaves the door open to future invitations. If the individual had no interest in attending or contributing, he or she might have ended the note with the simple goodwill statement such as, "I hope the event is a success."

Always review what you have written and revise it if necessary before sending it out. The last thing you want to do is send a negative message to the wrong person with the wrong

CHECKLIST

Items to check before sending a negative message:

- ☑ The name of the recipient is correct.
- ☑ The organization of the message prepares the reader for the news.
- ☑ The approach is appropriate for the situation.
- ☑ The facts are correct and the reason for the news is clearly stated.
- ☑ The tone of the message reduces bad feelings and conveys fairness.
- ☑ The language of the message does not create legal liability or responsibility for your organization.
- ☑ The closing clearly indicates whether further correspondence is necessary.

Exhibit 8-15 An E-mail Refusing a Request for Money

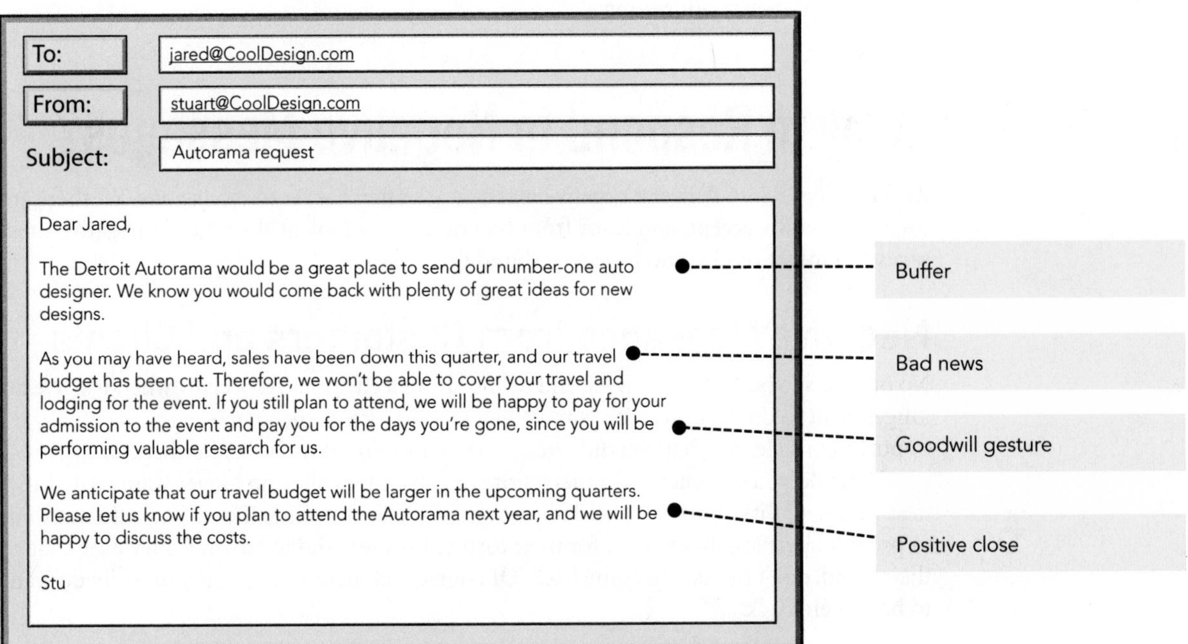

To: jared@CoolDesign.com

From: stuart@CoolDesign.com

Subject: Autorama request

Dear Jared,

The Detroit Autorama would be a great place to send our number-one auto designer. We know you would come back with plenty of great ideas for new designs.

As you may have heard, sales have been down this quarter, and our travel budget has been cut. Therefore, we won't be able to cover your travel and lodging for the event. If you still plan to attend, we will be happy to pay for your admission to the event and pay you for the days you're gone, since you will be performing valuable research for us.

We anticipate that our travel budget will be larger in the upcoming quarters. Please let us know if you plan to attend the Autorama next year, and we will be happy to discuss the costs.

Stu

Exhibit 8-16 Letters Declining an Invitation

No Interest Attending Now or in the Future	Interest in Attending in the Future
Dear Maggie, Thank you for inviting me to your firm's annual Toys for Tots fundraiser. I'm sorry I won't be able to attend the fundraiser. However, I have enclosed a small donation to support your cause. Sincerely, Jennifer Martinez	Dear Maggie, Thank you for inviting me to your firm's annual Toys for Tots fundraiser. I would love to attend the fundraiser, but I will be out-of-state visiting my parents for the holidays. I have enclosed a small donation to support your cause and would like to remain on your invitation list for next year's event. Sincerely, Jennifer Martinez

facts, the wrong tone, and wrong spelling and punctuation. Check the following before sending it out:

- That the name of the recipient is correct
- That the organization of the message prepares the reader for the news
- That the approach is appropriate for the situation
- That the facts are correct and the reason for the news is clearly stated
- That the tone of the message reduces bad feelings and conveys fairness
- That the language of the message does not create legal liability or responsibility for your organization
- That the closing clearly indicates whether further correspondence is necessary

Finally, put yourself in the shoes of the recipient as you read the message out loud. Does the message convey what it needs to convey? Is it written in a way that you would want to receive it? If the answers are "yes" to both questions, send the message. If you follow these guidelines, you will make a potentially painful experience more positive, both for you and for the people you're addressing.

4 What Is the Best Way to Respond to Negative Messages?

As difficult as it is to deliver a negative message, it's often harder to receive one. Yet there are ways to listen to, accept, and learn from bad news. Let's look at the types of negative messages you might receive and have to respond to.

Negative Messages from Customers and Clients

No one likes to be on the receiving end of "no" from a customer, especially when it's "We no longer want to do business with you." When you do receive such a message, it's actually an opportunity to learn what you did wrong so you can do things better in the future.

What do you say when customers write or call and say they no longer want to do business with you? First, find out why. This means asking for specifics. If customers do not want to provide specifics, thank them for their former business and tell them if they ever change their mind, don't hesitate to come back. Of course, tell them this only if you really do want to have them back.

REAL INSIGHTS from a Seasoned Professional

Name: *Gary Siedenburg*
Title: *Auto Claims Supervisor*
Organization: *Farmer's Insurance*
Location: *Fort Collins, Colorado*

WHAT IS THE FIRST THING you think when you hear the words "auto insurance claims adjuster"? Cars? Money? Accidents? The first thing Gary Siedenburg thinks about is listening, compassion, and understanding. After being an auto claims adjuster for 19 years, Siedenburg should know.

Siedenburg has always loved cars. While growing up, he spent time in his cousin's body shop working on his own Camaro, Duster, and El Camino. Once in college, he changed his major several times. He ultimately graduated with a degree in business, with an emphasis in marketing. Next came Siedenburg's post-college job search.

After his cousin closed his body shop and became a claims adjuster, Siedenburg decided that insurance appealed to him as well. He subsequently talked to his family's insurance agent and applied at Farmer's Insurance. No position was available, but he kept on calling and applying. Eventually an auto claims adjuster position opened up, and he got the job. Now, at age 47, he is an auto claims supervisor for Farmer's Insurance for the Mountain West region of the United States.

What does an auto claims adjuster do? When a car is damaged, an adjuster is assigned to the case. First, he or she contacts the owner to verify the information and explain the claims process. Next, the adjuster inspects the car, determines whether or not it is repairable, and re-contacts the owner with an estimate of damages and coverage.

The process of adjusting auto claims is usually straightforward, says Siedenburg. However, the interaction with owners often isn't. Sometimes Siedenburg delivers bad news to people who are upset, angry, or confused. How does he do this? Over the years, he's learned to really listen to people and allow them to vent their feelings. He makes sure he understands their concerns. Then he reviews the task at hand and explains what he can do for them. "I don't take it personally when people yell or cry—they're upset with the situation, not me," he explains.

Siedenburg is respectful and compassionate with all of his customers. He doesn't immediately begin talking numbers. Instead, he asks himself, "What would I say if this were my mother or a member of my family?" He has also learned the important skill of "reading" people. When he's talking to people face-to-face, he observes their facial and body language to determine how they are responding. If he's on the phone, he listens to their voices to gauge their reactions. If they say nothing, that tells him something as well. He always tries to deliver his news on the phone or in person and then follow up with a letter because e-mail and texting is simply too terse and impersonal.

Siedenburg says that even though he sometimes delivers bad news to people, as long as he keeps people informed and educated throughout the process, they are more accepting of the outcome. This type of communication typically involves three steps that keep expectations realistic and reduce objections:

1. Review any prior conversations. For example, "Remember when we discussed how the extra mileage on your car might reduce its value?"
2. Present the facts in a personal, but matter-of-fact way. For example, "Your car currently has 250,000 miles on it and has several electro-mechanical issues. However, your car does have a well taken-care-of interior, which I have made note of."
3. Discuss the end results and what you can do for the other person. For example, "Taking into consideration these issues, the value of your car is $3,000. I can get you an insurance company–issued check in as little as three days. Will that be all right?"

When Siedenburg isn't talking to people, he's writing to them. In fact, writing makes up 50 percent of his job, whether it's writing memos, reports, or letters. He admits that he wishes he had spent more time in college focusing on his writing skills but acknowledges that his writing skills have improved substantially over the years. He's learned to keep his materials friendly, yet professional, get to the point quickly, and avoid jargon. According to Siedenburg, communication is key especially when dealing with bad news. He says a good auto claims adjuster is simply someone who likes helping others, interacting with people on a personal level, and assessing and solving problems.

Questions

1. What does Siedenburg ask himself before he delivers bad news to someone? How does this help?
2. How does Siedenburg use the ability to "read" people to help him deliver bad news?
3. What does Siedenburg do to avoid objections when delivering bad news?
4. What are some methods Siedenburg uses to make sure his written messages are understood?

Source: Gary Siedenburg in discussion with the author, May 2010.

Exhibit 8-17
A Letter Responding to a Client's Negative Message

Pacific Insurance
3000 Wilshire Boulevard
Los Angeles, CA 90010
phone (213) 738-6937
fax (213) 738-6944
www.pacificinsur.com

January 7, 2012

Alex Montgomery
2051 Park Circle
Fort Worth, TX 76137

Dear Mr. Montgomery:

Thank you for your phone call. I was disappointed to learn that you want to switch to a different auto insurance agency. However, I do understand your need to reduce your expenses and your concern about the recent rate increase.

Ultimately, your satisfaction is very important to me. I would be more than happy to work with you to see if we can find another policy with our company that meets your needs. If you have not yet made up your mind to go with another agency, and you would like to hear what else we may be able to offer you, please give me a call.

Otherwise, I wish you success and hope that we can again do business with each other in the future.

Kind regards,

Sonja Bell

Sonja Bell
Agent

When clients are comfortable giving you specifics about why the contract was terminated, listen carefully and do not interrupt. You might have to ask for clarification from time to time, but let the customer do most of the talking. When the customer finishes, attempt to sum up what has been said to show that you listened and understood the concerns.

Acknowledge your part in their decision and apologize if you made a mistake. Then ask if there is anything you can do to keep the business (if that is important to you). If your customers agree to give you another chance, thank them and tell them that your goal is to meet their expectations. Ask them to be honest with you and keep you informed of how you're doing as you move forward.

If customers do not want to give you another chance, thank them for being valued customers and say goodbye. At this point it's wise to send a letter acknowledging the termination. **Exhibit 8-17** is a letter from an auto insurance agent responding to a client who wants to switch agents.

Negative Messages from Superiors

At one time or another, every employee experiences bad news from the boss. Perhaps you submitted a project proposal and it was rejected. What can you do in this case? Ask specific questions to find out what's wrong with the idea. By doing so, you can revise and resubmit the proposal if possible. The following is an example of responding to a proposal rejection.

> Thank you for reviewing my proposal. I'm sorry the proposal didn't meet with your expectations. However, I'm very interested in revising it so that it works for you. I would like to identify the proposal's shortcomings so I can figure out how to improve it.
>
> Are you open to meeting next week to discuss it further?

Or, perhaps you have been given a negative performance appraisal. If you have received a negative performance appraisal listen carefully to the message your manager is trying to get across before responding. When you respond, restate your manager's message to be clear you haven't misunderstood it. Then ask your manager what you can do to improve your performance in the future.

What if you are laid off? Most people experience a sense of disbelief, followed almost immediately by a sense of panic—"Oh no. What am I going to do? How am I going to make money? How am I going to pay the bills?" The person doing the laying off is probably just as uncomfortable with the situation.

If the situation allows for it, consider asking the following questions:

- Why am I being laid off?
- Is there anything I can do to stay?
- What are the procedures regarding severance pay?
- What are the rehiring practices?
- How do I claim the benefits I am due?
- How do I go about getting a letter of reference?

Layoffs are hard on survivors as well as the victims. Layoff survivors in the workplace often do the work of several people and operate under a cloud of fear that they will be next. They often feel guilty that they are still employed.

Getting fired is even harder because you are being told that you are not performing well enough to stay with the company. In general, composure during a firing is the key to getting through the event. Arguing won't save your job because the decision has already been made. If it will make you feel better, you can ask, "Why am I being fired?" However, if no answer is forthcoming, don't try to force any explanations. Do, however, try to learn from any mistakes you may have made so you don't repeat them in your next job.

Negative Messages from Peers

When someone gets upset with your actions, you have no control over the other person's feelings. All you can control is your own response and your own behavior.

It's important to listen to the person—really listen. Don't anticipate what you're going to say next or interrupt the person to defend yourself. Think of it as an opportunity to learn more about yourself and how others perceive you. It's also a chance to evaluate your behavior and change it so you're more effective. Once you're clear on the problem, ask the person what he or she would like you to do differently in the future. Work together with the other person to come up with a solution.

Consider Maria and Rosario, two coworkers who co-presented an idea to their managers. Maria was upset because she felt Rosario interrupted her. She was concerned that the people who attended the presentation would think of Rosario as the leader and her as the follower. Maria scheduled a short meeting with Rosario the next day. She told him how she felt. Rosario listened to Maria's concerns and answered her this way:

> "I had no idea you felt that way. You were so quiet in the meeting I thought you were feeling overwhelmed, so I decided to take over. I can see why you're upset. I bet people did think I was dominating the presentation. I'm really sorry.
>
> "Hey, how about we have a follow-up meeting and you can help me get better at not interrupting. If I start interrupting, just remind me by saying, 'Please let me finish.' If you do it enough, I just might get the message and won't bother other people as much either."

Disagreements are often caused by simple misunderstandings. If you find yourself in such a situation, talk to the other person as soon as possible before your resentment grows.

Negative Messages from Subordinates

Managers often find themselves in situations where team members do not agree with their decisions or opinions. For example, if, as a manager, you deliver a performance appraisal that is less than stellar, the employee receiving it will probably not agree with everything you

REAL INSIGHTS from a New Professional

Name: *Lauren Berger*
Title: *Business Development Manager*
Organization: *Superior Lexus North*
Location: *Kansas City, Missouri*

A SOLID FOUNDATION of writing skills and marketing insight has opened a galaxy of opportunities for Kansas City, Missouri, professional Lauren Berger. Just a handful of years removed from her undergraduate days at Illinois Wesleyan University, Berger has worked as an editor at women's e-zine *Girls Guide to the Galaxy;* hotel management staffer; freelance writer; social media strategist; conference planning manager; creative director; copywriter; and most recently, business development manager for a luxury auto dealership.

"I've met so many phenomenal people throughout the course of my career," Berger said. "That's one of the great things about business communication and marketing, particularly from the standpoint of a freelancer. I got to set up a Twitter account for a Missouri state senator. I got to do copywriting and writing for an alderman. On the other end of the spectrum, I got to meet a Grammy-winning DJ. The sky's the limit as far as the people you can meet and the experiences you can have."

An English literature and history grad, Berger is a go-getter with a craving for adventure and a passion for social media. She's a voracious reader, a lover of music, and a foodie. At age 19, she started STL Scene, Inc., a St. Louis arts and entertainment e-zine, and later founded V3 Creative, a marketing and communication firm. Romance led her west across I-70 to Kansas City, where she landed her current gig with Superior Lexus North. "I had absolutely no experience with the automotive industry, but marketing communications and customer service, I find, are transcendent of industries," Berger said. "The same principles apply when dealing with customers across the board."

One of Berger's preferred methods of customer interaction is through blogging and other social networking tools. STL Scene was somewhat of a pioneer in interactive online content, with quizzes, surveys, message boards, and chats attracting readers. At Superior Lexus, she hopes to take the dealership's Web presence in some powerful new directions. "You're taking advertising power, marketing power from the companies and handing it over to consumers," she said. "Instead of having one-way communication, you now have a dialogue. For instance, H&R Block now has a Facebook profile. It's a great example of how a company is doing social media right. People are interacting, they're excited about the brand, they're directing where the conversation is going. I see advertising power and marketing power being given to the consumer."

Berger's Lexus duties include overseeing Internet sales, tracking data metrics, maintaining customer accounts, handling the dealerships' Twitter and Facebook accounts, and fostering customer relationships. As a point person for customer service, Berger is involved first-hand in helping establish goodwill during both good and bad times. The luxury car buying experience is overwhelmingly a positive one, she stressed, but when customer concerns do come up, Berger said the company takes a direct approach with the customer. "We face situations head-on," Berger said. "What I like to do when dealing with dissatisfied customers is follow the formula of 'Apologize, emphasize, strategize.' We tell them, "I'm so sorry about this situation. I can understand how you feel. This is what we're going to do to address the situation."

No matter the industry, strong writing will help you succeed. Berger stresses mastering the basics of spelling and grammar; writing something every day to keep your ideas, vocabulary, and word recall fresh; and writing about what you love. "First and foremost," Berger said, "you're not going to be an effective writer unless you are enthusiastic and passionate about your content."

Questions

1. What three actions does Berger take when communicating negative news?
2. How does using a direct approach when dealing with customer concerns help to build goodwill?

Source: Lauren Berger in discussion with the author, August 2010.

say. In most companies, employees are allowed to dispute negative aspects of a performance appraisal by submitting their comments in writing. These comments go into their permanent records. Don't be alarmed if some of the comments do not reflect well on you—the employee is upset. Simply read the comments and decide if any of them require further discussion. As a manager, you often learn as much about yourself from performance appraisals as your employees do about themselves.

Managers also experience bad news when employees tell them they plan to apply for other positions. If you find yourself in such a scenario, don't assume the person is unhappy with you as a boss. Instead, ask the employee to share any reasons for applying for another position. Usually, employees are expected to be in their positions for two years. After that, you have the responsibility to promote their professional development, whether it means growing within the company, leaving the company, or gaining additional schooling or training.

If the employee who is resigning is a key part of your team and you would like the person to remain on the job, you can certainly ask why he or she is leaving on the off chance you can do something to persuade the person to stay. If you are unsuccessful, wish the employees the best of luck in their new endeavors and carry out following steps.

1. ***Time frame:*** Determine the person's time frame for changing positions.
2. ***Projects:*** Identify the projects the person is working on and the status of those projects.
3. ***Letter:*** Offer to write the person a letter of recommendation if you feel it is warranted.
4. ***Team communication:*** Let the person's team members know so they can adjust their project schedules and workloads to accommodate the person's absence.
5. ***Documentation:*** Make sure the person documents the work that he or she has been doing and passes on any important information to the rest of the team.
6. ***Training:*** If possible, pair up the individual who is leaving with another member of the team to train that team member to carry on the work.
7. ***Replacement search:*** If the budget permits it, make plans to search for a replacement employee. This typically involves writing a job description, asking for referrals from other team members, posting the description on job sites, and scheduling time to review résumés and conduct interviews.
8. ***Celebrate:*** It is often a good idea to plan a going away party just to acknowledge the individual's contribution and allow his or her teammates to say goodbye.

Summary *Synthesize What You Have Learned*

1. What is a negative message, and why is it important to plan one?

A negative message is any type of message that's considered bad news because it's not what the recipient wants to hear or see. This type of message might include a negative performance appraisal, a refusal of credit, a refusal of a request, or some type of criticism. Planning the message is important because people have a tendency to reject messages that deliver bad news. The tone, delivery method, and timing will affect how well the message is received.

2. How do you organize negative messages?

It is best to use the indirect approach to organize the message, which involves gradually revealing the bad news to the reader by using this method: buffer, reasons, bad news, and closing. This approach is best for news that is likely to shock or severely distress the reader.

3. What are the different types of negative messages?

Negative messages can be received and sent by customers, superiors, subordinates, peers, and external parties. Messages that deny customers' credit, inform a superior of a project delay, and inform employees about layoffs and terminations are among the many different types of negative messages.

4. What is the best way to respond to negative messages?

As a businessperson you will receive a variety of negative messages during your career. The messages might be from customers who are unhappy and terminating their contracts with you. Or, the messages might come from your superior, peers, or subordinates. When it comes to receiving negative messages, listen to the information, and don't get defensive or upset. Think of it as an opportunity to learn more about yourself and how others perceive you. It's also a chance to evaluate your behavior and change it so you're more effective. Try to clarify what exactly the person who delivered the news is trying to communicate. Once you're clear on the problem, ask the person what he or she would like you to do differently, if anything, in the future. Work together with the other person to come up with a solution and new plan for the future.

Know It *Reflect, Respond, and Express*

Build Your Critical Thinking Skills

Critical Thinking Questions

1. What are your responsibilities when you refuse a customer's claim against your organization?
2. What approach can you use when you receive a negative performance review? How can a negative performance review benefit your career?

Critical Thinking Scenario

Dmitri, an automobile loan processor with Toyota, helps people with their dreams every day. His favorite part of his job is being able to say "yes" to customers when their loans have been approved and they are able to buy vehicles. Unfortunately, Dmitri must also say "no" occasionally when loans are not approved. This happens to be one of those moments. Dmitri must deliver the bad news to a young couple. The couple did not have great credit or much of a down payment, but Dmitri hoped to help them. However, try as he might, he could not get the bank to approve the loan. Now, the young couple is sitting outside of his office.

Questions

1. What are the four steps Dmitri should remember when delivering bad news in person?
2. What responses should Dmitri prepare for? List at least three, as well as Dmitri's possible messages for each.
3. Name and explain four aspects Dmitri should keep in mind when preparing the tone of his message. Why are the four you chose important for this situation?

What about You?

4. Describe a time when you had to deliver bad news in person. How did you prepare to deliver it?
5. Looking back, how did it go? What could you have done, if anything, to improve the outcome?
6. Did the recipient's responses surprise you? Were you able to address the person's concerns?

Write It *Draft, Revise, and Finalize*

Create Your Own Success Story

1. Think back over the situations in the previous exercise. Now imagine you're delivering the news in print. Write the messages for each scenario on a separate sheet of paper.
2. Rewrite the following apology to accentuate the positive: "Your position has been terminated due to budget cuts. See Human Resources for information about worker displacement services."

3. Create effective e-mail subject lines for the following examples of negative messages:
   a. A negative performance review
   b. Your credit application has been denied
   c. The company is outsourcing the workforce
4. Using the direct approach to structuring a negative message, compose a brief paragraph explaining why a credit application has been denied because of a low credit score and not enough history on the credit report.
5. Using the indirect approach to structuring a negative message, compose a brief paragraph explaining a line of credit denial because of a low credit score and not enough history on the credit report.
6. What strategies should you use when delivering a negative performance review or a disciplinary notice to an employee? Compose a summary of methods to use to effectively convey the negative message.
7. Write a brief memo terminating a contract with a company you have worked with for over five years. As a chief financial officer, you discovered a more cost-effective company, so give specific details about when and why the contract has been terminated. Remember to thank the company for their service.
8. Use the same scenario from the previous question and write a response to the contract termination. How can you still offer your service? Remember to be courteous.

Speak It *Discuss, Listen, and Understand*

Build Your Leadership and Teamwork Skills

1. Pair up with another student to play the role of the deliverer of bad news and then the receiver of the same news. Ask a third student to observe the situation.
   - Walk through the scenario, switch roles, and then do it again. If you are the observer, pay attention to people's voices, body language, and facial expressions. At the end of the role play, give feedback to the deliverer and receiver. What did they do well, and what could they improve?

   Repeat the same process for the remaining scenarios.

   a. You are responding to a customer who is disappointed with the performance of an auto part he bought from your company. He wants a refund. You believe the customer damaged the part through misuse. You would be willing to provide a replacement part, but not a refund.
   b. You have to deliver a poor annual evaluation to a new employee. The individual is not achieving the goals you set. You are willing to cut the employee some slack, but you're concerned that the behavior problems are impacting the whole team and preventing projects from being completed.
   c. You are upset with the way a coworker spoke to you in a team meeting. You decide to explain why you thought the behavior was inappropriate, what the coworker should have done instead, and what you want the person to do in the future.

For the Deliverer	For the Receiver	For the Observer
• What did you keep in mind as you delivered your message? • Were you aware of your voice or body language? What did you notice? • Did you follow the chapter's four steps for delivering bad news in person? What was the effect?	• Did you follow the guidelines for how to receive a negative message in various roles as discussed in the chapter? • Were you listening and asking questions when appropriate? • What was the effect?	• What did you notice in terms of people's facial expressions, voices, and body language when they delivered the bad news? • How about when they received it?

2. In small groups, discuss the last time you had to tell someone disappointing news or deny a request. How did you word the message? How did you create goodwill with the other party involved?
3. In small groups, discuss the last time you were denied a request or received disappointing news. How did the content of the delivery affect your viewpoint of the sender of the negative message? What are the effects you have felt from the negative message?
4. What is the importance of preparing for objections to a negative message? In groups or as a class, discuss how you can create goodwill with the receiver of the message.
5. In groups or as a class, discuss the possible delivery methods for negative messages and how to determine which method is best. What guidelines will help you choose the best delivery methods?

6. In groups or as a class, discuss the "bad" methods of negative message delivery, such as through Twitter or a text message. How do the bad forms of delivery affect the timing of delivery? What options can you use for a message that must be delivered quickly?
7. In groups or as a class, discuss strategies for "damage control" when dealing with an upset customer. What experiences have you had when working with an upset customer, or even being the upset customer? How was the situation handled? What was the outcome?
8. In small groups, discuss and list ways to give a clear negative response without generating negative feelings.
9. In small groups or as a class, list the ways you can confront and discuss a conflict with a peer in the workplace. How can you prepare for the confrontation? How can you ensure both parties are satisfied with the outcome?

Do It *Document Your Success Track Record*

Build Your e-Portfolio

You have probably received various bad news messages throughout your life. In this exercise, you will have the opportunity to examine actual examples of bad news, analyze them, and rank them.

1. Form small groups to collect real examples of bad news from your lives. This will probably involve bringing in copies of e-mails or letters that deny credit, turn down a loan, reject a job application, or criticize something you did.
2. Create a "Bad News Examples" table like the one in the next column to keep track of the messages you collect; for example, credit rejections, loan rejections, job application rejections. (Note: We filled in the first line of the table with an example.)
3. Evaluate each example against the criteria you learned in this chapter. Rank it as follows:
   - ***Excellent:*** All criteria met, well written
   - ***Good:*** Most criteria met, well written
   - ***Fair:*** Some criteria met, not that well written
   - ***Poor:*** Few criteria met, poorly written

Pick some of the poor or fair examples and rewrite them.

Share your results with other groups. Are they similar? Different?

Bad News Examples

Type	To/From	Ranking & Notes
Loan rejection	From auto dealership to potential customer	Fair: Gave the bad news first without any buffer or reasons

Business in Action

Toyota Delay Tactics Lead to Deaths, Lawsuits, and Investigation

Is no news good news? Not when the news is delayed, denied, and discounted, which is what happened with Toyota in 2010.

According to *Motor Trend* magazine, Toyota's problems appeared to start with a single, horrifying car crash in southern California in August 2009. Off-duty patrol officer Mark Saylor was traveling on Highway 125 in Santee, California, with three family members, when his 2009 Lexus ES350 suddenly accelerated out of control to a speed in excess of 100 mph, hit another car, tumbled down an embankment and caught fire. All four people in Saylor's car were killed.

Later, after two separate recalls covering 7.5 million vehicles, Toyota was forced to announce it was suspending the sale of eight of its best-selling vehicles because of "unwanted acceleration," a move that would cost the company and its dealers a minimum of $54 million a day in lost sales revenue. Toyota's shareholders subsequently sued the company as did vehicle owners and their families. How did Toyota, the world's largest and most profitable automaker with a reputation for quality and dependability, find itself at the center of such a huge product recall and PR disaster?

As far back as 2003, Toyota internally dealt with an "unwanted acceleration" incident that occurred during production testing of the Sienna, a passenger van. However, Toyota did not report the incident to the safety officials at NHTSA (National Highway Traffic Safety Administration) for another five years.

From 2004 to 2007, the NHTSA investigated four speed-control incidents. The NHTSA suspected floor mats to be the culprit. However, at no time during those years of investigation did Toyota issue any news to customers about the problems.

More customer complaints, near-fatal accidents, and NHTSA investigations continued through October 2009, when Toyota finally issued a recall of 3.8 million vehicles on the grounds that floor mats could trap the accelerator pedal, causing sudden acceleration. It also publicly apologized to the NHTSA after reporting that "no defect exists." One month later, Toyota announced a plan to fix the floor mat problem by shortening the accelerators so they wouldn't get stuck against the floor mat. It also expanded the number of recalls to a total of 4.2 million. However, despite the floor mat recall, Toyota and federal safety officials continued to receive reports of unintended acceleration and stuck pedals, even in cases where the floor mats had been removed. A few months later, seven years after experiencing its own internal "unwanted acceleration" incident, Toyota informed NHTSA that the pedals themselves had a dangerous "sticky habit." The problem wasn't just the floor mats after all. Within 10 days Toyota recalled an additional 3.4 million vehicles because of pedal-entrapment problems and stopped selling eight models.

The president of Toyota, Akio Toyoda, later appeared before Congress to answer questions about the recall. Allegations were raised that Toyota knew about issues with unintended acceleration long before it began announcing recalls.

To these allegations, Toyoda responded, "I'm deeply sorry for any accident that Toyota drivers have experienced. [. . .]Toyota has, for the past few years, been expanding its business rapidly. Quite frankly, I fear the pace of which we have grown may have been too quick. [. . .] I would like to point out here that Toyota's priority has traditionally been the following: first, *safety*; second, *quality*; third, *volume*. These priorities became confused."

Toyoda offered his personal commitment to restore customers' trust in the company by working "vigorously and unceasingly" to correct problems with the recalled cars. However, the fact that his apology came so late in the game did little to renew customers' and shareholders' faith in the company. If Toyota had come clean and shared the bad news about the unintended acceleration problem at a much earlier date, money and lives might have been saved, along with the company's reputation.

Questions

1. Why do you think the NHTSA conducted so many investigations into customers' complaints about Toyota's "unexplained acceleration" problem? What do you think they could have done differently?
2. What do you think Toyota's biggest mistake was when it came to acknowledging its "unexplained acceleration" problem? What do you think they could have done differently?
3. Do you think there is anything that Akio Toyoda, president of Toyota, could have done to improve the situation?
4. Based on this story, what have you learned about delivering bad news?

Sources: Angus MacKenzie and Scott Evans, "The Toyota Recall Crisis," *Motor Trend*, January 2010 assessed at www.motortrend.com/features/auto_news/2010/112_1001_toyota_recall_crisis/index.html; Brett Emison, "Toyota Recall: A Time Line of Toyota's Checkered Safety History," *Injuryboard.com*, Feburary 10, 2010 assessed at http://kansascity.injuryboard.com/automobile-accidents/toyota-recall-a-time-line-of-toyotas-checkered-safety-history.aspx?googleid=278022; "Toyota Chief Apologizes for Recall," *Al Jazeera.net*, February 24, 2010 assessed at http://english.aljazeera.net/business/2010/02/2010224195918247230.html; David, Shepardson "Toyota Shareholders Sue Over Fallen Stock Price," by David Shepardson, *Detroit News*, March 21, 2010 assessed at www.detnews.com/article/20100321/AUTO01/3210331/1148/auto01/Toyota+shareholders+sue+over+fallen+stock+price.

Key Terms

Buffer. A neutral paragraph at the beginning of a negative message that engages the reader without stating the reason for the message. It should never contain negative words. *(p. 209)*

Claims. Demands for something customers feel are due them. *(p. 211)*

External parties. Anyone who works outside of your company (for example, vendors or customers). *(p. 220)*

Indirect approach. An approach to delivering bad news that reduces the impact of the negative news by providing explanations first. *(p. 209)*

Negative language. Words that convey unhappy and unpleasant thoughts, or predispose your reader to disagree with, or react poorly to your message. *(p. 205)*

Negative message. Any type of news construed as bad news because it's not what your audience wants to hear. It isn't necessarily terrible news; it can simply be a disappointing answer or a denied request. *(p. 204)*

Peer. A person who works at the same level in your firm's hierarchy as you do. *(p. 216)*

Subordinate. A person who works at a lower level in your firm's hierarchy than you do. *(p. 216)*

Superior. A person who works at a higher level in your firm's hierarchy than you do. *(p. 213)*

Review Questions *Test Yourself*

1. Define a negative message.
2. What are the four aspects to consider when presenting a negative message?
3. What are the three questions to ask yourself before you compose a negative message?
4. What strategies can you use to set the tone of a negative message?
5. What methods can you use to approach delivering a negative message in person?
6. When is the best possible time to deliver a negative message?
7. What goals should be considered when planning a negative message?
8. List the steps for how to structure a direct approach for a negative message. When is it best to use the direct approach for a negative message?
9. List the steps for how to structure an indirect approach for a negative message. When is the indirect approach the best approach to use for a negative message?
10. What strategies should be used when organizing a negative message to a superior, subordinate, or peer?
11. What goals should you have when writing a termination letter?
12. List four concepts that will help you receive and respond respectively to negative messages.
13. How do you approach a response to a terminated contract? What can you do to maintain goodwill with a client?

Grammar Review *Mastering Accuracy*

Commas

Section I

Each of the following sentences contains one or more common errors in word usage, grammar, or style. Identify the errors. If you have trouble finding the errors, review Sections 2.2.1. through 2.2.4. in the handbook (Appendix D) at the back of this textbook.

1. Because we stayed after class to help, grade exams, our instructor bought us dinner.
2. Mr. Davis brought his dog, Fluffy, for a demonstration, and, the dog promptly bit the supervisor.
3. John believed he has the correct course material, but, it turned out he purchased, the wrong textbook.
4. Jerry who works, in our corporate office has recently created standards for our current curriculum.
5. A violation of protocol will result in a thorough investigation, suspension without pay, and, possible termination.
6. Jogging, through the mist, to reach his car, Daniel suddenly realized he left his keys in his office.
7. The stern, overprotective, babysitter decided to send her charges to bed, without a snack, without television, and without a bedtime story.
8. Delivering his speech extemporaneously, Jack felt quite a sense of accomplishment, and peace.
9. Mr. Dobson, worked hard to eliminate all traces of the rat infestation in his neighbor's basement, but he remained, unsuccessful, in eradicating the stench.
10. Driving, while intoxicated, is a violation of the law, yet many people still try to get away with it.

Section II

On a separate sheet of paper, rewrite the following sentences so they are clearer, more professional sounding, grammatically correct, and goodwill oriented.

1. Campus policy dictates there is no running in the hallways, loud music, obnoxious behavior, or bad language permitted,
2. Someone left a mess for me to clean up this morning and I am sick of it: I'm telling the shift supervisor.
3. If the disclosure agreement is violated, the company will be sure to fold.
4. After the recent theft, Dave became extremely possessive of his desk's contents, not even allowing colleagues to borrow his stapler.
5. Close the door, as I don't want anyone to know what's going in here.
6. Don't use bad words—anyone might be nearby.
7. In order to listen like a pro, people should be on the ball and dedicated.
8. It's important to listen to other people's views and listen to them if you are a student or an instructor.
9. While there are certainly many additional ways in order to highly boost a student's professional standing, nothing will emerge as more of the utmost importance than the ability to assess one's own strengths and weaknesses.
10. In order to maintain the image appropriate for the business environment, all students should learn how to communicate like they want to have others communicate to them.

■ Extra Resources *Tools You Can Use*

Books

- Karr, Ron, and Don Blohowiak. *The Complete Idiot's Guide to Great Customer Service.* Indianapolis, IN: Penguin Group, 1997.
- Morgan, Rebecca. *Calming Upset Customers: Staying Effective During Unpleasant Situations,* 3rd ed. Canada: Crisp Publications, 2003.

Web Site

- "Apology Letters," *The Web's Premier Writing Site.*

“If I can get you to laugh with me, you like me better, which makes you more open to my ideas. And if I can persuade you to laugh at the particular point I make, by laughing at it you acknowledge its truth.” —John Cleese, actor

CHAPTER 9

Strategies for Persuasive Messages

Using the Right Words at the Right Time

LEARNING OBJECTIVE QUESTIONS

1. What are persuasive messages?
2. What makes a message persuasive?
3. What types of messages use persuasion?
4. How do you persuade ethically?

PEARSON **mybcommlab** Access interactive videos, simulations, sample documents, document makeovers, and assessment quizzes in Chapter 9 of **mybcommlab.com** for mastery of this chapter's objectives.

>>> **When** Theo finished college he knew right where he was going: Hollywood. As an aspiring screenwriter, Theo had already gained valuable experience during his time at New York University—he had held five internships and been involved in at least 25 student films. Once in Hollywood, Theo quickly learned the value of persuasion. While working on projects, Theo knew he had to remain enthusiastic to persuade his audience to adopt his screenplays and to maintain positive relationships with the influential figures in Hollywood. When it comes to selling his ideas, Theo always believed, "You've only got one shot. It had better be your best."

Theo also learned the importance of marketing his screenplays . . . by trial and error. When several of his projects flopped, Theo knew he had to revamp his approach. He started considering things like finding the right director, polishing the material, and figuring out what time of year the marketing might be most effective. By adopting this approach, Theo was able to make the most of his opportunities and better appeal to the needs of his audience. "Knowing where their focus is helps you reach them at the right time of year," Theo explained.

Today, Theo feels like his experience has paid off. "I sell something nearly every day—sometimes I'm selling the opportunity to read my work; sometimes I'm selling a film to a festival; and other times I'm selling a youth arts program to a sponsor," he says. All in all, whether marketing his work to a possible director or encouraging others to read his work, Theo knows how important persuasion is on a daily basis, and even more importantly, how to make it work for him.

Theo >>>

The business world emphasizes research metrics and data—getting the facts straight for your messages. However, what about the word choice, message structure, emotion, and tone of the messages? These elements are vital when you are trying to persuade people to change their minds or take a specific action.

■ For an interactive, real-world example of this topic, access this chapter's bcomm mini sim entitled Persuasive Messages, located at **mybcommlab.com**

PEARSON mybcommlab

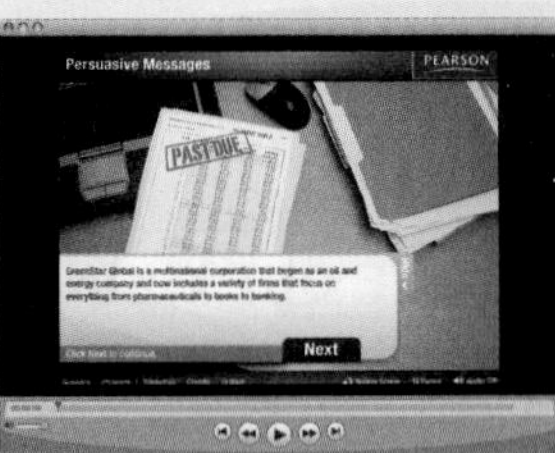

Persuasion plays a key role in business. Nowhere is this more apparent than in the entertainment industry. The entertainment industry encompasses a broad spectrum of businesses, such as film and television, music, gaming, the performing arts, and spectator sports. The music and movie businesses alone generate billions of dollars in revenues each year. People in the entertainment business all depend on words and images to obtain funding for their projects, generate publicity, and market and promote their products. Those products include movies, concerts, events, and the entertainers themselves.

Obtaining funding for these projects requires a bit more than pocket change. Director Clint Eastwood joked about one of his movies: "This film cost $31 million. With that kind of money I could have invaded a country." Consequently, people like Eastwood and others in the industry need to be very persuasive in their pitches to senior managers, venture capitalists, banks, and others that fund their ventures. Employees and entrepreneurs in the industry are constantly searching for innovative and effective ways to sell themselves and their clients and convince others of their worth.

The employment positions in the entertainment industry are as diverse as the products sold. They range from jobs for movie writers, producers and directors, agents and promoters, to musical composers and video game programmers. Many people who rise within the industry begin their careers as assistants. **Exhibit 9-1** describes some of the jobs that can be found in the industry. The individuals who do these jobs must be able to pitch their ideas in person and on paper.

Even if you don't pursue employment in the entertainment business, you will still need to be able to persuade people on the job. In this chapter, you will learn how to make your messages stand out and be convincing.

1 What Are Persuasive Messages?

A **persuasive message** is a message that persuades readers to change their beliefs or to take action. We all use persuasion at one time or another, whether we do so formally or informally. Parents persuade their children to go to bed. Teenagers persuade their parents to let them stay out later. Students persuade their teachers to reconsider their grades. Employees persuade their bosses to give them more time on assignments, better job assignments, and pay raises. Professionals persuade clients to hire them, and companies persuade customers to buy their products.

Exhibit 9-1 Jobs in the Entertainment Industry

Screenwriter	Director	Producer	Promoter	Agent
Writes screenplays for television and movies. Generally has to pitch ideas to directors.	Supervises all elements of a stage, film, or television production, such as the acting, location, staging, lighting, and soundtrack. Generally has to persuade actors to perform in ways that bring the screenwriter's screenplay to life.	Supervises and controls the finances, creation, and public presentation of a play, film, or program. Generally has to persuade others to finance the film.	In charge of putting on shows by working with agents, bands, and with concert venues to arrange for the show to take place. Generally makes sure information gets out about the show and that the show goes off smoothly.	Books talent. Agents approach promoters about shows, negotiate contracts for live performances, and make sure concert tours and shows go smoothly. Agents perform similar functions for authors, actors, and athletes.

❷ What Makes a Message Persuasive?

Persuasion is not trickery or fakery. It does not involve lying or coercion. It's an ethical way to let people know they have a choice, and to motivate them to make an informed decision—preferably in your favor. According to Steve Denning, an author and business leadership consultant, "True persuasion is not about any old idea, good, bad, or indifferent. Genuine persuasion is about an idea that is worthwhile in itself. If the idea is not worthwhile in itself and is being pursued for other reasons, such as career, prestige, money, power or simply the goal of winning, then it is unlikely to generate enduring enthusiasm in any audience."

One of the best ways to craft a persuasive message is through the use of the AIDA structure: **AIDA** is an acronym that stands for *attention, interest, desire,* and *action.* Let's now look at what each of these words entails when it comes to persuading people.

- ***Attention.*** Grab the attention of your audience members. Surprise them, question them, or confront them. An attention-getting opening ensures that a reader of a written message doesn't throw your letter in the trash or delete your e-mail. For example, suppose you want to persuade people not to send text messages while driving. You might start your message with a question such as the following:

  Would you drive your car the length of a football field with your eyes closed?

  That's the distance your car typically travels at 55 miles per hour when you take your eyes off the road for five seconds to text a message.[1]

  Metaphors are a useful way to grab people's attention. A metaphor is a figure of speech comparing two unlike things that actually have something in common. The following sentence contains a metaphor:

  The actor sank his talons into the script and ripped into his lines.

  In the metaphor, the actor is being compared to a bird of prey. Visualizing an eagle or raptor tearing into its prey helps the reader get a much better sense of the actor's intensity. Metaphors conjure up images in the reader's mind, making the information more powerful and memorable.

  Sometimes people use **shock tactics** to get audience attention. For example, consider the billboard in the following photo, which was paid for by SpeakUpOrElse, a Web site devoted to the fight against reckless driving. The bottom of the billboard reads: "If your friends drive recklessly, say something."

Source: Courtesy of The Advertising Council.

Some messages use shock tactics to persuade.

  The idea behind the use of shock tactics is that the audience reacts at an emotional level. Such gut-level responses are rarely long lasting and do not necessarily result in long-term change. Use shock tactics sparingly and only after you assess your audience. Let your audience be the deciding factor as to whether or not you use a shock tactic.

- ***Interest.*** Once you have your audience's attention, your message needs to build interest by appealing to both logic and emotion (more about this later in the chapter).

Facts, expert opinions, and examples work well because they appeal to people's logic. Testimonials and stories work well for emotional appeals. Stories in particular are entertaining, and people relate to them. People also remember stories better than they do facts or figures and are more likely to take action when they have been told a story.

For example, when Apple CEO Steve Jobs spoke at the Stanford University's commencement in 2005, he structured his talk around three simple stories of his life. Jobs talked about 1) dropping out of college and then 2) dropping back into classes just for fun. He also spoke about 3) being fired from Apple at the age of 30 and the trials and opportunities that accompanied this event. (He was rehired by Apple a few years later.) "Stay hungry, stay foolish," Jobs urged the Stanford graduates. Jobs' personal stories undoubtedly made his message far more memorable and persuasive than if he had shared long lists of facts or advice for graduates.

- ***Desire.*** The next step is to get your receivers to want, or desire, what you are presenting. First, explain what's in your message for them. You might even try explaining what's "not in it for them" if they don't act upon what you are suggesting. The threat of losing time, money, or reputation actually motivates some people more than the thought of gaining those things. To overcome resistance, lay out well-reasoned facts and arguments that address the receiver's objections. By admitting that objections exist and dealing with them, you also boost your credibility.
- ***Action.*** Always end your message with a "call to action." Motivate the receiver to take action by making a reasonable, precise request—to call you, e-mail you, make a purchase or donation, and so forth. With no call to action or a poor call to action, the reader is likely to read your message and then do nothing. **Exhibit 9-2** illustrates ineffective versus effective calls to action.

Exhibit 9-2
Calls to Action

Too Pushy	"If you don't respond by Friday, we're putting the project on hold."
Too Weak	"We hope to hear from you by Friday."
Too General	"Your feedback is important to us."
Effective	"Your feedback is important to us. Please respond by Friday so we can proceed with the project."

Exhibit 9-3 shows an example of how the AIDA approach was used to pitch a screenplay idea to an agent. As you have learned, taking certain steps will help you persuade people. However, it's difficult to persuade anyone of anything if you don't come across as trustworthy or credible.

Creating Trust and Credibility

Trust is absolutely essential when it comes to persuading your audience of anything. Your audience must trust you and have confidence in you before they will believe what you say. Think long and hard about the people you're trying to persuade with your messages. Do they believe you're a credible source, or do you need to share your credentials with them? Are they familiar with the product, idea, or plan you're sharing, or do you need to think "education" before "persuasion"?

Credibility refers to how your audience perceives you—whether or not they find you believable. People are more easily persuaded by someone they perceive as a truthful expert. To build your credibility, do the following:

- ***Be factual.*** Don't exaggerate. Don't lie.
- ***Be specific.*** Don't just say that something is good, say how good. Be specific about the benefits, savings, profits, or improvements your audience can expect from the idea you're proposing. People will take you seriously.

Exhibit 9-3 A Screenplay Pitch Developed Using the AIDA Approach

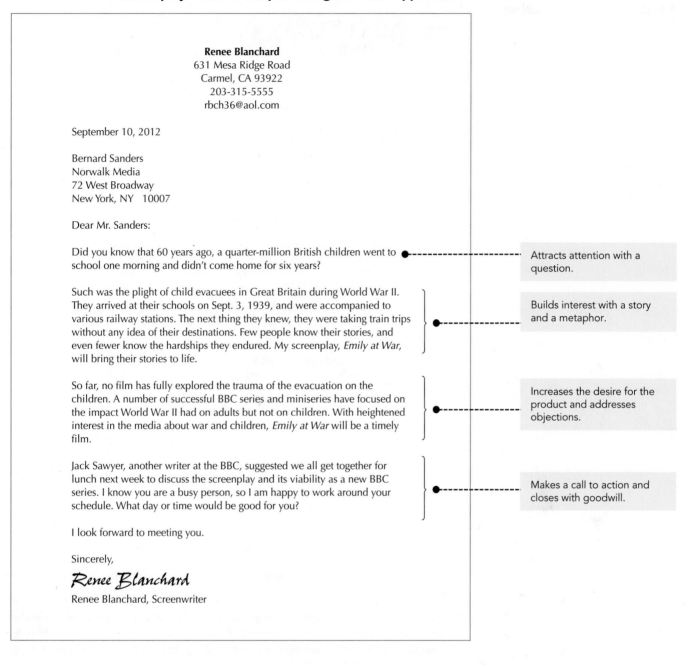

Renee Blanchard
631 Mesa Ridge Road
Carmel, CA 93922
203-315-5555
rbch36@aol.com

September 10, 2012

Bernard Sanders
Norwalk Media
72 West Broadway
New York, NY 10007

Dear Mr. Sanders:

Did you know that 60 years ago, a quarter-million British children went to school one morning and didn't come home for six years?

Attracts attention with a question.

Such was the plight of child evacuees in Great Britain during World War II. They arrived at their schools on Sept. 3, 1939, and were accompanied to various railway stations. The next thing they knew, they were taking train trips without any idea of their destinations. Few people know their stories, and even fewer know the hardships they endured. My screenplay, *Emily at War,* will bring their stories to life.

Builds interest with a story and a metaphor.

So far, no film has fully explored the trauma of the evacuation on the children. A number of successful BBC series and miniseries have focused on the impact World War II had on adults but not on children. With heightened interest in the media about war and children, *Emily at War* will be a timely film.

Increases the desire for the product and addresses objections.

Jack Sawyer, another writer at the BBC, suggested we all get together for lunch next week to discuss the screenplay and its viability as a new BBC series. I know you are a busy person, so I am happy to work around your schedule. What day or time would be good for you?

Makes a call to action and closes with goodwill.

I look forward to meeting you.

Sincerely,

Renee Blanchard

Renee Blanchard, Screenwriter

- ***Be reliable.*** Be up front with your audience. If you think something will take longer or cost more than you first suspected, tell your audience immediately. Keep them informed and make them part of the process.

Take the time to develop an ongoing relationship with your audience. When you do this, your audience will see you as credible and trustworthy and be more likely to consider your message. As people, we tend to trust those who are interested in our needs as long as their efforts seem sincere. **Exhibit 9-4** is an example of a credible reference letter from a television studio regarding a staff writer who left the studio to work in the film industry.

Setting the Right Tone

Once you are considered credible, your audience will be more willing to listen to your message. At this point, how you say something is just as important as what you say. The

Exhibit 9-4
A Credible Reference Letter

Alliance Television

7629 Clybourn Street
Sun Valley, California 91352

November 4, 2010

Madison Film Company
4400 El Camino Real
Los Angeles, CA 91608

To Whom It May Concern:

This letter regards Tyrone William. Tyrone came to Alliance three years ago as a freelance television writer with a spec script for our popular drama, *Oxidation*.

Unlike the hundreds of spec scripts we receive each year, this one was good. In fact, it was better than good. It was great. Tyrone's script imitated our style perfectly, and simultaneously introduced a sense of raw emotion and quirky humor that was never there before.

We took one look at the script and drew up a contract. Tyrone immediately joined the team as a staff writer for Alliance Television. However, it soon became apparent that he had another talent. He was a great "script doctor" for several of our other shows. He intuitively knew how to perk up boring dialog, speed up sluggish action, and tighten the entire story. Better yet, he never missed a deadline, and the crew and cast loved him.

We are sorry to see him go, but respect his desire to further his career. He will be an amazing asset to any film company that hires him.

Sincerely,

Joshua Tremaine

Joshua Tremaine, Producer

how depends on the tone of the message, which you learned about in Chapter 1. In particular, avoid these three tones: parental, arrogant, and stuffy.

1. ***Parental.*** When you write to people inside or outside your organization, use a friendly, open tone. A **parental tone** scolds or tells readers what to do. If you know the people, you can also use humor, as long as it is not insulting. **Exhibit 9-5a** contains an example of a memo from a director to his cast and crew.

Exhibit 9-5a
Correcting a Parental Tone

Parental Tone	Improved Tone
We are way over budget and running out of time. Therefore, I expect everyone on the set and ready to shoot by 7:30 A.M. each day. That means full makeup, costume, and lines memorized. There will be no retakes!	We are presently running over budget. However, I have confidence that if we put in slightly longer days, we will be able to finish the film on time. Please arrive on the set each day by 7:30 A.M., ready for the shoot in full costume and makeup. Have your lines memorized. We do not have time for retakes.

2. ***Arrogant.*** An **arrogant tone** is one that is condescending, which quickly alienates your audience. Instead, communicate with people in a reasonable and direct manner.

Exhibit 9-5b shows a section of a letter sent to Pennzoil's marketing firm, the Kerry Group, from a new NASCAR team requesting Pennzoil to sponsor it.

Exhibit 9-5b
Correcting an Arrogant Tone

Arrogant Tone	Improved Tone
We may be the new guys on the track, but with our Sprint Cup record, our experienced pit crew, and the points we've earned, this NASCAR team is superior to any other. NASCAR President Mike Helton recently called us "the team to watch." So do yourself a favor and sponsor us. You won't be sorry!	We may be the new guys on the track, but we've racked up almost 4,000 points in the Sprint Cup standings this year and have our eyes set on the checkered flag. NASCAR President Mike Helton recently called us "the team to watch." Helton suggested that Pennzoil would benefit from being a sponsor of the team. Please find attached detailed statistics about our performance. We look forward to talking to you in Illinois.

3. ***Stuffy.*** A **stuffy tone** is one people sometimes mistakenly use to make their messages sound more important. **Exhibit 9-5c** illustrates a stuffy tone and how it can be improved.

Exhibit 9-5c
Correcting a Stuffy Tone

Stuffy Tone	Improved Tone
Per your inquiry regarding the magicians represented by our agency: A list of their names, acts, and fees is attached for your reference. Your timely response is much appreciated.	We have attached a list of the names, acts, and fees of the magicians our agency represents, as you requested. We look forward to hearing from you. Our goal is to find the perfect entertainer for your venue.

Now that you know what tone not to use, what's the right tone to use?

- ***Be enthusiastic.*** Enthusiasm instills confidence. Let your personality come through as well. It will make your message more real, and receivers will be more likely to respond in a favorable way. People respond best to messages that are framed positively, regardless of their actual content.
- ***Be likeable.*** When people relate to you and like you, they are much more likely to agree with you and respond positively to your request. Being likeable means giving other people the benefit of the doubt and trying to see things from their perspective.
- ***Soften your words to persuade your superiors.*** When you need to persuade someone above you in the corporate hierarchy, you may have to tread lightly by making your request sound more like a suggestion than a demand. It also means using phrases such as "It might be a good idea to . . ." or "I recommend that we . . ." or "My research shows that . . ." Phrases such as these show that you are aware that the individual you are communicating with is still the person in charge.

Additionally, avoid bringing problems to your superiors without offering solutions to them. Outlining a problem and then offering a solution is a good way to persuade people, and a technique that savvy communicators frequently employ. Do the same when your firm's customers are experiencing problems with your company. Offering solutions to their problems is a good way to persuade them to remain your customers.

❸ What Types of Messages Use Persuasion?

So far in this chapter, we have outlined the general principles related to creating persuasive messages. Now let's examine specific types of persuasive messages you could be asked to write in the workplace: requests for favors and action, sales messages, and press releases.

REAL INSIGHTS from a Seasoned Professional

Name: *Scott Carter*
Title: *Executive Producer,* Real Time with Bill Maher *(HBO),* Curb: The Discussion *(TV Guide Network)*
Organization: *Efficiency Studios*
Location: *Los Angeles, California*

AS AN EXECUTIVE PRODUCER OF PROGRAMS like the political talk show *Real Time with Bill Maher,* Scott Carter needs to network with producers, please guests, and appeal to audiences in order to produce interesting and successful programs. Much of his success is due to his ability to envision what might sell and use this insight to communicate a persuasive plan.

Early in Carter's entertainment career, his persuasion skills helped open doors for both himself and his fellow crewmembers. While working on a show in New York, some of Carter's executives went away for a few days, leaving the crew with little to do. Carter saw the opportunity and persuaded a secondary executive to use the crew to shoot a new pilot, which would be shown to the other executives upon their return.

To win over the secondary executive, Carter outlined how shooting a new pilot would be cost effective, inventive, and would make the executive look good to his bosses. By relating his message directly to his audience, Carter tapped into his persuasive side—and it worked. From this convincing argument, the pilot for *SportsMonsters* was shot and bought by the impressed executives. The program continued to run for more than two years on Comedy Central.

Carter credits the more recent success of *Real Time with Bill Maher* to the fact that "talk shows run on goodwill." In other words, he laid the groundwork for persuading people to appear on the often controversial show. According to Carter, people need incentive to want to appear on a talk show, whether it is to enjoy the experience or to promote a movie or project. Using that knowledge, Carter ensures the guests' appearances are successful, which helps generate support for the show among other celebrities who might be interested in appearing on it. However, a show must also have a following. With this in mind, Carter takes the time to envision what his audience members want from the show, which helps him steer the direction of the featured guests and topics. This captures viewers and keeps them watching.

In the end, Carter attributes his success as an executive producer to his ability to shape his message to the needs of his audience. As he puts it, the powers of persuasion often begin with discovering "what would make everyone happy" and putting this knowledge into practice.

Questions

1. How did Carter persuade executives to shoot a second pilot? Using emotion? Using facts? Or both?
2. What methods did Carter use to persuade people to be on his show and watch his show?
3. When you try to persuade people, do you tend to use emotion or facts? Which have you found to work better?

Source: Scott Carter in discussion with the author, June 2010.

DID YOU KNOW?

How much money will you make and how far will you advance in your career? Did you know that the answers to those questions will depend, in part, on your ability to communicate with people and persuade them? The higher you climb in an organization, the more you will be asked to speak to and to persuade people.[2]

Requests for favors or actions are messages asking people to make decisions or take some action. For example, in the entertainment industry, the request might involve asking a director to read your client's screenplay or asking a radio or television station to host a music-awards event. Or, perhaps you are a music promoter who wants to put on a music and magic festival in a local park. However, first you need to approach the city and request a special permit to do so. This will involve writing a request for an action.

External Requests

The messages we just discussed are examples of **external requests,** or requests made of people and firms outside your organization. The AIDA approach is good for formulating external messages that are designed to be persuasive. For example, suppose you are a publicist for an entertainment company that represents illusionists, like magicians, mentalists, and escape artists. A new casino just opened in Las Vegas, Nevada, and you want one of your top acts to be the headliner for the debut. **Exhibit 9-6** is the letter you might write to the owner of the casino, persuading him or her to feature your illusionist as the headline act.

Exhibit 9-6 An External Request

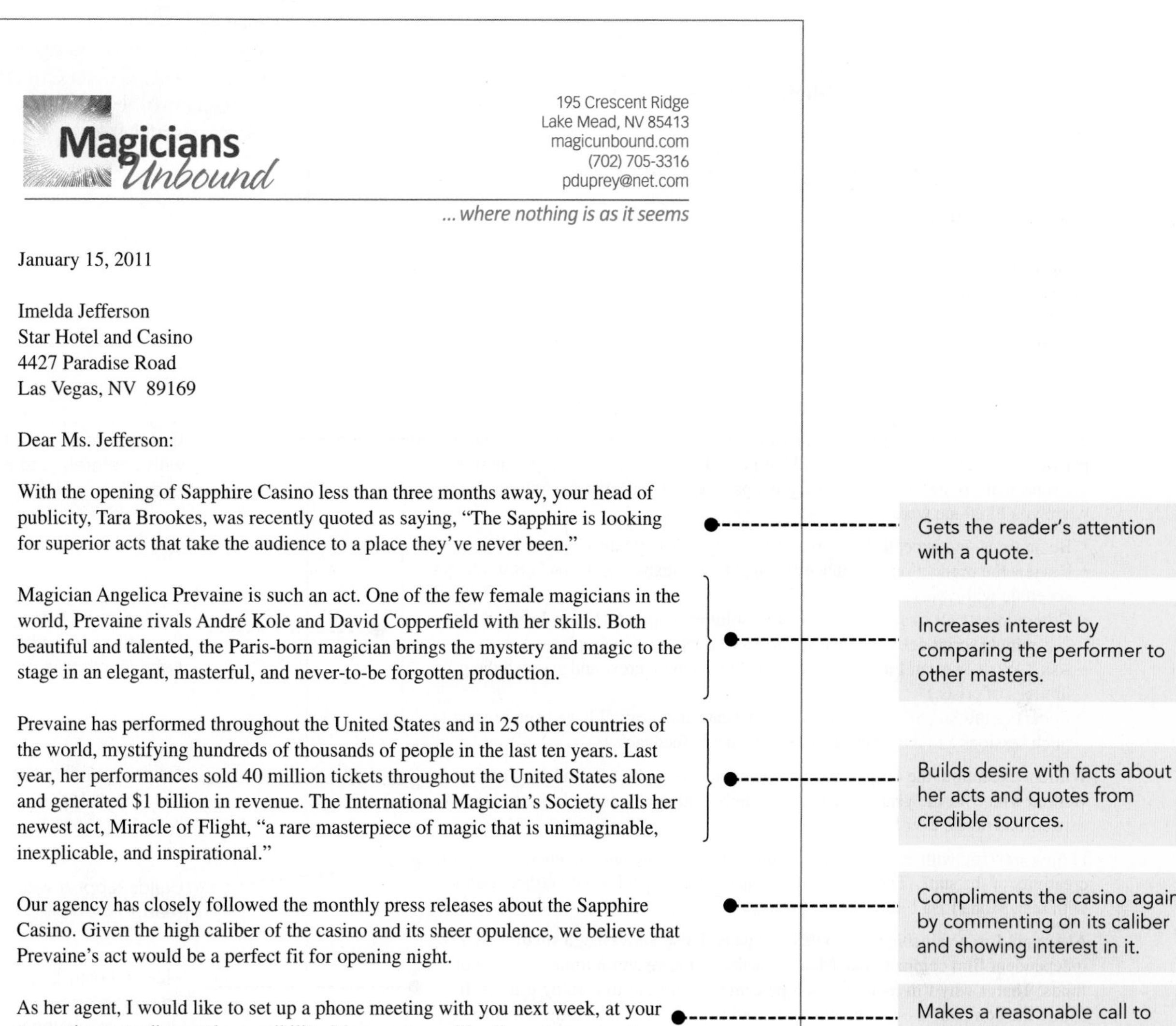

Magicians Unbound

195 Crescent Ridge
Lake Mead, NV 85413
magicunbound.com
(702) 705-3316
pduprey@net.com

... where nothing is as it seems

January 15, 2011

Imelda Jefferson
Star Hotel and Casino
4427 Paradise Road
Las Vegas, NV 89169

Dear Ms. Jefferson:

With the opening of Sapphire Casino less than three months away, your head of publicity, Tara Brookes, was recently quoted as saying, "The Sapphire is looking for superior acts that take the audience to a place they've never been."

Magician Angelica Prevaine is such an act. One of the few female magicians in the world, Prevaine rivals André Kole and David Copperfield with her skills. Both beautiful and talented, the Paris-born magician brings the mystery and magic to the stage in an elegant, masterful, and never-to-be forgotten production.

Prevaine has performed throughout the United States and in 25 other countries of the world, mystifying hundreds of thousands of people in the last ten years. Last year, her performances sold 40 million tickets throughout the United States alone and generated $1 billion in revenue. The International Magician's Society calls her newest act, Miracle of Flight, "a rare masterpiece of magic that is unimaginable, inexplicable, and inspirational."

Our agency has closely followed the monthly press releases about the Sapphire Casino. Given the high caliber of the casino and its sheer opulence, we believe that Prevaine's act would be a perfect fit for opening night.

As her agent, I would like to set up a phone meeting with you next week, at your convenience, to discuss the possibility. My secretary will call you tomorrow to make arrangements.

Sincerely,

Paul Duprey

Paul Duprey, Owner-Agent

Gets the reader's attention with a quote.
Increases interest by comparing the performer to other masters.
Builds desire with facts about her acts and quotes from credible sources.
Compliments the casino again by commenting on its caliber and showing interest in it.
Makes a reasonable call to action with a specific time frame.

Internal Requests

Internal requests are requests made within an organization. Typically they flow upward (to a superior), downward (to a subordinate), or laterally (to a coworker).

Upward Requests

We have already described the type of tone you should use when sending persuasive messages to your superiors. **Exhibit 9-7** shows a letter from a film production assistant to her manager in an effort to obtain a raise.

Downward Requests

Trying to persuade people who report to you in the corporate hierarchy is a bit different. By virtue of your position, you probably already have their attention and interest. However, you

Exhibit 9-7 A Request for a Raise

mybcommlab

Apply Exhibit 9-7's key concepts by revising a new document. Go to Chapter 9 in mybcommlab.com and select Document Makeovers.

Sheila Waters

410 Mesa Drive
Culver City, CA 90230
Phone: 310-545-3849 • Fax: 310-545-3850 • swaters324@sbcglobal.net

November 15, 2010

John Savage
Mona Lisa Films
1350 Elm Street
Los Angeles, CA 90065

Dear John:

This letter is a follow-up to our discussion yesterday. Your compliments about my performance made me think long and hard about my experience as a production assistant with Mona Lisa Films during the past year. Recall that the criteria you set when you hired me were as follows:

- Be on time—no exceptions. (I'm usually early and stay late.)
- Review the production schedule every night. (On many occasions I co-wrote the schedule with you.)
- Communicate all issues promptly with a solution in mind. (I have handled last-minute script deliveries and found new talent in unlikely places.)
- Ask, "What else can I do?" (I have helped the camera crew and assisted the grips in times of crisis.)
- Behave professionally at all times with the cast and crew. (I have been present at pitch sessions and have always offered valuable feedback.)

Without exception, the 10-plus production managers in the film industry I have worked with over the years have each privately told me I was the best production assistant he or she ever had.

I enjoy working with every member of this film company and am energized by the creativity of the staff. There's no film company for which I would rather contract with than Mona Lisa Films.

Although, I'm a valuable asset to this company, I also know that a small independent film company like Mona Lisa doesn't have an unlimited amount of funds. That is why I'm requesting a 5 percent raise for our upcoming project. It shows the company's commitment to me and is in line with the project's current budget.

If you would be so kind as to send me an e-mail acknowledging that you have received this letter and let me know the best time we could discuss the contract, I would appreciate it.

Thank you. I look forward to meeting with you.

Regards,

Sheila Waters

Sheila Waters
Production Assistant

Gets the reader's attention with a reference to a recent event.

Lists facts that demonstrates the writer's credibility and helps overcome objections.

Gains credibility and points out the writer's desirability within her field.

Builds rapport with the reader.

Makes a specific request with an understanding tone that demonstrates the writer's awareness of the reader's situation.

Makes a clear call to action.

never want to come across as demanding or threatening. Rather, you want to come across as someone who cares and understands the other person's situation. **Exhibit 9-8** shows a memo sent out to all of the members of an electronics production line, requesting they increase their output.

Direct Sales Messages

Many companies spend a good deal of their budgets on direct sales messages. **Direct sales messages** are used to sell goods and services to a large number of customers without the help of a salesperson. Direct sales messages typically go out by letter or e-mail to their tar-

Exhibit 9-8 A Request for Overtime Cooperation

MEMO

To: Line C Staff Members
From: Maria Abrerra
Date: May 9, 2010
Subject: Increased production for the Wii CPU

Avalon Electronics is the sole producer of the CPU for Nintendo's Wii. For the past three years Avalon Electronics has met and exceeded production schedules set by Nintendo. However, the General Manager of Nintendo of America in Redmond, Washington, contacted me yesterday. He is concerned that our current CPU production schedule will not meet the increased demand for Wiis.

States the problem without creating alarm.

Rather than find another vendor, he wants to continue Nintendo's relationship with Avalon because of our three-year work history and superior product quality. He needs us to increase our CPU production by 25 percent to meet the increased demand. I assured him that we were capable of doing this and could open another production line to accommodate his needs. He offered to pay a special expediting fee on all additional parts.

Provides details.

This is a terrific opportunity to show Nintendo what we can do, and lock in a long-term contract with Nintendo of America. Increased production will require additional hours for all members of the current production staff until we hire more workers. I anticipate that each of you will be working an extra four hours per week, possibly on Saturdays, for the next month.

Makes a request.

The extra work will not go unnoticed: You will receive time-and-a-half pay for your efforts. If you cannot work the extra hours due to family or other commitments, please let me know ahead of time so I can create an appropriate work schedule.

Exhibits goodwill.

Please plan to attend the production planning meeting Monday, July 5, from 10 A.M. to 11:30 A.M. in the Quartzite Room to discuss this new situation.

Makes a clear call to action.

Thank you for your efforts.

get audience. They also can be effectively sent via Twitter. The computer maker Dell, for example, sells millions of dollars of goods annually by "tweeting" followers on Twitter about special deals.

Direct Sales Letters

Most people consider direct sales letters to be much less invasive, or annoying, than unsolicited phone calls. However, letters are easy to throw away. Consequently, the more persuasive direct sales letters are, the better. **Exhibit 9-9** shows an example of a direct sales letter promoting a line of CDs to truck-stop owners.

In Chapter 7, you learned about writing everyday messages. Now you will learn how to write effective sales letters and sales e-mails. Most people who write sales letters and other sales materials have spent years analyzing the markets they write for and developing mailing lists of potential customers. In this chapter, we will simply touch on a few points to help you feel more comfortable with sales letters:

1. Study the product you are writing about to make sure you understand it.

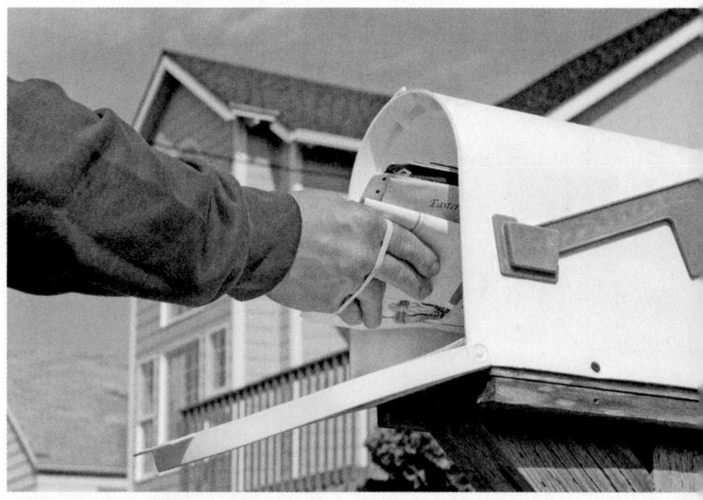

Direct sales letters are a popular way to sell goods and services. However, they have to be persuasive or they will quickly be thrown in the trash.

2. Be clear about who your audience is and what their needs are. Understand how your audience's needs can be met by the goods or services you are selling.
3. Identify your central selling points, or features, that provide important benefits to your audience.
4. Craft your letter using the AIDA method you learned about earlier:
   - ***Get attention.*** Try an offer, a promise, or a question. Sometimes an interesting or little-known fact works well. A testimonial from a previous buyer of the product can be effective.
   - ***Build interest.*** Describe the product or service clearly and simply using the selling points you earlier identified. Make sure that you appeal to the reader's emotions, and then build the appeal with facts.
   - ***Increase the reader's desire and reduce his or her resistance to act.*** Demonstrate how the product or service can improve the reader's life—either his or her savings,

Exhibit 9-9 A Direct Sales Letter

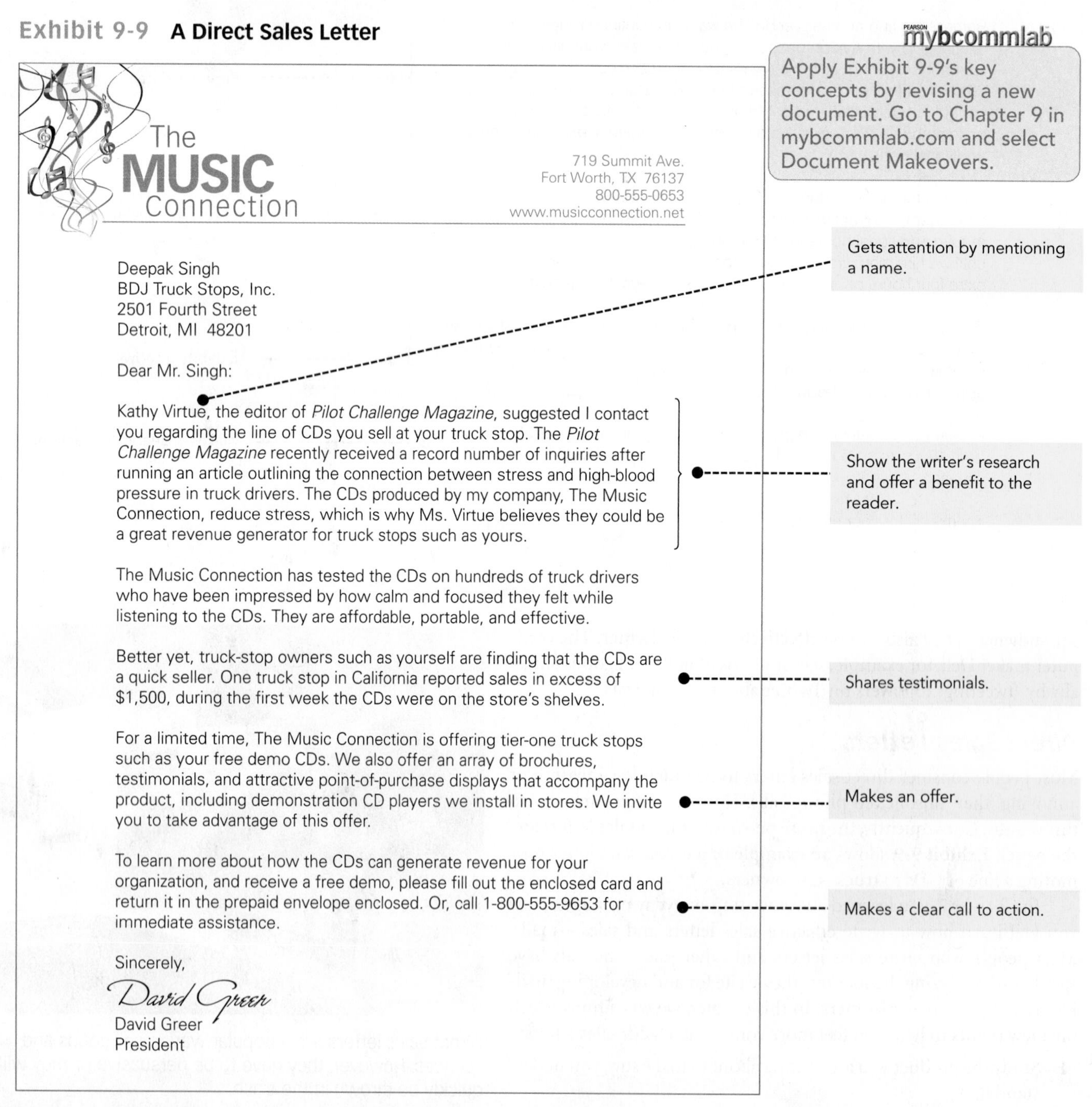

The MUSIC Connection

719 Summit Ave.
Fort Worth, TX 76137
800-555-0653
www.musicconnection.net

Deepak Singh
BDJ Truck Stops, Inc.
2501 Fourth Street
Detroit, MI 48201

Dear Mr. Singh:

Kathy Virtue, the editor of *Pilot Challenge Magazine*, suggested I contact you regarding the line of CDs you sell at your truck stop. The *Pilot Challenge Magazine* recently received a record number of inquiries after running an article outlining the connection between stress and high-blood pressure in truck drivers. The CDs produced by my company, The Music Connection, reduce stress, which is why Ms. Virtue believes they could be a great revenue generator for truck stops such as yours.

The Music Connection has tested the CDs on hundreds of truck drivers who have been impressed by how calm and focused they felt while listening to the CDs. They are affordable, portable, and effective.

Better yet, truck-stop owners such as yourself are finding that the CDs are a quick seller. One truck stop in California reported sales in excess of $1,500, during the first week the CDs were on the store's shelves.

For a limited time, The Music Connection is offering tier-one truck stops such as your free demo CDs. We also offer an array of brochures, testimonials, and attractive point-of-purchase displays that accompany the product, including demonstration CD players we install in stores. We invite you to take advantage of this offer.

To learn more about how the CDs can generate revenue for your organization, and receive a free demo, please fill out the enclosed card and return it in the prepaid envelope enclosed. Or, call 1-800-555-9653 for immediate assistance.

Sincerely,

David Greer

David Greer
President

Gets attention by mentioning a name.
Show the writer's research and offer a benefit to the reader.
Shares testimonials.
Makes an offer.
Makes a clear call to action.

PEARSON mybcommlab

Apply Exhibit 9-9's key concepts by revising a new document. Go to Chapter 9 in mybcommlab.com and select Document Makeovers.

health, confidence, attractiveness, income, or any other positive aspect. Get your reader interested and wanting the item before you mention the price. You can also share customer testimonials or offer a free trial, coupon, or money-back guarantee to help reduce resistance.

- ***Make a call to action.*** The call to action in a direct sales message often gives buyers an incentive to purchase before a certain deadline. The incentives can include discounts, free gifts, and rebates.

Direct Sales E-mails

Like direct sales letters, direct sales e-mails are sent to a list of potential buyers. The company either collects the e-mail addresses or purchases them from another organization. Constructing a direct sales e-mail is similar to constructing a direct sales letter. However, there are two main differences:

- ***Subject Line.*** The subject line of the e-mail needs to be crafted very carefully so readers don't delete the message as soon as they see it in their in-boxes. The subject is the hook. It should grab the reader's attention. Pay attention to the words you use in the subject line. Messages that contain certain words and phrases, such as *free*, *half off*, and *you're a winner*, will automatically be filtered and sent to a SPAM folder. **Exhibit 9-10** shows a list of some of the words that can cause an e-mail to be filtered.
- ***Length.*** Direct sales e-mails should be considerably shorter than direct sales letters. Don't force the reader to scroll down his or her computer screen to finish reading the e-mail. Typically the layout should be simpler than a letter and contain few or no photos. Complicated layouts and graphics increase the size of the e-mail, causing it to take longer for people with slower Internet connections to open. Additionally, some people's e-mail systems cannot display special formatting. Some companies send recipients two versions of a direct sales e-mail: one in plain text and one with a more complex layout. Other companies avoid that situation by sending plain text messages with links to their Web sites, where photos and special layouts appear.

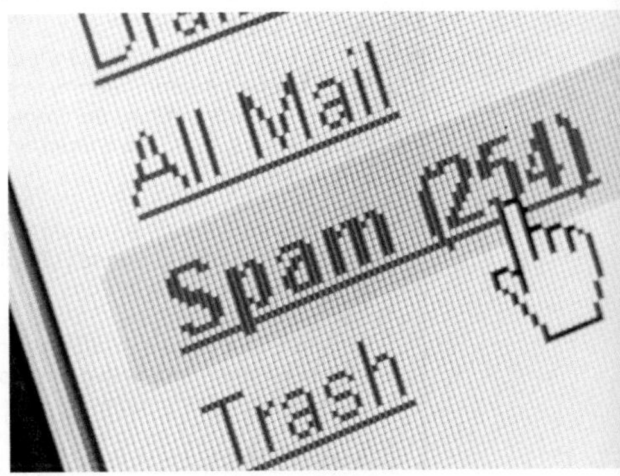

You are undoubtedly familiar with direct-sales e-mails. Which ones do you open versus send to your trash bin? Why?

Exhibit 9-10
Words and Phrases That Can Trigger E-mail Filters

A – D	E – N	O – W
100% satisfied	Extra income	One time
Accept credit cards	Free leads	Opportunity
Act now	Free membership	Order now
All natural	Free offer	Order today
All new	Free preview	Order status
Bargain	Get it now	Performance
Buy direct	Guarantee	Please read
Call	Information you requested	Potential earnings
Call free	Money	Preapproved
Click to remove	No gimmicks	Risk free
Compare rates	No hidden fees	Satisfaction guaranteed
Congratulations	No-obligation	Save $
Dear friend		Serious cash
Do it today		Special promotion
		Work at home

Exhibit 9-11 shows the earlier sales letter written in plain text for e-mail. You will notice that the message is shorter and contains no company letterhead, logo, or uncommonly used fonts.

Exhibit 9-11 A Direct Sales E-mail

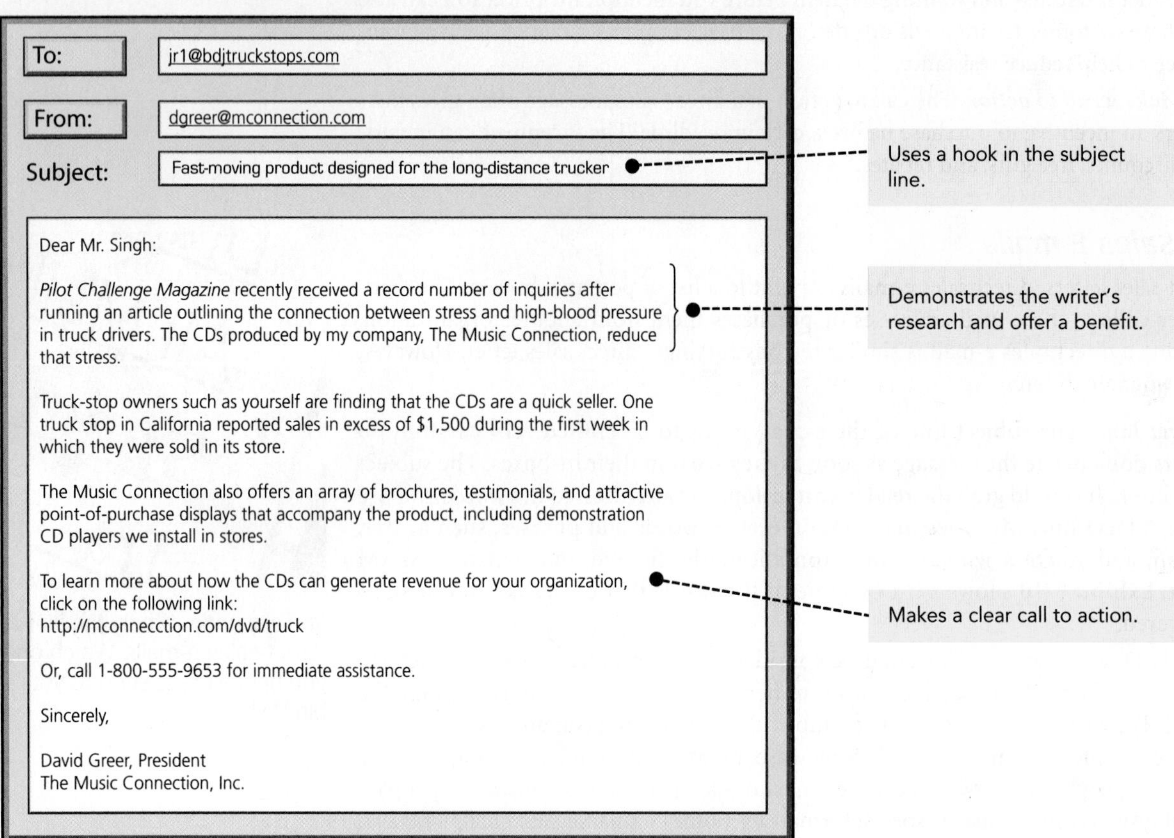

To: jr1@bdjtruckstops.com

From: dgreer@mconnection.com

Subject: Fast-moving product designed for the long-distance trucker

Dear Mr. Singh:

Pilot Challenge Magazine recently received a record number of inquiries after running an article outlining the connection between stress and high-blood pressure in truck drivers. The CDs produced by my company, The Music Connection, reduce that stress.

Truck-stop owners such as yourself are finding that the CDs are a quick seller. One truck stop in California reported sales in excess of $1,500 during the first week in which they were sold in its store.

The Music Connection also offers an array of brochures, testimonials, and attractive point-of-purchase displays that accompany the product, including demonstration CD players we install in stores.

To learn more about how the CDs can generate revenue for your organization, click on the following link:
http://mconnecction.com/dvd/truck

Or, call 1-800-555-9653 for immediate assistance.

Sincerely,

David Greer, President
The Music Connection, Inc.

Uses a hook in the subject line.
Demonstrates the writer's research and offer a benefit.
Makes a clear call to action.

Exhibit 9-12 on the next page shows an e-mail from a local theater business manager soliciting interest in a comedy boot camp for teens.

Selling via Social Networks

The popularity of social networks makes them a good way to reach out to potential customers or clients. Jennifer Wakefield of the Metro Orlando Economic Development Commission uses social networking to target the film and media industries saying, "We have green nearly 365 days out of the year here in Orlando." To advertise the ideal location for film shoots, Wakefield created profiles for metro Orlando on both Facebook and MySpace. In conjunction, Suzy Spang Allen, the commission's vice president of film and digital media development, posts tweets on Twitter to connect with people at film industry events such as film festivals. Wakefield reports that the number of producers scouting the Florida metropolis has more than doubled as a result.[3]

Press Releases

A **press release** is an announcement about your company to the media. The announcement resembles a news article. The information in the press release might include details about your firm's new CEO, product, location, or major initiative it is undertaking. Why is a press release considered persuasive writing? The purpose of a press release is to create interest about your company so that the media either publishes or airs the information or does a follow-up story on it. A press release is typically sent electronically to newspapers, magazines, or other media organizations, including Web sites like Google. It often appears on your company's Web site as well.

The setup of a press release is exactly the same as a news story. It begins by answering the questions *who, what, when, where, why,* and *how?* The most important information appears at the beginning of the release, so that if the receiver reads only the first

To: KathTomas@gmail.com

From: dgreer@mconnection.com

Subject: Recruiting for Duct Tape Theatre's Boot Camp

Dear Kathy:

You have proven in the past to be a supporter of both the arts and children. Consequently, I would like to ask if you would be willing to pass on this e-mail about the Duct Tape Theater's new Standup Comedy Boot Camp.

Standup Comedy Boot Camp, which takes place July 7 through August 25 at Florida State University, is an outstanding nonprofit venture. It includes an eight-week class taught by the 20-year comedy veteran Gene Moore, with special guest teachers from local radio stations and comedy clubs. The kids learn it all: the art, the history, the actual writing and telling of jokes, and they get to open a show for a professional comic.

If you know or teach a teen between the ages of 13 and 18 who would be interested or should be interested in this program, please forward this e-mail to him or her. If you have a classroom with a wall where you can post this e-mail, please be so kind as to do so and pass on the word.

Thank you for your help.

Tracy Charles, Business Manager
Duct Tape Theatre
(912) 492-8831
tcharles@ducttapetheatre.com
www.ducttapetheatre.com

Exhibit 9-12
A Request to "Pass on the Word"

paragraph, he or she will have a good sense of whether or not the item is newsworthy. The press release always ends with the name and contact information of the organization that produced it. Keep in mind that reporters are not interested in helping you make money or driving visitors to your company's Web site. They are interested in stories that will be interesting to their readers.

Exhibit 9-13 shows a typical press release posted on the Web site of a sports marketing firm. Explanations for the numbered callouts in the exhibit are as follows.

1. ***Document title.*** The words "Press Release" always appear at the top of the document.
2. ***Headline.*** The headline needs to be eye-catching and concise. It is typically used in the subject line if you're sending the press release by e-mail.
3. ***Release date.*** The release date indicates when the press release can go out to the public. In a Web press release, the date typically appears after the headline or at the beginning of the lead paragraph. In a print release, the date typically appears under the words "Press Release." The date is important, because the timing of the release can affect its impact and persuasiveness.
4. ***Lead paragraph.*** The lead paragraph is the most important paragraph in the press release. It should answer the questions who, what, when, where, and why—everything a media outlet would need to run the story as it is written.
5. ***Body.*** The body of the release should accurately support the claims made in the lead paragraph. Shorter is better. Try to say what you need to say in one page or less.
6. ***Boilerplate.*** The boilerplate is a standard block of text about the organization releasing the information. It appears in all of the firm's press releases.

Exhibit 9-13 A Press Release

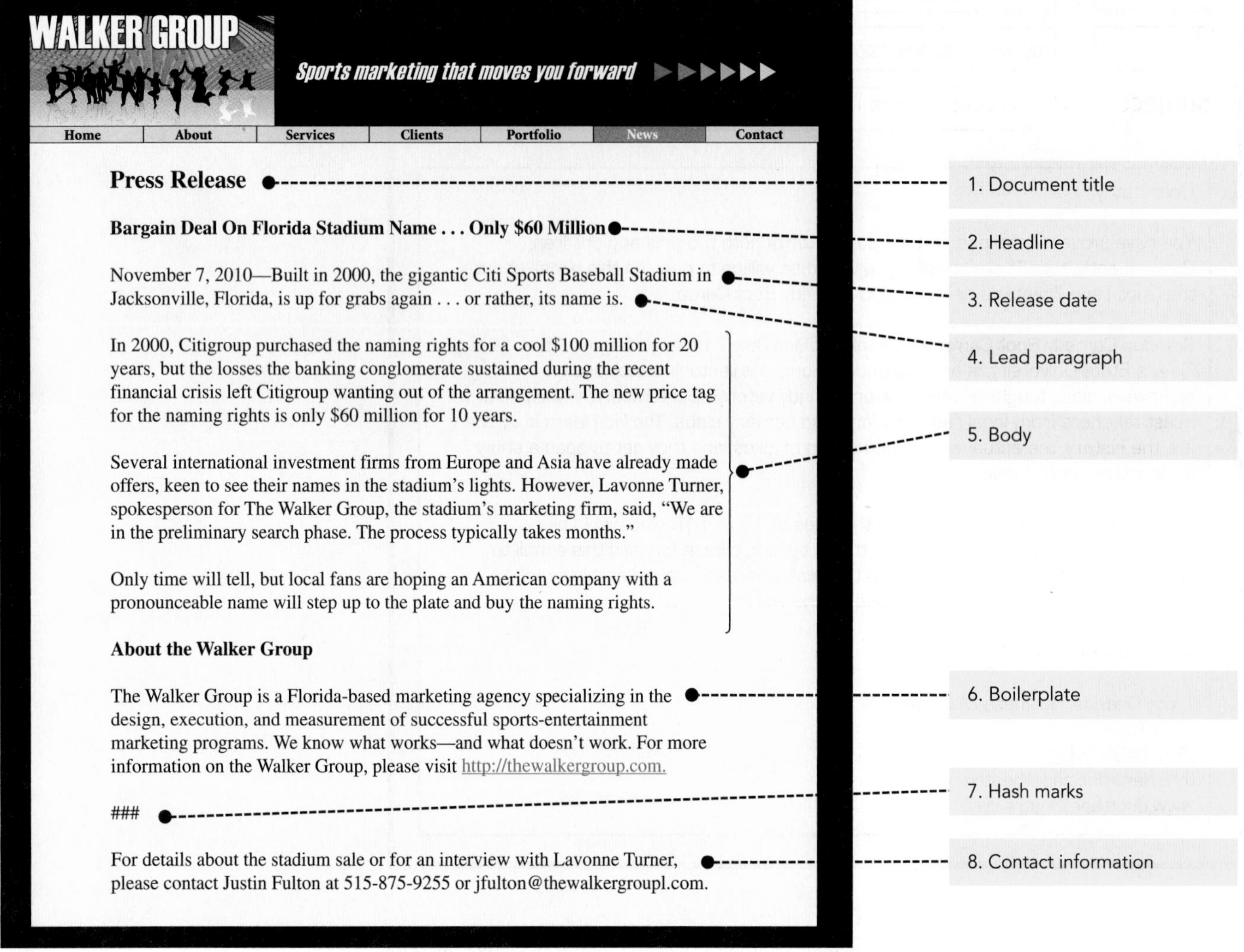

Press Release

Bargain Deal On Florida Stadium Name . . . Only $60 Million

November 7, 2010—Built in 2000, the gigantic Citi Sports Baseball Stadium in Jacksonville, Florida, is up for grabs again . . . or rather, its name is.

In 2000, Citigroup purchased the naming rights for a cool $100 million for 20 years, but the losses the banking conglomerate sustained during the recent financial crisis left Citigroup wanting out of the arrangement. The new price tag for the naming rights is only $60 million for 10 years.

Several international investment firms from Europe and Asia have already made offers, keen to see their names in the stadium's lights. However, Lavonne Turner, spokesperson for The Walker Group, the stadium's marketing firm, said, "We are in the preliminary search phase. The process typically takes months."

Only time will tell, but local fans are hoping an American company with a pronounceable name will step up to the plate and buy the naming rights.

About the Walker Group

The Walker Group is a Florida-based marketing agency specializing in the design, execution, and measurement of successful sports-entertainment marketing programs. We know what works—and what doesn't work. For more information on the Walker Group, please visit http://thewalkergroup.com.

###

For details about the stadium sale or for an interview with Lavonne Turner, please contact Justin Fulton at 515-875-9255 or jfulton@thewalkergroupl.com.

7. ***Hash marks.*** The hash marks (###) indicate the end of the release.
8. ***Contact information.*** The contact information explains who the media should contact with questions or to schedule interviews.

❹ How Do You Persuade Ethically?

We mentioned earlier that persuasion is not trickery. The most persuasive message is one that is true, objective, and fair. People who receive your message want to make an informed choice. If they suspect you're manipulating, misleading, or lying to them, you and your organization will lose credibility.

What can you do to make sure your persuasive messages are responsible? The following list contains some suggestions.

1. ***Stick to the facts.*** As we explained earlier in the chapter, don't distort the facts to get your point across.
2. ***Avoid circular reasoning.*** When you cite a reason for a statement, make sure the reason is not simply repeating the statement.

Circular Reasoning	Logical Reasoning
Mona Lisa's latest film project, *Emily at War,* is a guaranteed success because it's a sure thing.	Mona Lisa's latest film project, *Emily at War,* is a guaranteed success because it already has the backing of two successful production companies and an endorsement from the BBC.

3. ***Don't mischaracterize the cause and effect.*** Don't make statements indicating one event caused another just because the first event occurred before the second. Make sure there was an actual link between the events. In other words, be sure the first event actually caused the second.

Artificial Cause and Effect	Actual Cause and Effect
The first episode of *Emily at War* aired on BBC last Saturday and BBC's ratings soared.	The first episode of *Emily at War* aired on the BBC last Saturday, and response from viewers was quite positive. Interestingly, the BBC's ratings soared around the same time. However, several other new shows aired the same evening, which could have contributed to the spike in ratings.

4. ***Include the evidence.*** You have probably seen TV commercials that make outlandish claims about products over and over again. The idea behind such a sales tactic is that if you say something often enough, it becomes a fact. Not true. Stating an unsubstantiated claim over and over does not make it true; it just makes you repetitive and irritating. Always back up your claims with solid evidence.

Claim without Evidence	Claim with Evidence
Members of the Evacuee Reunion Association of Great Britain say the new BBC series, *Emily at War,* is their favorite series of the season.	Nine out of 10 members of the Evacuee Reunion Association of Great Britain say the new BBC series, *Emily at War,* is their favorite series of the season.

5. ***Avoid overselling.*** **Overselling** is promising more than can you can deliver. Some people will immediately know if a product is being oversold and resist buying it. Others will give in, only to regret their decision later. This could possibly result in negative word-of-mouth for your firm. **Exhibit 9-14** is an excerpt of a message that demonstrates overselling versus a measured approach to promotion.
6. ***Avoid manipulation.*** When asked "What is the difference between persuasion and manipulation?" Bob Burg, a noted business author and consultant, answered, "On a surface level, we could actually say . . . 'nothing.'" However, when you look beneath the surface, there is a big difference. **Manipulation** is the process of influencing people in unfair or devious ways. Manipulative messages often prey upon people's fears or their ignorance. Compare the right-hand side of **Exhibit 9-15** with the left-hand side, which shows how fear and unsupported claims are being used to sell a product.
7. ***Avoid euphemisms.*** A **euphemism** substitutes a mild or vague expression for a potentially negative or offensive one. In his book *Crazy Talk, Stupid Talk,* author Neil Postman defines a euphemism as an "exalted term used in place of a down-to-earth term, or an attempt to give a prettier term to an uglier reality."[4] Ethical messages have power

CHECKLIST

To create ethical messages:

- ☑ Stick to the facts.
- ☑ Avoid circular reasoning.
- ☑ Don't mischaracterize the cause and effect.
- ☑ Include the evidence.
- ☑ Avoid overselling.
- ☑ Avoid manipulation.
- ☑ Avoid euphemisms.

Exhibit 9-14 Overselling versus Appropriate Selling

Overselling	Appropriate Selling
The "Girl Power" concert is going to be the greatest concert ever. You won't believe all the different musicians we have lined up—everyone from Miley Cyrus, Beyonce, and Whitney Houston, to the Jonas Brothers, U2, and Elton John ... plus dozens more!	The "Girl Power" concert is stacking up to be one of the best concerts ever to hit the metro area. The show's terrific musical entertainment acts include Miley Cyrus, Beyonce, and Whitney Houston, as well as the Jonas Brothers, U2, Elton John ... and more!
Amazingly, every artist agreed to donate his or her time! Plus, we've got mega-sponsors, like Nike, Gatorade, and Coca Cola. This is going to be the biggest event of the decade—don't miss it!	All of the entertainers agreed to donate their time and a number of international companies, including Nike, Gatorade, and Coca-Cola have stepped up to the plate as sponsors. We are well on our way to raising $10 million across the United States to help educate girls throughout Afghanistan and Pakistan.
We're going to raise more money benefiting schoolgirls throughout Pakistan and Afghanistan than you ever thought was possible. This concert is really going to make a difference. And all it costs for a ticket is $10.00. You can afford that, right?	We invite you to make a difference by attending the concert with friends and family. The tickets are priced affordably at $10.00, so we anticipate a large crowd. Buy early while tickets are still available!

Exhibit 9-15
Manipulation versus Persuasion

Manipulation	Persuasion
If you're already more than 50 pounds overweight, you could die tomorrow of high blood pressure, atherosclerosis, or heart attack.	Did you know cholesterol screening, healthy diet, and regular physical activity can greatly reduce your risk of heart disease and stroke?

to persuade and inspire. Don't cheapen them with vague euphemisms. Most euphemisms are so common that people see right through them. For example, when companies talk about downsizing or smart-sizing employees, we're not fooled. We know the companies are laying off workers. **Exhibit 9-16** shows some examples of euphemisms people use.

Exhibit 9-16
Examples of Euphemisms

Euphemism	No Euphemism
Downsized, right-sized	Fired employees
Lost their lives	Killed, died
Took legal action	Sued
Friendly fire	Killed by your own troops

Balancing Logic and Emotion

As we explained earlier, the best persuasive messages have both logical and emotional appeal. Next we look at how to create and balance the two.

Using Logic

When you use a logical appeal, you present facts and data. You can use any of the following devices to create a logical appeal: an analogy, inductive reasoning, or deductive reasoning.

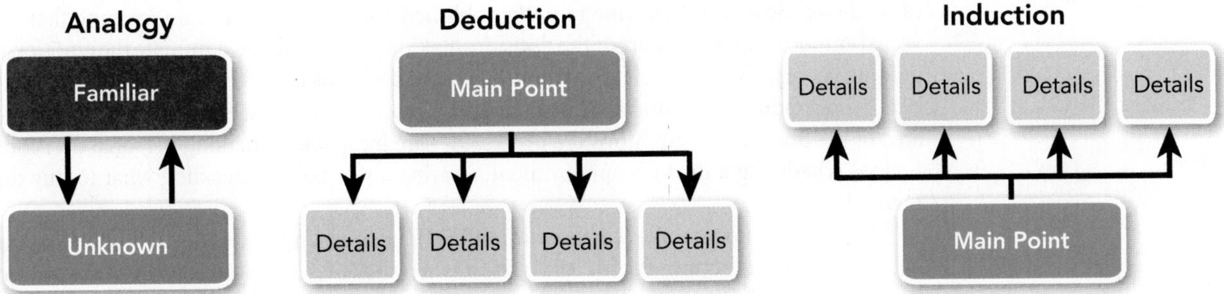

- ***Analogy.*** An **analogy** is a comparison between two ideas or things. Start with an example that your audience can relate to, and then compare it to something new. For example, suppose you are a music critic for the e-zine Celtic MP3s Music Magazine. You've just listened to a CD by a new group, Industrial Celtic, and want to persuade people to buy the CD. The following excerpt from your review attempts to convey the unique sound of the group using an analogy:

  We're all familiar with Celtic instruments—the harp, the pipes, and the drums. Now imagine a harp constructed from bent steel pipes and industrial wire. Then add a bodhrán drum that looks like a steel garbage can and a hammered dulcimer played with ball-peen hammers and lead pipes. The sound? Haunting Celtic melodies mixed with harsh industrial tones—that's Industrial Celtic.

- ***Deduction.*** **Deduction** is a reasoning process that begins with a general idea and moves toward a more specific conclusion. The following is another excerpt from the CD review you might write. Deductive reasoning is used to present the studio's unique location and its unusual instruments. Notice how the first sentence grabs the reader's attention and presents the main idea. The remaining sentences in the paragraph provide additional information.

  Recording tunes in an old, turn-of-the-century, abandoned Belfast linen mill, Industrial Celtic has carved out a unique niche for itself in the Celtic music world. The group's three siblings, Erinn, Siobhán, and Owen Dundas, chose the location because "it's big, it's cheap, and the acoustics are too fabulous to ignore." The group uses common industrial materials, like steel plates, wire, and concrete to create their oversized instruments. They have even rewired some of the ancient looms in the mill to become pseudo harps. No wonder they have to record their music in a factory—their instruments are too big and too heavy to transport to a studio.

- ***Induction.*** **Induction** is a process of reasoning that is the opposite of deduction. You begin with specific details and move toward a general conclusion. Such a structure can be quite useful if the conclusion of the message is somewhat negative. For example, suppose you may need to explain in your review that the concert schedule for Industrial Celtic is sparse, and the tickets to its concerts are expensive. You might decide to use inductive reasoning, as the following example shows. Notice how the last sentence is the main idea of the paragraph.

  The mill where the members of Industrial Celtic compose, practice, and record is also the same mill in which the group performs. More than a century old, it has been renovated and retrofitted with a modern stage and comfortable, intimate seating. The tall, narrow windows and numerous skylights provide fantastic natural lighting during daytime performances and display the night sky to its best advantage during evening concerts. The acoustics are indeed "out of this world." Because Industrial Celtic takes months to build new instruments and record new songs, concerts are few and far between. Consequently, tickets are expensive. However, experiencing an Industrial Celtic concert is well worth the wait and the price.

Increasing the Emotional Appeal of Messages

Business decisions are not always made based on factual data alone. They are also based on the emotional connection people feel to the ideas presented. There's scientific evidence to support the importance of the role emotions play when it comes to making decisions. The University of Rochester School of Medicine recently published a study based on brain imaging that revealed emotions are a vital part of the decision-making process. "If you eliminate the emotional guiding factors, it's impossible [for people] to make decisions in daily life," says Dr. Dean Shibata, who conducted the study.[5] Shibata says that people with damaged prefrontal lobes—the area of the brain where emotions are processed—are incapable of making personal decisions such as scheduling a doctor's appointment, wearing a seat belt, or deciding what to buy for themselves.

In Latin, the root of the word "emotion," is "to move." Emotions move people to make decisions and take action. People take action when they believe you understand them, and they trust your judgment. The words you use—nouns, verbs, and adjectives—therefore need to evoke the right emotions, preferably positive ones.

Suppose you are an event planner working on the annual Jerry Lewis MDA Telethon. You are contacting well-known entertainers to volunteer their time and talents for a telethon, in order to raise money for the Muscular Dystrophy Association. **Exhibit 9-17** shows the subtle difference between a straightforward request without much emotional appeal and a similar appeal that uses emotion-provoking words. The words are boldfaced. Look at the excerpts and ask yourself which one might produce better results.

Exhibit 9-17 Logic versus Emotions

Appeal with Logic Only	Appeal with Positive Emotions
You are one of the most popular singers in the nation and one of the few entertainers with a child suffering with muscular dystrophy.	Given your current concert schedule, we **understand** you are a very busy person. However, we also know of your **love** of children and your son's **battle** with muscular dystrophy.
That's why we're asking you to make a brief appearance on our Jerry Lewis MDA Telethon next Labor Day.	That's why we **hope** you might be available to make a brief appearance on our Jerry Lewis MDA Telethon next Labor Day.
Given your popularity around the world, we know that your presence on the telethon would raise the funds we need to help the 50,000 people who suffer from muscular dystrophy in the United States. Last year the telethon raised over \$60.5 million and 78.3 percent of that went directly to research, services, and education; the rest went to fundraising and administration.	Your voice brings **joy** to thousands of people around the world. We know that your presence on the telethon would raise much-needed funds. Last year the telethon raised over \$60.5 million, and 78.3% of that went directly to research, services, and education; the rest went to fundraising and administration. We believe that your **beautiful** voice and **stirring** story will bring **hope** to the more than 50,000 people who suffer from muscular dystrophy in the United States.
I will contact you early next week to find out if your schedule allows an appearance on the telethon.	I will contact you early next week to find out if your busy schedule allows an appearance on the telethon.

Words aren't the only tool people use to persuade others. Images can also be used effectively. Vision is the most powerful sense human beings have. Using images to persuade people is known as **visual communication** (or **visual rhetoric**), which is a burgeoning area of study. Messages created by the Humane Society typically show abused, hungry, or caged animals. The images drive home the society's message far better than words alone could, as **Exhibit 9-18** shows.

The placement, size, and subject of images have a tremendous impact on people:

- ***Placement.*** People in Western societies read from left to right and top to bottom. Consequently, images in the top-left or center of a page or TV or computer screen are most noticeable to us.
- ***Size.*** When we see a combination of images, we first notice large ones and then small ones.
- ***Subject.*** Most people respond to faces, so images that include faces are particularly powerful.

REAL INSIGHTS from a New Professional

Name: *Brooke Meacham*
Title: *Director's Coordinator*
Organization: *Omation Animation Studios*
Location: *Los Angeles, California*

FOR BROOKE MEACHAM, A DIRECTOR'S COORDINATOR for the California-based studio Omation Animation, persuasion isn't just another means of communication. It's the basis of her business.

While studying screenwriting in college, Meacham learned about an opportunity to intern with Omation, an animation studio that produces shows for Nickelodeon. She applied for the internship, was accepted, and worked with the company for six months. After graduating, the studio asked her to come back, again as an intern. Although some of her friends waited for the perfect job to come along, Meacham jumped at the chance to be an intern. It paid off. Within a short time, she was hired as a full-time employee. She was promoted several times before reaching the position of director's coordinator for the hit children's show *Back at the Barnyard.*

Among her many responsibilities, Meacham acts as a liaison between production crews and the director, assists with coordinating the director's schedule, works with the production manager to ensure that deadlines are met, and attends screenings a few times a month. With so many people vying for the director's attention, Meacham has to quickly discern which needs are most pressing while still keeping the mood upbeat among production personnel—a situation that requires her to positively persuade people every step of the way.

To Meacham, treating people with respect is a central part of persuasion, especially in her industry: "If the crew does not respect you, they will not work for you in the most efficient manner possible, which throws everyone off," she says. The stress of a deadline can sometimes derail a person's efforts to communicate in a positive and persuasive way. How does Meacham combat such a professional mishap? By recognizing that a production crew's time is every bit as valuable as her own: "I have to respect everyone's deadlines and communicate with them in ways that get both sides of the job done. Often, I wish I could add six more hours to the day just to get every issue addressed."

Looking back, Meacham attributes her quick rise to a seemingly simple skill: "I think one of the biggest reasons why I moved up so quickly is because I learned how to be an effective communicator."

Questions

1. According to Meacham, what is the key to her ability to successfully persuade others?
2. Based on Meacham's job description, what types of persuading do you imagine she does?

Source: Brooke Meacham in discussion with the author, September 2009.

Exhibit 9-18
An Example of Visual Communication, or Rhetoric

Six Additional Principles of Persuasion

If you use the techniques we have discussed to frame your messages in a positive and inspiring way, you will be well on the way to becoming a persuasive communicator. Assuming you utilize them ethically, you can also use the following six additional principles of persuasion developed by Robert Cialdini, the most-cited expert on persuasion and influence in the world:

1. ***Reciprocity.*** People like to work with people who help them.
2. ***Authority.*** People listen to others when they respect their judgment, actions, and results they get.
3. ***Scarcity.*** If people think something is unique or scarce, they will want it more.
4. ***Consistency and commitment.*** People follow through on their promises when they commit to them verbally or in writing.
5. ***Social proof.*** People are influenced by the behavior of others.
6. ***Liking.*** People are persuaded by those they like.

The Principle of Reciprocity

Think of the principle of reciprocity as "give and take." When someone gives us something for free, we tend to feel obligated to reciprocate. Conversely, if we give something to someone, they may feel inclined to give us something in return. Bribery, of course, is an unethical form of reciprocity. By contrast, consider the 2010 Hope for Haiti telethon. The telethon enlisted celebrities and musicians from all walks of life to perform, talk about the devastation the Haiti earthquake caused, and take calls from people pledging donations toward the relief effort. The lure of being able to talk personally on the phone with celebrities like George Clooney, Cindy Crawford, Reese Witherspoon, Drew Barrymore, and Julia Roberts caused many people to open their pocketbooks wider than they might have done otherwise. Talking to the celebrities made donors feel like they received something of value.

The Principle of Authority

According to conservative estimates, Americans are exposed to at least 250 advertisements a day. In order to process the information, we often defer to other people who are experts on certain subjects. If you have legitimate credentials in an area, make them known. People will be more likely to listen to you because of your expertise. Don't, however, exaggerate your level of expertise.

An extreme example of exaggerating one's expertise is depicted in the 2002 film *Catch Me If You Can,* starring Leonardo DiCaprio. The movie is based on the true story of Frank Abagnale Jr. In the 1960s, Abagnale forged millions of dollars worth of checks by posing as a number of "experts": a pilot, an attorney, and even a doctor. Eventually he was caught and sentenced to 12 months in a French prison, 6 months in a Swedish prison, and 12 years in a U.S. prison for his crimes. (Interestingly, Abagnale now runs his own fraud consultation company and is a lecturer at the FBI Academy.)

The Principle of Scarcity

Telling people there are only a few products left to be purchased is the idea behind the scarcity principle. Consumers are more likely to respond to messages that offer unique and limited opportunities. You have probably noticed that bands often announce their concert dates way in advance in an attempt to sell out on their shows. The public, in their haste to get tickets, often purchases so many seats the concerts sell out the first day. The bands' agents then schedule second and sometimes third nights for the bands to play. Do you have something that is truly scarce? If so, you can ethically use the principle of scarcity. Tell prospective employers about it during the job search process.

The Principle of Commitment and Consistency

The principle of commitment and consistency is probably the most difficult of the six to explain. One, it states that people like consistency and dislike contradictions. They prefer to rely on previous decisions when making new ones. Every Labor Day weekend, the *Jerry Lewis Telethon* uses the same format to raise money for kids who suffer from Muscular Dystrophy.

The consistent and predictable program is watched year after year by viewers who regularly donate to the cause. By consistently airing the show year after year, the *Jerry Lewis Telethon* has created an outlet for committed viewers to donate to an admirable cause they might otherwise fail to remember.

Second, the principle states that people are more likely to stick with their decisions when they commit to them publicly. Because they are more likely to follow through on them, asking people to write down their commitments is a very persuasive technique. In addition, small commitments tend to lead to larger ones, so ask for small ones first.

Good looks might persuade people, but there's a limit to how they should be used. Just ask Abercrombie & Fitch. The fashion leader was sued for purging sales associates when they gained weight, experienced a breakout, or simply didn't have the right look. The firm eventually agreed to a settlement with the plaintiffs.

The Principle of Social Proof

Social proof is the adult equivalent of peer pressure. According to the principle, people buy, do, or believe things when they see other people like them doing the same. Companies often use testimonials and images of happy customers in their marketing materials for this reason. You can use the principle of social proof ethically by discussing with others the positive interactions you have had with employees or customers. Many people do so on blogs, Facebook, and consumer-product rating Web sites.

The principle of social proof can be abused, though. Due to the negative attention it received, in 2008, R.J. Reynolds, the maker of Camel cigarettes, discontinued running magazine ads showing young people smoking in pool halls and other public places. It was not the first time the company had come under scrutiny for trying to influence teenagers to smoke.

The Principle of Liking

Most people are influenced by people they like. We like people who:

- are physically attractive (a situation that is unfair but true)[6]
- are similar to us
- praise us and show they like us

Look for similarities between you and your audience. Whether it's a coworker, a client, or a customer, get to know that person and find out what you have in common. By focusing on those commonalities, you foster a positive environment where you can better persuade. Be lavish with your praise in the workplace. If someone is doing a great job, say so. Put it in a memo as well; people love to see themselves praised in writing. Choose to like those who aren't necessarily likeable. Dig a little deeper with these people. If you do, you might discover someone who is quite likeable and whom you respect.

Summary *Synthesize What You Have Learned*

1. What are persuasive messages?

Persuasive messages persuade readers to change their beliefs or actions. Sometimes these messages request a special type of treatment or action. Planning a successful persuasive message involves knowing your purpose, your audience, the desired action or result, and your culture.

2. What makes a message persuasive?

The AIDA approach is very useful in structuring a persuasive message. AIDA is an acronym that stands for *attention, interest, desire,* and *action.* Additionally, creating trust makes you more persuasive. People must trust you before they will believe you. To create trust you must come across as credible. This means you must be factual, specific, and reliable. Finally, set the right tone. It's not just what you say; it's how you say it. The right tone is one that is not arrogant, parental, or stuffy. Instead, it's friendly, straightforward, and shows your enthusiasm for the subject and your respect for your audience.

3. What types of messages use persuasion?

Persuasive messages include external requests for favors or actions, internal requests for favors or actions (flowing upward), internal requests for favors or actions (flowing downward), sales letters, sales e-mails, and press releases.

4. How do you persuade ethically?

Remember that people make decisions based on emotion and then use facts to rationalize them. When you use facts, you can present your reasoning with analogies (comparisons), deduction (main point first, then details), or induction (details first, then main point). When you appeal to the emotions, focus on building trust, helping people feel comfortable with their decisions, and using words that evoke positive emotions.

Robert Cialdini's six principles of persuasion, if used ethically, can also be very persuasive.

1. ***Reciprocity.*** People like to work with people who help them.
2. ***Authority.*** People listen to others when they respect their judgment, actions, and results they get.
3. ***Scarcity.*** If people think something is unique or scarce, they will want it more.
4. ***Consistency and commitment.*** People follow through on their promises when they commit to them verbally or in writing.
5. ***Social proof.*** People are influenced by the behavior of others.
6. ***Liking.*** People are persuaded by those they like.

Know It *Reflect, Respond, and Express*

Build Your Critical Thinking Skills

Critical Thinking Questions

1. Visit a Web site for a major credit company such as Experian or TransUnion. Starting on the home page, analyze how the company tries to persuade the consumer using the AIDA structure. Explore the other pages linked to the Web site. How does the company attempt to gain your trust and build their credibility? What is the main persuasive message they present to consumers?
2. What affect can a testimonial have on a persuasive message? Find an advertisement that utilizes the testimonial approach and write an analysis about how the testimonial may work on a consumer and how the approach can be used in business communication.
3. Using a search engine such as Google or Bing, research examples of euphemisms and analyze them in terms of how each one is insincere or deceptive.
4. Imagine you are a manager who receives multiple complaints about a product from a customer. The customer has left phone messages and written e-mails. You suspect the issue is user error, not a problem with the product. How could you persuasively address the complaints? What possible solutions could you offer the customer?
5. Consider the idea of repetition and how it applies to ethical persuasive messages, specifically circular reasoning and presentation of evidence. What impression do you have of a company trying to persuade you with repetition rather than facts?

Critical Thinking Scenario

As a TV station manager, Nina sometimes has to deliver unwelcome information. Recently, it has come to her attention that one of her employees, a camera operator named Tobias, has been late to work repeatedly. Tobias is well known around the station as a funny guy and a competent worker. Whenever new employees have questions, Nina knows Tobias is more than happy to provide them with answers.

Hoping to make an impact on his work ethic but not lose him as an employee, Nina decides that a firmly written disciplinary notice would be the best way to both reinforce his value as a worker and let him know that such behavior is inappropriate. As she plans her message, what must she keep in mind? What should Nina avoid?

Now, imagine you are in Nina's shoes. Using AIDA, create a brief outline of Nina's message. Be sure to include the moment of goodwill, the action Tobias must take, as well as the consequence if he does not (firing). Then answer the following questions:

1. When organizing this message, why is an inductive approach better than a deductive one?
2. What's the benefit of creating goodwill?
3. How do trust and credibility affect the impact of Nina's message upon Tobias?

Write It *Draft, Revise, and Finalize*

Create Your Own Success Story

1. Here's your chance to put on your analyst's hat and review persuasive messages you find in ads, letters to the editor, or opinion blogs.
   - **a.** Find three messages that you feel are ineffective, obnoxious, offensive, or silly. What are their biggest mistakes?
   - **b.** Pick the worst message in the group and revise it according to the principles you've learned in this chapter.
2. Think of a change you would like to see happen in your current class, such as an extension for homework or more opportunity for group work in class. Choose a method of persuasion and write a memo addressed to either the class or your instructor, depending on the persuasive message. How would you organize the message? What would you use to appeal to your audience? What is the process you would need to present for the proposed change to be implemented?
3. Research the term "circular reasoning" on the Internet or in your library. List a few examples you find in your research and revise the statements to remove the circular aspects of the message.
4. Practice applying logical appeal using an analogy, inductive reasoning, and deductive reasoning. Develop an argument for a textbook rental service through your institution's bookstore and write a persuasive paragraph for each type of logical reasoning.
5. Write a short anecdote or story to use as an emotional appeal to inspire an audience to follow through with a task that is difficult, such as completing school. Exchange the anecdote or story with your classmates and refine the details in pairs.

Speak It *Discuss, Listen, and Understand*

Build Your Leadership and Teamwork Skills

1. Get into groups of three. Each person should come up with a quick idea for a movie and pitch it to two producers—your group members. Each pitch should be brief, to the point, and no longer than three minutes. Like all good persuasive messages, it should include some of these principles mentioned in the chapter:
   - Reciprocity
   - Authority
   - Scarcity
   - Commitment
   - Consistency
   - Social Proof
   - Liking

   When you're ready, present your idea to one another. Then discuss as a group which persuasion tools were used in each message and which could have been included or excluded.
2. In groups or as a class, list a few examples of persuasive messages you have delivered or received, such as students trying to persuade an instructor to postpone a test.
3. In small groups, discuss the importance of tone in a persuasive message. How do credibility, sincerity, and a positive framework affect the tone you use?
4. In small groups or as a class, discuss the three tones to avoid when writing persuasive messages. Compose a persuasive message attempting to convince your instructor to delay the start of class using the parental, arrogant, or

stuffy tone. Exchange your message with another group and revise the inappropriate tones.

5. In small groups, discuss the importance of trust when composing persuasive messages and how you can build trust with your audience.
6. In small groups, analyze the principle of liking. What three elements of this principle can you use in business communication? How do you use the principle of liking in your workplace? Write a brief summary of your findings to share with the class.
7. In groups or as a class, discuss the principle of commitment and consistency. Why do you think we are uncomfortable with contradictory statements? What is the difference between a small and a large commitment? How is taking a stand or position on a topic a commitment to that topic?

Do It *Document Your Success Track Record*

Build Your e-Portfolio

Think of a cause that you feel strongly about on campus. An example might be encouraging your school to conserve energy and paper, or addressing the issue of obesity with classmates.

1. Take some time and research the issue: who's against it, who's for it, and why. What will be difficult and/or controversial about pursuing these causes? Find out if there are programs aimed at accomplishing the task or if some need to be created.
2. Next, draft a letter to a well-known person in the media who could champion your cause. The letter should use at least some of the persuasion techniques laid out in the chapter. As you write, keep these questions in mind:
   - Who am I writing to and why? Does the person have a history of speaking out for causes like the one I am advocating?
   - Is my subject well known or does it require more explanation?
   - Am I using relevant persuasion techniques like social pressure or authority? Why should the receiver of my message listen to what I have to say?
   - What exactly do I want to have happen? Is there a clear call to action in my message?

Once you've written out your letter, go back over it for grammar, punctuation, and spelling errors. When you feel that you've gotten it as close to perfect as possible, turn it in to your professor for his or her comments. Then revise it accordingly and add it to your growing portfolio of professional business messages.

Business in Action

Tom Cruise Fails to Persuade Brooke Shields . . . and a Lot of Other People

As this chapter demonstrated, persuasion and the entertainment industry often go hand in hand. Generally, the connection is professional, such as screenwriters pitching stories. Sometimes, however, the connection is less formal and more personal.

Take the media event of actor Tom Cruise's attack on actress Brooke Shields a few years ago. Cruise was invited on the *Today* show to promote his latest movie, *War of the Worlds*. Instead, he got off-topic and decided to use his interview time with show host Matt Lauer to condemn Shields' use of antidepressants for her postpartum depression. Rather than talk about his movie, he chose to use his onscreen personality to persuade his audience that psychiatric drugs are not an acceptable treatment method for depression, and that the actress should have used vitamins instead. Was he successful? You be the judge.

In the interview,[7] Cruise made it clear that he did not condone psychiatric medicine as an effective therapy for mental illness. Initially, Cruise attempted to establish his credibility without concrete proof. According to the MSNBC show transcript, the actor said, "When I started studying the history of psychiatry, I understood more and more why I didn't believe in psychology." Later in the interview, he alienated his audience by shutting down the opposition when he said, "Here's the problem. You don't know the history of psychiatry. I do." Although he had no formal education in the study of psychiatry, he felt comfortable attacking his interviewer who suffered from the same lack of education. Behaving in a hypocritical manner destroys credibility and makes it difficult to persuade others of your opinion.

More than anything, Cruise missed an opportunity to effectively persuade his audience with real research and logical reasoning. By making extreme claims using words like *never* and *the only way,* Cruise left his audience feeling attacked and wary of his black-or-white attitude toward antidepressants. He provided no examples of cases where an alternative therapy had improved the effects of postpartum depression. He ignored Lauer's point that Shields had experienced a significant mood improvement from the antidepressants; and he frequently cut off the host to interject his own opinions.

When it came to using logic and emotion, Cruise lacked facts and showed no concern for the other person's point of view. His methods of persuasion were poor and he basically showed his audience the steps to losing a persuasive argument. In this instance, it becomes clear that unpersuasive arguments come at a price: for Cruise, he suffered a blow to his reputation, and his production company Cruise/Wagner Productions was eventually dropped by parent-company Paramount Pictures, an alliance with a 14-year history.

Eventually, Cruise called Shields to apologize for his comments. Hollywood, the entertainment Web site, states that he also made a second appearance on the Today show to discuss the first interview. "After looking at it," Cruise reflected, "it's not what I had intended. That's one of those things that you go, 'I could have handled that better.' I didn't communicate it the way that I wanted to communicate it. That's not who I am . . . I think I learned a really good lesson."

Questions

1. What were some mistakes Cruise made in terms of tone and persuasive methods?
2. What would you have done differently if you wanted to communicate Cruise's message?

Source: "Brooke Shields Blasts Cruise's "Ridiculous Rant'," *MSNBC,* June 25, 2005, http://www.msnbc.msn.com/id/8343368; "Cruise Slams Shields' Drug Use," *World Entertainment News Network,* May 25, 2005, http://www.hollywood.com/news/Tom_Cruise_Slams_Brooke_Shields_Drug_Use/2440860.

Key Terms

AIDA. Acronym that stands for *attention, interest, desire* and *action. (p. 237)*

Analogy. A comparison between two ideas or things, one of which is familiar to your audience. *(p. 253)*

Arrogant tone. A condescending and patronizing tone of voice that can alienate your audience. *(p. 240)*

Credibility. Refers to how your audience perceives you—whether or not they find you believable and trustworthy. *(p. 238)*

Deduction. A reasoning process that begins with a general idea and then moves toward a specific conclusion. *(p. 253)*

Direct sales messages. Letters or e-mails used to sell goods and services directly to a large number of customers without the help of a salesperson. *(p. 244)*

Euphemism. A mild or vague expression that is substituted for a potentially negative or offensive one. *(p. 251)*

External requests. Requests made of people and firms outside your organization. *(p. 242)*

Induction. A process of reasoning that begins with specific details to build toward a general conclusion. *(p. 253)*

Internal requests. Requests made within an organization. *(p. 243)*

Manipulation. The process of influencing people in unfair or devious ways. *(p. 251)*

Metaphor. A figure of speech comparing two unlike things that have something in common. *(p. 237)*

Overselling. Promising more than you can deliver. *(p. 251)*

Parental tone. Scolds or tells people what to do. *(p. 240)*

Persuasive message. A message that persuades readers to change their beliefs or actions. *(p. 236)*

Press release. An announcement about your company to the media. The announcement resembles a news article. The information in the press release might include details about your firm's new CEO, product, location, or major initiative it is undertaking. *(p. 248)*

Requests for favors or actions. Messages asking people to make decisions or take some action. *(p. 242)*

Shock tactics. A message that causes the audience to react on an emotional level. *(p. 237)*

Stuffy tone. A tone of voice that tries to make you or your message sound more important. The tone is usually overly formal. *(p. 241)*

Visual communication (visual rhetoric). Using images to persuade people. *(p. 254)*

Review Questions *Test Yourself*

1. Define a persuasive message.
2. Explain what the AIDA structure for persuasive messages is, and give a brief description of each step.
3. How can you build your credibility so as to be persuasive?
4. What questions can you ask yourself to clarify your intentions of a persuasive message? What does clarifying your intentions help you accomplish?
5. What are euphemisms? Why should you avoid euphemisms when creating a persuasive message?
6. What elements make up an effective persuasive message?
7. What are ways to ensure your persuasive message remains ethical?
8. List the three methods of using logic in persuasive messages and briefly describe each one.

9. How can stories with the right words affect a persuasive message?
10. Define the principle of reciprocity and explain how you can use it in the workplace.
11. Define the principle of authority and explain how you can use it in the workplace.

Grammar Review *Mastering Accuracy*

Colons and Semicolons

Section I

Each of the following sentences contains one or more common errors in word usage, grammar, or style. Identify the errors. If you have trouble finding the errors, review Sections 2.2. through 2.3. in the handbook (Appendix D) at the back of this textbook.

1. The sink in the lady's lavatory is not draining properly, therefore someone must volunteer to stay late to await the plumber.
2. The copier is malfunctioning - jammed and out of toner, and it's also missing staples!
3. We're focusing on several areas of organizational policy; goals, planning, implementation, assessment: and evaluation.
4. In *Less than Zero;* Bret Easton Ellis highlights the agony of bored, rich L.A. socialites suffering from anomie: the brutal, violent nature of drug dependency; and the pain of leading a directionless existence.
5. Douglas E. Winter: a lawyer and writer; understands how to relate real life experience to his novels; he often incorporates his knowledge of the law to form his characters.
6. It's important to be able to adapt to change in modern society, you will be more valuable: to your employer, as well.
7. The writers from Canton, Ohio, Chicago, Illinois, Seattle, Washington, and Tucson, Arizona, all gathered in the courtyard to discuss the next great American novel.
8. Remember to rehearse your presentation for, tomorrow's advisory meeting, the corporate advisors will be watching.
9. Our staff maintains an active presence, on campus, nevertheless, I would like all employees to be even more visible.
10. Since authorities have yet to name, a suspect, members of a local neighborhood committee formulated their own hypothesis; as to the arsonist's identity: me.

Section II

On a separate sheet of paper, rewrite the following sentences so they are clearer, more professional sounding, grammatically correct, and goodwill oriented.

1. Our corporate office would like all employees to get up to speed on this new crucial merger.
2. Chances are, the meeting will run over and we'll all have to stay later than we want.
3. Be ready to be on call tomorrow in case something stupid happens!
4. I kinda liked listening to your presentation; however, your voice was so shrill in the microphone!
5. Cynthia from Davenport, Iowa; Jonathan from Phoenix, Arizona; and Judy from Las Vegas, Nevada are the guys who bought the old warehouse to make it into a new deli.
6. All students everywhere should remember to continue to practice business communication, even after the end of the class, so as to remain aware and prepared for anything and everything.
7. The brand new administrator will hit our campus and all employees should get ready for her visit.
8. Sarah's credentials were kinda sketchy and called into question as her manager has still not received transcripts, recommendation, letters or a writing sample and this is not good for her image.
9. The University of Arizona, where I would like to teach, is well known for a number of famous writers, and poets, and has an established library of rare volumes, as well as an extensive selection of first editions.
10. All instructors in order to remaining good standing are required to complete their portfolios on time yet some do not and this will reflect poorly.

Extra Resources *Tools You Can Use*

Books

- Camp, Lindsay. Can I Change Your Mind? *The Craft and Art of Persuasive Writing.* London, UK: A&C Black, 2007.
- Davies, Roger H. B. *Mastering Communications: 10 Secrets to Fast, Clear, Persuasive Communications.* Toronto: McLuhan & Davies Communications, Inc., 2008.
- Goldstein, Noah J., Steve J. Martin, and Robert B. Cialdini. *Yes! 50 Scientifically Proven Ways to Be Persuasive.* New York: Free Press, 2008.
- Reiman, Tonya. *The Yes Factor: Get What You Want. Say What You Mean. The Secrets of Persuasive Communication.* United States: Hudson Street Press, 2010.
- Reina, Dennis and Michelle Reina. *Trust and Betrayal in the Workplace: Building Effective Relationships in Your Organization.* San Francisco: Berrett-Koehler, 2006.

Web Sites

- Abbott, Robert F, "Persuasive Communication in Business," *The Sideroad.*
- Marcus, Sander, "Top 7 Keys To Persuasive Writing," *Top7Business.*
- Thang, Jens, "How to Persuade More Effectively: 6 Principles to Help You Be More Persuasive Immediately," *TheNegotiation Guru.com.*
- "Persuasive Communication Workshop: Moving Between Metaphors," *MIT Tech TV.*

"So much to write—so little time—so much at stake!"[1]

— **Rachael McAlpine,** author and Web content consultant

CHAPTER 10

Writing Reports and Proposals

Compiling and Interpreting Business Information

LEARNING OBJECTIVE QUESTIONS

1. When do reports and proposals need to be written in the workplace and for whom?
2. What types of personal reports and logs do employees typically keep?
3. What types of informal progress reports do employees write?
4. What types of formal reports and proposals do employees write?
5. How are research reports written and organized?
6. What are feasibility reports and what do they consist of?

PEARSON mybcommlab Access interactive videos, simulations, sample documents, document makeovers, and assessment quizzes in Chapter 10 of **mybcommlab.com** for mastery of this chapter's objectives.

>>> **Brandon**, a recent college graduate with a degree in accounting, just got a job at a local bank in its finance and planning department. He wasn't sure if banking was for him. However, the people he met during the interview seemed friendly and passionate about their work, so he decided to accept the position.

Brandon has always loved working with numbers, which is why he got a degree in accounting. Then, at the end of his second week on the job, his boss asked him for a detailed status report. Brandon struggled to write it. Worse yet, his boss had a hard time understanding what he wrote.

A few weeks later the manager of the bank's loans department asked Brandon to contribute to an RFP (request for proposal). "RFP? What's that?" was all he could think to say. Next, a member of the bank's marketing team asked him to contribute material for a bank brochure designed to attract business customers.

"I don't get it," Brandon recently said to a friend, "I got into banking and accounting for the numbers, and all I'm doing is writing." Brandon quickly learned that writing is an integral part of doing business, no matter what field you're in.

<<< Brandon

In this chapter, you will move beyond composing personal e-mails and memos to writing reports and proposals. **Reports** typically discuss things that have already happened, whereas **proposals** discuss things that have not yet happened. The reports and proposals you write will vary by industry, and even by the company, department, or team in which you work. For example, accident reports are common in the insurance industry, whereas sales forecast reports are more common in the sales and marketing departments of retail or consumer goods companies. To keep things simple, the reports and proposals covered in this chapter are limited to those found in banking and finance.

There are a variety of job areas in banking and associated responsibilities, as **Exhibit 10-1** shows. According to the U.S. Department of Labor, the banking and finance industries are growing areas of employment. Nonetheless, as in all industries, the competition to gain new customers is always fierce. American Express is among the financial companies that have developed social networking sites to communicate with and attract new customers. American Expresss's site is designed to give small business owners a forum to discuss their problems while showcasing its finance-and-report-generating products that can help solve them.

Whether or not you choose a career in banking, written communication will become a vital part of your career. A well-written report could spell the difference between the success or failure of a project. A thoroughly researched report could mean a solution to a long-standing company problem as well as more respect and acknowledgement for you as the writer of the report.

Exhibit 10-1 Job Areas and Associated Responsibilities in Banking and Finance

Accounting
Analyze data, produce reports, and track profit and loss ratios.

Compliance
Ensure that a bank is in compliance with industry regulations on state and federal levels.

Data Processing
Process daily transactions related to checks, credit cards, debit cards, and deposits.

Human Resources
Get involved with recruiting and retaining personnel, managing their benefits, resolving employee conflicts, and sponsoring community events.

Loans
Help individuals and companies with loans for homes, cars, businesses, and construction.

Marketing
Come up with new ways to communicate the bank's services and products to reach new markets and increase revenues.

Personal Banking
Set up new accounts for individuals and businesses.

1 When Do Reports and Proposals Need to Be Written in the Workplace and for Whom?

Some reports are informal and for your eyes alone. Other reports and proposals are quite formal and designed to be read by many other people in the workplace as well as people outside of the organization:

- ***Peers.*** You will commonly write reports that your team members will read. The reports may be about research you have done, ideas you have, or suggestions for new ways of doing things.

- ***Your Manager.*** You will often write documents for your manager to read. The documents typically inform your manager of your progress on a project, problems you have solved, or accomplishments you're proud of.
- ***Other Departments.*** Occasionally you will be asked to contribute to reports that are distributed to other departments. Sometimes your reports will provide information that is important to an interdepartment project or cross-company initiative.
- ***Other Entities.*** You may be asked to contribute to reports and proposals that will be read outside of your company. They might be read by other businesses in your industry, government regulators, stockholders, or the general public.

The reader and the purpose of the document will affect its tone and content. Suppose you are writing a report for your manager about an initiative you took to solve a data processing problem in your firm's accounting department. Because your reader is a manager, you might decide to use a formal tone, provide hard facts about the problem and your solution, and highlight your contributions.

In general, you will write reports and proposals rather than make phone calls or send brief e-mails and memos when you need to 1) share a large amount of information that may include charts, tables, and illustrations, 2) distribute the information to a large number of people, and 3) provide a more formal way of documenting information. **Exhibit 10-2** shows

Exhibit 10-2 Typical Business Reports and Proposals

Reports and Proposals	Audience				
	Self	Peers	Your Manager	Other Departments	Other Entities
Personal Reports and Logs					
To-do list	X				
Daily log	X				
Progress Reports					
Weekly status report	X	X	X		
Monthly status report	X		X		
Annual accomplishments report	X		X		
Formal Proposals					
New project proposal			X	X	
Request for proposal (RFP)			X	X	X
Response to an RFP			X	X	X
Formal Reports					
Sales report		X	X	X	
Quarterly report		X	X	X	
Annual report	X	X	X	X	X
Research report		X	X	X	X
Feasibility report		X	X	X	X

the common reports and proposals you might be called upon to write in your career as well as who is likely to read them.

As a new hire, you probably won't write all of the reports and proposals listed in Exhibit 10-2. However, it's a good idea for you to get familiar with them. Also, many companies, departments, and teams have their own formats for the reports and proposals they create. If this is the case, you will need to learn to create reports and proposals that meet those standards.

2 What Types of Personal Reports and Logs Do Employees Typically Keep?

The personal reports and checklists mentioned in Exhibit 10-2 are brief, informal documents to help you keep track of your activities. Let's take a closer look at them.

To-Do Lists

A **to-do list** is a list of items you hope to accomplish on a given day. Some people like to make the list at the end of the day when they are thinking through the current day's events and planning the next day's tasks. Others like to make their list first thing in the morning. Keep the list handy throughout the day so you can check off completed tasks and add new ones as needed.

If the list gets too long, try prioritizing the items as A-B-C:

A) Must do
B) Need to do
C) Nice to do

DID YOU KNOW?

Pilots refer to checklists before takeoffs and landings so they don't forget any critical steps. The first checklist for pilots was developed in the 1930s by the jet-maker Boeing after the crash of a B-17 bomber.[2]

Once you decide what you must do on a given day, you can then decide which tasks you should do first. Many people use a system that management professionals recommend: the **shortest processing time (SPT) method.** With the shortest processing time (SPT) method, you do the task that is fastest to complete first—that is, the one with the shortest processing time. If you use the SPT method, you will be less likely to get bogged down with a lot of short tasks that stack up and overwhelm you. Tasks that do not get completed one day get moved to subsequent days or are perhaps dropped.

Amber Lopez, a senior loan processor at Seven Hills Bank, processes car loan applications submitted to the bank by car dealerships. She spends most of her day processing loans and identifying missing information, like insurance papers, signatures, and money disclosures. She also has a special project to find out whether the dealers that use the bank for their auto loans are satisfied with the bank's service. **Exhibit 10-3** shows Amber's to-do list.

Exhibit 10-3
A To-Do List

1. Read and respond to e-mail.
2. Process all incoming loans and identify issues.
3. Call Mary at ABC Motors to answer title questions.
4. Do insurance follow-up for Smith file.
5. Attend sales tax increase meeting at 3:00 P.M.
6. Research auto dealer satisfaction.

Daily Logs

Most people are aware that lawyers keep track of the hours they bill to clients. Companies that work with city, state, or federal government clients also require their employees to keep track of the time they spend on tasks so they can be billed properly to clients. Sometimes employees keep a **daily log (or planner)** to better manage their time. How often have you said to yourself, "I don't know where the day went?"

Exhibit 10-4 A Daily Log

Day	Date	Activity	Start	End	Hours
Tues.	3-23-2009	Listen to voice mail	8:30	8:45	0.25
		Read and respond to e-mail	8:45	9:30	0.75
		Follow up phone messages	9:30	9:45	0.25
		Break	9:45	10:00	0.25
		Attend department meeting for dealer event	10:00	11:00	1.00
		Read and respond to e-mail	11:00	11:15	0.25
		Process loans	11:15	12:00	0.75
		Lunch	12:00	1:00	1.00
		Check phone messages and e-mail	1:00	1:15	0.25
		Process more loans	1:15	2:45	1.50
		Read and respond to e-mail	2:45	3:00	0.25
		Attend sales tax increase meeting	3:00	4:00	1.00
		Break	4:00	4:15	0.25
		Call Mary at ABC Motors	4:15	4:30	0.25
		Do insurance follow-up on Smith file	4:30	4:45	0.25
		Organize and secure all loan materials	4:45	5:00	0.25

If you have problems finishing the items on your to-do list, try keeping a daily log. The log can be kept electronically or on paper. Use whichever format works best for you. **Exhibit 10-4** shows an example of a daily log. Above all, the log will help you prioritize your tasks.

3 What Types of Informal Progress Reports Do Employees Write?

Informal progress reports outline the progress employees and teams have made on various projects and activities. The reports are typically shared with their managers, who may incorporate some of the information into reports for their departments, other departments, or their managers.

Weekly Status Reports

A **weekly status report** like the one shown in **Exhibit 10-5** outlines the work you accomplished for the week. It can also include any problems you encountered and a brief overview of what you plan to do the following week. If you do not interact much with your manager, a weekly status report can be particularly helpful to him or her. It is also a good way for you

Exhibit 10-5
A Weekly Status Report

Weekly Status Report for: Amber Lopez
March 4–11, 2011

ACTIVITY	HOURS
Loan Processing	
Done: • Processed 150 loans. **Issues:** • 10 problems dealing with title searches, loan documentation, and insurance. **To Do:** • Resolve remaining issues. • Increase number of loans processed from 150 to 160.	30
Sales Research	
Done: • Called five auto dealers to find out whether they're satisfied with our services and, if not, why? What can we do better? • Summarized results of phone calls and sent e-mail to department. **Issues:** • None. **To Do:** • Call 5 more auto dealers to finish the study.	2
Meetings	
Done: • Attended weekly department meeting. • Attended sales-tax increase meeting. • Attended annual United Way meeting. **Issues:** Meetings cut into my loan processing time. **To Do:** • Attend only essential meetings.	3
Phone calls, e-mails, correspondence	
Done: • Responded to voice mail and e-mail as required. **Issues:** • Spending too much time on the phone and with e-mail. It cuts into my loan processing time. Any suggestions? **To Do:** • Follow up with e-mails and voice mails as necessary.	5
TOTAL	40

REAL INSIGHTS from a New Professional

Name: *Brianne Schmidt*
Title: *Associate*
Organization: *BMO Capital Markets*
Location: *Chicago, Illinois*

BY HER OWN ADMISSION, Brianne Schmidt used to be a bit of an introvert who loved numbers. Today Schmidt is a associate for BMO Capital Markets in Chicago, Illinois. BMO is a full-service North American financial services provider working with corporate, institutional, and government clients. "After working at BMO for the past one-and-a-half years, I'm more comfortable talking to people I don't know, more confident defending my ideas, and more persuasive in my business writing," she says.

Schmidt got into corporate banking because of her interest in finance and business. She interned with Hewlett-Packard's corporate finance department, and after graduation from the University of Notre Dame, she decided to interview with a variety of Chicago-based banks, including BMO. One of her friends worked at BMO and highly recommended the company. Schmidt wasn't sure what she wanted to do for the rest of her life, but she knew she wanted to live in the city and thought that BMO would be a good place to start.

Once she began working for BMO, Schmidt realized that banking was not just for people who were good with numbers. Bankers also needed good communication skills to establish relationships with corporate clients.

As an associate at BMO evaluating the credit profiles of healthcare clients, Schmidt has plenty of opportunities to fine-tune her verbal communication skills. She attends department meetings, mentors first-year analysts, and interacts frequently with clients. However, she has equal opportunity to work on her written communication skills. It's not uncommon for Schmidt to produce 15-page, credit-approval reports for potential customers. The reports are informative and persuasive documents that provide information about companies requesting loans. Such a write-up provides an overview of the company, presents its strengths and weaknesses, analyzes its historical financial situation, and defends its financial forecast. Schmidt must provide both soft and hard data to persuade BMO to give the company a loan.

Fifteen-page client write-ups aren't the only kinds of documents Schmidt writes. She puts to-do lists on her computer to keep her focused throughout the week. She compiles quarterly reports for credit executives who need to review high-risk accounts. She now keeps an Excel spreadsheet of her accomplishments so she can be prepared for her annual review. "The first year at BMO, I didn't keep track of my accomplishments and forgot about a lot of them. I won't make that mistake this year," she says.

Schmidt considers herself a much better communicator because of her work at BMO. She has learned how to write for business purposes. She knows how to organize information for her readers, present the right points, and pack more information into her reports while still keeping them concise. If she could offer a suggestion to college students, based on her experience at BMO, it would be this: "Write as much as you can, but when writing, keep your audience in mind. Only by writing for others can you learn how to persuade your readers to think the way you think."

Questions

1. What type of formal documents does Schmidt work on?
2. What type of informal checklists does Schmidt use to keep track of what she does?
3. How does Schmidt track her accomplishments? Why?
4. What does Schmidt think helps make people better writers?

Source: Brianne Schmidt in discussion with the author, June 2009.

to track your progress. Are you finishing all of your projects on time or just some of them? Are new projects coming up that prevent you from working on old ones?

Monthly Status Reports

Not all managers require weekly reports. However, many managers require monthly reports. You can consolidate your weekly status reports to create a monthly status report. **Exhibit 10-6** shows Amber's monthly status report. Besides tracking an employee's progress, monthly status reports track the progress of projects and teams. In this case, the accomplishments, issues, and plans are related to an entire project and its team, not just a single individual.

A monthly report identifies what you did during the month and issues that could affect your success.

Exhibit 10-6
A Monthly Status Report

Status Report: Amber Lopez
March 2011

Loan Processing

- Successfully processed 600 loan applications, which included resolving 20 exceptions.
- Currently have 15 loan applications outstanding.

Competitive Research on Dealer Loyalty

- Conducted phone surveys of 7 existing auto dealers for market loyalty.
- Produced a 10-page summary of the results and sent the summary to supervisor and department.

Process Improvements

- Noticed that dealers were complaining about loan turnaround times. Began to research ways to improve processing times.

PLANS FOR APRIL

Loan Processing

- Process at least 600 loan applications.
- Train processing intern to handle loan follow-ups to reduce my time on the phone and time with e-mail.

Competitive Research on Dealership Loyalty

- Plan a meeting and appreciation lunch for dealers to get more feedback on our services to them.

Processing Improvements

- Continue payment-improvement research.

Annual Accomplishments Reports

An **annual accomplishments report** like the one shown in **Exhibit 10-7** is an opportunity to identify the various projects you personally worked on during the year and write down what you have achieved. Doing so will be useful when you are preparing for a performance review. The report will also help you decide what new samples of work to put in your personal employment portfolio. Portfolios aren't just for artists. Everyone should keep samples of their best work.

Exhibit 10-7
An Annual Accomplishments Report

2011 Accomplishments for
Amber Lopez, Senior Loan Processor

1. Received 2,000 loans and processed 98 percent of them on time. Resolved all problems dealing with title, insurance, and income verification.

2. Initiated a dealer phone survey and followed up with a dealership luncheon. This resulted in greater dealer loyalty and a 2 percent increase in revenues earned from dealer-related loans.

3. Increased my efficiency by delegating loan processing follow-up duties to my assistant, whom I trained.

4. Put together and conducted a half-day training session for the department on reducing loan-processing times with online payments.

The accomplishments report should include the projects you worked on, your contributions, and the measurable end results to the company. Exhibit 10-7 shows an annual accomplishments list for Amber. Notice how she quantified the results of her work.

4 What Types of Formal Reports and Proposals Do Employees Write?

Formal reports and proposals are documents that are generally read by more people than just you and your manager and are widely distributed in organizations. Next, let's look at some of the most common reports and proposals you will encounter in the world of work.

New Project Proposals

Have you ever had to propose an idea on paper to persuade someone to go along with it? A **new project proposal** is a formal proposal for a new product, process, service, or job position a person or a team puts in writing for other people to read and consider. The proposal identifies a need, outlines how to meet that need, and explains the benefits of doing so. **Exhibit 10-8** on the next page shows a suggested outline for a typical project proposal.

■ For an interactive, real-world example of this topic, access this chapter's bcomm mini sim entitled Business Reports, located at **mybcommlab.com**

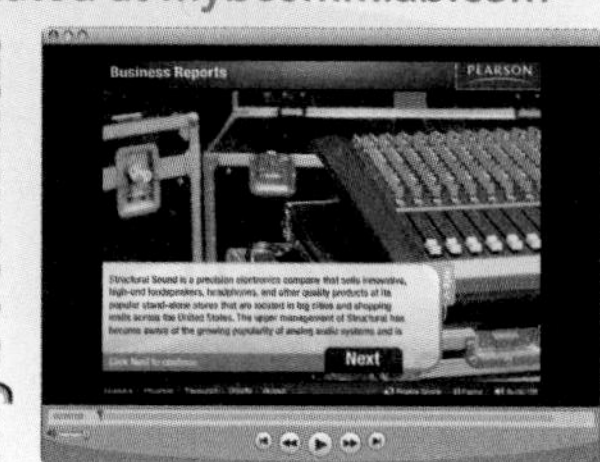

Consider James Desoto, a personal banker who put together a bank's FAQ sheet and posted it on the company's Web site. Six months later, James realized there were pieces of information still missing from the Web site that customers really needed, such as definitions of banking terms, details about the bank's financial strength, and more. He decided to propose the idea of an online "Community Banking Help Center" that would provide answers to customer questions about the bank, the security of their money, and the economy in general.

James sent the proposal to Maria Delgado, the head of the bank's finance and planning department. In the proposal, he followed a simple but effective structure. He a) provided background, b) explained the problem, c) presented a solution, and d) described the proposal's benefits as well as other details such as the team members in the best position to implement it and any risks it faced.

On page 275, **Exhibit 10-9a** shows the e-mail that James presented to Maria. The e-mail intrigued Maria enough that she read the attached proposal and loved it. **Exhibit 10-9b** shows the pages of the winning proposal. To read the actual project proposal, see Appendix 10A "Example Reports."

Requests for Proposals (RFPs)

A **request for proposal (RFP)** is a document an organization sends out inviting vendors to submit bids to provide the organization with a good or service. The RFP typically defines the product or service required and then asks for a response from vendors in a particular format. All vendors must develop their responses in the format so the organization can more easily compare the bids to determine which vendor should be awarded the job or contract. (For those of you in or considering careers in the nonprofit sector, writing a grant application package and instructions is very similar to writing an RFP.)

Structure of RFPs

The structure of an RFP varies by industry and organization. In general, government RFPs are longer and more detailed than private industry RFPs. The information for the RFP is typically gathered by a team of experienced people, each of whom is assigned a particular section. A technical writer then reviews the information to make the final RFP more understandable to the reader. The clearer and more precise the RFP is, the greater the chance that the resulting proposals from vendors will address the real needs of the organization. Once an RFP is finished, it is often posted on Web sites for contractors or is e-mailed to them. **Exhibit 10-10** on page 276 outlines the sections of a typical RFP that HUD or other government agencies might use.[3]

Some RFPs have far fewer sections than those shown in Exhibit 10-10. Others have more, especially if they come from the government. It is up to your company to decide just what needs to be put into an RFP to get responses from qualified vendors.

Exhibit 10-8
An Outline for a New Project Proposal

1. Title, Author, and Date

Provide the name of the proposal as well as your name and the date you are submitting it.

2. Table of Contents

List the topics and page numbers in the proposal.

3. Background

Give some background information describing the circumstances surrounding the problem that led to the proposal.

4. Problem

Outline the nature of the problem and state it as clearly as possible.

5. Suggested Solution

Write a brief overview of the solution you are suggesting.

6. Project Objectives

Explain how the project will affect your company's customers, operations, and finances. The objectives should be directly related to tangible outcomes such as customer satisfaction, efficiency, and revenue generation.

7. Project Team

Recommend the people or groups that should implement the proposed project.

8. Proposed Process

Outline the steps required to implement the project.

9. Assumptions and Constraints

Explain any assumptions made about the project and constraints or limitations it faces.

10. Risks and Concerns

Explain the risks or concerns associated with the project.

11. Benefits

Outline the benefits the organization will gain by implementing the project.

Responding to RFPs

If you are a member of a team responding to an RFP, the structure of your response will be dictated by the instructions in the RFP. Your team needs to carefully read the RFP, particularly the statement-of-work section, and then put together a response document that specifically addresses what is asked for. (In the nonprofit sector, applying for a grant and filling out a grant application package is very similar to writing a response to an RFP.)

The structure of an RFP response is dictated by the original RFP. Many companies assign the writing of RFP responses to technical writers who have expertise in specific industries. In fact, some writers specialize only in writing RFPs. However, small-business owners with no writers on staff must learn how to respond to RFPs themselves.

mybcommlab

Apply Exhibit 10-9a's key concepts by revising a new document. Go to Chapter 10 in mybcommlab.com and select Document Makeovers.

Exhibit 10-9a An E-mail Introducing a New Project Proposal

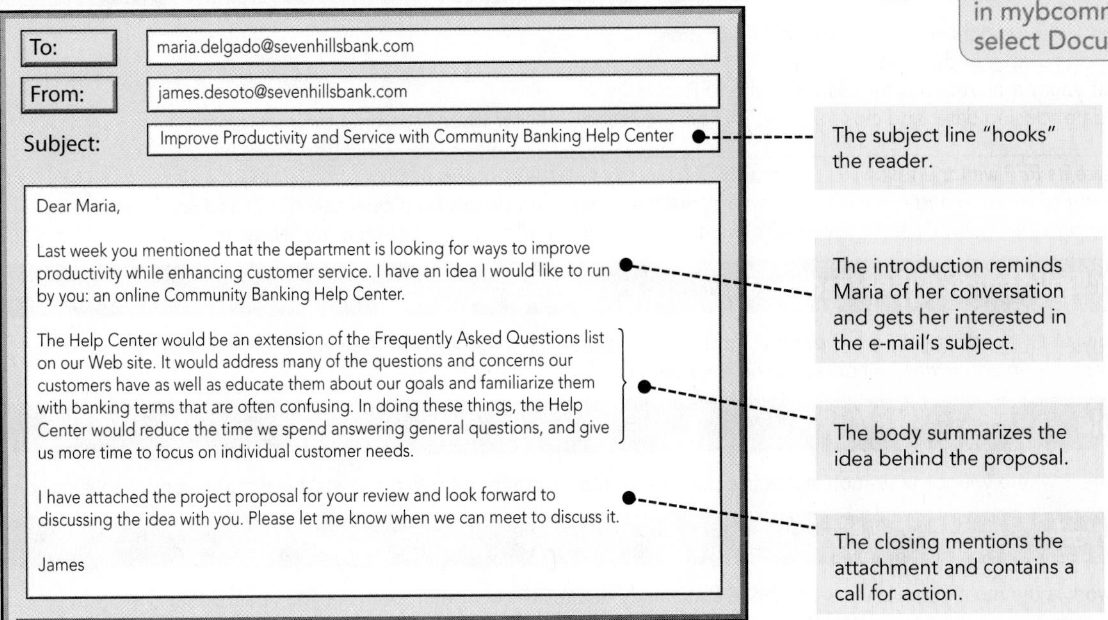

To: maria.delgado@sevenhillsbank.com

From: james.desoto@sevenhillsbank.com

Subject: Improve Productivity and Service with Community Banking Help Center

Dear Maria,

Last week you mentioned that the department is looking for ways to improve productivity while enhancing customer service. I have an idea I would like to run by you: an online Community Banking Help Center.

The Help Center would be an extension of the Frequently Asked Questions list on our Web site. It would address many of the questions and concerns our customers have as well as educate them about our goals and familiarize them with banking terms that are often confusing. In doing these things, the Help Center would reduce the time we spend answering general questions, and give us more time to focus on individual customer needs.

I have attached the project proposal for your review and look forward to discussing the idea with you. Please let me know when we can meet to discuss it.

James

The subject line "hooks" the reader.
The introduction reminds Maria of her conversation and gets her interested in the e-mail's subject.
The body summarizes the idea behind the proposal.
The closing mentions the attachment and contains a call for action.

Exhibit 10-9b A New Project Proposal

THE PROS AND CONS OF CREATING A
COMMUNITY BANKING ONLINE HELP CENTER

Prepared for
Seven Hills Bank Finance and Planning Department

Prepared by
James Desoto
Personal Banker
ext. 659

June 28, 2011

Table of Contents

Background	1
Problem	1
Suggested Solution	1
Project Objectives	1
Project Team	2
Proposed Process	2
Assumptions and Constraints	3
Risks and Concerns	3

Background

Two years ago Seven Hills Bank created a "frequently asked questions" (FAQ) list to better serve its customers. The list of questions grew and was later posted to our bank's Web site. Based in Web site statistics, more than 75 internal and external customers visit the FAQ page each day, spending 30 to 120 seconds on the page. The page is quite popular by statistical standards.

Problem

Customers are now starting to ask questions about the bank's financial security and the economy—questions that aren't really part of a traditional FAQ list. These questions are coming in the form of phone calls and in-bank visits. Additionally, the length of the FAQ list makes it difficult for Web site visitors to quickly find the information they need.

Suggested Solution

Adding an online "Community Banking Help Center" (hereafter referred to as "online Help Center"), which would be a sub-site of our current Web site, could potentially solve the problem. Launching such a site would give customers access to much-needed, up-to-date information with the click of a mouse, allowing Seven Hills Bank's staff to focus on other activities. The online Help Center would also publicize the bank's dedication to offering superior customer service, efforts to educate customers about good money management practices, efforts to improve the economy by lending to businesses and individuals, and reinforce optimism about the bank's financial strength.

The online Help Center would do so by providing the following information:

- **Glossary.** A glossary of common financial and banking terms.
- **FAQs.** Questions our customers typically ask.
- **Testimonials.** Success stories from customers that are related to the FAQs.
- **FDIC.** A clear explanation of FDIC insurance.
- **Financial Strength.** A discussion of our conservative management style, including the fact that Seven Hills Bank has never made subprime loans.
- **Our Mission and the Economy.** How we are helping the community during a difficult economy.

Project Objectives

The objectives of the online Help Center are as follows:

Customers

- Provide one-stop shopping for customers and potential customers with questions.
- Increase our customers' understanding of the bank's financial security.
- Reduce fears about mortgage and loan rates, foreclosures, and bank closings.
- Reduce the number of information questions our bankers deal with on the phone or in person to increase the amount of time available for dealing with specific customer needs (opening accounts, getting loans, understanding their statements, and so forth).

Operations

- Gradually transition Web site maintenance to the IT team, who is more experienced and efficient with Web sites than I am.

Sales

- Increase the number of new customers, new mortgages, and new loans by providing real-world answers and customer testimonials on the Web site.

Project Team

The following individuals have agreed to help implement the online Help Center, should the project be undertaken.

- James Desoto, Personal Banker (Project Leader)
- Aaron Kuntz, Public Relations Intern
- Maria Delgado, Director of Finance and Planning
- Casey Han, IT Specialist

Proposed Process

1. Aaron Kuntz will interview members of each department to find out what questions are most often asked by customers. Kuntz will also compile a list of potential terms customers need to know for an online glossary.
2. The project team will contact members of the executive staff to gather information about Seven Hill's Bank financial strength and the economy.
3. The project team will also create a site map identifying the potential Web pages for the online Help Center and how they will be organized.
4. The team will also develop a schedule with milestones, based on the size and structure of the Web map, as well as the volume of information collected.
5. I will review and revise the material Aaron provides me and pass it to my manager, Maria Delgado, for final approval.
6. The project team will also collectively develop layouts for the Web pages that follow corporate branding guidelines.
7. The final content for the Web site will be converted into plain text format and then given to the IT department, along with the mockups illustrating the layouts of each Web page.
8. The IT department will build the pages and post the information to a beta site for final review by the executive committee and our project team, which will test all of the links.
9. We will collect comments from the executive committee and project team, mark up the plain text files with those comments, and pass them on to the IT department for final implementation.
10. Paper and e-mail announcements will be distributed to all internal and external customers announcing the online Help Center and how to access it.

Note: Throughout the process, management will be kept apprised of the project's progress with regular status reports.

Assumptions and Constraints

Based on an initial analysis of the information customers try to find online, by phone, or in person, the online Help Center will consist of an estimated 7–10 Web pages. The amount of time each team member will spend to plan and implement the site should not exceed two hours per week. This level of commitment should not interfere with the members' normal job duties.

Risks and Concerns

The team's analysis might uncover the need for a more comprehensive online Help Center. However, if this is the case, we could readily launch the smaller, 7–10 page Web site and enhance it at a later date. This will allow us to gather feedback from customers before we consider expanding the site.

Exhibit 10-10 An Outline of an RFP Sent Out by HUD or Another Government Organization

1. Introduction

The introduction provides vendors with the following information:
- Title and identifying number of the RFP.
- Overview of what your organization is requesting in the RFP.
- The RFP's issue date, closing date, and closing time. This ensures vendors know when to submit their responses.

HUD might introduce its RFP with the following paragraph:
"The U.S. Department of Housing and Urban Development (HUD) is seeking proposals from qualified banks and credit unions in the United States to provide financial services to HUD's clients: low-income and minority, first-time homebuyers."

2. Standard Form: Solicitation, Offer, and Award

The standard form typically contains your organization's contact information, an area in which the vendor provides its contact information, and information about who will be awarding the contract.

3. Pricing Schedule

The pricing schedule is where your organization states the duration of the contract and lists the costs it wants the vendor to supply.

4. Statement of Work

The statement of work is the most important part of the RFP. It clearly defines the scope of the work you need done. The section begins with an objective to help vendors understand why your organization needs assistance. Then it itemizes the specific tasks that need to be done. The tasks vary by company but often include: services, training, testing, and inspection.

A HUD RFP would itemize the specific financial services HUD is looking for.

5. Vendor Qualifications

Information is requested about the vendor's specific qualifications and capabilities.

A HUD RFP might ask vendors questions such as the following:
- *How long have you been in business?*
- *What is your history of serving low-income families?*
- *How many branches do you have? Where are they located? Are any of them in low-income areas or near public transportation?*
- *What percentage of your loans are less than $200,000?*
- *Do you provide special programs for low-income families?*
- *What government programs do you participate in?*

(Continued)

Keep in mind that the organization that issued the RFP needs help. Your response needs to convince the organization that your team or company has the knowledge and experience needed to provide the right solution. The following guidelines will help ensure that yours are successful.

1. ***Organize your response correctly.*** Organize your response according to the outline provided in the RFP.
2. ***Include the right information.*** Include only information that specifically addresses items requested in the RFP. Do not skip any items, and do not add any items.
3. ***Write with the reader(s) in mind.*** Your team's document will typically be read by a team of reviewers, with each person reading a particular section. The readers usually have little time, so keep your document clear and to the point.
4. ***Edit for one voice.*** Have one member of the team review the entire response to the RFP and edit it so it sounds like one person wrote it.
5. ***Hold a group review.*** Before you send out the response, have it reviewed by a small group of people who are similar to those who will be reading it. You might ask managers to review it who are unfamiliar with the solution you are proposing. Doing so will give you a better idea about whether the recipients of the RFP will be able to understand it or not.
6. ***Proofread the document.*** Don't give your readers any excuse to turn down your response. Before sending a response, do the following:

6. Personnel Requirements

Vendors are asked to describe their personnel and provide their résumés in this section.

HUD might ask for the résumé of a bank's underwriter to see if the underwriter is certified to underwrite different types of government-sponsored loans.

7. Deliveries and Performance

When you expect vendors to deliver their goods and services (if awarded a contract), how your company plans to evaluate the vendor's performance, and what ongoing reports will be required from the vendor to track its progress are outlined.

8. Contract Administration

In the contract administration section, how your company will pay the vendor after the contract is awarded is explained.

9. Special Contract Requirements

Special requirements for winning the contract are outlined.

HUD might require a bank to have special computer or electronic equipment.

10. Instructions, Conditions, and Notices to Vendors

This portion of the RFP tells vendors exactly how to respond to the proposal.

11. Evaluation Factors for Award

How your company will evaluate vendors to make a decision about the award of the contract is explained here.

12. Attachments

Additional information to help the vendor better understand your organization's needs can be included as an attachment.

A HUD RFP might include standard job descriptions for required personnel or standard templates for résumés.

- ***Check for typos.*** Misspelled words can cause your document to be discarded by your readers.
- ***Format the document correctly.*** The instructions in an RFP are often very precise. They even go so far as to specify the font types, sizes, and margins that should be used. Follow the instructions exactly.

Sales Reports

Sales reports compare actual sales with projected sales. They are usually in a spreadsheet format and broken down by product or product category and include summary paragraphs to clarify objectives and action items. The sales numbers are usually shown by quarters, where Q1 is quarter 1 (January through March); Q2 is quarter 2 (April through June); Q3 is quarter 3 (July through September); and Q4 is quarter 4 (October through December). **Exhibit 10-11** on the next page shows a template for an annual sales report that needs to be completed for multiple products. The creator of the report then fills in the name of each product and its sales number in the "value" fields for each quarter.

Some sales reports are generated automatically by a company's data processing system. Other sales reports require data to be collected manually from different departments, the information analyzed, and then consolidated and formatted. Members of accounting, finance, or marketing departments typically perform this type of work.

Quarterly Reports

A **quarterly report** is much like a scorecard. Departments collect data on a quarterly basis and submit the information to upper-level managers. The managers then compile the data into a

Exhibit 10-11 A Template for an Annual Sales Report

	2011 Sales							
	Q1		Q2		Q3		Q4	
	Projected	Actual	Projected	Actual	Projected	Actual	Projected	Actual
Product A	value	value	value	value	value	value	value	value
Product B	value	value	value	value	value	value	value	value
Product C	value	value	value	value	value	value	value	value
Product D	value	value	value	value	value	value	value	value
Total Sales for Quarter:	Sum	Sum	Sum	Sum	Sum	Sum	Sum	Sum
							Projected Sales for 2011:	Sum
							Actual Sales for 2011:	Sum

report that represents the performance of the entire organization for that quarter. The information typically includes business and operation issues, audit results, and detailed performance tables. Upper-level executives typically read these reports to get a sense of how well the company is achieving its objectives. **Exhibit 10-12** shows a partial quarterly performance summary report for state banks insured by the FDIC (Federal Deposit Insurance Corporation). The figures in the report shown in the exhibit reflect the third-quarter performance of the banks for the years 2009 through 2011.

Annual Reports

An **annual report** is a federally required report published and distributed annually by a publicly traded company to its employees, customers, shareholders, the government, and the public. The annual report provides information about how well the firm met its objectives for the year, how well the business is doing financially, upcoming changes projected for the following year, and a list of the company's top managers. Hospitals, colleges, and many nonprofits also publish annual reports in print or online.

Quarterly reports help track a company's performance each quarter.

At a minimum, an annual report must include the following:

- The firm's balance sheet
- A report from an independent auditor certifying the veracity of the financial information in the report
- The firm's income statement
- A general report on the company's operations

The beginning of an annual report generally begins with a letter to the firm's stockholders and a discussion of the direction in which the company is moving. For quick and easy reading, the firm's basic financial information, such as its earnings and stock price, are often formatted as graphs like the ones shown in **Exhibit 10-13** and placed toward the front of the report. More detailed financial figures appear in small type toward the end of the report. Annual reports also provide information about the firm's chief executives and board members, including their contact information.

Most companies use their annual reports as marketing tools as well. The reports discuss the history of the industries in which the companies operate, along with emerging trends. Often the information is presented in magazine-style articles with colorful illustrations. Typically the reports are posted on the Web sites of companies and are also available in a

Exhibit 10-12 A Partial Quarterly Performance Report[4]

	Commercial Banks National September 30, 2011			Commercial Banks National September 30, 2010			Commercial Banks National September 30, 2009		
(dollar figures in millions)	All institutions	Assets less than $100 million	Assets greater than $100 million	All institutions	Assets less than $100 million	Assets greater than $100 million	All institutions	Assets less than $100 million	Assets greater than $100 million
Number of institutions reporting	6,911	2,588	4,323	7,146	2,882	4,264	7,303	3,132	4,171
Total employees (full-time equivalent)	1,889,422	44,228	1,845,194	1,952,753	51,350	1,901,403	1,955,958	58,711	1,897,247
AGGREGATE CONDITON AND INCOME DATA									
Net income (year-to-date)	8,064	166	7,899	37,712	632	37,080	90,117	1,107	89,011
Total assets	11,866,395	142,938	11,723,457	12,050,118	156,350	11,893,768	10,791,768	166,579	10,625,189
Earning assets	10,147,135	130,721	10,016,414	10,112,593	143,457	9,969,136	9,285,489	152,997	9,132,492
Total loans & leases	6,537,296	89,758	6,447,538	6,941,675	100,444	6,841,231	6,380,737	105,006	6,275,731
Other real estate owned	31,474	867	30,607	18,035	496	17,540	7,217	279	6,938
Total deposits	8,178,219	119,031	8,059,187	7,778,554	127,635	7,650,920	7,010,179	136,580	6,873,600
Equity capital	1,296,350	17,265	1,279,085	1,164,534	20,044	1,144,490	1,100,241	22,267	1,077,974

print form. You will rarely be involved in writing an annual report, although your manager might ask you to do some research to provide the figures that go into it.

5 How Are Research Reports Written and Organized?

Firms often conduct research when they're considering new strategic plans, products they want to offer, or processes they want to improve. A **research report** is designed to share research you have done on a particular problem or topic with other people. They may be your coworkers, your manager, corporate executives, professional organizations, or the general public. A research report is often a logical successor to a proposal because the ideas in the proposal need to be researched to flush out the details. More than one person can be involved in conducting the research or contributing to the report.

Defining Your Purpose

Understanding your purpose is the first step in any writing assignment. A research report is no exception. There's a saying that a research problem half defined is a problem half solved. Defining the problem of a research project involves pinpointing exactly what the project is supposed to accomplish versus something else. In other words, know clearly what problem you are researching and focus on solving *only* that problem and not another related problem. The problem or purpose, once clearly defined, will then drive the sources that you research for information.

Gathering Information

When gathering information for your report, you can use primary sources, secondary sources, or both. As you learned in Chapter 4, primary sources are sources of information you gather firsthand. The information can be obtained by interviewing and surveying customers, gathering your firm's sales data, and conducting studies or experiments that provide empirical data. Secondary sources are sources of information already gathered by other people and organizations.

Many researchers find it cheaper and faster to start with existing data from secondary sources such as books, publications, the Internet, or companies that specialize in gathering data and sell it. If necessary, the researchers then turn to primary sources, such as interviews

Research is how companies move their businesses forward, and you may be asked to help.

Exhibit 10-13
Financial Highlights Formatted as Graphs for an Annual Report

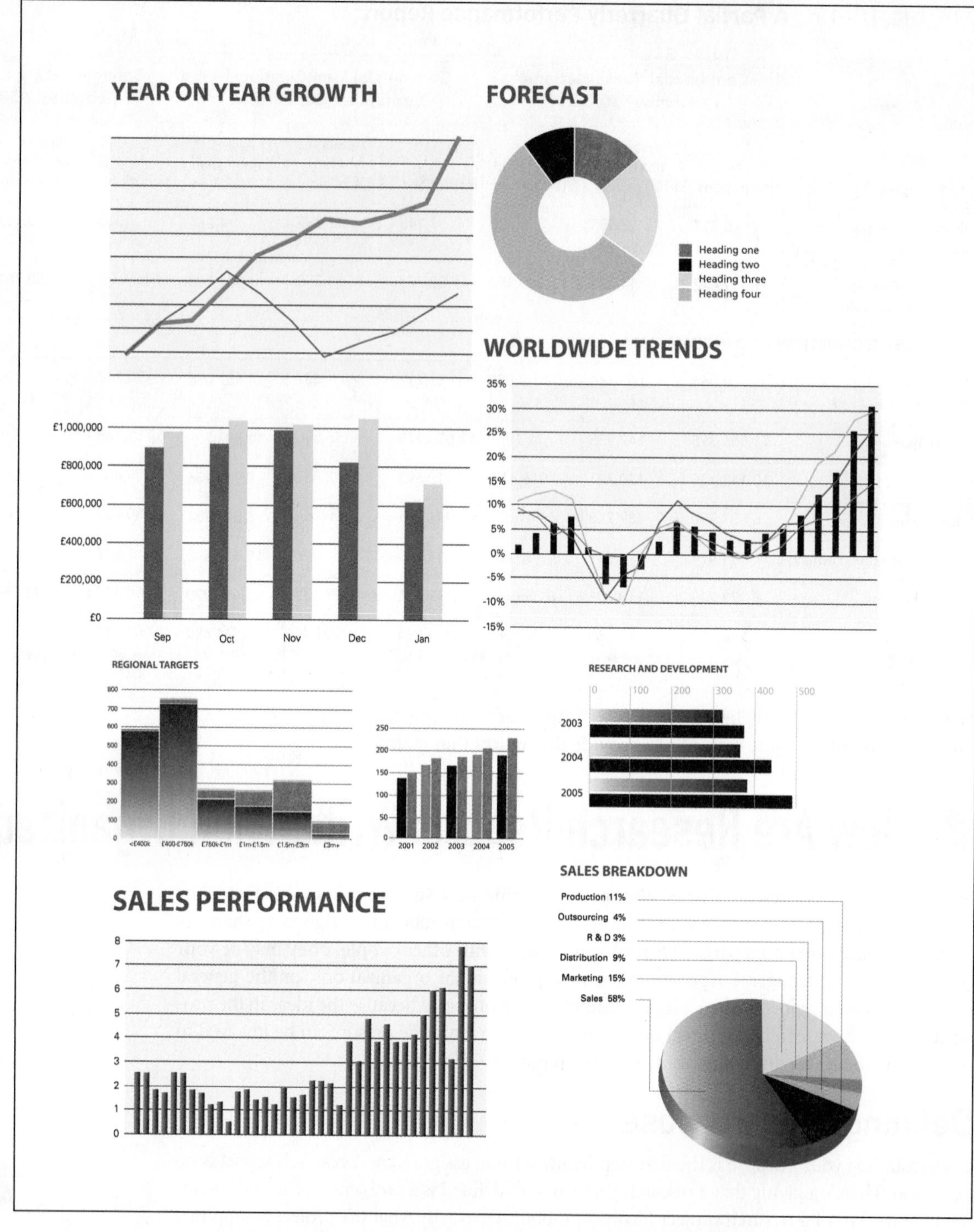

or surveys they conduct themselves. **Exhibit 10-14** describes the two types of sources and some of the ways to access them.

As you collect your data, keep an open mind so you don't skew your answers toward the outcome you want. For example, survey questions should be written in an unbiased, neutral way that doesn't lead respondents to answer one way or another. Don't mislead them about the purposes of your research. Refer back to Chapter 4 to assess the credibility of secondary sources, and review the copyright infringement and plagiarism guidelines presented.

Interpreting Your Findings

Interpreting data requires good analytical skills as well as ethics. Stay as objective as possible and try not to interject your own opinions into the research findings. **Exhibit 10-15** lists some tips for staying objective and to avoid introducing human errors into a research report.

Exhibit 10-14 Primary and Secondary Sources

Primary Sources	Secondary Sources
Interviews Interviews are one-on-one conversations with individuals to gather information. You will typically compile a list of questions and read them to respondents in person or over the phone. Some people prefer to e-mail respondents the questions and then follow up with them by phone.	**Books and Publications** Public and university libraries offer a wide array of books, newspapers, magazines, trade journals, and academic journals with a wealth of information. Reference librarians can help you begin your search for information and navigate through it.
Original Documents Original documents include records produced by your firm and its employees. The documents can include financial information such as sales and financial data, operations data, letters, memos, diaries, and films.	**Online Databases** Libraries typically provide databases that offer access to newspapers, magazines, and journals. Check with your reference librarian for the best one for your purposes.
Surveys Surveys are carefully prepared questions provided by mail or e-mail to a number of respondents. There are a number of Internet survey tools you can use, including Web sites such as SurveyMonkey, Zoomerang, and Insightify. The sites let you create a survey, identify your audience, distribute the survey to a large number of people, and process and report the information quickly and easily.	**Internet** Search engines such as Google can help you find sources all over the world. However, search engines cannot search restricted-access databases and not all Internet sources contain accurate and credible information.

Exhibit 10-15 Tips for Interpreting Research Findings

1. **Stick to the facts.** Avoid distorting or ignoring facts, even if they don't support your initial proposition.

2. **Don't mischaracterize the cause and effect.** Don't make statements indicating one event caused another just because the first event occurred before the second. Ensure there was an actual link between the two.

3. **Do not compare data that cannot be compared.** Just as "apples" and "oranges" can't be compared, certain types of data cannot be compared.

4. **Make sure your data are relevant and reliable.** Beware of oddities in the data gathered, which could indicate errors or bias on the part of the collector. Good reports start with good data.

5. **Do not oversimplify.** Most problems you research are not simple, so why oversimplify your data? If you do, you risk distorting what the information actually shows.

6. **Draw your conclusions from the data.** Use your findings to drive your conclusion, not the other way around. Study the data and make sure they support your conclusion, or adjust your conclusion accordingly. If no conclusion can be drawn from the data, or more or different research is necessary, state as much in your report.

Organizing the Report

Exhibit 10-16 shows the typical sections of a research report and how they should be laid out. Because research reports can be quite long, an executive summary is typically provided. An **executive summary** is a one to two page "mini-report" that summarizes your research report. Because they are extremely busy, high-level managers often prefer to read the executive summary rather than the complete report. In fact, the executive summary may be the only part they read.

Exhibit 10-17a shows a sample executive summary in memo form introducing Amber Lopez's research report on dealer loyalty. The research report follows the same structure as the executive summary but is more detailed. **Exhibit 10-17b** shows selected pages from the report. To read the report in its entirety, see Appendix 10A.

Exhibit 10-16 The Layout of a Typical Research Report

1. Front Matter

Consists of material that appears before the actual report begins. The front matter includes:

- Title of the report. The title should be clear so the audience understands at first glance what the subject is.
- Date. The date the report was finalized.
- Writer(s). The names, job titles, and possibly the departments of the people who contributed to the report.
- Table of contents. A list of the main sections of the report and their associated page numbers.
- List of illustrations. A list of the figures and tables in the report. Include this section if there are many of them.

2. Executive Summary

A one-page summary that a high-level executive can quickly scan. It is essentially a mini-version of the entire report.

3. Background

Information that demonstrates why the research report was written.

4. People Involved in the Research

An explanation of who conducted the research. Who were your research subjects? Was an outside research firm recruited to help with the task?

5. Methodology

How the research was conducted. Was it via phone, live interviews, an e-mail survey, or some other method?

6. Data Collected

A summary of the data collected for the ease of reading and decision-making purposes. Do not include all of the data. They can go into an optional reference appendix for people who want to look at them.

7. Conclusions

Conclusions that can be drawn from the data.

8. Recommendations

Next steps you recommend your organization to take based on the research report.

9. Appendices

Reference material, such as your sources, a bibliography, endnotes, and the raw data collected for the report. If the data encompass many pages, you can indicate in the report that they are available to readers upon request. Include information as to whom should be contacted for the data.

Exhibit 10-17a The Executive Summary of a Research Report (Memo)

To: The Finance and Planning Department
From: Amber Lopez, Senior Loan Processor
Date: February 10, 2011
Subject: Executive Summary: Dealer Loyalty Research Study

Executive Summary
This summary is for members of upper-level management who are concerned about the declining number of auto dealerships that use our bank for loan processing. The summary outlines the research performed, the basic findings, and recommendations for regaining auto dealer loyalty at Seven Hills Bank.

Background
When it comes to dealership loyalty, do we have it? Our bank depends on auto dealers in our region to send business our way, in the form of auto loans. We believe that those dealers continue to do business with us because we process loan applications quickly and provide the services they need. Their loyalty matters. During the last year, Seven Hills Bank processed 1,376 auto loans from four auto dealers in the region, resulting in $191,560 in revenue. However, the year before, the number of dealerships was seven and the revenue was more than $266,000. What caused the decline?

Methodology
Over the past two years, auto loan data from auto dealerships that were current clients, or who had been our clients in the past were studied. The dealerships included Cal's BMW Center, Delvecchio Chevrolet, Highland Ford, King's Autoplex, Markley's Minis, Northern Nissan, and Thompson's Toyota.

Findings
During the interviews, it was discovered that three of them transferred their business to other banks for these reasons (listed in priority order):

1. Slow loan-processing times
2. Higher interest rates
3. Poor customer service. Specifically, questions aren't answered by phone, tellers are slow, and the online preapproval of loans isn't allowed.

Recommendations
As a result of this research, I recommend we first address our number one problem—slow processing times—by considering a new vendor for electronic transfer and by providing preapproval capabilities online. Additionally, the interest rates offered by competitors should be examined, and we need to work on improving our customer service problems. Conducting a feasibility study of these recommendations would be a good next step.

If you have additional questions, please feel free to contact me at ext. 652. I look forward to talking to you about the recommendations at our next staff meeting.

Cite your secondary sources in your report with either footnotes or endnotes. **Footnotes** appear at the bottom of the same page in which the quote or cited information appears. **Endnotes** appear at the end of the document. The three most commonly used styles for formatting citations are the Modern Language Association (MLA) style, the American Psychological Association (APA) style, and the *Chicago Manual of Style* (CMS) format. Appendix C at the back of the book explains the differences between the three.

Illustrating and Polishing Your Report

Your job as a writer is to help readers understand the information you present. Visuals such as images, charts, graphs, tables, diagrams, and photos can help summarize information and make it clearer to readers. Chapter 12 discusses these items in detail so you can learn to choose the right visuals in your report.

If the report was written by multiple people, have one person write or edit the report so it sounds like one person wrote it. Doing so will make the writing style of the report less distracting and easier to read. Always carefully proofread your work. Scarcely anything will undermine your credibility more in the workplace than a research report riddled with mistakes.

A picture is worth a thousand words, especially when it comes to explaining something highly technical or conceptual.

Exhibit 10-17b Selected Pages from a Research Report

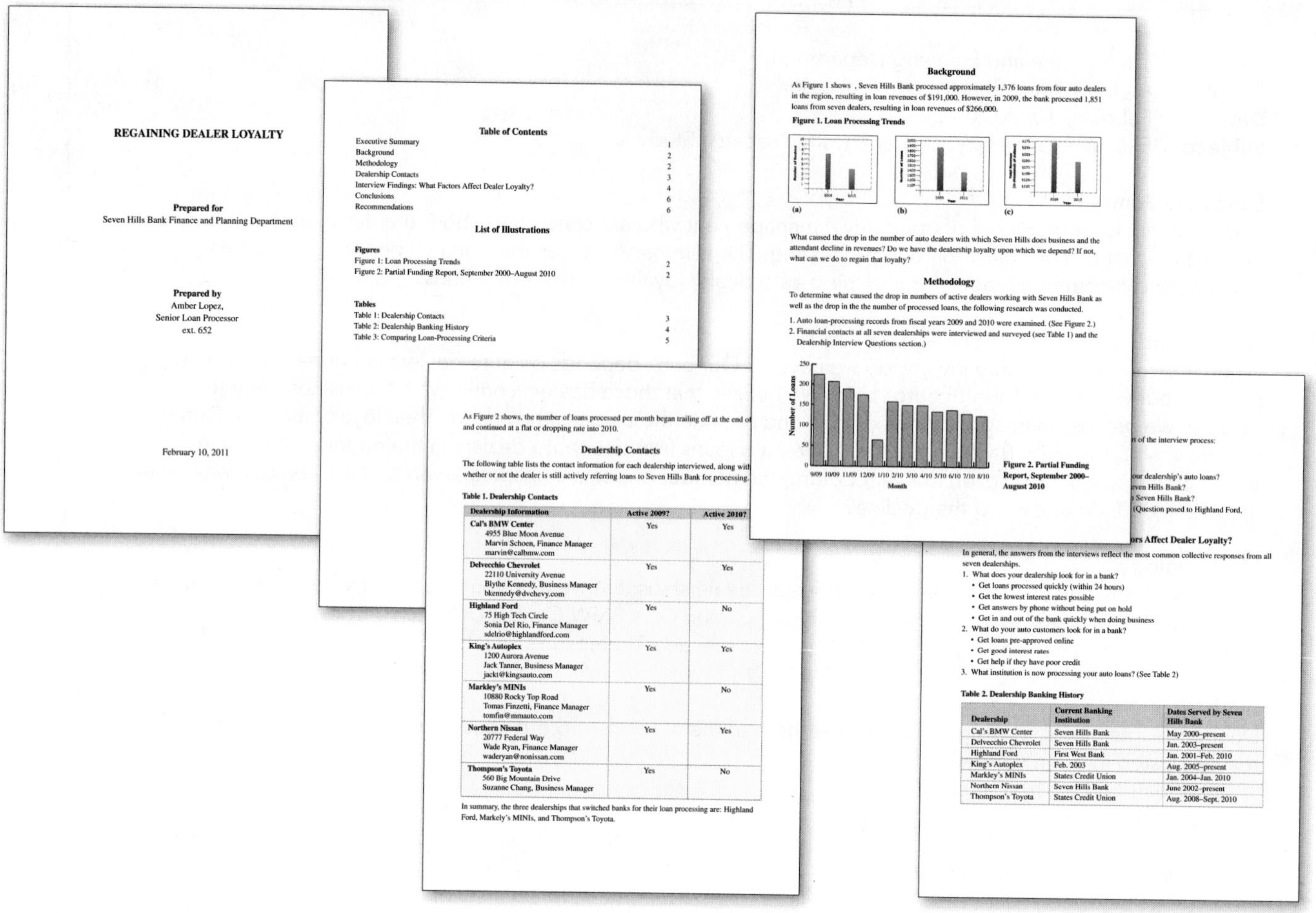

REGAINING DEALER LOYALTY

Prepared for
Seven Hills Bank Finance and Planning Department

Prepared by
Amber Lopez,
Senior Loan Processor
ext. 652

February 10, 2011

Table of Contents

Executive Summary 1
Background 2
Methodology 2
Dealership Contacts 3
Interview Findings: What Factors Affect Dealer Loyalty? 4
Conclusions 6
Recommendations 6

List of Illustrations

Figures
Figure 1: Loan Processing Trends 2
Figure 2: Partial Funding Report, September 2000–August 2010 2

Tables
Table 1: Dealership Contacts 3
Table 2: Dealership Banking History 4
Table 3: Comparing Loan-Processing Criteria 5

Background

As Figure 1 shows , Seven Hills Bank processed approximately 1,376 loans from four auto dealers in the region, resulting in loan revenues of $191,000. However, in 2009, the bank processed 1,851 loans from seven dealers, resulting in loan revenues of $266,000.

Figure 1. Loan Processing Trends

(a) (b) (c)

What caused the drop in the number of auto dealers with which Seven Hills does business and the attendant decline in revenues? Do we have the dealership loyalty upon which we depend? If not, what can we do to regain that loyalty?

Methodology

To determine what caused the drop in numbers of active dealers working with Seven Hills Bank as well as the drop in the the number of processed loans, the following research was conducted.

1. Auto loan-processing records from fiscal years 2009 and 2010 were examined. (See Figure 2.)
2. Financial contacts at all seven dealerships were interviewed and surveyed (see Table 1) and the Dealership Interview Questions section.)

Figure 2. Partial Funding Report, September 2000–August 2010

As Figure 2 shows, the number of loans processed per month began trailing off at the end of and continued at a flat or dropping rate into 2010.

Dealership Contacts

The following table lists the contact information for each dealership interviewed, along with whether or not the dealer is still actively referring loans to Seven Hills Bank for processing.

Table 1. Dealership Contacts

Dealership Information	Active 2009?	Active 2010?
Cal's BMW Center 4955 Blue Moon Avenue Marvin Schoen, Finance Manager marvin@calbmw.com	Yes	Yes
Delvecchio Chevrolet 22110 University Avenue Blythe Kennedy, Business Manager bkennedy@dvchevy.com	Yes	Yes
Highland Ford 75 High Tech Circle Sonia Del Rio, Finance Manager sdelrio@highlandford.com	Yes	No
King's Autoplex 1200 Aurora Avenue Jack Tanner, Business Manager jackt@kingsauto.com	Yes	Yes
Markley's MINIs 10880 Rocky Top Road Tomas Finzetti, Finance Manager tomfin@mmauto.com	Yes	No
Northern Nissan 20777 Federal Way Wade Ryan, Finance Manager waderyan@nonissan.com	Yes	Yes
Thompson's Toyota 560 Big Mountain Drive Suzanne Chang, Business Manager	Yes	No

In summary, the three dealerships that switched banks for their loan processing are: Highland Ford, Markely's MINIs, and Thompson's Toyota.

...t of the interview process:

...our dealership's auto loans?
...even Hills Bank?
...Seven Hills Bank?
...(Question posed to Highland Ford,

...ors Affect Dealer Loyalty?

In general, the answers from the interviews reflect the most common collective responses from all seven dealerships.

1. What does your dealership look for in a bank?
   - Get loans processed quickly (within 24 hours)
   - Get the lowest interest rates possible
   - Get answers by phone without being put on hold
   - Get in and out of the bank quickly when doing business
2. What do your auto customers look for in a bank?
   - Get loans pre-approved online
   - Get good interest rates
   - Get help if they have poor credit
3. What institution is now processing your auto loans? (See Table 2)

Table 2. Dealership Banking History

Dealership	Current Banking Institution	Dates Served by Seven Hills Bank
Cal's BMW Center	Seven Hills Bank	May 2000–present
Delvecchio Chevrolet	Seven Hills Bank	Jan. 2003–present
Highland Ford	First West Bank	Jan. 2001–Feb. 2010
King's Autoplex	Feb. 2003	Aug. 2005–present
Markley's MINIs	States Credit Union	Jan. 2004–Jan. 2010
Northern Nissan	Seven Hills Bank	June 2002–present
Thompson's Toyota	States Credit Union	Aug. 2008–Sept. 2010

- For an interactive, real-world example of this topic, access this chapter's bcomm mini sim entitled Business Data, located at my **mybcommlab.com**

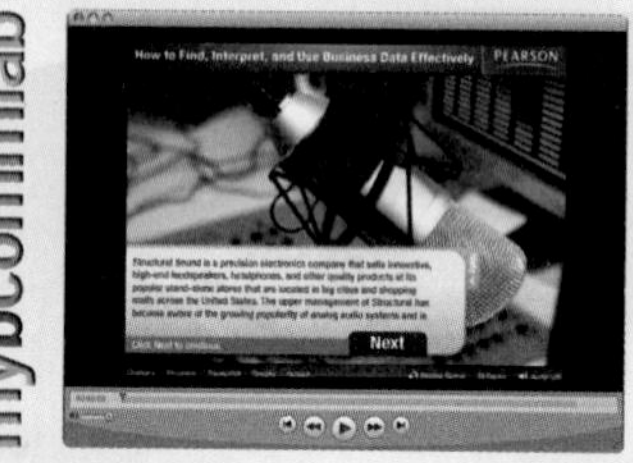

Delivering the Report

When the report is ready, deliver it electronically or on paper to the people who need it. If you are delivering it on paper, include a cover letter consisting of two paragraphs. The first paragraph should explain what the report is and why you are sending it to the person. The second paragraph should tell the person whether or not you expect him or her to offer you feedback on the report and when those comments are due back to you. If you send the report electronically, put the contents of the letter in an e-mail, and include the report and any additions as attachments. If the report is going outside the company, make sure the addresses are correct and the envelopes have enough postage.

Depending on the importance of the report, you might want to follow up with recipients either with a phone call or an e-mail to make sure they received the report. Doing so can be useful if you have worked with recipients who tend not to read or respond to their mail or e-mail in a timely fashion and you require their feedback. If you expect feedback, remind your reviewers as the due date approaches.

If you do decide to post your report on the Web, you can convert it to a PDF file. Your readers will be able to view the report as well as print it. However, they will not be able to mark it up with any feedback. Alternately, post your report to one or more Web pages, which will require more work because the information will need to be converted into an Internet programming language such as HTML or XHTML. Chapter 6 provided a number of tips for writing content for Web pages, which you can review.

6 What Are Feasibility Reports and What Do They Consist Of?

A **feasibility report** explores the possible financial and logistical ramifications of decisions a manager, department, or company is considering prior to the decision. The report is typically published after a proposal and research report have been presented. Feasibility reports are typically written by people at the management level and shared with those who will be affected by the decision for their comment.

The elements of a typical feasibility report are as follows:

1. An overview of the current situation
2. An analysis of the current situation
3. Competitive information
4. The pros and cons of the proposed idea versus the current situation
5. A conclusion about whether or not to implement the proposed idea

A feasibility report helps a company make a go/no-go decision about a proposal with confidence.

Exhibit 10-18 shows an outline of a feasibility report that James Desoto is currently researching. The complete feasibility report can be found in Appendix 10A on page 299. Roman numerals I through VII in the exhibit identify the typical items that make up a feasibility report. The outline will help Desoto put together a comprehensive report examining the feasibility of increasing his bank's hours to increase its traffic and revenues. However, his research is not yet done, as you can see by the questions and the empty tables in the outline. The finished report will then go to his branch manager and the bank's other executives, and they will examine its ramifications and make a decision.

In this chapter, you learned about the reports you are most likely to encounter in the workplace. **Exhibit 10-19** describes a few of the other types of reports you might encounter.

Exhibit 10-18 An Outline for a Feasibility Report

I. Overview

The three branches of Seven Hills Banks, currently serves a population of approximately 125,000 people. Our downtown branch is located in the most densely populated area of the city, surrounded by the greatest concentration of businesses. The workday population in the area is approximately 50,000 people.

Theoretically, the traffic at the bank should be greater than our other branches, and it is, but just barely. After studying our own bank traffic patterns and visiting our competitors, it appears our bank hours are the problem. Many people who visit us work in the downtown area but do not get off work until at least 5:00 P.M. Some of them are unable to visit us before work because we open our doors at 9:00 A.M., and many cannot come during the lunch hour because of other obligations.

The remainder of this report will provide data and analysis to gauge the feasibility of increasing the bank's hours by 1.5 hours (from 8:30 A.M. to 6:00 P.M.) and associated issues.

II. An Analysis of Seven Hills Bank's Downtown Location

Does the downtown location provide enough business to support increased bank hours?

Physical Demographics

- 40 percent industrial buildings
- 50 percent retail buildings
- 10 percent living accommodations (homes, condos, and apartments)

Human Demographics

During the hours of 6 A.M. to 6 P.M., there are approximately 50,000 people in the downtown area. After 6 P.M., the population drops to approximately 10,000. During the day, what is the breakdown of the population?

Age	Number of Customers
20–30	
31–40	
41–50	

Age	Number of Customers
51–60	
61–70	
71–80+	

(Continued)

III. Traffic and Parking

- Need to research the traffic levels in downtown during the day (display in a graph by hour).
- Need to research parking areas and capacities (display in a table).
- Need to research whether an adequate number of anchor stores (grocery stores and large retail) exist to draw people (display in a table with addresses).

IV. Downtown Customer Needs

Need to conduct interviews or surveys to identify typical needs of downtown customers in terms of:

- What hours do they bank? When would they like to bank?
- What banking services do they use? What other services do they want?
- Are they satisfied with the type of customer service they receive? Why or why not?
- What mode of transportation do they use to get here?
- Is the parking adequate?
- What type of physical environment do they prefer?
- What amenities do they expect (snacks in the lobby, holiday giveaways, etc.)?

V. Competitive Information

Need to gather research to find out the hours, services, parking, types of buildings, and amenities that our competitors provide.

	Seven Hills Bank	Competitor 1	Competitor 2	Competitor 3
Hours				
Services				
Parking				
Building				
Perks				

VI. Current Hours of Operation vs. Proposed Hours of Operation

Need to gather the following information in a table format.

Information	Current Hours (9:00 A.M. to 5:00 P.M.)	Expanded Hours (8:30 A.M. to 6:00 P.M.)
Number of current tellers and their shifts		
Labor costs for tellers and managers		
Average number of customers		
Average volume of transactions handled per day		
Utility costs		

VII. Conclusion

The research shows that it is feasible to increase our banking hours. The increased revenue will more than compensate the increased costs of extra tellers and utility usage.

REAL INSIGHTS from a Seasoned Professional

Name: *Karen Travis*
Title: *President and CEO*
Organization: *Sigma Performance Solutions, Inc.*
Location: *Baltimore, Maryland*

THE UNDERGRADUATE DEGREE KAREN TRAVIS earned in business management and marketing from Cornell University 23 years ago proved to be a great launching point for her career. While working in corporate America, Travis not only obtained a master's in applied behavioral science (also known as organizational psychology) from Johns Hopkins University but founded her own company and eventually acquired Sigma Performance Solutions, Inc. Sigma Performance Solutions, which is based in Baltimore, Maryland, is a consulting firm dedicated to improving the customer-service skills of technical professionals.

As the owner of a consulting firm, it's not surprising that Travis has crafted many business reports and financial proposals. She says she got her first taste of entrepreneurship in 1990. Her manager in the New York University administrative computing group kept her on as a consultant after she made financial operations so efficient that her staff position was no longer required. "From that entrepreneurial experience, I figured out that I loved the consulting gig," she says.

Travis says she really enjoys listening to people to find out what they need, coming up with solutions for them, and acquiring new knowledge. She has learned that when it comes to creating proposals and getting her work done effectively, good business communication and people skills are just as important as the technical skills. To illustrate the role business communication skills play, Travis displays a diagram of a bicycle. The back wheel of the bike represents a company's technical expertise—for example, a bank's ability to communicate information about its basic financial service products. However, the bicycle can't go far, go fast, or steer without the front wheel, which represents the bank's front-end contacts and relationships with internal and external customers. Training professionals to develop their front-wheel skills is where Travis and Sigma Performance Solutions excel.

As an example, Travis points to the business-communication solutions her company provided a major global investment firm. The firm was experiencing a lag in sales and asked Travis to take a look at its proposals. Travis found that the firm's service proposals contained all the necessary specifications: the right financial acronyms and lingo, legally-approved forms, and so forth. In other words, the investment firm had the right back-wheel expertise. What the proposals were missing was front-wheel expertise—content that made a connection to the customer's needs.

For example, the firm's financial offerings include tax-sheltered college funds. Although the proposals recommending these funds would list them and their specifications, they failed to explain the benefits of starting a tax-sheltered college fund for a young child and how the fund could grow over time and help families.

After conducting multiple interviews with the investment firm's managers and its personnel, Travis's solution included offering a comprehensive writing workshop for employees. The workshop covered an important precursor to writing proposals: writing and formatting basic business messages, including clear e-mails with effective links to information. The part of the workshop that covered proposal writing included not only information about the basics of writing and formatting documents but also interviewing techniques to uncover the needs of customers.

Following the training, the investment firm reported that more of its proposals were being accepted, and the company's call centers were experiencing a higher rate of effectiveness because the proposals were answering many more of the customer's questions. "By making better connections with their customers' needs, they were getting [the proposals] right the first time," Travis says. However, there is no "cookie cutter" proposal, she says. "Each one must be customized for the customer." "It's all about the customer's point of view. If they are pleased, it's a sale."

Questions

1. What role do front-wheel skills play when you are writing a plan or proposal?
2. Explain why business documents such as reports and proposals need to consist of more than just facts.

Source: Karen Travis in discussion with the author, September 2010.

Exhibit 10-19 **Other Types of Reports**

Report	Description
Meeting minutes	Documents the purpose of a meeting, who attended, what was discussed, and what actions are to be taken and by whom.
Auditing report	Verifies the accuracy of a company's financial information.
Compliance report	Documents how well or how poorly a company complies with certain regulations, such as financial, safety, or health regulations.
Operational report	Communicates the operational performance of a company, or departments within that company, over time (usually quarterly).
Health and safety report	Documents health-related statistics such as injuries, illnesses, and fatalities, and communicates health and safety tips to employees.

Summary *Synthesize What You Have Learned*

1. When do reports and proposals need to be written in the workplace and for whom?

Reports typically discuss things that have already happened, wheresas proposals discuss things that have not yet happened. In general, you will write reports and proposals rather than make phone calls or send brief e-mails and memos when you need to (1) share a large amount of information that may include charts, tables, and illustrations, (2) distribute the information to a large number of people, and (3) provide a more formal means of documenting information.

2. What types of personal reports and logs do employees typically keep?

To-do lists and daily logs are two types of logs employees keep.

To-do lists help you plan your day and prioritize activities. Daily logs help you keep track of work done and time spent so you can better manage your time.

3. What types of informal progress reports do employees write?

Some common informal progress reports include weekly status reports, monthly status reports, and annual accomplishment reports. Weekly and monthly status reports make your manager aware of your activities and help you plan your activities in future periods. An annual accomplishments list reminds you of what you have accomplished during the year and provides evidence of your contributions to your company.

4. What types of formal reports and proposals do employees write?

Common formal proposals include new project proposals and requests and request for proposals. A new project proposal is a proposal written by an individual or team proposing an idea for a new product or service. A request for proposal (RFP) is a document written by a team that invites vendors to bid on providing a particular product or service. Common formal reports include sales reports, quarterly reports, annual reports, research (investigative) reports, and feasibility reports.

5. **How are research reports written and organized?**

Organize a research report as follows: 1) background about the issues prompting the research, 2) explanation of how the research was conducted, 3) list data collected, 4) conclusions drawn from data, and 5) recommended course of action.

6. **What are feasibility reports and what do they consist of?**

A feasibility report explores the possible financial and logistical ramifications of the decisions a manager, department, or company is considering prior to the decision. The report is typically published after a proposal and research report have been presented. The report is generally organized as follows: 1) overview of the current situation, 2) analysis of the current situation, 3) competitive information, 4) pros and cons of the proposed idea versus the current situation, and 5) conclusion about whether or not to implement the proposed idea.

PEARSON **mybcommlab**™ Are you an active learner? Go to **mybcommlab.com** to master Chapter 10's content. Chapter 10's interactive activities include:

- Customizable Study Plan and Chapter 10 practice quizzes
- Two Chapter 10 Simulations, Business Reports *and* Business Data, that help you think critically and prepare to make choices in the business world
- Flash cards for mastering the definition of chapter terms
- Interactive Lessons that visually review key chapter concepts
- Document Makeovers for hands-on, scored practice in revising documents

Know It *Reflect, Respond, and Express*

Build Your Critical Thinking Skills

Critical Thinking Questions

1. Consider the various audiences present in your institution. How do the various audiences discussed in your textbook mirror the audiences in your institution? For example, your peers will be the same as the peer audience level in the text. How do the different levels affect the tone you use in any form of communication? What are the different types of communication you have with the various levels? What experience do you have communicating with the various levels?
2. Review the different purposes of the reports and proposals you will write for various audiences. What are the similarities and differences across the different levels?

Critical Thinking Scenario

Let's look at a case study of Amber Lopez, the loan processor you followed throughout this chapter. Lopez joined Seven Hills Bank when she was 27 years old. She was a single mother who needed to make more money. Her friend told her about a receptionist position at the bank and she jumped at the opportunity. She did her homework, learned more about the bank, and then studied the requirements for the position. Then she updated her résumé, emphasizing her personal interaction and problem-solving skills. Lopez dressed professionally, showed up early for her interview, and got the job.

As a receptionist, Lopez had the opportunity to talk to many people on the phone and in person. She also got to know all the departments in the bank because she was constantly transferring phone calls and sending people to other departments. She visited managers in other departments to ask questions and get the right answers. Every new question gave her an excuse to do more research—talking to other departments or studying bank documents. She kept her manager informed of her work with regular status reports.

Lopez's research allowed her to get to know various department managers and better understand what their departments did. She decided she wanted to work for the Finance and Planning manager as a loan processor—she liked the idea of helping people get auto financing. She talked to other loan processors and studied every loan document she was allowed to look at. She even developed a question and answer document just for loans. Her manager thought it was good enough for the Marketing Department to make into a customer brochure.

When it was time for Lopez's annual review, she had her accomplishments document ready, pointing out the self-initiated projects she worked on during the year, her self-study of loan processing, and her successful interaction with customers. She then shared a letter she had written requesting the opportunity to become a loan processor. Her manager was impressed and talked to the Finance and Planning manager who supervised the loan processors. The Finance and Planning manager, who was well acquainted with Lopez, decided to give her a chance as a junior loan officer.

As you learned in this chapter, several years later, Lopez went on to become a senior loan officer. In that capacity, she conducted auto dealer research, hosted a dealer appreciation event, introduced the idea of electronic deposits for dealers, and conducted training classes for new loan processors. She carefully documented her ideas and her accomplishments with status reports and proposals.

Questions

1. What kind of research did Lopez do at Seven Hills Bank—primary? Secondary?
2. What types of documents did Lopez write at Seven Hills Bank? Why did she write them and what would they accomplish?
3. Have you ever asked questions and shared the answers with others to improve a situation? Did you write down the questions and answers or share them orally?
4. Have you ever been in a situation where you saw a problem and decided to figure out how to solve it, even though no one asked you to? What was it?
5. Have you ever persuaded someone to go along with an idea that you presented on paper? How did you do that?
6. Based on what you learned in this chapter, what types of documents are you most familiar with from your own experience?

Write It *Draft, Revise, and Finalize*

Create Your Own Success Story

1. Reflect on everything you have accomplished over the past year. Write an annual accomplishment report based on your reflections. Include the following parts: name the specific projects you have completed, what skills and talents you used toward your contributions, and the results of your work and the resulting benefits. Use document design elements such as headings and lists to organize the presentation of your information.
2. In small groups, compose a new project proposal for a new service at your institution. Identify a need for the service, outline how your proposal will meet that need, and explain the benefits of the service. Use a memo format and document design to structure your proposal and submit the completed project to your instructor.
3. In small groups, write a response to an RFP you find on Grants.gov. Organize your response according to the request's guidelines, include only the pertinent information requested, write the response with the reader in mind, edit for one voice, hold a group review, and proofread the document carefully before submitting it to your instructor.
4. Choose a nonprofit organization to research online and locate the annual report posted on its Web site. Within the annual report, find the organization's balance sheet, an independent auditor's report certifying the veracity of the financial information, the organization's income statement, and a general report on the organization's operations. How is the organization using the annual report as a marketing tool, or how could they? Write a summary of an analysis of the report's design.
5. Write a research report about a software program or environmentally friendly product your institution could use to attract more students or enhance the current student experience. The report should contain the following components:
   a. Cover letter
   b. Title page
   c. Table of contents (based on headings and subheadings you use throughout the report)
   d. Executive summary
   e. Introduction
   f. Background information about the need for the program or product
   g. Data collected (keep track of all your sources and cite them)
   h. Conclusions
   i. Recommendations
6. Using your library, explore the various online databases available to you, such as Academic Search Premier, and search for a specific term. Write a brief paragraph of what you find. Next, use an Internet search engine to search for the same term and write a paragraph of your findings. How are the two search methods similar? What are the differences between the two? Which type of search offers more credible sources? Write a third paragraph comparing and contrasting the two different types of secondary sources.

Speak It *Discuss, Listen, and Understand*

Build Your Leadership and Teamwork Skills

1. As you learned in this chapter, it's wise to look for ways to improve a situation. Can you think of a proposal that would help make your home, school, or workplace a better environment for learning and growth?

   Perhaps your family could implement a family night where everyone eats together, discusses problems they had during the week, brainstorms solutions, and then watches a movie as a reward. Perhaps you and your school could implement a comprehensive recycling program to handle all paper, cardboard, glass, aluminum, and plastics throughout the campus. Or perhaps your business could initiate a flex-time program so employees could come to work at different times of the morning and leave at different times of the evening to better accommodate families and traffic.

Pair up with another person and take the following steps to get your proposal off the ground:

- Make a list of ideas you would like to propose to your school. Then, choose the one that you think has the most merit.
- Create an outline for the proposal and write it.
- Read the proposal to one another out loud and edit it as you see fit.
- Now, as a team, present the proposal to your class.
- After all of the proposals have been read, ask the class to decide which are the most compelling. Then, after making any necessary improvements, present the idea to your school's student government.

   a. What problems did you encounter coming up with an outline? How did you resolve them?
   b. How was teamwork necessary to complete the task? Was there leadership involved as well? How so?
   c. What method did you use to organize your proposal?
   d. What did you notice about the proposal when you read it aloud to your partner?
   e. How did your audience respond to the proposal?
   f. Did the audience members make points that you can incorporate to strengthen your proposal?

2. Discuss the ways a to-do list and daily log can aid in composing informal reports, such as the weekly status report. How are the purposes of the different reports similar? What are the differences?
3. Visit the Web site Grants.gov and search for Requests for Proposals based on a topic or government organization. Bring a copy of the request to class to discuss the different requests and discuss the different types of materials you would need to research to respond to the request. What tone does the request use? Analyze the content as well as the structure.

Do It *Document Your Success Track Record*

Build Your e-Portfolio

- In this exercise you will create an accomplishments report and add it to your e-portfolio. Think back over the last six months. Now imagine you're going to have a performance review based upon what you accomplished during those six months. What have you achieved? Have you gotten good grades? A new job? Landed an internship? What could you have done better? Did you miss a few credit card payments? Were you often late to class? As you consider these aspects, begin drafting your report.
- Write an accomplishments report in preparation for the review. The accomplishments can be related to school, work, or your personal life.
- Format the report as professionally as possible. Feel free to use the report in this chapter as an example.
- Have a friend, family member, or instructor read it when you're finished and discuss their comments.
- After you have considered any improvements or additions, review your report once more for sense, grammar, punctuation, spelling, and so forth. When you're sure the document is flawless, add the report to your e-portfolio.

1. As you wrote your accomplishments report, did anything surprise you?
2. How did your readers react to the report? Were you surprised?
3. Have you ever documented your accomplishments before? How did the report make you feel?

Business in Action

AIG's Reporting Practices Underscore the Importance of Ethical Communication

Businesses routinely create many types of reports, including financial statements, progress reports and even reports of worker's compensation claims. Ethical business communication through accurate reporting is essential to building and maintaining trust between a company and its shareholders, investors, employees, and customers.

The insurance giant American Insurance Group (AIG) gained notoriety for its faulty financial statements, exaggerated progress reports, and unethical reporting practices regarding workers' compensation claims. In an effort to look good to analysts, the firm entered into sham transactions that made its balance sheet look better, but did not change the fact that its reserves were declining at an unforeseen rate. Financial reports were manipulated to make the firm appear financially sound when it wasn't. Many of these reports eventually led to lawsuits against the company, ultimately costing the company millions of dollars.

AIG suffered both financial losses and a loss of credibility because of its inaccurate reports. Unreliable reports shook the faith of the firm's investors, employees, and customers, many of whom took their business elsewhere. Additionally, following the financial crisis that erupted in 2010, the government bailed out AIG several times with taxpayer money—money that could have been saved had AIG not needed to spend it on lawsuit settlements.

Although AIG is still considered one of the world's foremost authorities on insurance and financial services, its reputation has undoubtedly suffered greatly because of its poor reporting practices. AIG executives claim the firm is "dedicated to maintaining [its] well known underwriting discipline and providing value to policyholders, agents, and other business partners who are central to [its] success." However, is it dedicated to producing valid financial reports? Analysts and the public is not so sure. Sadly, AIG has lost its trustworthiness—a characteristic that it must eventually restore to be successful.[5]

Questions

1. Why do you think AIG tried to falsify its financial reports?
2. What effect does falsifying company reports have on a company's clients and the general public?

Key Terms

Annual accomplishments report. A report that serves as a reminder of what you accomplished and contributed to your organization in a given year. *(p. 272)*

Annual report. A federally required report for publicly traded companies outlining their finances and operations. *(p. 278)*

Daily log (planner). A log that keeps track of what you work on each day and how much time is spent on each item. *(p. 268)*

Endnotes. Source documentation that appears together at the end of a document. *(p. 283)*

Executive summary. A one- to two-page "mini-report" summarizing a longer research report for high-level managers. *(p. 282)*

Feasibility report. A report that explores the possible financial and logistical ramifications of decisions a manager, department, or company is considering prior to the decision. *(p. 285)*

Footnotes. Source documentation that appears at the bottom of the page on which the quote or cited information appears. *(p. 283)*

New project proposal. A formal proposal for a new product, process, service, or job position a person or a team puts in writing for other people's consideration. *(p. 273)*

Proposal. A document that proposes a particular course of action be taken. *(p. 266)*

Quarterly report. A report that helps track a company's financial performance each quarter. *(p. 277)*

Reports. Documents that discuss past happenings. *(p. 266)*

Request for proposal (RFP). A document an organization sends out inviting vendors to submit bids to provide the organization with a good or service. *(p. 273)*

Research report (investigative report). A report that researches a particular problem or topic. *(p. 279)*

Sales report. A report that compares actual sales with projected sales. Sales reports are usually in spreadsheet format and broken down by product or product category. The numbers are typically shown by quarter. *(p. 277)*

Shortest processing time (SPT) method. A work-completion method whereby you complete your fastest tasks first. *(p. 268)*

To-do list. A prioritized list of items to complete each day. *(p. 268)*

Weekly status report. A report that lets your manager know what you have been working on each week. *(p. 269)*

Review Questions *Test Yourself*

1. Explain the difference between reports and proposals.
2. Who are your audience members for both reports and proposals?
3. What type of reports will you alone see? What types of reports and proposals are written for your various audience members?
4. Describe the shortest processing time (SPT) method and how it can help you manage a to-do list.
5. What information should you include in an annual accomplishments report? How can you keep track of the information you need?
6. What is a new project proposal and what information does it include?
7. Explain what an RFP is and describe the components one contains.
8. What guidelines will ensure your success when responding to a request for proposal?
9. Describe what makes up a sales report and how the information is collected.
10. Explain the differences between quarterly and annual reports. How is information collected for each? Who makes up the primary audiences?
11. Describe the purpose for a research report and its required components.
12. What is the purpose of a feasibility report? Who authors this type of report? Who is the intended audience?

Grammar Review *Mastering Accuracy*

Exclamation Points, Periods, and Questions Marks

Section I

Each of the following sentences contains one or more common errors in word usage, grammar, or style. Identify the errors. If you have trouble finding the errors, review Sections 2.1.1., 2.1.2., and 2.1.3. in the handbook (Appendix D) at the back of this textbook.

1. What offers a complete description and overview of your job? The employee handbook, of course!
2. Your job description is listed on page 68 of our departmental manual; and yet, however, I'm not sure if this is the most recent version?
3. I can't believe you think I said that!?
4. John issued a statement indicating how we are to implement the new policy?
5. Julia did a really awesome job spearheading the committee: she raised over $20,000 for cancer research.
6. Say what you're thinking: I can't read your mind, you know!
7. Someone nominated Steven for employee of the month!
8. Please Dr Jones, close the door behind you!
9. Mrs. Henderson wrote an award-winning essay in defense of recent policies enacted by N.A.T.O.

Section II

On a separate sheet of paper, rewrite the following sentences so they are clearer, more professional sounding, grammatically correct, and goodwill oriented.

1. Did you even notice how hard I worked not to dustroy the documents on our employee portal?
2. If Davide has an impairment, he should report this to our Student Services department.
3. All employees have signed non-disclosure agreement: therefore, you shouldn't be talking about top secret company information!
4. "Is this your time of the month?" John jokingly asked Laura before she stormed from the room.
5. The copy machine is such a piece of junk! If you want to even get to it you have to sign up on a sheet.
6. I am smarter than the average Joe, really popular since lots o' people tell me they like me, and I have five years' experience within the medical field doing all sorts of stuff?
7. Many of my co-workers have a bad outlook! We all know a positive attitude is one of the many essential components employers consider when hiring!
8. Until my most recent gig as team head honcho, I had little management experience.
9. So you don't look like a spoilsport, consider the many volunteer and club opportunities on campus.
10. There is plenty of room to move; however, you will have to let your supervisor know which positions you want.

Extra Resources *Tools You Can Use*

Books

- Abell, Alicia, and Aspatore Books Staff. *Business Grammar, Style & Usage: The Most Used Desk Reference for Articulate and Polished Business Writing and Speaking by Executives Worldwide.* Boston: Aspatore Books, 2003.
- Appleman, Jack E. *10 Steps to Successful Business Writing* (10 Steps). Alexandria, VA: ASTD Press, 2008.
- Blake, Gary, and Robert W. Bly. *The Elements of Business Writing: A Guide to Writing Clear, Concise Letters, Memos, Reports, Proposals, and Other Business Documents.* New York: Longman, 1992.
- Davidson, Wilma. *Business Writing: What Works, What Won't.* New York: St. Martin's Griffin, 2001.
- Gewirtz, Adina Rishe. *How To Say It® Business Writing That Works: The Simple, 10-Step Target Outline System to Help You Reach Your Bottom Line.* New York: Prentice Hall Press, 2007.

Web Sites

- LaRocque, Paula, "Fourteen Tips for Clear and Graceful Writing," *Writing Tips.*
- McAlpine, Rachel. "List of Articles about Writing for Web content," *Quality Web Content.*

Appendix 10A *Example Reports*

Exhibit 10A-1 A New Project Proposal

THE PROS AND CONS OF CREATING A COMMUNITY BANKING ONLINE HELP CENTER

Title the report clearly so the audience knows the subject at first glance.

Prepared for
Seven Hills Bank Finance and Planning Department

Include the name of the recipient.

Prepared by
James Desoto
Personal Banker
ext. 659

Include the names, job titles, and possibly departments of the people who contributed to the report.

June 28, 2011

Provide the date the report was finalized.

Exhibit 10A-1 **(Continued)**

Table of Contents

Background 1

Problem 1

Suggested Solution 1

Project Objectives 1

Project Team 2

Proposed Process 2

Assumptions and Constraints 3

Risks and Concerns 3

List the topics and page numbers in the proposal.

ii

Exhibit 10A-1 **(Continued)**

Background

Two years ago Seven Hills Bank created a "frequently asked questions" (FAQ) list to better serve its customers. The list of questions grew and was later posted to our bank's Web site. Based in Web site statistics, more than 75 internal and external customers visit the FAQ page each day, spending 30 to 120 seconds on the page. The page is quite popular by statistical standards.

Describe the circumstances that motivated you to propose a solution to the problem.

Problem

Customers are now starting to ask questions about the bank's financial security and the economy—questions that aren't really part of a traditional FAQ list. These questions are coming in the form of phone calls and in-bank visits. Additionally, the length of the FAQ list makes it difficult for Web site visitors to quickly find the information they need.

State the problem.

Suggested Solution

Briefly outline your suggested solution.

Adding an online "Community Banking Help Center" (hereafter referred to as "online Help Center"), which would be a sub-site of our current Web site, could potentially solve the problem. Launching such a site would give customers access to much-needed, up-to-date information with the click of a mouse, allowing Seven Hills Bank's staff to focus on other activities. The online Help Center would also publicize the bank's dedication to offering superior customer service, efforts to educate customers about good money management practices, efforts to improve the economy by lending to businesses and individuals, and reinforce optimism about the bank's financial strength.

The online Help Center would do so by providing the following information:

- **Glossary.** A glossary of common financial and banking terms.
- **FAQs.** Questions our customers typically ask.
- **Testimonials.** Success stories from customers that are related to the FAQs.
- **FDIC.** A clear explanation of FDIC insurance.
- **Financial Strength.** A discussion of our conservative management style, including the fact that Seven Hills Bank has never made subprime loans.
- **Our Mission and the Economy.** How we are helping the community during a difficult economy.

Project Objectives

Explain how the project will affect the company by providing objectives that will yield tangible results.

The objectives of the online Help Center are as follows:

Customers

- Provide one-stop shopping for customers and potential customers with questions.
- Increase our customers' understanding of the bank's financial security.
- Reduce fears about mortgage and loan rates, foreclosures, and bank closings.
- Reduce the number of information questions our bankers deal with on the phone or in person to increase the amount of time available for dealing with specific customer needs (opening accounts, getting loans, understanding their statements, and so forth).

1

Operations

- Gradually transition Web site maintenance to the IT team, who is more experienced and efficient with Web sites than I am.

Sales

- Increase the number of new customers, new mortgages, and new loans by providing real-world answers and customer testimonials on the Web site.

Project Team

The following individuals have agreed to help implement the online Help Center, should the project be undertaken.

Give your recommendation of who should implement the proposed project.

- James Desoto, Personal Banker (Project Leader)
- Aaron Kuntz, Public Relations Intern
- Maria Delgado, Director of Finance and Planning
- Casey Han, IT Specialist

Proposed Process

Give an overview of the steps needed to take to implement the project.

1. Aaron Kuntz will interview members of each department to find out what questions are most often asked by customers. Kuntz will also compile a list of potential terms customers need to know for an online glossary.
2. The project team will contact members of the executive staff to gather information about Seven Hill's Bank financial strength and the economy.
3. The project team will also create a site map identifying the potential Web pages for the online Help Center and how they will be organized.
4. The team will also develop a schedule with milestones, based on the size and structure of the Web map, as well as the volume of information collected.
5. I will review and revise the material Aaron provides me and pass it to my manager, Maria Delgado, for final approval.
6. The project team will also collectively develop layouts for the Web pages that follow corporate branding guidelines.
7. The final content for the Web site will be converted into plain text format and then given to the IT department, along with the mockups illustrating the layouts of each Web page.
8. The IT department will build the pages and post the information to a beta site for final review by the executive committee and our project team, which will test all of the links.
9. We will collect comments from the executive committee and project team, mark up the plain text files with those comments, and pass them on to the IT department for final implementation.
10. Paper and e-mail announcements will be distributed to all internal and external customers announcing the online Help Center and how to access it.

Note: Throughout the process, management will be kept apprised of the project's progress with regular status reports.

2

Exhibit 10A-1 **(Continued)**

Assumptions and Constraints

Based on an initial analysis of the information customers try to find online, by phone, or in person, the online Help Center will consist of an estimated 7–10 Web pages. The amount of time each team member will spend to plan and implement the site should not exceed two hours per week. This level of commitment should not interfere with the members' normal job duties.

Explain realistic assumptions and constraints the team may face.

Risks and Concerns

The team's analysis might uncover the need for a more comprehensive online Help Center. However, if this is the case, we could readily launch the smaller, 7–10 page Web site and enhance it at a later date. This will allow us to gather feedback from customers before we consider expanding the site.

Outline any risks and concerns associated with the project.

3

Exhibit 10A-2 **A Feasibility Report**

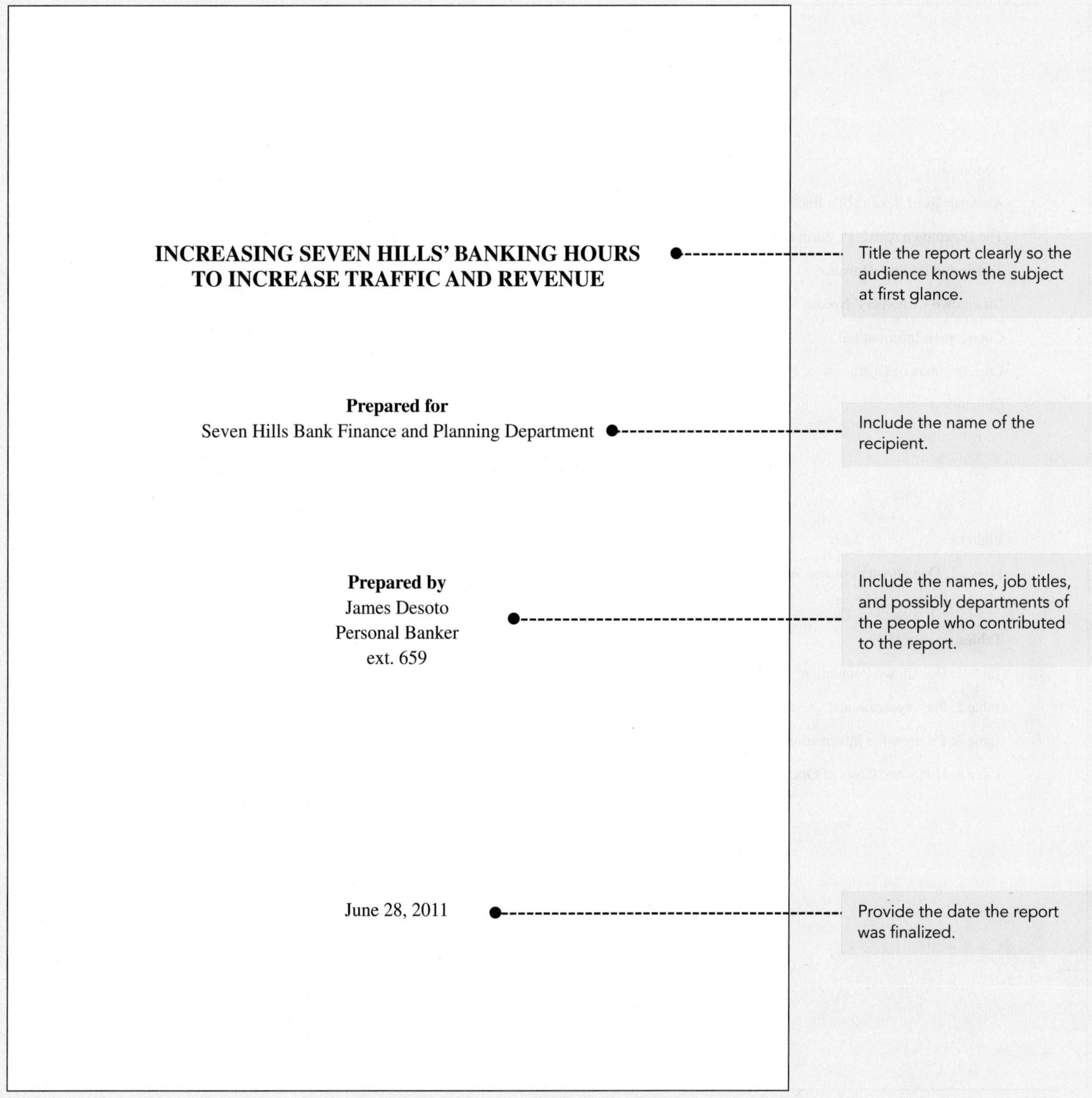

INCREASING SEVEN HILLS' BANKING HOURS
TO INCREASE TRAFFIC AND REVENUE
Prepared for
Seven Hills Bank Finance and Planning Department
Prepared by
James Desoto
Personal Banker
ext. 659
June 28, 2011
Title the report clearly so the audience knows the subject at first glance.
Include the name of the recipient.
Include the names, job titles, and possibly departments of the people who contributed to the report.
Provide the date the report was finalized.

Exhibit 10A-2 **(Continued)**

Table of Contents

Overview 1

An Analysis of Seven Hills Bank's Downtown Location 1

The Downtown Area's Physical and Human Demographics 1

Traffic and Parking Downtown 2

Downtown Customers' Needs 3

Competitive Information 4

Current Hours of Operation vs. Proposed Hours of Operation 5

Conclusion 5

List the topics and page numbers in the report.

List of Illustrations

Include a list of the figures and tables in the report.

Figures

Figure 1: Downtown Foot and Vehicle Traffic 2

Tables

Table 1: Downtown Population 2

Table 2: Parking Areas and Capacities 3

Table 3: Competitive Information 5

Table 4: Hours and Costs of Operation 5

ii

Overview

Seven Hills Bank, with its three branches, currently serves a population of approximately 125,000 people. Our downtown branch at 510 Grandstone Avenue is located in the most densely populated area of the city. It is surrounded by the greatest concentration of businesses, and has a workday population (6 A.M. to 6 P.M.) of approximately 50,000 people.

Provide an overview of the company's current situation.

Theoretically, the traffic at the bank should be greater than that of our other branches, and it is, but just barely. After studying our own bank traffic patterns and visiting our competitors, it appears our bank hours are the problem. Many people who visit us work in the downtown area but do not get off work until at least 5:00 P.M. Some of them are unable to visit us before work because we open our doors at 9:00 A.M., and many cannot come during the lunch hour because of other obligations.

The remainder of this report will gauge the feasibility of increasing the bank's hours by 1.5 hours (from 8:30 A.M. to 6:00 P.M.). Note that other issues besides bank hours can affect customer traffic, but they will not specifically be covered in this feasibility report.

An Analysis of Seven Hills Bank's Downtown Location

To examine the feasibility of increasing our banking hours, we need to first determine whether our downtown location provides enough business to support such a move. To do so, we will look at three types of information:

1. **Physical and human demographics.** What types of businesses are in the downtown area? How many people work in the downtown area, and when are they there?
2. **Traffic and parking.** How often do people travel past our bank on foot or in vehicles? Are there enough parking areas around the bank to support an expanded customer base and extended hours?
3. **Customer needs.** What do our current customers want and need when it comes to our hours and services?

The Downtown Area's Physical and Human Demographics

Presently, the downtown area consists of industrial, retail, and residential buildings:

- **40 percent industrial buildings.** The businesses in these buildings are typically open from 9 A.M. to 5 P.M. Some open at 8 A.M.
- **50 percent retail buildings.** The businesses in these buildings are typically open from 9 A.M. to 5 P.M. Less than one-third, most of which are restaurants, are open until 9 P.M.
- **10 percent living accommodations (homes, condos, apartments).** People in downtown residences typically work and shop in the downtown area.

Expand on the analysis by providing statistics and measurable data.

During the hours of 6 A.M. to 6 P.M., there are approximately 50,000 people in the downtown area. After 6 P.M., the population drops to approximately 10,000. According to last year's Seven Hills Downtown Business Report, the breakdown of the downtown population is shown in Table 1.

1

Table 1. Downtown Population Demographics, Weekdays

		Percentage of Population Downtown	
Age Group	Average Annual Income	From 6 A.M. to 6 P.M. (50,000 total)	After 6 P.M. (10,000 total)
20–30	$25,000	15%	33%
31–40	45,000	25	27
41–50	50,000	20	23
51–60	40,000	21	10
61–70	25,000	13	<5
71–80	20,000	5	<1
80+	18,000	1	<1

Use tables and charts to list similiar data efficiently.

According to the data, the larger population during the day consists of people ages 31 through 60, who also have the larger incomes. This could indicate they would be more likely to use our banking services. Moreover, because they are in the area until 6 P.M., extended banking hours would seem logical.

Traffic and Parking Downtown

Even if the population seems to support extended business hours, Seven Hills Bank would need to ensure there is adequate foot or vehicle traffic passing near the bank to support those hours. Because foot traffic often depends on other nearby stores, research related to surrounding stores is necessary. In addition to adequate foot traffic, the bank needs to ensure there is an adequate amount of parking in the area to accommodate vehicle traffic. The data for Figure 1 and Table 2 was gathered from last year's *Seven Hills Downtown Business Association Report.*

Reference upcoming tables and figures to make navigating the information easier for the reader.

Figure 1. Downtown Foot and Vehicle Traffic

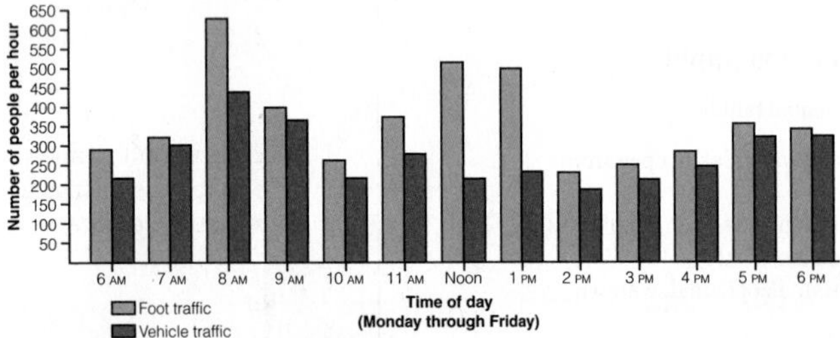

Insert the visual as close as possible to the text that discusses it.

The graph shows that the highest level of foot traffic occurs in the early morning (around 8 A.M.), followed by mid-day (between noon and 1 P.M.), followed by early evening traffic (after 5 P.M.). The high level of foot traffic in the morning is probably due to commuters arriving early in the downtown area to get to work. If we took advantage of this early morning traffic, we could increase our revenues.

2

The following nearby parking garages, lots, and parking spaces are found within the 30 square blocks (6 × 5 block area) that make up the downtown area.

Table 2. Parking Areas and Capacities

Table and figure titles should clearly describe the information presented.

Name	Capacity/Hours	Address	Distance from Bank
Central Parking	1,314 cars Open 24 hours	411 Lodi Avenue	3.0 blocks
City Center Parking	1,452 cars Open 7 A.M. to 5 P.M.	700 Grandstone Avenue	2.0 blocks
Downtown Parking Center	2,107 cars Open 24 hours	425 Lakepark Drive	2.5 blocks
Superior Parking	1,155 cars Open 7 A.M. to 5 P.M.	724 Mapleton Street	5.0 blocks
Val's Park 'n Shop	925 cars Open 7 A.M. to 10 P.M.	503 Oak Drive	1.0 block
On-street parking spaces	2,167 cars	Throughout downtown area	1 to 6 blocks

Downtown Customers' Needs

In May and June, 200 of Seven Hills Bank's current customers were surveyed about their needs as far as banking hours are concerned, levels of satisfaction with the bank's services, and the adequacy of the area's parking. All 200 customers filled out a survey form. Fifty of them were interviewed in person.

The following specific questions were asked. The answers were tabulated and appear below each question:

Use bulleted and numbered lists to break up details and highlight important information.

1. What hours do you bank?

- 30 percent banked between 9 and 10 A.M.
- 35 percent banked between 12 and 1 P.M.
- 15 percent banked between 4 and 5 P.M.
- 20 percent banked at other hours

  Note: Customers banking in the late afternoon indicated they typically get off work between 5 and 5:30 P.M., so if possible, they would prefer to bank between 5:00 and 6:00 P.M.

2. What hours would you like to bank?

- 40 percent wanted to bank before work (before 9 A.M.)
- 25 percent wanted to bank at lunch
- 20 percent wanted to bank after work (between 5 and 6 P.M.)
- 15 percent had no preference

  Note: Based on the answers to items 1 and 2, it appears that most people are banking at lunch because they have to, not because they want to. They would prefer to come in before work to do their banking.

3

3. Are you satisfied with the type of customer service you receive? Why or why not?
Ninety-six percent of our customers rated our service as "Excellent." They cited a number of qualities responsible for this rating:

- Friendly tellers who know people's names
- Staff members' attention to detail and willingness to help
- Staff members' knowledge of banking
- Staff members' assistance with mortgages and loan applications
- The bank's wide variety of services and products, such as business and personal checking, savings accounts, CDs, IRAs, health savings accounts, financial workshops, loans, mortgages, identity theft protection programs, and others

4. What mode of transport do you use to get to the downtown branch?

- Public Transportation: 25 percent
- Car: 25 percent
- Foot: 50 percent

5. If you drive, is parking adequate?
For those who drive to the bank, the answer to this question was a resounding "yes," thanks to the large number of parking garages and lots in the vicinity.

6. What type of physical banking environment do you prefer?
Most customers wanted an area where they can sit down (comfortable chairs or sofas), adequate space to wait in line, and private areas for talking to bank personnel so their financial conversations are not overheard. According to the survey respondents, the downtown branch has a nice "homey" feeling. In particular, clients commented about the bank's big-screen televisions, comfortable seating, and warm colors of the walls and furniture.

7. What perks, if any, do you expect from your bank (for example, snacks in the lobby, holiday giveaways, and so forth)?
The majority of our clients did not expect any perks. Quality service by friendly staff members and low wait times were most important to them. Roughly 15 percent mentioned that they liked our holiday giveaways, snacks, seasonal decorations, local business promotions, and contests. Eight percent of customers indicated that they liked the bank's free financial workshops and plan to utilize them.

Competitive Information

Data about our competitors' hours and services and how theirs compare to ours are shown in Table 3. "Complete services" refers to those services listed earlier: business and personal checking, savings accounts, CDs, IRAs, Health Savings Accounts, financial workshops, loans, mortgages.

Show the competitive intelligence you gathered by providing information about other companies.

4

Table 3. Competitive Information

	Seven Hills Bank	U.S. Bank	Rocky Mountain Bank	First Bank
Hours	9 A.M.–5 P.M.	8 A.M.–5 P.M.	9 A.M.–5 P.M.	8 A.M.–5 P.M.
Services	Complete services	No free workshop	No health savings accounts	No free workshops and long teller lines
Parking	Yes	Yes	Yes	Yes
Building	Homey and warm	Industrial and cold	No private offices for personal bankers	Cramped lobby
Perks	Holiday giveaways, snacks, promotions, new customer gifts, free financial workshops	Holiday giveaways, new customer gifts	Holiday giveaways, promotions, new customer gifts, free financial workshops	Holiday giveaways, new customer gifts

We appear to be doing better than average with our services. U.S. Bank and First Bank serve customers earlier, but do not extend their hours after 5:00 P.M., which is something our customers want.

Current Hours of Operation vs. Proposed Hours of Operation

Table 4 shows cost data gathered from Seven Hills Bank's Human Resources and Maintenance departments.

Expand on the analysis by providing statistics and measurable data.

Table 4. Hours and Costs of Operations

Information	Current Hours (9:30 A.M. to 5:00 P.M.)	Expanded Hours (8:30 A.M. to 6:00 P.M.)
Number of current tellers and their shifts	4 tellers	4 tellers
Labor costs for tellers and managers	$8,000 per month	$8,000 per month
Average number of customers	400	650
Average number of transactions and handled per day	$10,000 per month	$20,000 per month
Utility costs per month	$750	$850

Conclusion

Objectively state the conclusion the data points to, even if it doesn't bolster your position.

Based on the data collected, our customers are very satisfied with Seven Hills Bank's services. However, a significant percentage of them (4o percent) would prefer extended banking hours. According to the research conducted, the downtown area's demographics and traffic will support the extended hours. It is also feasible to increase our banking hours without unduly increasing costs. As Table 4 shows, the total number of tellers and shifts would not have to change if expanded hours were implemented. Instead, the bank could rearrange the shifts and hours so that tellers continue to work the same number of total hours. This means there would be no increase in payroll and no need for additional employees. At the same time, the potential number of customers would almost double, as would total revenue.

5

Exhibit 10A-3 A Formal Research Report

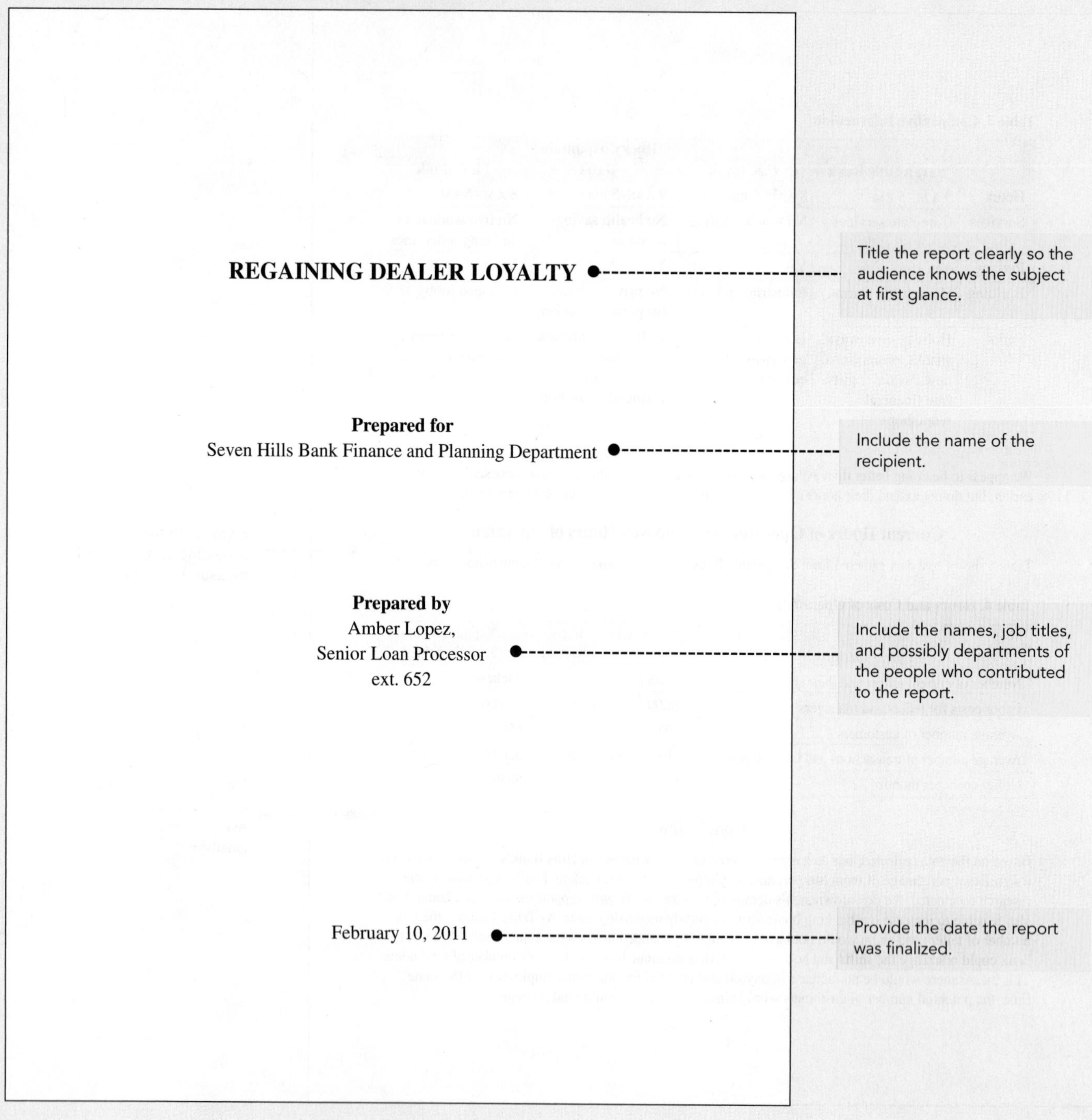

REGAINING DEALER LOYALTY
Prepared for
Seven Hills Bank Finance and Planning Department
Prepared by
Amber Lopez,
Senior Loan Processor
ext. 652
February 10, 2011
Title the report clearly so the audience knows the subject at first glance.
Include the name of the recipient.
Include the names, job titles, and possibly departments of the people who contributed to the report.
Provide the date the report was finalized.

Exhibit 10A-3 (Continued)

Table of Contents

Executive Summary 1
Background 2
Methodology 2
Dealership Contacts 3
Interview Findings: What Factors Affect Dealer Loyalty? 4
Conclusions 6
Recommendations 6

Use the same wording as the subheadings found in the body of the report.

List of Illustrations

Include a list of the figures and tables in the report.

Figures

Figure 1: Loan Processing Trends 2
Figure 2: Partial Funding Report, September 2000–August 2010 2

Tables

Table 1: Dealership Contacts 3
Table 2: Dealership Banking History 4
Table 3: Comparing Loan-Processing Criteria 5

ii

Exhibit 10A-3 **(Continued)**

Executive Summary

The following summary outlines the research performed, the basic findings, and recommendations for regaining auto dealer loyalty at Seven Hills Bank.

Background

When it comes to dealership loyalty, do we have it? Our bank depends on auto dealers in our region to send business our way in the form of auto loans. We believe those dealers continue to do business with us because we process loan applications quickly and provide the services they need. Their loyalty matters.

During the last year, Seven Hills Bank processed 1,376 auto loans from four auto dealers in the region, resulting in $191,560 in revenue. However, the year before, the number of dealerships for which the bank processed loans was seven, and the revenue generated from them was more than $266,000. What caused the decline?

Methodology

Two years worth of auto-loan data from seven dealerships was studied. The dealerships included Cal's BMW Center, Delvecchio Chevrolet, Highland Ford, King's Autoplex, Markley's Minis, Northern Nissan, and Thompson's Toyota.

Findings

Three of the seven dealers transferred their business to other banks during the course of two years. Their reasons for doing so were as follows (listed in priority order):

1. Slow loan-processing times
2. Higher interest rates
3. Poor customer service

Recommendations

Seven Hills Bank should address the most acute problem—slow processing times—by considering a new vendor for electronic transfer and by providing preapproval capabilities online. Additionally, the interest rates offered by competitors should be examined, as should our customer service quality.

1

The executive summary is a one-page summary of the entire report and is intended for a high-level executive to scan.

Insert a blank space between sections to help the reader distinguish which heading is correlated with the text.

Exhibit 10A-3 **(Continued)**

Background

As Figure 1 shows, Seven Hills Bank processed approximately 1,376 loans from four auto dealers in the region, resulting in loan revenues of $191,000. However, in 2009, the bank processed 1,851 loans from seven dealers, resulting in loan revenues of $266,000.

Figure 1. Loan Processing Trends

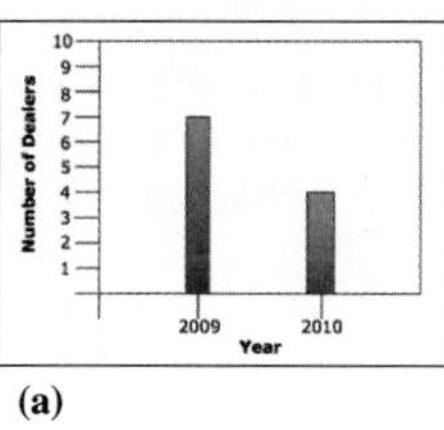

(a)

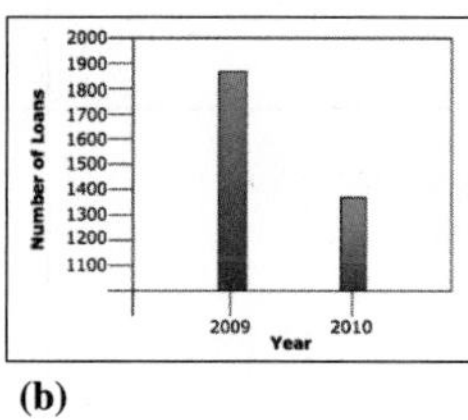

(b)

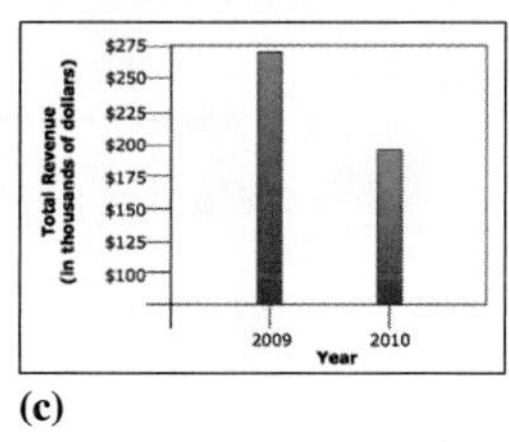

(c)

What caused the drop in the number of auto dealers with which Seven Hills does business and the attendant decline in revenues? Do we have the dealership loyalty upon which we depend? If not, what can we do to regain that loyalty?

Methodology

To determine what caused the drop in numbers of active dealers working with Seven Hills Bank as well as the drop in the the number of processed loans, the following research was conducted.

Auto loan-processing records from fiscal years 2009 and 2010 were examined. (See Figure 2.) Financial contacts at all seven dealerships were interviewed and surveyed (see Table 1 and the Dealership Interview Questions section.)

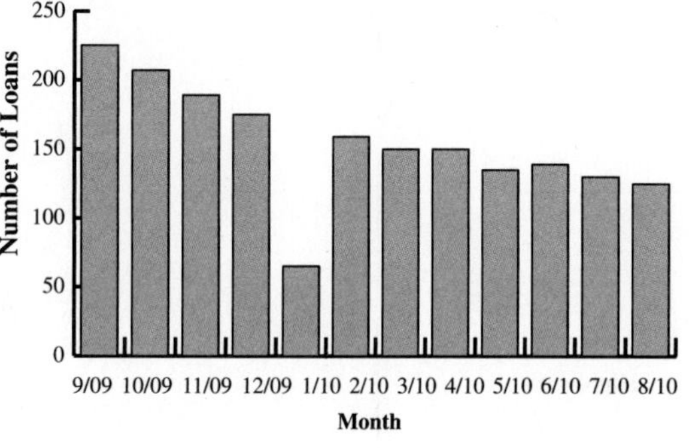

Figure 2. Partial Funding Report, September 2000–August 2010

2

Provide information about why research report was written.

Figure titles should clearly describe the graphics presented.

Insert the visual as close as possible to the text that discusses it.

Explain the way in which the research was conducted.

Exhibit 10A-3 **(Continued)**

As Figure 2 shows, the number of loans processed per month began trailing off at the end of 2009 and continued at a flat or dropping rate into 2010.

Dealership Contacts

The following table lists the contact information for each dealership interviewed, along with whether or not the dealer is still actively referring loans to Seven Hills Bank for processing.

Table 1. Dealership Contacts

Table titles should clearly describe the information presented.

Dealership Information	Active 2009?	Active 2010?
Cal's BMW Center 4955 Blue Moon Avenue Marvin Schoen, Finance Manager marvin@calbmw.com	Yes	Yes
Delvecchio Chevrolet 22110 University Avenue Blythe Kennedy, Business Manager bkennedy@dvchevy.com	Yes	Yes
Highland Ford 75 High Tech Circle Sonia Del Rio, Finance Manager sdelrio@highlandford.com	Yes	No
King's Autoplex 1200 Aurora Avenue Jack Tanner, Business Manager jackt@kingsauto.com	Yes	Yes
Markley's MINIs 10880 Rocky Top Road Tomas Finzetti, Finance Manager tomfin@mmauto.com	Yes	No
Northern Nissan 20777 Federal Way Wade Ryan, Finance Manager waderyan@nonissan.com	Yes	Yes
Thompson's Toyota 560 Big Mountain Drive Suzanne Chang, Business Manager schang@thompsontoyota.com	Yes	No

In summary, the three dealerships that switched banks for their loan processing are: Highland Ford, Markley's MINIs, and Thompson's Toyota.

3

Exhibit 10A-3 (Continued)

Interview Questions

Each of the following six questions were asked as part of the interview process:

1. What does your dealership look for in a bank?
2. What do your auto customers look for in a bank?
3. What bank are you currently working with to process your dealership's auto loans?
4. What do/did you like about doing business with Seven Hills Bank?
5. What do/did you dislike about doing business with Seven Hills Bank?
6. Why did your dealership leave Seven Hills Bank? (Question posed to Highland Ford, Markley's MINIs, and Thompson's Toyota only.)

Interview Findings: What Factors Affect Dealer Loyalty?

In general, the answers from the interviews reflect the most common collective responses from all seven dealerships.

1. What does your dealership look for in a bank?
   - Get loans processed quickly (within 24 hours)
   - Get the lowest interest rates possible
   - Get answers by phone without being put on hold
   - Get in and out of the bank quickly when doing business
2. What do your auto customers look for in a bank?
   - Get loans pre-approved online
   - Get good interest rates
   - Get help if they have poor credit
3. What institution is now processing your auto loans? (See Table 2)

Table 2. Dealership Banking History

Dealership	Current Banking Institution	Dates Served by Seven Hills Bank
Cal's BMW Center	Seven Hills Bank	May 2000–present
Delvecchio Chevrolet	Seven Hills Bank	Jan. 2003–present
Highland Ford	First West Bank	Jan. 2001–Feb. 2010
King's Autoplex	Feb. 2003	Aug. 2005–present
Markley's MINIs	States Credit Union	Jan. 2004–Jan. 2010
Northern Nissan	Seven Hills Bank	June 2002–present
Thompson's Toyota	States Credit Union	Aug. 2008–Sept. 2010

4

Use numbered lists when the order of the items must appear in sequence.

Provide information about what the data showed.

Use tables and charts to list similiar data efficiently.

Exhibit 10A-3 **(Continued)**

In summary, all four of our active dealers have been clients with Seven Hills Bank for more than seven years.

4. What do/did you like about doing business with Seven Hills Bank?
   - Friendly staff
   - Accuracy of loan processing
   - Comprehensive reports
   - Good follow-up
   - Single point of contact for loan processing
5. What do/did you dislike about doing business with Seven Hills Bank?
   - Slow processing time
   - High interest rates
   - Length of time to get questions answered by phone
   - No way to get loans pre-approved online
   - Long lines in the bank

The complaints listed in conjunction with Question 5 are shown in Table 3. Also shown are comparable statistics for First West Bank, Mountain States Credit Union, and other banks now serving the dealerships that left Seven Hills Bank. Table 3 compares various criteria associated with loan processing for Seven Hills Bank and the other banks.

Use bullet points to improve the report's readability and break up long text.

Table 3. Comparing Loan-Processing Criteria

	Seven Hills Bank	First West Bank	Mountain States Credit Union
Loan-processing time	36 hours	24 hours	24 hours
Interest rates	As low as 5.4%	As low as 5.19%	As low as 4.99%
Average phone wait time per call	Five minutes	Three minutes	Two minutes
Availability of online loan pre-approval	No	Yes	Yes
Average bank-line wait time per visit	Five minutes	Five minutes	Two minutes

6. Why did your dealership leave Seven Hills Bank?

   The following summarizes each dealership's reasons for ceasing to do business with Seven Hills Bank.

   - **Highland Ford:** Highland Ford was one of Seven Hills Bank's long-term customers, having started business with us almost 10 years ago. Finance Manager Sonia Del Rio explained that two years ago Highland customers began complaining that they could not get pre-approved for their loans online. In Del Rio's opinion, the extra paperwork and phone time required for pre-approval extends the total

5

Exhibit 10A-3 **(Continued)**

processing time for most auto loans. She also mentioned that even though our customer service representatives are very friendly, they can't readily answer all of her questions without putting her on hold for an average of five-to-seven minutes per auto customer.

- **Markley's MINIs:** Markley's Minis was Seven Hills Bank's newest customer. The organization specializes in selling MINI Coopers and hard-to-find small sports cars. Finance Manager Tomas Finzetti claims that 75 percent of Markley's auto customers want to use the Internet as a primary tool for loan processing. Our bank's lack of online preapproval for loan processing was incomprehensible to most customers, according to Finzetti. The lack of online preapproval added an entire day to the total loan processing time. Finzetti commented that in some cases the extra time allowed auto customers to rethink the financial feasibility of their purchases, and the dealership actually lost some sales. He also mentioned that Seven Hills' interest rates for auto loans were among the highest of the banks he personally researched.
- **Thompson's Toyota:** Thompson's Toyota began conducting business with Seven Hills Bank about seven years ago after being referred by Northern Nissan. Business Manager Suzanne Chang regretted breaking our contract but stated that a 36-hour loan approval time was no longer acceptable in her business. She suggested we look into online loan preapproval capabilities. Chang also mentioned that our interest rates seemed higher than those of other regional banks. Of less concern to Chang, but still worth mentioning, is her perception that her wait times in our bank lines are more than five minutes per visit.

Conclusions

The funding report revealed that the number of loans processed per month began trailing off at the end of 2009 and continued at a flat or dropping rate into 2010. This trend, the interview feedback collected, and data analysis conducted as part of this study suggest that the following three reasons explain why Seven Hills Bank's dealer loyalty has suffered:

- Slow loan-processing time, possibly linked to the lack of online loan preapproval
- Higher interest rates than many regional banks
- Poor customer service in the area of phone response times and perhaps bank-line wait times

Recommendations

Based on the conclusions of this study research, I recommend four initiatives be undertaken to regain dealer loyalty:

1. Reduce loan-processing times to a minimum 24-hour turnaround.
2. Offer lower interest rates for at least some loans.
3. Improve Seven Hills Bank's customer service, particularly in the area of customer response times.

Conduct a feasibility study to determine the costs and benefits of each of the aforementioned recommendations.

6

Provide information that has already been presented. Do not include new information in your conclusions.

Distinguish between the conclusion and recommendations by dividing them into two separate sections. However, if the report is short, the material can be placed in one section titled: "Conclusions and Recommendations."

List your recommendations for the organization to take based on the research report.

"Making a presentation is an opportunity to make a small difference in the world."
—**Garr Reynolds,** author

Business Presentations

Making an Impact

LEARNING OBJECTIVE QUESTIONS

1. What are the three basic types of presentations?
2. How do you plan a presentation?
3. How can you be a better presenter?
4. How should different types of audiences be handled?
5. What is the key to making a successful team presentation?

mybcommlab Access interactive videos, simulations, sample documents, document makeovers, and assessment quizzes in Chapter 11 of **mybcommlab.com** for mastery of this chapter's objectives.

>>> **Phong** has been working in the accounting department of Molly Fae Products—a national company known for everything from diapers to cleaning supplies. Although he likes his job, he's always been interested in moving into a more creative role. However, as a single father, Phong has had to juggle his time between his job and his son, Chen, and hasn't been able to focus on developing his skills.

Phong's chance has finally come. Recently, Molly Fae Products announced a contest for employees. In the contest, employees would have the opportunity to present a new product to the company's research and development team with the chance of having it developed and incorporated in the Molly Fae lineup of products. When Phong heard about the contest, he immediately knew what he would show: a new line of organic, aloe vera–based baby wipes—a concept he had come up with when dealing with his son's diaper rash. Phong believed the product could be a success because it would appeal to both environmentally conscious consumers and new parents alike. The only problem was the presentation. Phong hadn't given a presentation since high school and is terrified of public speaking.

Knowing that this might be his only opportunity to impress his superiors and move out of his department, Phong knew he had to give it a shot. Between work and taking care of Chen, Phong searched the Web for some help on how to give business presentations. After stumbling across several videos on good presentation habits, Phong started taking notes. Over the next few weeks, he planned his presentation, put together a visual aid, and practiced in front of the mirror, some friends, and even his son.

When it came time to bring the presentation before the research and development team, Phong felt nervous but not underprepared. In the end, his presentation went smoothly, and he could tell he had impressed the team. When Phong got the call a few weeks later announcing that he had won the contest, he felt sure that he had gained much more than an opportunity at a new career: He had gained a new skill and a new level of confidence.

Phong >>>

Making presentations is practically a way of life in most businesses. Being able to make a good presentation will enhance your credibility and make you more valuable to your employer. It will also help you and your coworkers understand and embrace your firm's common objectives and plans. Lastly, a presentation that calls others to action can help you guide your company in new strategic directions.

This chapter discusses the messages conveyed in presentations, from planning and developing, to delivering them. (Chapter 12 discusses developing visual aids for presentations, including slideshows.) The examples and scenarios in this chapter are built around the consumer products industry. Consumer products are typically merchandise or items used on a daily or frequent basis by consumers like toothpaste, laundry detergent, and deodorant. Consumer products companies spend large amounts of money researching and developing new products, and even larger amounts of money marketing those products to consumers. Some businesses such as Proctor & Gamble are creating online communities. Members are given products to sample and in return, give companies their feedback, marketing ideas, and so on.

■ For an interactive, real-world example of this topic, access this chapter's bcomm mini sim entitled Business Presentations, located at mybcommlab.com

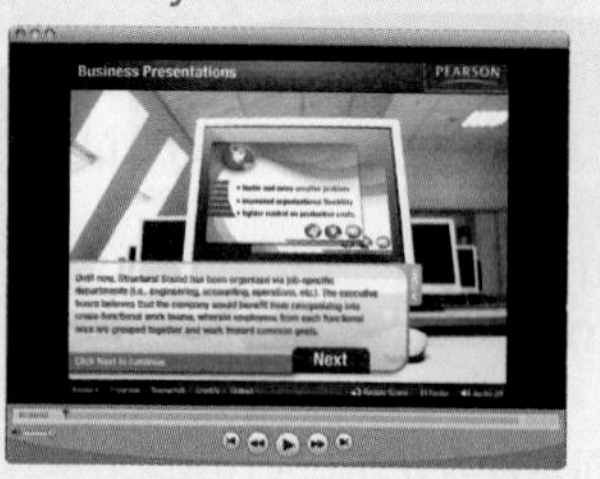

In many consumer products companies, presentations are used daily to inform, persuade, and solicit business. Landing and keeping a job in the industry may depend on a person's ability to plan and deliver effective presentations. With practice anyone can become an effective presenter. This chapter will tell you what you need to know to plan and deliver effective presentations that get your point across, keep your listeners engaged, and get them to take action.

1 What Are the Three Basic Types of Presentations?

Many workplace presentations are internal to the company. They are typically made to a small group of employees, such as your coworkers, peers, or superiors. You might make a small-group presentation to explain a procedure, provide status on a project, or pitch an idea. However, some presentations are external to the company. They can be made to small or large groups and are typically used to update an audience about new products and programs. Some external presentations are made to win a contract or sell products.

There are three primary types of presentations: persuasive, informative, and educational. Let's look at each.

Persuasive Presentations

Persuasive presentations are perhaps the most common types of business presentations. Their purpose is to convince the audience to do something. Typical persuasive presentations include:

- Sales presentations
- Business plan presentations
- New product development proposals

The key to making a persuasive presentation is communicating value to your listeners. Rick Robinson is the vice president of marketing at Vision Research, a company that manufactures high-speed cameras and accessories. Robinson has over 30 years of experience delivering presentations to colleagues, senior executives, and customers. He says, "In any presentation meant to persuade, you are actually engaging in a 'trade of value'—in return for delivering the content of the presentation, you expect something of value in return (a decision, a purchase, funding, and so forth). To get value, you must give value. So, think about how to make the presentation as valuable as possible."[1]

Informative Presentations

In an **informative presentation**, you might be asked to explain new policies and procedures to your coworkers, or offer training to new employees. At the highest level, you may be asked to present your findings to the executive members of your company.

According to Robinson, an informative presentation should captivate your audience, make them care about what you have to say, and leave them with key points they need to remember. Speakers making informative presentations sometimes provide their audience members with handouts so they can follow up on the detailed information later. For example, suppose your team is presenting a new cavity-preventing snack for children. You have conducted focus groups, developed a prototype, and taste-tested it with children, ages 4–6.

You might want to provide a handout with data about the focus group and taste-test results, as well as basic nutritional information, and color photos of the snack. That way, your audience has something to study after the presentation.

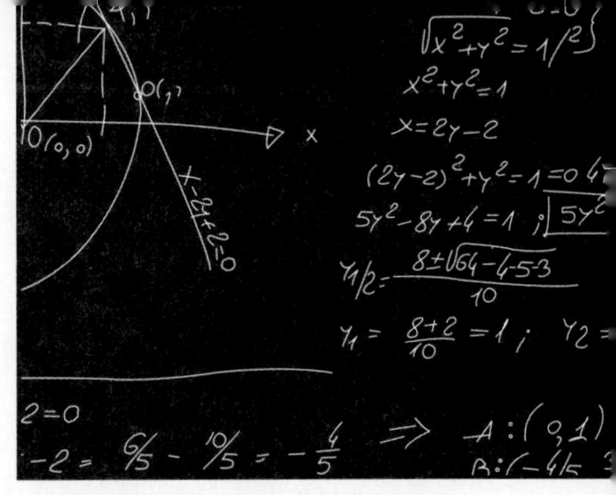

Educational Presentations

Sometimes you will be asked to give an **educational presentation**—a presentation used to teach your coworkers how to perform a task at which you are an expert. You might even become a trainer who teaches others about your company's products or technologies. For example, imagine you are a member of the research team at Procter & Gamble (P&G), and you need to teach a new group of scientists about P&G's research process and show them how new formulas are developed for detergents and fabric softeners. Of course, you need to present this information in a way that shows you respect their intelligence and realize that they are experts in their field.

Keep in mind that people—even highly-educated scientists—learn best when they are given information in "bite-sized" chunks. Don't overwhelm your audience with too much information in one sitting. Instead, share some information. Then ask questions and share some more. In addition, take breaks. They are a welcome relief for your audience.

DID YOU KNOW?

The average adult's span of attention is 20 minutes. If your audience members are doodling, looking at their laptops, reading papers, or dozing, you know you have lost their attention.[2]

2 How Do You Plan a Presentation?

Different presentations require different levels of planning. For example, preparing for a routine 10-minute status update probably requires very little preparation, especially after you have done one or two of them. However, a great deal of preparation is required for the presentation of a business plan or strategic plan for your firm.

According to Nancy Duarte, the president and CEO of Duarte Design (the design firm that created the slides Al Gore used in his Oscar-winning 2006 film, *An Inconvenient Truth*), a common rule of thumb for developing a presentation is 30 hours of preparation for every hour of presentation.[3] The number might be much lower for a simple status report where you're already familiar with all the information, or much higher for a formal presentation that involves much research and the development of visual aids.

Preparation is the key to giving a successful presentation. Preparing involves the following steps: identifying your audience, determining your purpose, brainstorming, collecting facts, and organizing your information.

Understand Your Audience

In Chapter 1 you learned some basic questions to ask about your audience. Now consider asking the seven more detailed questions shown in **Exhibit 11-1** to better get to know your audience.[4]

1. ***What are they like?*** Knowing the demographics of the audience members—where they are from, what parts of the country, their ages, genders, and so forth—is a great start, but connecting with them will require understanding them on a more personal level. Take a walk in their shoes and describe what their lives look like. Do some research on the Internet or talk to people who represent your audience so you can hear their stories and learn more about them.
2. ***Why are they here?*** What do they think they are going to get out of your presentation? Why did they come to hear you? Are they willing participants or mandatory attendees? You don't want audience members to think, "So what?" after you finish your presentation.
3. ***What motivates them?*** Everyone has concerns and frustrations. Let audience members know you empathize with them. This is often as easy as sharing a story or experience—anything that shows you understand their concerns.
4. ***How can you solve their problem?*** What's in it for the members of the audience? How are you going to make their lives better or other jobs easier? Offer solutions to their problems.
5. ***What do you want them to do?*** Make sure there's clear action for your audience to take.

Exhibit 11-1
Seven Questions to Ask about Your Audience

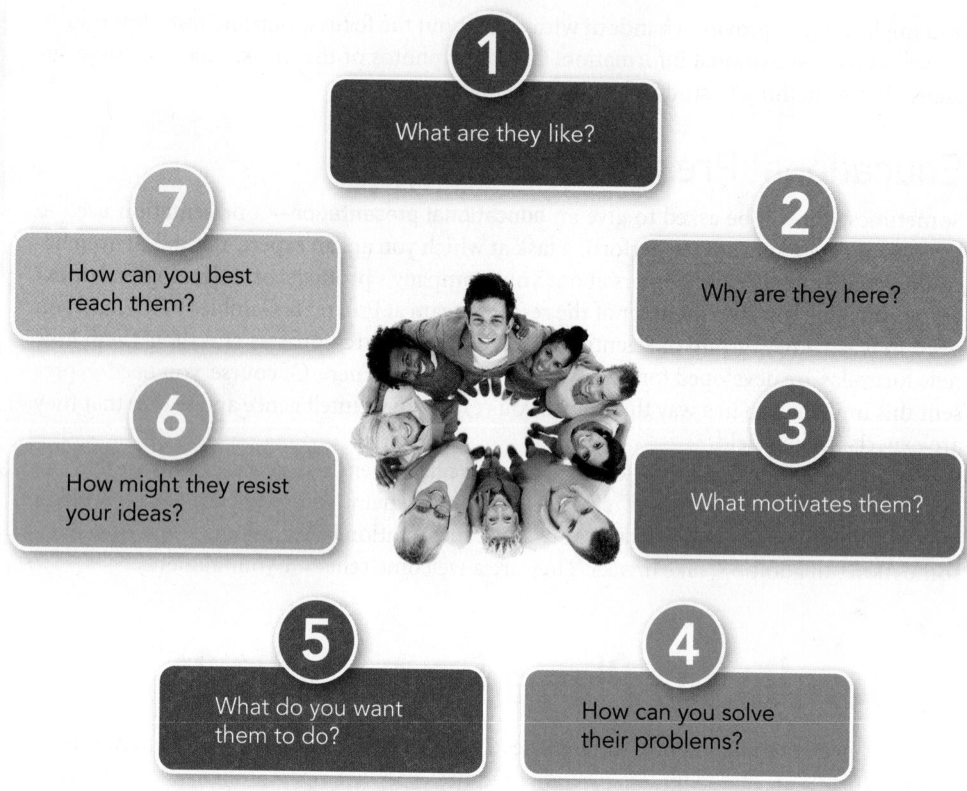
1
What are they like?
2
Why are they here?
3
What motivates them?
4
How can you solve their problems?
5
What do you want them to do?
6
How might they resist your ideas?
7
How can you best reach them?

6. ***How might they resist your ideas?*** What will keep the audience from agreeing with your message and carrying out your call to action?
7. ***How can you best reach them?*** People vary in how they prefer to receive information. This can affect everything from the setup of the room in which you are presenting to the availability of materials after the presentation. Give your audience members what they want in the way they want it.

Learning Styles

Finally, consider people's **learning styles**—the different ways people learn—to make sure your presentation accommodates as many of them as possible. **Exhibit 11-2** lists the different types of learners and their preferred styles of learning.

If you're wondering how to incorporate all of the learning styles into one presentation, you don't have to. You just have to use a few of the styles and be aware of the rest. For example, consider telling a short story and showing pictures to illustrate the ideas from the story. Then convey some facts and explain how they pertain to the story. Interact with the participants, if you can. Ask them questions and coax them to share their own stories. Ask them to practice what they have learned. If you do so, you will have met the needs of active, reflective, sensing, intuitive, visual, verbal, sequential, and global learners alike. Now that you know your audience, let's look at the purpose of your presentation.

Determine the Presentation's Purpose

Before you begin thinking about what you want to say to your audience, you need to ask yourself, "What is the purpose of my presentation?" The following three questions can help you target your goals:

1. Why would anyone want to listen to the presentation?
2. What would the audience have to gain by attending the presentation?
3. What do you want the audience members to do after they leave the presentation?

For example, suppose you are giving a presentation about aromatherapy and essential oils to the research and development (R&D) team at Procter & Gamble. You would like the

Exhibit 11-2 Types of Learning Styles

Type of Learner	Description
Active learners	Learn best by doing.
Reflective learners	Like to think it through first before acting.
Visual learners	Remember pictures, diagrams, flow charts, tables of data, and physical demonstrations.
Verbal learners	Get the most out of spoken words or written explanations.
Sensing learners	Tend to enjoy facts and data.
Intuitive learners	Prefer possibilities and relationships.
Sequential learners	Tend to gain understanding through a linear, step-by-step process, which is logical and systematic.
Global learners	Need to see the big picture before they tackle the details. A sudden flash of understanding characterizes their approach to learning.

team to launch an aromatherapy line of laundry products. **Exhibit 11-3** shows how you might answer the three questions to develop a purpose for your presentation.

Exhibit 11-3 Defining Your Presentation Purpose for the P&G Research Team

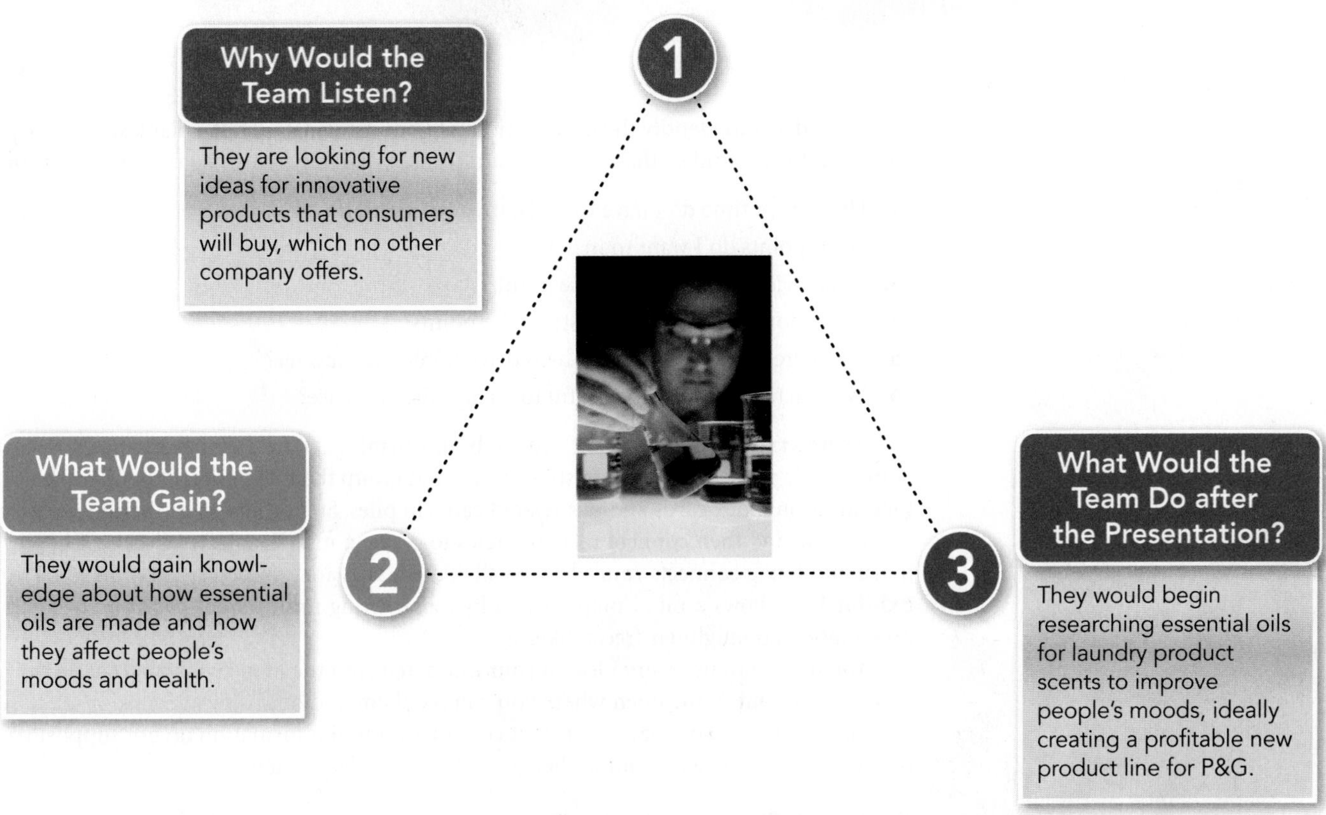

1
Why Would the Team Listen?
They are looking for new ideas for innovative products that consumers will buy, which no other company offers.
2
What Would the Team Gain?
They would gain knowledge about how essential oils are made and how they affect people's moods and health.
3
What Would the Team Do after the Presentation?
They would begin researching essential oils for laundry product scents to improve people's moods, ideally creating a profitable new product line for P&G.

Brainstorm to Gather Ideas for Your Presentation

Once you have the purpose and the audience clearly in mind, you can work backward to decide what information will achieve that purpose.

Exhibit 11-4 A Mind Map Used to Develop a Presentation

Gluten-free cookies presentation

Background
What is celiac disease?
Anecdote about cousin
Ask audience
How many people suffer from celiac disease?
Chart
Ask audience

Logistics
45-min. talk
15-min. questions
50 people
R&D
Marketing
Focus group

Business philosophy
Address special-needs customers
Quotes from customers
Quotes from doctors
Expand our market
What do celiacs want?

Moving forward
Recipes
Ideas from audience
Advertising
Free samples

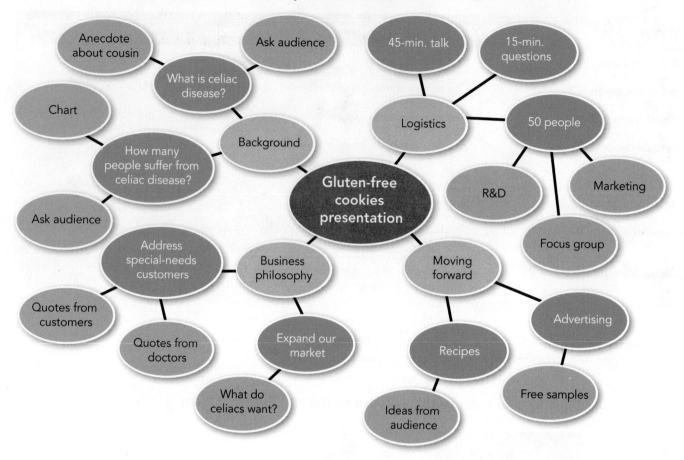

A good way to identify the information is to brainstorm. Pull out a blank sheet of paper and write down any ideas that come to mind. Get ideas by answering the following questions:

1. How much time do I have to make my presentation?
2. What points do I want to make?
3. What evidence supports those points?
4. What stories can I tell to illustrate the points?
5. Are there quotes I can use to help drive home my message?
6. What activities would be useful to engage the audience?

There are no bad ideas when you are brainstorming. Write down every idea you have. Some people write their ideas on sticky notes and group them together. Other people write their ideas on index cards and put related cards in piles. Still others write their ideas down, circle them, and then connect related circles to create a mind map. Recall from Chapter 4 that a mind map connects your ideas, so all related ideas are grouped together in some way. **Exhibit 11-4** shows a mind map created by a marketing professional planning to make a presentation about gluten-free cookies.

You might not use every idea on your mind map, but the map gives you a chance to get all your ideas out in the open where you can see them and how they are connected. Based on your mind map, you may decide that certain groups of information do not support your purpose or resonate with your audience, and you can delete them.

Collect Supporting Facts

Once you have mapped out your main ideas, research some facts to support them. For example, if you believe that developing a new product will increase your company's profit, gather data on new product introductions from the past and their impact on the bottom line. The research phase of your preparation will often be the longest phase.

Common ways to collect information include:

- Interviewing people in person, by phone, or by e-mail. Firsthand information is always best.
- Reading books, newspapers, or magazines on the subject.
- Performing an Internet search using key words related to your topic. When you get a list of results, click through them to find legitimate sources.
- Reading blogs related to the subject, but make sure they are truly written by experts. Review Chapter 4's discussion of legitimate research sources.

Decide on the Presentation's Level of Interaction

Before you move on to organizing your presentation, consider the amount of interaction you should have with the audience. The more interaction the better, when it comes to holding people's attention and ensuring they remember what you talk about. However, the level of interaction often depends on the amount of time you have, your topic, the presentation's level of formality, and the number of people to whom you are speaking. **Exhibit 11-5** illustrates the different levels of interaction between speakers and audiences in different types of presentations.

- ***Monologue.*** A **monologue** is when you speak virtually without interruption, and the audience waits until the end of the presentation to ask questions. This type of presentation is common for large groups. Delivering a monologue requires the most skill because you have to hold the attention of an audience that is relatively uninvolved. However, most good speakers still find ways to engage the audience.
- ***Interactive presentation.*** An **interactive presentation** is when you speak approximately 70 percent of the time, and the audience participates 30 percent of the time. An interactive presentation is good if you want the audience to engage in activities, ask questions, and discuss topics. It works well for groups of fewer than 25 people.
- ***Guided discussion.*** A **guided discussion** is when you speak 50 percent of the time and the audience actively participates 50 percent of the time. A guided discussion works well for small groups that have a series of specific issues they need to discuss and want you to lead the discussion.
- ***Facilitated discussion.*** A **facilitated discussion** is different from a guided discussion because you are not leading the discussion; your audience is. The audience members actively participate more than 60 percent of the time, while you act as a coach to keep them on track. If your presentation is educational rather than informational, facilitation might be the best way to deliver your message. Participants who create, discover, demonstrate, present, summarize, or discuss during a facilitated presentation learn more than if they are told the same information by the presenter.

DID YOU KNOW?

The larger your audience is, the more formal and structured your presentation should be. The structure keeps you on track and keeps your audience in sync with what you are saying.

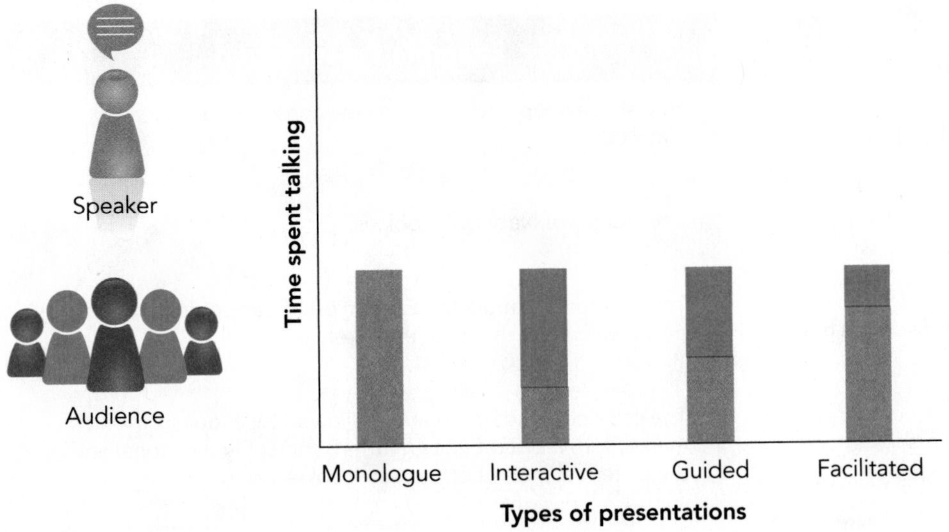

Exhibit 11-5
Time Spent Speaking in Different Types of Presentations

Decide on the Presentation's Location

Are you speaking to a large, formal group, or a small informal group? If you can, check that the seating arrangement is appropriate for your presentation. If you have no control over the seating arrangement, remain flexible and do your best.

- **Classroom seating** is typical for large audiences. All chairs or desks face forward. The arrangement does not lend itself to audience interaction.
- **Conference table seating** is typical for small meetings. Audience members sit around a large table with the presenter at the head of the table. The arrangement makes it easy for audience members to interact but may isolate the presenter at one end of the table.
- **U-shaped seating** is useful for small meetings because it allows the audience members to interact with one another, and the presenter can walk around and interact with the audience.
- **Café seating** is useful for meetings in which the audience will be doing group activities. Members of the audience sit around a number of tables and work together.

Synthesize and Organize Your Information

There are a number of ways to organize your information so it makes sense to your audience. **Exhibit 11-6** shows some common methods along with brief examples of each.

Some methods work better for certain topics than others. For example, research-based presentations lend themselves to the procedural or the chronological approach. For persuasive presentations, the simple-to-complex or general-to-specific formats work well.

Whatever method you choose, capturing your audience's attention and engaging them so they remember what you say is key. In the book *Made to Stick: Why Some Ideas Survive and Others Die*, authors Chip and Dan Heath explain why including information that "sticks," or resonates, with audiences is so important:

> Business managers seem to believe that, once they've clicked through a PowerPoint presentation showcasing their conclusions, they've successfully communicated their ideas. What they've done is shared data. If they're good speakers, they may even have created an enhanced sense, among their employees and peers, that they are "decisive" or "managerial" or "motivational." But the surprise will come when they realize that nothing they've said had impact. They've shared data, but they haven't created ideas that are useful and lasting. Nothing stuck.

Exhibit 11-6 Methods of Organizing Information for Presentations

Method	Example Presentation
Procedural Explains how to do something, step-by-step.	How to develop and launch a new consumer product at Nabisco.
Chronological Presents the topic along a time line, from the past to the present.	The history of Nabisco's cookies.
Simple-to-Complex Presents a specific example and then discusses how it relates to a broader topic.	The scientific formula for a new type of cookie, followed by how it will affect the cookie market.
General-to-Specific Presents general information, and then shows how it applies to a specific topic.	The cookie market in general, followed by a look at the market for Nabisco Oreos, NutterButters, Fig Newtons, and the potential market of the new cookie being developed.

To make your ideas stick, present your information in a way that will make your audience members do the following:

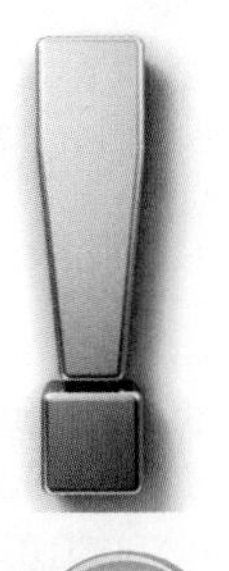

Pay attention
They need to be learning something new and interesting.

Understand and remember
The message must be clear and concrete.

Agree or believe
The message must be credible.

Care
You must touch their emotions by tying your ideas to a bigger ideal.

Act on the message
Make sure your presentation affects their lives.

There are a number of ways to make a presentation stick. Startling statistics and worst- and best-case scenarios often capture people's attention. Demonstrations are extremely effective because they involve motion and engage the senses. Science teachers use demonstrations all the time to help students understand scientific laws—throwing balls, launching objects into space, and blowing things up.

You don't have to be a scientist to give a demonstration. For example, consider Vyomesh Joshi, the one-time head of HP's printer division. In 1991, Joshi determined that the only way HP could stay competitive was to build a new line of printers that could be manufactured for less than the least expensive printer at the time, and retail for around $100. After listening to employees say it was impossible to build such an inexpensive printer, he decided to do something to get his point across: he put an HP printer on the floor and jumped on it (all 200 pounds of him). The printer wasn't damaged. That's when everyone at the presentation got the message. Joshi's physical demonstration clearly conveyed the fact that HP printers were over-engineered. They did not need to be constructed to serve as step stools. The extra engineering, material, and manufacturing costs made them too expensive. In the end, HP managers delivered a line of printers that was produced on time for a mere $49.

REAL INSIGHTS from a Seasoned Professional

Name: *Lynette Luis*
Position: *Technology Sales and Marketing*
Organizations: *Major computer makers*
Location: *Round Rock, Texas*

AFTER 25 YEARS IN TECHNOLOGY sales and marketing for computer companies, Lynette Luis has become an expert on engaging audiences during her presentations. "I find the method chosen for a presentation is not usually as important as how the message is delivered," Luis explains. In other words, media used—slides, flipcharts, and so forth—is far less important than the presenter's passionate delivery.

While earning her bachelor's degree in management and marketing, Luis decided to pursue technology sales and marketing because of the expansive career opportunities in the field and the rapid growth of the consumer products industry. After finishing college, Luis worked her way up from technology inside sales, became a product manager, and eventually an account executive for major computer companies. In these positions, she has worked for such companies as Fujitsu, IBM, and Dell.

When it comes to making business presentations, Luis sees each presentation as a chance to communicate a message and reach out to new contacts. When a presentation involves a product demo, Luis always tests the product first to make sure it works properly before beginning her presentation. She also recommends using visual aids to engage her audience.

"One time, I was speaking to an audience about the 'direction' they should take," she recalls. "I started out with a story about a friend of mine who got lost hiking and how she could have found the right direction with the aid of a compass. I had the compass with me in the presentation. I used it as a prop when I discussed how we could act as a compass for the audience members and help them find the direction to be more successful. Stories are much more engaging than reading words off of a PowerPoint presentation."

Luis' presentation style has evolved with the times, too. "When I started in this business, the Internet did not exist. Access to the Internet and communication methods like e-mail have changed everything," she says. Nevertheless, she warns that technology is not the answer to all business communication. Developing effective communication skills—oral and written—is critical for success. If your skills are lacking in this area, it is worth investing some extra time, Luis suggests.

Currently Luis presents material to clients and other executives on a weekly basis. She provides updates and information on products and her own work within her company. She also conducts quarterly business reviews for clients. However, Luis looks beyond the scope of computer manufacturing when considering her presentation skills. "Regardless of the industry you are in, the way you communicate impacts the first impression you make—and how effective you are on an ongoing basis."

Questions

1. What method does Luis like to use to engage her audience?
2. According to Luis, what skills are vital to making successful presentations?

Source: Lynette Luis in discussion with the author, June 2009.

Similes often stick in people's minds because they compare two very unlike objects using the words *like* and *as.* The following sentences include similes:

> "Life is like an onion: You peel it off one layer at a time, and sometimes you weep." Carl Sandburg
>
> "Humanity, let us say, is like people packed in an automobile which is traveling downhill without lights at terrific speed and driven by a four-year-old child. The signposts along the way are all marked 'Progress.' "—Lord Dunsany[5]

Humor can do wonders for a presentation. When your audience laughs, they are responding emotionally to your presentation. Emotional memories are deeper memories because our brains are hardwired to remember things associated with surprise, pleasure, shock, and discovery as opposed to dry facts. Be sure the humor is relevant to the presentation, comes from your own experience or those near you, and is not offensive.

Stories are another way to make presentations stick. Your audience might not remember every word of the story, but they will get the basic idea. Good stories resonate with audiences.

As we end this section, think of your presentation as a road trip. Once you know your destination, you can map out a route with scenic stops on the way, including rest stops. The destination is your presentation goal. The route is your presentation's organization. The scenic stops are all the stories and examples you share to make the presentation interesting and memorable. The rest stops are where you pause to gauge the interest level of your audience members and let them process what they have heard.

❸ How Can You Be a Better Presenter?

A successful speaker is one who is confident, enthusiastic, and credible. To become a successful presenter, you need to convey to your audience the following six points:

- I will make good use of your time.
- I know who you are.
- I am well organized.
- I know my subject.
- Here are my most important points.
- Feel free to ask me to clarify anything.

How do you convey this information? Through your delivery. **Exhibit 11-7** explains the steps you can take to make your delivery the best it can be.

Dress appropriately for your audience.

Get Ready

1. ***Prepare yourself for the presentation.*** Practice is important. Practice your presentation in front of a mirror, in front of friends, or by recording yourself. If you get a chance to practice in the room where you will deliver the presentation, you will be even more successful. The room will feel familiar to you, and you will be less likely to feel nervous.

   Your attire is important. Don't dress so lavishly that audience members focus on your appearance. You want them to remember your words, not how you looked. Do dress a little better than your audience. You want the audience to relate to you, but you don't want to appear overly casual. Dressing appropriately shows respect for your audience.

Exhibit 11-7 Steps to Delivering a Professional Presentation

2. ***Make sure you have all the materials you need and your presentation devices work.*** There's nothing worse than realizing your projector doesn't work, your microphone is full of static, or someone forgot to make copies of your handouts. Arrive early to make sure everything is as it should be.
3. ***Practice your own calming routine prior to making the presentation.*** Most people get nervous prior to making a presentation. It's normal. On the one hand, a little nervousness can keep you energized, sharp, and focused. On the other hand, extreme nervousness can prevent you from getting your point across, and worse, it can make your entire audience nervous. Taking a short walk and deliberately taking some deep breaths are among some of the things you can do to help calm yourself.

In the Beginning

4. ***Make a good entrance.*** Stand tall, walk with purpose, and greet the members of the audience before you begin your talk. Doing so will help you shake off some of your nervousness. Stop at the podium or front of the room and look at your audience.
5. ***Use an attention-grabbing opening.*** You are standing in front of your audience. It is time to say something, but what? Novice presenters often make the mistake of saying something like the following:

   "Hello, my name is [name], and I'm going to talk to you today about [topic]."

   There's nothing wrong with such an introduction except that it's boring. Instead, try to say something that will grab people's attention. Start with a question (real or hypothetical), an unusual fact, a short story, or a "did you know" type of fact to get people listening. Once you know they are listening, tell them your name and your topic.

   For example, suppose you work for the marketing department of Burger King. You do some more research and decide that a gluten-free hamburger bun just might open up the Whopper market to people with gluten intolerance. You plan to present your idea to Burger King's vice president of marketing. How do you start your presentation, with Version A or Version B?

   Version A: "I've been talking to Dr. Sorenson, the Senior Food Scientist in Research, and he tells me that 1 in 133 people in the U.S. suffers from gluten intolerance and cannot eat any foods made from wheat, since wheat contains gluten. People who suffer from gluten intolerance cannot eat our hamburger buns because buns are made of wheat flour, and wheat contains gluten . . ."

   -OR-

   Version B: "Did you know that 1 out of 133 people in the U.S. can't eat a hamburger bun because they're allergic to wheat? That's 2.3 million people a year who will never eat at Burger King. How much money does this cost Burger King annually? More than $298 million, assuming people eat one burger a week. Hundreds of millions of dollars go unearned simply because we don't offer a gluten-free hamburger. What's a gluten-free hamburger? That's what I'm here to explain."

   Did you choose Version B? The vice president of marketing is certainly more likely to listen to you if you choose this introduction.

PEARSON mybcommlab

Apply these key concepts by revising a new document. Go to Chapter 11 in mybcommlab.com and select Document Makeovers.

6. ***Start with the "PAL" approach.*** Once you have the attention of the members of the audience, set their expectations by sharing three important pieces of information about your presentation. The **PAL approach** stands for:
   - Purpose
   - Agenda
   - Length

   Telling the audience these three pieces of information takes very little time. It's as simple as saying: "Hi, I'm [your name]. Thank you for having me. I'm here to talk about ABC [your purpose]. I'm going to cover X, Y, and Z [the agenda]. We should be able to do this in X minutes [the length], depending on how many questions you have."

During the Presentation

7. ***Use positive body language in your delivery.*** Many people do not realize the impact their body language has on an audience. Stand up straight with your legs slightly apart so you don't lose your balance or rock back and forth. Keep your hands out of your pockets to avoid jingling your keys or loose change. Avoid wearing bracelets that jingle when you move your hands around. Keep your arms relaxed and at your sides. Crossing your arms conveys defensiveness to your audience. Smile from time to time when the situation warrants it. If you smile all of the time, the members of the audience could get the impression that you are insincere. However, if you never smile, they may find you cold.

   Move around. A presenter who stands as still as a statue is not very interesting to watch. Don't pace, but do walk around a bit. Express your passion for your topic by moving your arms and hands.

8. ***Maintain appropriate eye contact.*** Look at the entire audience in different parts of the room. Look at the back of the room, look at the right side of the room, and look at the left side. Do this in a natural way so your head doesn't look like a camera scanning the room.

   Make eye contact to establish rapport. Some presenters like to pick out a few people around the room and look at them for a few seconds. (Don't look at them for too long, or the audience members might get the impression you are staring at them.) If you are uncomfortable looking into people's eyes, look just above their foreheads for about three seconds. It will appear as if you're looking at them, and you won't feel uncomfortable.

9. ***Use your voice to your advantage.*** Do not read your presentation. Make sure you know it well enough that you can simply glance at your notes now and then and talk as if you were having a conversation. Some speakers prefer to write out their entire presentations and refer to them as needed. Others prefer clear, succinct outlines they can glance at. Still others use talking points or phrases. If you are using a slide show as part of your presentation, a printout of the slides can serve as your notes. However, don't simply read your slides. Instead, refer to them periodically as you speak.

   - ***Don't talk too fast or too slow.*** If you are not sure about your natural speaking speed, try recording and listening to yourself. If you still don't know if you are talking too fast or too slow, ask someone else to listen to the recording. You don't want to sound like you are racing to finish. Nor do you want to speak as if you are putting the audience into a trance. If necessary, alter your speed and record yourself again. With practice, you will get the speed just right. If you have an accent, practice in front of people who aren't familiar with it. Have them stop you if they become confused. You may need to speak more slowly or pronounce some words differently.
   - ***Make sure you're heard.*** If you are naturally soft-spoken, you will have to increase your volume. Have a friend stand at the back of the room and ask if he can hear you.
   - ***Keep your voice interesting.*** **Modulation** is the way your voice goes up and down. No one responds well to a monotone voice. It tends to put people to sleep. If your natural speaking voice is a monotone, you will have to deliberately raise and lower it.

10. ***Involve your audience.*** A good presentation is the same as a conversation, but your audience is larger. Think about it: In a conversation, would you do all the talking and never do any listening? Hopefully not.

    To make your presentation seem more like a conversation, build a relationship with your audience by including them. Ask questions, have a discussion, or use activities to engage your audience. In smaller groups in which interaction is easy to manage, hands-on activities and discussions are useful. In larger groups, it will likely be too difficult to manage such a level of interaction. However, you can still raise questions periodically during your presentation to get your audience thinking. Even **rhetorical questions,** which are questions asked purely for effect rather than to elicit answers, will help.

    For example, suppose you work for Procter & Gamble and are making a presentation about a new, lavender-scented bath soap. Instead of bombarding your listeners with statistics about the impact of scent on the brain, and how it relaxes or invigorates, you might consider including the following simple activity to engage a large or small audience.

Body language tells people a lot about you, especially during a presentation.

CHECKLIST

Before, during, and after your presentation:

Before

- ☑ Prepare yourself for the presentation.
- ☑ Make sure you have all the materials you need and your presentation devices work.
- ☑ Practice your own calming routine prior to making the presentation.

During

- ☑ Make a good entrance.
- ☑ Use an attention-grabbing opener.
- ☑ Start with the PAL approach.
- ☑ Use positive body language in your delivery.
- ☑ Maintain appropriate eye contact.
- ☑ Use your voice to your advantage.
- ☑ Involve your audience.

After

- ☑ Provide a definite wrap-up of your presentation.

REAL INSIGHTS from a New Professional

Name: *Michelle Aleti*
Title: *Brand Manager of Gillette*
Organization: *Procter & Gamble*
Location: *Boston, Massachusetts*

"THERE IS NO TYPICAL DAY," says Michelle Aleti of her job at Procter & Gamble. Aleti is a brand manager for the company, which means she manages products, not people. Her job includes everything from supervising product launches to developing marketing plans for products.

Aleti began her career with a series of internships. Including the internship with her current employer, Procter & Gamble, Aleti completed eight internships before she was able to narrow down her interests. In school, she gravitated toward marketing and psychology before realizing that she was "really interested in consumer insights and team building." After earning her bachelor's degree in finance and working as a marketing consultant, Aleti returned to school with an eye on her passion: marketing and strategy.

Aleti is expected to think critically about the marketing and strategy recommendations she makes to her employer. She must back up any solution she devises with rock-solid facts before presenting her ideas to large groups. When creating a presentation, she asks herself these questions: What is my recommendation? What is my rationale behind it? What are the risks?

When Aleti is ready to present her findings, she follows the same steps she recommends to others:

1. Keep the presentation simple.
2. Present the message in bite-sized chunks.
3. Be objective and help the audience digest the message.
4. Follow your logic.

"Clear presentation communicates clarity of thought," says Aleti. During a recent presentation to a group of venture capitalists, she used PowerPoint slides to supplement her speech. She had a passion for the topic and was confident of her own knowledge of the material. "I got a lot of head nods. A lot of eye contact," she remembers. When she asked for questions mid-presentation, several people spoke up. The questions built on one another, and the conversation remained relevant to the topic. The level of interaction showed Aleti her audience was following her. She highly recommends that speakers "take cues from questions."

In the end, Aleti's advice for giving presentations is simple: "Be 'in the moment' as much as you can. If you stay in the moment, you will stay with your audience."

Questions

1. What questions does Aleti ask herself before putting together a presentation?
2. According to Aleti, how can presenters gauge the interaction of their audience members?

Source: Michelle Aleti in discussion with the author, June 2009.

First you paint the scene for your audience:

"I want you to close your eyes and imagine you have been flown to Provence, France, where you're staying in a beautiful villa, free of charge.

You step out on the balcony in the early morning and sit back in a comfortable chair. You gaze out over acres and acres of lavender fields. All you see is a never-ending blanket of intensely purple flowers, glowing in the sun. All you smell is the heavenly aroma of clean, calming lavender. How does that make you feel?" Even if some of your audience members weren't interested in lavender before, they are listening now.

Stories and imagery can help engage an audience.

As you involve your audience, pay attention to how the members react, especially their nonverbal actions. Do people look confused? Hostile? Sleepy? Pay attention and adjust your voice, volume, examples, and delivery accordingly. (The next section provides some tips for handling audience members who are hostile, shy, bored, or who ask a lot of questions.)

At the End

11. ***Provide a definite wrap-up of your presentation.*** Summarize what you have talked about to reinforce your presentation. If appropriate, make a call to action that encour-

ages your audience to do something. For example, you could say, "Now that you know how we bake our cookies, I hope you will reach for them in the store the next time you shop."

It's always nice to thank your audience and end your presentation with a short story or quote. Your goal is to leave your audience members wanting more. You can also mention books, Web sites, and reports they can consult for more details or invite them to other presentations in which they might be interested.

4 How Should Different Types of Audiences Be Handled?

We have mentioned how important it is to engage the members of your audience and interact with them. The profile you just read about Michelle Aleti demonstrates as much. Let's look at ways to deal with different kinds of audiences.

How to Handle a Hostile Audience

As a presenter, you may be confronted by a heckler or an audience member who is genuinely hostile. Such a situation is uncomfortable for both the presenter and the audience. Most hecklers just want to be heard. Address their concerns but don't get caught up in their emotional turmoil. The following process will help you deal with a hostile audience.

- ***Take a deep breath before saying anything.*** When a hostile audience member asks you a question, it can feel like an attack. Taking a deep breath gives you a chance to compose yourself. Then take a small step toward the person with your palms open. This shows you are not running away (as a step back would indicate) or threatening them (as a pointing finger or hand would do). Don't appear defensive by crossing your arms.
- ***Rephrase the question and address the entire audience.*** For example, you might say, "It sounds like you're very concerned about the amount of time you spent on hold when you tried to reach a representative by phone. Then you didn't get an answer that made any sense to you and the representative didn't seem to care. Did I capture your concerns correctly?"
- ***Respond to the question, not the emotion.*** This can be difficult to do. It's easier if you remember that the audience member has a valid concern but is so upset that his or her emotions are getting in the way of communicating clearly. Remember, the person's emotions have nothing to do with you and may not really be directed at you.
- ***Make eye contact with the entire audience, not just the heckler, as you address the question.*** Do not engage in a one-on-one conversation with the heckler. Talk to the entire audience. For example, say "I'm sure all of you have had a similar problem when you have called a company and tried to get a question answered over the phone. Long waits on the phone feel like forever."
- ***Show the person respect.*** Even if the person is rude or aggressive, do not respond in the same way. Resist the impulse to lash out or be defensive. If you act that way to one member of the audience, the rest of the audience members will assume you would do the same to them. As a result, they will be less likely to trust you and less receptive to your message.

How to Handle a Shy Audience

A shy audience can be just as difficult to handle as a hostile one. People in a shy audience sit quietly, never say a word, and seem to resist any attempt to be engaged. Consequently, you have no idea whether you are getting your ideas across to them or not. The following are some suggestions for dealing with a shy audience:

- ***Share a short story.*** Then ask if anyone has experienced something similar.
- ***Ask a rhetorical question.*** "Did you know that 100 to 150 people die each year from peanut allergies?" is an example of a rhetorical question.[6]

- ***Ask a question and begin to answer it.*** Then ask someone else to finish. You might say, "OK, I'm planning my presentation. What do I do first? First, I need to identify my audience. Then what?"
- ***Ask an open-ended question.*** Ask questions that may not have any right or wrong answer. This avoids making shy people anxious about providing the wrong answer. You might say something like, "Can someone tell me about a time that they got exactly what they asked for?" There is no correct answer to the question—anyone's answer is fine.
- ***Ask for help.*** Even the shyest person can't resist the opportunity to help someone else. For example, you might say, "Hmmm, I may not have been explaining this in a way that makes sense to everyone. Can anyone help me out?"

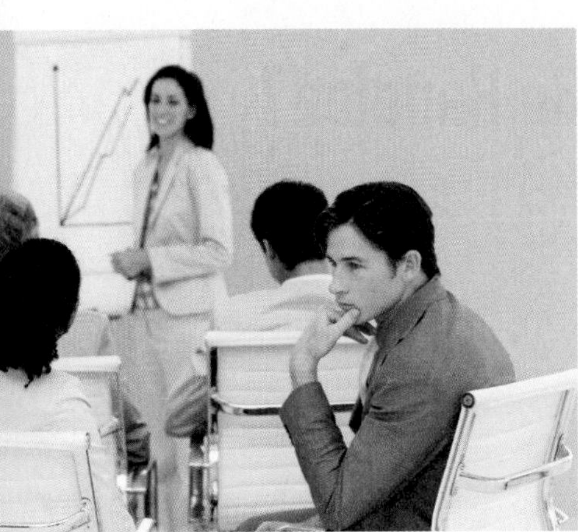

A bored audience is an unengaged audience.

How to Handle a Bored Audience

A bored audience is somewhat similar to a shy one in the sense that the audience members don't want to interact with you. Audience members are often bored when you have not done a proper analysis of purpose and audience. You may be telling your audience things they already know, in which case you have lost their interest and they don't want to listen anymore. Or, you may be telling them things they cannot comprehend, in which case you have confused them so much that they don't understand what you're saying and have tuned you out.

To deal with a bored audience, you must first recognize they're bored. If people are shuffling papers, have their eyes closed (are sleeping), or are looking downward (perhaps sending text messages or checking their phones), they are bored. You will also hear a bored audience, because the members tend to whisper to each other and fidget.

What can you do? The following suggestions can help you tell if there are aspects of your presentation your audience members don't understand as well as help you re-engage them:

- ***Ask questions.*** Asking questions can help wake up a bored audience.
- ***Tell a short story.*** For example, you might say, "I think these facts and figures might make more sense if I tell a story."
- ***Explain by using an example.*** For example, you might say, "It's a little tough to grasp this concept, so let me give you an example." You might also combine such a statement with a question: "This is a tough concept to explain. Anyone else want to jump in and give it a try?"
- ***Demonstrate something.*** Any kind of physical activity is likely to wake up your audience. You can perform a demonstration, ask audience members to participate, or simply ask your audience to stand, stretch, or move with you. Sometimes boredom is nothing more than fatigue brought on by remaining sedentary for too long.

How to Handle a Questioning Audience

Questions indicate that your audience is paying attention and they are interested. However, staying on track during a presentation is difficult when audience members ask a lot of questions, and you do not want to abruptly cut them off. The following are some suggestions for dealing with questions:

- ***Build time into your presentation to handle questions.*** Let your audience know how you are going to handle questions. For smaller audiences and situations in which you have the option of extending the length of your presentation, let the audience members ask questions whenever they have them. For larger audiences or tighter time frames, ask people to jot down their questions and hold them until the end of the presentation.
- ***When someone asks a question, always repeat it.*** Other people might not have heard the question, especially if the person who asked it spoke softly. By repeating the question, you also ensure that you understood it correctly.
- ***Never laugh at a question or talk down to the person who asked it.*** If you do this to even one member of the audience, no one else will feel comfortable asking you questions.
- ***Stay on target and hold your explanations to a minimum.*** If the question is too specific, answer it in a general way and offer to go into detail after the presentation. If the question is not relevant, again, offer to answer it after the presentation. If you get too

many questions, write them down and then compile a list of frequently asked questions (FAQs). You can e-mail the FAQs and their answers, post them on the Internet, or print them in a report for the audience.

- ***If you don't know the answer to a question, admit it and offer to find out the answer.*** Sometimes all it takes is a quick phone call or conversation with a content expert to find the answer. If more research is required, you can always get back to your audience later.

Regardless of the type of audience you're presenting to, avoid holding a one-on-one conversation with any one member of the audience. Always address everyone to make all attendees feel included.

5 What Is the Key to Making a Successful Team Presentation?

Making a **team presentation**—two or more people presenting—will alleviate some of the pressure you might feel during a presentation. Because you're sharing the podium with someone else, the entire presentation no longer rests on your shoulders alone. Any of the interaction styles you learned earlier in the chapter can be used in a team presentation as well. Take the following steps to make your presentation a success:

- ***Organize the presentation.*** Divide up the work evenly when it comes to preparation and planning. Decide who's going to research what and who's going to present what. Develop a time line so everyone knows when to finish his or her part of the work on the presentation. Make sure the time line allows for review and changes. Have each person create his or her part of the presentation, but choose one person to put it all together so it has a common voice and a common look.
- ***Practice the presentation.*** Practice the presentation, and time each person's part. Figure out transitions from one person speaking to another. At the end of your part, summarize what you talked about, give the name of the new presenter, and introduce that presenter's topic. For example, imagine a team presentation on a new line of chocolate truffles. When the first speaker finishes, she might say, "Now that I've explained how we create those interesting shapes and flavors, it's time for Ethan to describe our unique packaging techniques."
- ***Deliver the presentation.*** Introduce all of the members of the team and explain what each person will talk about. Share the floor with your co-presenters. Do not interrupt your co-presenters, and don't take over for them unless they ask for help. Do not talk too much and dominate the presentation. Be sure you (and your team members) stick to your time limit.
- ***Handle questions.*** Allow time for questions. Have one person field questions and turn over the right questions to the right presenters. When one of your teammates is answering a question, do not interrupt. Instead, ask permission to add your insights to an answer.

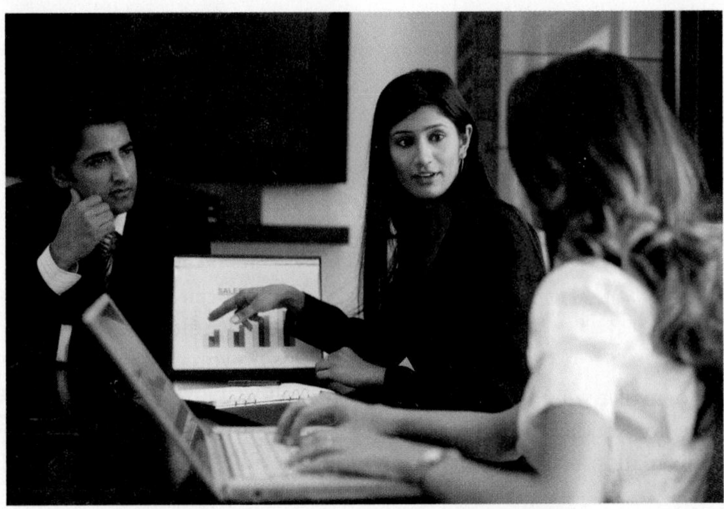

Team presentations have their own unique set of challenges.

Summary *Synthesize What You Have Learned*

1. What are the three basic types of presentations?

The three basic types of presentations are informative, which convey information to a group; persuasive, which convince a group to believe or do something; and educational, which teach a group to do something.

2. How do you plan a presentation?

Six factors you must consider when planning presentations are identify your audience, determine your purpose, brainstorm, collect facts, decide on the level of interaction for delivery, and synthesize and organize.

3. How can you be a better presenter?

Good ways to prepare for and polish a presentation are to prepare or practice, check your materials and equipment, perform your personal "anti-nervousness" routine, make a good entrance, provide an attention-grabbing opener, use good body language, make eye contact, be aware of voice volume and pitch, involve your audience, and provide a definite wrap-up and call to action.

4. How should different types of audiences be handled?

To handle a hostile audience, listen to the message, not the emotion. Restate the individual's concern, then address the entire audience, not just the individual who is upset. Gain a shy audience's trust with open-ended questions, stories, and requests for assistance. Similarly, gain a bored audience's trust with stories, questions, and examples. Lastly, manage a questioning audience by addressing questions as they come or all together at the end. Keep answers short and provide details later.

5. What is the key to making a successful team presentation?

To make a successful team presentation, divide up its preparation, practice it as a group, and time yourselves. Introduce all of the team members during the presentation and take turns speaking. As a group, field questions from the audience.

PEARSON **mybcommlab**™ Are you an active learner? Go to **mybcommlab.com** to master Chapter 11's content. Chapter 11's interactive activities include:

- Customizable Study Plan and Chapter 11 practice quizzes
- Chapter 11 Simulation, Business Presentations, that helps you think critically and prepare to make choices in the business world
- Chapter 11 Video Exercise, Effective Oral Presentations, which shows you how textbook concepts are put into practice every day
- Flash cards for mastering the definition of chapter terms
- Interactive Lessons that visually review key chapter concepts
- Document Makeovers for hands-on, scored practice in revising documents

Know It *Reflect, Respond, and Express*

Build Your Critical Thinking Skills

Critical Thinking Questions

1. Describe some techniques you can use to involve your audience in your presentation. What effect does audience involvement have on the retention of information regarding your message?
2. Analyze the importance of using your voice during a presentation. How would you define the right tempo? What assumptions do you make about someone who speaks too fast or too slow? How do volume and a person's accent affect your reception to a presentation? How can you use modulation to place emphasis on important elements in your presentation?

3. Type in the term "team presentation" to YouTube.com and find two examples of team presentations: one effective presentation and one ineffective presentation. What is the difference in the preparation levels of the two different presentations? How effectively or ineffectively did each group present their information?

Critical Thinking Scenario

Chad, a writer and trainer for the Kimberly-Clark Corporation, was responsible for making a presentation about a new brand of diapers to an audience of about 100 people. The presentation was taking place in a large conference room. Chad arrived early and made sure everything in the room was in working order. He then put his handouts on every chair. Soon the room was packed and the audience was eager. In fact, all of the audience members were looking through Chad's handouts.

Chad introduced his subject matter with a rhetorical question that everyone could answer and then told a short story about something most of his audience could relate to—babies, diapers, and potty accidents. Everyone laughed.

Having made a connection with the audience, he started discussing his topic and walking through his slides. The slides had interesting pictures and just enough text to keep the audience attuned. Then the unthinkable happened—the power went out. No projector. No slides. Just darkness.

Questions

1. After the lights went out, what could Chad have done to release the tension in the room and reassure the audience?
2. Suppose the lights came back on, but Chad's laptop and projector didn't work. How could Chad have continued his presentation?
3. How did preparation affect Chad's situation? Are there dangers associated with being so rehearsed?
4. Think of at least two things that could go wrong during a presentation. What could you do about them?
5. What would you feel comfortable doing to get your audience engaged?
6. How do you plan to practice your presentation?

Write It *Draft, Revise, and Finalize*

Create Your Own Success Story

1. Prepare a very short, informal presentation for a small group. (You will be giving the presentation in the next section, "Speak It.") The topic can be about anything you're interested in or are familiar with. Follow these steps:
   a. Think of a list of possible topics and write them down.
   b. Select the topic that appeals to you the most and that you think would interest the audience.
   c. Create a mind map with all of the ideas you would like to put in the presentation. Remember to circle each idea and connect it with related ideas.
   d. When you're done, cross out any ideas that you think don't fit.
2. Determine which type of learning style best describes your approach to learning. Are you a visual learner? Sequential? Write a description of your learning style and the types of presentation techniques that hold your attention.
3. Analyze the lecture you heard in this class or another class recently. Does the lecture fulfill the components needed for creating an effective, informative presentation? Did the instructor captivate your attention, make you care about the information covered, and leave you with the key points to remember? Write a brief explanation of your findings and suggestions for improvement if the components of an informative presentation were not fulfilled.
4. What experience do you have with being a part of the different types of problematic audiences? Write an explanation of the different types of audiences of which you have been a part and analyze how the presenter handled the situation.
5. Find your institution's student policies on the school's Web site or in a student handbook. Choose a group of students to work with to prepare a presentation of one of the policies for the class. How do you divide labor for tackling the research and compiling the information? What organization will best convey the policy you choose? How do you deliver the information—as a group or by choosing a group representative? Who do you designate to answer audience questions? After you have completed the presentation, write a reflection of your experience working as a team member for a presentation.
6. What issues can arise from presenting as a team? What issues do you need to address before you begin researching the material to present? How much time do you allow for practice? How can group dynamics affect the project overall? Write a summary of your answers and what you would expect from working on a team presentation.

Speak It *Discuss, Listen, and Understand*

Build Your Leadership and Teamwork Skills

1. This exercise is designed to help you deal with three problems presenters face: keeping an audience interested, coping with hecklers, and fielding questions. The steps in the exercise should be done in front of a small group of 5–10 people. For each step, use any information you want from the mind map you created in the "Write It" section of this chapter.

As the speaker

   a. Come up with an interesting opening for the topic from your mind map. Try it out on your audience.
   b. Take an idea from your mind map and share it with your audience in a story form.
   c. Try to accomodate your audience and respond appropriately to questions asked.

As an audience member

   d. "Heckle" the speaker.
   e. Ask the speaker a lot of questions.

After the presentation

   f. Answer and discuss the following questions with the speaker following the presentation:
      - Did the presenter have good posture? What did the person do with his or her or hands? Was the person chewing gum?
      - Did the presenter make eye contact with different members of the audience? Did the eye contact seem too short? Too long? Or just right?
      - Did the presenter vary his or her pitch to avoid sounding monotonous? How was the person's tone? Was it friendly or arrogant? Condescending?
      - How did the presenter interact with the audience? Did the presenter tell interesting stories? Ask questions? How did he or she handle boredom?
      - How did the presenter interact with hostile audience members? Did the person listen to the message rather than the emotion and restate any concerns audience members might have had?
      - How did the presenter handle questions? Were the answers short and relevant? Did the presenter answer questions as they were asked or wait until the end of the presentation? How effective was this approach?

2. In small groups or as a class, discuss how the different types of presentations (monologue, interactive, guided, and facilitated) relate to the presentation's location (classroom, conference table, U-shaped, and café seating). How is the formality level a factor in type and location considerations? How can both the type and location give you the tools for an effective presentation?
3. In small groups, develop a five-minute sales presentation for one of your supplies, such as your pen, pencil, or notebook. How can you add value to your presentation and convince the class/audience to use the supply?
4. In small groups, discuss the different techniques for making a presentation stick with an audience. What is your goal in using the different techniques? What examples of these techniques can you recall from different presentations you have seen?
5. Discuss how the suggestions for handling different types of audiences relate to one another. How are the strategies different? How are they similar? Discuss how the strategies can lead to an effective presentaiton when there are no audience issues.
6. Analyze the strategies for handling a questioning audience. How can you encourage questions from your audience without being interrupted? How can you address a question without having a one-on-one conversation with the questioner? Discuss different strategies with the class.
7. Select a section of Chapter 11 to present to the class. Prepare an educational presentation that divides the section into chunks of information rather than one lecture. Interact with the audience—remember that asking questions that require answers elicits commitment in your audience members.

Do It *Document Your Success Track Record*

Build Your e-Portfolio

In the "Speak It" section, you just had a chance to deliver a short, informal speech in front of a small group. Now you're going to prepare a short, but slightly more formal presentation for your entire class.

First, organize your basic ideas into a simple outline. You can either use the topic from your practice speech or choose a new topic. However, if you choose a new topic, consider creating a new mind map to help you synthesize and organize your ideas before you create the outline.

Next, draft your presentation by filling in the outline for the following presentation plan on a separate piece of paper. When you finish, put the plan in your e-portfolio to use during the next chapter.

- General Information (title, purpose, audience)
- Opening (come up with an interesting question, quote, or story)
- Outline (main points, questions to ask, or activity ideas)
- Wrap-Up (sum it up, call to action, and possible quote or story)

Business in Action

IDEO—Making Business Presentations the Unconventional Way

IDEO refers to itself as "a global design consultancy." "Everything except nature is designed," IDEO founder Dave Kelley said in a 1999 Nightline interview. Since the design firm's inception in 1987, IDEO has created or improved consumer products in every imaginable way—many of which began with something as simple as a presentation. Indeed, the firm's success has been unstoppable: In 2009, Fast Company magazine ranked IDEO fifth on its list of Top 10 Most Innovative Companies.

IDEO brings people from different specialties together to gain new insights, identify problems, and create efficient solutions for common consumer products. By doing so, IDEO has improved everything from scales to cleaning supplies, to bikes and water pumps for third-world countries. With an extensive list of innovations and successful products, IDEO works quite differently than other companies. Just look at the IDEO meeting room. It's populated with Nerf guns, which designers are encouraged to play with as they think up ideas and communicate them. During meetings, Kelley stresses the importance of freely offering and accepting input. In fact, Kelley wears a bell on his wrist like a watch, and a sharp ring fills the room if designers start putting down one another's ideas.

Within each meeting, there is actually a handful of small, informal presentations happening. From suggesting a new idea, to building on top of an old one, designers are constantly offering their thoughts to the group to try and find the most innovative products. By creating a supportive atmosphere (complete with a "bell-watch") where brainstorming is encouraged and stimulated, IDEO serves as a fertile soil for concrete, plausible ideas to grow out of mini-presentations.

Outside the meeting room, IDEO teams pitch their ideas to clients with formal, persuasive presentations. With a laugh, Kelley says the firm's playful atmosphere might be overwhelming for a traditional corporation. After all, IDEO is trying to sell its product ideas within the presentation, not scare off the customer. Though its methods may not always be traditional, its presentations are always informative, interesting, and innovative.

On the leading edge of design and innovation, IDEO doesn't just come up with creative ideas; it tailors every idea with efficiency and new consumers in mind. By providing a place for ideas to grow into designs, the company has taken simple presentations from their birth in the boardroom, to their place on the shelves of the industry and shown that presentations, no matter how small or informal, can lead to big ideas and bigger solutions.

If you want to see examples of IDEO presentations, workshops, and television ads, visit the IDEO Web site or visit YouTube and enter the key word IDEO.

Questions

1. What is unique about IDEO's meeting room and meetings?
2. What role do mini-presentations play in IDEO's meetings?

Sources: Linda Tischler, "IDEO's David Kelley on Design Thinking," *Fast Company,* February 1, 2009, accessed at http://www.fastcompany.com/magazine/132/a-designer-takes-on-his-biggest-challenge-ever.html; "The Deep Dive," *ABC News: Nightline,* ABC (New York: ABC, July, 13, 1999), accessed at http://www.youtube.com/watch?v=oUazVjvsMHs/.

Key Terms

Café seating. Seating in which the audience sits at small tables and works in groups. *(p. 322)*

Classroom seating. Seating in which the audience sits in chairs or desks facing forward. *(p. 322)*

Conference table seating. Seating in which the audience sits around a large table with the presenter at the head. *(p. 322)*

Educational presentation. A presentation that teaches. *(p. 317)*

Facilitated discussion. A presentation in which the audience members actively participate more than 60 percent of the time, while you act as a coach to keep them on track. *(p. 321)*

Guided discussion. A presentation in which you speak 50 percent of the time and the audience actively participates 50 percent of the time. Often used for small groups. *(p. 321)*

Informative presentation. A presentation that explains new policies, procedures, or presents the status of a project to others. *(p. 316)*

Interactive presentation. A presentation in which you speak approximately 70 percent of the time, and the audience participates 30 percent of the time. Often used for groups of fewer than 25 people. *(p. 321)*

Learning styles. The different ways by which people learn. *(p. 318)*

Modulation. The pitch of your voice. *(p. 327)*

Monologue. A presentation in which you speak virtually without interruption, and the audience waits until the end of the presentation to ask questions. Often used for large audiences. *(p. 321)*

PAL approach. Stands for "purpose," "agenda," and "length," which are three important pieces of information you should tell your audience after opening your presentation. *(p. 326)*

Persuasive presentation. A presentation intended to convince the audience to do something. *(p. 316)*

Rhetorical questions. Questions asked only for effect, not to elicit answers. *(p. 327)*

Similes. A comparison of two different concepts using the words *like* and *as*. *(p. 324)*

Team presentation. A presentation made by two or more people. *(p. 331)*

U-shaped seating. Seating in which the audience sits in a semicircle around the presenter. *(p. 322)*

Review Questions *Test Yourself*

1. What are three purposes of presentations?
2. What is the purpose of a persuasive presentation? What is the key to giving persuasive presentations? Give a few examples of types of persuasive presentations.
3. Describe what components make an informative presentation effective.
4. What are the six factors that will help you prepare for any presentation?
5. What are the seven questions that will help you know your audience better?
6. What are three questions to help you figure out your purpose of presenting?
7. List a few common organizational methods for presenting information and briefly explain each type.
8. What are six messages you want to convey to your audience as you present?
9. Describe the importance of practice and how to do so for presentations.
10. Explain what the PAL approach is and how you can use it in a presentation.
11. What process can you use to handle a hostile audience?
12. How can you pull a shy audience out of its shell?
13. What strategies can you use to liven up a bored audience?
14. How do the strategies differ for solo versus team presentations?
15. What are the four steps to a successful team presentation?
16. On what three aspects will your audience always judge you?

Grammar Review *Mastering Accuracy*

Dashes and Hyphens

Section I

Each of the following sentences contains one or more common errors in word usage, grammar, or style. Identify the errors. If you have trouble finding the errors, review Sections 2.7.1. and 2.7.2. in the handbook (Appendix D) at the back of this textbook.

1. Tasha decided a move to the South-Carolina border might provide more financially-rewarding job opportunities.
2. It appears there might be a printer issue as - a yellow gray - smudge appears on the bottom of all recently-copied documents.
3. John's music was too loud – therefore, his colleagues complained to his new-supervisor.
4. Maria's distinct personality traits, such as her bubbly-enthusiasm and sense-of-humor, are guaranteed to help her in this business.
5. Candidates who dress professionally: such as business-suit, will make a better impression.
6. The most relevant sections of the handbook; page-46, the most overlooked page – will be included on tomorrow's applicant test.
7. Vanessa, Jacob, - and Isabella – these are the candidates I will need to interview next-week.
8. Exercise caution on the east-stairwell, there is a loose-railing.
9. Please be aware – of the time – I wouldn't want you to miss – this meeting.
10. Remember to check your timecards: that is, we would not want to miss any hours you may have worked.

Section II

On a separate sheet of paper, rewrite the following sentences so they are clearer, more professional sounding, grammatically correct, and goodwill oriented.

1. Folks applying for the externship should arrive in a punctual fashion; that is, unless they want to be discounted immediately.
2. Try not to dress like a tramp for the seminar tomorrow – for example, I wouldn't wear a halter top.
3. It's rude to leave the light on - when you very well know - you are the last one out!
4. Stop panicking during fire drills – for example, don't make our department look foolish like you did last time by forgetting the exit strategies!
5. During the Jan.-1988 and Mar.-1988, our company increased efficiency levels by 66-percent.
6. Our VP-of-Security will be on the New-York—Paris flight tomorrow afternoon promptly after he checks in at the VIP counter.
7. The anti-Semitism message spray painted on the building is wrong and looks bad for the company.
8. The merger is taking a long time and it will take several weeks to complete and we want to send some thanks in advance for your un-wavering patience – and support.
9. There is a Web site all employees should visit in order to review the assessments of the microorganisms located in substation B.
10. The outside of our new building appears appealing and looks like the mall.

■ Extra Resources *Tools You Can Use*

Books

- Heath, Chip, and Dan Heath. *Made to Stick: Why Some Ideas Survive and Others Die.* New York: Random House, 2007.
- Hoff, Ron. *I Can See You Naked: America's Best Book on Making Presentations.* Kansas City, MO: Andrews McMeel Publishing, 1992.

Web Sites

- "A Funny Thing Happened on My Way to This Meeting," *The Total Communicator.*
- Boyd, Stephen, "Incorporate Humor in Your Next Presentation," *Presentation Magazine.*

"Vision trumps all other senses." —Dr. John Medina, author

CHAPTER 12

Effective Visual Aids in Presentations

Engaging the Audience and Commanding Attention

>>> **As a project** manager for a firm specializing in new communication technology, Yasmine works with five other people—all in other countries. Together, through video conferencing and document sharing over the Internet, Yasmine and her team put their heads together to come up with new products.

Last month, the team was asked to develop a new voice-activated headset for the firm's most popular smartphone and to present the product in a Web presentation to the company's worldwide marketing department. Though confident about their designs, Yasmine is nervous about making and leading a thorough, interesting presentation. She's done presentations in the past, but never virtually for so many people around the globe.

Concerned about the upcoming deadline, Yasmine gathered her team together for a video conference. Together, they considered different visual aid techniques for their slideshow. Using one another's cultural experiences, they decided on the visual aids to add to the presentation to engage the marketing department and effectively demonstrate the product's worldwide marketability. Jing, from the Philippines, suggested mentioning the product's beneficial impact on families, and Greg, from the U.K., suggested incorporating graphs to show the product's versatility in both rural and urban areas. By the end of the call, they had so many ideas on how to make the presentation a success, Yasmine could barely keep them all in her head.

LEARNING OBJECTIVE QUESTIONS

1. What types of visual aids are used in presentations?
2. What makes a slideshow effective?
3. How can you make your slides look professional?
4. How can you deliver your slideshow effectively?
5. How can the Web be used to make presentations?

PEARSON mybcommlab Access interactive videos, simulations, sample documents, document makeovers, and assessment quizzes in Chapter 12 of **mybcommlab.com** for mastery of this chapter's objectives.

Why bother including visual aids in your presentations? The answer is easy. As the opening quote in this chapter suggests, vision is our most dominant sense. Our brains are hardwired to remember visual information. Most people remember the pictures, colors, and patterns they are shown better than they remember what is said during a presentation.

The ability to create presentations using visual aids is important in any profession, but it is particularly vital to those working in the technology industry. Individuals working in technology fields spend a fair amount of time sharing what they know with their coworkers, managers, and customers. When it comes to presenting hard-to-understand technical knowledge, good visual aids provide a necessary boost by clarifying complicated concepts and keeping people from becoming bored during presentations.

As you might imagine, technology companies manufacture a wide variety of products from software and electronics, to communication devices and scientific instruments. Just as the products of technology continue to grow and adapt, so does the industry. Experts say that the $58.2 billion industry is expected to grow 38 percent between now and 2016. That translates to an estimated 1.3 million job opportunities for graduates interested in doing anything from computer software and electronic engineering, to information communication and sales and marketing.[1]

1 What Types of Visual Aids Are Used in Presentations?

Visual aids keep your audience interested and engaged. In the upcoming section, we will provide some insight into making live presentations that do not use slides such as PowerPoint. Later, we will look specifically at slide presentations.

You can use a variety of low-tech and high-tech visual aids including flipcharts, whiteboards, overhead projectors, digital visual presenters, handouts, demonstrations, and slide shows. Over time, as you make presentations, you will discover which visual aids you are most comfortable using and which are most effective given the type of presentation you are making.

Flipcharts

For smaller audiences, flipcharts provide an effective way to visually support your presentation. A **flipchart** is a large, portable pad of paper placed on an easel. A flipchart has several benefits:

- There is no overhead projector lightbulb to burn out.
- You can add or cross out points in the middle of your presentation.
- A flipchart invites comments and discussion from the audience.
- Flipping between pages gives your hands something to do so you look less nervous.

Many presenters write on flipcharts extemporaneously as they collect ideas from the audience. However, other presenters choose to prepare some of their flipchart pages in advance to avoid using note cards and save writing time.

When you write on flipcharts, do the following to help your audience see what you write:

1. ***Text size.*** Write in large letters that everyone can see (at least two inches tall).
2. ***Position.*** Stand to the side of the words as you write so you don't block your audience's view. You might have to practice writing on the board to make sure you write large enough and don't turn your back to the audience.
3. ***Talking.*** Be extra careful not to talk while your back is turned to the audience. People will not be able to hear you.
4. ***Pens.*** Use thick marking pens in dark colors. Blue, black, and purple are best because they are visible against a white background. Red and green are fine for accent colors but are not visible enough for writing the main content. Never use yellow or orange. They will make it hard for people to see what you're writing.

You can also tape or pin flipchart pages to the wall after you finish writing on them. The audience can then look at them during breaks or after the presentation.

The real power of the flipchart is when it's used as a **parking lot,** so to speak, which is a place to "park" the audience's questions or objections that you cannot address at the moment. If you have time at the end of your session, review the parking lot questions during a question-and-answer period. If you don't have time to answer all the questions, write down the names and e-mail addresses of the questioners and respond to them later.

Whiteboards

Dry-erase whiteboards are smooth, white porcelain-on-steel boards that replace blackboards. Instead of using chalk, you use special colored, dry-erase markers to write on the board. Whiteboards are useful for more casual, interactive presentations to smaller groups of people where you want to capture thoughts, erase them, and then generate more ideas. The nice thing about whiteboards is that many presentation rooms have them, so you don't have to bring any special equipment with you. Some whiteboards have a special mechanism that allows you to scan the text on the board and print it out on paper.

When you write on a whiteboard, follow the same rules that you use for writing on flipcharts, with these additions:

1. ***Position.*** Don't write on the very bottom of the board; no one will see what you have written.
2. ***Pens.*** Make sure your dry-erase pens have not dried up. Some presenters like to bring their own pens and erasers to ensure they don't face such a problem. Don't make the mistake of using permanent marking pens (the kind you use with flipcharts) when you write on a whiteboard. You will not be able to erase your writing, and you will probably have ruined the board because you won't be able to reuse it.
3. ***Colors.*** Be careful about the colors you choose. Black is the most visible color for text, but dark blue and purple are also easy colors to see. Red can work as an accent color, but it's difficult to see, as is green. As with flipcharts, never use orange and yellow on a whiteboard. The two colors are too hard to see.

Overhead Projectors

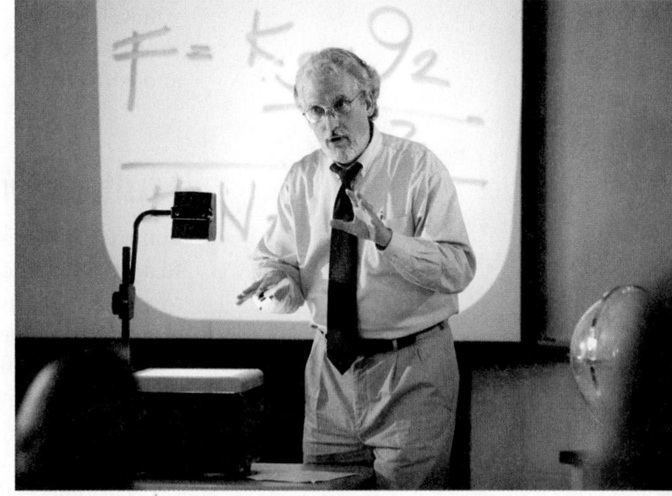

If you prefer to write on a horizontal surface, rather than a vertical one, you might consider using transparencies and an overhead projector. An **overhead projector** typically consists of a large box with a very bright lamp in it, a wide, flat lens above the lamp, and a mirror above the lens. You place a transparency on top of the lens, and the light travels through the transparency and is projected by the mirror onto a screen the audience can see. Anything printed or drawn can be copied onto a transparency. You can also handwrite your transparencies, add notes and comments to them as you make your presentation, and later erase them from the transparency.

Overheads serve as a good backup visual aid for slide presentations, should you have technical problems with your computer. Always bring an extra bulb in case the light on the projector burns out. If possible, keep the lights in the room on and move around as you speak to engage your audience. Do not "stay glued" to the projector. A dark room with an immobile presenter and the humming sound of a projector fan can easily put any audience to sleep.

Visual Presenters

A **visual presenter** is the high-tech version of an overhead projector. It consists of a stage (a pad where you put the object you want to project) and a camera head above the stage. You can place any three-dimensional object or flat document page on the stage. The

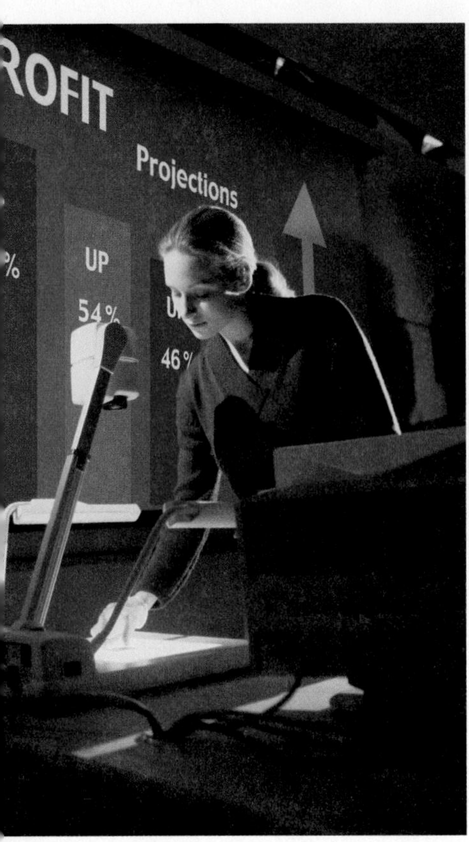

overhead camera captures it and sends it to a large LCD screen for the entire audience to see or to individual monitors in front of the audience members. Visual presenters let you show objects to your audience as well as scroll down or zoom in on them. In high-tech and educational environments, digital visual presenters are quickly becoming more popular than overhead projectors. However, visual presenters are typically expensive, so you might need to reserve one ahead of time if your organization has only a limited number of them.

Handouts

One of the biggest mistakes presenters make is trying to communicate too much information to the audience. Keep your presentation simple. Give your audience the big picture and then present more details. Don't explain everything.

If you're worried about not being able to provide enough details during your presentation, you can always provide them in a handout at the end. Of course, you could provide the handout during the presentation, but you would run the risk of people reading it instead of listening to you. Letting people know they can refer to the handout later for more detailed information helps them relax instead of feeling like they must desperately scramble to take notes about everything you say.

Some presenters like to provide audience members with brief handouts prior to presentations. The handouts include basic information with plenty of room for people to take notes. **Kinesthetic learners,** who are people who need to do something to learn (like move their hands and write), often appreciate handouts such as these. Note-taking handouts do not contain everything the speaker says; just major points that help guide audience members by showing them what is important. If you provide handouts during the presentation and expect your audience to take notes, make sure that pens or pencils are available in case some of members don't bring them.

Activities, Demonstrations, and Props

Hands-on activities are a good way to add life to your presentation. They can be actual activities people do in their seats by themselves or with others, such as answering questions, holding discussions, solving problems, or creating things. If you feel like doing an activity yourself, consider performing some type of demonstration. A **demonstration** often involves props such as objects, costumes, or books that help illustrate or reinforce a point, or help the audience recall an idea.

Multimedia Slides

Sometimes, flipcharts, whiteboards, and overheads are not adequate when you're speaking to a large audience, are presenting many graphics, or plan to post your presentation on the Web. In situations such as these, multimedia slides created using presentation software such as Microsoft PowerPoint, Apple Keynotes, and Corel Presentation can be useful. PowerPoint is the most commonly used presentation software.

Most presenters use visual aids such as PowerPoint because they have the following advantages.

- ***Portable.*** Unlike a flipchart, a slide presentation fits on a **memory stick** or **thumb drive,** which are portable memory storage devices. You can post the slides on the Web, allowing people who were unable to attend your live presentation to view them.
- ***Flexible.*** Slideshow presentations can be animated and contain audio. They also work well with other visual aids, like flipcharts and whiteboards. There's no need to use only slides in the presentations you give.
- ***Familiar.*** Most audiences are very comfortable with slideshow presentations—they have seen so many of them.

DID YOU KNOW?

If you are unfamiliar with PowerPoint, you can learn how to use it with books or tutorials on the Web. You will probably find a book easier to follow because you can read the book as you look at the PowerPoint window on your screen rather than trying to see the tutorial in your browser window and PowerPoint in another window. In other words, it can be hard to see both at the same time on a single computer screen. The Extra Resources section at the end of the chapter lists some good PowerPoint books you can refer to.

❷ What Makes a Slideshow Effective?

Slideshows work best to reinforce your message when you have organized your material well, practiced your presentation, and made your key points clear. If your material is poorly organized and you haven't critically and creatively thought through your points, don't expect your slideshow to save the day.

Using Storyboarding to Organize Your Presentation

Your slides should keep your audience focused on the main points of your presentation. So, as you put your slides together, don't start with the details. Instead, structure your presentation around the big picture, then support the key ideas with details.[2]

Storyboarding can help presenters organize their visual presentations. Animators, advertising agencies that create TV commercials, and filmmakers use **storyboarding** to tell a story visually, panel by panel, in sequence, kind of like a comic book. You can use the same method for your own presentations

With a storyboard, you jot down a few notes or sketch a quick graphic for each slide. Some people like to use index cards and sticky notes to create a storyboard (they are easy to rearrange). Other people prefer paper. Still others use downloadable templates. Review **Exhibit 12-1** to learn which type of storyboard you might prefer.

Exhibit 12-1 **Storyboard Materials**

Index Cards and Sticky Notes	Paper	Computer Templates
Each card or note represents a potential slide, which makes it easy to rearrange the order of your slides.	Divide graph or lined paper into several small "screens" with room for notes. This lets you see multiple slides on the same page.	Download a computer template that contains screens for you to fill in with notes. Free storyboard templates are available on the Internet.

Assembling Your Presentation

With your storyboard as your map, you can now assemble your presentation. Let's take a look at some slides while we walk through the steps to creating a successful presentation.

1. ***First slide.*** Make sure you have an attractive, attention-getting first slide that includes the title of your presentation and your name and organization. If you making a presentation within your company, list your department.

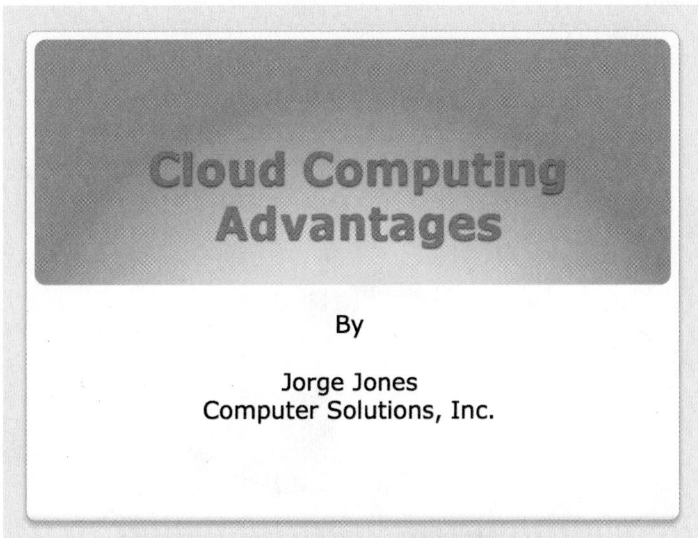

2. ***Introduction slide.*** Set the stage by providing an introduction slide that describes the purpose of the presentation and the points you plan to cover.

Cloud Computing Offers Customers

- Low costs
- Convenience (ease of use)
- Reliability
- Scalability

3. ***Main topic slides.*** Each slide should illustrate a main topic in your presentation to help the audience keep in mind what you're talking about.

Low Costs

- No equipment to buy
- No contracts
- Pay as go you
- Sign up and cancel immediately

4. ***Attention-getting slides.*** Include slides or activities to make sure people are paying attention.

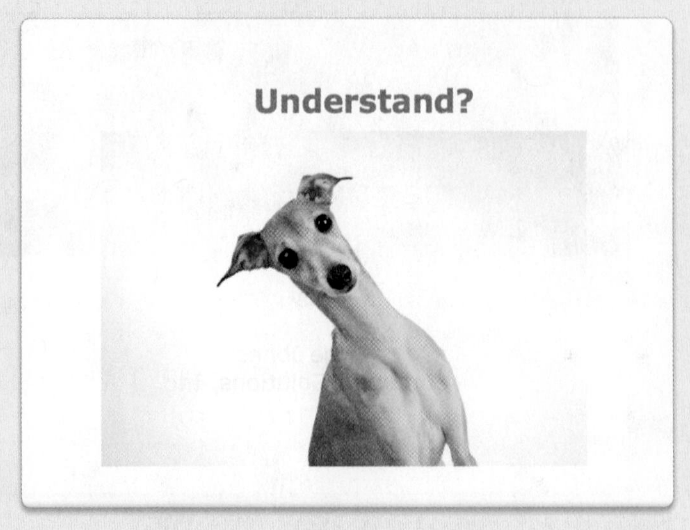

5. ***Summary slide.*** At the end of your presentation, provide a summary slide to remind the audience of the key points you presented.

Emphasize the Following to Close the Sale

✓The costs are minimal. No initial outlay required.
✓Nontechnical personnel can utilize system.
✓Customers don't have to worry about their networks going down.
✓Customers can increase and decrease their capacity immediately.

6. ***Final slide with your name and contact information.*** The final slide should include your name and contact information.

Contact Information

Jorge Jones
Business Development Manager

E-mail: jjones@compsolutions.com
Mobile: 469-222-7294
Site: www.compsolutions.com
Blog: blog.compsolutions.com

Using Pictures

The more difficult it is to explain a concept in words, the greater the need is for a picture. This includes photos, diagrams, and flowcharts.

Photographs

The photographs you use in your presentations should look professional. If you see a photo on the Internet you would like to use, you must seek the permission of the person or organization that originally took it. For a fee, you can typically purchase professional stock photos on the Internet at the following Web sites:

- ***iStockphoto.*** Provides good quality, reasonably priced images that usually cost anywhere from $1 to $20. You can search for images by keywords.
- ***Getty Images.*** Provides a tremendous variety of high quality, but expensive, images.
- ***Flickr.*** Provides mostly free images posted by members. You must give credit to the person who took the picture. Be sure to check the copyright information for each image to determine if there is a cost related to using the image.
- ***Stockxpert by Jupiter Images.*** Provides free images grouped by topic.

REAL INSIGHTS from a Seasoned Professional

Name: *Dave Bouwman*
Title: *Chief Technology Officer and Lead Software Engineer*
Organization: *DTS Agile*
Locations: *Colorado and Florida*

DAVE BOUWMAN IS THE CHIEF TECHNOLOGY OFFICER and lead software engineer at DTS Agile, a software and training company with offices in the Pacific Northwest, Midwest, South, and East Coast. Bouwman has been writing software code for 12 years, mostly in the geographic information system (GIS) industry. The software he writes helps create online maps that let people display roads, rivers, soil types, ecosystems, and more—just about anything anyone would ever want to see on a map.

If you work in a high-tech industry, it can be a struggle to keep up with new breakthroughs in technology. However, Bouwman has found that conferences are a great way to stay up-to-date with technology and make important contacts. Over the years, he's attended many conferences. Conferences are expensive, and most of the companies Bouwman has worked for are small and have tiny travel and training budgets. Early in his career he learned that the only way he could go to a conference was if the conference was free. However, he also learned that he could attend an expensive conference without paying if he agreed to be a presenter. Initially the idea of making presentations to hundreds of people scared him—a lot. But the opportunity to go to a conference for free was too good to pass up.

Bouwman admits his first presentations were terrible. They were full of slides with lots of text and lots of bullet points. "I used to kill people with bullets," he jokes. "It's amazing anyone left my presentations alive. People slept. People left the room. It was terrible."

But then Bouwman stumbled upon an animated video called "Change Happens", originally a PowerPoint presentation. The slides were bright and colorful, incorporating a clean design and simple graphics. They conveyed a great deal of information but without the ues of bullet points. Presenters were personable, funny, and told interesting stories while images flashed in the background. The audience responded with questions, laughter, and applause.

Bouwman started implementing these techniques. Although it took more time to prepare a talk, the audience response told him it was well worth the effort. After some early success, he purchased some books to help make his slides even better. He registered for an account with the online photo provider iStock and started buying photos for his presentation. He visited Web sites where he watched professional speakers making presentations.

Bouwman soon came up with new slides, created new presentations, and attended new conferences. His presentations got better and better, full of more images and less text, until he created his own signature presentation style—a single photo on each slide with one or two interesting lines of text, supplemented by Bouwman's own witty narration. Soon people were asking him how he became such a good presenter.

Today Bouwman has moved up in the world. He is in a lead position in his company. He spends only 50 percent of his time writing code. He spends the other 50 percent giving presentations and coaching people. He creates slides, posts them online, and talks at conferences. He teaches other people who have difficulty giving presentations. From software developer to presentation guru—Bouwman's changing the world, one PowerPoint slide at a time.

Check out some of Bouwman's presentations at slideshare .net/dbouwman

Questions

1. Bouwman mentioned some mistakes he made with his early presentations. What were they? Have you ever made those kinds of mistakes?
2. When Bouwman finally had a chance to watch a really good presentation, what characteristics did he notice? In what way might you improve your presentations as well?
3. What resources helped Bouwman improve his presentations?

Source: Dave Bouwman in discussion with the author, June 2010.

Flowcharts

Flowcharts are line drawings that help illustrate complicated procedures. For a professional look, use a single, commonly used font (Times New Roman, Arial, and so forth) in an easy-to-read size. Don't use too many colors in flowcharts.

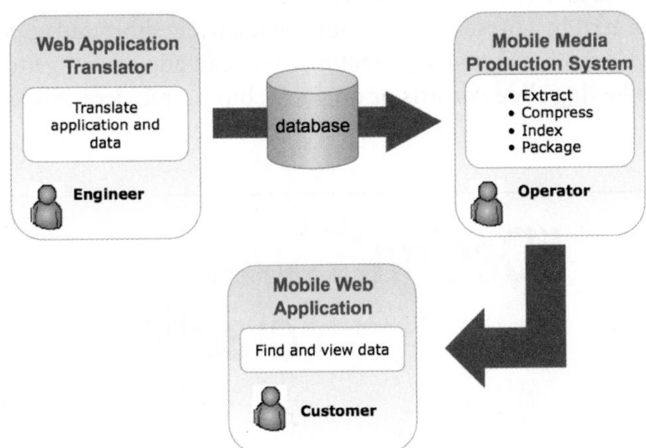

Drawings and Diagrams

Drawings and diagrams should be clear, attractive, and readable from a distance.

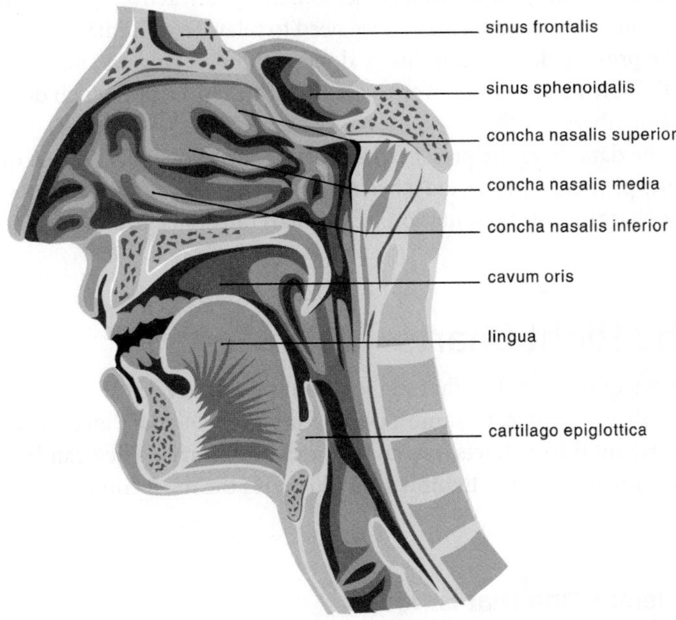

Avoiding Wordiness

The slides in a presentation should never contain every word you plan to say. Remember that you are the speaker, not the slide. If the slides are too wordy, your audience will be too busy reading them to listen or so overwhelmed by all of the information in the slides that they tune you out completely. If you're worried that your slides don't contain enough information, you can always distribute a handout at the end of the presentation to provide the audience with more details.

Some people like to insert **hyperlinks** in their presentation slides. Hyperlinks are links to Web pages. Include hyperlinks only if you are sure you will be able to connect to the Internet during your presentation and access the linked Web pages. If you print your slides, the hyperlinks will simply appear as underlined text, and readers will not be able to see the Web pages you have linked to.

Anchoring Your Points with Quotes

Quotes lend credibility and generate interest to presentations because they make audience members think. Do they agree with the quote or disagree? The audience's reaction to the quote can generate discussion. If the audience knows the person who made the quote, or if that person is an expert in the subject, even better.

The quotes used in a presentation should be relatively short and appear in a font that can easily be read from a distance. Sometimes you can add an image to get people's attention. The following slide consists of only text, but no pictures. Nonetheless, it's quite effective.

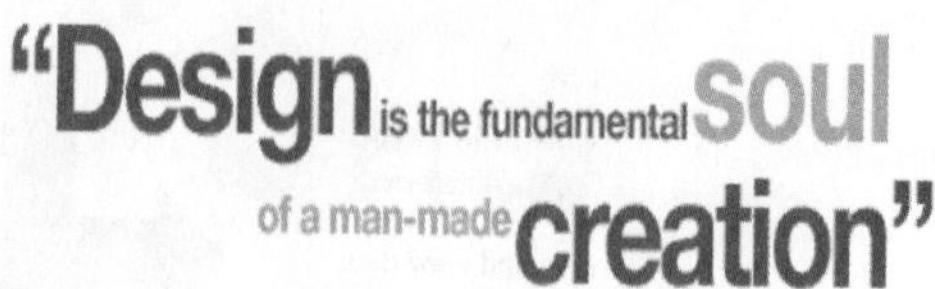

Presenting Data

As much as we would like to think otherwise, sometimes attractive photos and memorable quotes cannot convey all the information we need to relate to an audience. Sometimes hard facts have to be presented. How can this be done without boring an audience? Look at the two slides in **Exhibit 12-2**. They convey the same information, but which do you think audiences will remember?

Don't let the data drive the presentation. Just because you analyzed the quarterly sales of an electronics product and charted it beautifully over the past five years doesn't mean you should put the chart in your presentation. Add a chart only if it clarifies or reinforces a point that you're making.

Using the Right Charts

When you have acquired the data that support your points, present the information as simply and effectively as possible. Common charts for visualizing data include **tables, vertical bar charts, horizontal bar charts, pie charts,** and **line charts.** They can be used in both printed reports and slideshows. **Exhibit 12-3** illustrates the most common types of charts.

Exhibit 12-2 A Visually Compelling Slide versus One That Is Not

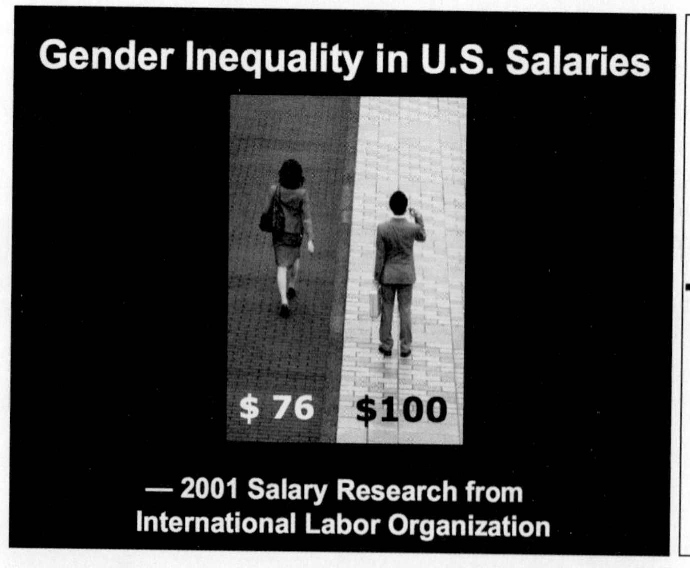

Exhibit 12-3 Common Types of Charts

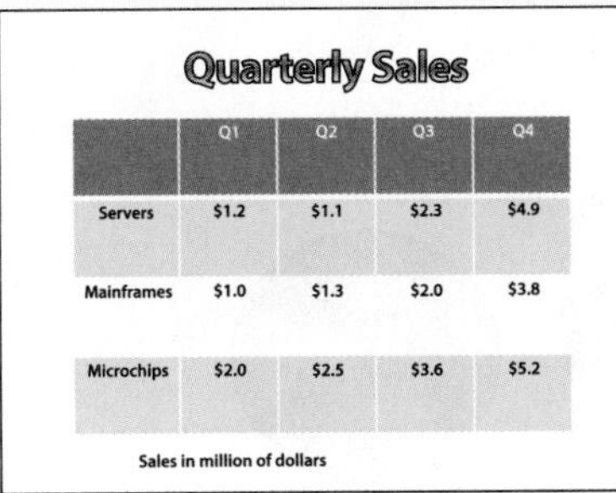

Quarterly Sales

	Q1	Q2	Q3	Q4
Servers	$1.2	$1.1	$2.3	$4.9
Mainframes	$1.0	$1.3	$2.0	$3.8
Microchips	$2.0	$2.5	$3.6	$5.2

Sales in million of dollars

(a) Table. Presents information in rows and columns for easy scanning. Tables are good for side-by-side comparisons of data but show information in a less dramatic way than charts.

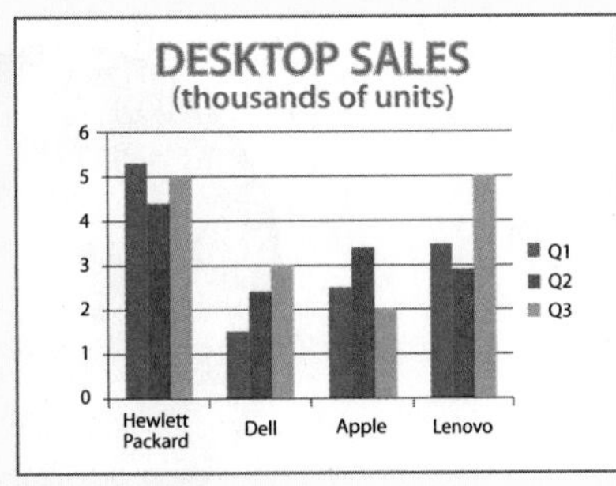

(b) Vertical bar chart. Shows changes in quantities over time. Use no more than four to eight bars in a single chart.

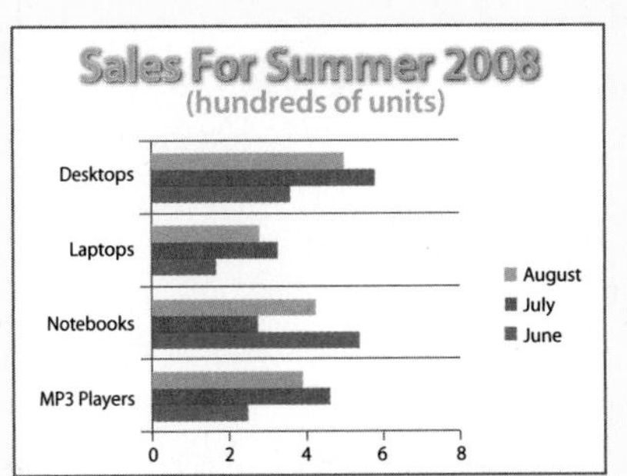

(c) Horizontal bar chart. Compares quantities—for example, sales figures among the four regions of a company.

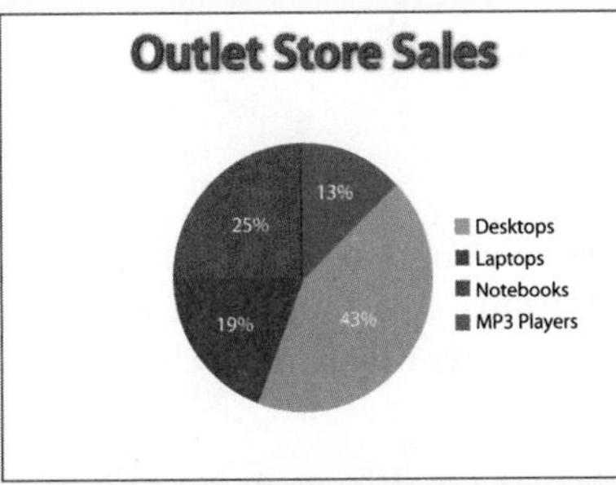

(d) Pie chart. Presents information as wedges of a circular "pie" to show percentages. Limit the slices to 4–6 and contrast the most important slice either with color or by "exploding" the slice.

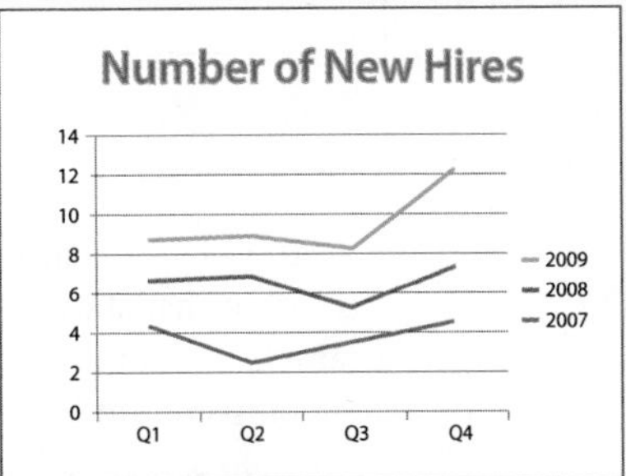

(e) Line chart. Presents information as a series of connected line segments. Line charts are used to demonstrate trends. A simple line chart can show whether a company's sales have gone up or down.

As Exhibit 12-3(e) shows, a chart or graph's x-axis (horizontal axis) often shows the time from left to right. Sometimes the x-axis shows quantities, as Exhibit 12-3(b) shows. The y-axis (vertical axis) of a graph often shows gains going up and losses going down.

On occasion, you might need a different type of chart that visually shows the relative size of things. This is when a bubble chart comes in handy. A **bubble chart** displays a set of numeric values as circles. The circles in a bubble chart represent different data values, with the area of each circle corresponding to a particular value—the bigger the circle, the bigger the value. The positions of the bubbles don't mean anything but are designed to pack the circles together with relatively little wasted space. A bubble chart is especially useful for data sets with dozens to hundreds of values or when the values differ by several orders of magnitude. **Exhibit 12-4** shows a bubble chart. The sizes of the circles (not their positions) indicate the number of people in different professions.

In addition to the charts you have just seen, there are also **organizational charts,** which are charts that typically illustrate how a company or a Web site is organized. **Exhibit 12-5a** is an organizational chart of a small high-tech consulting company. **Exhibit 12-5b** is the organizational chart of the company's Web site.

Exhibit 12-4
A Bubble Chart

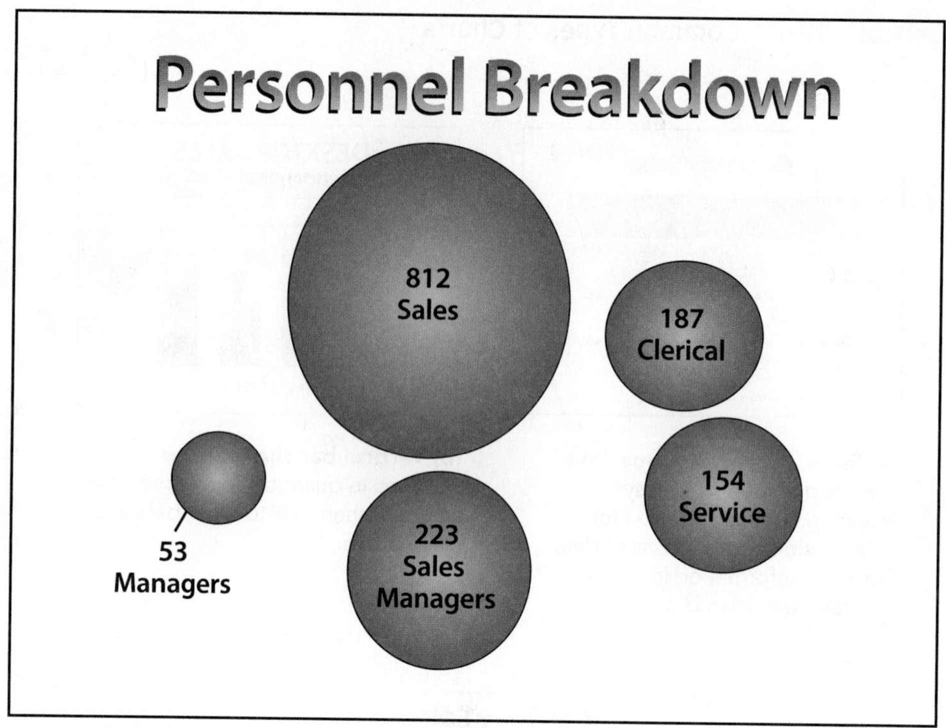

You can also combine the various charts we have discussed with images. The earlier illustration that showed how much people remember from words versus pictures is a good example of a combination chart. No matter what kind of chart you choose, keep the following points in mind:

1. ***Title the chart.*** Provide a title for your chart, including a figure number.
2. ***Label the contents.*** Label the contents of your chart, including units of measure, axes, column headings, and so forth.
3. ***Use readable fonts.*** Use a font big enough for people to read.
4. ***Use colors that are visible.*** Use colors that people can see from a distance.
5. ***Proofread the chart.*** Proofread your charts and get someone else to proofread them too.

Exhibit 12-5 **Organizational Charts**

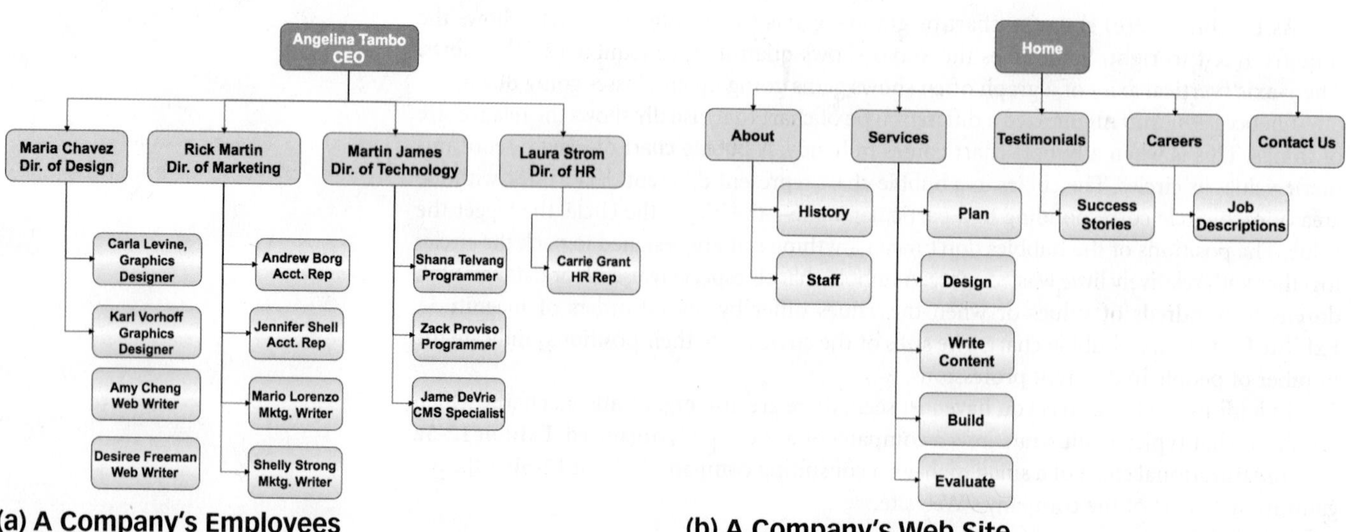

(a) A Company's Employees **(b) A Company's Web Site**

REAL INSIGHTS from a New Professional

Name: *Diandra Macias*
Title: *Creative Director*
Organization: *Duarte Design Inc.*
Location: *Mountain View, California*

DIANDRA MACIAS IS A LUCKY CAREER WOMAN. She's actually doing what she loves: combining stories and art in the form of high-tech presentations. As the creative director at California-based Duarte Design Inc., a high-tech design firm in Mountain View, California, the 37-year-old gets to work on some phenomenal projects. In fact, Macias' team created the presentation used by former U.S. Vice President Al Gore in his documentary, *An Inconvenient Truth*.

To understand Macias and the path that brought her to Duarte Design, you have to look back at her childhood. "Ever since I could remember, I was thinking about art. I was happiest getting my fingers into paint or Play Doh." Then, in her senior year of high school, her art teacher brought in a graphics specialist who created art with a computer. It was at that moment that her dream of becoming a graphics designer was born.

After graduating with a degree in multimedia design from a graphics design college in California, Macias joined Duarte. At the time, Duarte Design was a company that consisted of only four people. As a result, each of its employees had to do many different tasks. "In school, we weren't taught about presentations. We were taught the principles of design. I learned by doing, and I learned fast!" she says. As Duarte Design grew through the years, she worked her way up from designer to creative director.

Macias finds her job fun, challenging, and rewarding. Her primary focus is to inspire her coworkers by sparking their creativity. Highly creative individuals comprise the company's marketing group, who rely heavily on visual thinking skills—the ability to use images for critical thinking and communication. She feels the real secret of the success of any presentation is its story: "Presentations don't always equate to slides. Every interaction you have with another person is an opportunity to present your ideas, thoughts, and experiences through storytelling. If you don't get the story right, adding visuals would be like putting lipstick on a pig," she says. She knows that every good story appeals to both the emotional and analytical sides of the brain. When you hit both sides, your message is more likely to stick. She believes that the most memorable presentations are those that touch people's hearts as well as their minds.

Based on her experience at Duarte Design, Macias has a number of tips for novice presenters using visual aids. Narrow the goal of your presentation, she advises. Figure out what you want the audience to walk away with. Determine the main point and build your story around it, including facts and emotions. Get emotionally connected to your message. Then get into your audience's head and relate the story to them. Make sure your visuals support the story instead of distracting the audience. Moreover, never lose your passion.

Questions

1. How did Macias learn to create effective presentations?
2. Macias says that the story is the key to successful presentation and must appeal to what two parts of the brain?
3. What are some tips Macias offers to novice presenters?

Source: Diandra Macias in discussion with the author, April 2009.

3 How Can You Make Your Slides Look Professional?

At this point, you have seen examples of slides with quotes, stories, and graphics. However, you may still be asking yourself, "What can I do to get my slides looking really good?" The following are some guidelines to keep in mind.

Keep Your Slides Simple

- Present one concept per slide.
- Use no more than three bullet points on a slide.
- Keep your sentences short (two lines or less).
- Limit yourself to three-to-five lines of text per slide.
- A simple diagram or photo is often better than words.

Use Professional-Looking Images

- Use professional photos, not clip art.
- Try to match the background color of the image with the background of the slide.
- If possible, use large photos or full-size photos that fill the whole slide.

Use Consistent Fonts and Colors

Fonts

- Use only one or two font styles—one for headings and one for body text.
- Do not mix sans-serif fonts with serif fonts. Serif fonts include fonts like Times New Roman and Georgia. Sans-serif fonts include Arial and Verdana.
- Don't use unusual fonts. They might not appear correctly in different versions of PowerPoint or in other software or operating systems.
- The body text should be 14 points or larger for readability.
- The headings should be 4 points larger than body text.

San-serif font

Heading

Body text body text
body text body text

Serif font

Heading

Body text body text
body text body text

Colors

- Use dark text on a light background, which is easier to read than light text on a dark background. If you do choose to use light text on dark background, use white on black.
- For a professional look, do not use more than two colors of text.
- A significant proportion of people are red-green colorblind. Because they cannot differentiate between red and green, don't use the two colors next to one another.

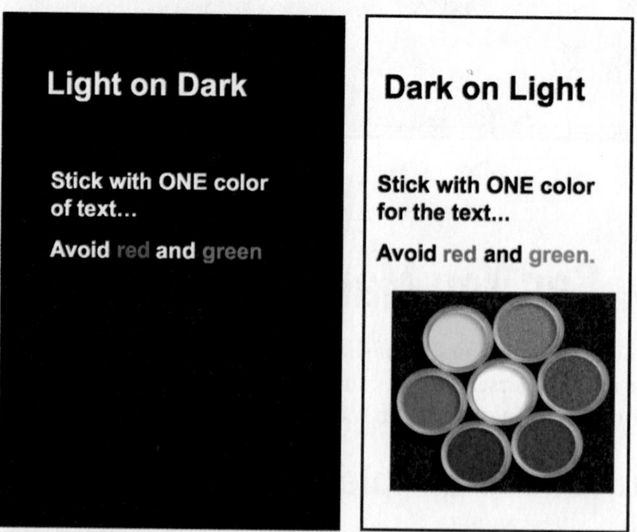

Light on Dark
Stick with ONE color
of text...
Avoid red and green
Dark on Light
Stick with ONE color
for the text...
Avoid red and green.

Make Your Slides Easy for the Audience to Scan Visually

Make sure you are clear on what you want people to notice first as you put together your slides. People will initially visually scan your slide.

To help them do so efficiently, keep the following points in mind:

- In Western cultures, peoples' eyes naturally travel from the top left of a slide to the bottom right.
- People are attracted to images first and text second.
- People see large objects first, followed by smaller objects.
- People naturally see patterns, so group related points together or use different colors to show the relationships.

Make Your Slides Easy to Read

Let's now look at the actual words on the slides and their formatting.

- Left-justify your text for easier reading (especially lists).
- Use active voice instead of passive voice.
- Number your lists when the order of the points is important.
- Use bullet points when the order of the points on a list is not important.
- Avoid long paragraphs. Instead, pull out the important points from the paragraph and insert bullets points in front of each.

Limit Music and Animation

If your presentation will be posted on the Web without your voice to accompany it, light music might be appropriate. If you plan to post your presentation on the Internet, be particularly careful with music and animation. Although viewers find music and animation interesting and entertaining, if overused, both can easily distract from the information you are attempting to present. For example, animations on the same page as text can make it difficult for viewers to focus on words they are trying to read. Use music and animation sparingly to enhance your presentation, not to distract from it.

Putting What You Have Learned into Practice

Exhibits 12-6 to **12-8** show the before-and-after versions of slides that are based on real-life presentations in the software industry. View the slides to see the concepts we have discussed put into practice.

PEARSON mybcommlab

Apply Exhibit 12-6's key concepts by revising a new document. Go to Chapter 12 in mybcommlab.com and select Document Makeovers.

Exhibit 12-6 Reducing Text and Adding Images

Why Should You Care About Software Usability?

Why spend the time up front to design easy-to-use software? What difference does it make?

Let's look at an example of poorly designed software used by 250 users:

Each user accesses 60 screens per day, while working 230 days per year, and being paid $15 per hour

Now imagine that the software is redesigned to reduce processing time by 3 seconds per screen:

3 sec/screen x 60 screens/day x 230 days/year x 250 users x $15/hour x 1 hour/3,600 sec =

$62,566 in savings for 250 users

The savings equals the salaries of two employees – all from redesigning the software screens for usability!

Well-Designed Software Saves Money

Imagine poorly designed software used by 250 users ...

Each user:

- Accesses 60 screens per day
- Works 230 days per year
- Is paid $15 per hour

Software is redesigned to reduce processing time by 3 seconds per screen ...

- 3 sec/screen x 60 screens/day x 230 days/year = **41,400 seconds saved per year for one user**
- 41,400 sec/user x 250 users x $15/hour x 1 hour/ 3,600 sec = **$62,566 in savings for 250 users**

Software redesign saves $62,566 — that's two employees' salaries!

Exhibit 12-7 Improving Contrast and Visual Appeal

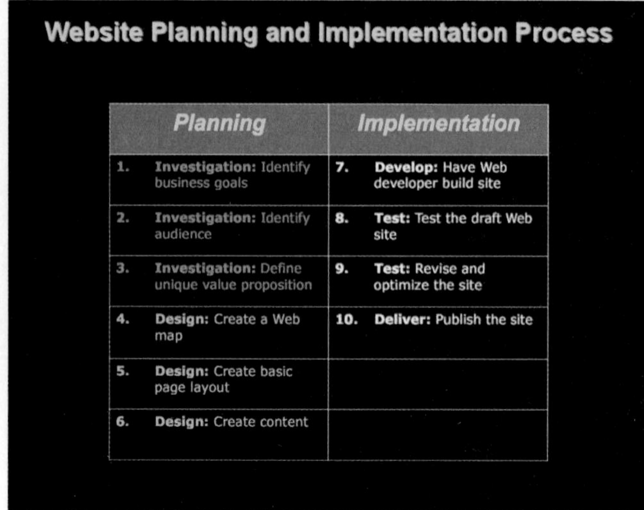

Planning	Implementation
1. **Investigation:** Identify business goals	7. **Develop:** Have Web developer build site
2. **Investigation:** Identify audience	8. **Test:** Test the draft Web site
3. **Investigation:** Define unique value proposition	9. **Test:** Revise and optimize the site
4. **Design:** Create a Web map	10. **Deliver:** Publish the site
5. **Design:** Create basic page layout	
6. **Design:** Create content	

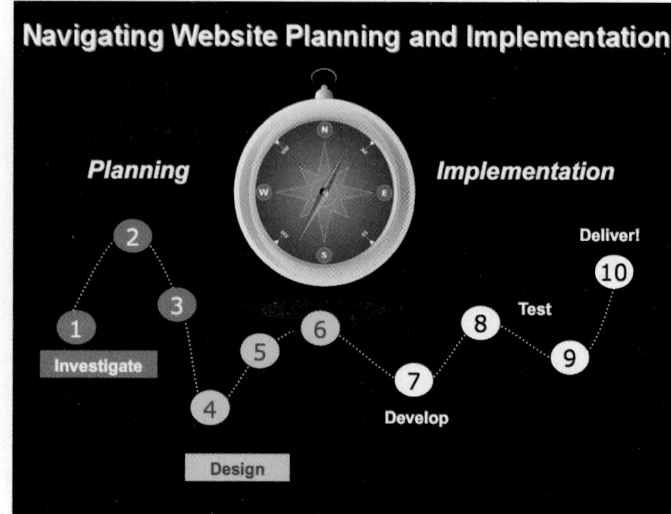

Exhibit 12-8 Improving Fonts and Alignment

Ideal customer

– > 5000 employees
– > $500 million in revenue
– End-users ARE finding issues
– Web-enabling or accessible applications
– Highly reactive
– Distributed applications and technology
– Users in many geographic locations
– Very little outsourced
– Familiarity with complex, alternative products

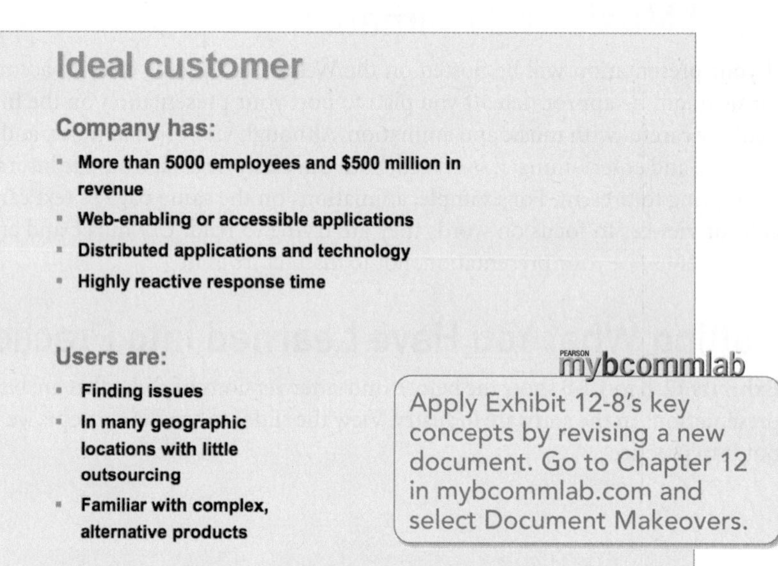

❹ How Can You Deliver Your Slideshow Effectively?

So far, you have heard a lot about the actual slides but not how to integrate them into your presentation. Let's now look at this aspect of delivering your slideshow.

Avoid Reading the Slides Word for Word

Have you ever attended a presentation in which the presenter chose to read every single word on the slides while the audience dozed off? As we have explained, you are the presenter, not the slideshow. You should know your presentation backward and forward and not rely on the slides to get you through it. The slides should keep you on track and remind you of key items. They are not meant to be read word for word. When you present a slide, glance at it to show you are moving to a new idea, and then look at your audience as you speak.

Exhibit 12-9 shows sample slides from a presentation made by Dave Bouwman, the seasoned professional we featured in this chapter.[3] What is unique about the slides is that none of them contain bullet points, yet they grab your attention. The presenter then fills in the missing information for the audience.

Exhibit 12-9
Sample Slides from a GIS Software Presentation

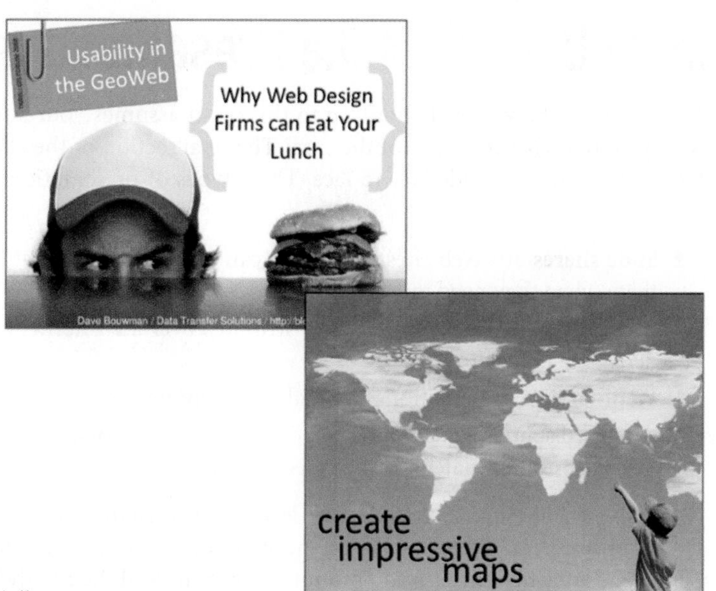

Source: David Bouwman/DTSAgile.

Avoid Rushing through the Slides

If reading slides is bad for your audience, so is rushing through them. Have you ever attended a presentation where there were so many slides the presenter had to flash them across the screen at breakneck speed while the audience struggled to keep up? You should always give your audience enough time to look at each slide while you discuss it.

Presenters often rush through their slides because they are trying to present too much information. If you know the purpose of your presentation and have carefully organized your information, you won't need a million slides to make your point. As you learned earlier, your slides are merely a backdrop for your message. They are not the message itself.

To avoid rushing through your slides, practice your presentation ahead of time to determine the timing. As you practice the presentation, time its length by asking some questions at strategic places and then answering them yourself. If you cannot get through your presentation in the allotted time without talking at the speed of light, you are trying to cover too many points. Reduce the number of points and eliminate some slides.

Other Tips for Delivering a Successful Slideshow Presentation

The following are some additional points to remember for delivering a slideshow effectively:

1. Have an introduction, whether you introduce yourself or someone else does. Introducing yourself quickly tells your audience who you are, what you're going to talk about, and why you're qualified to talk about it. Include an interesting quote, short story, or question to get people interested in what you have to say.
2. Don't block your visuals with your body. Also, don't speak with your back turned to your audience.
3. To avoid being tethered to your computer during a slide presentation, try using a remote control. This allows you to walk around the room and engage your audience. Even if you don't have a remote control, you should still move away from your computer from time to time to discuss points with your audience.
4. At the end of the presentation, always thank your audience members and give them your contact information, if it's appropriate to do so. Some presenters prefer to bring business cards to hand out after presentations.

CHECKLIST

Final points to remember: before, during, and after your presentation

- ☑ Check your slides for typos.
- ☑ Practice and time your presentation.
- ☑ Have a contingency plan in case your technology fails.
- ☑ Don't block your visuals with your body.
- ☑ Have an introduction, whether you introduce yourself or someone else does.
- ☑ Try using a remote control.
- ☑ Break up the presentation.
- ☑ Thank your audience.

❺ How Can the Web Be Used to Make Presentations?

Everything we have talked about up to this point assumes your audience is in the room with you. But what if that's not the case? The final section of the chapter looks at presentations that are not made face to face. These types of presentations typically include the following:

- **Slide shares** are Web sites where you can post your presentation so others can view them when they need to.
- **Podcasts** are audio presentations distributed over the Internet for playback on mobile devices or computers.
- **Webinars** are presentations you make to a remote audience over the Web.
- **Video presentations** are presentations you make to a live audience, while being recorded. You can later put the videos on the Web.

Web presentations do not have the level of personal interaction that in-person presentations provide. It is difficult to gauge the attention, interest, or understanding of the members of the audience because you cannot see them to read their body language. Instead, you must anticipate their questions and build that anticipation into your presentation.

Slide Shares

Slide shares are Web sites that allow you to upload and publicly or privately share your slides. Some Web sites are for the general public, such as SlideShare. Others are designed for particular industries, such as SlideLive (the education industry) and SecondSlide (the pathology industry). When you use a slide-share site, you will not be physically present to explain your ideas to viewers. Viewers will have only your slides as a reference. In addition, anyone who visits the site can view your slides unless you designate them as being private. (If you are posting information you don't want your competitors to see, you definitely want to designate the slides as being private.)

What can you do to make your slides easier to understand remotely without revising your entire presentation? If the information in your slides is basic yet comprehensive, you can leave the slides alone. Some PowerPoint slide presentations are self-explanatory. If the viewer has to "fill in the blanks" to understand the presentation, you should add more explanatory text to the slides, supplement with additional slides, or provide a downloadable handout people can read as they view the slides. You can also walk through the slides yourself and record an audio voiceover or narrative. As people view each slide, they will hear your explanation. If appropriate, you can add background music (no vocals).

Podcasts

Most presentations we have mentioned up to this point are visual ones, but what about audio presentations? This is where podcasts come in. Podcasts allow speakers to digitally record their presentations and make them available on their Web sites or through "really simple syndication" (RSS) feeds.

The beauty of podcasts is that they are short in length and can be downloaded any time. Many professional bloggers and presenters use podcasts as a way to share information on a regular basis. Visitors can listen to the conversations in their homes or offices or on their personal computers. Or, if they have a mobile device, they can listen to the podcasts anywhere.

Webinars

The cost of travel often prevents companies from sending their employees to seminars, workshops, or training classes in other cities, states, or countries. Instead, the companies depend on Webinars to teach their employees new skills and concepts. One or two people make the presentation using slides. The remote audience watches the presenter(s) and the visual presentation on their computers. **Exhibit 12-10** illustrates what participants would see on their computers during a Webinar.

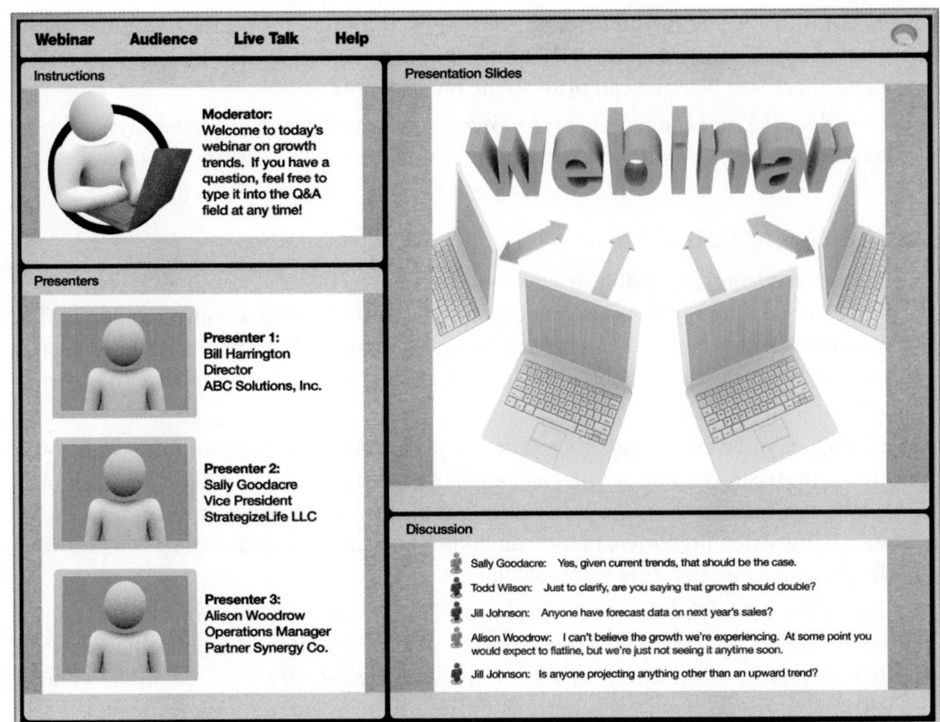

Exhibit 12-10
What Webinar Participants See on Their Computer Screens

Some Webinars show only slides. No presenter(s) are visible. Attendees listen to the presentation via computer or over the phone by dialing into a toll-free number. People watching the Webinar have only the visuals to watch, augmented by the voice of the presenter(s). If the visuals are not interesting, the audience will get bored, stop watching, and log off.

Webinars work well for introductory-level topics that do not require a lot of interaction and can be presented visually. Limiting the coverage to an introductory level is important because Webinars are typically only 30–45 minutes long and allow only a short period of time for questions and answers at the end of the presentations. Most questions are submitted by e-mail or some other online method.

Take time zones into account when giving a live Webinar to a geographically dispersed audience so that people can attend during their work hours. For example, suppose you work for a software company in Los Angeles, and the company also has offices in New York City, London, Moscow, and Tokyo. You have been tasked with developing a Webinar for sales representatives in all of the offices. Because of time zone differences, you plan to hold one Webinar at 8:30 A.M. in Los Angeles, so representatives in New York can watch it at 11:30 A.M., while representatives in London can watch it at 3:30 P.M. You plan to hold a second Webinar at 8:30 P.M. the same day so representatives in Moscow and Japan can watch it the next morning at 7:30 A.M. and 11:30 A.M., respectively. Some companies opt to present Webinars only once and then later post them on a Web site so they are available to people who attended the presentation as well as those who did not. The following are tips for conducting successful Webinars:

Prior to the Presentation

1. ***Handouts.*** Consider sending handouts ahead of time. If your presentation covers a lot of new material, provide detailed handouts that your audience can refer to before, during, or after your presentation. That way, you can focus on the major points of the presentation and refer your audience to the handouts for more details.
2. ***Slides.*** Your slides should be professional looking and contain quality images. Keep the slides as simple as possible. Break complicated concepts into manageable chunks presented on several slides. Consider how your slides will appear to members of your audience on their computer screens.

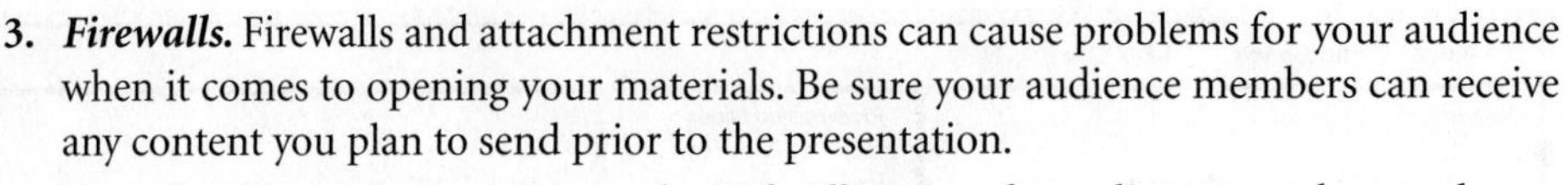

3. ***Firewalls.*** Firewalls and attachment restrictions can cause problems for your audience when it comes to opening your materials. Be sure your audience members can receive any content you plan to send prior to the presentation.
4. ***Downloading and connecting to the Web.*** Allow time for audience members to download and get familiar with any software they might need to view the Webinar.

During the Presentation

1. ***Team presenting.*** If possible, use two people to present and have them talk back and forth to one another like newscasters or two people having a conversation do. The presentation will be more interesting, but it will require both people to have a script and to have practiced it. Follow the standard team presentation etiquette you learned in Chapter 11.
2. ***Timing.*** As you walk through each slide and point at items with your mouse, move your mouse more slowly than normal and explain each move as you make it. For example, tell the audience, "Now we're going to look at the top-right corner of the slide where we see . . ." Too often presenters race through the slides, and the audience has no idea what the presenters are pointing at or clicking on.
3. ***Questions.*** Let attendees know when you will be addressing questions (usually at the end of the Webinar) and how they can submit their questions. Usually attendees type their questions into a question area on the Web site or call a toll-free phone number with them. If you do allow questions during the presentation, ask for feedback frequently. This is one of the best ways to find out whether people are having any difficulty understanding you. Remember, you won't be able to see your audience members to gauge how well they comprehend the presentation. When you answer questions, always repeat the question and tell the audience who asked the question and where that person is located.

After the Presentation

1. ***Additional materials.*** Tell attendees where they can download the slides after the presentation, and let them know if other materials are available to them.
2. ***FAQs.*** Document the questions asked and send a list of frequently asked questions, with answers, to all attendees.

Video (Recorded) Presentations

Some presentations are made live in front of large audiences and recorded. The recordings are then posted on the Web. If you plan to make your live presentation available as a video, be aware of the following:

1. ***Slides.*** Project the slides on a large screen so they are highly visible to the live audience and the remote audience.
2. ***Eye contact.*** Look at the live audience as well as the camera. Once the video is made, the remote audience members who watch on the Web will feel like you are looking at them when you face the camera.
3. ***Clothes and hair.*** Make sure your clothing, hair, and makeup are professional but not extreme. Avoid wearing clothing with small stripes or patterns because they appear to vibrate when recorded. White clothes reflect too much light and appear to glow. Wear rich, dark colors.
4. ***Methods.*** Follow the presentation methods described earlier in Chapter 11.
5. ***Questions.*** Always repeat questions so your live audience, and later, your Web audience, can hear the questions.
6. ***Editing.*** Have a professional editor clean up any background noise so your Web audience will easily hear you.

7. ***Studying.*** Study high-quality live presentations that are recorded and posted on the Web. A good Web site for viewing professional presentations is Technology Entertainment Design (TED).

Summary *Synthesize What You Have Learned*

1. **What types of visual aids are used in presentations?**

   Flipcharts, whiteboards, overhead projectors and transparencies, visual presenters, handouts and hands-on activities, demonstrations, and multimedia slides are among the most common types of visual aids used in presentations. Consider the purpose of your presentation and the size of your audience when choosing a visual aid. Visual aids, if used properly, can keep your audience engaged.

2. **What makes a slideshow effective?**

   Slides are useful because they are a portable, familiar, and flexible medium. Organize your slides as follows: an attention-getting first slide, followed by a slide that describes the purpose and objectives of your presentation, followed by slides illustrating your main points and keeping people's attention. Remember to include a summary slide and a slide that thanks your audience and provides your contact information.

3. **How can you make your slides look professional?**

   Avoid wordiness, interject stories illustrated by slides, use quotes, and include professional images (photos, flowcharts, diagrams, charts, etc.). Keep the presentation simple and limit the number of items on the slide. Use large fonts, along with contrasting text and background colors. Left-justify text, use active voice, number your lists in order of importance, use bullets when order isn't important, and avoid long paragraphs.

4. **How can you deliver your slideshow effectively?**

   Check your slides for typos. Time and practice your presentation. Ensure your equipment works. Don't read the slides word for word, and don't block the slides with your body. Don't rush, and take a breather from slides with activities or stories. Finally, thank the audience.

5. **How can the Web be used to make presentations?**

   You can deliver presentations on the Web through slide share, podcasts, Webinars, and videos. Slide shares are Web sites where you can post your presentation so others can view them when they need to. Podcasts are audio presentations distributed over the Internet for playback on mobile devices or personal computers. Webinars are presentations you make to a remote audience over the Web. Video presentations are presentations you make to a live audience, while being recorded. You can later put the videos on the Web.

PEARSON **mybcommlab**™ Are you an active learner? Go to **mybcommlab.com** to master Chapter 12's content. Chapter 12's interactive activities include:

- Customizable Study Plan and Chapter 12 practice quizzes
- Chapter 12 Video Exercise, Ehancing Presentations with Slides and Other Visuals: Orange Photography, which shows you how textbook concepts are put into practice every day
- Flash cards for mastering the definition of chapter terms
- Interactive Lessons that visually review key chapter concepts
- Document Makeovers for hands-on, scored practice in revising documents

Know It *Reflect, Respond, and Express*

Build Your Critical Thinking Skills

Critical Thinking Questions

1. Consider the non-PowerPoint visual aids used in presentations you have witnessed. Which types of visual aids were the most effective? What visual aids do you recall after the presentation was over?
2. Find a PowerPoint slideshow presentation on the Internet or through your library that uses animation or sound to enhance the information. What effects do the extras have on the message of the presentation? What could the author have used instead? Is the use of animation and sound appropriate for the message?
3. Make a list of different contingency plans to use in case the equipment discussed in this chapter does not work. What other types of visual aids could you use? Why are contingency plans important to have for each type of equipment?

Critical Thinking Scenario

Jeff is a senior software developer in the geographic information system (GIS) industry. After seeing some of Jeff's work on a recent project, Jeff's supervisor asked him to be a presenter at an upcoming technology conference. Jeff had never given a presentation to such a large audience. Plus, his supervisor wanted him to incorporate visuals into his presentation—something Jeff had little experience with.

Jeff asked a few friends to watch him rehearse his presentation. His speech was clear and his posture was good, but his presentation was full of slides with lots of text and too many bullets. His friends had trouble following the points and keeping up with his ideas. His images weren't well-related to the topics he was discussing and the light-on-dark layout of his slides was distracting.

Questions

1. Pick two of Jeff's presentation problems. How could he improve those aspects?
2. If Jeff were unable to use PowerPoint to make his presentation compelling, what other tools could he use to give an effective presentation?
3. Suppose Jeff decides to use PowerPoint. What five slides must he include? Why are they essential?
4. Why do visual aids help your audience retain information? Have you experienced a time when they were used in such a way? What information do you remember?
5. Describe a time when you gave a presentation. What visual aids did you use? How effective were they? Looking back, what could you have done to make your presentation even better?
6. What visual aids do you feel most comfortable using in presentations? Why? What visual aids are you not as comfortable using, but are interested in trying? Keep this list handy during the next few exercises.

Write It *Draft, Revise, and Finalize*

Create Your Own Success Story

1. Remember the presentation you made at the end of Chapter 11? You are now going to create a storyboard to outline a set of 12 or more visual aids to accompany the presentation.
   - Create 12 large rectangles to represent your presentation.
   - Sketch your idea for each slide in each rectangle. Make sure your presentation includes a) a title slide, b) an introductory slide, c) slides that illustrate main points (pictures, quotes, and phrases), d) a slide to get attention or an activity to break up the presentation, e) a summary slide, and f) thank you and contact information. (Make copies of the next page if you need more slides.)
   - Gather the necessary images for your slide sketches and create the presentation using PowerPoint or any presentation software available on Windows, Mac, or Linux operating systems.
   - If you do not have access to computer software, create the slides on transparencies or draw them on flipchart pages.
   - Make note of any places where you plan to use props or demonstrate.

   a. What medium did you choose: Slides? Transparencies? Flipchart pages? Other? Why?
   b. What problems did you have coming up with ideas for visual aids?
   c. What problems did you have when it came to developing text for your visual aids?
   d. If you developed slides, what Web site(s) did you visit to find photos? Why?
   e. If you developed slides, did you have any problems finding images for your slides? What kind of problems?
   f. If you did not develop slides, what problems did you encounter with your visual aids?
   g. Did you decide on any props or demonstrations? Why?
2. In PowerPoint or a comparable program, create a slideshow containing two slides. On one slide, write your name and use text animation to present the information. On the sec-

ond slide, find a sound bite or a small section of video to include on the slide. E-mail the completed slideshow to your instructor.

3. In PowerPoint or a comparable program, open a slideshow with at least four slides. Place text or pictures on each of the slides. Using the page setup or print option, view your slideshow all at once. Print a copy of your slideshow in storyboard format. After reviewing the appearance, determine if you would prefer to take notes on separate note cards or on the space available on your printed sheet. How would using notes with a storyboard version help you avoid wordiness when presenting your slideshow? Write a memo to your instructor explaining your findings.
4. Compose a slideshow on a topic you are interested in by using the suggested assembly of organized slides within Chapter 12. Include a first slide, introduction slide, two main topic slides, an attention slide, summary slide, and final slide. Print out the slideshow, or e-mail it to your instructor if you use animation or hyperlinks throughout the presentation.
5. Convert the following information into the appropriate type of chart: Of the current student body, 3,357 are engineering majors, 569 are business management majors, and 409 are humanities majors. Create a chart that visually represents the 4,335 students.
6. Create the appropriate chart to visually represent the following information: During the last quarter, The Coffee Company sold 5,889 house coffees, 967 caramel lattes, 433 mocha lattes, and 232 chai teas.
7. Create the appropriate chart to visually represent the following information: During 1999, the Whole Tread Tire Company sold 11,764 tires. That number steadily rose to 11,980 tires in 2000 and 12,546 tires in 2001. A drop occurred over the next couple of years to 10,958 in 2002 and 10,224 in 2003. As of the last quarter in 2004, they sold 10,678 tires.
8. Develop an idea for a "breather" exercise your instructor could use in class to break up a lecture and improve the class's alertness and ability to remember the lecture. Write a proposal in memo format to your instructor proposing the idea with an explanation of how it would benefit the entire class.
9. Visit the Web site SlideShare and choose a slideshow to view and critique. What is the design of the slideshow? How does the author integrate the design suggestions within Chapter 12 to create an aesthetically pleasing slideshow? What does the author do to prepare for questions from the audience online? Write a short analysis of the slideshow you watch.
10. Find a video recorded presentation that uses a slideshow using the Technology Entertainment Design Web site. Are the slides projected so both the live and remote audience can see them? Does the presenter look at the live audience and the camera to make eye contact with the remote audience? How does the speaker physically present himself or herself? Does the speaker repeat any questions so all audience members can understand? Write a summary of your findings after you view the presentation, including the full source citation material for the video you analyzed.
11. Explore the following photograph Web sites: iStock Photo, Getty Images, Flickr, and Stock Xpert by Jupiter Images. Find the terms and conditions of usage and write a brief summary of the guidelines set up by each Web site. Next, analyze the quality of the images available from each. Which one has the best value and quality? Finish your summary with recommendation for which Web site would be best to use for PowerPoint slideshows.
12. Open up PowerPoint or a comparable program and explore the setup. Start a basic slideshow using three slides total. Write your class title and name on the first slide, insert a visual from the clip art section on the second slide, and write about the ease of using the program on the third slide. Print the slideshow.
13. Design a handout to accompany a demonstration presentation for tying a fishing knot, using an ATM machine, or logging on to a computer. What type of information will you include on your handout? Would you distribute the handout before or after your presentation? How much room on the page would you leave for notes to be taken? Include a brief description of your design decisions with the handout.

Speak It *Discuss, Listen, and Understand*

Build Your Leadership and Teamwork Skills

1. Now that you have created your visual aids, it's time to make your presentation in front of your class.

Gather Your Visual Aids

- If you decided to use any props or demonstrations, make sure you have the items you need.
- If you created transparencies, use an overhead projector or document camera.
- If you created flipchart pages, use a flipchart.
- If you created PowerPoint slides, use an electronic projector. If you do not have access to an electronic projector or do not know how to use one, print your slides in color on transparencies. Or print your slides in color on paper, enlarge them, and use them on a flip chart. You could also make a packet of the slides to duplicate and hand them to audience members so they can follow along.

Practice your presentation. You don't need to memorize the material, nor should you read it word for word. You should, however, have a strong enough handle on it so questions from the audience, hostile members, and unexpected changes don't catch you off-guard.

Present and evaluate. Have your audience time you and evaluate you during a dry run.

- **a.** Did you find it easier or more difficult to give the presentation using visual aids?
- **b.** Which visual aids worked particularly well with your audience? Which did not?
- **c.** Did you find yourself reading the slides or did you stay focused on your audience?
- **d.** Do you think that handouts could have helped?
- **e.** Could your audience see your visual aids easily?
- **f.** If you gave a demonstration or used props, did you run into any difficulties?
- **g.** Did your audience ask any questions? What did they have difficulty understanding?
- **h.** What would you do differently next time? Make a list of changes you need to make to your slides and to your verbal presentation.

2. In small groups, discuss suggestions for delivering a slideshow presentation. What impression do you get of the speaker if each slide is read verbatim to you? How can you avoid the curse of knowledge that can plague a speaker? What techniques can you develop to take breathers during a PowerPoint slideshow? Develop a list of standards for the class to use when using PowerPoint slideshows. Compile your lists as a class to use as guidelines for presentations.
3. Create a PowerPoint slideshow using three slides to present what your schedule looked like during the past three days, dedicating each day to one slide. Write a full narrative for each day. Present the slideshow to the class and discuss what tools, such as bulleted lists or charts, could help organize the information. As a class, analyze the effect of viewing slides with just text.
4. In small groups, discuss Webinars, particularly their usage now and how you see them being used in the future. What elements are necessary to create a successful Webinar? What aspects do you need to consider when creating a Webinar? How are Webinars useful in today's business world? How will Webinars affect business communication in the future? Compile a list of your answers to discuss with the class.
5. What types of visual aids are available for you to use in the classroom? Explore the capabilities of the visual aids, taking turns with your classmates to use the aids available to you. Familiarize yourself with how the projector runs or practice writing on the chalkboard. Which aid is the least intimidating to use? The most intimidating? Discuss with the class the aids available to you.
6. In small groups, discuss your experience with viewing PowerPoint slideshows. What qualities create effective slideshows? What was ineffective about the presentations? Make notes of your discussion to share with the entire class.
7. Create a PowerPoint slideshow using three slides to experiment with color and font. On the first slide, use only one type of color and font style, on the second slide use two colors and font styles, and on the third slide use three colors and font styles. Present the slideshow to the class and discuss how the different number of font colors and styles affects the readability and aesthetics of the slideshow.

Do It *Document Your Success Track Record*

Build Your e-Portfolio

In this exercise you are going to post your presentation online for potential employers, others students, and the rest of the world to see.

1. Incorporate the feedback you received following your live presentation and practice the presentation until it flows as smoothly as possible.
2. Next, ask a friend or teacher to help you record yourself giving the presentation. If you used some type of presentation software, like PowerPoint, you should be able to record your voice while giving the presentation. You will not appear in the slides, but your voice will be audible. Review the earlier section in the chapter about how to give Web and video pre-s-entations, which require additional skills and planning.
3. Save a digital copy to your computer or flash drive and burn a copy onto a CD.
4. Upload a copy to one of the following sites:
   - YouTube
   - SlideBoom
   - SlideLive
5. Finally, e-mail a copy of the link to your classmates and teacher along with these questions:
   - How effective were you at presenting the subject matter?
   - Were your visuals compelling? How well did they work with the medium used?
   - Did your demonstrations or props go over well with the audience?
   - What could you do to improve this presentation?
   - What worked well in your presentation?
6. Consider their responses as you prepare future presentations. When finished, place the CD copy in your e-portfolio to show potential employers.

Business in Action
Engaging Audiences with iClickers

How can teachers engage their students in the classroom? This was the question University of Illinois professors contemplated when they designed the original iClicker. The iClicker—also known as an Audience Response System—is a handheld device much like a remote control that makes visual aids interactive. The iClicker allows students or audience members to provide instant feedback to a presentation or answers on a quiz by clicking different buttons corresponding to options on a screen. Once they respond to a question or prompt, the audience's answers are instantly viewable in the form of a graph or chart. This allows audience members to become directly involved with the presentation by making their responses a part of the visual aids used.

After almost a decade of development, inventors Tim Stelzer and Mats Selen began marketing the iClicker in 2006. The positive response in education was enormous and immediate. Approximately 700 educational institutions and 1 million students use iClickers in North America alone. However, businesses noticed the new technology as well, realizing it could be used in a variety of business presentation situations.

In addition to obtaining demographic information about their audiences, many companies have found other uses for the iClicker. During presentations, speakers are able to take immediate polls and save the data for later research, which is helpful for marketing professionals. Speakers can also ask interactive questions while recording the most common responses. During bigger events like conferences, companies can use the invention to gauge which speakers have been most effective and which might need more training. Additionally, presenters can use the iClicker to send a preliminary question to audience members before a presentation and then receive an immediate response. This is almost like a text message or a "tweet" on Twitter, but with a more specific audience.

In contrast to other electronic visual aids like PowerPoint, the iClicker uses technology to combat waning participation and encourage interaction with the speaker. Audience members are no longer content to just sit through a progression of slides, and wait for the end to come. With innovative tools like the iClicker, presentations are becoming more two-sided and are connecting the speakers of today with the audiences of tomorrow by making them an integral part of the visual aid process.

Questions

1. What is an iClicker?
2. How do presenters use iClickers to increase audience interaction? What else can they use it for?

Sources: Louis Lipschultz, "Developing Better Presentations with an Audience Response System," *Ezine Articles,* accessed November 6, 2010, at http://ezinearticles.com/?Developing-Better-Presentations-With-an-Audience-Response-System&id=2160038; Sarah Martin "Loyola University Chicago Selects iClicker's Classroom Response System," *New Media Consortium (NMC),* March 19, 2009, accessed at www.nmc.org/news/partner/loyola-university-chicago-selects-i-clicker-s-classroom-response-system.

Key Terms

Bubble chart. A chart that displays a set of numeric values as circles. The bigger the circle, the bigger the value. *(p. 349)*

Demonstration. The act of physically showing or explaining a concept. *(p. 342)*

Dry-erase whiteboards. Smooth, white porcelain-on-steel boards that replace blackboards. You write or draw on them with colorful dry-erase markers. *(p. 341)*

Flipchart. A large, portable pad of paper placed on an easel. You can write or draw on the paper, and also tear off the paper pages and attach them to the wall, as necessary. *(p. 340)*

Flowcharts. Line drawings or diagrams that show the flow of information or the steps in a procedure or process. *(p. 346)*

Horizontal bar chart. A chart with horizontal bars that are proportional to the data being displayed. *(p. 348)*

Hyperlinks. Clickable links on a slide that take the viewer to another Web page or Web site. *(p. 347)*

Kinesthetic learners. People who need to do something physically in order to learn. *(p. 342)*

Line chart. A chart that presents information as a series of connected line segments. Often used to demonstrate trends. *(p. 348)*

Memory stick. A removable flash memory card. *(p. 342)*

Organizational chart. A series of connected rectangles that illustrates how a company or a Web site is organized. *(p. 349)*

Overhead projector. A device upon which you place a transparency to project an image or text onto a screen. *(p. 341)*

Parking lot. A portion of a flipchart used to "park" the audience's questions or objections that cannot be addressed at the moment. *(p. 341)*

Pie chart. A chart that presents information as slices of a circular "pie" to show percentages of a whole. *(p. 348)*

Podcast. Audio presentations distributed over the Internet for playback on mobile devices or personal computers. *(p. 356)*

Slide share. A Web site where people can post slide presentations and Webinars for viewing. *(p. 356)*

Storyboarding. A method of visually telling a story, panel by panel, in sequence, using notes and visuals (similar to frames in a comic book). *(p. 343)*

Table. A graphic that presents information in rows and columns for easy side-by-side comparisons of data. *(p. 348)*

Thumb drive. A portable memory storage device. *(p. 342)*

Vertical bar chart. A chart with vertical bars that are proportional to the data being displayed. *(p. 348)*

Video presentations. A presentation made to a live audience, recorded, and posted on the Web. *(p. 356)*

Visual presenter. A device that projects 2-D and 3-D images onto a large LCD screen. *(p. 341)*

Webinar. A Web presentation in which viewers typically watch a slide presentation and listen to the presenter's voice. *(p. 356)*

Review Questions *Test Yourself*

1. Why are visual aids important in creating effective presentations?
2. What are the different types of visual aids you can use for presentations?
3. What should you consider when using flipcharts and whiteboards?
4. What are the advantages of using PowerPoint slides?
5. Explain what storyboarding is and explain how it can be used to create effective slideshows.
6. How can you effectively and ineffectively use text in a slideshow?
7. What general rules should be followed for any type of chart you use in a presentation?
8. Explain what a bubble chart is and explain what type of data it supports.
9. Explain what an organizational chart is and the type of data it supports.
10. List some suggestions for keeping your slideshows simple and professional in appearance.
11. What are some suggestions to ensure font and color consistency in your slideshows?
12. How can you relax and avoid rushing through slides during your presentation?
13. What types of presentations can be delivered without being face to face with your audience?
14. Describe slide shares and explain how you can transform a presentation to make it ready for the Web.
15. What tips can you follow prior to, during, and after a Webinar to create a successful presentation?
16. Why should you avoid reading a slideshow word-for-word when you present it?

Grammar Review *Mastering Accuracy*

Quotation Marks, Parentheses, Apostrophes, and Italics

Section I

Each of the following sentences contains one or more common errors in word usage, grammar, or style. Identify the errors. If you have trouble finding the errors, review Sections 2.5., 2.6., and 2.7. in the handbook (Appendix D) at the back of this textbook.

1. We will enforce the NO FOOD OR DRINK policy in all classrooms.
2. Parking is plentiful at all of our companys' facilities.
3. The vending machine's do not except coins from other countries.
4. Bella is currently reading Better_Business_Practices . . . moreover, she plans to apply the material she learns.
5. Please turn in all your (business) receipts (to Margaret) by the end of the week (or by the end of next week) if you have scheduled weekend travel.).
6. Please keep umbrellas closed . . . inside . . . the building.
7. Our vending machines' contain snack's that are sugar-free and cheap.
8. "Please remember to follow all policies while in the building, Tony reminded the new recruits."
9. Joshua announced, sternly with "quarterly report deadlines looming, the secretarial . . . pool will be working extended hours," he said.
10. Please, slow down! "I don't want anyone hurt" said, our next-door neighbor.

Section II

On a separate sheet of paper, rewrite the following sentences so they are clearer, more professional sounding, grammatically correct, and goodwill oriented.

1. Effective right now, . . . time cards must be signed by supervisors before you think of processing them.
2. The old sink knobs, "on the second floor" will be replaced with electric eyes.
3. Before being issued a badge, visitors must sign_in 'with security' at the front desk.
4. Please do not act funny, actually, everyone should act normal when accreditation visits next week.

5. Go get the office manager and grab his key to the supply closet.
6. David said, "Rhonda asked, 'What's the rules again to this game before we start the game?"
7. We would'nt wanna start the biz talk without Mr. Jones' input.
8. It would not be wise to lowball this candidate: she seems on the up and up.
9. I wish you would have asked for help before things got so bad!
10. Deborah will communicate our needs to the Pittsburgh office and also I seem to think she will be charge of chatting with the Chicago office.

Extra Resources *Tools You Can Use*

Books

- Cox, Joyce. *Microsoft® Office PowerPoint® 2007 Step by Step.* Redmond, WA: Microsoft Press, 2007.
- Duarte, Nancy. *Slide:ology: The Art and Science of Creating Great Presentations.* Sebastopol: CA: O'Reilly Media, 2008.
- Lowe, Doug. *PowerPoint® 2007 for Dummies.* Hoboken, NJ: Wiley, 2006.
- Medina, John. *Brain Rules: 12 Principles for Surviving and Thriving at Work, Home, and School.* Seattle, WA: Pear Press, 2008.
- Reynolds, Garr. *Presentation Zen: Simple Ideas on Presentation Design and Delivery.* Berkeley, CA: New Riders, 2008.
- Tufte, Edward R. *The Cognitive Style of PowerPoint.* Cheshire, CT: Graphics Press, 2006.
- Tufte, Edward R. *The Visual Display of Quantitative Information,* 2nd ed. Cheshire, CT: Graphics Press, 1992.
- Williams, Robin. *The Non-Designer's Design Book: Design and Typographical Principles for the Visual Novice,* 3rd ed. Berkeley, CA: Peachpit Press, 2008.

Web Sites

- *Presentation Zen*
- *TED: Ideas Worth Spreading*

"If opportunity doesn't knock, build a door." —**Milton Berle**, comedian and actor

CHAPTER
13

Career Exploration and the Job Search

Starting Out on the Path to Future Success

LEARNING OBJECTIVE QUESTIONS

1. How can you pinpoint your best skills to use professionally?
2. How can networking and research help you target a career and a company?
3. What can make you a desirable employee?
4. How do you effectively search for a job?
5. What steps can you take in a difficult job market?

PEARSON **mybcommlab** Access interactive videos, simulations, sample documents, document makeovers, and assessment quizzes in Chapter 13 of **mybcommlab.com** for mastery of this chapter's objectives.

>>> **Toby Nadir** began school unclear about his major. He spent his freshman year taking the core classes required for all incoming students. He gave little thought to the future, figuring he'd have his career plan in place by the time he graduated. Once Toby discovered his passion for history, he focused on that as his major. However, he wasn't really sure what he could do with a history degree after graduation.

Toby earned his spending money during summer breaks and worked weekends during the school year when he needed extra cash. When it came time to graduate, Toby's uncle offered him a position as a salesman in his office furniture and supplies store. Toby accepted the position. After all, he needed the money.

>>> **Benita Gonzalez** began her freshman year also unsure of her major. She was passionate about art and fashion, but had no idea how she could develop her love of clothing into a career. She dreamed of becoming a stylist to the stars but knew there were many other more realistic alternatives she needed to explore.

Benita visited her college's career services center and made appointments to explore her options with a professional career advisor. Benita then took personality and skills assessment tests, which revealed that she was a "driver," someone focused on getting results. Benita vowed to turn her strengths and abilities into a career. The question was, how?

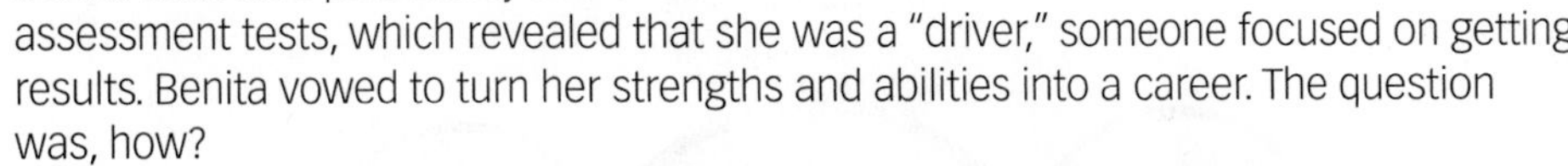

Finding the right internship became Benita's priority. She wasted no time building her network of contacts. By contacting her school's alumni association, Benita was referred to an alum working at Stilet-toes, a shoe company based in New York City. The alum informed her that the company was about to place a job posting online for summer advertising interns. With the alum's help, Benita was accepted for the position.

During her internship, Benita realized that she loved the advertising aspect of fashion. When she returned to school, she took more advertising classes and joined the Marketing Club, an organization that brought students together to critique each other's ideas and work and hosted guest speakers. At graduation time, Benita felt clear about her direction. She was proud that, due to her hard work, Stilet-toes was interested in hiring her as an advertising associate.

If your approach to college resembles Toby's, your employment options upon graduating could be limited. As businessman and columnist Harvey Mackay advises, "Dig your well before you're thirsty." In other words, don't wait until you've graduated to start planning for your future. Starting early gives you time to change course, refine your ideas about your future, and leave college better equipped for professional life.

All people need to find meaningful work to survive and thrive in the world. There are no exceptions. Students need to prepare to find jobs long before graduation. Your time in college gives you a chance to explore your interests and challenge yourself with opportunities to engage in teamwork, accept leadership roles, and sometimes operate outside your comfort zone. These experiences, along with a college degree, can provide you with both a practical and academic foundation for your future career in whatever industry you choose.

In this chapter, we will discuss the fashion and apparel industry, which includes the design, manufacturing, and sales of clothing, accessories, shoes, and jewelry. The fashion design and merchandising industry took a real hit between 2000 and 2010 due to the economic downturn and outsourcing of many key positions to third-world countries. In fact, many experts predict that U.S. job opportunities in the fashion and design field will continue to decline during the next few years.

Nonetheless, there are still opportunities in this industry for creative and enterprising graduates. The opportunities include jobs in fashion design, retail and wholesale buying, sales, and fashion media, including Web sites and publications. In coming years, there will likely be stiff competition for these jobs, and positions will go to passionate candidates who have laid a foundation for their success.

Determining your career path requires a job search that is both strategic and tactical. An effective job search begins by determining how your strengths and skills can be applied to your area of interest. It then includes exploring various career opportunities. Finally, it involves starting your job search. This chapter addresses all three aspects: the questions students must ask themselves about their personal and professional direction, the ways to network and learn more about potential careers, and the nuts and bolts of job hunting.

1 How Can You Pinpoint Your Best Skills to Use Professionally?

How well do you know yourself? Think about who you are and where you are headed . . . do you like what you see? In *Majoring in the Rest of Your Life,* by Carol Carter, readers are invited to complete the following sentences.[1] How would you complete them?

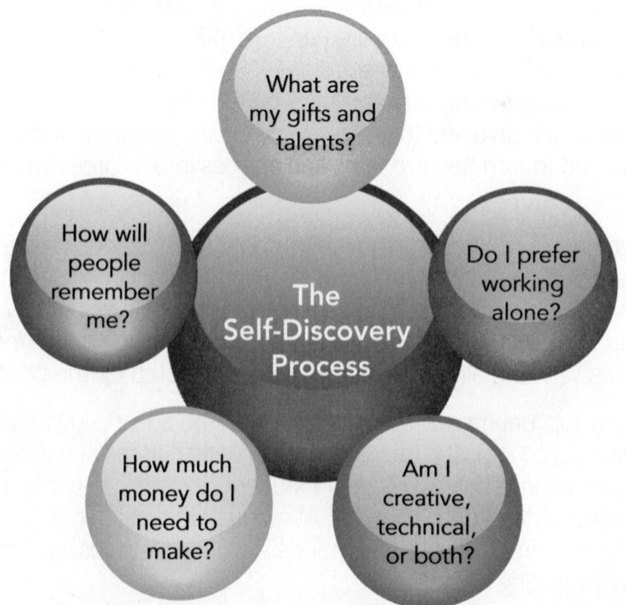

Source: Reprinted with permission from Carol Carter, Majoring in the Rest of Your Life, LifeBound, 2005.

- I like ________________.
- I want to accomplish ________________.
- When I die, I want to be remembered for ________________.
- In life, I value these things the most ________________.
- Contributions I want to make to the world include ________________.
- Things that give me peace of mind are ________________.

Try answering these additional questions:

- What are your gifts and talents?
- What activities inspire you?
- What did you want to be when you "grew up"?
- Do you prefer working alone or with others?
- What are your convictions?
- Do you like to travel?
- Are you creative or technical?
- What type of lifestyle do you enjoy?
- What are your "must-haves" in life?
- How important are your surroundings?
- Are you active or sedentary?
- How much money do you need to make?
- How important is your legacy, or how will people remember you?
- Do you want to live in the city or the country?

If you don't know the answers to those questions, start the process of self-discovery now. The most rewarding careers will be the ones that align with your interests and talents, and college is a great time to start defining them. In the workforce, you have less time and opportunity to gain leadership experience, study abroad, make connections, experience various employment environments, and participate in an academic community.

While you're engaging in self-exploration, there is no such thing as failure. For example, participating on an environmental board, only to discover you don't want a related career, does not make the experience a failure. On the contrary, you have narrowed your focus, fostered new relationships, practiced professional communication skills, and gained clarity about your life's direction. Keep your focus on progress, not perfection, so you can celebrate success, make mistakes and learn from them, and appreciate life. Let's take a look at some ways to help you gain clarity about your own gifts and talents, and the careers they might be suited for.

When students use college as a way to stretch themselves beyond their perceived limitations, they feel extremely empowered. Not only do they learn more about themselves and others, but they gain experience and confidence while building their professional portfolios.

Take Online Personality Tests

Personality tests and skill-set tests, like the Emotional Quotient test in Chapter 2, are suggestive rather than determinative.[2] View taking them as an opportunity to explore your likes, dislikes, strengths, and opportunities for growth. As you review the results, see which ones resonate with you. Ask yourself, "Are there themes in the various tests I've taken that can help me make a career decision?" In addition to the tests administered by your career services center, there are many career and personality tests you can take online at various Web sites, such as *CareerPath*, *JobDiagnosis*, *MyPlan*, and *LiveCareer.*

Use Career-Related Reference Books

There are countless books available on exploring how your gifts and talents apply to the world. As mentioned earlier, *Majoring in the Rest of Your Life* discusses the discovery of gifts and talents, effective networking, and understanding employer expectations in the working world. It also has sections for journaling ideas and inspirations. There are many other resources available on career exploration in your local bookstore or library. Ask for suggestions from your career advisor or internship coordinator or see the list of books at the back of this chapter.

DID YOU KNOW?

The Occupational Outlook Handbook, published by the U.S. Department of Labor and available for free on the Web, contains information on hundreds of positions. Using the handbook can help you determine the education and training needed for a position, its responsibilities, working conditions, and salary.

Visit Your College's Career Services Center

Most schools have a career services center on campus, some with an internship center. Form relationships with the people working in your school's career services center by setting periodic appointments during your college career. The staff typically consists of trained professionals accustomed to helping college students determine a career path. Their services are generally free to students. By contrast, graduates can spend thousands of dollars for similar assistance in the working world.

Career advisors in the center have access to personality tests, skill tests, and other interpersonal inventories that can help you match your strengths with various careers. The advisors can also outline career paths pursued by other students with similar aspirations, as well as keep you informed of job openings posted with the center. Finally, career advisors know when job fairs and on-campus interviews are occurring, so stay connected to these people.

Ask your career advisor to put you on any e-mail lists regarding career fairs, career events, and résumé workshops hosted on campus. As you prepare your résumé, set an appointment with the career advisor to review it and offer suggestions. Your advisor will likely provide suggestions for internships or recommend specific employment. Be sure to keep a folder of the material, tests, and data you receive. If your career advisor suggests an industry that might appeal to you, find out if the advisor has contacts in any related companies. Then, reach out to those contacts using correspondence like that shown in **Exhibit 13-1**.

Consider your relationship with your career advisor a professional relationship and treat it as such. Follow up on *all* opportunities presented to you with correspondence like that shown in **Exhibit 13-2**. Before determining that an opportunity doesn't fit your criteria, take the time to explore it and make connections within that organization.

Finally, send a thank-you card to your career advisor after receiving a lead. Doing so will make a lasting professional impression. Remember, campus career advisors are in contact with companies. If you stand out as being especially professional, advisors will remember you and tell their company contacts about you.

Exhibit 13-1 An E-mail Requesting Internship Information

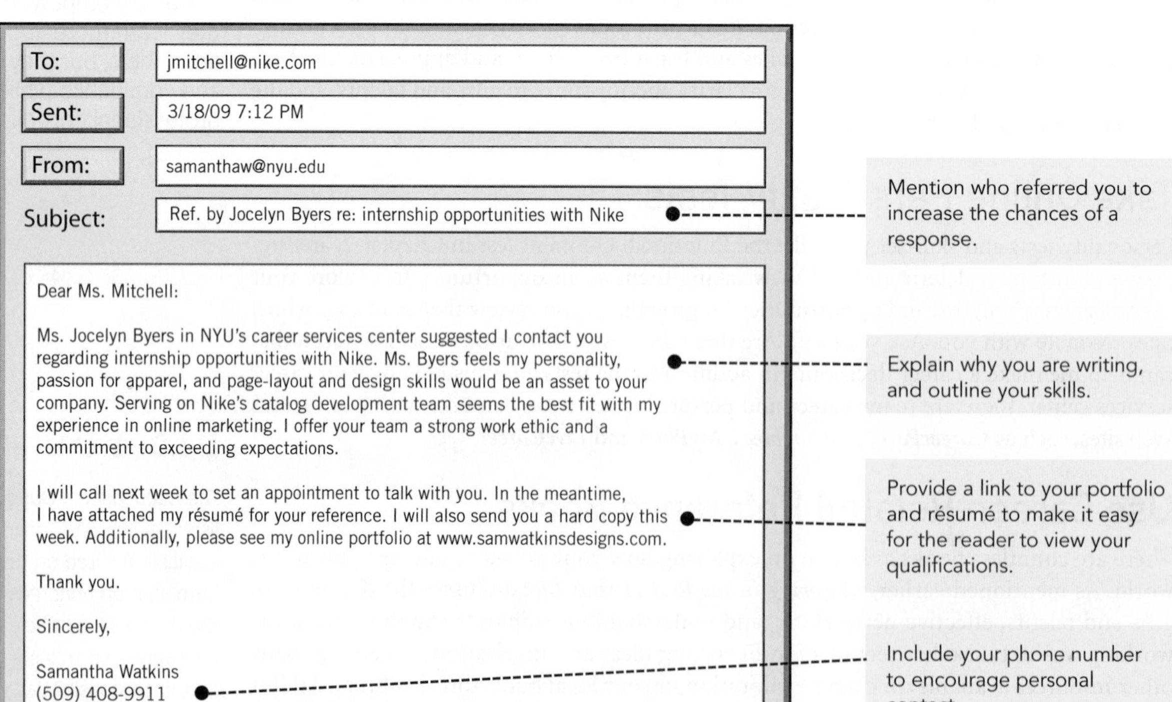

To: jmitchell@nike.com

Sent: 3/18/09 7:12 PM

From: samanthaw@nyu.edu

Subject: Ref. by Jocelyn Byers re: internship opportunities with Nike

Dear Ms. Mitchell:

Ms. Jocelyn Byers in NYU's career services center suggested I contact you regarding internship opportunities with Nike. Ms. Byers feels my personality, passion for apparel, and page-layout and design skills would be an asset to your company. Serving on Nike's catalog development team seems the best fit with my experience in online marketing. I offer your team a strong work ethic and a commitment to exceeding expectations.

I will call next week to set an appointment to talk with you. In the meantime, I have attached my résumé for your reference. I will also send you a hard copy this week. Additionally, please see my online portfolio at www.samwatkinsdesigns.com.

Thank you.

Sincerely,

Samantha Watkins
(509) 408-9911

Exhibit 13-2 An E-mail Request for an On-Campus Interview

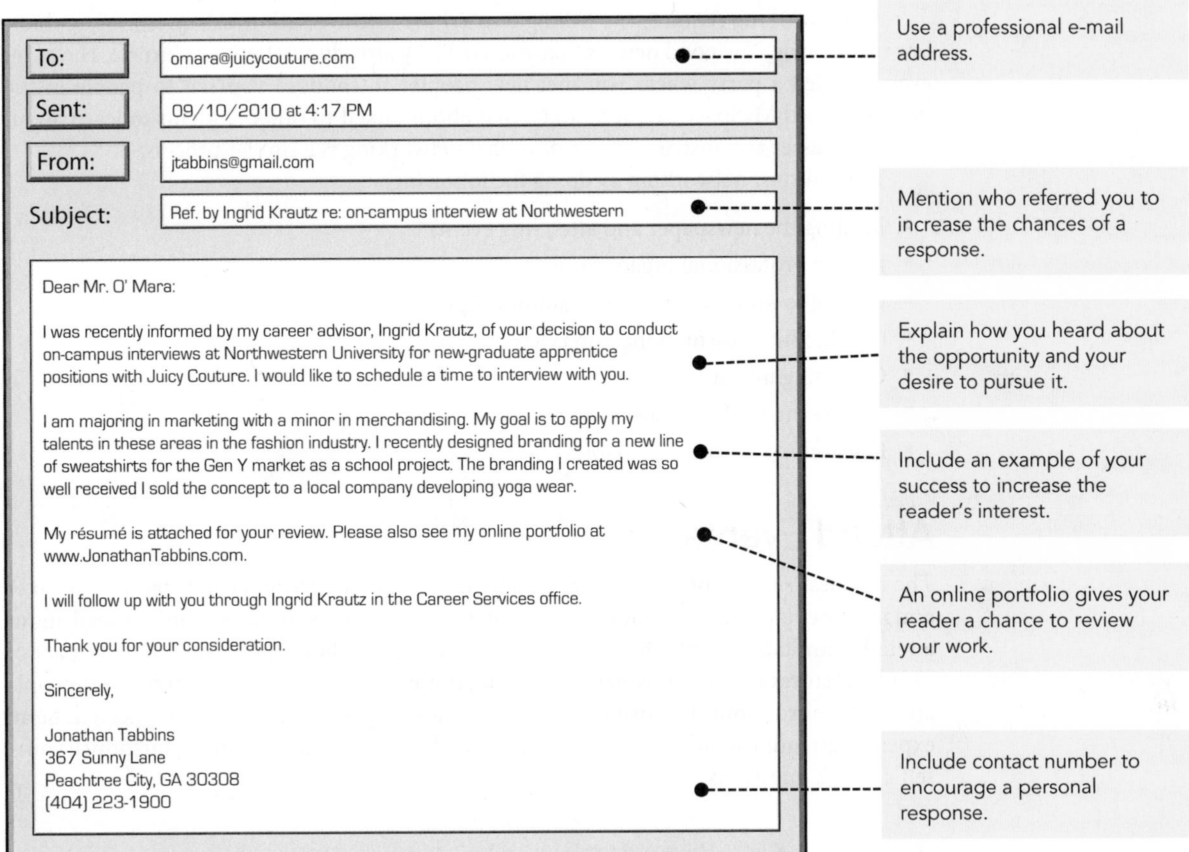

To: omara@juicycouture.com

Sent: 09/10/2010 at 4:17 PM

From: jtabbins@gmail.com

Subject: Ref. by Ingrid Krautz re: on-campus interview at Northwestern

Dear Mr. O' Mara:

I was recently informed by my career advisor, Ingrid Krautz, of your decision to conduct on-campus interviews at Northwestern University for new-graduate apprentice positions with Juicy Couture. I would like to schedule a time to interview with you.

I am majoring in marketing with a minor in merchandising. My goal is to apply my talents in these areas in the fashion industry. I recently designed branding for a new line of sweatshirts for the Gen Y market as a school project. The branding I created was so well received I sold the concept to a local company developing yoga wear.

My résumé is attached for your review. Please also see my online portfolio at www.JonathanTabbins.com.

I will follow up with you through Ingrid Krautz in the Career Services office.

Thank you for your consideration.

Sincerely,

Jonathan Tabbins
367 Sunny Lane
Peachtree City, GA 30308
(404) 223-1900

Use a professional e-mail address.

Mention who referred you to increase the chances of a response.

Explain how you heard about the opportunity and your desire to pursue it.

Include an example of your success to increase the reader's interest.

An online portfolio gives your reader a chance to review your work.

Include contact number to encourage a personal response.

PEARSON mybcommlab

Apply Exhibit 13-2's key concepts by revising a new document. Go to Chapter 13 in mybcommlab.com and select Document Makeovers.

Notice that Exhibits 13-1 and 13-2 are both e-mails. However, you could have sent letters instead. You may wonder which form is most appropriate. As you learned in Chapter 7, timing often dictates the method of correspondence you use. E-mails encourage a prompt response because the recipient can easily hit "reply." However, if you are an "unknown" sender, the corporate firewall could send your message to the recipient's junk file. Such filters are particularly common in large corporations. In these cases, following up with a hard copy referencing your e-mail is advised. After sending attachments, following up with a paper copy is a good idea because it keeps your name in front of the recipient.

A letter is more formal and can be quite effective if you have paper examples of your work to include. Regardless of whether you send an e-mail or a letter, you must follow up. People are often busy and might not get to your e-mail or letter for a while. Or they might forget about you after they read your correspondence. That's why it's important to follow up with a phone call after sending correspondence. Jog your contact's memory by saying something such as, "Mr. Jones, I am just following up on my e-mail regarding internships in your department. Is this a good time to talk?"

2 How Can Networking and Research Help You Target a Career and a Company?

There's no better way to learn about a career than to talk to people who are already in it. The practice of **networking** refers to the simple act of talking to people you know directly, or people you know through others, about the work they do, the industry they are in, and how they got into that line of work. Of course, it also involves telling them something about yourself. Networking lets you "cast a wider net" among contacts.

All networking requires is a willingness to have a conversation, ask questions, and follow up on leads. The good news is that you are likely already a networking expert. Have you ever attended a party where you met new people? Introduced yourself to people in the dorms? Joined MySpace or Facebook? What about talked to other students to learn about different classes and instructors? Professional networking is a similar process.

You can start networking by doing the following:

- Reading the newspaper and attending events
- Joining professional organizations
- Getting to know your college's alumni center
- Conducting informational interviews
- Obtaining internships
- Shadowing professionals
- Researching specific companies

Attend Events

The business section of newspapers usually lists events where you can listen to a speaker and meet people in a profession you are interested in. For example, you might read about a retail roundtable event where owners of local clothing boutiques discuss the impact of "big box" stores on their business. Attending these events is a way for you to meet people and learn more about the business you are considering as a career. You don't need to be an expert to attend. You just need to be an interested listener who is willing to introduce yourself and ask questions.

Join Professional Organizations

Every field has its own professional organizations, and their local chapters are usually thrilled to have student members. By joining such an organization, you automatically expand your network to include a wide number of people in the same profession. For example, in the fashion industry, there are organizations associated with footwear, leather, sewing, fabrics, and more: American Apparel Manufacturers, American Apparel Producers' Network, American Sewing Guild, and National Association of Retail Merchandising Services, to name a few. Additionally, there is a myriad of online groups at the Web site Meetup you can join to find other people who share your interests. See Meetup's site for more information. Most professional organizations typically offer special membership rates for students and often enlist students as volunteers for different activities that can give you experience in your field.

Visit Your College's Alumni Center

Don't overlook your college's alumni center as a means of networking. If you are interested in a few fields, ask the alumni coordinator to arrange introductions with alumni working in those fields. Some of your school's alumni may be prominent professionals more than willing to offer career advice.

Remember, students and alumni share a common interest—their school. Active alumni have already demonstrated a commitment to their alma mater. They may also take an active interest in helping students. By connecting with alumni in your prospective field, you are likely to forge relationships that will open doors in the future. Those alumni might be willing to write letters of recommendation on your behalf and keep you informed of opportunities within their own companies. **Exhibit 13-3** is an example of an e-mail requesting an informational interview by telephone with an alum. Informational interviews are discussed in detail in the next section.

Remember, when someone has helped you by providing an informational interview, follow up with a thank-you card. See **Exhibit 13-4** for an example of a follow-up thank-you card.

Exhibit 13-3 An E-mail to an Alumni Requesting a Telephone Interview

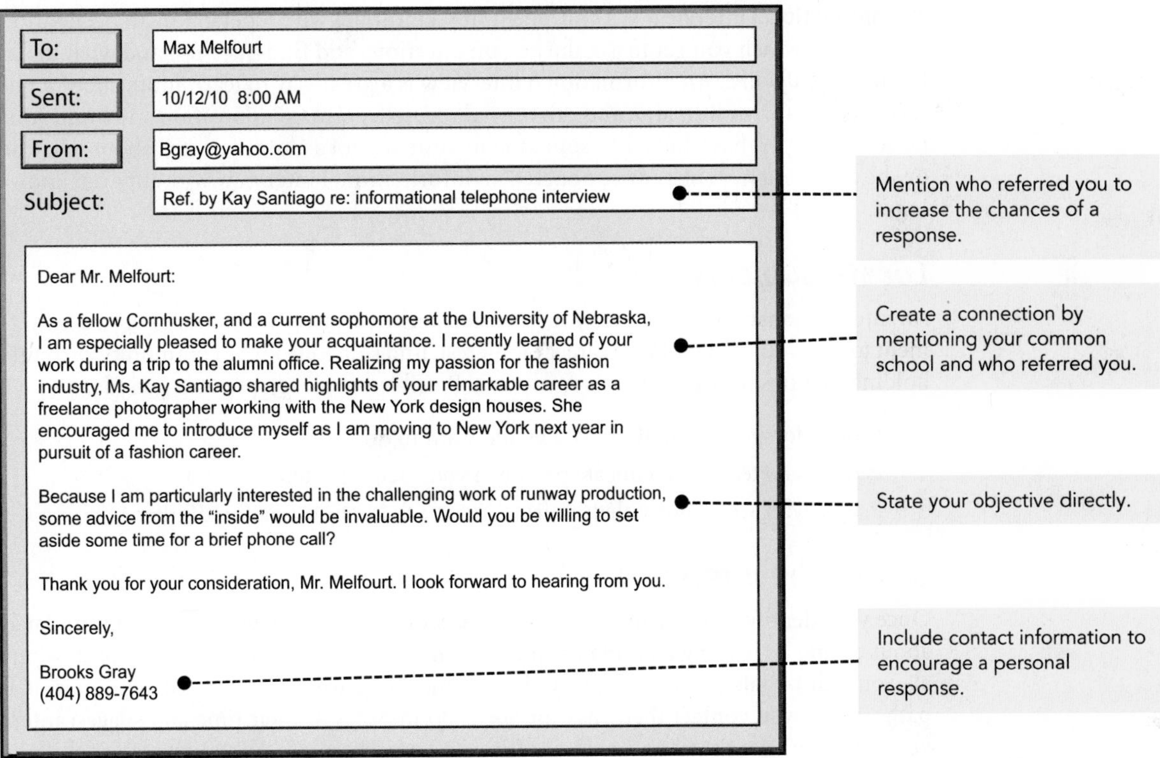

To: Max Melfourt

Sent: 10/12/10 8:00 AM

From: Bgray@yahoo.com

Subject: Ref. by Kay Santiago re: informational telephone interview

Mention who referred you to increase the chances of a response.

Dear Mr. Melfourt:

As a fellow Cornhusker, and a current sophomore at the University of Nebraska, I am especially pleased to make your acquaintance. I recently learned of your work during a trip to the alumni office. Realizing my passion for the fashion industry, Ms. Kay Santiago shared highlights of your remarkable career as a freelance photographer working with the New York design houses. She encouraged me to introduce myself as I am moving to New York next year in pursuit of a fashion career.

Create a connection by mentioning your common school and who referred you.

Because I am particularly interested in the challenging work of runway production, some advice from the "inside" would be invaluable. Would you be willing to set aside some time for a brief phone call?

State your objective directly.

Thank you for your consideration, Mr. Melfourt. I look forward to hearing from you.

Sincerely,

Brooks Gray
(404) 889-7643

Include contact information to encourage a personal response.

Exhibit 13-4 A Thank-You Card Following an Informational Interview

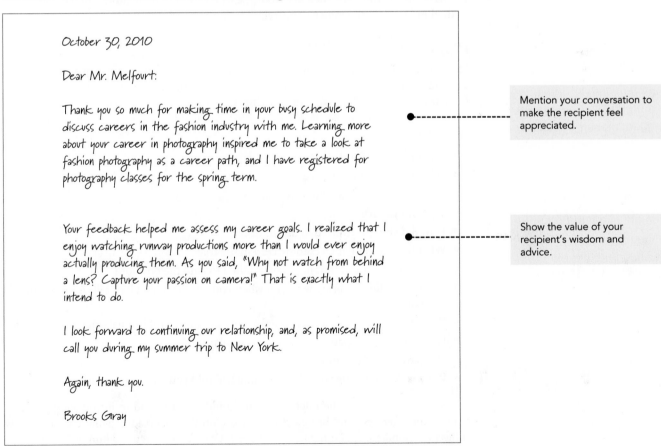

October 30, 2010

Dear Mr. Melfourt:

Thank you so much for making time in your busy schedule to discuss careers in the fashion industry with me. Learning more about your career in photography inspired me to take a look at fashion photography as a career path, and I have registered for photography classes for the spring term.

Mention your conversation to make the recipient feel appreciated.

Your feedback helped me assess my career goals. I realized that I enjoy watching runway productions more than I would ever enjoy actually producing them. As you said, "Why not watch from behind a lens? Capture your passion on camera!" That is exactly what I intend to do.

Show the value of your recipient's wisdom and advice.

I look forward to continuing our relationship, and, as promised, will call you during my summer trip to New York.

Again, thank you.

Brooks Gray

Conduct Informational Interviews

An **informational interview** is a conversation you initiate with a person in an occupation or career in which you get to ask the person questions and find out firsthand what his or her job is really like. An informational interview is a great way to learn more about a position, company, or industry, and can open doors to a permanent position and build your network.[3] If you have talked to someone in your school's alumni center about what he or she does, you have already conducted an informational interview without even knowing it.

Locate Subjects

An informational interview gives you an inside peek at a career without making a commitment to it. If you've identified a career of interest, find someone in the community currently holding that position and introduce yourself. Possible people to approach include:

- People doing jobs you think you would want to do
- People who teach and educate people in your field of interest
- People who are responsible for hiring in your field or occupation of interest

Set Up the Interview

Once you identify possible interview subjects, set up the interview. Don't feel intimidated about calling or sending an e-mail requesting an informational interview. The professionals you will be talking to probably did the same thing when deciding their professional paths. When you contact them, ask for about 30 minutes of their time and suggest interviewing them over the phone, at their office, or somewhere else. You might consider inviting the person to lunch or coffee. Make it clear that you are not seeking employment, just information and advice, and let the person know who referred you to them.

Exhibit 13-5 shows an e-mail requesting an informational interview. As you read through the text, notice that Abigail, the student, is still deciding the direction of her career. From the information provided, she would be wise to have several informational interviews, both in menswear and women's apparel.

Prepare for the Interview

Start by researching your area of interest so you have a basic understanding of the industry and can ask intelligent questions. Try to learn something about the person you will be interviewing so you can build rapport with him or her when you meet. Most importantly, prepare a list of questions to ask the person whom you are interviewing. The following are some suggestions:

- What is your official title?
- What is your typical day like?
- What do you like best about working as a ________?
- What do you like least?
- How did you get involved in this industry?
- What do you think it takes to succeed in the role?
- What education and training were required to land the position?
- What skills did you bring with you when you got the job? What skills have you developed on the job?
- What are some of the greatest mistakes you see young professionals make in your field?
- How can I best prepare for success in a similar role?
- How strong is the industry?
- What is the one thing you wish someone had told you when you were starting out?

Since you asked for the interview, you should take the lead in introducing yourself, guiding the interview, and bringing it to a close on time. Consider giving your interview subject a reminder call or e-mail a day before your meeting to remind him or her of it.

Exhibit 13-5 An E-mail Requesting an Informational Interview

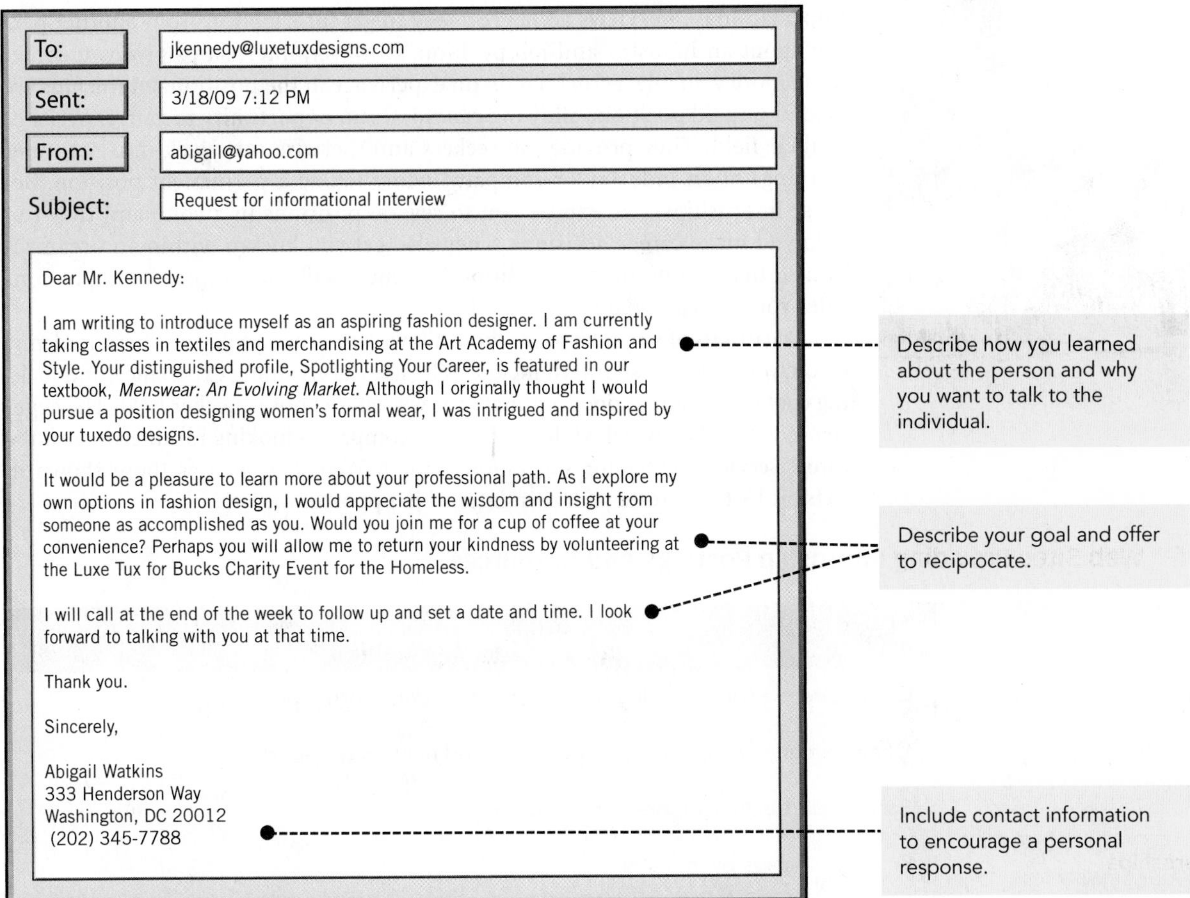

To: jkennedy@luxetuxdesigns.com

Sent: 3/18/09 7:12 PM

From: abigail@yahoo.com

Subject: Request for informational interview

Dear Mr. Kennedy:

I am writing to introduce myself as an aspiring fashion designer. I am currently taking classes in textiles and merchandising at the Art Academy of Fashion and Style. Your distinguished profile, Spotlighting Your Career, is featured in our textbook, *Menswear: An Evolving Market*. Although I originally thought I would pursue a position designing women's formal wear, I was intrigued and inspired by your tuxedo designs.

It would be a pleasure to learn more about your professional path. As I explore my own options in fashion design, I would appreciate the wisdom and insight from someone as accomplished as you. Would you join me for a cup of coffee at your convenience? Perhaps you will allow me to return your kindness by volunteering at the Luxe Tux for Bucks Charity Event for the Homeless.

I will call at the end of the week to follow up and set a date and time. I look forward to talking with you at that time.

Thank you.

Sincerely,

Abigail Watkins
333 Henderson Way
Washington, DC 20012
(202) 345-7788

Describe how you learned about the person and why you want to talk to the individual.
Describe your goal and offer to reciprocate.
Include contact information to encourage a personal response.

Conduct the Interview

When you first meet your interview subject, greet him or her by name, give your name, and thank the person for coming. Next, review why you are conducting the informational interview—to gather information that will help you in your career search. Explain why you are interested in talking to the person and let the individual know that you will be asking a lot of questions over the next 30 minutes or so. Ask if the person minds you taking notes or recording him or her. Taking notes is less off-putting than recording a person or typing notes into a laptop. The laptop screen puts a barrier between you and your subject, and the sound of clicking keys can be annoying. Some people feel intimidated being recorded and are less likely to open up as a result.

An informational interview is different than a job interview. Do not put the interviewee on the spot and ask for a job. You will alienate the person and probably put a quick end to the interview. As you conduct the interview, be aware of the time. If you are reaching the time limit, start wrapping up your questions. When you finish, always ask your subject if there is someone else with whom you might talk. Finally, thank your interview subject, ask for his or her business card, and give out your contact information.

After the Interview

It is crucial to send the person you interviewed a thank-you note—preferably handwritten. After all, that person took time out of a busy day to talk to you. If you contact the individual in the future, he or she will be more likely to remember you. Also, if you discovered you had rapport with the person during the interview, you might consider asking the person to act as a mentor to you.

Obtain Internships

Informational interviews are a great way to get information from another person about an industry and job position. However, internships give you something more valuable: actual hands-on experience in the position. **Internships** are paid or unpaid positions allowing candidates an opportunity to gain experience in their field. They provide job seekers an otherwise rare peek into the inner workings of an industry or company before taking a permanent position. Because internships may expose you to several positions in a company, they can help you make career decisions. They also get you known within an organization so that if a permanent position becomes available, employers might consider you as a candidate.

Regardless of whether your school allows you to accept pay or offers academic credit, your goals as an intern include self-discovery, gaining experience, and making contacts. Again, it does not matter if you later choose another field. The experience will still be worthwhile. To research companies looking for interns, visit the career services center for suggestions, search Web sites such as those shown in **Exhibit 13-6**, or create your own internship opportunities.

Exhibit 13-6 Web Sites Providing Internship Postings and Resources

Web Site	Types of Information
CareerRookie	Offers career advice, employment postings, and internship postings.
CollegeGrad	Offers career advice, internship postings, and new-grad opportunities.
InternAbroad	Posts opportunities for internships abroad.
RisingStarInternships	Posts internships by industry.

Although Web sites are an excellent place to start looking for a career, use caution when searching for jobs online. Beware of work-from-home opportunities. A large percentage of these offers are scams. They usually require applicants to pay a small "registration fee" before applying for jobs. After the fee is paid, applicants rarely hear back from the companies.

Before applying for an internship, clarify your goals for the proposed time of service. Check your school's policies regarding acquiring credit and accepting compensation. The following questions will help guide you to the right internship:

- Which industries do I want to know more about?
- What skills do I need to land a job in this industry?
- What can I do to obtain those skills as an intern?
- What do I want to accomplish while working for this company?
- What training would I like to receive during this internship?
- What sacrifices am I willing to make as an intern (personal time, weekends, monetary income, and so forth)?
- Will I be compensated financially or earn school credit for interning?
- How will I be managed during my internship (weekly or monthly meetings) and by whom?

Approaching a company or organization with your own internship idea is a great way to take responsibility for your professional growth. If you choose this route, create a brief proposal outlining your proposed activities, contributions, and measurements for success. Doing so shows a company your dedication to your career. Before proposing your internship idea, have a career advisor review your proposal and make suggestions for improvements. Confirm that your proposal complies with your school's internship policies. See **Exhibit 13-7** for an example of an internship proposal.

Exhibit 13-7 An E-mail Proposing an Internship Position with a Growing Company

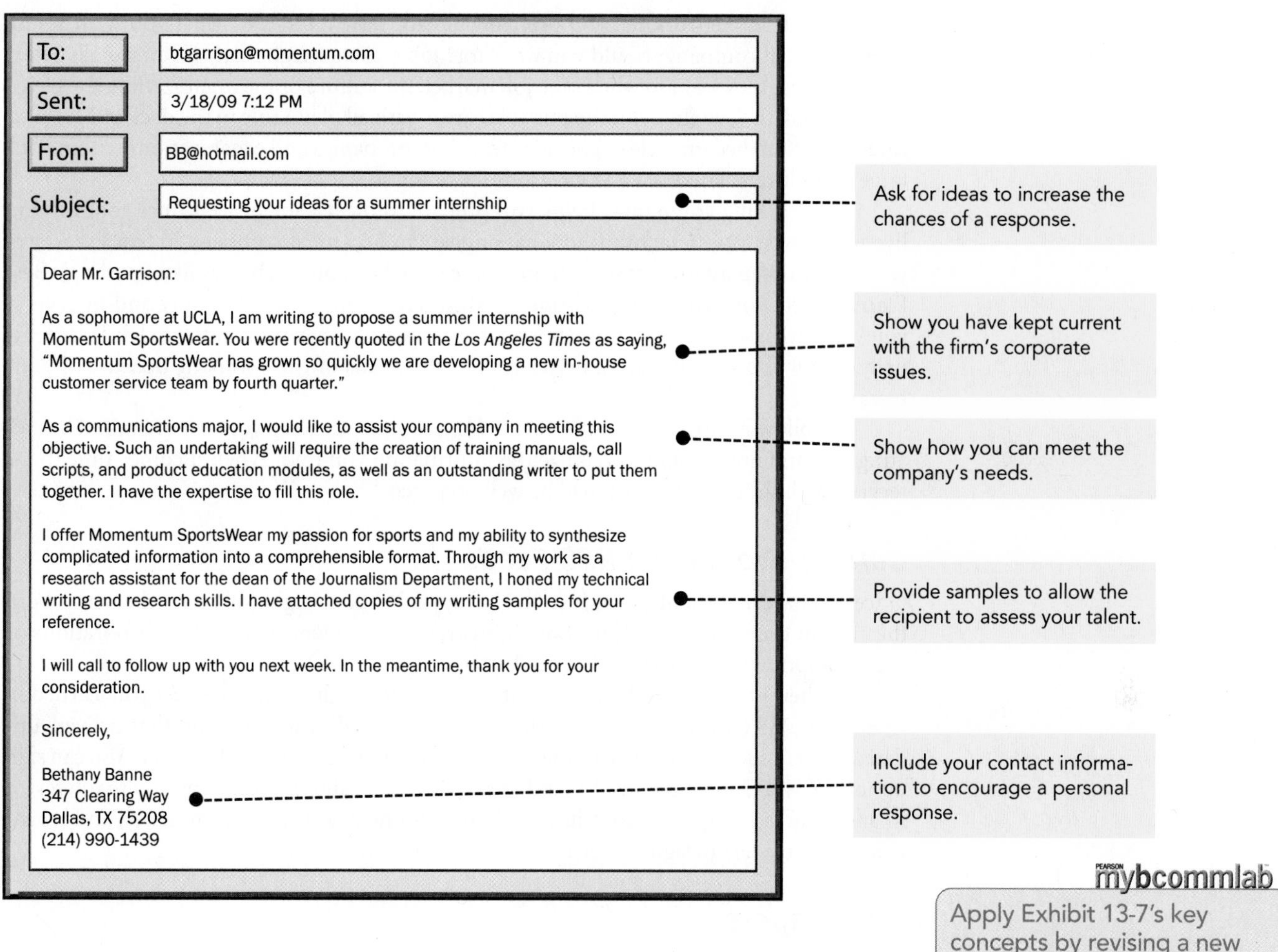

To: btgarrison@momentum.com

Sent: 3/18/09 7:12 PM

From: BB@hotmail.com

Subject: Requesting your ideas for a summer internship

Dear Mr. Garrison:

As a sophomore at UCLA, I am writing to propose a summer internship with Momentum SportsWear. You were recently quoted in the *Los Angeles Times* as saying, "Momentum SportsWear has grown so quickly we are developing a new in-house customer service team by fourth quarter."

As a communications major, I would like to assist your company in meeting this objective. Such an undertaking will require the creation of training manuals, call scripts, and product education modules, as well as an outstanding writer to put them together. I have the expertise to fill this role.

I offer Momentum SportsWear my passion for sports and my ability to synthesize complicated information into a comprehensible format. Through my work as a research assistant for the dean of the Journalism Department, I honed my technical writing and research skills. I have attached copies of my writing samples for your reference.

I will call to follow up with you next week. In the meantime, thank you for your consideration.

Sincerely,

Bethany Banne
347 Clearing Way
Dallas, TX 75208
(214) 990-1439

mybcommlab

Apply Exhibit 13-7's key concepts by revising a new document. Go to to Chapter 13 in mybcommlab.com and select Document Makeovers.

Ask for ideas to increase the chances of a response.
Show you have kept current with the firm's corporate issues.
Show how you can meet the company's needs.
Provide samples to allow the recipient to assess your talent.
Include your contact information to encourage a personal response.

Shadow Professionals

Shadowing is an alternative to interning. It involves observing someone in his or her own work environment to better understand the individual's roles and responsibilities. Some people shadow a professional for a few hours. Others do so for an entire day or multiple days. During a shadowing, your objective is merely to observe unless otherwise instructed. This means sitting quietly, watching and listening, or following the person around. It may involve occasionally asking questions. Just make sure that your presence does not negatively affect the other person's productivity.

The benefits of this type of experience are more personal than professional. Because shadowing provides only a limited snapshot of what the position really requires, it cannot be added to your résumé. However, if financial constraints make long-term internships unrealistic, shadowing is an effective way to gather immediate information about a particular career.

Volunteer

Volunteering is another great way to get hands-on experience in a field and build your résumé. When you volunteer with an organization, you meet new people and expand your network. Even if the volunteering project has nothing to do with a future career direction, you will gain new skills, get exposed to different types of work, and meet people who could be key to pointing you to future jobs. Additionally, volunteer positions sometimes transition into paid positions.

Research Companies

If you have been networking, you probably already have an idea of what you want to do. However, what company should you work for? Job seekers weigh many factors when determining where they want to work. The job market, the culture of the organization, the training provided, the benefits, and the possible career path all play a role in the decision. As your career direction becomes clear, consider tracking companies and organizations within your targeted industry. There are a few reasons for doing so.

First, tracking companies helps you prepare to meet your professional goals. If you live in Billings, Montana, but find what appears to be a great company in San Francisco, you need to prepare for a cost-of-living increase. Check out Web sites like Sperling's Best Places for cost of living comparisons. Next, when it comes time to apply and interview, you will have a solid idea of how those companies are performing in the marketplace. Finally, you will probably have a better idea of the needs of the company because of your research.

The following are resources for researching companies. Keep yourself organized by creating files and notebooks to organize the information you find. When it comes time to interview with the company, you will be well prepared.

Current Events and RSS Feeds

Once you have an idea of the industries that appeal to you, begin following the news about the current events and trends in those industries. If you identify desirable corporations or organizations within those fields, even better.

Another way to research various companies is through an RSS feed. As you learned in Chapter 7, RSS (really simple syndication) is a Web-feed of information that delivers updated content such as recent headlines about a company, person, or other topic. You can sign up to receive a Google RSS feed that disseminates news about a company you're interested in and what is being said about it. Like Google, some newspapers, companies, and magazines allow readers to sign up for RSS feeds on their Web sites.

Newspapers

The business section of a newspaper is an excellent source of information about local and regional companies: Who's hiring? Who isn't? What companies are new to the area? What companies are moving out? Who's expanding? Who's laying off workers? Read pertinent articles for the latest news about a company's products, work environment, and financial situation. Then check the company's Web site or blog. If you are researching companies outside your geographical area, read newspapers online from the cities where these firms are located.

Family, Friends, and Associates

Use your personal contacts and social networking sites such as LinkedIn and Facebook to find contacts in your targeted companies. Ask these people about their positions. Find out what it is really like to work for their companies. Better yet, ask them to identify needs within their companies. Understanding these needs will help you tailor your cover letter or résumé for the company, as well as prepare for interviews (more about this in Chapter 14).

Corporate Web Sites and Blogs

A corporate Web site not only lists job openings but also can help you find out who a firm's key clients are and its mission statement, while giving you a sense of its corporate culture. Reading corporate or independent blogs and newsletters about a company or an industry can give you an inside scoop and help you develop rapport with interviewers. Social media is also a good source of information on companies. For example, Proper Cloth, a high-end custom shirt maker, posts photos of its clothing through FanBook on Facebook for people's feedback. CEO Tom Skerrit's Twitters and podcasts are available for download on iTunes. Likewise, Zappos' CEO Tony Hsieh has a blog and a Twitter fan base you can follow.

REAL INSIGHTS from a New Professional

Name: *Jenna Drobnick*
Title: *Stylist*
Organization: *Freelancer*
Location: *San Francisco, California*

JENNA DROBNICK HAS CREATED A LIFE for herself many fashion industry students only dream of living. Drobnick, who attended Colorado State University, is now a stylist in San Francisco. Part of her job includes choosing the wardrobe and accessories that models and celebrities wear in photo shoots and runway productions.

After consulting with her clients about their advertising concepts, Drobnick spends time shopping for the necessary items to create "the look" her clients want. Her keen eye for fashion and design help her bring the client's vision to life during a shoot. On event day, she works with art directors, makeup artists, hair stylists, and photographers to ensure they achieve the desired effects. Among her clients are the magazines *Teen Vogue* and *Marie Claire* and retailers and clothing manufacturers such as Macy's, Bebe, Adidas, Nike, and Target.

Drobnick is the first to admit her dream job didn't fall in her lap. "I always loved fashion, and figured I would become a designer. In college, I didn't even know what a stylist was." Knowing she'd need design experience, she began researching internships in her industry, but was unimpressed. Drobnick decided to create her own. Having long admired Donna Karan's work, she sent a cover letter, résumé, and portfolio for the company's internship coordinator to review. She worked as a waitress and saved money to make her move to New York possible while waiting for a response. Soon, she was offered a position and heading off to start her career.

As an intern, Drobnick worked on the design floor, assisting top designers with sketches and fabric choices. "While it was exciting, it wasn't always glamorous," says Drobnick. "Being an intern meant handling a lot of 'grunt work.' I often ran errands for designers in the Garment District and handled tasks others had no interest in doing." In addition, working as an intern meant working for free. "I was so broke," she remembers. At one point, she took a part-time job in the evenings as a waitress to make ends meet. "I remember eating rice one Thanksgiving, because I had no money."

Drobnick now sees the return on her one-year internship investment. In fact, that internship was a pivotal point in her career. "The contacts I made in the Garment District while interning led to a design position." She remained open to learning other aspects of the industry before finding her calling as a stylist. "At every turn, I committed to doing the best job I could and learning as much as possible."

When asked to give advice to new graduates, Drobnick responds, "First of all, your reputation is everything. It always catches up to you. In my position, you're only as good as your last job, so you always have to give your best. Secondly, treat everyone with respect, regardless of his or her position. Many people once subordinate to me in other positions have been promoted. Those people are now my clients."

Questions

1. Drobnick knows she cannot rest on her laurels since her reputation is "only as good as her last job." What would past employers and teachers say about you? Although you cannot change the past, are there things you can do to improve people's perceptions of you?
2. Drobnick points out that everyone should be treated with respect. How can you demonstrate respect for the people with whom you work via the way you communicate with them? Refer to Chapter 2 if you have trouble answering this question.

Soure: Jenna Drobnick in discussion with the author, June 2009.

Annual and Quarterly Reports

In addition to publishing and distributing printed annual and quarterly reports, publicly traded companies and privately held companies often make them available on their Web sites. Reports such as these not only disclose the financial health of an organization but also its initiatives and risks to its success. Reading through a company's annual and quarterly reports is probably the best way to learn about a company's priorities. When a company highlights its goals or initiatives in its annual report for all of its shareholders to see, you can bet the firm's executives are committed to accomplishing those goals.

3 What Can Make You a Desirable Employee?

Part of preparing for your future requires taking responsibility for current and past actions. Consider the fact that every job application form asks, "Have you ever been convicted of a felony?" Companies also conduct background checks before hiring a candidate. The check can involve looking at credit reports, criminal records, transcripts, and meetings with personal and professional contacts.[4]

Stop Any Recreational Drug Use

Many companies require mandatory drug testing before they will hire you. Others spontaneously and randomly test employees for drug use throughout their course of employment. Sometimes any involvement with recreational drugs will permanently close the door on an opportunity.

Improve Your Credit Rating

A **credit score** is a number reflecting the level of risk involved in entering a financial or financially dependent business relationship with someone. A consumer who has a high credit score is perceived as financially responsible and a low risk. These consumers are more apt to receive loans, lower interest rates, and lines of credit. A low credit score reflects the opposite.[5]

Companies may conduct credit checks on potential employees for a variety of reasons. Employees who will be handling money and using corporate credit cards for business expenses are frequently subjected to credit checks before they are hired. Many managers believe that a candidate in financial trouble is more likely to steal from the company. Because your credit score can impact your employment options, guard it carefully by making sound financial decisions, keeping your borrowing to a minimum, and paying all of your bills on time.

If you are not sure what your credit score is, contact any of the three major credit agencies in **Exhibit 13-8** and request a free credit report. You can order a credit report by going to their Web sites. By law you are entitled to one free report from each agency each year. Read over your report and look for signs of concern. Mistakes on your report can be corrected with some effort. If you have trouble reading the report, schedule an appointment with your financial aid office and request assistance.

Lastly, don't waste time dwelling on your financial mistakes. Instead, create a plan to get on track. Cut up your credit cards and set goals for paying off your debts. Most employers respect job seekers who acknowledge their mistakes and devise plans to correct them.

Avoid Internet Indiscretions

Increasing numbers of employers perform Google, MySpace, or Facebook searches to get a clearer picture of candidates. Oftentimes, they discover far more than the candidate revealed during the hour-long interview. A candidate with a negative online image may lose job opportunities.

Even after being hired, maintaining a professional online image is important.[6] Colleagues might want to connect on your page. What will they see? Will it damage your credibility or hurt your chances of promotion? If you intend to use your Facebook account as a way to advertise yourself to potential employers, make sure its content is professional and

Exhibit 13-8
Major Credit Agencies

Agency	Web Addresses
Experian	experian.com
Equifax	equifax.com
TransUnion	transunion.com

not embarrassing. Other people's postings on your page can also shed a negative light on you. Consider a wall-to-wall Facebook post that reads as follows:

Sherri:
Another crazy party . . . couldn't make the first three classes! Hey, C's get degrees!

Emily:
No kidding. Rest up . . . it starts all over again tonight!

What impression does this post say about these women's lifestyles, work ethic, and commitment to excellence?

You might be wondering, "What constitutes inappropriate material?" Consider any of the following as off-limits:

- Pictures of you drinking, partying, or smoking, even if you are of legal age.
- Revealing pictures of you, including wearing a bathing suit.
- Any posts that disparage others, especially past employers.
- References to your dating life.

Keep in mind that if your page reveals a minute-by-minute replay of your life or if your social networking page contains a large number of posts, employers might wonder about your work ethic. "What does this person actually *do* all day?" a hiring manager might wonder. Many social networking sites have security settings that allow you to restrict who can view your page. Use these features. Likewise, be careful what you say in a blog. Never disparage an employer or bad mouth anyone online.

Assess Your Attitude

The true test of a person's character occurs not in times of victory, but in times of adversity. Job searches offer opportunities to experience both. Many job seekers face adverse circumstances such as a bad economy, steep competition, and rejection before accepting the right position. The difference between those who break down and those who break through is attitude. Fortunately, having a positive or negative attitude is a matter of choice.

People with positive attitudes speak words of encouragement to others and find solutions rather than dwell on problems. Conversely, negative people complain about everything, make excuses, feel entitled, and indulge in self-pity. Which kind of person would you rather be?

Your attitude impacts every communication you have—business and otherwise. A negative attitude becomes a habit, and that habit forms your character. You might not be able to control the circumstances around your job hunt, but you can certainly control your reaction to them. Doors open unexpectedly when you are positive.

4 How Do You Effectively Search for a Job?

The term **talent acquisition** refers to the process of hiring new employees. The process of acquiring talent has changed with technology. Newspapers were once the ideal place to post job openings, but today, online ads are significantly cheaper. As a result, the number of job postings in newspapers has declined. The benefit of posting jobs online, of course, is the Web's expanded reach. The downside is increased competition for the posted positions.

Employers are strategic in their approach to finding the best candidates. Some use software that "trolls" social networking sites for qualified candidates. Using the Web, companies can find talented professionals who, although happy in their current positions, might be wooed away to greener pastures. Likewise, job seekers have also become more strategic. They are no longer bound by geography. They can look for the best jobs anywhere in the world. With the availability of telecommuting, people may not need to relocate to accept a position.

Tap the Hidden Job Market

When a job is advertised in classified ads or online, it becomes public knowledge. Jobs such as these represent only 20 percent of available jobs. The **hidden job market** refers to the other 80 percent of the job openings that haven't been advertised or made public yet. Most companies dislike searching for new employees as much as employees dislike searching for new jobs. Companies often prefer to get references from their own employees, their employees' families, friends, or vendors to find people to fill open positions.

Make a List

Create a list of people—friends, family, business acquaintances, and members of civic organizations you belong to—who you think might be willing to talk to you about your job search. Then contact them. Ask them if they know other people to whom they could refer you. Then follow up with those people. Share your aspirations with your professors. Professors may know of symposiums, lectures, events, and openings through their connections in the industry. Ask them to keep you informed.

Carry Business Cards

You can find Web sites that let you create business cards either for free or for a nominal charge. Keep the motif professional and include your name, address, phone number, and e-mail address. If you are a professional blogger or have a professional page or online portfolio, include the online addresses as well. For information about online business cards, visit VistaPrint, GigglePrint, and BizCard.

Develop an "Elevator Pitch" for Introductions

You never know whom you will meet or where. An **elevator pitch** is a short verbal message designed to generate interest in what you have to offer. You should be able to deliver the message in the amount of time an elevator ride takes (about 30 seconds). If you were to meet the CEO of a company in the elevator, what would you share about yourself? An elevator pitch should sum up your career objective and highlight your strengths. The following is an example:

> "It's very nice to meet you, and quite a coincidence . . . I just applied for a position in the sales department of Just Beachy Swimwear. I am very enthusiastic about the opening because I want to apply my sales strategy experience in the retail sector."

Practice your pitch often so it sounds natural. Doing so ensures that you are prepared in the event of a serendipitous business encounter. Then make a point of introducing yourself to as many new people as you can. During your discussions, let people know about your job search, and use your elevator pitch to be as specific as possible about what you are looking for.

Volunteer

You already know that volunteering can help you learn more about a career. Volunteering is a great way to gain experience and build a network. Often, companies support organizations by sending their employees to volunteer at that organization's events. The firms usually mention their support of certain organizations on their corporate Web sites. Taking the time to volunteer at those events can forge relationships with prospective employers. Always include the experience on your résumé, especially before sending it to the specific company.

Search Newspapers

Companies still post job advertisements in the newspaper. Candidates are often able to search the "want ads" for positions either in the paper or online. Sometimes newspapers partner with an online job board so the advertisement is posted in both the paper and on the job board's Web site.

Join Associations and Chambers of Commerce

Companies sometimes post open positions on professional association Web sites or with their local chambers of commerce. Periodically check these sites for new postings. For a list of associations, visit Weddles.

Network Online

Not all networking needs to be done in person. You can do a lot of preliminary networking online. The following are some tips for networking online.

Check Corporate Web Sites for Jobs

Check the corporate Web site periodically for job postings. If given the option to upload a résumé in the company résumé bank, do so, but keep a list of sites to which you have uploaded your résumé. As you update it, you will want the most current version posted on corporate Web sites.

Join Online Communities Related to Your Industry

Participate in online discussions and work on becoming a recognizable contributor. Ask good questions, if you feel you don't have the expertise to contribute. Of course, always be respectful when commenting on another person's viewpoint. By staying involved you may learn of openings within the community.

Introduce Yourself Online

Social networking sites such as LinkedIn and Facebook allow you to make introductions to others with site accounts. LinkedIn is such a popular social networking site that it adds a member a minute, many of whom are job-seeking.[7] Take advantage of the opportunity, but follow the etiquette guidelines shown in **Exhibit 13-9**.

1. If you find a contact while on a friend's Facebook page, ask the friend to introduce you to the contact first—or at least inform your friend of your intention to correspond with the contact.[8]

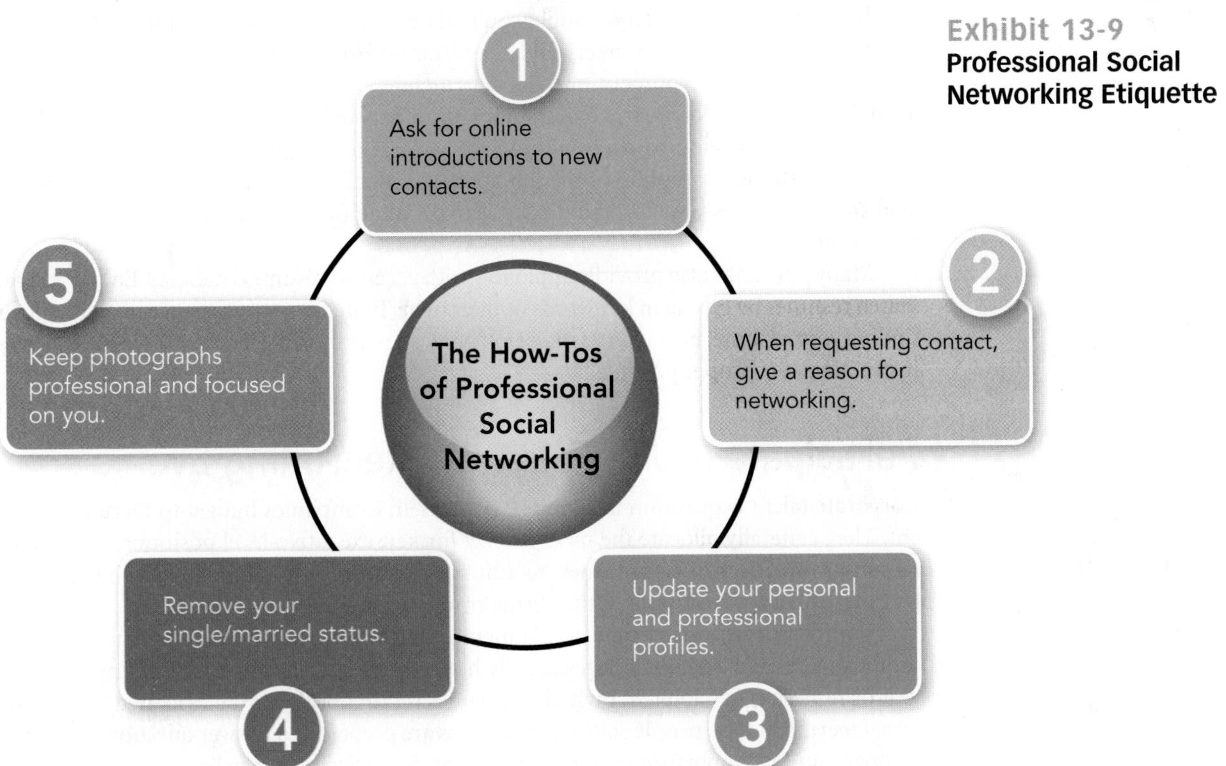
The How-Tos of Professional Social Networking
1
Ask for online introductions to new contacts.
2
When requesting contact, give a reason for networking.
3
Update your personal and professional profiles.
4
Remove your single/married status.
5
Keep photographs professional and focused on you.

Exhibit 13-9
Professional Social Networking Etiquette

2. Indicate why you are reaching out to that person, rather than just inviting them as a "friend" or connection. For instance, "Marcus Hooper suggested I send you a message introducing myself. I am entering the job market as a fashion designer. I would like to invite you to coffee and learn more about your firm." If possible, set up a face-to-face meeting. You will be far more memorable if you connect in person.
3. Make sure that your professional information and personal information is updated on all social networking sites. Your professional profile may read as an abbreviated résumé. Take the time to draft your statements carefully because they can be seen by anyone. Review job descriptions of coveted positions before building your profile, and incorporate key words from those descriptions, when applicable, into your profile.
4. Keep information about your "status"—that is, whether you are single, married, looking for friends, and so forth—off of your profile. It appears juvenile and unprofessional.
5. Post professional pictures of yourself on your profile—not your kids, dog, or goldfish. After all, you are marketing yourself.

Blog about Current Events and Changes Affecting Your Industry

If your writing skills are strong, consider starting a blog about relevant issues pertaining to your industry. If you are already a member of an online community, you might already have a ready-made audience. Writing a blog will force you to keep informed and involved. It may also get you noticed by hiring managers reading your thoughts and ideas.[9]

Post Your Résumé with Online Job Banks

Companies pay a fee to post open positions on job bank sites, but job seekers are generally not required to do so. **Online job banks** typically allow seekers to search by title, company, and location. Employers solicit résumés directly through the job banks or by providing directions for application. Many job banks also provide employers with access to résumé databases. Employers can search résumés by typing in keywords of their own. To increase your chance of an employer finding your résumé, post it on as many job bank sites as possible. Each site will have its own instructions for proper posting. The job bank site might prompt you to enter information about your industries of interest. The site will then send automatic e-mail updates to you when suitable positions become available. As stated earlier, keep a list of all Web sites to which you posted your résumé. Should you update it, you will want to post the latest version.

Sites such as Monster, CareerBuilder, and Yahoo HotJobs dominated the job-bank sector, but they now have competition. New sites include niche and college graduate job boards as well as Craigslist. Job boards should not trump networking, however. Using a social networking site to develop contacts within an organization might be time better spent.[10] See **Exhibit 13-10** for a sampling of the job boards available. Because new job boards are created constantly, it is wise to periodically search online for new sites that might pertain to your industry.

Many job banks also provide employers with access to résumé databases. Employers can search résumés by typing in key words of their own. To increase your chance of an employer finding your résumé, post it on as many job bank sites as possible. Each site will have its own instructions for proper posting.

Participate in Job Fairs and Recruiting Events

Corporate talent acquisition is an industry in itself. Companies budget to recruit new talent. They generally allocate the most money for key, executive-level positions. For various reasons, some firms outsource their recruiting by working with agencies and independent recruiters on a contract basis. Other firms employ an internal recruiting team.

Companies typically send internal members of their recruiting teams to job fairs and campus recruiting events. Colleges usually host at least one job fair or recruiting event per year or semester. At a **job fair**, invited companies set up booths or tables staffed by their internal recruiters. The people staffing the booths are prepared to answer questions about the company and its opportunities for employment. Sometimes, if they have immediate open-

Site	Types of Positions Posted
CareerBuilder	Positions posted for all levels
Monster	Positions posted for all levels
Yahoo! HotJobs	Positions posted for all levels
Career Rookie	College and recent college grad specific
College Grad Job Hunter	College and recent college grad specific
Student Jobs	College and recent college grad specific
MonsterTrack	College specific
Indeed	An aggregation of jobs pulled from various websites
Jobster	An aggregation of jobs pulled from various websites
SimplyHired	An aggregation of jobs pulled from various websites
SnagAJob	Part-time and retail positions emphasized
Work in Retail	Retail positions posted
Cool Works	Seasonal employment emphasized
Career One Stop	Job search and career advice offered and positions posted
Craigslist	Forum with employment posting section

Exhibit 13-10
Online Job Boards

ings, they will perform on-the-spot interviews—or **on-campus interviews**—but these are typically initial-screening events.

Because so many students attend job fairs, it is vital that you distinguish yourself. Recruiters at job fairs travel to many campuses across the nation. They see many "students," but not many "professionals." Stand out by being professional. The following are ways to come across as such.

Be Informed

Learn which companies are participating in the fair and do your research on them beforehand. Read through their Web sites and familiarize yourself with their current successes. Also, look at the openings that fit your qualifications so you can discuss them with the representatives.

Be Prepared

Prepare a few intelligent questions prepared in advance of the fair. They might be questions you prepared earlier for informational interviews. Because the representatives will be in demand and unable to devote a great deal of time to one person, quality trumps quantity. After doing some preliminary research, prepare three questions that will distinguish you from the pack. For example, ask, "What are three professional traits you look for in a fashion line buyer?" or, "What growth path can an account executive pursue at your company?"

Bring copies of your résumé and your business cards to pass out to participating companies. This may be the only direct contact you have with someone in a company, unless you're invited to interview. Make the most of it.

Dress the Part

Surrounded by a sea of sweatshirts, jeans, and shorts, corporate representatives at a career fair will remember a professionally dressed student. How you dress when meeting other professionals may communicate more than the first words out of your mouth. As discussed later in Chapter 15, dressing professionally does not necessarily mean spending a fortune on suits.

Clean, pressed, professional clothing does not have to be expensive. Avoid baggy, casual clothing and revealing, too-tight, or too-short clothing. You want the recruiter to take you seriously. When in doubt, it is better to dress more formally for a career fair than not. Feel good in your clothes, and you will exude confidence.

Get Information

Because a job fair is a unique opportunity, make the most of it and be bold. Whenever possible, ask who the hiring managers are for specific positions. Uncover details about the interview process and time line for making hiring decisions. Above all, never leave a booth without obtaining the contact information of the representative with whom you spoke. Politely let the person know of your intention to follow up. For instance, "Thank you, Ms. Harkins. I see there is a line forming and I don't want to monopolize your time. I will follow up next week when you are back in the office." By getting a name you can address a real person, not just "Dear Sir" or "To Whom It May Concern," on a cover letter you later send.

Campus recruiting events can sometimes be more targeted than job fairs. Some firms solicit résumés in advance and schedule interviews before arriving on campus. Therefore, it is important to know what companies are coming to your campus. Contact the college career services office to find out in advance the deadlines for submitting your résumé.

Follow Up

Follow up with the contacts you made at an on-campus job fair. This is one of the best ways to stand out from the other students interviewed nationwide. Not many students take the time to send thank-you cards or letters for the casual introductions made at a career fair. Because communications such as these are so rare, they will be remembered.

Work with Recruiters, Temporary Agencies, and Permanent Placement Agencies

Job seekers should always take a multistrategy approach to find their desired position, especially in a competitive market. Working with independent recruiters and agencies may not be for everyone, but they can expand a candidate's reach.

Independent Recruiters and Permanent Placement Agencies

Independent recruiters and **permanent placement agencies** (which are sometimes referred to as *headhunters*) contract with corporations to fill permanent open positions. They don't charge the job seeker for their services. Instead, the company searching for candidates pays a fee when a candidate is hired. The payment is often based upon certain standards the company and agency have agreed upon in a contract. For instance, the contract might require that the new hire remain with the company for a certain number of months.

There are advantages and disadvantages to working with a recruiter. On one hand, recruiters develop relationships within the companies they represent. Consequently, they have direct access to hiring managers. If a recruiter is impressed by you, he or she will recommend you by passing on positive insights about you and forwarding your résumé to the decision maker. A recruiter with strong client relationships can greatly impact your chance of securing an interview.

On the flipside, companies pay recruiters as much as 30 percent of a hired applicant's salary for recruiting services.[11] Therefore, some companies use recruiters sparingly. For this reason, when considering equally qualified candidates, a hiring manager might prefer hiring the nonrepresented candidate to the one working with an independent recruiter. Additionally, if you are a good networker with an extensive network, you probably do not need a recruiter.

REAL INSIGHTS from a Seasoned Professional

Name: Paul Rosengard
Title: President of Menswear
Organization: Li & Fung USA
Location: New York, New York

PAUL F. ROSENGARD IS THE PRESIDENT of menswear at Li & Fung USA. Although he's made quite a splash in his chosen field, he did not start out thinking he was destined for the apparel business. His path to fashion took a few twists and turns.

Graduating in 1980 with a degree in economics from Brandeis University, Rosengard worked in educational publishing at Prentice Hall, followed by a short stint in motion picture finance at Delphi Corp. The communication and finance skills he gained at Prentice Hall and Delphi Corp made him a natural at marketing and sales, which is how he got into the apparel industry.

In 1987, he joined Randa Corporation, a small, independent neckwear company, and during a 17-year span he eventually rose to the level of executive vice president. By directing global sales, marketing, licensing, and merchandising, Rosengard helped the family-owned business grow into the world's largest men's accessories company.

At that point, it seemed only natural for Rosengard to use his portfolio of accomplishments to reach out to an even larger apparel firm. His expertise in building successful companies was already established and his credibility was unquestioned. So in 2005, Rosengard joined Perry Ellis International as Group President of Premium Brands. He came on board with a commitment to rebuild the legacy of the brand Perry Ellis, which had lost its "luster" over the years. In 2010, he left Perry Ellis International to broaden his horizons at Li & Fung USA, a dominant supply-chain company engaged in aggressive growth via an acquisition strategy.

Rosengard has accomplished his goals by building unified teams with consistent marketing-driven messages. His consumer-centric motto says it all: "One brand, one vision, one voice." One embraced, this results in a corporate paradigm shift. Says Rosengard, "An apparel company's design, sales, and planning teams need to work in harmony to create fashion product in response to the market, not in search of a market."

When asked to what he attributes his success, Rosengard says, "Talent, luck, and hard work." He emphasizes that the key is ". . . maximizing the one variable over which you have the most control—hard work. I find that the harder I work, the luckier I get. Becoming president of a public company was always his goal, so Rosengard made choices and sacrifices that positioned him for that outcome. "I worked nights and weekends building contacts with high-level industry executives, including donating my time to specific industry organizations fraternized by those people. I eventually accepted positions of leadership within those organizations, where I was seen as a rising star and ultimately accepted as a peer."

A persuasive and driven executive, Rosengard offers this advice to graduating students looking for career success: "Think big. Start small. Show value. Recognize that colleagues don't want to hear about your problems. They want and need to hear about your proposed solutions. Don't look at the glass as half full or half empty. Instead, look at the glass and ask yourself two questions: What size does the glass need to be; and how can I help fill it if it needs filling?"

Questions

1. What transferable skills launched Rosengard into the apparel business?
2. What portfolio of skills and accomplishments do you think Rosengard has built during his career? What portfolio of skills have you built that will help you in your future career?
3. Rosengard attributes much of his success to hard work. What role does hard work play in your life?
4. Rosengard advises graduates to assess what needs to be done and how they can assist in the process. Is there a need you've recognized in the community? If so, how can you assist in meeting it? How would doing so build your portfolio and persuade others of your value?

Source: Paul Rosengard in discussion with the author, December 2010.

Temporary Agencies

Temporary agencies provide **temporary placement** for job seekers, which gives them the opportunity to learn about how different companies do business. Companies enlist the help of temporary agencies for various reasons. A short-term project might demand more employees than the company has on staff, or a staff member might be on extended leave and the firm needs help. A temporary agency matches the skills of candidates with those needed for positions. Successful agencies may even have enough contracts with firms to keep candidates consistently working. A temporary employment position can also help you make connections within a company and give you a chance to impress the people there. It is not uncommon for companies to make permanent placement offers to temporary employees who perform their responsibilities well.

⑤ What Steps Can You Take in a Difficult Job Market?

Whether economic problems are making jobs scarce or you need more training before you're qualified for a position, effective job seekers stay creative in tough times. Remaining innovative and positive can make all the difference when the next opportunity arises.

Stay Attentive

When a market is in decline, scarce jobs go to the most qualified candidates. It bears repeating that preparation begins before graduation. If you find yourself searching for a job during a difficult economic time, don't give in to the idea that there is "nothing out there." Difficult times pass, and the job seeker who uses the interim wisely will find employment.

A hiring freeze is a temporary condition. If you like the company, make sure your interviewer remembers you by staying in touch until the "thaw" occurs.

Make Progress during Hiring Freezes

It is discouraging to learn that the company you targeted for employment has a hiring freeze. A **hiring freeze** is a situation in which a company decides not to hire anyone for a period of time, even if positions within the company become available. Sometimes candidates are well into the interview process when a company learns it cannot extend offers.

The key is to remain at the top of the candidate list until the "thaw" occurs. Stay connected with the people you've interacted with by occasionally sending notes of continued interest to them. A clever way of keeping your name in front of a decision maker is to send the person relevant articles about his or her industry with a note saying, "I thought you might find this interesting."

Don't be afraid to ask a hiring manager how you can prepare for the position during the interim. For instance:

> "Mr. Randall, I was disappointed to learn the company is on a hiring freeze. As you know, I would really like to work for Just Jeans. What do you suggest I do to best prepare myself for getting hired when the freeze ends? When the opening becomes available again, I want to make sure I'm the most qualified candidate."

Hiring managers will respect and appreciate your drive, initiative, and commitment. Of course, follow up as you proceed with the advice given. For example:

> "Thank you for your sound advice, Mr. Randall. Reading the book *Innovative Marketing* was very inspiring. In fact it gave me some ideas for Just Jean's messaging. Perhaps we could meet for lunch."

Even after graduation, consider interning for a specified period of time or assisting on a project. Although you might not have the financial ability to do so full-time, taking action like that keeps you on a company's radar for future employment.

Adjust Your Pay Expectations

Chapter 15 in this book discusses salary negotiations in further detail. Be advised that difficult economic times sometimes mean you have to make compromises. However, those compromises can be made strategically. For instance, consider offering to accept lower pay for a set number of months before ramping up to your desired pay scale, or offer to work on a part-time basis. Although dividing your workweek between two part-time positions might not be ideal, you will still gain valuable experience. Negotiate an option for the first permanent position should one arise.

Explore Freelance Opportunities

Freelancing as an alternative to permanent employment can be very beneficial. A **freelancer** is not an employee but someone who often works with several companies on a contract basis. Determine what skills you can offer an employer on a freelance or contract basis. During an economic downturn, companies are often more open to freelance or contract workers than permanent employees. Companies appreciate people who are willing to work for themselves and offer their services at reasonable rates.

Companies contract for all kinds of services including writing, design, editing, sales, legal services, and accounting. Post yourself as a freelance specialist on free sites such as Craigslist, or contact companies directly. When an opening for a permanent position arises, you will have experience and possibly a portfolio of material for the employer's review.

Attain Certifications or Higher Degrees

Take the time during an economic slump to increase your marketability. Certifications and higher degrees will increase your marketability when jobs become available. If you're approaching graduation during a downturn, consider taking these steps, even while working part-time.

Research Strong Industries and Shift Your Focus

Industries weakened by economic difficulty are often offset by industries that remain vital. Focus on attaining transferable skills in a different industry than you had originally targeted so you can apply those skills later on in your ideal position. During future interviews, you can explain that your decision to temporarily take a job in another industry was a strategic one.

Consider Alternative Employment Opportunities

Many young professionals, particularly following college graduation, opt to postpone or even forgo corporate life. Consider the following alternatives.

International Employment

As corporations become increasingly global, candidates with experience handling diverse cultural matters will have an advantage over their counterparts. Some graduates seize the opportunity to travel and work in foreign countries early in their career when they are unencumbered by other commitments.

If you are interested in pursuing international employment, consider the following questions:

- Would you feel comfortable living internationally on your own? If not, do you have friends who might also have international interests?
- Can you speak another language?
- How long can you commit to living in another country?
- Do you have the resources to move to a country and look for a work opportunity there?
- What do you hope to gain from the experience, and how will it help you achieve your goals?
- What will you need to do to prepare yourself for the experience (language lessons, networking online, studying the culture, and so on)?
- How will you handle homesickness?

Service Organizations

Some students opt to use their skills to better the lives of others both domestically and abroad. If you are this type of person, consider service organizations such as Peace Corps and Teach For America. These organizations require you to commit your service to them for a specified period of time. In exchange, you gain skills, increase marketability, and under some circumstances, offset your student loan repayment.

Exhibit 13-11 lists some service organizations that promote international opportunities such as these. Many professionals today look back on their careers and regret the time they spent trying to get ahead instead of choosing their own paths. Consider all opportunities before choosing your path.

Exhibit 13-11 Examples of Service Organizations and International Opportunities

Organization	Description
Teach For America	Organization offering new graduates teaching positions in inner cities
Peace Corps	Organization offering international volunteer experiences
AmeriCorps	Organization offering opportunities to work with local and national nonprofit groups.
Idealist	Web site posting nonprofit and international experiences

Ask the Question, "How Can I Improve My Skills and Qualifications?"

Questioning your qualifications doesn't mean you have a bad attitude about your job search. Honestly assess any weaknesses you may have and build on your strengths. For example, if a coveted position requires public speaking skills and you have none, participate in a group like Toastmasters, a nonprofit educational organization that teaches public speaking and leadership skills. Toastmasters has chapters in cities all over the world. Or volunteer to give presentations for a cause you support. Keep updating your résumé as you improve your skills.

Be Patient

Expect delays during the job search. The hiring manager who promises to call you with a decision by Friday might not call you until Monday morning because an urgent matter took precedence.

Don't spend the weekend obsessing about the status of an application. Realize upfront that companies often take their time when choosing employees. However, do follow up after a week just to find out the status of the hiring process, and continue to check up on the process if you do not hear back. It is better to be the "squeaky wheel" than to be forgotten.

Use Your Time Efficiently

Treat your job search like a job. Distractions will abound. Although it may be tempting to send out a few résumés before settling in to watch TV, that approach will not lead to employment, only discouragement.

An effective job search requires discipline and attention. Block out hours of time dedicated to performing your search, and allow for some breaks. The blocks of time should be spent strategically. In other words, all actions taken during those blocks should lead you closer to employment. Activities such as networking, attending professional meetings, informational interviews, online searches, and tailoring résumés and cover letters to fit particular positions, will all lead you closer to your goal.

Create Your Own Opportunities

Never count on one particular job offer coming through. Rather, create options for yourself. Having many "irons in the fire" will help you avoid feeling like your search is futile when delays occur or letters of rejection arrive. Having multiple options when you do get a job offer can be liberating during the negotiation process. When one employer says "No," the effective job seeker with multiple offers thinks, "Next!" In addition, some job seekers decide to create their own businesses as covered in Chapter 4.

Don't Take Rejection Personally

It takes courage to risk rejection. Many job seekers who experience the disappointment of rejection tend to berate themselves and their abilities. During your job search, protect yourself from feelings that drag you down. Whether it's going for a run, repeating an affirmation, or meeting a friend for coffee, develop nurturing activities to keep yourself on track.

Also, remember that how you handle the rejection can make a difference. Companies that reject candidates often contact them later when other positions open up or when other candidates decline their offers. Always follow up after receiving a rejection letter with a thank you. (Chapter 15 will show you how to respond to a rejection.)

Help Others and Express Kindness

Taking a "what can I do for you?" attitude not only expands your network of friends and makes you feel good, it prompts discussions, yields invitations to events, and inspires reciprocity in others. Simply put, people want to help people they like. Taking the time to express your gratitude and assist others will make your job search more enjoyable.

Remember, Your Starting Point Is Not Your Ending Point

Realize that your first job will not likely be your last job. Focusing on making the perfect choice about your career, position, and company can lead to "analysis paralysis." Instead, focus on the skills you can gain in a position and how transferable they may be. Many people end up in careers they never dreamed they would have. Often, they did not "land" in those positions. They "arrived" after having worked in other positions, soul searching, and assessing their goals.

CHECKLIST

Job search basics:

- ☑ Ask the question, "How can I improve my skills and qualifications?"
- ☑ Be patient.
- ☑ Use your time efficiently.
- ☑ Create your own opportunities.
- ☑ Don't take rejection personally.
- ☑ Help others and express kindness.
- ☑ Remember, your starting point is not your ending point.

Summary *Synthesize What You Have Learned*

1. How can you pinpoint your best skills to use professionally?

There are many resources available to students looking for the right application for their skills and talents. The resources include career services centers, alumni centers, books, and Web sites. Additionally, students can take action by conducting informational interviews, shadowing, participating in internships, and taking personality and professional assessments to determine the best fit.

2. How can networking and research help you target a career and a company?

Assessing your values can help you choose a career and the best place to work. Attending events, networking with professionals, conducting informational interviews with them, and job shadowing can give you insight about different careers and organizations. Each company has a unique culture and finding your fit is important. Candidates can research a company by reading articles, visiting the corporation's Web site, researching annual reports, and talking with friends and family working for that company.

3. What can make you a desirable employee?

Part of preparing for your future means taking responsibility for your current and previous actions that communicate as much as the spoken word. For example, experimenting with recreational drugs can close the door to some opportunities completely. Take the time to check your credit reports and remove from all social networking sites any unprofessional messages and pictures that could cast you in a negative light. Lastly, be the kind of employee you'd like to hire by communicating a great attitude.

4. How do you effectively search for a job?

Networking is the key to an effective job search. Your job search effort requires establishing a presence online and within your physical community. Job seekers should establish an online presence through job banks, blogging, and social and professional networks. Offline, job seekers should attend charity events, volunteer, and network with professors to establish face-to-face connections with potential job contacts. You can meet internal recruiters by attending job fairs and recruiting events. Take these events seriously by dressing for an interview, having a résumé prepared, researching the companies in advance, and following up with a thank-you card. You might consider working with external recruiters as well if you are trying to break into an industry that has few openings.

Temporary placement agencies are a good way to gain experience and learn about different industries and companies.

5. What steps can you take in a difficult job market?

Look for ways to improve your skills and qualifications. Be patient, and don't take rejection personally. Continue to use your time wisely to search for a job. Realize, too, that there are many options available to you beyond the corporate world. You may decide to opt for international work experience or work for a service organization or nonprofit or start your own business. The career services center on your campus will likely have information on both. Additionally, refer to the Web sites mentioned in this chapter to uncover opportunities.

Know It *Reflect, Respond, and Express*

Building Your Critical Thinking Skills

Critical Thinking Questions

1. Imagine you are a prospective employer who wants to know more about a job candidate—you. Search for yourself using Google, Facebook, or MySpace. (Use quotation marks around your name or the Advanced Search option.) What information is available about you on the Internet? Also perform a deep Web search for yourself using pipl.com. What impressions would a prospective employer have about you based on your findings? What information did you discover is on the Internet about you? What type of impression would it leave on a potential employer?
2. Search for freelance work within your field on the Internet using a search engine. What types of work match your skills? What type of experience would you gain from each that you could add to your skills base?

Critical Thinking Scenario

Marco, an extremely talented young designer, just graduated from the prestigious School of Fashion in New York City. Unfortunately, upon graduation, Marco discovers that since he started school four years earlier, the once blossoming job market has declined immensely. Jobs are now scarce. Nervous and strapped for cash, Marco is unsure how to survive the economic downturn while preparing himself for the eventual upswing.

Questions

1. What are Marco's next steps? Describe at least three things Marco can do to continue to market his abilities, given his skills and the industry in which he is seeking employment. Explain why each choice would be beneficial for someone in Marco's position.
2. In all likelihood, you will experience some sort of economic downturn during your professional career. Given your interests and talents, what steps will you take to continue to market yourself during those times? Once you have answered this question, consider how your steps might differ from Marco's. What does this say about the relationship between a person's marketability and the industry in which he or she is looking for work?

Write It *Draft, Revise, and Finalize*

Create Your Own Success Story

1. Identify three companies where you would like to intern. Research those companies by reading their Web sites, news articles, and annual reports. Choose the company that interests you the most and identify someone within the company to contact. Draft an e-mail to that person, indicating what your research shows and how you could help meet a company need as an intern. Close the e-mail with a request to meet. Have your career advisor review the letter and make editing suggestions.

2. Write brief answers to the following questions to start your path to self-discovery: What are your gifts and talents? What activities inspire you? What did you always dream of being when you "grew up"? Do you prefer working alone or with others? What are your convictions? Do you like to travel? Do you want to live in the city or country? Are you creative or technical? What type of lifestyle do you enjoy? What are your "must-haves" in life? How important are your surroundings? Are you active or sedentary? How much money do you need to make? How important is your legacy?
3. Locate your institution's career center and set up an information appointment with a career counselor. What tools are available to you as you discover your career interests? What services are available to you as a current student as well as a graduating student? Write a memo to your instructor summarizing your findings.
4. Determine a prospective company for which you would like to work and subscribe to the company's RSS feed. After a week of your subscription, write a summary of the information you have learned about the company through the RSS feed alone.
5. Find a corporate Web site for a company you are interested in working for. What can you tell about the company's key clients? What is the company's mission statement? What is your impression of the corporate culture? Write a summary of your analysis.
6. On a prospective employer's Web site, locate the annual or quarterly report. Find the initiatives and risks the company is taking to succeed as a business. What can you determine about the company's priorities through the annual or quarterly report? How do your qualifications match the goals of the company? Write an e-mail to a job position contact within the company inquiring about any open positions and explaining how you would fit into the company's culture based on the information you find in the report.
7. Sign up for a LinkedIn or Facebook account in order to broaden your marketability. Follow the guidelines and How-Tos of Professional Social Networking discussed in the chapter when adding the content. Print a copy of your profile to submit to your instructor.
8. Research possible volunteering opportunities within your community. Compile a list of services to which you would be willing to donate your time and include a brief explanation of your interest with each one. Include at least five opportunities in a memo addressed to your instructor expressing plans to volunteer in the future.
9. Visit your institution's career center and sign up for the next job fair offered. Prepare for the fair by researching the possible companies that will attend, getting your résumé and other job documents in order, and dressing professionally to meet potential employers. Find out as much information as you possibly can and follow up with any representatives you speak to. Write a summary of your experience.
10. Compose an e-mail to a fictitious hiring manager asking for the qualifications that would help make you a viable candidate for a position once a hiring freeze is lifted. Remember to be courteous and thankful when attempting to make contact with a possible employer.
11. Complete a job search online for international jobs available in your field and make a list of the opportunities you discover. What are the required degrees for the positions you find? Where are the jobs located? What materials would you need to gather before applying for an international position? Summarize your answers and expectations and bring them to class to discuss.
12. Research various service organizations, such as Teach For America or the Peace Corps, to discover the possibilities they offer. Compile a list of the opportunities open to your job field, where they are located, and the length of time you would be required to commit to the organization. Write an analysis of what skills you would gain from the experience.
13. Visit one of the major job search Web sites such as Monster or TheLadders. Find at least five positions for which you are (or will be) qualified and write them down. Write an analysis of each position and what would interest you about each job. Include what qualifications you would need to pursue each opportunity.

Speak It *Discuss, Listen, and Understand*

Build Your Leadership and Teamwork Skills

1. Get in groups of two. Imagine you are campus recruiters for the clothing company, Planet Style. Now imagine meeting the following two candidates at a campus recruiting event. Be prepared to answer questions about the impressions they communicate to you and about their marketability.

Student #1:

Amy approaches your booth confidently. Her hair is neatly pinned behind her ears and she is sporting the most up-to-date outfit with matching accessories. You immediately notice that one of those accessories is the pair of sunglasses she's still wearing—indoors. As she picks up a flier for Planet Style she blows a bubble with her gum.

"So what's this place all about?" she asks casually. As you begin to explain, she flips her hair over her shoulder and says, "Oh, I remember this place. The jeans I bought from you guys ripped within a week."

Then, just as you're about to tune her out, she says, "You know, I heard about this amazing new form of Lycra that would probably really help the life of your clothes. I actually read a study on how it performed over several years and would love to show it to someone in your company."

As she leaves, Amy flips her hair again and pops another bubble before saying, "Thank you so much for your time. I'll definitely prepare my résumé and send it over along with a copy of that article I was telling you about. Thank you again, and I look forward to speaking with you next week."

Student #2:

Eric watches your booth for a few minutes before approaching. He walks up quietly, stepping quickly between oncoming people before edging up to the side of the table. While he is not dressed in designer clothing, he respectfully wore a suit and tie.

You ask him if he's ever heard of your company. He shakes his head and picks up some marketing material. As you begin to tell him a little about Planet Style you notice that his eyes start to light up. When you ask him if he's ever considered a career in the fashion industry, he nods enthusiastically and pulls out some drawings from his backpack.

"I'd like to work as a designer actually. These are some of the sketches I drew up last week after seeing a runway show that my roommate had on TV," he says. "See how the colors reflect the leaves right now? I just think these colors will be really big all throughout the fall and winter."

As Eric prepares to leave, he shoves the fliers and drawings back in his bag without bothering to fold them. He shakes your hand enthusiastically and says, "Thanks for talking with me. I don't want to monopolize your time. I know you're busy. I would like to learn more about the opportunities at Planet Style. I have some other questions for you. I really think Planet Style could be a great place for me."

a. Based on what you noticed as the students approached your booth, what do you think of them? Could they be potential employees?

b. What does the body language and overt attitude of the students tell you about their motivations? Do you think that's what they're trying to portray?

c. What do the questions they ask and the conversation they make lead you to believe about their abilities and potential as employees?

d. How about their closing statements? Are they professional and courteous? What's the lasting impression you get as each student leaves?

e. Would you interview either student as a potential hire for your company? Why or why not?

f. Both students forgot to ask a very important question after indicating their interest in getting back in touch with Planet Style. What did they forget?

2. Visit one of the following Web sites and take a career or personality test: careerpath.com, jobdiagnosis.com, myplan.com, or livecareer.com. Analyze the results and discuss them in teams. Are they accurate?
3. In groups or as a class, discuss how credit scores and reports can affect employment opportunities. Analyze ways to help build your credit and handle any debt. Write a memo to the class offering your suggestions.
4. In groups or as a class, discuss ways your attitude and perspective of a situation can affect your marketability as an employee. Reflect on a positive person you know and discuss your overall impression of that person based on attitude/perspective. Also discuss a person you know with a negative attitude and how that attitude affects your opinion of that person.
5. Develop an "elevator pitch" in order to prepare a strong statement you can use to introduce yourself to a prospective employer. Share your pitch with a classmate and analyze the strength of your statement.

Do It *Document Your Success Track Record*

Build Your e-Portfolio

Use the different job search and self-marketing techniques listed under the "Networking and Community Presence" section to map out a plan for your job search.

Include the following:

1. Draw up a design of your personal business card. What would it look like? What information should be on it? Then, research free business-card sites online and order some.
2. Draft an elevator pitch and practice giving it to at least five people, while handing out your business card.
3. Pick an industry you are passionate about and want to focus on in your job search. Imagine you are creating a blog about the current state of this industry. Write up the first two posts you would publish to your readers. Assume your future hiring manager is one of your readers. How will you effectively convey your knowledge and opinions about this industry in your blog posts?

Business in Action

Bonobos Founders Created Their Own Opportunities—and Some for Others

Some people grumble about a problem; others look for the solution. While finding solutions can take some work, the effort often pays off, both in problem resolution and in cash. Just ask Brian Spaly and Andy Dunn, two former Stanford University students. Their menswear company, Bonobos, projected $1.2 million in revenue for 2008. Bonobos hires stylists, technical designers, and other go-getter positions called "Ninjas."

It all started with Spaly's search for well-fitting pants. He couldn't find any so he set out to make his own. The pants he made for himself fit better than any others, so he began making them in different sizes for other people. As a hobby, he began selling the pants online. That is, until his friend from business school, Andy Dunn, proposed solving another problem: shopping difficulty. As Dunn said, "... not only is there a market need for great pants, but there's also a market need for an easier way to shop, especially for guys." Dunn realized that the pants sold well on Spaly's Web site due to the no-risk return policy. He created a business model with an emphasis on both customer service and personality. A partnership was born.

Although Spaly and Dunn bring different gifts to the table, they leverage each other's strengths. Says Spaly, "... we both admire the other person for supplying the piece that we didn't have on our own.... We don't ever forget that."

The two credit their success, in part, to taking risks. The venture required both courage and entrepreneurship. Says Spaly, "... we realized that what's going to make us happier and more excited about going to work every day is trying to build our own thing."

Even the hiring process at Bonobos is engaging and personal. The company wants to know what potential employees read and look at online. The company's interviewers want to know how graduating students view Bonobos' competitors in the market. They want applicants to communicate what Bonobos should do differently to become an even better company.

Questions

1. Spaly and Dunn were willing to take risks if it meant feeling passionate about their work. What risks are you willing to take in order to feel creative, capable, and joyful as you think about your career? What changes do you see in your communication style when you are passionate about what you are doing in school and out?
2. Clearly Spaly and Dunn don't let their egos get in the way of running a business. Instead, they respect each other's individual talents. How do you show that you respect others' gifts and talents in class, during group projects, or in your study group outside of class? Do you become defensive or combative if your ideas are challenged? How can you keep your ego from interfering in business communication in college, your part-time job, and in your leadership activities?
3. How can the act of identifying a need or gap in your life lead you to some conclusions about your job search and how to communicate your skills effectively?

Source: "Fashion, Done Right," *Bonobos.com,* accessed August 17, 2010 at http://bonobos.com/about/founders/; Brian Pettrucelli, "A Perfect Pair," *Entrepreneur.com,* July 24, 2008, accessed at http://www.entrepreneur.com/startingabusiness/successstories/article195864.html.

Key Terms

Credit score. A numeric rating assessing the risk of extending credit to an individual. *(p. 380)*

Elevator pitch. A 30-second presentation given by a job seeker to outline his or her career goals and strengths as a candidate. *(p. 382)*

Freelancer. A person who is not an employee of a company but works on a contract basis to accomplish projects. *(p. 388)*

Hidden job market. A saying that refers to the 80 percent of jobs that are not available to the general public, have not been advertised, or made public yet. *(p. 382)*

Hiring freeze. A situation in which an organization ceases its recruiting efforts until the economic or corporate climate becomes more favorable. *(p. 388)*

Independent recruiters. Professionals who contract with corporations to fill permanent positions. *(p. 386)*

Informational interview. An interview where a job seeker interviews someone to learn about that person's position, company, or industry. *(p. 374)*

Internships. Nominally paid or unpaid positions that give students and job candidates an opportunity to gain experience in their fields. *(p. 376)*

Job fair. A forum made up of several representatives from various companies, gathering to meet and recruit prospective employees. *(p. 384)*

Networking. The practice of introducing yourself and establishing multiple personal and professional relationships. *(p. 371)*

On-campus interview. An interview where a corporate representative visits a college campus to recruit employees. *(p. 385)*

Online job banks. Internet sites where companies post positions, accept résumés from candidates, and search for candidates. *(p. 384)*

Permanent placement agencies. Agencies that match candidates to permanent positions with organizations. *(p. 386)*

Shadowing. The process whereby someone observes an individual at work for the purpose of understanding the roles and responsibilities associated with the individual's position. *(p. 377)*

Talent acquisition. The process of recruiting and retaining talented employees. *(p. 381)*

Temporary placement. The process of matching candidates to positions for predetermined amounts of time. *(p. 387)*

Review Questions *Test Yourself*

1. What is *The Occupational Outlook Handbook* and what information does it offer?
2. Explain what an informational interview is and how you can use it in your search for a career.
3. What is an internship and how can you find one?
4. What circumstances play a role in determining where you want to work?
5. What are four different resources you can use to research a company?
6. What are the benefits of researching a company at which you are interested in working?
7. What information do background checks explore in prospective employees?
8. What actions can you take to alleviate any issues that could hinder the possibility of you obtaining employment?
9. What items constitute inappropriate material online?
10. Define the term *talent acquisition* and how technology has changed it.
11. List the different ways you can network within your career field.
12. What guidelines should you follow when posting information to an online profile?
13. List the ways you can prepare for a job fair or recruiting event.
14. What are the advantages and disadvantages of working with recruiters, temporary agencies, and permanent placement agencies?
15. What are a few strategies you can use to search for employment in a tough job market?
16. List a few questions to ask yourself if you are considering international employment.
17. How can a service organization help you in building your career portfolio?
18. What are additional tips to consider when performing a job search?

Grammar Review *Mastering Accuracy*

Numbers

Section I

Each of the following sentences contains one or more common errors in word usage, grammar, or style. Identify the errors. If you have trouble finding the errors, review Section 3.2. in the handbook (Appendix D) at the back of this textbook.

1. Professor Riley had 17 students in his class, but only sixteen were present.
2. Several business associates gathered to split the check four different ways.
3. 6 candidates are to be hired today, with at least 5 beginning a new shift on Monday.
4. Janice still believes that her padded business suit from the 80's will be popular once again.
5. Our annual revenue is expected to surpass 745376 dollars this year.
6. My supervisor stated that she prefers to read 19th century literature, but I did see her reading the new Anne Rice novel from Twenty-01.
7. Our guidelines are strict, so we need all participants in this year's bake-sale to use no more than 1 cup of two-percent milk in each recipe.
8. Our department believes thirty-six percent of our students may be involved in gang activity.
9. We expect a full report of the day's activities by 7 P.M. this evening.
10. Her classroom has 9- 6 year olds, but only 4 seven year olds.

Section II

On a separate sheet of paper, rewrite the following sentences so they are clearer, more professional sounding, grammatically correct, and goodwill oriented.

1. Something like 8 million people were hit by the earthquake.
2. Several reports indicated that Ms. Henderson was the victim of a completed suicide attempt.
3. This 1st report is not difficult; are you mentally-challenged?
4. You should demolish all of those documents when you're done reading them.
5. Those reports are top-secret, so don't let anyone outside our department see them!
6. Was it our last supervisor or current supervisor who said something like, "Please look at the departmental manual?"
7. We think we knew that a ransom note had likely been created demanding only just one thing; but, as of the day of the week on Tuesday, the public did not know the note's contents.
8. Campus security guards and agents will investigate all shady vehicles; additionally, be ready to show your id badge when the cops ask.
9. I firmly and realistically believe that for this case, it is not pertinent nor advisable to wave your right to council.
10. You should totally let your executive committee member know weather or not you will be effected by the whether conditions.

Extra Resources *Tools You Can Use*

Books

- Ackley, Kristina M. *100 Top Internet Job Sites: Get Wired, Get Hired in Today's New Job Market.* Manassas Park, VA: Impact Publications, 2000.
- Bolles, Richard Nelson. *Job-Hunting on the Internet.* Berkeley, CA: Ten Speed Press, 2001.
- Carter, Carol. *Majoring in the Rest of Your Life.* Denver, CO: LifeBound, 2005.
- Dixon, Pam. *Job Searching Online for Dummies.* Foster City, CA: IDG Books Worldwide, 2000.
- Doyle, Alison. *The About.com Guide to Job Searching.* Avon, MA: Adams Media, 2006.
- Farr, Michael, and Laurence Shatkin, PhD. *50 Best Jobs for Your Personality.* St. Paul, MN: Jist Works, 2009.
- Fry, Ron. *101 Smart Questions to Ask on Your Interview.* Florence, KY: Cengage Learning, 2006.
- Graham, Bridget, and Reidy, Monique. *Working World 101.* Avon, MA: Adams Media, 2009.
- Kennedy, Joyce Lain. *Cover Letters for Dummies.* Hoboken, NJ: Wiley, 2009.
- Krueger, Brian. *College Grad Job Hunter.* Avon, MA: Adams Media, 2008.
- Loveland, Elaina. *Creative Careers.* Belmont, CA: SuperCollege, 2007.
- Pierson, Orville. *Highly Effective Networking.* Franklin Lakes, NJ: Career Press, 2009.
- Smith, Rebecca. *Electronic Résumés and Online Networking.* Franklin Lakes, NJ: Career Press, 2000.
- Tieger, Paul D., and Barbara Barron. *Do What You Are.* New York City: Little, Brown and Company, 2007.

"To find out your real opinion of someone, judge the impression you have when you first see a letter from them." — **Arthur Schopenhauer,** German philosopher

The Tools for Finding a Job

Cover Letters, Résumés, and Portfolios

LEARNING OBJECTIVE QUESTIONS

1. What makes up a winning application packet?
2. What are the different types of cover letters?
3. How can you make your cover letter stand out?
4. Which résumé formats are most common?
5. How do you write a winning résumé?
6. How does technology affect résumé writing?
7. How can you create an impressive portfolio?

PEARSON **mybcommlab** Access interactive videos, simulations, sample documents, document makeovers, and assessment quizzes in Chapter 14 of **mybcommlab.com** for mastery of this chapter's objectives.

>>> **Robert** is a manager in charge of hiring at Sun TeleComm, a telecommunications company. A week ago, a key player on his team announced that she was moving across the country, leaving an opening on his team. Robert managed to post a job description as quickly as possible and is now spending the evening looking through the first responses to the posting.

It is now 7:55 P.M. and Robert sits staring at a pile of résumés forwarded to him by his firm's human resources department. The task seems daunting. He picks up the first résumé and starts reading. Robert is looking for direct, clear evidence that the person who sent the résumé has the qualities, skill, experience, and stamina that could help his team immediately and in the future.

At first the process is painfully slow. Résumé after résumé is too short, too long, unfocused, or too specialized. Although some candidates have attended prominent colleges and have a lot of professional experience, they seem unable to follow the simple directions in the job posting. Or, they have written generalized cover letters that tell Robert the applicants aren't really serious about the opportunity.

It's quite late when Robert finally stumbles across something that looks promising. The applicant is a recent graduate of a nearby community college. Her cover letter is the correct length and is obviously personalized to fit the position. According to her résumé, she's held several internships during college and volunteered at some of Sun TeleComm's community events. Even better, her résumé and cover letter are spotless: no grammar problems or spelling mistakes. Feeling confident, Robert turns to his computer and begins typing her an e-mail requesting an interview.

Robert >>>

Managers in all industries struggle to find the right people for the right jobs. An effective résumé and cover letter makes the task much easier. This is certainly true in the Internet services industry. The Internet services industry is an industry that encompasses Internet publishing and broadcasting, as well as Internet service providers, hosting companies, Web communication firms, and search portals. The companies perform many activities. They provide access to the Internet, develop search engines and navigation tools, and prepare, transform, and publish information on the Internet in text, audio, video, and multimedia formats. Knowing how to present and sell your abilities and talents effectively through résumés, cover letters, and portfolios can be a first step in the door of this industry. Your written communication skills could give you a chance to work with Internet and media giants such as Google, Yahoo, AOL, Microsoft, EarthLink, Verizon, Comcast, and SBC, just to name a few.

1 What Makes Up a Winning Application Packet?

■ For an interactive, real-world example of this topic, access this chapter's bcomm mini sim entitled Cover Letters and Résumés, located at **mybcommlab.com**

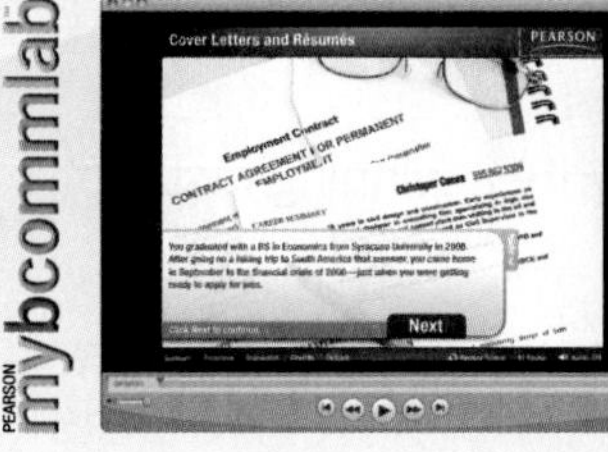

As the saying goes, "You never get a second chance to make a first impression." Your cover letter and résumé determine the first impression a company gets of you during the job-hunting process. A computer program may be used to scan your documents for key words and phrases relevant to the position. Then, human resources screeners take a second look. They want to see a professional submission—relevant work experience and no typos, grammatical errors, or design flaws. If the résumé meets a company's human resources department's standard, it is forwarded to a manager doing the hiring. These managers make the distinction between ordinary and extraordinary candidates quickly. From a stack of 500 résumés, they might conduct a phone interview of a dozen or so candidates and then interview about half of them in person.

Managers who hire new employees are responsible for making sound corporate investments, especially when it comes to a company's greatest asset—its employees. It's been estimated that the average cost of hiring a new employee is $4,000.[1] The expense includes human resources–related efforts, new-hire training, lost productivity during a new hire's probationary period, and candidates' travel expenses. Because of the high costs of recruiting, some companies evaluate and compensate managers, at least in part, on their acquisition and retention of high-performing employees. After all, every new hire is possibly the company's next future director or CEO.

What Do Managers Look for in Applicants?

Because sloppy correspondence affects a company's credibility, managers filter out applicants whose cover letters have misspellings. Likewise, a poorly formatted résumé creates the impression that the applicant will overlook details and take shortcuts. Hiring managers assume that you will approach your next position in the same way you did your application for employment. Make it your goal to create an outstanding **application packet** you can show employers. The packet should include your 1) cover letter, 2) résumé, 3) professional portfolio, and 4) letters of recommendation.

You want these documents to leave a manager asking, "When can this person start?"

Organizing and Tailoring Your Application Packet

Open positions draw competition from many applicants. Savvy job seekers tailor their application packets to their audiences rather than send the same cover letters and résumés to everyone. For example, consider Amanda, a double marketing and computer sciences major. Amanda is currently applying for a position as a marketing associate with an Internet service provider. During college she followed trends in multimedia via Google RSS feeds. Through her research she learned that many Internet service providers target the growing number of Hispanic businesses as potential clients. One article specifically mentioned the firm to which Amanda is applying. As she prepares her cover letter, Amanda acknowledges

Exhibit 14-1 Questions to Ask Yourself When Tailoring an Application Packet

Topics to Tailor	Question
Industry Trends	What is relevant to the company's industry today?
Research	What is important to this company's business?
Skills	What transferable skills did I master that would make me successful in this position?
Leadership	How have I demonstrated leadership and taken initiative?
References	Who will be the most compelling reference for this particular job?
Awards	What did I contribute? What awards have I won? How have I excelled? Example: "I was the first African-American student awarded the Young Playwright's Scholarship."
Quantifiable Success	Can I quantify my success? Example: "I increased student participation in the Human Rights Matter organization by 200 percent."
Activities	What job-relevant activities have I participated in?

the firm's initiative, its strategy for successful search engine optimization, and highlights her fluency in Spanish. Her focus on the company's goals distinguishes her from other applicants who have not done their homework.

Before preparing your application packet, identify and rank your accomplishments by how relevant and impressive they would be to the organization to which you are applying. Start with the most recent ones and work backward. Hopefully, as you prepare this information, you will feel proud of the things you have accomplished. Many students and younger job seekers are surprised at their accomplishments and find them to be real confidence boosters. As you review your accomplishments, conduct a gap analysis. In other words, evaluate areas of your professional skills and experience that might need work. Then seize every opportunity to gain experience, education, training, and skills. See **Exhibit 14-1** for some questions to ask yourself as you tailor an application packet. Answering them will help you include the key points you want to emphasize in your packet.

2 What Are the Different Types of Cover Letters?

Sending a résumé or portfolio without a cover letter clearly communicates, "I really don't care about this job." **Cover letters** are a critical component of an application packet.[2] Not only do they introduce the job applicant to a prospective employer, they also grab attention, showcase the applicant's writing proficiency and demonstrate critical thinking skills. Your cover letter is what will make someone decide to read your résumé.

When writing a cover letter, start with the job posting itself. Compare the experience required in the posting with your own. In many cases, hiring mangers actually draft job postings themselves. Using the same terminology in your cover letter that you saw in the posting is a good way to get a manager's attention.

The Application Cover Letter

A job seeker sends an **application cover letter** to a prospective employer as a means of introduction. You typically provide prospective employers this letter with your résumé, portfolio, and letter(s) of recommendation. **Exhibit 14-2** is an example of an application cover letter that responds directly to a job posting. Because representatives of the company posted the position and solicited applicants, they expect to receive application packets.

Exhibit 14-2 Application Cover Letter

EMILY YORK
8900 Pearl St.
Carlton, NJ 08501
EY@hotmail.com; (609) 356-7865

June 19, 2012

Mr. Jay Quinton
Vice President of Sales
Video Stream Resources, Inc.
346 Michigan Avenue
Chicago, IL 60089

Dear Mr. Quinton:

Please accept my application for the position of territory developer for Video Stream Resources, Inc. in response to your online ad. I was excited to learn from a June 2, *Chicago Tribune* article that Video Stream Resources streamed the Olympic highlights online.

The introduction shows the candidate has researched the company.

Having previously worked as a videographer, I am not only very experienced in selling streaming video services, but I have an extensive book of business contacts as well. Those contacts, along with my technical expertise, make me an ideal candidate for Video Stream Resources.

The body shows the applicant is genuinely interested in the firm and has experience needed for the position.

I welcome the opportunity to discuss my qualifications further. In the meantime, enclosed are my résumé and a letter of recommendation from my former employer. I will follow up next week with you in an effort to schedule an interview.

The close references the applicants résumé and letter of recommendation.

Thank you for your consideration.

Sincerely,

Emily York

Emily York

The Prospecting Cover Letter

A proactive job seeker sends prospecting cover letters like the one shown in **Exhibit 14-3**. A **prospecting cover letter** is a letter you send to a company for which you are interested in working, whether or not a position has been advertised. Although a company might not be hiring, it is entirely possible to create a position by addressing a company need, providing a solution, and proving your value. The prospecting cover letter introduces the job seeker and her ideas.

The Networking Cover Letter

Successful professionals network proactively regardless of their employment status. They send networking cover letters like the one shown in **Exhibit 14-4** on page 404. A **networking cover letter** introduces you to a contact, explains why you are writing to that individual, gives him or her a chance to review your résumé, and invites further communication. Focus on the mutual benefits to be gained. If someone offers to assist you, always suggest ways that you can reciprocate his or her kindness. For instance, you might offer to help with some office work or draft some necessary documents for the person's business. Your thoughtfulness will always be remembered. The new connections you make while networking result in new ideas, mentors, synergistic partnerships, and even clients.

Exhibit 14-3 A Prospecting Cover Letter

2367 Greenbay Road
Merrifield, MN 56465

December 15, 2012

Ms. Anita Gonzalez
Vice President of Program Development
Translate Your Circle, Inc.
2356 World View Way
San Diego, CA 92101

Dear Ms. Gonzalez:

My name is Amir Pasha, and I am graduating this May from your alma mater, Lake Hills College. I was prompted to contact you after learning how Translate Your Circle has broadened the reach of social media with automatic foreign language translation in addition to basic language skills. I subsequently created an online strategy that will promote your company's reach and reduce your expenses. If it impresses you, I would like to spearhead the project as a member of your team.

The opening shows the applicant has researched the company and the contact and has something to offer the firm.

As a student attending a semester abroad in Salamanca, Spain, Translate Your Circle helped prepare me for studying abroad, and I now use it to teach English as a second language on a volunteer basis in a small orphanage of middle-school–aged kids.

The body shows the applicant's commitment to the company's mission.

My extensive language experience, my love of foreign culture, and my ability to see new potential for growth opportunities make me a good fit for your organization. I have included my résumé for your review and will be in San Diego in three weeks. I will call to arrange a time to meet. If you would like to reach me, I am accessible by international cell phone at (217) 998-3465. In the meantime, thank you for your consideration.

The close refers to the applicant's résumé and includes a follow-up plan.

Regards,

Amir Pasha

Amir Pasha

3 How Can You Make Your Cover Letter Stand Out?

The purpose of a cover letter, regardless of its type, is to pique your reader's interest so he or she will look at your résumé. Remember the AIDA approach you learned about in Chapter 9? A good cover letter should create interest in the introduction, desire in the body, and call for action in the closing. Let's now take a closer look at how you can accomplish this.

The Introduction

You will likely be one of several applicants. Consequently, you need to distinguish yourself immediately.

Address the Recipient by Name

Whenever possible, winning cover letters address the recipient by name. Many job postings exclude the names of the managers doing the hiring to protect them from an onslaught of phone calls from applicants. However, if you call the company's receptionist, he or she will often give you the name you need. If that approach doesn't work, check the company's Web site or perform a Google search using the individual's title. Always confirm that your information is accurate with a phone call. For instance, "I would like to confirm that

Exhibit 14-4 A Networking Cover Letter Sent by E-mail

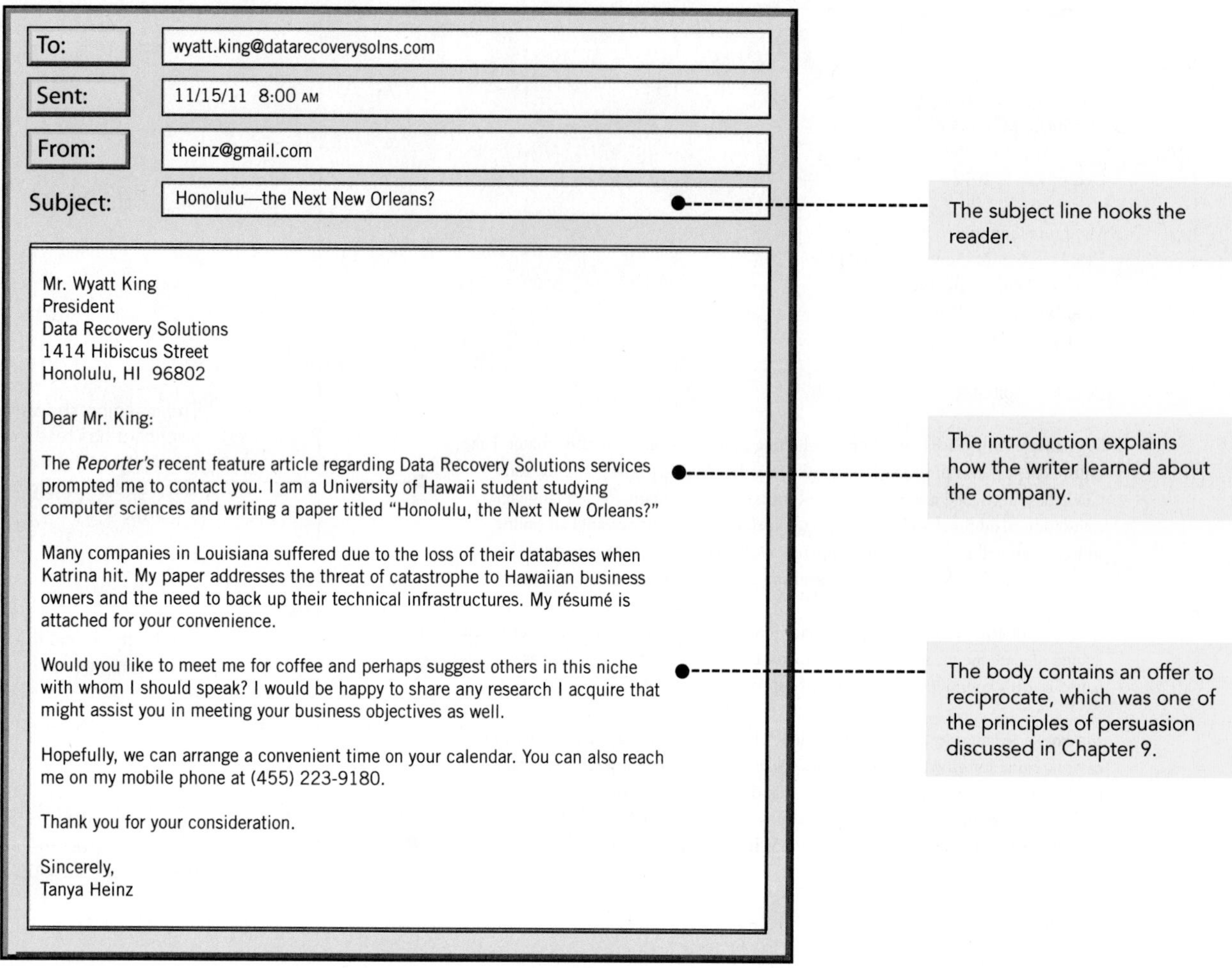
To: wyatt.king@datarecoverysolns.com
Sent: 11/15/11 8:00 AM
From: theinz@gmail.com
Subject: Honolulu—the Next New Orleans?

Mr. Wyatt King
President
Data Recovery Solutions
1414 Hibiscus Street
Honolulu, HI 96802

Dear Mr. King:

The *Reporter's* recent feature article regarding Data Recovery Solutions services prompted me to contact you. I am a University of Hawaii student studying computer sciences and writing a paper titled "Honolulu, the Next New Orleans?"

Many companies in Louisiana suffered due to the loss of their databases when Katrina hit. My paper addresses the threat of catastrophe to Hawaiian business owners and the need to back up their technical infrastructures. My résumé is attached for your convenience.

Would you like to meet me for coffee and perhaps suggest others in this niche with whom I should speak? I would be happy to share any research I acquire that might assist you in meeting your business objectives as well.

Hopefully, we can arrange a convenient time on your calendar. You can also reach me on my mobile phone at (455) 223-9180.

Thank you for your consideration.

Sincerely,
Tanya Heinz

The subject line hooks the reader.
The introduction explains how the writer learned about the company.
The body contains an offer to reciprocate, which was one of the principles of persuasion discussed in Chapter 9.

Meredith Katz is still the company's IT director." When in doubt, address your letter with "Dear Hiring Manager," "Dear Sir or Madam," or "Dear [company_name] Representative."

Explain How You Learned about the Position

Companies often invest a great deal of money in recruiting top talent. Hiring managers appreciate when you explain how you learned about a job opening. For example, "I am very enthusiastic about the executive assistant position your company posted on CareerBuilder.com." Such a statement lets the manager know which postings are the most effective.

Grab Attention and Show Your Knowledge

A good cover letter grabs the reader's attention and creates interest within the first paragraph. This is often accomplished by a friendly, professional opening that mentions how you heard about the company, who referred you, or a recent event that spurred you to write the letter. Whenever it's possible and impressive to do so, quantify your success. For instance, "Under my leadership, efficiency increased 75 percent." If you learned about the open position from a friend, indicate the person's name in your letter. "I was prompted to write you by Michelle Taggart, host of *Today's General Counsel,* who called me when the opening on your team arose. She thought my qualifications were perfect for success in the role." Mentioning a mutual contact can attract your reader's interest.

If you are writing a prospecting cover letter, your first paragraph should explain your intentions quickly: "After learning of Content Delivery Live's challenges in training international employees, I designed a system to streamline the process. I would like to discuss it with you." Mentioning a company's successes or challenges can pique the reader's interest.

Networking cover letters should take a slightly different spin. For instance, "I am writing to introduce myself. I was recently talking to our mutual friend Bart Gilbertson, and mentioned my desire to find an accomplished mentor in the field of online consulting. Your name came immediately to his mind. He said you are blogging on the subject and suggested I contact you." In this instance, the introduction doesn't reference a position. However, it still states the writer's purpose and addresses a matter of interest to the reader.

Always refer to accompanying documents in your cover letter. It would be a shame if a glowing letter of recommendation written by the company's top client was lost in the shuffle. A simple, "Please find my résumé and a letter of recommendation attached for your consideration" or "I have outlined my extensive journalism experience in my accompanying résumé," lets the recipient know to look for more. Some applicants choose to reference information about their attachments in the last paragraph. This is acceptable. Just don't forget to include the information. **Exhibit 14-5** shows a simple way to make sure your introduction catches your reader's attention and keeps his or her interest.

Exhibit 14-5
Three Steps to Writing a Riveting Cover Letter Introduction

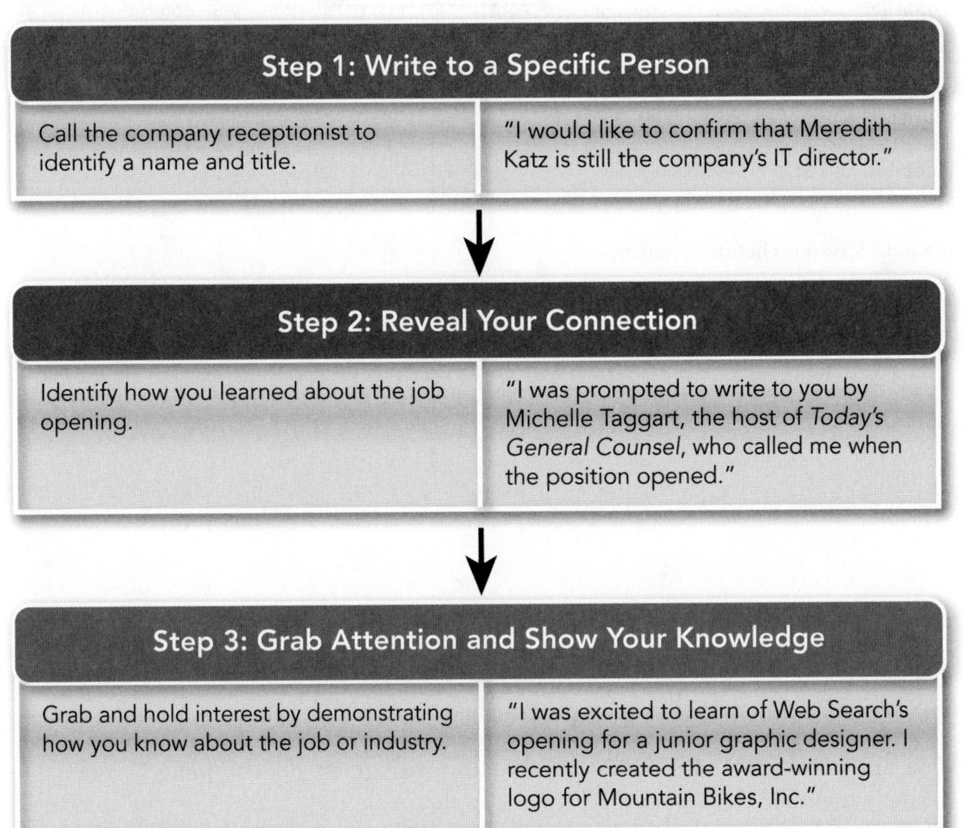

Step 1: Write to a Specific Person
Call the company receptionist to identify a name and title.
"I would like to confirm that Meredith Katz is still the company's IT director."
Step 2: Reveal Your Connection
Identify how you learned about the job opening.
"I was prompted to write to you by Michelle Taggart, the host of Today's General Counsel, who called me when the position opened."
Step 3: Grab Attention and Show Your Knowledge
Grab and hold interest by demonstrating how you know about the job or industry.
"I was excited to learn of Web Search's opening for a junior graphic designer. I recently created the award-winning logo for Mountain Bikes, Inc."

The Body

The body emphasizes the experience and interpersonal skills that make the applicant an ideal hire. People don't like others who "blow their own horn" without cause. The body should include some concrete examples of your success in either similar roles or within parallel areas of responsibility. A candidate stating, "I am a strong leader" without providing supporting evidence is only announcing his self-worth.

The body of the cover letter is the place to present yourself as the answer to a company need. Your key and most relevant qualifications should be demonstrated within the body, making the reader eager to see the details within your résumé.

The Close

The close should emphasize action by stating your desire to meet, and request an appointment. It could also include your intention to follow up with a phone call.

Exhibit 14-6 An Ineffective Cover Letter

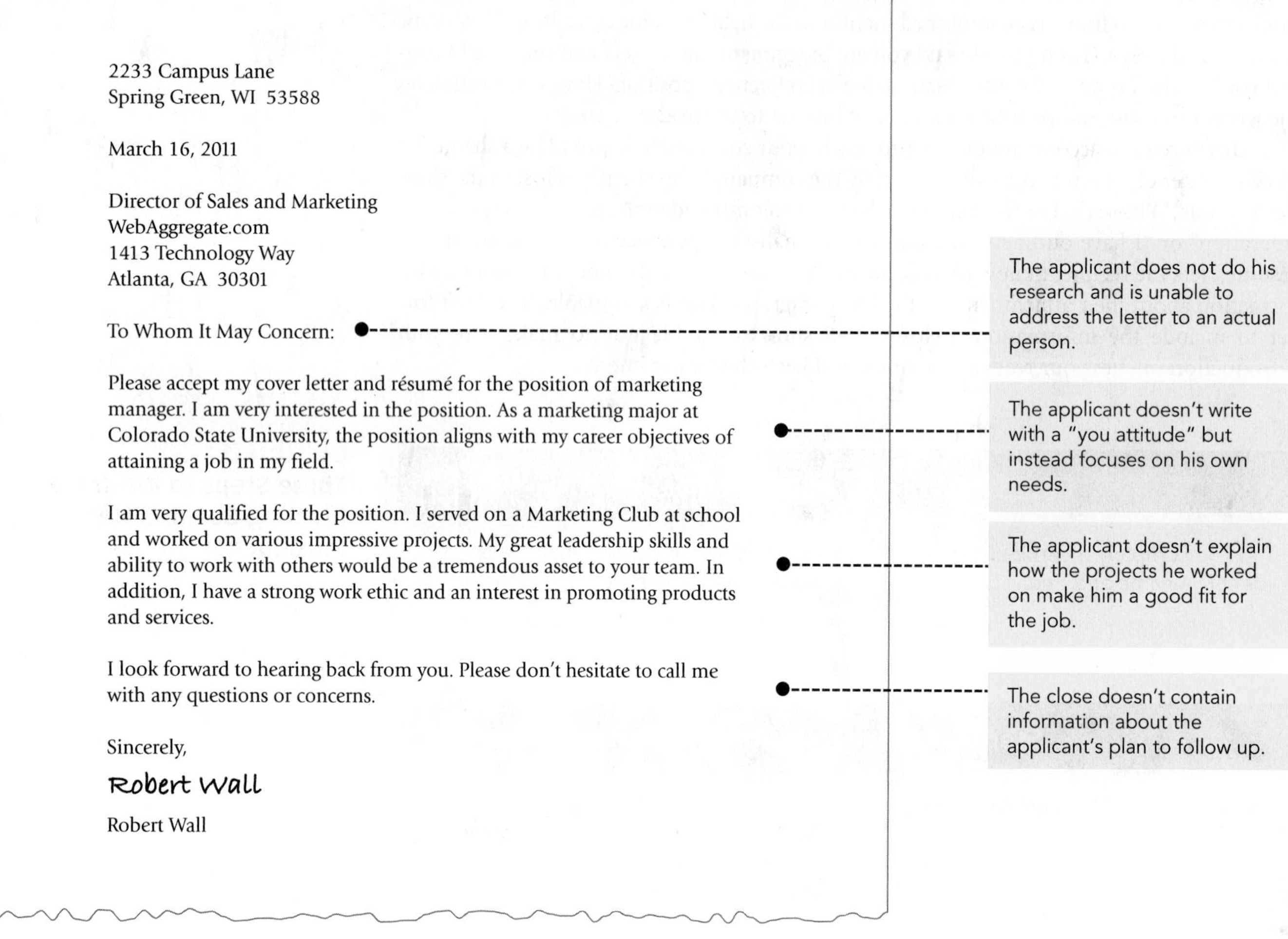
2233 Campus Lane
Spring Green, WI 53588

March 16, 2011

Director of Sales and Marketing
WebAggregate.com
1413 Technology Way
Atlanta, GA 30301

To Whom It May Concern:

Please accept my cover letter and résumé for the position of marketing manager. I am very interested in the position. As a marketing major at Colorado State University, the position aligns with my career objectives of attaining a job in my field.

I am very qualified for the position. I served on a Marketing Club at school and worked on various impressive projects. My great leadership skills and ability to work with others would be a tremendous asset to your team. In addition, I have a strong work ethic and an interest in promoting products and services.

I look forward to hearing back from you. Please don't hesitate to call me with any questions or concerns.

Sincerely,

Robert Wall

Robert Wall

The applicant does not do his research and is unable to address the letter to an actual person.
The applicant doesn't write with a "you attitude" but instead focuses on his own needs.
The applicant doesn't explain how the projects he worked on make him a good fit for the job.
The close doesn't contain information about the applicant's plan to follow up.

To illustrate the components of an effective cover letter, let's return to the manager facing a stack of application packets. Read through the cover letters in **Exhibits 14-6** and **14-7**, paying attention to the impressions each might leave on the manager.

Most managers would not continue reading past the introductory paragraph of the first applicant's cover letter. The introductory paragraph does nothing to grab the reader's attention. It focuses entirely on the applicant's agenda, rather than the objectives of the manager.

Furthermore, in the body, the first applicant mentions he has desirable qualities but does not provide evidence supporting his claim. Since managers doing the hiring often take a "prove it to me" approach, job applicants must back up their statements about qualifications with bona fide accomplishments or risk losing credibility.

Finally, the close is weak. It doesn't contain a call to action or refer to a résumé to prompt the reader to look at it. Additionally, the close provides no contact information in case the reader did want to get in touch with the applicant.

It probably wouldn't surprise you to learn that the second applicant's cover letter made it to the "schedule an interview" pile. The second applicant's letter grabs the manager's attention immediately. The extensive experience mentioned in the first paragraph demonstrates that the applicant already exceeds expectations. The manager wants to read more, and the body of the letter doesn't disappoint. The examples within the body clearly prove that the second applicant has initiative and leadership abilities.

The second applicant also includes a proactive follow-up plan in her close. This is far more impressive than the "wait and see" attitude the first applicant took. Finally, the second applicant remembers to thank the manager for his or her consideration, whereas the first

CHECKLIST

How to make your cover letter stand out:

- ☑ Address the recipient by name.
- ☑ Explain how you learned about the position.
- ☑ Grab attention and show your knowledge.

Exhibit 14-7 An Effective Cover Letter

VALERIE AGASSI

14577 Mascot Blvd.
Boise, ID 83701
Valerioagassi@gmail.com
(208) 222-8768

May 16, 2011

Ms. Michelle Watson
Director of Sales and Marketing
WebAggregate.com
1413 Technology Way
Atlanta, GA 30301

Dear Ms. Watson:

Attached is my résumé in response to your posting for a marketing manager on Monster.com. Not only do I have the fundamentals requested in your ad, I also have experience creating Web-based marketing strategies. In fact, the blog I created as an intern for Metro Man Clothing increased the company's Web site traffic by 200 percent.

In the opening, the applicant quantifies her success and shows how her skills and talents will be useful to the company.

As a member of the Boise State's Marketing Club, I honed leadership skills necessary for corporate work. In one of our projects I spearheaded a green-campus marketing initiative. This included galvanizing a team, creating a Web site promoting our mission, garnering university support through presentations, and tracking the success of our efforts. So successful was our plan, students at Tulsa University recently adopted the model for their own environmental initiative.

If hired, I would deliver WebAggregate.com the same passion and tenacity. My résumé, letters of recommendation, and work examples are attached for your review. I will call you at the end of this week to follow up on my application.

Thank you for your consideration.

The close references the applicant's résumé and letters of recommendation and outlines a follow-up plan.

Sincerely,

Valerie Agassi

Valerie Agassi

did not. **Exhibit 14-8** contains a sample cover letter used to apply for a promotion at a person's current place of employment.

4 Which Résumé Formats Are Most Common?

Just as a cover letter is crafted to grab a hiring manager's attention, a résumé must do the same. Ask yourself, why is this company hiring? Who are they looking for right now? What priorities are at the forefront in the hiring manager's mind? A winning résumé makes managers eager to interview you. It advertises your experience, education, activities, and qualifications while promoting you as an excellent fit for the job and the company.

The next step is determining which type of résumé to use. Traditionally, there are two kinds of résumés; chronological and functional (see **Exhibit 14-9** on page 390 and **Exhibit 14-10** on page 391). Some candidates create a résumé that is a hybrid of the two styles (see **Exhibit 14-11** on page 392). Still others use a video résumé, although there are some pros and cons to

Exhibit 14-8 An Internal Posting Cover Letter E-mailed Internally

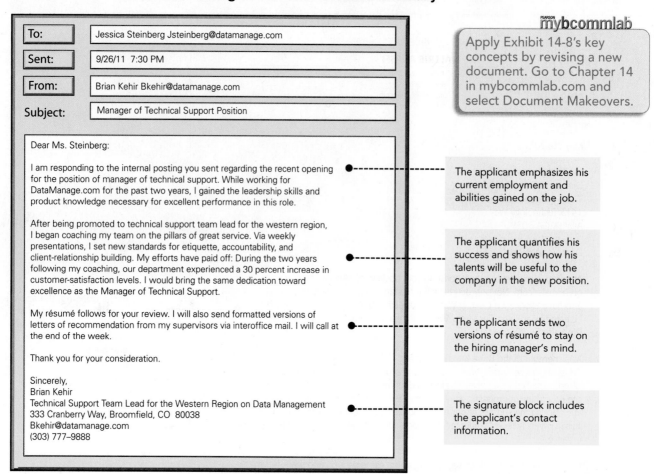

To: Jessica Steinberg Jsteinberg@datamanage.com

Sent: 9/26/11 7:30 PM

From: Brian Kehir Bkehir@datamanage.com

Subject: Manager of Technical Support Position

Dear Ms. Steinberg:

I am responding to the internal posting you sent regarding the recent opening for the position of manager of technical support. While working for DataManage.com for the past two years, I gained the leadership skills and product knowledge necessary for excellent performance in this role.

> The applicant emphasizes his current employment and abilities gained on the job.

After being promoted to technical support team lead for the western region, I began coaching my team on the pillars of great service. Via weekly presentations, I set new standards for etiquette, accountability, and client-relationship building. My efforts have paid off: During the two years following my coaching, our department experienced a 30 percent increase in customer-satisfaction levels. I would bring the same dedication toward excellence as the Manager of Technical Support.

> The applicant quantifies his success and shows how his talents will be useful to the company in the new position.

My résumé follows for your review. I will also send formatted versions of letters of recommendation from my supervisors via interoffice mail. I will call at the end of the week.

> The applicant sends two versions of résumé to stay on the hiring manager's mind.

Thank you for your consideration.

Sincerely,
Brian Kehir
Technical Support Team Lead for the Western Region on Data Management
333 Cranberry Way, Broomfield, CO 80038
Bkehir@datamanage.com
(303) 777–9888

> The signature block includes the applicant's contact information.

mybcommlab

Apply Exhibit 14-8's key concepts by revising a new document. Go to Chapter 14 in mybcommlab.com and select Document Makeovers.

consider with this format, as we discuss later in the chapter. Each type of résumé has similar information, but the content is presented in a different way. After reading about the different types of résumés, you should be able to determine the best format for your particular situation.

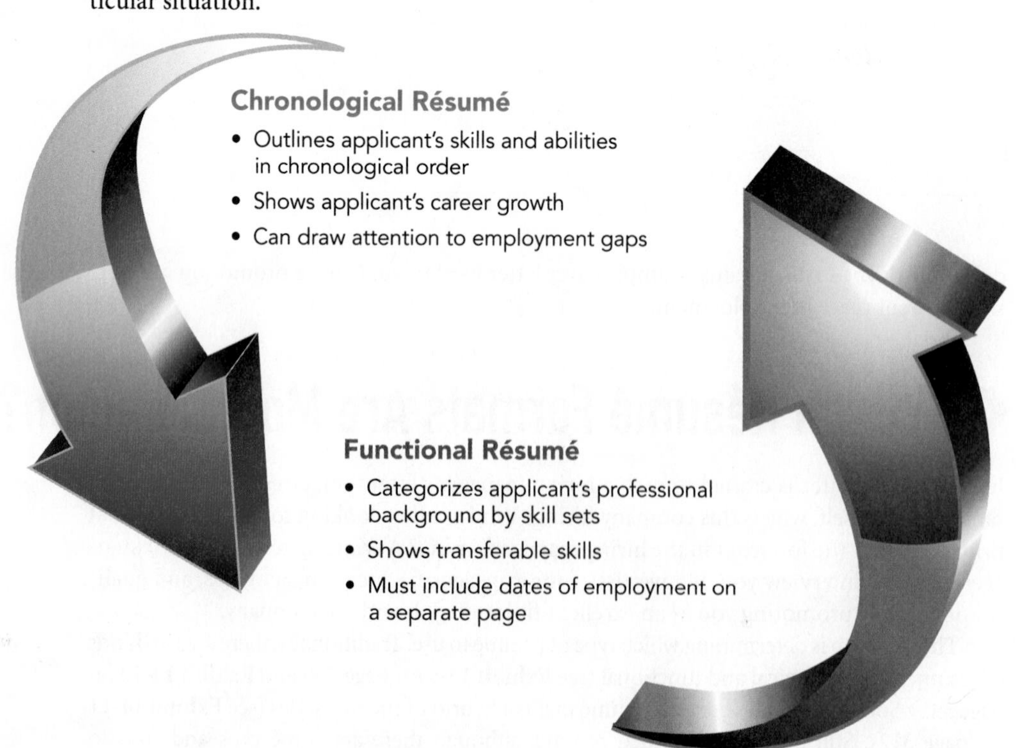

Chronological Résumé
• Outlines applicant's skills and abilities in chronological order
• Shows applicant's career growth
• Can draw attention to employment gaps
Functional Résumé
• Categorizes applicant's professional background by skill sets
• Shows transferable skills
• Must include dates of employment on a separate page

REAL INSIGHTS from a New Professional

Name: *Jessica Bennett*
Title: *Human Resources Coordinator*
Organization: *Organic People, Inc.*
Location: *Denver, Colorado*

JESSICA BENNETT HAS TACKLED HER SHARE OF CHALLENGES. She's dueled against the powerhouses in women's college soccer. She's trekked across Africa in a camper van with her entrepreneur parents and fellow adopted siblings, where she saw firsthand the heartache caused by AIDS and malaria. She has also confronted the intimidating post-college obstacle of writing a cover letter.

A 2006 Hiram College graduate, Bennett also faced learning disabilities as she embarked on her job search. She has dyslexia and attention-deficit hyperactivity disorder, challenging her reading and focusing abilities. "The cover letter was definitely difficult. The dyslexia caused me to jump around in my thoughts. A lot of people helped me with it," she says. After numerous revisions, an effective cover letter combined with personal networking and an aggressive approach in the interviewing process resulted in Bennett getting a position as a human resources coordinator with Denver-based Organic People, Inc. Organic People is a telecommunications firm specializing in billing systems for corporations such as Comcast and Time-Warner.

"Because I was out of college for just a year or so, my résumé was pretty minimal," says Bennett. "However, I had a strong willingness to learn, and I had to convey that in my cover letter. I stressed that I was a hard worker, and I had experience as an undergraduate working on a team, working with people, and experience with my college's fraternity and sorority council learning how to manage people."

She also learned a thing or two about business communication after she landed the job. "One thing I had to learn was business writing style: writing that is more formal than casual and that isn't stiff or cold," Bennett says. "Clarity is extremely important as is getting to the point, stating what's relevant, and clearly conveying it."

Bennett is now on the other end of the job search spectrum, evaluating résumés and cover letters to recruit top talent to Organic People. "First I look at whether there would have to be a lot of training or if it would be a pretty easy transition into this company. I look at their skill sets, and how they might complement the rest of us in the office. I also look at if they ask for the close—if they appear to want the job."

She's seen résumés seven pages long. "Get to the point," Bennett stresses. "What does the candidate have to contribute, versus everything they've done for the past 25 years? I want to see a résumé that says, 'These are the skills I have, and this is what I can bring to this company.'"

Questions

1. Bennett stresses that you should state the skills you have to offer the company. What skills do you have to offer? How can you portray those skills and link them to a company's needs in a cover letter?
2. Study your résumé and a recent cover letter, and think back to Bennett's advice. How can you revise the documents to provide an employer a professional overview of your skills and talents—one that will get you an interview?

Source: Jessica Bennett in discussion with the author, July 2010.

Chronological Résumés

A **chronological résumé**, like the one shown in Exhibit 14-9, outlines a person's education and experience beginning with the most recent event and working backward. This type of résumé is easy for your potential employer to scan because it shows how your career has progressed over time: the skills you have gained, your promotions, and the achievement of your goals. Notice in Exhibit 14-9 that the applicant does not have experience working for an Internet service provider, but she focused on her transferable skills relating to her desired position. **Transferable skills** are skills gained in one position that relate to those required by another.

The downside of a chronological résumé is that it shows frequent job changes as well as gaps in employment. These gaps are often "red flags" for managers doing the hiring—gaps you will have to account for in your cover letter and when you are interviewed. If you have gaps, you might have to offer an explanation such as the following: "Between my employment with Books Unlimited and Paper Text, I did my own fundraising as a volunteer for Clean Water for All.

Exhibit 14-9 A Chronological Résumé for a New Graduate

Chandra Vashti
333 Newtown Circle, Slyvania, GA 30467
Sirlitav@hotmail.com
(229)-235-7756

OBJECTIVE
To apply my public relations experience working as a public relations assistant for a high-profile Internet service provider.

EDUCATION
BA, Cornell College
- Graduating May 2011
- Public Relations Major, Psychology Minor
- 3.0 GPA

EXPERIENCE
Cornell College, Mount Vernon, IA 08/2010–12/2011
Student Ambassador
- Nominated by a board of college professors and administrators for a public relations role interacting with prospective students and their parents.
- Promoted Cornell College as a college of choice to applying high school students by giving presentations on campus life and visiting families.
- Facilitated Q&A sessions for the parents of incoming freshman.
- Created a welcome packet placed in dorms for incoming freshmen.
- Hosted a dinner for summer-prep students to welcome them to campus.

Cornell College, Mount Vernon, IA 07/2009–07/2010
Resident Hall Advisor, Brown Hall
- Entrusted as an advisor to the largest dormitory on campus; served as advisor to 20 residents, most of whom were away from home for the first time.
- Coordinated outings for students and activities to foster dorm relationships.
- Spearheaded a program called Brown Hall Reaches Out designed to promote community volunteering in residents; 95% participation among residents.
- Named "Advisor of the Year" by peers and supervisors.

WGTO Campus Public Radio, Mount Vernon IA 06/2009–07/2011
Radio Talk-Show Host
- Hosted a talk show targeting a large 20–30-year-old demographic.
- Handled on-the-air questions regarding various campus matters.
- Interviewed key campus and community officials.

The objective is clearly stated.

The applicant lists skills relevant to the job.

The applicant quantifies her success.

The applicant demonstrates her speaking ability, a necessary skill for the job.

Functional Résumés

A **functional résumé** like the one in Exhibit 14-10 is organized by skill sets, rather than job history. You extract skills and accomplishments from your entire job history (and personal experience related to it) and feature them in your résumé instead of particular jobs. For example, the major skill sets for a trainer position might include the following: management experience, curriculum development and training, or writing skills. When you have diverse experience, many employment gaps, or have done freelance work with a variety of clients, the functional résumé is an effective format to use because it shows how your past accomplishments lend themselves to the job at hand.

Exhibit 14-10 A Functional Résumé for a New Graduate

MARIA FERNANDEZ
3570 Pinion Way
Santa Fe, NM 87501
(505) 876-3321

OBJECTIVE
To secure a position as a graphic designer for Collocation Connex.

SKILLS
Technical Skills
- Proficient with Microsoft Office Suite, Adobe CS4, Dreamweaver, and Flash.
- Trained in Web site and blog creation; conducted training sessions on campus for professors.
- Experience with updating and modifying existing Web page layouts.

Communication Skills
- Well-versed in making presentations to audiences of 20 to 50 people.
- EffectiveCrisis hotline volunteer; employed strong active listening skills, problem-solving skills and resourcefulness; trained to handle various crisis situations and solve critical problems at a moment's notice.

CREATIVE EXPERIENCE
- Illustrated *The Three Golden Ducks* by Weifield Publishing.
- Designed an event poster for a statewide campaign by Stop Abuse, a community nonprofit organization.
- Won a package design contest for Delishie Chocolate's Happy Face Candy line; the design is now used on candy bar packaging and point-of-sale stands.
- Created corporate logos, business cards, letterhead, and Web pages for two local start-up companies.

EDUCATION
- Washington State University, BA, earned May 2011
- Graphic Design

ACTIVITIES & AWARDS
- Received "Top 20 Under 20" award given to young leaders under 20 years of age for leadership in the Seattle community.
- Elected social chairman of Washington State University's Kappa Kappa Gamma Sorority, 2010–2011.

DATES OF EMPLOYMENT
- Delishie Chocolates, Branding Intern 06/2010–12/2010
- Freelance Work: 08/2009–05/2011
  Applekins, Stop Abuse, Catwalk Clothing, and Mom's Mission Safety Products

The skills section focuses on what the applicant does best.

The creative experience section lists diverse freelance activities that would not work as well in a chronological.

The activities and awards section demonstrates the applicant's leadership.

A functional résumé does not necessarily show career progression and dates of employment. Since most managers still want to see this information, you can include it in a separate section titled *Work History* or *Dates of Employment*. The section lists your work history and the time you spent at each job, without specifying the tasks you performed. At some point during the application process, be prepared to discuss the chronology of your employment history. If it doesn't come up in an interview, it certainly will on a standard job application form used for reference checks.

Hybrid Résumés

A **hybrid résumé** like the one in Exhibit 14-11 contains elements of both the functional and chronological résumé. It includes a section that highlights your skills, as well as a section that

Exhibit 14-11 A Hybrid of a Chronological Résumé and a Functional Résumé

CALEB TOLSON
111 Swan Lake Drive
Anderson, IN 46001
(765) 245-1190; CTolson@gmail.com

OBJECTIVE
To apply my award winning writing skills as a technical writer for WebSeek.com.

SUMMARY OF QUALIFICATIONS
- Proficient with LexisNexis and Westlaw databases.
- Experienced with Word, PowerPoint, Excel, and AutoCAD.
- Able to create messages in varying voices depending on assignment.
- Received a Technical Writer's Certificate of Proficiency from the Institute of Technical Writing.

WRITING EXPERIENCE
- Created Indiana University *Newcomer's Guide*, a 50-page document distributed to all freshmen.
- Reported campus events for the university's online paper, *The Campus Post*, a paper receiving 1,000 Web site hits a day.
- Published two magazine articles in *Young Writer's Journal*: "Blogging for Cash" and "Technology in the Classroom."
- Wrote lesson plans for psychology professor by synthesizing textbook material into a daily instructional format.

The applicant lists his writing experience near the top of the résumé.

EDUCATION
BS and BA, Indiana University
- Double major in business and journalism
- Graduated 2011

AWARDS
Young Writer Rising Star Award, presented by Writer's Guild for Most Promising Young Writer in 2010

PROFESSIONAL EXPERIENCE
Kate and Nate's Cupcake Shoppe, Bloomington, IN 2009–2011
Manager
Baked cupcakes and balanced books for local bakery.

Because it doesn't show writing experience, the professional experience section appears toward the bottom of the résumé.

University of Indiana, Bloomington, IN 2009–2010
Teacher's Assistant
Performed research, held office hours, and assisted with writing plans and grading papers.

Password-protected portfolio available upon request.

The résumé mentions the applicant's portfolio abilities.

DID YOU KNOW?

A 2001 paper by the Association for Job Search Trainers revealed that the majority of recruiters prefer chronological résumés and that they review them in 10 to 30 seconds.

details your work history. The hybrid format is good to use when you are applying for a job that is different from what you have done in the past or a job in a different industry. The format lets you highlight your experience in other areas that is relevant to the job for which you are applying.

Video Résumés

Video résumés have become more popular among candidates looking for creative ways to present themselves. A **video résumé** is a short one- to three-minute video that describes an applicant's skills and qualifications. Typically it supplements a traditional résumé. Some candidates use video résumés as a way to demonstrate their enthusiasm for a particular type of work as well as showcase their personalities. However, not all companies accept video résumés. Because video résumés visually show candidates, some human resource representatives worry that they could lead to claims of bias or discrimination.[3] To be on the safe side, never provide a video résumé in lieu of a traditional one. Instead, consider providing a link to your video résumé, which allows recipients the option of viewing it. Always mention your first and last name, talk about your professional endeavors, not your personal ones, discuss what you can do for the company, and thank the viewer for considering you for employment. In terms of how you dress and act, follow the guidelines for presenters discussed earlier in Chapter 11.

Video résumés can be downloaded and e-mailed to other people. So, even if you remove your copy of the résumé from a Web site, it can remain in cyberspace for a long time. Consider what your video résumé includes. Is it appropriate material for the position and culture of the company? Not all employers will appreciate a video résumé that is offbeat or appreciate humor at the interview stage. Keep the video professional and tailor it to the position for which you are applying.

5 How Do You Write a Winning Résumé?

A résumé should be succinct and include only your relevant experience, not your whole life history. Always tailor your résumé. For example, suppose you are a good public speaker who would easily excel in a training and sales position. If you apply for a training position, your résumé should emphasize your ability to convey information in a clear and engaging manner. If you are applying for a sales position, your résumé should highlight your revenue generating abilities. The best résumés are limited to one page (or two if you have extensive experience) with impressive and specific examples of your abilities.

Effective versus Ineffective Résumés

What makes a résumé good or bad? Imagine you are a manager reviewing applications for a marketing manager. You are currently looking at a résumé from a graduating college senior named Katherine Smith. Your thoughts might be similar to those shown in the highlighted boxes in **Exhibit 14-12.**

Now imagine that the same candidate revised her résumé as shown in **Exhibit 14-13.** What are your impressions? The difference in quality between the two résumés is stark. The same candidate, with some attention to persuasiveness and professionalism, casts herself in a much better light.

Sometimes the difference between a good and bad résumé is obvious. Other times it is subtle. Winning résumés include several sections, and attention to detail must be given to all of them. Next, let's look at the sections that make up a résumé.

Contact Header

The **contact header** is the section of a résumé with the candidate's contact information. Microsoft Word provides résumé templates, all of which create the header for you. If you want to create a unique format, remember that your name should be the first thing the reader sees. Include it at the top of the résumé in a larger font than the rest of the page. Your name should appear in the same font as the rest of the headings. Also include your contact information: phone number, address, and e-mail. Don't use nicknames or cutesy e-mail addresses. Keep your header formal. If necessary, create a professional e-mail account just for your job search. For instance: sandyj.taber@gmail.com, rather than skiqueen@aol.com.

Professional Objective

The **professional objective** section of a résumé is where you succinctly state the type of job you are seeking. This section often includes the type of work you want to do or the job title, the skills you want to use, and the environment where you want to use them. For instance, the objective of a candidate applying for a sales position might be, "Use my sales skills to drive revenue and develop a sales territory for a leading Internet services provider."

Exhibit 14-12 A Poorly Written Résumé

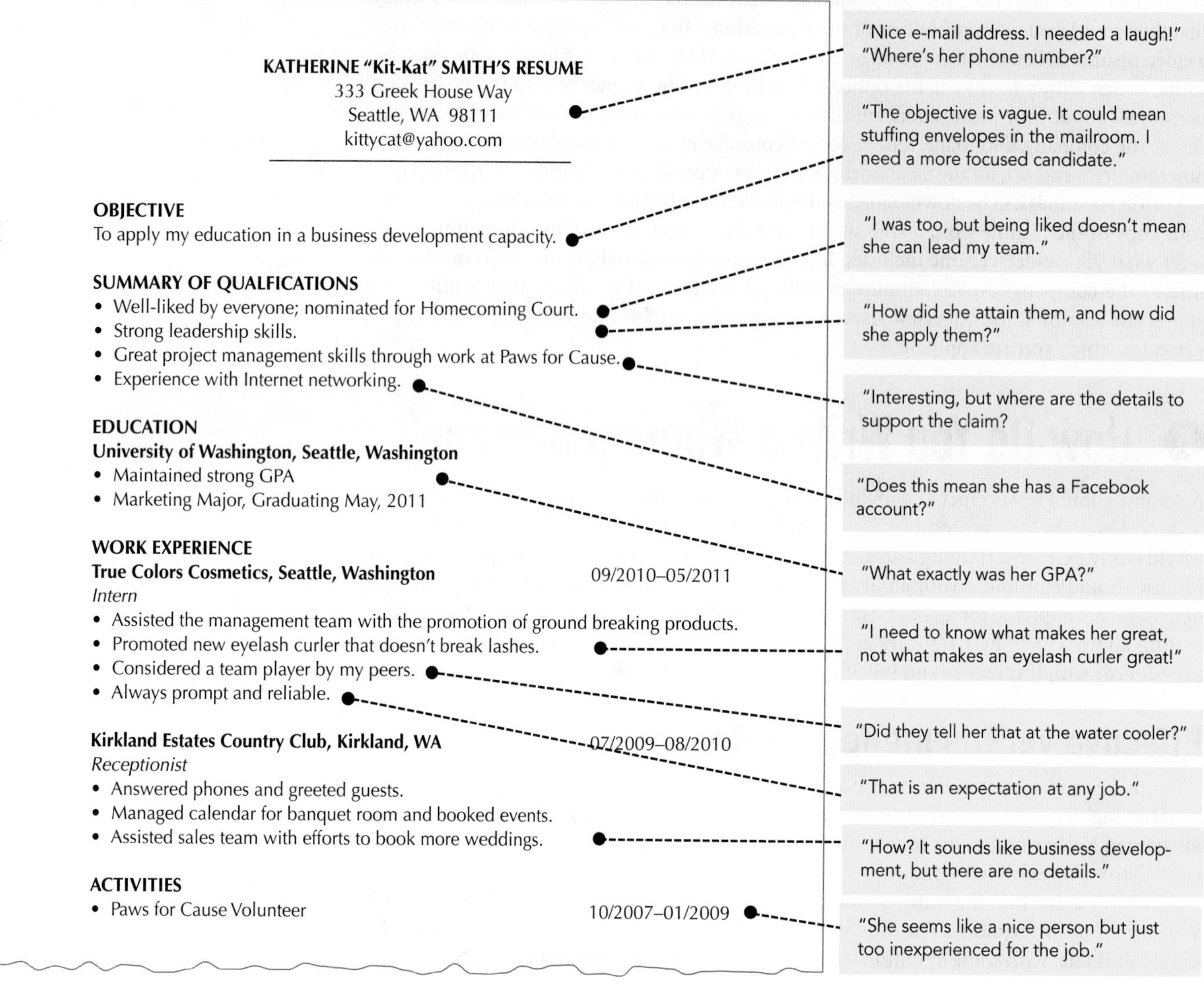
KATHERINE "Kit-Kat" SMITH'S RESUME
333 Greek House Way
Seattle, WA 98111
kittycat@yahoo.com

OBJECTIVE
To apply my education in a business development capacity.

SUMMARY OF QUALFICATIONS
• Well-liked by everyone; nominated for Homecoming Court.
• Strong leadership skills.
• Great project management skills through work at Paws for Cause.
• Experience with Internet networking.

EDUCATION
University of Washington, Seattle, Washington
• Maintained strong GPA
• Marketing Major, Graduating May, 2011

WORK EXPERIENCE
True Colors Cosmetics, Seattle, Washington 09/2010–05/2011
Intern
• Assisted the management team with the promotion of ground breaking products.
• Promoted new eyelash curler that doesn't break lashes.
• Considered a team player by my peers.
• Always prompt and reliable.

Kirkland Estates Country Club, Kirkland, WA 07/2009–08/2010
Receptionist
• Answered phones and greeted guests.
• Managed calendar for banquet room and booked events.
• Assisted sales team with efforts to book more weddings.

ACTIVITIES
• Paws for Cause Volunteer 10/2007–01/2009

"Nice e-mail address. I needed a laugh!" "Where's her phone number?"
"The objective is vague. It could mean stuffing envelopes in the mailroom. I need a more focused candidate."
"I was too, but being liked doesn't mean she can lead my team."
"How did she attain them, and how did she apply them?"
"Interesting, but where are the details to support the claim?"
"Does this mean she has a Facebook account?"
"What exactly was her GPA?"
"I need to know what makes her great, not what makes an eyelash curler great!"
"Did they tell her that at the water cooler?"
"That is an expectation at any job."
"How? It sounds like business development, but there are no details."
"She seems like a nice person but just too inexperienced for the job."

Job seekers with extensive experience often choose to omit professional objectives to make additional room for their qualifications. Others may not want to limit their opportunities. An employer may, after all, determine that your skill set is best suited for another department also hiring. However, some employers appreciate an objective because it tells them what you are interested in. So, if you are a multi-talented person whose skills could be used in a number of jobs, you may want to omit a specific job title in your objective, but still indicate the skills you want to use. For example, you might write: "Use my professional writing skills in the Internet industry to promote, educate, and inform." This objective would be appropriate for a marketing, training, or technical writing position. State your objective in active voice, as Exhibit 14-13 shows, and tailor the objective to the position for which you are applying.

Summary of Qualifications

The **summary of qualifications** section highlights a few of a jobseeker's most relevant qualities as they pertain to the position applied. Lengthy paragraphs on a résumé are not read. Instead use either short statements or bullet points. Include only qualifications that are measurable, verifiable, or supported by your work experience. For instance:

- Citrix-certified
- Proficient in Access, Excel, Word, PowerPoint, and WordPress
- Five years of military service
- Fluent in Mandarin Chinese

Exhibit 14-13 A Well-Written Résumé (Chronological)

KATHERINE TINA SMITH

333 Greek House Way Seattle, WA 98111 Tinaksmith@gmail.com (206) 789-0000

OBJECTIVE

To serve as a marketing assistant for Internet Conference by using my communication skills to develop successful online promotional strategies.

SUMMARY OF QUALIFICATIONS

- Executive board service on three college committees
- Spanish fluency
- Two years project management experience running events for Paws for Cause, a charitable organization that benefits community animal shelters
- Creation of three Internet marketing strategies for local businesses

EDUCATION

University of Washington, Seattle, WA

- Major: Marketing; Minor: Computer Science
- 3.7 GPA; Graduating May 2011
- Semester in Florence, Italy, studying international marketing
- President of French Club; Secretary of Chi Omega Sorority, and Student Director of Human Rights Advocacy Group

PROFESSIONAL EXPERIENCE

Marketing Intern, True Colors Cosmetics, Spring Green, WI 09/2010–05/2011

- Performed market research on target demographics for the promotion of a new cosmetics line; wrote a comprehensive report on the findings.
- Managed all print promotions related to the launch of the new product, including the design, budget, and release.
- Recognized with an "Above and Beyond Award" given by colleagues to the best team player.
- Created a blog targeting women in their twenties to gather market feedback; the blog has surpassed the number of total hits on the company's Web site.

Receptionist, Kirkland Estates Country Club, Kirkland, WA 07/2009–08/2010

- Planned and coordinated all aspects of the club's Winter Festival, including vendor selection, volunteer coordination, staffing, and public relations.
- Managed the executive calendars of six employees as well as the company's banquet-hall agenda.
- Designed an event marketing strategy as an initiative for improving lagging banquet sales; the banquet hall sold out after its implementation and banquet sales doubled.

HONORS, AWARDS, AND ACTIVITIES

- Paws for Cause Volunteer (10/2007– 01/2009)
- Honored as Volunteer of the Year (2009) for raising $100,000 of in-kind donations for Paws for Cause's annual silent auction

Large and small capital letters in a standard font are easier to read and more professional than all capital letters.

Laying out all contact information horizontally saves space.

The objective shows the applicant is a fit for the position.

The summary shows skills needed for the job and highlights the applicant's language abilities, which could be useful to the firm.

The education section demonstrates that the applicant is a well-rounded candidate.

The professional experience section outlines the applicant's skills related to the job, quantifies her success, and ability to work well with other people.

Use parallel construction for the bulleted list, as you learned in Chapter 5.

Not all applicants include a summary of qualifications on their résumés. However, including a brief opener of this type gives the résumé reader a point of reference. From there, the goal is to present content in a format that casts you in the best light.

Education

For students, the **education and training** section should appear earlier in the résumé. (After you have been in the workforce full time for two to three years, you can move the education section on your résumé to follow your professional experience.) Indicate your major,

minor, high grade-point average, any experience you have had studying abroad, and your anticipated graduation date. If your coursework slants toward a specific focus, include it. For example:

Business major with an emphasis in prelaw courses

Employers in technical fields often need to see specific classes you have taken. However, don't list all the courses. Limit yourself to a handful of upper division courses in your major that are relevant to the position you're applying for. You can list them in two bulleted columns to save space. For example:

- Web Programming
- Web Infrastructure
- Web Usability
- Web Design Project

If you received training outside of school, label the section "Education and Training," rather than "Education" so you can include your nonacademic education. For instance:

- Bachelor of Arts, School of Business; Graduated May 2010
- Attended the Young Entrepreneur's Boot Camp, a six-week intensive program for business majors
- Graduated from the Leading Leaders three-day training program
- Attended the Cutting Edge Technology and Its Impact on Business Symposium, May 2009

Professional Experience

Skills you pick up in one job are often very useful in different jobs.

The **professional experience** section is the area where you list the positions you have held. They can be paid or unpaid, such as internships or volunteer positions, and you can present these chronologically or functionally. *Note:* A professional who has been in the workforce for a year or more should list his or her professional experience section before education section.

Some new graduates lament, "If experience is required to get experience, how in the world does anyone get a job?" You often do not need the *exact* experience required for a posted position to get the job. Sometimes your transferable skills satisfy the experience requirements.

For example, suppose you are applying for an IT support position with an Internet software company. When customers encounter difficulties, they call the support line and the support technician answers their questions. Although you do not have experience working at a software company, you do have volunteer experience working in the computer lab at your college, where you answered students' questions. Your volunteer experience would probably have provided you with excellent transferable skills needed for the job.

When listing your professional experience, begin with your most recent job and work backward. List your employer (or organization where you volunteered or interned), dates of employment, city and state in which you worked, and your title. Then list the most relevant responsibilities and accomplishments within the position. As you describe each task, consider using this formula:

A + P = R
A = the action you took
P = a problem you faced
R = the results you got

For example, rather than saying:

- Developed a frequently asked questions list for a computer-lab's Web site.

You might say:

- Developed frequently asked questions list for computer-lab's Web site, which reduced the number of repetitive questions asked during lab sessions and resulted in higher assignment completion rates by students.

DID YOU KNOW?

A recent survey of professional recruiters conducted by Kathy Sweeney, the president of The Write Résumé, a résumé consulting firm, revealed that 91 percent of those completing the survey wanted résumés that had "position descriptions with a good mix of duties and accomplishments." Sixty-five percent of the respondents stated they wanted cover letters with "specific accomplishments or results."

Use Quantitative Examples

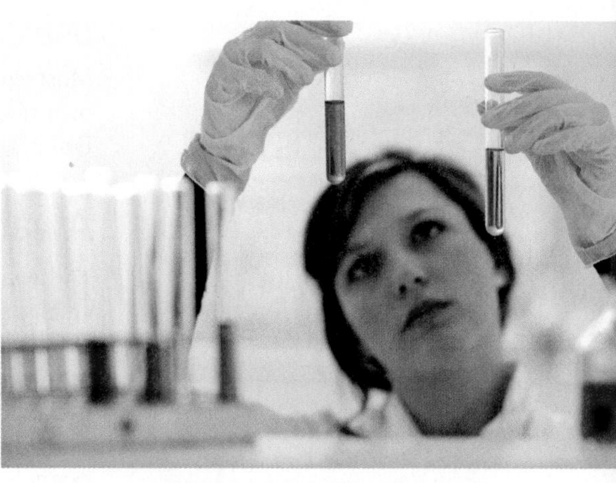

Quantitative examples carry more weight with résumé reviewers.

The difference between qualitative examples and quantitative examples is the difference between stating your value and proving it. A **qualitative example** states what you did. A **quantitative example** states what you did and measures how well you did it. Hiring managers can easily measure your performance if it's based on numbers, so include numbers when possible. Which of these two examples sounds more effective?

"Successfully recruited participants for the Breast Cancer Awareness Run." (qualitative)

-OR-

"Increased participation in the Breast Cancer Awareness Run by 97 percent through aggressive recruitment efforts." (quantitative)

You probably found the second example more persuasive. This quantitative statement includes a percentage (quantity) that objectively demonstrates a person's success.

Use Active Voice Instead of Passive Voice

Résumés written with active-voice verbs rather than passive-voice verbs create a stronger impression. Consistently use active verbs at the start of each bullet. For example, say:

"Trained 250 community members."

-INSTEAD OF-

"Was responsible for training 250 community members."

Exhibit 14-14 shows a list of active verbs.

Exhibit 14-14 **Active Verbs for Résumés**

accentuated	contributed	exercised	outlined	resumed
accomplished	controlled	exerted	oversaw	revealed
achieved	cooperated	exhibited	participated	revived
adhered to	coordinated	expedited	performed	schemed
administered	created	featured	persisted	secured
adopted	delegated	formed	planned	seized
advanced	demonstrated	fulfilled	pointed out	shared
applied	derived	generated	pooled	showed
apprehended	designated	handled	practiced	specialized
assimilated	designed	helped	prepared	sponsored
assisted	developed	implemented	prevailed	stressed
assumed	devised	indicated	produced	succeeded
attained	directed	invested	programmed	supervised
authorized	discharged	made	progressed	supported
built	dispatched	maintained	projected	surpassed
carried out	displayed	managed	promoted	sustained
caused	earned	mapped	prompted	synchronized
charted	effected	mastered	proposed	synthesized
checked	emphasized	merited	pursued	transacted
collaborated	employed	mobilized	qualified	understood
combined	empowered	modeled	regulated	undertook
commanded	enforced	negotiated	remained	used
commissioned	engineered	obtained	represented	utilized
conducted	established	operated	resisted	ventured
constructed	exceeded	organized	resolved	verified
continued	excelled	originated	restored	withstood

Source: Courtesy of Marquette University's Career Services Center.[4]

Use Consistent Fonts and Align Bullet Points

Most templates have styles for pre-aligned bullet points and margins. If you're creating your own résumé, make sure that your bullets align and your fonts are consistent throughout. Doing so creates a clean look and makes the résumé easy to read.

Awards, Honors, and Activities

The **awards, honors, and activities** section should include any awards you were given, scholarships and contests you won, and other types of recognition you received. The section can also include your participation in a sorority or fraternity, student council, athletic organizations, clubs, and volunteer groups relevant to the job or career field you're pursuing. Especially highlight those activities demonstrating leadership.

When you're listing an award or honor, explain why you received it. The following is an example: "Mentor Extraordinaire Award (required nomination by ten community members to qualify) given to young college students making substantial contributions to the lives of disadvantaged children." See Exhibit 14-13 for an example of effectively written honors.

Once you have written your résumé, there are still a few other aspects to consider: the appearance of the résumé (formatting) and a list of references. A professional appearance enhances the credibility of your résumé content. A list of people who can serve as references enhances your credibility. However, do not list references on your résumé. Prepare a separate list that you can supply if directly asked.

Using Templates to Format Your Résumé

You might find it easier to use a template as a starting point for your résumé. If you visit Microsoft's Web site and search for "résumé templates," you will find a wide variety of free ones you can download. Templates are nice because you do not have to do as much formatting. The drawback could be that your résumé will look like those of other applicants. You can prevent this from happening by using the template only as a guideline and then modify your résumé somewhat to make it unique. There are also excellent books on the market containing the résumés of real-life professionals working in various fields. (See the "Extra Resources" section at the end of this chapter.) Looking at other résumés will give you many ideas for formatting your own.

Getting References

Your list of references should include people with whom you have worked professionally, such as professors, volunteer directors, respected leaders within the company, and work supervisors. Choose people who are familiar with your performance, so they can provide specific examples to back up their statements. You want people who are familiar with the industry and able to intuitively speak to your strengths and weaknesses.[5] **Exhibit 14-15** is a sample list of references a student might provide a potential employer when requested.

Never list someone as a reference without first asking his or her permission. If the person agrees to be listed, you might consider asking if he or she will write you a letter of recommendation. Offer to provide your references with copies of your résumé for their

Exhibit 14-15 A List of References

REFERENCES FOR JANELLE SANTIAGO
August 2011
Phone: 360-867-3343, **E-mail:** jsantiago49@sbcglobal.net

- Raphael Blanco, Lab Assistant, Computer Science Department, Evergreen State College, Olympia, WA, rblanco@evergreen.edu, 360-867-3977
- Renee Dupres, Head of Student Services, Evergreen State College, Olympia, WA, rdupres@evergreen.edu, 360-867-3950
- Dr. Martin Jordon, Professor of Computer Science, Evergreen State College, Olympia, WA, mjordan@evergreen.edu, 360-867-3966
- Heather Anderson, Tutoring Center, Evergreen State College, Olympia, WA, handerson@evergreen.edu, 360-867-3979

REAL INSIGHTS from a Seasoned Professional

Name: *Frank Jedlicka*
Title: *Technical Sales Representative for Strategic Accounts*
Organization: *Adtran, Inc.*
Location: *Denver, Colorado*

IN THE TELECOMMUNICATIONS INDUSTRY, where change is a constant, academic and career accomplishments take a backseat to skills and adaptive thinking. Frank Jedlicka is a technical sales representative for Adtran, Inc., which engineers and manufactures electronics for phone, cable, fiber-optic, and other communications companies. A 17-year veteran of the telecom industry, he stays current with technological advancements and is a clear, convincing communicator.

"One of the most interesting aspects of the telecommunications industry is that it's a constant evolution," Jedlicka says. "It never stops. It's had its economic peaks and valleys, but the technology continues rolling on and evolving to the point where people in businesses and companies need to take advantage of the newest, latest, least expensive, most efficient technologies to run their businesses well and succeed." He says the current forecast is strong for telecommunications jobs. Candidates with engineering or computer technology degrees are in demand, but there are huge opportunities for graduates with marketing, sales, and administrative backgrounds.

"One of the qualities that has allowed me to be most successful in my own job is an ability to grasp a technical concept and communicate that to audiences of all technical levels," he explains. "I have a good ability to 'dumb it down' for a complete novice or get as technical as an engineer while still maintaining the message of the topic." Jedlicka's written communication often follows this model: Build a strong case. Make your main point. Elicit action. "I try to get people to buy in before I ever ask for the action," he says.

Early in his career, Jedlicka relocated from St. Louis to Colorado without a solid job offer in place. It was then that his persuasive writing skills were put to the test. His job-search strategy included creating cover letters that showed he knew his industry and the top companies and professionals within it. "I had some semblance of a cover-letter skeleton, which I would then customize for every job opportunity I sought," he says. "I would do a fair amount of investigation on Web sites or talk to anybody I knew to understand the company's motives, competencies, and core mission so as to drive home that message in my cover letter." He says it's also important to present and deliver a résumé in an up-to-date format and to share drafts of it with your peers, friends, and family for feedback.

However, you're not finished once you get the job. Instead, you need to continually seek out avenues for self-improvement, Jedlicka says. "The way you present yourself both in person and in writing is so important. It's not just your formal education that can win you a good job. It's also the other areas in which you seek enlightenment by doing additional reading, getting to know the industry you're interested in, getting to know the people within the industry, and really query them. Ask them where they see things going."

Questions

1. How did Jedlicka prepare his cover letters? How could you tweak his technique to use in your own job hunting?
2. Think about the industry you are interested in, how can you continually seek out avenues for self-improvement once you have your foot in the door. Where would you start?

Source: Frank Jedlicka in discussion with the author, August 2010.

information. Describe the job, or jobs, you are applying for and the skills required. Doing so will help the person decide what to focus on when writing the letter or what to talk about during a conversation with a potential employer.

Your Portfolio

Potential employers might want to see samples of work you have done. Rather than sending them the material, include this phrase at the bottom of your résumé:

"Portfolio available upon request."

-OR-

"Password-protected portfolio available upon request." (for e-portfolios only)

You will learn more about the contents of a portfolio later in this chapter.

Contact your references before you begin interviewing, and they will serve you well throughout your job search.

What *Not* to Include on Résumés

Many first-time résumé writers make the mistake of including information usually saved for an application form. **Application forms** are used internally by human resources departments for background checks and by small business owners for hiring purposes. If you are invited to interview, you might be asked to fill out an internal application while you wait for the interviewer. On an application form, you are typically asked to supply full addresses of your employers and schools you attended. You might also be asked for salary information and the reasons why you left your previous jobs. If a company requests your permission for a background check, you will probably be asked for your social security number. This is the only time you should offer it.

Your résumé, however, is not the place for application-form information. Limit employers' addresses to the city and state. Indicate only the months and years of your employment. In addition, never include information about your children, race, national origin, health status, or religion on a résumé or an application form.

To prevent anyone from altering your information, save your résumé as a PDF before sending it. Finally, never include dishonest information on your résumé. Lying about your work experience or degrees attained is a dangerous move for applicants. Not only does it compromise your integrity, but your "fibs" might not survive a background check. Even if you were hired, employers would soon see you lacked the experience to do the job well and they could terminate you if they discovered that you had lied on your résumé.[6]

6 How Does Technology Affect Résumé Writing?

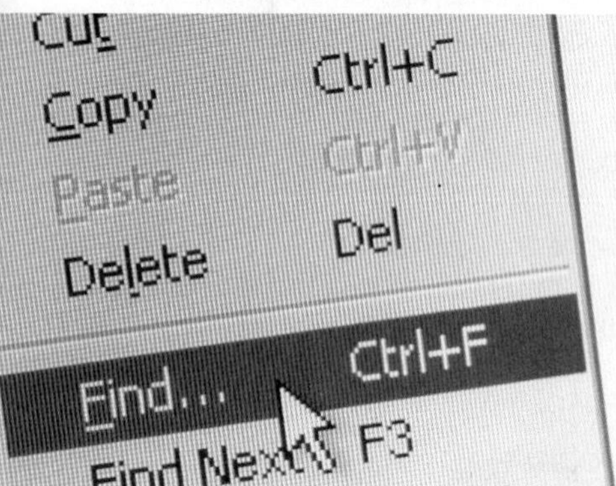

The most important thing about a résumé is actually getting it in front of the right people. As we mentioned earlier, in today's world, résumés are usually first "seen" by computers. Although computers are unbiased, they are also unforgiving. Job seekers must format their résumés in a way that passes both computer and manager screening.

Key Words

Because most companies post job positions on their Web sites and on Internet job boards, human resource managers are often inundated with résumés. To manage the flow, computer software is commonly used for initial screenings. The software searches for key words within a résumé. **Key words** are specific words pertaining to a position.

If the key words are found during a computer scan, the résumé is accepted. For instance a résumé for a sales position might be scanned for words such as *cold-calling, prospecting, revenue, quota, account management, territory, business development,* and *commission.* A job's key words might also describe interpersonal qualities such as *assertive* and *diplomatic,* or skills such as *certification required.* Review job postings for their key words and include them in your résumé. Your résumé is more likely to be accepted following a computer screening, which means a human will soon be reading it.

Scannable Résumés

Printed résumés are ideal for a hand-delivered presentation. However, they might not scan well because the screening software used by companies often can't read them unless they are formatted appropriately. **Scannable résumés** typically have very little formatting and font styles. Although they have less aesthetic appeal, they are more easily read by a computer.

Use sans serif fonts, such as Verdana and Arial, rather than serif fonts, such as Times New Roman or Georgia. Don't use bullets, boldface, or italics. Scanners also have difficulty reading condensed versions of fonts because the letters are pushed so close together. For example, look at the differences in the following fonts:

- ***Easy to Scan:*** This sentence is written in Verdana, a sans serif, uncondensed font.
- ***Difficult to Scan:*** *This sentence is written in Arial Narrow, a sans serif, condensed font.*

Exhibit 14-16 shows a résumé in scannable format. Notice the difference in fonts, formatting, and spacing. The words that appear in yellow in the exhibit are key words. However, they should not be highlighted in an actual résumé.

Exhibit 14-16 A Scannable Résumé

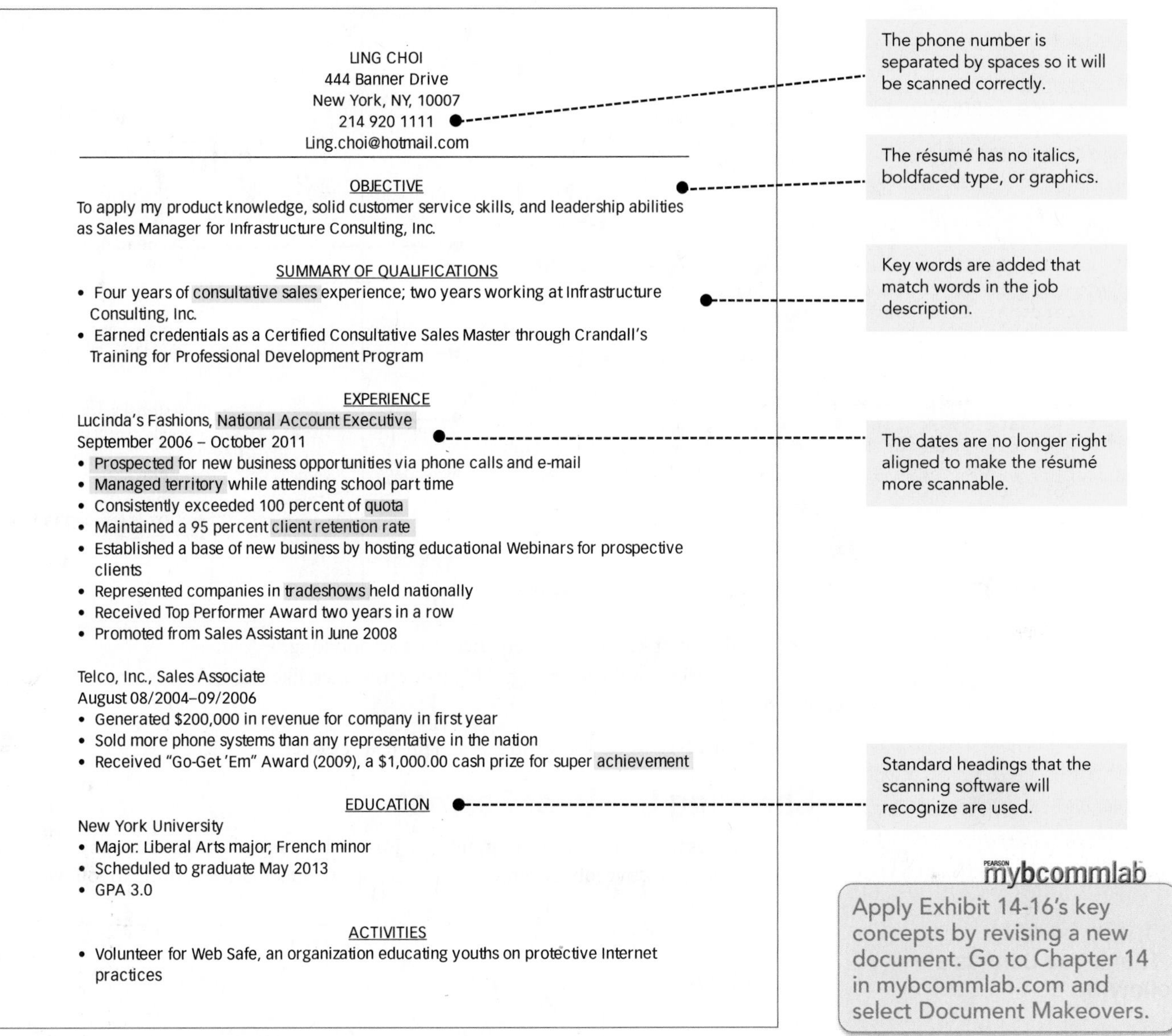

LING CHOI
444 Banner Drive
New York, NY, 10007
214 920 1111
Ling.choi@hotmail.com

OBJECTIVE

To apply my product knowledge, solid customer service skills, and leadership abilities as Sales Manager for Infrastructure Consulting, Inc.

SUMMARY OF QUALIFICATIONS

- Four years of consultative sales experience; two years working at Infrastructure Consulting, Inc.
- Earned credentials as a Certified Consultative Sales Master through Crandall's Training for Professional Development Program

EXPERIENCE

Lucinda's Fashions, National Account Executive
September 2006 – October 2011

- Prospected for new business opportunities via phone calls and e-mail
- Managed territory while attending school part time
- Consistently exceeded 100 percent of quota
- Maintained a 95 percent client retention rate
- Established a base of new business by hosting educational Webinars for prospective clients
- Represented companies in tradeshows held nationally
- Received Top Performer Award two years in a row
- Promoted from Sales Assistant in June 2008

Telco, Inc., Sales Associate
August 08/2004–09/2006

- Generated $200,000 in revenue for company in first year
- Sold more phone systems than any representative in the nation
- Received "Go-Get 'Em" Award (2009), a $1,000.00 cash prize for super achievement

EDUCATION

New York University

- Major: Liberal Arts major; French minor
- Scheduled to graduate May 2013
- GPA 3.0

ACTIVITIES

- Volunteer for Web Safe, an organization educating youths on protective Internet practices

The phone number is separated by spaces so it will be scanned correctly.
The résumé has no italics, boldfaced type, or graphics.
Key words are added that match words in the job description.
The dates are no longer right aligned to make the résumé more scannable.
Standard headings that the scanning software will recognize are used.

PEARSON mybcommlab

Apply Exhibit 14-16's key concepts by revising a new document. Go to Chapter 14 in mybcommlab.com and select Document Makeovers.

Plain-Text Résumés

Many people send formatted résumés as attachments to e-mail messages. However, e-mail recipients often worry about viruses associated with attachments. To reduce their concern, consider pasting your résumé directly into the e-mail message. However, when you do this, you must use a **plain-text résumé**—a résumé saved in a .txt file that has no special formatting, fonts, or layout. Otherwise, your recipient's e-mail system and scanning software might not interpret the formatting correctly.

To create a plain text résumé, save the word processing version of your résumé as an ASCII file (plain text). During the conversion, the plain-text version will not distinguish justification, tabs, fonts, hyphens, italicizing, underlining, and graphics. Nor will it interpret boxes, graphics, and columns. Plain-text format is a "bare bones" presentation. Its sole purpose is to survive a computer scan and avoid word processing software incompatibilities.

The résumé might look rather strange with its formatting removed, in which case you will have to edit it somewhat. The following are some tips for doing so:

- Consider using equal signs or dashes to create lines that separate sections (====== or ------------).
- Change bullets points to * or + signs.
- Do not use tabs or margin justification to align sentences; instead, use spaces.

Exhibit 14-17 A Section of a Plain-Text Résumé

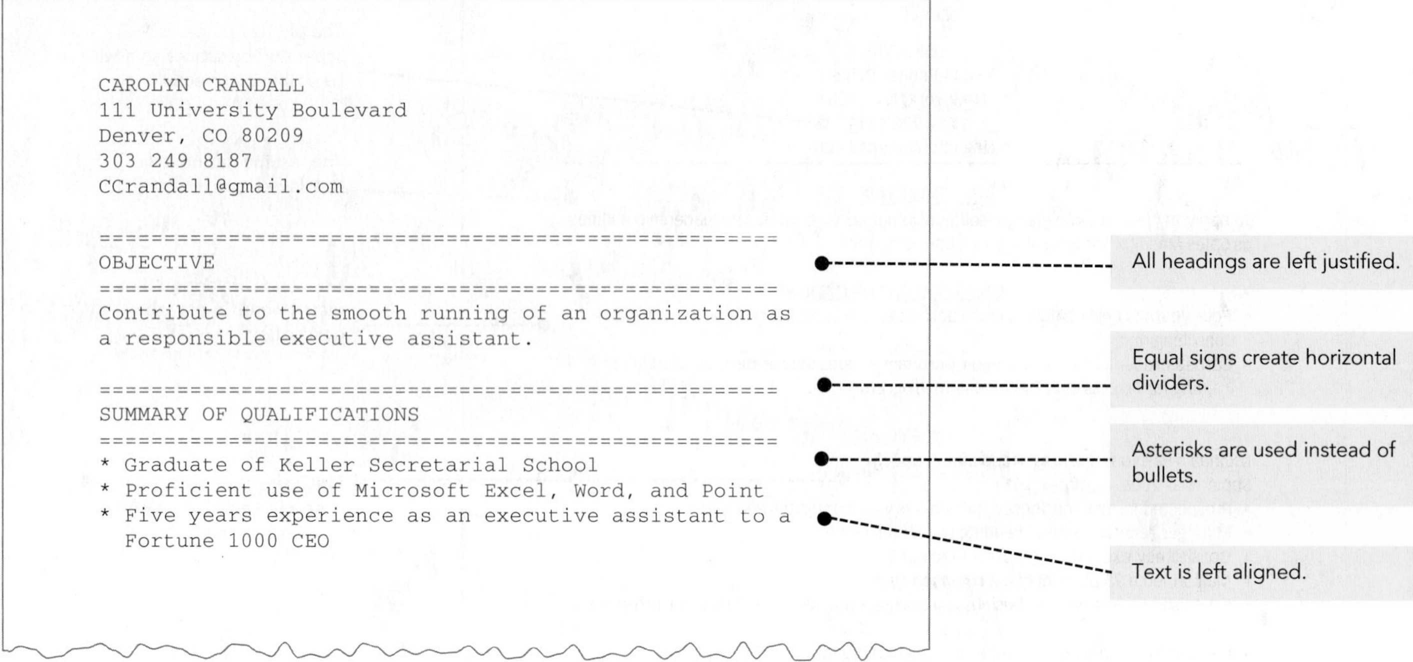

```
CAROLYN CRANDALL
111 University Boulevard
Denver, CO 80209
303 249 8187
CCrandall@gmail.com

=====================================================
OBJECTIVE
=====================================================
Contribute to the smooth running of an organization as
a responsible executive assistant.

=====================================================
SUMMARY OF QUALIFICATIONS
=====================================================
* Graduate of Keller Secretarial School
* Proficient use of Microsoft Excel, Word, and Point
* Five years experience as an executive assistant to a
  Fortune 1000 CEO
```

All headings are left justified.
Equal signs create horizontal dividers.
Asterisks are used instead of bullets.
Text is left aligned.

- Use the Enter key to break sentences that are too long.
- Begin all lines at the left margin. Plain-text résumés, like scannable résumés, can exceed one page.

See **Exhibit 14-17** to view a section of a plain-text résumé.

Choosing the Best Format

When you respond to a job posting, use the format best suited to the company's system. However, as a proactive job seeker, send a paper copy of a formatted résumé to follow-up. If

Exhibit 14-18
A Thank-You Card as a Follow Up

May 11, 2011

Ms. Hartford:

Thank you again for considering my application for the position of Sales Manager. I am very enthusiastic about the position. As promised in my e-mail, I have enclosed a formatted version of my résumé and cover letter for your review.

I will follow-up with you next week with the goal of scheduling an interview.

Sincerely,

Ling Choi

you e-mailed your résumé in text format, let the recipient know you will send a formatted version via standard mail. Then, send the hard copy immediately with a copy of your cover letter and a handwritten note on quality, professional card stock. The note, such as the one in **Exhibit 14-18**, reminds your contact of your earlier correspondence. For tips on making print-based and text résumés look their best, refer to **Exhibit 14-19**.

Exhibit 14-19 **Tips for Formatting and Sending a Résumé**

	Hard Copy Formatted Résumé	Scannable or Plain Text Résumé
Format	Create a Word document and save as a PDF file.	Create an ASCII version of your résumé by saving it as a .txt file.
Paper	Use résumé-grade paper (off-white or cream).	For a scanned résumé: Use 8 ½" by 11" nontextured paper (white).
Style	Use different fonts, boldface, underlines, italics, graphics, boxes, and columns to create an easy-to-read résumé with aesthetic appeal.	Do not use different fonts, boldface, underlines, italics, graphics, boxes, or columns because they will not scan. Use a lot of white space for an easy-to-scan résumé.
Font	Use a traditional font.	Do not use a condensed font. The closer the letters are, the greater the risk is the words will not scan well.
Bullet Points	Use bullet points to call attention to your accomplishments.	Use asterisks (*) or plus (+) signs to call attention to your accomplishments. Bullets do not scan well.
Alignment and Margins	Align and justify the text and margins to create a clean presentation.	Do not justify the text, use tabs, or align the margins. For scanning purposes, use spaces to align the text.
Length	Stick to one page. Keep your résumé succinct and relevant.	Employers understand that text-formatted résumés often exceed one page.
Sending Method	Mail both a text version of your résumé for scanning and a formatted version for reading.	If you are e-mailing your résumé, indicate the position and reference number (found on the job ad) in your subject line. Use a text version of your résumé in the body of your e-mail, and inform the recipient that you are sending a hard copy in Word by regular mail.
Key Words	Use the key words found in job postings because they indicate the exact qualities that managers want. Do not abbreviate any words. Diversify your action and descriptive words to showcase all of your abilities.	Use key words in your résumé so they are scanned. Write out all words and eliminate hyphens and dashes.

7 How Can You Create an Impressive Portfolio?

A **portfolio** is a collection of your best work. Portfolios are not just for artists. They are an effective way set you apart from the crowd. The examples in your portfolio should be relevant to the job you are applying for and support any claims you made in your résumé and cover letter. Organize your examples in professional binders that you can bring with you to interviews and share with potential employers.

A portfolio provides potential employers actual examples of your success.

E-portfolios, or portfolios in an electronic format, are becoming increasingly popular. You can store them on a USB drive or post them on a Web site. For certain jobs, such as a Web-design position, e-portfolios are a must. The person interviewing will need to view the material online, see and hear all of the online effects, and interact with it. However, it is still wise to print out sample color copies of your work to share. They will also come in handy in case of an equipment failure. Delivering an impressive portfolio or e-portfolio is a three-step process. Next, we discuss each step.

Collect Materials

If you haven't spent much time in the workforce, you might believe you have nothing to put in a portfolio. Not true. Your portfolio can include materials associated with your activities, education, training, personal projects, and internships, as long as those materials are evidence of the skills and experience for the position you're applying for. The following are some ideas for your portfolio:

- Awards you have received
- Copies of your diplomas and certificates
- Copies of your transcripts
- Samples of your work related to the position or transferrable to it
- News articles related to your accomplishments
- Evidence of your military experience
- List of references and letters of recommendation
- Your résumé

Assemble Your Portfolio

Begin grouping your material into categories. Then decide which categories are applicable to the job or industry you are pursuing. Some people keep a "master portfolio" of all of their materials and then select items out of that portfolio, targeted to the job they are pursuing.

For a printed portfolio, prepare a professional-looking cover sheet for the front of your binder with your name and contact information. Within the binder, use clear protector sheets for your examples and tabs to separate the categories of material. You can add brief captions for photos, articles, or anything that needs explanation. Keep your portfolio simple, but elegant. It should contain *samples* of your work, not everything you have created in the course of your career or college years. Hiring managers do not have time to examine every piece in your portfolio, and you will typically have only a brief amount of time to review the portfolio with them.

If you choose an electronic portfolio, you might need to scan in some of your work. Or, you might decide to combine parts of multiple documents into a single file. Additionally, you may have links to actual Web sites. In any case, convert your portfolio to PDF format so it cannot be tampered with. For additional security, consider using a key and password to protect your portfolio. (Provide the key and password only upon request.)

Send Your Portfolio

Sending a portfolio that consists of hard copies to every company is hardly feasible or even advisable. Imagine the space it would take up in a manager's office, not to mention the cost to you. It is never good practice to send your portfolio with your résumé. Instead, provide your hardcopy portfolio only when a manager requests it. Include the line, "Portfolio available upon request" at the bottom of your résumé.

If you send an e-portfolio to an interested manager, send it via thumb drive or as a link to your Web site. In your e-mail, include a list of the contents and instructions for viewing the portfolio's contents. Instructions are particularly important if your portfolio requires extra steps to review, such as clicking on the proper files, loading a disc, and so forth.

Finally, remember that an online portfolio can be viewed by anyone. If you include examples of work performed while working for a former employer, do not post it without the employer's permission. Your work product belongs to the company that employed you during the work's completion. If the work is proprietary, there could be legal ramifications for posting it. Due to the risk of identity theft, never include your social security number on anything posted on the Internet, and make sure your social security number is blacked out on transcripts or other records.

You should now have a well-crafted cover letter, professional résumé, and quality portfolio at your fingertips. Before you share the packet with a potential employer, review the following tips to ensure your success.

There are many more than two ways to send your portfolio.

- ***Get a "second set of eyes."*** After spending a great deal of time on a document, it is easy to miss errors, problems with alignment, and misspellings. Have a professional, preferably one in a hiring role, critique the contents of your application packet. Prepare to edit your résumé and cover letter more than once.
- ***Avoid technical glitches.*** Send your résumé electronically to a trusted friend first. Can your friend read it easily? Do attached documents open without issue? This simple step can make all the difference in your job application process.
- ***Be your own PR manager and circulate your material.*** Once you have a résumé and cover letter, consider all the people who may be able to help you get noticed. Professors, family friends, relatives, employers, volunteer coordinators, and coaches are probably just a few of the people who would be willing to lend a hand. Share your résumés and selected contents of your portfolio with them. Make sure they understand what your skills and experience are and the type of work you are looking for. They can promote you to others and expand your network.
- ***Get your résumé and application packet to the right person.*** Finding the right person to send your résumé and application packet to is often the most critical part of your job hunt. What happens if no contact person is listed for a job opening? In today's world of nameless, faceless, global job postings, it's highly likely that the only contact you will find is a general human resources or information e-mail address—not the name of a human being. In this case, get ready for some detective work and networking. You can certainly call the company or visit the Web site to try and find the right person to receive your résumé. Or, you can use your own network of contacts to find the right person.
- ***Start with your teachers and people from the career center.*** Span out to people you have met during internships and while in volunteer positions. Network with your alumni association or other people you know who work for the company where you want to apply. Perhaps one of them knows someone who knows the hiring manager.

Summary *Synthesize What You Have Learned*

1. What makes up a winning application packet?

An application packet should contain evidence of a candidate's skills and abilities. It consists of a résumé, cover letter, letters of reference, and a portfolio. The portfolio itself may contain documents of achievement, awards, transcripts, artwork, writing samples, and stellar academic projects.

2. What are the different types of cover letters?

Depending on your job-seeking approach and purpose, choose between three types of cover letters: 1) application cover letter, 2) prospecting cover letter, and 3) networking cover letter. An application cover letter responds to a specific job advertisement or posting. A prospecting cover letter is useful for proactive job seekers. Use it when you identify a company that you believe needs your skills. The letter introduces you to a company, identifies a need, and proposes your skills or strategy as a solution. A networking cover letter is a way to connect with professional contacts. After you identify a professional you want to meet, the letter extends an introduction and requests an appointment to talk.

3. How can you make your cover letter stand out?

A winning cover letter must capture a hiring manager's attention and make him or her interested in reviewing the résumé. The letter has three components: 1) introduction, 2) body, and 3) closing. The introduction is the first paragraph of a cover letter. It should inspire a hiring manager to keep reading. This section introduces the applicant, lets the reader know to which position the applicant is applying, and where the applicant learned of the position. It should also refer to the applicant's accompanying résumé. The body is the second part of the cover. It highlights an applicant's experience and explains why the applicant is a good fit for the position. A job seeker must first research the company and industry in order to tailor both the cover letter and the résumé. The closing is the final paragraph. It includes a plan of action, informing the reader how the applicant plans to follow up on the status of his application.

4. Which résumé formats are most common?

There are three typical résumé formats: 1) chronological, 2) functional, and 3) hybrid. The most commonly used résumé formats are chronological and functional. A chronological résumé outlines a candidate's skills and abilities and the progression of his or her career in chronological order. However, it tends to easily highlight a candidate's employment gaps. A functional résumé is organized by skill sets rather than job history. A hybrid résumé is a combination of chronological and functional résumés. Video résumés have become more popular among candidates looking for creative ways to promote themselves.

5. How do you write a winning résumé?

The components of a winning résumé include 1) professional objective, 2) summary of qualifications, 3) education, 4) professional experience, and 5) honors and awards. The professional objective is a short statement indicating your career aspiration. The summary of qualifications identifies key qualities and skills you have that pertain to the position in question. The education section focuses on your degrees, certificates attained, instructional courses completed, and your GPA if it is impressive. The professional experience section outlines the jobs you held. The honors and awards section lists accolades you received for your work.

6. How does technology impact résumé writing?

Using key words that are relevant to the position you are applying for and will be picked up by screening software will help get it accepted. Create both a plain text résumé as well as a formatted résumé (in PDF format). The plain text résumé can be pasted into an e-mail or into an online job application form without any problems. It is easily scanned. The PDF version of your résumé will be more attractive to the reader and can be sent as an attachment or printed and mailed.

7. How can you create an impressive portfolio?

A portfolio is an organized collection of best work. Include any awards you have received; copies of your diplomas and certificates; copies of your transcripts; news articles related to your accomplishments; evidence of your military experience; a list of references and letters of recommendation; and your résumé. Organize your examples in professional binders that you can take with you to interviews and share with potential employers. E-portfolios, or portfolios in an electronic format, can be stored on a USB drive or posted on a Web site. Provide the person interviewing you with a list of its contents and instructions for viewing the portfolio.

PEARSON mybcommlab™ Are you an active learner? Go to **mybcommlab.com** to master Chapter 14's content. Chapter 14's interactive activities include:

- Customizable Study Plan and Chapter 14 practice quizzes
- Chapter 14 Simulation, Cover Letters and Résumés, that helps you think critically and prepare to make choices in the business world
- Chapter 14 Video Exercise, Building Careers and Writing Résumés: Giant Robot Magazine, which shows you how textbook concepts are put into practice every day
- Flash cards for mastering the definition of chapter terms
- Interactive Lessons that visually review key chapter concepts
- Document Makeovers for hands-on, scored practice in revising documents

Know It Reflect, Respond, and Express

Build Your Critical Thinking Skills

Critical Thinking Questions

1. Research a company you would like to work for through the company's Web site and any other sources of information you can find. What is the corporate culture of your chosen company? What different types of people and environments would you be working with? How can you gain more knowledge about the company?

Critical Thinking Scenario

You are Jenny Bear's student mentor, and she has approached you for some professional advice. Jenny is an ambitious student with aspirations of securing a position as a business development executive with an Internet multimedia company. She would eventually like to obtain an MBA from Harvard. She loves volunteering and is an avid baker. As a sophomore, Jenny sees her graduating friends struggle to find jobs or get into graduate programs. Jenny is worried that she too will have difficulty finding employment when she graduates.

Jenny knows that her résumé must demonstrate leadership, service, and critical thinking skills. She needs your help to form a strategy for success.

Questions

1. Come up with a community service project for Jenny that uses both her business and baking skills.
2. Write a networking cover letter to a nearby charity proposing the community service project and requesting a time to discuss it in detail.

Write It Draft, Revise, and Finalize

Create Your Own Success Story

1. In this exercise you will create a "Goal Résumé." First think about your ultimate dream job. Then imagine you have the training, funding, and experience to land the job you have always dreamed of in your field.

   By creating an imaginary "Goal Résumé" you are learning to visualize a path to your ultimate job. This résumé helps clarify where you might need to work, whom you might need to meet, and what you might need to learn to fulfill your dreams. You may never work at those exact jobs, but seeing them on a résumé will help you chart your course.

   a. Start at the "end." Imagine you have achieved your dream position. What is the title of the position? What tasks does it involve? What skills and education does it require? Do the necessary research to find the answers, if you are unsure.

   b. Next, come up with at least three imaginary jobs that you held before getting your dream position. What were they? What did they involve? Again, do research if you need to.

   c. Now create a résumé that outlines the path that got you to your dream position. Use a hybrid format with these components:

   - ***Objective.*** List your dream objective.
   - ***Core Skills.*** Provide a quick summary of your skill areas.
   - ***Education and Training.*** List any degrees or certifications you might need.
   - ***Professional Experience.*** List at least three jobs you held, along with the tasks you performed and your accomplishments. The dates you indicate on your résumé should correlate with your possible goals for achievement.

2. Revise the following sentences from cover letters to get rid of the grammar and punctuation errors.

   a. I will follow-up next week with you in an effert to schedule a interview.

   b. I am writting to express my interest in you're job posting.

   c. My qualifications is a perfect match for your jobs' required qualifications.

3. Answer the questions in Exhibit 14-1 to evaluate the areas of your professional development and experience. After writing down your answers, evaluate the different aspects that need more attention or development. Create a to-do list for the areas you want to develop as you complete your degree.
4. Write an application cover letter that answers a specific job listing. Practice writing in business letter format, so include your address, the date, a greeting, the content, and a closing.
5. Write a networking cover letter to someone you consider a mentor in your field, such as an employer or your instructor. Introduce yourself and reason for writing, why you are writing the specific person, and invite the mentor to communicate with you further. Include an offer to help the reader in some way, so you create goodwill and mutually benefit from a meeting.
6. Write a cover letter in which you express your interest in a position and why you feel you are the best candidate for it. Revise the letter with a "you" attitude, focusing on the recipient of the letter (specifically a hiring manager). Analyze what changes you made to direct your letter to a specific audience and include a summary with the two drafts.

7. Locate a job posting online or in a local newspaper that includes a contact person for the job position. Write a prospecting cover letter to the company. Don't forget to include how you learned about the position and why you feel you are the best candidate, giving specific examples for the description of your abilities.
8. Locate a job posting that does not have a contact person listed within the description. Using either the Internet or by contacting the company, find out the contact's name for the job description and write a targeted cover letter for the position.
9. Write professional objectives for the following positions. Remember to keep them job-specific and action oriented.
   a. Sales Manager
   b. Accountant
   c. Technical Writer
10. Create a chronological résumé with the following information and headings: your contact information, an objective, your education, experience, and references statement (upon request or something similar). Remember to use reverse chronological order for both your education and employment listings.
11. Create a functional résumé with the following information included: your contact information, at least three skill sets and your experiences listed with the appropriate section, your education, and a references statement.
12. Create a hybrid résumé using both the chronological and functional formats. Include the following information: your contact information, your employment experience using skill sets or not, your education, and a references statement.
13. Practice formatting the experience section of your résumé using different designs for the information you present. Include the company name, your job title, the times you worked there, the location of the company, and two to three job duties for each position. Write the job duties in active voice and as transferable skills that could be used for different types of positions. Emphasize your accomplishments. For example, you could use "Maintained cleanliness of the facility" as a job duty for a busboy at a restaurant. Use different text designs such as italics or bold to help organize your information. Include at least three different examples.
14. Format the education section at least three different ways using various types of text design to help the information stand out. Include your major, minor, GPA if 3.0 or above, the institution name and location, and graduation date.
15. Compile a list of 15–20 key words that pertain to your degree and desired career. Look at a job posting if you need some ideas. Compare your list to your classmates' lists.
16. Format your résumé into a scannable format using the example in the chapter as a guide. Do not use underline, bold, or italics, and use consistent headings throughout the document.
17. Generate a text-formatted résumé to create a plain text version you can paste into an e-mail. Save your résumé as an ASCII file, use a common font like Courier, do not use bold, italics, or underlines, use asterisks or plus signs for bullet points, and align all information left.
18. Choose three people from whom you solicit recommendations, such as professors or employers. Write a brief e-mail to each person inquiring if they would write the recommendations. Volunteer to give each person a copy of your résumé. Copy your instructor on the e-mail. Collect the letters you receive and place them in your portfolio.
19. Write your personal mission statement that reveals your personal values. It should be a single statement that describes you and your approach to your chosen career. Add your personal mission statement to your portfolio.

Speak It *Discuss, Listen, and Understand*

Build Your Leadership and Teamwork Skills

1. Identify a specific position you would be interested in and draft a cover letter and résumé tailored to it.
   a. Get into groups of four. Then, in pairs, review each other's résumés and cover letters. Be sure to share the position you chose with your group members. Critique each document by answering the following questions:
      - Did your partner have an attention-grabbing first paragraph in his or her cover letter?
      - What was mentioned in the cover letter that sparked interest in seeing the résumé?
      - Were the cover letter and résumé tailored to meet the position?
      - What suggestions could you offer your partner to better prepare for the position?
      - Did the résumé have active verbs? Did it quantify your partner's success?
      - Did the examples in the résumé best showcase your partner's abilities?
      - Would your partner's résumé distinguish him or her from other candidates?
      - As an employer, would you ask your partner to interview based on the information provided?

   b. When you're finished, switch partners and follow the same steps as before.
   c. After each person's résumé has been reviewed by at least two different people, discuss the following as a group:
      - Name something you admire about one of the résumés or cover letters you critiqued. What makes the information effective?
      - Who best showcased their talents in their résumé? Explain why.
      - Whose cover letter had the most impact and why?

   d. Now revise your own résumé and cover letter based on what you learned in this exercise.

2. Find a job description online or in a local newspaper and write down the job qualifications required for the position. Create a couple of sentences that would answer those qualifications and describe how you fit the position. What is the importance of using the same terminology in your letter that is in the job posting? Bring to class the job description and your examples. In teams, critique how well you described your fit with the position.

Do It *Document Your Success Track Record*

Build Your e-Portfolio

In this exercise you will research a company, develop a specific way in which you can make a difference in an entry-level job, and write a prospecting cover letter to accompany it. For example, if you are applying to be a customer service representative in telecommunications, write a cover letter describing how you would improve sales through better customer response. Also, describe how you would enlist happy customers to connect you with other clients. The purpose of this exercise is to develop an example of your critical thinking skills for your portfolio.

1. Research a company in your industry of choice. Read news articles, annual reports, and press releases on the firm's Web site. Identify a problem they need solved, or a strategy for implementing one of their goals.
2. Create an outline for improving the business. The business outline identifies the problem, provides a solution, and includes a plan for implementation. As you prepare the outline, consult with professors and even people you know working for the company.
3. Draft a prospecting cover letter to accompany the business outline.
4. Once you complete the business strategy and cover letter, get honest feedback. Update the strategy and letter accordingly. They might be useful in the future to secure a job or internship.

Business in Action
How Does Google Attract and Retain the Best?

Up to this point, you have heard a lot about how job seekers attract attention through well-written résumés and cover letters. However, you haven't heard much about how companies attract qualified job seekers. Here's your chance to hear "the other side" of the story.

To most of us, Google is a user-friendly Internet search engine that helps us find information on a daily basis. The leader in its industry, Google keeps improving and developing new services by investing in people with top talent and creative minds. So how does Google attract and retain its employees? They use both traditional and creative methods for recruiting.

To start, when people love their jobs, word travels fast. Employee referrals play a big role in Google's recruitment process, along with professional networking sites such as LinkedIn. Google uses these methods because professional communication and networking-generated leads are highly valued in today's job market. College recruitment efforts and internships also play a part in Google's recruiting strategy.

Additionally, Google uses its own advertising platform, AdWords, to post job ads. The ads pop up when Internet visitors type certain search words. Google also holds contests, one of which is a software writing competition with $50,000 in prizes, plus a job offer for the winner. The company also posts brainteasers on billboards that attract mathematically minded people to the Google's recruiting Web site.

Why would Google go to all of that trouble? Obviously, the company sees its employees as an investment, so much so that it offers incomparable benefits to keep them. These benefits include free breakfast, lunch, and dinner; free yoga and massages onsite; running trails and free recreation; valet parking; a casual work environment; and a "bring your dog to work every day" policy. All these perks help make up for the fact that Google employees often work very long hours onsite.

If all of that leaves you asking, "How do I get a job in a place like that?" rest assured you are not alone. Coveted places of employment such as Google attract thousands of applicants. In short, if you want to work for the best, commit yourself to being the best.

Questions

1. To find the best employees, Google goes out if its way to develop creative recruiting strategies. What are some of the recruiting strategies employed by the companies you want to work for? To be "found" by these companies, what specific adjustments will you make to your job-searching tools?
2. What method do you think would be best for submitting your application packet to Google, if you wanted to interview with the company?

Sources: "A Look Inside the Google Talent Machine," *Human Resources,* July 25, 2006, accessed at http://www.humanresourcesmagazine.com; "Benefits," *Google .com,* accessed September 29, 2010 at http://www.google.com/intl/en/jobs/lifeat google/benefits/index.html.

Key Terms

Application cover letter. A letter sent along with a résumé, portfolio, and letter(s) of recommendation in response to a job posting. *(p. 401)*

Application forms. Documents used internally by Human Resources departments for background checks, and by small business owners for hiring purposes. *(p. 420)*

Application packet. A collection of documents including a résumé, cover letter, professional portfolio, and letters of recommendation used as an application for employment. *(p. 400)*

Awards, honors, and activities section. The section of a résumé presenting an applicant's awards, honors, and activities, especially those indicating leadership. *(p. 418)*

Chronological résumé. A résumé outlining a job seeker's work experience and education in chronological order. *(p. 409)*

Contact header. The section of a résumé providing a job seeker's contact information. *(p. 413)*

Cover letters. A letter sent by a job seeker to a prospective employer, accompanying a résumé, portfolio, and letters of recommendation, as a means of introduction. *(p. 421)*

Education and training. The section of a résumé presenting an applicant's academic and professional education. *(p. 415)*

E-portfolio. An electronic portfolio stored on a thumb drive or Web site. *(p. 424)*

Functional résumé. A résumé categorizing a job seeker's work experience in skill categories rather than by date. *(p. 410)*

Hybrid résumé. A résumé that contains elements of both functional and chronological résumés. *(p. 411)*

Key words. Specific words pertaining to an employment position in a résumé that can be read by applicant screening program. *(p. 420)*

Networking cover letter. A cover letter is sent by professionals to introduce themselves to a potential contact and proposing a meeting. *(p. 402)*

Plain-text résumé. A résumé saved in ASCII format as a .txt file. It has no special formatting, fonts, or layout. *(p. 421)*

Portfolio. A collection of relevant work samples that support statements made in a job seeker's résumé and cover letter. *(p. 423)*

Professional experience. The section of a résumé highlighting specific professional accomplishments for each position. *(p. 416)*

Professional objective. The section of a résumé providing a succinct statement of the job seeker's goals. *(p. 413)*

Prospecting cover letter. A letter sent by a job seeker when prospecting for an unadvertised position. This letter proposes the job seeker as a candidate for employment. *(p. 422)*

Qualitative example. An example that states what you did. *(p. 417)*

Quantitative example. An example that states what you did and measures how well you did it. *(p. 417)*

Scannable résumés. Résumés that are easily read by computers due to little formatting and font styling. *(p. 420)*

Summary of qualifications. The section of a résumé highlighting a job seeker's most relevant qualities as they pertain to the position applied. *(p. 414)*

Transferable skills. Skills gained in one position that relate to those necessary for another position. *(p. 409)*

Video résumé. A short video that accompanies a physical résumé and is used to demonstrate an applicant's interest and passion for a particular type of work. *(p. 412)*

Review Questions *Test Yourself*

1. What documents go into an application packet?
2. How should you rank your accomplishments as you start writing your application packet?
3. What are the three types of cover letters?
4. What information can you include in a prospecting cover letter that could help you create a job for yourself?
5. What methods can you use to discover a contact name if it is not listed with a job ad?
6. What are the three steps to writing a riveting cover letter?
7. What information should be included in the closing paragraph of a cover letter?
8. What is a chronological résumé and how does it highlight your qualifications?
9. What is a functional résumé and how does it highlight your qualifications?
10. Describe a video résumé and explain its advantages and disadvantages.
11. What information should you include in a contact header section and how should it be formatted?
12. What are transferable skills and how can they help the professional experience section of your résumé?
13. What are key words with regard to résumés, and how can you decide which ones are best to use in your résumé?
14. What is a scannable résumé and how do you format it?
15. What is a text-formatted résumé and how do you format it?
16. What information should you include in a portfolio?

Grammar Review *Mastering Accuracy*

Common Preposition and Pronoun Errors

Section I

Each of the following sentences contains one or more common errors in word usage, grammar, or style. Identify the errors. If you have trouble finding the errors, review Sections 1.1.4. and 1.3.4. through 1.3.5. in the handbook (Appendix D) at the back of this textbook.

1. The handbook is located on my desk among the manila folder and electric pencil sharpener.
2. The meeting will be held among the hours of 7:00 P.M. and 8:00 P.M. and be between numerous faculty and staff; however, they will be invited, as well.
3. Even as it grew dark, we continued to walk between the flowers.
4. He negotiates as if they was a trained businessman.
5. Like your immediate supervisor that I am, I must tell you to dress for tomorrow's meeting like your career depended on it.
6. She treats all employees fairly, like they were a part of her immediate family.
7. Nancy might of left a detailed message with instructions on how to handle this situation.
8. I value your opinion as a colleague; moreover, I wished I would of listened to you more often.
9. As an obsessed teenager might, John, who is old enough and should of known better, used the telephone at work for an abundance of personal phone calls.
10. I could of been a rock star, if only I had learned how to play an instrument.

Section II

On a separate sheet of paper, rewrite the following sentences so they are clearer, more professional sounding, grammatically correct, and goodwill oriented.

1. I feel like diving in to the pile of papers on my desk, just to see if anyone comes to my rescue.
2. During the meeting, Daniel bumped in to the projector several times, causing many of us to wonder if he knew what he was doing.
3. Steven walked back into talk to the shop owner, noticing that several customers were in line to purchase the exact same sweater he intended to buy.
4. Sasha referred to the new clothing line, insinuating it's customers were unfashionable, like they had no taste.
5. Its bad enough Greg is talking behind our backs as if were still in high school, but to get caught smoking in the break room was just a dumb move.
6. Return this document to it's rightful owner; moreover, cease and desist snooping through papers, that do not belong to you, and tossing them about in an unruly manner.
7. French, although it is a difficult language that I never studied, seems like it might be exceptionally difficult to learn.
8. They're are an unusually high number of accidents this year, that might indicate a general lack of awareness between the village population.
9. We insist all members of the assembly return to there seats in an orderly manner.
10. Remember to look over they're documents before shipping them to there destination.

Extra Resources *Tools You Can Use*

Books

- Enelow, Wendy S., and Louise M. Kursmack. *Expert Résumés.* Indianapolis, IN: JIST Works, 2007.
- McKay, Dawn Rosenberg. *The Everything Get a Job Book: The Tools and Strategies You Need to Land the Job of Your Dreams.* Cincinnati: Adams Media, 2007.
- Karsh, Brad, with Courtney Pike. *How to Say It on Your Résumé: A Top Recruiting Director's Guide to Writing the Perfect Résumé for Every Job.* Upper Saddle River, NJ: Prentice Hall, 2009.
- Mackay, Harvey. *Use Your Head to Get Your Foot in the Door: Job Search Secrets No One Else Will Tell You.* New York: Portfolio Publishers, Hardcover, 2010.
- Nobel, David. *Gallery of Best Cover Letters: A Collection of Quality Cover Letters By Professional Résumé Writers.* Indianapolis, IN: JIST Works. 2007.
- Satterthwaite, Frank, and Gary D'Orsi. *The Career Portfolio Workbook: Using the Newest Tool in Your Job-Hunting Arsenal to Impress Employers and Land a Great Job.* New York: McGraw-Hill, 2003.

Web Sites

- Hill, Cathy H. "How to Design a Winning Job Portfolio," *eHow.*
- "Common Résumé Writing Mistakes," *5min.*
- "How to find a job using Twitter," *Mashable.*
- "44 Résumé Writing Tips," *Daily Writing Tips.*

"Choose a job you love and you will never have to work a day in your life."

— **Confucius,** Chinese philosopher

Job Interviewing

Securing a Position and Negotiating Your Salary

LEARNING OBJECTIVE QUESTIONS

1. How do you respond to or set up an interview?
2. What types of interviews do employers utilize?
3. How do you prepare for an interview?
4. What should you do on the day of the interview?
5. How do you close an interview?
6. How should job offers, job rejections, and resignations be handled?

mybcommlab Access interactive videos, simulations, sample documents, document makeovers, and assessment quizzes in Chapter 15 of **mybcommlab.com** for mastery of this chapter's objectives.

>>> **Small World Resorts** is an international resort company that caters to corporate clients planning end-of-year incentive trips for their high performers. The company is looking for a new salesperson. The hiring manager is willing to hire and train a college graduate in exchange for the graduate's dedication and results. Robert Kratin and Lucy Ming are two candidates who leave very different impressions with Shawntelle, the hiring manager.

>>> **Robert Kratin**

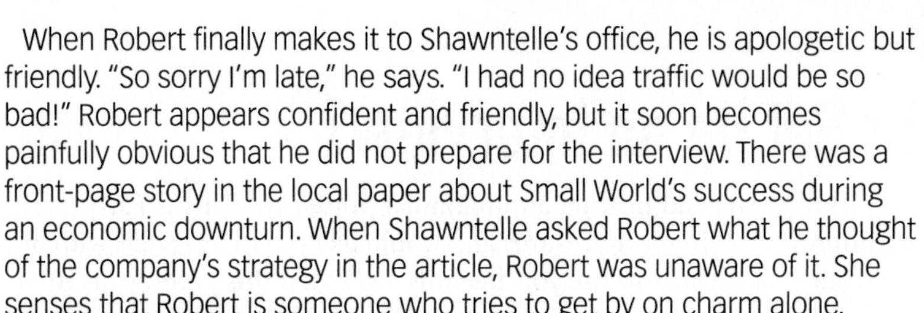

It is 10:10 A.M., and Shawntelle is wondering why the first candidate, Robert Kratin, has not arrived. Shawntelle was hoping to introduce the candidate to the company's vice president of sales before she leaves town for four weeks, but that's not going to happen now.

When Robert finally makes it to Shawntelle's office, he is apologetic but friendly. "So sorry I'm late," he says. "I had no idea traffic would be so bad!" Robert appears confident and friendly, but it soon becomes painfully obvious that he did not prepare for the interview. There was a front-page story in the local paper about Small World's success during an economic downturn. When Shawntelle asked Robert what he thought of the company's strategy in the article, Robert was unaware of it. She senses that Robert is someone who tries to get by on charm alone.

>>> **Lucy Ming**

The next interview begins much better. This candidate is Lucy Ming. When Shawntelle's assistant calls, she tells Shawntelle, "Ms. Ming will be ready promptly at 11:00. She is just finishing her job application." Shawntelle is glad Lucy has arrived on time.

Lucy arrives in the office dressed in a suit and carrying a portfolio. "Thank you for this opportunity," she says, while shaking Shawntelle's hand firmly, smiling, and looking her in the eye. "I am very impressed with Small World Resorts." The interview has not even begun, yet Shawntelle feels like Lucy is polished, genuine, and professional.

Notice that in both interview scenarios, it did not take long for Shawntelle to form an impression. In fact, both candidates made an impression before even meeting her, and Shawntelle had already started to make a choice.

The scenarios described are not far-fetched, nor is the imaginary company, Small World Resorts. The hospitality and tourism industry is one in which the professionals focus on vacation, travel, and entertainment, but they hardly have jobs of leisure. In fact, professionals in this industry work very hard to put the needs of others first. Regardless, this highly competitive field draws candidates with a passion for service and fun.

The largest portion of the hospitality and tourism industry is the accommodations field, which grosses $46 billion a year. Accommodations are the portion of the industry that provides services for travelers such as transportation, vacation planning, food, and lodging. The leisure and hospitality industry as a whole is expected to grow 5 percent by the year 2018.[1]

The employment opportunities in the industry include travel blogging, finance and administration of facilities, travel agencies, and lodging management. Although the positions in hospitality and tourism vary, most of them require employees to interact directly with customers. As a result, employees must be at their best at all times—just like people need to be during job interviews.

Job interviews allow companies to determine whether you are a good fit for a position and the company. The interviews also help you determine whether the company is a good fit for you, your skills, and career goals. Perhaps you are unsure whether you want to work for the company. You might still be learning about the firm's corporate culture and the position's responsibility. Is the culture formal or informal? Is it collaborative or competitive? Likewise, you will want to know about your prospective manager's style. Does this person have a structured management style or a looser approach? Would you like to work for the person? What training will you receive? Of course, compensation and location are other considerations. Is the position near your home, or will you have to commute or relocate?

■ For an interactive, real-world example of this topic, access this chapter's bcomm mini sim entitled Interviewing, located at **mybcommlab.com.**

PEARSON mybcommlab

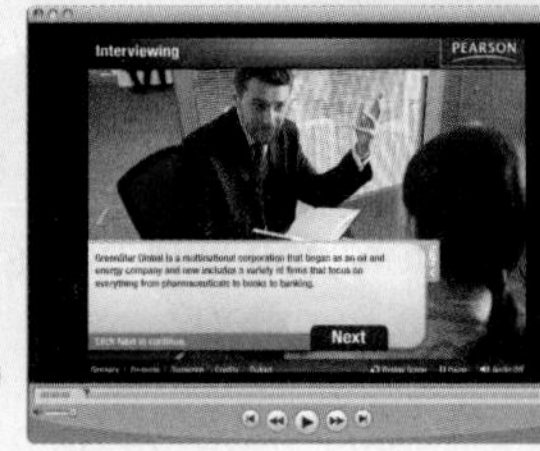

On the other side of the equation, representatives from the company will evaluate you. Candidates might meet with one person or several people from the company over a period of time. The hiring process can take anywhere from a few days to a couple of months. Some interviewers even assign candidates a project or ask for a presentation as part of the interview process, which the interviewer can use to evaluate a candidate's critical thinking and communication skills.

This chapter covers the entire interview process: setting up an interview, understanding different types of interviews, getting ready for them, making a good impression during an interview, and handling both being accepted or rejected for a position. Knowing what to expect during an interview will alleviate your anxiety so you perform at your best.

1 How Do You Respond to or Set Up an Interview?

Imagine answering your phone and hearing an unfamiliar voice say, "This is Patty Grant with Five Star Vacations. We received your résumé and would like you to interview with our vice president of account management. Are you free this week?" At this point, your interview has begun. Mumbling "Uh, okay . . . I guess I can do it next Thursday" will not leave a favorable impression. In the event you are unavailable to take the call, what will the caller hear on your voice mail? Does your voice mail sound professional? Is there music blaring in the background? Employers hire polished candidates. A voice mail message saying, "Yo, dude! I'm not here" will leave a lasting impression—and not a good one.

Avoid these scenarios. Instead, express your gratitude and leave a professional impression by saying, "Thank you for the opportunity. I would like that very much. I am available on Wednesday morning or Thursday afternoon. Will either time work?" Then get the necessary information about the people conducting the interview. Write their names and titles down, which will help you in your interview preparation, as we will discuss later. If you receive more than one name, ask whether you will meet with everyone in a group or separately. Also, depending on the type of position for which you applied, you might be asked to take a skills assessment test before interviewing (more about this later). Ask whether you should arrive early to complete any paperwork. For legal and other reasons, companies often ask candidates to fill out applications.

When scheduling time, be as available and flexible as possible. If you appear too busy for an interview, the company could get the impression you're not very interested in the job.

Offer some times that work on your calendar. Also, when setting an appointment for a phone interview, confirm the time zone from which your interviewer will call. For example, "A phone interview at 10 A.M. Eastern Time works well for me."

Opening Your Own Doors for an Interview

If you don't yet have an interview secured, open your own doors by being proactive. After submitting your résumé, follow up by expressing your interest and offering the company something of value. For instance, you might say, "Mr. Redmond, I am following up on my application for the position of event coordinator at your hotel. I subsequently drafted a strategy for scheduling more winter events after the holiday season. I'd like the opportunity to share that strategy with you."

2 What Types of Interviews Do Employers Utilize?

Companies conduct different types of interviews to field candidates. Become familiar with the types so you know what to expect.

In-Person Interviews

The in-person interview is the most common type of interview employers rely upon when hiring people. In-person interviews typically take place at a company's facility and involve employees and managers who ask a variety of questions of the interviewee. The number of interviews and employees involved varies with the job and the company.

One-on-One Interviews

A **one-on-one interview** involves only one candidate and one interviewer. The type and number of interviews may vary as a candidate progresses through the hiring process. A candidate might meet with one interviewer during the first meeting and multiple interviewers during the second. Or, the candidate might interview with a lower-level manager as a screening procedure during the first interview and a higher-level manager during the second interview.

Group Interviews

When a company wants an interviewee to meet as many people as possible, the company often uses group interviews. **Group interviews** simply involve more than one person. Sometimes hiring managers ask members of their staff for assistance with an interview. Group interviews can leave candidates feeling outnumbered. However, the more people you meet during an interview, the greater your potential impact can be. You will typically be asked only one question by one interviewer at a time, so the process is not as overwhelming as you might assume.

- ***Greet Each Person and Wait to Be Seated.*** Greet each of the interviewers and shake everyone's hands. Always wait to be seated. Usually interviewers will gesture to your seat. Traditionally, sitting at the head of the table establishes dominance, which is an inappropriate position for an interviewee. However, your interviewers might invite you to sit at the head spot, so that everyone in the room can easily interact with you. If instead you are seated across the table from many people, don't be intimidated. Take advantage of the fact that you will easily be able to make eye contact with everyone from this position.
- ***Make Eye Contact with Everyone.*** Make eye contact with all of the interviewers. It is easy to focus on people with whom we feel most comfortable, but others present may perceive it as disrespectful. Since your main focal point will be the person who is asking the question, connect with other participants by occasionally looking at them as well.
- ***Get the Names of Everyone.*** If the people participating in the interview don't give you their business cards, write down all of their names. You can later look up their titles online or call the company's receptionist to find out. Having those names will be useful later when it is time to write thank-you cards. During the interview, address each person by name.

DID YOU KNOW?

According to the Best-Job-Interview Web site, when talking with one interviewer, you should maintain eye contact with the person for at least 10 seconds before looking away and then reestablishing eye contact.

Phone Interviews

A hiring manager might choose a **phone interview** versus a face-to-face for many reasons. For instance, if a position requires telephone sales, the hiring manager might want to get a sense of the candidate's "phone presence." Some human resources representatives use phone interviews to screen candidates and save time for hiring managers. Other times the interviewer or candidate is simply in another town, state, or country and can't initially meet face to face.

Phone interviews have pros and cons. On the one hand, you might feel more comfortable talking from your home or another location of your choice. You can keep an outline of points you would like to cover nearby without the interviewer being aware of it. On the other hand, the interviewer will not have the benefit of seeing your nonverbal cues, poise, and professional appearance. Nor will you have the benefit of seeing his or hers. In most cases, however, an in-person interview follows a phone interview that goes well.

To prepare for a phone interview, do the following:

- ***Have Your Notepad, Pen, and Résumé Ready.*** Note the key points covered during the interview. Since the interviewer will discuss your work experience, have your résumé readily available. Before the interview begins, in the margins of your résumé, jot down the key points and your qualifications you want to cover. You literally need to be "on the same page" as your interviewer.
- ***Choose a Quiet Place.*** Find a place where you can speak uninterrupted for at least an hour while the interview takes place. Allow yourself additional time beforehand to collect yourself and review points you would like to make. Turn off timers, mobile phones, alarms, and other devices that might interrupt your call. Request some private time from roommates or friends who might interrupt.
- ***Charge Your Phone.*** The interviewer will likely call you on a number you provide. Provide a landline number or charge your cell phone in advance, so your battery will not fail mid-interview.
- ***Begin and End the Call with Gratitude.*** Thank the interviewer at the beginning and end of the call. By saying, "Thank you for the opportunity to speak with you today. I have been looking forward to it," you will express both your gratitude and interest in the position.
- ***Use Your Voice.*** Since the interviewer does not have the benefit of seeing your nonverbal cues, your voice inflection is especially important. Don't sink into your most comfortable couch when you take the call. Instead, establish a "ready for business" mindset by sitting upright at a table or by standing. Smile as you speak—it will come through in your voice. Also, dress in a suit or professional clothing for a phone interview to help put you in the right mindset.[2]

Videoconference Interviews

Videoconferencing services allow participants to see and hear each other via computer technology. If you're not accustomed to this technology, you might feel uncomfortable. Treat a **videoconference interview**—a remote interview telecast through computers—as an in-person interview by dressing the part and maintaining eye contact during the conversation. Focus on what is being asked so that you are not distracted by the occasional freeze frames or blurriness that can occur with videoconference technology.

Check your computer, video equipment, or Webcam ahead of time to make sure you are ready for the interview. Remember that not only can the interviewer see you, he or she can see your surroundings as well. Clear away any clutter that is within viewing range. Don't attempt to perform other tasks, such as texting or answering phone calls during the interview, which will come across as rude.

Stress Interviews

Sometimes interviewers will purposely create a stressful environment for the purpose of seeing how a candidate responds under pressure. Employers sometimes conduct **stress interviews** when they are trying to fill high-pressure positions and want to hire candidates who can think and act quickly. Examples might be a job as an air traffic controller or a 911 operator.

A stress interview can come in the form of a surprise group interview or a request for an impromptu presentation. Other times, one interviewer appears kind, whereas another interviewer appears to be exceedingly gruff. Stress interviews can involve tough questions. Later in the chapter, you will learn how to handle tough questions.

When participating in a stress interview, keep your sense of humor and your wits about you. Remember, you have handled stress before and survived. This will be no different. Interviewers realize you are under pressure and will take this into account when evaluating your answers—if you maintain your composure.

Social Setting Interviews

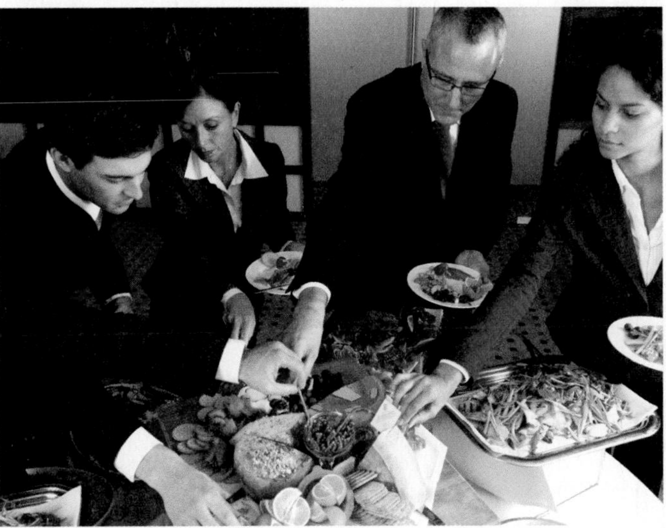

To get a sense of an applicant's social skills, etiquette, and personality, employers sometimes conduct a **social setting interview**. For example, an interviewer might suggest meeting over lunch. Alternatively, an interviewer might suggest a cocktail event or a golf meeting and ask very few questions during the interview but focus instead on how well the candidate socializes with other people. The social environment chosen usually mirrors social settings that occur on the job.

Keep the following in mind during a social setting interview:

- ***Regularly Practice Rules of Etiquette.*** Review the basic rules of etiquette, particularly dining etiquette. Practice them in your everyday life so they become second nature to you.
- ***Remember That You Are a Guest.*** As a guest you are not expected to pay, nor should you offer to do so. Instead, accept the invitation graciously. After the event, thank your interviewer. You will, however, want to remember to bring cash for coat checks, restroom attendants, and valets you encounter during the interview.
- ***Follow Your Interviewer's Lead.*** When in doubt about the proper way to handle a situation, follow the interviewer's lead. If you're invited to a country club, call ahead and ask about the club's dress code for the golf course, tennis courts, and dining areas, depending upon the activity in which you will be engaging.
- ***Learn the Purpose of the Event.*** If you're invited to a charity event, learn as much as possible about the event, the cause supported, and the attendees. Find out which of the firm's clients will be there. For instance, tell the interviewer, "Thank you for the invitation to the 'Resorts with a Cause' gala. I would love to attend. Should I be aware of any clients in attendance?" Then, research those clients just like you researched the company. As you meet the company's clients, you can then mention their successes. For example, "I'm pleased to meet you, Mr. Billings. Congratulations on ZComm's acceptance of the Community Favorite Award."
- ***Talk to Everyone.*** Make a point of giving a firm handshake, and smiling at everyone in the room. Leave a positive impression with everyone you meet.
- ***Limit or Abstain from Alcohol Consumption.*** There are varying opinions on when it is appropriate to drink on a social interview. As a rule, never order a drink unless the interviewer does, and never drink at a lunch interview, regardless of who else does. Always limit yourself to one glass per occasion. Never consume alcohol if you are underage or it's against your principles. Simply request a nonalcoholic beverage. You need not explain why you are not drinking alcohol.
- ***Follow Up with New Contacts.*** Introductions can become a blur when you meet many people at once. Repeat each person's name as you meet him or her, and ask for a business card if you speak with someone for an extended period of time. Having a card makes following up with the person easy. After a social interview, follow up within 24 hours with your new contacts so they keep you in mind. Notice that Tyrone, the candidate writing the letter in **Exhibit 15-1**, not only followed up with an e-mail, but searched the Web for a relevant article addressing his contact's concerns.

Exhibit 15-1 A Follow-Up E-mail to a Contact after a Social Interview

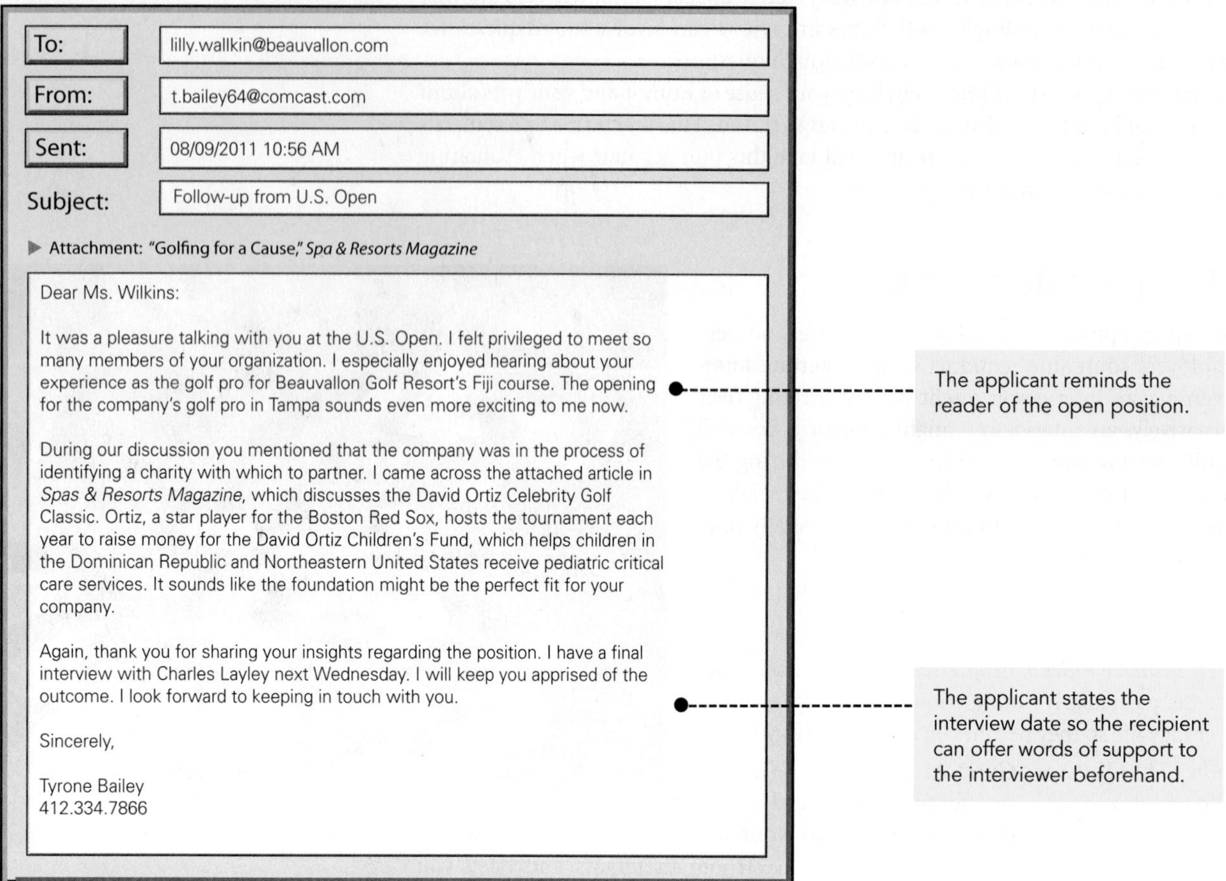

To: lilly.wallkin@beauvallon.com

From: t.bailey64@comcast.com

Sent: 08/09/2011 10:56 AM

Subject: Follow-up from U.S. Open

▶ Attachment: "Golfing for a Cause," *Spa & Resorts Magazine*

Dear Ms. Wilkins:

It was a pleasure talking with you at the U.S. Open. I felt privileged to meet so many members of your organization. I especially enjoyed hearing about your experience as the golf pro for Beauvallon Golf Resort's Fiji course. The opening for the company's golf pro in Tampa sounds even more exciting to me now.

During our discussion you mentioned that the company was in the process of identifying a charity with which to partner. I came across the attached article in *Spas & Resorts Magazine*, which discusses the David Ortiz Celebrity Golf Classic. Ortiz, a star player for the Boston Red Sox, hosts the tournament each year to raise money for the David Ortiz Children's Fund, which helps children in the Dominican Republic and Northeastern United States receive pediatric critical care services. It sounds like the foundation might be the perfect fit for your company.

Again, thank you for sharing your insights regarding the position. I have a final interview with Charles Layley next Wednesday. I will keep you apprised of the outcome. I look forward to keeping in touch with you.

Sincerely,

Tyrone Bailey
412.334.7866

The applicant reminds the reader of the open position.

The applicant states the interview date so the recipient can offer words of support to the interviewer beforehand.

❸ How Do You Prepare for an Interview?

Hiring managers assess both a candidate's skill and value. They ask themselves, "Do I want to hire this person?" and "What pay level is this person worth?" You have only a few minutes to make a lasting impression. Demonstrating that you are not only familiar with the corporation's goals and challenges but also dedicated to bringing value to it will also help you receive compensation on the higher end of the pay scale.

Taking time to research and stay up to date on a company's activities will result in a more successful interview.

Brush Up on Your Research of the Firm

If you followed the instructions in Chapter 13, by interview time you have already researched the applicable industry. Focus your attention specifically on the company with which you will be interviewing by brushing up on the most current news and events related to the company. Read through all progress reports on the company's Web site, along with all of its quarterly and recent annual reports. To uncover recent news about the firm, type the company's name into a search engine.

In addition to finding current information on the company, research the people who are conducting your interview. Wouldn't it be nice to know in advance whether the hiring manager went to your high school? Wouldn't you want to know if he or she previously worked for a company where you interned? Knowledge such as this is invaluable and can be easily obtained through social networking sites. For instance, if your interviewer is a member of LinkedIn, you can view his or her abbreviated professional history by typing

REAL INSIGHTS from a New Professional

Name: *Rebecca Cummings*
Title: *Editor/Production Manager*
Organization: *Aloha Guide*
Location: *Honolulu, Hawaii*

TODAY REBECCA CUMMINGS IS AN EDITOR AND PRODUCTION MANAGER for *Aloha Guide,* a travel publication based in Honolulu, Hawaii. An experienced lifeguard, snorkeling instructor, and windsurfing teacher, she began her career in the hospitality industry at the Pacific Islands Club resort in Guam.

Because of the distance between Guam and her residence on the United States East Coast, Cummings was unable to have a formal face-to-face interview with the Pacific Islands Club when she initially applied with the company. Instead, she was asked to make a "visual presentation" of herself in the form of a collage that would best show off her personality. Cummings embraced the assignment and showcased through video and pictures both her friendly and welcoming sides, as well as her snorkeling and windsurfing skills.

Since hospitality and tourism positions often require a person to work in foreign or exotic locations where there may be barriers of language or culture, Cummings highlighted her experience working with diverse populations. For instance, she emphasized her work with disadvantaged children at the local community center and her time spent abroad in France. Although she had never worked in Guam before, she drew parallels from the experiences she did have.

The approach worked. After a successful telephone interview, Cummings was hired as an activity leader, ensuring that all of the resort's guests were comfortable and having fun during the excursions she led. Cummings says her experience in Guam has made her comfortable "in an interview, a business meeting, or at networking events," regardless of the country she is in. In fact, Cummings learned so much about herself and the people of Guam that she says, "I know I will always have a home in Guam if I return."

Questions

1. What qualities do you think Cummings displayed that helped her get her first job at the Pacifics Island Club? How do you think her experience is helping in her new position at the *Aloha Guide?*
2. Cummings did not have direct experience working abroad in tourism, yet was able to clearly show how her skills transferred well into such a role. Can you think of a position you might be interested in but do not have direct experience with? How could you show that your current skills are transferable?
3. What benefits can you see in working abroad at the start of your career? What are some of the skills a graduate might learn working overseas?

Source: Rebecca Cummings in discussion with the author, July 2010.

the individual's name into the LinkedIn Web site. Some Web sites require you to create a personal profile of yourself before searching for other members.

Do you need to go to every social networking site? It doesn't hurt to do so. However, you can also "Google" your interviewer. Using the popular search engine, type in the interviewer's name and company. This search alone can turn up information about the interviewer such as the person's quotes in news articles and his or her professional history. The search can also direct you to the social networks in which the interviewer participates.

Get the "Inside Scoop" on the Interview

Having insight into an interviewer's approach and the interviewing process will give you an advantage. At this stage it is wise to contact anyone you know who formerly or currently is employed by the company—even a contact who merely interviewed there before. Explain your interest in the position and your desire to be well prepared. If your contact reported directly to the interviewer, also ask about the interviewer's management style. **Exhibit 15-2** suggests questions you might ask your contact in order to get inside information.

Exhibit 15-2 Questions to Ask Your Contact

1. How many people participated in your interview with the company?
2. What were the steps in the hiring process?
3. What were some of the questions the interviewer asked you?
4. Are you aware of any specific things the interviewer is looking for in a candidate?
5. Why is the interviewer looking to fill a position? Was the employee who previously held the job promoted or did she resign?
6. What is the interviewer's managing style?
7. How long do the interviews generally last?

Practice makes perfect when it comes to preparing for an interview.

Practice Responses to Different Types of Interview Questions

Interviewing is an art. Some candidates will occasionally avoid interviewing with their favored companies until they sharpen their interviewing skills.[3] Practicing with companies that are your second choice will help you interview more effectively with companies that are your first choice, as will mock interviews with an advisor or friend.

Interviewers' questions can be categorized fairly easily. Once you understand the motives behind an interviewer's questions, you will be able to provide effective responses to them. Next we discuss the types of questions you are likely to be asked and how you should respond to them.

Background and Interest Questions

Background questions are nonthreatening because they pertain to a subject you know well: yourself. See **Exhibit 15-3** for a sample list of background questions. Whereas background questions focus on your past experiences, **interest questions** focus on your personal interests. Sometimes an interviewer will ask, "Why are you interested in our company?" This is where your research on the company comes into play. For instance, you might tell the interviewer the following: "I want to work for a company that gives back. I am impressed that Coastal Adventures donates 10 percent of its profits to disadvantaged families."

Exhibit 15-3
Sample List of Background and Interest Questions

1. How did you choose your major?
2. What inspired your change in majors?
3. Tell me about your college experience.
4. What brought you out to San Francisco from Miami?
5. Explain the gaps between employment terms.
6. Why did you choose the hotel industry?
7. Why the Ritz Hotel?
8. What do you do in your free time?

Sometimes background questions are very open-ended. For instance, interviewers often say to candidates, "Tell me about yourself." Because this question is wide open, keep your answer brief and relevant. For example, although it's appropriate to discuss what motivated you to major in a particular field, don't delve too deeply into personal matters. Compare the following candidates' responses.

Johanna: "Well, I grew up in Chicago, before moving to San Diego in the sixth grade. It was really hard to leave the city, but I'm a Scorpio, and we're really resilient. Anyway, the move to San Diego made me realize how much I love sunshine, travel, and the beach. That's why my boyfriend said I should apply here. I would really like to work for Sail Away USA."

Matt: "I am a senior at UCLA, graduating this May. I chose to major in hospitality after interning with your company two years ago. The Sail Away staff made a lasting impression on me. I respected their dedication to providing guests with exceptional service. I found I really enjoyed ensuring the guests had the time of their lives. It was then I realized that I wanted to be a part of the Sail Away team."

Johanna expresses passion, but her response is unprofessional. Notice that she does not mention anything about her professional aspirations. She includes irrelevant information about her personal life and refers unnecessarily to her relationship with her boyfriend. Matt's response shows clear direction and commitment to his career. It is professional, relevant, and succinct.

Behavioral Questions

Behavioral questions inquire about a candidate's past experiences and behaviors on the job. **Exhibit 15-4** lists some typical behavioral questions. Interviewers use the responses as a predictor of future performance on the job. The interviewer assumes a candidate will respond and behave similarly if hired.

Exhibit 15-4
Sample List of Behavioral Questions

1. Have you ever had a conflict with coworkers? How did you handle it?
2. What was your greatest challenge on your last job? How did you overcome it?
3. Have you ever had to deal with a difficult client? How did you handle the situation?
4. What is your greatest success? How did you achieve it?
5. How have you planned for success in previous positions?
6. Walk me through one of your previous projects from start to finish.
7. Share a time when you failed to reach your goal. What happened?
8. Discuss a time you felt overwhelmed. How did you handle the stress?
9. Have you ever worked on a team project? What role did you play?
10. Have you ever had difficulty with a manager's decision? How did you handle it?

When answering behavioral questions, give a quick synopsis of the situation, the actions you took, and the results you attained. It is always best to focus on a positive outcome without dwelling on the negative situation. The following candidates answered in ways that demonstrated their ability to turn challenges into opportunities.

Lori: "I remember dealing with a difficult client in the past. While I was working as a banquet manager at Sand Castle Spa, a bride preparing for her wedding became irate when a busboy served her tap water. I realized she was just under a lot of stress, so I stepped in. I gave her an opportunity to express her frustration. I extended an apology and sent several bottles of mineral water to her suite, along with a complimentary fruit plate for her and her attendants. We received a glowing thank-you card and several client referrals as a result."

Kojo: "Yes. I had difficulty with a manager in the past. Because he was on the road a great deal, I had a challenging time as a new employee understanding my responsibilities. I handled it by arranging a phone conference at his convenience. I expressed my concerns and proposed having weekly phone meetings with him. I also sent him mid-week status reports by e-mail. This let me touch base with him until my training ended. That plan made all the difference. He gave me a stellar recommendation."

Situational Questions

Situational questions present candidates with hypothetical challenges. After setting the scene, the interviewer then asks the candidates what actions they would take under the same circumstances. The hypothetical situation often mirrors circumstances that actually occur in the job for which the candidates are applying. **Exhibit 15-5** lists some typical situational questions.

Exhibit 15-5 Sample List of Situational Questions

1. What would you do if a hotel guest believed his room charges were excessive? Suppose he was loud and irate in airing his complaints in a hotel lobby full of other guests?
2. What would you do if you realized the receptionist double-booked the ocean view suite for two prominent clients?
3. How would you handle a conflict between two salespeople regarding their ownership of an account and the commission attached to the sale?
4. How would you motivate a team with low morale and poor performance?
5. As a manager, what would you do if a member of your staff called in sick minutes before a shift?
6. What would you do if you saw a coworker stealing from the company?
7. What would you do if a client complained about her service, but you had nothing to do with the service she received?

Avoid difficult questions by addressing an interviewer's concerns about your background before he or she asks.

When it comes to handling situational questions, remember the mnemonic device *HALO:*

- ***Honesty.*** Propose actions that are lawful and truthful. If you witness theft or dishonesty on a job, for instance, it is your responsibility to report the offense.
- ***Accountability.*** When the hypothetical situation involves a personal mistake, demonstrate your accountability. For instance, tell the interviewer, "In that situation, I would apologize to the client for my accounting error. If approved by management, I would also offer the client free dessert in the restaurant as a gesture of my remorse."
- ***Leadership.*** Hiring managers appreciate answers demonstrating a candidate's leadership ability. For instance, "I don't tolerate negativity on the job. I confront people who complain on the job and encourage them to find ways to motivate their teammates rather than bring them down."
- ***Outcomes.*** When answering a situational question, demonstrate that you are outcome driven. For instance, "Under the circumstances you described, I would promote the Angler's Fly Fishing Ranch by marketing it to families holding reunions. My goal would be to deliver at least a 50 percent increase in third quarter revenue."

Difficult Questions about Your Background

Interviewers will often ask tough questions. The following are examples:

- "You spent only six months in your previous position. Why was that?"
- "Your grade point average is less than stellar. Can you explain why?"

See **Exhibit 15-6** for some examples of difficult questions. One way to handle these concerns is to address them before the interviewer does. Point out that missteps are often our greatest teachers and what you learned from the experience, good or bad. How did the mistakes make you a better person and potential employee?

Exhibit 15-6
Examples of Difficult Questions about Your Background

1. "It appears you weren't a very serious student. Why did you receive such poor grades?"
2. "Why should I hire you, when I have three candidates who are more qualified?"
3. "Why would a person interested in a career in journalism major in business?"
4. "Why are there gaps in your employment?"
5. "Why weren't you more involved in extracurricular activities?"
6. "How can someone with no experience relate to our clientele?"

Illegal Questions

Illegal questions are questions regarding your race, color, sex, religion, national origin, birthplace, age, disability, or marital/family status that are against the law for interviewers to ask.[4]

Illegal Question	Legal Question
"Are you married with children?"	"Are you able to travel 50 percent of the time?"
"Your accent sounds Middle Eastern. Is it?"	"Are you a U.S. citizen?"
"You're in your 40s, right?"	"You have had at least ten years' sales experience, correct?"
"Are you a member of any transgender organizations?"	"How do you network for business purposes?"
"Is that neck brace the result of a disability?"	"Can you lift the weight required for the position of bellman?"

Exhibit 15-7
Legal and Illegal Questions

Sometimes questions are worded in such a way that the candidate volunteers information that would otherwise be illegal for an interviewer to ask. However, it is legal for interviewers to ask you related questions when they pertain to the job's responsibilities. Compare and contrast the legal and illegal questions in **Exhibit 15-7**.

Some interviewers ask illegal questions unwittingly. For example, interviewers might discuss their children and innocently ask if you have any. You can avoid answering the question or decide there is no harm in doing so. If you truly feel there is a discriminatory motive behind the questions, however, you can file a claim with the U.S. Equal Employment Opportunity Commission (EEOC).[5]

CHECKLIST

To prepare for an interview:

- ☑ Brush up on your research of the firm.
- ☑ Get the "inside scoop" on the interview.
- ☑ Practice responses to different types of interview questions.

4 What Should You Do on the Day of the Interview?

On the day of your interview, you will want to keep your stress to a minimum. The tips in this section will help avoid some of the stressors that crop up before interviewing.

Dress for Success

People communicate a great deal with their choice of clothing. Your interview clothing should portray you as professional, respectful, and serious about the prospect of working for the company. Despite varying dress codes, it is wise to err on the side of formality. Formality, however, does not mean breaking the bank to impress your interviewer. There is nothing wrong with finding a well-fitted suit or dress at a consignment store or borrowing one from your roommate for the big day. See **Exhibit 15-8** for guidelines on dressing for interviews. Lastly, is your hair in place? Is there food or lipstick on your teeth? Do you have a run in your hosiery? Look in a mirror, and check yourself from front to back.

Bring the Right Materials

Interviewers juggling many responsibilities and interviewing multiple candidates might not have your résumé readily available. These people will appreciate the copies you provide them. Also, bring a folder with references to give to the interviewers if they are requested. If you have an online portfolio, consider bringing your laptop in case the interview takes place in a conference room in which there is no computer. Carry your materials in a professional looking case or binder, and bring a notepad and pen to take notes.

Aside from the items you need for your interview, leave everything else in your car or at home. Walking into an interview laden with "stuff" leaves an unpolished impression. Remember to turn off your cell phone. For some interviewers a ringing cell phone is a deal breaker. Another deal breaker is to bring a relative or a friend with you to an interview. Believe it or not, some people do so.

Exhibit 15-8 Guidelines on Dressing for Interviews

Dress Point	Men	Women
Hygiene	Always shower or bathe before an interview.	
Hair	Get a haircut a few days in advance of the interview. For longer hair, pull it back with a ponytail holder during the interview. Avoid excessive hair products such as hairspray or gel.	Wear your hair pulled away from face and avoid excessive hair products. Dry your hair completely—do not attend an interview with damp hair.
Cologne	Use scent sparingly, or not at all. Do not smell like smoke.	
Nails	Make sure your nails are clean.	Make sure your nails are clean. Avoid excessively long or colored nails.
Makeup	Men traditionally do not wear makeup on job interviews.	Keep makeup to a minimum.
Jewelry	Remove obvious piercings, and keep chains and rings to a minimum.	Keep jewelry to a minimum. Stud earrings are best for an interview. Wear understated, rather than large jewelry.
Tattoos	Cover tattoos for an interview.	
Belts	If you have belt loops, wear a belt. Always tuck your shirt in for an interview.	If you have belt loops, wear a belt. Always tuck your shirt in for an interview.
Pants	Pressed and hemmed. Choose a dark color.	
Suits	Dry cleaned.	Dry cleaned. Skirted suits should never rise above the knee.
Shirt	Pressed. Always wear a tie when interviewing unless the office is very informal. In that case, wear a sport coat. Choose a color that does not make you look pale.	Pressed. Do not wear a low-cut shirt. Choose a color that does not make you look pale.
Shoes	Polished dress shoes or loafers for an informal interview. Matching socks. Do not wear athletic shoes.	Polished, closed-toed shoes are advised for interviews. Avoid stiletto heels. Hosiery is required in formal offices.

Arrive at the Right Time

If you were told you would need to fill out paperwork before the interview, arrive 15 minutes early. If you are unfamiliar with the location of the interview, get driving directions from a Web site such as MapQuest or Google Maps, or request them from the human resources representative at the time the interview is scheduled. Know where you're going and where to park by taking a trip to the location in advance of your interview. Allow additional time for traffic, parking, and completing a job application.

Complete the Application Correctly

Since application forms require specific information not included on résumés, arrive prepared to provide the full addresses of your schools, places of employment, names of supervisors, and relevant phone numbers. The form will also require you to provide specific dates of employment and possibly professional references. When filling out an application, never write "please refer to résumé." Fill in all of the information that is requested. The document is used for background checks and is a necessary part of the hiring process.

Be Prepared to Take Pre-Employment Tests

Pre-employment testing is particularly common for jobs that require specific skills, such as technical jobs, jobs involving data or numeric processing, or writing and editing jobs. The tests are used to gauge both mental aptitude and personality dimensions associated with the job. The following are some common types of pre-employment tests and the attributes they are intended to measure:

- ***Skills and knowledge tests.*** What general skills and knowledge do you already have that would be useful in the job for which you are applying?
- ***Cognitive ability and general problem solving tests.*** How well can you think, analyze, and solve problems?
- ***Specific ability tests.*** What specific job-related skills do you currently have? How good are they?
- ***Personality tests.*** Is your personality suited to the job for which you are applying?
- ***Situational judgment tests.*** How well would you think and behave in situations that might occur on the job? **Exhibit 15-9** shows some of the tests that might be used to screen candidates for certain jobs in the tourism industry.

DID YOU KNOW?

According to the *2010 Global Assessment Trends Report* by Sarah S. Fallaw and Andrew L. Solomonson, 86 percent of all companies surveyed use some type of testing (either online or pencil-and-paper) as part of the hiring process for jobs within their organizations.

Exhibit 15-9 **Examples of Employment Tests**

Job	Type of Test
Marketing Writer	A writing competency test to evaluate a candidate's vocabulary, spelling, organization, written communication, and editing skills.
Hotel Cashier	A math competency test to evaluate a candidate's money counting and change-making skills.
Concierge and Tour Guide	A knowledge test to evaluate the candidate's awareness of city, events, and locations; a personality test to evaluate the candidate's, flexibility, interpersonal communication, and organizational skills.
Sales Representative	A personality test to evaluate a candidate's energy, assertiveness, communication, motivation, and competitiveness.

Avoid Distracting Behaviors

Some behaviors people engage in, either consciously or unconsciously during an interview, can be distracting and even disqualify a candidate. Don't, for example, glance at your watch or continually adjust your hair or clothing. Don't chew gum or jingle your keys, jewelry, or pocket change. Behaviors such as these communicate that you are not interested in or serious about the position, are bored, or are extremely nervous.

Avoid Gaffes

Can you remember a time when you really put your foot in your mouth? Maybe you were on a date and told a joke that fell flat or you were unprepared when giving an answer in class. Unfortunately, in a job interview putting your foot in your mouth may result in more than mild embarrassment—it can cost you the position.

Never Talk Badly about a Former Employer

Rather than discussing the negative qualities of a former supervisor or position, focus on the positive aspects of your experience. Your prospective employer may respect your former employer, or even be friends or relatives with the individual. Discuss instead what you learned while working for your former employer and the skills you attained: for instance, "Working for a demanding manager taught me the value of anticipating the needs of others and responding to them without being asked. This was probably my best preparation for work in the hospitality industry. It made me realize I enjoy exceeding the expectations of others."

Don't Ask Inappropriate Questions

A job seeker's questions could be the very thing that impress a manager—or offend him or her. Let's look at questions that could be considered inappropriate by a manager.

- ***Questions about time off or the possibility of working from home:*** Asking questions about time-off *before* you have received an offer calls your work ethic into question. If you are offered the job, you can discuss vacation time with your prospective employer during the negotiation phase. Do not discuss it during the interviewing process. Likewise, if you tell an employer in an initial interview that you expect to work from home when it's clear the position is an in-office job, your work ethic is likely to be questioned. **Exhibit 15-10** contains a list of inappropriate questions along with how they can better be phrased.
- ***Questions you could easily have answered yourself had you done some research:*** The worst thing an interviewer can ask mid-discussion is, "Have you been to our Web site?" A hiring manager will never question your preparation if you are asking intelligent questions.

After reading up on the current events and news related to the industry and company with which you are applying, form a list of probing questions. **Probing questions** invite elaboration rather than just a simple explanation. For example, **Exhibit 15-11** shows questions asked by three different candidates. The thoughts of the hiring manager appear on the right side of the diagram. Compare and contrast the effectiveness of each question. Is it a probing question? Could the candidate have easily ascertained the answer?

All of the questions addressed the company's goals, but Camy and Troy have a distinct advantage. By mentioning the company's specific objectives, they act as company insiders and align themselves with the interviewer. By comparison, Jesse's question positions him as an "outsider." His question requires a full-blown explanation, rather than elaboration.

Troy's question is superior because it synthesizes corporate information with current global events. Doing so demonstrates he is informed and has good critical thinking skills.

Exhibit 15-10 Inappropriate Questions Asked by Candidates

Question	Interviewer's Perception	A Better Question
"Does this job require long hours?"	This person is unwilling to go the extra mile. This person is unwilling to do extra work.	"Your Web site indicates your company strives to provide its employees with a good work-life balance. Could you elaborate, please?"
"When do people get raises?"	People don't "get" raises in this company. They earn them. This person already has a sense of entitlement.	"Are there opportunities for advancement in this position? What do you see as the career path from this position?"
"Can I work from home?"	An entry-level candidate should be more interested in learning to do the job well, rather than working from home.	"Does your company allow high-performing employees to work remotely?" This question is usually not appropriate in a first interview.
"How much vacation time do employees get?"	This employee is discussing vacation before we have even made an offer. Instead, she should be trying to impress me with her work ethic.	"How can an employee exceed your expectations?"
"Can I wear jeans to work?"	Is the dress policy really the most relevant issue right now?	"Would you describe your company's corporate culture? What is your managerial style?"

Exhibit 15-11 Evaluating Probing Questions

Which Is the Most Probing Question?

Jesse's Interview

Jesse's question:	Manager's thoughts:
"What's the company's direction for the coming year?"	"That would be a great question if the answer weren't already available in our annual report on our Web site. He should have been more prepared."

Camy's Interview

Camy's question:	Manager's thoughts:
"I understand from reading your annual report that Spa Destinations plans to focus on marketing overseas, but few details were given. Why are international markets a priority for your company?"	"This is the first candidate today who actually referenced our annual report. I am impressed. Clearly, she did her research."

Troy's Interview

Troy's question:	Manager's thoughts:
"I understand from reading your annual report that Spa Destinations plans to focus on marketing overseas, but few details were given. Were international markets targeted due to the euro's increasing strength, or was there another motivation?"	"This is a critical thinker. This candidate not only prepared and knows our priorities, he clearly follows global economics. I like his strategic thinking."

Ask Questions

Asking nothing at all is just as bad as asking inappropriate questions. An interviewer may perceive a candidate without questions as disinterested or unprepared. **Exhibit 15-12** on the next page offers some ideas for questions to ask during an interview. At the very least you can always ask the interviewer to elaborate on something already mentioned.

Don't Discuss Sensitive Topics

Avoid discussing politics and religion during an interview, unless the position you are applying for is religious or political in nature. It's also unwise to share details of your personal life that do not relate to the job. Of course, during your discussion with an interviewer, you might find the two of you share things in common. In such a situation, a brief, superficial discussion about your favorite sports teams or something similar could build rapport. However, an extended discussion about your former girlfriend is inappropriate. Keep the focus on your qualifications for the position.

Postponing Salary Discussions

Sometimes interviewers ask about your salary requirements and expectations during the interview. A wise candidate postpones the salary discussion until he or she has all details about a job, knows the responsibilities it entails, and has been extended a job offer. **Exhibit 15-13** lists some ways to postpone a salary discussion during an interview. Notice how the candidate politely deflects the question while gathering more information. If the interviewer persists, you can always suggest a salary range, but not before researching the marketplace.

Exhibit 15-12 Ideas for Questions to Ask Interviewers

Employee Expectations
How long does it typically take new employees at your company to finish training?
What training does a new employee receive?
How do you measure the performance of your employees?
How is the team currently performing? To what do you attribute their success (or failure)?
If I'm hired, how can I best prepare myself for success?
Hiring Manager's Management Style and Expectations
How do you describe your management style?
What do you value most in an employee?
What extent of interaction do you like to have with your team members? For example, do you conduct weekly calls or hold daily meetings?
How many people in your department are exceeding your expectations and how are they doing that?
Job Responsibilities
What are your immediate objectives and priorities for this job?
Will I be working closely with other people or mostly independently?
Will I be given a list of clients or will I prospect for them? (for a sales position)
What level of interaction will I have with the media when writing and distributing press releases? (for a sales and marketing position)
What do you think are the greatest challenges of this position? How have successful employees overcome them in the past?

Exhibit 15-13 Sample Answers Used to Postpone a Salary Discussion

Question: What Are Your Salary Expectations?

Possible Answers:

- "My expectations about compensations depend on the responsibilities of the position. I am looking forward to learning more about the job."
- "Of course I want compensation commensurate with my skills and education. In addition, I am also factoring in the corporate culture, training provided, and benefits. Could you please tell me about the training offered?"
- "I am committed to providing a return on the company's investment in me. I will give the matter more consideration."
- "I am confident a company with a reputation like that of Hotel Seasons compensates its employees fairly. I am interested in learning more about the career paths available with this position. Could you please elaborate on them?"

5 How Do You Close the Interview?

The close occurs at the end of the interview. At this stage you have already fielded background, interest, behavioral, and situational questions. As the interview winds down many candidates hold their breath and hope for the best, rather than ask questions about the hiring process or the interviewer's possible concerns. Taking a direct approach earns respect. At closing time, your goals are to 1) determine the next steps of the hiring process, 2) handle any objections regarding your qualifications, and 3) ensure you will proceed in the process.

Ask about the Interviewer's Concerns

Before the interview concludes, ask your interviewers if they have any concerns regarding your qualifications. Doing so gives you the opportunity to address them.

When an interviewer gives you candid feedback, don't become defensive. Instead, express appreciation for his or her candor and provide evidence to the contrary. Offer to supply additional copies of work or give an example of experience addressing the issue. For instance, "Thank you for your candor, Mr. Richards. While I don't have professional management experience, my leadership role as the student director for Campus Travelers required comparable skills. In that role, I managed 100 student volunteers, ensuring the group complied with the regulations of all universities and international sites. After that experience, managing a team of 10 would be a welcomed change." **Exhibit 15-14** provides a set of sample questions you can ask interviewers to help address any concerns they might have.

Exhibit 15-14 Sample Questions Addressing Interviewers' Concerns

1. "You mentioned that Ms. Taylor makes the final decision. Are you comfortable referring me to her for an interview?"
2. "Do you have any concerns about advancing me in the interviewing process?"
3. "In the beginning of the interview, you mentioned qualities of a perfect hire. After talking to me, do I fit the bill?"
4. "Do you have any questions or concerns that would keep me from advancing in the hiring process?"
5. "Can I offer you any more assurances of my abilities and commitment?"

Find Out What the Next Steps in the Hiring Process Are

Determining the next steps in the hiring process helps you avoid suffering from the "unknown" in the days and weeks following your interview. Wouldn't it be nice to know when the interviewer plans to make a decision or when the company wants the new hire to start? **Exhibit 15-15** provides a list of sample questions that can help you better understand the hiring process.

Exhibit 15-15 Questions to Ask about the Next Steps in the Hiring Process

1. What does the rest of the hiring process entail?
2. What is your timeline for making a decision?
3. Are there additional steps in the interviewing process?
4. Are there additional people I should meet?
5. Can you explain how you will proceed in making your decision?

State Your Desire to Continue Participating in the Hiring Process

Always thank the interviewer when ending the meeting and shake his or her hand. You might at this point provide a list of references as a closing gesture. Moreover, let the person know you are interested in the job and enthusiastic about the possibility of being hired. Simply say, "Thank you for this opportunity. I am very interested in continuing in the process. The position sounds like a great fit for me."

Notice the difference in how the candidates in **Exhibit 15-16** end their interviews for the same sales position. (The interviewer's thoughts appear in the boxes.) Unlike Sari, Katie never had the opportunity to overcome objections and concerns, simply because she never

Exhibit 15-16 A Bad versus a Good Closing to an Interview

Interview closing with Katie Maestas

The hiring manager sees it is time to wrap up. "We discussed some of your questions regarding the company and the position. Are there any other questions you have?" he asks.

"No. I think you've answered all of them," Katie says. "When do you expect to make a decision?"

"Within the next three weeks," says the hiring manager. Katie's cell phone rings in her purse.

"Ok. Well, thank you for your time. I hope I hear from you," says Katie.

"I'm surprised she didn't make sure her phone was off. A ringing phone would be really embarrassing in a client meeting, especially when she's closing a sale."

"I'm surprised she doesn't want to know whether she qualifies for another interview. She seems nice, but hoping to get somewhere won't get her hired or close deals with our clients."

Interview closing with Sari Lakshman

The hiring manager sees it is time to wrap up. "We discussed some of your questions regarding the company and the position. Are there any other questions you have?" he asks.

"Yes, thank you for asking. I do have a few questions about the interview process," Sari says. "Can you please tell me what the rest of the process entails? Are there other interviews?"

"Actually, I planned to schedule second interviews with our vice president of sales" the hiring manager says.

"Do you feel comfortable advancing me in the process?" Sari asks.

"Actually, Sari, I am concerned that you might not have experience responding to requests for proposals. It's a big part of the job," says the hiring manager.

"Thank you for your candor," Sari replies. "I would like to alleviate those concerns by drafting such a response for your review. I am very interested in this position. I believe after seeing additional samples of my work, you will find I am well-qualified. Do you have any other concerns?"

"No," says the hiring manager. "I would be happy to see your writing samples. Please e-mail them to me, and I will follow up with you in the next week."

"I'm glad she is bold when it comes to trying to answer any concerns I have. This is something she will have to do on the job when talking to clients."

"She is a strong candidate. This is the perfect way to handle objections. If her work is good, she's going to meet the vice president of sales."

asked if the interviewer had any. She will likely have to wait weeks before learning of the hiring manager's decision.

Send a Thank-You Card or Letter

When you arrive home, immediately follow up with a thank-you card or letter. Your thank-you card should refer to the position, your gratitude for the interview, and your desire to continue in the process. See **Exhibit 15-17** for an example of a thank-you letter following an interview.

Exhibit 15-17 A Thank-You Letter Following an Interview

Theodore J. Wilkens
444 Long Horn Trail
Hastings, NE 88766

April 17, 2011

Mr. Conrad Tygart, President
Dudes and Dolls Horse Ranch
3345 Indian Trail
Billings, MT 59105

Dear Mr. Tygart:

Thank you for the opportunity to interview for the position of entertainment director for Dudes and Dolls Horse Ranch. I am very interested in continuing in the hiring process for this position.

After learning more about your ideas for the coming tourist season, I created a sample calendar of activities I would implement if hired as entertainment director. My research shows these activities are great crowd-pleasers.

I will call you next week to follow up. In the meantime, please accept my appreciation.

Sincerely,

Theodore Wilkens

Theodore Wilkens

The applicant refers to the position for which he interviewed.

The applicant demonstrates initiative and a plan to follow up after the interview.

mybcommlab

Apply Exhibit 15-17's key concepts by revising a new document. Go to Chapter 15 in mybcommlab.com and select Document Makeovers.

6 How Should Job Offers, Job Rejections, and Resignations Be Handled?

At some point you will be notified about the interviewer's employment decision. If it is an offer, you will enter a whole new world of strategic decision making regarding your compensation package. If rejected, you will be better prepared for the next interview. Remember, in the case of a rejection, a winning motto is, "*Next*!"

Evaluating a Job Offer

An offer is generally made in person or over the phone and later followed by an **offer letter** confirming the details regarding the position's start date, benefits, and compensation. Preparation is key when it comes to evaluating and negotiating the best compensation package possible.

To evaluate a job offer, you should have already formulated a budget for your own cost-of-living expenses. From there, research what other professionals with your education and experience make in the same position in your geographic area. Web sites such as *Salary.com* are a good place to start. If you are considering moving to another area for a position, investigate how your living costs would differ in the new locale at a Web site such as *Payscale*

After determining what you need for survival, prioritize your professional objectives. While a higher salary may be tempting, consider the following factors in your decision:

- Does the company offer health benefits?
- What is the potential for advancement?
- How reputable is the company?

REAL INSIGHTS from a Seasoned Professional

Name: *David Secunda*
Title: *Founder and Program Director*
Organization: *Avid4 Adventure*
Location: *Denver, Colorado*

AS THE FOUNDER AND PROGRAM DIRECTOR of Avid4 Adventure, a company that runs youth-centered outdoor excursions like rock climbing and canoeing, David Secunda must employ a rigorous interview process. After all, when taking groups of kids into the "great outdoors," you need the right staff in place. A candidate interested in joining Avid4 Adventure must be prepared for both physical and mental challenges. To ensure he makes the right hiring decisions, Secunda uses a three-step interview process.

The first step is a phone interview. Although Secunda cannot gauge an applicant's rock-climbing abilities with a phone interview, he uses it to assess personality. When working with a young population, many of whom are testing perceived limitations, a team member must have both patience and a sense of humor. Therefore, Secunda looks for evidence of these traits during his initial conversation. In Secunda's business, the personality of candidates is just as important as their experience.

When it comes to relevant experience, Secunda believes that candidates who handle themselves well during the second step, the face-to-face interview, will probably be able to handle themselves on a mountain. This includes being able to provide Secunda with any training certifications needed for the job. Secunda wants evidence that a candidate is proactive, prepared, and confident, all of which are essential traits for Avid4 Adventure employees.

During the third step of the interviewing process, Secunda tests an applicant on the "job site" to measure physical skills. Above all, Avid4 Adventure employees must keep the kids safe. One way of testing an applicants' ability to do that is by observing him or her in action in a wilderness setting. Although field interviews are physically taxing and mentally challenging, they are a good opportunity for candidates to learn more about Avid4 Adventure while the company learns more about them.

As Avid4 Adventure employees know, a successful interview requires more than just a firm handshake. Candidates must be prepared to demonstrate social intelligence, knowledge, and skill. Your next interview might not take place in the wilderness, but prepare accordingly, and you will be ready for anything.

Questions

1. What kind of preparation is necessary for each of the three types of interviews you would experience at Avid4 Adventure?
2. Which 21st century communication skills are going to make a positive impression on an interviewer looking for the qualities sought by Secunda?

Source: "Staff Hiring and Jobs," *Avid4 Adventure*, June 9, 2009, accessed at http://www.avid4.com/StaffHiring.html.

- Which company exposes you to networking opportunities?
- Which company provides the most responsibility?
- Where will I have the best work-life balance? How important is that to me initially?

Negotiate the Offer

Negotiating your salary is a common part of the job acceptance process.

Few people feel comfortable negotiating salaries, especially women. Many employees make the mistake of accepting a low starting salary with the intent of "fixing it" later with raises. However, raises are usually incremental, and may be scarce and small. The time to obtain a desirable salary is before accepting a job.[6]

If the employer originally indicated a salary range and the amount you desire is somewhere within the range, it is appropriate to negotiate. Before you enter into a salary negotiation, be clear on what you're willing to negotiate—salary, benefits, vacations, training, or retirement plans. Be tactful, patient, and firm during negotiations. Your goal should be to create a "win-win" outcome that works for you and your employer. **Exhibit 15-18** offers some tips for how to negotiate your starting salary.

Remember, high salaries are earned. Candidates requesting high salaries must demonstrate their worth. After an interviewer brings up the issue of compensation, a candidate might say, "I understand that the median income for position of activities director is

Exhibit 15-18 Tips for Negotiating Your Starting Salary

1. Convey your enthusiasm for the job and your desire to work for the company.
2. Communicate that you don't want money to be an obstacle to accepting the position.
3. Use "we" statements to create a feeling of partnership with the person offering you the position.
4. Mention the salary range you desire rather than specifying a particular salary, and be prepared to negotiate.

$35,000. However, because I also have certificates in CPR and recreational training, I am asking $38,000." If you request a salary at the higher end of the pay range, prepare to negotiate it. Always support your claims for more money by proving you have additional or superior education or experience.

Accepting a Job Offer

If you have negotiated and the offer is a fit, accept it. Once you accept a job offer in person or by phone, and your start date has been set, both you and your future employer should confirm the agreement in writing. **Exhibit 15-19** shows an example of an offer letter. **Exhibit 15-20** shows an example of an **acceptance letter** sent by a candidate to an employer accepting an offer of employment.

Exhibit 15-19
An Offer Letter

Vail Ski Resorts
444 Eldorado Lane
Vail, CO 81657

December 1, 2010

Ms. Lisa Gilmore
314 Navajo Way
Denver, CO 80210

Dear Ms. Gilmore:

To follow up on our conversation, I am pleased to offer you the position of assistant director of Vail Resorts' Ski School. Both your teaching and ski skills are exceptional, and we are excited to welcome you to our team. As we discussed, the salary for the position is $40,000, and includes an annual, two-week paid vacation. The medical and dental coverage associated with the job is outlined in the enclosed Employment Package.

Your start date is January 15, 2011. We look forward to receiving your written acceptance. If you have any questions, please call me at 907.232.1899.

Sincerely,

Chase Wicker

Chase Wicker
Director

Enclosure

Declining a Job Offer

Generally, when a candidate declines an offer for employment, it is polite to respond with both a phone call thanking the interviewer for the offer and a **letter of decline.** The letter can be sent as a formal business letter, but a handwritten note is also appropriate. See **Exhibit 15-21** for an example of a letter declining an employment offer.

Exhibit 15-20
A Written Acceptance of a Job Offer

mybcommlab

Apply Exhibit 15-20's key concepts by revising a new document. Go to Chapter 15 in mybcommlab.com and select Document Makeovers.

314 Navajo Way
Denver, CO 80210

December 5, 2010

Mr. Chase Wicker
Director of Vail Resorts
444 Eldorado Lane
Vail, CO 81657

Dear Mr. Wicker:

Thank you for your kind offer to work as the assistant director of Vail Resorts' Ski School. The employment package outlining the details of compensation and benefits arrived today. I am pleased to accept your offer. Working for such a fine establishment in this capacity is a great privilege.

As we discussed on the phone, I look forward to starting work on January 15, 2011. Again, thank you.

Cordially,

Lisa Gilmore

Lisa Gilmore

Exhibit 15-21
A Letter Declining an Offer

314 Navajo Way
Denver, CO 80210

December 5, 2010

Mr. Chase Wicker
Director of Vail Resorts
444 Eldorado Lane
Vail, CO 81657

Dear Mr. Wicker:

Thank you for your kind offer to work at Vail Resorts as your Ski School's assistant director. As we discussed on the phone, I made the difficult decision to work internationally at the Swiss Ski School for Young Adults. In doing so, I hope to return to the states with even more management experience.

I do hope that an opportunity presents itself for future employment at Vail Resorts. I would be honored to work for such a well-respected ski school. Please accept my gratitude and best wishes for your team.

Sincerely,

Lisa Gilmore

Lisa Gilmore

Tactfully Resigning from Your Current Job

Although starting a new position is thrilling, be tactful when resigning from your current responsibilities. After all, your current job likely provided the experience you needed for the new position. Exit the position with an attitude of gratitude.

Traditionally, two weeks is acceptable notice. "Finish strong" is the motto of many athletes. The same holds true for professionals. Give your employer your best during your final two weeks by finishing any outstanding projects. If completing them is impossible, prepare them to a point where a colleague can easily resume your work. If you are replaced by someone internally, provide the person with checklists and tips for the job. Document the location of your files and provide instructions to your team members about your work.

Finally, always provide your current employer with a written **resignation letter**. The letter should thank your employer for the opportunity the job provided you and diplomatically state your decision to leave. See **Exhibit 15-22** for an example of a resignation letter.

Your coworkers should never learn of your resignation before your supervisor. Once you inform your supervisor of your decision to leave, ask how he or she would like it announced to the team. He or she may prefer to send an e-mail or make the announcement personally. When explaining your decision to leave, never boast about the higher pay or better working conditions you might receive as part of your new job.

Exhibit 15-22 A Letter of Resignation

6654 Northern Lane
Anchorage, AK 99501

September 1, 2011

Ms. Jessica Iota
Director of Hospitality
Garden Hotel
897 Orchard Blvd.
Anchorage, AK 99501

Dear Ms. Iota:

Please accept this letter as notice of my resignation effective September 14, 2011. Serving as Garden Hotel's night clerk provided me a great deal of valuable experience for which I am so grateful. I especially appreciate your mentorship over the past two years.

In the weeks before my departure, I will help you make the transition as seamless as possible. I have outlined my responsibilities in writing for my successor and am available to assist with the person's training.

The employee demonstrates his professionalism by offering to make the transition following his departure easier.

Thank you for giving me the opportunity to work for Garden Hotel and the wonderful professional experience you have provided me.

Sincerely,

Julian Ralston

Julian Ralston

Accepting Rejection

Being rejected for a job, especially one you really wanted, is disappointing. Generally, if you are rejected for a job, you will receive a **rejection letter**. However, if you have progressed far enough in the interview process, the hiring manager might call you directly. Unfortunately, some companies neglect contacting rejected candidates entirely. If you aren't contacted after two weeks, call or e-mail the firm's human resources department to check the status of your application.

Speak with the Interviewer

Whenever possible, speak with the interviewer. Use the opportunity to understand his or her reasons for choosing someone else. Always request candor. For example, tell the manager, "Mr. Reynolds, thank you for taking my call. I wondered if you would share your reasons for choosing an alternative candidate. I am very impressed with Weekend Stays, Inc. and would like to better prepare myself for the next opening. I welcome your candid feedback."

Never argue with interviewers who provide you with feedback or attempt to change their minds. Instead, listen to what they have to say and solicit suggestions for your improvement. Always thank them for their assistance and honesty. However, do not be surprised if an interviewer declines to give you feedback on your interview. Legal reasons or personnel policies could prevent the interviewer from doing so.

After being rejected for a position, never say anything disparaging about the company or interviewer. Disparaging words have a way of circling back to their sources with damaging results. By contrast, demonstrating your appreciation for the opportunity to interview, even if you are rejected, shows both maturity and professionalism and could also put you in the running for future jobs with the company. **Exhibit 15-23** shows an example of a thank-you card sent following a rejection.

Exhibit 15-23
A Thank-You Card Following a Rejection

December 15, 2010

Dear Mr. Rodriguez:

Thank you for the opportunity to interview for the position of tour director with Peru Guided, Inc. Although I am disappointed that I was not chosen to fill this opening, it was a pleasure meeting you and learning more about your company.

I hope that you will keep me in mind when the next position opens at Peru Guided. In the meantime, I intend to improve my Spanish, as you suggested, by taking an advanced conversational Spanish course. I will be well prepared to lead the next Amazon Adventure trip, should the need for a knowledgeable and friendly tour director arise again.

Until then, thank you again for your consideration.

Sincerely,

Stephanie Stauber

Summary *Synthesize What You Have Learned*

1. How do you respond to or set up an interview?

When you receive a call for an interview, be prepared by writing down the interviewers' names and titles. Be certain you have directions, dates, and the time (including time zone) for your interview.

2. What types of interviews do employers utilize?

Interviews take many forms. Phone interviews are generally used for screening purposes before one-on-one interviews takes place. The process can take a few weeks to several months. Videoconference interviews are becoming increasingly popular. Stress interviews help a company gauge how well a candidate responds under pressure. Social interviews help a company gauge how well a candidate responds in a certain social situation.

3. How do you prepare for an interview?

Preparing for an interview should begin long before it is scheduled. A candidate should have prepared a portfolio and a résumé reflecting his or her applicable skill sets. The candidate should also research the firm's industry on an ongoing basis. Once an interview is scheduled, the candidate must prepare by updating his or her research on the company and the industry. The candidate must also research information about the interviewer. It is wise to investigate the hiring process and the types of questions likely to be asked in an interview. Finally, the candidate should practice responding to potential interview questions.

4. What should you do on the day of the interview?

On the day of the interview, keep your stress to a minimum. Have your driving directions ready, along with copies of your résumé and the dates and addresses of the schools you attended and employers for whom you have worked. When dressing for the interview, err on the side of formality. Keep tattoos and multiple earrings covered and makeup and perfume to a minimum. Bring your résumé, portfolio, and references in a professional-looking case or binder. Turn off your cell phone.

As you answer questions, avoid distracting behaviors, such as chewing gum, fiddling with your hair, or jingling your pocket change. Never make disparaging remarks about an interviewer, about the company, or about any former employees. Finally, postpone any salary discussions until after a job offer is made.

5. How do you close the interview?

As the interview draws to a close, always ask the interviewer about the next steps and any concerns he or she might have. Then state your desire to continue in the hiring process. When you arrive home, send a thank-you note.

6. How should job offers, job rejections, and resignations be handled?

If you are rejected, consider the interview good practice. Then honestly assess your interviewing skills. Always follow up by sending thank-you cards to your interviewers, even if they have rejected you. Call the interviewer personally for feedback. Never disparage someone who has interviewed you.

If you receive an offer, evaluate all aspects of the hiring package, as opposed to just the job's salary. Consider where the job will take you in the long run. If necessary, negotiate your salary. When accepting an offer, always follow up with a written acceptance letter. Once you have accepted a position, resign from your current position tactfully. Prepare a resignation letter and inform your boss of your resignation before sharing the news with any of your coworkers. Never brag about the pay or benefits you will receive as part of your new job.

PEARSON **mybcommlab**™ Are you an active learner? Go to **mybcommlab.com** to master Chapter 15's content. Chapter 15's interactive activities include:

- Customizable Study Plan and Chapter 15 practice quizzes
- Chapter 15 Simulation, Interviewing, that helps you think critically and prepare to make choices in the business world
- Chapter 15 Video Exercise, Interviewing Skills, which shows you how textbook concepts are put into practice every day
- Flash cards for mastering the definition of chapter terms
- Interactive Lessons that visually review key chapter concepts
- Document Makeovers for hands-on, scored practice in revising documents

Know It *Reflect, Respond, and Express*

Build Your Critical Thinking Skills

Critical Thinking Questions

1. How do you think body language can affect a job interview, even if the interview is over the phone?
2. Analyze the time each person arrives to class every day, even the instructor. What impressions do your classmates give you by arriving early, on time, or late? Discuss the assumptions you make about your classmates' work ethics based on the times they arrive to class.
3. Imagine you are an employer who is ready to start interviewing for an open position. What type of interview do you use to help learn the most about potential employees? Do you use different types for different levels of interviews? Would you base your decision on one interview type only?
4. Listen to your voice mail or answering machine message. What does the current message say? What impression would you make on a prospective employer based on the message? How can you revise your message to make it sound more professional?
5. Write a list of ways to prepare for difficult or illegal questions. How can you still make a good impression when you are asked an illegal question you don't want to answer?

Critical Thinking Scenario

Tom, a graduating student, just learned of an opening as a tour guide for Safari Trekking, a company hosting guided tours to Africa. The position calls for a personable and informed guide. Tom has never been to Africa, but he has worked at a local theme park guiding families through the attractions. He has also studied African history and read many essays and articles on the subject. Tom is described by everyone as a "people-magnet." His stories and sense of humor draw people in.

The hiring manager at Safari Trekking has reluctantly agreed to interview Tom, as a favor to a family member. How can Tom overcome the perception that he does not have the global experience needed for the job? Consider these additional facts about Tom:

- Tom is a photographer. On a family trip to the Grand Canyon, he took pictures that are now showcased in a campus coffee shop.
- During high school, Tom spent several months in Beijing, China, as a foreign-exchange student. His family hosted foreign exchange students as well.
- Tom taught ESL (English as a Second Language) as part of a community volunteer project.

Questions

1. How should Tom prepare for his interview? How should he go about researching Safari Trekking, the tourism industry, and Africa specifically? How can he best present his knowledge about Africa?
2. What should Tom include in his portfolio for presentation at the interview? How could Tom use his writing samples, past experience, and references to make his case? How could Tom demonstrate his qualifications with media, such as a blog or video?
3. What "tough questions" can Tom expect? How can he overcome them?

Write It *Draft, Revise, and Finalize*

Create Your Own Success Story

1. Read through the following scenarios and determine how to best respond to them in writing. You can choose a formal business letter, an e-mail, or a handwritten note. Consider the propriety of both the message and form of communication, and whether you should include attachments or enclosures with it.

   a. While out with friends, you meet Jeff Williams, a tennis pro who works for a hotel where you have applied for a position. Because you have an interview with the hotel next week, you would like to leave a professional impression by following up with Jeff. In fact, Jeff told you he reports directly to the manager interviewing you. Jeff gave you his business card, so you have all necessary contact information. How will you connect with Jeff?

   b. You have just interviewed with College Cruises, a cruise company specializing in trips for people in their twenties. The interview went well. During the interview, the hiring manager mentioned that he really wants a better understanding of his market's priorities. You want to follow up immediately by thanking him in a way that also demonstrates that you would make a significant contribution to the College Cruises as an employee. How would you go about doing this?

   c. You just received a disappointing rejection for the position of sous chef for a ski lodge in the Rocky Mountains. The hiring manager indicated that you are skilled, but the lodge is entering the busy season and he needs someone with more experience. You would really like to work at that particular lodge in the future. How should you respond?

Once you determine the best method and manner to respond to each situation, pick the one you're most interested in and draft your response. The messages don't have to be very long, only effective.

2. Imagine you are applying for a specific position of your choosing at your institution or a local company. Explore the company or school's Web site to find out as much as possible about the position. Develop at least five probing questions about the institution and the position.
3. Make a list of all the materials you would need to bring with you to an interview to serve as a checklist. Write a summary of how you could bring all the materials and still present yourself professionally.
4. Write an acceptance letter for a fictitious job within your career field. Refer to the employment packet you have been offered to confirm you accept the terms, and remember to be gracious with your response. Now recast it as talking points for a telephone acceptance to be followed by a formal letter.
5. Write a letter declining a job within your career field, either in business letter format or hand-written. Be gracious and include a brief reason as to why you have declined the job.

Speak It *Discuss, Listen, and Understand*

Build Your Leadership and Teamwork Skills

1. Using the job you applied for in the Do It exercise in Chapter 14, prepare a list of questions you think an interviewer might ask using the examples from this chapter. Then, pair up with a classmate for mock interviews. If possible, schedule these mock interviews ahead of time in order to allow you and your classmate to prepare and dress for the event. If this exercise is spontaneous, just describe to your classmate what you would be wearing, and what documents and tools you would bring with you.
   a. Take turns playing the role of the candidate and the interviewer. Using the interview practice form that follows, critique each other's interview performance. Give candid feedback in order to hone each other's interviewing skills.
   b. When you and your partner have had a chance to be both the interviewer and the interviewee, pick one of the two interviews to role play in front of the class. The class will use the same Interview Practice Form to critique your conduct and responses.

Practice Interview Form
First Impression
1. Was the candidate dressed appropriately?
2. Did the candidate make eye contact well?
3. Did the candidate seem at ease?
4. Was the candidate on time?
5. Did the candidate come prepared with the necessary materials?
6. Comments:
Candidate Skill Set
1. Does the candidate have the requisite experience for the position? Explain.
2. How well did the candidate demonstrate an aptitude for the job by referring to past experience? Did the candidate provide relevant examples of his or her success?
3. How well did the candidate demonstrate his or her knowledge of the company's objectives and challenges? Did the candidate reference articles or news reports about the company?
Candidate Interaction
1. How did the candidate respond to tough questions? How well did the candidate maintain his or her composure?
2. Did the candidate inquire about the interview process?
3. Did the candidate ask about your (the interviewer's) objections or concerns?
4. How well did the candidate respond to your objections and concerns?
5. Did the candidate ask to advance in the interview process?
6. Additional comments:

2. In groups or as a class, discuss your experience with interviews. Create a list of positive experiences you have had and a list of aspects you would approach differently now.
3. In small groups or as a class, discuss the different types of interviews you have experienced. How were they different? Which ones were you most comfortable in? What different

strategies did you use? What similar strategies did you use for the different types?

4. In groups or as a class, discuss ways to prepare for the close of an interview. Make a list of questions you can ask the employer when given the opportunity.
5. In pairs, use the background and behavioral sample questions in Exhibits 15-14 and 15-16 to interview each other. Then refine your answers to increase their appeal to an employer.
6. Create a list of questions to ask interviewers for a specific position, such as accountant or salesperson. Compose at least three questions for each of the following topics: Employee Expectations, Hiring Manager's Management Style, and Job Responsibilities. Exchange questions with a classmate to see how your questions could be interpreted by another person.
7. Wear a professional, interview-ready outfit to class based on your chosen career. Compare and contrast your outfit with your classmates. Did everyone follow the guidelines in Exhibit 15-8? What types of careers would allow for variations of an interview dress code? How can you represent your personality in your appearance and still follow the basic professional dress guidelines?

Do It *Document Your Success Track Record*

Build Your e-Portfolio

One of the best ways to get a good understanding of your interviewing skills is to watch yourself during an interview. Repeat the mock interview you did with your partner in the Speak It exercise, but this time, video-record one another. Since you will be familiar with the questions asked in the last exercise, have your partner come up with at least three new "hard-ball" questions you weren't asked in the prior exercise.

1. After the interview, watch the recording of yourself and answer the following questions:
   - When it came to answering tough questions, did you use the HALO (Honesty, Accountability, Leadership, Outcomes) technique?
   - Did your body language indicate that you wanted the job?
   - How was your delivery? Were you obviously nervous, speaking too quietly, or speaking quickly without listening?
   - Did you use qualitative answers to back up your experience?
2. Overall, what aspects of your interview behavior need work?
3. Keep copies of your practice interviews so you can see your own progress. The videos will provide a starting point for your interview training as you enter the job market realm. Make it a point to address the parts of your interviewing behavior that still need work. After all, your interview may be the very reason you land or get passed over for your dream job.

Business in Action
Interview Tips from Zest Recruitment

What's the secret to a successful interview? This is one of the many questions Zest Recruitment, an Australian-based recruiting company for the hotel and tourism industries, asks every day. After all, getting candidates hired and getting companies staffed is the company's specialty.

According to Jerry Pinder, director of Zest Recruitment, the company caters to businesses such as cruise lines, sport stadiums, hotels, restaurants, resorts, clubs, festivals, and other events. The company's goal is to find temporary and permanent employees for these businesses. Candidates come from a variety of locations around the world, including New Zealand, India, China, Singapore, Fiji, and Malaysia.

As you might expect, interviewing practices are not always the same in different countries. To help bridge the gap, Zest Recruitment provides its interview candidates with helpful hints about interviewing in the hotel and tourism industry. Many of these tips apply to multiple industries in countries around the world.

Because the hotel and tourism industry promotes relaxation and hospitality, Zest Recruitment suggests that above all, interviewees should relax. "Feel confident. Look alert," and of course, "Smile." One of Zest's tips is: "Without being arrogant or presumptuous, you should work on the assumption that it is perfectly natural that you will be given the job. After all, you know that you can do it well, and it is merely a matter of allowing the client to see that, too."

Other tips provided by Zest include how to dress for the interview. For both men and women, Zest encourages applicants to wear a "conservative two-piece business suit" in either dark blue or gray, a "conservative long-sleeved shirt" in white or pastel colors, and "clean, polished, conservative shoes." Furthermore, Zest warns against carrying anything in your pockets (because you might have a tendency to fiddle with it when you're nervous); wearing strong cologne or perfume (because you don't want your fragrance to overshadow your personality); and having visible tattoos, piercings, or anything else that might distract from what you have to offer the company.

In the end, Zest Recruitment helps provide people with jobs, companies with employees, and interviewees with lessons that can change their world. What's the last step to succeeding in a job interview? Zest Recruitment says, "Be yourself."

Questions

1. The Zest Recruitment company profile mentions that interviewees tend to fiddle with things in their pockets when nervous. What nervous traits do you have? How do they detract from the way you would like to be perceived? What can you do instead to communicate confidence?
2. Zest Recruitment identified the traits "relaxed and confident" as those necessary for someone working in hospitality. What traits are necessary for the positions you are seeking? How can you demonstrate those traits in your interviews?
3. The hotel and tourism industry sells entertainment and leisure. Why does it recommend that job interviewees dress conservatively?

Source: Interview with Jerry Pinder, June 29, 2009, in "Interview Skills" from Zest Recruitment.

Key Terms

Acceptance letters. A letter or e-mail sent by a candidate to an employer accepting an offer of employment. *(p. 453)*

Background questions. Interview questions that focus on both a candidate's personal and professional background. *(p. 440)*

Behavioral questions. Interview questions regarding a candidate's past behavior. The responses are taken as a predictor of the person's future performance on the job. *(p. 441)*

Group interviews. An interview with multiple interviewers at one time. *(p. 435)*

Illegal questions. Questions about a candidate's race, color, sex, religion, national origin, birthplace, age, disability, and marital or family status that are against the law to ask. *(p. 442)*

Interest questions. Interview questions that gauge a candidate's interest in a company, industry, and position. *(p. 440)*

Letter of decline. A letter or note written by a candidate declining an offer of employment. *(p. 453)*

Offer letter. A letter or e-mail sent by an employer to a candidate outlining a job's salary, benefits, and start date as an offer of employment. *(p. 451)*

One-on-one interviews. Interviews involving just the candidate and an interviewer. *(p. 435)*

Phone interview. An interview conducted over the phone, generally as an initial or screening interview. *(p. 436)*

Probing questions. Questions candidates ask interviewers that require elaboration as opposed to simple explanation. *(p. 446)*

Rejection letter. A letter sent by a corporate representative informing a candidate of his or her rejection for a position. *(p. 455)*

Resignation letter. A letter written by an employee to inform his employer that he is resigning from a position. *(p. 455)*

Situational questions. Interview questions that ask candidates to provide solutions to hypothetical challenges. *(p. 441)*

Social setting interview. An interview that takes place in a social setting to gauge a candidate's social skills. *(p. 437)*

Stress interview. An interview under stressful conditions created by the interviewer for the purpose of testing a candidate's responses under pressure. *(p. 436)*

Videoconference interview. A remote interview telecast through computers. *(p. 436)*

Review Questions *Test Yourself*

1. What should your first response be to an interview offer?
2. What information should you request about the interview?
3. What considerations do you need to make when scheduling an interview?
4. Define a phone interview and how you can best prepare for one.
5. Define a group interview and how you can effectively present yourself to everyone involved.
6. What guidelines you can follow before and during a social interview?
7. What should you research to prepare for an interview?
8. What information is an employer trying to obtain by asking background and interest questions to a job candidate?
9. How does the mnemonic device HALO help you answer situational questions?
10. What topics should you avoid when given a chance to ask questions in an interview?
11. Define a probing question. How will asking it help you in an interview?
12. Why shouldn't you ask questions about time off or the possibility of working from home? How does an employer interpret those questions?

13. What information do you supply on an application, and what is the application's importance?
14. List some basic guidelines for dressing for an interview, such as how to wear your hair. Why is dress such an important consideration for an interview?
15. What items should you bring to an interview?
16. When should you discuss the salary, and what factors should you consider when negotiating a final salary offer?
17. What considerations should you show a current employer when resigning from your position before you move on in your career?

Grammar Review *Mastering Accuracy*

Accurate Word Choices

Section I

Each of the following sentences contains one or more common errors in word usage, grammar, or style. Identify the errors. If you have trouble finding the errors, review Section 4.4. in the handbook (Appendix D) at the back of this textbook.

1. Whose the number one candidate for this position?
2. Who's decision warrants debate?
3. We will offer no acceptations for late arrivals.
4. Please except our congratulations on your recent promotion.
5. We will offer complementary poolside service to those who wish to compliment their celebratory afternoon!
6. It will be difficult not to loose your lose change.
7. Our roll in the company is to role out the best peace of product in the industry.
8. Business principals dictate that you should be honest and fare with all clients.
9. Remain discrete when addressing difficult members of the organization.
10. Our advanced technology is daring and completely discreet from the competition.

Section II

On a separate sheet of paper, rewrite the following sentences so they are clearer, more professional sounding, grammatically correct, and goodwill oriented.

1. Remember to site your sources in all essays; it makes you look bad if you don't.
2. Our sister says she was an awful victim of prosecution at school when she was younger; however, it would be pointless to try and persecute her torturers now that she is a big-shot lawyer.
3. Visit our websight fore more information on ways to improve your site reading abilities.
4. Weather or not you except the position, don't be rude.
5. Remember too haggle when you go in there!
6. Our employee health plan states we should workout twenty minutes everyday.
7. Deborah for some reason insists on coming to work in her tennis shoes.
8. Offer advise only when you have the know-how to correctly advice a person or situation.
9. Their our too moor meetings today, which is still mercifully less than yesterday.
10. You so need this assistance more then me, so I want you to really take a look at all options before admitting you are disinterested.

Extra Resources *Tools You Can Use*

Books

- Beshara, Tony. *Acing the Interview: How to Ask and Answer the Questions That Will Get You the Job.* New York: AMACOM, 2008.
- Burns, Dan. *The First 60 Seconds: Win the Job Interview before It Begins.* Naperville, IL: Sourcebooks, Inc., 2009.
- Cohen, Herb. *You Can Negotiate Anything: The World's Best Negotiator Tells You How to Get What You Want.* Secaucus, NJ: Bantam, 1982.
- Oliver, Vicky. *301 Smart Answers to Tough Interview Questions.* Naperville, IL: Sourcebooks, Inc., 2005.
- Powers, Paul. *Winning Job Interviews.* United States: Career Press, 2010.

Web Sites

- Doyle, Alison, "Interview Questions and Answers," *About .com.*
- Giordano, Louise, "The Ultimate Guide to Job Interview Preparation," *QuintCareers.com.*
- Campbell, Gloria Dixon, "How to Reject a Job Offer," *eHow*
- Doyle, Alison, "How to Prepare for a Job Interview," *About .com.*

"Communication is the real work of leadership." —Nitin Nohria, Richard P. Chapman professor of Business Administration, Harvard Business School

CHAPTER 16

Becoming a World-Class Employee and Leader

Communicate Your Own Success Story

LEARNING OBJECTIVE QUESTIONS

1. How do good communication skills help organizations succeed?
2. How do you find and keep your passion for your work?
3. Why is it important to establish healthy boundaries at work?
4. How do you exceed expectations on the job?
5. How can you advance your career with communication?
6. How can feedback improve your professionalism?
7. What is the key to ethical communication in the business world?
8. How do you know when your job is no longer a good fit?

PEARSON **mybcommlab** Access interactive videos, simulations, sample documents, document makeovers, and assessment quizzes in Chapter 16 of **mybcommlab.com** for mastery of this chapter's objectives.

>>> **Hans** always loved nature. Growing up near the woods, he felt a special connection to the natural world and developed a heartfelt desire to keep it intact for future generations. Combined with a business sense he inherited from his father, he decided to do something proactive. Along with a few close friends, Hans founded Forever Forest, an environmental nonprofit that teaches the benefits of nature to young people around the world.

Because he had never started a business before, Hans felt a little overwhelmed at first. There was so much to do and so many decisions to make. Hans began researching and absorbing everything he could about starting a successful business. He spoke to business owners he knew and attended seminars on nonprofits where he learned how to obtain funding. He read news articles on his industry and took notes when he read stories about businesses that had failed.

Within a year, Hans opened the doors of Forever Forest's first office. He and his small staff set up appointments with school counselors and principals to present the organization's services. Pretty soon, they were maintaining a small group of clients.

Hans' organization started out small but kept growing. Six years later, Hans was well known in the nonprofit community and a celebrated small-business owner. When others asked how he came by his success, he answered, "I stuck it out and never stopped learning. Everyone has something they can teach you to make you a more successful version of yourself. Keep your ears and eyes open, and you will never be far from your goal."

Hans put his passion, interests, and communication skills to work in his own nonprofit in order to make the world a better place. You can do the same. This chapter will take you beyond the search for successful employment to show you how all of the 21st century communication skills you have learned so far will serve you in college, your career, and your life. You will learn how good communication skills add value to nonprofit organizations and positively affect others. You will learn how to maintain passion for your work and avoid burnout. Finally, you will learn to exceed expectations and remain highly ethical as you become a real contributor and leader in your field.

Hans >>>

Your ability to communicate as a paid employee or volunteer for a nonprofit can dramatically affect your success and the success of the organization.

Once you land the job of your dreams, or the job that is a stepping stone to the job of your dreams, that is just the beginning—not the end. Your career is not a destination. It's a journey, so enjoy the trip and be mindful of the process. Many people find themselves taking detours and side roads along the way. Some even start their own nonprofits as Hans did. Most people get involved with nonprofits because they want to give back. Some do so because they have a passion for a cause.

Habitat for Humanity, the United Way, the Red Cross, Peace Corps, and the World Wildlife Fund are examples of nonprofit organizations. These organizations don't distribute their profits to shareholders like corporations do. Instead, they reinvest the money in their organizations to expand the work they do.

The nonprofit sector is expected to grow substantially in the coming years. Consequently, the opportunities within it are significant. These include executive-level positions, research jobs, accounting, marketing, and public relations jobs, board member and volunteer opportunities, and other positions—positions in which your ability to communicate clearly and competently will affect your effectiveness. In addition, nonprofits offer competitive salaries and benefits packages that are often on par with traditional for-profit businesses.

Nonprofits appreciate volunteers who can perform a wide variety of functions including writing letters and grant proposals, planning fundraising events, making phone calls or training other volunteers, and making speeches to the public. Nonprofit work is a great way to strengthen your business abilities and increase your business network, while making a difference.

Now let's look at qualities that will keep you employable, promotable, and help you make a difference in the world, whether you work for a nonprofit or a for-profit organization.

1 How Do Good Business Communication Skills Help Organizations Succeed?

Although you may never move to a developing country to work for a nonprofit, you may volunteer for a cause that means a lot to you—or several causes during your life. In this capacity, you will have many chances to influence action through your communication skills. If you volunteer with a local homeless shelter, you might write up what the shelter needs from donors in a formal report to the organization's board members. You might end up writing a compelling reason for neighbors to open up their homes as part of the homes-tour benefit for your local grade school.

If your business communication—oral and in writing—is not clear and direct, then the people you want to help the most may not get the assistance they need. Your ability to convey your message successfully will directly affect the success of your cause and so will your ability to maintain a passion for what you do.

2 How Do You Find and Keep Your Passion for Your Work?

What are you enthusiastic and passionate about? Use Exhibit 16-1 to help you find out and pursue a related career.

Passion and enthusiasm go a long way in both the corporate and nonprofit world. For example, consider SurfAid International, a medical aid organization working to improve the health of the indigenous people of the Mentawai Islands in Indonesia. A passion for surfing and helping others is the reason why this organization exists. The aid group was founded by surfers who visited the islands to enjoy their sport and discovered that the people living beyond the beautiful shores of the island suffered severe health and poverty problems. SurfAid International efforts work toward malaria prevention, providing clean water and sanitation, disaster preparedness, and developing community health programs. In 2007, the organization won the Humanitarian Award from the World Association of Non-Governmental Organizations (WANGO).

People who like what they do are fun to be around, and they inspire others to do and be their best. Additionally, employers prefer people who like what they do because they tend to perform their jobs well, are highly productive, and motivate others. Take time to review the questions in **Exhibit 16-1** to find out if you are pursuing your passion.

Exhibit 16-1 Finding Your Passion: Questions to Ask Yourself

1. How do you feel about your current stage of life—do you like what you are doing?
2. Are you energized by the path of study you have chosen? If not, what are you enthusiastic about? Are you gathering information and soliciting advice so as to change your study path?
3. What interests and excites you? How do you plan to integrate your interests into your career?
4. When you graduate, will your first full-time job be a step toward your dream career or simply a job to get you from point A to point B?
5. Are you looking forward to the challenges of the working world?
6. What is standing between good and great for you?

When it comes to passion for your work, consider Antonio, a young man who loved building things ever since he was a child. At the age of four, Antonio built his first bookend, and graduated to a crooked three-piece side table at the age of five. From there it was birdhouses, doghouses, a Victorian dollhouse for his sister, and a series of forts and tree houses. In high school he volunteered at Habitat for Humanity, learning all he could about conventional building. He was ready to go into the construction trade straight out of high school, but his parents urged him to try at least two years at a community college.

During those two years, Antonio took general education courses and continued working with Habitat for Humanity during the summer. Part of his general education curriculum included an anthropology and sociology course, which exposed him to other cultures. He was particularly interested in sustainable building and the earthen architecture in villages in Africa and the Middle East.

As luck would have it, a local university offered a degree in sustainable building. Antonio couldn't wait to transfer. During his junior year, he took two off-campus workshops on building straw-bale and rammed-earth homes. Then he applied for an internship with the Cal-Earth, the California Institute of Earth Art and Architecture. His love of building, experience with Habitat for Humanity, and passion for rammed-earth homes, got him hired. That summer he made a stipend that barely covered his room and board, but he loved every minute of it. The experience was invaluable, and his passion for earthen homes was rekindled every day.

Your passion may start with an interest, but it needs to be nurtured and sustained. Many people find their passion is sustained by the ability to pursue what they love, the chance to stretch themselves, the opportunity to help others, and the feeling of being valued and rewarded for a job well done.

3 Why Is It Important to Establish Healthy Boundaries at Work?

No matter where your interests take you, you will still need to set boundaries in the workplace to maintain healthy relationships with your coworkers. In Chapter 1, you explored how good interpersonal communication skills start with good intrapersonal communications skills. In this section we discuss tips to encourage you to set personal limits and stay on a productive track during the business day so that your life at work and outside of work can be rewarding.

Avoiding Burnout

You have probably heard about job **burnout.** Burnout is not necessarily a single incident of a meltdown that occurs during a person's career. Burnout can also manifest itself in smaller ways each day. Daily signs of burnout include becoming irritated or unproductive, no longer thinking clearly, and being unable to verbalize your thoughts effectively. It's been said that burnout

Exhibit 16-2 Tips for Managing Burnout

Burnout Management Technique	Actions to Take
Establish a system of balance.	Listen to the nonverbal ways your body communicates its need for a break. Is your head throbbing? Are your eyes glazing over? Do you get tense in your neck and shoulders? If so, this is another sign that you need to balance periods of hard work with breaks.
Change your state and take a "think break."	If you are sitting, try standing while you go about your business. If you have been standing, sit down and relax. Or, take a short walk, even if it's inside the building. Take a stretch break to reactivate your blood flow.
Know when you need to refuel.	Refueling involves more than just a short break. Make time to eat, rest, breathe deeply, exercise, and interact with others or take some time alone.

is nature's way of telling you that you have been going through the motions—that your "soul has departed."[1] **Exhibit 16-2** offers some tips for managing small bouts of burnout.

Communicating under Pressure

One of the most difficult situations in the working world is communicating under pressure. Once you become aware of the pitfalls of hurried communication you can communicate successfully even under duress. Three common pitfalls of communicating under pressure are 1) undergoing personality changes, 2) sacrificing relationships to get the job done, and 3) becoming paralyzed by your emotions or over-analysis. Let's look at how to deal with each pitfall.

Pitfall #1: Undergoing Personality Changes

In extreme circumstances of crisis or deadline, people have the potential to shift into **back-up behavior,** a sort of "coping" mode. Back-up behavior manifests itself differently across each personality type you studied in Chapter 2. Thinkers can withdraw and withhold information. Givers may become passive-aggressive. Organizers might become controlling and autocratic, while Adventurers can explode or lay blame.

How do you deal with these changes? First, learn to recognize back-up behaviors in others and in yourself. Next, think before you speak and act. Become aware of your own back-up tendencies and learn how to manage them.

Pitfall #2: Sacrificing Relationships to Get the Job Done

Although your first instinct under pressure may be to charge forward and take action, you still need to preserve relationships in the process. To do this, you must continue to communicate with key players. This collaboration will provide a checks-and-balances system in terms of the solution your group decides upon. Hash out options in an impromptu meeting, assign actions with everyone present agreeing to them, and then charge forward on your piece of the solution.

Pitfall #3: Becoming Paralyzed by Indecision

Nothing will slow you down more than letting yourself become overwhelmed by personal and professional quagmires and analyzing whether or not you performed perfectly. What's the best way to deal with feeling overwhelmed? Do something to relax, like going for a walk, talking to someone, listening to music, or engaging in a mindless activity such as doodling. No one makes the right decisions all of the time. If you admit as much and keep your communication positive, the repercussions of any mistakes you make will probably be minor. Other people realize that mistakes are how people learn, and they will know you are doing your best. That is all anyone can ask.

Friends versus Coworkers

Another aspect of healthy workplace boundaries is workplace friendships. When you work with people every day, it's easy to start over-communicating personal information. You may need to set limits on friendships so they do not get in the way of working relationships. Instead of being friendly and communicating with everyone, some people spend too much time developing friendships and communicating with people who have the same personality traits as them. As a result, they don't take into account other people's points and view. This hurts their work relationships and decision-making ability. It also hurts their chances for promotion because other people don't see them as employees who are able to listen to and lead a diverse group of people.

4 How Do You Exceed Expectations on the Job?

Do you really want to be successful in the workplace? Then consider this: a successful employee is more than someone who shows up for work, works long hours, receives good evaluations, and moves up the corporate ladder. Truly successful employees are those who consistently look for ways to improve the environment in which they work, seek opportunities to stretch their abilities, and pay attention to the work at hand and the people they work with.

Instead of thinking about what the company can do for you, think more about what you can do for the company. This means switching gears from "How can I make more money?" or "How can I get more attention?" to "What more can I do?" and "How can I make a difference?" Ask yourself, "What contributions can my gifts and talents produce?"

Paying Your Dues

It's not unusual for new college graduates who haven't been in the workforce before to have unrealistic views of what to expect on the job. Some graduates enter the workplace with a sense of entitlement. They believe that because they have a degree, they should automatically be making the "big bucks" and have executive responsibilities when they land a position. Be willing to pay your dues and don't think you're above the entry-level jobs where you learn the most. Entry level jobs are the foundation of most people's careers. Your skills and talents will develop over time, and your experience will increase the longer you work. Taking a lower-paying job to start is often a great way to break into a field and gain both experience and confidence.

Let's look at an example of how a college student's can-do attitude and willingness to go the extra mile helped her create a positive, professional image that attracted the respect and attention of others: Katrina is a university student who volunteers as a coffee-stand server at a day shelter. She would eventually like to run a business of her own. Although Katrina doesn't plan to become employed in the coffee business or a homeless relief agency, she recognizes that relating to customers at the coffee stand is good practice for relating to customers in future businesses. She interacts brightly with customers. She also makes a point to cater to the special needs of her customers. For example, a man with a bad cold will have different needs than a woman taking care of small children. Regular customers look forward to being served by Katrina, and new customers appreciate her help.

The fact is, every type of work you do, whether volunteer or paid, is a stepping stone to the next move in your future career. Communication is the outward expression of your performance. Additionally, your instructors and supervisors will be evaluating your performance. Not only that, but they will be writing your professional references for tomorrow's opportunities. The professionalism Katrina exhibited while working at the day shelter served her well in another position as a volunteer fundraiser for a political campaign. The fundraising manager was glad to write her the letter of reference shown in **Exhibit 16-3.**

DID YOU KNOW?

To get a good job or be admitted to a school of higher learning, you will probably need one or more letters of recommendation from your college professors or employers.

Exhibit 16-3 A Letter of Recommendation

The Hope Foundation
51 Sleeper St # 200
Boston, MA 02210-1121

May 23, 2011

Ms. Delia Sonari
Development Director
Hands Across the Nation
45 M Street SW
Washington, DC 20024-3622

Dear Ms. Sonari:

It is my pleasure to recommend Katrina Martin for your fundraising coordinator's position at your organization. I see from the description of the position that you are looking for a candidate who exhibits solid business and communication skills, shows initiative, is persistent, and has fundraising experience.

The introduction mentions the candidate's name and desired position.

Katrina approached me one year ago to volunteer for our spring fundraising drive with our nonprofit. She immediately demonstrated her leadership skills by introducing a novel and timely pledge package distributed via social media networks. The package increased pledges by 20 percent the day it was launched.

Katrina returned to work for us during our fall fundraising drive after our fundraising coordinator fell ill. She recognized our fundamental business dilemma and took the initiative to apply her outstanding communication skills. She then proceeded to work three extra shifts a week managing a team of live phone operators accepting donations. This act of going above and beyond allowed us to keep our call processing rate steady despite the coordinator's absence.

In summary, I think Katrina would be a wonderful fit for Hands Across the Nation's fundraising coordinator's position. In my opinion, she has a strong understanding of business principles, leads by communicating well with both senior-level managers and peers, and is fully dedicated to all aspects of fundraising.

The close summarizes the candidate's business attributes needed for the job.

Sincerely,

Ron Yoder

Ron Yoder
Development Director

mybcommlab

Apply Exhibit 16-13's key concepts by revising a new document. Go to Chapter 16 in mybcommlab.com and select Document Makeovers.

Going the Extra Mile

When you're hired for a job, you're hired with certain expectations—that you can skillfully and effectively meet your employer's job requirements. However, don't limit yourself to your job description. Work to exceed your job's requirements so you're seen as someone who goes the extra mile to add value to the company. Adding value—or going the extra mile—refers to what you personally bring to your job that is beyond your employer's expectations and unique to your personality and style. It does not necessarily mean working harder; it means working smarter and contributing to the company's success in creative, imaginative, and useful ways. You can practice this right now by going the extra mile in class and during college.

If you see a problem that needs solving, but it's not a direct part of your job, get involved if you think you can contribute. All companies have problems—including communication and process problems—some of which they are not even aware. It's a good idea to learn as much as you can about your company so you can contribute on all levels beyond your basic job function. If you tactfully bring up a problem, show genuine interest in solving it, and offer to work on it, your manager will definitely stand up and take notice. Assume that others are doing their best and want to work well with you to solve problems and make decisions.

Take time to consider how your actions might impact the bigger picture. An average worker says, "I'm just one person. What can I do?" An exceptional worker says, "I'm just the person to make a difference." For example, suppose you notice that some departments are unaware of what other departments are doing, which means a lot of duplication of effort and loss of productivity. You could volunteer to act as an interdepartmental communicator, sharing information between departments. Go out of your way to help others at work. Just a little extra time on your part could make a big difference in the company.

As you start offering assistance in areas outside your job description, people will begin to notice you. You will be educating them about who you really are and what you are capable of. It's a great way to get known and make a difference. Ask yourself the questions in **Exhibit 16-4** to identify areas where you can go the extra mile.

Exhibit 16-4
Paying Your Dues and Going the Extra Mile: Questions to Ask Yourself

1. Do I look for problems to solve?
2. Do I look for opportunities to take a leadership role?
3. Do I ask for assignments no one else wants or no one else can take on?
4. Do I offer to assist my coworkers with their projects?
5. Do I give others credit?
6. Do I get involved with projects outside of work?

Developing Your Game Face

Your game face—or your poker face—relates to your ability to keep a professional outlook and communicate positively even though you may be working through personal difficulties or setbacks. To be a true professional, you need to understand what the business world expects of you. The way you communicate with others—your social and emotional abilities—says as much as the actual actions you take and job goals you achieve. Business professionals today are successful because of their behaviors, attitudes, and relationships. They have a positive, confident "game face" even when they are privately stressed, discouraged, or agitated.

The behaviors you exhibit in the workplace are simply an extension of the communication behaviors you exhibit in college, on the job, and in activities to which you belong. Do you show up on time for class? Do you wear grubby sweats and a baseball cap, or do you dress like an aspiring business professional? Do you ask thoughtful questions during a lecture? Do you make eye contact with your professor and communicate with your classmates in a helpful way?

Exhibit 16-5 lists professional behaviors to embrace and unprofessional behaviors to avoid. As you examine the list, notice which column in the table represents your typical behavior, and determine whether you need to shift the ways you behave to become more professional in today's workplace.

5 How Can You Advance Your Career with Communication?

Paying your dues, going the extra mile, and adopting a professional attitude can take you far. In Chapter 2, you learned how to approach and communicate with people who have different work personalities. In Chapter 7, you learned how to communicate up the company hierarchy to superiors, across the hierarchy to peers, and down the hierarchy to subordinates. Now is your chance to put it all together so you communicate effectively with people at all levels of an organization you might join after graduating.

Exhibit 16-5 Professional Behaviors Required and Rewarded in the 21st Century

Practice These Behaviors	Replace These Behaviors
Time Management	
Be punctual. Stick to the schedule so others can rely on you.	**Rarely show up on time.** This is not only rude but communicates that your time is more valuable than everyone else's.
Meet your deadlines. Don't view deadlines as negotiable. Recognize that others depend on you to complete your part so they can do theirs. Don't give your colleagues and boss the idea that they cannot count on you.	**Miss your deadlines.** Your colleagues and boss will learn that they cannot count on you and will consider you undependable.
Interpersonal Communication	
Treat others as they would like to be treated. This is basic courtesy. You won't necessarily like everyone you work with, but you should always communicate professionally with them.	**Do unto others before they do unto you.** This is an attitude that will make enemies and lose you friends (not to mention, promotions).
Earn respect. Don't expect instant rewards. You must prove you are worthy of them. Be patient. Your professional communication and behavior will earn others' respect over time.	**Expect instant respect and rewards.** You must prove you are worthy of them.
Admit your mistakes and share your successes. Take personal responsibility for mistakes and learn from them. Share what you have learned with others. Don't forget to share responsibility for your successes as well.	**Accuse others of being wrong and claim all of the credit.** Few people will want to work with you, and managers will not be impressed.
Don't take people for granted. Don't assume that coworkers owe you their time. Instead, encourage them to communicate with you and give you their time when they have a chance. Express gratitude for their help.	**Act entitled.** By assuming your coworkers owe you their time, you come across as self-centered.
Respect those with more experience. By ignoring and not communicating with these people you lose out on valuable knowledge and an opportunity to learn from them. Look for a mentor and learn all you can. Value what seniority can bring to the workplace.	**Disrespect people older than you or with more experience.** By ignoring these people you lose allies in the workplace and the opportunity to learn from them.
Control your emotions. Restrain yourself emotionally when you communicate with another person. Behaving in an over-emotional way sends a message that you can't be trusted to "keep your cool" under stress when you are communicating with customers, coworkers, and managers.	**Show extremes of emotion.** By behaving this way, you alienate others and earn a reputation as an unprofessional bully or crybaby. Worse, you run the risk of alienating others and negatively affecting your future.
Be flexible. Study up on communication style differences and be flexible so you can learn to meet others where they are.	**Be rigid and judgmental.** Don't expect everyone to be just like you. Don't judge coworkers because they perform tasks differently than you do.
Professional Communication Behavior	
Remember to proofread. Take the time to check over all workplace communication, whether written or electronic.	**Never check your work.** It's not enough to only show passion in your work, you must also take the time to check your form.
Speak with a professional tone and vocabulary. Be your own censor.	**Speak as you would with your buddies.** It is inappropriate to use slang, and tell about wild weekend escapades.

Exhibit 16-5 Professional Behaviors Required and Rewarded in the 21st Century, *(continued)*

Avoid distractions. Persevere to meet business goals by purposefully avoiding distractions. While most employers won't mind if you check your e-mail now and then, don't waste time checking it every 10 minutes or hanging out on social networking sites.	**Allow yourself to get distracted.** Don't respond to every personal text, Facebook chat, and e-mail. Don't play games, shop online, or spend time on networking sites.
Professional Attitude	
Take the initiative. Look for ways to reduce costs, streamline operations, improve communications, and increase efficiency. Taking the reins will show that you can handle responsibility.	**Always wait for direction.** Self-motivated people tend to be more valued in organizations.
Adopt a "can-do" attitude. Be part of the solution, not the problem. If something is bothering you, share it, but also share a possible solution. Use phrases like, "I can," "I will," and "I'll figure it out."	**Be negative.** Negative people seem to suck the energy out of the room. If you find yourself saying "I can't" or "I don't know," or "It will never change," you are in danger of becoming a naysayer and someone to avoid.
Appearance and Actions	
Express your individuality appropriately. Show you are unique through your contribution to the professional workplace.	**Express your individuality inappropriately.** Refrain from showing you are unique through your visible tattoos and piercings.
Dress professionally. Differentiate the attire you wear to work from your personal attire, even on casual (dress down) Fridays. What you wear reflects the way you feel about your job. Take a cue from coworkers and managers to see what's appropriate.	**Dress unprofessionally.** Don't wear whatever you want to work. Flip-flops, low-cut shirts, ripped jeans, or baseball caps are not appropriate for the office, even on casual days.

Communicating Clearly and Effectively

One key to effective communication is to be genuine. If you are true to yourself, chances are that other people will enjoy working with you and respond more positively to your ideas. Part of being genuine is learning how to communicate *clearly* and *thoroughly* with those for whom you work, and those whom you may eventually supervise.

Consider Jaden, an independent writing contractor in San Francisco. Jaden is working with a nonprofit arts foundation with offices in San Francisco and Chicago. She is sending Web site copy to the foundation's Web designer, Dan, located at the organization's Chicago office. Jaden is aware that Bob, the foundation's vice president who hired her, wants the question-and-answer portion of the copy to appear in a special Frequently Asked Questions (FAQ) section. She also knows he wants users to be able to navigate to that page quickly and easily.

It's 4:00 P.M. in San Francisco, and Jaden is getting ready to leave for five days of vacation the next morning. She forwards a copy of the e-mail to Dan with the note shown in **Exhibit 16-6a.**

This brief e-mail brings up several communication issues. Jaden sends the message at 4:00 P.M. San Francisco time, which is 6:00 P.M. Chicago time. Dan has already left for the day. Jaden is headed out on vacation, and she hasn't left Dan a concrete way to contact her in case he needs to follow up or ask her a question. The note also doesn't tell Dan about the request for the FAQ section, which is very important to Bob. Nor does the e-mail provide any details about where or how the FAQ section is supposed to look in the Web site.

Exhibit 16-6a
An Unclear E-mail Message

To: dan.ortega@artfortherestofus.org
Sent: 12/18/2011 1:30 PM
From: jaden.collins@artforththerestofus.org
Subject: Status on glazier

Dan,
Attached is the Web site copy. Bob has approved it all. Please put the FAQ on the home page. I will be back in the office next Wednesday.

Jaden

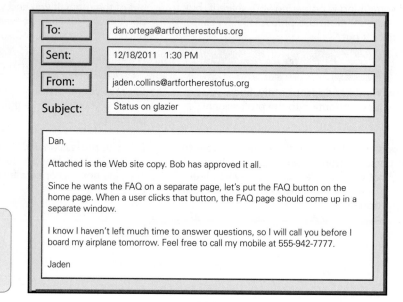

Exhibit 16-6b
A Clear E-mail Message

To: dan.ortega@artfortherestofus.org
Sent: 12/18/2011 1:30 PM
From: jaden.collins@artfortherestofus.org
Subject: Status on glazier

Dan,

Attached is the Web site copy. Bob has approved it all.

Since he wants the FAQ on a separate page, let's put the FAQ button on the home page. When a user clicks that button, the FAQ page should come up in a separate window.

I know I haven't left much time to answer questions, so I will call you before I board my airplane tomorrow. Feel free to call my mobile at 555-942-7777.

Jaden

PEARSON mybcommlab

Apply Exhibit 16-6b's key concepts by revising a new document. Go to Chapter 16 in mybcommlab.com and select Document Makeovers.

Dan doesn't feel he can finish the FAQ portion of the Web site until Jaden returns from vacation. During this time, Dan receives an e-mail from Bob, asking about the progress on the Web site. How does Dan respond? Jaden's actions have jeopardized the project, perhaps her job, and possibly Dan's as well.

If Jaden had improved the clarity and detail of her communication to Dan, things would have gone differently. **Exhibit 16-6b** shows how her improved e-mail might read.

In this e-mail, Jaden explains to Dan exactly what Bob wants. She also indicates her intention to follow up with Dan so she can check with him for understanding. Once she gets him on the phone, she can use the perceptive listening skills from Chapter 1 to make sure from his voice that he is clear about her directions. If Bob e-mails Dan while she is gone, Dan will be able to show Bob the FAQ button, maintain the schedule, and get the tasks completed on time.

Communicating Upward (to Superiors)

When you communicate with someone who has supervisory responsibility for you or your manager, you are **communicating up.** Your relationship with your manager or supervisor will be even more interactive than the relationships you have with most college instructors. Although you will encounter many different management styles within a single company, your communication responsibility remains the same: communicate with respect, and communicate to gain your manager's trust.

Brooke works for the nongovernmental organization (NGO) Doctors Without Borders. She has been sent to the Democratic Republic of Congo's Katanga province to assess the health benefits of extending existing water lines out to refugee camps. During her sec-

Exhibit 16-7 Checklist: Communicating Upward

- ☐ I communicate regularly and appropriately with my manager.
- ☐ I set realistic goals for myself, and obtain written and verbal agreement about them from my manager.
- ☐ If my goals do not seem realistic, I share my concerns with my manager.
- ☐ I ask for my manager's input on a few "stretch" goals—goals that are slightly out of my reach.
- ☐ I use weekly and monthly reports to inform my manager about my formal progress.
- ☐ I evaluate my resources and ask my manager when I need additional resources.
- ☐ I ask for frequent feedback in the early stages of my relationship with a new manager.
- ☐ I anticipate problems and identify issues early so I can ask for assistance from my manager in a proactive manner.
- ☐ I talk to my manager the minute I know I may have trouble meeting a deadline.
- ☐ I use electronic communication to notify my manager of routine updates or changes.
- ☐ I document all my major actions and decisions by creating a "communication trail" folder where I keep all e-mails or notes related to my goals.
- ☐ I copy my manager on all goal-related written communication.
- ☐ If I can't meet one of my goals, I let my manager know as soon as possible, either by phone or face to face.
- ☐ As Chapter 8 explained, I alert my manager to any deadline crises that appear on the horizon.

ond day at the investigation site, she discovers a cracked pipe that could pose an environmental or health threat to the whole water system. Rather than waiting to include this discovery on her weekly report, Brooke immediately sends a courier message to her site supervisor, Easton, who then drives over to her location to assess the situation. Once Easton studies the pipe, he phones an emergency contact at Doctors Without Borders to request additional labor for pipe replacement. Without Brooke's prompt and timely upward communication, it may have been days before Easton returned to her community, possibly just long enough for the pipe to burst or for contaminant levels to rise.

Review **Exhibit 16-7** for upward communication skills that will maximize your dependability and minimize the surprises your superiors experience. You will also set a high communication standard for your coworkers. Check off the behaviors you exhibit in your current internship, volunteer position, or part-time job.

Downward (to Subordinates)

Sometimes you will **communicate down** to subordinates, who may include coworkers with less experience than you. No matter where those workers are located in the organization, they can help you meet your goals. To figure out what motivates a coworker or subordinate to do his or her best, you can ask such open-ended questions as:

- What are your responsibilities here?
- What do you like best about this job?
- What kind of recognition is important to you?
- How can I assist you to help you do your job better?

Through their answers, people will give you clues about how to work with them and what tasks they enjoy most. For example, make note of the job duties in which they seem to take the most pride. Determine whether the recognition they prefer is external: Do they prefer awards, letters of recommendation, or bonuses? Or are the employees more internally motivated: Do they enjoy appearing knowledgeable and seeing their suggestions put into action?

When you arm yourself with knowledge of what your employees value and understand how they want to be rewarded, you will be able to attract and motivate people who can help you meet your goals. In turn, you can help them achieve their goals. Let's look at an example of successful downward communication.

In the middle of June each year, the U.S. Department of State sends a mandate to global student-exchange organizations. The mandate clearly states that all international high

Exhibit 16-8 Checklist: Communicating Downward

- ☐ I communicate with people in the manner in which they would like to receive communication.
- ☐ I treat each person with respect, no matter what his or her position is within the organization.
- ☐ I ask open-ended questions to engage my fellow employees.
- ☐ I listen perceptively.
- ☐ I delegate appropriately.
- ☐ When I delegate, I check for understanding on the part of the person to whom I delegated the responsibilities.
- ☐ I communicate trust in people's abilities.
- ☐ I communicate my values to others.

school students waiting to travel to the United States in August must know of their U.S. addresses by August 31. As a result, all high school placement personnel must accelerate their student placements to finish on time.

Jose is the western regional manager for the Council for Educational Travel USA, a global exchange organization that coordinates school and home stays for international students. Jose decides to ask his community coordinator, Madison, who has already met her placements goal, to place yet one more student. Rather than sending Madison an e-mail, which is less personal, he calls her on the phone, which is more personal. He describes the situation, and asks for her reaction. (He can tell by her response that she is surprised.) Then, instead of telling Madison she must place one more student (authoritative communication), he asks if he can count on her to do so (motivation-based communication). Coincidentally, Madison has just discovered that one of the local high schools would like to enroll more exchange students. She tells Jose she will go investigate possibilities there. Review **Exhibit 16-8** for tips regarding effective downward communication. How many of the following skills do you currently employ with coworkers and subordinates?

Communicating Sideways (with Peers)

As you learned in Chapter 2, collaboration involves working together in teams. Communication is, of course, the main way in which people collaborate. When you join a work group, you become part of a team trying to achieve an organization's goals. **Communicating sideways** (or lateral communication) is a way to reach out to the others on your team so that, as a group, you make a difference in your organization. Let's look at an example of successful sideways communication.

Darnell, a music professor at a fine arts college, petitions his school's artistic director for a state-of-the-art piece of equipment that is not itemized in the fiscal year budget. The artistic director, Charissa, finds a grant that could cover three-quarters of the cost of the piece, but the grant deadline looms in three weeks. Charissa puts together a volunteer team of grant writers, made up of two graduate students in nonprofit studies and Darnell. This team meets every other day during the first week, each member tossing out his or her ideas for writing an effective grant. The team supplies Charissa with progress reports and drafts of the grant, which have been written by the students and approved by Darnell. Charissa reads through the material and offers advice based on her experience with grant writing. The team submits a well-written grant by the deadline. Review **Exhibit 16-9** and check off the lateral communication skills you have used to encourage a team to achieve optimally when working together.

Exhibit 16-9 Checklist: Communicating Sideways

- ☐ I ask for input from all of the team's members.
- ☐ I create settings where all members of the team are heard and all their ideas are considered.
- ☐ I copy everyone on all progress updates and reports.
- ☐ I am aware of how my communication might affect others.

REAL INSIGHTS from a New Professional

Name: *Aron Rosenthal*
Title: *Executive Director*
Organization: *Orbis Institute*
Location: *Colorado and China*

MEET ARON ROSENTHAL, THE EXECUTIVE DIRECTOR of Orbis Institute, a nonprofit organization in China that specializes in youth leadership. During college at the University of Colorado Denver, Rosenthal was an avid reader of newspapers and magazines. He noticed that articles about China were everywhere. He hoped that one day he would have a chance to see "the Asian giant" for himself.

In his senior year, Rosenthal got his wish. His father introduced him to the wife of a coworker, a woman from a small town in the Henan province, deep in China's interior. From her, he learned that a group of public schools were looking for a native English speaker . . . would he be interested?

Of course he was interested, and a few months later Rosenthal arrived in the small town of Hebi. He worked in the countryside, and eventually in the Henan capital of Zhengzhou. He worked for various public and private schools teaching English as a second language where he developed a "profound respect for what it means to be an educator." Rosenthal discovered it was crucial to speak some Mandarin to do simple tasks. He says, "I was almost always accompanied by a bilingual colleague native of Henan and never expected my audience to understand much if any English."

One year later Rosenthal returned to the U.S. and almost immediately was introduced to the founder of Orbis Institute. The organization works with high school and college age leaders providing them with a broader scope of international leadership through experiential learning. The organization had programs in Denver and Central Europe and wanted to start a new program in China. Rosenthal volunteered his time for several months to help develop a plan of action. Orbis then sent him to China to lay the groundwork for the new program. Eventually he became the executive director of Orbis Institute, where he helped create a Chinese subsidiary so the organization could legally operate in that country.

Rosenthal says that his world-view was forever changed by his experience in China. More importantly, his interest in the "Asian giant" and his experience there eventually allowed him to lead others in a nonprofit organization. His passion and communication skills have indeed made a difference in the world.

Questions

1. How did Rosenthal's professionalism in college pave the way for realizing his dream in China?
2. Given that Rosenthal had teaching experience in China, why did he donate his time to the Orbis Institute before taking a paid position?
3. Rosenthal had a passion for China and a love of learning that served him well when he became executive director of Orbis Institute. What passions do you have that could move you closer to your career goals?

Source: Aron Rosenthal in discussion with the author, June 2010.

Communicating with Customers

Nonprofits rely on funding from their *constituents*—or donors, members, or sponsors. These people and groups are a nonprofit's customers, so to speak, and as customers, they need to feel that the nonprofit values them. You are a mouthpiece for your organization whenever you interact with its constituents. You have perhaps heard the saying, "The customer is always right." Why is the customer always right? One reason is that someone who is subjected to poor customer communication is likely to tell 10 to 14 other people about his or her bad experience—regardless of whether the customer or the organization was at fault. Pamela Hawley, founder and CEO of UniversalGiving, has learned from her years in nonprofit work that "service is how you treat people . . . it's how you listen, serve, help, and even build together with others."[2] Review the checklist in Exhibit 16-10 to make sure you communicate professionally with customers.

Exhibit 16-10 Checklist: Communicating with Customers

- ☐ I establish regular communication with my customers, by newsletter, e-mail, or Facebook page update.
- ☐ I communicate any organizational changes that will affect my customers.
- ☐ I communicate my organization's needs with sincerity and professionalism.
- ☐ I keep my communication positive, even when customers are in a poor mood or have a complaint.
- ☐ When working directly with dissatisfied customers, I ask how I can help them with their problems, and offer them solutions.
- ☐ I listen perceptively for the real message my customer is communicating.
- ☐ I explain what I think he or she is feeling: Pleased with the progress? Curious? Confused? Frustrated? Angry?
- ☐ If there is a complaint, I immediately state that I'm working to resolve the problem.
- ☐ If my organization is at fault, I communicate a concession I can make to help alleviate the negative experience.

6 How Can Feedback Improve Your Professionalism?

Whether you work for a nonprofit or for-profit company, you will be constantly interacting with other people, as well as giving and receiving feedback. As you learned in Chapter 8, giving and receiving feedback allows for a continued process of growth and improvement. You will be head and shoulders above your peers if you learn to give and receive feedback in a professional manner.

Receiving Feedback

At most companies, you will receive an annual performance review to let you know what you are doing well and where you need to improve. **Exhibit 16-11** provides a quick list of tips to ensure that you handle your first performance appraisal professionally.

Exhibit 16-11
Performance Appraisal Tips

1. Respectfully accept feedback and avoid being defensive. It is far more valuable to gracefully accept criticism than to believe you have no weaknesses and deserve only praise.
2. Remember that meeting expectations means you are doing your job well.
3. Ask for clarification on areas for improvement and how to work on those areas.
4. Ask what you would be doing if you were exceeding all expectations.

Don't wait for a performance appraisal to find out how you are doing. Actively solicit feedback from those who can give you information that will help you improve your performance. This includes asking your supervisor how you can be more effective. You can also ask your customers and clients. In fact, doing so is the foundation for most customer satisfaction surveys.

Different companies have different performance appraisal process forms, but the forms tend to have common components, including a ratings section and an explanation of the ratings. In addition, the forms usually have a section in which supervisors write their overall evaluation of employees. Sometimes the forms contain an employee comments section. You are generally required to sign the form to acknowledge that you have read the review.

Giving Feedback

In Chapter 8, you also learned how to effectively give feedback, even when it is negative. As a manager, your ability to develop the best employees and produce positive results will be helped or hindered by your ability to give constructive feedback to your staff members. As a team member, you will be respected and valued for your ability to point out ways to improve a process, product, or performance. **Exhibit 16-12** reviews some general tips for giving feedback so that it will be understood and better accepted.

Exhibit 16-12
Successfully Giving Feedback

1. Make sure your employees understand your expectations.
2. Get everyone on the same page regarding desired outcomes.
3. Use the "feedback sandwich" technique to provide negative feedback.
4. Provide a performance improvement plan that allows three to six months for the employee to show a positive change in performance.

In general, if employees do not show improvement within the period of time specified in their performance improvement plan, they are usually terminated or asked to leave. Another important aspect of providing feedback is to always look for the positive in addition to areas for improvement. One feedback technique for doing so is the **feedback sandwich.** It is made up of constructive feedback or criticism sandwiched between two pieces of positive information. **Exhibit 16-13** provides an example.

In Exhibit 16-13, Amy's supervisor confronted her for not involving her team members more when making decisions. However, her supervisor was able to make the corrective message into a positive one by emphasizing Amy's good traits.

Exhibit 16-13
A Feedback Sandwich

Positive Feedback
"Amy, you have remarkable ability to solve problems."

Constructive Criticism
"However, you really need to work harder to sell your ideas to your coworkers rather than charging ahead without consulting them."

Positive Feedback
"Once you do that, you are going to be well on your way to becoming a leader in this company."

7 What Is the Key to Ethical Communication in the Business World?

Good ethical communication—making the right communication choices given the circumstances—makes good business sense. Organizations that communicate ethically develop better reputations, reduce their legal risks, and in some industries become less subject to government regulations. If you're not 100 percent clear a behavior is ethical, ask yourself this question: If your coworkers or people outside your organization were to see the choices you're making, would they approve or disapprove?

Not only do you risk running afoul of the law if you or your organization communicates in ways that are unethical, such communication can be hazardous to your business career in the long term or to your company's ability to do business. For example, in 2001, the plant owner of Peanut Corporation of America, Stewart Parnell, communicated to FDA health inspectors that he would correct plant problems and fix faulty equipment.[3] Apparently Parnell misrepresented the plant's intentions. Eight years later, federal inspectors shut

DID YOU KNOW?

Formal ethics codes exist for accountants, court reporters, administrative professionals, and many other professions. Most of these codes can be found online.

down the plant because of unsanitary conditions and a salmonella outbreak that infected roughly 600 people, presumed to be caused by the conditions.

You will face ethical communication dilemmas in the business world. It's not always clear in business what you should and should not say or write. Consider the situation faced by an organization that monitors TV programming. The organization, the Parents Television Council (PTC), discovered what it believed to be dangerous behavior shown in a wrestling program called *SmackDown.* The organization felt a social responsibility to take action against the show's producer. However, in doing so, several PTC members made unsupported statements to the media claiming that young children died when older children practiced dangerous wrestling moves on them—moves they had seen on *SmackDown.*[4] The PTC was later forced to issue an apology for the incident, stating that the statements were premature and not backed by evidence. The PTC's parent company also had to pay $3.5 million in damages to the producers of the show. Stretching the truth can be costly.

To some extent, your organization's policies will dictate what you say and do. Ultimately, though, how you behave in these situations is up to you. You will have to keep your own counsel. Sometimes your ethics may be stronger than those of your boss or your company, and understanding some of the most common legal violations will certainly help you avoid communication mistakes the PTC experienced.

Legal Violations

Certain forms of communication can be harmful and illegal. They include *libel, slander,* and *copyright infractions,* which we will discuss next. In addition there may be industry-specific communication laws and regulations you must abide by, such as specific documents that must be created and filed with the government for an organization to legally become and remain a nonprofit.

Libel and Slander

Defamation, which covers libel and slander, is the legal term for any false statement that harms an individual's reputation. **Libel** occurs when purposeful false and defamatory communication appears in a widely dispersed written form, such as newspapers, magazines, books, television (text), Web pages, or Internet documents. **Slander** occurs when a person or entity is overheard knowingly or recklessly speaking false statements that damage the reputation of another person or entity. These statements might be made in person, on television or radio, or on the Internet. The laws governing libel and slander are complex. With libel, the victim must prove the message was widely dispersed or published, which is not the case for slander.

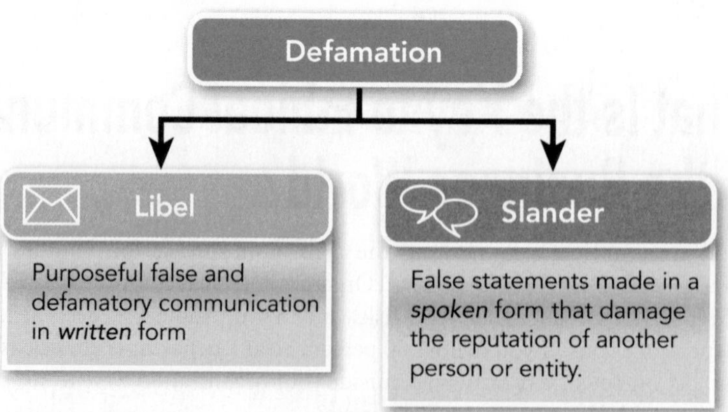

Exhibits 16-14a and 14b provide examples of libel and slander, respectively.

Three factors make the behavior in these two examples bait for a lawsuit: 1) the statements are false, and the maker of the statement either knows as much or should have reason to believe they are; 2) the statements harm someone's reputation, and 3) the statements were heard by others.

Exhibit 16-14a
An Example of Libel

The writer of a newsletter maliciously prints a false statement about a local political candidate (that he didn't pay his taxes). The candidate has to deal with a barrage of questions from community members.

Exhibit 16-14b
An Example of Slander

Without any evidence, a woman sitting in the first row of a college basketball game accuses a university basketball coach of abusing his players. Other people at the game overhear her.

Consider the following ethical dilemma: You work for the fundraising arm of a non-profit, and you repeatedly witness nonstandard accounting procedures on the part of your manager. You have an ethical responsibility to your organization, yet you don't want to falsely accuse your manager in a way that will harm her reputation. One solution would be to write a letter to the organization's board of directors—one that simply requests validation of the organization's accounting standards as you understand them. The letter could (and should) send a signal to the board to investigate if the organization is following the standards. Also, be aware that any message recorded in any way, either on paper or electronically, can be subpoenaed as legal evidence. Electronic communications include e-mails, chat rooms, instant messages, voice messages, and text messages. For this reason, many organizations try to monitor both the messages that come into their organizations and those that go out of them.

Copyright Violations

A **copyright violation** is a legal offense that occurs when someone wrongly republishes material owned by another person or organization. Under a legal guideline referred to as **fair use,** people and organizations have a right to use a limited amount of copyrighted material without seeking permission from the material's owner. However, fair use is not easy to define. How much is a limited amount? Only a court can decide. Courts make this decision, in part, based upon the amount of material that was borrowed from the original source and whether or not it was fair to use it without the owner's permission. Did the person who borrowed the material give the owner credit or was he or she basically passing it off as his or her own work? A diligent business communicator will always research the need to obtain permission to use other people's material. You can check a copyright online with the U.S. Copyright Office.

Copyright laws also extend to the Internet. **Exhibit 16-15** provides two different examples of what happens when a photograph is reused on a Web site. In both examples, Jeremy, a college student, has been asked to write a post on his humanitarian organization's blog about a hunger project partnership between the organization and his university alma mater. On his university's Web site, Jeremy finds a recently copyrighted photograph of students and company employees volunteering at a project worksite. He believes he's found the perfect picture.

Exhibit 16-15 Copyright Violation or Not?

Violation	No Violation
Jeremy posts the photo on his company blog without getting authorization from the copyright owner (in this case, someone at the university). Under these circumstances, Jeremy and his company could be fined for copyright violation.	Jeremy calls the university's media relations director and is granted permission to use that photograph as long as he posts a credit to the photographer. If he posts the photo and the photo credit as requested, this situation would not be considered copyright violation.

False Marketing Claims

Marketing is one aspect of business that is particularly vulnerable to litigation-prone language. Marketing professionals are in the business of making claims about their products. However, sales and marketing messages are illegal if they falsely advertise prices, performance capabilities, quality, or other product characteristics. For example, household products and appliances can earn an Energy Star certification by meeting strict energy efficiency guidelines set by the EPA and U.S. Department of Energy. Scot Case, of the environmental consulting firm TerraChoice, claims that many Americans (including himself) have been "greenwashed."[5] Case found out that his Energy Star–rated refrigerator actually used twice as much energy as advertised, and he reported this to a House of Representatives committee. Later, the company that manufactured the refrigerator issued a letter stating that in its process of "self-certification" it had strayed from the efficiency guidelines set by the Department of Energy. In the end, a simple rule to follow is that your organization must be able to document that the product or service actually delivers what your marketing language and promotion promises.

Ethical Leadership

Businesses that pay attention to and place a stated value upon ethical communication and ethical conduct throughout the organization can be recognized for their ethical leadership. For example, businessmen and professors William F. Baker and Michael O'Malley have awarded kudos to many companies who are displaying a new way of managing. These two men traveled across the U.S. seeking the kindest companies and leaders, and published their findings in the book *Leading with Kindness: How Good People Consistently Get Superior Results.* Their thesis states that some of the world's most successful companies are realizing that the better they treat their employees, the more productive they become.

The Juilliard School earned public recognition for its "applause culture" in which employees openly praise and value one another.

College opportunities, flexible schedules, advanced health care plans, and transparency between ranks are only a few examples of the phenomenon Baker and O'Malley call "leading with kindness." Excellent communication skills are essential to all of these organizational initiatives. Employees, managers, and boards of directors need to communicate to set and understand goals, launch new company programs, change cultural mindsets, and execute the deliverables that go along with each phase of their process. Communicating these ethical practices becomes a catalyst for standards and outcomes throughout the organization and with customers and suppliers.

Leading with Kindness recognized the nonprofit Juilliard School of Dance, Drama, and Music—one of the nation's most prestigious performing arts universities—for its excellence, respect, flexibility, and commitment. Excellence relates not only to an expected level of performance, but also to the excellence of human values. Respect is communicated through supportive dialogue and praise for each other's endeavors. Imagine what it would be like to work in what one of Julliard's directors calls "an applause culture," where employees overtly praise and value each other. Julliard's managers also respect the personal growth of each staff member, communicated by allowing staff to take time off to pursue personal excellence. The managers show their commitment to staff by listening to each request for teaching projects, new equipment, and other departmental needs. Creating a positive, productive work culture is part of making a great company. Adhering to high ethical standards is the other part.

DoTheRightThing and other sites have brought the ethical debate to social networking. Users submit stories about companies that are then voted on by others based on whether the company is "good" or "bad." The idea is that companies will notice their "scores" and realize people pay attention to nonfinancial effects on society, hopefully causing companies to change bad behaviors.

8 How Do You Know When Your Job Is No Longer a Good Fit?

People often wonder how long they should stay in one job before moving on to the next. A job is not about showing up and collecting a paycheck. It's about expressing yourself, using your skills, learning new abilities, and impacting others. It takes time to do this. A good rule

REAL INSIGHTS from a Seasoned Professional

Name: *Vanessa Evans*
Title: *Associate Director*
Organization: *Ron Brown Scholar Program*
Location: *Charlottesville, Virginia*

VANESSA EVANS HAS BEEN IN THE WORKFORCE for 17 years, with exactly half those years spent in her current position as the associate director of the Ron Brown Scholar Program. This program was established in 1996 to provide academic scholarships, service opportunities, and leadership experience for young African Americans of outstanding promise.

Because Evans works for a nonprofit organization with a small staff, she has the opportunity to wear many hats. "We like variety, and we have to be flexible," she says. "I am able to use all my skills in one place, such as writing, oral communication, counseling, admissions, and program planning." Evans loves her job and literally wakes up "looking forward to every day."

She has shown initiative by learning new skills in the areas of finance and development even though she wasn't required or hired to do so. "I thought it was best for me to understand and know the whole picture," which wasn't complete without these two disciplines. Evans highly recommends young professionals to take on new things and be open to new ideas.

Evans' undergraduate degree in marketing from James Madison University in Virginia and her graduate degree in college personnel administration from the same institution, prepared her well for the workforce. During and after her master's work she held positions in student affairs and admissions at James Madison University and The College of William and Mary. "I thought at one point that I might work in business, but I discovered my passion was in education," she says.

Evans "fell into" her current position through the college admissions network she had built. Another recruiter admired her presence and her people skills. He recommended her to the Ron Brown Program. Her work experience combined with her interpersonal skills, commitment to community, and open-mindedness landed her the position.

"One of the biggest business communication challenges in the workforce is the soft skills you have to use, such as the interpersonal skills that must change with each person you interact with and meet," says Evans. She coaches students to better understand who they are in order to have a baseline to evaluate themselves and how to work with others. "Understanding who you are is an ongoing and valuable process for young professionals," she says.

In fact, students' abilities to express who they are and how they want to impact their communities are key written and verbal communication skills required of students to advance as candidates for a Ron Brown Scholarship. Applicants start the qualification process by submitting several written essays and a résumé. Semifinalists often speak with staff at which point they are looking for students who want to be part of a connected family of like-minded individuals dedicated to leadership and public service.

Finally, the Ron Brown Scholar Program flies the finalists to Washington D.C., where they interview with three different panels. "We are looking for bridge builders and team players who will be able to foster relationships and work with a diverse group of people in communities around the world," says Evans. "Since we want our Scholars to become part of our lifelong family, we look for individuals who want and will stay connected with the Program."

The Ron Brown Scholar Program supports all of its Scholars to build their interpersonal and leadership skills throughout the college years and beyond. Evans herself provides coaching and counseling to new Scholars and alumni alike. "We interact with our Scholars constantly to discuss what they are doing and what they hope their public service impact will be," she says. "We also direct them toward specific tools to help improve point areas of communication, such as college writing labs, career and academic advising centers or personality assessment tools."

Evans relishes her work with the Ron Brown Scholar Program community because she can share her experience in a community that really does feel like a family. She says her top three communication tips learned over the years are "to be concise, to know what you want to communicate, and to be open to new ideas and a variety of personalities."

Questions

1. What business advantages did Evans realize by pushing herself to learn about finance and development during her work at the Ron Brown Scholar Program? When is the last time you took the initiative to learn something you weren't required to learn?
2. Evans remarks that one of the biggest business communication challenges for young professionals is applying their interpersonal skills. What can you do right now to gain experience communicating well with different personalities?

Source: Vanessa Evans in discussion with the author, September 2010.

Exhibit 16-16
Signs That It's Time to Look for a New Job

1. I am doing the same things over and over with little opportunity for change or to learn or stretch myself.
2. I'm not paid what I'm worth.
3. My personal philosophy and values no longer match those of the company.
4. The company's processes or lack of them interfere with my ability to do my work.
5. I am unable to produce the quality of work I am capable of, and do not feel pride in what I do.
6. I no longer enjoy the people I work with or the tasks that I do.

of thumb is to stay at least two years. You need this amount of time to understand the culture of your company, communicate effectively within it, learn, gain new skills, and prove yourself. Only then can you honestly assess whether it's time to move on.

Exhibit 16-16 provides a list of statements that people often make when a job is no longer a fit. If you find yourself making many of the statements in the exhibit, it may be time to leave. However, before you decide to do so, it's smart to do whatever you can to improve the situation. This usually involves changing your own perceptions and perhaps communicating differently on the job than you had been. **Exhibit 16-17** provides tips for improving your work situation.

If you do decide that your job is no longer a fit and you have done all you can to improve your work situation, it's time to leave. Part of your career evolution involves endings, as well as beginnings. When it's time to go, you'll know it. Don't delay. Develop an exit date and plan, and then write a letter of resignation. It's generally acceptable to give two weeks' notice. Stay upbeat and positive in your letter (refer to Exhibit 15-22 in Chapter 15 for an example of a good resignation notice).

Finally, it's good to secure a new job before you leave your old job. Unless you have a trust fund, lots of savings in the bank, or are willing to live meagerly for a period of time it's wise to go from one solid job to another with no gaps in your résumé or your paycheck.

Armed with your well-developed business communication skills you have learned in this book, you will be able to navigate the choppy waters of the world around you. You will be able to excel at work as a contributor and a leader. You will be able to troubleshoot issues that occur in your personal life, such as helping a friend write a letter to a healthcare provider, or clearly communicating with a real estate agent what you want in a home. The business communication skills you have learned in this book are invaluable because they provide the tools to solve any problem you may encounter. The connection between 21st century skills and college, career, and life has never been so important.

The global business world is filled with opportunities that await you. Will you choose a career in one of the industries mentioned in this book? Will you work with a nonprofit organization or forge a path of your own? No matter what path you choose, you can always rely on your communication abilities to unite your personal leadership aspirations with your professional goals. With communication talents in your professional toolbox, you will have every advantage to become an empowered, effective, and passionate world-class employee.

Exhibit 16-17 Tips for Improving a Work Situation[6]

1. Identify things you do enjoy about your job. Can you put more focus and attention into these things?
2. Speak with your manager and ask if you can design your job duties differently to better match your values and skills.
3. Practice communication skills with your coworkers and manager by expressing what you really enjoy doing and what kind of opportunities you would like to have more of.
4. Tactfully share the process or behaviors that make things difficult for you, and suggest ways to improve them.
5. Delegate something you don't like to do to someone who does (with management approval).

As the author Thomas Friedman put it in his book *The World Is Flat*, "... the world needs you to be forever the generation of strategic optimists, the generation with more dreams than memories, the generation that wakes up each morning and not only imagines that things can be better but also acts on that imagination every day."

Summary *Synthesize What You Have Learned*

1. How do good communication skills help organizations succeed?

Nonprofit and for-profit organizations need people with solid business skills, especially the abilities to set objectives, lead or participate in teams, communicate clearly, and meet deadlines. Without these skills, plans cannot be made, work cannot be done, funds cannot be raised, and results cannot be achieved.

2. How do you find and keep your passion for your work?

Pursue work that you like and are interested in. People who like what they do are generally admired by those around them because they are fun to be around and they inspire others to do their best. Additionally, employers prefer people who like what they do because they tend to do their jobs well, are highly productive, and motivate others.

3. Why is it important to establish healthy boundaries at work?

Avoid burnout by changing your state, taking a think break, establishing a system of balance, and knowing when to refuel. Learn how to communicate under pressure by understanding people's "back-up" behaviors and staying under control, maintaining your relationships with people, and concentrating to block out distractions. Don't over-share information, and resist the temptation to cultivate personal friendships instead of professional ones.

4. How do you exceed expectations on the job?

Instead of thinking about what the company can do for you, think about what you can do for the company. Successful employees are those who look for ways to improve the environment in which they work and to augment their abilities.

5. How can you advance your career with communication?

Go the extra mile and look for ways to make a difference. If you see a problem that needs solving, but it's not part of your job, get involved if you think you can contribute. Tactfully offer to work on problems, and always refrain from being critical or arrogant as you do so.

Always communicate clearly, thoroughly, and appropriately.

6. How can feedback improve your professionalism?

Receive feedback with an open mind, asking yourself, "What can I learn from this?" and look for ways to improve. Give feedback the way you would appreciate receiving it: start with something positive, then introduce the "negative" feedback, and end with something positive.

7. What is the key to ethical communication in the business world?

Good ethical communication—making the right communication choices given the circumstances—makes good business sense. To some extent, your organization's policies will dictate what you say and do. Ultimately, though, how you behave in these situations is up to you; you will have to keep your own counsel. Avoid defaming people with libelous writing or slanderous comments. Respect copyrights. Avoid false marketing claims. Treat others with respect.

8. How do you know when your job is no longer a good fit?

You typically know your job is no longer a good fit when you feel like you're doing the same thing over and over, you no longer enjoy the people you work with, your philosophy and values no longer match the company's, you have little opportunity to stretch and grow, you do not feel valued or respected, and you don't feel you're being paid what you're worth.

PEARSON **mybcommlab**™ Are you an active learner? Go to **mybcommlab.com** to master Chapter 16's content. Chapter 16's interactive activities include:

- Customizable Study Plan and Chapter 16 practice quizzes
- Flash cards for mastering the definition of chapter terms
- Interactive Lessons that visually review key chapter concepts
- Document Makeovers for hands-on, scored practice in revising documents

Know It *Reflect, Respond, and Express*

Build Your Critical Thinking Skills

Critical Thinking Questions

1. Recall a time you experienced burnout. What were your physical symptoms during your burnout? What signaled you that you needed to step away from the project or take a break? In what ways did your body communicate that you were burned out?
2. Analyze how goals can help you maintain a positive and professional image in the workplace.
3. Think of a time you received critical feedback and describe the situation. Was the feedback valuable? Did you learn anything about how or how not to communicate critical feedback? If so, what did you learn?

Critical Thinking Scenario

Jiang's world is spinning. His job with the nonprofit organization Big Hearts, Big Helpers is taking up all of his waking hours. He recently lost two full-time employees and has been playing catch-up ever since. Because the company's annual marathon is coming up, several board meetings are in the works, and he is short of help. He's been working more than 60 hours a week for almost a month. What's worse, he's not going to have a chance to interview, hire, and train anyone else for at least two more weeks!

Questions

1. What "communication under pressure" pitfalls should Jiang watch out for, considering the stress he's under? List at least three pitfalls and describe a way to avoid each.
2. What burnout-reduction actions might help Jiang's stress? (See Exhibit 16-2.)
3. Because he's lost several employees, the importance of teamwork for Jiang cannot be overstated. What skills must he keep in mind for "communicating sideways"?

Write It *Draft, Revise, and Finalize*

Create Your Own Success Story

1. Using the plan you created in the last activity, map out your writing strategy for a press release, a high impact flyer, or a strong memo. This includes identifying your audience, creating goodwill, using proper tone, and anything else that applies to the type of message you are creating. When you feel confident about your plan, start writing.
   a. After you complete your first draft, revise it. Edit the document for readability, grammar, punctuation, and spelling.
   b. Next, format the document using good design principles for layout, fonts, and colors.
   c. When you are done, print the document and proofread it for typos and layout mistakes.
   d. Correct the errors and turn in the final document to your instructor.
2. Answer the following questions: How do you feel about your current stage in life? Are you energized by the path of study you have chosen? Are you satisfied with your current path of study? When you graduate, will your first full-time job be a step toward your dream career or simply a job to get you from point A to point B? Are you looking forward to the challenges of the working world? What is standing between good and great for you? Summarize how your answers affect your overall attitude toward work and life.
3. Revise the following statement to clarify any details that are vague, highlighting the information you put into the document.

   I put the thing for that presentation in your office so you could have enough time to look it over beforehand. I know a couple hours will do you good. Let me know if you have questions about it.

4. Revise the following statement to a supervisor. Use proper grammar and punctuation in order to communicate respectfully.

   i'm not gonna be able to make that first meeting tomorrow—you gotta do it solo. i have big plans that work just cant be my focus. I should be in after I get up at some point.

5. Simulate a performance review by evaluating your instructor's performance based on the following criteria: use of class time, presentation of materials, availability for students, and knowledge of the course information. Rate your instructor from 1 to 5 for each category, with 1 being least effective and 5 the most effective. Write a brief summary of your opinion for each item. Leave room under each item for the instructor to respond.

6. Imagine you are a manager and one of your employees is constantly late to work. The employee is great with customers and one of your best presenters, but comes in 15 minutes late to work every day—sometimes later. Write a brief e-mail to your employee confronting the tardiness but also explaining how you value the work the employee does.

7. Using your library or the Internet, find a recent lawsuit involving defamation. Write a brief summary of the case you find and explain how the incident could have hurt, or not hurt, the party claiming defamation.

8. Using your library or the Internet, find an example of a marketing claim that was proven to be false, such as the Energy Star example discussed on page 482. Write a summary of the claim, the research, and the outcome of the situation.

Speak It *Discuss, Listen, and Understand*

Build Your Leadership and Teamwork Skills

1. Get into groups of five. Imagine you and your team members represent the board of directors for a nonprofit recreation company. Your company specializes in providing outdoor adventures for children with life-threatening illnesses and diseases. Normally operations run pretty smoothly, but a few days ago, your organization received some bad news—the name and logo it currently uses were previously copyrighted by another recreation company. Worse, that firm is threatening to sue your organization for copyright infringement.

   As a team, prepare a response to the situation by answering the following questions:

   a. How can your company prevent copyright infringement problems in the future?

   b. As a group, design a new name and logo for your company. Describe three ways you can ensure that the new name and logo are not copyrighted.

   c. Next, map out a strategy for distributing your new name and logo to investors and customers, while tactfully explaining why the name and logo changed. Create a memo, letter, or phone message in the event that you employ all three. Include specifics because you will use this information in the next activity.

2. In groups or as a class, discuss the phrase "The customer is always right." Why is this statement true for any type of business? Review the skills checklist in Exhibit 16-10 for building trust and preventing negative perceptions of your company or organization. What are the common themes in the skills? What basic values and attitude should you have when working with customers?

3. In small groups, discuss a time you experienced burnout at work or school. List the ways you remedied the burnout. How did you get back on track? Compile a list of remedy strategies to share with the rest of the class.

4. In groups or as a class, discuss how social networks such as Facebook or Twitter are affected by copyright laws. What are the privacy and usage settings for Facebook or Twitter? Do these networks need to obtain your permission to share your information with marketing or advertising firms? Should the networks gain your permission since users willingly post information to the sites?

5. In small groups, discuss a time you felt pressure when communicating and how you handled the situation. How did you control (or not control) your emotions? What was the reaction of those around you? Compile a list of methods you used (or should have used) to effectively communicate under pressure.

Do It *Document Your Success Track Record*

Build Your e-Portfolio

Topics covered in this textbook appear on the following page. For each topic, write down a point you want to remember that's related to the topic. The points should be tips you believe will help you become a better communicator. These points will form your own personal "Successful Communication Tips" document. When you're done, add the document to your e-portfolio and use it as a guide during your job search and throughout your career.

1. Leadership:
2. Cultures:
3. Planning before writing:
4. Writing:
5. Revising:
6. Everyday messages:
   - Memos:
   - Letters:
   - Electronic communication:
7. Persuasive messages:
8. Negative messages:
9. Reports:
10. Proposals:
11. Making presentations:
12. Visual aids:
13. Networking and job searching:
14. Job aids:
    - Cover letters:
    - Résumés:
    - Portfolios:
15. Interviewing:
16. Business ethics:
17. Communicating at different levels:

Business in Action

Goals Lead a Former Cattle Herder to Achieve Her Dreams

When Jo Luck, a representative of nonprofit organization Heifer International, gave an inspirational talk to a group of poor, village women in Zimbabwe, she had no idea what the impact would be on one young lady in particular.

Tererai Trent, then in her early twenties, attended the talk and was amazed to hear Luck tell her that her dream of gaining an education was very achievable. So Trent wrote down her dreams:

- To study abroad in the United States
- To earn a BA
- To earn an MA
- To earn a doctorate

She scribbled these dreams on a piece of paper, put the scribbled paper into an old tin box, and buried it deep beneath a pile of rocks.

Those goals were visionary and lofty for a female cattle herder who had less than one year of elementary school education and had been married off at the age of 11 to a husband who regularly beat her. Lofty or not, those written goals took Trent on an amazing journey.

Trent began raising money to leave her village, partly through the sale of milk from a goat Heifer gave to her aunt. Because of its mission to work with communities to end hunger and poverty, Heifer International continued its presence in Trent's rural village. Trent began to work for Heifer and also for several Christian organizations as a community organizer. She used some of her income to enroll in correspondence courses to further her education and saved the rest to help her meet her future goals.

In 1998, Trent was accepted to Oklahoma State University. With $4,000 cash wrapped in a stocking and tied around her waist, Trent carted her husband and all five children with her to the United States. Things didn't go as planned. Trent's family was soon hungry, her husband refused to do housework, and he continued to beat her. Trent herself would sometimes eat from trashcans. She almost gave up on her educational dreams, but she could still see her written goals in front of her. She knew that her actions stood for something, and she knew that other African women could derive hope from what she was doing.

Luckily a university official intervened on her behalf and swayed both Oklahoma University faculty and the local community to support Trent's family with food and donations. With this type of support behind her, Trent was able to have her husband deported back to Zimbabwe.

By now, Trent was middle-aged and had advanced to a PhD program at Western Michigan University. She began working as a program evaluator with Heifer International, the organization that originally inspired her to do something with her talents. In December 2009, she received her PhD. What a celebration it was when Trent checked off the very last of her four goals written on that old, worn paper—an impressive conclusion to a lifelong journey and her mid-life goals.

Questions

1. Trent's story is a reminder that talent is universal, yet opportunity does not always knock. What leadership qualities did Trent exhibit that allowed her to convert her talents and dreams into reality?
2. Trent visualized her goals by writing them down. What value did the written goals have for her? If you were to write down four goals for your future, what would they be?

Sources: Nicholas D. Kristof, "Triumph of a Dreamer," *New York Times* (op-ed), November 14, 2009, accessed at http://ww.nytimes.com/2009/11/15/opinion/15kristof.html; "Hope in a Box," *The Oprah Show*, October 1, 2009, accessed at http://www.oprah.com/world/Tererai-Trents-Inspiring-Education/1; Cindy Tickle, "Education Ended the Cycle of Poverty for Tererai Trents," *Examiner.com*, October 9, 2009, accessed at http://www.examiner.com/oprah-in-national/education-ended-the-cycle-of-poverty-for-tererai-trent.

Key Terms

Back-up behavior. A coping behavior that different personality types exhibit under stress. *(p. 468)*

Burnout. A situation in which you become irritated or unproductive, can no longer think clearly, or effectively verbalize your thoughts on the job. *(p. 467)*

Communicating down. Communicating with your subordinates, including coworkers who may have less experience than you. *(p. 475)*

Communicating sideways. Communicating with your peers and in team settings. *(p. 476)*

Communicating up. Communicating with your superiors. *(p. 454)*

Copyright violation. A legal offense that occurs when someone wrongly republishes material owned by another person or organization. *(p. 481)*

Defamation. A legal term for any false statement that harms an individual's reputation. *(p. 480)*

Fair use. A legal guideline that allows people and organizations to have a right to use a limited amount of copyrighted material without seeking permission from the material's owner. *(p. 481)*

Feedback sandwich. A technique for providing feedback in which you first say something positive, then provide negative feedback, and end with another positive statement. *(p. 479)*

Libel. A legal offense that occurs when purposeful false and defamatory communication appears in written form including in newspapers, magazines, books, on television, and the Internet. *(p. 480)*

Slander. A legal offense that occurs when a person or entity is overheard knowingly or recklessly speaking false statements that damage the reputation of another person or entity. *(p. 480)*

Review Questions *Test Yourself*

1. What are a few questions you can ask yourself to ensure you are developing a positive, professional image while you are in school?
2. In what ways can your attitude help you create a positive, professional image?
3. How can having a "no excuses" attitude help you maintain a positive attitude?
4. What techniques can you use to communicate clearly and thoroughly?
5. What is work-related burnout?
6. What are a few burnout management techniques you can use to maintain professionalism and a positive attitude?
7. What guidelines can you follow to help you communicate under pressure?
8. What are some points to keep in mind when you receive feedback from a performance review?
9. What essentials should you keep in mind when providing someone with feedback?
10. What is ethical communication and how can it benefit a company or organization?
11. What are defamation, libel, and slander and how can these legal violations harm a business?
12. What constitutes a copyright violation? What constitutes fair use?

Grammar Review *Mastering Accuracy*

Wordiness

Section I

Each of the following sentences contains one or more common errors in word usage, grammar, or style. Identify the errors. If you have trouble finding the errors, review Section 1.1.2. in the handbook (Appendix D) at the back of this textbook.

1. Really, do you think we'll find the right version of this file that we'll need for the upgrade?
2. All day long, we needed to refer to the pricing guide for other, additional alternatives to our manager's request.
3. Without a doubt I will certainly attend the meeting that is in close proximity to our Vancouver office.
4. Before returning to work, it is essential that all employees decide to wash their hands.
5. Having just given birth to a pair of twins, Mary will take a leave of absence under the FMLA policy and return to that shift's regular routine next week.
6. Even the tiniest speck of dust is enough to make me have sneezing fits.
7. Please return your textbooks by 7:30 AM in the morning for the benefit of all individuals of the general public using the library.
8. The board room was filled to capacity when the final end results of our 8:30 PM in the evening deliberation were announced.
9. I didn't know that that was the day we'd have the meeting.

10. To whom do you wish to speak to that you think really be able and might help you?

Section II

On a separate sheet of paper, rewrite the following sentences so they are clearer, more professional sounding, grammatically correct, and goodwill oriented.

1. This has really been quite a relatively long meeting.
2. Well, I firmly and wholeheartedly believe that this is an excellent film.
3. SenTech is the technology firm that hired Jim during the summer.
4. Provide some advance notice of the meeting already, will you?
5. I fully and completely understand our company's new technology platform.
6. Our newest student, who dresses in old clothes, will visit the department that houses our financial aid tomorrow.
7. All of our academic advisors graduated from Harvard, that school for really smart people.
8. Deborah certainly feels that she will need to heavily prepare for that presentation which is due tomorrow.

Extra Resources *Tools You Can Use*

Books

- Cappelli, Pete, Harbir Singh, Jitendra Singh, and Michael Useem. *The India Way: How India's Top Business Leaders Are Revolutionizing Management.* Boston: Harvard Business Publishing, 2010.
- Cohen, Ed. *Leadership Without Borders: Successful Strategies From World Class Leaders.* Singapore: John Wiley & Sons, 2007.
- Maurer, Rick. *Feedback Toolkit: 16 Tools for Better Communication in the Workplace.* New York: Productivity Press, 1994.
- Pearce, Craig L., Joseph A. Marciariello, Hideki Yamawaki. *The Drucker Difference: What the World's Greatest Management Thinker Means to Today's Business Leaders.* New York: McGraw-Hill, 2010.
- Tedlow, Richard S. *Denial: Why Business Leaders Fail to Look Facts in the Face—and What to Do About It.* New York: Portfolio Publishing, 2010.

Web Sites

- Rutherford, Richard, "Becoming a Great Employee—The 10 Top Traits." *EzineArticles.*
- Widener, Chris, "Top 7 Steps to Becoming a Great Leader." *Top7Business.*

Appendix A

Social Networking and Media

Getting the Word Out in the 21st Century

In numerous chapters throughout this book, we mentioned social networking as a way to connect and communicate with others as well as to explore career opportunities and promote yourself. In this appendix, we will provide you with more details about the nuts and bolts of social networking and social media as they relate to businesses. Let's start with some formal definitions.

- ***Social networking*** means connecting with a community of people in your online network through services like LinkedIn, Facebook, and Twitter with various methods of online interaction.
- ***Social media*** relates to the tools for sharing and discussing information.[1] The term refers to the online media such as blogs, podcasts, videos, and news feeds. This type of media allows participation through comments and ratings. Social media is generated "by the people and for the people" with content created by anyone with a voice, from people who know nothing to experts in their fields.[2] As a result, the media content may not always be accurate or trustworthy.

If you think about it, social networking has always been a part of our personal and professional culture. Today, much of our "social networking" still occurs in person. It's the way we meet and get to know people and share information. For example, when you talk to your friends, family, and business associates about what's going on in your life, that's a form of social networking. When businesses hold conferences to share their products and services and get to know their customers, that's a form of in-person social networking as well. In addition, when companies spend millions on ad campaigns in print, television, and radio campaigns, that's still social networking, as long as customers provide some feedback.

In this appendix, we will focus on online social networking and the media involved by doing the following:

- Briefly covering the history of social networking
- Describing different types of social media
- Walking through the process of planning your social media strategy
- Sharing best practices for each type of social media
- Discussing the possible future of social networking

When you finish reading this appendix, you will be able to navigate the sometimes stormy waters of social networking without a problem.

A Short History

More than 2,500 years ago, the Chinese philosopher Confucius said, "*. . . tell me and I will forget. Show me and I may remember. Involve me and I will understand . . .*" Today that philosophy is more important than ever in business communication, and it applies directly to social networking.

Social networking allows people to get involved. It allows companies and consumers to interact with one another. It's a way for people to share their values, experiences, opinions, knowledge, and expertise with mass audiences. The ability to participate in local and global conversations has created a phenomenon where consumers don't have to be blasted by traditional business messages anymore. They can now interact with businesses to create higher levels of loyalty and understanding so as to establish better connections with them.

For the first time in marketing history, consumers trust the words of other consumers on the Web more than they trust the words of companies. Today, consumers are looking at testimonials, blog posts, and online comments to help them with buying decisions rather than depending on company advertisements.[3]

How did the phenomenon of social networking get started? In the 1970s and early 1980s Bulletin Board Systems (BBS for short) were online meeting places where hobbyists could download files or games and post messages to one another. The first recognizable social network site, SixDegrees, launched in 1997. The site allowed users to create profiles, list their Friends, and surf their Friends lists. SixDegrees promoted itself as a tool to help people connect with and send messages to others.

From 2003 onward, many new social networking sites were launched, targeting an unlimited number of niche audiences and range of subject matter. Indie-rock bands began creating profiles on MySpace, and local promoters used the site to advertise VIP passes for popular clubs. Soon, teenagers began joining MySpace. Some joined because they wanted to connect with their favorite bands; others were introduced to the site through older family members. LinkedIn targeted a different crowd: professionals in the 25- to 65-year-old category. Headhunters, job seekers, and professionals attempting to increase their business networks found a new home with this social networking site. Facebook began in 2004 as a Harvard University–only social networking site. To join, users had to have a Harvard e-mail address. Facebook then began supporting users at other schools. In 2005, Facebook expanded to include high school students, professionals inside corporate networks, and eventually everyone.

As social networking sites evolved, so did blogs. As early as 2001, blogging was enough of a phenomenon that how-to-blog manuals began appearing, primarily focusing on technique. Since 2002, blogs have gained increasing notice and coverage for their role in breaking, shaping, and spinning new stories. By 2004, political consultants and candidates were using blogs for outreach and opinion forming. In 2006, microblogging entered the scene as Twitter caught the attention of the general public, celebrities, and businesses alike. Suddenly individuals could send short messages called "tweets," in real-time, to anyone in their network.

Today, there are no reliable data regarding how many people use social networking sites, although marketing research indicates they are growing in popularity worldwide. This growth has prompted many corporations to invest time and money in creating, purchasing, promoting, and advertising social networking sites. At the same time, other companies are blocking their employees from accessing the sites. The U.S. military banned soldiers from accessing MySpace, and the Canadian government prohibited employees from accessing Facebook. Additionally, the U.S. Congress has proposed legislation to ban youth from accessing social networking sites in schools and libraries.

Exploring Social Media

Different industries often use different types of social media tools. In general, the more channels (types) of social media a company uses, the faster it reaches people. However, using multiple social channels typically requires more time and effort on the part of businesses, which costs more in terms of time and resources. The trick is figuring out the best channel(s) of social media tool to use. This section will help you assess each type and determine how it can (or cannot) aid you and your business.

Social Networking Sites

Regardless of the purpose or audience for different social networking sites, they share similar characteristics: Users can set up accounts with user names and passwords and create profiles that tell other people about them. Once they are on the system, they then identify with others people or entities with whom they want to have a relationship. These entities are typically called "Friends," "Contacts," and "Fans," and the sites provide ways for them to leave messages for one another on the network.

Aside from these characteristics, social networking sites vary greatly in terms of their features and users. Some sites have photo-sharing or video-sharing capabilities; others have built-in blogging and instant messaging technology. Many target people from specific geographical regions or linguistic groups. Some sites are designed with specific ethnic, religious, sexual orientation, political, or other identity-driven categories in mind. There are even social networking sites for dogs (Dogster) and cats (Catster), although their owners must manage their profiles.[4]

Let's look at two of the most popular social networking sites used by businesses: LinkedIn and Facebook.

LinkedIn

LinkedIn has more than 70 million registered users, spanning more than 200 countries and territories worldwide.[5] Launched in 2003, this social networking site helps professionals advance their careers by connecting with past and present colleagues and discovering job openings and business opportunities. LinkedIn users often join special-interest groups, such as groups consisting of writers, computer programmers, and marketing professionals. By doing so, they are able to meet other professionals in their field, widen their networks, and ask or answer questions related to their professions. Many firms "troll" LinkedIn profiles searching for individuals with the skills and experience they need. That's why it's so important for LinkedIn users to keep their profiles up-to-date. Companies also post job openings on LinkedIn.

Almost everyone can benefit from LinkedIn. If you are employed, unemployed, or a freelancer, you can have a professional presence on the Web through LinkedIn. If you do not have a Web site, your LinkedIn page can serve as a personal Web page. Keep in mind, however, that the profile you create of yourself on the site is public. Anyone can view it, whether or not the viewer is a member of LinkedIn. Make sure your profile contains only information you want the public to see. Ensure it is up-to-date, so the people who view it are not looking at outdated information. If you join a lot of groups on the site, you are likely to receive a large amount of e-mail from members asking questions or responding to them. Reading the e-mail and responding to it can take up a large amount of time. Use discretion when deciding what, if any, groups to join. For more information, see the section titled "Social Media Best Practices" later in this appendix.

Facebook

Facebook is the largest global online social network in the world with more than 300 million users worldwide, which is roughly equivalent to the entire population of the United States. Many companies use the site to promote their brands. Other companies use it to help individuals and groups within their firms get to know each other and to facilitate internal communication.

Who doesn't need to be on Facebook? People and companies who are not interested in constant updating or uploading of photos, or sharing of personal information, will probably do better with LinkedIn. The users of Facebook also need to understand the site's privacy policies.

Web Sites

A Web site provides an online presence for an individual or company, promoting its products and services to people who visit the site. Almost everyone can benefit from a Web site. It gives potential customers a place where they can find more about you or your company, discover how you can help them, and see examples of your work. The site might simply be one page that identifies who you are, what you do, and how you can be contacted. For large companies, the site might consist of hundreds of pages, complete with product descriptions and customer testimonials.

A well-designed Web site targets specific audiences and focuses on what the members of those audiences want to find or accomplish on the site, rather than what the owner of the Web site wants to say. Highly visited sites are those where people can find the information they are looking for and understand it. The sites are organized to make navigation easy, and their colors and fonts are optimized so visitors do not struggle to read tiny text or strain

Good blogs like this one, which was created by the author of this book, regularly provide people with useful information in which they are interested.

to see text against strangely colored backgrounds. Their content is developed for readability, with words that resonate with the readers, presented in bite-sized chunks for easy reading and retention. As Steve Krug, author of *Don't Make Me Think*, says of poorly designed Web sites, "If it's hard to use, it will hardly be used."[6]

The most common Web pages for a standard Web site include the following:

- ***Home page.*** A site's home page is the first page visitors are expected to "land on." It is usually quite eye-catching and gives visitors in 10 seconds or less the information they need to continue to navigate the site.
- ***About page.*** The About page gives visitors a sense of who the site's owner is, what the person or organization does, and how long the organization has been in operation.
- ***Products or services pages.*** These pages identify in detail what the company that owns the site makes or the services it provides.
- ***Contact page.*** The contact page tells visitors how to get in touch with the organization or site owner. It usually includes a physical address, phone number, and e-mail.
- ***Shopping Cart.*** You are probably familiar with the shopping cart on sites from which you can buy items. The shopping cart indicates the items you want to purchase. Visitors can usually make adjustments to the number of items, continue shopping, or check out.

A Web site can have far more pages than those we have listed, depending on the company's size, customer-base, and the needs of its visitors. Planning, building, and maintaining a site requires time, skills, and money. Before you build a Web site, you must do some planning to determine its objectives, target audience, business value, and how it will be organized. Once the planning is done, you must be able to write the content and build the site, or hire someone who can. In addition, a Web site requires you make a commitment to maintain and monitor the site. Luckily, there are companies that specialize in designing, building, and optimizing sites.

Blogs

If you think of a Web site as a novel, then consider a blog to be a short story, in terms of size. As we explained earlier in the book, the word *blog* actually stands for "Web log." A blog is typically part of an existing Web site or its own Web site. On the blog, an individual posts commentaries, reviews products, describes events, gives advice, or shares best practices. Blog posts are typically displayed in reverse-chronological order. Readers can then comment on the posts.

A successful blogger develops content that consistently interests a dedicated following of readers who will be inspired to spread the word to even more readers. The more people who read the blog, the more people get to know the blogger, his or her company, and its products and services. In fact, many corporate blogs point readers to a company Web site to learn more about the company or read news related to the company.

The downside of a blog is that it must be maintained on a regular basis with fresh entries every day, or at least once a week. This can be time-consuming. Bloggers often spend a minimum of an hour a day researching and writing blog posts. Companies often hire bloggers who may or may not work for the company to post blogs on their sites on a regular basis. If you do not have the time or interest to come up with engaging messages or share information on a daily or weekly basis, blogging is not for you. If you lack good writing skills or don't have someone who can review your posts, avoid blogging. Additionally, people who read blogs sometime find themselves spending hours each day reading blog posts, which detracts from time doing actual work or maintaining personal relationships.

Microblogs (Twitter)

If a blog is a short story, then a microblog is a sentence or two from that story. A microblog entry typically consists of nothing but a short sentence fragment, an image, or a link to an embedded video or Web page.

The most famous microblog today is Twitter, which has more than 60,000,000 active users each month, including individuals, businesses, celebrities, and politicians. Twitter allows users to broadcast 140-character tweets. In a business environment, these tweets can convey important news and opinions, and help build relationships with people who read the tweets.

Tweets are publicly visible by default; however, senders can restrict their messages to their Friends lists. Users also can subscribe to tweets from specific people—this is known as "following" and the subscribers are known as "followers."

The jury is out right now on who needs Twitter. However, individuals who already have a following, such as authors, celebrities, and politicians, often send tweets to inform their followers about current and upcoming events, books, films, and political issues they need to be aware of. (These usually involve a link to another Web site.) The celebrity homemaker Martha Stewart uses Twitter to inform her followers about where she will be signing new books she has published, and followers show up at the events in droves. Some companies and people use Twitter as a way to help others by posting tips and links to helpful Web site articles, videos, and interviews.

Many people use Twitter for purely personal reasons that have nothing to do with their professional lives. For some Twitter authors, posting tweets becomes a form of narcissism that allows them to brag to others about what they are doing every minute of the day. For some Twitter followers, reading the posts becomes a time-consuming form of voyeurism. Essentially these people are watching others go about their daily lives.

Online Forums

An **online forum** is an online discussion site. You can think of online forums as interactive blogs. Rather than one author posting short articles for people to read, one person posts an idea and starts an online discussion. Others join in and respond. **Exhibit A-1** shows an example of an online forum.

Instead of a single, cohesive blog post, an online forum has many statements and responses (dialogs) that go in different directions. Forums help people with similar interests come together to learn more about one another and their projects. They are particularly popular in high-tech and hobby industries where people are working on projects of their own and want to get feedback from others.

Forums are an excellent social media for companies or individuals who are trying to encourage activities among their audience or the sharing of knowledge and experiences. Forums help companies better understand what people are wondering about, what they are having problems with, or what they are excited about.

Forums often help companies come up with ideas for new products and services. Procter & Gamble has started online forums with customers to help it develop products. The forum participants provide the company with ideas and feedback, which has helped the company speed up its development and marketing of new goods.

An online forum requires Web-based software to manage the user-generated content as well as an administrator to set up the forum and provide technical maintenance. A set of discussion rules for participants, called a "policy," is generally established. The policy is usually created by the individuals who started the forum. Finally, the forum needs a moderator to make sure those rules are enforced and that offensive or harassing posts are removed from the site. By doing so, they keep the forum a friendly place.

Exhibit A-1 An Online Forum

HUMAN RESOURCES MANAGEMENT	TOPICS	POSTS	LAST POST
General Discussion Debate and discussion of general human resourses management topics. **Moderator: HRM Team**	2483	12440	by Cas21 Mon Jul 26, 2010 3:00 pm
HRM strategy Debate and discussion about human resources role when it comes to an organization's strategy development. **Moderator: HRM Team**	2214	10425	by mdwyer Mon Jul 26, 2010 7:54 pm
Labor Relations Discussion of all aspects of labor relations and labor laws. **Moderator: HRM Team**	2158	6721	by Rjmk Mon Jul 26, 2010 6:37 pm
Compensation Discussion of employee compensation and benefits. **Moderator: HRM Team**	832	7816	by Cas21 Sat Jul 24, 2010 1:45 am
Training and Development Employee training programs discussed. **Moderator: HRM Team**	634	4288	by blyga Mon Jul 26, 2010 10:40 pm
Recruiting Recruiting, screening, interviewing, and testing discussed. **Moderator: HRM Team**	872	892	by blyga Mon Jul 26, 2010 7:33 pm

Companies and individuals who have limited time should think twice before launching an online forum. It requires computer savvy, technical knowledge, regular maintenance, and personnel to read every post and moderate the discussions. Forums can become hostile places when moderators cannot keep things under control. And, of course, participants have been known to disparage a company and products on forums. Consider General Motors. In 2006, the company started a Web site that allowed readers to make their own commercials online by selecting backgrounds, video shots, and inputting text in order to win prizes. However, some "rogue" surfers created satirical ads casting the company and its products in a bad light. Domino's Pizza experienced a similar problem on YouTube after some employees posted a video of themselves doing nasty things to customers' pizzas while cooking them. As you can see, because it's two-way, social media can be a double-edged sword and hard to control. To prevent people from posting disparaging messages on her Facebook page, political celebrity Sarah Palin has hired professionals to remove them as soon as possible.

RSS Feeds

As we explained earlier in the book, RSS stands for really simple syndication. It is a mechanism for delivering regularly changing Web content to readers who want it. Free software lets you read RSS feeds. Many news-related sites, blogs, and other online publishers offer late-breaking news on events and products via RSS feeds. If you are interested in finding out the moves your competitors are making, subscribing to their feeds can help. RSS feeds are also an excellent way to collect information when you are doing research about your industry, company, or trend-setters.

Podcasts

A podcast is a non-streamed Webcast consisting of a series of audio MP3 files people can listen to on their iPods (hence the "pod") or on other MP3 audio players. The term "podcasting" was selected to rhyme with "broadcasting."

Podcasting lets individuals and organizations publish radio shows and other audio information that interested listeners can subscribe to. Before podcasting existed you could record a radio show or other audio and put it on your Web site. However, podcasting now allows people to automatically get the podcasts on their MP3 players without having to go to a specific site and download them.

Individuals or companies that focus on informing or educating people can benefit from podcasts. An example is the Web site GrammarGirl, which provides quick tips for improving a person's writing through daily podcasts. Podcasts are also a good way to "give to get." For example, suppose your company is putting on a conference. You might consider publishing free podcasts of some of the events after the conference to get people interested in the following year's conference. Finally, people in the public eye who get interviewed frequently can use podcasts to keep their fans happy.

If you don't have the time to come up with interesting topics, are unable to write your own podcast scripts, or never do interviews, podcasts might not be for you, however. If you do not provide a service that requires that you regularly "talk" to your audience, there is no need to worry about podcasts.

A couple of points to be aware of: Good podcasts require quality MP3 files. They need to be recorded in a quiet place so that background noise does not interfere with what the podcaster is saying. Additionally, unscripted podcasts can sound rambling and amateurish.

Social Media Strategy

Individuals and businesses often make the mistake of launching social networking activities without having a plan in mind or figuring out which social media is best for their purposes. Don't let technology and hype drive your decision to use social media. Instead, begin by doing the following:

1. Identify your objectives.
2. Profile your audience.
3. Pick the media that fits both your audience and purpose.
4. Design the media for usability and readability.
5. Implement the media.
6. Assess and maintain the tool.

Step 1: Identify Your Objective

During this step, you ask what you want to achieve with a social networking strategy. Are you trying to:

- Increase revenue?
- Attract more customers?
- Raise awareness?
- Develop new products and services?

Let's now look at the firm Eclectic Music Company (EMC). EMC provides vintage and contemporary music for the general public, as well as music for professionals and film students to use in media projects. Additionally, the company works with film directors to compose custom music for movies.

EMC's Objectives

After much discussion, EMC comes up with the following objectives for its social media:

- Learn more about issues that film directors face regarding theme music.
- Find out the type of projects film students are working on and problems they face getting music for their projects.
- Provide an easy way for the general public to download inexpensive but unusual singles. Also, find out the types of music that they are downloading most often.
- Share film music composition tips with other composers.
- Increase the general public's awareness of vintage music CDs.
- Increase the film industry's awareness of EMC's music for film and media projects.
- Increase the company's sales by 15 percent.

Step 2: Profile Your Audience

Next, ask yourself who your audience is and how you can connect to them. Profiling an audience involves identifying the characteristics of the different audience types. Each type is referred to as a "persona." A persona is a real-life description of an imaginary person in the audience who encapsulates the qualities of a particular group of people.

To develop a persona, you must collect information. The easiest way to do this is by talking to people whom you believe make up your audience, in person, by phone, or by e-mail. Another way would be to conduct online surveys or focus groups.

A complete persona typically consists of the following types of information about a particular audience:

- ***Type:*** What type of audience does this persona represent: A customer? An analyst? A supplier?
- ***Description:*** What is the gender, age, location, and background of the audience?
- ***Tasks:*** What tasks is the persona trying to accomplish (for example, find a product, get information, or connect with others)?
- ***Motivations and frustrations:*** What might motivate the persona to use social media? What might frustrate him or her?
- ***Online behavior:*** When it comes to social media, is this persona likely to be a contributor, infrequent visitor, or information collector?
- ***Comments:*** What do you already know about what this persona is saying about your company? You can often gather this information from the persona's e-mails, online comments, and blogs, or from online forums and news feeds.

Example: EMC's Personas

The social media objectives for the EMC have already been identified. But what about the type of people the company hopes to reach? EMC has identified several personas that represent different types of customers it wants to reach in the following order of importance: 1) film directors, 2) film students, 3) professionals looking for background music for presentations, and 4) music lovers who want vintage or unusual music.

The following is an example of the first persona, the film director. The persona is written as if it were an actual individual to make it easier for Eclectic Music Company to visualize this type of customer as a real person.

Persona: Jack, the Film Director

Jack grew up in Hollywood and fell in love with movies at an early age. As a child, he saved enough money to buy an old movie camera and soon realized he was born to be a director. He then began experimenting with filmmaking. His growing obsession eventually led him to film school in New York, where he learned the tools of the trade. He realized he had a gift for making documentaries and found his niche doing exactly that.

Jack now receives grant money from government agencies and other institutions to make short films and documentaries on many diverse subjects. He travels the world filming documentaries, often on a limited budget. Therefore, he frequently has to rely on friends who are musicians and will help him out by letting him use their music. He also uses prerecorded music that he likes, or has heard somewhere, that will fit seamlessly to-

gether with his film projects. Thanks to the Internet, he can now simply download an extremely wide variety of music for a reasonable price.

Jack's Needs

- He needs to access and be able to listen to a wide variety of music quickly.
- He needs excellent, affordable music that falls within the limits of his budget.
- Or, he needs to work with a composer who understands his needs and can tailor fit his music to Jack's films. This option is usually the most ideal and original.

Jack's Frustrations

- He cannot find incredibly fantastic, wonderful, romantic, and moving music without having to hire a big-name film composer who is way out of his price range.
- His musician friends are all out of town. He needs a way to find other musicians.
- He is running out of time, his film is due, and he's beginning to worry about getting it finished.
- He needs a way to connect with other documentary film directors and find out what they are doing music-wise.

Step 3: Pick the Media That Fits Both Your Audience and Purpose

It would be a waste of time to use a form of social media that your audience won't use. Creating your personas first will help you learn what they want to do online and understand their online behavior.

Example: EMC's Social Media Channels

EMC examines all the social media channels and identifies the ones that would best appeal to its potential customers and help the company achieve its objectives. The channels are listed in the order of their priority.

1. ***Web site.*** EMC's number-one priority is to develop a Web presence that allows people to learn more about the com-

pany. It decides that a Web site with a modern appearance, cutting-edge music, and witty content will be just the thing to promote both the company's music and composition services. The firm decides to keep its Web site fairly simply by limiting it to six pages:

- An eye-catching home page to capture people's attention
- An intriguing "About Us" page sharing the company's musical history
- A "Music CDs" page where people can listen to sample tracks and then purchase the CDs
- An "Electronic Download" page for people who want to listen to music samples and download them for purchase
- A "For Directors Only" page to promote the company's film-music composition services
- A standard "Contact Us" page so people can get in touch with the firm

2. ***Blog.*** The company decides it wants to take some small steps to launch a blog. The CEO (or her assistant with exceptional writing skills) might decide to post a weekly blog about breaking news in the film industry. The blog might highlight aspects of the industry that Eclectic Music Company is involved in, such as theme music or special-effects music or provide tips for musicians trying to break into the industry. People who read the blog might want to learn more about the CEO and the company and tell others about it, thereby driving more people to the company's Web site.
3. ***Forum.*** After a year or so, if the blog becomes a success, the company would like to try an online forum to learn even more about its audience and what they need. Suppose the CEO invites musicians to participate in an online discussion about composing music for movies. One musician might start the discussion by talking about a project he's working on. A second musician might respond with some questions. A third musician might attempt to answer those questions and so on.
4. ***Twitter.*** At some point in the future, the company might encourage its musicians on staff to tweet daily about new music the company is producing, film projects it is working on, a particular musician's tour schedule, or links to unusual musical events.

Step 4: Design the Media for Usability and Readability

Once you decide on the media, you will need to do some up-front design work, a step that is particularly important for Web sites and blogs. The following are some tips for designing a Web site or a blog:

- Based on the tasks you know your online audience will be doing on your Web site or blog, identify the pages you will need. Doing so will force you to think about only the content your audience needs and the type of pages necessary to convey that content, and keep your site from getting too large.
- Create a Web map that shows how the pages will be organized. A Web map looks like a business organization chart. **Exhibit A-2** shows an example of one. A Web map can prevent you from developing a site that's too complicated or large, where people will get lost.
- Decide on a layout for the Web pages. It should be relatively uncluttered to allow readers' eyes to move about the pages in a natural fashion (usually from top-to-bottom and left-to-right).

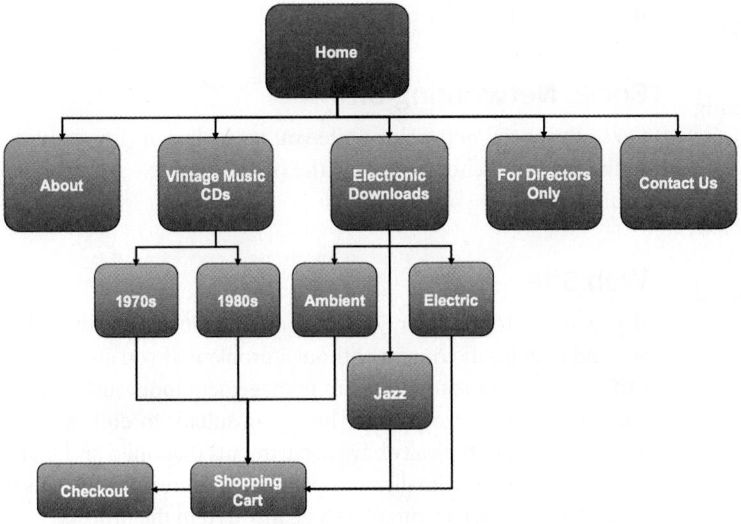

Exhibit A-2 A Web Map

Exhibit A-3
A Mockup of a Home Page

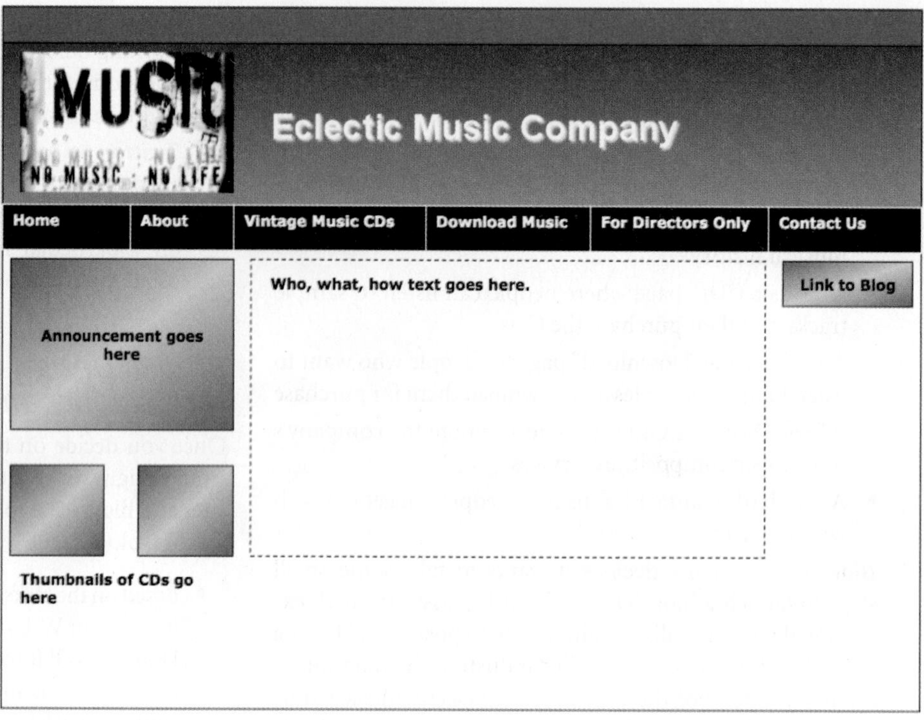

- Decide on your colors. They should be easy on the eyes and should not interfere with reading.
- Decide on your fonts and font sizes. They should be standard fonts that are easy to read using all browsers.
- Create a "Style Guide" that documents all your design decisions such as the font types, colors, menu bar locations, and so forth.
- Create mockups of your home page and other typical pages to illustrate the layout and color. **Exhibit A-3** shows an example of one.

Once you have specified your design, you can begin writing the content for the Web site or blog. The following are tips for readable content for Web sites and blogs:

- Create a single file that contains all your content. Clearly identify what content goes on each Web page.
- If you are developing a blog, write up a series of posts ahead of time.
- Keep your text short, clear, and engaging.
- Limit the length of sentences and paragraphs.
- Use words that resonate with your audience.
- Use headings that grab people's attention.

Readability is equally important for tweets, which can only be 140 words in length.

- Put the subject or most important information at the beginning of the tweet.
- Write in active voice.
- Remove filler words.
- Watch for typos.
- Keep your message short and positive.

Step 5: Implement the Media

If you or the company you work for has carried out steps 1–4, implementing the social media tool(s) you have chosen should not be too difficult or costly.

Social Networking Site

Go to the social networking site you have chosen (for example, LinkedIn or Facebook), follow the instructions to set up an account, and enter your profile.

Web Site

If you are a programmer, you can probably build your own Web site and manage its content without a problem. If you are not, you can use free open-source content management tools, such as Drupal, Joomla, or TangoCMS, or hire a consultant to do it for you. Large companies typically have departments that build and maintain their Web sites. Smaller companies often hire outside firms to do so. Graphics artists might also be involved in the process.

Regardless of whether you are an individual, a small company, or a large one, have your style guide, mockups, and text ready. This will save you time and money because it will allow the Web site developers to immediately begin creating pages that look like your mockups and then paste in your text.

Blog

Pick a blogging tool that is easy to use, such as Blogger, WordPress, or Xanga. If you are the person who is going to be doing the blogging, make sure you know how to use the tool.

Next, retrieve the list of posts you prepared ahead of time and review the first entry before you post it. People often use their cell phones to post messages to blogs, forums, and social networking sites. If you are one of these people, be careful. Carelessly written messages, in all lower-case, with no punctuation and misspellings are not taken seriously. Worse, those messages live on forever on the blog, for all to see.

Twitter

Go to Twitter and follow the instructions to set up an account, post your profile, and start tweeting.

Forum

Decide on your forum tool. There are plenty of free, open-source tools, such as Zoho Discussions, Vanilla Forums, and Monkey Boards. In fact, there is even a Web site where you can compare and contrast the latest open-source forums: ForumMatrix. Assign an administrator and a moderator and develop an agreed-upon policy before you start.

Step 6: Assess and Maintain the Tool

You just launched your Web site, blog, or forum. You are now the host of an ongoing conversation, which means you will need to gauge people's reactions, ask questions, give honest answers, and assess the results of your efforts.

How do you assess your success, or lack of success? Some individuals and companies choose to do their own monitoring to see how they are doing in the social networking scene. The following are some free tools commonly used to measure the reaction of the public to social media efforts.[7]

- ***Google Reader.*** Use the Google Reader tool as your home base for collecting and reading all the various sources of information you collect. It's Web-based, fast, and easy to use.
- ***Technorati.*** Use this tool to find out what people are saying about your company, your competitors, and other individuals. Go to Technorati and put the name of your company, product, or brand into the search bar. Then do the same for your competitors, individuals of interest, or any products or industry terms you are interested in. You have now created "listening searches," the results of which you will be able to read with Google Reader.
- ***Google Blog Search.*** Go to Google Blog Search and do the same thing you did with Technorati. There will be some overlap, but it's important to capture as much information as possible from both.
- ***Summize.*** If some of your customers are using Twitter, go to Summize and put your search terms there. Tweets that contain those terms will then be accessible to you on Google Reader.
- ***Link Checker.*** SEO Pro provides a free link checker that tells you who is linking to your Web site or blog and what link text they clicked on to land on your site. This helps you understand how people are finding out about you.
- ***Crazy Egg.*** If you want to see what people are doing on your Web site, Crazy Egg is the tool for you. It's full of visualization data, including "heatmaps," which show you what areas of a page people are looking at and how long they are staying there. This is a good way to find out if people are paying attention to what you want them to read or being distracted and looking elsewhere on the Web pages.

Many companies choose to hire a firm to maintain and monitor their Web sites, blogs, and other social media. For example, companies like Hubspot.com do it all: They design and publish Web sites, set up blogs, assist with content on social media sites, and analyze blog and Web site activity. They also provide Web-based software to perform those tasks.

Regardless of who does the measuring or monitoring—you or another firm—once the results are in, you need to act on them. If they are not good, you'll need to adjust your tools and possibly your overall strategy.

Social Media Best Practices

When businesses use social media, instead of merely broadcasting information in one direction, they can give and receive information. They can talk to customers directly and really find out what they need and how to fill those needs.

Even small companies or individuals who cannot offer huge discounts, contests, or prizes can make customers feel they're cared for by using social media to interact with them. Social media becomes a way to build stronger relationships between people and businesses, as long as the messages are honest and sincere.

That's why it's important to follow best practices when your channels of social media are in place. No matter what channel of social media you choose, there are some general rules you need to be aware of, as well as media-specific rules. We will first look at the general rules.

General Rules

Many of the rules of social networking are common sense. They revolve around being authentic and interacting respectfully with your audience.

Give to Get

Successful social media marketing programs center around the idea of your giving something of value to other people before expecting anything in return. Quit trying to sell. If you post a link that offers tips, make sure it leads to a page that provides the information you promised, not a pushy sales pitch. Share your expertise, insights, wisdom, and assistance.

Listen

Take time to listen. How can you learn about anything if the information is flowing only one way? Social networking is not just about broadcasting; it's about listening. It's been theorized that when it comes to social media, 90 percent of what you hear comes from less than 10 percent of your audience, and 90 percent of that information is negative.[8] If your organization is a business, what this means is that most of the time you are hearing from customers who have complaints. That's why it's important to focus on your audience you don't hear from. These are the people who are either neutral or happy about you and your company. Avoid being blinded by the vocally discontented minority.

Participate

Welcome participation and feedback. Use your blog, podcasts, and tweets to develop relationships with the social networking community. Comment on content, engage in conversations (on and offline), and attend local meetups so you can meet people face-to-face.

Commit the Right Resources

Actively listening and building relationships in online communities is a full-time job. How many hours and how many people are you going to need to manage your social networking strategy? You might want to start small and branch out. Managing a Web site or forum, updating a blog on a regular basis, sending out tweets, and monitoring activity is time-intensive. Make sure you have the time and staff for it. If you don't, scale back.

Be Transparent

Be transparent with your intentions for your social media or you may alienate your audience. For example, make sure people know why you have a Facebook page, what the purpose of your blog is, and why you are tweeting. Don't waste people's time with hidden agendas. Be up front.

Be Authentic

Be yourself. Be real. If you lack sincerity, social media is not the best medium for you. People will see right through your motives. Being sincere in your messages will increase your credibility and increase the attention that your audience gives your messages.

Be Professional

Use profiles, posts, Web content, and messages in professional ways. Online, present yourself in a way that makes potential clients and employers realize your value. Limit the personal information you provide, yet keep the information friendly.

Be Polite

It pays to lurk a bit in social communities to learn more about them and their unwritten "rules of engagement." How do they speak with one another? What words do they use? Regardless of the community, remain polite. This means, control yourself: Don't slam people or insult them, don't swear, and don't lie. Treat people the way you would like to be treated if you were talking to them face-to-face.

Communicate Clearly

Many members of online communities use their cell phones to send messages. This often results in messages that are in all lowercase letters (or ALL CAPS), with no punctuation, and lots of misspellings. This makes it difficult for others in the community to read the messages and understand them. Take the time to use punctuation, capitalize the beginnings of sentences, and check your spelling. Your readers will appreciate it, and you will be viewed as a professional—someone who knows what he or she is doing.

Be Consistent

Every tweet, blog post, Web page, and forum comment should communicate who you are or what your company is about. Consequently, your blog and Web page should use similar colors and fonts, so visitors know they are related. In other words, create a look that communicates your brand. It also means you should use the same user name and photo for all your blog comments, forum posts, and tweets. That way, people get to know you.

Ask for Help

Ask for help when you need it. People like to help other people, so tap into the community and be prepared for unexpected results. Thank those who help you and reciprocate when possible by helping others when you can. Social media is about getting help and giving help.

Measure Your Effectiveness

Don't forget to measure return on investment (ROI) when it comes to social networking. Assess the time and money you are spending on maintaining a Web site and blog, running a forum, and publishing podcasts. Is it worth it? Are you getting the results you want? If not, revisit your social media strategy and decide if you need to reduce your involvement and spend the time in other areas instead.

Specific Rules

With the general rules under your belt, let's take a look at rules that are specific to different types of social media.

Rules for Personal Social Networking Sites

- Add only people you really want as part of your network.
- Take a careful look at your own profile. Is there any content you would not want to share during an in-person discussion with a future business contact or employer? Is your profile simple and easy to read?
- Limit the photos you post. Keep them professional.
- Exercise common sense when you interact with an online community because anyone can access what you have posted. It is wise to limit the amount of personal information you share when using social media in a business setting.

Rules for Web Sites

- Know your unique business value and share it throughout the site.

- Use key words on your Web pages that visitors are likely to use when performing an online search. Key words will make it easier for search engines to find your site.
- Make sure your pages are easy to read and mean something to your visitors.
- Make your site easy to navigate. The links on your Web site should make sense to your visitors. Don't force them to click to find out where a link takes them and then have to return because it's not where they expected.
- Monitor your site. Companies spend tens to hundreds of thousands of dollars on designing Web sites but often forget to use the simplest listening tools to find out what visitors are doing on them.

Rules for Blogs

- Write for your audience. Your blog posts need to reflect topics your audience is interested in (not just you), in words they understand.
- Don't join so many online social networks that you can't keep up with them. Choose one, stick with it, and keep at it.[9]
- Keep your content fresh. Post daily, if possible, or at least weekly to keep readers interested.
- Whatever you post, always evaluate its accuracy. If you do make a mistake, admit it, retract it, and correct it.
- Make sure your blog has a good search tool and a well-organized table of contents with categories for your posts. Readers often have difficulty finding information that was posted several months in the past. If you have particularly popular blog posts, you might want to convert them to articles and post them on your Web site where people can find them more easily.

Rules for Microblogs

- Write for your followers, not for you. Make sure your post has value to your readers.
- Make your posts count. Don't make a post if all you can provide is a blow-by-blow description of every minor task you are presently engaging in. Few people care.
- Provide links to Web sites and articles your followers will appreciate.

Rules for Forums

- Visit a particular forum for a while to find out what it is about, what people are saying and doing on the forum, and how they interact.
- Start a discussion if you have something to say you think others will find interesting.
- Join in a discussion for a reason, not just to see your words online.
- Answer people's questions and don't be afraid to ask your own.
- Avoid flame wars. Do not argue, yell, or swear at others online. Treat other forum members with respect, as if they were in the same room with you.
- Take issues offline if they cannot be resolved in the forum. Most forums provide private instant-messaging tools so you can communicate directly with an individual without involving other forum members. If things don't go well with the individual via instant messaging, you may have to contact him or her by phone to resolve the matter.

Driving Customers Your Way

Social media won't guarantee your success. Do not imagine that "if you build it, they will come." A Web site, blog, or online profile does not guarantee an onslaught of customers, online contacts, or followers.

You must still use a variety of methods to make people aware of your online existence.

For example, suppose you have a quality Web site. How do you make people aware of it?

- If you have a blog that is independent of the site, you might blog about the new Web site and direct people there. Or, if you have a Twitter following, you might direct people to the site that way. If you belong to an onsite forum, you might also tell people on the forum about your site.
- If you don't have a blog, don't tweet, and don't belong to a forum, there is still good old-fashioned word-of-mouth advertising: Tell people about your site.
- Another simple and cheap way to make people aware of your Web site is to send e-mails to friends, business associates, and family, letting them know of your online presence. Ask them to visit your Web site, share its URL with others, and tell you what they think.

Perhaps you are just starting a blog and want to gain a following.

- Once again, you can e-mail people, feature the blog in a prominent position on your Web site, or mention it on a forum you belong to.
- You can tweet about it as well.

Or maybe you just joined a social network. You can make people aware of you by any of the following methods:

- Invite people to join your network.
- Join some online groups and ask and answer questions.
- Provide a link to your Web site.

Once people find you, if they like what they read, they will be back, and they will tell others about you. More important, you will still have to maintain your interpersonal skills because not all interaction will be done via cyberspace. At some point, expect to talk to contacts on the phone or in person.

You might think you already have a handle on social media and networking. But guess again—it's a moving target. It's hard to know what's next with social networking. It has already come a long way since the late 1990s, and will continue to evolve. Prepare yourself to evolve with it.

Formats for Business Documents

You have learned about various business documents and how they are formatted throughout the text. This appendix is a quick guide you can refer to when you need to format letters, memos, e-mails, and reports.

In Chapter 3, you learned that business conventions vary around the world. The same is true for the formats of business documents. The formats can also differ from industry to industry and firm to firm. Many firms develop their own standards for business documents. If you work in such a firm, follow its guidelines.

Letters

Business letters should be printed on 8½" × 11" paper that has a weight of between 16 and 20 pounds. (Paper that is 16–20 pounds is not as heavy as résumé paper but not as light as paper you put in your printer.) White paper is most commonly used, but light shades of grey and pastels are occasionally used. Consider the message you are trying to send when you choose the color of your paper. If you are an interior designer, a light peach-colored paper might be a fine choice. However, if you are in a conservative field such as engineering, choosing white paper would be preferable.

For their business letters, most companies use stationery printed with their letterheads. Recall from Chapter 7 that the letterhead includes the company's logo (if there is one), name and address, and sometimes the firm's phone number, fax number, and Web address. When writing on behalf of your company, always use your organization's letterhead. Conversely, if you are writing a personal message, don't put it on your company's letterhead. Doing so could confuse the reader and create problems for you within your company. If you are sending a personal business letter and you lack stationery with a letterhead, you can create one by typing your name and contact information at the top of the page. Or, you can simply type your address at the top left margin of the page above the date.

Standard Letter Formats

Business letters can be written in block style or modified block style. In block style letters, all elements—the date, signature, and so forth—begin at the left-hand margin. In modified block style letters, the date and closing lines are aligned near the center of the page. **Exhibit B-1** shows the two styles. Paragraphs can either be indented or justified at the left margin. Although both formats are acceptable, the block style is more common in U.S. correspondence and easier to use.

Well-formatted letters are centered vertically and horizontally on the page. Use at least 1-inch margins. Lines should be single-spaced and ragged-right. Don't justify the type because, as you learned in Chapter 6, doing so can make the copy hard to read.

Exhibit B-1 Format of a Block Style Letter versus a Modified Block Style Letter

Block Style

Modified Block Style

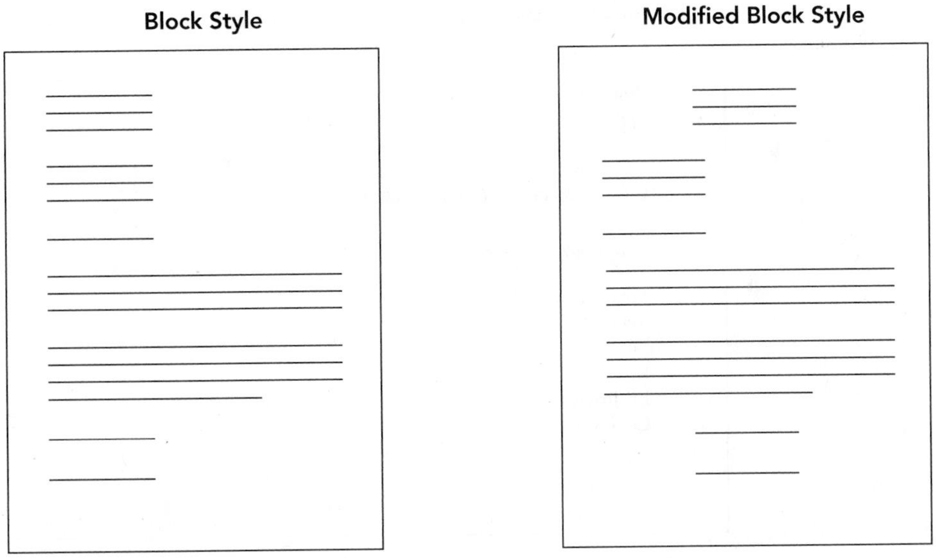

Elements of Business Letters

The basic elements of a business letter are shown in **Exhibit B-2a**. Notice that the letter is formatted using the block style. **Exhibit B-2b** shows an actual business letter with these elements and their spacing.

Return Address

The return address is your address if letterhead isn't being used. If you aren't using letterhead, type it roughly four to six lines down from the top of the page. Be prepared to increase or decrease the space as necessary to center the letter vertically on the page.

Date

Position the date at least one blank line below the letterhead or return address. If you need to vary the space for better vertical alignment of the letter on the page, you can do so. (See Exhibit B-2b.) In a block letter, the date should be left-justified. In a modified block letter, it should begin near the center of the page. Type out the full month, followed by the day and a comma, followed by the year. Don't abbreviate the month and don't add letters such as *th*, *nd*, *rd*, and *st* to the date. For example, type:

March 8, 2011
not
March 8th, 2011

Many word processing programs will automatically insert the date for you. If you are sending a letter to another country, use the appropriate date format for the culture. (See Chapter 3.)

Inside Address

A letter's inside address consists of the recipient's title, complete name, company name, if there is one, and address. Leave at least one blank line between the date and the inside address. You can adjust the amount of space to center the letter vertically on the page after you have completed it.

Exhibit B-2a Elements of a Business Letter

Return Address Line 1
Return Address Line 2

Date (Month, Day, Year)

Mr./Mrs./Ms./Dr. Complete Name
Title/Position of Recipient
Company Name
Address Line 1
Address Line 2

Dear Ms./Mrs./Mr. /Dr. Last Name:

Subject: Title of Subject

Body paragraph 1 . . . .

Body paragraph 2 . . . .

Body paragraph 3 . . . .

Closing (*Sincerely, Cordially,* etc.)

Your Signature

Your Name
Your Title

Reference initials (writer and typist's)
Enclosures
Copies

Exhibit B-2b Completed Business Letter

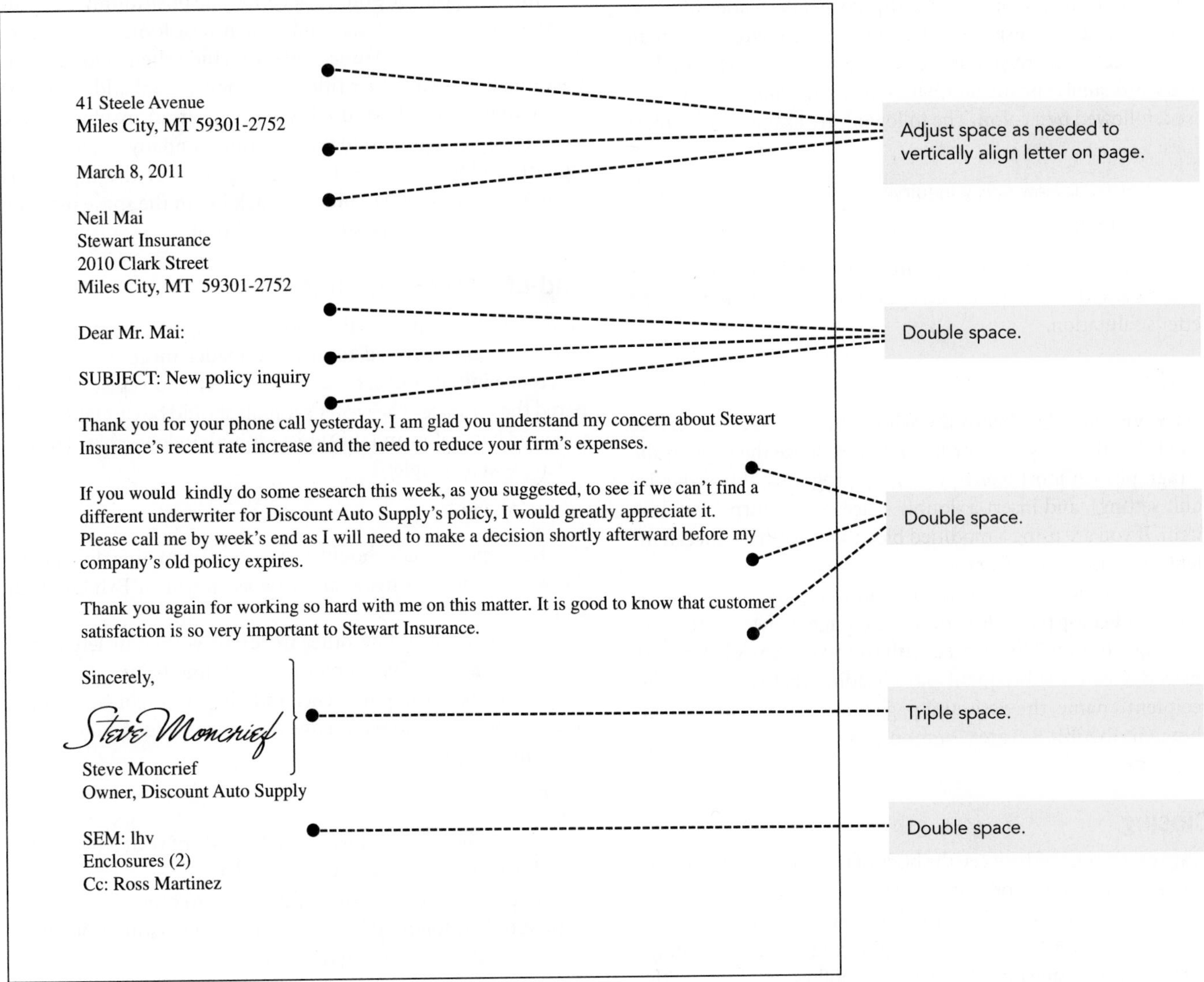
41 Steele Avenue
Miles City, MT 59301-2752

March 8, 2011

Neil Mai
Stewart Insurance
2010 Clark Street
Miles City, MT 59301-2752

Dear Mr. Mai:

SUBJECT: New policy inquiry

Thank you for your phone call yesterday. I am glad you understand my concern about Stewart Insurance's recent rate increase and the need to reduce your firm's expenses.

If you would kindly do some research this week, as you suggested, to see if we can't find a different underwriter for Discount Auto Supply's policy, I would greatly appreciate it. Please call me by week's end as I will need to make a decision shortly afterward before my company's old policy expires.

Thank you again for working so hard with me on this matter. It is good to know that customer satisfaction is so very important to Stewart Insurance.

Sincerely,

Steve Moncrief
Owner, Discount Auto Supply

SEM: lhv
Enclosures (2)
Cc: Ross Martinez

Salutation

The salutation is a letter's greeting followed by the recipient's title and last name (*Dear Ms. Jones*). However, if you know the person well, and the situation is not particularly formal, you can address the person by his or her first name (*Dear Robin*). Find out the title by which the person prefers to be addressed, such as *Dr., Mr., Ms., Mrs.,* or *Miss.* If the recipient is a woman, and you don't know her, it is best to use *Ms.* as the salutation. If you are unsure whether or not the person is a man or woman, and he or she goes by no other title that you aware of (such as *Dr.*), omit the title.

If you are unsure whether the recipient is a man or woman, simply type the person's first and last names (*Dear Robin Jones*). If you only know the person's title, you can use it in full or in part (*Dear Director* or *Dear Personnel Director*). If you cannot determine exactly to whom the letter should be addressed, use the person's position such as *Personnel Director.* If you are addressing a group of people, *Ladies and Gentlemen* is an acceptable salutation.

Type the salutation one blank line down from the inside address and insert a colon after it, if you are using mixed punctuation. When mixed punctuation is used, a colon is placed after the salutation, and a comma is placed after the closing line at the end of the letter. When open punctuation is used, no punctuation is used after either the salutation or the close. Mixed punctuation is the more common of the two in U.S. correspondence.

Attention Line

If, rather than an individual, you are directing a letter to an organization as a whole or a department within it, use an attention line in the first line of the inside address. This will help direct the letter to the right person in the organization. Then use a salutation such as *To Whom It May Concern,* or *Ladies and Gentlemen.* The following is an example:

Attention: Returns Department
Surfware Inc.
52 Santa Monica Blvd.
Santa Monica, CA

To Whom It May Concern:

Subject Line

Some people use a subject line to quickly tell the reader what the letter is about. For example, the subject line might refer to an earlier piece of correspondence or an order or invoice number. The word *subject* or the abbreviation *re* (meaning *regarding*) is used, followed by a colon. The following are examples of subject lines:

SUBJECT: New policy inquiry

Re: Invoice no. 225

Subject lines can be capitalized or boldfaced to get the reader's attention. They should appear one blank line below the letter's salutation.

Body

Leave one blank line below the salutation or subject line before beginning the body of your letter. Single-space the copy in the paragraphs (in most word-processing programs, this is the default setting), and insert a double space (two returns) between them. If you are using a modified block style format, you can indent the paragraphs (five spaces is standard).

If your letter requires more than one page, use the same grade and color paper for the second page. However, the second page shouldn't be printed with your company's letterhead. Instead, create a subsequent-page heading that consists of the recipient's name, the date, and page number. The two formats shown in **Exhibit B-3** are commonly used for subsequent-page headings.

Closing

Leave one blank line between the body of the letter and the closing. Use a standard one-word closing such as *Sincerely, Cordially,* or *Respectfully.* If you are using a modified block format, the closing should begin near the center of the page and be aligned with the date. If you are using mixed punctuation, follow the closing with a comma. If you are using open punctuation, use no punctuation.

Signature Block

Align and type your name and title three blank lines down from the closing. Both your name and title can appear on the same line. Or, if your title is long, you can put your name on the first line and your title on the second. The positioning depends on the length of the letter and how it best looks from top to bottom on the page. Some writers include their phone numbers one line below their titles, and their e-mail addresses one below that. If you have used letterhead or an inside address, there is no need for you to type in your company's name in the signature block because it already appears at the top of the page. Sign your name in blue or black ink in the space between the closing and your typed name and title.

End-of-letter Notations

Notations that appear at the bottom left-hand corner of a business letter are provided to give the reader more information. Reference initials indicate both the writer and typist who prepared the message. The writer's initials should be capitalized and followed by a colon and the typist's initials in lowercase. The following is an example:

NEM: lhv

Reference initials should appear one blank line down from the writer's printed name and title as shown in Exhibits B-2a and B-2b.

If you are including other materials with your letter, type *Enc., Enclosure,* or *Enclosures* one blank line below your name and title or below any reference initials you might be using. If you are enclosing more than one document, add the number of enclosures in parentheses:

Enclosures (2)

Always mention enclosures in the body of your letter so that they don't get overlooked by your reader.

If you are sending copies of the letter to other readers, type *cc,* or simply *c,* followed by a colon and the person or people to whom you are also sending the letter:

c: Ross Martinez, Chandra Singh

The copy line should appear one line below any reference initials and enclosure designations. If there are no reference initials and enclosure designations, the copy line should appear one blank line below your name and title.

Exhibit B-3 Formats for Second Pages of Business Letters

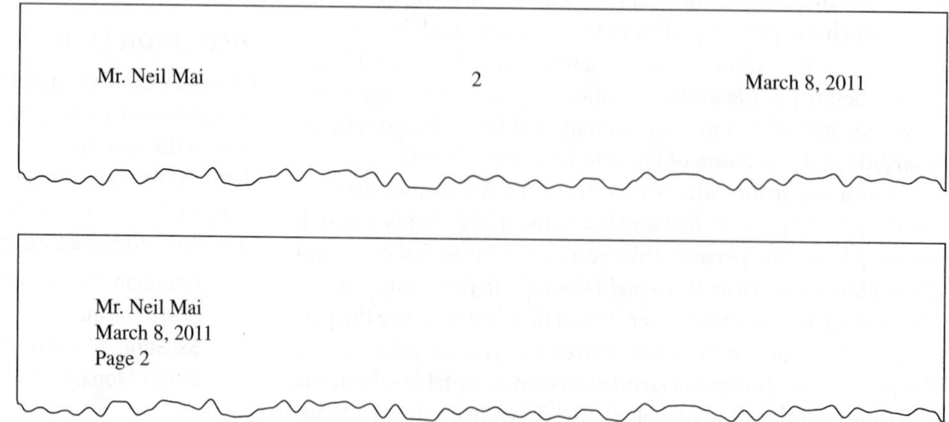

Mr. Neil Mai 2 March 8, 2011

Mr. Neil Mai
March 8, 2011
Page 2

Exhibit B-4 The Right Way to Fold a Business Letter and Insert It into an Envelope

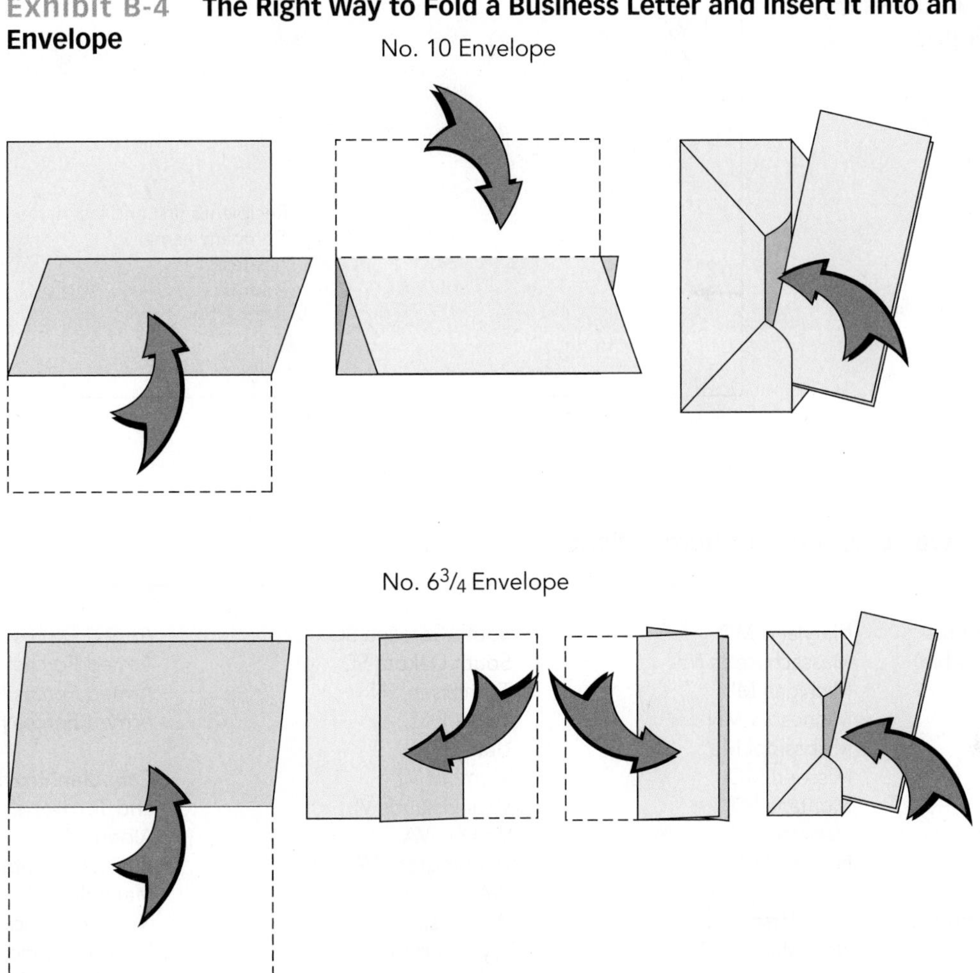

Avoid adding the *P.S.* notations and information to the bottom of business letter. Doing so could give the reader the impression that you didn't plan your letter well, so you forgot to include some information in the letter's body. The exception is direct-sales letters designed to get readers to take action. *P.S. Don't forget to mail your application by November 1* is an example.

Envelopes

Fold the letter into thirds as shown in **Exhibit B-4**. Then, place the letter into a No. 10-sized business envelope, which is 4⅛" long by 9½" wide. Place the bottom fold of the letter into the bottom fold of the envelope with the open flap of the letter facing outward.

Address Format

Single-space the information on the envelope. Type the recipient's name, company, if there is one, delivery address, city, state, and ZIP code onto the scannable area of the envelope, which is the shaded area shown in **Exhibit B-5**. However, you don't need to include the recipient's title on the envelope.

The U.S. Postal Service prefers all capital characters and no punctuation be used on envelopes because the format is easiest for its optical character readers to record the information. The postal service also prefers senders use the newer, nine-digit ZIP codes (ZIP + 4) rather than the older five-digit zip codes. You can find the ZIP + 4 code for a recipient by entering the person's street address and city/state in the postal service's "ZIP Code Lookup" screen on its Web site.

All of the lines of the recipient's address should be typed flush left halfway across the envelope in the scannable area. Use the two-letter state abbreviation and include the ZIP code. The two-letter abbreviations for U.S. states, Canadian provinces, the U.S. armed services, and various American possessions, commonwealths, and territories are shown in **Exhibit B-6**. For information on how to address mail sent abroad to different countries or to U.S. military personnel, see the U.S. Postal Service's Web site.

Your return address should be typed flush left in the upper left-hand corner of the envelope. Most companies have envelopes that are already printed with their return addresses. Any on-arrival, delivery information for the recipient, such as *Personal* or *Confidential,* should appear four lines below the return address. Special mailing instructions meant for the post office, such as *Registered* and *Do Not Bend,* should appear below the stamp but at least three lines above the recipient's address.

Exhibit B-5 Addressing Business Envelopes

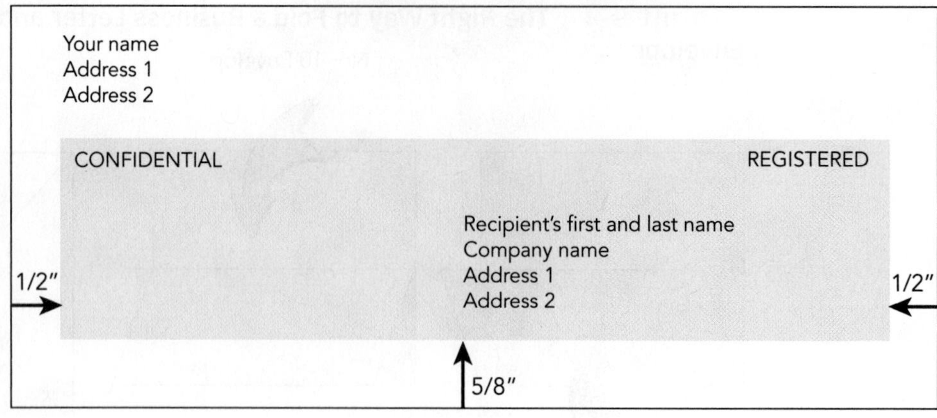

Exhibit B-6 Two-Letter Postal Abbreviations

U.S. States (and the District of Columbia)
Alabama AL
Alaska AK
Arizona AZ
Arkansas AR
California CA
Colorado CO
Connecticut CT
Delaware DE
District of Columbia DC
Florida FL
Georgia GA
Hawaii HI
Idaho ID
Illinois IL
Indiana IN
Iowa IA
Kansas KS
Kentucky KY
Louisiana LA
Maine ME
Marshall Islands MH
Maryland MD
Massachusetts MA
Michigan MI
Minnesota MN
Mississippi MS
Missouri MO
Montana MT
Nebraska NE
Nevada NV
New Hampshire NH
New Jersey NJ
New Mexico NM
New York NY
North Carolina NC
North Dakota ND
Northern Mariana Islands MP
Ohio OH
Oklahoma OK
Oregon OR
Palau PW
Pennsylvania PA
Puerto Rico PR
Rhode Island RI
South Carolina SC
South Dakota SD
Tennessee TN
Texas TX
Utah UT
Vermont VT
Virgin Islands VI
Virginia VA
Washington WA
West Virginia WV
Wisconsin WI
Wyoming WY

U.S. Territories, Possessions, and Commonwealths
American Samoa AS
Federated States of Micronesia FM
Guam GU

U.S. Armed Services
Armed Forces Africa AE
Armed Forces Americas AA
Armed Forces Canada AE
Armed Forces Europe AE
Armed Forces Middle East AE
Armed Forces Pacific AP

Canadian Provinces and Territories
Alberta AB
British Columbia BC
Manitoba MB
New Brunswick NB
Newfoundland and Labrador NL
Northwest Territories NT
Nova Scotia NS
Nunavut NU
Ontario ON
Prince Edward Island PE
Quebec QC
Saskatchewan SK
Yukon YT

Memos

Memos are reserved for messages sent within an organization. Managers often use memos when they must present important messages in a formal manner such as changes in policy.

All memos include *Date, To, From,* and *Subject* headings at the top. (Sometimes *Re* is used instead of *Subject.*) The headings generally are typed flush with the left-hand margin and are capitalized. However, they can appear in different order. Most companies supply their employees with preprinted memo paper or word processing templates set up like memos that they can then fill out and print. If you lack such a template, you can either choose one from your word processing program or create one on blank paper. If you create one on blank paper, leave an adequate amount of margin space around the document and type the word MEMO in all capital letters at the top center of the page, as shown in **Exhibit B-7**. Double-space the *Date, To, From,* and *Subject* lines to make them easier to read.

You don't need to include the recipient's title in the *To* line—only his or her first and last name. You can also address the memo to a group of people or an entire department, as Exhibit B-7 shows. Just be sure everyone in the group or department receives a copy.

Begin the body at least two lines below the last heading at the top of the memo (generally the subject) line. Single-space the copy, but double-space between paragraphs. If the memo is

Exhibit B-7 **Formatting a Memo**

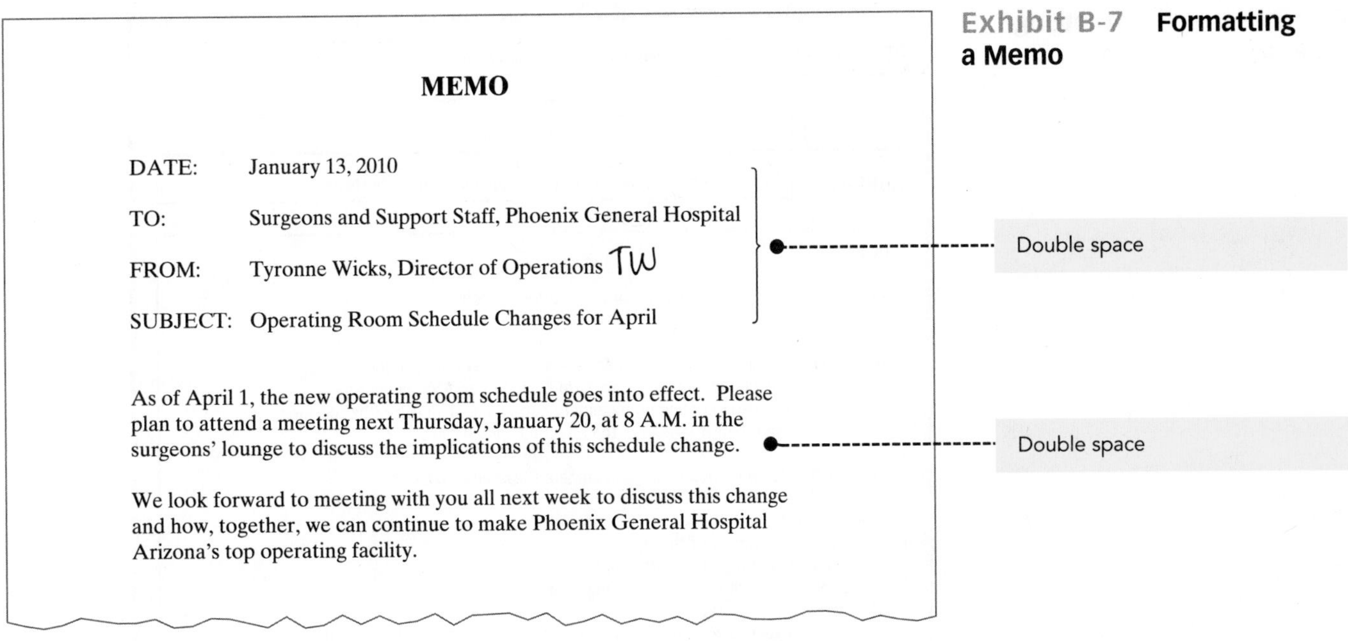
MEMO

DATE: January 13, 2010

TO: Surgeons and Support Staff, Phoenix General Hospital

FROM: Tyronne Wicks, Director of Operations TW

SUBJECT: Operating Room Schedule Changes for April

As of April 1, the new operating room schedule goes into effect. Please plan to attend a meeting next Thursday, January 20, at 8 A.M. in the surgeons' lounge to discuss the implications of this schedule change.

We look forward to meeting with you all next week to discuss this change and how, together, we can continue to make Phoenix General Hospital Arizona's top operating facility.

long or detailed, you can create heads, subheads, and lists to make it easier for readers to skim. If you wish, you can indent the paragraphs, although most writers don't. If the memo runs to a second page, create a second-page heading like those that are created for letters. (See the "Letters" section in this appendix.) Print the second page on the same color and grade of paper.

You don't need to create a complimentary close or use a signature block on a memo because your name already appears at the top of it, so it's clear. However, many senders write their initials next to their names in the *From* line. Doing so helps assure readers that the memo was indeed authorized by the sender and not written and distributed by someone else.

E-mails

For many organizations, e-mails have replaced memos as the primary form of internal written communication. E-mails are similar to memos but less formal. They are quick to send, inexpensive, easy to distribute around the globe, and they don't create a lot of paper waste. Like letters, firms also send e-mails externally to people such as customers and suppliers.

Elements of E-mails

The various elements of an e-mail are shown in **Exhibit B-8** and outlined next.

From

Unless you have permission from your manager, be sure to use your work e-mail address rather than your personal e-mail address for all business correspondence.

To

Type the recipient's e-mail address in the *To* line. To avoid sending e-mails to the wrong people, consider completing this line after you finish writing your message. You can't accidentally send an e-mail without the *To* line completed.

Subject

Busy employees often have to read through hundreds of e-mails a day, so include a clear and specific subject line.

Cc

Copy others who need to be informed about the discussion.

Bcc

Bcc stands for "blind courtesy copy." Complete the Bcc line when you want to send an e-mail to a third party but you do not want your reader to know the third party has been copied on it. However, before you use this feature, check with your manager. Many employees and managers dislike the use of blind copies because it implies the writer is unwilling to communicate openly with the person being blind copied.

Salutation

Greet your reader with a simple salutation. The following examples are all acceptable:

- Dear Ms. Rivers:
- Hello:
- David:

If you are sending an e-mail to a close colleague, you can be less formal and use greetings such as:

- Hi, Jasmine,
- Good morning, Michael.

Body

Single-space the paragraphs and insert a double space between them. You have the option of indenting paragraphs if you like, but it's easier and more common to simply start them flush left. Avoid sending long e-mails. If your e-mail contains

Exhibit B-8 Formatting an E-mail

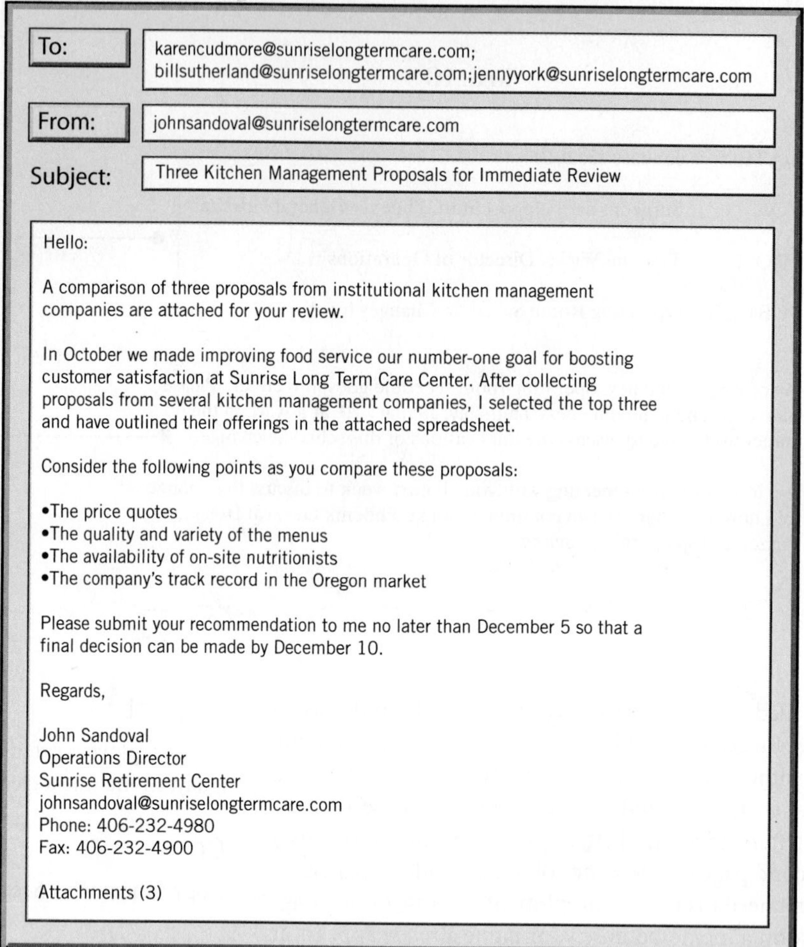

To: karencudmore@sunriselongtermcare.com; billsutherland@sunriselongtermcare.com;jennyyork@sunriselongtermcare.com

From: johnsandoval@sunriselongtermcare.com

Subject: Three Kitchen Management Proposals for Immediate Review

Hello:

A comparison of three proposals from institutional kitchen management companies are attached for your review.

In October we made improving food service our number-one goal for boosting customer satisfaction at Sunrise Long Term Care Center. After collecting proposals from several kitchen management companies, I selected the top three and have outlined their offerings in the attached spreadsheet.

Consider the following points as you compare these proposals:

•The price quotes
•The quality and variety of the menus
•The availability of on-site nutritionists
•The company's track record in the Oregon market

Please submit your recommendation to me no later than December 5 so that a final decision can be made by December 10.

Regards,

John Sandoval
Operations Director
Sunrise Retirement Center
johnsandoval@sunriselongtermcare.com
Phone: 406-232-4980
Fax: 406-232-4900

Attachments (3)

detailed information that needs to be conveyed, use heads, subheads, and lists to make the copy easier to skim and read.

Close

Close your message with a simple expression such as one of the following, followed by a comma:

- Regards,
- Best wishes,
- Thank you,
- Cordially,
- Sincerely,

The one you choose should reflect the formality of the situation. *Sincerely* and *Cordially* are more formal than *Regards* and *Best wishes.*

Signature Block

Follow the closing information with your name, title, company's name, and your contact information, including your e-mail address. Some people also like to include their companies' Web site addresses. Most e-mail applications allow you to create a personalized signature block that automatically appears at the bottom of every e-mail message you send.

Attachments

Send attachments with your e-mail message when your information:

- Is longer than a page or two.
- Has complicated formatting such as detailed outlines, multiple subheadings, or varied margins.
- Consists of a non-text file such as an "html" file or PowerPoint file.

Some Internet providers have spam and virus detectors that reject e-mails with large files attached or files with certain extensions, such as .zip files. If you are sending an attachment that is somewhat uncommon, you may need to follow up with your recipients to make sure they received it.

Formal Reports

The format of formal reports can vary, depending upon their content. Most word processing applications, including Microsoft Word 2007, offer templates you can use to help you format different reports. The report in **Exhibit B-9** was created using such a template.

Whether you use a template or not, you need to understand the basic setup of reports. Why? Suppose you print your report but

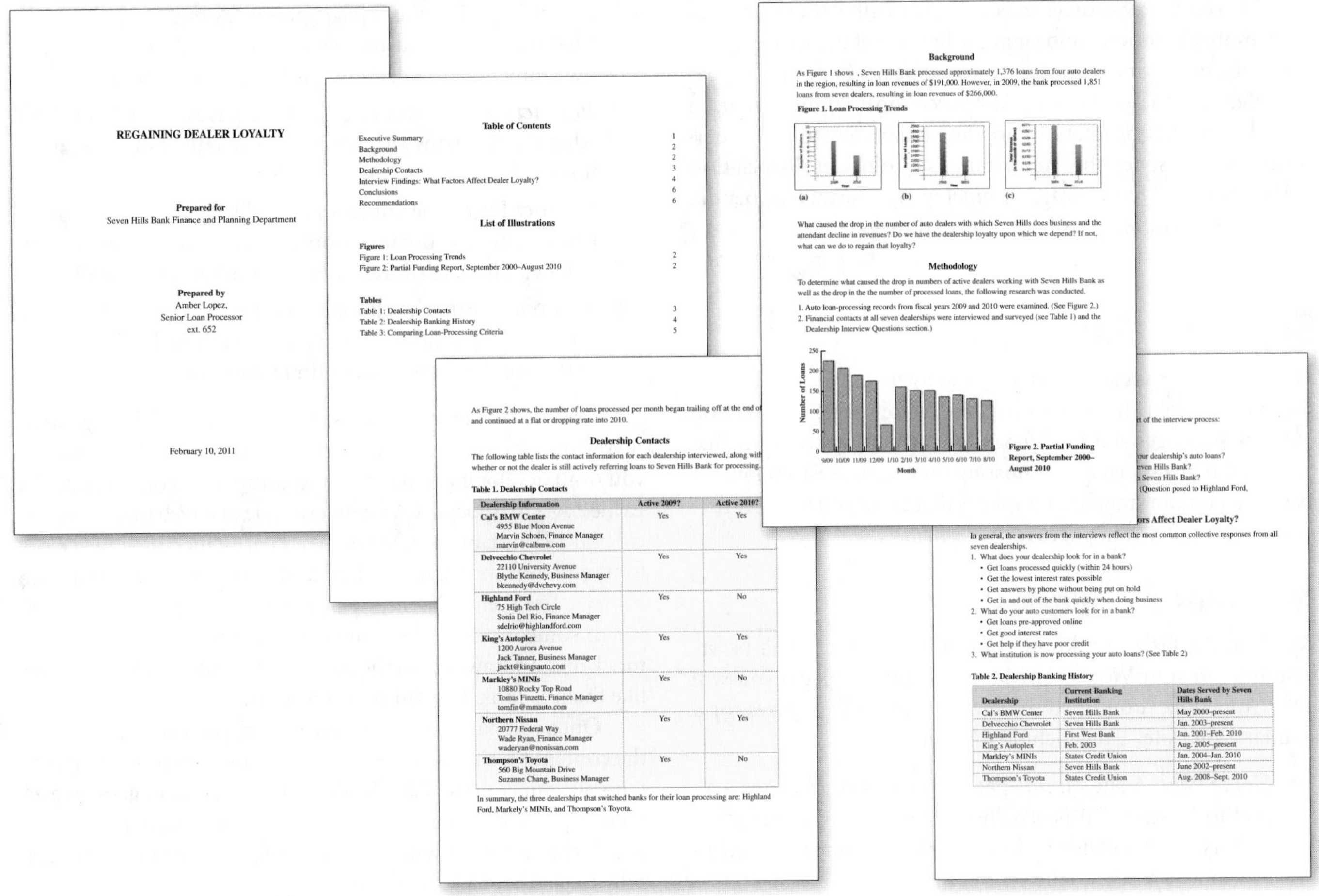

REGAINING DEALER LOYALTY

Prepared for
Seven Hills Bank Finance and Planning Department

Prepared by
Amber Lopez,
Senior Loan Processor
ext. 652

February 10, 2011

Table of Contents

Executive Summary	1
Background	2
Methodology	2
Dealership Contacts	3
Interview Findings: What Factors Affect Dealer Loyalty?	4
Conclusions	6
Recommendations	6

List of Illustrations

Figures

Figure 1: Loan Processing Trends	2
Figure 2: Partial Funding Report, September 2000–August 2010	2

Tables

Table 1: Dealership Contacts	3
Table 2: Dealership Banking History	4
Table 3: Comparing Loan-Processing Criteria	5

Background

As Figure 1 shows , Seven Hills Bank processed approximately 1,376 loans from four auto dealers in the region, resulting in loan revenues of $191,000. However, in 2009, the bank processed 1,851 loans from seven dealers, resulting in loan revenues of $266,000.

Figure 1. Loan Processing Trends

(a) (b) (c)

What caused the drop in the number of auto dealers with which Seven Hills does business and the attendant decline in revenues? Do we have the dealership loyalty upon which we depend? If not, what can we do to regain that loyalty?

Methodology

To determine what caused the drop in numbers of active dealers working with Seven Hills Bank as well as the drop in the the number of processed loans, the following research was conducted.

1. Auto loan-processing records from fiscal years 2009 and 2010 were examined. (See Figure 2.)
2. Financial contacts at all seven dealerships were interviewed and surveyed (see Table 1) and the Dealership Interview Questions section.)

Figure 2. Partial Funding Report, September 2000–August 2010

As Figure 2 shows, the number of loans processed per month began trailing off at the end of and continued at a flat or dropping rate into 2010.

Dealership Contacts

The following table lists the contact information for each dealership interviewed, along with whether or not the dealer is still actively referring loans to Seven Hills Bank for processing.

Table 1. Dealership Contacts

Dealership Information	Active 2009?	Active 2010?
Cal's BMW Center 4955 Blue Moon Avenue Marvin Schoen, Finance Manager marvin@calbmw.com	Yes	Yes
Delvecchio Chevrolet 22110 University Avenue Blythe Kennedy, Business Manager bkennedy@dvchevy.com	Yes	Yes
Highland Ford 75 High Tech Circle Sonia Del Rio, Finance Manager sdelrio@highlandford.com	Yes	No
King's Autoplex 1200 Aurora Avenue Jack Tanner, Business Manager jackt@kingsauto.com	Yes	Yes
Markley's MINIs 10880 Rocky Top Road Tomas Finzetti, Finance Manager tomfin@mmauto.com	Yes	No
Northern Nissan 20777 Federal Way Wade Ryan, Finance Manager waderyan@nonissan.com	Yes	Yes
Thompson's Toyota 560 Big Mountain Drive Suzanne Chang, Business Manager	Yes	No

In summary, the three dealerships that switched banks for their loan processing are: Highland Ford, Markely's MINIs, and Thompson's Toyota.

In general, the answers from the interviews reflect the most common collective responses from all seven dealerships.

1. What does your dealership look for in a bank?
   - Get loans processed quickly (within 24 hours)
   - Get the lowest interest rates possible
   - Get answers by phone without being put on hold
   - Get in and out of the bank quickly when doing business
2. What do your auto customers look for in a bank?
   - Get loans pre-approved online
   - Get good interest rates
   - Get help if they have poor credit
3. What institution is now processing your auto loans? (See Table 2)

Table 2. Dealership Banking History

Dealership	Current Banking Institution	Dates Served by Seven Hills Bank
Cal's BMW Center	Seven Hills Bank	May 2000–present
Delvecchio Chevrolet	Seven Hills Bank	Jan. 2003–present
Highland Ford	First West Bank	Jan. 2001–Feb. 2010
King's Autoplex	Feb. 2003	Aug. 2005–present
Markley's MINIs	States Credit Union	Jan. 2004–Jan. 2010
Northern Nissan	Seven Hills Bank	June 2002–present
Thompson's Toyota	States Credit Union	Aug. 2008–Sept. 2010

Exhibit B-9 An Example of a Report Formatted Using a Word Processing Template

there are some "bugs" with your template or the application itself. The report, therefore, doesn't look right. Your credibility could be seriously affected, even if the content of your report is terrific.

Spacing

Reports can either be double- or single-spaced. Traditionally, they have been double-spaced. To save paper and preserve the environment, today more firms are opting to single-space their reports. If you single-space your report, double-space between paragraphs so it's clear where one ends and the other begins. If you double-space your report, don't triple-space between the paragraphs. Instead, indent them so it's clear where one ends and the other begins.

Margins

The margins of the report should be at least 1 inch. If you plan to bind the report, increase by a half-inch the margin on the side of the page where the binding will appear. Bindings take up space. If you don't leave room for the binding, the copy on the side of the bound page will be too close to the edge of the page or perhaps even cut off by the binding.

Page Numbers

All of the pages in the report should be given a page number. The introductory pages such as the title of the report, the table of contents, and list of illustrations are labeled with Roman numerals (i, ii, iii, iv, v, and so on) beginning with *i*. By contrast, the pages in the main body of the report are labeled with Arabic page numbers (1, 2, 3, 4, and so on.) The textbook you are now reading is set up this way. Notice that all of the pages prior to Chapter 1 have Roman-style page numbers. There is one exception: the title page (first page) of the report. The page number for the title page is page *i*, but the number shouldn't actually appear on the report. Notice that the title page at the front of this textbook doesn't have a number either.

The word-processing program you use can help you automatically fill in the page numbers for your table of contents and list of illustrations. For example, if you add content and a section of your report moves from one page to another, your table of contents will automatically change to reflect the change.

Headings

Be consistent with the headings you use in your report. All main headings should be set in the same font. The same is true for all second-level headings and all third-level headings as well as the spaces you leave above and below them. Also, the spaces you leave above heads should be larger than the spaces you leave below them. That way, the heads appear to be associated with the text to which they refer, rather than to the previous text in the document.

Cite secondary sources in your report with either footnotes or endnotes. Footnotes appear at the bottom of the same page in which the quote or cited information appears. Endnotes appear at the end of the document. The three most commonly used styles for formatting citations are the Modern Language Association (MLA) style, the American Psychological Association (APA) style, and the *Chicago Manual of Style* format. Appendix C explains the differences between the three.

Social Media

The formats for social media vary widely from Web site to Web site, blog to blog, and Twitter page to Twitter page. This section outlines some general guidelines for formatting social media. Note that many social media hosting sites, such as Facebook, for example, contain standard templates that allow you to easily format social media Web pages for your firm's use.

Web Sites and Blogs

Based on the tasks you know your online audience will be attempting on your Web site or blog, identify the pages you will need. Appendix A outlined the most common Web pages for a standard Web site. They include the following:

- ***Home Page.*** A site's home page is the first page visitors expect to "land on." It is usually quite eye-catching and gives visitors in 10 seconds or less the information they need to continue to navigate the site.
- ***About Page.*** The about page gives visitors a sense of who the site's owner is, what the person or organization does, and how long the organization has been in operation.
- ***Products or Services Pages.*** These pages identify in detail what the company that owns the site makes or the services it provides.
- ***Contact Page.*** The contact page tells visitors how to get in touch with the organization or site owner. It usually includes a physical address, phone number, and e-mail.
- ***Shopping Cart.*** The shopping cart indicates the items visitors want to purchase. Visitors can usually make adjustments to the number of items, continue shopping, or check out.

Create a Web map that shows how the pages will be organized. A Web map looks like a business organization chart. It can prevent you from developing a site that's too complicated or too large. See Exhibit A-2 in Appendix A for an example of a Web map. Then decide on a layout, or look, for the Web pages, including the colors, fonts and font sizes. Use standard fonts that can be read using any browser. Use them consistently from page to page.

If someone else is building your site for you, you can create mock ups, or drawings, of the pages so they know how you would like them to look. **Exhibit B-10** shows an example of a mock up.

Once you have specified your design, you can begin writing the content for the Web site or blog. Create a single file that contains all your content. Clearly identify what content goes on each Web page. Keep your text short, clear, and engaging and use words that resonate with your audience. Use heading strategically to get the reader's attention.

Exhibit B-10 A Mock-Up of a Web Page

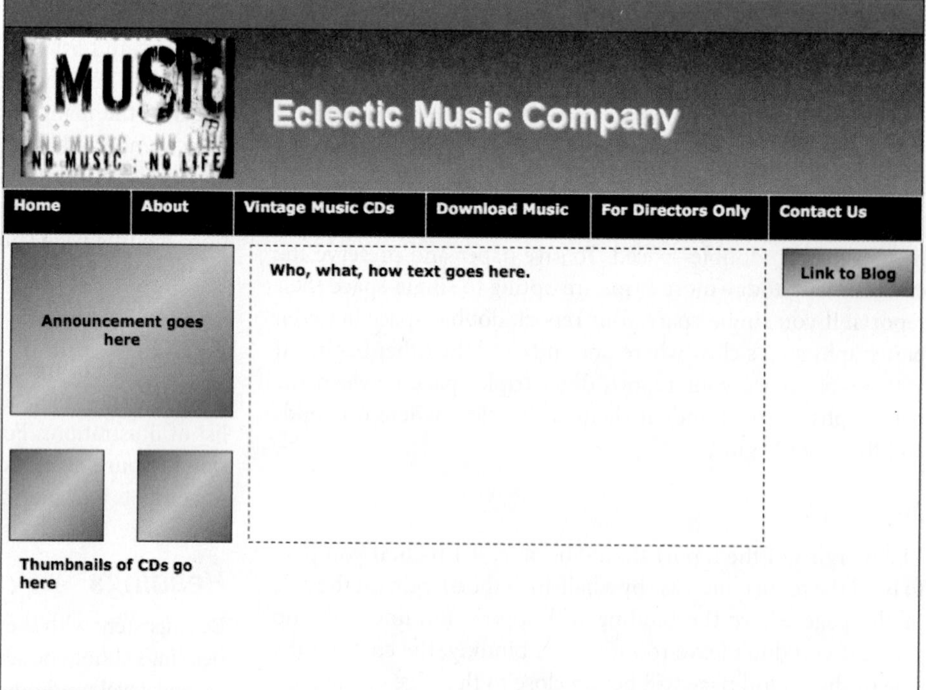

Microblogs (Twitter)

If your business decides to use Twitter, you won't have to do much design work because Twitter has a standard template you can use. When you sign up for a Twitter, you will be asked to create an account. If you're creating a company account, type the name of your company in the "Full name" field, which will help customers locate your company on Twitter. Then type your company's location and Web site address in the appropriate fields.

The "Username" field is a "handle," or short nickname, that will appear on your tweets. For example, the handle for National Association for Stock Car Auto Racing (NASCAR) is *NASCAR Hometracks.*

After you have signed up for an account, your browser will automatically take you to your firm's account page. This is where you will create the "look" of your site and provide more information to people who want to follow your firm on Twitter.

1. Click on "Settings" and follow the instructions. In the "Bio" field, fill out a description of your company. You have 160 characters in which to do so. The Bio field will appear on your Twitter page and give the reader an idea about what your organization does. The Bio field for NASCAR is as follows:

   The official NASCAR twitter for its touring and weekly series

   You can also include the names of the people twittering on your firm's behalf as well as additional contact information for them, such as their e-mail addresses.

2. Click on the "Picture" tab and upload your company's logo or an image used in your firm's advertising or on its Web page.
3. Click the "Design" tab to upload a background image for your Twitter page. You can also adjust the background colors of your Twitter page under this tab.

The background on NASCAR's home page on Twitter has the look and feel of a race, and the organization's logo is prominently displayed when followers search for the organization on Twitter.

Readability is equally important for tweets as it is for any business communication. So is brevity because messages can be only 140 words in length. The following are tips for writing Twitter messages:

- Put the subject or most important information at the beginning of the tweet.
- Write in active voice.
- Remove filler words.
- Watch for typos.
- Keep your message short and positive.

Exhibit B-11 shows the Twitter page for Carol Carter, the author of this book. Notice how Carter's messages to her followers are succinct, grammatically correct, positive, and inspiring.

Exhibit B-11 An Example of a Twitter Homepage

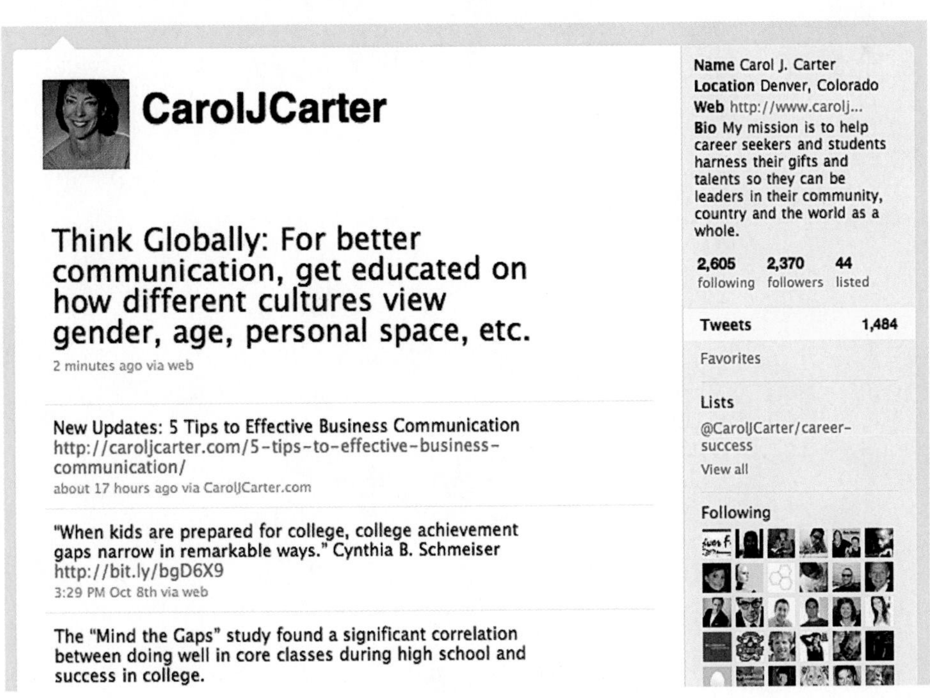

Appendix C

A Basic Guide to Documenting Sources

If the ideas and information you put forth in your writing are not entirely your own, you must document the sources from which they were drawn. Documenting your sources and giving credit where it is due is not only ethical but, as Chapter 16 explained, legally required. Whether you use a direct quote, paraphrase a quote, or summarize information you gathered from your source, you need to cite it. The same is true for tables, photos, and graphics drawn from other sources. In addition, you may need to seek permission from the publisher of the material in order to use it.

Types of Style Guidelines

There are a variety of different style guidelines writers and publishers adhere to. The guidelines specify not only the format of source notes, but also how words and numbers and many other details too numerous to mention here should appear in print. For example, newspaper publishers follow the styles outlined in the *Associated Press Style Book.* Book publishers generally follow the guidelines outlined by *The Chicago Manual of Style.*

Undergraduate students are often asked to adhere to one of the following styles in their papers and publications:

- American Psychological Association (APA) style. The *Publication Manual of the American Psychological Association* is most commonly used to cite sources within the social sciences and physical sciences.
- Modern Language Association (MLA) style. The *MLA Handbook for Writers of Research Papers* is most commonly used by writers in the liberal arts and humanities areas, such as English, the languages, history, and philosophy.
- *The Chicago Manual of Style (CMS).* Like MLA style, CMS is often used in the area of humanities and liberal arts.

Some organizations have their own style guidelines for the materials they produce. Pearson, the publisher of this book, is one such organization. For example, Pearson does not include complete Web site addresses in its textbooks except in source notes. If you work for an organization with specific guidelines, follow them.

In addition, just as the English language changes, so do style guidelines. Guidelines for citing electronic sources are a case in point: They are much different today than they were originally. For example, the MLA no longer requires the use of uniform resource locators (URLs) in its citations because they tend to change and can appear in different databases on the Web, each with different URLs. Instead, readers are encouraged to type the author, title, or other information into a search engine such as Google to find the source. Check to see if your citations conform to those in the latest edition of the style book you use.

MLA Style

The MLA provides two different ways to cite sources. One method is via short parenthetical citations within the text followed by a complete list of the works cited in the document at its end. The other method is via footnotes (or endnotes). The parenthetical citation method is most commonly used by students, so we will focus on it in this appendix.

Using the parenthetical system, you simply insert the source's name and the page number, or numbers, you are citing. No punctuation should appear between the two pieces of information:

> Greater banking regulation won't necessarily head off crises within the Internet banking industry (Schwan 414).

When citing the page ranges for triple-digit numbers, conserve space by dropping the first number from the last page in the range. For example, the page range *303-305* should be shortened to *303-05.* (Also, use hyphens to indicate page ranges.) Notice in the above example how the parenthetical citation appears at the end of the sentence. This is generally the norm. However, if part of the sentence contains your own ideas, place the citation mid-sentence, closest to the copy sourced:

> Greater banking regulation won't necessarily head off crises within the Internet banking industry (Schwan 414), although some experts believe there may be ways to contain the crises.

If the author's name is mentioned in the text, you need not include it in the in-text citation because it's obvious. Instead, just list the page number:

> Schwan contends that greater banking regulation won't necessarily head off crises within the Internet banking industry (414).

To cite two sources for one sentence, put both sources in one set of parentheses separated by a semicolon:

> Greater banking regulation won't necessarily head off crises within the Internet banking or international banking industries (Gregoriou 42; Schwan 414).

Exhibit C-1 shows how to format parenthetical references following MLA style.

Of course, citing this information alone isn't enough. You must provide the complete citations at the end of your document. At the end of your document, start a new page and center the title "Works Cited." Then left-align the text and type the full citations of the references you cited in your paper. **Exhibit C-2** shows a partial works cited section. Notice how the authors' last names appear first, and the subsequent lines of the individual citation entries are indented. All of your entries should be formatted sim-

Exhibit C-1
Formats for Parenthetical References (MLA)

Source Example	Parenthetical Reference
Single author	(Schwan 12)
Single author, multiple pages	(Schwan 15-17) or (Schwan 15, 221)
Two authors	(Schwan and Ramirez 74)
Three to five authors	(Schwan, Ramirez, and Schmidt 847)
Corporate or organizational author	(Pfizer 31)
Book with no author	*Use the first descriptive word in the title*: (Letters 274)
Journal or newspaper article with no author	*Use the first descriptive word in the title*: ("History" 11)
Web site with no page numbers	*(Maskell, par. 3)*

Exhibit C-2
A Partial Works Cited Section (MLA)

Works Cited

Gregoriou, Greg N. *The Banking Crisis Handbook.* Boca Raton: CC Press, 2009. Print.

Lewis, Michael. *The Big Short: Inside the Doomsday Machine.* New York: Norton, 2010. Print.

Schwan, David. "Regulation in the Internet Banking Industry." *International Journal of Bank Marketing* 23.5 (2005): 414-37. Print.

ilarly. They should then be alphabetized. Alphabetizing them allows readers to quickly skim through the list for the complete citations for which they are looking. When the author's name is not known, alphabetize the source by the first major word in its title. Ignore articles such as *A*, *An*, and *The* at the beginning of the title for this purpose. List only the city of the publisher, followed by the publisher's name. In most cases, you can shorten the publisher's name to the first major word to conserve space. For example, *W.W. Norton* can be shortened to *Norton*. However, there is nothing wrong with including the full name of the publisher, especially if it eliminates ambiguity.

Note that the works cited section is not the same as a bibliography. A bibliography is a list of publications you encourage a reader to look at for further reading. However, they aren't meant to specifically document the sources you used. To learn how to create a bibliography using MLA style, refer to the 7th edition of the MLA handbook.

The format for the works cited entries varies slightly depending upon the type of source cited. **Exhibit C-3** shows some of the more common types of citations you will refer to and how to format them. For an article in a periodical, on the Web, or a distinct work that appears in a book (such as a poem in an anthology), cite the entire page range. Also, list the medium of the sourced material you consulted—for example, whether you found it on the Web, in print, on a CD, and so forth.

As we mentioned at the beginning of this appendix, MLA no longer requires you to include the URL for Internet sources. However, you do need to include two dates in the following order: (1) the date the Web page was last updated, if there is one, and (2) the date you accessed the copy. If you cannot find the date on the Web page, type in *n.d.*, which stands for "no date." If you cannot find the publisher of the information, type in *n.p.*, which stands for "no publisher."

APA Style

APA style provides two different ways to cite sources. One method is via short parenthetical citations within the text followed by a complete list of the citations in the document at its end. The other method is via footnotes (or endnotes). Because parenthetical citations are more commonly used by students, we will focus on that system in this section.

Using the parenthetical system, you simply insert the author, the year of publication, and the page number, or numbers, from the sourced material as shown in the following example. (If the date of publication is unknown, use the designation *n.d.*, which stands for "no date.")

> Greater banking regulation won't necessarily head off crises within the Internet banking industry (Schwan, 2005, p. 414).

Exhibit C-3 Formats for References in a Works Cited Section (MLA)

Blog Posting

Krugman, Paul. "It's Demand, Stupid." *The Conscience of a Liberal.* NYTimes.com. 15 Sept. 2010. Web. 21 Sept. 2010.

Book, Single Author

Lewis, Michael. *The Big Short: Inside the Doomsday Machine.* New York: Norton, 2010. Print.

Book, Two or More Authors

Bullock, Richard H., Maureen Daly Goggin, and Francine Weinberg. *The Norton Field Guide to Writing with Readings and Handbook.* 2nd ed. New York: Norton, 2009. Print.

Book, Four or More Authors

Bear, Donald R., et al. *Words Their Way: Word Study for Phonics, Vocabulary, and Spelling Instruction.* 4th ed. Upper Saddle River: Prentice Hall, 2007. Print.

Book, Corporate or Organizational Author

American Medical Association. *American Medical Association Manual of Style: A Guide for Authors and Editors.* 9th ed. Philadelphia: Williams, 1998. Print.

Book, Online

Gladwell, Malcolm. *The Tipping Point.* New York: Back Bay, 2002. Web. 12 Feb. 2010.

Brochure (Pamphlet)

TourTexas. *Visit Big Bend.* Austin: AJR Media, 2009. Print.

Essay (or Short Story, Poem, or Other Work) in an Anthology

Walton, Susan. "The Cautious and Obedient Life." *Short Essays.* Ed. Gerald Levin. Fort Worth: Harcourt, 1992. 9-13. Print.

CD

Fortinash, Katherine M., and Patricia A. Holoday Worret. *Virtual Clinical Excursions for Psychiatric Mental Health Nursing.* 4th ed. St. Louis: Mosby, 2007. CD.

Government Document

Business Systems Modernization: The Internal Revenue Service's Fiscal Year 2008 Expenditure Plan. Washington: Government Accountability Office, 2008. Print.

Journal Article with Volume Number Only

Maklan, Stan, Simon Knox, and Lynette Ryals. "New Trends in Innovation and Customer Relationship Management: A Challenge for Market Researchers." *International Journal of Market Research.* 50 (2008): 221-38. Print.

Journal Article with Volume and Issue Numbers

Schwan, David. "Regulation in the Internet Banking Industry." *International Journal of Bank Marketing.* 23.5 (2005): 414-37. Print.

Magazine Article

Kita, Joe. "White Coat Confessions." *Reader's Digest.* Oct. 2010: 86-97. Print.

Newspaper Article

Birchall, John. "Greener Apple Helps Clean Up." *Financial Times.* 24 Mar. 2009: 11. Print.

(continued)

Exhibit C-3 **(Continued)**

Personal Interview
Carter, Scott. Personal interview. 3 Mar. 2010.
Podcast
Freudberg, David. "Barely Getting By: Stories of America's Working Poor." *Humankind.* Human Media. Web. 27 Aug. 2010.
Speech
Obama, Barack. "Speech On Iraq." n.p. Oval Office, Washington, DC. 31 Aug. 2010. Address.
Television and Radio
"Explosion Rocks San Bruno Neighborhood." *KCBS News.* CBS. KCBS, San Francisco, 13 Sept. 2010. Television.
Web Site
Staff, "Patagonia's Clothing Recycling Program: Lessons Learned, Challenges Ahead," *GreenerDesign.* 9 Mar. 2009. Web. 15 Sept. 2010.
Web Site, No Date
Waters, Shari. "Shoplifting Prevention 101." *About.com.* n.d. Web. 15 Sept. 2010.

You can also cite an entire book by listing just the author's name and the publication date as follows:

> Greater banking regulation won't necessarily head off crises within the Internet banking industry (Schwan, 2005).

If you make a general reference to an entire study or a book in your copy, move the reference up:

> One study (Schwan, 2005) found that greater banking regulation won't necessarily head off crises within the Internet banking industry.

If the author's name is mentioned in the text, you need not include it in parentheses because it's obvious. Instead, list the year after the name of the author, and then put the page number at the end of the sentence:

> Schwan (2005) contends that greater banking regulation won't necessarily head off crises within the Internet banking industry (p. 414).

However, if part of the sentence contains your own ideas, place the page number closest to the copy sourced rather than at the end of the sentence:

> Schwan (2005) contends that greater banking regulation won't necessarily head off crises within the Internet banking industry (p. 414), although some experts believe there may be ways to contain the crises.

To cite two sources for one sentence, put both sources in one set of parentheses separated by a semicolon. Use commas before and after the dates of publication:

> Greater banking regulation won't necessarily head off crises within the Internet banking or international banking industries (Gregoriou, 2009, p. 42; Schwan, 2005, p. 414).

Exhibit C-4 shows how to format parenthetical references using APA style.

Of course, citing this information alone isn't enough. You must provide the complete citations at the end of your document. At the end of your document, start a new page and center the title "References." Then left-align the text and type the full citations of the references you cited in your paper. Include the complete information about the references so readers can easily refer to the material you cited. **Exhibit C-5** shows a partial references section. Notice how the authors' last names appear first and the subsequent lines of the individual entries are indented. All of your entries should be formatted similarly. They should then be alphabetized. Alphabetizing them allows readers to quickly skim through the list to find citations for which they are looking. When the author's name is not known, simply alphabetize the source by the first major word in the title. Ignore articles such as *A, An,* and *The* at the beginning of the title. List both the city and state of the publisher using the U.S. Postal Service's two-letter zip code for the state.

Note that the references section is not the same as a bibliography. A bibliography is a list of publications you encourage your readers to look at for further reading. However, the publications in the bibliography don't specifically document the sources you used. To learn how to create a bibliography using APA style, refer to the 6th edition of the APA manual.

Exhibit C-4 Formats for Parenthetical References (APA)

Source Example	Parenthetical Reference
Single author	(Schwan, 2005, p. 12)
Single author, multiple pages	(Schwan, 2005, pp. 15–17) or (Schwan, 2005, pp. 15, 221)
Two authors	(Schwan & Ramirez, 2006, p. 74)
Three to five authors	*First reference:* (Schwan, Ramirez, Schmidt, & Fox, 2005, p. 22) *Subsequent references:* (Schwan et al., 225, p. 22
Six or more authors	*First and subsequent references:* (Schwan et al., 225, p. 492)
Corporate or organizational author	(Pfizer, 2010, p. 31)
Book, no author listed	*Use the first descriptive word in the title:* (Letters, 2005, p. 274)
Journal or newspaper article, no author listed	*Use the first descriptive word in the title:* ("History," 2005, listed p. 11)
Personal communication	(personal communication, April 4, 2010)
Web site with no page numbers	(Maskell, 2006, para. 3)

References

Bear, D. R., et al. (2007). *Words their way: Word study for phonics, vocabulary, and spelling instruction* (4th ed.). Upper Saddle River, NJ: Prentice Hall.

Bullock, R. H., Daly Goggin, M., & Weinberg, F. (2008). *Norton field guide to writing with readings and handbook* (2nd ed.). New York, NY: Norton.

Lewis, M. (2010). *The big short: Inside the doomsday machine.* New York, NY: Norton.

Exhibit C-5
A Partial References Section (APA)

The format for the references section entries varies slightly depending upon their type. **Exhibit C-6** shows some of the more common types of citations you will refer to and how to format them. For an article in a periodical, on the Web, or a distinct work that appears in a book (such as a poem in an anthology), cite the entire page range in the references section.

For documents on the Internet that are unlikely to change, you don't need to provide a retrieval date. However, you do need to include a URL. If the URL is not stable, which is often the case with databases and newspapers, use the home page of the site you retrieved the work from. See the entry for the online book in Exhibit C-6 for an example. Don't include periods after the URLs. If you have to break a URL into two lines, insert the line break before a slash or other punctuation mark. Sometimes journals and other publications have what's called a digital object identifier (DOI). When an article has a DOI, include that information instead of the URL. For undated works, include the date the resource was retrieved and its URL. See Exhibit C-6 for examples of each scenario.

CMS

The Chicago Manual of Style outlines two systems for citing sources. One of the systems is similar to the MLA and APA parenthetical systems we discussed. However, the more widely used system utilizes footnotes or endnotes. This style, which is covered extensively in the manual, accommodates a variety of different types of sources that don't work as well with the parenthetical system. In addition to citing sources, the notes can be used to explain information the writer doesn't want to cover in detail in the main body of the document. We will discuss this system to illustrate how it differs from parenthetical systems.

Businesses often prefer to use footnotes or endnotes in their publications because they alleviate the need for a reader to flip back and forth to the end of a document to see the complete information for sources. Because the information in the notes is complete, no additional works cited or references section needs to be included, unless the writer wants to add one. If you want to add a bibliography, you can do so. To learn how to create a bibliography, consult the 16th edition of *The Chicago Manual of Style.*

Exhibit C-6 Formats for Sources in a References Section (APA)

Blog Posting

Krugman, P. (2010, September 15). It's demand, stupid [Blog]. Retrieved from http://krugman.blogs.nytimes.com/2010/09/15/its-demand-stupid/

Book, Single Author

Lewis, M. (2010). *The big short: Inside the doomsday machine.* New York, NY: Norton.

Book, Two Authors

Bullock, R. H., Daley Goggin, M., & Weinberg, F. (2008). *Norton field guide to writing with readings and handbook.* (2nd ed.). New York, NY: Norton.

Book, Three to Seven Authors

Bear, D. R., Invernizzi, M., Templeton, S., & Johnston, F. (2007). *Words their way: Word study for phonics, vocabulary, and spelling instruction.* (4th ed.). Upper Saddle River, NJ: Prentice Hall.

Note: When there are more than seven authors, list the first six, insert an ellipsis, and then add the name of the last author.

Book, Corporate or Organizational Author

American Medical Association. (1998). *American Medical Association manual of style: A guide for authors and editors.* (9th ed.). Philadelphia, PA: Williams & Wilkins.

Book, Online

Gladwell, M. (2002). *The tipping point.* New York, NY: Back Bay Books. Retrieved from http://books.google.com/

Brochure (Pamphlet)

TourTexas. (2009). *Visit Big Bend.* [Brochure]. Austin, TX: AJR Media Group.

CD

Fortinash, K. M., & Holoday Worret, P. A. (2007). *Virtual clinical excursions for psychiatric mental health nursing* (4th ed.) [CD]. St. Louis, MO: Mosby.

Government Document

U.S. Government Accountability Office. (2008). *Business systems modernization: Internal Revenue Service's fiscal year 2008 expenditure plan.* Washington, DC: U.S. Government Accountability Office.

Journal Article with Volume Number Only

Maklan, S., Knox, S., & Ryals, L. (2008). New trends in innovation and customer relationship management. *International Journal of Market Research, 50,* 221–238.

Journal Article with Volume and Issue Numbers

Schwan, D. (2005). Regulation in the Internet banking industry. *International Journal of Bank Marketing, 23*(5), 414–437.

Journal Article with a DOI

Urban, G. L. (2005, Spring). Customer advocacy: A new era in marketing? *Journal of Public Policy and Marketing, 24,* 155–159. doi:10.1080/11417549836275585

Magazine Article

Kita, J. (2010, October). White coat confessions. *Reader's Digest,* 86–97.

Exhibit C-6 **(Continued)**

Newspaper Article
Birchall, J. (2009, March 24). Greener apple helps clean up. *The Financial Times*, p. 11.
Personal Interview
Personal interviews and correspondence aren't included in the references section. Use only the parenthetical references. (See Exhibit C-4.)
Podcast
Freudberg, D. (2010, August 27). Barely getting by: Stories of America's working poor. *Humankind.* Human Media [Audio podcast]. Retrieved from http://www.humanmedia.org/catalog/ program.php?products_id=280
Speech
Obama, B. (2010, August 31). President Obama's Oval Office speech on Iraq. Address at the Oval Office, Washington, DC.
Television or Radio Program
Perret, L. (Director). (2010, September 13). Explosion rocks San Bruno neighborhood. [Television broadcast]. *KCBS News*. San Francisco: KCBS/CBS.
Web Site
Staff. (2009, March 9). *Patagonia's clothing recycling program: Lessons learned, challenges ahead.* Retrieved from http://www.greenbiz.com/news/2009/03/09/patagonias-clothing-recycling-program-lessons-learned-challenges-ahead
Web Site, No Date
Waters, S. (n.d.). *Shoplifting 101.* Retrieved September 21, 2010, from http://retail.about.com/od/lossprevention/a/ stopshoplifting.htm

The format of the footnotes (or endnotes if you choose to put your citations at the end of your document) varies slightly depending upon their type. **Exhibit C-7** shows some of the more common types of citations you will refer to and how to format them. Regardless of whether you use footnotes or endnotes, insert a superscript number immediately after the sentence that contains the information you are sourcing.

In the note itself, indent the first line as you would a paragraph, and begin with the note number (full-sized) followed by a period. I include all of the information related to the source, including the page numbers you are citing, unless you are citing a newspaper article. No page numbers are required for newspaper articles. When citing the page ranges for triple-digit numbers, conserve space by dropping the first number from the last page in the range. For example, the page *303–305* should be shortened to *303–05.* List the city and state of the publisher using the U.S. Postal Service's two-letter zip codes for the state. For major cities, you need not include the state abbreviation. In most cases, you can shorten the publisher's name to the first major word to conserve space. For example, *W.W. Norton* can be shortened to *Norton.* However, there is nothing wrong with including the full name of the publisher, especially if it eliminates ambiguity. If you cite the same source again in your document, you can use a shortened version of the longer footnote that includes the last name of the author, a shortened title, and the relevant page numbers:

1. Michael Lewis, *The Big Short: Inside the Doomsday Machine* (New York: Norton, 2010), 63–64.
2. Lewis, *Big Short,* 112.

If you cite the same source and page numbers two or more times consecutively, use the term "Ibid." If you use the same source but cite a different page number, use "Ibid." followed by a comma and the new page number or numbers:

2. Lewis, *Big Short,* 112.
3. Ibid.
4. Ibid., 114.

For electronic sources, include as much of the following information as you can: the author, the title of the article, the owner or sponsor of the site, and the article's URL followed by a period. If the URL is not stable, which sometimes occurs with articles in databases and newspapers, use the home page of the site from which you retrieved the work. See the entry for the online book in Exhibit C-7 for an example. If you have to break a URL into two lines, insert the line break before a slash or other punctuation mark. Include a period at the end of the URL. Some

Exhibit C-7 Formats for Footnotes and Endnotes *(Chicago)*

Blog Posting

1. Paul Krugman, "It's Demand, Stupid," *The Conscience of a Liberal* (blog), *New York Times*, September 15, 2010, http://krugman.blogs.nytimes.com/2010/09/15/its-demand-stupid/.

Book, Single Author

1. Michael Lewis, *The Big Short: Inside the Doomsday Machine* (New York: Norton, 2010), 63–64.

Book, Two or More Authors

1. Richard H. Bullock, Maureen Daly Goggin, and Francine Weinberg, *The Norton Field Guide to Writing with Readings and Handbook*, 2nd ed. (New York: Norton, 2008), 200–203.

Book, Three or More Authors

1. Donald R. Bear et al., *Words Their Way: Word Study for Phonics, Vocabulary, and Spelling Instruction*, 4th ed. (New York: Prentice Hall, 2007), 17–21.

Book, Corporate or Organizational Author

1. American Medical Association, *American Medical Association Manual of Style: A Guide for Authors and Editors*, 9th ed. (Philadelphia: Williams & Wilkins, 1998), 4–5.

Book, Online

1. Malcolm Gladwell, *The Tipping Point* (New York: Back Bay Books, 2002), 36, http://books.google.com/.

Brochure (Pamphlet)

1. TourTexas, *Visit Big Bend* (Austin, TX: AJR Media Group, 2009).

CD

1. Katherine M. Fortinash and Patricia A. Holoday Worret, *Virtual Clinical Excursions for Psychiatric Mental Health Nursing*, 4th ed. (St. Louis: Mosby, 2007), compact disc.

Government Document

1. Government Accountability Office, *Business Systems Modernization: Internal Revenue Service's Fiscal Year 2008 Expenditure Plan* (Washington, DC: Government Accountability Office, 2008), 13–14.

Journal Article with Volume Number Only

1. Stan Maklan, Simon Knox, and Lynette Ryals, "New Trends in Innovation and Customer Relationship Management," *International Journal of Market Research* 50 (2008): 221–238.

Journal Article with Volume and Issue Numbers

1. David Schwan, "Regulation in the Internet Banking Industry," *International Journal of Bank Marketing* 23, no. 5 (2005): 414–437.

Journal Article with a DOI

1. Glen L. Urban, "Customer Advocacy: A New Era in Marketing?" *Journal of Public Policy and Marketing* 24 (Spring 2005): 155–159, doi:10.1080/11417549836275585.

Magazine Article

1. Joe Kita, "White Coat Confessions," *Reader's Digest*, October 2010, 86–97.

Exhibit C-7 (Continued)

Newspaper Article

1. John Birchall, "Greener Apple Helps Clean Up," *Financial Times*, March 11, 2009, 11.

Personal Interview

1. Carter, Scott (executive television producer) in discussion with the author, December 2010.

Podcast

1. David Freudberg, "Barely Getting By: Stories of America's Working Poor," *Humankind* (podcast), Human Media, August, 27, 2010, http://www.humanmedia.org/catalog/ program.php?products_id=280.

Speech

1. Barack Obama,"Speech on Iraq" (speech, Oval Office, Washington, DC, August 31, 2010).

Television or Radio Program

1. "Explosion Rocks San Bruno Neighborhood," *News*, CBS (San Francisco: KCBS, September 13, 2010).

Web Site

1. "Patagonia's Clothing Recycling Program: Lessons Learned, Challenges Ahead," *GreenerDesign*, March 9, 2009, http://www.greenbiz.com/news/2009/03/09/patagonias-clothing-recycling-program-lessons-learned-challenges-ahead.

Web Site, No Date

1. Shari Water, "Shoplifting 101," *About.com*, accessed September 21, 2010, http://retail.about.com/od/lossprevention/a/stopshoplifting.htm.

journals and other publications in digital databases have what's called a digital object identifier (DOI). If an article has a DOI, include that information instead of the URL.

As you have perhaps discovered, electronic sources don't always include page numbers. If the work is short (such as a blog entry), you need not list page numbers. However, if it is long, you can include a paragraph number, section heading, or even a chapter number to guide the reader to the information you are citing. If the electronic source doesn't include a date, include an access date. The last entry in Exhibit C-7 shows the format for such a citation.

Brief Handbook of Grammar, Punctuation, Mechanics, and Conventions

Contents

Sentence-Level Skills Diagnostic Test p. D-3
Sentence-Level Skills Assessment p. D-5
Brief Handbook p. D-5

1.0. Sentences p. D-5

1.1. Parts of Speech p. D-5

1.1.1. Naming Words: Nouns and Pronouns p. D-5
- Types of Nouns
- Types of Pronouns
- Possessive Case

Grammar in Context: Nouns and Pronouns p. D-8

1.1.2. Action and Being Words: Verbs p. D-8
- Tense, Person, Number, Voice, and Mood
- Expletives

Grammar in Context: Verbs p. D-9

1.1.3. Modifying Words: Adjectives and Adverbs p. D-9
- Adjectives
- Adverbs
- Positive, Comparative, and Superlative Forms

Grammar in Context: Adjectives and Adverbs p. D-10

1.1.4. Connecting Words: Prepositions and Conjunctions p. D-10
- Prepositions
- Coordinate, Correlative, and Subordinate Conjunctions

Grammar in Context: Prepositions and Conjunctions p. D-10

1.1.5. Exclaiming Words: Interjections p. D-10

Grammar in Context: Interjections p. D-11

1.2. Sentence Parts and Patterns p. D-11

1.2.1. Subjects and Predicates p. D-11
- Simple Subject and Predicate
- Complete Subject and Predicate
- Objects and Complements

Grammar in Context: Subjects and Predicates p. D-11

1.2.2. Phrases and Clauses p. D-12
- Phrases
- Independent and Dependent Clauses

Grammar in Context: Phrases and Clauses p. D-12

1.2.3. Sentence Types p. D-13
- Simple
- Compound
- Complex
- Compound-Complex

Grammar in Context: Sentence Types p. D-13

1.3. Common Sentence Errors p. D-13

1.3.3. Sentence Fragments p. D-13

Grammar in Context: Sentence Fragments p. D-14

1.3.2. Run-On (Fused) Sentences and Comma Splices p. D-14

Grammar in Context: Run-On (Fused) Sentences and Comma Splices p. D-14

1.3.3. Subject-Verb Agreement p. D-15

Grammar in Context: Subject-Verb Agreement p. D-16

1.3.4. Pronoun-Antecedent Agreement p. D-16

Grammar in Context: Pronoun-Antecedent Agreement p. D-17

1.3.5. Vague Pronoun Reference p. D-17

Grammar in Context: Vague Pronoun Reference p. D-17

2.0. Punctuation p. D-17

2.1. End Punctuation p. D-17

2.1.1. Periods p. D-17

2.1.2. Question Marks p. D-18
- Direct and Indirect Questions
- Polite Requests

2.1.3. Exclamation Points p. D-18

Punctuation in Context: End Punctuation p. D-18

2.2. Commas p. D-18

2.2.1. Between Clauses p. D-18

Punctuation in Context: Commas with Clauses and Phrases p. D-19

2.2.2. Between Adjectives p. D-19

2.2.3. Between Items in Series p. D-19

Punctuation in Context: Commas with Coordinate and Serial Elements p. D-19

2.2.4. Around Clauses, Phrases, or Words p. D-19
- Nonrestrictive and Restrictive Clauses and Phrases
- Appositives
- Direct Address and Other Parenthetical Elements

Punctuation in Context: Commas with Restrictive, Nonrestrictive, and Parenthetical Elements; That, Which, *and* Who *p. D-20*
- Dates and Places
- Direct Quotations
- Salutations

Punctuation in Context: Commas in Dates, Places, Direct Quotations, and Salutations p. D-20

2.3. Semicolons p. D-21
- Between Independent Clauses
- Between Items in Series

2.4. Colons p. D-21
- Preceding a List
- Preceding an Explanation or Illustration
- Preceding a Rule, Formal Quotation, or Subtitle

Punctuation in Context: Semicolons and Colons p. D-21

2.5. Quotation Marks and Italics p. D-22

2.5.1. Quotation Marks p. D-22
- Direct Quotation
- Titles
- Words as Words or Used in a Special Sense
- Punctuation of Quotations

2.5.2. Italics p. D-22
- Titles
- Letters, Numbers, Words Used as Words, Foreign Words, etc.
- Emphasis

Punctuation in Context: Quotation Marks and Italics p. D-22

2.6. Apostrophes p. D-23
- Possessive Case
- Contractions

Punctuation in Context: Apostrophes p. D-23

2.7. Other Punctuation Marks p. D-23

2.7.1. Parentheses, Dashes, Brackets, and Ellipses p. D-23

Punctuation in Context: Parentheses, Dashes, Brackets, and Ellipses p. D-24

2.7.2. Hyphens p. D-24

Punctuation in Context: Hyphens p. D-24

3.0. Mechanics and Business Conventions p. D-25

3.1. Capitalization p. D-25

3.1.1. First Words and Pronouns p. D-25

3.1.2. Proper Nouns versus Common Nouns p. D-25
- Proper Nouns and Adjectives
- Places and Directions
- Brand and Product Names, Organizations and Institutions
- Titles, Offices, Positions, and Abbreviations
- Organizations and Parts of Organizations
- Courses, Academic Subjects, Majors, and Degrees
- Days of the Week, Months, Holiday, Holy Days and Names
- Historic Events, Periods, Documents, and Seasons
- Title of Works

Mechanics and Conventions in Context: Capitalization p. D-26

3.2. Numbers p. D-26

3.2.1. Words versus Figures p. D-27

3.2.2. Consecutive Numbers p. D-27

3.2.3. Related Numbers p. D-27

3.2.4. Indefinite or Approximate Numbers p. D-27

3.2.5. Numbers at Beginning of Sentences p. D-27

3.2.6. Fractions and Ordinals p. D-27

3.2.7. Decimals and Percentages p. D-27

3.2.8. Money p. D-27

3.2.9. Dates and Times p. D-27

3.2.10. Measurements and Compound-Number Adjectives p. D-28

3.2.11. Addresses and Telephone Numbers p. D-28

Mechanics and Conventions in Context: Numbers p. D-28

3.3. Abbreviations, Acronyms, and Initialisms p. D-28

3.3.1. Definitions, Forms, and Functions p. D-28

3.3.2. When to Use Abbreviations—or Not p. D-28
- Titles before Names
- Titles Appearing Independently or Following Names
- Academic Degrees and Professional Certifications
- Company Names
- Names of People, Countries, States, Place Names, Days
- Months and Holidays, Organizational Units, Academic Subjects
- Units of Measurements, Times, Dates

3.3.3. Spacing and Punctuation of Abbreviations p. D-29

Mechanics and Conventions in Context: Abbreviations, Acronyms, and Initialisms p. D-29

4.0. Spelling p. D-29

4.1. Four Rules of Thumb for Adding Endings p. D-30
- Suffix Added to One-Syllable Words
- Stress on Final Syllable
- Final *-e* Dropped
- Final *-y* Changed to *-i*

4.2. Memory Aids for *ie* and *ei* p. D-30

Spelling in Context: Rules of Thumb and Memory Aids p. D-31

4.3. Commonly Misspelled Words p. D-31

Spelling in Context: Commonly Misspelled Words p. D-32

4.4. Commonly Confused Words p. D-32

Spelling in Context: Commonly Confused Words p. D-34

The Brief Handbook begins with a diagnostic test to help you identify strengths and weaknesses in your sentence-level writing skills. Identify the areas that you need to work on to become the best possible business communicator. Then, use the Brief Handbook to refresh yourself on the rules, to check your writing, and correct any mistakes.

The numbered sections of the handbook cover the basics of grammar, punctuation, mechanics, and conventions in written business communication. Headings such as **GRAMMAR ALERT!** and **PUNCTUATION ALERT!** draw attention to especially common writing errors. **Grammar in Context** exercises appear at the end of major sections, so you can assess your ability to spot and correct common errors in continuous discourse, just as you would on the job. The answers to the Grammar in Context exercises appear at the end of the handbook.

Brief Handbook

Sentence-Level Skills Diagnostic Test

The following test covers common sentence-level errors. After you have completed the test, ask your instructor for the answer sheet, and score your answers. Use the **Skills Assessment** table following the test to record your scores in each category. The assessment will identify the skill areas you need to strengthen, and their location in the handbook.

Use and Formation of Nouns and Pronouns

Each of the following sentences is either correct or contains an error. If the sentence is correct, write "C" in the blank. If the sentence contains an error, underline the error and write the correct form in the blank.

1._____ Our supervisor wanted George and I come in early on Tuesday.

2._____ If your sure that everyone has left, turn out the lights.

3._____ I will speak with whoever is in the office this morning.

4._____ For three months in a row this Dealership had the highest sales.

5._____ There are fewer jobs and less employments during a recession.

Use and Formation of Adjectives and Adverbs

Each of the following sentences is either correct or contains an error. If the sentence is correct, write "C" in the blank. If the sentence contains an error, underline the error and write the correct form in the blank.

6._____ Most consumers prefer the least costly of the two service plans.

7._____ He sees badly in the dark because of his cataracts.

8._____ Remember to drive slow in a school zone.

9._____ Wasn't it snowing real hard last evening?

10._____ The timing of the winter sale was absolutely perfect.

Sentence Fragments, Run-On (Fused) Sentences, and Comma Splices

Each of the following sentences is either correct or incorrect. If the sentence is correct, write "C" in the blank. If it is incorrect, insert the punctuation and/or wording that would make the sentence correct. Adjust capitalization as necessary.

11._____ When people enjoy their jobs. They usually perform better.

12._____ Many younger employees rate job satisfaction over high salary, they want meaningful work.

13._____ Baby boomers, on the other hand, have spent their lives working to get ahead their goal has been to reach the top.

14._____ Finding the right balance between work, family, and leisure that fits a person's personal and professional goals.

15._____ Women usually have a more difficult time than men, however, achieving this balance.

Subject-Verb Agreement and Pronoun-Antecedent Agreement

Each of the following sentences is either correct or contains an error. If the sentence is correct, write "C" in the blank. If the sentence contains an error, write the correction in the blank.

16._____ Each generation defines their relationship to work.

17._____ There is sometimes considerable differences in attitudes.

18._____ Members of one generation believes in "living to work."

19._____ Conversely, the goals and philosophy of the next generation is "working to live."

20._____ To be satisfied, everybody has to find what works best for them.

Commas

Each of the following sentences is either correct or incorrect in its use of commas. If the sentence is correct, write "C" next to it. If it is incorrect, insert or delete punctuation to make it correct.

21._____ Many cultures value recreation, and family time highly and business practices reflect these norms.

22._____ In Europe for example workers get at least a month of vacation in the summer.

23._____ Although some businesses stay open many are closed for most of August.

24. _____ Posting an "On Vacation" sign in the window collecting the family and gassing up the car business owners across the continent head for the beach or the mountains.

25. _____ This practice of closing up shop and going on vacation for a month which annoys Americans traveling abroad in August is considered "therapeutic and necessary for good physical and mental health" says Doris Pernegger an Austrian travel agent.

Commas and Semicolons

Each of the following sentences is either correct or incorrect in use of commas and semicolons. If the sentence is correct, write "C" next to it. If it is incorrect, insert or delete punctuation to make it correct.

26. _____ In France the workweek is 35 hours; but most Americans still work a 40-hour week.

27. _____ The number of hours one can work is set by national law in many countries, however U.S. labor laws allow for variations among employee categories.

28. _____ Many U.S. companies classify workers as "exempt" employees, who may work extra hours without extra pay, "non-exempt" employees, who must be paid a minimum wage and receive higher overtime pay for extra hours, and part-time employees, who may be covered by minimum-wage laws but who are not necessarily being paid a higher wage for overtime.

29. _____ The average worker in Germany spends about 1,500 hours on the job per year; the average worker in India annually spends about twice that number on the job.

30. _____ The most leisure time contrary to popular belief was enjoyed by prehistoric hunter-gatherers, not modern humans.

Other Punctuation Marks

In each of the following sentences insert or delete colons, end punctuation, apostrophes, parentheses, quotation marks, dashes, and hyphens as needed. If a sentence is correct, write "C" next to it.

31. _____ Some of the benefits of a four day workweek may be: improved levels of education (extra time for classes), improved health less stress, and money saved on transportation.

32. _____ If we dont have to drive to work as often, we reduce carbon related automobile emissions.

33. _____ Some economists argue that unemployment will decrease if the workweek is shortened a big if.

34. _____ This is the theory: People working fewer hours will create a demand for additional workers in order to produce the same amount of goods and services.

35. _____ The old expression work smarter, not harder describes my philosophy.

Capitalization

In each of the following sentences insert or delete capital letters as needed. If a sentence is correct, write "C" next to it.

36. _____ In the Western world the workweek for many employees is Monday through friday.

37. _____ Of course, doctors and nurses, people with md or rn after their name, as well as public safety and hospitality employees often work weekend shifts.

38. _____ the workweek in a number of muslim countries is Sunday through Thursday or Saturday through Wednesday, because Friday is a Holy Day.

39. _____ My Mother says Washington's and lincoln's birthdays used to be celebrated separately, but they have been lumped together to create presidents' day, giving many employees a three-day weekend in mid-february.

40. _____ We say "tgif," meaning "Thank Goodness It's Friday," to salute the end of the workweek.

Numbers

Each of the following sentences is either correct or incorrect in the way numbers are expressed. If the sentence is correct, write "C" next to it. If it is incorrect, insert the necessary changes.

41. _____ South Koreans average thirty-four percent more work hours per year than U.S. workers.

42. _____ Most South Koreans start work at eight A.M., take a break for dinner, and don't leave work until after 10 o'clock at night.

43. _____ 2004 marked the end of the 6-day workweek in South Korea; before then, everyone worked Saturdays.

44. _____ A South Korean accountant averaged about twenty-seven hundred dollars a month in 2005; the average annual income was 22,928 dollars, or 18,544,199 Korean wons.

45. _____ Since Korean employees are expected to stay at their desks until their superiors leave, we really shouldn't complain about our measly 5 8-hour days.

Spelling

In each of the following sentences correct spelling as needed. If a sentence is correct, write "C" next to it.

46. _____ Before making a judgement about excepting a job offer, you might want to explore what "work" means in that company's culture.

47. _____ Some people find it inconcievable that they are expected to wear a suit and tie to work; its tee shirts and flip-flops for them.

48. _____ Does the employer have a flextime policy, leting you come and go as you please as long as you meet your deadlines and attend meetings?

49._____ What seems like a miner inconvienence when your first hired may be a major hurdle after you have been on the job awhile.

50._____ Ask yourself weather you can acommodate the company policies and expectations or if you would be happyer and more productive in a different inviroment.

In the grid below, record the number of questions you answered incorrectly in each category. If you got more than two answers wrong in any category, it is likely that you are making similar errors in your writing. Review the relevant sections of the Brief Handbook and complete the exercises. If you are still having trouble with sentence-level errors in any category, you may want to seek additional help at your college writing center or writing lab.

QUESTIONS	SKILL AREA	NUMBER OF INCORRECT ANSWERS	HANDBOOK SECTION(S)
1–5	Nouns and Pronouns		1.1.1., 3.1.2.
6–10	Adjectives and Adverbs		1.1.3.
11–15	Fragments, Run-On (Fused) Sentences, Comma Splices		1.2.2., 1.3.1., 1.3.2.
16–20	Subject-Verb Agreement, Pronoun-Antecedent Agreement		1.1.2., 1.3.3., 1.3.4.
21–25	Commas		2.2. –2.2.4.
26–30	Commas and Semicolons		2.3.
31–35	Other Punctuation Marks		2.4.–2.7.
36–40	Capitalization		3.1.–3.1.2.
41–45	Numbers		3.2. –3.2.11.
46–50	Spelling		4.0

Brief Handbook

1.0. Sentences

A sentence is often described as a group of words that expresses a complete thought. True, but a sentence does more than that. Sentences convey information and establish relationships between ideas. Your ability to communicate well—effectively manage sentences and their parts—will have a great deal to do with your success in the workplace.

1.1. Parts of Speech

Words in sentences belong to categories that describe their function within the sentence. Just as particular departments within a business have particular functions—accounting, sales, shipping and receiving—words are categorized according to the functions they serve in sentences. These categories are commonly called the **parts of speech.** Knowing the names and functions of the parts of speech enables people to talk about how sentences work—or don't work—when there are errors.

FUNCTION	PART OF SPEECH	EXAMPLES
naming	nouns pronouns	computer, IBM, e-mail I, you, itself, hers, everyone
showing action or being	verbs	e-mail, was, will hire, has run
modifying	adjectives adverbs	expensive, clear, legal quickly, really, well
connecting	prepositions conjunctions	in, under, after, of, to, on, and, but, although, since
exclaiming	interjections	oh, well, hey, indeed Ouch! Help! Stop! Wow!

As you can see from the examples above, the same word (e.g., *e-mail*) may serve different functions, depending on its use in a sentence.

1.1.1. Naming Words: Nouns and Pronouns

Nouns name persons, places, things, and concepts. They can be classified as follows.

TYPE OF NOUN	FUNCTION	EXAMPLES
Common nouns	refer to general groups, people, places, things, and ideas. They are not capitalized.	intern, street, company, soda, capitalism
Proper nouns	refer to particular people, places, things, and ideas. They are capitalized.	Monica, Wall Street, Progressive Insurance Company, Coca-Cola, Marxism
Count nouns	refer to people, places, and things that can be counted individually. Count nouns have singular and plural forms.	two interns, 15 insurance companies, one customer, $3 million, raindrops, job
Mass nouns (noncount nouns)	refer to things that cannot be counted individually but that exist in a mass or aggregate. Thus, they take singular verbs. Mass nouns do not usually have plural forms.	rain, coffee, steel, money, overstock, employment The *coffee is* ready.
Collective nouns	refer to groups that are singular in form but, depending on context, may be singular or plural in meaning.	committee, team, sales force, board of directors, faculty, staff, herd, flock The *staff* [collectively] *is* meeting this afternoon. The *staff* [individually] *are* registering for the conference.
Abstract nouns	refer to intangible conditions, qualities, or ideas.	wealth, illness, technology, sound, capitalism
Concrete nouns	refer to things perceived by the five senses.	euros, diabetes, sonogram, applause, stockholder

Many nouns form the plural **regularly** by adding *-s* or *-es* at the end: *report, reports; expense, expenses.* Some nouns have an **irregular** plural form, often formed by a change in vowel: *man, men; mouse, mice; goose, geese.*

Pronouns replace or refer to nouns. The word that a pronoun replaces or refers to is called its **antecedent** (meaning "to go before"): *Shanice* said *she* received the memo. *She* is the pronoun; *Shanice* is the antecedent. Like nouns, pronouns can be classified.

TYPE OF PRONOUN	FUNCTION	EXAMPLES
Personal pronouns	refer to specific persons, places, things	I, me, you, she, her, he, him, it, they, their, them
Indefinite pronouns	do not refer to specific persons, places, things; do not require antecedents. Pronouns indicating individuals are singular: any, each, every, -body, -one, -thing, no. Pronouns indicating several are plural: all, many, most, some.	all, any, anyone, anybody, both, each, everyone, everybody, everything, many, most, none, no one, nobody, nothing, some, somebody, something *Everybody hopes* for a raise. *Some are* counting on it.
Relative pronouns	introduce subordinate clauses that refer to a noun or pronoun the clause modifies.	that, who, whom, whose, which The vice president *who gave the presentation* used to be my boss.
Interrogative pronouns	introduce questions.	what, who, whom, whose, which *What* happened next?
Demonstrative pronouns	identify particular people or things.	this, that, these, those *Those* are the most recent sales figures available.
(a) Intensive pronouns (b) Reflexive pronouns	(a) emphasize the antecedent. (b) refer to the receiver of an action who is the same as the performer of the action.	Same form for both types: myself, yourself, himself, herself, itself, ourselves, yourselves, themselves (a) The *president himself* will attend the conference. (b) *We* congratulated *ourselves* on a job well done.
Reciprocal pronouns	refer to separate parts of a plural antecedent.	each other, one another The new *employees* introduced themselves to *each other.*

Pronouns show their function in a sentence by means of **case: subjective, objective,** or **possessive case.**

PERSONAL PRONOUNS: SPECIFIC PERSONS, PLACES, THINGS	PRONOUN SUBJECTS, AND AFTER "BE" VERBS (IS, ARE, WAS, WERE, HAVE BEEN, HAD BEEN)	PRONOUN OBJECTS: OBJECTS OF VERBS, VERBALS, AND PREPOSITIONS	PRONOUN POSSESSION: OWNERSHIP
SINGULAR	**SUBJECTIVE CASE**	**OBJECTIVE CASE**	**POSSESSIVE CASE**
First person (denotes person speaking)	I *I* sent an e-mail.	me Rob sent an e-mail to *me*.	my, mine *My* mailbox was full.
Second person (denotes person or thing spoken to)	you Were *you* the recipient?	you Mae saw *you* in the lobby.	your, yours Did you find *your* ticket?
Third person (denotes person or thing spoken of)	he, she, it *It* came in the mail.	him, her, it I found *it* on the desk.	his, her, hers, its The storm ruined *his* travel plans.
PERSONAL PRONOUNS PLURAL	**SUBJECTIVE CASE**	**OBJECTIVE CASE**	**POSSESSIVE CASE**
First person (persons speaking)	we When *we* arrived, the meeting had already started.	us Let *us* know the date.	our, ours *Our* flight was canceled.
Second person (persons or things spoken to)	you As new employees, *you* have temporary security clearances.	you I wish *you* the best of luck.	your, yours *Your* supervisors will distribute the new software.
Third person (persons or things spoken of)	they It was *they* who completed the project.	them The department head recommended *them* for a raise.	their, theirs They earned *their* reward.
RELATIVE OR INTERROGATIVE PRONOUNS	**SUBJECTIVE CASE**	**OBJECTIVE CASE**	**POSSESSIVE CASE**
Singular and plural forms are the same	who Lee was the person *who* phoned.	whom To *whom* am I speaking?	whose Please tell me *whose* turn is next.

GRAMMAR ALERT! MISUSE OF PRONOUN CASE

If a pronoun is in the wrong **case,** the sentence will be grammatically incorrect.

Use the objective case for the object of a transitive verb (a verb that passes the action to a recipient—or object—of that action).

Incorrect The division manager asked him and *I* to report our findings. (Incorrect use of subjective case: *I* is not the subject of the sentence.)

Correct The division manager asked him and *me* to report our findings. (Correct use of objective case: The pronoun *me* is the object of the verb *asked.*)

Use the subjective case with intransitive verbs such as linking or being verbs.

Incorrect The principal researchers on the project were *him* and *me.* (Incorrect use of objective case: the subject antecedent, *researchers,* and pronouns referring to it are linked by a "be" verb—*were*—so both are subjective case.)

Correct The principal researchers on the project were *he* and *I.*

Use the subjective case when answering a caller's question, "Is [your name] there?"

Incorrect This is *me.* (Incorrect use of objective case; *me* renames the subject *this,* which refers to the antecedent subject [your name] in the question, so use subjective case.)

Correct This is *she.*

(continued)

(continued)

Sometimes you can hear the correct case if you turn the sentence around and start with the pronoun(s) in the subject spot: *He* and *I* were the principal researchers on the project. Another test is to switch to the plural: The division manager asked *us* to report our findings. *Us* sounds (and is) correct, so the corresponding singular objective form, *him and me*, will be correct.

SPELLING ALERT! MISUSE OF APOSTROPHE

Do not confuse there/their/they're, your/you're, or its/it's. Possessive pronouns are never formed with an apostrophe, but contractions ending in -*s* always are.

They're the lawyers who handle corporate mergers in *their* law firm. (contraction of *they are*; possessive pronoun)

Your application is due if *you're* interested in being considered for the job. (possessive pronoun; contraction of *you are*)

You can't tell a book by *its* cover, although *it's* tempting to try. (possessive pronoun; contraction of *it is*)

Grammar in Context: Nouns and Pronouns

The following paragraph contains 10 errors in use or formation of nouns and pronouns, one in each sentence. Find and correct them. The answers are located at the end of the handbook.

Whomever answers the phone may be the only contact a caller has with a business. Everyone has their own personal preferences. However, find out how your employer wants the telephone answered, what your expected to say. When you pick up the phone, its important to speak politely and provide identifying information. Clearly state the company's name and you're name. Should you identify the Department, too? These are the kinds of question's to settle before the phone rings. If the caller asks for you by name, say, "This is me." Don't leave the caller wondering who he or she has reached. Remember that when on the telephone at work, you are the Company.

1.1.2. Action and Being Words: Verbs

Verbs express action, occurrence, or state of being.

Action	Stock prices *rose* in late December.
Occurrence	That often *happens* at the end of the year.
State of Being	The phenomenon *is known* as the "year-end bump."

Time	present, past, future (tense)	The stock market *rose* 58 points. Prices *will increase.*
Person	first, second, third	*You and I think* it is a bull market. *He thinks* it is a bear market.
Number	singular, plural	A rising *tide raises* all boats, but ill financial *winds raise* many fears.
Voice: Active voice	Subject performs action of verb.	Corporate losses *caused* a market decline.
Passive voice	Subject receives action of verb.	The market decline *was caused* by corporate losses.
Mood: Indicative Imperative Subjunctive	Indicates whether action expresses a fact or question (indicative), gives a command (imperative), or expresses a condition contrary to fact (subjunctive).	Indicative: She *saves* part of every paycheck. *Does* she *save* part of every paycheck? Imperative: *Save* part of every paycheck. Subjunctive: If she *were saving* part of every paycheck, she would be financially secure. [But the fact is she is not saving, so she is not secure.]

Verbs change form to show **time (tense), person, number, voice, and mood.**

GRAMMAR ALERT! SUBJECT-VERB AGREEMENT ERROR

Verbs must agree with their subjects in person and number. The subject cannot be in a prepositional phrase. Find the true subject and make the verb agree.

Incorrect	The members of the Federal Reserve Board *sets* interest rates. (Verb *sets* is incorrect because subject *members* is plural.)
Correct	The *members* of the Federal Reserve Board *set* interest rates.

Contractions should be separated and matched with the correct person.

Incorrect	He *don't* want to be late, and I don't either. (Verb form *don't* or *do not* disagrees with third-person singular subject *he*.)
Correct	He *doesn't* want to be late, and I don't either.
Or	He *does not* want to be late, and I *do not* either.

Also see "Subject-Verb Agreement" in *Common Sentence Errors.*

Expletives are introductory words such as *there* or *it* followed by a linking verb (*is, are, was, were*).

It is probable that Jean won't attend.

There are 50 pamphlets in this set.

Expletives function more as signal expressions used for emphasis than as true conveyers of content. For example, *There were six people on the conference call* could as easily be expressed *Six people were on the conference call.* Examine your writing to eliminate expletives, when possible. Although they can be used effectively to manage the pace and emphasis in a sentence, expletives can also add words that may not be necessary.

Wordy	It is probable that Jean won't attend.
Revised	Jean probably won't attend.

GRAMMAR ALERT! AGREEMENT ERROR WITH *THERE*

When a sentence begins with the expletive *there,* the verb is singular or plural depending on the number of the noun or pronoun that follows it. In other words, the verb must agree with the true grammatical subject of the sentence; *there* is an adverbial modifier and cannot be a grammatical subject.

Incorrect	There was two possible solutions.
Correct	There were two possible solutions.

To check for correct agreement between subject and verb, try putting the sentence in subject-verb word order: Two possible *solutions were* there.

Grammar in Context: Verbs

The following paragraph contains 10 errors in use or formation of verbs. Find and correct them. The answers are located at the end of the handbook.

If my first boss had ran his businesses the way he answered the phone, he would have went broke long ago. Usually he grabbed the receiver and growls, "Barker." The person at the other end probably thought, "That don't that sound like a human, more like a rottweiler." If George Barker was a dog, he would probably be more courteous on the phone. No doubt there was lots of offended customers. The other day he asked my co-worker, Jess, and me to stop by his office. He still answer the phone the same way. George's phone offenses amounts to quite a long list. Instead of "barking," here is several other things he could say. "Hello, Barker Contracting" or "This is George Barker" make a better impression.

1.1.3. Modifying Words: Adjectives and Adverbs

Adjectives modify nouns and pronouns: Put the expense report in the *tall, gray filing* cabinet. Adjectives answer the questions *which one? what kind of?* or *how many?*

"Modify" means to identify, describe, limit, or qualify in some way. For example, the *tall, gray filing* cabinet describes the height, color, and type of cabinet, differentiating it from the low, white equipment cabinet next to it.

Adverbs modify verbs, adjectives, other adverbs, and occasionally prepositions, conjunctions, or even whole sentences: I *quickly* located the cabinet but *unfortunately* could *not* pull *open* the *very firmly stuck* drawer. Adverbs answer the questions *how? when? where? why? to what extent?* or *to what degree?*

Many adjectives and adverbs change form to indicate three degrees of **comparison:**

- ***positive*** (nothing being compared)
- ***comparative*** (higher or lower degree when comparing two)
- ***superlative*** (highest or lowest degree when comparing three or more).

The changes in form are indicated three ways.

1. By adding *-er* or *-est* to the positive form of a one-syllable adjective or adverb or an adjective that ends in *-ly*: *tall, taller, tallest; few, fewer, fewest; fast, faster, fastest; friendly, friendlier, friendliest*
2. By adding the prefix words *more* and *most* or *less* and *least* to the positive form of adjectives with three or more syllables or adverbs with two or more syllables: expensive, *less* expensive, *least* expensive; simply, *more* simply, *most* simply.
3. By using an irregular form: *good, better, best; bad, worse, worst*

Some adjectives are considered **absolute,** not comparable. Absolute adjectives include *perfect, unique, square, straight, endless,* and *dead.* Something cannot be *more dead* than something else; it can, however, be *almost* or *nearly dead.*

GRAMMAR ALERT! MISUSE OF *BAD* AND *GOOD*

Use adjectives, not adverbs, with linking verbs (*be, become, is, are, was, were*) and verbs of the senses (*feel, smell, taste, look, appear, seem*). One of the most common adjective/adverb errors is confusion of *good* and *well, bad* and *badly.*

Incorrect	He *looks well* in that suit. (An adjective should be used instead of the adverb *well,* because it describes the subject, *he.*)
Correct	He *looks good* in that suit.
Incorrect	She *felt badly* about missing the appointment. (The "sensing" verb *felt* requires an adjective, not an adverb, because it describes the subject, *she.*)
Correct	She *felt bad* about missing the appointment.
But	Because her fingers were numb with cold, she *felt badly* and couldn't tell her car key from her house key. (The adverb form *badly* is correct because it describes the verb, her ability to feel or touch.)

Grammar in Context: Adjectives and Adverbs

The following paragraph contains 10 errors in use or formation of adjectives and adverbs, one in each sentence. Find and correct them. The answers are located at the end of the handbook.

> Does your telephone etiquette speak good of you? Because most people answer their own phones at work, poor phone manners make both you and your company look badly. Which greeting will make the best impression: "How may I help you?" or "What do you want?" It is important to sound cheerfully on the phone. Even if you don't feel well, try to respond positively. A more simple way to sound positive is to smile when speaking. Smiling actually does make a person seem more friendlier over the phone. Some people like to have the most unique telephone greeting in the office: "Yo, super service representative Skip speaking!" A greeting like that just makes "Skip" seem real unprofessional. Instead of being named "Best Employee of the Month," he is likely to be awarded "Worse Phone Manners of the Year."

1.1.4. Connecting Words: Prepositions and Conjunctions

Prepositions connect a noun or pronoun (called the "object" of the preposition) to some other word in a sentence. These prepositional "phrases" usually function as modifiers, describing the words to which they are connected: The office *on the left* belongs to the corporate lawyer. Common prepositions include *in, out, up, down, before, behind, over, under, to, from, above, below, on, off, by, through, around.* Although we sometimes end sentences with prepositions in conversation ("Where are you from?"), try to avoid these "danglers" in writing. Follow the preposition with a noun or a pronoun as the object, unless doing so makes the sentence unusually awkward.

> **GRAMMAR ALERT!** AGREEMENT ERROR WITH PREPOSITIONAL OBJECT
>
> The object of a preposition cannot be the subject of a sentence. Consequently, the verb should not be made to agree with it but rather with the true subject of the sentence.
>
> Incorrect — The box of name badges are on your desk. (The subject is not *badges; badges* is the object of the preposition *of.*)
>
> Correct — The *box* of name badges *is* on your desk. (The subject is *box;* the verb *is* agrees with the subject.)

Conjunctions connect words, phrases, or clauses to show relationships between them: **coordination, correlation,** or **subordination.**

TYPE	FUNCTION	EXAMPLES
Coordinating conjunctions	join words, phrases, or clauses of equal grammatical rank.	and, but, or, nor, for, so, yet
Correlative conjunctions	work in pairs to join words, phrases, or clauses of equal grammatical rank.	both/and, either/or, neither/nor, not/but, not only/but also
Subordinating conjunctions	join clauses that are not of equal rank and cannot stand by themselves as sentences.	after, although, as, because, before, if, since, rather than, that, unless, when, where, whether, while
Conjunctive adverbs	join independent clauses only, clauses that can stand by themselves as sentences.	however, therefore, nevertheless, furthermore, instead, besides, consequently, then, meanwhile, thus

Note that some conjunctions also function as other parts of speech. For example, *after* can be a preposition or a conjunction, depending on whether it is followed by a noun or pronoun as an object or begins a phrase or clause containing a verb form.

Prepositional Phrase	Jason returned to the office *after* lunch. (*Lunch* is a noun.)
Conjunction Joining Independent Clauses	Jason returned to the office *after* he finished lunch. (*He finished lunch* is a clause.)

Grammar in Context: Prepositions and Conjunctions

In the following paragraph, identify the prepositions (P), coordinating conjunctions (CC), correlative conjunctions (CorC), subordinating conjunctions (SC), and conjunctive adverbs (CA). There are a total of 10 prepositions and conjunctions. Count correlative conjunction pairs as one. Before you begin, you may find it helpful to read "Phrases and Clauses" and "Sentence Types" in this handbook. The answers are located at the end of the handbook.

> The way you begin a business call is very important; however, the conclusion is equally important. Have you ever been caught in an awkward spot, wondering who should end the call? If you initiated the call, the convention is for you to conclude it. After you have obtained the information you need, thank the person you called and then say good-bye. The person at the other end either can just say good-bye or can end with a pleasantry: for example, "I'm glad I could help."

1.1.5. Exclaiming Words: Interjections

Interjections are considered a part of speech, but their only function is to express strong feeling. While a few interjections can be interpreted as single-word commands with understood subjects or objects (*Help! Stop!*), most are grammatically unconnected to the rest of the sentence. An interjection may be accompanied by an explanation mark if the emotion is to be interpreted as particularly strong: "*Ouch!* I just got a paper cut from that file folder."

Interjections are common in speech, so they may be appropriate (if used with discretion) in written business communications that are more informal and conversational, such as e-mail. Conversely, they are seldom appropriate in formal business writing, unless used for instructions that must grab the reader's attention.

Spoken Conversation	*Hey,* Lynn, do you have a minute?
Informal E-Mail	*Wow!* I was impressed by her accomplishments.
Written Instructions	*Attention!* Set the brake before starting the engine.

Be aware that interjections that might be appropriate for texting friends will create an unprofessional, immature tone in business correspondence.

Grammar in Context: Interjections

The following paragraph is a proposed e-mail and text message alert to be sent to college students and employees, announcing a tornado warning and giving safety instructions. Cross out any interjections that you think are unnecessary or inappropriate. The answers are located at the end of the handbook.

> Hey! Attention! The campus is under a tornado warning. A tornado has been spotted over Lambert Heights. Stop! Go to the nearest shelter. Now! In buildings take cover in basements, or inner hallways or bathrooms on the lowest floor. For heaven's sake, stay away from windows and doors. Oh, if you are outdoors and cannot get to a safe building, lie in a ditch or depression. Stay in a sheltered area until you hear the "all clear" horn (two blasts repeated) or receive an "all clear" text message.

1.2. Sentence Parts and Patterns

As the old song says, "The knee bone's connected to the thigh bone," not to the heel bone or the toe bone. Understanding the components that make up a sentence and how they work together can help writers and speakers create effective, error-free communications.

1.2.1. Subjects and Predicates

The largest structural parts of sentences are their subjects and predicates. The **subject** explains who or what the sentence is about, who is performing or receiving the action described in the sentence. The **predicate** states the action or state of existence. A sentence can be as short as two words—one word for the subject, and one word for the predicate: *Prices rose.* If the sentence is a command with an understood subject, it can even be just one word: *Run!* Usually sentences are longer, their subjects and predicates composed of more words, more information: *The prices for new homes rose in the third quarter.* However, every sentence can be pared down to its essential elements, the **simple subject** (noun, pronoun, or noun equivalent) and **simple predicate** (verb): *Prices rose.*

The simple subject along with all its modifiers is called the **complete subject.**

> *The **prices** for new homes* rose in the third quarter.

Similarly, the simple predicate along with all its modifiers is the **complete predicate.**

> The prices for new homes ***rose** in the third quarter.*

In addition to the verb, a complete predicate may include modifiers of the verb: *rose **in the third quarter**.*

The complete predicate may also include a **direct object** that receives the action of the verb: We *bought **a house**.* It may include an **indirect object,** telling to or for whom or what the action occurred: The real estate agent *sent **us** the contract.* Verbs that take an object are called transitive verbs. If the predicate has a linking verb, it may include a **complement**—a noun, pronoun, or adjective that "completes" the verb, renaming or describing the subject: The house *is **a two-story colonial**.* The price *was **reasonable**.* Verbs that do not take an object are called intransitive verbs; linking verbs are one type of intransitive verb. Complete verbs are the second intransitive type, and, as the name suggests, they make a complete statement without the help of any other word: Prices ***rose**.*

Inverted word order can sometimes make locating the subject and predicate difficult. For example, questions have inverted word order, in which the verb (or part of a verb phrase) precedes the subject. In the following questions, the simple predicates are *did rise* and *are.* The simple subjects are *prices* and *they*: ***Did** home prices **rise*** last month? ***Are** they* still reasonable?

Grammar in Context: Subjects and Predicates

In the following paragraph underline the complete subject once and the complete predicate twice. Then circle or highlight the simple subject and the simple predicate. Before you begin, you may find it helpful to read "Phrases and Clauses" and "Sentence Types" in this handbook. The answers are located at the end of the handbook.

> A survey of chief information officers at companies with 100 or more employees was conducted by Robert Half Technologies. The survey focused on the use of cell phones, BlackBerries or PDAs, wireless earpieces, and headphones at work. Have breaches in workplace "tech-etiquette" increased, decreased, or remained the same? Twenty-two percent felt that poor etiquette had "increased significantly." The votes for "remained the same" were 42 percent. Only two percent of chief information officers voted for "decreased significantly." Robert Half Technologies named five main types of tech-etiquette offenders. The "misguided multitasker" and the "e-mail addict" were the first two. Others on the list included the "broadcaster," the "cyborg," and the "distractor." Exactly how had these employees offended in their handling of technology? In most cases they failed to pay attention to the people or circumstances around them.

1.2.2. Phrases and Clauses

Phrases are word groups that may contain a subject or a predicate, but not both. They function as a single part of speech.

FUNCTION OF PHRASE	EXAMPLE	EXPLANATION
Functions as noun	*Remembering all my computer passwords* is difficult.	Noun phrase takes subject position in sentence.
Functions as verb	I *have been writing* them on sticky notes.	Verb phrase takes verb position in sentence.
Functions as adjective	Dozens *of these notes* are stuck to my computer.	Adjectival prepositional phrase modifies noun *dozens*, telling what kind.
Functions as adverb	I can't seem to remember my password *from one day to the next.*	Adverbial prepositional phrase modifies verb *seem to remember*, telling when.

Clauses are word groups that have both a subject and a predicate. The subject and predicate may contain no modifiers or many; they may contain no phrases or many.

Prices rose. (no modifiers)

Prices *for new homes* rose *in the third quarter.* (two modifying phrases)

An **independent clause** (main clause) can stand by itself as a complete sentence, but a **dependent clause** cannot stand alone.

Independent Clause *I can't remember my passwords* because I have too many of them. (Italicized words can stand alone.)

Dependent Clause I can't remember my passwords *because I have too many of them.* (Italicized words cannot stand alone.)

Dependent clauses (also called subordinate clauses) add information to the main idea, but they are incomplete without the main clause to which they are attached. You can identify an adverbial dependent clause by the subordinating conjunction that connects it to the main clause (see "Connecting Words"). You can identify an adjectival subordinate clause (also called a relative clause) by the relative pronoun (*who, whom, whose, that,* or *which*) or the relative adverb (*when, where,* or *why*) that connects it to the main clause.

PUNCTUATION ALERT! SENTENCE FRAGMENT

Do not punctuate a **dependent clause** as if it were a sentence. Doing so creates a sentence fragment (see "Common Sentence Errors: Sentence Fragments").

Incorrect My computer doesn't work. Although the technician checked it. (*Although the technician checked it* is a dependent clause—a sentence fragment, not a complete sentence.)

Correct My computer doesn't work although the technician checked it.

Grammar in Context: Phrases and Clauses

In the following paragraph circle or highlight each phrase. Underline each dependent clause once and each independent clause twice. There are a total of 10 dependent and independent clauses and a total of 15 phrases. Before you begin, you may find it helpful to read "Sentence Types" in this handbook. The answers are located at the end of the handbook.

In the list of tech-etiquette offenders, the "misguided multitasker" may be the worst, although the "broadcaster" is a close second. Holding their BlackBerries under the table, multitaskers send e-mail or text messages during meetings. The nonverbal message that they are sending to everyone else is that the meeting is not important to them. Broadcasters use their cell phones anytime, anywhere, and they apparently don't mind being overheard by others. On a crowded elevator, they will discuss the intimate details of a medical procedure or talk loudly about confidential business matters.

1.2.3. Sentence Types: Simple, Compound, Complex, Compound-Complex

Sentences can be classified according to the number and types of clauses they contain. Good communicators take advantage of these sentence types to express their ideas most effectively. From simple to complex, at its best, sentence structure can help create and reinforce meaning.

SENTENCE TYPE	STRUCTURE	EXAMPLES
Simple	One **independent** clause; no *dependent* clauses	**People want to save for retirement.**
Compound	Two or more **independent** clauses; no *dependent* clauses	**People want to save for retirement,** but **they seldom do it.**
Complex	One **independent** clause; one or more *dependent* clauses	*Although people want to save for retirement,* **they seldom do it voluntarily.**
Compound-Complex	Two or more **independent** clauses; one or more *dependent* clauses	**People say** *that they want to save for retirement,* but **they seldom do it** *while they are young.*

Subjects and predicates may have compound elements, but those compound elements do not necessarily make the sentence itself compound. For example, a simple sentence with a compound verb is still a simple sentence: People ***live*** longer *but* ***save*** less.

PUNCTUATION ALERT! MISUSE OF COMMA

Do not punctuate a simple sentence with a compound subject or compound predicate as if it were a compound sentence. Before putting a comma in front of *and* or *but,* check to make sure it connects two independent clauses.

Incorrect I turned off my computer, and then went to get the mail.
(This is a single independent clause with a compound predicate.)

Correct I turned off my computer and then went to get the mail.

Correct I turned off my computer, and then I went to get the mail.
(Each clause is independent, so the comma is required.)

Grammar in Context: Sentence Types

In the following paragraph label the 10 sentences as either simple (S), compound (C), complex (CX), or compound-complex (C-CX). Before you begin, you may find it helpful to review "Phrases and Clauses" and "Connecting Words" in this handbook. The answers are located at the end of the handbook.

The blinking Bluetooth headset or iPod earbuds of the "cyborg" can be very distracting to other people at work. Because no one else can hear their music or ringing phone, cyborgs think that they are being courteous. Actually, the earpieces signal something else entirely. The nonverbal message is loud and clear. "I am not available," or "Don't bother me." If you are always plugged in at work, you may be a cyborg behaving badly. You can't see the earpiece, perhaps have forgotten all about it, but the people looking at you can see it, and they will infer that your first priority is whatever comes over the headset. They may hesitate to interrupt, even with something important. Signal your availability to your coworkers. Take the earbuds out unless you are working alone in your office.

1.3. Common Sentence Errors

The most frequent sentence errors are **fragments, run-ons** or **fused sentences, comma splices,** and **agreement errors.** The first three errors occur because the writer has incorrectly indicated where one sentence stops and another begins. These errors can play havoc with readers understanding the meaning the writer intended. Although our daily speech is full of these "not sentence" constructions, listeners have many more cues to help determine meaning—including the opportunity to ask questions. Business writers need to get it right the first time, or they may cause serious miscommunication.

1.3.1. Sentence Fragments

A sentence contains at least one independent clause, having a subject and a verb, and can stand alone as a complete thought. When a word group (phrase or dependent clause) lacking these characteristics is punctuated as if it were a sentence, a **fragment** results. A fragment can be corrected by rewriting it as a complete sentence: joining the fragment to the sentence before or after it or supplying the missing subject or verb to make the fragment an independent clause.

Incorrect	People would rather have rewards now. Than wait patiently for rewards in the future. (phrases punctuated as a sentence)
Correct	People would rather have rewards now than wait patiently for rewards in the future.
Incorrect	Behavioral economists say people choose immediate rewards. Because they overly discount the future. (dependent clause punctuated as a sentence)
Correct	Behavioral economists say people choose immediate rewards because they overly discount the future.
Incorrect	People buying things on credit that they can't afford. (phrases and dependent clause punctuated as a sentence)
Correct	People buy things on credit that they can't afford.

Compound predicates (joined by *and, but, or, yet,* and so on) are sometimes punctuated as complete sentences in informal correspondence and e-mail, but this type of fragment should generally be avoided in more formal business writing.

Incorrect	Sometimes people have to run up their credit card bills. But they shouldn't make a habit of it.
Correct	Sometimes people have to run up their credit card bills, but they shouldn't make a habit of it.

A polite request or command may appear to be missing a subject, and therefore be a sentence fragment; however, the sentence is complete because the subject is the understood pronoun *you.*

Incorrect	Hope to hear from you soon. (Because the understood subject is not *you,* and, therefore, cannot be omitted, this is a fragment.)
Correct	Please send your response as soon as possible. (The understood subject is *you.*)

Grammar in Context: Sentence Fragments

The following paragraph contains 10 sentence fragments. Find and correct them. The answers are located at the end of the handbook.

> You may get a person's voice mail. When making a business call. If you have to leave a message. Decide beforehand what to say. Identify yourself first. Then state your message clearly, making it brief and to the point. Not a million details. Rambling messages, in addition to trying the listener's patience. Very likely he or she will forget what you said. Everybody thinks, "My message is really important." But the listener may have many messages to play. What about yours? Your message has to compete for attention. With all the rest. And don't presume the person at the other end has caller ID. Consequently, can see your phone number. You should say your telephone number slowly and clearly. No mumbling. The listener has to be able to hear, to understand, and to write down the number in order to return your call.

1.3.2. Run-On (Fused) Sentences and Comma Splices

Run-on or **fused sentences** are independent clauses joined together without a connecting conjunction.

Classical economists believe humans rationally weigh costs and benefits **conversely, behavioral economists point out humans' irrational decision making.**

Comma splices are independent clauses joined together by a comma.

Rational humans are marvelous in theory, **in reality they do not exist.**

Run-ons and comma splices are both incorrect, and both can be fixed in one of five ways:

1. Connect the independent clauses with a comma and a coordinating conjunction.

   Classical economists believe humans rationally weigh costs and benefits, **but** behavioral economists point out humans' irrational decision making.

2. Connect the independent clauses with a semicolon.

   Rational humans are marvelous in theory; in reality they do not exist.

3. Make a separate sentence of each independent clause.

   Classical economists believe humans rationally weigh costs and benefits. Conversely, behavioral economists point out humans' irrational decision making.

4. Change one independent clause to a dependent clause.

   Although rational humans are marvelous in theory, in reality they do not exist.

5. Change one independent clause to a phrase.

   Marvelous in theory, rational humans do not exist in reality.

Grammar in Context: Run-On (Fused) Sentences and Comma Splices

The following paragraph contains 10 run-on or fused sentences and comma splices. Find and correct them. The answers are located at the end of the handbook.

> One business etiquette consultant believes that good telephone manners begin in childhood, children should be taught how to answer the phone courteously and take messages. Diane Eaves says, "I work with a lot of people who are technically ready for work however, they apparently missed a lot of the teaching of manners." For instance, asking who is calling can be taught in childhood then it will be a habit. Parents know how annoying it is to have a child report that "somebody called and wants you to call back" Sonny doesn't remember who it was and didn't write

down the number. Thank goodness for caller ID it can be a big help, nevertheless, children should be taught to ask for and write down names and numbers. It's surprising how many people don't identify themselves when they make business calls, they expect listeners to recognize their voice. That may be OK if you speak frequently with the caller on the other hand it's mystifying when a voice you don't recognizes launches right into a subject. It is the caller's responsibility to identify himself or herself, if he or she doesn't you can politely say, "Excuse me, I didn't catch your name."

1.3.3. Subject-Verb Agreement

Subjects and verbs need to agree in number and person. If the subject of a clause is singular, the verb must be singular as well; if plural, it must be plural. If the subject is in third person, the verb must reflect that. (Also see "Action and Being Words: Verbs.") Agreement errors are most common in the following instances.

- ***Words and phrases between subject and verb.*** Locate the subject and verb and make them agree, ignoring everything in between.

  The *aroma* of baking cupcakes *convinces* me to start my diet tomorrow.

  (The verb *convinces* should agree in number with the subject *aroma,* not with *cupcakes,* the object of the preposition *of.*)

  Even though words such as *with, together with,* and *as well as* suggest plural meaning, they are not part of the subject. When they follow singular subjects, use singular verbs.

  Temptation, as well as immediate sweet rewards, *undermines* my willpower.

- ***Indefinite pronouns as subjects.*** Use singular verbs with indefinite pronouns indicating one: *another, each, either, much, neither, one,* and all pronouns ending in *-one, -body,* and *-thing.*

  Everybody believes in doing what is best for the future; nevertheless, *each* of us often irrationally *gives* in to immediate gratification.

  Use plural verbs with indefinite pronouns indicating more than one: *both, few many, others,* and *several.*

  Many behave irrationally, but *few view* their choices as irrational.

  The indefinite pronouns *all, any, most, more, none,* and *some* take either a singular or a plural verb, depending on whether the noun to which they refer is singular or plural.

  Some people are good at delaying gratification, but *none find* it very easy. (*None* refers to *people* and so requires the plural verb *find.*)

  Most of the cake is gone, but some is still on the plate.

  (*Most* and *some* refer to one item—most of it and some of it.)

- ***Collective nouns as subjects.*** Collective nouns are singular in form but name a group of persons or things: *committee, crowd, jury, team, task force.* Use a singular verb when the group is considered as a unit acting collectively as one. Use a plural verb when the members of the group are acting separately as individuals.

  The *task force has* reported its findings to the director.

  (*Task force* is considered a unit acting collectively.)

  The *task force have* agreed to conduct follow-up studies in their own departments.

  (Individuals on the task force are acting separately.)

  OR The task force *members have* agreed to conduct follow-up studies in their own departments.

- ***Plural forms that have singular meanings.*** Some nouns are plural in form but singular in meaning: *economics, mathematics, news, measles.* Use a singular verb with these.

  Behavioral *economics explains* why consumers can't resist a sale.

  However, some nouns in plural form, such as *athletics, politics, statistics,* and *acoustics,* may be singular or plural, depending on whether they refer to a singular or plural idea.

  The Republican Party's *politics is* generally conservative, although members' *politics reflect* a wide spectrum of views.

> **GRAMMAR ALERT!** DATA
>
> A singular verb is often used with the word *data: The data appears in the appendix.* However, people in technical and scientific fields typically think of data as plural, as compilations of separate pieces of numerical information. Therefore, they usually prefer plural verbs: *The data appear in the appendix.* Follow the practice of the business, industry, or field for which you are writing. If the word *data* is considered plural in meaning, use a plural verb: The *data are* reliable. Her *data show* that more testing should be done. The singular form is *datum,* or you can write about an individual *data point.*

- ***Subjects joined by coordinating conjunctions* and, or, *or* nor.** Use a plural verb when two or more subjects are joined by *and,* unless the parts of the compound subject refer to the same thing.

  Our *wants and* our *needs are* often not the same thing.

  The *son and executor* of the estate *has signed* the documents.

  When *each* or *every* precedes a compound singular subject joined by *and,* the subject is considered singular and takes a singular verb.

  Every employee and his or her guest *has been issued* an identification badge.

  When subjects are joined by *or, nor,* or *not only / but also,* the verb should agree in number with the subject that is nearer.

  Neither the employee *nor* her *guests have been issued* badges, so either the receptionist *or* the *department head has to call* Security for clearance.

  Neither the guests *nor* the *employee has been issued* badges.

- ***Relative pronouns* who, which, *and* that *as subjects.*** When the relative pronoun *who, which,* or *that* is the subject of a dependent clause, make the verb agree with the pronoun's antecedent.

Please give me a list of the *guests who need* badges.

(*Who* refers to the antecedent *guests,* so the verb must be plural.)

- ***Inverted word order.*** Be sure to check agreement when the verb comes before the subject. Test for correctness by putting the subject first. (Also see "Expletives.")

After a vacation *comes* the *reality* of an overflowing in-box.

(The *reality* of an overflowing in-box *comes* after a vacation.)

There *appears* to be no *end* to the e-mails.

(No *end* to the e-mails *appears* to be there.)

- ***Quantities.*** Total amounts are usually considered a single unit and thus take singular verbs.

Two weeks is not enough vacation, according to Europeans.

I think *$100 is* outrageous for weekly parking.

If the individual parts of a unit are being emphasized, choose a plural verb.

Twenty-four grams of fat *have* to be spread over three meals, not eaten in a single sitting.

If a percentage refers to things that are plural and countable, the verb should be plural.

Thirty percent of the engine parts *do* not pass quality standards.

If a percentage refers to something that is singular, the verb is singular.

Ten percent of his income *goes* to charity.

The number takes a singular verb, but *a number* takes a plural verb.

A number of faulty parts *were found,* although *the number* of returns *was* low.

- ***Business names, products, titles, and words used as words.*** Even if the form of a business name or product or the title of a work is plural, it takes a singular verb because it is a single thing. The same is true for words discussed as words.

I think *Twinings makes* the best cup of Earl Grey tea.

Hot, Flat, and Crowded by Thomas Friedman *has* sold millions of copies.

Geese is the plural of *goose.*

Grammar in Context: Subject-Verb Agreement

The following paragraph contains 10 subject-verb agreement errors. Find and correct them. The answers are located at the end of the handbook.

> When making a business call, being put on hold for countless minutes fray even patient people's nerves. Having to wait, as well as not knowing for how long, are upsetting. Each of us have our own way of coping with this irritant. *The Sounds of Silence* not only apply to the Simon and Garfunkel song but also to endless minutes on hold. Three minutes feel like forever to the person waiting. If you must put someone on hold, there is several things you should do. First, ask, "May I put you on hold?" and then give the caller an estimate of the probable waiting time. The person on the other end might be one of those callers who really need to know how long the wait might be. The unknown number of minutes are what drive people crazy. Data collected by Hold On America, Inc. shows that callers become frustrated after 20 seconds. After 90 seconds, 50 percent of callers hangs up.

1.3.4. Pronoun-Antecedent Agreement

Pronouns must agree in number with their antecedents, the words to which they refer. Most agreement situations are obvious: The *interns* received *their* orientation yesterday. However, the following situations can be tricky.

- ***Indefinite pronouns.*** As the word "indefinite" suggests, these pronouns do not refer to specific persons, places, or things: for example, *some, all, many,* and *anyone* are indefinite pronouns. Although people tend to use plural pronouns when speaking, in writing use singular pronouns to refer to indefinite pronoun antecedents such as *person, one, any, each, either,* and *neither* and indefinite pronouns ending in *-one, -body,* and *-thing,* such as *anybody, someone,* or *everything.*

Incorrect	*Everybody* knows *they* should dress appropriately for a job interview.
Correct	*Everybody* knows *he or she* should dress appropriately for a job interview.

- ***Collective nouns.*** Use a singular pronoun if the antecedent is a group being considered as a unit. Use a plural pronoun if the members of the group are being considered individually.

The review *panel* started *its* tour of the laboratory at 9:30 A.M.

(The panel toured as a group.)

The review *panel* asked many questions when *they* met with the research director.

(Individual members of the group asked questions.)

- ***Compound antecedents.*** Antecedents connected by *and* take plural pronouns. Pronouns referring to compound antecedents connected by *or* or *nor* should agree with the antecedent closer to it.

Incorrect	If you ask either Jenny or Paul, they will help you.
Incorrect	If you ask either the supervisors or Jenny, they will help you.
Correct	If you ask *Jenny and Paul, they* will help you.
Correct	If you ask either *Jenny or Paul, he or she* will help you.
Correct	If you ask either the supervisor*s or Jenny, she* will help you.
Correct	If you ask either Jenny *or the supervisors, they* will help you.

When a compound antecedent is introduced by *each* or *every*, or when it refers to a single person or thing, use a singular pronoun.

Each hospital and clinic has *its* own evacuation plan.

The president and CEO delivered *his* annual state-of-the-company speech.

Grammar in Context: Pronoun-Antecedent Agreement

The following paragraph contains 10 pronoun-antecedent agreement errors. Find and correct them. The answers are located at the end of the handbook.

Everybody has preferences about their communication tools. A person may prefer e-mail rather than telephone, so they might respond to a voice-mail message by sending an e-mail instead of returning the call. If you ask either of my managers, Jenny or Kurt, they will tell you that I would rather e-mail them. Business professionals will often choose the one with which he or she is most at ease. Considering its total number of calls versus e-mails per month, the sales team obviously would rather talk than write. Each of these communication media has their advantages and disadvantages. Text messages and e-mail may be best because it will be delivered whether the recipient is there or not. On the other hand, someone who leaves a voice-mail message probably assumes you will call them back, not send a text. Otherwise, they would have texted you instead of calling.

1.3.5. Vague Pronoun Reference

The antecedent to which a pronoun refers should be clear. Pronouns should refer to

- only one antecedent. It may be plural or compound, but it should be only one.
- an antecedent that is nearby. Readers generally assume the antecedent is the closest previous noun or noun substitute.
- a specific antecedent, not an implied person or thing or the general idea of a preceding clause or sentence. A pronoun should refer to a noun or noun substitute that exists in a previous phrase or clause. Revise if *this, that,* or *which* refers to the general idea of a preceding clause or sentence.

Vague We need to survey more customers. *This* will give us better data, so we can develop better products. *They* will benefit in the long run.

(*This* vaguely refers to the whole idea in the previous sentence. *They* could refer to customers, data, or products; the closest noun, *products,* doesn't make sense.)

Clear We need to survey more customers. A bigger sampling will give us better data, so we can develop better products. Customers will benefit in the long run.

Grammar in Context: Vague Pronoun Reference

The following paragraph contains 10 vague pronoun references. Revise the sentences so that pronoun references are clear. The answers are located at the end of the handbook.

Text messages have their own rules of business etiquette; however, they may not be well understood. Students who are used to texting friends and family wherever-whenever may not be aware that this is considered rude during a business meeting or presentation. As Brian tapped out text messages while President Jackson welcomed the new summer interns, he didn't know he was being videotaped. The camera operator panned the audience for reaction shots during the speech, and there he was, thumbing away on his cell-phone keypad. When the president saw it, he asked Brian's department manager who that was and what he was doing. Brian certainly made lasting impression on the chief executive, which should be a lesson for all of us. That spelled the end of Brian's brief but memorable career at Jackson Ltd.

2.0. Punctuation

Punctuation marks fall into four basic categories: **end punctuation** that marks the beginnings and endings of sentences and indicates their character; **internal punctuation** that shows the relationship of individual words or sentence parts to the rest of a sentence; **direct-quotation punctuation** that indicates speakers and changes of speaker as well as where words have been added or omitted from the original text; and **word punctuation** that indicates words or letters having a special use. These functions are illustrated in the sections that follow.

2.1. End Punctuation

The punctuation at the ends of sentences signals where ideas start and stop. It marks the beginning and ending of complete grammatical units that can stand alone. End punctuation also indicates whether the sentence is to be understood as a statement, command, or polite request (**period**), question (**question mark**), or strong expression of emotion (**exclamation point**).

Examples:

I will now ask your name.

Tell me your name.

Will you please state your name?

What is your name?

What a wonderful name!

2.1.1. Periods

Periods mark the ends of statements and commands. They also are normally used with initials and with abbreviations ending with lowercase letters.

Dr. Janice Brown Sen. Ben Cardin St. Jerome Mr. Kim

Academic degrees and professional certifications in some fields omit the period from abbreviations; for example, PhD, RN, or MD may appear without periods. Consult the style manual of the profession if in doubt. Your company may also have a style manual that specifies how abbreviations are to be handled in company correspondence and publications.

2.1.2. Question Marks: Indirect Questions and Polite Requests

Direct questions are punctuated with a question mark: *What time is the meeting? She asked me, "What time is the meeting?"* However, indirect questions and polite requests end with a period. An **indirect question** implies a question but does not actually ask one: *She asked me what time the meeting was.* One clue that the previous sentence is not a direct question is the word order: the subject and verb are not inverted in indirect questions, as they are in a direct question (what time *was the meeting*). A **polite request** may be phrased like a question, but it is really a command stated nicely. Thus, it is often punctuated with a period rather than a question mark: *When you have scheduled the meeting, would you please let me know.*

Deciding whether a sentence is a polite request or a question may also have to do with who is making the request. A polite request that is a command from a supervisor would require a period: *"Will you please attend the meeting for me."* A polite request for a favor from a coworker would require a question mark: *"Will you please attend the meeting for me?"*

2.1.3. Exclamation Points: Use and Misuse

Interjections and sentences that require strong emphasis or express extreme emotion are punctuated with exclamation points: *Attention! Fire on the third floor! Evacuate the building using the stairs!*

Unfortunately, many people have adopted the habit of sprinkling their communications liberally with exclamations, particularly in text messages and e-mails: *OMG!! Guess who showed up at the company party?!* More formal business communication should contain few if any exclamation points. Overusing exclamations either diminishes their effect or makes the writing sound hysterical and immature. In some fields, such as court reporting, exclamation points are never used.

Punctuation in Context: End Punctuation

The following paragraph contains 10 errors in the use of periods, question marks, and exclamation points. Find and correct them. The answers are located at the end of the handbook.

> What about voice-mail greetings. They are a form of business communication, but people frequently overlook their importance! If you cannot answer the phone, won't your voice-mail greeting create a new caller's first impression of you and your company. I've wondered if greetings that are overly long and detailed don't waste listeners' time? Some voice-mail greetings, like "This is Dr Allen's office. The office is closed, but if you are calling for a referral, blah, blah, blah, blah," seem to go on forever, don't they. Voice-mail systems that allow callers to skip the greeting are great! The greeting should include your name, your company's or department's name, a statement that you cannot take the call right now, and an invitation to leave a message. Also, would you please give the number of whom to contact for immediate assistance, if appropriate? It isn't necessary to say you are out of the office! A greeting that demonstrates good telephone etiquette will end with "thanks for your call" or "thanks for calling?" A person who has to suffer through to a poor voice-mail greeting is not going to "have a nice day"!

2.2. Commas

Commas separate parts of a sentence, guiding readers through complex constructions, indicating modifiers, series, and generally ordering things into understandable units of meaning. Although there are many rules for using commas, most business communications rely on a fairly limited number. Think of commas as markers that signal changes in the road.

2.2.1. Between Clauses

- ***Independent clauses joined by coordinating conjunctions and, but, or, nor, for, so, yet.*** The comma before the coordinating conjunction linking the clauses signals that one complete thought is finished and another is about to begin.

  I prepared the slides, *and* Mavis printed the handouts.

  The comma can be omitted between very short clauses if there is no possibility of confusion: You drive *and* I'll navigate.

  Do not use a comma with a coordinating conjunction linking compound predicates (verbs plus objects and modifiers). Check to be sure the conjunction links independent clauses.

Incorrect	I prepared the slides for the meeting, and then printed the handouts.
Correct	I prepared the slides for the meeting, and then I printed the handouts.
Or	I prepared the slides for the meeting and then printed the handouts.

  Also see "Sentence Types: Simple, Compound, Complex, Compound-Complex."

- ***Dependent clauses and phrases preceding the independent clause.*** The comma following an introductory dependent phrase or clause signals that the main clause containing the main idea is about to begin. It helps the reader differentiate modifying information from the meat of the sentence, announcing "OK, now pay attention. Here comes the most important stuff."

  When the presentation was finished, the speaker answered questions.

  Having missed the first 15 minutes, I was a bit confused.

  If it will not cause misreading, the comma can be omitted after very short introductory clauses or phrases.

Clear	*After lunch* we returned to the office.
Confusing	*Before long* smears appeared on the glass.
Clear	*Before long,* smears appeared on the glass.
Confusing	*After she ate* lunch was served to the rest of us.
Clear	*After she ate,* lunch was served to the rest of us.

Punctuation in Context: Commas with Clauses and Phrases

The following paragraph contains 10 errors in the use of commas with independent clauses and dependent clauses and phrases. Find and correct them. The answers are located at the end of the handbook.

Although most final job interviews are face to face telephone interviews have become common for screening interviews. Employers find that phone interviews are not only economical but they are also an effective way to determine which candidates merit a closer look. While you are on the job market a potential employer or networking contact might call, and ask, "Do you have a few minutes to talk?" Being interviewed over the phone isn't easy, so you need to be prepared. What initially seems like an informal conversation about a job might actually be the first round of screening or the first test of your communication skills. After the initial introductions and pleasantries let the caller take the lead, and guide the conversation. When you answer questions keep your responses short and to the point. The caller will ask follow-up questions if necessary, and will bring the interview to a close.

2.2.2. Between Adjectives

- ***Coordinate and cumulative adjectives.*** If each adjective in a series modifies the noun separately, they are **coordinate** and need commas between them.

  The *personable, youthful* guide led the way.

  If any adjective in a series modifies the total concept, they are cumulative and do not need commas.

  International currency exchange rates are posted on the Internet. (Currency exchange rates is a total concept.)

  To test for coordinate adjectives, see if the adjectives can be rearranged and if *and* can be inserted between them without altering the basic meaning: *knowledgeable and youthful and personable* guide. If the result is nonsense, the adjectives are cumulative, interdependent, and should not be separated from each other by commas: *international currency exchange rates* must appear in that order, or the statement makes no sense.

2.2.3. Between Items in a Series

Three or more words, phrases, or clauses in a series are said to be **serial** or **coordinate.** Their equal importance is indicated by their equal grammatical rank and parallel grammatical form.

- ***Serial words, phrases, or clauses.*** Serial items are differentiated from one another by the commas between them.

  Many U.S. companies have found that outsourcing call-center jobs *cuts costs, increases productivity, and allows 24-hour global service.*

  Although writing in newspapers, magazines, and Web sites often omits the comma before the conjunction, use it in business communications to prevent misreading—which could be not only confusing but costly.

Confusing	Charge the plane tickets for the vice president, board chairwoman and president and CEO to the corporate account. (Three tickets or four?)
Clear	Charge the plane tickets for the vice president, board chairwoman, and president and CEO to the corporate account. (Three tickets, because the president and the CEO are the same person.)

Punctuation in Context: Commas with Coordinate and Serial Elements

The following paragraph contains 10 errors in the use of commas with coordinate and cumulative adjectives and with serial words, phrases, and clauses. Find and correct the errors. Each missing or unnecessary comma counts as one error. The answers are located at the end of the handbook.

After you have sent out résumés and applied for jobs, be ready willing and able to handle a telephone interview. Keep your résumé a pad and pen and a bottle of water near the phone. You will need your résumé for reference the pad and pen to take notes and the water in case your throat gets dry. Is your cell phone, service, provider reliable, or do you have to worry about dropped calls? If so, consider using a landline. Send roommates, friends, spouses, children and pets from the room when a potential employer calls. You want to be completely calmly focused and undistracted during a telephone interview.

2.2.4. Around Clauses, Phrases, or Words

- ***Nonrestrictive and restrictive clauses and phrases.*** If the information in a modifying clause or phrase can be omitted without changing the basic meaning of a sentence, it is **nonrestrictive** and is set off by commas. If readers would be unable to understand the sentence's core meaning without the modifying information, it is **restrictive** and is not set off by commas. Restrictive modifiers limit meaning to a particular set within a category and thus are crucial to the sentence.

Nonrestrictive	The sales award went to McKenzie, *who landed six new accounts.* (The clause provides additional information about McKenzie, but without it we would still know who got the award.)
Restrictive	Everyone *who has been with the company for three years* is eligible for profit sharing. (The clause restricts who qualifies; otherwise, the company would have to include all employees in profit sharing.)

GRAMMAR ALERT! *THAT AND WHICH*

That and *which* are not interchangeable. Use *that* to introduce restrictive clauses and *which* to introduce nonrestrictive clauses: The retirement plan *that I chose* is split between annuities and stock funds. The stock funds, *which are invested in Fortune 500 companies,* showed a good return last year. Remember that nonrestrictive clauses, *which are set off by commas,* can be removed without destroying the basic meaning of the sentence. Most of the time, if you use *that,* you will be making the correct choice.

Use *who,* not *which* or *that,* when referring to people; use *which* or *that* when referring to things or ideas.

Incorrect Dr. Phillips is the only veterinarian *that* keeps Sunday hours.

Correct Dr. Phillips is the only veterinarian *who* keeps Sunday hours.

- ***Appositives.*** An appositive is a noun, with or without modifiers, that identifies the noun immediately preceding it. Appositives can be nonrestrictive or restrictive, accordingly written with or without commas.

  Mnemonics, *memory aids,* can help you learn things.

  The mnemonic *"every good boy does fine"* refers to the musical notes E, G, B, D, and F.

  I learned that mnemonic from Mr. Glonner, *my third-grade music teacher.*

- ***Direct address and other parenthetical elements.*** If you insert the name of the person to whom you are speaking or writing into a sentence, you are using **direct address.** Set these names off with commas: Thank you, *Leela,* for closing the door. *Committee members,* are we ready to vote?

  Parenthetical elements such as interjections, transition words, words expressing contrast, and other interrupting words that are unrelated to the grammatical structure of a sentence should also be set off with commas.

  Yes, everyone is present and ready to vote. We shall, *therefore,* proceed. *Oh,* before we do, someone needs to second the motion. Parliamentary procedure, *unlike the consensus method,* requires a second.

Punctuation in Context: Commas with Restrictive, Nonrestrictive, and Parenthetical Elements; That, Which, and Who

The following paragraph contains 13 errors in the use of commas with restrictive, nonrestrictive, or parenthetical words, phrases, or clauses. There are also two mistakes in the use of *that, which,* or *who.* Find and correct the errors. Each missing or unnecessary comma counts as one error. The answers are located at the end of the handbook.

Anyone, who has been through an employment interview, knows it is nerve-wracking. A telephone interview which provides none of the nonverbal cues available in a face-to-face situation can be even trickier. The interviewer's word choice, tone of voice, and level of enthusiasm may therefore be important indicators. The interviewee the person that is being interviewed must listen carefully. The advice, "sit up and pay attention," certainly applies in this situation. Companies, who use telephone interviews for employment screening, have heard it all everything from bad grammar to burping.

- ***Dates and places.*** Dates and places in sentences are treated similarly to parenthetical elements. In general, place a comma after each element. Exceptions: Do not put a comma between the state and zip code. If there is no day-date, do not put a comma between the month and year. If the date is written day-month-year, use no commas.

  October 29, 1929, is known as Black Tuesday, the day the New York stock market crashed.

  No American will forget *11 September 2001.*

  Isn't NBC's headquarters at *30 Rockefeller Plaza, New York, NY 10112,* in midtown Manhattan?

  The annual convention will be held in *Boise, Idaho,* next year and *Toronto, Canada,* the year after that.

- ***Direct quotations.*** Direct quotations are set off with commas. Any comma at the end of a quotation **always** goes inside the quotation marks. Also see "Quotation Marks."

  The manager told the sales associates, "We need better customer service."

  "I'm hearing too many complaints," she explained, "and we're losing business."

  Use a question mark at the end of the quotation if it is a question.

  "Does anyone have a suggestion?" she asked.

- ***Salutations.*** In formal business correspondence, punctuate the salutation or greeting with a colon, not with a comma. Commas should be reserved for informal e-mails and personal, social correspondence written on personal stationery. Follow this convention even if you know the recipient and use his or her first name in the salutation.

Not Dear Dr. Spaulding, or Dear Jerry,

But Dear Dr. Spaulding: or Dear Jerry:

The colon announces that the subject of the correspondence is business. Conventions are somewhat more flexible for business e-mail. Make your decision based on the content of the e-mail and your relationship with the recipient. You might use a comma in the salutation of an e-mail to a coworker, but probably not in one addressed to senior executives.

Punctuation in Context: Commas in Dates, Places, Direct Quotations, and Salutations

The following paragraph contains 10 errors in the use of commas with dates, places, direct quotations, and business salutations. Find and correct the errors. The answers are located at the end of the handbook.

Often a potential employer will arrange the phone interview date and time in advance. That way you won't be in Dallas or Phoenix Arizona or Paris France, when the call comes. However, you may receive an interview call at an inconvenient time. In that situation, ask "Can we set up another time to talk?" Let's look at the case of Tia Clark, who got a surprise interview call from Mr. Jordan. "I'm just leaving to pick up my daughter from school", she said "so may I call you back in an hour?" They rescheduled the conversation for another date, and Tia wrote in her daily planner: Jordan phone interview on March 12, 2011 at 10:00 A.M. After the interview, she knew she should send a thank-you note to Jordan within 24 hours if possible but no later than 14, March, 2011. Good business etiquette makes a good impression no matter whether the interview is face to face or by phone. Tia typed *Dear Mr. Jordan,* and then reiterated how enthusiastic she was about working for his company.

2.3. Semicolons

In a sentence, a semicolon is the equivalent of a period. It signals the end of one complete thought and the beginning of another. A period could be used in its place; however, reserve semicolons for sentences in which the thoughts in the independent clauses are closely related, where a period would signal too strong a disconnection between ideas.

- ***Joining independent clauses.*** Use a semicolon between grammatically independent clauses that are closely related in thought. When the second clause is introduced by a conjunctive adverb (*however, moreover, therefore, consequently*), place a comma after the conjunctive adverb. Do not use a semicolon between independent clauses joined by coordinating conjunctions (*and, but, so, for*), unless the clauses are quite long or internally punctuated.

Incorrect	Pollution threatens air quality; and everything that breathes is at risk.
Correct	Pollution threatens air quality; everything that breathes is at risk.
Correct	Pollution threatens air quality; consequently, everything that breathes is at risk.

- ***Between items in a series that contains internal commas.*** Use semicolons between serial items if any parts of the series have internal commas. The semicolons help readers sort things into the appropriate subsets and prevent misreading.

  International negotiations about global emission standards have had varied results, including the Montreal Protocol of 1989; the Kyoto Protocol adopted on December 11, 1997; and the largely unsuccessful Copenhagen Climate Conference held December 7–18, 2009.

2.4. Colons

A colon signals that what follows will explain, clarify, or illustrate preceding information.

- ***Preceding a list.*** Use a colon after phrases such as *the following* or *as follows* to signal the beginning of a list or series.

  Businesses can be "greener" and also save money by taking *the following steps:* insulate the building well, switch to fluorescent lighting, and recycle disposable items.

- ***Preceding an explanation or illustration.*** Use a colon between explanatory material and the independent clause that introduces it.

  Polluting industries that balk at stricter standards usually offer one reason: the expense of compliance.

- ***Preceding a rule, formal quotation, or subtitle.***

  Carpenters follow this advice: to cut once, measure twice. (rule)

  The Declaration of Independence assumes inherent human rights: "We hold these truths to be self evident." (formal quotation)

  The World is Flat: A Brief History of the Twenty-First Century (subtitle)

PUNCTUATION ALERT! MISUSE OF COLONS.

Be sure that a complete sentence, not a partial statement, precedes the colon—even if the clause ends with *including* or *such as*. Do not put a colon between a verb and its object or complement or between a proposition and its object.

Incorrect	Our office does "green" things including: recycling soda cans and toner cartridges.
Correct	Our office does "green" things, including recycling soda cans and toner cartridges.
Incorrect	I try to cut down carbon emissions by: biking to work, combining errands, and driving a hybrid car.
Correct	I try to cut down on carbon emissions by biking to work, combining errands, and driving a hybrid car.

However, if the items following a verb or preposition are presented as a vertical list, use a colon.

Correct Signs that the planet is warming include:
- melting glaciers
- invasive tropical species in temperate zones
- more frequent violent weather systems

Punctuation in Context: Semicolons and Colons

The following paragraph contains 10 errors or omissions in the use of semicolons and colons. Find and correct them. The answers are located at the end of the handbook.

In the on-line article "How to Give a Professional Voicemail Greeting The Business Etiquette of Voicemail Greetings," author James Bucki asks, "What would I want to know from the voicemail greeting?" The greeting may be perfectly clear to you however, the caller may be mystified. His advice create the greeting as if you were the listener at the other end. As a general rule, the length of a voicemail greeting should be: no longer than 20–25 seconds. Some of the most annoying greetings are: long introductions, greetings that are too casual or personal, and background music of any kind (especially music that drowns out the message). Avoid endings that are not business related (such as "have a blessed day"); because they may strike customers and clients as presumptuous. Here is an example of a bad voicemail greeting; "Hi. This is Accounting. Leave me a message." Callers have no idea whether they have reached the right person; nor do they know if they even have the right company. Too little information is bad, conversely, so is too much information. Business callers don't want personal details, including: the fun spot where you are vacationing; or that you are out sick with the flu.

2.5. Quotation Marks and Italics

Quotation marks and italics indicate that words are being used in a distinct way, most commonly to identify direct address, titles, and special meaning or emphasis.

2.5.1. Quotation Marks

Quotation marks signal that language has been reproduced exactly as someone spoke or wrote it.

- ***Direct quotation.*** Use double quotation marks for direct quotations from speech or writing. Use single quotation marks for a quotation within a quotation.

  According to this morning's news, "The president reminded his audience that economic recessions can be partly psychological. President Roosevelt said, 'We have nothing to fear but fear itself.' You know, he was right."

- ***Titles that are part of longer works.*** Use quotation marks around titles of short stories, poems, chapters, articles, sections, songs, or episodes that are part of whole works. The title of the complete work in which a shorter work appears is italicized. Also see "Italics."

  The article "Putting Green Technology into Bricks" in *The Wall Street Journal* makes the point that venture capital investment in the "green" building sector has nearly doubled in the past year.

- ***Words as words or words used in a special sense.*** Quotation marks signal that a word is being used in a special way. In the previous example, the quotation marks around "green" in *"green" building sector* alert the reader that "green" doesn't mean buildings painted green but green in the sense of "ecologically friendly."

- ***Punctuation of quotations.*** According to American punctuation usage, periods and commas always go inside single and double quotation marks—no exceptions. Question marks, exclamation points, semicolons, colons, and other punctuation marks go either inside or outside, depending on whether the punctuation is part of the quotation or part of the sentence in which the quotation appears.

  "Shouldn't we recycle these computer printouts?" Marge asked.

  Did Marge say, "We should recycle these computer printouts"?

  I am sick of hearing the expression "waste not, want not"!

  He said, "I thought my grandmother invented the expression 'waste not, want not'; I guess I was wrong."

2.5.2. Italics

Italics are used to distinguish titles of whole works from parts of works and for emphasis.

- ***Titles.*** Place titles of works in italics; place title of parts of works in quotation marks: One of my favorite "On Language" columns is William Safire's discussion of the Yiddish word *schlep,* which appeared in *The New York Times Magazine.* If the word *The* is part of the title, some style guides say to capitalize and italicize it, and others say not to (the *New York Times*).

  Some well-known titles of works are not italicized: religious works such as the Bible (and books of the Bible), the Koran, and the Talmud, and founding governmental documents such as the Declaration of Independence, the Bill of Rights, the Magna Carta, and the U.S. Constitution.

- ***Letters, numbers, words used as words, foreign words, names of ships and aircraft.*** Italics are used to signal that a letter, number, or words is being identified as such: To an American, a *7* written by a German looks more like the number *1.* In the example under "Titles," the word *schlep* is italicized to emphasize that it is being discussed as a word. Italics are also used to identify foreign words that have not been accepted into English (*schlep* is Yiddish). Words that have become part of the English language need not be italicized: bourgeois, milieu, zeitgeist, fiesta. Names of ships and aircraft are italicized but not the abbreviations that precede them: U.S.S. *Saratoga,* H.M.S. *Bounty,* the space shuttle *Atlantis.*

- ***Emphasis.*** Italics can also be used for special emphasis: This is absolutely the *last* time we can accept a late shipment. However, as with exclamation points, in business writing emphasizing too many words soon becomes tiresome to readers. It is like crying wolf; soon no one is paying attention, even when the wolf really is at the door. Use italicized emphasis sparingly.

Punctuation in Context: Quotation Marks and Italics

The following paragraph contains 10 errors or omissions in the use of quotation marks and italics. Find and correct them. Count pairs of quotation marks as one. The answers are located at the end of the handbook.

It's a *good* idea to review the voice-mail greeting on your personal phone, especially if potential employers might call. As part of his greeting, my friend Joe recorded John Cleese speaking lines from the *Dead Parrot Sketch* from the British television comedy "Monty Python's Flying Circus." His friends all thought it was really funny, using the words hilarious and clever to describe the greeting. One afternoon he retrieved a phone message that said, You really should use a more professional greeting. The voice continued, I called to offer you a job interview, but I've changed my mind. Joe thought, 'I wouldn't want to work for someone who didn't understand the humor in the "Dead Parrot Sketch", anyway. Sounds like this guy just doesn't get it.' Maybe not, but Joe's chances with that company are kaput.

2.6. Apostrophes

Apostrophes have two main functions in business writing: to show possession and to indicate the omission of a letter.

ADD 'S TO SHOW POSSESSION	SINGULAR NOUNS	PLURAL NOUNS NOT ENDING IN -S	INDEFINITE PRONOUNS
Examples	my child's education the boss's office an individual's rights a person's income Dow Jones's sales James's paycheck	his children's education the mass media's influence the people's choice the mice's mutations	another's misfortune someone's benefit nobody's fault

- ***Possessive case of singular nouns, plural nouns that do not end in* -s, *and indefinite pronouns.*** Also see "Pronoun Case." In compounds, make only the last word possessive.

  his brother-in-law's mortgage (singular possessive)

  mothers-in-law's Christmas gifts (plural possessive)

  somebody else's parking space

  the writer-in-residence's latest one-act play

- ***Possessive case of plural nouns ending in* -s.** Add the apostrophe after the *-s.*

  the presidents' terms in office

  the stocks' dramatic rebound after the sell-off

  the pharmaceutical companies' profits

  the auto workers' union

- ***Joint possession.*** Make the last noun possessive. In cases of individual possession, make both nouns possessive.

  Beth and Earl's project is due tomorrow. (joint possession)

  Beth's and Earl's offices are on different floors. (individual possession)

- ***Possessive case of personal pronouns.*** Do not use an apostrophe to form the possessive of personal pronouns. The pronouns *his, hers, its, ours, yours, theirs,* and *whose* are possessive as they stand.

  Ours is the second house on the right.

  Its expiration date is past.

  Be especially careful not to confuse *its* (possessive form of *it*) and *it's* (the contraction for *it is*) or *whose* (possessive form of *who*) and *who's* (contraction for *who is*).

- ***Omission of a letter: contractions.*** Apostrophes in contractions show where letters or numbers have been omitted.

  can't = cannot they're = they are o'clock = of the clock

  it's = it is won't = will not the crash of '29 = the crash of 1929

Punctuation in Context: Apostrophes

The following paragraph contains 10 errors or omissions in the use of apostrophes. Find and correct them. The answers are located at the end of the handbook.

> Practicing for a telephone interview will give you confidence that you wont blow the real thing. Ask one of your parents' or a friend to conduct a mock interview with you. Have him or her phone you and ask an interviewers questions. Its also helpful to get a spouses' or father's-in-laws critique of your answers. Ask one of them to listen in, or, whats even more useful, tape record the mock interview for later analysis. Pay attention not only to the content of your answers, but also to the vocal quality. Is your's clear, without too many "uhms," "you knows," and "likes"? The practice sessions payoff is your improved interviewing skills.

2.7. Other Punctuation Marks

The following punctuation marks are used less frequently in business writing than internal punctuation such as commas, semicolons, and colons. However, when they are called for, it is important to use them correctly.

2.7.1. Parentheses, Dashes, Brackets, and Ellipses

Parentheses, dashes, brackets, and ellipses signal that words are being inserted or being left out.

- ***Incidental or nonessential information.*** Set off incidental information with **parentheses.**

  Mortgages that are "underwater" (meaning the property is worth less than the amount owed on it) have resulted in numerous foreclosures.

  The findings of the study (pp. 12–14) are quite surprising.

- ***Emphasis and abrupt shifts in sentence structure or thought.*** If you want more emphasis for inserted incidental information, use an **em dash** instead of parentheses. An em dash is a long dash. It is not a hyphen. To insert an em dash using Microsoft Word, for example, click on the "Insert" tab followed by the "Symbol" icon on your toolbar. You will see an em dash listed among the symbols.

  Wilkins missed the start of the meeting—again—and so didn't hear about the new deadline.

Be careful not to overuse dashes, however. They are seldom appropriate in formal business documents and can give writing a breezy, chatty tone that is better reserved for e-mail and notes to close associates.

- ***Editorial remarks or information inserted into direct quotations.*** If you insert information, explanation, or comment into quoted material, use **brackets** to indicate that the words are not those of the quoted speaker or writer. To make a quotation grammatical when you insert it into your writing, you may sometimes have to add or change a word. These additions or changes should also be bracketed.

  "Innovation is not necessarily discovering new things, but discovering how to use old things [in a new way]," he said.

- ***Omitted words.*** When quoting an author or speaker, you may choose to use only part of the material. You need to be honest with your readers and let them know that you have omitted some words or sentences. Use **ellipses,** spaced periods, to show the omission. If you are leaving out words within a sentence, use three ellipsis marks. If the omission comes at the end of a sentence, use three ellipses followed by whatever is the punctuation mark at the end of the quoted sentence.

  "While the rest of the industry has retreated . . . green construction has actually grown," says Paul Holland, a partner at venture firm Foundation Capital. He continues, "Why wouldn't smart contractors promote green construction for schools, shopping centers, office buildings . . .?"

  If you find that the quotation is lengthy and you are removing words at more than one or two spots, it is better to summarize or paraphrase the ideas rather than butchering the original passage. Remember that you need to cite the source of paraphrases and summaries, just as you do for quotations.

Punctuation in Context: Parentheses, Dashes, Brackets, and Ellipses

Insert parentheses, dashes, brackets, and ellipses in the following paragraph. There are 10 omissions. Consider pairs of parentheses or brackets as a single omission. In cases where there is more than one possibility, be ready to explain your choice. Answers are located at the end of the handbook.

> The time to research a potential employer is before not after the job interview. Interviewers expect job applicants to know something about a company's products goods or services its markets local, national, international and its operating locations. Job applicants can begin their research on an Internet search engine Google or bing. Career advisor Martin Reis writes on his blog, "A company's URL Uniform Resource Locator is the gateway to a wealth of information new products, financial statements, press releases, the corporate mission statement can be found . . ." There is something else a company's Web site may reveal its corporate culture. Web page photos can provide clues about dress standards casual or traditional, employee diversity ethnicity, gender, age, and community involvement.

2.7.2. Hyphens

Hyphens are used to form compound words, to form some numbers expressed as words, and with some prefixes and suffixes. A hyphen may also be used when it is necessary to divide a word at the end of a line. In this case, divide the word between syllables as shown in a dictionary. Most word processing programs take care of this issue by "wrapping" the word to the next line.

- ***Forming compound words.*** Hyphens are used to join words into a single concept: *second-string* quarterback. Most hyphenated compounds are adjectives: *well-known* company, *back-ordered* items. Omit the hyphen when the first word is an adverb ending in *-ly*: *slowly rising* temperature, *previously paid* bill.

> **PUNCTUATION ALERT!** MISUSE OF HYPHENS
>
> When a compound modifier follows the word it modifies, the hyphen is omitted: The company is *well known* for its progressive policies. Your items have been *back ordered.* Compound nouns used as adjectives before another noun are not hyphenated either: *data processing* software; *high school* reunion; *income tax* return; *life insurance* policy.

- ***Numbers as words.*** Use a hyphen to form fractions and compound numbers twenty-one through ninety-nine when they are spelled out as words: *two-fifths, one-third, twenty-six.*
- ***With some prefixes and suffixes.*** Use a hyphen with the prefixes *all-*, *self-*, *ex-*, and the suffix *-elect*: *all-important, self-evident, ex-mayor, president-elect.* Do not capitalize *ex-* or *-elect*, even when it is part of a title that precedes a name: *ex-President* George Bush, *Councilwoman-elect* Betsy M. Clark. Do not use hyphens with prefixes such as *anti-*, *extra-*, *inter-*, *non-*, *pre-*, *pro-*, *re-*, and *un-*: *interoffice* memorandum, *pretrial* motion. The exception is if the prefix occurs before a proper noun or the first letter of the root word is the same as the last letter of the prefix: *anti-American* demonstration, *non-negotiable* demands.

  Some words have changed over time from a hyphenated form to a single word. For example, *co-worker* has lost its hyphen and is now commonly written as *coworker.* When in doubt about whether a prefix is hyphenated, consult an up-to-date dictionary.

Punctuation in Context: Hyphens

The following paragraph contains 10 errors or omissions in the use of hyphens. Find and correct them. Use a dictionary if necessary. The answers are located at the end of the handbook.

> Personal calls made during business hours are a well known problem. People resent it when a co-worker spends time on personal calls instead of attending to business. According to Computerweekly.com, sixty five percent of office workers admit they gossip about people who make personal phone calls. It's hard not to over-hear when the guy at the next desk is talking about his ex wife's alimony payments. Although some

personal calls are necessary, such as an after school call to a child home alone or arranging a dentist appointment, they should be reserved for decidedly-important matters rather than chit-chat. The need to check on a sick family member is self explanatory, but long distance calls to college buddies no doubt violate company policy.

3.0. Mechanics and Business Conventions

Written English has many conventions, standard ways of doing things that developed over time: "It's just the way things are." Business writing has some of its own conventions that differ from standard, written English and from writing in the sciences or the humanities. Where these differences are important, they will be noted in the following sections.

3.1. Capitalization

Text messaging and other social media have spawned communications that feature little or no capitalization. In these cases, the technology drives the behavior: it is difficult to capitalize on a small keypad where each key functions for several letters. However, the correct use of capital letters is still important for clarity in business letters, memos, reports, and e-mails. Capital letters signal beginnings as well as differentiate between the particular and the general.

3.1.1. First Words and Pronouns

- ***First words of grammatically independent structures.*** Capitalize the first word of a sentence, a direct quotation, a complete sentence enclosed within parentheses or brackets, and a complete sentence following a colon.

    Job interviews can be nerve wracking. (sentence)

    He said, "*Please* have a seat." (direct quotation)

    Sales for the last three quarters have been flat. (*See* Table 2 for specific figures.) (sentence in parentheses)

    There are two alternatives: *We* can raise prices, or we can cut costs. (complete sentence following colon)

3.1.2. Proper Nouns versus Common Nouns

Proper nouns name particular persons, places, and things: Steve Jobs, Grand Hyatt, Honda Accord. Common nouns name general categories of persons, places, and things: investor, hotel, automobile.

- ***Proper nouns and adjectives formed from them.*** The names of particular persons, places, and things are capitalized, as are nicknames, adjectives, and abbreviations formed from them. Foreign countries and languages are always capitalized. The words Internet and Web are always capitalized, but do not capitalize *intranet,* or *site* in *Web site.*

    William Jefferson Clinton prefers to be called *Bill.*

    How many people know that *IBM* is the abbreviation for the *International Business Machine Corporation*?

    The *National Cathedral* stands on the highest point in *Washington, D.C.*

    Claire took a job with a *French* pharmaceutical company.

    I did most of the research on the *Internet.*

    Post your résumé on your *Web* site.

- ***Places and directions.*** Places deserve special mention because the conventions governing their capitalization can be confusing. Should it be Accounting Department or accounting department? If it is the actual name of the department in your organization or you know it is the actual name of the department in another organization, then it is capitalized. Otherwise, don't capitalize department names:

    Send your résumé to our Human Resources Department.

    He sent his résumé to their personnel department.

    In business organizations, follow the style of the organization: If the standard practice in your company is always to capitalize a word, you should, too. If there is no apparent company style, follow the conventions of standard American English:

    - Official place names are capitalized.
    - Common nouns that are part of official place names are also capitalized.
    - Place names that simply refer to a general category are not capitalized.

OFFICIAL PLACE NAME: CAPITALIZE	GENERAL CATEGORY: DON'T CAPITALIZE
West Virginia	the western Virginia plateau
Woodrow Wilson High School graduate	high school graduate
Miami International Airport	the Miami airport
Seattle is in the Pacific Northwest.	Is Seattle northwest of Tacoma?
The Office of the Vice President is on the third floor of the Arnold Administration Building.	The vice president's office is on the third floor of the administration building.

Directions are capitalized if they serve as recognized names of regions or are part of an official name: the *South* of France, *Northwest* Airlines. They are not capitalized when they refer to points of the compass: the *east* side of town, a *westerly* breeze. Some directional nouns and adjectives may appear either way: the southern hemisphere, the Southern Hemisphere. When in doubt, check a dictionary.

- ***Brand and product names, organizations, and institutions.*** The brand names of products and the names of organizations and institutions are proper nouns and therefore are capitalized: Jell-O, Post-it notes, Citibank, General Electric Company, Chicago Cubs, Google, the National Science Foundation, the Mayo Clinic, the United States Senate.

  Take care to capitalize and spell brand names correctly. Most of them are registered trademarks, even though they may be widely used as generic terms. A generic term following a brand name is not capitalized.

Incorrect	post-its, jello, realtor, xerox, kleenex, ipod
Correct	Post-it notes, Jell-O, Realtor, Xerox, Kleenex tissues, iPod
Correct	sticky notes, gelatin, real estate agent, photocopy, tissues, portable media player

- ***Titles, offices, positions, and abbreviations.*** Capitalize titles, offices, and positions when they precede a proper name. Capitalize abbreviations of professional certificates and degrees when they follow a proper name.

  Secretary of State Clinton Dr. Snow Professor Okpala

  Bridget Brennan, CPA Ty Ray, RN Chairman Bill Gates

  Do not capitalize a title, office, or position that follows a name unless the office is one of high distinction.

Incorrect	Bill Gates is Chairman of Microsoft Corporation.
Incorrect	Bill Gates, Chairman of Microsoft Corporation
Correct	Bill Gates, chairman of Microsoft Corporation
Correct	John Roberts, Chief Justice of the United States

- ***Organizations and parts of organizations.*** Names of specific organizations are capitalized, as are the official names of parts of organizations: *Clark Equipment Company, Off-Road Vehicles Division, Department of Internal Affairs.* When the organization or a part is being referred to in a general way, do not capitalize: the *dealership*, the *internal affairs department.* When writing about your own company or organization, observe its capitalization conventions. Many organizations capitalize words that would not be capitalized in standard usage. Consider, for example, this sentence from a Ford Motor Company annual report: "We believe we are on track for the total Company and North American Automotive pre-tax results. . . ." Although contrary to standard convention, Ford's documents always capitalize *Company,* even when the word stands alone. The words *North American Automotive* refer to the official title of a Ford business unit and thus conform to standard capitalization conventions.
- ***Courses, academic subjects, majors, and degrees.*** Capitalize the abbreviation of a degree and the names of specific courses, but not majors or general areas of study.

  Patrick needs business law, *Intermediate Chinese,* and *Economics 315* to complete his bachelor's degree. He hopes his B.S. with a major in international business will help him land a job with a global company.
- ***Days of the week; months; holidays; holy days and names; historic events, periods, and documents; and seasons.***

Tuesday	Easter	Labor Day	the Great Depression
November	Ramadan	Yom Kippur	the Fourth of July
Black Friday	Allah	Treaty of Versailles	the Middle Ages

  Do not capitalize seasons: *summer* vacation, last *spring, midwinter* doldrums, *fall* foliage.
- ***Titles of works.*** Capitalize the first word of a title and all other words except articles (*a, an, the*). Some style guides also recommend capitalizing prepositions of fewer than five letters (for example, *for, to, in, from*). The first word following the colon in a subtitle is also capitalized.

  The Wealth of Nations *The Wall Street Journal*

  Business Week "Why China Is No Match for the Internet"

  Predictably Irrational: The Hidden Forces That Shape Our Decisions

Mechanics and Conventions in Context: Capitalization

The following paragraph contains 30 errors or omissions in the use of capital letters. Find and correct them. The answers are located at the end of the handbook.

> Robin thompson, owner of etiquette network and Robin Thompson charm school, says, "personal phone calls are fine, so long as you limit them and choose the appropriate time." She also believes cell phones should be turned off at work; If you are at work, that means you have a desk phone and can be reached at that number most of the time. Cell phones and pagers don't belong in business meetings, either, she says. Would you interrupt your Vice President to answer your cell phone? (you wouldn't if you want to keep working for the Company.) Of course, when you are flying to Corporate Headquarters on the West Coast from the Regional Office in north Dakota, a cell phone can be a life saver. Because you had to take your daughter to her spanish lesson, you've missed your plane. The head of the division of specialty products wants that report by 5 p.m., president McMillan is expecting you for lunch, and your son forgot to order his date's corsage for the High School prom tonight. Note to self: text son about picking up tuxedo. Instead of a Master's Degree in business, you're thinking maybe you should have majored in Emergency Management. Thank heavens you have a blackberry.

3.2. Numbers

The conventions for expressing numbers vary from field to field. Historians spell out numbers from one to 100; psychologists spell out only those less than 10. Lawyers may follow a number expressed as a word with the figure in parentheses; business people do not. Chemists use decimals instead of fractions to indicate parts of a whole. As a general rule, the more numbers are used in a field, the more likely they are to be expressed as figures rather than words. Business is such a field.

3.2.1. Words versus Figures

Amounts expressed as figures in a sentence are usually easier to read than amounts expressed as words. Consequently, business writers generally express isolated numbers of nine or less as words, and numbers 10 and greater as figures: *four* customers, *24* orders.

Use commas in numbers of four figures or more: *2,400; 76,000,000*

Numbers of one million or more can be expressed in a combination of words and numbers: *12 billion* light years, *6.2 million* people.

NUMBER ALERT! FIGURES IN PARENTHESES

Do not follow a number expressed as a word with a parenthetical figure for the same number.

Incorrect	We are shipping three (3) printers by UPS.
Revised	We are shipping three printers by UPS.

Although technical and legal writing sometimes follow this practice, business writing does not. The repetition is unnecessary.

3.2.2. Consecutive Numbers

Unrelated numbers that appear next to each other should be separated by a comma to avoid confusion.

The report stated that in 2010, 468 orders were delayed.

Of the 10, two shipments were damaged.

3.2.3. Related Numbers

Related numbers appearing in the same sentence or same paragraph should be expressed in the same way. Opinions differ regarding whether to use figures or words. However, readers appreciate simplicity: if any of the numbers is greater than 10, use figures.

NASA employees over age 60 outnumber those under 30 by about 3 to 1.

Nearly one of every four NASA employees will be eligible to retire in five years.

3.2.4. Indefinite or Approximate Numbers

Spell out numbers that express approximate quantities: *hundreds* of tickets, *tens* of *thousands* of gallons, *millions* of dollars.

3.2.5. Numbers at the Beginning of Sentences

Always spell out a number that begins a sentence, even if it would ordinarily be written as a figure.

Fifty thousand students from India are studying in the United States today.

If spelling out the number makes the sentence awkward, rewrite it so that another word comes first.

Awkward	Two-thousand seven was the beginning of a severe economic recession.
Revised	A severe economic recession began in 2007.

3.2.6. Fractions and Ordinals

Express fractions as words, unless the fraction is a mixed number (a whole number and a fraction).

Only one-third of the members were present, so we did not have a quorum.

The administrative staff is 1 1/2 times larger than it was last year.

Express ordinals (*first, second, tenth,* and so on) as words, unless they are longer than one word.

The board always meets on the fourth Tuesday, which is the 25th of this month.

3.2.7. Decimals and Percentages

Express decimals and percentages as figures. To avoid misreading, place a zero before the decimal if there is no whole number.

The odometer read 388.4 miles, so the gas station was only 0.6 miles from where we ran out of fuel.

More than 2.8 million bachelor's degrees in science and engineering were awarded worldwide in 2003; Asian students earned 1.2 million of them.

Express percentages as figures, followed by the word *percent.* Use the % symbol only in tables, charts, and graphs.

Science and engineering jobs are increasing 5 percent per year.

3.2.8. Money

Express precise amounts of money in figures, but do not use decimals and zeros with whole amounts: *$14.25*; a *$50* check (not a $50.00 check); *$5* worth of quarters (not $5.00 worth); a condominium priced at *$389,000.*

Express indefinite or approximate amounts of money in words: *almost thirty* pesos; a *few hundred* euros; *over a trillion* dollars.

Express amounts of money of one million or more by combining figures and words: *$2.5 million*; *€30 billion.*

3.2.9. Dates and Times

In U.S. business documents, dates are usually written month, day, year. Place a comma before the year when a date stands alone, and also place one after the year when the date occurs in a sentence. Months followed by years have no commas. Many other countries use international style: day, month, year. In either case, express dates in figures, spelling out the month.

June 14, 2009   June 2009   June 14   14 June 2009

The contract was signed on June 14, 2009, after all parties had agreed to terms.

Express hours and minutes as figures when using A.M. and P.M. Use words with fractional times and with *o'clock.* Times on the hour do not require zeros unless the sentence contains another time in hours and minutes.

10:45 A.M.   eleven o'clock   half past eight

from 4:00 P.M. to 5:30 P.M.   from 4 P.M. to 5 P.M.

3.2.10. Measurements and Compound-Number Adjectives

Express precise units of measurement in figures. Ordinarily, spell out the word for a unit within a sentence, rather than abbreviating it: the room measured *12 feet* by *18 feet.* In the case of compound-number adjectives, when quantities and units are next to each other, write one number as a word and the other as a figure to avoid confusion. Spell out the first of the two or the shorter of the two.

six 10-foot poles   24 twelve-liter bottles   8 two-ton trucks

For isolated numbers, spell out numbers less than 10: my car ran out of gas because the tank held *two* gallons less than I thought.

3.2.11. Addresses and Telephone Numbers

Follow the style of an address if you have direct correspondence such as letterhead stationery or envelope, the signature block with address from an e-mail, an example from a Web site, and so forth. Lacking direct information, use the following guidelines.

Express street numbers from one through nine in words; use figures for those higher than nine. Express building numbers as figures, except for the number one. Ordinarily in formal business correspondence, words that are part of the address, such as *street, avenue, boulevard, place, way, terrace,* and compass points (*north, west,* and so on) are not abbreviated.

305 Fourth Avenue   One West 16th Street   1437 Wooten Parkway

Use figures for highway numbers: I-80, U.S. 17, A-5.

Telephone numbers are always expressed as figures. Although the U.S. style is to place a hyphen between the parts of a telephone number, with the globalization of business the trend is to adopt international style, which places one space between the international code, country code, city code, and number.

U.S. Style	1-505-555-4523
International Style	001 505 555 4523

Mechanics and Conventions in Context: Numbers

The following paragraph contains 15 errors in the use of numbers. Find and correct them. The answers are located at the end of the handbook.

20 years ago mobile phones were novel and expensive. In the nineteen-eighties cellular telephones, luxury items used only by top executives, cost almost $4,000 and weighed 2 pounds. Today, of course, even 10-year-olds have them, and the lightest ones weigh two.65 ounces. Some people have more than one mobile phone; imagine carrying 2 2-pound phones in your purse. The International Telecommunications Union estimates that there are approximately 4,6000,000,000 mobile telephones in use worldwide. That amounts to about sixty percent of the world's population. China ranks number 1 with a little over 57 percent of Chinese using cellular telephones. India ranks 2nd, adding more than six (6) million subscribers a month. According to *The Washington Post,* with more than 6 million subscribers added per month, nearly 1/2 of the Indian population has wireless service—3 times the number of landlines in the country. The United States ranks third, with 91% of us using cell phones.

3.3. Abbreviations, Acronyms, and Initialisms

Abbreviations, acronyms, and initialisms are a kind of shorthand, allowing writers to avoid awkward, laborious repetition of lengthy names and terminology. They work fine when everyone knows what they mean, when they do not create confusion, and when writers follow generally accepted guidelines.

3.3.1. Definitions, Forms, and Functions

An **abbreviation** is a shortened version of a word or series of words, usually formed by cropping or contracting the word or by combining the first letter of each word: *Dr.* (doctor), *Mrs.* (mistress), *Pres.* (president), *etc.* (et cetera).

An **acronym** is an abbreviation formed from the first letters of a series of words, with the combination pronounced as a word: scuba (self-contained underwater breathing apparatus), OSHA (Occupational Safety and Health Administration), UNICEF (United Nations Children's Emergency Fund).

An **initialism** is an abbreviation formed from the first letters of a series of words, but the letters are pronounced separately: CIA (Central Intelligence Agency), MIT (Massachusetts Institute of Technology), p.m. (post meridiem), UPS (United Parcel Service), CEO (chief executive officer), ROI (return on investment), mph (miles per hour).

3.3.2. When to Use Abbreviations–or Not

Within the text of business documents, generally do not use abbreviations unless they are well known to your readers. Remember that abbreviations common to a particular business or subject may be unfamiliar to readers outside that field. In general, save abbreviations for tables, charts, graphs, and other places where space is limited.

When you feel an abbreviation is appropriate (to avoid repetition of a lengthy name or term, for instance), always spell out the term in its first use and write the abbreviation in parentheses unless it is commonly understood, and cannot be confused with some other term. For example, AMA can stand for either the American Management Association or the American Medical Association, so it needs to be spelled out at the first use: *He is a member of the American Management Association (AMA). He became president of the AMA last year.* In some cases, an abbreviation may be more widely recognized than the name for which it stands and thus not require being spelled out on first use: for example, NAACP (National Association of Colored People). Assess your audience, and act accordingly. When in doubt, provide the parenthetical information.

The following guidelines will help you decide how and when to abbreviate.

- ***Titles before names.*** Except for *Mr., Mrs., Ms.,* and *Dr.,* courtesy and professional titles are generally spelled out in formal business writing.

Ms. Eames	Dr. Sanchez	Senator Lewkowski
President Lee	Lieutenant Wells	Professor Jones

- ***Titles appearing independently or following names.*** Academic, religious, military, and civilian titles that follow a proper name or stand alone should not be abbreviated or capitalized: John Wells, the *lieutenant* who handled the arrest, appeared as a witness for the prosecution. However, when a title is used in place of a name in direct address, it should be capitalized: So are you saying, *Lieutenant*, that you actually witnessed the assault?
- ***Academic degrees and professional certifications.*** Degrees and certifications are abbreviated when they follow a proper name. These abbreviations can also stand by themselves. However, do not use both a professional title before a name and the equivalent degree after it.

Incorrect	Dr. Lenora Sanchez, MD, also holds a PhD from Stanford.
Correct	Lenora Sanchez, MD, also holds a PhD from Stanford.
Correct	Dr. Lenora Sanchez also holds a PhD from Stanford.

- ***Company names.*** Use abbreviations for only those words that the company itself abbreviates: Eli Lilly and *Company*, but Barnes *&* Noble, *Inc., IBM, AT&T.*
- ***Names of people; countries, states, and place names; days, months, and holidays; organizational units; and academic subjects.*** Ordinarily, spell out first names. Use initials if that is what the individual uses professionally or prefers: *I. F.* Stone, Dr. *H. C.* Brown. Countries and states may be abbreviated when part of mailing addresses, but should be spelled out in the text of documents. Days and months are often abbreviated in informal notes and e-mails but should be spelled out in more formal documents. Similarly, organizational units (such as departments and divisions) as well as academic subjects should be spelled out.

Incorrect	Chas. was transferred to our biochem div. in the UK during Mar. but he e-mailed his report last Tues. in time for the BOT meeting.
Correct	Charles was transferred to our biochemistry division in the United Kingdom during March, but he e-mailed his report last Tuesday in time for the board of trustees meeting.

- ***Units of measurement, times, and dates.*** Use abbreviations for units of measurement when they are expressed as figures: 13 *oz*, 28 *mpg*, 6 *ft* 2 *in.* The abbreviation *in.* is the only one that is followed with a period because it could otherwise be misread as the preposition *in.* Use abbreviations for exact times and dates: 9:30 A.M., 4:00 P.M., 800 *B.C., A.D.* 1603

3.3.3. Spacing and Punctuation of Abbreviations

For most **lowercase abbreviations** that stand for multiple words, put a period after each letter of the abbreviation with no spaces between them: *A.M., P.M., i.e., e.g., c.o.d.*

Exceptions are lowercase abbreviations for precise units of measurement following figures. These are abbreviated without periods with one space between the figure and the abbreviation: for example, *23 mpg, 65 mph, 90 wpm, 10 ft, 7 in., 3 yd, 5 gal, 40 km, 3½ tsp, 2 mg.* Note that the singular and plural forms are the same when used with figures: 3 *yd*, not 3 *yds.*

Most **capitalized abbreviations** do not use periods or internal spaces: *MD, RN, CPA, ACLU, IRS, SEC.* Opinions differ on whether abbreviations for academic degrees such as Ph.D., M.S., and B.A. should contain periods; however, the trend is toward omitting them: *PhD, MS, BA.* The all-capital abbreviations *P.O., A.D.,* and *B.C.* retain periods, without spaces, in general usage.

Mechanics and Conventions in Context: Abbreviations, Acronyms, and Initialisms

The following paragraph contains 10 errors or omissions in the use, formation, or punctuation of abbreviations, acronyms, and initialisms. Find and correct them. The answers are located at the end of the handbook.

> In 1989 the United States (US) Congress passed a law that stated the value of an employee-provided cell phone must be included in the employee's gross income. That means the IRS considers the value of the cell phone taxable along with the rest of the employee's income. Keeping the call records to prove that employees are using these phones for business wastes costly hrs. and mins. that could be spent more productively. Everyone, including the IRS, wants the law changed or repealed. Reps. Sam Johnson of TX and Earl Pomery of N. Dakota sponsored a bill to repeal it. Although the bill passed the House of Representatives, it failed in the Senate. Sens. John Kerry and John Ensign later introduced a similar bill in the Senate. The Pres. will no doubt sign the bill if it comes to his desk. Even phone companies such as American Telephone and Telegraph think it's time to get rid of the law. Lawmakers should work through the p.m. to repeal this out-dated legislation.

4.0. Spelling

Use your computer's spell checker to help edit your work. However, it is important to proofread documents carefully and more than once. Spell checkers will not catch homonyms (words that are similar in sound but different in meaning: *council, counsel; to, two*), misspelled proper names, dropped endings, and other errors. The following "rules of thumb" can help you deal with some of the spelling questions that occur most often.

4.1. Four Rules of Thumb for Adding Endings

- ***Suffix added to one-syllable word.*** Double the final consonant before the suffix if a vowel precedes the consonant and the suffix begins with a vowel. Do not double the final consonant if the suffix begins with a consonant.

VOWEL PRECEDES CONSONANT	SUFFIX BEGINS WITH VOWEL: DOUBLE FINAL CONSONANT	VOWEL PRECEDES CONSONANT	SUFFIX BEGINS WITH CONSONANT: DO NOT DOUBLE FINAL CONSONANT
stop	stopp*ing*	live	live*ly*
drop	dropp*ed*	fit	fit*ness*
put	putt*ing*	ship	ship*ment*

- ***Stress on final syllable.*** Double the final consonant before a suffix if the last syllable is accented: *submit, submitted; occur, occurrence; regret, regretted; propel, propeller.* Note that for suffixes added to *program*, the *-m* may or may not be doubled. Both are considered correct: *programmed, programed; programming, programing.* Just make the spelling consistent throughout the document.
- ***Final* -e *dropped.*** For words ending in *-e*, drop the *-e* before the suffix if the suffix begins with a vowel but not if the suffix begins with a consonant.

ROOT FORM	SUFFIX BEGINS WITH VOWEL: DROP FINAL *-E*	ROOT FORM	SUFFIX BEGINS WITH CONSONANT: RETAIN FINAL *-E*
locate	locat*ion*	manage	manage*ment*
use	us*able*	use	use*ful*
come	com*ing*	sure	sure*ly*

The *-e* is retained after a soft *c* or *g* before *a* or *o*: *noticeable, changeable.* It is dropped in some words taking the suffix *-ful, -ly,* or *-ment*: *awe, awful; due, duly; true, truly; judge, judgment; acknowledge, acknowledgment.*

- ***Final* -y *changed to* i.** For words ending in *-y*, change the y to *i* unless the suffix begins with *i.*

ROOT FORM	SUFFIX BEGINS WITH LETTER OTHER THAN *I*: CHANGE -Y TO *I*	ROOT FORM	SUFFIX BEGINS WITH *I*: RETAIN FINAL -Y
mercy	merc*iful*	comply	comply*ing*
ninety	ninet*ieth*	rectify	rectify*ing*
company	compan*ies*	thirty	thirty*ish*
deny	den*ial*	deny	deny*ing*

4.2. Memory Aids for ie and ei

The rhyming jingle heading the following table will help you remember whether to choose *ie* or *ei.*

WRITE *I* BEFORE *E*	EXCEPT AFTER *C*	OR WHEN SOUNDED LIKE A AS IN *NEIGHBOR* AND *WEIGH*
relief	conceive	eight
believe	ceiling	freight
yield	deceive	reign
wield	receive	vein

The exceptions to this rule are captured in the following sentence attributed to Christopher W. Blackwell:

> N*ei*ther sover*ei*gns nor financ*ie*rs forf*ei*t the h*ei*ght of th*ei*r surf*ei*t l*ei*sure to s*ei*ze the w*ei*rd counterf*ei*ts of f*ei*sty for*ei*gners.

Spelling in Context: Rules of Thumb and Memory Aids

The following paragraph contains 10 misspelled words. Use the "four rules of thumb" and "memory aids" to find and correct the misspellings. The answers are located at the end of the handbook.

> Cellular telephones have made a noticable difference in the way people do business. "Can you hear me now?" is not just an advertisement tag line but also a common question in this world of droped calls and phone dead zones. However, many people are so commited to their cell phones that they lack good judgement about when and where to use them. A call recieved doesn't have to mean a call personaly answered. When engaged in a face-to-face business conversation with someone, you can let the call go to voice mail rather than being rude by dismissivly puting the person in front of you "on hold." Even if you say "excuse me while I take this call," that person is bound to feel a little wierd and uncomfortable. If you are expecting an emergency call, warning your companion beforhand is the courteous thing to do.

4.3. Commonly Misspelled Words

Spelling a word correctly from memory is still faster than using a spell checker. All of us have personal spelling challenges that we simply have to keep working on throughout our careers. The following list contains words that are frequently misspelled in business communications. Renew your efforts to master the ones that are problems for you.

absence
accessible
accommodate
achieve
acknowledgment
advisable
advantageous
aggressive
alignment
all right
amateur
among
analyze
annually
apparent
argument
assistant
attendance
bankruptcy
believable
benefited
bulletin
bureau
calendar
campaign
canceled
catalog
ceiling
changeable
collateral
column
committee
competitor
concede
conceive
congratulations
consensus
convenient
courteous
criticism
debt
deceive
definitely
description
desirable
develop
dilemma
disappoint
disbursement
discrepancy
dissatisfied
efficient
eighth
eligible
embarrassment
emphasis
entrepreneur
environment
emphasize
especially
exaggerate
existence
extraordinary
familiar
fascinate
feasible
flexible
foreign
forty
fourth
freight
government
grateful
guarantee
harass
hors d' oeuvre
illegible
immediate
incidentally
independent
indispensable
irresistible
itinerary
jewelry
judgment
knowledgeable
labeling
legitimate
leisure
license
maintenance
manageable
mileage
misspell
mortgage
necessary
negligence
negotiable
ninety
noticeable
occasional
occurrence

omission
omitted
opportunity
paid
parallel
pastime
perceive
permanent
personnel
persuade
precede
prerogative
privilege
procedure
proceed
profited
pursue
questionnaire
receipt
receive
recommend
remittance
repetition
restaurant
rhythm
ridiculous
secretary
seize
separate
sergeant
sincerely
succeed
suddenness
surprise
tenant
thorough
truly
unanimous
until
usable
usage
vacuum
volume
weird
yield

Spelling in Context: Commonly Misspelled Words

The following paragraph contains 10 commonly misspelled words. Find and correct the misspellings. The answers are located at the end of the handbook.

> Text messaging has overtaken voice calls in terms of percentage of mobile phone useage. Some people estimate that 74 percent of all mobile phone calls consist of text messages, but this figure may be exagerated. Although teenagers send the most phone-to-phone text messages, entrepenuers have been quick to see the advantagous oppertunities. In most of the world sending a text is less than half the cost of a voice message, an excellent arguement for commercial use. Text messages can also accomodate video and graphics, adding even more impact. Businesses find bulk text messaging to be a profittable way garuanteed to reach large numbers of potential customers at a much cheaper cost than direct-mail advertising. However, consumer surveys and questionaires reveal that as it increasingly fills up people's phone message boxes, this type of marketing may soon be regarded as spam.

4.4. Commonly Confused Words

The following words are homonyms, or near homonyms—words that sound the same but have different spellings and meanings. Spell checkers won't catch these confusions. Check your writing to be sure you have chosen the correct word and spelling for the meaning you intend.

accede	to agree to
exceed	to go beyond
accept	to receive
except	to exclude
access	to gain admittance
excess	too much, more than enough
advice	(noun) a suggestion
advise	(verb) to suggest
affect	to influence
effect	(verb) to bring about; (noun) result
aid	(verb) to help
aide	(noun) an assistant
allowed	permitted
aloud	audible, out loud
all ready	prepared
already	previously, by now
ascent, ascending	rising
assent	agreement
biannual	occurring twice a year
biennial	occurring every two years
capital	money or wealth; seat of government
capitol	building housing state or national governing body
choose	(present-tense verb) to select
chose	(verb) past tense of *choose*
cite	to quote or refer to
sight	to see, the ability to see
site	location
coarse	rough in texture, not delicate
course	route taken, movement in a direction, duration
complement	to add to or complete
compliment	to flatter
conscience	sense of right and wrong
conscious	aware, alert
council	governing body or advisory group
counsel	(verb) to advise; (noun) advice, a lawyer
defer	to put off until later
differ	to be different from; to disagree
desert	to abandon; arid wasteland
dessert	last course of a meal, usually sweet
device	a mechanism or instrument
devise	to plan, create, arrange
disburse	to pay out
disperse	to scatter
discreet	careful, circumspect

discrete	separate, individual
do	to perform, fulfill, complete
due	payable, debt owed
elicit	to draw out
illicit	illegal, unlawful
eligible	qualified, worthy
illegible	not legible, impossible to read
ensure	to make certain
insure	to protect from financial loss
assure	to inform confidently
envelop	to surround
envelope	container for a letter
everyday	ordinary
every day	each day
farther	a greater distance
further	additional
forth	forward
fourth	ordinal form of the number four
holey	full of holes
holy	sacred
wholly	entirely, completely
hear	(verb) to perceive by ear
here	at or in this place
human	characteristic of humans
humane	kind
incidence	frequency
incidents	events, occurrences
imply	to express indirectly, to suggest
infer	to conclude from evidence, deduce
instance	example, case
instants	brief moments, seconds
interstate	between states
intrastate	within a state
its	possessive form of *it*
it's	contraction for *it is*
later	afterward
latter	the second or last of two
lay	to place, put down
lie	to recline
lead	chemical element, metal; (verb) to guide
led	(verb) past tense of lead, guided
lean	to rest at an angle
lien	a claim against property for debt
loose	not tight; (verb) to free
lose	to misplace, to be deprived of
miner	a person who works in a mine
minor	a person who is not of legal age; something comparatively less
moral	virtuous, good character; lesson of a story or tale
morale	state of mind, sense of well-being
overdo	to act in excess
overdue	past the due date, unpaid
passed	(verb) to move, go around, hand out
past	(noun, adjective) time before the present
patience	willingness to wait, perseverance
patients	recipients of medical treatment
peace	absence of conflict
piece	a portion, fragment
pedal	a foot lever
peddle	to sell
persecute	to torment
prosecute	to bring legal action
personal	individual, private
personnel	employees
populace	the population, the people
populous	densely populated
precede	(verb) to come before
proceed	(verb) to move ahead, advance
principal	chief or main; leader or head; sum of money
principle	basic law or general rule
right	correct
rite	ceremony
write	to form words on a surface
role	a part that one plays
roll	(noun) a list; (verb) to tumble
stationary	fixed, not moving
stationery	writing paper
than	as compared with
then	at that time
their	(pronoun) possessive form of *they*, belonging to them
there	(adverb) in that place
they're	contraction for *they are*
to	(preposition) suggesting "toward"
too	(adverb) also, an excessive degree
two	the number
vain	futile, useless; excessive pride in appearance or achievements
vein	tubular, branching vessel; bed of minerals; line of thought or action
waist	area between rib cage and pelvis
waste	(verb) to use carelessly (noun) undesirable by-product
waive, waiver	to set aside; intentional relinquishment of right or claim
wave	a swell of water; a sweeping gesture
weather	atmospheric conditions
whether	if
who's	contraction for *who is*
whose	possessive form of *who*
your	possessive form of *you*
you're	contraction for *you are*

Spelling in Context: Commonly Confused Words

The following paragraph contains 10 incorrect homonyms or near homonyms. Find these commonly confused words and replace them with the homonym that correctly fits the meaning. The answers are located at the end of the handbook.

> Businesses rely on text messaging for many things besides advertising. Texting can compliment other forms of communication and surpass some for speed and affectiveness. To site one example, let's consider instant communication between a stockbroker and investor. The broker can council the investor about the movement of a stock price and get a "buy" or "sell" decision quickly. Vendors can confirm deliveries, customers can track shipments, and contractors can tell there on-sight crews to precede with construction. Another principle advantage of text messages is the ability to communicate silently. In situations where speaking may be awkward or impossible but immediate communication is important, texting makes more sense then a phone call. Instead of searching in vein for a place to take a call, a person can simply tap out a reply, waving the need for privacy.

Grammar in Context Answer Key

1.1.1. Grammar in Context: Nouns and Pronouns

The 10 correct answers are highlighted in color and listed in the order they appear in the paragraph. See Section 1.1.1. for explanations.

Whoever answers
Everyone has his or her own
what you're expected
the phone, it's important
and your name.
identify the department
kinds of questions to settle
"This is I."
wondering whom he
you are the company.

1.1.2. Grammar in Context: Verbs

The 10 correct answers are highlighted in color and listed in the order they appear in the paragraph. See Section 1.1.2. for explanations.

If my first boss had run
have gone broke
he grabs the receiver
"That doesn't sound
Barker were a dog,
there were lots
still answers the phone
offenses amount to
there are several
George Barker" makes a better impression.

1.1.3. Grammar in Context: Adjectives and Adverbs

The 10 correct answers are highlighted in color and listed in the order they appear in the paragraph. See Section 1.1.3. for explanations.

speak well
look bad.
make the better impression
sound cheerful
feel good,
A simpler way
more friendly
have the unique
seem really unprofessional.
"Worst Phone Manners

1.1.4. Grammar in Context: Prepositions and Conjunctions

The prepositions and conjunctions are identified as follows: prepositions (P), coordinating conjunctions (CC), correlative conjunctions (CorC), subordinating conjunctions (SC), and conjunctive adverbs (CA). The 10 prepositions and conjunctions are highlighted in color and listed in the order they appear in the paragraph. Correlative conjunction pairs are counted as one. See Section 1.1.4. for explanations.

important; however (CA),
caught in (P) an awkward spot
If (SC) you
is for (P) you
After (SC) you
called and (CC) then
person at (P) the other
either (CorC) can . . . or (CorC) can
with (P) a pleasantry
for (P) example

1.1.5. Grammar in Context: Interjections

The five unnecessary or inappropriate interjections are crossed out and highlighted in color. See Section 1.1.5. for explanations.

~~Hey!~~
~~Stop!~~
~~Now!~~
~~For heaven's sake,~~
~~Oh,~~

1.2.1. Grammar in Context: Subjects and Predicates

The complete subjects are underlined once, and the complete predicates are underlined twice. The simple subjects are highlighted in red, and the simple predicates are highlighted in blue. See Section 1.2.1. for explanations.

A survey of chief information officers at companies with 100 or more employees was conducted by Robert Half

Technologies. The survey focused on the use of cell phones, BlackBerries or PDAs, wireless earpieces, and headphones at work. Have breaches in workplace "tech-etiquette" increased, decreased, or remained the same? Twenty-two percent felt that poor etiquette had "increased significantly." The votes for "remained the same" were 42 percent. Only two percent of chief information officers voted for "decreased significantly." Robert Half Technologies named five main types of tech-etiquette offenders. The "misguided multitasker" and the "e-mail addict" were the first two. Others on the list included the "broadcaster," the "cyborg," and the "distractor." Exactly how had these employees offended in their handling of technology? In most cases they failed to pay attention to the people or circumstances around them.

1.2.2. Grammar in Context: Phrases and Clauses

The phrases are highlighted in color, with the type of phrase (P/preposition; V/verb or verbal) indicated in parentheses. The dependent clauses are underlined once, and independent clauses are underlined twice. There are a total of 10 dependent and independent clauses and a total of 15 phrases. See Section 1.2.2. for explanations.

In the list (P) of tech-etiquette offenders (P), **the "misguided multitasker"** may be (V) the worst, although the "broadcaster" is a close second. Holding their BlackBerries (V) under the table (P), multitaskers send e-mail or text messages during meetings (P). Broadcasters use their cell phones anytime, anywhere, and they apparently don't mind being overheard (V) by others (P). On a crowded elevator (P), they will discuss (V) the intimate details of a medical procedure (P) or talk loudly about confidential business matters (P).

1.2.3. Grammar in Context: Sentence Types

The 10 sentences are labeled either as simple (S), compound (C), complex (CX), or compound-complex (C-CX). See Section 1.2.3. for explanations.

The blinking Bluetooth headset or iPod earbuds of the "cyborg" can be very distracting to other people at work. (S) Because no one else can hear their music or ringing phone, cyborgs think that they are being courteous. (CX) Actually, the earpieces signal something else entirely. (S) The nonverbal message is loud and clear. (S) "I am not available," or "Don't bother me." (C) If you are always plugged in at work, you may be a cyborg behaving badly. (CX) You can't see the earpiece, perhaps have forgotten all about it, but the people looking at you can see it, and they will infer that your first priority is whatever comes over the headset. (C-CX) They may hesitate to interrupt, even with something important. (S) Signal your availability to your coworkers. (S) Take the earbuds out unless you are working alone in your office. (CX)

1.3.1. Grammar in Context: Sentence Fragments

The 10 sentence fragments are highlighted in color in the first paragraph. They are corrected in the second paragraph. See Section 1.3.1. for explanations.

Fragments Identified

You may get a person's voice mail. When making a business call. If you have to leave a message. Decide beforehand what to say. Identify yourself first. Then state your message clearly, making it brief and to the point. Not a million details. Rambling messages, in addition to trying the listener's patience. Very likely he or she will forget what you said. Everybody thinks, "My message is really important." But the listener may have many messages to play. What about yours? Your message has to compete for attention. With all the rest. And don't presume the person at the other end has caller ID. Consequently, can see your phone number. You should say your telephone number slowly and clearly. No mumbling. The listener has to be able to hear, to understand, and to write down the number in order to return your call.

Fragments Corrected (answers will vary)

You may get a person's voice mail when making a business call. If you have to leave a message, decide beforehand what to say. Identify yourself first. Then state your message clearly, making it brief and to the point. Don't give a million details. Rambling messages, in addition to trying the listener's patience, very likely will make him or her forget what you said. Everybody thinks, "My message is really important," but the listener may have many messages to play. What should you do about your own voice-mail message? Your message has to compete for attention with all the rest. Don't presume the person at the other end has caller ID and, consequently, can see your phone number. You should say your telephone number slowly and clearly. Don't mumble. The listener has to be able to hear, to understand, and to write down the number in order to return your call.

1.3.2. Grammar in Context: Run-On (Fused) Sentences and Comma Splices

The 10 run-on (fused) sentences and commas splices are highlighted in color in the first paragraph. They are corrected in the second paragraph. See Section 1.3.2. for explanations.

Run-Ons (RO) and Comma Spliced Identified (CS)

One business etiquette consultant believes that good telephone manners begin in childhood, (CS) children should be taught how to answer the phone courteously and take messages. Diane Eaves says, "I work with a lot of people who are technically ready for work (RO) however, they apparently missed a lot of the teaching of manners." For instance, asking who is calling can be taught in childhood (RO) then it will be a habit. Parents know how annoying it is to have a child report that "somebody called and wants you to call back" (RO) Sonny doesn't remember who it was and didn't write down the number. Thank goodness for caller ID (RO) it can be a big help, (C) nevertheless, children should be taught to ask for and write down names and numbers. It's surprising how many people don't identify themselves when they make business calls, (CS) they expect listeners to recognize their voice. That may be OK if you speak frequently with the caller (RO) on the other hand it's mystifying when a voice you don't recognizes launches right into a subject. It is the caller's responsibility to identify himself or herself, (CS) if he or she doesn't you can politely say, "Excuse me, (CS) I didn't catch your name."

Run-Ons and Comma Splices Corrected (answers will vary)

One business etiquette consultant believes that good telephone manners begin in childhood. Children should be taught how to answer the phone courteously and take messages. Diane Eaves says, "I work with a lot of people who are technically ready for work; however, they apparently missed a lot of the teaching of manners." For instance, asking who is calling can be taught in childhood; then it will be a habit. Parents know how annoying it is to have a child report that "somebody called and wants you to call back." Sonny doesn't remember who it was and didn't write down the number. Thank goodness for caller ID. It can be a big help. Nevertheless, children should be taught to ask for and write down names and numbers. It's surprising how many people don't identify themselves when they make business calls. They expect listeners to recognize their voice. That may be OK if you speak frequently with the caller. On the other hand it's mystifying when a voice you don't recognizes launches right into a subject. It is the caller's responsibility to identify himself or herself. If he or she doesn't, you can politely say, "Excuse me. I didn't catch your name."

1.3.3. Grammar in Context: Subject-Verb Agreement

The 10 subject-verb agreement errors are highlighted in color in the first paragraph. They are corrected in the second paragraph. See Section 1.3.3. for explanations.

Agreement Errors Identified

When making a business call, being put on hold for countless minutes fray even patient people's nerves. Having to wait, as well as not knowing for how long, are upsetting. Each of us have our own way of coping with this irritant. *The Sounds of Silence* not only apply to the Simon and Garfunkel song but also to endless minutes on hold. Three minutes feel like forever to the person waiting. If you must put someone on hold, there is several things you should do. First, ask, "May I put you on hold?" and then give the caller an estimate of the probable waiting time. The person on the other end might be one of those callers who really need to know how long the wait might be. The unknown number of minutes are what drive people crazy. Data collected by Hold On America, Inc. shows that callers become frustrated after 20 seconds. After 90 seconds, 50 percent of callers hangs up.

Verbs Corrected

When making a business call, being put on hold for countless minutes frays even patient people's nerves. Having to wait, as well as not knowing for how long, is upsetting. Each of us has our own way of coping with this irritant. *The Sounds of Silence* not only applies to the Simon and Garfunkel song but also to endless minutes on hold. Three minutes feels like forever to the person waiting. If you must put someone on hold, there are several things you should do. First, ask, "May I put you on hold?" and then give the caller an estimate of the probable waiting time. The person on the other end might be one of those callers who really needs to know how long the wait might be. The unknown number of minutes is what drives people crazy. Data collected by Hold On America, Inc. show that callers become frustrated after 20 seconds. After 90 seconds, 50 percent of callers hang up.

1.3.4. Grammar in Context: Pronoun-Antecedent Agreement

The 10 pronoun-antecedent agreement errors are highlighted in color in the first paragraph. They are corrected in the second paragraph. See Section 1.3.4. for explanations.

Agreement Errors Identified

Everybody has preferences about their communication tools. A person may prefer e-mail rather than telephone, so they might respond to a voice-mail message by sending an e-mail instead of returning the call. If you ask either of my managers, Jenny or Kurt, they will tell you that I would rather e-mail them. Business professionals will often choose the one with which he or she is most at ease. Considering its total number of calls versus e-mails per month, the sales team obviously would rather talk than write. Each of these communication media has their advantages and disadvantages. Text messages and e-mail may be best because it will be delivered whether the recipient is there or not. On the other hand, someone who leaves a voice-mail message probably assumes you will call them back, not send a text. Otherwise, they would have texted you instead of calling.

Agreement Errors Corrected

Everybody has preferences about his or her communication tools. A person (people) may prefer e-mail rather than telephone, so he or she (they) might respond to a voice-mail message by sending an e-mail instead of returning the call. If you ask either of my managers, Jenny or Kurt, she or he will tell you that I would rather e-mail her or him. Business professionals will often choose the one with which they are most at ease. Considering their total number of calls versus e-mails per month, the sales team obviously would rather talk than write. Each of these communication media has its advantages and disadvantages. Text messages and e-mail may be best because they will be delivered whether the recipient is there or not. On the other hand, someone (people) who leaves (leave) a voice-mail message probably assumes you will call him or her (them) back, not send a text. Otherwise, he or she (they) would have texted you instead of calling.

1.3.5. Grammar in Context: Vague Pronoun Reference

The 10 vague pronoun references are highlighted in color in the first paragraph. They are corrected in the second paragraph. See Section 1.3.5. for explanations.

Vague Pronoun References Identified

Text messages have their own rules of business etiquette; however, they may not be well understood. Students who are used to texting friends and family wherever-whenever may not be aware that this is considered rude during a business meeting or presentation. As Brian tapped out text messages while President Jackson welcomed the new summer interns, he didn't know he was being videotaped. The camera operator panned the audience for reaction shots during the speech, and there he was, thumbing away on his cell-phone keypad. When the president saw it, he asked Brian's department manager who that was and what he was doing. Brian certainly made lasting impression on the chief executive, which should be a lesson for all of us. That spelled the end of Brian's brief but memorable career at Jackson Ltd.

Vague Pronoun References Corrected (answers will vary)

Text messages have their own rules of business etiquette; however, these rules may not be well understood. Students who are used to texting friends and family wherever-whenever may not be aware that texting is considered rude during a business meeting or presentation. As Brian tapped out text messages while President Jackson welcomed the new summer interns, Brian didn't know Jackson was being videotaped. The camera operator panned the audience for reaction shots during the speech, and there Brian was, thumbing away on his cell-phone keypad. When the president saw the video tape, he asked Brian's department manager who Brian was and what the intern was doing. Brian certainly made lasting impression on the chief executive, an impression that should be a lesson for all of us. The incident spelled the end of Brian's brief but memorable career at Jackson Ltd.

2.1.1.–2.1.3. Punctuation in Context: End Punctuation

The 10 correct end punctuation marks are highlighted in color and listed in the order they appear in the paragraph. The reason is given in parentheses. See Sections 2.1.1. through 2.1.3. for further explanations.

What about voice-mail greetings? (direct question)
their importance. (statement)
your company? (direct question)
listeners' time. (indirect question)
don't they? (direct question)
greeting are great. (statement)
if appropriate. (polite request)
out of the office. (statement)
"thanks for calling." (statement)
"have a nice day." (statement)

2.2.1. Punctuation in Context: Commas with Clauses and Phrases

The 10 correct uses of commas are highlighted in color and listed in the order they appear in the paragraph. The reason for each is given in parentheses. See Section 2.2.1. for further explanations.

Although . . . face to face, telephone (introductory dependent clause)
economical, but they are (independent clauses joined by coordinating conjunction)
While . . . job market, a potential employer (introductory dependent clause)
might call and (compound predicate requires no comma)
isn't easy, so you (independent clauses joined by coordinating conjunction)
screening or the first test (compound complement requires no comma)
pleasantries, let the caller (long introductory phrase)
take the lead and guide (compound predicate requires no comma)
When you answer questions, keep (introductory dependent clause)
if necessary and will bring (compound predicate requires no comma; "if necessary" requires no special emphasis)

2.2.2.–2.2.3. Punctuation in Context: Commas with Coordinate and Serial Elements

The 10 correct uses of commas are highlighted in color and listed in the order they appear in the paragraph. The reason for each is given in parentheses. See Sections 2.2.2.–2.2.3. for further explanations.

ready, willing, and able (coordinate adjectives)
your résumé, a pad and pen, and a bottle (serial elements)
your résumé for reference, the pad and pen to take notes, and the water (serial elements)
cell phone service provider (cumulative adjectives: no commas)
spouses, children, and pets (serial nouns)
completely, calmly focused (coordinate adverbs)

2.2.4. Punctuation in Context: Commas with Restrictive, Nonrestrictive, and Parenthetical Elements; *That, Which,* and *Who*

The 13 errors in the use of commas with restrictive, nonrestrictive, or parenthetical words, phrases, or clauses and the two mistakes in the use of *that, which,* or *who* are highlighted in color. The reason for each is given in parentheses. Each missing or unnecessary comma counts as one error. See Section 2.2.4. for further explanations.

Anyone who has . . . interview (restrictive clause identifies who and requires no commas)
interview, which provides . . . situation, can (nonrestrictive clauses requires commas) may, therefore, be (parenthetical element)
interviewee, the person who is being interviewed, must (nonrestrictive appositive requires commas; *who* is the correct pronoun for referring to a person, *interviewee*)
advice "sit up and pay attention" (restrictive appositive requires no commas)

Companies that use telephone interviews for employment screening (restrictive clause requires no commas; *that* is the correct pronoun for referring to a thing, *companies*) have heard it all, everything (nonrestrictive appositive explaining *all* requires comma)

2.2.4. (continued) Punctuation in Context: Commas in Dates, Places, Direct Quotations, and Salutations

The 10 correct uses of commas are highlighted in color and listed in the order they appear in the paragraph. The reason for each is given in parentheses. See Section 2.2.4. for further explanations.

Phoenix, Arizona, or Paris, France, (elements of places: cities, states or countries)
In that situation, ask, "Can we (introducing direct quotation)
from school," she said, "so may I (direct quotations; comma inside quotation marks)
March 12, 2011, at (elements of month/day/year dates)
14 March 2011 (no commas in day/month/year dates)
Dear Mr. Jordan: (colon rather than comma for business letter salutation)

2.3.–2.4. Punctuation in Context: Semicolons and Colons

The 10 correct uses of semicolons and colons are highlighted in color and listed in the order they appear in the paragraph. The reason for each is given in parentheses. See Sections 2.3.–2.4. for further explanations.

"How to . . . Voicemail Greeting: The Business . . . Greetings" (preceding subtitle)
clear to you; however, (independent clause introduced by conjunctive adverb)
His advice: create the greeting (preceding an explanation or rule)
greeting should be (delete colon) no longer (no colon between verb and object)
greetings are (delete colon) long introductions (no colon between verb and object) blessed day") (delete semicolon)
because they ("because" clause is dependent)
voicemail greeting: (colon preceding an illustration)
is bad; conversely, so (independent clause introduced by conjunctive adverb)
details, including (delete colon) (not preceded by a complete statement)
vacationing (delete semicolon) or (not followed by an independent clause)

2.5.1.–2.5.2. Punctuation in Context: Quotation Marks and Italics

The 10 correct uses of quotation marks and italics are highlighted in color and listed in the order they appear in the paragraph. The reason for each is given in parentheses. Pairs of quotation marks count as one error. See Sections 2.5.1.–2.5.2. for further explanations.

It's a good idea (the word needs no special emphasis)
"Dead Parrot Sketch" (title of a segment, part of a longer work)
Monty Python's Flying Circus (title of television program, complete work)
using the words "hilarious" and "clever" (direct quotation)
"You really . . . greeting. " (direct quotation)
"I called . . . my mind. " (direct quotation
"I wouldn't . . . in the 'Dead Parrot Sketch,' anyway . . . doesn't get it." (quotation within a quotation)
are *kaput*. (foreign word)

2.6. Punctuation in Context: Apostrophes

The 10 correct uses of apostrophes are highlighted in color and listed in the order they appear in the paragraph. The reason for each is given in parentheses. See Section 2.6. for further explanation.

you won't (contraction of *will not*)
parents (plural but not possessive)
an interviewer's (singular possessive)
It's also (contraction of *it is*)
spouse's (singular possessive)
father-in-law's (singular possessive)
what's (contraction of *what is*)
Is yours (possessive form of *you*)
practice session's (singular possessive)

2.7.1. Punctuation in Context: Parentheses, Dashes, Brackets, and Ellipses

The 10 correct insertions of parentheses, dashes, brackets, and ellipses are highlighted in color and listed in the order they appear in the paragraph. The reason for each is given in parentheses. Pairs of parentheses or brackets are considered a single insertion. Answers may vary. See Section 2.7.1. for further explanations.

before—not after—the job interview. (emphasis)
a company's products, (goods or services), its markets (local, national, international), and its operating locations. (incidental information)
search engine—Google or Bing. (emphasis on inserted information)
company's URL [Uniform Resource Locator] (editorial information inserted into direct quotation)
can be found . . . ." (words omitted from end of direct quotation)
may reveal—its corporate culture. (emphasis)
dress standards (casual or traditional), employee diversity (ethnicity, gender, age), and community involvement. (incidental information)

2.7.2. Punctuation in Context: Hyphens

The 10 correct uses of hyphens are highlighted in color and listed in the order they appear in the paragraph. The reason for each is given in parentheses. See Section 2.7.2. for further explanation.

coworker (prefix not hyphenated)
sixty-five (compound number)
overhear (prefix not hyphenated)
ex-wife's (prefix *ex-* hyphenated)
after-school call (compound adjective)
decidedly important matters (first modifier is adverb ending in *-ly*)
chitchat. (word no longer hyphenated)
self-explanatory (prefix *self-* is hyphenated)
long-distance calls (compound adjective)

3.1. Mechanics and Conventions in Context: Capitalization

The 30 correct uses of capital letters are highlighted in color and listed in the order they appear in the paragraph. The reason for each is given in parentheses. See Section 3.1. for further explanation.

Robin Thompson, owner of Etiquette Network and Robin Thompson Charm School (proper nouns: name of person; name of companies)
"Personal (first word of sentence)
work; if you (first word of dependent clause requires no capital)
your vice president (common noun)
(You wouldn't (first word of complete sentence in parentheses)
the company.) (common noun)
corporate headquarters common nouns)
regional office (common nouns)
North Dakota (proper noun: state)
Spanish lesson (adjective formed from proper noun: language)
Division of Specialty Products (proper noun: official name of part of organization)
President McMillan (proper noun: official title or position)
high school prom (common noun)
Note to self: Text son (first word of grammatically independent structure)
master's degree (common nouns: generic degree name)
emergency management (common noun: academic major)
BlackBerry (proper noun: brand/product name. This product name illustrates "camel case" or "medial capitals," compound proper nouns in which the first letters of the parts are capitalized. Names using camel case should always be capitalized as branded or trademarked—for example, PowerPoint.

3.2.1.–3.2.11. Mechanics and Conventions in Context: Numbers

The 15 correct uses of apostrophes are highlighted in color and listed in the order they appear in the paragraph. The reason for each is given in parentheses. See Sections 3.2.1.–3.2.11 for further explanations.

Twenty years (word, not figure, at beginning of sentence)
In the 1980s (year date)
almost four thousand dollars (approximate amounts of money)
weighed two pounds. (measurements; words versus figures)
10-year-olds (words versus figures)
2.65 ounces. (measurements; decimals)
two 2-pound phones (measurements, compound-number adjectives)
approximately 4.6 million (decimals; words versus figures)
about 60 percent (words versus figures)
number one (words versus figures)
ranks second (one-word ordinal number)
more than six million (words versus figures; do not use parenthetical figure)
one-half of (fraction that is not a mixed number)
three times (words versus figures)
with 91 percent (*percent* as word when part of paragraph, not graphic)

3.3.2.–3.3.3. Mechanics and Conventions in Context: Abbreviations, Acronyms, and Initialisms

The 10 corrections in the use, formation, or punctuation of abbreviations, acronyms, and initialisms are highlighted in color. The reason for each is given in parentheses. See Sections 3.3.2.–3.3.3. for further explanations.

United States (delete US) Congress (unnecessary abbreviation)
the IRS (commonly used, well-understood initialism)
hours and minutes (no units of measurement given, so abbreviation inappropriate)
Representatives Sam Johnson (spell out titles before names)
Texas (spell out state names)
North Dakota (spell out state names)
Senators John Kerry (spell out titles before names)
The president (spell out title; capitalize only if it is immediately before person's name)
AT&T (company uses this initialism)
the evening (no unit of time given, so abbreviation inappropriate)

4.1.–4.2. Spelling in Context: Rules of Thumb; Memory Aids for *ie* and *ei*

The 10 corrected misspellings are highlighted in color and listed in the order they appear in the paragraph. The reason for each is given in parentheses. See Sections 4.1.–4.2. for further explanations.

noticeable difference (*e* retained after soft *c*)
dropped calls (suffix of one-syllable word begins with vowel: double final consonant)
committed to (stress on final syllable: double final consonant)
judgment about (exception to "*e* retained after soft *c*" rule)
received doesn't (*i* before *e* except after *c*)
personally answered (all letters of root word and suffix retained; no rules of thumb apply)
dismissively (suffix begins with consonant: retain final –*e*)
putting the person (suffix of one-syllable word beings with vowel: double final consonant)
weird and (exception to "*i* before *e* except after *c*" rule)
beforehand is (suffix begins with consonant: retain final –*e*)

4.3. Spelling in Context: Commonly Misspelled Words

The 10 corrected common misspellings are highlighted in color and listed in the order they appear in the paragraph. See Section 4.3. for an extended list of commonly misspelled words.

phone usage
be exaggerated
entrepreneurs have
the advantageous
opportunities
excellent argument
also accommodate
profitable way
guaranteed to reach
questionnaires reveal

4.4. Spelling in Context: Commonly Confused Words

The 10 correct homonyms are highlighted in color and listed in the order they appear in the paragraph. See Section 4.4. for an extended list of commonly confused words and their meanings.

can complement
and effectiveness
To cite
can counsel
tell their
on-site
to proceed
Another principal
in vain
reply, waiving

Commonly Used Revision and Proofreading Symbols

The first part of this appendix contains information about editing symbols commonly used to mark up copy that needs to be rewritten. Perhaps the material is awkward or negative sounding. Or, perhaps it includes jargon that needs to be revised so the reader doesn't become confused.

The second part of this appendix contains information about how to mark up copy as you proofread it. For example, you might find spelling errors, missing punctuation, or typos in your material. The proofreading symbols in this appendix will help you flag these mistakes so you can quickly correct them.

Revision (Editing) Symbols

When instructors edit students' writing, they often use the abbreviations shown in **Exhibit E-1**. If your instructors use revision abbreviations, Exhibit E-1 will help you understand how they want you to rewrite your material. You can also use the abbreviations to mark up your own copy as you edit it for revision purposes.

Proofreading Symbols

Exhibit E-2 shows the basic proofreading symbols used to mark spelling, grammar, and typographical mistakes. **Exhibit E-3** shows how they are used in an actual document, and **Exhibit E-4** shows the corrected document.

If you find typographical and other mistakes that need to be fixed in the business documents you create, both mark them and correct them. Don't simply mark the copy and deliver it to the recipient thinking the handwritten corrections will suffice. Doing so looks unprofessional and makes it appear that you don't care enough about your writing or your reader to completely fix it.

Exhibit E-1 Commonly Used Revision Abbreviations

Abbreviation	Meaning
Ab	Abbreviation error. Verify the correct abbreviation to use.
Agr	Agreement error. Check the subject-verb or pronoun-antecedent pairs for agreement.
Awk	Awkward-sounding copy. Rewrite for clarity.
Cap	Capitalization error. Verify proper capitalization usage.
Chop	Choppy-sounding copy. Combine sentences or create transitions between them.
Con	Condense. Rewrite the material so that it's shorter and more to the point.
CS	Comma splice. Use a period, semicolon, or colon rather than a comma.
Dev	Develop. Explain the material in greater detail.
DM	Dangling modifier. Move the modifier so that it describes the subject.
Dir	Use the direct approach. Don't use passive voice.
Frag	Fragment. Make the material a complete sentence.
Gram	Grammar error. Revise for correct grammar usage.
Jar	Jargon. Use language understood by a more general audience.
LC	Lowercase. Don't capitalize.

(continued)

Exhibit E-1 (Continued)

Log	Logic. Check the development of your argument to be sure it is rational.
Neg	Negative-sounding copy. Rewrite to make the copy positive.
Obv	Obvious. Eliminate the amount of detail surrounding the point.
Org	Organization. Reorganize the material for better flow.
P-A	Pronoun-antecedent agreement error. Correct for agreement.
Par	Parallel. Use parallel construction.
Rep	Repetitive. Delete because the idea has already been stated.
Red	Redundant. Delete because the point is already clear. No more information is needed.
RO	Run-on sentence. Separate the material with a period, semicolon, or conjunction.
Sp	Spelling error. Correct the spelling.
Stet	Let the original copy stand. Don't change it.
S-V	Subject-verb agreement error. Correct for agreement.
SX	Sexist. Use gender-neutral language.
Tone	Improve the tone.
Wdy	Wordy. Eliminate extra words to make the copy more concise.
WW	Wrong word choice. Choose a more appropriate word to get the point across.

Exhibit E-2 Commonly Used Proofreading Symbols and Their Meanings

Symbol	Meaning
ℯ	Delete copy
∧	Insert copy
∧ with ,	Insert a comma
∨ with ’	Insert an aprostrophe
∨“ ∨” or ∨‘ ∨’	Insert quotation marks
¶	Start a new paragraph
∽	Transpose (reverse)
/	Lowercase (do not capitalize)
≡	Capitalize
⊙	Add a period
][	Center copy horizontally
⊔ ⊓	Center copy vertically
[	Move copy left
]	Move copy right
#	Insert a space
⁐ ‿	Close up space
‖	Align copy vertically
=	Align copy horizontally
bf	Use boldfaced type
ital	Italicize
wf	Wrong font
(sp)	Spell out
stet	Let it stand (don’t make marked change after all)

Exhibit E-3 Copy Hand-Marked with Proofreading Symbols

Dear Cherie,
Ms. White:

My Technical Journalism Instructor, Dr. Ashfield, told everyone in class about you internship.

I am currently a Junior in the Technical Journalism program at Wesley College. During hte summer of my freshman year, I had the opportunity to proofread sections of text books for two professors at Wesley—one in the biology department and one in the archeology department. Not only did I gain valuable experience identifying spelling, grammar, and punctuation errors, I also learned a lot about Biology and Archeology.

During the summer of my sophomore year, i worked with the same Professors; this time helping them put together lecture materials and presentations. I found that I really enjoyed learning about new subjects and figuring out how to present them to students in exciting ways. Both Professors said my assistance was invaluable in getting their text books finished on time and making sure their lecture materials were top quality. I visited your Web site and was very impressed by the books you've published and the coaching you provide to students and teachers. You are definitely making a difference in education, on book at a time and I want to be a part of that difference.

With my writing, editing, proofreading, love of learning, i think I'm an excellent candidate for your internship. I've attached my résumé, writing samples, and letters of recommendations from the 2 professors I worked with. Feel free to contact them with any questions. Their contact information is in the letters

I hope to hear from you soon.

Exhibit E-4 Corrected Copy

Dear Ms. White:

My Technical Journalism instructor, Dr. Ashfield, told everyone in class about your internship.

I'm currently a junior in the Technical Journalism program at Wesley College. During the summer of my freshman year, I had the opportunity to proofread sections of textbooks for two professors at Wesley—one in the Biology Department and one in the Archeology Department. Not only did I gain valuable experience identifying spelling, grammar, and punctuation errors, I also learned a lot about biology and archeology.

During the summer of my sophomore year, I worked with the same professors again; this time helping them put together lecture materials and presentations. I found that I really enjoyed learning about new subjects and figuring out how to present them to students in exciting ways. Both professors said my assistance was invaluable in getting their textbooks finished on time and making sure their lecture materials were top quality.

I visited your Web site and was very impressed by the books you've published and the coaching you provide to students and teachers. You are definitely making a difference in education, one book at a time. I want to be part of the difference you are making.

My writing, editing, and proofreading experience as well as my love of learning make me a good fit for the internship. I've attached my résumé, writing samples, and letters of recommendation from the two professors I worked with. Feel free to contact them if you have any questions. Their contact information is in the letters.

I hope to hear from you soon.

Glossary

A

Acceptance letters A letter or e-mail sent by a candidate to an employer accepting an offer of employment.

Acronyms Acronyms are formed from the first letters of the words for which they stand. An acronym is usually pronounced as a word rather than as individual letters: POTUS (President of the United States).

Active voice A sentence in which the subject performs the action of the verb.

Adapted for the audience Involves knowing your audience and adjusting your message accordingly.

AIDA Acronym that stands for *attention, interest, desire,* and *action.*

Analogy A comparison between two ideas or things, one of which is familiar to your audience.

Annotated outline An outline with additional notes, quotes, and reference information that can aid a writer in creating a first draft.

Annual accomplishments report A report that serves as a reminder of what you accomplished and contributed to your organization in a given year.

Annual report A federally required report for publicly traded companies outlining their finances and operations.

Application cover letter A letter sent along with a résumé, portfolio, and letter(s) of recommendation in response to a job posting.

Application forms Documents used internally by Human Resources departments for background checks, and by small business owners for hiring purposes.

Application packet A collection of documents including a résumé, cover letter, professional portfolio, and letters of recommendation used as an application for employment.

Arrogant tone A condescending and patronizing tone of voice that can alienate your audience.

Assumptions Beliefs that are typically based on stereotypes and negatively impact our perceptions of other people.

Awards, honors, and activities section The section of a résumé presenting an applicant's awards, honors, and activities, especially those indicating leadership.

B

Back-up behavior A coping behavior that different personality types exhibit under stress.

Background questions Interview questions that focus on both a candidate's personal and professional background.

Behavioral questions Interview questions regarding a candidate's past behavior. The responses are taken as a predictor of the person's future performance on the job.

Block style A letter style in which the basic elements (the date, signature, and so forth) begin at the left-hand margin.

Blog A shortened expression for the two words *Web log.* A blog is a Web site upon which a writer posts informative messages on a daily or frequent basis. People who read the blog can then post their follow-up comments on the site.

Body text Text that makes up the majority of a document.

Body The largest section of the message. Here you identify and discuss points you must make to achieve your purpose.

Boldface A typeface that appears thicker than regular text.

Brainstorm The process of capturing as many ideas about a given topic without censoring your ideas.

Bubble chart A chart that displays a set of numeric values as circles. The bigger the circle, the bigger the value.

Buffer A neutral paragraph at the beginning of a negative message that engages the reader without stating the reason for the message. It should never contain negative words.

Burnout A situation in which you become irritated or unproductive, can no longer think clearly, or effectively verbalize your thoughts on the job.

C

Café seating Seating in which the audience sits at small tables and works in groups.

Chain of command An organization structure that determines the communication channels for sending and receiving messages from supervisors and those reporting to you.

Chronological résumé A résumé outlining a job seeker's work experience and education in chronological order.

Claims Demands for something customers feel are due them.

Classroom seating Seating in which the audience sits in chairs or desks facing forward.

Clause A related group of words containing a subject and a verb.

Close-mindedness The characteristic of having absolutely no interest in learning.

Closing An element at the end of a message that tells your reader what you will do or what the reader should do.

Collaborative writing software Software that allows multiple people to work on the same document together.

Color contrast The contrast between the background color and the foreground text.

Comma splice When a comma joins, or splices, two independent clauses in a sentence without a conjunction.

Communicating down Communicating with your subordinates, including coworkers who may have less experience than you.

Communicating sideways Communicating with your peers and in team settings.

Communicating up Communicating with your superiors.

Complex sentence A sentence consisting of a major idea in the independent main clause and one or more minor ideas in one or more dependent clauses.

Compound sentence A sentence consisting of two main clauses connected by a conjunction such as *or, and,* or *but.*

Conference call Simultaneous phone conversation between all team members.

Conference table seating Seating in which the audience sits around a large table with the presenter at the head.

Conjunction A word such as *or, and, but, because, although,* or *whereas* that connects one clause to another clause.

Contact header The section of a résumé providing a job seeker's contact information.

Copyright violation A legal offense that occurs when someone wrongly republishes material owned by another person or organization.

Cover letter A letter or message that accompanies other material to explain what it consists of and who sent it.

Credibility Refers to how your audience perceives you—whether or not they find you believable and trustworthy.

Credit score A numeric rating assessing the risk of extending credit to an individual.

Culture Includes all the socially transmitted behavior patterns of a particular society, such as language, religion, eating, greeting, business, and public behavior, treatment of people based on age and gender, perception of time, and acknowledgement of personal space.

D

Daily log (planner) A log that keeps track of what you work on each day and how much time is spent on each item.

Dangling participle An action word or phrase that appears to be performed by the subject but actually has nothing to do with the subject.

Deduction A reasoning process that begins with a general idea and then moves toward a specific conclusion.

Defamation A legal term for any false statement that harms an individual's reputation.

Default settings The settings that are automatically in place when you open a new document on your computer.

Demonstration The act of physically showing or explaining a concept.

Dependent clause The minor idea of a complex sentence. It cannot stand on its own and is not a complete sentence.

Detractors Team members who do not support a group's leader and can be derisive or coercive.

Direct approach An approach that presents the main point of the message at the beginning so readers understand its purpose as quickly as possible.

Direct paragraph A paragraph that begins with the main sentence, followed by supporting sentences.

Direct sales messages Letters or e-mails used to sell goods and services directly to a large number of customers without the help of a salesperson.

Diversity (both visible differences and nonvisible) Things about people that differ, such as their races, genders, skill levels, professional backgrounds, differing work habits, and cultural values.

Dovetailing A sentence that serves as a bridge between one paragraph and the next by repeating words.

Dry-erase whiteboards Smooth, white porcelain-on-steel boards that replace blackboards. You write or draw on them with colorful dry-erase markers.

E

e-portfolio An electronic portfolio stored on a thumb drive or Web site.

e-zines Electronic magazines delivered by e-mail to subscribers.

Education and training The section of a résumé presenting an applicant's academic and professional education.

Educational presentation A presentation that teaches.

Elevator pitch A 30-second presentation given by a job seeker to outline his or her career goals and strengths as a candidate.

Emotional intelligence The ability to monitor and control your emotions, thoughts, and feelings, while remaining sensitive to and aware of others' feelings.

Emotional quotient (EQ) The measurement of one's emotional intelligence; much like the intelligence quotient (IQ) is a measurement of one's intellectual intelligence.

Endnotes Source documentation that appears together at the end of a document.

Ethnocentrism The belief that your own culture is superior to all others and is the standard by which all other cultures should be measured.

Euphemism A mild or vague expression that is substituted for a potentially negative or offensive one.

Executive summary A one- to two-page "mini-report" summarizing a longer research report for high-level managers.

External parties Anyone who works outside of your company (for example, vendors or customers).

External requests Requests made of people and firms outside your organization.

F

Facilitated discussion A presentation in which the audience members actively participate more than 60 percent of the time, while you act as a coach to keep them on track.

Fair use A legal guideline that allows people and organizations to have a right to use a limited amount of copyrighted material without seeking permission from the material's owner.

Feasibility report A report that explores the possible financial and logistical ramifications of decisions a manager, department, or company is considering prior to the decision.

Feedback sandwich A technique for providing feedback in which you first say something positive, then provide negative feedback, and end with another positive statement.

Filler words Words that have little or no meaning but merely fill gaps in conversation.

Flat chain of command An organization structure that gives staff members easier access to their superiors because there are fewer levels of hierarchy above them.

Flipchart A large, portable pad of paper placed on an easel. You can write or draw on the paper, and also tear off the paper pages and attach them to the wall, as necessary.

Flowcharts Line drawings or diagrams that show the flow of information or the steps in a procedure or process.

Font A typeface.

Footnotes Source documentation that appears at the bottom of the page on which the quote or cited information appears.

Formal research Defined ways to gather information for longer, more complex writing projects. See *qualitative* and *quantitative research*.

Four-step communication model Four steps involved in communicating with others: (1) the messenger formulates the idea to be communicated; (2) the messenger delivers the message through a channel; (3) the recipient receives and interprets the message; (4) the recipient provides the sender with feedback.

Free-write A method of writing whereby you write whatever comes to your mind without mentally censoring your ideas

Freelancer A person who is not an employee of a company but works on a contract basis to accomplish projects.

Full-justified Text that is flush against both the right and left margins.

Functional résumé A résumé categorizing a job seeker's work experience in skill categories rather than by date.

G

Gatekeeper Someone who controls or monitors access to someone else—usually an administrative staff member who screens phone calls and e-mails.

Generation A particular age group, usually consisting of people born within the same 25-year time period.

Goodwill The value a company creates for itself by developing positive business relationships, demonstrating loyalty to its customers, employees, and community, and committing to conscientious business practices.

Grid A temporary table with vertical and horizontal lines that help a person line up text and illustrations on a page.

Group interviews An interview with multiple interviewers at one time.

Groupthink The phenomenon where members of a group begin to tacitly agree with one another's ideas to avoid conflict—even when they might silently object to those ideas. Everyone appears to think alike.

Groupware Software that allows users to hold meetings and collaborate over the Web. As they work, they can see one another's screens and collaboratively use their software applications.

Guided discussion A presentation in which you speak 50 percent of the time and the audience actively participates 50 percent of the time. Often used for small groups.

H

Headings Phrases that identify major sections in a document and act like newspaper headlines.

Hidden job market A saying that refers to the 80 percent of jobs that are not available to the general public, have not been advertised, or made public yet.

Hiring freeze A situation in which an organization ceases its recruiting efforts until the economic or corporate climate becomes more favorable.

Homonyms Two words that sound alike but have completely different meanings and spellings.

Hook An interesting phrase or sentence that begins a paragraph and gets the reader "hooked" into reading the rest.

Horizontal bar chart A chart with horizontal bars that are proportional to the data being displayed.

Hybrid résumé A résumé that contains elements of both functional and chronological résumés.

Hyperlinks Clickable links on a slide that take the viewer to another Web page or Web site.

I

Idiom Expressions that mean something other than the actual words being used.

Ignorance The failure to understand a culture due to lack of experience with the culture or lack of education about it.

Illegal questions Questions about a candidate's race, color, sex, religion, national origin, birthplace, age, disability, and marital or family status that are against the law to ask.

Independent clause The major idea of a simple or complex sentence; it can stand on its own as a complete sentence. Compound sentences have two or more independent clauses.

Independent recruiters Professionals who contract with corporations to fill permanent positions.

Indirect approach An approach that waits to mention the main purpose until the body of the message, and uses the introduction to "build up" to the main point.

Indirect approach An approach to delivering bad news that reduces the impact of the negative news by providing explanations first.

Indirect paragraph A paragraph that begins with supporting sentences and ends with the main sentence.

Induction A process of reasoning that begins with specific details to build toward a general conclusion.

Informal research Informal ways to gather information, such as asking questions, referring to company files, and talking with colleagues, for smaller or daily writing tasks.

Informational interview An interview where a job seeker interviews someone to learn about that person's position, company, or industry.

Informative presentation A presentation that explains new policies, procedures, or presents the status of a project to others.

Inside address Consists of the recipient's name, title, and address.

Instant messages (IM) Messages that are electronically distributed directly to a recipient computer in real time.

Interactive presentation A presentation in which you speak approximately 70 percent of the time, and the audience participates 30 percent of the time. Often used for groups of fewer than 25 people.

Interest questions Interview questions that gauge a candidate's interest in a company, industry, and position.

Internal requests Requests made within an organization.

Internships Nominally paid or unpaid positions that give students and job candidates an opportunity to gain experience in their fields.

Interpersonal communication Communication you have with others to exchange ideas. This communication includes words, gestures, and tone.

Intrapersonal communication Communication you have with yourself, such as internal thoughts and conversations. The way you think about and talk to yourself affects how you think about and talk to others.

Introduction Information at the beginning of a message that informs readers about its purpose of the document.

Italics Characters set in rightward-leaning type.

J

Jargon Language that is particular to a culture, profession, or group. Jargon often consists of acronyms.

Job fair A forum made up of several representatives from various companies, gathering to meet and recruit prospective employees.

Justification The vertical alignment of the text.

K

Keirsey Sorter personality types Four common types of personalities that exhibit certain strengths and weaknesses. The types are giver, thinker, adventurer, and organizer.

Key words Specific words pertaining to an employment position in a résumé that can be read by an applicant screening program.

Kinesthetic learners People who need to do something physically in order to learn.

L

Leader An individual (or, rarely, a set of individuals) who significantly affects the thoughts, feelings, and/or behaviors of a significant number of individuals.

Learning styles The different ways by which people learn.

Left-aligned (left-justified) Text that is flush against the left margin.

Letter of decline A letter or note written by a candidate declining an offer of employment.

Letterhead The heading at the top of a piece of stationery that contains the sender's name and contact information.

Libel A legal offense that occurs when purposeful false and defamatory communication appears in written form including in newspapers, magazines, books, on television, and the Internet.

Line chart A chart that presents information as a series of connected line segments. Often used to demonstrate trends.

Listening for meaning You listen on a deeper level to process words and extract meaning from the message. This involves asking questions to confirm that you are correctly interpreting the message. This is mid-level listening, requiring more effort on your part.

Listening A process of actively gathering information through hearing and reading nonverbal cues.

M

Manipulation The process of influencing people in unfair or devious ways.

Margins The white space at the top, bottom, and sides of a page.

Memory stick A removable flash memory card.

Metaphor A figure of speech comparing two unlike things that have something in common.

Microblog A short blog posting of small amounts of text, images, and videos sent to people in a restricted group.

Mind map An idea-generating device whereby you write a main idea in a circle. As new ideas are triggered from this idea, you draw offshoots to record them.

Mission statement A statement that usually consists of several sentences summarizing the purpose and goals of a company, while highlighting its overarching philosophies and values.

Modified block style A letter style in which date and signature are aligned to begin at the center of the page.

Modulation The pitch of your voice.

Monologue A presentation in which you speak virtually without interruption, and the audience waits until the end of the presentation to ask questions. Often used for large audiences.

N

Negative language Words that convey unhappy and unpleasant thoughts, or predispose your reader to disagree with, or react poorly to your message.

Negative message Any type of news construed as bad news because it's not what your audience wants to hear. It isn't necessarily terrible news; it can simply be a disappointing answer or a denied request.

Networking cover letter A cover letter is sent by professionals to introduce themselves to a potential contact and proposing a meeting.

Networking The practice of introducing yourself and establishing multiple personal and professional relationships.

New project proposal A formal proposal for a new product, process, service, or job position a person or a team puts in writing for other people's consideration.

Nonnative English speaker A person in or from another country learning English as a second language.

Nonrestrictive clauses A clause that adds information, but is not essential to meaning.

O

Object A person, place, or thing that receives the action of the verb.

Objections Negative reactions to a message.

Offer letter A letter or e-mail sent by an employer to a candidate outlining a job's salary, benefits, and start date as an offer of employment.

On-campus interview An interview where a corporate representative visits a college campus to recruit employees.

One-on-one interviews Interviews involving just the candidate and an interviewer.

Online chat A form of instant messaging and e-mails for quick, everyday written correspondence.

Online job banks Internet sites where companies post positions, accept résumés from candidates, and search for candidates.

Organizational chart A series of connected rectangles that illustrates how a company or a Web site is organized.

Outline A guide that lists the topics you plan to write in the order you plan to write them.

Overhead projector A device upon which you place a transparency to project an image or text onto a screen.

Overselling Promising more than you can deliver.

P

PAL approach Stands for "purpose," "agenda," and "length," which are three important pieces of information you should tell your audience after opening your presentation.

Parallel construction Words or phrases using the same grammatical form to establish coherence, particularly in lists.

Parental tone Scolds or tells people what to do.

Parking lot A portion of a flipchart used to "park" the audience's questions or objections that cannot be addressed at the moment.

Passive voice A sentence in which the subject receives the action of the verb.

PDF An acronym for Portable Document Format. A PDF is essentially a photo of the original document that retains all special fonts and formatting.

Peer A person who works at the same level in your firm's hierarchy as you do.

Perceptive listening You are fully present and actively listening for meaning by looking for nonverbal cues, interpreting body language, and considering the timing, tone, and context of the message. This is the deepest level of listening, requiring the most effort on your part.

Permanent placement agencies Agencies that match candidates to permanent positions with organizations.

Personal space The space immediately surrounding a person's body; the size of someone's personal space influences how he or she interacts with others.

Persuasive message A message that persuades readers to change their beliefs or actions.

Persuasive presentation A presentation intended to convince the audience to do something.

Phone interview An interview conducted over the phone, generally as an initial or screening interview.

Pie chart A chart that presents information as slices of a circular "pie" to show percentages of a whole.

Pivoting paragraph A paragraph that starts with a sentence that offers a contrasting or negative idea before delivering the main idea.

Plain-text résumé A résumé saved in ASCII format as a .txt file. It has no special formatting, fonts, or layout.

Podcast Audio presentations distributed over the Internet for playback on mobile devices or personal computers.

Point A unit of measure for font sizes. A point is about 1/72 of an inch.

Portfolio A collection of relevant work samples that support statements made in a job seeker's résumé and cover letter.

Positive, everyday messages Messages sent on a daily basis. They deliver either good news or neutral news.

Press release An announcement about your company to the media. The announcement resembles a news article. The information in the press release might include details about your firm's new CEO, product, location, or major initiative it is undertaking.

Primary sources Information you gather firsthand.

Probing questions Questions candidates ask interviewers that require elaboration as opposed to simple explanation.

Professional experience The section of a résumé highlighting specific professional accomplishments for each position.

Professional objective The section of a résumé providing a succinct statement of the job seeker's goals.

Proofreading A detailed read-through of a document for the purpose of finding typos, formatting, grammar, punctuation, and spelling errors.

Proposal A document that proposes a particular course of action be taken.

Prospecting cover letter A letter sent by a job seeker when prospecting for an unadvertised position. This letter proposes the job seeker as a candidate for employment.

Purpose Involves knowing why you are communicating and what you want the communication to achieve.

Q

Qualitative example An example that states what you did.

Qualitative research Informal, firsthand surveys of small groups of people.

Quantitative example An example that states what you did and measures how well you did it.

Quantitative research Formal surveys of large groups of individuals, the results of which are statistically calculated.

Quarterly report A report that helps track a company's financial performance each quarter.

R

Ragged Text that is not vertically aligned and has an uneven edge.

Reference initials Initials that indicate both the writer and typist who prepared the message. They should appear one blank line down from the writer's printed name and title.

Rejection letter A letter sent by a corporate representative informing a candidate of his or her rejection for a position.

Religion A specific, fundamental set of beliefs and practices generally agreed upon by a number of persons or sects.

Reports Documents that discuss past happenings.

Request for proposal (RFP) A document an organization sends out inviting vendors to submit bids to provide the organization with a good or service.

Requests for favors or actions Messages asking people to make decisions or take some action.

Research report (investigative report) A report that researches a particular problem or topic.

Resignation letter A letter written by an employee to inform his employer that he is resigning from a position.

Restrictive clauses A clause that deliberately limits the scope of the noun and is essential to meaning.

Return address The sender's typed address on a letter. It appears below the letter's date and above the recipient's address.

Rhetorical questions Questions asked only for effect, not to elicit answers.

Right-aligned (right-justified) Text that is flush against the right margin.

RSS An acronym that stands for *really simple syndication.* An RSS feed allows subscribers to electronically receive updated information from specific Web sites without having to check their e-mail inboxes.

Run-on sentence A fused sentence that results when two independent clauses are fused together without punctuation or a conjunction.

S

Sales report A report that compares actual sales with projected sales. Sales reports are usually in spreadsheet format and broken down by product or product category. The numbers are typically shown by quarter.

Salutation The greeting that begins a letter.

Sans-serif A typeface style that does not have a serif (a vertical or horizontal mark, sometimes called a "tail") at the end of the stroke.

Scannable résumés Résumés that are easily read by computers due to little formatting and font styling.

Secondary sources Information that was already gathered by others and is already published or accessible. It might include information in databases, libraries, trade books, or other reference material.

Self-awareness The ability to understand how you process information, read the signals other people are sending, and express yourself as perceived by others.

Sentence fragment A grammatically incomplete sentence lacking either a subject, a verb, or both.

Serif A typeface style that has a small feature called a serif (a vertical or horizontal mark, sometimes called a "tail") at the end of the stroke.

Shadowing The process whereby someone observes an individual at work for the purpose of understanding the roles and responsibilities associated with the individual's position.

Shock tactic A message that causes the audience to react on an emotional level.

Shortest processing time (SPT) method A method of completing tasks whereby you do the task that is fastest to complete first.

Signature block A set of information containing the name, title, and contact information of a message's sender.

Similes A comparison of two different concepts using the words *like* and *as*.

Simple sentence A sentence consisting of a subject (person, place, thing, or idea) and a verb (action).

Situational question Interview questions that ask candidates to provide solutions to hypothetical challenges.

Slander A legal offense that occurs when a person or entity is overheard knowingly or recklessly speaking false statements that damage the reputation of another person or entity.

Slide share A Web site where people can post slide presentations and Webinars for viewing.

Social networking The act of using a Web site or a network of Web sites that allows people with common interests to communicate with one another.

Social networking site A Web site that allows people to connect with one another online for personal or professional reasons.

Social setting interviews An interview that takes place in a social setting to gauge a candidate's social skills.

Storyboarding A method of visually telling a story, panel by panel, in sequence, using notes and visuals (similar to frames in a comic book).

Stress interview An interview under stressful conditions created by the interviewer for the purpose of testing a candidate's responses under pressure.

Stuffy tone A tone of voice that tries to make you or your message sound more important. The tone is usually overly formal.

Styles Formatting applications in word processing applications that specify fonts, sizes, justification, and boldface.

Subheadings Phrases that indicate subsections in a document.

Subject A person, place, or thing that performs the action of a sentence.

Subordinate A person who works at a lower level in your firm's hierarchy than you do.

Summary of qualifications The section of a résumé highlighting a job seeker's most relevant qualities as they pertain to the position applied.

Superior A person who works at a higher level in your firm's hierarchy than you do.

Supporters Team members who support the leader and show their commitment by meeting deadlines, coming up with new and original ideas, and creating a culture and an environment that is positive and affirms the leader's goals and vision.

Surface listening You appear to be listening, but are probably thinking about other things or planning your response. This is superficial listening, requiring very little effort on your part.

T

Table A graphic that presents information in rows and columns for easy side-by-side comparisons of data.

Talent acquisition The process of recruiting and retaining talented employees.

Team presentation A presentation made by two or more people.

Templates Special documents with a predefined layout, sample text, and built-in styles.

Temporary placement The process of matching candidates to positions for predetermined amounts of time.

Text messages Short text messages that are sent by phone to a recipient in real time.

Thumb drive A portable memory storage device.

To-do list A prioritized list of items to complete each day.

Tone The attitude conveyed by the writer, either consciously or unconsciously. The best messages are both businesslike *and* friendly. Typical tones include conversational, informal, and formal.

Toxic team members Team members that behave poorly and negatively impact the performance of the team. Toxic members include Lone Ranger, Know-it-All, Passive Aggressive, Intimidated, Gossip, Taker, Slacker, Seat Filler.

Transferable skills Skills gained in one position that relate to those necessary for another position.

Transition A word, phrase, or sentence that serves as a bridge between the previous idea and the next idea.

U

U-shaped seating Seating in which the audience sits in a semi-circle around the presenter.

Underlining A typeface often used to highlight Internet links in electronic documents. It is rarely used in print documents.

V

Verb The action of a sentence.

Vertical bar chart A chart with vertical bars that are proportional to the data being displayed.

Vertical chain of command An organization structure with numerous levels of hierarchy, which can make it harder for staff members, managers, and executives to access and communicate with one another.

Video presentations A presentation made to a live audience, recorded, and posted on the Web.

Video résumé A short video that accompanies a physical résumé and is used to demonstrate an applicant's interest and passion for a particular type of work.

Videoconference interview A remote interview telecast through computers.

Videoconferencing Technology that allows team members to see and hear one another, such as when they hold a conference call.

Virtual team A team that is not physically in the same location and relies on technology to communicate.

Visual communication (visual rhetoric) Using images to persuade people.

Visual presenter A device that projects 2-D and 3-D images onto a large LCD screen.

Voice over Internet protocol (VoIP) Technology that transfers audio signals to digital data and transmits the data over the Internet.

W

Web conferencing The process of conducting live, real-time meetings where each member uses his or her computer to connect through the Internet. Attendees see and hear one another with Webcams, and typically use groupware to collaborate.

Webcasts On-demand or live presentations streamed over the Internet. Webcasts are typically formal presentations made to large, dispersed audiences.

Webinar A Web presentation in which viewers typically watch a slide presentation and listen to the presenter's voice.

Weekly status report A report that lets your manager know what you have been working on each week.

White space The part of the document that is blank and does not contain text, images, or graphics.

Wikis Web sites that allow workers to collaborate on documents and projects by directly editing them online.

Writer's block A state of mind in which you believe you cannot think of anything to write.

Y

"You" attitude A way of writing that makes the reader feel as if you are speaking directly to him or her, in terms that are meaningful to the reader. Your attitude shows that you have taken into account the reader's point of view. This typically involves using words like *you* and *your* more than *I, me, mine, we, us,* and *ours*.

References

CHAPTER 1

1. "Communication Skills Start Here," *MindTools.com*, accessed June 15, 2009, at www.mindtools.com/CommSkll/CommunicationIntro.htm.
2. James Bennett and Robert Olney, "Executives Priorities for Effective Communication in an Information Society," *Journal of Business Communication*, 23 no. 5 (1986): 13–22.
3. Paul M. Bauer and R. Bruce Hutton, "Guided by a Compass," *ICOSA* 2, no. 3 (2009), accessed at www.icosamag.com/media/Edocs/Issue_3_Daniels_College_of_Business.pdf.
4. Joseph Lieberman, "Offshore Outsourcing and America's Competitive Edge: Losing Out in the High Technology R & D and Services Sectors," *United States Senate*, May 11, 2004, accessed at http://lieberman.senate.gov/documents/whitepapers/Offshoring.pdf.
5. Alan S. Binder, "How Many US Jobs Might be Offshorable?" CEPS Working Paper, 142, March 2007.
6. Bureau of Labor Statistics, *Occupational Outlook Handbook, 2009–2011 Edition* (Washington DC: U.S. Bureau of Labor Statistics, 2010), accessed at www.bls.gov/oco/oco2003.htm.
7. "Graduate Jobs," *TheBigChoice.com*, accessed June 15, 2009, at www.thebigchoice.com/Careers/Graduate/Graduate_Job_Skills.html.
8. Dominic Donaldson, "Discover the Importance of Effective Communication in Business," *BestManagementArticles.com*, January 23, 2009, accessed at http://management-communication.bestmanagementarticles.com/a-31317-discover-the-importance-of-effective-communication-in-business.aspx.
9. Accenture Communications and High Tech Solutions, "Big Trouble with 'No Trouble Found' Returns: Confronting the High Cost of Customer Returns," *Accenture*, 2008, accessed at www.accenture.com/NR/Rdonlyres/8119AEE6-0442-4EOD-94AA-E5A2163D07DB/0/22701_ReturnsRepairsRvn_v04lr.pdf.
10. Robert Ulmer, Timothy Sellnow, and Matthew Seeger, *Effective Crisis Communication: Moving from Crisis to Opportunity*, (Thousand Oaks, CA, Sage Publications, 2007)
11. Edward R. Murrow, "Edward R. Murrow Quotes," *BrainyQuote*, accessed June 17, 2009, at www.brainyquotes.com/quotes/.../e/edward_r_murrow.html.
12. Guy Harris, "Listen More, Speak Less – 5 Steps to Better Listening," 2006, *Inside Indiana Business*, accessed June 17, 2009, at www.insideindianabusiness.com/contributors.asp?id=718.
13. Michael Webb, "Eliminate Barriers to Effective Listening," *Agile Advice*, April 24, 2006, accessed at www.sklatch.net/thoughtlets/listen.html.

CHAPTER 2

1. Dean Foust, "The BusinessWeek 50," *BusinessWeek*, April 6, 2008, pp. 60–61.
2. "30 Top Team Building Quotes," *Leadership with You*, accessed June 23, 2009, at www.leadership-with-you.com/team-building-quotes.html.
3. Mitch McCrimmon, "Leadership & Teamwork: Why Great Leaders are Team Players," April 4, 2008, accessed at http://businessmanagement.suite101.com/article.cfm/leadership_and_teamwork.
4. Census Bureau, *Advance Monthly Retail Trade and Food Services Survey* (Washington DC: U.S. Census Bureau), accessed June 18, 2009, at www.census.gov.
5. Cary Cherniss and Daniel Goleman, *The Emotionally Intelligent Workplace* (San Francisco, CA: Jossey-Bass, 2001) pp. 13–26.
6. M. K. Smith, "Bruce W. Tuckman – Forming, Storming, Norming, and Performing in Groups," *The Encyclopedia of Informal Education*, accessed December 3, 2010 at www.infed.org/thinkers/tuckman.htm.
7. I. L. Janis, *Victims of Groupthink: A Psychological Study of Foreign Policy Decisions and Fiascos* (Boston: Houghton Mifflin Company, 1972).
8. Howard Gardner, "Howard Gardner's Definition of Leadership," *New Horizons for Learning Online Journal* (Fall 2003), accessed at http://www.newhorizons.org.html.
9. John Maxwell, *The 21 Irrefutable Laws of Leadership: Follow Them and People Will Follow You* (Nashville, TN: Thomas Nelson, 1998).
10. Henry Ford, "Henry Ford Quotes," *BrainyQuote*, accessed April 27, 2009, at www.brainy quote.com/quotes/henryford121997.html.

CHAPTER 3

1. "Measuring Green Jobs," *Occupational Outlook Handbook, 2009–2011 Edition* (Washington DC: U.S. Bureau of Labor Statistics, 2009), accessed at http://www.bls.gov/green/.
2. Connie Glaser, *Gender Talk Works* (New York: Windsor Hall Press, 2007).
3. Deborah Tannen, *You Just Don't Understand* (New York: Ballantine Books, 1991).
4. "Enthnocentrism," *The American Heritage® New Dictionary of Cultural Literacy*, 3rd ed. (Houghton Mifflin Company, 2005), accessed December 3, 2010 at http://dictionary.reference.com/browse/culture.
5. Laura Higgins Florand, "Stop Ethnocentrism—A Case for Armchair Multiculturalism," *Transitions Abroad* (September–October 2002), accessed at www.transitionsabroad.com/publications/magazine/0209/ethnocentrism.shtml.
6. Zeeya Merali, "Exploding the Myth of Cultural Stereotypes," *New Scientist*, October 6, 2006, accessed at www.newscientist.com/article/dn8111.
7. Jodi Weber, Center Director, ESL Language Center, Southern Oregon University, in discussion with the author, March 2009.
8. Thomas R. Dewar, "Thomas Dewar, 1st Baron Dewer." *Wikipedia.com*, accessed December 3, 2010 at http://en.wikipedia.org/wiki/Sir_Thomas_R._Dewar,_M.P.
9. Hal Amen, "12 Things You Don't Want to Get Caught Doing in Foreign Lands," *Traveler's Notebook*, December 2008. Retrieved from http://thetravelersnotebook.com/destination-guides/12things-you-dont-want-to-be-caught-doing-in-foreign-lands/#respond.
10. See Note 7.
11. Greg Hammill, "Mixing and Matching Four Generations of Employees," *FDU Magazine* (Winter–Spring 2005), Fairleigh Dickinson University, accessed at www.fdu.edu/newspubs/magazine/05ws/generations.htm.
12. See note 11.
13. See note 11.
14. See note 11.

CHAPTER 4

1. Jacke Swearingen, "How Social Networking Can Build Business." *Portfolio.com*, February 1, 2009, accessed at www.portfolio.com/resources/insight-center/2009/02/01/Social-Networking-and-Business/.
2. Robert W. Fairlee, "Kauffman Index of Entrepreneurial Activity 1996-2007," *Kauffman Foundation*, April 24, 2008, accessed at http://sites.kauffman.org/kauffmanindex/.
3. Leslie Kwoh, "Business Owners Lead in Workplace Happiness," *NJ.com*, October 10, 2009, accessed at www.nj.com/business/index.ssf/2009/09/business_owners_lead_in_workpl.html.

4. "Frequently Asked Questions About Small Business," *Small Business Administration,* September 2009, accessed at www.sba.gov/advo/stats/sbfaq.txt.
5. Miranda Marquit, "Surprising Entrepreneur Facts," *EveryJoe,* September, 22, 2009, accessed at http://everyjoe.com/work/surprising-entrepreneur-facts/?utm_source=everyjoe&utm_medium=web&utm_campaign=b5hubs_migration.
6. "Writing: A Ticket to Work . . . or a Ticket Out, a Survey of Business Leaders," College Entrance Examination Board, September 3, 2004, accessed at www.collegeboard.com/prod_downloads/writingcom/writing-ticket-to-work.pdf.
7. J. R. Hayes and L. S. Flower, "Writing Research and the Writer," *American Psychologist,* 41 (1980): 1106–1113.
8. Amanda Avallone, Andrew Gorman, et al., "Validity on the Internet," *The Center for Lifelong Learning and Design,* October 10, 2009, accessed at http://l3d.cs.colorado.edu/∼agorman/educ6804/validity/overview.htm.
9. U.S. Copyright Office, *Fair Use* (Washington, DC: U.S. Copyright Office), accessed Marh 27, 2009, at www.copyright.gov/fls/fl102.html.
10. "Splenda Settles Lawsuit Over 'Sugar' Claim," *MSNBC,* May 11, 2007, accessed at www.msnbc.msn.com/id/18618557.
11. See note 8.

CHAPTER 5

1. Arelene Dohm and Lynn Shniper, "Bureau of Labor Statistics: Employment Outlook: 2006-16," *Monthly Labor Review* (November 2007): 116.
2. "Writing: A Ticket to Work . . . Or a Ticket Out," *Report of The National Commission on Writing* (New York: College Board, September 2004), accessed at www.writingcommission.org/prod_downloads/writingcom/writing-ticket-to-work.pdf.
3. *Keys to Home Ownership* (Silver Springs, MD: National Foundation for Credit Counseling, 2001).
4. Ellen Roddick, *Writing That Means Business: How to Get Your Message across Simply and Effectively* (New York: Collier Books, 1986) p. 78.
5. Richard Nordquist, "Writers on Rewriting," *About.com,* accessed April 26, 2009, at http://uwf.edu/writelab/advice/documents/wa-goodgram1.
6. See note 2.

CHAPTER 6

1. "Sans-serif," *Wikipedia,* accessed May 11, 2009, at http://en.wikipedia.org/wiki/Sans-serif.
2. Gerry McGovern, "Writing Killer Web Headings and Links," *New Thinking,* April 13, 2009, accessed at www.gerrymcgovern.com/nt/2009/nt-2009-04-13-web-headings-links.htm.
3. Catherine S. Hibbard, "Improving the Appearance of your Technical Document," *Cypress Media Group,* accessed May 11, 2009, at www.cypressmedia.net/pages/article21.htm.
4. Eric Schaffer, "Ask Eric," *Human Factors International,* December 9, 2002, accessed at www.humanfactors.com/downloads/askericdesign.asp.
5. Jakob Nielson, "Right-Justified Navigation Menus Impede Scanability," *Jakob Nielson's Alertbox,* April 28, 2008, accessed at www.useit.com/alertbox/navigation-menu-alignment.html.
6. *Occupational Information Employment and Training Administration, Salary information: O Net Online* (Washington, DC: U.S. Department of Labor), accessed May 26, 2009, at www.online.onetcenter.org/.

CHAPTER 7

1. Eve Tahmincioglu, "Health Care Industry Offers Rich Opportunities." *MSNBC,* March 18, 2007, accessed at www.msnbc.msn.com/id/176345961.
2. Brian Gardiner, "Apple Kills Think Secret: Publisher Nick Ciarelli Talks," *Wired,* December 20, 2007, accessed at http://www.wired.com/epicenter/2007/12/apple-and-think/
3. Laura Aronsson, and Bianca Male, "Is Your Target Audience on Twitter, Facebook, Or LinkedIn?" *Business Insider War Room,* February 19, 2010, accessed at www.businessinsider.com/is-your-target-audience-on-twitter-facebook-or-linkedin-2010-2.
4. See note 3.
5. Matt Richtel, "Read This and Cost Your Company Dough," *The New York Times,* December 22, 2008, accessed at http://bits.blogs nytimes.com/2008/12/22/read-this-and-cost-your-company-dough/.

CHAPTER 8

1. The Associated Press, "RadioShack Layoff Notices are Sent by E-Mail," *The New York Times,* August 31, 2006, accessed at www.nytimes.com/2006/08/31/business/31radio.html.
2. Curtis Sittenfeld, "Good Ways to Deliver Bad News," *Fast Company,* December 19, 2007, accessed at www.fastcompany.com/magazine/23/buckman.html.
3. Stephen A. Glickman, "Wrongful Termination Claims," *FindLaw,* July 3, 2009, accessed at http://employment.findlaw.com/employment/employment-employee-job-loss/employment-employee-wrongful-termination.html.

CHAPTER 9

1. Beth Hale, "How Texting as You Drive Increases Your Risk of Crashing by Up to 23 Times," *Mail Online,* July 28, 2009, accessed at www.dailymail.co.uk/motoring/article-1202771/How-texting-drive-increases-risk-crashing-23-times.html.
2. John Boe, "Small Business Selling Skills: Principles of Persuasion," *Small Business Success,* accessed at December 3, 2010 at www.smallbusinesssuccess.biz/articles_week/principles_persuasion.htm.
3. Jake Swearingen, "Social Networking for Business," *BNet, CBS Interactive Business Network,* accessed December 3, 2010 at www.bnet.com/2403-13070_23-219914.html.
4. "Pretty Names for Unpleasant Realities of Life," *Entertaining Euphemisms,* accessed December 3, 2010 at www.squidoo.com/entertaining_euphemisms.
5. Walter Neary, "Personal Decisions Exercise the Emotional Part of the Brain," *University of Washington News,* November 26, 2001, accessed at http://uwnews.org/article.asp?articleID=2728.
6. Dahlia Lithwick, "Our Beauty Bias Is Unfair," *Newsweek,* June 14, 2010, p. 20.
7. "Cruise Slams Shields' Drug Use," *Hollywood.com,* May 25, 2005, accessed at www.hollywood.com/news/Tom_Cruise_Slams_Brooke_Shields_Drug_Use/2440860.

CHAPTER 10

1. Rachel McAlpine, "Crash Course in Corporate Communications." *CC Press,* accessed at www.ccpress.info/cccc.htm.
2. David Weliver, "Checklists for a Successful Life," *Money Under 30,* March 29, 2007, accessed at www.moneyunder30.com/checklists-for-a-successful-life.
3. U.S. Department of Housing and Urban Development, "Request for Proposals R-PHI-01002," July 18, 2008, accessed at www.hud.gov/offices/cpo/contract/phi01002.pdf.
4. Federal Deposit Insurance Corporation, *State Banking Performance Summary: FDIC-Insured Institutions, Commercial Banks–National–September 30,* (Washington, DC: FDIC Office of Inspector General, 2009), accessed at www2.fdic.gov.
5. "The AIG Financial Crisis: A Summary," *AIG,* accessed December 3, 2010 at http://www.aig.com/Our-Commitment_3105_136429.html.

CHAPTER 11

1. Rick Robinson, vice president of marketing at Vision Research, in discussion with the author, (November 15, 2009).
2. Bradley Vander Zanden, "Preparing an Effective Presentation." *Department of Computer Science* (Knoxville, TN: The University of

Tennessee), March 12, 2009, accessed at www.cs.utk.edu/∼bvz/presentation.html.
3. Nancy Duarte, *Slide:ology* (Sebastopol, CA: O'Reilly Group, 2008).
4. See note 3.
5. "Simile," *About.com,* July 4, 2009, accessed at http://grammar.about.com/od/rs/g/simileterm.htm.
6. Delia Lloyd, "Parents, Rejoice: Peanut Allergy Cure Within Sight, British Study Finds," *PoliticsDaily.com,* February 22, 2010, accessed at www.politicsdaily.com/2010/02/22/parents-rejoice-peanut-allergy-cure-within-sight-british-stud/.

CHAPTER 12

1. U.S. Department of Labor, *Occupational Outlook Handbook, 2009* (Washington, DC: U. S. Department of Labor, 1999), p. 3.
2. Garr Reynolds, "Takeaways & Quotes from Dr. John Medina's Brain Rules: What All Presenters Need to Know," *Presentation Zen,* accessed December 3, 2010 at www.presentationzen.com/presentationzen/2008/05/brain-rules-for.html.
3. Bouwman, Dave, "Usability in the GeoWeb," *Slideshare,* accessed December 3, 2010 at www.slideshare.net/dbouwman/usability-in-the-geoweb-presentation.

CHAPTER 13

1. Carol Carter, *Majoring in the Rest of Your Life* (Denver, CO: LifeBound, 2005).
2. Susan Britton Whitcomb, *Job Search Magic* (St. Paul, MN: Jist Works, 2006).
3. Dawn Rosenberg McKay, *Everything-Get-A-Job Book* (Cincinnati, OH: Adams Media, 2000).
4. See note 1.
5. Tatiana Morales, "Understanding Your Credit Score," *CBS News,* April 4, 2003, accessed at www.cbsnews.com/stories/2003/04/29/earlyshow/contributors/raymartin/main551521.shtml.
6. Kim Hart, "Teaching the Facebook Generation the Ways of Washington," *The Washington Post,* March 30, 2009, accessed at www.washingtonpost.com/wpdyn/content/article/2009/03/29/AR2009032901877.html.
7. Laura M. Hoson, "On the Job, But on the Lookout for Work," *The New York Times,* April 8, 2009, accessed at www.nytimes.com/2009/04/09/fashion/09networking.html?_r=1&emc=eta1.
8. Kelly Whitt, "The Dos and Don'ts of Social Networking Online, *Suite101,* March 10, 2009, accessed at http://social-networking-tagging.suite101.com/article.cfm/facebook_etiquette_tips.
9. David Claus, "Should You Recruit on Social Networking Sites?" *HR World,* January 24, 2008, accessed at www.hrworld.com/features/Should-you-012408/.
10. See note 9.
11. Kimberly Schenk, "Great Options for Recruiters," *Articlesbase,* July 9, 2008, accessed at www.articlesbase.com/human-resources-articles/recruiter-career-great-options-for-recruiters-478022.html.

CHAPTER 14

1. Erika Welz Prafder, "Hiring Your First Employee," *Entrepreneur,* accessed at www.entrepreneur.com/humanresources/hiring/article83774.html.
2. Phyllis Korkii, "A Cover Letter Is Not Expendable, *The New York Times,* February 14, 2009, accessed at www.nytimes.com/2009/02/15/jobs/15career.html?_r=1&scp=1&sq=cover%20letter%20&st=cse.
3. Lisa Takeuchi Cullen, "It's a Wrap. You're Hired," *Times,* February 22, 2007, accessed at www.time.com/time/magazine/article/0,9171,1592860,00.html.
4. *Action Words: Resume and Cover Letter Writing* (Marquette, MI: Marquette University Career Services Center, 2005), accessed at www.marquette.edu/csc/students/documents/ResumeandCover-LetterWriting12_04_05.pdf.
5. Marci Alboher, "How to Pick the Ideal Reference," *The New York Times,* February 25, 2008, accessed at http://shiftingcareers.blogs.nytimes.com/2008/02/25/how-to-pick-the-ideal-reference/?scp=1&sq=How%20to%20pick%20the%20ideal%20reference&st=cse.
6. Floyd Norris, "Radio Shack Chief Resigns After Lying," *The New York Times,* February 21, 2006, accessed at www.nytimes.com/2006/02/21/business/21radio.html.

CHAPTER 15

1. Bureau of Labor Statistics, *Hotel and Other Accommodations* (Washington, DC: U. S. Bureau of Labor Statistics, 2009), accessed at www.bls.gov/oco/cg/cgs036.htm.
2. Ryan Stewart, "Zen and the Art of Mastering the Phone Interview," *WorkBloom.com,* accessed at http://workbloom.com/articles/interview.aspx.
3. Phyllis Korkki, "Lining Up Interviews Is Just the Beginning," *The New York Times,* March 29, 2009, p. 14.
4. Ronald L. Krannich, "38 Illegal, Sensitive and Stupid Interview Questions . . . and how to Respond," *The Wall Street Journal,* April 11, 2007, accessed at www.washingtonpost.com/wp-dyn/articles/A8963-2003Apr11.html.
5. U.S. Equal Employment Opportunity Commission, "Filing a Charge," EEOC.com, accessed May 27, 2009, at www.eeoc.gov/facts/howtofil.html.
6. Heather Joslyn, "Closing the Gap: Tips for Negotiating a Robust Starting Salary," *The Chronicle of Philanthropy,* March 20, 2003, accessed at http://philanthropy.com/article/Closing-the-Gap-Tips-for/50036/.

CHAPTER 16

1. Sam Keen, "Sam Keen Quotes," *Thinkexist.com,* accessed July 18, 2009, at http://thinkexist.com/search/searchquotation.asp?search=Burnout+is+nature%27s+way+of+telling+you.
2. Marshall Goldsmith, "Profile of a Social Entrepreneur," *Business Week,* December 24, 2008, accessed at www.businessweek.com/print/managing/content/dec2008/ca20081224_387821.htm.
3. Brett J. Blackledge and Ricardo Alonso-Zaldivar, "FDA: Plant Knew Peanuts Laced with Salmonella," *The Associated Press*, 2009, accessed at http://abcnews.go.com/print?id=6825713.
4. "World Wrestling Entertainment Settles Lawsuit with Parents Television Council; PTC Founder Brent Bozell Issues Apology," *Business Wire,* 2002, accessed at www.thefreelibrary.com/World+Wrestling+Entertainment+Settles+Lawsuit+With+Parents+Television...-a088554235.
5. Suzanne Goldenberg, "American Shoppers Misled by Greenwash, Congress Told," *Guardian.co.uk,* accessed at www.guardian.co.uk/world/2009/jun/21/green-environment-ecology-congress-us-supermarkets.
6. Lucy Miller, *Career Development Strategies* (Fort Collins, CO: Weston Distance Learning, 2008).

Photo Credits

CHAPTER 1

Pixland/Thinkstock; s26/Shutterstock; Meder Lorant/Shutterstock; Pixotico/Shutterstock; Stephan Coburn\Shutterstock; Medio-images/Photodisc/Thinkstock; Thinkstock/Nick White/Photodisc; Elena Elisseeva/Shutterstock; Stockbyte\Thinkstock; Stephen Coburn/Shutterstock; Andreser/Shutterstock.

CHAPTER 2

Goodshoot/Thinkstock; Pixland/Thinkstock; Yuri Arcurs/Shutterstock; Comstock/Thinkstock; Comstock/Getty Images/Jupiterimages/Thinkstock; Comstock/Getty Images/Jupiterimages/Thinkstock; Pixland/Thinkstock; DPAPhotos/Newscom; Moodboard\Alamy Images Royalty Free.

CHAPTER 3

Mario7\Shutterstock; Goodshoot/Getty Images/Juiterimages/Thinkstock; JinYoung Lee\Shutterstock; Lightspring\Shutterstock; Brand X Pictures/Getty Images/Jupiterimages/Thinkstock; jamaican\Shutterstock; Taipan Kid\Shutterstock; jamaican\Shutterstock; Taipan Kid\Shutterstock; 21thDesign\Shutterstock; jamaican\Shutterstock; Graphic design\Shutterstock; Yuri Arcurs\Shutterstock; Yuri Arcurs\Shutterstock; Stephen Coburn\Shutterstock.

CHAPTER 4

Piotr Marcinski\Shutterstock; Robert Kneschke\Shutterstock; Orange Line Media\Shutterstock; Yellowj\Shutterstock; Gunnar Pippel\Shutterstock; Stockbyte\Thinkstock; Susan Chiang\Shutterstock; Pixotico/Shutterstock; Meder Lorant/Shutterstock; deMatos\Shutterstock; s26/Shutterstock; Joanne Harris and Daniel Bubnich\Shutterstock; Christopher Robbins\Thinkstock; Dmitriy Shironosov\Shutterstock.

CHAPTER 5

Diego Cervo\Shutterstock; Dmitriy Shironosov\Shutterstock; Thinkstock; George Doyle\Thinkstock; John Teate\Shutterstock; Stockbyte\Thinkstock; Miroslav Hlavko \Shutterstock; Stephen Orsillo\Shutterstock; zimmylws\Shutterstock.

CHAPTER 6

Stephen Coburn\Shutterstock; Jennifer Stone\Shutterstock; RTImages\Shutterstock; Workmans Photos\Shutterstock; Anatoily Samara\Shutterstock; PHOTOCREO Michal Bednarek\Shutterstock; Refat\Shutterstock; Lagui\Shutterstock; PaulPaladin\Shutterstock; Shutterstock; Dmitriy Shironosov\Shutterstock.

CHAPTER 7

Olly\Shutterstock; EDHAR\Shutterstock; StockLile\Shutterstock; Yuri Arcurs\Shutterstock; Zhukov Oleg\Shutterstock; Rudy Umans\Shutterstock; mostafa fawzy\Shutterstock; Rob Marmion\Shutterstock; Hemera Technologies\Getty Images – Thinkstock; Andresr\Shutterstock.

CHAPTER 8

rSnapshotPhotos\Shutterstock; Rick Becker–Leckrone\Shutterstock; Mindy w.m. Shung\Shutterstock; Monkey Business Images\Shutterstock; Olaru Radiam-Alexandru\Shutterstock; Patrick Ryan\Thinkstock; Dean Mitchell\Shutterstock; Jupiterimages\Thinkstock.

CHAPTER 9

Jules Studio\Shutterstock; mjay\Shutterstock; Lim Yong Hian\Shutterstock; Yuri Arcurs\Shutterstock; Kuzma\Shutterstock; Benis Arapovic\Shutterstock; Comstock\Thinkstock; Alex Roz\Shutterstock.

CHAPTER 10

Goerge Doyle\Thinkstock; Nick White\Thinkstock; Picsfive\Shutterstock; Banana Stock\Thinkstock; Digital Vision\Thinkstock; More Similiar Images\Shutterstock; Pokomeda\Shutterstock; Yarygin\Shutterstock; Zentilia\Shutterstock; Nataliia Natykach\Shutterstock; Pokomeda\Shutterstock; Patrick Ryan\Shutterstock; Kaspri\Shutterstock; Digital Vision\Thinkstock; Goodshoot\Thinkstock; joingate\Shutterstock; Nataliia Natykach\Shutterstock.

CHAPTER 11

hfng\Shutterstock; Jacob Wackerhausen/iStockphoto ekler\Shutterstock; lightpoet\Shutterstock; Zenteilia\Shutterstock; MilaLiu\Shutterstock; More similiar images\Shutterstock; twentyfourweekd\Shutterstock; astudio\Shutterstock; Creatas images\Thinkstock; Hemra Technologies\Thinkstock; Andreas G. Karelias\Shutterstock; Sean Prior\Shutterstock; getty images\Thinkstock; Comstock/Jupiterimages/Getty Images/Thinkstock; Yuri_Arcurs\iStockphoto.com; Mark Aplet\Shutterstock.

CHAPTER 12

comstock\Thinkstock; James Steidl \Shutterstock; stockbyte\Thinkstock; getty images\Thinkstock; Thinkstock; Thinkstock; ss_serg\Shutterstock; Digital Vision\Thinkstock; Thinkstock/Goodshoot/Jupiterimages/Getty Images; iQoncept\Shutterstock; jallfree\iStockphoto.com.

CHAPTER 13

Phase4photography\Shutterstock; Andresr\Shutterstock; Andresr\Shutterstock; Lisa F. Young\Shutterstock; jupiterimages\Thinkstock; Thinkstock; stockbyte\Thinkstock; Michael Blann\Thinkstock; jovannig\Shutterstock; Comstock images/Thinkstock/Getty Images.

CHAPTER 14

Valua Vitaly\Shutterstock; Andresr\Shutterstock; Noel Hendrickson\Thinkstock; Benis Arapovic\Shutterstock; Monkey Business images\Shutterstock; Hemera Technologies/Thinkstock/Getty images; Jupiterimages/Thinkstock/Getty images; Jupiterimages/Thinkstock/Getty images; Arunas Gabalis\Shutterstock; Stephen Coburn\Shutterstock.

CHAPTER 15

bikeriderlondon\Shutterstock; Christopher Robbins/Thinkstock/Getty images; Anton Prado PHOTO\Shutterstock; stockbyte\Thinkstock; Yuri Arcurs\Shutterstock; Graca Victoria\Shutterstock; Creatas Images\Thinkstock; Digital Vision\Thinkstock; Thinkstock; SVLuma\Shutterstock; Comstock\Thinkstock; Konstantin Chagin\Shutterstock; Stephen Coburn\Shutterstock.

CHAPTER 16

Wallenrock\Shutterstock; Jupiterimages/Thinkstock/Getty images; Karl Weatherly\Thinkstock; Jason Stitt \Shutterstock; Stockbyte\Thinkstock; Edyta Pawlowska\Shutterstock; Kevin Britland\Shutterstock; Sean Prior\Shutterstock; SoleilC\Shutterstock; Tracy Whiteside\Shutterstock; Stephen Coburn\Shutterstock; Thinkstock/Creatas/Jupiterimages/Getty Images.

APPENDIX

ARENA Creative\Shutterstock.

Index

An e after page numbers refers to exhibits.
Book titles are in italics.

A

Abercrombie & Fitch, 257
Academic Coaching Co., 103
Acceptance letter, 453, 454e, 461
Accuracy, in grammar, 489–490
Acronyms, 117, 139
Action, in persuasive messages
  defined, 238
  examples of, 239e, 243e–244e, 245e, 246e, 248e
Active voice, 119, 139
Activities, for presentations, 342
Adams, Bob, 218
Adams, John Quincy, 28
Adapted, for audience, 81, 108
Adjectives, adverbs, 109, 116, 140
Adjourning, 37
Adobe Reader, 162
Adult-education instructor, 144
Adventurer type, 34–35
Adverbs, 140
Age, 60, 62, 116
Aging suits, 60
AIDA, 237–238, 239e, 261, 403
AIG, 291–292
Aleti, Michelle, 328
Alignment, of text, 155
Allen, Suzy Spang, 248
Aloha Guide, 439
Alumni centers, 372–373
Analogy, 253, 261
Angelica's Organic Coffee, 85
Annotated outline, 113–114, 139
Annual accomplishments reports, 272–273, 292
Annual reports, 278, 279, 280e, 292
Appearance, actions, 473e
Appendices, 282e
Apple Computers, 191, 238
Application cover letter, 401–402, 430
Application forms, 400, 430
Application packet, 399–400, 425, 430
Aquino, Carmen and Arturo, 111–112
Archiving, of messages, 189, 194
Arrogant tone, 240–241, 261
Assumptions, 65, 76
Attachments, to e-mail, 186
Attention, for persuasive messages, 237, 239e, 243e–244e, 246e
Attitude, and employment, 381
Audience
  adapting message to, 81–82
  for business presentation, 317–318
  engaging, 324
  interpretation by, 60–62
  knowing, 72
  types of, 329–332
Audience Response System, 363
Auditing report, 288e
Authoritarian model, 38
Authority, 256, 258
Avid4 Adventure, 452
Awards, honors, activities, in résumés, 418–419, 430

B

Background questions, in interview, 440–441, 442, 461
Back-up behavior, 468, 489
Back-wheel skills, 287
Bad news, in negative message
  defined, 209
  examples of, 210e–212e, 214e–216e, 219e–221e
Baker, William E., 482
Behavior, 63
Behavioral questions, in interview, 441, 461
Bennett, Jessica, 409
Berger, Lauren, 226
Berle, Milton, 366
Bias-free language, 116–117
Blinder, Alan S., 6
Block style, for letters, 178–179, 200
Blogging
  advantages, disadvantages of, 194
  as a business, 107–108
  defined, 200
  and job searching, 384
  purposes for, 189–191
  and research, 378
BMO Capital Markets, 271
Body
  of letter, 99, 108, 209, 275e, 405, 426
  of message, 181, 186
  of text, 150, 168
Body language, 68
Boilerplate, 249–250
Boldface, 148, 168
Bonobos, 395
Boundaries, establishing at work, 467–469, 485
Bouwman, Dave, 346, 354–355
Brainstorming, 94–95, 108, 319–320
Brunetti Language School, 167–168
Bubble charts, 349–350, 363
Buckman, Robert, 207
Buffer, for message
  defined, 209, 231
  examples of, 210e–212e, 214e–216e, 219e–221e
Bulleted list, 128, 154
Burg, Bob, 251
Burnout, 467–468, 489
Business, and public behavior, 63
Business cards, 382
Business climate, 6
Business messages
  and blogging, 107–108
  in business plans, 79–80
  and knowledge of company, 84–86
  legality, ethics of, 98
  medium for, 90–91, 99, 104
  objections to, 88–90, 91e, 99, 104, 108
  organizing for, 94–98, 104
  planning for, 80–82, 103
  purpose of, 86–87, 90e–91e, 98, 104
  research for, 95–98
  structuring, 98–101, 111–112
  target for, 86–89, 90e–91e, 99, 104
  templates for, 90e–91e
  timeframe for, 87–88, 90e–91e, 99, 104
  and writer's role, 83–84
  See also Negative messages; Persuasive messages; Positive, everyday messages; Writing, writing skills
Business presentations
  beginning of, 326
  bored audience for, 330, 332
  during, 327–328
  educational, 317, 332, 335
  end of, 328–329
  examples of, 315–316
  hostile audience for, 329, 332
  informative, 316–317, 332
  keys to successful, 331, 332
  making them "stick," 322–324
  persuasive, 316, 332, 336
  planning, 317–324, 332
  preparing for, 325–326, 332
  questioning audience for, 330–331, 332
  shy audience for, 329–330, 332
  See also Slideshows; Visual aids
Business Source Premier, 96

C

Café seating, 322, 335
Campus Advantage Inc., 112
On-campus interviews, 385, 396
Capitalization, 150, 201
Care2, 60
Career City, 218
Career exploration
  books for, 369–370
  examples of, 367–368, 387
  networking and research for, 371–379, 391
  pinpointing skills, 368–371, 391
  See also Interviews; Job Search
Career services centers, 370
CareerBuilder, 168
Carter, Carol, 368

Carter, Scott, 242
Case, of pronoun, 130
Cause and effect, 251
Centered text, 156
Chain of command, 83, 108
Chambers of Commerce, 383
Charts, types of, 348–350
Checklist, 268
Chronological organization, 322e
Chronological résumés, 407–410, 430
Chua, Sacha, 13
Cialdini, Robert, 256, 258
Claims, 211, 212, 231
Claremont McKenna College, 196
Classroom seating, 322, 335
Clauses, 121–122, 130–131, 140
Cleese, John, 234
Close-mindedness, 66, 76
Closing
  contents of, 99, 405
  defined, 108
  examples of, 275e, 406e
  style for, 181, 186
Coda Coffee Co., 89
Collaborative writing software, 43–44, 45, 55
Colons, 262
Color, for text, 148–149, 168
Columns, 153
Comma splice, 133, 140
Commas, 232, 364–365
Commitment, consistency, 256–257, 258
Communication
  in the 21st Century, 7
  advancing career with, 471–478, 485
  affecting success, failure, 7–8
  breakdowns in, 11–12
  clear, effective, 473–474
  as collaboration, 62
  with customers, 477–478
  downward, 475–476, 489
  elements of exchange for, 22
  energy, passion in, 13, 466–467, 485
  ethical, 478–480
  between generations, 70–72
  importance of skills for, 4–5, 10, 21, 147, 466, 485
  with international partners, 20, 21
  interpersonal, intrapersonal, 8–9, 25
  and legal violations, 480–482
  model of, 10–11, 25
  oral vs. written, 92–94, 104
  positive impact in, 18–19
  under pressure, 468
  professional vs. personal, 195–196, 197
  sideways, 476, 489
  Skype's influence on, 25
  upward, 474–475, 489
  See also Business messages; Intercultural communication
Communications officer, 144
Competition, global, 6
Complex sentence, 122, 140
Compliance report, 288e
Compound sentence, 121, 140
Concise sentences, 118–119
Conclusions, 282e
Conference call, 31, 55
Conference table seating, 322, 335
Conferencing, 55
  See also Online chat; Skype; Videoconferencing; Webcasts
Conflicts, in teams, 46–49
Confucius, 432
Conjunctions, 121, 140, 169
Consensus model, 38
Contact header, 413, 430
Contact information, 250
Conversational tone, 18
Copies, of letters, 183
Copyeditor, 144
Copyright infringement, 18, 97–98
Copyright violation, 481, 489
Corporate trainer, 144
Cover letter
  for application, 401–402, 425
  contents of, 135–136
  defined, 140, 430
  effective, 403–407, 425–426
  ineffective, 406e
  networking, 402, 404e, 405, 425
  prospecting, 402, 403e, 425
Credibility, 96–97, 239, 240e, 261
Credit score, 380, 395
Crisis management, 10
Critical thinking
  on business messages, 105
  for business presentation, 332–333
  on intercultural communication, 73–74
  and job interviewing, 458
  and job searching, 392
  for message design, proofreading, distribution, 165
  on negative messages, 228
  and passion for career, 486–487
  for persuasive messages, 258–259
  on positive, everyday messages, 197–198
  on report, proposal writing, 289–290
  for résumés, 427–428
  and slideshows, 360
  on strategic thinking, 23
  on teamwork, leadership, 53
  and writing skills, 137
Cruise, Tom, 260–261
Culture, 62, 68, 76
  See also Intercultural communication
Cummings, Rebecca, 439
Cypress Media Group, 151

D

Daily log (planner), 268–269, 292
Dangling participle, 130–131, 140
Dashes, 336–337
Data collection, 282e
Date, for letter, 180
Date, number differences, 70
Deduction, 253, 261
Defamation, 480–481, 489
Default settings, 157, 168
Demonstrations, in presentations, 323, 342, 363
Denning, Steve, 237
Dependent clauses, 122, 140
Design, of message
  fonts, point sizes for, 145–150, 164
  graphic elements for, 155, 164
  headings, white space for, 150–154, 164
  layout, alignment for, 156–157, 164
  technology shortcuts for, 157–159
Desire, in persuasive messages, 238, 239e, 243e–244e
Detractors, 51, 55
Direct approach, for message, 99–100, 108
Direct paragraph, 123, 140
Direct sales message, 244, 261
Disability bias, 116–117
Distribution, 160–164
Diversity, 5–6, 25
Dobra, Elaine, 218
Dohr, Amy, 178
Domain extensions, 97e
Dovetailing, of paragraphs, 124–125, 140
Downward requests, 243–244
Draft revision
  and conciseness, 126–127
  editing grammar, 129–133
  exercises for, 138
  and goals, 126
  and impact, 136–137
  and readability, 127–128
Drobnick, Jenna, 379
Dry-erase whiteboards, 341, 363
D'Souza, Derrick, 207
DTS Agile, 346
Duarte, Nancy, 317
Duarte Design, 317
Duarte Inc., 351
Dunn, Andy, 395
Dunsany, Lord, 324

E

Eastwood, Clint, 236
Eating behavior, 63
Editing, 129–133
Education, and perspective, 61
Education, training, in résumés, 415–416, 430
Educational administrator, 144
Educational presentations, 317
Elevator pitch, 382, 395
E-mail
  clear, effective, 474
  direct sales, 247–248
  filter triggers for, 247e
  formatting for, 149e
  for negative messages, 207, 208
  for positive, everyday messages, 185–188, 193–194
  requesting internships, 377e
  requesting interviews, 370e, 371e, 373, 375e
  rules for, 20
Emotion, and persuasion, 252–254
Emotional intelligence, 31–33, 55
Emotional quotient (EQ), 31, 55
Enclosures, 182
Endnotes, 283, 292

Entertainment industry, 235–236, 242, 255
Entrepreneurs, and communication, 79–81
Envirofit, 76
E-portfolio
and business presentations, 334–335
composition of, 19–20
defined, 430
intercultural skills for, 75
job description for, 24
and job interviewing, 460
and job searching, 394–395, 429
leadership, teamwork skills for, 54
for message design, proofreading, distribution, 166–167
mission statement for, 107
negative message for, 230
persuasive message for, 260
positive, everyday message for, 199
recommendation for, 139
report, proposal writing for, 291
successful communication tips for, 487–488
and visual aids, 362
Ethics
and AIG, 291–292
and business communication, 478–480, 485
of business messages, 98, 250–252, 258
Ethnicity, racism, 62, 116
Ethnocentrism, 65, 76
Etiquette, in teams, 38–40
Euphemism, 251–252, 261
Europe Through the Back Door, 68
Evans, Vanessa, 483
Events, professional, 372
Exclamation points, 293
Execu-Fleet, 203
Executive Planet web site, 63, 70
Executive summary, 282e–283e, 292
Expectations, exceeding, 469–471, 485
External parties, 220, 231
External requests, 242–243, 261
E-zines, 193, 194, 200

F

Facebook
about, 191–192
in business communication, 41, 112, 226
ethical use of, 195
internal, 45
making contacts through, 378, 383
seen by employers, 380–381
Face-to-face meetings, 92e
Facilitated discussion, 321, 335
Fair use, 481, 489
Fairlie, Robert W., 80
False marketing claims, 482
Family, and communication, 62
Family, friends, as resources, 378
Farmer's Insurance, 223
Fear, 67
Feasibility reports, 285–286, 289, 292, 299–305
Feedback
and communication breakdown, 12
giving, 477–478, 485
and message response, 137
receiving, 477, 485
sandwich, 478, 489
on writing, 135–136
Filler words, 69, 76
Firewalls, 358, 371
Flat chain of command, 83, 108
Flipcharts, 340–341, 363
Flowcharts, 346, 363
Focus (research) groups, 28
Follet, Ken, 126
Fonts, 145–150, 168, 188
Footnotes, 283, 292
Ford, Henry, 78
Ford Motor Co., 191
Forever Forest, 465
Formal research, 96, 108
Formal tone, 18
Formats, for résumés, 422–423, 426
Forming, 37
Four-step communication model, 10, 25
Framework for 21st Century Learning, 7e
Freelancer, 388, 395
Free-writing, 95, 108, 114
Front matter, 282e
Front-wheel skills, 287
Full-justification, 156, 168
Functional résumé, 410–411, 430

G

Gallup-Healthways Well-Being Index, 80
Game (poker) face, 471
Gandhi, Indira, 17
Gardner, Howard, 49–50
Gatekeeper, 87, 108
Gates, Bill, 51
Gender, 61, 62, 116–117
General-to-Specific organization, 322e
Generations, 60, 70–72, 73, 76
GIF file, 155
GiftTRAP, 80
Giver type, 34–35
Globetrekker, 68
Goals, achieving, 488
Going the extra mile, 470–471
Goleman, Daniel, 31
Goodwill
in business message, 82
in closing, 177
creating, 17, 22
defined, 25
gesture, in negative message, 220e
in persuasive message, 245e
Google, 429
Google Docs, 42, 43–44
Gossip team member, 48
Grammar
accuracy of, 489–490
adjectives, 109
adverbs, 140
capitalization, 201
colons, semicolons, 262
commas, 232
dashes, hyphens, 336–337
editing, 129–133
exclamation points, periods, question marks, 293
nouns, 26–27
numbers, 396–397
prepositions, pronouns, 431
prepositions and conjunctions, 169
pronouns, 56–57
quotation marks, parentheses, apostrophes, italics, 364–365
verbs, 77
word choices, 462
Green industry, 59–60
Green Line Food Distributors, 46–47, 48
Greeting behavior, 63
Grid, 156–157, 168
Group deciders model, 38
Group interviews, 435, 461
Groupthink, 46, 52, 55
Groupware, 43, 55
Guided discussion, 321, 335

H

Habitat for Humanity, 467
Hall, Edward, 37
Handouts, 342, 357
Hanley Wood, 139
HarperCollins Children's Books, 147
Hashmarks, 250
Hawley, Pamela, 477
HBO, 242
Headhunters, 386
Headings, 150–151, 168
Health, safety report, 288e
Health care-related organizations, 172
Health educator, 144
Heath, Chip and Dan, 322
Heifer International, 488
Hewlett-Packard, 323
Hibbard, Catherine S., 151
Hidden job market, 382, 395
Hiring freeze, 388, 395
Ho, Cliff, 67
Homonyms, 133, 140
Hook, 123, 140, 248e, 275e
Horizontal bar charts, 348–349, 363
Humor, in presentations, 324
Hybrid résumés, 391, 430
Hyperlinks, in slides, 347
Hyphens, 336–337

I

"I" attitude, 18
Iacocca, Lee, 30
iClicker, 363
IDEO, 335
Idioms, 117–118, 140
Ignorance, 66–67, 76
Illegal questions, in interview, 442–443, 461
Independent clause, 122, 140
Independent recruiters, 386, 395
Index cards, for outline, 113
Indig, Chaim, 200
Indirect approach, for message, 99–101, 108, 209–210, 231

Indirect paragraph, 124, 140
Indiscretions, online, 380–381
Induction, 253, 261
Informal research, 96, 108
Informal tone, 18
Information Overload Research Group (IORG), 192
Informative presentations, 316–317, 336
Inside address, for letter, 181, 200
Instant messaging (IM), 43, 188–189, 194, 200, 208
Instructional coordinator, 144
Instructional designer, 144
Interaction, for presentation, 321
Intercultural communication
  barriers to, 64–67, 73
  components of, 62–63, 72–73
  facilitating, 68–70, 73
  insights on, 64, 67
  and marketing plans, 76
Interest, for persuasive messages, 237–238, 239e, 243e–244e
Interest questions, in interview, 440, 461
Internal requests, 243–244, 261
International employment, 389, 390e
International Furniture Express Inc., 85–86
Internship flyer, changes to, 146, 151, 154, 158
Internships
  defined, 376, 395
  obtaining, 376–377
  requesting, 370e, 371e
Interpersonal communication, 8–10, 25, 472e
Interviews
  application for, 444
  behavior during, 445–446, 457
  on-campus, 385
  closing, 448–449, 450e, 457
  dressing for, 443, 444e, 457
  examples of, 433–434, 439
  follow-up for, 449–450
  gaining, 434–435, 456
  informational, 374–375, 395
  material for, 443
  one-on-one, 435, 457, 461
  in person, 435–436
  phone, 436, 457, 461
  practicing for, 440
  pre-employment testing in, 445
  questions for, 446–447, 448e
  requesting, 370e–371e, 372e
  research for, 438–440, 457
  and salary questions, 447, 448e
  in a social setting, 437–438, 461
  stress, 436–437, 461
  thank-you for, 450–451
  timing for, 444
  typical questions for, 440–443
  videoconference, 436, 461
Intimidated team members, 48
Intrapersonal communication, 8, 9e, 25
Introduction, of letter
  in cover letters, 403–405
  defined, 99, 108, 425–426
  examples of, 275e
Italics, 148, 168, 364–365

J

Janis, Irving, 46
Jargon, 117, 140
Jeffes, Steve, 142
Job search
  application packet for, 400–401
  desirable employees for, 380–381, 391
  in difficult markets, 388–391, 392
  elements of, 368
  examples of, 399–400, 409
  and fairs, recruiting events, 384–386
  and networking, 383–384, 391–392
  recruiters, agencies, 386–387
  résumés for, 407–423
  tapping hidden markets, 382–383
  See also Career exploration; Interviews
Jobs
  fairs, recruiting events for, 384–386, 395
  leaving, 483–485, 485
  offers for, 451–454, 457
  rejections, 455–456, 457
  resignation from, 455, 457
  See also Interviews; Job search
Jobs, Steve, 51, 238
Johnson & Johnson, 10
Joshi, Vyomesh, 323
JPEG files, 155
Justification, 156, 168

K

Katz, Susan, 147
Kaufman Index of Entrepreneurial Activity, 80
Keirsey Sorter test, 32–33, 55
Kellet, Nick, 80
Kelley, Dave, 335
Key words, 420–422, 423e, 430
Kinesthetic learners, 342, 363
Know-It-All team member, 48
Kraft Foods, 55

L

Language
  active, passive voice for, 206–207
  bias-free, 116–117
  differences in, 65–66
  familiarity with, 68
  fluency in, 62
  negative, positive, 205, 231
  texting, 69
  word types, 115–119
Lateral requests, 243
Law, and communication, 18, 134
Leader, defined, 49, 55
Leadership
  and business messages, 106–107
  and business presentations, 334
  and communication channels, 199
  in crisis, 487
  ethical, 482
  intercultural, 75
  and job interviewing, 459–460
  and job searching, 393–394
  and negative messages, 229–230
  and persuasive messages, 259–260
  in report, proposal writing, 290–291
  and résumés, 428–429
  in teams, 49–52
  and teamwork skills, 24, 54
  and visual aids, 361–362
  and writing skills, 138
Leading with Kindness: How Good People Consistently Get Superior Results, 482
Learning styles, 318, 319e, 336
Left-alignment (justification), 155, 156, 168
Letterhead, 179, 200
Letters
  of acceptance, 453–454, 454e
  of decline, 453–454, 461
  direct sales, 245–247
  following up e-mails, 371
  for negative messages, 208
  for positive, everyday messages, 193–194
  of recommendation, 469–470
  of rejection, 455–456, 461
  of resignation, 455, 461
  thank-you, 373e, 375, 386, 422e, 450–451, 456
  uses, types of, 178–183
Li & Fung USA, 387
Libel, 480–481, 489
Liking, principle of, 257, 258
Line charts, 348–349, 363
Line spaces, 152–153
LinkedIn, 191–192, 378, 383, 439–440
Lipa, Gia, 107–108
Listening
  active, 68
  barriers to, 15e
  defined, 25
  levels of, 13–15, 22
  for meaning, 14, 25
  perceptive, 14, 25
  surface, 14, 25
Listmaking, 95
Lists, in text, 128–129
Live-Radio.net, 65
Location, of presentation, 322
Logic, and persuasion, 252–254
Lone Ranger team member, 47
Luis, Lynette, 324

M

Macias, Diandra, 351
Mackay, Harvey, 368
Made to Stick: Why Some Ideas Survive and Others Die, 322
Majoring in the Rest of Your Life, 368
Majority rules model, 38
Manipulation, 251, 252e, 261
Margins, 151–152, 168
Martin, Joe, 103
Matteson, Rich, 30–31
McAlpine, Rachael, 264
McNeal Nutritionals, 98
Meacham, Brooke, 255
Meaning, listening for, 14, 25
Medina, John, 338
Meeting minutes, 288e
Meetup, 372

Mehlman, Cole, 20
Memory stick, 342, 363
Memos, 184–185, 194
Message
designing, 143–159
distributing, 160–164
proofreading, 159–160
simplicity of, 69
See also Business messages; Negative messages; Positive, everyday messages
Messenger, in communication, 10–11, 22
Metaphor, 237, 261
Methodology, 282e–283e
Metro Orlando Economic Development Commission, 248
Micro-blogs, 192–193, 200
Mind mapping, 95, 108, 320e
MindMeister, 112
Misplaced modifier, 130–131
Mission statement, 85–86, 107, 108
Modified block style, for letters, 178, 180e, 200
Modulation, of voice, 327, 336
Molly Fae Products, 315–316
Monologue, 321, 336
Monthly status reports, 271–272
Morsch, Laura, 168
Multimedia slides, 342

N

Neely, Heather, 72
Negative messages
to customers, clients, 211–213, 214f, 215f
from customers, clients, 222, 224
defined, 227, 231
delivering in person, 207
delivering in print, 208
to external parties, internal employees, 219–222
organizing, 208–210, 227
responding to, 227–228
rules for presenting, 204–205
to subordinates, peers, 217–219, 220e
from subordinates, peers, 225, 227–228
to superiors, 213, 214–216
from superiors, 224–225
timing for, 208
tone for, 205–207
Networking, 371–372, 396
See also under Job search
Networking cover letter, 402, 404e, 405, 430
New projects proposals
about, 273
defined, 292
examples of, 274e, 275e, 294–298
New Teacher University, 103
Newspapers, 378, 382–383
The Next Wave of Young Workers, 72
Nielsen Co., 97
Nohria, Nitin, 464
Nonnative English speaker, 62, 65–66, 69–70, 76
Nonprofit organizations, 465–466, 483
Nonrestrictive clauses, 130–131, 140
Norming, 37
Nouns, 26–27
Numbered list, 128
Numbers, 396–397

O

Object, 132, 140
Objections, to message, 88–90, 91e, 104, 108
Odyssey International, 20
Offer letter, 451, 453e, 461
Oltersdorf, Dan, 112
O'Malley, Michael, 482
Omation Animation Studios, 255
One-on-one interviews, 435, 457, 461
Online chat, 43, 45, 55
Online job banks, 384, 396
Operational report, 288e
Oral communication, 92–94, 104
Orbis Institute, 477
Organic Chips, 44
Organic People Inc., 409
Organization, for presentation, 322–325
Organizational charts, 349–350, 363
Organizer type, 34–35
Outline, 98, 108, 113–114
Outsourced, 68–69
Overhead projectors, 341, 363
Overselling, 251, 252e, 261

P

Packer, David, 50
PAL approach, in presentations, 326, 336
Paragraphs, 122–125, 128, 136, 140
Parallel construction, 128–129, 140
Parental tone, 240, 261
Parentheses, 364–365
Parents Television Council, 479
Parking lot, on flipchart, 341, 363
Parnell, Stewart, 478–479
Partnership for 21st Century Skills, 7
Passion, discovering, 466–467, 485
Passive Aggressive team member, 48
Passive voice, 119–120, 140
Paying dues, 469, 471e
PDF files
about, 161–163
defined, 168
for privacy, 208, 420, 424
for reports, proposals, 284
Peanut Corporation of America, 478–479
Peers, 216, 231, 266, 476
Perceptive listening, 14, 25
Performing, 37
Periods, 293
Permanent placement agencies, 386, 396
Personal space, 63, 76
Personality tests, 369
Personality types, 33–36
Persuasive messages
AIDA structure for, 237–238, 239e, 257
defined, 236, 257, 261
and direct sales, 244–250
and ethics, 250–252, 258
examples of, 235–236, 260–261
external, internal requests, 242–244, 245e, 258
and logic, emotion, 252–254
principles of, 256–257
tone for, 239, 240–241
trust, credibility for, 238, 239, 240e
Persuasive presentations, 316
Phone calls, 92e, 93b
Phone interviews, 436, 457, 461
Phreesia, 200
Physical abilities, disabilities, and perspective, 61
Pie charts, 348–349, 363
Pinder, Jerry, 460–461
Pivoting paragraph, 124, 140
Pizza Hut, 41
Plain-text résumés, 421–422, 430
PNG files, 155
Podcasts, 356, 363
Point size, 148, 168, 188
Portfolio, 423–425, 426, 430
See also E-portfolio
Positive, everyday messages
blogging for, 189–191, 194
choosing best channel for, 193–195, 197
defined, 196, 200
effective writing for, 175–177, 197
e-mails for, 185–188, 193–194
instant messaging (IM) for, 188–189, 194
letters for, 178–183, 193–194
memos for, 184–185, 194
online technologies for, 192–193, 194
professional vs. personal, 195–196, 197
and social media, 191–192, 194
texting for, 189
types of, 171–175
Positive, powerful words, 115
Positive close
defined, 210
examples of, 211e–212e, 214e–216e, 219e–221e
Postman, Neil, 251–252
Preemployment tests, 445
Prepositions, 169, 431
Press releases, 248–250, 261
Primary sources, 96, 108
Probing questions, in interview, 426, 461
Procedural organization, 322e
Procter & Gamble, 328
Professional attitude, 473e
Professional communication behavior, 472e
Professional experience, in résumés, 416–418, 430
Professional objectives, 413–414, 430
Professional organizations, 372, 383
Pronouns, 56–57, 130–132, 431
Proofreading, of message, 159–160, 161e, 162e, 168
Proposal, 266, 292
Props, for presentations, 342
Prospecting cover letter, 402, 403e, 430
Punctuation, 133
Puri, Ritika, 196
Purpose, of communication exchange, 16, 22, 81–82, 108
Purpose, of presentation, 318, 319